The HANDBOOK of COUNSELING

To all who promote scholarship, research,
professionalism, and excellence in counseling
—*The Editors*

To Marjorie, Tonya, and Regina for
your continuing love and support
—*Don C. Locke*

To Tom for the love and encouragement
he so freely shares with others
—*Jane E. Myers*

To Pat, Alicia, Amber, and Christopher Herr
in gratitude for their love, support, and individual
professional achievements
—*Edwin L. Herr*

The HANDBOOK
of COUNSELING

Editors

Don C. Locke • Jane E. Myers • Edwin L. Herr

Sage Publications
International Educational and Professional Publisher
Thousand Oaks ▪ London ▪ New Delhi

For information:

 Sage Publications, Inc.
2455 Teller Road
Thousand Oaks, California 91320
E-mail: order@sagepub.com

Sage Publications Ltd.
6 Bonhill Street
London EC2A 4PU
United Kingdom

Sage Publications India Pvt. Ltd.
M-32 Market
Greater Kailash I
New Delhi 110 048 India

Printed in the United States of America

Library of Congress Cataloging-in-Publication Data

The handbook of counseling / edited by Don C. Locke, Jane E. Myers, and
Edwin L. Herr.
    p. cm.
Includes bibliographical references and index.
   ISBN 0-7619-1993-7 (hardcover: alk. paper)
  1. Counseling. I. Locke, Don C. II. Myers, Jane E. III. Herr, Edwin L.
   BF637.C6 H365 2001
   158'.3—dc21

                               00-012633

01 02 03 10 9 8 7 6 5 4 3 2 1

Acquiring Editor:	Nancy S. Hale
Production Editor:	Diana E. Axelsen
Editorial Assistant:	Victoria Cheng
Typesetter/Designer:	Rebecca Evans
Indexer:	Rachel Rice
Cover Designer:	Michelle Lee

CONTENTS

PREFACE

Counseling as a unique and definitive profession emerged during the latter half of the 20th century. The chief markers of the profession—a body of knowledge, recognized and accredited training programs, supervised clinical training, credentialing of practitioners, legal recognition and licensure, professional organization of peers, and a code of ethics—all were firmly in place by the year 2000. The milestone of the new millennium created an opportunity both for reflection and for developing a vision of the future. With this dual emphasis in mind, this handbook evolved as an attempt to accomplish three main objectives: to capture the rich legacy of the evolution of counseling as a profession, to define the state of the art in counseling as it exists at this point in time, and to project the trends and issues that comprise our challenges for the next decade and beyond.

As editors, we recognized the tremendous diversity within our profession and devoted considerable effort to the task of determining how best to reflect that diversity in the pages of one text. We sought both the topics and the expertise of experienced authors to define the best in our field. The cooperation and enthusiasm of each of the chapter authors resulted in content that we believe will be of value not only to students and others new to our field but also to experienced counselors and counselor educators. Our request of all authors to envision the future, and to include within the chapters their perspectives on what lies ahead, makes this book unique and helps to provide a sense of direction for the years ahead.

Also unique is the cooperative relationship between Chi Sigma Iota (CSI), the International Counseling Honor Society, and Sage Publications as partners for this project. The three editors share a common experience as president of CSI, an organization with a single mission—the promotion of excellence in counseling. That mission resulted not only in CSI's endorsement of this handbook but also in the consensus decision of the editors and authors to donate the proceeds of the book to CSI to be maintained in a special fund earmarked for projects that promote excellence in our field.

The chapters in this handbook are organized into six major areas. Part I, "The Profession of Counseling," consists of six chapters. The first chapter chronicles the historical development of the field and, in particular, the factors that resulted in the emergence of counseling as a profession separate and distinct from clinical and counseling psychology. The roles of specialties, professional associations, standards, and credentials are described; ethical and legal issues are considered; and advocacy for counseling is broadly defined and described in the remaining five chapters of this section.

Part II consists of 11 chapters that present the "Foundations of Counseling." Eight of these chapters provide succinct yet in-depth introductions to theories commonly used by counseling practitioners: cognitive-developmental stage theories, cognitive-behavioral theories, humanistic theories, existential theory, Adlerian theory, systems theories, constructivist theories, and integrative theories. Basic counseling skills; counselor roles; and issues in assessment, diagnosis, and treatment are additional foundation issues covered in subsequent chapters of this section.

"Settings and Interventions" in which counselors commonly work are described in Part III. These include schools, colleges and universities, community agencies, private practice, and medical settings. "Counselor Education and Supervision," described in Part IV, is addressed through three chapters dealing with descriptive characteristics of the size and scope of counselor education, the processes and desired outcomes of counselor training and counselor supervision, and multicultural counseling training.

The importance of "Research in Counseling" is the focus of Part V. The chapters in this section include common epistemological and methodological issues as well as approaches to quantitative and qualitative research design. In addition to a comprehensive summary of the trend toward identifying and incorporating evidence-based counseling practices, practitioner-based and outcome research is discussed and program evaluation is defined and described.

Part VI, "Critical Issues and Emerging Topics," provides analyses of the major challenges facing the profession as we enter the new millennium. It begins with the changing demographics of society and an overview of issues affecting people at risk, including substance-abusing individuals. The changing demographics of the profession and how these affect the future are explored, and the importance of professional identification of counselors is examined. Strategies for defining and responding to ethnic and racial diversity as well as gender, sexual, and religious diversity are considered. The emergence of spirituality as a central issue in clinical work, the importance of character and personal responsibility, and strategies for optimizing behavior and promoting wellness are considered. The use of technology in counseling, evolving delivery systems for the provision of needed counseling interventions, and the cost-benefit of counseling services are addressed in the concluding chapters of this section.

In the "Conclusion" (Part VII), we summarize the issues facing the profession in the future and the collective challenges to be addressed as we attempt to respond to what lies ahead. In developing this summary, we attempted to incorporate the best thinking of the authors of each of the 43 separate chapters as well as our own ideas based on more than 100 years of collective experience as professional counselors. We invite the reader to think with us, to envision with us, and to work with us to create a future where the counseling profession continues to grow in strength and stature and where the services provided by practitioners combine to build a legacy of optimal human growth and development across the life span for all individuals.

Don C. Locke
Jane E. Myers
Edwin L. Herr

ACKNOWLEDGMENTS

There are many individuals who have contributed to the development and success of this handbook. It was Mark Kiselica who suggested the project to Sage Publications and my involvement as an editor. Jim Nageotte and Kassie Gavrilis nurtured the idea, and Nancy Hale saw the project to completion. I owe a great deal to the chapter authors, who willingly accepted our request to write in their specialties and who completed their tasks enthusiastically and on time. I doubt that a better team of co-editors can be found than Jane and Ed, two of my mentors, who continued their mentoring throughout this process. Annis Lytle always was eager to offer her assistance for the project. Eugene McDowell was quick with an encouraging comment when it seemed that the project was too overwhelming. D. J. Peck was efficient as copy editor. My counselor education colleagues and dean, Joan J. Michael, at North Carolina State University were very supportive of my efforts. My sincere thanks go to all of you.

—*Don C. Locke*

I want to express special thanks to the authors of the chapters of this handbook, who have eagerly shared their expertise, ideas, and enthusiasm for this volume. Their thoughts, research, and visions for the future reflect both the legacy and promise of our profession. In addition, I am grateful to many of these authors as well as other professionals in our field who have mentored and encouraged me through the years, persons too numerous to list but who have left their own legacy through any work that I do. I also am grateful to my students, whose constant thirst for knowledge challenges me to continue to grow as a counselor and as a counselor educator. Matt Shurts has been especially helpful in literature searches for my co-authored chapters for this book. Finally, to my family and friends, I again extend my appreciation for simply being there for me, for freely sharing the joys and sorrows on this journey of experiences toward a life fully lived.

—*Jane E. Myers*

My thanks go to my family and to the many authors of chapters in his handbook who, in their individual ways, have supported the process by which ideas become realities. In addition, it is important to acknowledge that this book is very much a product of the legion of pioneer and contemporary theorists, policy makers, researchers, and practitioners who have given shape and substance to counseling and to counselor education over the past 100 years. It is this latter group of visionaries, humanists, and statespersons for counseling and counselor education on whose legacy this volume rests.

—*Edwin L. Herr*

PART I

The Profession of Counseling

CHAPTER ONE

Counseling

Historical Origins and Philosophical Roots

THOMAS J. SWEENEY

Counseling has a unique place among the helping professions. Although the profession is not unique in the provision of counseling per se, it is a creation of both human and societal needs and our response to them as an evolving dynamic amalgam of individuals and organizations. Professionally trained counselors have come to share a common body of knowledge, a philosophical basis, and competencies suited to work with individuals, couples, families, groups, and organizations across the life span. Although doctoral preparation provides the recipient with greater in-depth research, consultation, supervision, counseling, and counselor education preparation, the master's-level practitioner has proven effective and is accepted as the entry level for the profession.

As a result of efforts by individuals and organizations, counseling has attained the status of a profession through national preparation standards, accreditation of preparation programs, credentialing of practitioners through both state legislative means and national certification, ethical standards for its membership, advancement of its knowledge base through research and scholarly publications, and professional development of its membership through continuing education. This chapter discusses the events and persons that made this possible.

A brief overview of the historical antecedents of counseling as a profession is essential to understanding how it has evolved to its present state. In this chapter, for example, some of the major societal needs and priorities that have helped to shape the nature of the profession are referenced. The educational nature and foundation of counseling as a profession is illuminated. This emphasis on our educational roots is somewhat unique in that our history often is portrayed as chiefly associated with vocational guidance, psychological testing, and mental health. And yet, we owe much to the pioneers in school guidance for helping us to stand apart from other disciplines that also use counseling as an intervention. As a consequence, a number of the references cited are from works earlier in the 20th century. The blending of other disciplines in the preparation and practice of counseling is acknowledged, but the emphasis is on how the counseling profession has distinguished itself from other professions historically through an emphasis on optimal human development over the life span for all individuals, families, and groups.

The hallmarks of a profession and how counseling meets them are presented in other chapters in this handbook. References to these hallmarks in this chapter are presented principally to highlight the interdisciplinary challenges that provided both impetus for and clearer definition of counseling as distinct from that of other professions. I am both a product and a participant in this era of our history. As a consequence, I hope to share a perspective on the internal and external forces that have helped to shape the profession until the present time.

We are indebted to far more individuals than any history can appropriately identify, but there are some persons whose vision, leadership, and personal commitment to the profession deserve recording for posterity. Some of the early unsung pioneers of the profession as it evolved over the past half century are identified for their contributions. Finally, the chapter concludes with a summary of current societal needs and priorities that are likely to influence the profession during the 21st century.

Early Antecedents: Education

The history of the counseling profession necessarily intersects with societal events and issues, as well as responses to these events and issues, by social institutions including government, business and industry, education, and related professions. As Herr (1989) noted, counseling services must be understood in a sociopolitical and cultural context. For us, the foundation for the counseling profession is established within the Bill of Rights and fortified by the Constitution and system of government of the United States (Hutson, 1968). Although imperfect in their full implementation even at this point in our 200-plus years as a nation, these documents are the philosophical basis of an individual's right to "life, liberty, and the *pursuit of happiness.*" As will be noted subsequently, our urgent need to address issues of diversity within present-day practice is directly related to the promise of these "inalienable rights." As a profession, we are further fortified by the premise that an educated citizenry is necessary for good government.

Jessie B. Davis has been identified by historians as the first individual to attempt to make guidance a systematic part of the school curriculum (Brewer, 1942; Miller, 1961). Davis had been an administrator in one of the growing industrial centers of this country, Detroit, between 1898 and 1907. He was struck by the significant social and vocational problems of his students resulting from the dramatic changes brought on by industrialization. When Davis moved to a high school in Grand Rapids, Michigan, in 1907, he decided that every English composition class would devote time to help each student develop "a conception of himself as a social being in some future occupation, and from this viewpoint the appreciation of his duty and obligation toward his business associates, toward his neighbors, and [toward] the law" (Davis, 1914, p. 17). So it was that educators like Davis and others (e.g., Eli W. Weaver, Lightner Witmer) were the early advocates for what became school guidance and counseling. In fact, there is no doubt that there are far more individuals like Davis than historians have captured for posterity. Those who are noted, however, generally were effective spokespersons for change of the type still sought today.

The famous 19th-century educator Horace Mann articulated forcefully the benefits of an educational system for all our citizenry. Furthermore, he believed that it was through education that society could be reformed. His position made the incorporation of what became guidance and counseling in schools during the 20th century an appropriate and needed component of a good educational system. However, John Dewey (1859-1952) probably was the most influential intellectual to lay the technical and philosophical foundation for accepting counseling as an integral part of education in the broadest sense. His was the "progressive" movement of that era.

Hickman and Alexander (1998) noted, "Dewey's insights into the problems of public education [and] immigration, the prospects of democratic government, and the relation of faith to science are as fresh today as when they were first published" (p. ix). *The New York Times* credited Dewey with being "America's Philosopher" (p. ix). There were those who believed that for a generation, until Dewey had spoken, no major issue had been fully clarified. He is perhaps best known for his "pragmatism" and emphases on creating a learning environment that respects the unique qualities of children while preparing them for the real world into which they were born. Furthermore, Dewey called on teachers to withstand the efforts of forces that would "fragment the national culture by fostering fear and hatred of minorities, immigrants, and others who have traditionally been targets of such demagoguery" (p. xii). Finally, in the midst of the Great Depression of the 1930s, he called for what he termed a "radical liberalism," one that made it clear that intelligence is a social asset and that it is social cooperation, and not what he called "ragged individualism," that is essential to progress. With such an articulate and influential intellectual espousing counterpoints to many traditional philosophical and practical concepts of both educational and social consequence, the advocates for guidance services no doubt felt supported.

During the early 1930s, Arthur J. Jones, a professor of secondary education at the University of Pennsylvania, published the second edition of what has become a classic text on the *Principles of Guidance*. In his first chapter, he states his view on the need for guidance:

> Guidance is based upon the fact that human beings need help. To a greater or lesser degree, we all need the assistance of others. The possibility of education, as well as the necessity for it, is

founded upon the essential dependence of people upon one another. Young people, especially, are not capable of solving life's problems successfully without aid. Many critical situations occur in our lives, situations in which important and far-reaching decisions must be made, and it is very necessary that some adequate help be provided in order that decisions may be made wisely. (Jones, 1934, p. 3)

We find within these simple and yet profound statements a consistency with both Dewey and current philosophical positions of counselor education. First, we note the pragmatic nature of all human existence: We need one another as social beings. All must make decisions about life. With help, we hope to make them more "wisely." Although Jones (1934) noted that children "especially" need help, implicit within his statements is the need that we all have for some assistance throughout our lives. He assumes that human development is facilitated by such help. Therefore, human development, facilitated throughout the life span by deliberate positive assistance, is needed and normal in the course of human existence.

Jones (1934) went on to elaborate on the "present demand for definite provision for guidance." The conditions that he enumerated include changing conditions of the home, changing conditions of labor and industry, changes in population (urban vs. rural), decreasing birth rate, changing standards of living (higher), increase in the demand for general education, elimination from school (dropout rates), leisure time (more available), moral and religious conditions (weakening), and leadership (successful democracy requires educated citizenry). Although the statistics and discussion would necessarily vary, Jones's topics still are relevant today as a part of the basis for counseling services.

From Education and Guidance to Counseling

The historical connection of counseling with education is revealed in part by early literature concerned with the further definition of "guidance" as a function of education. John Brewer's early 1930s work, *Education as Guidance,* espouses a position that guidance be infused into the total curriculum and that every teacher share the responsibility for its implementation (Brewer, 1932). Later in the same decade, others proposed that guidance be a part of, but not synonymous with, education. For example, Hamrin and Erickson (1939) felt compelled to note,

> *Guidance* is a term appearing with increasing frequency in education literature and as a topic of discussion at meetings of professional organizations. Some writers and speakers use the term *guidance* synonymously with the term *education;* others identify and characterize as guidance only those activities that are concerned with the vocational aspects of life. (p. v, italics in original)

During the succeeding decades, the term *guidance* went through its own acceptance as suitable for what "guidance counselors" did in schools to a term no longer considered adequate for the professional preparation, practice, and identity desired by those who earned advanced degrees in "*counselor* education." In fact, the work of professional counselors both inside and outside of educational settings became too complex to be subsumed under rubrics such as "guidance" or "personnel."

The significance of terms may be best illustrated by the name changes of what was first the American Personnel and Guidance Association (APGA), established in 1952, subsequently the American Association for Counseling and Development (AACD) in 1983, and finally the American Counseling Association (ACA) in 1992. Such name changes did not take place easily. Philosophical and emotional attachments to the terms *guidance, personnel,* and *development* underscore the significant, if not dramatic, changes that accompanied the final three decades of the 20th century. Long before *counseling* came into common use, *guidance* was the accepted term for all that counselors do including counseling. To be a "guidance" or "personnel" worker was the norm. "Personnel work" in both schools and colleges was considered appropriate terminology.

Those who worked in colleges and universities in 1924-1925 established, first, the National Association of Appointment Secretaries and, subsequently, the National Association of Placement and Personnel Officers and, finally in 1931, the American College Personnel Association (ACPA). To this day, ACPA is composed in large measure of deans of students and other related administrative personnel. As one of the founding associations of APGA, it is no surprise that the name change process from APGA, to AACD, and finally to ACA was a difficult one for many ACPA members. Although college counselors affiliated with ACPA, their interests were different from those for the majority of members. Therefore, when ACPA disaffiliated from what became ACA in 1992, the college counselors created a new organization, the American College Counselors Association (ACCA). Indeed, identity as a profession distinct from those from which it sprang is at the heart of current issues for counselors and the organizations that represent them. School and rehabilitation counselors, for example, may be pulled in two different directions by competing organizations.

School counselors historically were associated with teacher education. For many years, school teaching was universally seen as a prerequisite to becoming a "guidance counselor," and affiliation with teacher organizations to represent the interests of school counselors with school boards and legislators was expected. Although fewer states and school systems now require teaching certificates or school teaching experience as a requisite to being a counselor, there still are those states that do. Research study results to the contrary, there remains a strong vocal group among those who believe that only teaching experience is sufficient to prepare someone for work in schools. As a consequence, the National Education Association (NEA), for example, still has an affiliate organization for school counselors, even though the American School Counselors Association (ASCA) was one of the earliest divisions of what was APGA during the early 1950s.

Although school counseling has changed dramatically since the first half of the 20th century, many school counselors still find a comfortable home within education as a part of their identity. Other school counselors, however, have been influenced by the development of counseling as a separate discipline. The setting still is an essential part of their identity, but they are professional counselors with specialized skills working in schools. There are other counselors in rehabilitation settings, for example, who share this same view (Gladding, 2000).

Wright (1980), whose text *Total Rehabilitation* is itself a classic, thoroughly detailed the history of rehabilitation counseling including significant legislation to serve persons with disabilities, the evolution of rehabilitation counselor preparation, and methods of rehabilitation counseling. For example, he reported that rehabilitation counseling has the unique distinction of being the only profession established by congressional legislation in Public Law 565 of the 83rd Congress in 1954. He also provided an explanation of how rehabilitation counselors choose professional affiliations with or between APGA/ACA and the National Rehabilitation Association (NRA). He noted that, much like school counseling described earlier, rehabilitation counselors have a common body of knowledge with other professional counselors but through the settings and persons they serve have developed unique methods and techniques to be most effective with them. Likewise, some rehabilitation counselors prefer affiliation with others who identify first with rehabilitation, rather than counseling, as a discipline. So, as we attempt to understand current issues in counseling such as why school counselors do not agree on the need for teaching experience for school counselor certification and why the Council for Accreditation of Counseling and Related Educational Programs (CACREP) and the Council on Rehabilitation Education (CORE) are separate agencies that accredit counselor preparation programs in the same department or university, the historical antecedents may prove all the more helpful.

Early Antecedents: Vocational Guidance

There may be no name more easily identified with what was termed "guidance" than Frank Parsons. At the turn of the 20th century, industrialization, immigration, out-of-work farmers, Southerners seeking greater pay in the North, youths seeking excitement in the cities, and injustices rampant through abuse by those with growing wealth and power called out for reform (Aubrey, 1977). Parsons became a re-

former with a mission. Unlike Davis, an educator, Parsons was an engineer, a lawyer, and a social worker who saw the need for assisting youths in their search for suitable work. He shared the desire to see his work located in schools, but his Vocational Bureau in Civic Service House in Boston was the first such effort to institutionalize vocational guidance (Ginzberg, 1971). His book, *Choosing a Vocation* (Parsons, 1909), was published posthumously, and his efforts were further recognized in 1910 when the first conference of what became the National Vocational Guidance Association (NVGA) met in Boston. NVGA was established in 1913 in Grand Rapids, Michigan. Descendant members in 1952 helped to establish what is now ACA (formerly APGA). NVGA has since been renamed the National Career Development Association (NCDA), illustrating again the shift from "guidance" as well as "vocation" to a more inclusive "career" and "development" emphasis. During the intervening years, a number of events affected not only counseling but closely related disciplines as well.

Both world wars increased the need for better means to assess the capabilities of men for the armed services. Alfred Binet and others helped to advance methods and techniques that strengthened the scientific basis for guidance. As a consequence, the postwar years during the 1920s saw increased research and development of measurement techniques. In addition, the adequacy of placement within the school curricula and an evaluation of the end results brought educational guidance into greater prominence. The depression years of the 1930s also contributed to the perception that vocational guidance was an important need for our citizenry. A number of local, state, and federal programs sponsored by efforts such as President Roosevelt's New Deal legislation resulted in counseling services as adjuncts to health, social, employment, and educational concerns.

Hoyt (1974) reported that prior to 1938, the counseling and guidance movement grew slowly and principally at the local level. The George-Dean Act of 1938, however, created the Vocational Education Division of the U.S. Office of Education and an Occupational Information and Guidance Service headed by Harry A. Jager, a former high school principal. This, in turn, led to the creation of state supervisor of guidance positions in state departments of education throughout the country. All of these positions were located within divisions of vocational education. World events entered the picture once more to influence the development of the profession.

World War II again brought into sharper focus the need to use personnel in the most efficient manner possible. Testing and placement of personnel very much like the Parsons model of matching people to occupations still was the function of "guidance." Postwar business and industry continued this interest by investing in testing programs to identify and place personnel within their growing structures.

In schools, however, the George-Barden Act of 1946 provided funds through the U.S. Office of Education (USOE) for partial support of state supervisors of guidance and counselor educators. This act provided vocational education funds to reimburse counselor training institutions. Jager then moved to encourage state certification of school counselors through his network of state supervisors. As a consequence, state school counselor certification preceded other forms of counselor credentialing, even though it lacked the national standards needed to create uniformity.

There were 80 colleges and universities purportedly training school counselors during the late 1940s. Half of the programs were at the undergraduate level. Hoyt (1974) recalled that undergraduate programs in counselor education were discouraged by Jager's decision during the early 1950s not to fund them under the George-Bardon Act. This no doubt had a profound effect on the university programs at that time, which had undergraduate emphases.

Also of consequence to counselor professionalization, Jager's unit published a series of eight reports on counselor preparation (six on course content and two on in-service education). The final report was titled, "Supervised Practice in Counselor Preparation." These reports were prepared by state supervisors of guidance and counselor educators who were reimbursed by the USOE for this purpose. It is Hoyt's (1974) recollection that these reports set the pattern for school counselor education and heavily influenced other forms of counselor education during the period from 1946 to 1958.

Hoyt (1974) went on to note, for example, that when federal legislation provided for the preparation of vocational rehabilitation counselors in 1955, those responsible decided that it was more appropriate to train rehabilitation counselors at the same level and in ways analogous to school counselor training. As a result, most vocational rehabilitation programs were placed in colleges of education where the master's degree was considered an appropriate entry-level degree. Likewise, Jager's and the USOE's influence on courses appropriate for counselor preparation no doubt helped to shape preparation for rehabilitation counselors as well. The initiative for advancement of the profession was about to shift, however, from government to the professionals themselves.

By the late 1950s, the stage was set for counselor educators, state supervisors, and practitioners to take the leadership for national preparation standards for school counselors. However, another major societal event and congressional actions no doubt created greater urgency for such action.

National Defense Education Act of 1958

Perhaps the most important legislation associated with the counseling profession's ascendancy on university campuses came with the passage of Public Law 85-864, the National Defense Education Act of 1958 (NDEA). This act provided funds for guidance and counseling institutes, provided funds for fellowships in counselor preparation, and expanded guidance and testing programs in schools. The origin of the legislation and its intended purposes are important as well. In 1957, the Soviet Union launched a successful space capsule. American leadership in rocket and space technology was in serious question. National pride and national defense against the Communist Soviet Union were uppermost in the minds of congressional leaders. Congress decided that schools needed to identify, prepare, and "guide" the most gifted and talents youngsters into engineering and other technical careers important to our "space race" with the Soviets. Testing programs were quickly assembled and put into schools throughout the country. Teachers were identified by their principals as promising guidance counselors and sent off to summer or academic-year institutes, with all expenses paid including stipends.

Within a matter of a few short years, the number of counselors in schools would quadruple and the ratio of counselors to students would decrease from 1 to 960 in 1958-1959 to 1 to 450 by 1966-1967 (Shertzer & Stone, 1971). Not surprisingly, the number of universities training counselors and the number

of counselor educators also increased dramatically.

Dugan (1961) reported that between 1958 and 1961, the number of counselor education *programs* grew from 175 to 475. In 1964, the Department of Education's *Directory of Counselor Educators* listed 706 counselor educators and 327 preparation *institutions* at that time (cited in Hollis, 1997). In 1967, just 3 years later, this same directory listed 1,119 counselor educators (a 58% increase) and 372 institutions offering programs (a 14% increase).

Hoyt (1991) was one of a few counselor educators who helped to identify which programs would receive federal funding under the NDEA. He recalled that Harold McCully, deputy to the director of the Counseling and Guidance Institutes Programs, Title VB, noted that 90% of the persons listed as "directors" of the 300 new programs never had been counselors. As a staff member of several institutes, I recall that staff tended to come from one of two disciplines: education and psychology. Although some could speak of their experience as school counselors, they were the exceptions rather than the rule. Nevertheless, the need for national guidelines for counselor preparation was evident to the leaders intent on the professionalization of counseling.

National Standards for Preparation

Dugan (1961) of the University of Minnesota, Hill (1967) of Ohio University, and Robert Stripling of the University of Florida were instrumental in the development of national standards. With Stripling's leadership (Stripling & Dugan, 1961), the Association for Counselor Education and Supervision (ACES) made a decision to adopt national standards for the preparation of secondary school counselors in 1964

(Hoyt, 1991). This was done after several years of collaboration with ASCA. Stripling's legacy to the profession continues to this day through the work of CACREP.

It was Stripling, especially, who advocated for 2 years of graduate study in counselor preparation. This was a major issue during the 1960s (Hoyt, 1991). To understand the magnitude of such a proposal, it is necessary to acknowledge that most school counseling programs required 30 semester hours of preparation at the time. More than a few disagreed with Stripling's position, but in time, he lived to see his proposal adopted. In addition to his publications and passionate presentations to colleagues on the necessity for national standards, Stripling subsequently chaired the ACES committee on doctoral standards that also were adopted by CACREP during its formative stage.

Another who firmly advocated for implementation of national standards was George E. Hill. Under Hill's mentorship, Ohio University faculty developed and implemented one of the first institutional self-studies in counselor education. He also chaired the ACES committee making recommendations for secondary school guidance counselor preparation. Hill was reported in the ACES journal anniversary issue to be the most prolific contributor during its first 25 years (Hosie, Poret, Lauck, & Rosier, 1986). He published foundation textbooks (Hill, 1967, 1974) including one of the early texts on elementary school counseling (Hill & Luckey, 1969). In addition, Hill helped to recruit me to Ohio University when he retired in 1972. Based on a program history of service to the profession, and encouraged and supported by the faculty in the Hill tradition, I was able to prepare and help to implement the APGA adopted positions on both licensure (APGA, 1974) and accreditation (APGA, 1981). This included chair-

ing both the first APGA Licensure Committee (Sweeney, 1991) and CACREP through its first 6 years as the official accrediting body for counseling. During the latter assignment, Joe Wittmer (University of Florida), the first CACREP executive director and a colleague of Stripling's, and I (Sweeney & Wittmer, 1983, 1984) helped CACREP to achieve recognition by the Council on Postsecondary Accreditation (COPA) when even Stripling had doubts that it could be done (Stripling, 1978). I believe that Hill's influence in creating a faculty commitment to professional leadership and service at Ohio University is a part of his legacy to the profession. Yet, nothing either Stripling or Hill did had greater impact than helping to spearhead the school counselor standards initiative, which became the prototype for both the core requirements and specialty standards used today in counselor education accreditation.

The Great Society's War on Poverty

President Lyndon Johnson might be best known for his pursuit of the war in Vietnam, but it was his war on poverty that propelled a significant shift in the destiny of counseling practitioners. During President Kennedy's administration, the Community Mental Health Services Act of 1963 established community mental health centers throughout the country. This act provided funds for a variety of mental health workers, including counselors, to deliver services to those in need at the grassroots level. Johnson, however, had long been an advocate for what he considered to be the underdog in our society. As a result, he successfully lobbied Congress to pass the Economic Opportunity Act of 1964 (Public Law 88-452). This was one of his efforts designed to create "a war to eliminate poverty." This act was intended to expand opportunities for youths, stimulate communities to attack the roots of poverty, help destitute rural families, expand small business activities in poor areas, improve adult education, encourage states to use public assistance programs to help the poor help themselves out of poverty, and recruit and train volunteers to help staff programs. At the very time school counseling programs and school counselor education were experiencing the full impact of NDEA funding, new legislation shifted the focus from schools to communities and from the gifted and talented to the disadvantaged and poor. This was the beginning of what would be a shift from school counseling preparation to a community counseling emphasis.

During the 1960s, philosophically developmental guidance (Peters & Farwell, 1967; Wrenn, 1962) still was being promoted, but for many, the call to save those who were destitute and in crises became more urgent. So, it was in 1976 that Jim Messina and Nancy Spisso, two Florida counselors, saw the need for a mental health counseling organization. The result was the American Mental Health Counselors Association (AMHCA), which subsequently affiliated with APGA in 1978. Shortly after joining APGA, AMHCA ambitiously instituted a national certification for mental health counselors. That certification now is administered by the National Board of Certified Counselors (NBCC). It is noteworthy that although this new group of members responded to the same urgent message for serving the needs of persons in mental health crises, they chose to define the essence of mental health counseling as that of promoting healthy lifestyles, eliminating stressors that detract from such lifestyles, and preserving or restoring positive health (Seiler & Messina, 1979). Adherence to this philosophical position is one of the defining distinctions that mental health counselors bring to any community or interdisciplinary team. Professional counselors are not alone in this position now, however, as others embrace the value of prevention and enhancement of optimal health. Counseling psychology, for example, established its place among psychologists in the same way (Wright, 1980).

Counseling and Counseling Psychology

No overview of the evolution of counseling as a profession would be complete without acknowledging counseling's relationship with another relatively new specialty, counseling psychology. Hoyt (1974) noted that it was the Veterans Administration that initiated doctoral programs in counseling psychology during the period from 1946 to 1952 after World War II. At the same time as APGA was being formed in 1952, Counseling Psychology was taking form as Division 17 of the American Psychological Association (APA). Counseling psychologists sought a place within the discipline of psychology as a specialty concerned with serving the normal adjustment needs of individuals, as compared to clinical psychology, which seeks to address the needs of those individuals with chronic and severe disorders. They, too, embraced the idea of optimal human development as a goal for counseling psychologists working with "normal" clients. So, it might seem that a natural bond would be established between counselor education and counseling psychology.

Several of the same persons helped to initiate both APGA and Division 17 of APA. Certainly, Donald Super (Super, 1955), a president of both associations, and Gilbert Wrenn (Wrenn,

1962) are among them (VanHoose & Pietrofesa, 1970). Wrenn was president of NVGA (1946-1947) and ACPA (1947-1949). He also was president of the Division of Counseling and Guidance of APA in 1951 when it changed its name to Counseling Psychology and subsequently became Division 17 of APA in 1952. Both were prolific scholars and were widely read by students and colleagues of each organization, and both served Division 17 and APGA in various capacities. They helped to shape the philosophical basis for practitioners in each field. They were among those who espoused a developmental, humanistic orientation that promoted optimal functioning regardless of individual differences. What most historical accounts of counseling fail to note, however, is the connection between the guidance and counseling movement in education and its pervasive influence on present-day counselor education and, quite likely, counseling psychology.

The preponderance of counselor educators are graduates of colleges and departments of education (Hollis, 2000). Those of us who attended NDEA programs during the 1950s and 1960s became the faculty who prepared the succeeding generations of counselors and counselor educators. While in our counselor education doctoral programs, we were encouraged to have preparation in counseling psychology where we studied much of the same literature as the counseling psychology majors. Our philosophical foundations, however, grew out of our educational discipline. It might only be coincidental that counseling psychology chose to align itself with the same orientation as counseling, but the most cited statements on this topic are by Super (1955). Super was on the faculty of Teachers College at Columbia University. To what extent he was influenced by his colleagues or the literature in education is unknown. Clearly, Super was a friend to counselors and counseling psychologists alike. Unfortunately, marketplace politics, at least for the time being, have interfered with the interface between the organizations and members in some significant ways.

Historically, membership in both APGA and APA was not at all unusual as many counselor educators affiliated with Division 17 and state psychology associations. Nevertheless, in 1967, many counselor educators were completely unaware that APA adopted an initiative to aggressively establish state legislation that would limit the practice of counseling to doctoral-trained psychologists or those under their supervision (Sweeney & Sturdevant, 1974). By the early 1970s, these efforts were being established in both legislative and administrative actions within the states. A fundamental difference between psychology and counseling emerged in both legislation and member organizations.

Psychology (APA) holds that only doctoral training in psychology is sufficient to practice psychology or hold the title of "psychologist." Likewise, membership in APA requires a doctorate. Even a master's degree in psychology is not sufficient. Professional membership requiring a master's degree was instituted by ACA for the first time in 1991. Prior to that time, membership was open to persons of any discipline, so that they could network with persons of similar interest through the organization. For example, many members of NVGA/NCDA, like those of ACPA, were not trained counselors per se. Many saw this lack of counseling experience as a strength of APGA because it was inclusive. Lobbyists for professional counseling legislation during the 1980s, however, were quick to point out the disadvantages when legislators and others asked about criteria for membership in the professional counselors association (Barstow, 1998). Thus, the need arose for ACA to adopt membership criteria requiring at least a master's degree or greater in counseling or a closely related field. These criteria, of course, still are inclusive for those with "related degree," including degrees in psychology. In fact, counseling psychologists continue to publish in ACA journals and present at ACA conferences extensively (Weinrach, Lustig, Chan, & Thomas, 1998).

The tension between counseling psychologists and counselor educators (i.e., those not prepared in psychology departments) becomes most pointed when employment issues are discussed. Psychology departments are expected by their accrediting agency to hire psychologists to teach in their programs. CACREP has made no such distinction, and as a consequence, doctoral graduates in counselor education have been disadvantaged in seeking teaching positions in higher education other than in counselor education programs. Although some counseling psychologists acknowledge the commonalities and tensions between counseling and counseling psychology, none has made an effort to rectify the discrepancy in hiring practices in higher education.

Until CACREP rectifies the inequity between counselor education and counseling psychology hiring practices in counselor education, no change is likely in the foreseeable future. To do so, CACREP will need to institute the same policies as do other disciplines, including psychology, that is, requiring that counselor education faculty have their preparation from counselor education programs. In the meantime, some master's degree programs in particular have few counselor education graduate faculty members (if any), and in other programs, few faculty members have a strong identity with counseling themselves, preferring, for example, a "therapist" title of some sort. How this and related facts affect the professional identity of those being prepared in such programs has been the focus of discussion and action by two national conferences (Chi Sigma Iota, 1998).

Advocacy for professional counselors and those they serve has received growing attention during recent years (Barstow, 1998). At the heart of many such efforts is motivating both students and practitioners to become their own best advocates. Professional counselors who understand the value of their historical roots, can articulate the efficacy of their interventions, and reveal pride in their chosen profession will earn the respect they deserve. Clarification of what makes counselors special as members of an interdisciplinary team or community practice may help to sharpen the focus on how we are different and how counselors add value to services in schools, communities, and businesses.

What Is Unique About Counseling?

So, what is it that makes counseling unique as a separate discipline? The answer to this question is multifaceted and includes our national standards, philosophical orientation, master's degree entry into the profession, professional identity, state and national credentials, and national leadership.

Standards

First, we must note differences in preparation of counselors and other practitioners. The standards for preparation by other disciplines (e.g., psychology, marriage and family therapy, social work) are substantively different, although not entirely so. The core areas of counselor education require preparation in areas not required of other disciplines such as marriage and family therapy and social work (e.g., career development, group procedures). Whereas psychologists must study the history and systems of psychology, counselor education students have professional orientation and social and cultural foundations required of all majors.

Psychologists preparing for clinical work must take some of the same course work as counselors. Counselors are prepared in the theories and techniques of counseling, with particular attention paid to clinical skill and ethical decision making. Although not to the same extent as marriage and family therapists, counselors must learn about families and interventions for them. Counselors prepared at the doctoral level are more likely to have the same types of research and statistical methodology courses as do psychologists in addition to preparation for teaching, supervision, consultation, and/or counseling related to their areas of specialty.

One difference in doctoral programs concerns clinical experience. Most doctoral programs in counselor education and supervision require post-master's experience prior to admission to doctoral study. Most psychology programs admit for both the master's (or its equivalent) and doctoral degrees without clinical experience before the doctoral internship. Clinical experience makes a qualitative difference in what doctoral students perceive they require in the way of advanced preparation and how they approach planning their doctoral programs with faculty. Less experienced students must depend on faculty in large part or wholly, whereas experienced clinicians expect to help design the types of program that they require for future career responsibilities.

Equally important, the collective professional and clinical experience of one's cohort group in graduate preparation becomes an essential part not only of broadening fellow students' educations but also of enriching the entire program at the master's level and enhancing the development of the faculty as they interact with the doctoral students. As a result, the clinical experience that doctoral students in counseling bring to both the doctoral and master's programs enriches the educational opportunities of all students as well as the faculty.

Philosophical Orientation

Graduates of each discipline approach even similar topics from a different perspective. For example, although counseling psychology has many of the same historical roots as does counseling, the former is steeped in psychology as its fundamental identity. Counseling shares some of these roots (Beers, 1908; Parsons, 1909; Super, 1955) but likewise has strong roots in educational philosophy, methods, and practices. Those of us who came out of the ranks of teacher education during the NDEA era of rapid expansion in counselor education programs and growth in numbers of faculty were retooling ourselves during the shift to community and mental health counseling during the 1970s. As a consequence, we retained a strong attachment to the human development and educational philosophy approach to counseling. Indeed, counseling is a learning activity in which the subject is the individual seeking education about himself or herself, life, and how to live with others.

We can see that counseling and counselor education have had their historical roots in a developmental, life-span, facilitative approach to intervention and human growth since the early part of the 20th century (Hickman & Alexander, 1998; Jones, 1934). Before "wellness" and holistic approaches to helping were in vogue, guidance and counseling literature contained the philosophy and values now embraced by many in the helping professions (Cottingham, 1956; Hill & Luckey, 1969; Hutson, 1968; Miller, 1961; Peters & Farwell, 1967). Indeed, the failure of our health care system to adequately address the needs of the American public is predicated in large part on the mistaken concept that until one's health is diseased or injured, no care is required (Myers, Sweeney, & Witmer, 2000).

In education, we know that developmental stages require transitions. This is normal, but not everyone moves through the stages chronologically or smoothly. Educational experiences, including guidance and counseling, are most effective when needs are anticipated, are facilitated, and enhance the learners' capacity to change and grow. This is a fundamental belief of counseling that predates others who have since embraced its value. However, we welcome colleagues of other disciplines who share these values and seek to further them for the benefit of those we serve.

Professional Identity

Professional identity is reflected in one's terminal graduate degrees, preferred professional credentials, primary organizational affiliations, and preferred professional sources of knowledge (e.g., journals, books). When I was a neophyte to the profession during the late 1950s

and early 1960s, my graduate advisers for both the master's and doctorate expected me to join and participate in the work of APGA and its affiliate branches and divisions. All of my cohort members were expected to do the same. By the 1970s, state licensure for psychologists required many doctoral counselors to acquire a psychology license to practice what we were prepared to do as counselors. About the same time, the American Association of Marriage and Family Counselors (AAMFC) changed its name to American Association of Marriage and Family Therapy (AAMFT) and created a credential with a similar identity that many counselor educators sought while counselor licensure still was in its infancy. This was all taking place while the shift in emphasis in counselor education went from schools to community and mental health counseling.

In a few short years, many counselor educators, including those teaching the professional orientation classes, either made no mention of joining professional organizations or presented their favorites as most desirable, that is, not necessarily APGA/AACD/ACA. Likewise, their university offices would show credentials and memberships from a variety of organizations representing their interests. Not infrequently, counseling associations never were mentioned.

Chi Sigma Iota Counseling Academic and Professional Honor Society International (CSI) came into being in 1985 in large part as a response to the consequences of lost identity of many young professionals to our field. As a past president of APGA and ACES, I witnessed the confusion that students and graduates experienced while we geared up to establish CACREP, NBCC, and state licensure such as it exists today. The frustration of being told that a professional counselor must work as a "psychologist's assistant" or in a state system where bachelor's degree social workers were preferred to master's degree counselors was intolerable. In the absence of a clear and positive identity as a profession, we lost many competent professionals to other disciplines in their doctoral studies or to other organizations with identities different from that of counseling.

Today, CSI speaks to the need that existed and the readiness for it to be filled. More than 200 university chapters exist in this country and abroad. More than 30,000 persons have accepted an oath of excellence in all that they do personally and professionally as members. About 40% of the membership are practitioners, supervisors, and counselor educators. The remaining 60% are students at the entry level (master's degree) or advanced doctoral level. CSI's mission is to promote excellence in counseling. This is best done by helping all members and chapters to be their best. Pride in the profession, the careers that they have chosen, and the services that they render is a byproduct.

Programs with a strong identity with counseling as a profession increase the likelihood that their graduates will be advocates for a lifespan, human development, facilitative approach to intervention. As a consequence, students in counselor education learn to distinguish themselves from other practitioners with similar competencies and knowledge, for it is not the competencies or knowledge that will distinguish them from others but rather the values and how they share them in professional actions.

Professional counselors are not "just like" or "as good as" some other professional discipline; instead, we add value to the educational and health care systems. The leaders of mental health counseling realized this from the inception of their movement toward professionalization. Although many in mental health counseling today have been coerced into the crisis-oriented, pay-for-pain intervention system, the official philosophical and value orientation of the AMHCA leadership has been firmly grounded in a wellness, developmental orientation to helping since its inception (Seiler & Messina, 1979). As members of interdisciplinary teams, both master's and doctoral counselors have much to offer and will benefit from advertising their professional identity in a clear and unequivocal way. As we now know, advocacy for the profession must start with each member (Barstow, 1998).

Master's Degree Entry Level

Counseling celebrates the competence, contributions, and value of its entry-level professionals. There is no doubt that there is more to learn about human behavior, intervention strategies, and the settings in which we work as helpers than one can master in 2 or even 4 years of full-time study. It is one of the great challenges and questions for both accrediting bodies and university program faculty: How much is enough education to begin practicing in vivo? In the absence of outcome data, critics have reason to question the relevance of standards based on opinion, ratios, and hours that result in universities receiving registration fees and filling classes (Hoyt, 1991). Equally challenging are data suggesting that peers and paraprofessionals are as effective at helping as are those with advanced preparation (Hattie, Sharpley & Rogers, 1984).

However, outcome data exist to demonstrate that counselors' services make a positive difference for their clients (Sexton, Whiston,

Bleuer, & Walz, 1997). Likewise, preparation at the master's degree level has been found to result in better services, for example, to rehabilitation clients (Szymanski, Linkowski, Leahy, Diamond, & Thoreson, 1993). The issue is not so much whether master's-level practitioners can be effective as what greater benefit is derived by more advanced preparation.

Unlike the case with paraprofessionals or self-help facilitators, ethical judgment, accountability for standards of care, and other legal considerations have become critical areas for expertise with professional helpers. These are complex issue areas as well. One area of professional obligation is having evidence of adequate preparation. As a consequence of the growing correlation between the substance of our national standards and the content of counselor preparation, confidence in national standards becomes all the more significant.

Counselor education faculty show that they value the national standards promulgated by CACREP as they continue to seek accreditation under them, and over the years, many more have requested copies for their universities' internal reviews. In short, professional counselors have reason to celebrate the services they provide and feel secure in the knowledge that the foundation they receive in graduate school is both necessary and sufficient for entry into the profession.

State and National Credentials

Counseling is fortunate to have begun its accreditation and state and national credentialing initiatives a number of years after some other disciplines, the problems noted earlier notwithstanding. We learned by their successes and failures. By design and deliberate effort, APGA initiated accreditation, pursuit of licensure legislation in all states, and national certification within a relatively short time span beginning during the late 1970s and early 1980s (Sweeney, 1995). As a result, there has been excellent articulation on all three initiatives. Because state legislatures and Congress—not citizen groups such as counselors—make laws, state laws vary from one legislature to the next. Nevertheless, there is more uniformity among states than might have existed had our leaders not agreed, for example, to use the national preparation standards as a guide in developing model legislation for licensure. Likewise, NBCC's decision to incorporate the core areas of the standards into its national examination and its criteria for credentialing counselors facilitated and strengthened all three initiatives. At the present time, counselors in all but a few states have access to both state and national credentials through a single examination process administered by NBCC.

As noted earlier for all professional disciplines, continuing education is both expected and necessary for the foundation provided by graduate preparation to remain adequate beyond the entry level, regardless of the degree earned. Our state and national boards reinforce the expectation of continued professional education so as to meet credential renewal requirements.

National Leadership

Counseling has been richly blessed with a variety of able leaders who have selflessly donated their time, energy, and resources to the professionalization of counseling. Some of these persons were identified earlier, but there are others who deserve mentioning because, unlike university professors, they did not publish articles or books that others could cite. They were the supervisors or counselors who served in offices, chaired committees, and planned conferences where others could meet, discuss, and formulate policy. Although there are a number of other persons who could be listed, I have chosen to limit those listed to leaders who have since died but deserve mentioning.

Among them are three state and county supervisors of counseling:

Dolph Camp. Camp was a state supervisor and president of the National Association of Guidance Supervisors and Counselor Trainers (later to become ACES) from 1946 to 1948. He organized the first program of guidance services in the state of Arkansas. While serving at the state level, he administered the first program to reimburse school counselor salaries from state funds earmarked for vocational education. Later, under the NDEA, other states followed a similar reimbursement plan. He also served 10 years in the USOE during the growth of school guidance (Sheeley, 1978).

Anna R. Meeks. The elementary guidance movement had a solid advocate in the person of Meeks. She was a supervisor of guidance in the Baltimore County Schools (Maryland) during the late 1940s and became a president of ASCA in 1956-1957. While serving the Baltimore schools, she helped with the early foundation of relations between ASCA and APGA. She subsequently joined the counselor education staff at Oregon State University.

Bill VanHoose. VanHoose was a local director of pupil personnel services in Ohio who cre-ated a model program of services by his vision, power of persuasion, and dynamism. He left county supervision to work in the Ohio State Department of Education, Division of Guidance and Testing, as a school guidance supervisor under the direction of John Odgers, an outstanding leader recognized for program innovation and initiative throughout the country. He later turned to teaching in counselor education at Virginia Polytechnic Institute and University. He continued contributing through publications (VanHoose & Pietrofesa, 1970), teaching, and service. He served as chair of the ACES Commission on Standards Implementation. As noted earlier, there were many who resisted the movement toward national accreditation. We had to have a solid leader negotiating what was to become the ACES accreditation initiative. VanHoose was just such a leader. He and his committee laid the foundation for what ACES needed to move us forward toward national accreditation (VanHoose, 1978).

Counselor educators who have not served as supervisors have been prominent in our history as well. Although many could be listed, the following four persons clearly illustrate the energy, commitment, career dedication, and leadership that served to create significant change in the profession:

David K. Brooks. Brooks is the most junior of all those mentioned here because of an untimely illness and early death. However, his contributions are no less notable. As a graduate student at the University of Georgia, he was appointed to serve on the APGA Licensure Commission in 1975. He dove into the work with a vigor that sometimes only youth can provide. In fact, he continued his interest in licensure and was himself the commission chair after his graduation. An author and eloquent spokesperson for mental health counselors, he served on the ACA Governing Council, on CACREP, and as president of AMHCA. His influence reached far beyond mental health counseling, for as a counselor educator at Syracuse University and Kent State University, he was, first and foremost, a professional counselor.

Harold Cottingham. Cottingham was a professor of counselor education at Florida State University. He served as president of NVGA (1962-1963) and APGA (1964-1965) and authored books on school counseling (Cottingham, 1956). He was very intense in all that he did, and he worked from deeply held values and beliefs. He worked passionately for the profession and believed deeply in its worth. He was active long after his NVGA and APGA offices, for example, as a member of the first APGA Licensure Committee. He considered no job too small or insignificant if it benefited others.

Willis (Bill) E. Dugan. Dugan died only recently. His career included a number of professional and leadership positions as well as being a frequent author and spokesperson for the profession. In addition to being a school counselor and counselor educator, he was a professor and a director of counselor education at the University of Minnesota prior to becoming the executive director of APGA from 1966 to 1971. He was urged to accept the position with APGA at a time critical in its history (Sheeley, 1978). Under his leadership, APGA modernized its operations and focused on building state branches and member services. He came to the executive director position after serving as president of two APGA divisions of that day (Student Personnel for Teacher Education

[SPATE]/Counseling–Association for Humanistic Education and Development [C-AHEAD] [1950-1952] and ACES [1961-1962]) and of APGA (1963-1964). His contributions to the profession, including those mentioned earlier relating to our professional standards, are too numerous to mention. They are nonetheless a legacy from which we all benefit today.

Robert Hoppock. A professor at New York University, Hoppock served as president of NVGA in 1949-1950. He is best known for his work on occupations. He developed one of the first job satisfaction scales used in a variety of studies. He initiated the Occupational Index, the first periodical indexing pamphlets, books, and magazine articles. His text, *Occupational Information* (Hoppock, 1967), published first in 1957, went through several editions as a main text in what was a core course on occupational and education information. He was particularly pleased with his text *Group Guidance* (Hoppock, 1949), published in 1949. This was so because at that time, and for several years thereafter, many counselor educators debated the idea of "multiple" counseling of counselees. So deeply ingrained was the idea of "one-to-one" counseling relationships that group counseling seemed a contradiction in terms for some counselors. Hoppock was not limited by convention, and he delighted in being correct.

Herman J. Peters and Gail F. Farwell. Peters (Ohio State University) and Farwell (University of Wisconsin) published texts together (Farwell & Peters, 1960; Peters & Farwell, 1967) and were equally committed to the profession of counseling. They espoused a developmental view of guidance throughout their careers (Peters & Farwell, 1967). Peters was president of ACES in 1960-1961 and ranked among the most frequent contributors to the ACES journal in its 25th anniversary issue (Hosie et al., 1986). Farwell was treasurer and then president of APGA in 1968-1969, during a time when strong leadership was needed to help the national headquarters operation. Both Peters and Farwell directed NDEA institutes that later proved to be the source of several doctoral graduates who contributed to both the literature and leadership of counseling.

The list of persons to whom we owe much continues today. There are many more whom I can recount from personal and professional affiliations. I have attempted to identify historically significant persons who might otherwise be lost in the editorial practice of using only references of persons published during recent times. It always is a great risk when some persons are recognized and not others. For failing to mention some leaders who no doubt are deserving as well, I hope that a second edition will permit their inclusion. (But given my stated criterion that only those now deceased may be mentioned, I hope that few of the leaders of our profession soon meet the criteria!)

Challenges to Our Future

Herr (1989) provides a succinct and still relevant summary of what lies before us as a profession in this new century:

> Perhaps, in the last analysis, the ultimate challenge to counselors will be that of continuing self-definition as professionals, commitment to lifelong learning to constantly hone and add to their competencies, and the willingness to read widely and experience life fully to stay current with the trends and conceptual models that signal the need for and the processes of behavioral change. . . . In

the future, counselors will need to give more attention to who they are and the influence they have as professionals in a nation of growing pluralism, changing family structures, shifting work conditions and technostress, as well as a society abundant in risk factors and conditions that create personal vulnerability. (pp. 389-390)

I wish to focus on three of these future needs for counseling both as a profession and for us as members of it: self-definition, growing pluralism, and coping with risk factors. Subsequent chapters in this handbook address others as well.

Self-Definition as Professionals

There are two entry points for self-definition. One concerns the profession as a whole, and the other concerns each of us as an individual. Regarding the first, ACA represents the single largest membership organization of professional counselors. Its affiliated divisions address specialty interests of its membership and serve as a common ground based on setting, clientele, or topic. No one division is sufficiently large in numbers to have the same effect in lobbying Congress or federal and state agencies on matters of mutual interest. Likewise, colleagues in other disciplines are more amenable to collaboration with organizations equal to or greater in size of membership.

Originally established during the early 1950s by four distinct organizations representing vocational, school, college personnel, and counselor educators and supervisors, the founders of APGA hoped to reduce administrative overhead, provide their membership with better services, and lobby more effectively as a unified group. I believe that these still are worthy goals today. As we move into the coming decade, unity in our message, our methods, and use of our resources will be critical to providing the leverage needed to effect change on behalf of those we serve.

On the matter of self-definition from an individual practitioner's point of view, I am reminded of Sam Gladding's introduction of himself to a new group or audience: "Hi, I'm Sam, I'm a counselor." What better way to clear up one's identity crisis! In some ways, it is just that simple to decide, but it is not sufficient to stop there. One does not become "professional" simply by graduating or earning a professional credential.

Professionalism is a process. There are milestones along the way, and graduation is one of them. Earning a credential as a professional counselor is another. Participating in local, state, and national organizations of professional counselors is another. In many settings, counselors are a minority on a staff. Through affiliations with other professional counselors, there is opportunity for continuing education, service, and affirmation in one's chosen career. In addition, there is more political influence in numbers. Otherwise, the job setting may define who one is, what one can do, and how long one will be permitted to do it.

Growing Pluralism

I do not wish to overgeneralize, but I do believe that one of the greatest challenges to us as a profession starts with each of us as a person. We are more than scientists using knowledge to manipulate other persons for their own greater good. We are living, dynamic humans in our own state of evolving. We are just as enmeshed in the trials of our own lives as our clients are enmeshed in the trials of their lives. We must be students of ourselves as well. We live in an increasingly diverse society. As Dewey admonished during the early 20th century, let us "withstand the efforts of forces that would fragment the national culture by fostering fear and hatred of minorities, immigrants, and others who have traditionally been targets of such demagoguery" (quoted in Hickman & Alexander, 1998, p. xii). And as Martin Luther King, Jr., prayed so eloquently, let the majority who have been silent find their voice for what is right. So, how do we do that as a profession and as individuals?

I think that we should expect our professional leaders to model appropriate concern and sensitivity to issues of diversity. Although there are pitfalls to advocacy such as overzealousness, there is less likely to be such concern when proactive attention is addressed in planning and execution of events and activities (Locke, 1998). Members can foster an expectation that, as a profession founded on the premise of social equality and the right to pursue happiness for all, we expect no less for our members or for those they serve.

We have excellent resources available to help us in the process (Lee & Richardson, 1991; Locke, 1998; McFadden, 1993). Under the leadership of an effective facilitator at a local, state, or national conference or workshop, our learning can be accelerated immensely. We have an ethical responsibility to make the effort.

Coping With Risk Factors

Two thirds of all deaths in this country are the result of lifestyle factors (Myers et al., 2000). In this time of managed care, counselors no less than those in other disciplines are being pressed to intervene at crisis points in the lives of clients when prevention would have been far more effective and less costly, economically and in terms of emotional pain. It is sad but true that many counselors have had to capitulate to these pressures and compromise their own best judgment about needed care for their clients.

As a profession, counseling must ask itself if it wants to continue as a part of the problem of our health and educational systems or collaborate with others in moving it toward change. Prevention and pressing for optimal wellness of all persons sounds far-fetched to many persons. But insurance companies, businesses, and some government agencies are convinced that to reduce health care cost and the violence in schools and communities, and to realize the untapped potential of many that live outside of the "American dream," a new plan and set of policies are needed. Other disciplines already are claiming that they should be among the brokers of a new system.

The history of counseling reflects a sound basis for counselors as particularly well suited to participate in initiatives designed to promote human development over the life span. Efforts can be instituted at all levels—local, state, and national (CSI, 1998, 1999). At least as important as our national organizations taking a proactive stand nationally to join those who wish to redirect our schools and health care systems to a wellness developmental focus, each of us must attend to the admonition "Counselor heal thyself"; that is, we must model our personal commitment to a wellness approach to life.

Professional counselors are no less at risk than their clients unless they practice what they are taught to "preach." Even though we are a profession based on the value of promoting optimal human development for all persons, counselors are in a high-stress occupation. The past half century has resulted in greater stress for all persons (Herr, 1989). Technology has initiated instant communications that create a sense of immediacy where it did not exist before. Open spaces in time and living environment are precious. As a consequence, a deliberate effort must be made to moderate the effects of such stress.

There is compelling scientific evidence regarding the attitudes, values, and behaviors of those persons who live long and well (Myers et al., 2000). Managing our own lives so as to model this for our clients and students, however, is a constant challenge. We, like them, need a confidant, a trusted friend—someone with whom to share joys and sorrows, triumphs and setbacks. Like them, our physical, emotional, and spiritual well-being is essential to our quality of life. Like them, we require encouragement to monitor our openness and readiness for change (Herr, 2000; Prochaska, Norcross, & DiClemente, 1994). To be responsible, to act ethically, all of us will strive to be our best selves. No one can or should ask more.

Conclusion

I have traced the dominant roots of counseling during the 20th century. These include the profound influence of societal events surrounding the industrialization of our economy and two world wars. Each contributed to the apparent need for vocational guidance and tools such as measurement to be more effective. The plight of those in need of mental health care was first highlighted near the turn of the 20th century. It was not until the latter half of the 20th century that national legislation created a need for community counselors and, subsequently, mental health counselors as a specialty within counseling. History shows, however, that it is the developmental, life-span orientation of counseling that is most fundamental to its philosophical basis.

Counseling historically has been a part of education both as a discipline and within its institutions. Schools and educators were the first to embrace guidance and counseling as a vital function for all people at all levels of education. Counselor preparation programs are located principally in colleges and schools of education as a result of this historical connection. Psychology, sociology, anthropology, and demography all have been important to counselor preparation, as noted in our earliest national standards (ACES, 1979). Counseling psychology, however, has the closest relationship to counseling through shared literature, philosophical orientation, and membership in ACA. The tensions between those in counseling psychology and those in counselor education are attributable in large measure to marketplace issues between psychologists and counselors in general, not (in my opinion) to substantive differences in goals or means for serving our clients.

The future of counseling might better be portrayed as a matrix rather than as a linear design. We are emerging in a global economy where "enemies" are quickly becoming customers and vendors, where violence is prevalent at every level from genocide to murder in the schools. Breakthroughs in medicine promise complete codes for all of our human conditions with a promise for cures or reengineering in the future. Our health care system and schools have been under scrutiny—some would say attack— for failing to meet the most basic needs of our citizenry. The list could go on.

What I have suggested in the concluding part of this chapter is setting a priority on that part of the future over which we have some measure of control. I have noted that the profession and each of us as a part of it can help by being proud of and clear about our professional identity. We have reason to do so. Second, we must address the increasingly pluralist nature of our society for the sake of sanity and social equality. We can best do this by ensuring that our professional associations are themselves inclusive and reflect the diversity in our society. Coercion is the least desirable way in which to win cooperation. So, by education and opportunity to interact with persons of different cultural backgrounds, I believe that we can have a more sensitive, truly caring community of professional helpers. This starts with all of us making a genuine and persistent effort to appropriately confront our ignorance and share our insights on these matters.

Third, we as a profession still have a window of opportunity to participate in redirecting our health care and educational institutions toward a preventive wellness orientation. The longer we delay, however, the less available the opportunity will be. Leadership at the national and state levels is required. If all of us consider this a priority for ourselves, then there is greater likelihood that we will advocate such services for our clients and students.

Finally, "Counselor, heal thyself." The pursuit of wellness is a choice each of us can make. Excuses are what we see when we take our eyes off of our goals. We should not ask less of ourselves than we do of our students and clients. Subsequent chapters share more about these and other issues before us in the near- and long-term future. None is beyond our means to address. Together, we have accomplished a great deal in just a few short decades of the past century. Now, we have all of this new century to realize the balance of our potential.

References

American Personnel and Guidance Association. (1974). *Counselor licensure: A position statement.* Falls Church, VA: Author. (Adopted in 1975)

American Personnel and Guidance Association. (1981). *Alternatives for counselor preparation accreditation* (adopted March 1981). Falls Church, VA: Author.

Association for Counselor Education and Supervision. (1979). *Standards for preparation in counselor education.* Falls Church, VA: American Personnel and Guidance Association.

Aubrey, R. F. (1977). Historical development of guidance and counseling and implications for the future. *Personnel and Guidance Journal, 55,* 288-295.

Barstow, S. (1998). Challenges and opportunities of counselor advocacy. *Exemplar, 13*(3), 1-2.

Beers, C. (1908). *A mind that found itself.* New York: Longman Green.

Brewer, J. M. (1932). *Education as guidance.* New York: Macmillan.

Brewer, J. M. (1942). *History of vocational guidance.* New York: Harper & Brothers.

Chi Sigma Iota. (1998). Counselor advocacy leadership conferences. *Exemplar, 13*(2), 1.

Chi Sigma Iota. (1999). Counselor advocacy conference II. *Exemplar, 14*(1), 3, 5.

Cottingham, H. F. (1956). *Guidance in elementary schools.* Bloomington, IL: McKnight & McKnight.

Davis, J. (1914). *Vocational and moral guidance.* Boston: Ginn.

Dugan, W. (1961). Critical concerns of counselor education. *Counselor Education and Supervision, 1,* 5-11.

Farwell, G. F., & Peters, H. J. (Eds.). (1960). *Guidance readings for counselors.* Chicago: Rand McNally.

Ginzberg, E. (1971). *Career guidance.* New York: McGraw-Hill.

Gladding, S. T. (2000). *Counseling a comprehensive profession* (4th ed.). Upper Saddle River, NJ: Merrill/Prentice Hall.

Hamrin, S. A., & Erickson, C. E. (1939). *Guidance in the secondary school.* New York: Appleton-Century.

Hattie, J. A., Sharpley, C. F., & Rogers, H. J. (1984). Comparative effectiveness of professional and paraprofessional helpers. *Psychological Bulletin, 95,* 534-541.

Herr, E. L. (1989). *Counseling in a dynamic society: Opportunities and challenges.* Alexandria, VA: American Association for Counseling and Development.

Herr, E. L. (2000, March). *The quest for personal excellence.* Paper presented at the meeting of the American Counseling Association, Washington, DC.

Hickman, L. A., & Alexander, T. M. (1998). *The essential Dewey pragmatism, education, democracy* (Vol. 1). Bloomington: Indiana University Press.

Hill, G. E. (1967). The profession and standards for counselor education. *Counselor Education and Supervision, 6,* 130-136.

Hill, G. E. (1974). *Management and improvement of guidance* (2nd ed.). Englewood Cliffs, NJ: Prentice Hall.

Hill, G. E., & Luckey, E. B. (1969). *Guidance for children in elementary schools.* New York: Appleton-Century-Crofts.

Hollis, J. W. (1997). *Counselor preparation 1996-98: Programs, faculty, trends* (9th ed.). Washington, DC: Taylor & Francis.

Hollis, J. W. (2000). *Counselor preparation 1999-2001: Programs, faculty, trends* (10th ed.). Philadelphia: Accelerated Development/Taylor & Francis.

Hoppock, R. (1949). *Group guidance.* New York: McGraw-Hill.

Hoppock, R. (1967). *Occupational information.* New York: McGraw-Hill.

Hosie, T. W., Poret, M., Lauck, P., & Rosier, B. (1986). Contributions to *Counselor Education and Supervision* for Volumes 0-25, 1961-1986. *Counselor Education and Supervision, 25,* 284-288.

Hoyt, K. B. (1974). Professional preparation for vocational guidance. In E. L. Herr (Ed.), *Vocational guidance and human development* (pp. 502-527). Boston: Houghton Mifflin.

Hoyt, K. B. (1991). Concerns about accreditation and credentialing: A personal view. In F. O. Bradley (Ed.), *Credentialing in counseling* (pp. 69-80). Alexandria, VA: Association for Counselor Education and Supervision.

Hutson, P. W. (1968). *The guidance function in education* (2nd ed.). New York: Appleton-Century-Crofts.

Jones, A. J. (1934). *Principles of guidance* (2nd ed.). New York: McGraw-Hill.

Lee, C. C., & Richardson, B. L. (1991). *Multicultural issues in counseling: New approaches to diversity.* Alexandria, VA: American Association for Counseling and Development.

Locke, D. C. (1998). *Increasing multicultural understanding: A comprehensive model.* Thousand Oaks, CA: Sage.

McFadden, J. (Ed.). (1993). *Transcultural counseling.* Alexandria, VA: American Counseling Association.

Miller, C. H. (1961). *Foundations of guidance.* New York: Harper & Brothers.

Myers, J. E., Sweeney, T. J., & Witmer, J. M. (2000). Counseling for wellness: A holistic model for treatment planning. *Journal of Counseling and Development, 78,* 251-266.

Parsons, F. (1909). *Choosing a vocation*. Boston: Houghton Mifflin.

Peters, H. J., & Farwell, G. F. (1967). *Guidance: A developmental approach*. Chicago: Rand McNally.

Prochaska, J. O., Norcross, J. C., & DiClemente, C. C. (1994). *Changing for good: A revolutionary six-stage program for overcoming bad habits and moving your life positively forward*. New York: Avon Books.

Seiler, G., & Messina, J. J. (1979). Toward professional identity: Dimensions of mental health counseling in perspective. *AMHCA Journal, 1*, 3-8.

Sexton, T., Whiston, S. C., Bleuer, J. C., & Walz, G. (1997). *Integrating outcome research in counseling practice*. Alexandria, VA: American Counseling Association.

Sheeley, V. L. (1978). *Presidential reporting: Echoes abound from APGA leaders*. Scottsville, KY: Gerald Printing Service.

Shertzer, B., & Stone, S. C. (1971). *Fundamentals of guidance*. Boston: Houghton Mifflin.

Stripling, R. O. (1978). Standards and accreditation in counselor education: A proposal. *Personnel and Guidance Journal, 56*, 608-611.

Stripling, R. O., & Dugan, W. E. (1961). The cooperative study of counselor education standards. *Counselor Education and Supervision, 1*, 34-35.

Super, D. E. (1955). Transition: From vocational guidance to counseling psychology. *Journal of Counseling Psychology, 42*, 132-136.

Sweeney, T. J. (1991). Counselor credentialing: Purpose and origin. In F. O. Bradley (Ed.), *Credentialing in counseling* (pp. 1-12). Alexandria, VA: Association for Counselor Education and Supervision.

Sweeney, T. J. (1995). Accreditation, credentialing, professionalization: The role of specialties. *Journal of Counseling and Development, 74*, 117-125.

Sweeney, T. J., & Sturdevant, A. D. (1974). Licensure in the helping professions: Anatomy of an issue. *Personnel and Guidance Journal, 52*, 575-580.

Sweeney, T. J., & Wittmer, J. (1983). *Council on Postsecondary Accreditation preapplication Phase I: Demonstration of need*. Unpublished manuscript, Council for Accreditation of Counseling and Related Educational Programs.

Sweeney, T. J., & Wittmer, J. (1984). *Council on Postsecondary Accreditation preapplication Phase II: Demonstration of capacity*. Unpublished manuscript, Council for Accreditation of Counseling and Related Educational Programs.

Szymanski, E. M., Linkowski, D. C., Leahy, M. J., Diamond, E. E., & Thoreson, R. W. (1993). Validation of rehabilitation counseling accreditation and certification knowledge areas: Methodology and initial results. *Rehabilitation Counseling Bulletin, 37*(2), 109-122.

VanHoose, W. H. (1978, March). *1978 Commission on Standards Implementation Report: Association for Counselor Education and Supervision*. Paper presented at the meeting of the American Personnel and Guidance Association, Washington, DC.

VanHoose, W. H., & Pietrofesa, J. J. (Eds.). (1970). *Counseling and guidance in the twentieth century: Reflections and reformulations*. Boston: Houghton Mifflin.

Weinrach, S. G., Lustig, D., Chan, F., & Thomas, K. R. (1998). Publication patterns of the *Personnel and Guidance/Journal of Counseling and Development: 1978-1993*. *Journal of Counseling and Development, 76*, 427-435.

Wrenn, C. G. (1962). *Counselor in a changing world*. Washington, DC: American Personnel and Guidance Association.

Wright, G. N. (1980). *Total rehabilitation*. Boston: Little, Brown.

CHAPTER TWO

Counseling

Evolution of the Profession

RICHARD W. BRADLEY
JANE A. COX

When considering the evolution of this profession, one must recognize that the word *counseling* seldom is used by itself. For example, one is not just a counselor but also works as a college counselor, mental health counselor, or school counselor. The position is modified by an agency or a setting. Others prefer to recognize a type of counseling such as academic, rehabilitation, or career. Still others identify themselves as counselors of a particular population (ranging in age from youth to geriatric groups) or disorder (ranging from attention deficit to visual impairment disorders). A final example might be counselors associated with a particular academic training orientation such as counselor education or college student personnel. Each of these modifiers has some unique aspects while being intertwined with the whole.

Thus, the history of counseling might be thought of as a ball of multicolored yarns. The ball has a unified structure while also being made up of various individual strands or themes. The green strand could be labeled *career counseling*. It has a history of its own that can be described and chronicled as a single entity as it wraps around other strands or themes. Another strand might be red and labeled *college counseling*. It, too, is distinct but wraps with and binds to the green, yellow, and blue threads. Our endeavor is to describe how some of these strands or themes intertwine to make the whole.

The profession of counseling has been and is being shaped by people and events that preceded us. Historians usually separate the people and events into personalistic and naturalistic approaches. The former, often called the "great person" view, holds that major contributions are the function of innovative or revolutionary ideas. Sigmund Freud's contribution of talk therapy is an example of this view. "The naturalistic view, on the other hand, asserts that prior cultural change must prepare a climate of receptivity for a radically new conception or movement" (Borow, 1990, p. 266). Thus, persons such as Freud and other pioneers must be placed in the cultural context of their times. To have a major impact on the profession, these persons reacted to cultural change. Therefore, this brief history of counseling focuses more on events than on people. As Borow (1990) noted, "To have had a significant impact on the course of history, they will have had to be moving with the prevailing tide" (p. 266). To begin this look at the evolution of counseling, the context of this evolution is considered, followed by discussions of the strands of career, school, mental health, and family counseling. Finally, we speculate about evolving perspectives during the next decade.

The Context

Although history does not repeat itself, in some respects there are parallels between the ends of the 19th and 20th centuries. For a contemporary audience, we would like to sketch the evolution of counseling as a tale of two centuries. Counseling, as we think of it today,

evolved from the guidance movement at the end of the 19th century somewhat as a reaction to social change. Counseling still is a profession that adjusts so as to remain responsive to the effects of social change on people.

In the United States, the mid- and late 1800s were marked by a devastating civil war from which the country redefined itself. The mid- and late 1900s were marked by a divisive "cold war" from which much of the world still is redefining itself. Social orders changed. Old ethnic and religious differences festered. Persons who participated in these wars returned to, or in many cases left, their homes changed.

Similar to the changes wrought by war were two revolutions. The industrial revolution initiated an abrupt shift from a self-sufficient agrarian society to one focused on manufactured goods. Today, only 1% of society is actively involved in producing the food we eat. Now, multinational corporations handle food production and distribution. Coca-Cola and Pepsi are everywhere, and the world's biggest food company, Nestlé, does business virtually everywhere in the world. The second revolution, a technology-driven one, began taking place at the end of the 20th century. The so-called information revolution changed work and society as much as did the industrial revolution. Television, personal computers, cell phones, and pagers are altering the ways in which people deal with each other today, just as 19th-century power-driven looms made spinning wheels museum pieces. Even though there was the telegraph at the end of the 19th century, most information still traveled at the speed of a horse. Now, it travels at the speed of light.

While totally different in a technological sense, these revolutions have had some similar impacts on workers. During the 19th century, machines rapidly displaced workers, many of whom had trouble adjusting. Time-honored skills became obsolete. Today, a similar pattern is occurring as computers and corporate restructuring displace some workers and cause others to acquire new job skills.

Demography of the country also is important to consider. The population more than tripled from slightly less than 80 million in 1900 to an estimated 275 million in 2000. Along with this increase, industrialization was a decided movement from rural to urban settings. Cities grew and grew throughout the 20th century, and in 1950 the census bureau noted that more than half of the population lived in urban centers. A new term, *megalopolis,* was coined to describe the urban sprawl that stretched along the East Coast, the West Coast, and south of the Great Lakes. But these population centers continued to change. Steel-producing and automobile-manufacturing cities of the industrial revolution turned into a "rust belt." New cities grew around information technology and were labeled "silicon valleys." City centers experienced rapid demographic shifts such as social and ethnic alterations. Similar to the long-established European enclaves in major cities (e.g., Irish in Boston, Polish in Chicago), large ethnic communities sprung up (e.g., Cubans in Miami, Koreans in Los Angeles).

The nation's diversity helps to make us progressive. Immigrants continue to provide stimulation and entrepreneurship (Stanley & Danko, 1996). Yet, as a diverse nation, we still have problems integrating persons from a variety of cultural backgrounds including those who have been here for centuries as well as the newly arrived. Race is a good example. At the end of the 19th century, former slaves were trying to find their place in society. Segregation

was challenged by the civil rights movement. Integration moved forward with momentum during the last half of the 20th century, but unfortunately, there still is racism in America.

Career Counseling: Moving Beyond Matching

With the 1909 posthumous publication of *Choosing a Vocation* (Parsons, 1909/1967), Frank Parsons often is given credit as the "father of guidance" (Aubrey, 1977). See Table 2.1 for a listing of additional major events in the history of counseling during the 20th century. Penner's (1967) introduction in the reprinted edition states, "Parsons is rightfully regarded as the first modern practitioner and theorist of the profession" (p. v). Rockwell and Rothney (1961) called him a "utopian social reformer" because of the breadth and social significance of his writings. Although Parsons' principles for vocational guidance are quite simple, they have had a pervasive influence on the profession. His three-point method for choosing a vocation was as follows: (a) understand self, (b) understand the world of work, and (c) apply reason to match these understandings (Parsons, 1909/1967).

Similar thinking seems to have been around since the first division of labor. Several contemporary authors have identified Parsonian-type ideas in works published centuries earlier. Chambless and Zytowski (1987) located the principal elements in a Renaissance Southern European work of 1468 titled *Mirror of Human Life.* Carson and Altai (1994) presented evidence showing how the basic tenets of Parsons' matching model can be located in the Arabic text translated as *Treatises of the Brothers of*

TABLE 2.1   Major Events in the History of Counseling During the 20th Century

Year	Event
1909	Parsons' *Choosing a Vocation* published
1910	First National Conference on Vocational Guidance held in Boston
1913	National Vocational Guidance Association founded
1915	First professional guidance journal, the *Vocational Guidance Bulletin,* published
1935	Teachers College of Columbia University formed Division of Individual Development and Guidance
1939	*Dictionary of Occupational Titles* published (U.S. Employment Service, 1939)
	E. G. Williamson published *How to Counsel Students: A Manual of Techniques for Clinical Counselors,* which became primer for "directive" therapy (Williamson, 1939)
1941-1945	World War II ensued
	Audiotape recorders became available for use in training counselors
1942	G.I. Bill established
	Within 4 years of passage of Public Laws 16 and 346 by Congress, 415 colleges and universities established veterans guidance centers, which were forerunners of college counseling centers
1942	Carl Rogers published *Counseling and Psychotherapy,* which became primer for "nondirective" (later called "client-centered") therapy (Rogers, 1942)
1945	Teachers College of Columbia University formed Department of Guidance
1946	Counseling and Guidance established as a founding division of the American Psychological Association
	Veterans Administration Counseling Services established
1952	National Vocational Guidance Association merged with American College Personnel Association to form American Personnel and Guidance Association (now called American Counseling Association)
1954	Vocational rehabilitation amendments provided grants to prepare rehabilitation counselors
1958	National Defense Education Act passed
1958-1966	National Defense Education Act Training Institutes for school counselors conducted
1963	Community Mental Health Centers Act passed
1965	First computer-based guidance prototype developed
1972	Council on Rehabilitation Education founded to accredit rehabilitation counselor education
1975	Virginia passed first regulatory act for professional counselors
1976	Virginia became first state to license counselors
1981	Council on Accreditation of Counseling and Related Educational Programs created
	National Board for Certified Counselors established
1983	American Personnel and Guidance Association changed name to American Association for Counseling and Development
1992	American Association for Counseling and Development changed name to American Counseling Association

Purity, probably written around 955 A.D. in what now is southern Iraq. Although not specifically relating their work to Parsons (1909),

Dumont and Carson (1995) went back even further in time. They argued that as societies became complex, there was a need to differentiate among individuals for the infrastructure to work. They suggested that Eastern Mediterranean Egyptians, Semites, and Greeks, as well as Eurasian Chinese societies, possessed the basic elements of vocational psychology thousands of years ago.

One challenging point regarding these cultures and today's multiculturalism involves the role of individuals. Dumont and Carson (1995) pointed out how Eastern Mediterranean societies, especially the Greeks, placed extreme importance on individual accomplishment. Plato's *Republic,* for example, was based on the meritocracy of individuals. Career counseling today, from a Parsonian tradition, would place responsibility for career decision making on the individual. Cheatham (1990) challenged this as a Eurocentric orientation that values competition, individuation, and mastery over nature. In opposition, he thinks that the African tradition has no central emphasis on the individual. The African, according to Cheatham, is authenticated in terms of others. This argument sounds quite similar to what Gilligan (1982) suggested for North American women.

Miller (1973) translated Parsons' three steps into the modern counseling terminology of appraisal, providing occupational information, and providing counseling. From Parsons' time until about World War II, vocational guidance consisted primarily of giving information about occupations. If individuals received help in appraisal, then it usually was in assessing some trait such as interests. If assistance was provided with the reasoning process, then it was oriented toward the notion of matching persons with jobs.

It was mid-century before major reconceptualizations of vocational guidance came into focus. Miller (1973) identified three themes. First "was an increasing recognition of the basic importance of personality dynamics in vocational choice and adjustment" (p. 11). The National Vocational Guidance Association (1949), for example, recommended "counseling on problems of personal-social development" as one of the objectives for vocational guidance. There were multiple antecedents for this change, but it was clearly exemplified in efforts to provide assistance to veterans returning from World War II. The advising of these veterans under programs of the Veterans Administration (VA) probably was the most extensive single guidance effort undertaken in the United States. The VA for the first time authorized personal adjustment and rehabilitation counseling and changed its name from "advisement and guidance" to "counseling services." Aside from the direct services to veterans themselves, there also were important effects on educational programs. Funds were made available on a contractual basis to public and private institutions for counseling services. Many colleges started their counseling centers and counselor education programs with these funds.

The second major change in conceptualization was a move away from the notion of matching persons with jobs toward a view that individuals move through stages of career development. This was evidenced by a shift in the National Career Development Association's definition of *vocational guidance,* a shift away from what is to be chosen and toward the characteristics of the chooser (e.g., developmental characteristics), reducing the effects of a pure trait and factor approach (Herr & Cramer, 1996). The concept of using stages to describe development permeated much of psychology during the 1950s and 1960s. Developmental tasks were described by Robert Havighurst, Erik Erickson evolved psychosocial stages, and Jean Piaget described cognitive stages of development. For the vocational field, it was Eli

Ginzburg who first introduced stage theory in *Occupational Choice* (Ginzberg, Ginzburg, Axelrad, & Herma, 1951). Ginzberg and colleagues found occupational choice to be a process that took place over 6 to 10 years, during which individuals progressed through a fantasy stage, became tentative, and finally moved into a realistic period. During the late 1950s, Donald Super and colleagues expanded career development theory to include the total life span rather than limiting it to childhood and adolescence. Also during this period and into the 1960s, the term *vocational* was replaced by *career* in counseling and guidance.

The third reconceptualization that Miller (1973) noted was a gradual change in the meaning of work. Previously, work had been given Western European religious and social class connotations. Members of religious orders performed certain manual tasks, or individuals spoke of a religious calling to some professional position. And European feudal class distinctions still reflected differences between the commoner and the landed gentry. By mid-century, work had become secularized rather than a "calling"; World War II had transformed orientations toward work. Ordinary men and women, not just sons and daughters of the landed gentry, were drawn together overseas and on the home front with unity of purpose. Brokaw (1998) called these men and women the "greatest generation." They overcame obstacles in war and transferred the "I can do it" attitude to the economy. Wartime Americans were forced to confront their beliefs regarding who can do what work and discrimination by gender and race. Although discrimination remains an unresolved challenge in society, the war experience accelerated solutions.

The children of the "greatest generation," born between 1946 and 1964, were dubbed the "baby boomers." Their combined orientation toward consumerism and affluence continued to change the orientation toward work in the last half of the century. And their identity was defined not so much by the work they did as by what work provided for them. Yet, the baby boomers converse, the so-called underclass, brought to light our society's have and have-not reality that career counselors of the 21st century must address.

During the past several decades, rapid changes in science, technology, and society have caused many to question long-held assumptions about the existence of an objective reality. The rise of theories such as chaos theory, which recognizes the complexity and unpredictability in what once were viewed as stable systems, has challenged beliefs about absolute truths. Similarly, conceptualizations of career counseling have continued to evolve, and the positivist assumptions underlying much of career theory have been challenged. Logical positivists attempt to "extract knowledge from reality and validate it against theory" (Savickas, 1995, p. 364). As Savickas (1995) noted, this is evidenced when a career counselor considers career variables in isolation, apart from the client's context, with the focus on quantifying such variables using assessment instruments. By contrast, social constructivists assume that knowledge is the result of social interaction and negotiation. Therefore, career counselors pay more attention to clients and the "stories" they tell rather than giving primary attention to the results of assessment instruments.

Social constructivist concepts have many implications for career counseling. Of particular importance, they broaden the boundaries around what may be thought of as career counseling by challenging counselors to consider clients more holistically and in context. But as

Krumboltz (1993) noted, the term *career counseling* is problematic in and of itself because it distinguishes career counseling from personal counseling, thus limiting a more holistic view of the client. Yet, personal and career concerns are inextricably woven together. Therefore, career counselors must attend to the complexity of the whole person.

Undoubtedly, the assumptions underlying career counseling, and even the definition of what constitutes *career,* will continue to evolve. Yet, no one can ignore or dismiss that work will continue to be a part of life. Parsons (1909/1967) thought that individuals had the capacity to know themselves, understand the world of work, and make reasonable choices. We continue to affirm his beliefs.

School Counseling: From Moral Education to National Defense

Although Parsons' early work focused on young people not in school, he hoped that "vocational guidance would become a part of the public school system in every community" (Aubrey, 1977, p. 289). As early as 1906, vocational guidance was introduced to the New York City schools by a principal named Eli Weaver. By 1910, he reported at the First National Conference on Vocational Guidance that "every high school in the city of New York had a committee of teachers who were actively attempting to aid boys and girls to discover what they could do best and how to secure a job in which their abilities could be used to the fullest advantages of both employer and employee" (Rockwell & Rothney, 1961, p. 352). Also at the turn of the century, another school principal, Jesse B. Davis, in Grand Rapids, Michigan, had English students write themes on topics such as "what I

will do when I grow up." He advocated what historians called the social gospel, which was essentially an attempt to bring church views into the schools. Rockwell and Rothney (1961) described Davis's view of counseling as preaching to students "about the moral value of hard work, ambition, honesty, and the development of good character" (p. 350). Much of early school guidance involved an infusion of self-help ideas into the curriculum initiated by social reformers.

Educational opportunities were expanding for the poor and immigrant groups. Leadership of our emerging profession came primarily from idealistic and committed reformers. There was a slow and steady expansion of vocational guidance in schools. By 1910, 35 U.S. cities had or were working on plans, and by 1937, half of the cities with populations of 10,000 or more had vocational guidance programs in their schools (Aubrey, 1977). But the actual number of school counselors, as we think of them today, was low. For example, it was estimated that there were only some 50 school counselors in 1917.

Although vocational guidance was stimulated by the changing patterns of industrialization, a major economic depression during the 1930s clearly slowed growth. Yet, as the numbers of children and adolescents attending public schools grew, schools had to adapt. Guidance workers in schools often took titles such as dean of boys or girls. Over the half century from 1908 until 1958, the number of school counselors grew to 12,000.

During the late 1950s and early 1960s, a remarkable shift occurred in the concept of education that affected school counseling. The Cold War with the Soviet Union made Americans deeply suspicious of the Russians. When the Soviets launched a satellite in 1957, education became an instrument of national defense. Congress passed the National Defense Education Act of 1958 (NDEA), which provided a springboard for the rapid development of the counseling profession. Title V-A of the NDEA provided monies to support school counseling programs, and Title V-B established funds to support the training of secondary school counselors. Congress charged educational institutions with responsibility for identifying and nurturing talented students, particularly those with scientific abilities. The training programs, called NDEA Guidance and Counseling Institutes, were to be operated separately from other academic programs at state universities. These institutes created a revolution in counseling (Bourne, 1988). Although designed to train school counselors, the institutes enhanced and improved counselor education programs across the country by setting training standards and by serving as the training programs for the next generation of counselor educators.

In less than a decade, the number of school counselors quadrupled and the counselor-to-student ratio decreased from 1 to 960 in 1958 to 1 to 450 by 1966-1967 (Aubrey, 1977). By 1999, this ratio had grown to 1 to 513 nationwide, with great variation among states. California had the highest ratio (1 counselor for every 1,182 students), followed by Minnesota, Utah, Arizona, Illinois, Ohio, Mississippi, Michigan, Tennessee, and Colorado, whereas Vermont had the lowest ratio (1 to 313) ("100,000 New Counselors," 1999; Schmitt, 1999).

What will it take to lower the school counselor-to-student ratios? Historically, the biggest single event was federal legislation, casting education as national defense in 1958. The June and September 1999 issues of *Counseling Today* contained several articles about legislation

to fund 100,000 new elementary and secondary counselors. The Russians' launching a satellite named *Sputnik* was an impetus for the NDEA in 1958. It is unfortunate that high school names and towns (from Heath High School in Paducah, Kentucky, to Columbine High School in Littleton, Colorado) may be the watchwords for legislation to increase the number of school counselors for the next generation of students. Yet, protecting children from violence and killings in schools is a type of national defense. School counselors are vital to this endeavor.

From Freud's Couch to Mental Health Centers

Tracing the strands of our multicolored ball of yarn called *counseling* becomes a matter of choice. Not all the histories will be unraveled, but one fascinating story is the process of making talk therapy available to the general public. Most often, this tale begins with Freud's psychoanalysis.

Torrey (1992), in a not particularly complimentary book titled *Freudian Fraud* and subtitled *The Malignant Effects of Freud's Theory on American Cultural Thought,* used a dramatic metaphor. For nearly half a century, according to Torrey, Freud's ideas were nurtured, or grown, like exotic house plants in a few select hothouses such as Vienna, Berlin, and New York. But after World War II, the theory and practice of psychoanalysis grew like cultural kudzu on the American landscape. Although American intellectuals of the 1930s and 1940s were attracted to the ideas of Karl Marx, Torrey claimed that the phenomenal spread of Freud's ideas shifted their interest from socialism to psychoanalysis. Although psychoanalysis of the

1930s was an unusual and little-known theory of the importance of childhood sexual experiences on adult personality, by the 1950s Freud became a quasi-religious figure sent to redeem his children by confessional and transference. During the late 1950s, popular press articles about analysis were rampant, from "How I Got Caught In My Husband's Analysis" in *Good Housekeeping* to "Psychoanalysis Broke Up My Marriage" in *Cosmopolitan* (as reported in Torrey, 1992, p. 120). Margaret Mead, a respected cultural anthropologist, used many Freudian notions in her work, including the column she wrote in *Redbook* from 1961 to 1979. The impact of Freud's notions were everywhere in the American popular culture, from plays by Tennessee Williams, Eugene O'Neill, and T. S. Eliot to Alfred Hitchcock movies. Benjamin Spock became a missionary on the pediatric frontier, and Karl Menninger was a proponent of how early childhood influenced criminal behavior. Even at the end of the 20th century, the insanity defense in the U.S. legal system was directly related to Freud.

Although pervasive, psychoanalysis never was widely used by the masses. It generally was time-consuming and costly. Patients benefiting most from analysis were middle-aged men and women oppressed by a sense of futility and searching for meaning in life. Today, we would speak of these persons in existential terms. Yet Freud, after his death, revolutionized counseling.

In this country, prior to the Freudian revolution, guidance was the norm. There were a few hothouses where select orientations to guidance were encouraged. Parsons' Vocational Guidance Bureau in Boston, Davis's social gospel in Michigan schools, and Reed's social Darwinism in Seattle schools were examples (Rockwell & Rothney, 1961). If counseling, as we think of it, occurred at all, it generally was offered from a parental/expert orientation; counselors were authorities who had the skill and knowledge to determine what was most helpful for their clients (Aubrey, 1977, p. 291).

During the 1930s and 1940s, counseling often was linked to testing. It was hoped that psychometric assessment would provide a scientific base for understanding individuals' capabilities, interests, strengths, and limitations. The underlying trait-factor philosophy took a firm hold over counseling. The model that evolved became known as directive counseling or, as practiced by some, test-and-tell counseling.

This model began to erode during the 1940s with individuals' greater desire for freedom and personal autonomy. "It was abetted by the newly founded affluence following the war, a full employment market, the opportunities offered to returning veterans by the GI Bill, and as a general extension of education to hitherto denied audiences" (Aubrey, 1977, p. 292). The spirit of freedom, combined with a willingness to change one's life after the war and the programs offered by the VA, created a revolution in counseling. Services were available to the masses. Yet, directive counseling did not fit, and although psychoanalysis was helping to popularize individuals' search for meaning in the magazines, movies, and plays of the 1940s, 1950s, and 1960s, it was simply too long and expensive for wide application. However, Freud's lineage may, more important, be linked to a generation of brilliant young thinkers trained as psychoanalysts who rejected his approach and moved in different directions. Albert Ellis, Victor Frankl, William Glasser, and Carl Rogers are four such persons. Of these, it was Rogers who influenced the greatest paradigm shift.

Rogers's (1951) *Client-Centered Therapy* turned the profession around. It went from a directive (i.e., tell the clients what to do) to a new directive (i.e., follow the clients' phenomenology). Guidance, for all intents and purposes, was replaced by counseling—not counseling with a client on the couch free associating but rather counseling with an active responsible participating coequal. Sure, guidance models hung around for another 30 years. Schools in particular were slow to change, and many continued to employ ex-teachers with little or no training as their guidance counselors, but the remainder of the profession moved beyond the directive, trait-factor-driven orientation. Emphasis shifted to refinements in the counseling process. By the 1960s, refinements had become a proliferation of tools and techniques. On the one hand, this enriched the field; on the other, students of counseling were faced with a gauntlet of competing methodologies. And counseling has not been immune to charlatans proselytizing their ideas.

NDEA-trained counselors were filling the available school counselor positions during the 1960s. Concurrent with the proliferation of available educational counselors was the passage of the Community Mental Health Centers Act of 1963. This legislation authorized the establishment of community mental health agencies and the employment of counselors outside of educational settings. Much like the availability of public education across the country, tax-supported public mental health centers were established across the country. Counseling was made available to the masses as an outgrowth of President Lyndon Johnson's "Great Society" programs.

During the latter part of the 20th century, many "strength-based" theories of counseling gained prominence. Up until that point, counseling had been largely problem focused; counselors served as expert guides while helping clients to identify problems and delving into the "core" reasons for these problems. They focused strongly on clients' limitations. But with the rise of more strength-oriented types of counseling, some counselors began to attend more to clients' resources and successes.

Examples of such strength-oriented types of counseling include solution-focused and narrative therapies. Solution-focused therapists, such as Insoo Kim Berg and Steve de Shazer, propose that it is more helpful to identify and expand on clients' strengths than to concentrate on their problems. Therefore, solution-focused counselors work to discover satisfying *exceptions* to problems (e.g., times when clients might have typically experienced their problems but the problems did not arise), how clients were able to create these exceptions, and how clients can expand these exceptions to become commonplace in their lives (DeJong & Berg, 1997).

Similarly, narrative therapists such as White and Epston (1990) help clients to identify "unique outcomes" or times when clients are free of their identified problems. They attempt to do this by separating the problems from the persons ("externalizing" the problems) rather than viewing the problems as part of the persons. Narrative therapists encourage clients to remember times when they had some control or influence over their identified problems and then work with them to increase clients' influence over problems. Ultimately, narrative therapists help clients to re-author their "problem-saturated" stories by inviting them to change not only problematic actions but also the associated meanings held by clients that might be causing them distress.

Solution-focused counselors, narrative therapists, and other strength-oriented therapists (e.g., Harlene Anderson and Harold Goolishian in their work with language systems in therapy, William O'Hanlon's use of "possibility" therapy) focus on clients' strengths, competence, and exceptions to problems rather than on the problems themselves. These therapists work in a collaborative fashion with clients; clients, not counselors, are seen as the experts on their own lives. Consistent with a postmodern perspective, there is recognition that there are a variety of truths and realities, and it is the clients' goals and reality that drive the counseling process. Some have criticized these strength-based therapies as being quick, ineffective fixes that overlook important client issues. Yet, these therapies continue to gain in popularity and have challenged the profession to examine basic assumptions about the focus of counseling and the role of the counselor.

Family Counseling: From Systems Theory to Family Stories

Family counseling adds many strands to our ball of counseling yarn, thus increasing both the size and the complexity of the ball. In some cases, established strands were interwoven to produce new colorful fibers. That is, historical threads were spun together to produce a variety of theories and techniques of family counseling. But to allow for the appearance of the new hues of family counseling, some older rigid strands had to become more flexible.

One such strand was the notion that counseling was effective only when the counselor worked with a client individually. During the first half of the 20th century, inclusion of other family members in counseling usually was viewed as a disruption to the client-counselor relationship. For example, psychoanalysts excluded parents from therapy sessions for fear that they would hinder "the development of the transference neurosis . . . necessary [for] successful therapy" (Corsini & Wedding, 1989, p. 458). Behaviorists also excluded the client's family members from therapy, although for a different reason. They viewed the "identified patient" as the problem and saddled the client with the responsibility for change, contrary to the systemic notion that all family members influence the aggravation or abatement of a problem.

In contrast to this focus on the individual in therapy, several events occurred during the first half of the 20th century that set the stage for the emergence of family counseling. These included the child guidance movement, the emergence of marriage counseling, research on schizophrenia within families, social workers' history of involvement with families, and studies on small group dynamics (Nichols & Schwartz, 1995). These and many other events, both in society and in the field of psychotherapy, intertwined to encourage the development of family counseling and ultimately led to the dramatic paradigm shift toward systemic theory.

This movement toward the use of systems theory to explain family functioning was a radical departure from the traditional linear model for behavior. Proponents of this linear model assumed that causality moved in one direction. So, when a child acted out and a father scolded, the acting out "caused" the scolding in this linear model. By contrast, systemic thinkers envisioned families as systems of interdependent members with circular causality; each family member was interconnected with, and had some influence on, other family members. The child acting out and the father scolding had reciprocal effects on one another, and they were stuck in a repeated pattern or system of interacting. Other family members also contributed to and were affected by the father-child interaction.

This move toward systemic thinking opened up new possibilities for family therapy. Positive change anywhere in the family (as opposed to simply with the identified patient) might reduce the problems presented by the family. Systemic concepts became foundational to many of the therapeutic models that emerged during the 1960s and 1970s including structural, strategic, and systemic models of family therapy.

During the last few decades of the 20th century, the "truth" behind stories such as systemic theory and other concepts long held as reflective of people and their lives (e.g., developmental stage theory [Steenbarger, 1991]) has been challenged. Such challenges have stemmed from postmodern philosophy, a major assumption of which is that there is no established reality or truth. Rather, people construct realities or "stories" of their lives. Social constructionism is a school of thought that has emerged from this notion and shares some assumptions of the previously discussed social constructivism. (Note that the literature is inconsistent in its definitions of *social constructivism* and *social constructionism*. At times, the terms appear to be interchangeable; at other times, they appear to be quite distinct. See Gergen [1994] for a discussion of his ideas about the differences between these theories.) Social constructionism proposes that people create realities through social processes that are closely tied to language (McNamee & Gergen, 1992). As stated by Freedman and Combs (1996),

[Social constructionism's] main premise is that the beliefs, values, institutions, customs, labels, laws, divisions of labor, and the like that make up our social realities are constructed by members of a culture as they interact with one another from generation to generation and day to day. That is, societies construct the "lenses" through which their members interpret the world. (p. 16)

Gergen (1985), a leading social constructionism theorist, noted that the descriptions and meanings that people ascribe to the world will result in certain implications and actions. Therefore, changes in descriptions may change actions, and counselors coauthor such changes with their clients.

So how has the emergence of postmodern theories influenced family therapy? Nichols and Schwartz (1995) noted several effects of these theories on modern counselors (and their clients) who put these theories into practice. First, there was liberation from the belief that there was one "right" way in which to work with families; "family therapy, like the culture in general, became more pluralistic" (p. 121). Also, the expertness of the family therapist has been replaced with a collaborative approach, with the counselor and family members all being expert in some realm. And there has been emphasis on how clients make meaning in their lives rather than a strong focus on behavior. Finally, and perhaps most important, issues of gender, race, sexual orientation, social class, and disability have been given long overdue attention, and a multiplicity of voices (e.g., feminist family therapists) have entered an arena long dominated by European American men.

Perspectives: The Next Decade

While attending a World Futurist Association convention in Washington, D.C., several decades ago, the first author was struck by the absence of crystal ball speculation about the future. Projections were speculative only so far as assumptions based on present trends did in fact continue. So, what does this mean for our counseling ball of yarn? We will leave the reader with four thoughts for the future based on present observations.

1. Career counseling, the oldest identified counseling service, is expanding to incorporate a more holistic view of clients. Although the trait-factor mentality still persists, the profession has begun to embrace more contemporary philosophies such as social constructivism. Much has been written about these changing philosophies, but less has been explored about how to integrate these philosophies into practice (Young & Chen, 1999). A need exists in the profession to further develop helpful strategies of applying postmodern ideas to career counseling.

2. The history of counseling has been shaped by social policies. Examples include programs of the VA (e.g., its Counseling Services), NDEA counselor training institutes, and President Johnson's Great Society programs. These social policy initiatives enacted into laws helped to form people's lives and the counseling profession.

Today's issues are as dramatic as, or more dramatic than, those addressed by past social policies. War metaphors often are used in our culture when addressing social policy and national issues. The United States won the Cold War. It is losing the "war on drugs"; the United States incarcerates a larger proportion of its population than does any other country, with many convictions associated with sales and use of illegal substances. A war against violence is in place. Some social policy initiative like the NDEA is needed. The infusion of counselors was dramatic after the NDEA. Not only in schools (which have disproportionate counselor-to-

student ratios such as California's ratio of 1 counselor to 1,182 students) but also in every mental health and rehabilitation facility, more counselors are needed.

Passing legislation, such as the American Counseling Association's (ACA) "100,000 new school counselors" campaign, is not enough. Counselor educators must continually strive to improve their training programs, preparing practitioners who will provide and evaluate quality services both inside and outside of educational institutions.

3. Not only are more counselors needed, but high school guidance workers also need to become counselors. There is a need to attend to educational planning and programming with students. But does one need a master's degree in counseling to do much of this work? We believe that employment of administrators to accomplish administrative tasks, freeing school counselors to counsel, is a better expenditure of money than is employing armed guards in schools.

4. The ACA, the largest association representing professional counselors, certainly is reflective of our metaphor of the counseling profession being like a ball of multicolored yarn; the 17 divisions within the ACA add significant strands to the counseling profession. However, do we focus primarily on keeping these strands tightly wound and melded together, or do we focus more on affirming and accommodating the colorful variety in the threads? Our history suggests that we have concentrated on the former. Aubrey (1977) wrote more than 20 years ago, at the conclusion of his history article celebrating the American Personnel Guidance Association's (the former name of the ACA) 25th anniversary,

We still need to "search for a system" to unify our members under common and mutually agreed upon purposes. This message is perhaps the greatest legacy we possess from the past and represents our most vital mission for the future. (p. 299)

During recent years, such efforts at unification have been challenged. There have been moves toward dissociations from the ACA confederation, and a few divisions, in a figurative sense, have partially unwound themselves from the ball. These divisions apparently were not finding the larger organization accommodating to their differences. Perhaps, in a postmodern era, the "search for a system" could better incorporate difference as well as commonality. The counseling profession no longer needs a melting pot to unify its membership. Like multiculturalism, counseling needs to celebrate its diversity.

References

Aubrey, R. F. (1977). Historical development of guidance and counseling and implications for the future. *Personnel and Guidance Journal, 55,* 288-295.

Borow, H. (1990). Counseling psychology in the Minnesota tradition. *Journal of Counseling and Development, 68,* 266-275.

Bourne, B. (1988). Making ideas work: Ralph Bedell and the NDEA institutes. *Journal of Counseling and Development, 67,* 136-142.

Brokaw, T. (1998). *The greatest generation.* New York: Random House.

Carson, A. D., & Altai, N. M. (1994). 1000 years before Parsons: Vocational psychology in classical Islam. *Career Developmental Quarterly, 43,* 197-206.

Chambless, H., & Zytowski, D. G. (1987). Occupational outlook in the 15th century: Sanchez de Avevalo's mirror of human life. *Journal of Counseling and Development, 66,* 168-170.

Cheatham, H. E. (1990). Africentricity and career development of African Americans. *Career Development Quarterly, 38,* 334-346.

Corsini, R. J., & Wedding, D. (1989). *Current psychotherapies* (4th ed.). Itasca, IL: F. E. Peacock.

DeJong, P., & Berg, I. K. (1997). *Interviewing for solutions.* Pacific Grove, CA: Brooks/Cole.

Dumont, F., & Carson, A. D. (1995). Precursors of vocational psychology in ancient civilizations. *Journal of Counseling and Development, 73,* 371-378.

Freedman, J., & Combs, G. (1996). *Narrative therapy: The social construction of preferred realities.* New York: Norton.

Gergen, K. J. (1985). The social construction movement in modern psychology. *American Psychologist, 40,* 266-275.

Gergen, K. J. (1994). *Realities and relationships.* Cambridge, MA: Harvard University Press.

Gilligan, C. (1982). *In a different voice.* Cambridge, MA: Harvard University Press.

Ginzburg, E., Ginzburg, S. W., Axelrad, S., & Herma, J. L. (1951). *Occupational choice: An approach to a general theory.* New York: Columbia University Press.

Herr, E. L., & Cramer, S. H. (1996). *Career guidance and counseling through the life span: Systematic approaches* (5th ed.). New York: HarperCollins.

Krumboltz, J. D. (1993). Integrating career and personal counseling. *Career Development Quarterly, 42,* 143-148.

McNamee, S., & Gergen, K. J. (1992). *Therapy as social construction.* London: Sage.

Miller, C. H. (1973). Historical and recent perspectives on work and vocational guidance. In H. Borow (Ed.), *Career guidance for a new age* (pp. 3-39). Boston: Houghton Mifflin.

National Vocational Guidance Association. (1949). Report of the Policy Committee. *Occupations, 27,* 270-272.

Nichols, M. P., & Schwartz, R. C. (1995). *Family therapy: Concepts and methods* (3rd ed.). Boston: Allyn & Bacon.

"100,000 new counselors" amendment voted on. (1999, June). *Counseling Today,* pp. 1, 10.

Parsons, F. (1967). *Choosing a vocation.* New York: Agathon. (Original work published in 1909)

Penner, E. (1967). Introduction. In F. Parsons, *Choosing a vocation* (pp. v-ix). New York: Agathon. (Original work published in 1909)

Rockwell, P. J., & Rothney, J. W. M. (1961). Some social ideas of pioneers in the guidance movement. *Personnel and Guidance Journal, 40,* 349-354.

Rogers, C. R. (1942). *Counseling and psychotherapy.* Boston: Houghton Mifflin.

Rogers, C. R. (1951). *Client-centered therapy.* Boston: Houghton Mifflin.

Savickas, M. L. (1995). Constructivist counseling for career indecision. *Career Development Quarterly, 43,* 363-373.

Schmitt, S. M. (1999, September). School counselors' role may be in "transition." *Counseling Today,* pp. 28-29.

Stanley, T. J., & Danko, W. (1996). *The millionaire next door.* Atlanta, GA: Longstreet Press.

Steenbarger, B. N. (1991). All the world is not a stage: Emerging contextualist themes in counseling and development. *Journal of Counseling and Development, 70,* 288-296.

Torrey, E. F. (1992). *Freudian fraud: The malignant effects of Freud's theory on American cultural thought.* New York: HarperCollins.

U.S. Employment Service. (1939). *Dictionary of occupational titles.* Washington, DC: Author.

White, M., & Epston, D. (1990). *Narrative means to therapeutic ends.* New York: Norton.

Williamson, E. G. (1939). *How to counsel students: A manual of techniques for clinical counselors.* New York: McGraw-Hill.

Young, R. A., & Chen, C. P. (1999). Annual review: Practice and research in career counseling and development—1998. *Career Development Quarterly, 48,* 98-141.

CHAPTER THREE

Specialties in Counseling

JANE E. MYERS

THOMAS J. SWEENEY

Hollis (2000) reviewed the criteria that generally must be met for the establishment of a profession. These include having a specific body of knowledge with recognized training programs, a professional organization of peers, accreditation of training programs, supervised clinical training, credentialing of practitioners, and legal recognition and licensure. In addition, professional behavior is guided by a code of ethical behavior. Consistent with these criteria, as Sweeney described in Chapter 1 of this volume, counseling emerged as a profession during the last half of the 20th century. The profession continues to grow, and according to the *Occupational Outlook Handbook* (*OOH*) (U.S. Department of Labor, 2000), the outlook for new positions in the field exceeds the average for all professions through 2008.

The *OOH* clarifies that this projection applies "only to vocational and educational counselors," noting that future job conditions for "rehabilitation and mental health counselors" are discussed in a subsequent section. If one reads on, the *OOH* describes the outlook for additional parts of the field, referring the interested reader to the American Counseling Association (ACA) for information on "counseling specialties such as school, college, multicultural, marriage and family, gerontological." Whether these specialties also meet the criteria to define a unique profession is a question of interest for the field. Recent articles in our professional literature suggest that some of these specialties do, indeed, define themselves as separate professions (Fong, 1990; Palmo, 1990; Szymanski, 1985; Throckmorton, 1996) while simultaneously claiming to be part of the broader profession of counseling. Other specialties document some, if not most, of the criteria for a profession but make no claims to be other than specialties in counseling (Myers, 1995; Page & Bailey, 1995). No doubt, claims such as these are a source of confusion to those outside of the counseling profession as well as to novice counselors and many with considerable experience and expertise in the field.

In this chapter, an attempt is made to present some of the issues related to professional unification and specialties. The context for this discussion is a historical overview of the existing specialties within the field. This overview is followed by a review of definitions of counseling and counseling specialties. The chapter concludes with a discussion of future trends and challenges relative to specialties.

The Evolution of Counseling and Counseling Specialties

Although the historical roots of counseling may be traced to the 19th and early 20th centuries, clearly a major historical event underlying the development of the profession was the establishment in 1952 of the American Personnel and Guidance Association (APGA), the forerunner to ACA. Of course, the founding organizations that came together to form APGA did not do so with the intent of establishing a new profession. The National Vocational Guidance Association (NVGA; now called the National Career Development Association [NCDA]), the American College Personnel Association (ACPA), the National Association of Guidance and Counselor Trainers (NAGCT; now called the Association for Counselor Education and

Supervision [ACES]), and the Student Personnel Association for Teacher Education (SPATE; now called the Counseling Association for Humanistic Education and Development [C-AHEAD]) established APGA in the hope that unification would result in an association with the professional strength to reach goals impossible to achieve for smaller special interest groups. ACA's founders, however, were not ready to completely surrender the autonomy of their individual associations. The groups that had merged to form APGA became divisions, each with its own bylaws, officers, committees, and publications (ACA, 1999).

APGA functioned as an umbrella agency for its constituents, providing a headquarters office and staff to assist the divisions with tasks such as financial and membership record keeping, membership recruitment, and publications. All members of the four divisions were required to join the parent organization, APGA, in order to join and affiliate with a division. Thus, although the divisions represented special interests that were independent, the requirement for all members to be part of APGA enforced a type of unification within the membership. Membership within APGA (ACA), however, was not a professional membership as it is now. In fact, the second president of APGA, Donald Super, wrote,

The question of professional membership in APGA, rather than just NVGA as at the present time, is occasionally raised and must be thought through. There is strong feeling in some quarters that if APGA is to be viewed by others as a truly professional association, we must have membership standards that mean something. This feeling is reinforced in some members who are touched by medical efforts to limit the practice of psychodiagnosis and psychotherapy to physicians, by related efforts of psychologists to define the practice of psychology and obtain licensing for psychologists, and by the work of others interested in the curbing of quacks. They fear that, as an interest association without professional standards, our voice will not be heard in medical, psychological, social work, or licensing or certification efforts. . . . What is our stand here? And why do we have professional membership in one division, professional requirements in another, and none (other than employment) in others? We may want to give these matters thought. (Super, 1953, p. 498)

The answer to this question of whether APGA would have professional membership was not answered affirmatively until 1991. As Sweeney noted in Chapter 1 of this volume, this amalgam of organizations with memberships across client, interest, and employment settings hardly projected a clear professional identity. As a consequence, the seeds of discontent were embedded in the very fabric of the structure of ACA from its inception as an organization (APGA). The challenge of diversity and unity has been a theme across the decades of ACA existence as a result (Herr, 1985; Hoyt, 1967, 1971; McDaniels, 1964; Myers, 1995b; Peer, 1982; Smith, 1990; Sweeney, 1982, 1990).

An interesting development occurring concurrently with the formation of APGA/ACA was the creation of Counseling Psychology as a division of the American Psychological Association (APA) by Super, Gilbert Wrenn, and others who also were instrumental in the organization and leadership of APGA and its divisions. Membership in APA and, consequently, Counseling Psychology required a doctorate. We might speculate that the need for a strong professional identity was satisfied for some of these early leaders through APA, whereas APGA/ACA represented an "interest" membership sharing

both academic and practitioner/client interests. For many members, APGA/ACA's inclusiveness was an asset for involvement with university and college administrators, for those interested in vocational guidance in nonacademic settings, and for bringing practitioners and educators together.

Other groups soon sought representation and affiliation within APGA's umbrella. The American School Counselors Association (ASCA) joined APGA in 1953 after deciding during the previous year that NVGA did not represent the breadth of school counselor interests (Minkoff & Terres, 1985). Since that time, 14 more organizations have affiliated, many of which evolved through the APGA membership rather than external to it. Table 3.1 provides a summary of the divisions of ACA as it now exists, along with the date of chartering for each one and the dates of name changes for the division, if any.

A review of the divisions of ACA reveals at least four possible sources for the definition of a division: work setting (e.g., schools, colleges), clientele (e.g., addicted individuals, adults, older adults), type of intervention (e.g., group counseling), and intent or purpose (e.g., social justice). Clearly, there is considerable diversity in these definitions. Further exploration of divisions according to levels and types of activity within the divisions reveals even more differences.

Several of the divisions have been the impetus for development of competency statements for practitioners or supervisors (e.g., NCDA, Association for Adult Development and Aging [AADA], ACES, Association for Spiritual, Ethical, and Religious Values in Counseling [ASERVIC]). Others have developed specific sets of competency-based training standards

TABLE 3.1   Divisions of the American Counseling Association and Dates of Initial Chartering or Affiliation

Acronym	Title of Division	Date of Affiliation
ACES	Association for Counselor Education and Supervision	1952
NCDA	National Career Development Association (1985), formerly National Vocational Guidance Association	1952
C-AHEAD	Counseling Association for Humanistic Education and Development (1999), formerly Association for Humanistic Education and Development (1974), formerly Student Personnel Association for Teacher Education	1952
ACPA	American College Personnel Association	1952
ASCA	American School Counselor Association	1953
ARCA	American Rehabilitation Counseling Association	1958
AAC	Association for Assessment in Counseling (1992), formerly Association for Measurement and Evaluation in Counseling and Development (1984), formerly Association for Measurement and Evaluation in Guidance	1965
NECA	National Employment Counseling Association (1992), formerly National Employment Counselors Association	1966
AMCD	Association for Multicultural Counseling and Development (1985), formerly Association for Non-White Concerns in Guidance	1972
ASERVIC	Association for Spiritual, Ethical, and Religious Values in Counseling (1977), formerly National Catholic Guidance Conference	1974
ASGW	Association for Specialists in Group Work	1973
IAAOC	International Association for Addictions and Offender Counseling (1990), formerly Public Offender Counselors Association	1972
AMHCA	American Mental Health Counselors Association	1978
AADA	Association for Adult Development and Aging	1986
ACEG	Association for Counselors and Educators in Government (1994), formerly Military Educators and Counselors Association	1984
IAMFC	International Association of Marriage and Family Counselors	1989
ACCA	American College Counseling Association	1991
AGLBIC	Association for Gay, Lesbian, and Bisexual Issues in Counseling	1996
CSJ	Counselors for Social Justice	1999

(e.g., American Mental Health Counselors Association [AMHCA], American Rehabilitation Counseling Association [ARCA]). Although these statements and standards reflect commonalities, they also reveal significant differences in content, emphasis, and skills for the practitioners in specialty areas.

Many of the divisions also sponsor representatives to the Council for Accreditation of Counseling and Related Educational Programs (CACREP), some of which have the specific task of advocating for specialty preparation standards. It is noteworthy here that CACREP accredits counseling specialties, not the generic

TABLE 3.2 ACA Divisions, CACREP Specialty Accreditation Areas, and NBCC Specialty Certifications

Division	CACREP Accreditation	NBCC Certification
ACES	Counselor education and supervision (doctoral standards)	Approved clinical supervisor (ACS)
NCDA	Career counseling	National certified career counselor (NCCC) (dropped in 1999)
C-AHEAD		
ACPA	a	
ASCA	School counseling	National certified school counselor (NCSC)
ARCA	b	c
AAC		
NECA		
AMCD		
ASERVIC		
ASGW		
IAAOC		Master addictions counselor (MAC)
AMHCA	Mental health counseling	Certified clinical mental health counselor (CCMHC)
AADA	Gerontological counseling	National certified gerontological counselor (NCGC) (dropped in 1999)
ACEG		
IAMFC	Marriage and family counseling	d
ACCA	College counseling/student development	
AGLBIC		
CSJ		
	Community counseling	

NOTE: ACA = American Counseling Association; CACREP = Council for Accreditation of Counseling and Related Educational Programs; NBCC = National Board for Certified Counselors. See Table 3.1 for full titles of ACA divisions represented by acronyms.

a. ACPA withdrew from ACA in 1991.

b. Rehabilitation counseling training programs are accredited by the Council on Rehabilitation Education (CORE).

c. Rehabilitation counselors are certified by the Council on Rehabilitation Counselor Certification (CRCC).

d. Marriage and family therapists are certified by the National Academy for Certified Family Therapists (NACFT).

preparation of professional counselors. However, the National Board for Certified Counselors (NBCC) certifies generalists (i.e., national certified counselors [NCCs]) as well as specialists. Table 3.2 provides a list of the ACA divisions, CACREP specialties, and NBCC certifications, with comparable areas of specialty across the three associations indicated. Two of the NBCC certifications (NCCs and national certified gerontological counselors [NCGCs]) were discontinued in 1999 due to the low numbers of certificants and a lack of new applicants for such certification.

Divisions Versus Separate Professions

From this brief review of facts about ACA divisions, it is clear that some of their areas of expertise or interest meet Hollis's (2000) criteria for an established profession, yet not all claim to be separate professions. Throughout the history of ACA, various divisions at various times have expressed dissatisfaction with their relationship with ACA and/or the other divisions of the association. Disagreements have ranged from mild to acrimonious, with mutual agreements reached through means such as discussion, dialogue, and legal intervention. ACA often has been compared with a family, one whose constituents relate in dysfunctional ways. Such comparisons negate the relatively smooth relations that exist between ACA and most of its divisions most of the time. However, when disagreements persist between ACA and its larger divisions, all of the constituencies are affected.

At least five ACA divisions historically or consistently have considered their primary missions to be most closely aligned with their specialty constituencies rather than with a more generalist profession. These five divisions are ACPA, ASCA, AMHCA, NCDA, and ARCA. Most of these divisions have had large numbers of members; thus, perceptions that the umbrella association was not meeting the needs of those specialty members as closely as possible understandably have arisen. ACPA, itself an umbrella organization for a diverse constituency of college and university personnel, withdrew its membership in ACA in 1991. Since that time, significant discussions have been held in the other four organizations concerning possible disaffiliation. ASCA, AMHCA, NCDA, and ARCA each effected a physical separation of its headquarters personnel from the ACA headquarters during the late 1990s, and ASCA

and AMHCA instituted separate procedures for collecting membership dues.

Internal disagreements and dissension within ACA came to a head in 1997 when the Governing Council of the association made an unprecedented decision to allow membership in ACA without joining a division. Prior to that time, it was assumed by many members and leaders that counselors joined ACA as the avenue to affiliation with like-minded persons in their divisions. Now that division membership is not required, virtually all divisions have suffered losses of members while ACA has gained in membership. The turmoil of the 1990s in ACA and its divisions consumed considerable energy and shifted the focus of leadership from advocacy for professional issues to issues of structure and governance. This movement followed two decades of significant professionalization chronicled by Sweeney in Chapter 1 of this volume. Although not the only reason for membership changes within ACA, a review of changing membership statistics certainly provides a reason to pause and wonder about the future of the profession as a whole as well as the specialties that historically have comprised the counseling profession as we know it. These statistics are provided in Tables 3.3 and 3.4.

Definitions and Defining Moments

Sweeney (1995) suggested,

Specialties within counseling are synonymous with the development of professional preparation standards, accreditation, and credentialing. . . . In fact, were it not for the efforts of specialties within counseling, there would be little more than a smattering of events to report on the topic of professionalization. And yet, no single specialty has the equivalent influence and strength that

TABLE 3.3 Membership in the American Counseling Association, 1953-2000

Year	Total Number of Members
1953	6,086
1960	13,030
1970	27,336
1980-1981	40,311
1981-1982	39,440
1982-1983	40,327
1983-1984	41,470
1984-1985	43,085
1985-1986	47,845
1986-1987	55,526
1987-1988	56,658
1988-1989	55,385
1989-1990	55,974
1990-1991	57,822
1991-1992	59,009
1992-1993	56,562
1993-1994	58,138
1994-1995	56,176
1995-1996	55,603
1996-1997	53,386
1997-1998	50,539
1998-1999	51,826
1999-2000	51,236

TABLE 3.4 Membership in the Divisions of ACA, 1990 and 2000

Division	Membership in 1990	Membership in March 2000
ACES	2,898	2,552
NCDA	5,804	3,063
C-AHEAD	2,681	841
ACPA	7,862	a
ASCA	12,539	12,000[b]
ARCA	2,698	1,043
AAC	1,701	1,199
NECA	1,699	839
AMCD	2,776	2,302
ASERVIC	3,971	3,060
ASGW	5,262	2,415
IAAOC	911	1,844
AMHCA	11,970	5,380[b]
AADA	1,936	1,256
ACEG	693	409
IAMFC	2,132	4,300
ACCA	c	2,069
AGLBIC	c	943
CSJ	c	249

NOTE: ACA = American Counseling Association. See Table 3.1 for full titles of ACA division acronyms.

a. Left ACA in 1991.

b. ASCA and AMHCA maintain their own membership statistics separate from ACA. These figures are approximate based on information provided to the ACA library from the offices of these two divisions.

c. ACCA, AGLBIC, and CSJ were chartered in 1992, 1996, and 1999, respectively.

comes from the united effort called professionalization. Although each specialty has significant positive attributes and historical roots in the political and economic marketplace, one should know that the saying "united we stand, divided we fall" is more than just a slogan. (p. 117)

Myers (1995) noted, "The question of whether the counseling profession is a *unified* profession continues to be postulated by professional leaders and members, both within and outside of ACA" (p. 115, italics in original). In

this context, a "defining moment" occurred for us, and for others, at an historical meeting held in 1991. In spite of tremendous momentum toward professionalization, ACA had not had in place a clearly defined, comprehensive plan to define and promote the emergence of counseling as a profession. A Professionalization Directorate was established that year, with one of the authors serving in the capacity of president of ACA and the other as chair of the directorate. This directorate convened a meeting of all ACA divisions and credentialing groups (e.g., CACREP, Council on Rehabilitation Education [CORE], NBCC, Council on Rehabilitation Counselor Certification [CRCC]) with the intent of developing such a plan. Turf issues and a history of not working together laid a foundation in which the potential for accomplishing the purpose of the meeting was tenuous at best. This foundation changed rapidly, however, with the introduction of the first speaker.

In attendance at the professionalization meeting was an invited guest from the National Institute for Mental Health (NIMH), a psychiatrist and leading administrator working within the institute. After he had explained the NIMH programs and policies, he was challenged by a division representative to explain why, after 10 years of concerted efforts and political lobbying, counselors had not been able to be recognized as providers of mental health training. His response was simple yet direct: If you have been trying for 10 years and it has not worked, then you need to try another way. He went on to say,

> You have to decide one fundamental question: Are you a group or a group of groups? If you come to me as 3,000 rehabilitation counselors, or 10,000 school counselors, or 12,000 mental health counselors, or 4,000 career counselors, I really don't need to listen to you. But if you come to me as 50,000 professional counselors, then you will get my attention.

In that short span of time, the NIMH administrator, who was not a member of the counseling profession, defined our essential problem. We needed to define who we were and then use that definition as a basis for professional advocacy.

No one—legislators, policy makers, or administrators—would care to listen to us unless we first were clear about who we were as a profession.

Subsequent to that professionalization meeting, a number of positive steps have been taken toward unifying our profession and defining who we are. Notable among them was the adoption by ACA (1997) of definitions of professional counseling and professional counseling specialty. These definitions read as follows:

> *The Practice of Professional Counseling:* [This is] the application of mental health, psychological, or human development principles through cognitive, affective, behavioral, or systemic intervention strategies that address wellness, personal growth, or career development as well as pathology.
>
> *Professional Counseling Specialty:* A professional counseling specialty is narrowly focused, requiring advanced knowledge in the field founded on the premise that all professional counselors must first meet the requirements for the general practice of professional counseling.

Although not perfect, these definitions provide a foundation for advocacy and allow those within our profession, as well as others, to better understand what a professional counselor is and does and what is meant by a specialty within our field.

Perspectives on the Future

Any discussion of unity for the profession of counseling inevitably results in consideration of the role of specialties. Myers (1995) emphasized that our specialties are at once a rich heritage and a strong force for fragmentation. Articles such as "ACA Divisions Split Counseling

Profession" (Robinson, 1993) and "Survival of the Profession Depends on Unity" (Breasure, 1995) underscore the need for the profession as a whole to clarify the role of specialties and find a means to meet the needs of specialties within a broader structure or to seek a new structure and definition as the basis for a strong profession of counseling. Herr (1985) appropriately defined a major strength of the counseling profession as our respect for the diversity that exists within our membership and, at the same time, suggested that we can best achieve unity through building on the strengths that derive from our diversity. How to do so seems to be elusive at best and impossible at worst. Clearly, a major challenge for the new century lies in finding a way for professional counselors to coalesce around our common identity while encouraging the uniqueness that arises from our diversity of competencies, training, methods, and interests.

Although ACA has proposed an official definition for the profession of a counseling specialty, the process by which a specialty is defined remains elusive. Is a specialty only something a group of counselors believes to be important, or is it something defined by the profession as a whole? During the past 5 years, two new ACA divisions—the Association for Gay, Lesbian, and Bisexual Issues in Counseling (AGLBIC) and Counselors for Social Justice (CSJ)—have been approved by the ACA Governing Council. NBCC has added a new specialty credential for approved clinical supervisors (ACSs) (Bernard, 1998). A review of the counseling literature provides additional areas that claim to be emerging as specialties including Christian counseling (Carter, 1999), sports counseling (Miller & Wooten, 1995), and adoption counseling (Janus, 1997). In addition, special populations are being identified as new challenges for counselors. Examples include sex offenders (Glennon, 1996), Chicanos (Gonzalez, 1997), and children with attachment disorder (Parker & Forrest, 1993). These examples suggest that any new setting, client population, or method may give rise to yet another "specialty." How many can we afford to support while remaining viable as a unified profession? What we propose is a means to clarify and better define *specialty* as opposed to *special interest*.

Common criteria cited for what constitutes a profession include having a specific body of specialized knowledge, recognized training programs, a professional organization of peers, accreditation of training programs, supervised clinical training, credentialing of practitioners, and a code for ethical decision making. If we apply these same criteria to specialties, then the number of specialties becomes more coherent.

As noted by the ACA definitions, all counseling specialties begin with a common body of knowledge. CACREP's core areas of preparation are required of all specialties. CORE has similar (but not identical) basic requirements for rehabilitation counselor preparation, but it uses a different process of accreditation determination. What constitutes an organization of peers becomes another issue. Historically, APGA/ACA had required that new divisions applying for recognition first must meet a critical mass of 1,000 individuals who joined them in order to petition for division status. This requirement came into being after years of larger divisions financially carrying the smaller organizations that never realized the potential promised by their founders. For political reasons internal to ACA governance, this criterion was dropped during the past several years, and much smaller groups have been and are recognized as a part of ACA's structure (Table 3.4). This requirement still seems to be a reasonable criterion for the purpose of establishing sufficient size to merit consideration for a specialty. Five divisions do not meet the criterion of 1,000 members at this time. Nevertheless, without effective discriminating criteria, if any small but ambitious group of "special interest"-minded individuals came together and created a professional "specialty," then proliferation of specialties could be a very real possibility (Sweeney, 1995).

Recognized training programs represent another area of confusion, although one that still is useful for definition purposes. Whereas CACREP encourages institutions to identify their graduate programs using the accreditation rubrics (e.g., community counseling, mental health counseling), it is just as common to find training programs in counseling using other titles including variations on psychology, therapy, and human services. Because there is no association of "community counselors," such a "specialty" does not have advocates. As a type of counselor preparation, the community counseling emphasis is second ($N = 204$) only to school counseling ($N = 314$) regarding number of graduate programs (Hollis, 2000). Such are the anomalies of counselor preparation. School, rehabilitation, mental health, and marriage and family counseling, however, all have graduate programs accredited by CACREP and/or CORE. At the doctoral level, CACREP accredits programs in counselor education and supervision that include preparation for practice, research, consultation, supervision, and teaching. CACREP also has specialty preparation standards for career, college, and gerontological counseling.

School, rehabilitation, mental health, and marriage and family counseling, as well as ca-

reer, college, and gerontological counseling, all require supervised clinical experience. Only school, rehabilitation, mental health, marriage and family, and addictions counseling have national and/or state credentials with titles specific for them. NBCC now certifies an ACS, but it does not require a doctorate per se and requires no preparation for, or teaching experience in, counselor education. As yet, there have been no references to a "specialty" in counselor education, in part because higher education does not require state or national credentials for teaching. If a specialty is to be defined, however, then counselor education graduates of CACREP-accredited programs likely would be the greatest benefactors given that CACREP doctoral standards are used to guide doctoral preparation in counselor education. Likewise, it should be such standards that would guide those who developed specialty credentials. All of the other criteria for a specialty are met for counselor education.

All of the four areas—school, rehabilitation, mental health, and marriage and family counseling—also have setting- or client-specific codes of ethical conduct. This is true for counselor education and supervision as well.

If it is appropriate to suggest that a "specialty" in counseling requires meeting the preceding criteria, then school, mental health, rehabilitation, and marriage and family counseling meet all of these criteria both historically and by way of membership at the present time. Although addictions counseling is considered a specialty by those in the field, the leaders have chosen not to develop national accreditation standards, thereby omitting a key criterion even by the ACA definition. In addition, unlike the other areas listed previously, addictions counselors have no specific code of professional conduct related to their work. Both of these oversights still could be addressed. Similarly, counselor education could become a specialty with attention to a national credential based on the national preparation standards.

Might there be other new specialties in the future? This is possible, but only if advocates for the specialties commit to the same level of rigor and persistence as do those for the preceding member groups. This should in no way detract, however, from the value and benefits derived through membership groups by setting, clientele, or interest such as have existed within ACA since its inception. Unity still is possible through diversity.

Conclusion

The *OOH* (U.S. Department of Labor, 2000) estimated that there were more than 182,000 practicing counselors in the United States in 1998. This figure included only educational and vocational counselors and did not include mental health and rehabilitation counselors. Adding these to the total would easily bring the estimate to more than 200,000 professional counselors. Yet, only one fourth of these individuals are members of the major professional association, ACA. Certainly, a challenge for the future lies in finding a way in which to make affiliation with others in the profession not just a priority but also a professional imperative. Advocacy for counselors and those we serve will be most successful if based on a clearly defined profession that is able to express strength through numbers as well as through effective services.

References

American Counseling Association. (1997). *Definitions of professional counseling and professional counseling specialty*. Alexandria, VA: Author.

American Counseling Association. (1999). *ACA history: 1999*. Alexandria, VA: Author.

Bernard, J. M. (1998, July). Approved clinical supervisor: A new NBCC credential. *Counseling Today*, p. 19.

Breasure, J. M. (1995, November). Survival of the profession depends on unity. *Counseling Today*, p. 5.

Carter, R. B. (1999). Christian counseling: An emerging counseling specialty. *Counseling and Values, 43*(3), 189-198.

Fong, M. L. (1990). Mental health counseling: The essence of professional counseling. *Counselor Education and Supervision, 30*, 106-113.

Glennon, B. (1996). Sex offenders in prisons, jails, and other inpatient facilities: A contemporary challenge. *IAAOC Newsletter, 21*(6), 2-3. (International Association of Addictions and Offender Counselors)

Gonzalez, G. M. (1997). The emergence of Chicanos in the twenty-first century: Implications for counseling, research, and policy. *Journal of Multicultural Counseling and Development, 25*(2), 94-106.

Herr, E. L. (1985). An association committed to unity through diversity. *Journal of Counseling and Development, 63*, 395-404.

Hollis, J. W. (2000). *Counselor preparation 1999-2001: Programs, faculty, trends* (10th ed.). Philadelphia: Accelerated Development/Taylor & Francis.

Hoyt, K. P. (1967). Attaining the promise of guidance for all. *Personnel and Guidance Journal, 45*, 624-630.

Hoyt, K. P. (1971). Cherish or perish. *Personnel and Guidance Journal, 49*, 431-438.

Janus, N. G. (1997). Adoption counseling as a professional specialty area for counselors. *Journal of Counseling and Development, 75*, 266-274.

McDaniels, C. (1964). *The history and development of the American Personnel and Guidance Association*. Unpublished manuscript, American Counseling Association.

Miller, G. M., & Wooten, H. R. (1995). Sports counseling: A new counseling specialty area. *Journal of Counseling and Development, 74*, 172-173.

Minkoff, H. B., & Terres, C. K. (1985). ASCA perspectives: Past, present, and future. *Journal of Counseling and Development, 63*, 424-427.

Myers, J. E. (1995a). Specialities in counseling: Rich heritage or force for fragmentation? *Journal of Counseling and Development, 75*, 115-116.

Myers, J. E., (Ed.). (1995b). Professional counseling: Spotlight on specialities. [special issue]. *Journal of Counseling and Development, 74*(2).

Page, R. C., & Bailey, J. B. (1995). Addictions counseling: An emerging counseling specialty. *Journal of Counseling and Development, 74*, 167-172.

Palmo, A. J. (1990). Mental health counseling: Definitely a profession unto itself. *Counselor Education and Supervision, 30*, 114-119.

Parker, K. C., & Forrest, D. (1993). Attachment disorder: An emerging concern for school counselors. *Elementary School Guidance and Counseling, 27*(3), 209-215.

Peer, G. (1982). APGA today: A closer analysis. *Personnel and Guidance Journal, 60*, 517-519.

Robinson, G. (1993, November). ACA divisions split counseling profession. *Guidepost*, p. 16. (American Counseling Association)

Smith, H. (1990). AACD may have outlived its usefulness. *Counselor Education and Supervision, 29*, 134-141.

Super, D. E. (1953). Promises and performance. *Personnel and Guidance Journal, 34*, 496-499.

Sweeney, T. J. (1982). Peer's view: Creative tension or just plain trouble? *Personnel and Guidance Journal, 60*, 521-522.

Sweeney, T. J. (1990). AACD: A case for unity. *Counselor Education and Supervision, 29*, 141-147.

Sweeney, T. J. (1995). Accreditation, credentialing, professionalization: The role of specialties. *Journal of Counseling and Development, 74*, 117-125.

Szymanski, E. M. (1985). Rehabilitation counseling: A profession with a vision, an identity. *Rehabilitation Counseling Bulletin, 29*(1), 2-5.

Throckmorton, W. (1996). Mental health or professional counseling: Home is where the heart is. *AMHCA Advocate, 20*(1), 15. (American Mental Health Counselors Association)

U.S. Department of Labor. (2000). *Occupational outlook handbook*. Washington, DC: Author. Available: www.stats.bls.gov/oco/ocos067.htm

CHAPTER FOUR

Professional Associations, Standards, and Credentials in Counseling

BROOKE B. COLLISON

Professional counselors are active members of a professional association designed to serve their needs, have been educated in programs that met preparation standards for their specialty, and are credentialed for the work they do. This chapter elaborates on those three components and will explain how both students and practicing professionals can use the components to their best advantage as well as to the advantage of the clients they serve. This chapter also includes some speculation about the future of the three components: professional associations, accreditation standards, and credentialing in counseling.

The three components are independent but interrelated. Professional associations help to define and modify standards and have been instrumental in creating the accrediting bodies that work to apply the standards. Standards for preparation programs reflect and shape the education needed to prepare professional counselors. Credentials—certificates or licenses—provide visible demonstration that counselors have met standards of preparation and ensure the quality of practice that accredited programs have prepared people to deliver. Each component is dependent on the other two components, yet each component stands alone in its governance and operation as well as in its effect on the other two.

Professional Associations

The discussion of professional associations emphasizes the American Counseling Association (ACA) because it is the primary association for professional counselors. This section includes discussion of the association and the divisions within it, ethics and standards of practice, liability insurance for practitioners, how associations work for practitioners through governmental lobby efforts, and the role that associations play in development and distribution of new knowledge in the profession. One segment describes how ACA is addressing issues related to multicultural and diversity concerns. In addition, this section includes some discussion of the role that associations play in facilitating the employment of professional counselors. Finally, the section discusses some information about associations that are related to ACA in some way as well as how honor societies serve the counseling professional.

American Counseling Association

ACA is the primary member association for professional counselors. Examining the ACA Web page (www.counseling.org) reveals a great deal of information for students and professional counselors alike. Whether one is an ACA member or not, the author recommends that readers scan the ACA Web site periodically for current and changing information of interest to professional counselors. At the outset, the Web site identifies ACA as the "largest organization representing professional counselors." A few

clicks of the cursor will take the interested reader to the association's mission statement, a definition of professional counseling, a discussion of membership benefits, a brief history of significant events, a complete copy of the ACA code of ethics and standards of practice, and procedures for contacting persons in the association.

ACA, like most membership organizations that serve professionals, is a not-for-profit organization that, according to a statement from the introductory section of the Web page, is "dedicated to the growth and enhancement of the counseling profession." It also could be said that the organization is dedicated to the growth and enhancement of the counseling *professional,* for members—both students and practicing professionals—should be involved in a program of continuous professional development or growth if they are to provide clients with the assurance that their practice is as effective as it could be. Like most member-based professional associations, ACA is organized on a number of different levels, with possibilities for member involvement at local, state, regional, and national levels. Professional counselors will find a level of involvement most appropriate for their own needs where they can both profit from active participation and contribute to the well-being of their colleagues. The author takes the position that counselors who work alone—whether in agencies, schools, or private practice settings—expose themselves and their clients to unnecessary risk when they do not have accessible professional colleagues available for frequent consultation. Counselors also need continuing supervision, regardless of their level of preparation or license. Professional associations provide one way for colleague groups to be formed. At the very least, professional associations provide the ongoing stimulation and informational content that assist counselors in remaining current with the requirements of their practice.

To illustrate the scope of ACA, the reader should know that there are more than 50,000 members of the association. There are 56 branches in the United States and its territories as well as 17 different divisions, each organized to serve the interests of professionals either in unique work settings, with specific job titles, serving particular populations, or having specialized interests that they pursue. For example, some divisions respond to the needs of professionals in public school or college work settings; other divisions serve persons with clinical identities such as mental health counselors and marriage and family counselors; and some divisions organize around interests or issues such as justice, spirituality, and multicultural concerns. A description of those divisions is included in an appendix to this volume (Appendix A).

Ethics and Standards of Practice

Much of the work of a professional association is designed to give definition and shape to the profession that the members practice. For example, ACA has developed a comprehensive set of ethical guidelines and standards of practice (available on the Web site). The ethical code has evolved over several years, and a group of qualified members within the association works continuously to revise the code as new practice situations arise. The advent of computer technology and the many electronic applications to counseling-related activity are examples of how changes in counseling practices and tools cause the ethical code for professional counselors to be revised periodically. When the ethics code

originally was written, the concept of client service was exclusively in the form of personal contact. Now, telephone and computer counseling are growing in popularity requiring new codes and standards to guide the practice of the professional and ultimately to provide protection to the public.

ACA not only developed the code of ethics in use but also maintains an active procedure for persons to file and process ethical complaints against members. ACA staff members who process complaints say that they always are discouraged when a member of the public or another professional counselor calls to register a complaint against a counselor and the staff member discovers that the person charged is not an ACA member. The complainant is left to pursue his or her issue in the only other venue available, the civil court. Although very few ACA members are charged with offenses, without membership in the association, there is little that can be done to remedy bad practice. On the other hand, members who are charged with ethical violations have access to association resources in their own defense through established procedures for processing complaints and through legal defense funds.

It often has been said in counselor education classes and other workshop settings that the only defense against charges of malpractice is that one practices "according to the standards of the profession" (Bertram & Wheeler, 1996). Without established written standards such as those developed by ACA, there is nothing for the counselor to point to from the witness stand to say, "These are the standards by which I practice." Professional association membership, therefore, is important both in establishing how one works and in defending that work against charges when they arise.

Liability Insurance

Professional counselors also protect themselves and their clients by maintaining adequate insurance coverage against claims and charges against them in their practice. The national culture has become much more litigious during recent years. Although counselors, as a professional group, are not sued frequently, it does happen. Adequate coverage is determined by the work setting and the nature of the client group with which one works, but most persons advise that some type of professional liability insurance is essential. ACA has worked to develop provisions for that coverage and to make insurance available for students and practitioners alike.

There generally are two types of liability insurance available for counseling professionals: "claims made" and "occurrence." In deciding which of the two is more appropriate for a counselor, it should be noted that, unlike the case with automobile insurance where the driver knows immediately that a collision has occurred, it sometimes takes years for a counseling client to know that he or she has been injured and perhaps even longer to decide to charge the counselor involved. As an example, suppose that a student received information from a counselor about probable success at college and, based on that information, decided against going to school. Several years later, the student might learn that the information was in error and that college enrollment would have been a very good choice. If the former student decided to bring malpractice charges against the counselor in question, then it would be important for the counselor to have the type of insurance that would cover him or her for charges brought several years after the action that caused the complainant to file the charges. If the counselor was covered by an occurrence policy during the year in which the original session was held, then a claim would be covered even if the charge was made several years later. If the counselor was covered by a claims made policy during the year in which the original session was held, then a claim would be covered only if the counselor had continued to purchase similar policies each year thereafter including the year in which the claim was filed. Occurrence policies tend to cost more per year because they cover the insured for events that may be reported at some time in the future. Claims made policies are less expensive during the first year because they cover claims made only during the year in which the insurance is in force, but the longer the insured is covered, the more the policies tend to increase in cost.

For most counselors, more than 95% of the claims are filed within 5 years of the events that trigger the claims (Paul Nelson, personal communication, August 1999). Even so, it is important for counselors to have protection for any foreseeable future that is probable. The period of time after the event and before the claim is filed is called a "tail" in insurance parlance, and counselors who explore liability coverage should ask agents about the length of the tail. Remember, a counselor might harm someone during one year, but the client might not realize it for several years and might take even longer to decide to bring charges.

Multicultural and Diversity Issues

Professional associations have struggled during recent years to find effective ways in which to serve both members and clients from multicultural and diverse populations. Although each

ACA division includes multicultural awareness in its program activities, one ACA division, the Association for Multicultural Counseling and Development (AMCD), is devoted to multicultural issues, primarily those related to persons of color. Another newer division, the Association for Gay, Lesbian, and Bisexual Issues in Counseling (AGLBIC), emphasizes issues related to gay, lesbian, bisexual, and transgender persons. One division, the Association for Adult Development and Aging (AADA), emphasizes matters related to adult development and aging. These divisions have developed as members of ACA have identified needs that were not being met by existing entities. When a significant number of persons affirm that they are committed to a particular issue or activity, there are procedures for them to become a recognized group and, ultimately, a freestanding division within ACA.

A special emphasis has been under way for the past few years that would develop a multicultural agenda for ACA. In response to concerns that the entire organization needed to become more responsive to matters of multicultural and diverse populations, a series of task forces has been at work under the leadership of Courtland Lee, past president of ACA, to identify issues and develop strategies for response. These strategies include structural and organizational changes as well as emphasis on content and procedures that each association entity should consider to be most effective in serving multicultural and diverse populations.

Lobby Efforts

Professional associations also provide counselors with a voice. ACA regularly invests a portion of its budget and both its professional staff and volunteer activities in lobbying efforts at local, state, and national levels. Because it is a tax-exempt organization—called a 501(c)(3) organization—there are limitations on the amount of member money that can be spent on governmental lobbying efforts, but the association maintains a continuing governmental presence. A single counselor may be heard by a congressperson with whom the counselor has a personal relationship, but issues that affect the profession are best addressed by association personnel who can represent several thousand members in a particular category. A description of ACA's lobbying efforts and text of public policy statements can be found on the association's Web page.

New Knowledge

A professional association such as ACA becomes the primary vehicle for disseminating new knowledge within the field of counseling. Traditional forms of dissemination—print journals and conference presentations—remain a central form of presenting new ideas to colleagues in the profession. New forms of disseminating knowledge use new technologies—electronic journals, videoconferences, chat rooms for members, searchable databases, and listservs. The ACA Web page has been cited several times thus far in this chapter; persons who access that Web page will note that some of the links may be accessed only by members.

The traditional information sources—print journal articles and conference presentations—usually are subject to editorial review before distribution. Journal article manuscripts customarily are read by three persons qualified to judge the merits of the articles. These readers do not know the authors' identities; thus, the term *blind review* is applied to the editorial process. Journal articles published as a result of the blind review process generally are valued more highly than articles that are not reviewed. Persons in the profession are seeking procedures that will permit the more instantaneous publication and distribution of electronic manuscripts that meet the same rigorous review as those traditionally used with print media. Conference presentations that are blind reviewed by a panel or committee before acceptance generally are called *juried* or *refereed* presentations. These are procedures that the professional association uses to ensure quality of content and to avoid presentation of information or research that does not meet the standards required in the counseling profession.

Employment

Professional associations also are avenues for employment. Employers list position openings in different association publications in both print and electronic form. Conventions and conferences provide a setting for employment networking and job interviewing. Some employment procedures require nominal fees paid by prospective employers or employees; however, members of the association usually obtain the services at significant cost advantage.

Related Associations

Several other professional associations include a focus or an emphasis on counseling. The American College Personnel Association (ACPA) is a freestanding association that was one of the original ACA divisions. Its members emphasize college personnel issues including counseling matters. The American Vocational Association

(AVA) includes a counseling section and has been allied for many years with the personnel and guidance movement. AVA and the National Career Development Association (NCDA) have developed numerous cooperative activities over the years. Persons in social work and psychology have professional associations available to them that include counseling functions. The National Association of Social Work (NASW) and the American Psychological Association (APA) both have many members interested in counseling. Other associations that include an emphasis on counseling include the American Rehabilitation Counseling Association (ARCA), the American Association of Marriage and Family Therapists (AAMFT), the National Rehabilitation Association (NRA), the American Educational Research Association (AERA), and the International Association of Educational and Vocational Guidance (IAEVG).

Honor Societies

Another way that both students and practicing professionals have of forming colleague groups is through honor societies. Most higher education institutions have different honor societies available to students through either demonstrated academic performance or special interest activities. One major honor society is devoted to counseling, Chi Sigma Iota (CSI). Information about CSI is available from its printed materials or from its Web page (www. csi-net.org). Chapters have been organized on more than 200 college campuses. Each chapter might have a special focus that it has developed; however, CSI has identified counselor advocacy as a long-term, sustained commitment (see its Web page). To this end, position papers have been written and international conferences have been held to promote professional counseling. CSI has taken the position that it advocates for both counselors and their clients. Six themes have been presented that guide this advocacy approach: (a) *counselor education,* to ensure that all counselor education students graduate with a clear identity and sense of pride as professional counselors; (b) *intraprofessional relations,* to develop and implement a unified collaborative advocacy plan for the advancement of counselors and those they serve; (c) *marketplace recognition,* to ensure that professional counselors in all settings are suitably compensated for their services and are free to provide service to the public within all areas of their competence; (d) *interprofessional issues,* to establish collaborative working relationships with other organizations, groups, and disciplines on matters of mutual interest and concern so as to achieve advocacy goals for both counselors and their clients; (e) *research,* to promote professional counselors and the services they provide based on scientifically sound research; and (f) *prevention/wellness,* to promote optimal human development across the life span through prevention and wellness.

Like most honorary societies, CSI chapters develop their own activities, both professional and social. Many have raised funds that were used to support various persons and benevolent activities. Information about organizing a CSI chapter can be obtained from the CSI executive director, whose address can be found on the Web page cited earlier.

Preparation Standards

Colleges and universities use a variety of organizations and procedures for describing the quality of their educational programs. The most familiar to the general public probably are the weekly periodicals, such as *Newsweek* and *U.S. News and World Report,* that annually rank college programs. The rankings create much discussion. Colleges and universities that rank high on these popular press ratings use the information in recruiting materials and often quote the rankings in other presentations. Internally, university program faculty might quote the rankings to justify additional expenditures of money so that the universities can move up in future ratings. Those institutions that rank near the bottom of the quality indicator lists often release statements that the ratings are flawed or that they have failed to consider some of the more important characteristics of those particular institutions. There also are methods of ranking academic programs that frequently are published by researchers in scholarly journals such as the *Journal of Counseling and Development* and *Counselor Education and Supervision.* These articles might use degree production, faculty-student ratio, and scholarly production of the faculty as major criteria for ranking academic programs. For example, the frequency with which a university program's faculty are published or cited in scholarly journals is used as an indicator of quality.

Accreditation

The more traditional preparation standards are those developed by related professional associations through careful scrutiny and rigorous study. In counseling, the most important accreditation body is the Council for Accreditation of Counseling and Related Educational Programs (CACREP). CACREP, as an organization, exists independently of ACA but is influenced by ACA through cooperative procedures in the naming of board of director members, funding, and revision of the standards that are used in the accreditation process.

CACREP was formed in 1981 through the efforts of committed members of the counseling profession. The Association for Counselor Education and Supervision (ACES) cooperated with ACA over several years to develop initial standards for counselor education and supervision. Both organizations contributed resources to the development of CACREP. Accreditation processes from CACREP remain as voluntary efforts; institutions go through the rigorous standards review because they decide to do so (Sweeney, 1995). Additional information about CACREP can be obtained from its Web site (www.counseling.org/cacrep).

Development of standards, accreditation processes, licensure, certification, and the related changes in education programs and professional practice are in a constant state of dynamic tension; changes or modifications in one component affect all other components. These elements constantly evolve, even though that evolution appears to happen in jerks and starts. An adopted set of standards will be in force for several years before new standards come into play that reflect changes in theory, practice, education, or other applications. When the new standards or processes are implemented, the change is noted as a plateau jump rather than as a gradual evolution. All of the entities described in this chapter—professional associations, accrediting agencies, licensing agencies, educational institutions, and professional counselors—continually work to improve. The individual professional counselor serves the profession best by being involved in the changes

rather than just watching or ignoring them. A comprehensive discussion of professional counseling and related accreditation issues was described in a special issue of the *Journal of Counseling and Development* (Myers, 1995) and in Myers' chapter on specialties in this volume (Chapter 3).

To be accredited is to say to the public that an educational program has met or exceeded criteria of educational quality (CACREP, 1994). To become accredited by CACREP, an institution or a program (e.g., a counseling program) must (a) complete a thorough self-study following a prescribed content outline, (b) apply to and have persons from CACREP review the completed self-study document, (c) undergo a site visit by trained CACREP visitors who have reviewed the self-study, and (d) meet the standards defined by CACREP as determined by a vote of the governing body of the organization. The entire accreditation process may take 12 or more months to complete. The costs of the self-study and the accreditation site visit are substantial. The personnel and time costs to prepare the self-study also are significant.

The advantages to an institutional program of being accredited are listed in the CACREP (1994) manual. To the public, the listed advantages are (a) an assurance of external evaluation, (b) identification of those institutions that are willing to submit themselves to review, (c) improvement in professional services, and (d) a decreased need for intervention by public agencies. The advantages to students are listed as (a) assurance that the educational activities of the institutions have been found to be satisfactory; (b) assistance in transfer of credits; and (c) a prerequisite, in some instances, for entering the profession. The advantages to the institution are listed as (a) a stimulus for self-evaluation and program improvements, (b) strengthening of institutional and program evaluation, (c) application of established criteria to programs, (d) enhancing the programs and institutional reputations, and (e) providing some means to access programs of governmental aid. The same publication lists the advantages to the profession of accreditation to be that it (a) provides a means for the participation of practitioners in setting the requirements for entering the profession and (b) contributes to the unity of the profession by bringing together practitioners, teachers, and students in an activity directed at improving professional preparation and professional practice. The preceding lists have been paraphrased from the CACREP (1994) manual.

Persons considering enrolling in a graduate program in counseling would be advised to explore the accreditation status of the program. That information should be readily available from either the institution or CACREP itself. The CACREP Web page lists accredited institutions by state and indicates which of the institutions' programs meet CACREP specialty standards. In addition, if a program has failed to meet the standards or has some probationary status imposed, that information is available. Prospective students who eventually will seek some type of licensing on completing their studies also need to determine the relationship of graduation from an accredited program to the license processes in the states where they intend to practice. Because licensing is a function of the state, requirements may differ significantly from state to state, and students are advised to check requirements in advance of their graduate work. State licensing agencies frequently write their application criteria using CACREP accreditation standards as a guide.

CACREP Content

CACREP-accredited programs will have met standards in the following six categories: (a) institutional characteristics, (b) program objectives and curriculum, (c) clinical instruction, (d) faculty and staff, (e) organization and evaluation, and (f) program evaluations. For example, institutional characteristics will include adequacy of library holdings, whether the institution is accredited by other organizations, and how the counseling program is administered. Program objectives will include instruction in core areas—human growth and development, social and cultural foundations, helping relationships, group work, lifestyle and career development, appraisal, research and program evaluation, and professional orientation. Clinical instruction will include the number of hours of practicum and internship that students must complete and will describe both the quality of the supervision to be received and the number of hours per week in supervision required. Faculty and staff qualifications must meet standards in terms of appropriate degrees and professional experience as well as involvement in appropriate professional activities. The organization and administration of programs must comply with certain standards including how information is disseminated to students and whether faculty have reasonable teaching loads. Periodic program evaluations must be completed through data from graduates and employers.

CACREP Specialties

Institutions seeking CACREP accreditation also designate specific programs or specialties that they wish to have recognized. Separate standards in addition to the core standards are defined for each of the specialties. The 1994 standards listed the following specialties: (a) community counseling, (b) gerontological counseling, (c) marriage and family counseling/therapy, (d) mental health counseling, (e) school counseling, and (f) student affairs practice in higher education. As revisions in the CACREP standards are made, different specialties may be included. Changes proposed to be effective in 2001 include (a) career counseling, (b) college counseling and student affairs, (c) community counseling, (d) gerontological counseling, (e) marital/couple and family counseling/therapy, (f) mental health counseling, and (g) school counseling (CACREP, 1999). Note both the similarity of specialty and the slightly different wording of several of the specialties. These changes reflect the continuing effort of the CACREP board to ensure that the specialties and standards reflect current and future thinking in the profession. An additional specialty in counselor education and supervision is included at the doctoral level for those institutions that meet the requisite qualifications. For an expanded discussion of counseling specialties, see the special issue of the *Journal of Counseling and Development* (Myers, 1995) and Myers's chapter on specialties in this volume (Chapter 3).

Licensing and Certification

Two words are commonly used in describing counselor credentials: *license* and *certificate*. There are differences between them, but many people use these two words interchangeably. Licensing nearly always is a function of the state. Certification may be a function of the state or a function of an organization or board that exists independently of state governments. For example, states grant licenses to professional counselors; the National Board for Certified Counselors (NBCC) grants certificates to counselors. In some states, teachers and school counselors hold licenses to do their work; in other states, teachers and school counselors might have certificates that cover their qualifications. A certificate is an official statement that something is a fact—a verification that a counselor has met certain qualifications of education or a certain score on a specified examination. A license is permission to either do a particular thing or use a particular title. In many states, it might be that anyone can call himself or herself a counselor, but only persons who have applied to and met the requirements established by a state agency can call themselves licensed counselors (LCs) or licensed professional counselors (LPCs). Licenses may further define the functions a person may or may not perform, for example, who may prescribe medication, perform marriages, complete psychological diagnoses, conduct psychotherapy, or do counseling.

In 1976, Virginia was the first state to pass a counselor licensing law. Other states have added or modified license laws since then, with the most recent counselor license laws passed as recently as 1998. Counselor licensing continues to be a regular item on many state legislative agendas. Across the states, there are at least 16 different titles used for licensed or certified counselors, with LPCs being the most frequently used (30 states). Licensed mental health counselors (LMHCs) and certified professional counselors (CPCs) both are used in 5 states. Several states use more than one title for counselors in their state regulations. Updated information about state license status can be obtained from an NBCC Web site (www.nbcc.org/states/key.htm).

NBCC was incorporated in 1982 as a credentialing body. It administers a certification system for counselors and provides information to other counselors and the public about who has met the necessary education and examination requirements to be certified. NBCC traditionally has used the CACREP standards to define the educational requirements needed for a person who applies for status as a nationally certified counselor (NCC). Persons who meet those requirements are entitled to use the "NCC" initials to publicly indicate their certification status. To maintain that status, NCCs must pay an annual fee, meet annual continuing education requirements, and remain in good standing with the counseling profession. NBCC lists more than 28,000 counselors as NCCs and reports that 37 states and the District of Columbia use the National Counselor Examination (NCE) as part of their licensure processes.

Persons who hold the NCC designation can lose it in several ways. Other counselors or clients may bring charges against counselors. If the charges are found to be true, then various penalties may be imposed by NBCC including revocation of the certificate status. That information is publicly announced in NBCC publications, and if members of the public inquire about a counselor's status, they will be informed whether the person is or is not a certificate holder in good standing.

Both licensing and certification provide the public with assurances about counselors and with avenues for redress of grievances if they occur. Members of the public who work with unlicensed or noncertified counselors have only the civil or criminal courts to rely on if they believe that they have been treated unfairly or unprofessionally.

Specialty Certification

In addition to the NCC designation, there are several specialty certification designations available from NBCC for persons who meet the particular qualifications of each. Persons may apply for specialty certification as school counselors, clinical mental health counselors, or addictions counselors (NBCC, 1999). Each of those specialties has its own title, with accompanying initials as designators; school counselors become nationally certified school counselors (NCSCs), mental health counselors become nationally certified clinical mental health counselors (NCCMHCs), and addictions counselors become master addictions counselors (MACs). For several years, NBCC also certified career counselors (NCCCs) and gerontological counselors (NCGCs); however, new applications for those certifications have been suspended by NBCC. Only the persons who already held the designations may continue to have those certifications for their use. The plethora of initials that indicate degrees, certifications, associations, accrediting agencies, universities, and licenses are easily a source of confusion for consumers. Counseling professionals must make certain that they present themselves in a way that does not confuse, but rather informs, the consumer and the public.

Codes of Ethics

NBCC has developed a code of ethics for persons who become NCCs. A standard practice for professional counselors is to have that code displayed or easily available to clients as a means of informing them and the public of their rights and responsibilities as well as the rights and responsibilities of the counselors. In addition to the basic code of ethics, NBCC (1999) has been developing codes of ethics for the practice of counseling through the World Wide Web, for the ethical practice of clinical supervision, and for the ethical practice of career development facilitators. NBCC and CSI have collaborated to develop a statement of rights and responsibilities for both counselors and clients that can be displayed in an office or presented to clients.

The Future

During the next several years, we undoubtedly will see major changes in all of the components of professional counseling that have been discussed in this chapter. The practice of counseling will change, as will the professional associations that serve counselors, the educational institutions that prepare them, the accreditation standards that are used to evaluate those educational institutions, and the licenses and certificates that those professional counselors hold. A major force bringing change to these components will continue to be the rapid advance of technology, in particular, the changes to be found in electronic communication processes.

In 1990, I described a futuristic counseling scenario that involved a client-counselor interaction via holographic projections (Collison, 1990). In that scenario, the client and counselor appeared to be in the same room, but in actuality, they could have been miles apart. Holographic projections are not immediately available on the current scene, but video simulcasts are, and with even a modest investment one can mount a digital camera on top of a home personal computer that could be (and, in some instances, is) linked to that of a counselor in some remote location. At the time of this writing, this technology is very limited, and neither picture nor sound quality is good; however, with the speed of technological change that we experience, high-quality picture and sound transmission undoubtedly are on the immediate horizon.

Technological changes create a major shift in the way that personal communication takes place. Professional associations no longer have to assemble thousands of members in some central meeting place to exchange the newest ideas about the counseling profession. ACA already makes use of telephone conference calls to convene committees and governing bodies to make major decisions. National videoconferences have been held with multiple receiver sites scattered across the world, where participants interact visually and verbally with experts who might or might not be gathered at a single location.

The practice of counseling will change rapidly with various uses of Web-based communication, therapeutic chat rooms replacing group sessions, and supervision groups that meet online for regular discussion and viewing of counseling sessions. Questions of confidentiality, security, and ethical responsibility abound in these situations that will continue to escalate as the technology improves and, simultaneously, becomes less expensive and more accessible.

Preparation, licensure, and accreditation standards must change to meet the demands of technological advances. For example, supervision standards presently are written with face-to-face supervision as the only parameter. Obviously, those standards must be rewritten to allow for alternate meeting formats if the professional counseling research and literature demonstrate that supervision can, in fact, take place with effectiveness in something other than a face-to-face venue.

Electronic counseling applications also require new modes of certification and licensing. Licenses are granted by a state for a licensed counselor to practice in that state. With electronic communication processes, state boundaries have little meaning, so that a client could be in an east coast state and the counselor in a west coast state. Jurisdiction becomes a critical issue, as do matters of reporting abuse, complaints of malpractice, and standards of care. Do the licenses and laws of the state where the counselor practices apply to counseling, or is the client's state the jurisdictional determinant? Recently, I read a counselor's personal Web page that implied that client information could be shared with the counselor with impunity through the World Wide Web that possibly would have to be reported if the two met face-to-face in the state where the counselee lived.

Although it has not been a subject for this chapter thus far, the serious concerns about managed care and payment for services no doubt will continue to increase in the future. Each of the components discussed in this chapter has a bearing on how services are delivered and how they are reimbursed. The health care industry has not yet taken control of the accreditation or licensing of counselors, but that industry has made decisions that determine which counseling group will be allowed to provide service for fees. These will be hotly contested matters for professional counselors in the future. The contest will affect professional associations, preparation programs and standards, licensing, and all of the other components discussed thus far in this chapter.

Within professional associations, and within the profession, some struggles will continue to exist, new ones will emerge, and some will fade away. During recent years, ACA has undergone organizational struggles, with some divisions choosing to leave the association to operate more independently. One question this has represented is whether *counseling* has a single definition or whether there are multiple definitions. For example, is a school counselor a counselor who works in a school? Or, is a school counselor such a specialized person that he or she is not the same as a mental health counselor? Should the word *counselor* have a generic meaning or only specialized meanings? This same issue has surfaced in certification programs around the issue of general knowledge or specialty knowledge—and the subsequent preparations, certificates, and licenses that apply. NBCC experienced several years of what seemed like proliferation of specialties. During recent years, new applications for two specialties—NCCCs and NCGCs—have been suspended. The profession must resolve the issue of generalization versus specialization.

The ultimate question that must be answered for the future is how counseling will change and how all the different components of professional counseling will keep up with the changes that technological advance will trigger. The slow rate of change in traditional systems such as higher education, professional standards, and license laws has no comparison with the rate of change in technology, where one must hurry to unbox a new computer so that it will not be too far out of date by the time one turns it on. If associations and standards and license groups cannot keep up or lead, then they might take on the appearance of having less value, and that could lead to being either ignored or replaced. It clearly is an opportunity for members of the professional counseling community to be vigorous in pursuit of the matters that affect their lives.

References

Bertram, B., & Wheeler, N. (Speakers). (1996). *Risk management strategies* [Cassette recording]. Alexandria, VA: ACA Insurance Trust.

Collison, B. B. (1990). Counseling in the twenty-first century. In D. Capuzzi & D. Gross (Eds.), *Introduction to counseling: Perspectives for the 1990s* (pp. 469-486). Boston: Allyn & Bacon.

Council for Accreditation of Counseling and Related Educational Programs. (1994). *CACREP accreditation standards and procedures manual*. Alexandria, VA: Author.

Council for Accreditation of Counseling and Related Educational Programs. (1999, August). *CACREP standards revision process* [Online]. Available: www.counseling.org/cacrep/srprocess.htm

Myers, J. E. (Ed.). (1995). Professional counseling: Spotlight on specialties [Special issue]. *Journal of Counseling and Development, 74*(2).

National Board for Certified Counselors. (1999, May). *About NBCC: National Board for Certified Counselors, Inc.* [Online]. Available: www.nbcc.org/aboutnbcc.htm

Sweeney, T. J. (1995). Accreditation, credentialing, professionalization: The role of specialties. *Journal of Counseling and Development, 74*, 117-125.

CHAPTER FIVE

Legal and Ethical Challenges in Counseling

BARBARA HERLIHY
THEODORE P. REMLEY, JR.

It is critically important for counselors to have a thoughtful and up-to-date understanding of the legal and ethical dimensions of counseling. When people who are in emotional distress seek professional help, they place a great deal of trust in their counselors. As they tell their stories, and as they take risks in exploring painful feelings and trying out new ways of thinking and behaving, they make themselves vulnerable. Thus, counselors have considerable power in the therapeutic relationship, and this power must be used responsibly. Because clients have invested their trust in counselors, counselors must be trustworthy. They must respect the freedom and dignity of their clients and have the knowledge, skills, and judgment to provide effective services. These obligations form the foundations of ethical practice.

Although very few counselors have extensive legal training, they do need to have a working knowledge of the law as it applies to their practice. As Swenson (1997) noted, laws are having greater and greater influence on the behavior of mental health professionals, and psychological variables are becoming increasingly important within the legal system. Thus, Swenson argued, "cross-disciplinary knowledge is important for effective professional performance" (p. 4). But beyond the need for counselors to understand basic legal principles, it is vital for them to be able to recognize legal issues as they arise and know how to secure legal advice when needed.

The importance of law and ethics in the counseling profession is underscored by the fact that, in many jurisdictions, it is impossible for a counselor to begin practicing without having a demonstrable grasp of legal and ethical issues. The bodies that credential counselors, such as state licensing boards and national and state certification agencies, require the counselors they endorse to demonstrate knowledge in this arena. In some states, practicing counselors must keep current with legal and ethical issues so as to qualify for renewal of their licenses. Aside from these external forces, however, we would hope that professional counselors feel an internal push to practice in ways that are legally and ethically sound so as to promote the welfare of their clients and offer them the best possible services.

Although counseling is a relatively new mental health profession (at least in comparison to psychology and social work), counselors have achieved increasing recognition as legitimate providers of mental health services. Along with this recognition has come an increase in expectations. Counselors are being held to a higher standard of care by regulatory boards, in courts of law, and by more informed consumers. At the same time, the practice of counseling has become vastly more complex. Today's counselors grapple with complicated ethical and legal issues associated with developments such as managed care, genetic engineering, and families with a wide array of nontraditional configurations. More than ever before in the history of our profession, counselors must be informed and capable of dealing appropriately with the ethical and legal challenges of contemporary practice.

Law and ethics share some similarities, but they also are distinguished by some significant differences. Lawyers and mental health professionals both are called *counselors,* and they deal with people who are experiencing conflict and may be under considerable stress. Both see their roles as helping their clients to resolve problems, although they approach this task in very different ways. Legal proceedings take place within an adversarial system in which two opposing sides present their best arguments, with the outcome being that one side wins and the other loses. Professional counselors, by contrast, approach the resolution of conflicts between humans by searching for "win-win" solutions within a cooperative framework.

Law is an ancient discipline, whereas counseling is much more recent. Laws are a necessary means of social control without which we would have anarchy. Although we recognize the need for some measure of control to maintain an orderly society, Americans are quite adamant about preserving their individual freedoms. Thus, the law exists in a state of dynamic tension, with the rights of individuals balanced against the rights of society. Only those constraints that are deemed to be necessary are enacted into law.

Ethics is a discipline within philosophy that is concerned with human conduct, moral decision making, and how humans should treat each other. Applied to the counseling profession, ethics refers to conduct that is deemed to be good or right for counselors as a professional group. Professional counselors try to practice aspirational ethics, meaning that they strive to meet the highest possible standards of conduct. They look outward to established codes of ethics but also look inward and ask themselves whether they are doing their best for their clients.

How law and ethics are defined as disciplines is a reflection of some of the basic differences between them. Remley and Herlihy (2001) explained that laws dictate the minimum standards of behavior that society will tolerate. Applied to the counseling profession, they are the "musts" of behavior to which counselors must adhere. They are created by elected officials, enforced by police, and interpreted by judges. Ethics represent the ideals or aspirations of the counseling profession. They are the "shoulds" that guide counselors as they strive for the very best practices. Ethics are created by counselors themselves and are interpreted and enforced by ethics committees and licensure and certification boards. When legal or ethical problems arise, legal advice generally is aimed at protecting the counselors, whereas advice regarding ethical issues focuses on protecting the welfare of the clients.

Just as the law is an evolving human creation that changes constantly, codes of professional ethics are living documents that are revised periodically as knowledge expands and as consensus develops around emerging ethical issues (Remley & Herlihy, 2001). Therefore, counselors need to work constantly to stay abreast of legal and ethical developments that affect their work.

This chapter highlights the primary legal and ethical challenges facing contemporary counselors. Specific guidelines for meeting these challenges successfully are offered.

Recognizing Legal and Ethical Challenges

When counselors are faced with challenges to their practices, they often find it difficult to distinguish whether they have a legal concern or an ethical concern. Legal challenges are not always easy to recognize. Remley and Herlihy (2001) suggested that counselors should study their situations to see whether (a) legal proceedings of any type have been initiated, (b) they are vulnerable to having complaints filed against them for misconduct, or (c) attorneys are on the scene in some capacity. When counselors are practicing counseling and any of these situations apply, the counselors definitely are dealing with legal challenges.

Ethical challenges arise when counselors are faced with two or more equally desirable but incompatible possible actions to resolve a problem. In these instances, counselors can look to certain moral principles for guidance. There is general agreement among ethics scholars that these five moral principles undergird the helping professions: respect for autonomy, beneficence, nonmaleficence, justice, and fidelity. The principle of *respect for autonomy* refers to counselors' obligation to foster client self-determination and to decrease client dependency. *Beneficence* means to do good or to actively promote clients' mental health. *Nonmaleficence* means to do no harm. *Justice* means that counselors must be fair to all parties concerned in resolving an ethical dilemma. *Fidelity* means being faithful to promises made to clients.

Often, these principles compete with each other in a given situation, thus creating an ethical dilemma. For example, when a counselor is working with a teenager who might be suicidal, the principles of nonmaleficence and beneficence appear to suggest that the counselor enlist the assistance of the parents in keeping the teen safe from harm. This action, however, seems to violate the principles of respect for autonomy and fidelity in that notifying the parents would infringe on the client's autonomy and would breach the client's confidentiality if the teenager does not want the counselor to inform the parents.

Counselors find it unsettling and anxiety provoking when they receive subpoenas, when clients threaten to file complaints against them, when they must choose between two competing but equally desirable courses of action, and whenever they are confronted with legal or ethical challenges. Steps to take when responding to legal or ethical problems are discussed next.

Responding to Legal and Ethical Challenges

Counselors always are well advised to consult with others when they are uncertain about their best course of action in a professional situation. It is important, however, to choose an appropriate consultant.

Consulting With Attorneys

Counselors who are confronted with legal challenges never should ask fellow mental health professionals for advice regarding what to do. When counselors have legal problems, only attorneys have the legal knowledge needed to provide sound advice.

The next step for counselors is to formulate legal questions. A proper legal question asks a lawyer to explain whether there are statutes, case law, or common law principles that dictate a course of action in a particular situation. Legal questions should begin with phrases such as the following: "Does the law require . . . ?" "Is there a law that is relevant to the following situation . . . ?" and "Given this situation, am I prohibited by law to . . . ?" Legal questions that are formulated well avoid asking clinical opinions

or advice in professional judgment areas. For example, a counselor should not ask a lawyer whether a client's behavior means that he or she is at risk for suicide or whether a particular dual relationship boundary should be crossed.

Once counselors have formulated the legal questions they need answered, they should request legal advice. Counselors who are employed by agencies, schools, hospitals, or other organizations have the advantage of being able to take the questions to their supervisors and ask for assistance. The supervisors will, in turn, either answer the questions or take them to the attorneys who handle legal issues for their organizations. It is unlikely that supervisors will allow counselors direct access to the attorneys, for two reasons. First, counselors who are stressed over legal issues probably will want to tell the lawyers all the details of their situations, and most lawyers charge by the minute. Second, supervisors like to maintain their authority in making decisions that affect their employees.

When counselors ask their supervisors for help with legal concerns, the supervisors should be willing to provide the assistance. Employers have a legal obligation to provide their employees with the legal advice they need to perform their jobs adequately. Counselors may take some comfort in knowing that asking their supervisors for help with legal questions shifts the liability to their employers, even if the requested advice is not forthcoming. If advice is given, then the supervisors (or the attorneys who advised the supervisors) become responsible for that advice.

Sometimes, supervisors do not give counselors the answers they were hoping to hear. Counselors might even completely disagree with the advice. If they believe that the supervisors or attorneys have failed to understand important dimensions of their problems, counselors can express their concerns and attempt to clarify the issues. Once the supervisors or lawyers have given the advice, however, counselors should follow it precisely. This is the only way in which they can protect themselves from being held individually liable if their actions are challenged later. Employers will support counselors who follow their directives but might not be required to do so if counselors have ignored their advice.

Counselors in private practice do not have the same opportunities to obtain legal advice as do employed counselors. Self-employed counselors will need to find attorneys on their own initiative. Private practitioners should establish relationships with lawyers when they begin their practices in the same way as they establish relationships with accountants, bankers, and others who help them to run their businesses. If possible, they should look for attorneys who represent other mental health professionals in the community. Such lawyers already will have some familiarity with legal issues faced by counselors. If this is not possible, then attorneys who represent other health care professionals, such as physicians, might be viable choices.

Independent practitioners should make contact with potential attorneys, have conversations, and then determine whether they feel comfortable and confident with these people's representation. It probably will not be necessary to place attorneys on retainers, which can be costly. Rather, agreements usually can be reached in which the attorneys agree to be contacted when questions or problems arise. It is far better for counselors to have established relationships with attorneys than to search frantically for legal assistance after legal problems arise.

Consulting With Colleagues

In the previous section, we described an ethical dilemma as a situation in which a counselor must choose between two or more desirable but mutually exclusive actions. A counselor who finds himself or herself in such a situation might begin by gathering and organizing all relevant information that is available to him or her (Welfel, 1998). Then, it might be useful for the counselor to ask, "What do I want to see happen in this situation?" This helps to generate desired outcomes, and because most ethical dilemmas are complex, there usually will be several potential outcomes that could benefit the client and others involved.

Next, the counselor might generate a list of possible actions he or she could take that likely would lead to these outcomes. Some feminist scholars have suggested that counselors, in addition to asking themselves what they should do, should ask themselves who they want to be in the situation. In other words, these scholars believe that it is important to focus on the actor as well as the actions and to consider what is morally right or "virtuous" rather than focus exclusively on the possible consequences of the decision.

The initial steps in addressing ethical problems, as described previously, require the counselor to use a reflective process and rely primarily on his or her internal resources. There are helpful external resources as well, and primary among these is the counselor's code of ethics. Thus, an important step is to review the code carefully for guidance relevant to the question at hand.

Another vital element in resolving both ethical and legal questions is consultation. Again, choosing an appropriate consultant is key to making the consultation effective. Although a counselor might be tempted to ask advice from a friend whom the counselor expects to agree with his or her thinking, colleagues who practice in similar circumstances or who have similar training and experience are more likely to provide helpful perspectives on the problem. Other mental health professionals who have particular expertise, either in ethics or in a specialty area relevant to the situation, can be helpful as well. It usually is prudent for a counselor who has an ethical question to ask for more than one opinion. If there is consensus among the consultants, then the counselor should follow the advice given. It would be extremely difficult for the counselor, if challenged later, to explain why advice was sought and then ignored.

Finally, a counselor who is employed should seek administrative support for any actions taken that could be considered unusual and should document carefully. Documentation should include who was consulted and when, what advice was given, what actions were taken and the rationale for those actions, results, and follow-up.

Six Critical Legal and Ethical Challenges

Although there are a multitude of possible legal and ethical challenges to a counselor's practice, this chapter focuses on six that are critical. Legal challenges include dealing with clients who are a danger to themselves or others, responding to subpoenas, and operating private practices. Ethical challenges that are addressed include dealing effectively with boundary issues, obtaining informed consent from clients, and

determining one's level of competence. Keep in mind that none of these challenges is exclusively legal or exclusively ethical in nature. There are ethical considerations in each of the legal issues, and there are some legal aspects to each of the issues that are primarily ethical. Guidelines for meeting each challenge are offered.

Three Legal Challenges

Responding to Clients Who Are a Danger to Themselves or Others

Counselors take very seriously their confidentiality pledge to clients. They breach confidentiality only in limited circumstances. One situation that often requires breaching confidentiality is when clients, in the counselors' judgment, pose a danger to themselves or others. In these instances, the duty to protect the people in danger supersedes the obligation to maintain confidentiality.

As a result of the landmark *Tarasoff* court case (*Tarasoff v. Regents of University of California,* 1976), mental health professionals in some jurisdictions have a legal duty to warn identifiable or reasonably foreseeable victims of clients who pose a danger to others. Many similar cases have been decided since *Tarasoff,* and the courts have reasoned somewhat differently in each of them. It should be noted that not all states have accepted or applied what has come to be known as the "Tarasoff doctrine," that statutes vary considerably with respect to what actions mental health professionals are allowed or required to take when they determine that a danger exists, and that counselors are not always included among the mental health professionals who have a duty to warn. This makes it extremely difficult for counselors to know what their legal obligations are when any of their clients make credible threats to harm other people. It is essential that they learn whether a legal duty to warn applies to their practices. If so, they must understand what actions they are allowed and required to take.

Counselors must decide whether particular clients pose a clear and imminent danger to others in the absence of any scientific basis for making such decisions. It is not possible to predict human behavior accurately, yet this is what a duty to warn requires. Counselors can err by issuing unnecessary warnings or by inappropriately failing to warn. Both types of error can have excruciating consequences for the counselors. Counselors are not legally required to predict beforehand whether particular clients will harm themselves or others. Instead, counselors are required to assess their situations in a manner that a reasonable professionally competent counselor would have and to take actions that are warranted given the circumstances.

It could be devastating on a personal level for a counselor to determine that a client was unlikely to act on a threat, only to learn that the client had hurt or even killed someone. It is entirely possible that an ethics committee or a claimant in court, with the perfect vision that comes with hindsight, would question whether such a counselor could have or should have acted to prevent the harm. In the opposite scenario, a counselor might decide that a client does pose a danger to others and issue a warning. Then, if the client does not act in a harmful way, not only has the counseling relationship been destroyed, but the counselor has labeled the client as dangerous and could be accused of defamation of character, misdiagnosis, or violation of confidentiality (Remley & Herlihy, 2001).

Despite the difficulties involved, there are some methods of identifying clients who are most at risk for causing harm to others. Getting accurate histories is essential, as recent studies indicate consistently that the best predictor of violence is past violent behavior (Litwack, Kirschner, & Wack, 1993; McNeil & Binder, 1991; Mulvey & Lidz, 1995; Slovic & Monahan, 1995; Truscott, Evens, & Mansell, 1995). It is equally important to appraise clients' current behavior, decision-making skills, and social stability. Finn (1998) surveyed employee assistance professionals who worked with U.S. Postal Service employees. Participants in her study evaluated the following nine client characteristics as extremely important in assessing clients for risk of harm to others: history of violence, recent violent behavior, threats to harm others, access to a weapon, command hallucinations that command them to do something, a belief that they had nothing to lose, access to a victim, poor impulse control, and symptoms of psychopathology.

Although identifying clients who are at high risk for violence toward others remains an imprecise science, once counselors have made determinations that clients pose a danger to others, they are legally required to take action to prevent harm. The action taken must be the least disruptive steps that could be reasonably presumed to be effective (Rice, 1993). Counselors have a wide range of options from which to choose. Relatively unintrusive actions include having the clients promise not to harm anyone or persuading the clients to submit to psychiatric evaluations. An intermediate step might be to enlist the clients' families in keeping the clients under control. Highly intrusive measures, such as having the clients committed involuntarily to residential facilities and calling the police, should be taken only when counselors are quite convinced that the clients are in clear and imminent danger of harming others.

Consulting with other mental health professionals before taking action is highly recommended when the situation permits. This might be the best action counselors may have taken if their decisions are challenged later.

A duty to warn and protect applies not only to working with clients who are dangerous to others but also to those who pose a danger to themselves. Although counselors find it very stressful to work with suicidal clients (Corey, Corey, & Callanan, 1998), they must realize that, whatever their work setting, they are highly likely to encounter clients who express suicidal thoughts. They must be prepared to deal with these clients effectively. Precedent-setting court cases have established that counselors, as legitimate mental health professionals, must know how to accurately assess clients' risk for suicide. Counselors can be held liable for underreacting or overreacting to clients' potential for suicide (Remley & Herlihy, 2001).

When counselors suspect that clients' conditions might pose a danger to themselves, counselors' first step, as noted earlier, is to conduct risk assessments. It is vital to be aware of research findings. For example, it has been established that individuals who attempt suicide usually give certain cues such as giving away prized possessions. Counselors need to know the warning signs, and many resources are available including books, articles, and professional development workshops. Several commercial suicide risk assessment instruments are available and can be helpful, although counselors should not rely on them exclusively. Risk assessment

must be based on clinical observations, not just test results.

Once counselors have made the determinations that clients are at risk for suicide, they must take action to prevent harm and must use the least intrusive procedures that will be effective. Some less intrusive options might include requiring the clients to agree to be examined by mental health professionals who have expertise in assessing suicide risk and requiring the clients to see staff psychiatrists where the counselors are employed or psychiatrists at local hospitals. We do not recommend that counselors take no action other than entering into "no suicide" contracts with clients, although such documents might be therapeutically helpful. They might remind clients that mental health professionals should be contacted during crises. However, if clients do attempt or commit suicide, then documents such as "no suicide" contracts could be used to demonstrate that the counselors knew that the clients were at risk yet failed to take the necessary steps to prevent harm. Other possible actions range from working with clients to arrange for voluntary hospitalization, to involving clients' families or significant others in keeping the clients safe, to arranging for clients' involuntary commitment to psychiatric facilities. All of these interventions are disruptive to clients' lives and compromise the clients' confidentiality. Counselors' obligation to confidentiality is waived when their clients' conditions pose a danger to themselves. Nevertheless, it is important to limit disclosure to only that information that is necessary for someone else to be helpful.

It is impossible for counselors to be 100% certain when they make judgments regarding clients' potential for suicide. Thankfully, the law does not require that they always be correct in their assessments. Rather, the law requires that counselors make assessments that are based on current knowledge and that they do what other counselors with similar training and experience working in the same community would do. For this reason, it is essential that counselors consult with others when clients are at high risk for suicide. Of course, counselors should follow the advice of their consultants when there is consensus and should document actions taken.

Responding to Subpoenas

Counselors might feel anxious and intimidated when they receive subpoenas. This a natural reaction because subpoenas thrust counselors into the legal arena, with its unfamiliar rules and adversarial procedures. Subpoenas may request that counselors respond to written questions; turn over records; appear at a deposition, hearing, or trial; or appear and bring the records. Subpoenas, as official court documents, demand responses of some type. Counselors can get into trouble if they give confidential or privileged information in response to invalid subpoenas or if they fail to give information when the subpoenas are valid.

Counselors never should respond to subpoenas without first consulting attorneys. Counselors who are employed should notify their supervisors and request legal advice. Counselors who are self-employed should contact their own attorneys immediately after receiving the subpoenas. Counselors should feel free to explain to the attorneys any details of the cases that may be relevant to the subpoenas, as all conversations between them are privileged.

Only attorneys can determine whether subpoenas are valid. The attorneys will review the subpoenas and advise the counselors regarding how to respond. If counselors believe that the subpoenas are requesting information that is privileged, then the counselors should tell the attorneys (or the supervisors), who will research the issues and inform the counselors whether the subpoenas are invalid for that or any other reason. Attorneys also can assist counselors by initiating procedures such as asking the attorneys who issued the subpoenas to withdraw them or filing motions to quash the subpoenas.

Attorneys may advise counselors to comply with subpoenas. If that occurs, counselors should keep in mind several caveats. First, if records are subpoenaed, then counselors should provide copies—never the original records—and should provide only those records that are pertinent to the information requested. If the records contain information pertaining to individuals other than the clients involved, then attorneys usually will advise counselors to blank out those portions of the records. If counselors' records include any information given to the counselors by other professionals, then that information should not be produced. If counselors' testimonies are subpoenaed, then the counselors should not take their records to any legal proceedings unless the records also have been subpoenaed. The attorneys who issued the subpoenas sometimes will accept summaries prepared by the counselors rather than the actual case notes.

Counselors always should follow the advice of their attorneys or supervisors once they have asked for assistance in responding to subpoenas. If subpoenas include lists of written questions for counselors to answer (this form of subpoena is called an interrogatory), then the counselors should have the attorneys review the answers given. When subpoenas order counselors to appear at depositions, counselors should request that their attorneys accompany them to these proceedings. Depositions are taken before trials occur, usually in lawyers' offices, so there will be no judges present to rule on whether counselors should answer questions. Therefore, it is particularly important for counselors to have their attorneys present to advise them. When subpoenas direct counselors to appear at legal proceedings, counselors should ask their attorneys to tell them what to expect and should ask that the attorneys go with them to these proceedings, if possible.

Although appearing in court in response to subpoenas rarely is a pleasant experience for them, counselors can navigate the proceedings successfully by heeding the advice of attorneys, staying calm and nondefensive on the witness stand, and restricting their answers to only those questions that have been asked and that they have the knowledge or expertise to answer. Only counselors who are being paid as experts and who have been qualified by the presiding judge as expert witnesses should answer questions related to their professional opinions. If counselors who are not expert witnesses are asked their opinions, then they should decline to give them. A good response in such situations is that the counselor does not have enough information to form a professional opinion—which always is the case.

Operating Private Practices

There are a number of legal issues involved in operating private practices in counseling. It is important for counselors to realize that if they generate any income at all outside of their salaries, they are in business and have private practices (Remley & Herlihy, 2001). Depending on the state statutes and the nature of the services rendered that generated the income, counselors might need to be licensed by their state counselor licensing boards.

Counselors who generate income outside of wages or salaries must file a separate federal income tax form for income produced from a business. In states that have income taxes, similar forms sometimes must be filed at the state level as well.

There are numerous federal, state, and local requirements that must be addressed when counselors open their private practices. Haynsworth (1986) listed the following possible steps that might need to be taken:

- A federal tax identification number has to be obtained if there might be any employees.
- A professional license has to be obtained in some states.
- A business license must be applied for and obtained.
- Workers' compensation insurance or unemployment compensation insurance might have to be purchased.
- Employee bonds might be required.
- Liability, property damage, and/or other types of insurance might be needed.
- A fictitious or assumed name statute might need to be complied with.
- Other public filing requirements might exist.

Counselors with businesses must purchase business licenses from their local city halls or county courthouses (Alberty, 1989). Part of the process in purchasing a business license involves listing a business address. In most jurisdictions, zoning laws in some way prohibit or limit clients coming to residences. If residences are listed as the places of business, then counselors must indicate that no clients or customers come there for services. Each year, when business licenses are renewed, counselors must report their gross incomes and pay taxes to the city or county (Remley & Herlihy, 2001).

Counselors who generate income and fail to report that income on federal and state income tax forms, or fail to purchase and renew business licenses each year, are committing crimes. A number of counselors who are unaware of tax and business license requirements are in violation of these laws. Ignorance of legal requirements does not excuse those who violate them.

Counselors in private practice must set fees for their services. Although most professionals seek to establish the highest fees the market will tolerate, counselors are in a fiduciary relationship with clients. Therefore, they must set fees within a framework of basic fairness (Smith & Mallen, 1989).

Some counselors establish in their private practices the same "sliding scale" fee structure that is used by counseling centers supported by public funds or private charitable funds. A sliding scale fee structure sets the fee for services based on objective criteria such as amount of income and size of family. With sliding scales, individuals with more income and less financial burden pay more for the same services than do those with less income and more financial burden. Although a sliding scale seems more appropriate for nonprofit agencies than for private practices from a business perspective, counselors can adopt such a scheme for charging fees so long as they do not accept clients who receive health insurance reimbursement for the counselors' services. If counselors do participate in clients' receiving health insurance reimbursement for their services, then the only way in which they can have a sliding scale fee

structure is if they apply the formulas precisely for all clients, regardless of whether the clients have health insurance that reimburses them for the counselors' services (Remley & Herlihy, 2001).

Because of the exposure of their personal assets, it is essential that counselors purchase professional liability insurance for their practices. Counselors in private practice should purchase the best professional liability insurance available to them and should request the maximum coverage available. If possible, they should purchase policies that pay attorneys' fees and judgments, pay for legal representation if ethical complaints are filed against the counselors, pay for claims made for actions that occurred during the time the policy was in effect, and pay for claims against partners or employees.

Counselors in private practice also need insurance that covers injuries that might occur on their office premises (Schutz, 1990), the acts of omissions of those whom they might be supervising, and any other claims that might arise as a result of their businesses. This type of insurance is relatively inexpensive.

Three Ethical Issues

Dealing With Boundary Issues

Boundaries help to provide safety and structure in counseling by creating a border around the professional relationship that defines the roles and responsibilities of each member of the therapeutic dyad. A border is a "limit that promotes integrity" (Katherine, 1991, p. 4).

People often find it difficult to establish limits in their business, personal, and social lives. A wealth of literature exists to help people learn to set healthy boundaries, for example, books on assertiveness training, on helping teens deal with peer pressure, and on how to "fight fair" in a marriage. In the professional literature on counseling, discussion about boundaries has centered around the issue of dual or multiple relationships.

Dual or multiple relationships occur when counselors take on two or more roles simultaneously or sequentially with help seekers (Herlihy & Corey, 1997). A dual relationship is created whenever the role of counselor is combined with another relationship, which could be professional (e.g., professor, supervisor, employer) or personal (e.g., friend, close relative, sexual partner). Counselors generally are advised to make every effort to avoid these types of relationships because of their potential harm to clients. The American Counseling Association's (ACA, 1995) code of ethics requires counselors to be "aware of their influential position with respect to clients" and to "avoid exploiting the trust and dependency of clients" (Standard A.6.a). These phrases point to the primary risk factor in dual relationships. There is a power differential in the counseling relationship. As noted earlier in the chapter, clients who come seeking help make themselves vulnerable as they disclose their personal problems and struggles. Although intimate relationships develop, the intimacy is one-way. The counselors learn a great deal about the clients, but the clients learn little about the counselors. Counselors are obligated to recognize that they are in a position of power and that misusing that power would be exploitative and could cause serious harm to clients. Dual relationship issues apply not only to counseling relationships but also to other relationships in which counselors are in a power position. Examples of such relationships include those of professor-student and supervisor-supervisee.

Kitchener and Harding (1990) identified two factors that, in addition to the power differential, create a risk of harm in dual relationships. First, the help seeker has incompatible expectations of the counselor in the different roles that the counselor is playing. For example, let us assume that Sue and Angelina are friends and that Sue also has agreed to counsel Angelina. As a friend, Angelina always has expected that she is welcome to call Sue at home when she needs someone to listen to her problems and that she can invite Sue to go out to lunch with her. As a client, however, Angelina is informed that Sue's policy is that clients are to call her answering service rather than her home and that she does not socialize with clients.

Second, the counselor in a dual relationship is faced with incompatible responsibilities. To take another example, let us assume that Patricia is John's supervisor and that she also has entered into a counseling relationship with him. As a counselor, Patricia is accepting and holds an unconditional positive regard for John as he works through his problems. As his supervisor, however, she is responsible for evaluating his work performance, which is less than satisfactory because he is distracted by his personal problems.

It is easy to see how the clients in both of the scenarios just described could feel confused, hurt, or betrayed. In both instances, the dual relationships could have been avoided by sending the individuals who were seeking counseling to other counselors. But other dual relationships are difficult, if not impossible, to avoid. Counselors who work in isolated rural communities would have very few clients if they could not provide counseling services to people with whom they already are acquainted. Counselors who practice in small towns might have as their clients the local pharmacist, grocery store manager, mail carrier, principal of the school their children attend—the possibilities are almost endless. "Small worlds" can exist in an urban environment as well (Herlihy & Corey, 1997). Because clients often seek out counselors who hold similar values, counselors' cultural or ethnic identities, sexual orientations, substance abuse recovery status, and/or political activities can create a potential for dual relationships (Lerman & Porter, 1990). This can raise some difficult questions for the counselors involved. As an example, Jeremy is a substance abuse counselor who is in recovery. Can he attend the same 12-step meetings as his clients? Would it be reasonable to expect him to jeopardize his own recovery so as to avoid role overlap?

Much of the debate concerning dual relationships has focused on the propriety of counselor behaviors that do not by themselves constitute dual relationships but that have a potential for creating them. Some of these behaviors include bartering for goods or services, accepting gifts from clients, and touching or hugging clients. Each of these issues is briefly explored here.

The ACA (1995) code of ethics discourages but does not prohibit bartering. The code delineates three criteria that should be met for bartering to be acceptable: The client requests the arrangement, the relationship is not exploitative, and bartering is an accepted practice among professionals in the community (Standard A.10.c). The main problems with bartering lie in determining what goods or services are equal in value to counseling services and in satisfaction with the quality of goods or services exchanged. For example, a client who is a talented artist and whose hobby is glassblowing wants to pay for counseling by making a vase for the counselor. One problem would be to determine how many hours of counseling are equivalent to the value of the vase. Another problem could arise if the counselor does not particularly like the vase or if the client is dissatisfied with the counseling services. In either case, the feelings of resentment that would be created are likely to have a negative effect on the counseling relationship. For these reasons, counselors generally are prudent to avoid entering into bartering relationships.

Many counselors struggle with the issue of where to draw the line in accepting gifts from clients. They do not want to offend clients by refusing small token gifts, but they want to keep the relationships within proper professional boundaries. In one study, Borys (1988) found that 82% of mental health professionals believed that it never or only rarely was ethical to accept a gift worth more than $50, but only 16% felt the same way about gifts worth less than $10. The monetary value of the gift might be one factor for counselors to consider when deciding whether or not to accept gifts offered by clients. Other factors that might be considered are clients' motivation for offering gifts, counselors' motivation in wanting to accept or decline gifts, the cultural meaning of gift giving for clients, and the stage of the counseling relationship when the gifts are offered (Remley & Herlihy, 2001).

Mental health professionals' stance toward touching or hugging clients has varied over time. During the Freudian era, physical contact with clients was thought to have a negative impact on the transference and countertransference processes; therefore, therapeutic touch was prohibited (Smith & Fitzpatrick, 1995). Later, during the human potential movement of the 1960s, touch was a more widely accepted practice. By the late 1980s, 44% of mental health professionals who responded to one survey (Pope, Tabachnick, & Keith-Spiegel, 1987) believed that hugging a client never or only rarely was ethical. Today, it appears that the trend toward caution is continuing. Professional liability insurance carriers certainly are concerned that touching or hugging might be misinterpreted and form the basis for a lawsuit, and new counselors are being trained to be discerning about physical contact with clients.

There are no absolute right or wrong answers to questions of bartering, accepting gifts, and having physical contact with clients. None of these behaviors necessarily constitutes a harmful dual relationship. Each probably is more appropriately viewed as a "boundary crossing" rather than a boundary violation. In a boundary crossing, a counselor shifts the established boundary of the therapeutic relationship so as to meet the needs of a particular client at a particular moment. For example, a counselor might have a policy of not accepting gifts from clients yet might decide to accept a potted plant that a client brings to a termination session as a way of saying thank you for the work they accomplished together. Most counselors probably make occasional minor departures from their customary practices when they believe that clients will benefit. This is not problematic so long as such departures are infrequent and can be justified. Counselors need to take care, however, not to let boundary crossing become routine. If boundary crossings become part of a pattern of blurring the professional boundaries, then this can lead to dual relationships that are potentially harmful (Herlihy & Corey, 1997).

Sexual intimacies are a type of boundary violation that can be extremely harmful to clients. Clients who have been victimized in this way often suffer from "therapist-patient sex syndrome," manifesting symptoms similar to those found in posttraumatic stress disorder (Pope,

1988). The findings of one study (Bouhoutsos, Holroyd, Lerman, Forer, & Greenberg, 1983) indicated that at least 90% of clients who have been sexually involved with therapists are damaged by the relationships. It is not known how frequently such violations occur, given the limits of self-report data, but various studies suggest that approximately 9% to 13% of male therapists and 2% to 3% of female therapists have engaged in such activities. There is no single profile of a typical offending therapist, but there is clear evidence that offenses occur more frequently in male therapist-female client relationships and that most offenders are repeat offenders (Holroyd & Brodsky, 1977). The ACA code of ethics explicitly forbids sexual relationships with current clients and with former clients for at least 2 years after the termination of counseling relationships. Although some offenders have attempted to excuse their behavior by claiming ignorance or by blaming the clients for behaving seductively, there are no valid excuses for entering into sexual relationships with clients. It always is the responsibility of the professionals to set and maintain appropriate boundaries.

An issue about which there is little consensus is whether post-termination nonsexual relationships with former clients are acceptable. Although a friendship and a therapeutic relationship cannot exist simultaneously, the ACA code of ethics is silent on the question of post-termination friendships. Several risks in post-therapy friendships have been identified. These include the risks that (a) resolution of lingering transference issues may be disrupted, (b) the client is deprived of the opportunity to reenter counseling with the counselor who has become a friend, and (c) the power differential continues after termination because the counselor has unreciprocated knowledge of the former client's vulnerabilities (Gelso & Carter, 1985; Kitchener, 1992; Salisbury & Kinnier, 1996; Vasquez, 1991). Nonetheless, it appears that most counselors believe that post-therapy friendships could be acceptable (Salisbury & Kinnier, 1996). Counselors who are considering developing friendships with former clients should consider several factors in making their decisions, including the length and nature of the counseling relationships, client diagnoses or issues, circumstances of termination, the possibility that the clients might want to return to counseling, unresolved transference or countertransference issues, and whether any harm to the clients can be foreseen. Generally speaking, however, counselors should avoid getting their social needs met through clients or former clients.

All counselors, whatever their work setting or clientele, will encounter situations that could lead to dual relationships with clients. Herlihy and Corey (1997) suggested that in these situations, counselors first should determine whether or not the dual relationships can be avoided. If they are avoidable, then the next step is to determine whether the risks of entering these relationships outweigh the benefits or vice versa. If the risks are high, then counselors should decline to enter the dual relationships and should refer the clients if that is deemed necessary. If the potential benefits to the clients seem great and the risks of harm seem small, or if the dual relationships are unavoidable, then counselors have several safeguards that they can use to reduce the risks of harm. Counselors should have full discussions with the clients, exploring the potential problems and benefits and securing the clients' informed consent to proceed. Seeking consultation on an ongoing basis and getting supervision for the work with the

clients involved are excellent strategies for identifying the problems that can arise if the counselors lose objectivity. Finally, counselors who are involved in dual relationships should be conscientious in self-monitoring and should document the dual relationships and the steps they take to avoid harm.

Obtaining Informed Consent From Clients

The likelihood of attaining successful counseling outcomes is enhanced when clients are actively involved in their therapeutic journeys, making informed decisions throughout the process. The first decision that prospective clients must make (except for involuntary clients) is whether or not to enter into counseling and, if so, with whom. To make this decision prudently, clients have a right to know what counseling entails. They might have many questions and uncertainties when they first come for counseling. Therefore, counselors have an ethical obligation to provide clients with a full explanation of the counseling process. The ACA (1995) code of ethics spells out in considerable detail the elements that need to be included in obtaining informed consent from clients:

- The purposes, goals, techniques, procedures, limitations, and potential risks and benefits of the proposed counseling services
- The implications of any diagnoses made and the intended use of tests and reports
- Information about fees and billing arrangements
- Confidentiality and its limitations
- Clients' rights to obtain information about their records and to participate in their ongoing counseling plans
- Clients' rights to refuse any recommended services and to be informed of the consequences of refusal (Standard A.3)

In addition to these elements spelled out in the code of ethics, various writers (Bray, Shepherd, & Hays, 1985; Corey et al., 1998; Haas & Malouf, 1995; Welfel, 1998) have recommended that the following be discussed:

- The counselor's qualifications, including degrees held, licensure or certification status, specializations, and experience
- The counselor's philosophy of counseling or theoretical orientation, in language that the client can understand
- Information about insurance reimbursement and, if the client is under a managed care health plan, how that plan might affect the counseling process
- Information about alternatives to counseling such as self-help groups, books, and expressive therapies (e.g., art or music therapy)
- The client's recourse if dissatisfied with the counseling services provided

All of the preceding elements add up to a great deal of information, and it would be unreasonable to expect a client to absorb it all in a single intake or initial counseling session. In fact, if all of this information were discussed in detail in an initial session, the client might well feel overwhelmed, intimidated, and reluctant to enter such a complicated business relationship. It is preferable that counselors cover the information orally in general terms and have written disclosure statements that provide detailed information. Clients can take these written statements home, study them between sessions, and return with any questions that remain. Having written disclosure statements allows counselors to use face-to-face discussion to answer questions and assess clients' comprehension of the information.

Each client will be somewhat different in terms of the amount and types of information

that need to be covered at the outset of the counseling relationship. Just as it would be a mistake to inundate clients with too much detailed information, there is risk in giving too little. Problems can arise later if clients believe that their counselors have misled them or failed to explain what could happen in counseling. Counselors should be particularly careful not to guarantee absolute confidentiality. It is important to explain that there are certain exceptions including when clients' conditions pose a danger to themselves or others and when courts order counselors to disclose information. It is helpful to give specific examples that are relevant for clients' situations. For example, a high school counselor would want to alert teenage counselees if the school has a policy requiring the counselor to inform parents about suspected pregnancies.

Counselors should work to ensure that clients have realistic expectations for counseling. They never should guarantee "cures" or specific outcomes. Other errors that are potentially problematic include (a) allowing clients to have mistaken impressions of counselors' credentials, (b) using strategies that are experimental or that involve touch without first explaining the strategies and securing clients' permission to proceed, (c) changing fee arrangements after counseling has begun, and (d) failing to warn clients about the effects that assigning diagnoses might have on their future insurability or employment opportunities.

Informed consent discussions present an opportunity at the beginning of a counseling relationship for the counselor and the client to clarify their understanding of the shared journey that they are about to undertake. Counselors need to keep in mind, however, that securing clients' informed consent is not a one-time event. Rather, it begins with the first contact between the counselor and the client and continues throughout the counseling relationship. New questions and concerns undoubtedly will arise as counseling progresses, and counselors need to be prepared to revisit informed consent issues as needed.

Determining One's Level of Competence

By definition, *competence* means having the ability to perform a task at an acceptable level (Cramton, 1981). Competence in counseling is more difficult to define. Counseling is comprised of a complex set of tasks and is a very broad profession. No single counselor could possibly be competent to offer services to every possible client in all areas of practice. Competence exists along a continuum, with gross incompetence at one end and maximum effectiveness at the other (Remley & Herlihy, 2001). The vast majority of counselors function at various points between the two extremes. The ACA (1995) code of ethics states that counselors must "practice only within the boundaries of their competence" (Standard C.2.a). Staying within these boundaries is crucial because incompetence often is a significant factor in causing harm to clients.

Who determines whether a counselor is sufficiently competent to provide counseling services? Competence to enter the profession is monitored by gatekeepers—faculty in counselor education programs and supervisors of trainees. Once counselors have completed their required training and are licensed or certified to practice, they are responsible for determining their own competence. Counselors are autonomous professionals who are granted the privilege and responsibility for monitoring their own effectiveness.

It is not easy for counselors to determine where their boundaries of competence lie. Although it is important that counselors recognize their own limitations, if they are too modest about their competencies, then they unnecessarily restrict their scope of practice. The task for practitioners is to recognize when they are unable to serve prospective clients due to a lack of the needed skills or knowledge yet be willing to accept clients who will challenge them to grow and stretch their boundaries of competence.

When counselors question whether they should take on particular new clients, they should give honest consideration to the reasons for their hesitation. If they believe that they cannot provide competent services because they lack training or experience with the clients' particular concerns, then they probably are justified in declining to accept the clients. In these instances, they should provide appropriate referrals to other mental health professionals.

It is ethically appropriate for counselors to decline to accept clients whom they believe they cannot serve adequately. Yet, counselors who always refer clients when they have questions about their abilities will have few clients and are bound to stagnate. Instead, they can stretch their boundaries of competence by accepting clients and taking steps to protect the clients while they are learning. An initial step for counselors is to have discussions with the clients about their concerns. Honestly admitting that there are gaps in their knowledge or experience allows clients to make informed choices regarding whether to continue these counseling relationships. They often are willing to teach their counselors about their cultures or particular concerns or situations. Certainly, conscientious counselors will do research and reading between sessions to fill in the gaps in their knowledge. They would be well advised to seek regular consultations while working with the clients, to work under supervision, or even to co-counsel with other counselors who have more expertise in dealing with the clients' types of problems. To be prepared to serve similar clients in the future, they can seek out specialized training through reading, participating in continuing education workshops or seminars, taking university courses, and consulting with colleagues.

In today's society, it is particularly important for counselors to develop intercultural counseling competence. The U.S. population is becoming increasingly diverse, and counselors are encountering more clients who are culturally different from themselves. It would not be ethical for counselors to attempt to provide services to culturally diverse clients without appropriate training and experience. The ACA (1995) code of ethics requires counselors to strive actively to understand the diverse cultural backgrounds of their clients and to gain skills and current knowledge in working with diverse and special client populations (Standards A.2.b, C.2.f, and C.2.a). Recognizing the importance of counselor self-awareness, the code of ethics also obligates counselors to learn how their own cultural/racial/ethnic identities have an impact on their values and beliefs about counseling (Standard A.2.b). Although no one is completely free of bias or prejudice, self-awareness and a commitment to learning about diversity can help counselors to be interculturally competent practitioners.

Competence is not a static concept; counselors need to participate in continuing education activities to maintain their competence to practice. According to the ACA (1995) code of ethics, counselors are expected to recognize the need for continuing education to maintain awareness of current information (Standard C.2.f). In most states, counselor licensure boards mandate that counselors accrue certain numbers of continuing education credits to have their licenses renewed. Credits earned by attending continuing education seminars and workshops, however, are not sufficient to ensure continuing competence. Regularly engaging in peer consultation or participating in peer supervision groups can be an important factor in maintaining competence. Peer groups can provide objective feedback in dealing with countertransference issues, information on new techniques and research, assistance in dealing with difficult clients, and support and help in dealing with the stress and isolation sometimes experienced by counselors. The code of ethics requires independent private practitioners to seek peer supervision (Standard C.2.d).

Because counseling can be a stressful occupation, it is important for counselors to maintain a sense of efficacy. Unrelieved stress can lead to burnout, and burnout can lead to impairment. The competence of impaired counselors has diminished or deteriorated to the point where they are unable to perform their tasks adequately. Guidance regarding impairment is found in the ACA (1995) code of ethics in the statement that counselors must refrain from offering professional services when their physical, mental, or emotional problems are likely to harm clients or others. They must limit, suspend, or terminate their professional responsibilities if necessary to prevent that harm (Standard C.2.g). Counselors are exhorted to be alert for the signs of impairment and to seek assistance. Some ways in which to seek help include getting personal counseling, working under supervision, taking breaks or vacations, and participating in ongoing peer support groups.

Future Legal and Ethical Challenges in Counseling

If the recent past is any indication, then issues in mental health that have legal and ethical dimensions will change radically in a short period of time, and these changes will require counselors to adjust their ideas and practices substantially. For example, counselors were shocked about 25 years ago when the *Tarasoff* decision was handed down in California, requiring counselors in that state to warn intended victims of their clients who threatened harm to others. We remember counselors at the time predicting dire consequences to the profession and saying that it would be impossible to counsel clients unless absolute confidentiality existed. Instead, we have found that counselors and clients have incorporated the Tarasoff doctrine into their day-to-day practices and that the general public has accepted this exception to their privacy.

Probably the most surprising change in counseling has been the growing list of exceptions to confidentiality and privileged communication. Today's counselors and clients understand that statutes can require that suspected abuse be reported, that clients mandated by courts for counseling agree to have details of their sessions reported to court officials, and that the law does not protect the privacy of minors if parents or guardians demand information obtained in counseling sessions.

Another situation where privacy is being compromised is in the arena of managed health care. To receive mental health care benefits, consumers today are being required to waive their privacy rights. We believe that this trend not only will continue but actually will escalate. However, we are not as alarmed over this trend as are some of our colleagues. So long as health care records are handled in a professional manner, the personal privacy of individuals from a practical perspective is not compromised. However, the greater the number of individuals who have access to private information, the greater the chance that the information will be disclosed inappropriately.

We believe that exceptions will continue to be created to the principle of client privacy and that counselors and clients will accept these changes. It is possible that counselors might be more concerned about client privacy than are clients themselves, and this acceptance by clients of compromises to their privacy will bring changes to the counselor-client relationship that we could not even imagine at this time.

A positive change that we anticipate is the continuation of advancements that are being made by professional counselors in being recognized as legitimate mental health providers. States will continue to pass legislation ensuring that all licensed mental health professionals (including counselors) will be entitled to reimbursement for their services under health care plans. In addition, statutory restrictions on professional practices of counselors in areas such as the diagnosis and treatment of mental disorders and testing will be removed over time.

Finally, we believe that increasing numbers of ethical complaints and malpractice lawsuits will be filed against counselors. At this point, very few counselors are accused of wrongdoing in a formal manner. The price that counselors will pay for increased public recognition as legitimate mental health providers, coupled with the status and public attention that comes with that advancement, will be a higher demand from the public for competent services. As the public becomes more aware of the standards of practice that counselors have established for themselves, complaints and lawsuits will result as consumers attempt to enforce those standards.

Counselor preparation programs, licensure boards, and certification agencies are requiring more pre-service and continuing education in the areas of legal and ethical issues. It is anticipated that this increased attention will prepare counselors adequately for the legal and ethical challenges they face daily in their professional practices.

References

Alberty, S. C. (1989). *Advising small business*. Deerfield, IL: Callaghan & Company.

American Counseling Association. (1995). *Code of ethics and standards of practice*. Alexandria, VA: Author.

Borys, D. S. (1988). *Dual relationships between therapist and client: A national survey of clinicians' attitudes and practices*. Unpublished doctoral dissertation, University of California, Los Angeles.

Bouhoutsos, J., Holroyd, J., Lerman, H., Forer, B., & Greenberg, M. (1983). Sexual intimacy between psychologists and patients. *Professional Psychology, 14*, 185-196.

Bray, J. H., Shepherd, J. N., & Hays, J. R. (1985). Legal and ethical issues in informed consent to psychotherapy. *American Journal of Family Therapy, 13*, 50-60.

Corey, G., Corey, M., & Callanan, P. (1998). *Issues and ethics in the helping professions* (5th ed.). Pacific Grove, CA: Brooks/Cole.

Cramton, R. C. (1981). Incompetence: The North American experience. In L. E. Trakman & D. Watters (Eds.), *Professional competence and the law* (pp. 158-163). Halifax, Nova Scotia, Canada: Dalhousie University.

Finn, A. S. (1998). *Assessment by mental health professionals of client risk for harming others*. Unpublished doctoral dissertation, University of New Orleans.

Gelso, C. J., & Carter, J. A. (1985). The relationship in counseling and psychotherapy: Components, conse-

quences, and theoretical antecedents. *The Counseling Psychologist, 13*, 155-243.

Haas, L. J., & Malouf, J. L. (1995). *Keeping up the good work: A practitioner's guide to mental health ethics* (2nd ed.). Sarasota, FL: Professional Resource Exchange.

Haynsworth, H. J. (1986). *Organizing a small business entity*. Philadelphia: American Law Institute–American Bar Association Committee on Continuing Professional Education.

Herlihy, B., & Corey, G. (1997). Codes of ethics as catalysts for improving practice. In B. Herlihy & G. Corey, *Ethics in therapy* (pp. 37-56). New York: Hatherleigh.

Holroyd, J. C., & Brodsky, A. M. (1977). Psychologists' attitudes and practices regarding erotic and nonerotic physical contact with patients. *American Psychologist, 32*, 843-849.

Katherine. A. (1991). *Boundaries: Where you end and I begin*. New York: Simon & Schuster.

Kitchener, K. S. (1992). Posttherapy relationships: Ever or never? In B. Herlihy & G. Corey (Eds.), *Dual relationships in counseling* (pp. 145-148). Alexandria, VA: American Counseling Association.

Kitchener, K. S., & Harding, S. S. (1990). Dual role relationships. In B. Herlihy & L. Golden (Eds.), *Ethical standards casebook* (4th ed., pp. 145-148). Alexandria, VA: American Counseling Association.

Lerman, H., & Porter, N. (1990). The contribution of feminism to ethics in psychotherapy. In H. Lerman & N. Porter (Eds.), *Feminist ethics in psychotherapy* (pp. 5-13). New York: Springer.

Litwack, T., Kirschner, S., & Wack, R. (1993). The assessment of dangerousness and prediction of violence: Recent research and future prospects. *Psychiatric Quarterly, 64*, 245-273.

McNeil, D., & Binder, R. (1991). Clinical assessment of risk of violence among psychiatric inpatients. *American Journal of Psychiatry, 148*, 1317-1321.

Mulvey, E., & Lidz, C. (1995). Conditional prediction: A model for research on dangerousness to others in a new era. *International Journal of Law and Psychiatry, 18*, 129-143.

Pope, K. S. (1988). How clients are harmed by sexual contact with mental health professionals: The syndrome and its prevalence. *Journal of Counseling and Development, 67*, 222-226.

Pope, K. S., Tabachnick, B. G., & Keith-Spiegel, P. (1987). Good and poor practices in psychotherapy: National survey of beliefs of psychologists. *Professional Psychology: Research and Practice, 19*, 547-552.

Remley, T. P., Jr., & Herlihy, B. (2001). *Ethical, legal, and professional issues in counseling*. Upper Saddle River, NJ: Merrill/Prentice Hall.

Rice, P. R. (1993). *Attorney-client privilege in the United States.* Rochester, NY: Lawyers Cooperative.

Salisbury, W. A., & Kinnier, R. T. (1996). Posttermination friendship between counselors and clients. *Journal of Counseling and Development, 74,* 495-500.

Schutz, B. M. (1990). *Legal liability in psychotherapy.* San Francisco: Jossey-Bass.

Slovic, P., & Monahan, J. (1995). Probability, danger, and coercion: A study of risk perception and decision making in mental health law. *Law and Human Behavior, 19,* 49-65.

Smith, D., & Fitzpatrick, M. (1995). Patient-therapist boundary issues: An integrative review of theory and research. *Professional Psychology: Research and Practice, 26,* 499-506.

Smith, J. M., & Mallen, R. E. (1989). *Preventing legal malpractice.* St. Paul, MN: West.

Swenson, L. C. (1997). *Psychology and the law for the helping professions* (2nd ed.). Pacific Grove, CA: Brooks/ Cole.

Tarasoff v. Regents of University of California, 529 P.2d 553, 118 Cal. Rptr., 129 (1974), *vacated,* 17 Cal. 3d 425, 551 P.2d 334, 131 Cal. Rptr., 14 (1976).

Truscott, D., Evens, J., & Mansell, S. (1995). Outpatient psychotherapy with dangerous clients: A model for clinical decision making. *Professional Psychology: Research and Practice, 26,* 484-490.

Vasquez, M. J. T. (1991). Sexual intimacies with clients after termination: Should a prohibition be explicit? *Ethics and Behavior, 1,* 45-61.

Welfel, E. R. (1998). *Ethics in counseling and psychotherapy.* Pacific Grove, CA: Brooks/Cole.

CHAPTER SIX

Advocacy for the
Counseling Profession

DENNIS W. ENGELS

LORETTA J. BRADLEY

Promotion of human worth, dignity, unique-ness, and potential is the cornerstone of counseling. This prominent and ennobling dedication in the preamble to the American Counseling Association's (ACA, 1995) ethical standards differentiates ACA and counseling from other organizations and professions in powerful and compelling ways. What nobler focus, what greater value, what more empowering source of commitment could one find for a profession, a professional organization, or professional practice?

This chapter focuses on counselors' championing of human worth, dignity, uniqueness, and potential as a beacon to unify the counseling profession and empower counseling practice in promoting client wellness and development. Policy and practice implications arise from definitions and discussions of advocacy issues, opportunities, and obstacles, and a subsequent discussion covers internal and external implicaions and operational aspects of the key terms, *counseling* and *advocacy*. Emphases in this discussion emanate from our experience as state and national counseling organization presidents and selected aspects of three conferences: a University of North Texas (UNT)/ Texas Association for Counselor Education and Supervision (TACES) conference, "Counseling: A Profession at Risk," (Engels, 1996), and two Chi Sigma Iota (CSI) Counselor Advocacy Leadership forums held at the University of North Carolina at Greensboro (CSI, 1998, 1999).

Because *counseling* and *advocacy* may be variously defined, because recent ACA efforts to define counseling met with dismal results, because the CSI (1998, 1999) forums indicated that the profession needs a fuller operational definition of advocacy, and because definitions are fundamental to communication, initial discussion of each of the two major emphases, advocacy and counseling, starts with definitions. Following attempts at respective and mutually compatible professional and public definitions and initial discussions on each of those two topics, efforts are directed toward discussing advocacy for the counseling profession as a prerequisite to counselor advocacy for important causes. The focus then moves to counselor preparation and credentialing as major points of departure in strengthening the case for refined advocacy for the profession of counseling, concluding with attention to implications for professional advocacy.

Advocacy

Etymological definitions of *advocacy* afford some important insights; for example, from the Latin, *ad vocare,* comes a sense of calling or summoning by some entity larger and nobler than an individual or group for or toward a goal or purpose that is larger and nobler than the individual or group. Seen in this light, advocacy is inspired, dedicated, and noble. Related French and Latin origins of the term incorporate more contemporary notions of speaking and acting for or on behalf of a person, an idea, a principle, a cause, or a policy, concepts closely related to current dictionary definitions (Agnes, 1999; Simpson & Weiner, 1989). For counselors, advocacy generally seems aimed at benefiting clients and/or the profession. ACA's definition of advocacy emphasizes services to clients and promotion of public policy related to counseling (ACA, 2000).

Since its inception, the American Personnel and Guidance Association (APGA, now called ACA) has championed the worth, dignity, potential, and uniqueness of humans. ACA's support of individual and human rights issues has long been a hallmark of ACA, as recently illustrated in ACA's 1998-1999 presidential theme of human advocacy but also going back to the start, in 1913, of ACA's earliest founding organization, the National Vocational Guidance Association (NVGA). Recent examples of this advocacy for health, education, and other social justice issues include creation and distribution of fact sheets and briefing papers on school counseling and mental health counseling (ACA, 2000) and collaboration and/or endorsement of papers on these topics and on sexual orientation. A more immediate aspect of advocacy lies in directly helping an individual or a group, especially members of underrepresented populations such as those who are impoverished, homeless, ex-offenders, chemically dependent, or victims of physical or other abuse and oppression (Lewis & Bradley, 2000). For these populations, a counselor might need to offer direct service to bring a person to a point of embarking on a more common counseling journey toward self-help. A very poor person, for example, might need direct counselor help and intervention to meet basic food, clothing, shelter, hygiene, and social skill needs before the counselor and client begin working to help this person to help himself or herself. Although not without some internal controversy, ACA's record of advocacy for human justice and related health and human services issues is abundant and relatively consistent in terms of advocating and speaking out on behalf of popular and unpopular, but important, human causes.

In contrast to this long-standing record of advocacy for human services issues, ACA's record of advocacy for the counseling profession itself seems to have a much shorter lineage, going back to state counselor licensure initiatives during the mid-1970s. Ironically, the very special and intense dedication of counselors and the counseling profession in fostering and supporting social causes risks a perception of and guilt about seemingly blatant collective selfishness in terms of promoting the counseling profession (CSI, 1998, 1999). However, the latter also can be the pivotal key to the former. In a world and nation driven by public and private policy, professions that do not participate in the public policy process risk exclusion from the sanctions and opportunities that such policies provide. Without appropriate advocacy for the counseling profession, mental health legislation, managed care, and other public and private policies can severely restrict and jeopardize counselors' sanctions and responsibility to serve the public in general and any particular population or person, even to a point of professional extinction.

Because effects of public and private sector policy are so ominous and profound, it seems that counselors can help their various publics in major ways only if counselors first affect policy. In the long run, counselors can provide appropriate help only if they are included as providers for a wide array of private and public sector education, mental health, and related human services policies and programs. Seen in this light, advocacy for counseling or any profession is less an option than a mandate; counselors and counseling organizations must advocate for the profession. Counselors, who are so naturally altruistic, must fight for their own rights to practice if they are to have a vital part as acknowledged providers of health and related human services for various constituencies in a variety of environments.

Policy Accomplishments

To its credit, ACA has some major public and private policy accomplishments, for example, $20 million for the year 2000 Elementary School Counseling Demonstration Act appropriation (the largest single allocation ever for the counseling profession) and the U.S. Rehabilitation Services Administration's 1999 mandate that rehabilitation counselors must have master's degrees (J. Urbaniak, personal communication, February 25, 2000). But in view of the fundamental and pivotal importance of policy input for professional organizations now and in the future, more and more targeted strategic and specific action and resources are required, and the continued distractions of obstacles and disagreements work to undermine or even sabotage progress. Policy happens, and only those professions that help to formulate policy will be able to implement those policies in ways that positively affect humans.

A necessary prelude to continued, greater, and more frequent external advocacy campaigns is internal forums, consensus building, and decisions. Participation in private and public policy making, in formulating and advocating policies, and in implementing policy requires much in the form of ACA's internal dialogue and decision-making processes if ACA's external policy ventures are to bear abundant and robust fruit in the form of inclusion of counselors as mental health providers, parity with other licensed providers, and many other designations and opportunities for counselors.

The CSI (1998, 1999) and UNT/TACES (Engels, 1996) forums noted numerous factors on which to base advocacy for the counseling profession, such as national counselor preparation standards (Council for Accreditation of Counseling and Related Educational Programs [CACREP], 1994, 2000); more than 400 CACREP-accredited and other graduate counselor preparation programs; state and national professional counselor credentialing standards; state, regional, and national professional associations dedicated to advancing the scientific, educational, and philosophical foundations of the counseling profession and its members; and the need for counseling of individuals, couples, families, and organizations. Indeed, all of these elements of counselor competence and availability, standards of care, and public need require that the counseling profession strive for realization of the full potential of professional counselors including challenges to the scope of practice, equal opportunity to serve those who need and desire their services, equitable payment for services, counselors' right to practice, and the public's right to choose.

Thus, advocacy may be variously defined or based, yet there is relative professional and public consensus regarding these respective definitions. Moreover, advocacy for the counseling profession has achieved significant gains. For continued and fuller recognition and parity, however, counselors are obligated to define counseling—to clearly articulate what it is that counselors do, how counselor preparation programs prepare them to do competent work, and why counselors should be sanctioned and en-

trusted to do what they are prepared to do. Such clarity and articulation seem to require clear definitions of counseling.

Defining Counseling

Etymological and other dictionary definitions of counseling seem to afford little insight except to illustrate widely varying and relatively general and generic meanings of *counseling* and *counselor*, for example, *Webster's* definition: "anyone whose advice is sought" or "a person in charge of a group of children at a camp" (Agnes, 1999, p. 331). These and other long-standing contextual and conventional meanings of counselor or counseling make it difficult to define professional counseling. Whereas dictionary and colloquial definitions might not help to appropriately differentiate the counseling profession, historical, organizational, preparational, professional, and behavioral definitions might be better suited to this purpose.

History

Depending on where one starts and ends, history affords different perspectives of counseling. Whether one starts with ancient lessons and practices in various cultures or with the work of Frank Parsons or another counseling pioneer makes a major difference in defining our profession (Engels, 1980). Starting with Parsons' work, for example, affords a significant point of demarcation and a developmental direction in the evolution of the counseling profession (Piccioni & Bonk, 1980). Our short-term and immediate history suggests incrementally narrowing meanings, directions, philosophy, and practice within the counseling profession. For example, state licensure laws protect use of the title *professional counselor* and/or the practice of *professional counseling*. Internal and external tensions and nuances notwithstanding, the counseling profession has a rich and varied lineage, heritage, and historical record that serve to define the profession by affording contextual and ideological perspectives.

Counselor Preparation Programs

By stipulating a core curriculum, fundamental principles, clinical standards, and other general and specific requirements, accreditation standards afford a delimiting and potentially encouraging definition of curricular and clinical experiences required for entry into the counseling profession. In many respects, accreditation standards constitute a profession's internal definition as well as guidance and quality assurance for aspiring counselors and, ultimately, the publics whom aspiring counselors will serve. CACREP serves this definitive purpose for the counseling profession.

Work Behaviors and Counselor Credentials

General and specific knowledge, skill, and experience competencies emanating from accreditation standards, individual credentialing, professional literature, and observational and self-report studies of practitioners also afford a definition of counseling that can have substantial value for a variety of audiences (Engels & Dameron, 1990; National Board for Certified Counselors [NBCC], 1995). By specifying what it takes to obtain a license or certificate, state standards, laws, and rules governing counselor credentialing and practice may be the least equivocal and most widely disseminated means

of defining counseling for the public in a particular state. Unfortunately, however, state counselor licensure requirements vary widely. NBCC requirements also define counseling, but NBCC standards differ from ACA's 1995 model (licensure) legislation. Thus, although state and national counseling licensure and certification and accreditation requirements and procedures can be seen as the counseling profession's clearest (i.e., most explicitly definitive) public definitions of counseling, the variety and differences among and between these sources, as well as the lack of licensure portability, also add confusion.

Toward a Comprehensive Definition of Counseling

As noted in the preceding section, there are many ways in which to define counseling. Definitions of counseling and related concerns, however, have little or no intrinsic value. Rather, these abstractions derive their value from the wisdom, motives, and behaviors of counselors and the counseling profession. Combinations of all or some of the definitions of counseling listed earlier afford interpretations, explanations, and descriptions of the counseling profession's motivation, behavior, and identity, but it might be necessary to determine whether the definition is to be used internally or externally. Unfortunately, however, many obstacles impede a clear definition.

Obstacles to Defining Counseling

Failure of a recent concerted ACA effort to arrive at a clear, all-purpose, internal/external definition may be attributable, in part, to counseling specialties emphasizing differences and exclusive aspects of specialties rather than commonalities (Smith, 2000). We have no recollection of cardiologists working to restrict family practitioners or of board-certified personal injury attorneys denigrating other lawyers. Counseling's relative failure at definition seems to accentuate risks of overlooking commonalities as well as concomitant difficulties of creating appropriate multipurpose internal and external definitions for the counseling profession. There may be utility in protracted internal discussions, but there must be simple external clarity if the public and legislators are to understand what counselors are competent to do.

The CSI (1998, 1999) forums highlighted obstacles to clarity and consensus, even in the area of counselor preparation. CACREP (1994) accreditation standards permit faculty from other disciplines not only to teach but also to coordinate programs and chair departments of counselor education, thereby influencing hiring, promotions, and student admissions. Students/graduates also may receive mixed messages from faculty and colleagues regarding the adequacy of their preparation, where they should seek advanced preparation, and how they should describe counseling, for example, counseling and professional counselor versus therapy and therapist. Many counselors add to the confusion by identifying themselves by other titles, such as therapist and psychotherapist. Many members of counseling associations, including those who work in counselor education, are not professional counselors who share a collective passion for the counseling profession. In understating or ignoring common goals, philosophies, objectives, and collaborative successes while highlighting disagreements between organizations and among association officers' points of view and focusing on or-

ganizational and structural issues, counseling association officials may both confuse and discourage their memberships from reaching a common vision and direction for advocacy.

State counseling licensure is commonly available to other mental health providers, such as psychological associates and social workers, suggesting that others can do the work of professional counselors in addition to their primary professional disciplines. Although this list of obstacles could go on at some length, suffice it to say that there are many barriers to ideological and behavioral consensus and unity in counselor preparation and that the resultant confusion inhibits or undercuts the profession's basis for advocacy or assertiveness.

One central question asks whether all counselors have more education, knowledge, and skills in common than any group of counselors has in exclusion from other counselors. Making a clearly definitive case for the counseling profession seems difficult, if not impossible, if the profession chooses to adopt (or retain) the latter perspective.

Defining Counseling Advocacy

The preceding definitions suggest that the concept and process of advocacy for a profession can be readily and clearly defined, whereas defining counseling seems much more challenging, probably requiring separate internal and external definitions. Determining exactly what the counseling profession advocates, however, requires defining counseling. As counseling seeks to maintain or move beyond its current progress, difficulties in defining counseling may constitute a major problem in manifesting a consensus as to what to advocate. At some point in policy making, legislators require clear, unequivocal, definitive language. One basis for definitive clarity might concentrate on counselor preparation.

Counselor Preparation as a Pivotal Basis for Advocacy

Assuming that counselor education programs properly prepare counselors for ethical practice, counselor preparation standards and entry-level requirements may be primary means to define the profession and afford a central basis for refined advocacy. Accreditation standards could have great potential for informing public and private policy and credentialing discussions. To a great extent, CACREP (1994, 2000) accreditation standards constitute internal and external statements emanating from internal organizational member discussions and CACREP board decisions.

From 1996 through January 2000, for example, the most recent CACREP Standards Revision Committee drafted revisions and invited counselor, counselor educator, counseling supervisor, and public input through open forums at professional meetings and postings on the World Wide Web. Based on constituent input, many professional counselor identity quandaries and many of the hopes noted in the CSI (1998, 1999) forums have been added literally, or in spirit, to early drafts through Draft 3 of the 2001 CACREP standards (CACREP, 1999). Among those changes is a clear expectation for faculty and program coordinators who hold state and/or national counseling credentials; stay professionally active in state, regional, and national counseling associations; and offer professional orientation courses affording students knowledge of and respect for the counseling profession, ACA, and the ACA ethical standards.

In stipulating a 48-semester-hour master's degree, and in welcoming programs to use creativity in documenting how an approach meets the spirit of a particular standard, the CACREP standards serve as a beacon and an encouragement for all counselor education programs to work toward achieving accreditation. Ironically, those who argue for more credits than a master's degree and other increases in what they proclaim as added qualitative improvements certainly fly in the face of CSI recommendations of encouraging all programs to seek accreditation. In general, then, it appears that the CACREP process seeks and affords opportunities for member input, has considerable impact on selected aspects of credentialing, and constitutes a major basis for professional advocacy.

National Certification Standards

The CACREP standards, in turn, serve as part of the basis for the NBCC general and specialty examinations and credentials. Graduation from a CACREP program qualifies one for immediate NBCC examination and credentialing, with recent changes in examination format and content aimed at reflecting counselor work behaviors (Engels & Dameron, 1990; NBCC, 1994) within the CACREP core curriculum areas. NBCC's National Counseling Examination (NCE) constitutes the licensure examination in Guam, Washington, D.C., and 36 of the 46 states with licensure (NBCC's National Mental Health Counselor Examination is used in 6 additional states). Ironically, although CACREP graduates can sit for the NCE and obtain NBCC's national certified counselor (NCC) credential immediately on graduation, state licensure typically requires 2,000 or more hours of post-degree supervision. In addition, although most state licenses reflect the CACREP core curriculum and most states use the NCE, aspiring counselors must complete additional course work beyond the CACREP entry-level standards and/or post-degree, extra-institutional supervision requirements before attaining eligibility for counselor licensure in most states.

As noted earlier, laws and other credentialing standards and related rules may constitute the most definitive external articulation or definition of the counseling profession for the public. State laws and NBCC and CACREP standards can be seen to constitute the profession's best efforts at external definition and articulation—at informing legislators, other authorities, aspiring students, and the general public about all facets of counseling from formal preparation to practice. CACREP and NBCC standards and state statutes articulate much about counseling preparation and practice in ways that no other statements can, and they do so primarily as a means of protecting the public from inferior or harmful practices and practitioners.

Problems, Challenges, and Opportunities

While licensing statutes are respectively definitive within any one state, their wide variability nationally, in terms of licensing requirements and other elements, poses serious issues and problems for the counseling profession, practitioner, state and national policy makers, third-party payers and clients. Other problems add to the quandary, as well. Perhaps the most notable problem emanating from within the counseling profession is the ACA Legislative Licensure Model.

Problems Emanating From ACA Legislative Licensure Model. One major confounding fac-

tor that contributes to confusion about counselor identity and state licensure requirements that exceed the CACREP standards and NBCC process described previously is the ACA legislative licensure model. This model, at its origin, departed radically from the CACREP standards and NBCC credentialing process by recommending 60-semester-hour entry-level programs and 3,000-hour post-degree supervision prior to licensure. One apparent rationale for this model was to parallel social work licensure standards. Whether this near-term tactical approach to access is the most prudent long-term approach for counseling is not clear. In addition, it can be argued that this ACA legislative licensure model initially was adopted merely by being accepted as an ACA Professionalization Committee report (D. Coy, personal communication, August 29, 1997) without discussion by the ACA Governing Council. That licensure model is unlike the vast majority of counselor preparation program requirements, seems to have had little or no member input or opportunity for input, disregarded opposition voiced by the CACREP chair and executive director regarding the model's perversion of the CACREP standards (C. L. Bobby, personal communication, April 11, 1995), and paid no attention to the recommendation of the ACA 1995-1996 Advisory Council (division presidents and region chairs) that the model should parallel the CACREP standards. From one perspective, the burden of proof usually required of those advocating change to long-standing standards or practices was bypassed during a time of ACA organizational preoccupation with financial survival. Whatever the genesis and evolution of the ACA licensure model, its impact is readily evident in state licensure statutes amended or adopted since the early 1990s, with state licensure boards recommending counselor preparation requirements paralleling the ACA model while ignoring parallel aspects of the CACREP and NBCC standards.

Although rigorous educational and clinical standards already exist for CACREP accreditation and NBCC credentialing, the ACA licensure model advocates a massive number (3,000 hours) of post-degree, extra-institutional requirements for licensure. Although higher education institutions might have some shortcomings or bureaucratic excesses in preparing counselors, institutional safeguards are substantially lacking in extra-institutional supervision requirements. In advocating 3,000 hours of extra-institutional supervision, the ACA model creates a potential gold mine for supervisors at the possible expense of the profession and at the profound temporal and financial expense of aspiring counselors. Ironically, although the model advocates protecting the public, exclusive standards restrict underrepresented populations in the counseling profession and, in turn, keep vast numbers of the public from the services of licensed professional counselors (LPCs). One risk of the ACA licensure model is the possibility that state licensing boards will, in the not-too-distant future, succumb to the "psychology of more" (Looft, 1971) and align statutes accordingly, yielding a default victory for the ACA model and a quandary, or even a dilemma, for the future of the profession, to say nothing of a unilateral abandonment of counseling's roots, developmental philosophical core, and master's degree emphasis. With this central issue of credentialing as a pivotal focus, attention to related questions and implications seems in order.

Toward a Unified Public Definition of Counseling. Seen in light of this major contradiction about minimal requirements for entry into the profession, what might be a clear and consistent national definition for the public, emanating from the CACREP standards and NBCC examination and credentialing process, is at risk of considerable confusion and consternation in the form of state policy making and licensure requirements, and it readily interferes with advocacy for the profession. One inference for policy makers and the public is a sense of confusion within the counseling profession and a consequent disregard for what those representing counselors say during the policy-formulating process. How might the profession minimize the confusion without compromising the CACREP process and standards and the collective judgment manifest in the requirements of the vast majority of counselor preparation programs? If licensure requirements constitute a profession's clearest public definition yet contradict a profession's best collective internal philosophy and judgment manifest in accreditation standards, then how might the counseling profession reconcile these differences in the best interests of the profession and the public? Although some advocate additional quantitative and specialized increases in requirements, the vast majority of the 143 schools with accredited entry-level programs and nearly all nonaccredited counselor preparation programs remain at the master's degree level, requiring 48 or fewer credit hours (Hollis, 2000). Such an overwhelming majority of CACREP accredited counselor preparation programs constitutes a collective and definitive professional behavioral statement that the entry level CACREP standards are most appropriate for preparing qualified counselors. Seen in light of this overwhelming majority behavior, this collective definition allows for clear articulation as a basis for advocating for the counseling profession.

There seems little encouragement for faculty in nonaccredited programs to strive for accreditation if the minimal requirements are perceived as beyond the horizon of attainability. In addition, there are few material or other career incentives for individuals to endure substantial opportunity costs of extensive graduate education and very low pay during extensive postgraduate supervision requirements. Might those demanding more credits and post-degree supervision and other requirements be losing sight of the fact that credentials always are awarded based on minima? Ultimately, credentialing requirements stipulate the least that one must do to attain the credentials, and any program has the option of increasing its requirements beyond specified minima. Because professionals require continuing education to stay current with professional knowledge and practice and to maintain professional credentials, those advocating increased entry requirements might want to reconsider their stance on substantial front-loading.

Although the psychology of more holds that more of anything or any process is better, more might be far worse, and the more profound question ought to be one of quality, not quantity (Looft, 1971). In minimizing, downplaying, or not addressing quality of counselor preparation, those supporting quantitative increases miss a substantive issue while focusing on one or another immediate target such as current third-party reimbursement rules, comparison with other helping professions, or some other expedient. In fixating on quantity and not addressing quality of counselor preparation, and in using only or primarily an external locus of evaluation, the counseling profession risks losing its core identity including a humanistic, wellness-based master's degree, strong preparation standards, and a dedication to counseling for the masses. In addition, promoting a universal requirement for 3,000 hours of postdegree extra-institutional supervision says, in effect, that current preparation requirements in

the vast majority of programs and in the CACREP standards are so inferior as to require nearly as much time beyond graduation as is required in the formal preparation process. UNT/TACES (Engels, 1996) conference participants stated that 48 semester hours is sufficient time for preparing competent counselors and that 60 semester hours or 3,000 clock hours is not a desirable option for a variety of reasons. Participants said that quality preparation can occur in a 48-semester-hour format, and increasing the opportunity cost of preparation excludes people of low financial means while appearing to front-load the preparation process by demanding extensive requirements prior to credentialing rather than emphasizing a substantive generic preparation process followed by specialization opportunities attained through continuing education.

Front-Loading. In the face of countless testaments to the necessity of lifelong learning and continuing education (Secretary's Commission on Achieving Necessary Skills, 1991, 1992), it seems ridiculous to advocate expanding already rigorous entry-level standards. There never will be a complete turnkey or "set-it-and-forget-it" education in any profession. Yet, rather than advocate sound entry-level standards followed by a lifetime of continuing education, including continuing supervision, the ACA model advocates entry-level standards that go far beyond a master's degree. Gerstein and Brooks (1990) illustrated how increased opportunity costs ultimately drive practitioners to seek high pay in affluent urban areas where middle- and upper-middle-class clients can afford higher costs. This phenomenon, in turn, has immediate implications for access to professional counseling for the poor and very poor and for those in remote, rural, and other underserved communities as well as profound implications for the poor and very poor who might aspire to the counseling profession. Our profession's talk of inclusiveness and human advocacy rings hollow if the concept of counseling for the masses remains obscured by excessive opportunity costs for aspiring counselors, reduced counselor availability in remote locations, and ultimately higher costs for clients.

Additional Obstacles to Advocacy. The choice (or non-choice) of continuing to emphasize or exaggerate internal differences seems unlikely to help the profession and risks hurting it. In addition, capitulation to external loci of evaluation costs the profession prohibitively, even to a point of dilution or extinction. When one sorts through major points of internal contention, the major point of disagreement seems to be diagnosis. Certainly, the profession can find a way in which to help all counselors learn to diagnose and treat maladies in addition to counselors' historical developmental emphasis on case conceptualization.

Moving Toward Advocacy. Based on a discipline and common core of knowledge and skills, counselors provide competent essential professional services to many publics in a variety of settings in unique and profound ways. Yet, obstacles risk clouding the message and undercutting the effort of unified advocacy for the counseling profession. It is incumbent on all counselors to articulate and prize counselor competencies, credentials, right to practice and related issues discussed throughout this book. In spite of many past and present obstacles, professional counselors can and must find a unified means to clearly articulate in a unified voice our common heritage and our dedication to promoting the worth, dignity, diversity, unique-

ness, potential and capacity of all human beings. Based on this common and moving dedication, counselors need to clearly articulate a unified definitive message. To this end, the authors believe the entry level CACREP standards constitute a unified articulated platform which readily lends itself to advocacy for the profession.

Summary, Conclusion, and Implications

The CSI (1998, 1999) forums concentrated on six major common themes: counselor preparation, marketplace recognition, interprofessional issues, intra-professional issues, professional research, and client/constituency wellness. This chapter merely begins to highlight these vital issues. Those desiring more information on the CSI forums can find the reports and other points of contact on the World Wide Web (www.csi-net.org) or by writing CSI (School of Education, UNCG, P.O. Box 26171, Greensboro, NC 27402-6171).

One overriding theme of the UNT/TACES (Engels, 1996) and CSI (1998, 1999) discussions was that counseling is a distinguished and distinctive caring profession promoting the worth, dignity, uniqueness, and potential of all individuals including those in underserved, vulnerable, and oppressed populations and meriting equivalent status with other caring professions. To the counseling profession's credit, even in the face of numerous internal and external problems, disagreements, and other confusions, advocacy for the profession has resulted in many important accomplishments in a relatively short time. However great the accomplishments have been, the forums point out the need for new and stronger approaches to unity, consensus, and commitment in articulating our vision and mission as first steps to a renewed external push that moves beyond internal problems in maintaining and expanding policy gains to a next level of unified professionalism. These recent forums suggest that the counseling profession needs a concerted effort to clearly and democratically ascertain and unequivocally articulate and communicate a professional vision, mission, and goals that lend themselves to advocacy for the unified counseling profession.

Counseling's philosophical and scientific grounding in human growth and development, with concern both for prevention and optimal wellness across the life span and for assessment, case conceptualization, diagnosis, and treatment of dysfunction, distinguishes counseling from other mental health professions without compromising counselors' ability to provide an array of services to various types of clients in a variety of settings. CSI (1998, 1999) forum participant insights and findings noted high public regard for counseling as a part of normal human development activities as opposed to negative and dysfunctional connotations related to "illness" and "therapy." Again, this developmental heritage and philosophical grounding may hold the key to bringing counselors back together in a unified cause.

In addition, the 143 schools with nationally accredited counselor education programs, 65,000 state credentialed professional counselors, 45,000 nationally credentialed professional counselors, 110,000 members of state and national counseling associations, abundant evidence that counseling services help to alleviate and prevent both acute and transitional human development challenges, and unprecedented risks to health and safety all require that counselors combat persistent and substantial challenges to the right of professional counselors to provide services to individuals, couples, families, and organizations that need them, to be paid equitably for their services, and to be employed in a variety of settings. These assets and challenges require continued and renewed advocacy for the profession. General and specific ideas come to mind.

Bemak and Espina (1999) offered possibilities for near- and long-term policy and related action. Among their ideas are a national U.S. license based on the NCE, a federal mandate directing states to modify standards based on the NBCC standards or the ACA model legislation requirements, formation of a national repository for state license applications, and development of a model licensure law. Citing the importance of nationwide reciprocity, or portability, as a "critical next step" for counselors, and lamenting independent state credentials that ignore nationally established criteria, Bemak and Espina echoed the UNT/TACES (Engels, 1996) and CSI (1998, 1999) forums' call for cooperation among and between all state and national elements of ACA and state and national credentialing bodies to promote reciprocity and optimally protect the public and regulate practice. Unfortunately, Bemak and Espina paid minimal attention to the CACREP standards. Expanded attention to case conceptualization and treatment for all entry-level programs and specific diagnostic and treatment knowledge and skill requirements in the 48-semester-hour community counseling standards of the 2001 CACREP standards (CACREP, 2000) may serve as a unifying compromise on which to base future advocacy for the counseling profession.

If the vast majority of counselor preparation programs in more than 400 schools want to model consistency with what they advocates, then faculty and students in those programs might do well to encourage state licensing boards to parallel NBCC's credentialing process by waiving post-degree supervision requirements for CACREP graduates. Such a process might be a possible compromise for differences among the ACA licensure model, many state license requirements, and requirements of the vast majority of preparation programs. The near universality of state licensing board use of NBCC's NCE seems to add credence to states considering this NBCC policy of offering credentials to counselors on graduation from a CACREP-accredited program, and such a practice definitely could help the counseling career field to have realistic and reasonable opportunity costs without compromising quality.

UNT/TACES (Engels, 1996) and CSI (1998, 1999) participants recommended that counselors, counselor educators, and counseling associations reaffirm a developmental focus overall while also being market wise but not market driven. Because markets are profoundly fickle, and because repeated responses to fickle markets undercut long-term stability within a profession, possible compromise of fundamental underpinnings, and related problems, counselors need to find ways in which to accommodate market requirements without compromising their professional identity. A related implication from the conference deliberations suggests the potential harm of our profession seeking definition through comparisons with other professions and continued redefinition in terms of such comparisons and related external phenomena. At some point, ACA's licensure legislation model risks bringing counseling to a point where it is no different or little different from other mental health professions, most notably, counseling psychology and social work. If counseling moves to a point of virtual similarty with counseling psychology, then it becomes important to reassess whether there needs to be a counseling profession and coun-

seling organizations separate from other helping professions.

Another implication arising from the forum discussions is the need for counselors to articulate and become assertive in helping public and private policy makers to understand and appreciate the unique value of counselors as mental health professionals. One model for counselor advocacy might lie in aspects of the 15-year fight for recognition by chiropractors, *Wilk v. American Medical Association* (1987). In a prolonged and costly battle, chiropractors eventually prevailed and obtained professional recognition in laws and other domains without compromising their homeopathic philosophy and original dedication to promoting wellness (American Chiropractic Association, 1987). In contrast to this principled stance, asserting how and why chiropractors are appropriately and uniquely prepared for practice and must be allowed to practice, the counseling profession has tended to capitulate and defer rather than assert its identity.

Articulation. Counselors must articulate and assert what they do and document their effectiveness. The CSI (1998, 1999) and TACES (Engels, 1996) forums noted the need for counselors not only to believe in the value of their profession's preparation standards, graduate programs, credentialing requirements, and scope of services, but also to strive for consensus as a baseline for educating, informing, and promoting these elements to the general public and, most notably, to public and private policy makers, namely, legislators, employers, and third-party payers (CSI, 1998). All too often, in too many critical arenas, and with too little member input, counselors have resorted to an external locus of evaluation in adopting standards of other professions rather than advocating for counselor recognition and inclusion on the basis of the quality of counselor preparation programs (CSI, 1998, 1999; Engels, 1996; Smith, 2000). Outside the counseling profession, for example, who knows that counselor preparation credits in accredited programs are exclusively graduate credits (as opposed to a combination of undergraduate and graduate credits for social workers) and that counselors attain substantial clinical knowledge, skills, and closely supervised practice as part of a rigorous clinical component of their master's degree entry-level programs (CACREP, 2000)? In working to persuade legislators and health maintenance organization policy makers, counselors need to assert the high quality of this qualitative preparation process rather than merely pointing out how counselor preparation is similar to that in already approved professions, most notably, social work.

Seeking consensus and collaboration. Related implications emphasize the need to obtain member input through the widest means—through *Counseling Today,* the listserv CESNET (Counselor Education and Supervision Network), and related forums—in seeking member input before finalizing definitional delimitations, especially in the area of licensure. Democracy is expensive, especially in terms of time. But a democratic process can add integrity and save incredible time, energy, and confusion in the long run in ensuring consistency and continuity in both state and national legislative advocacy efforts. CSI (1998, 1999) forum participants recommended a 5- to 10-year plan, with widest opportunities for member and organizational input and eventual collaboration, noting that ACA's national and state family of professional associations and entities, such as CACREP, need to collaborate with each other and related relevant constituencies, such as NBCC, on matters

of advocacy on a regular and systematic basis including a comprehensive, collaborative advocacy plan for the profession. To this end, CSI forum participants called for a task force of counseling association representatives chosen for their scholarship, leadership, and experience in the counseling professionalization movement to develop a definition and rationale for a common identity to articulate and advocate publicly, most notably, in the areas of public and private policy.

Unity. Just as counselors can be seen to have more in common with one another than any group of counselors has in exclusion from other counselors, so, too, it seems that all mental health professions have more in common than surface differences and long-standing competition might suggest. Although all counseling associations most interested in advocacy already have agendas, committees, staff, and ongoing activities with proprietary senses of priorities, strategies, goals, and objectives, and although existing resources assigned to advocacy efforts are fully committed to a wide variety of objectives, there is a very real possibility that a new comprehensive emphasis on advocacy could be ambitious beyond what is reasonably attainable through present resources. Overcommitment, diffusion, or underfunding of efforts could result in unnecessary frustration, failure, or both. Through strategic plans and specific actions, counseling profession governing bodies and their officers need to find ways in which to collaborate in appropriately and prudently targeting resources and guiding ACA and state counseling association staff and volunteers in their efforts to ensure that professional counselors in all settings are free to provide service to the public within all areas of their competence and be suitably compensated for their services.

Research. Major research needs constitute another implication for the profession. Scientifically sound research, including multiple broad-based approaches to research (e.g., qualitative, quantitative, formative, summative, longitudinal, short term, case study), is needed to investigate, evaluate, and document many areas of the profession and practice, including outcomes of counselor preparation as they relate to graduates' ability to counsel, obtain employment, conduct research, manage businesses, and be effective advocates for the profession and clients. We also need evidence that master's-level practitioners are effective within areas of practice for which other professions require doctoral preparation (at more cost to employers and consumers) as well as renewed attention to formerly exclusive counselor domains such as school counseling, which now is being encroached by social workers and others. This effort also could assess counselor employability in terms of employment opportunities (e.g., federal/state levels), economic return on opportunity costs, and factors affecting retention in the counseling profession (e.g., job satisfaction, salaries, trends).

Advocacy. How can the profession come to agreement about what best articulates how counselors are prepared and what counselors are prepared to do? How might the counseling profession best educate the public and policy makers about the rigor of the CACREP preparation standards? More fundamentally, what might it take for members of the counseling profession to own and embrace the CACREP standards as a basis for policy formulation and credentialing? What are the policy and other professional costs of failing to find consensus?

Mature people can acknowledge and refine ill-conceived decisions, reconcile past real and perceived transgressions, and find unity. To the extent that counselors can formulate clear definitions internally, they can afford clarity and guidance to various external publics including legislators and private policy makers. To reiterate, we believe that the counseling profession has one point of virtually universal member consensus in the noble and profound statement of dedication in the preamble of ACA's (1995) ethical standards, where counselors say that they "recognize diversity in our society and embrace a cross-cultural approach in support of the worth, dignity, potential, and uniqueness of each individual" (p. 1). It seems most appropriate for counselors to reaffirm that counseling matters only as it supports and promotes these and related worthy goals.

How do we best capture/recapture the principles heritage and other aspects of our profession that unite us as a prelude to refining what and how we advocate for our profession? The journey is long and difficult, and the stakes are high (indeed vital), but the journey to and the destination of helping clients are too important for us to stay bogged down. Whatever our differences, our baggage, and our perspective, let us find harmony and join and inform the quest in clearly articulating and then advocating for the profession of counseling. Future professional counselors and our publics are depending on us.

References

Agnes, M. (Ed.). (1999). *Webster's new world college dictionary* (4th ed.). New York: Macmillan.

American Chiropractic Association. (1987). *American Medical Association issues revised ethics opinion on chiropractic as litigation on antitrust suit is concluded.* Arlington, VA: Author.

American Counseling Association. (1995). *Code of ethics and standards of practice.* Alexandria, VA: Author.

American Counseling Association. (2000). *Legislative advocacy for counselors institute handbook.* Alexandria, VA: Author.

Bemak, F., & Espina, M. R. (1999, Winter). Professional counseling licensure: Going from state to state. *Spectrum,* pp. 4-6, 11. (Association for Counselor Education and Supervision)

Chi Sigma Iota. (1998). *Counselor advocacy leadership conference proceedings.* Greensboro: University of North Carolina, School of Education.

Chi Sigma Iota. (1999). *Counselor advocacy leadership conference proceedings.* Greensboro: University of North Carolina, School of Education.

Council for Accreditation of Counseling and Related Educational Programs. (1994). *CACREP accreditation standards and procedures manual.* Alexandria, VA: Author.

Council for Accreditation of Counseling and Related Educational Programs. (2000). *CACREP accreditation manual: 2001 standards.* Alexandria, VA: Author.

Engels, D.W. (1980). Looking forward via hindsight: A rationale for reviewing our ideological roots. *Personnel and Guidance Journal, 59,* 183-186.

Engels, D. W. (1996). *Counseling: A profession at risk.* Unpublished manuscript, University of North Texas.

Engels, D. W., & Dameron, J. D. (1990). *The professional counselor: Competencies, performance guidelines, and assessment* (2nd ed.). Alexandria, VA: American Association for Counseling and Development.

Gerstein, L. H., & Brooks, D. K., Jr. (1990). Counselor credentialing and interprofessional collaboration. *Journal of Counseling and Development, 68,* 477-484.

Hollis, J. W. (2000). *Counselor preparation: 1999-2001: Programs, faculty, trends* (10th ed.). Philadelphia: Accelerated Development/Taylor & Francis.

Lewis, J., & Bradley, L. (2000). *Counseling and advocacy: Counselors, clients, and communities.* Greensboro, NC: ERIC/CASS.

Looft, W. R. (1971). The psychology of more. *American Psychologist, 26,* 561-565.

National Board for Certified Counselors. (1994). *Counselor work behaviors.* Greensboro, NC: Author.

Piccioni, A. P., & Bonk, E. C. (1983). *A comprehensive history of guidance in the United States.* Austin: Texas Personnel and Guidance Association.

Secretary's Commission on Achieving Necessary Skills. (1991). *Skills and tasks for jobs: A SCANS report for America 2000.* Washington, DC: U.S. Department of Labor.

Secretary's Commission on Achieving Necessary Skills. (1992). *Learning a living: A blueprint for high performance—A SCANS report for America 2000.* Washington, DC: U.S. Department of Labor.

Simpson, J. A., & Weiner, E. S. C. (Eds.). (1989). *Oxford English dictionary* (2nd ed.). New York: Oxford University Press.

Smith, H. (2000). Counselor advocacy: Promoting the profession. In H. Hackney (Ed.), *Practice issues for the beginning counselor* (pp. 153-169). Boston: Allyn & Bacon.

Wilk v. American Medical Association, U.S.D.C., N.D. East. Ill. (1987).

PART II

Foundations
of Counseling

Cognitive-Developmental Stage Theories for Counseling

NORMAN A. SPRINTHALL

SANDRA DeANGELIS PEACE

PATRICIA ANNE DAVIS KENNINGTON

In presenting our rationale for cognitive-developmental stage theories for counseling in this chapter, we discuss the failure of prior models for counseling and the need for a preventive-developmental framework. The cognitive-developmental paradigm, as opposed to previous models, is linked directly to comprehensive theory and major longitudinal and cross-cultural research. Ultimately, any effective counseling practice must reside on the broadest set of theoretical and empirical validations. It is insufficient, in our view, to base practice on perhaps interesting and speculative eclectic and/or "pop" psychology ideas. In-

stead, we present the assumptions linked to empirical cross-validation that outline a sequence of cognitive-developmental stages that humans employ when faced with difficult and problematic issues of development. We integrate theories of Loevinger, Kohlberg, Piaget, and others to describe the different preferred modes of cognitions that humans employ depending on their cognitive capacity to make meaning from experience. This is followed by a series of case studies to illustrate the crucial importance of selecting a counseling technique that matches the client's needs and then gradually mismatches within a zone of manageable dissonance. We also complement individual counseling with examples of social role-taking activities designed to shift the emphasis to primary prevention. We close the chapter with a discussion of implications for both counseling and counselor education. The cognitive-developmental model encompasses nearly all common techniques. As we note, the effective counselor employs systematic techniques such as behavior modification, rational emotive techniques, person-centered methods, and cognitive-behavioral methods selected and keyed to the current cognitive-developmental stage of the client.

Background: The Need for a Preventive and Developmental Approach

During the 1970s, applied psychology was confronted with a professional dilemma. Research had shown that traditional approaches of counseling and psychotherapy had, at best, achieved only very modest positive effects (Smith & Glass, 1977). In fact, much earlier research had shown no effect whatsoever (Bergin, 1963). Partly as a result of these findings, some leaders within the psychological establishment called for what then was viewed as a radical change. Miller (1969), in his American Psychological Association presidential address, urged that psychologists concentrate on giving their skills away to the lay public. He said that we should select principles and practices from the armamentarium of applied psychology and teach the public how to employ such knowledge and skills on its own behalf. At the same time, Kohlberg and his associates had completed a major review of child, adolescent, and adult development and reached a stark conclusion: "Put

bluntly, there is now research evidence indicating that clinical treatment of emotional symptoms during childhood leads to predictions of adult adjustment" (Kohlberg, 1974, p. 251). Kohlberg further noted, "The best predictors of the absence of adult mental illness and maladjustment are the presence of various forms of competence and ego maturity in childhood and adolescence rather than the absence of problems and symptoms" (p. 251).

This same theme was echoed by Albee's (1982) comments on the need for a primary preventive approach for applied psychology rather than after-the-fact treatment on an individual basis from the intrapsychic paradigm. The way in which to avoid mental illness was to promote psychological development; prevention always is more effective than a curative approach. Allport (1968) had consistently pointed out that most psychological theories of the day essentially conceptualized humans as reactive rather than proactive. And within counseling, there were a series of special journal issues devoted to a rationale for primary prevention such as those in the *Personnel and Guidance Journal* (Barclay, 1984) and, more recently, in *Elementary School Guidance and Counseling* (Paisley & Peace, 1995). Baker (2000) also has written extensively about the need for school counselors to achieve a balance of primary prevention and intervention programs with the same goal—healthy development for all students. The goal is applicable to other client settings as well.

Although all of these efforts are important as significant reasons for a preventive and developmental approach, it is instructive to examine just briefly the failures of many of the precursors. For example, Super (1955) attempted to create such a model with his concept of "hygiology," presumably a variant of the mental hygiene movement or Alschuler's (1970) concept of a "Eupsychian psychology" or even van Kaam's (1965) model of a "positive existentialism." These attempts were no more successful than parallel ventures to revise psychoanalytic models to include a positive and proactive conflict-free sphere for ego development as a target for counseling (Hartmann, 1958).

It might be somewhat of an overgeneralization, but nearly all of these prior attempts to form an adequate model for development and primary prevention were unable to resolve the theory-research-practice gap. For example, psychoanalytic ego theory and van Kaam's (1965) positive existentialism were brilliant theoretical discourses, yet they lacked a research base and had only very broad guidelines for practice. Similarly, other models for prevention may display an opposite set of problems, namely, a major focus on practice and perhaps research without adequate conceptual frameworks. From one of our allied fields, in teacher education, Katz and Raths (1985) referred to this as the "Goldilocks problem," with the slender Goldilocks slipping and sliding in the overly spacious beds of the papa and mama bear. Theory is too broad to fit practice. At the other extreme, we could denote the problem as the "Procustean" difficulty. That mythical Greek robber would simply stretch a short victim or lop off the limbs of a tall victim to force a fit between the person and his or her bed, for example, a theory too narrow bereft of research as a framework for practice.

The Retreat to Eclecticism

The result of all these well-meaning but misguided attempts created the conditions for an eclectic model for counseling, and quite unfortunately, that has merely replaced one set of problems with an equal set of new problems for prevention. As documented by program analyses of Hollis (1997), no single theory with a research base provides an adequate basis for practice. The solution at this point in the phases of intellectual history is to reject ideological purity and adopt eclecticism. Counselor education programs, for example, now are apt to provide a variety of deliberately different theories and practices. These form a broad repertoire of counseling models. The counselor then is expected either to develop the ability to pick and choose from among these competing alternatives and find one that fits or to use different methods with equal competence—sometimes referred to in the literature as "happy eclecticism." Even recent integrative models (Ivey, 1986; Lazarus, 1981; Meichenbaum, 1991) lack a central theoretical rationale for selecting techniques in a meaningful fashion. The assumption is that somehow the counselor will be able to make these choices prudently and that clients will benefit. Does this mean that we have reached the end point in the journey of intellectual development for counseling practice?

One of the most glaring problems is that eclecticism actually creates more and varied practices rather than providing a disciplined focus for the practitioner. New "therapies" emerge almost overnight and perhaps even faster than a small group of proponents can gather, form themselves into a group, and seek legal certification. Creating new counseling "guilds" through such proliferation avoids requisite theory and research and promotes what Barclay (1984) referred to as an "endless flow of 'gimmicky' techniques" (p. 476). Without theory and research, eclecticism expands randomly using the anecdotal and the idiosyncratic

(Brabeck & Welfel, 1985). Practice is simply a series of fads, fables, and folklore wandering in a zone between the trivial and the cosmic without distinguishing one from the other. Thus, it is with a sense of urgency that we turn toward an elaboration of a cognitive-developmental model for counseling as a careful synthesis of theory, research, and practice, resting equally on all three components.

The Cognitive-Developmental Model

The cognitive-developmental model rests on a series of assumptions that themselves have been tested out through extensive research. The most important of these are as follows:

1. Humans create meaning from experience—a cognitive process. "Meaning is not given to us but by us" (Duckworth, 1996, p. i). These cognitive structures form into a stage of development.
2. Cognitive stages form a hierarchical and invariant sequence of meaning making from the less complex to increasingly greater levels of complexity of thinking (Kohlberg, 1984).
3. Stage growth is determined by interaction between the person and the environment including cultural, ethnic, and racial backgrounds (Lewis, Lewis, Daniels, & D'Andrea, 1998). It is neither unilateral nor automatic and is a lifelong process.

Since at least the 1960s, there have been literally thousands of studies documenting these aspects of the developmental model in a variety of domains including cognitive, moral reasoning, and ego development. Stages of cognitions have been studied in the classic work of Piaget (1964, 1972) and confirmed many times over by the recent work of Case (1992) and King

and Kitchener (1994) and cross-culturally by Ginsburg and Opper (1988). Stages of moral judgment were validated first on males by Kohlberg (1975) and then longitudinally on both males and females by Kohlberg (1984) and Rest (1986) and cross-culturally by Gielen (1996) and Snarey (1985). Stages of ego development were documented by Loevinger and Wessler (1970), confirming in many ways the theoretical propositions of Erikson (1959) and cross-culturally and within cultures by Hy and Loevinger (1996) and Faubert, Locke, Sprinthall, and Howland (1996). The Loevinger measure of ego stages has been translated into at least 11 languages for other cultures and demonstrates similar growth patterns across the stages in these cultures.

We should add that there are some developmental theories that do not agree with these basic assumptions. For example, both Ivey (1986) and Noam (1988) suggested that developmental stages are nonhierarchical. A close examination of these claims reveals a lack of significant longitudinal and cross-sectional empirical research in support of these views. Also in our view, these theorists might have confused developmental multilevelness as an indicator of a lack of age-stage growth. Current theory based on many of the studies cited previously indicates that cognitive stage growth occurs across a series of semi-independent areas, for example, cognitive, self (ego), moral, interpersonal, and affective domains. There may be systematic gaps in development across these domains according to experience and significant role-taking opportunities. This horizontal decalage (i.e., systematic gaps in development) results in patterns of uneven development that may give the appearance of a lack of a hierarchical stage and sequence (Loevinger, 1987a). In reality, however, such a decalage is an indicator of different stages within each individual. From a counseling standpoint, the usual presenting problems are systematic gaps in the personal and interpersonal domains when compared to stage functioning in academic/intellectual areas. The current state of the art along with a robust research base, then, supports the stage sequence framework as well as the problems presented by uneven development across different domains.

Also, the most recent evidence indicates that none of these cognitive-developmental frameworks by Piaget, Kohlberg, Rest, and other developmentalists is biased against women. In fact, the most current outcome from a large number of studies by Rest and Narvaez (1994) documented a recent trend in stages of moral development indicating that women consistently score higher on justice issues than do men. These findings also were confirmed by Lind (1993) in Germany; by Stewart, Sprinthall, and Siemienska (1997) in Poland; and by Daniels, D'Andrea, and Heck (1995) in Hawaii. Loevinger (1987b) originally normed her stage theory on an exclusively female population and subsequently cross-validated the scheme with male samples. Morrow (1993) examined the Loevinger system in a sample of lesbian women and found no bias by sexual orientation. The distribution by stage from Morrow's sample was exactly parallel to that from Loevinger's normative female and male samples. From all of this, and in spite of the commentary by critics such as Gilligan (1982), we can document the lack of bias across these developmental stage theories.

As a result of this extremely large set of basic research studies, it can be concluded that humans do exhibit the characteristics of cognitive-developmental growth as they confront problems of living in a complex and diverse society.

Cognitive-Developmental Stage and Behavior: Is There a Link?

From a counseling standpoint, of course, the question of stage theory does not end with the theoretical and cross-cultural validations noted earlier. Far more important is the stage-behavior connection. Namely, do humans behave differently and in accordance with these stages? The results here are not as clear-cut, yet the trends are highly consistent. Humans who process experience at higher stages of development are more likely to act in humane and altruistic modes than are cohorts who function at less complex stages. These results were summarized by Sprinthall, Sprinthall, and Oja (1998) in studies of resisting cheating, whistle-blowing situations, resisting obedience to arbitrary authority, aiding a bystander in distress, and returning an important questionnaire. Studies reviewed by Rest and Narvaez (1994) documented the relationship between higher stages and fraud detection by certified public accountants; between higher stages and skilled professional performance by physicians, veterinarians, dentists, and nurses; and the opposite by those professionals functioning at lower stages. Goleman (1998) documented similar findings for business executives. Peace (1995), in her review, showed clear relationships between stage of development and professional performance in areas such as teaching and counseling.

In summary, we can conclude that as each stage of development is transcended, individuals increase their competence in a wide variety of domains (Heath, 1991). These include greater effectiveness in problem solving and even problem finding, interpersonal sensitivity, recognition of individual differences, valuing cultural diversity, decision making in accord with democratic principles of equity and fairness, ego strength to withstand unjust criticism, and self-knowledge and -awareness.

Cognitive-Developmental Stage: Counseling Goals and Strategies

The overall process of counseling, either through primary prevention or by individual and small group work, starts with the current stage level of functioning of the client. Then, the counselor creates a slightly more challenging interaction that results in a constructive mismatch so as to promote developmental growth (Hunt, 1974). All developmentalists agree that growth is not automatic, unilateral, or without some pain. The accommodation-assimilation disequilibrium is inevitable given that growth toward greater effectiveness requires the person to give up his or her "old" and ineffective methods of problem solving. Thus, with any developmental strategy, there needs to be a careful balance between support and challenge. Each stage, then, is not fixed or permanent as a special education label; rather, the stage represents the current preferred mode of problem solving. The goal is to aid the growth process, step by step, to a system that is toward more complex functioning at both the cognitive and affective levels. This is based on Vygotsky's (1962) theory of the zone of proximal development. It is important to remember that no one is completely "in" one stage; rather, there are elements of both higher and lower cognitive process. The counseling dictum is to connect with

the current mode and then facilitate development to the slightly higher and more complex mode. Our case studies in subsequent sections illustrate this "plus one" concept given that effective growth always is a gradual and graduated process.

Having established the research and theory base for stage as a predictor of different levels of behavior (e.g., lower stages produce less complex problem-solving strategies and vice versa), we now can outline a general synthesis of stage level and strategies to promote client growth. Early work on this model first was suggested by D'Andrea (1984), Ivey (1986), Loevenger and Wessler (1970), Swensen (1980), and Young-Eisendrath (1988). Paisley and Hubbard (1994) and Vernon (1999) also incorporated developmental theories into counseling strategies for children and adolescents. The current model, described in the following paragraphs, is a further elaboration of those initial efforts. Also, we have expanded and integrated the stage definitions of Loevinger, Kohlberg, and others as a means of providing broad definitions of human functioning across domains of cognitive, affective, and interpersonal functioning. For background purposes, a brief overview of Loevinger's and Kohlberg's stages is outlined in Table 7.1.

We now provide a few sample strategies at each level of functioning in two modes: (a) individual/group counseling and (b) primary prevention role-taking strategies. First, given the importance of primary prevention, we do wish to emphasize the need for the role-taking mode as a genuine complement to the more traditional methods. This idea of incorporating both counseling strategies and preventive social role-taking methods originated with a colleague, Jean Williams (personal communication, April

TABLE 7.1   Kohlberg's Stages of Moral Development and Loevinger's Stages of Ego
Development

Moral Development		*Ego Development*	
Stage/Level	*Characteristics*	*Stage/Level*	*Characteristics*
1	Obedience, avoidance of punishment orientation	1-2	Impulsive, fear of retaliation
2	Satisfying individual's needs; others' needs considered only if individual also benefits	Delta	Self-protective, externalized blame, fear of being caught
3	Social conformity, orientation to approval of others	3	Conformity to external rules, shame/guilt for breaking rules
4	Orientation to showing respect for authority, decisions based on legal sanctions	4	Conscientious, self-evaluated standards, self-critical, guilt for consequences
5	Rules upheld because of the social contract, agreement to guarantee as many individual rights as possible	5	Autonomous, toleration, coping with conflicting inner needs
6	Following universal principles of justice	6	Integrated, reconciling inner conflicts

SOURCES: Adapted from Kohlberg (1975) and Loevinger (1987a).

1993). A key element in using a cognitive-developmental framework to create person-environment interactions to promote growth is social role-taking, first suggested by Mead (1934). Assuming a complex new role such as peer mentoring, tutoring, counseling, teaching, child care, or companions to older persons can facilitate the ability to take another's perspective, comprehend a wider worldview, and tolerate ambiguity (Sprinthall, 1994). Significant role-taking experiences in a person's contextual setting combined with guided reflection has been shown to promote more complex levels of thinking and reasoning (Boss, 1994; Sprinthall, Reiman, & Thies-Sprinthall, 1993). More details on the conditions needed for designing successful role-taking activities are discussed in a subsequent section.

Sample Strategies for Each Level of Functioning

Delta/Delta Three Level

Table 7.2 outlines the client characteristics common at a highly concrete and low level of psychological integration along with the corresponding counseling techniques. For example, Loevinger's stage definitions, unfortunately, somewhat mix the numerical and the conceptual. Thus, her lower stages of functioning, the equivalent of Stages 1 and 2, are denoted as Delta/Delta Three levels. The individual does not differentiate ideas and feelings and exhibits impulse control problems, sees the world in a narrow-minded dichotomy of right and wrong, and focuses on materialistic gain for self. This

TABLE 7.2   Client Characteristics for Loevinger Delta/Delta Three and Corresponding
Counseling Techniques: Loevinger Delta or Delta Three Level of Ego Integration

	Cognitive	*Interpersonal*	*Character*
Characteristics	• Dualistic thinker (right or wrong, black or white) • Fantasy, exaggerated thinking to very literal, concrete • Lacks ability to be self-critical • Overgeneralizes (lack of differentiating ability) • Limited vocabulary	• Self-oriented • Control and advantage in relationships • Does not understand feelings of others • Lack of perspective-taking ability • Competitive • Physical response as problem-solving method • Impulsive	• Pleasure oriented (follows rules to obtain rewards) • Opportunistic ("Look out for Number One") • "It's okay if I don't get caught" • Self-protective
Problem areas	• Lack of differentiation between thoughts and feelings, so problem with impulse control	• Difficulty in establishing intimate relationships • Pattern of needing to control • Inability to understand others' feelings and needs • Blames others during times of conflict; does not take responsibility • Feels victimized without logical reasoning • Self at the center of all decisions, with little or no regard for impact on others	• Lacks self-discipline • Needs strong external order imposed or has difficulty in adapting (sees what he or she can get away with)
Techniques	• Behavior modification, concrete activities and rewards • Modeling and positive behavioral reinforcement • Gradual elaboration of feelings for self and understanding of feelings in others • Reality therapy, a concrete view of the relationship between means and ends	• Facilitate other-directedness through group affiliations	• Focus on behaviors and consequences • Look at new behaviors and outcomes • Explore feelings (might have to identify feelings)

SOURCE: Adapted from Loevinger and Wessler (1970).

sometimes is referred to as the impulsive/self-protective stage.

Counseling strategies initially would focus very directly on the concrete, for example, a behavior modification system set up and managed by the counselor. The individual at that level is not capable of consistent self-management. This also means that the counselor needs to employ high structure with minimal ambiguity using immediate, concrete, and meaningful rewards through positive reinforcement. At the same time, the counselor stresses the concrete connection between the individual's current maladaptive behavior and consequences (means connected to ends). This also indicates that the counselor would be very active in the process—to set up, maintain, and comment on the reinforcement schedules. Because client self-understanding is very limited, there will be only a rudimentary consciousness of level of emotions in self and others. This would mean a very limited discussion of feelings, perhaps only an acknowledgment and naming of a few. Use of expressive arts, such as drawing, photography, music, and drama (Gladding, 1998), could be effective when strictly verbal modes fail.

Social role-taking through a peer helping model would be highly concrete and highly structured. For example, at the school level, high school students could be taught to use almost a paint-by-the-numbers approach to transmit a health education curriculum to elementary school students, complete with easy-to-follow transparencies and worksheets. Also, the counselor then would facilitate short and structured discussions with the helpers after each session. The counselor would present a few words describing feelings that the helpers might have experienced and would ask them to pick out one or two and write them down in a journal. This will gradually expand the ability to process experiences of the helpers and then later to begin to process the feelings of the elementary school students. A similar format could be used with adults working out of a community setting (e.g., women's center, church outreach program, sheltered workshop, retirement home). For example, the client could be taught how to teach retirement home residents simple skills such as crafts and exercise.

Stage Three Level

Table 7.3 presents characteristics of clients functioning at the Stage Three level of integration. The main problem at this level is the lack of individuation and autonomy. The person is largely "other directed" and caught in constant need for social conformity, with abundant use of clichés and a ready acceptance of stereotypes concerning race and gender. An appropriate counseling mode needs to emphasize assertiveness training, complete with cognitive-behavioral "self-talk." This should occur in a sequence of modest steps to ensure success. After a period of initial successes, it also might be possible to employ a few of Ellis's (1994) rational emotive behavior therapy techniques, particularly the "worst-case scenario" approach. Group counseling could employ a moral dilemma discussion method to increase clients' perspectives (Claypoole, Moody, & Peace, in press; Powell, Locke, & Sprinthall, 1991).

The social role-taking method could focus directly on one aspect of excessive social conformity: Have the individuals learn how to use

TABLE 7.3   Client Characteristics for Loevinger Level Three and Corresponding Counseling
Techniques: Loevinger Level Three of Ego Integration

	Cognitive	*Interpersonal*	*Character*
Characteristics	• Relies on structure • Dualist (right or wrong, black or white) • Rarely sees alternatives • Limited self-analysis, lack of self-examination • Easily frustrated by failure	• Simple categories for humans (stereotyping, generalizing) • Strong need for acceptance to fit in • Clichés • Superficial relationships • Limited vocabulary for feelings • Feels guilty about disagreements with friends	• What is valued or right is what is accepted by society • Other-directedness • Social conformity • Social etiquette is confused with democratic principles • External rules and guidelines
Problem areas	• Poor planning orientation (externally oriented, go with the flow) • Denies reality (nostalgia, myths, imaginary audience, personal fable phenomenon) • Learned helplessness (independent coping skills not developed) • Can easily be distracted from tasks • Short-term solutions • Appearance and "fitting in" are critical	• Superficial awareness of self in relation to others • Fears of group being dissolved are very great • Needs lots of support • May look for careers where he or she will be taken care of	• Externally motivated • External frame of reference • Accepts stereotypes (gender, race) • Behaves in accordance with those around him or her • Opinions and values the same as the group's opinions and values
Techniques	• Cognitive behavioral self-talk • Self-directed behavioral contract • Teach planning and decision making (homework) • Examine the "why's" • Rational emotive behavior therapy, focus on fears and worst-case scenarios • Set reachable goals and celebrate victories • Start concrete	• Peer helping (role-taking) • Use of role models • Assertiveness training	• Focus on dissonant feelings when "sticking one's neck out" or being different from the group

SOURCE: Adapted from Loevinger and Wessler (1970).

"I-messages" and then teach either peers or others how to use the techniques, a small yet significant step out of social conformity and a lack of individuation. We have found that this Stage Three level is very common with adolescents and with a rather large number of both young and middle-aged adults (Sprinthall, 1993). The content of the conformity may be different, but the structural process is highly similar. A survey of our community counseling center at North Carolina State University indicated that at least 50% of the adults seeking help still functioned at that level. Quite unfortunately, most were women who had been "treated" previously only with drugs to handle their depressive feelings (Sprinthall, 1993).

Stage Four Level

Table 7.4 describes the characteristics at Stage Four as well as the problem areas most associated with that level. McClelland (1980) identified this as a level with a high need for achievement—a rational problem solver and a moderate risk taker—as opposed to the previous Stage Three, where the strong need is for affiliation and relationship. Thus, at Stage Four, there is an important developmental gain, namely, individuation and self-directed decision making. However, such individuality carries with it an identifiable set of concerns such as overachievement, a lack of mutuality in relationships, a narrow rationalism, and perhaps an aloofness to anyone less fortunate. As a result, concerns for others might be low. Objectivity might be so high that there is no room for subjectivity.

Counseling, then, would focus on expanding emotional awareness. Goleman (1998) referred to this as "emotional intelligence." Because individuals here are self-directed, self-managed behavioral contracts could be negotiated, keeping track of how the person and cohorts feel in everyday situations. Similarly, self-managed systematic relaxation modes could be followed to further expand the range and complexity of human emotions. These procedures would help the person to loosen up and not worry quite so much about linking self-esteem to his or her most recent grade point average or some other criterion. Written reflection, through journals or poetry writing, also could prompt emotional expression and fresh insights. The counselor could enhance client development by guiding the reflection process through asking questions, reflecting feelings, and using positive reinforcement (Sprinthall et al., 1993).

Role-taking here would focus on leading groups in peer helping, teaching active listening and accurate empathy. Learning empathy by teaching it to others, such as peers (e.g., mentors, tutors, residence hall advisers in schools and colleges) or paraprofessional helpers in community centers, would be the most obvious choice of role-taking (Delworth & Aulepp, 1976). Keeping journals on self and discussing how the "helpee" felt would expand interpersonal and intrapersonal perspective taking. These leadership role-taking experiences could be graduated in levels of complexity according to how quickly the person learns from the helping experiences (Sprinthall, 1994).

Stage Four/Five to Five Level

Table 7.5 presents the characteristics of a very high stage of development, Stage Four/Five to Five. Of course, the first question that always is asked is why anyone who functions at that level would need help. Swensen (1980)

TABLE 7.4   Client Characteristics for Loevinger Stage Four and Corresponding Counseling
Techniques: Loevinger Level Four of Ego Integration

	Cognitive	*Interpersonal*	*Character*
Characteristics	• Self-directed as a learner • Planning orientation • Some rigidity • Rational achiever • Introspection mostly rational • Controlled problem solver • Abstract thinker	• Limited interpersonal relationships, many friendships functional • Delays gratification • Generally polite • Pragmatic	• Conscientious, strong feelings of loyalty and laws • Autonomous ("master of my fate") • Highly responsible • Self-critical • Accepts conflicting views • Makes some allowances for exceptions
Problem areas	• Difficulty in distinguishing between objective and interpersonal problem solving • Responds to "shoulds/oughts" with submerged guilt feelings • Limited understanding of range of emotions	• May be overly respectful of authority • High ego strength and high expectations for self may be transferred to others • Difficulty in asking for help	• May be too self-sacrificing • May be a workaholic or an overachiever • Excessive expectations for self • For culturally devalued groups, "Have I sacrificed my cultural roots?"
Techniques	• Lengthy exploration to articulate multiple feelings (Myers-Briggs Type Indicator can bring out feelings) • Deal with immediate transference issues • Authenticity • Self-managed behavioral model • Readings, films • Rogerian "immediate atmosphere" • Relaxation, meditation • Journaling	• Role-taking experiences • Leading peer-helping groups	• Search for balance/bigger picture • Learn how to have fun in work

SOURCE: Adapted from Loevinger and Wessler (1970).

quipped something to the effect that if a counselor runs into anyone at that level, then one should reverse roles and request help. However, Loevinger (1987b) made it clear that higher stages are not necessarily happier ones.

In fact, the real problems at this level are those that appear as endemic to our society—the twin evils of racism and sexism. How can a person relax and experience joy when there are so many societal problems at the doorstep? How,

TABLE 7.5 Client Characteristics for Loevinger Stage Four/Five to Five and Corresponding Counseling Techniques: Loevinger Level Four/Five to Five of Ego Integration

	Cognitive	*Interpersonal*	*Character*
Characteristics	• Abstract • Draws a variety of meanings from a variety of experiences • Can articulate counterarguments to own view • Accepts discomforts with new tasks • Committed relativist • Deals well with ambiguous issues • Uses metaphor and humor in analysis	• Understands and appreciates diversity • Can process multiple feelings in self and others simultaneously • Articulates knowledge of self as a complex person • Accurate empathy • Rich interpersonal relations with a few very close friends • Understands different impacts that he or she may have on others • Extensive descriptive vocabulary • Existential humor	• Understands democratic principles • Sees issues in terms of policies, the greatest good, and individual rights • Possible history of protest, standing up for unpopular but democratic causes • Self-fulfillment more important than career achievement • Offended by greed and materialism • Focused on a complex philosophy of life • Sees life's paradoxes
Problem areas	• Feels unchallenged in career • Feels stuck in a rut • Sees variety of possibilities and dimensions but stops short of taking action • Wheel spinner	• May feel some isolation from significant others • May have some difficulty in valuing own needs in decisions with others • Career conflict (being in helping profession but not in full charge) • Conflict over marriage, family, career	• Sometimes struggling to really liberate self from a materialistic society
Techniques	• Review carefully and in detail for the intellectual, affective components of current concern • Homework (films, readings) • Address feelings at different levels of intensity • Journaling with focus on feelings • Promote openness to current experiencing as a guide to action	• Support and grounding • Help to identify own support system • Support spiritual search	• Humor (help see bigger picture and see the irony) • Metaphors

SOURCE: Adapted from Loevinger and Wessler (1970).

in an existential sense, can a person accept his or her limits and avoid what often is called a "messianic complex"?

Probably the counselor with such a client needs to facilitate an examination of the client's strengths and emotional investment that are aligned with pressing societal concerns. The counselor may help the client prioritize how time will be spent in altruistic actions. Also, the counselor can continue to help the client reframe the problems and concerns in a careful balance of seriousness and humor. Readings, particularly Frankel's (1939) compelling discussion on meaning and purpose under horrendous conditions or other such accounts, would promote perspectives for a balance between one's obligation to society at large and one's obligation to self and private life. Quite obviously, the counseling interactions would become much more of a peer dialogue at this level. Helping the client to integrate a spiritual dimension could help with questions about life's purpose and meaning (Burke & Miranti, 1992).

The social role-taking component likely would involve creating a support system, that is, a common concerns and (interests-based) dialogue group with others in the community. This would reduce the isolation and increase the resources for each individual as he or she struggles with these central life issues. The personal, work, and societal dilemmas could be the context for a searching examination toward actualizing a holistic approach to life including physical, psychological, spiritual, and emotional aspects. As Loevinger and Wessler (1970) noted, at this level, all the complexities of life are evident, and seemingly irreconcilable issues are confronted (e.g., rational passion, commitment, relativism). This is one of the tasks of the generativity stage described by Erikson (1959)

or, in the words of Allport (1968), becoming "whole hearted yet half sure" (p. 320).

Conditions for Social Role-Taking Activities

In addition to using traditional individual and group counseling strategies, the counselor needs to be intentional about incorporating social role-taking activities as part of the counseling process. For optimal success in promoting client development, the following conditions for designing and implementing role-taking activities are necessary.

Significant role-taking experiences. These are complex situations in which the client feels fully involved with others, requiring the client to construct new ways of thinking and behaving in response to the new demands of the role. As opposed to role-playing in a counseling session, a significant new helping role triggers empathy as the client actively cares for another and perspectives increase. The counselor matches client characteristics of developmental stage with an appropriate level of social role-taking such as the examples described earlier.

Guided reflection. It is important to provide ongoing opportunities to examine the new role-taking experiences through journal writing and discussions. These forms of reflection help the client to process his or her thoughts and feelings and to understand experiences from different perspectives. The counselor can monitor client progress and guide the growth process by responding to the client's written reflections with systematic feedback, differentiated based on developmental level (Sprinthall et al., 1993).

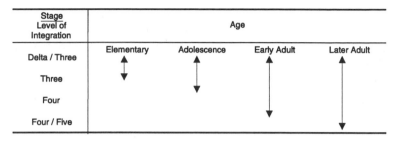

Figure 7.1. Age-Stage Relationships Across the Life Span

Balance between reflection and experience. Programs must be carefully planned to allow for sequences of experiential activities balanced with regular cycles of reflection and self-analysis. This interplay of action and reflection ideally should occur on a weekly basis so that there is an ongoing examination of one's adjustment to the new role.

Support and challenge. Complex new roles create a challenge for people. Psychological support is needed when clients enter a state of disequilibrium as they give up old cognitions for newer and more complex methods of problem solving and understanding. The goal is to manage an appropriate ratio of support and challenge, which varies for each individual.

Continuity. For cognitive structural change to take place, the role-taking experience and the other conditions described previously have to be continuous—preferably weekly—and span 6 to 12 months.

Age and Stage Issues

On an overall basis, then, the framework becomes a guiding format for the counselor. Each stage represents a consistent cognitive problem-solving system. The stage structures how we as individuals derive meaning from experience. It is important to note the qualitative differences between the less complex and more complex stages. This also means that the stage system can be more significant than age. For example, a 30-year-old who employs a Stage Three social conformity mode finds a parallel in a 17-year-old who also solves problems at Stage Three. The same would hold for a 45-year-old and a 25-year-old Stage Four conscientious achiever. No one, however, is ever completely "in" a single stage. There always is overlap across the earlier and later stages juxtaposed with the current modal system. Figure 7.1 depicts very crudely some of the age-stage relationships across the life span. Note that as age increases, the modal stages also increase. This represents primarily an integration of longitudinal studies from Loevinger (1987a) and Kohlberg (1984) and other developmental researchers.

Transitions

From a counseling viewpoint, the age-stage question is more complicated than depicted in Figure 7.1. Transitions from stage to stage usually are created by a crisis in problem solving and interaction with the environmental press

(Ivey & Bradford Ivey, 1998). The current system is literally jammed, and anxiety follows as the person begins to confront the reality that the current mode is inadequate to the new task. An obvious example occurs at the Stage Three level when one struggles with how to please everybody or the crisis created when a concrete dualistic thinker confronts an essay exam requiring symbolic interpretation. One of us still remembers hearing a college student bitterly complaining about why a professor kept talking about Herman Melville's symbolism. After all, he said, "Why spoil a good sea story with Melville's complexes?" Kegan (1982) reminded us that a modal stage is only a temporary "evolutionary truce" (p. 108) that may shatter when confronted with a more complex task. During such periods, of course, the individual may be most inclined to seek counseling assistance given that a common response to a more complex task involves feelings of despair, retreat, and withdrawal or the opposite (e.g., anger, acting out). Thus, it is during these periods of transition that the emotional agenda will be most apparent and most accessible to an alert counselor.

Assessment Issues

Certainly, one of the keys to the developmental approach concerns assessment. It is clear that the choice of individual treatment and the complementary social role-taking activity is guided by an assessment of the current level of functioning. There has been some advocacy for using formal developmental testing methods to guide counseling strategies to promote growth (D'Andrea & Daniels, 1992). We have found that a less formal method of using the counselor's listening skills represents the starting point. The counselor bears in mind the problem-solving strategies common to each stage (as noted in Tables 7.2 to 7.5 on client characteristics and problem areas) and listens and questions during an initial interview or two. This generally will provide at least an initial approximation of stage level. The counselor needs to remain open to adjustments to this initial view if further discussion yields important new insight. It is good to remember that we need to know what the modal level is during difficult situations. Metaphorically, it is similar to assessing the competence of a sailor during a storm versus being safely at anchor in a peaceful harbor. An appropriate level of support through accurate empathy is particularly important during the emotionally charged transition periods. Consequently, assessment is an ongoing process of listening and revising when necessary to gradually get an accurate fix on present cognitive stage process.

Case Studies

As a means of illustrating the assessment intervention strategies, we present a few examples of a person's seeking counseling assistance and then present some sample strategies for short-term counseling and social role-taking suggestions.

Case 1. The client is a 34-year-old male with a history of underachievement in school and career. His characteristics include the inability to see long-term consequences and the desire to solve problems exclusively from an intuitive perspective. He seems easily swayed by popular opinion. All of this results in a low planning orientation toward problem solving. Despite an attractive personality and strong social skills, he has failed to get promoted and remains an assistant sales manager. He switches companies, but the career pattern repeats itself. During counseling, the client says that it might be time to figure out what is getting in the way of being successful. He talks about himself in a very cliché manner.

The chief characteristics of this client are the following: low planning, low rationality, high social skills, and reliance on stereotypes and clichés. This would lead to an initial assessment of a Stage Three system. From this, the counselor would choose some assertiveness training and decision making, emphasizing contracting and similar activities to promote self-direction and self-management. Social role-taking could involve volunteer work as a school mentor to middle school students using one of the career decision-making curricula.

Case 2. The teenager, a 15-year-old, has a record of being a real "cut-up" in school and has had multiple minor scrapes with the police. She shows a very short attention span in counseling and class discussions. The student seems to understand self and ideas at a concrete level. She is easily distracted, with grades heading toward a dropout level. There is little in-depth insight. She indicates a desire to do better in school but does not know where to start.

The characteristics of this client are obvious: impulsive behavior, acting up, concrete thinking, and low on self-awareness/insight. These fit closely with the Delta/Delta Three level and will require high levels of counselor directedness. Behavioral contracts directed by the counselor focused in rudimentary study skills represent the starting point. After an initial period with positive reinforcement for small successes, the counselor could arrange for the teenager to "help" some elementary school students in Grades 1 and 2 to improve their reading skills as an appropriate role-taking activity.

Case 3. The client, a 60-year-old at the community counseling center, has just learned that his company has folded as a result of a heavily leveraged buy-out. He has 30 years experience with the company as an accountant but has heard that the new firm might not fully honor his retirement plan. He has been a "company man" all his life and says, "I always figured that I'd work there til retirement at [age] 70." At this point, he appears confused and depressed as he reflects, "It's something I never thought I'd have to confront." He concludes, "I always thought good work and loyalty was enough."

In this situation, the client actually exhibits segments of two stages. There are characteristics of Stage Four, including conscientious achievement. Stage Three is represented by his loyalty to the company and his assumption that "they" would take care of him together with a lack of self-direction and assertiveness. The counselor could well choose to build on the Stage Four elements, for example, a planning orientation along with supporting exploration for career options. Simultaneously, the counselor needs to expand the client's emotional repertoire because this apparently is his first major crisis.

Journal writing assignments can encourage expression of feelings and thoughts. The counselor can guide the written reflection by providing feedback and reflecting feelings. Social role-taking eventually could include volunteer work at a senior center in setting up a tax advising service.

These cases are necessarily brief to simply illustrate aspects of the process of assessment and strategies for both counseling and social role-taking. Also, we need to point out that research supporting these approaches does vary. Because the counseling model is relatively new, positive results have been reported in the form of case studies by Ivey (1986) and Kegan (1982) and from our practice in supervising graduate students in a community-based counseling center. However, the research base for the social role-taking procedures has been widely researched over the past 25 years across age groups (children, adolescents, young adults, and older adults) and different geographical, social, and racial groupings (Sprinthall, 1994; Sprinthall et al., 1993). The meta-analysis shows a consistent positive effect size (circa +1.0) in promoting developmental stage growth for those helpers who participated in the peer programs. Also, such studies have shown the importance of varying the amount of responsibility and structure in relation to different developmental stages. Hedin's research (as reported by Sprinthall, 1994), in particular, demonstrated how to employ three different role-taking strategies for adolescents who themselves presented three different levels from Delta/Delta Three to Stage Four. Each group then improved within its own stage as a result of the helping activity.

Implications

For Counseling Practice

We have outlined the importance of creating a counseling system based on the developmental stage characteristics of individuals. The following are a few of the major implications for counselors:

- Learn to tune in and listen for the structure of the problem-solving strategies and successively review the client's current mode of stage cognitions, an ongoing process.

- Select strategies that are most apt to match and slightly mismatch the current mode of stage cognitions.

- Be particularly alert to transition periods in modes because of heightened anxiety and stress. Monitor level of support and challenge.

- Remember that a stage is not fixed or permanent but rather the current mode with abilities both slightly higher and slightly lower than the current stage.

- Keep a balance between counseling strategies and preventive social role-taking activities because the latter has so clearly achieved a solid research base for developmental growth.

- Remember that an extremely broad research base has clearly demonstrated that there is no bias toward women, a person's sexual orientation, or ethnically diverse persons. The scheme is fair by gender, culture, and sexual orientation.

- The use of a cognitive-developmental framework through social role-taking represents a comprehensive model for differing sociopolitical, cultural, ethnic, and racial contexts.

For Counselor Education

Traditionally, counselor education programs have placed great emphasis on remedial and individual therapeutic paradigms of how change takes place (Lewis et al., 1998). This limits many counselors' understanding of primary prevention and developmental interventions. Training in an expanded developmental model should aim to do the following:

- Provide a base in theory and research as a basis for practice, avoiding atheoretical eclectic modes

- Outline a framework that broadly encompasses strategies such as those of Rogers and Ellis and cognitive-behavioral, behavioral contracting, and preventive modes that avoid singularity of intervention (Peace & Sprinthall, 1998)

- Become rooted in development in a manner that allows us as a profession to regain our distinctiveness and separation from clinically oriented therapy including replacing the non-researched base of the *DSM-IV* (*Diagnostic and Statistical Manual of Mental Disorders* [American Psychiatric Association, 1994]) with a developmental understanding of persons (Ivey & Bradford-Ivey, 1998)

In fact, those of us who made dire predictions (Sprinthall, 1990) as to the difficulties of forsaking a developmental model for clinical private practice have, perhaps unfortunately, seen these predictions borne out. The gold of third-party reimbursement has turned out to be fool's gold as headlines in the *National Psychologist* announced, "Average Income of Psychologists Has Dropped Notably" (1998) and "Psychology Told to Put 'House in Order' Before Seeking Prescription Privileges" (1998).

Perspectives on the Future

The demands and expectations placed on counselors continue to grow in complexity and degree (Lewis et al., 1998). Factors such as continuing demographic changes, new immigrants, economic discrepancies, disenfranchised adolescents, and managed care require counselors to broaden their ideas about helping. The developmental framework described in this chapter can guide counselors' work to respond to future client and societal issues. By meeting clients where they are and gradually applying challenging conditions, not only are their presenting issues addressed, but there also is potential for clients to be transformed to a new way of being. Counselors can play an important role in promoting the development of people to increasing levels of empathy, to be better citizens, and to negotiate the intricacies of interacting with diverse populations. In this sense, counselors also can contribute to addressing societal problems.

Likewise, future challenges provide a rationale for restructuring counselor education programs to focus as much attention on enhancing counselors' cognitive development as on acquiring skills (Peace & Sprinthall, 1998). The need for counselors to develop higher levels of thinking, problem solving, and ethical actions is greater than ever. Competent counselors have to be described as those with the ability to see the social and political implications of their actions and to use their skills to promote greater equality, justice, and humane conditions inside and beyond their work settings. Counselors can use their training to help clients manage and alter their environments and to assist others in viewing situations from multiple lenses and from an ethical perspective. There are many opportunities for counselors to provide a compassionate voice and to serve as advocates on behalf of clients and policy reform (Kennington, 1999).

References

Albee, G. (1982). Preventing psychopathology and promoting human potential. *American Psychologist, 32,* 1043-1050.

Allport, G. (1968). *The person in psychology.* Boston: Beacon.

Alschuler, A. (1970). *Teaching achievement motivation.* Middletown, CT: Educational Ventures.

American Psychiatric Association. (1994). *Diagnostic and statistical manual of mental disorders* (4th ed.). Washington, DC: Author.

Average income of psychologists has dropped notably. (1998, July-August). *National Psychologist,* p. 1.

Baker, S. B. (2000). *School counseling for the twenty-first century.* Upper Saddle River, NJ: Merrill/Prentice Hall.

Barclay, J. R. (Ed.). (1984). [Special issue]. Primary prevention in schools]. *Personnel and Guidance Journal, 62,* 443-495.

Bergin, A. (1963). The effects of psychotherapy: Negative results revisited. *Journal of Counseling Psychology, 10,* 244-250.

Boss, J. (1994). The effect of community service work on the moral development of college ethics students. *Journal of Moral Education, 23,* 183-198.

Brabeck, M., & Welfel, E. (1985). Counseling theory: Understanding the trend toward eclecticism from a developmental perspective. *Journal of Counseling and Development, 63,* 343-348.

Burke, M. T., & Miranti, J. G. (Eds.). (1992). *Ethical and spiritual values in counseling.* Alexandria, VA: American Association for Counseling and Development.

Case, R. (1992). *The mind's staircase.* Hillsdale, NJ: Lawrence Erlbaum.

Claypoole, S., Moody, E., & Peace, S. D. (in press). Moral dilemma discussion groups: An effective form of psychoeducational groups for juvenile offenders. *Journal for Specialists in Group Work.*

D'Andrea, M. (1984). The counselor as pacer: A model for the revitalization of the counseling profession. In R. Hayes & R. Aubrey (Eds.), *New directions for counseling and human development* (pp. 22-44). Denver, CO: Love.

D'Andrea, M., & Daniels, J. (1992). Measuring ego development for counseling practice: Implementing developmental eclecticism. *Journal of Humanistic Education and Development, 31,* 12-21.

Daniels, J., D'Andrea, M., & Heck, R. (1995). Moral development and Hawaiian youth: Does gender make a difference? *Journal of Counseling and Development, 74,* 90-93.

Delworth, U., & Aulepp, L. (1976). *Training manual for paraprofessionals and allied professional programs.* Boulder, CO: Western Interstate Commission for Higher Education.

Duckworth, E. (1996). *The having of wonderful ideas.* New York: Teachers College Press.

Ellis, A. (1994). *Reason and emotion in psychotherapy revised.* New York: Carol.

Erikson, E. (1959). *Identity and the life cycle* (Psychological Issues, Monograph 1). New York: International Universities Press.

Faubert, M., Locke, D., Sprinthall, N., & Howland, W. (1996). Promoting cognitive and ego development of African-American rural youth: A program of deliberate

psychological education. *Journal of Adolescence, 19,* 533-543.

Frankel, V. (1939). *Man's search for meaning: An introduction to logotherapy.* Boston: Beacon.

Gielen, U. P. (1996). Moral reasoning in a cross-cultural perspective: A review of Kohlbergian research. *World Psychology, 2,* 313-334.

Gilligan, C. (1982). *In a different voice.* Cambridge, MA: Harvard University Press.

Ginsburg, H., & Opper, S. (1988). *Piaget's theory of intellectual development.* Englewood Cliffs, NJ: Prentice Hall.

Gladding, S. (1998). *Counseling as an art: The creative arts in counseling.* Alexandria, VA: ACA Publications.

Goleman, D. (1998). *Working with emotional intelligence.* New York: Bantam.

Hartmann, H. (1958). *Ego psychology and the problem of adaptation.* New York: International Universities Press.

Heath, D. (1991). *Fulfilling lives: Paths to maturity and success.* San Francisco: Jossey-Bass.

Hollis, J. W. (1997). *Counselor preparation 1996-1998: Programs, personnel, trends* (9th ed.). Washington, DC: Taylor & Francis.

Hunt, D. E. (1974). *Matching models in education.* Toronto: Ontario Institute for Studies in Education.

Hy, L., & Loevinger, J. (1996). *Measuring ego development.* Mahwah, NJ: Lawrence Erlbaum.

Ivey, A. (1986). *Developmental counseling and therapy.* San Francisco: Jossey-Bass.

Ivey, A., & Bradford Ivey, M. (1998). Reframing DSM-IV: Positive strategies from developmental counseling and therapy. *Journal of Counseling and Development, 76,* 334-350.

Katz, L., & Raths, J. (1985). Dispositions as goals for teacher education. *Teaching and Teacher Education, 1,* 301-307.

Kegan, R. (1982). *The evolving self.* Cambridge, MA: Harvard University Press.

Kennington, P. D. (1999). The ethical and social justice dilemma of managed behavioral health care. *Alabama Counseling Association Journal, 24,* 26-40.

King, P., & Kitchener, K. (1994). *Developing reflective judgment: Understanding and promoting intellectual growth and critical thinking in adolescents and adults.* San Francisco: Jossey-Bass.

Kohlberg, L. (1974). Counseling and counselor education. *Counselor Education and Supervision, 14,* 250-256.

Kohlberg, L. (1975). The cognitive-developmental approach to moral development. *Phi Delta Kappan, 56,* 671-675.

Kohlberg, L. (1984). *Essays on moral development* (Vol. 2). New York: Harper & Row.

Lazarus, A. A. (1981). *The practice of multimodal psychotherapy*. New York: McGraw-Hill.

Lewis, J. A., Lewis, M. D., Daniels, J. A., & D'Andrea, M. J. (1998). *Community counseling: Empowerment strategies for a diverse society*. Pacific Grove, CA: Brooks/Cole.

Lind, G. (1993). *Moral und bildung*. Heidelberg, Germany: Roland Asanger Verlag.

Loevinger, J. (1987a). *Ego development: Conceptions in theories*. San Francisco: Jossey-Bass.

Loevinger, J. (1987b). *Paradigms of personality*. New York: Freeman.

Loevinger, J., & Wessler, R. (1970). *Measuring ego development* (Vols. 1-2). San Francisco: Jossey-Bass.

McClelland, D. (1980). Motive dispositions: The merits of operant and respondent measures. *Review of Personality and Social Psychology, 1*, 10-41.

Mead, G. A. (1934). *Mind, self, and society*. Chicago: University of Chicago Press.

Meichenbaum, D. (1991). Evolution of cognitive-behavior therapy. In J. Zeig (Ed.), *The evolution of psychology* (Vol. 2). New York: Brunner/Mazel.

Miller, G. (1969). Psychology as a means of promoting human welfare. *American Psychologist, 24*, 1063-1075.

Morrow, D. (1993). *Lesbian identity development through group process: An exploration of coming out issues*. Unpublished doctoral dissertation, North Carolina State University.

Noam, G. G. (1988). Self-complexity and self-integration: Theory and therapy in clinical developmental psychology. *Journal of Moral Education, 17*, 230-245.

Paisley, P. O., & Hubbard, G. T. (1994). *Developmental school counseling programs: From theory to practice*. Alexandria, VA: ACA Publications.

Paisley, P. O., & Peace, S. D. (Eds.). (1995). [Special edition]. Developmental issues. *Elementary School Guidance and Counseling, 30*, 81-159.

Peace, S. D. (1995). Addressing school counselor induction issues: A developmental counselor mentor model. *Elementary School Guidance and Counseling, 29*, 20-31.

Peace, S. D., & Sprinthall, N. A. (1998). Training school counselors to supervise beginning counselors: Theory, research, and practice. *Professional School Counseling, 1*, 2-8.

Piaget, J. (1964). *Judgment and reasoning in the child*. New York: Viking.

Piaget, J. (1972). Intellectual evolution from adolescence to adulthood. *Human Development, 15*, 1-12.

Powell, R. E., Locke, D. C., & Sprinthall, N. A. (1991). Female offenders and their guards: A program to promote moral and ego development of both groups. *Journal of Moral Education, 20*, 191-203.

Psychology told to put "house in order" before seeking prescription rights. (1998, July-August). *National Psychologist*, p. 1.

Rest, J. (1986). *Moral development: Advances in research and theory*. New York: Praeger.

Rest, J., & Narvaez, D. (1994). *Moral development in the professions: Psychology and applied ethics*. Hillsdale, NJ: Lawrence Erlbaum.

Smith, M., & Glass, G. (1977). Meta-analysis of psychotherapy outcome studies. *American Psychologist, 32*, 752-760.

Snarey, J. (1985). Cross-cultural universality of social-moral development: A critical review of Kohlbergian research. *Psychological Bulletin, 97*, 202-232.

Sprinthall, N. A. (1990). Counseling psychology from Greyston to Atlanta: On the road to Armageddon? *The Counseling Psychologist, 18*, 455-463.

Sprinthall, N. A. (1993). [Unpublished raw data]. Lab report, North Carolina State University.

Sprinthall, N. A. (1994). Counseling and social role-taking: Promoting moral and ego development. In J. Rest & D. Narvaez (Eds.), *Moral development in the professions* (pp. 85-100). Hillsdale, NJ: Lawrence Erlbaum.

Sprinthall, N. A., Reiman, A. J., & Thies-Sprinthall, L. (1993). Role-taking and reflection: Promoting the conceptual and moral development of teachers. *Learning and Individual Differences, 5*, 283-300.

Sprinthall, R., Sprinthall, N. A., & Oja, S. (1998). *Educational psychology: A developmental approach*. New York: McGraw-Hill.

Stewart, D., Sprinthall, N. A., & Siemienska, R. (1997). Ethical reasoning in a time of revolution: A study of local officials in Poland. *Public Administration Review, 57*, 445-453.

Super, D. (1955). Personality integration through vocational counseling. *Journal of Counseling Psychology, 2*, 217-226.

Swensen, C. H. (1980). Ego development and a general model for counseling and psychotherapy. *Personnel and Guidance Journal, 58*, 382-387.

van Kaam, A. (1965). Counseling from the viewpoint of existential psychology. In R. Mosher, R. Carle, & C. Kehas (Eds.), *Guidance: An examination* (pp. 66-81). New York: Harcourt Brace & World.

Vernon, A. (1999). *Counseling children and adolescents*. Denver, CO: Love.

Vygotsky, L. (1962). *Thought and language*. Cambridge: MIT Press.

Young-Eisendrath, P. (1988). Making use of human development theories in counseling. In R. Hayes & R. Aubrey (Eds.), *New directions for counseling and human development* (pp. 66-84). Denver, CO: Love.

CHAPTER EIGHT

Cognitive-Behavioral Counseling

JANICE MINER HOLDEN

> The key to personal freedom lies in understanding the factors that influence our behaviors and accepting responsibility for controlling [those factors].
>
> —*Spiegler and Guevremont (1998, p. 40)*

> We are what we think.
> All that we are arises with our thoughts.
> With our thoughts we make the world.
>
> —*The Buddha (Byrom, 1976, p. 1)*

Counseling addresses not only remediation of psychological problems but also prevention of such problems, augmentation of coping strategies for normal developmental challenges, and enhancement of the quality of life. Although nothing has prevented mental health professionals from applying cognitive-behavioral strategies to the latter three foci of counseling, they have developed and continue to apply these strategies primarily to remediation. Nevertheless, in the Western philosophical, social, and economic climate of the turn of the 21st century, including the valuing of empirical evidence that supports the efficiency and effectiveness of psychotherapeutic approaches, every counselor is prudent to be knowledgeable about, if not competent in the use of, cognitive-behavioral counseling strategies.

Regarding efficiency, the cognitive-behavioral approach is inherently a form of brief therapy. From its inception, its practitioners have focused on specific problems and have pursued solutions through the use of specific interventions. Thus, this approach is useful not only in community agency and private practice settings but also in settings where client-counselor contact may be time limited such as in K-12 schools and in colleges and universities. Even religiously oriented counselors have adapted cognitive-behavioral principles for use in religiously and spiritually based counseling (Holden, 1993; Holden, Watts, & Brookshire, 1991; Propst, 1980, 1988, 1996; Propst, Ostrom, Watkins, Dean, & Mashburn, 1992; Richards & Bergin, 1997, p. 240).

Regarding effectiveness, the clearest support for cognitive-behavioral strategies comes from a recent major research endeavor. In 1993, the Clinical Psychology division of the American Psychological Association created a task force to identify psychotherapeutic approaches validated by research to be effective or probably effective. Members of the task force established criteria including a minimum number of studies with acceptable research designs that had involved the use of standardized treatment manuals and had yielded statistically significant results. Then, they surveyed the vast psychotherapy research literature.

In a list of examples of treatments identified by the task force, approximately 75% of empirically validated treatments and 65% of probably effective treatments were cognitive, behavioral, or cognitive-behavioral. These included cognitive therapy for depression; behavioral interventions for enuresis (bed-wetting), headache, obsessive-compulsive disorder, female orgasmic dysfunction, male erectile dysfunction, marital distress, and developmental disabilities; and cognitive-behavioral therapy for panic disorder with or without agoraphobia, generalized anxiety disorder, social phobia, irritable bowel syndrome, chronic pain, and bulimia (Crits-Christoph, 1998).

Considering the plethora of psychotherapeutic modalities that mental health practitioners currently are using, and even narrowing the focus to the approximately 10 modalities that most practitioners use (Jensen, Bergin, & Greaves, 1990) and that are covered in most counseling theories texts (e.g., Corey, 1996; Sharf, 2000), cognitive-behavioral approaches are disproportionately represented in the task force's findings. This overrepresentation probably is not the result of bias (Crits-Christoph, 1998). However, the criterion that a study must have involved the use of a treatment manual clearly favored more systematic approaches, such as cognitive and behavioral approaches, and might have unilaterally eliminated some approaches from even being considered.

Indeed, authors of more broad-based literature reviews have identified several generic aspects of psychotherapy that predict positive client outcomes. These aspects include client variables (e.g., severity and chronicity of problems) and counselor variables (e.g., level of empathy). In this regard, Lambert and Cattani-Thompson (1996) concluded, "A body of evidence for the particular effectiveness of specific techniques as applied to particular problems does exist. However, there is more evidence for the conclusion that there is little difference between schools of counseling in their ability to produce effect" (p. 604).

True as this may be, cognitive-behavioral principles and strategies can play an enhancing, if not a crucial, role in a counselor's therapeutic repertoire. Not only is it brief and has it been shown to be effective, but it is the treatment of choice of managed care providers, and its techniques can be incorporated into other theoretical perspectives such as in the reorientation phase of Adlerian counseling and in addressing the thinking aspect of total behavior in reality therapy.

In this chapter, the history, principles, and techniques of the cognitive and behavioral approaches to counseling are reviewed; the extent to which cognitive and behavioral approaches have become inextricably integrated is described; and some of the most current resources to which the reader may turn for further information are provided. Behavioral counseling is presented first because historically it developed prior to cognitive counseling.

Behavioral Counseling

Historically, the roots of behaviorism date back to the 1st century A.D. (Spiegler & Guevremont, 1998). Current behaviorism emerged during the 1860s and reached its first peak of popularity during the 1920s (Mills, 1998). *Behavior therapy,* the application of the principles of behaviorism to counseling and psychotherapy, saw its heyday during the 1950s and 1960s, after which cognitive approaches became increasingly prominent. Among the people most often credited with pioneering contributions to behaviorism and behavior therapy are Ivan Pavlov, John B. Watson, Mary Cover Jones, Hobart and Willie Mowrer, Edward Thorndike, B. F. Skinner, Joseph Wolpe, Arnold Lazarus, and Albert Bandura.

What distinguishes behavioral counseling from other approaches is its foundation in behavioral learning theory. Learning is defined in behaviorism as a relatively permanent observable change in behavior that results from experience or practice. Behaviorists believe that learning occurs by one of two processes: classi-

cal or operant conditioning. These two types of conditioning are reviewed next, followed by a discussion of principles that apply to both processes and implications for counseling.

Classical Conditioning

Classical conditioning is the process whereby involuntary behavior (i.e., behavior that one cannot instantly produce by an act of will) is learned. Pavlov is credited with discovering this process while studying digestion in dogs. The following explanation of classical conditioning employs a human example more relevant to counseling.

The classical conditioning process involves four components. The first two components comprise the foundation of the process: the *unconditioned* (unlearned) *stimulus* and the *unconditioned response*. These are unlearned in the sense that the response is *innate* in the presence of the stimulus. For example, a newborn infant will startle in response to a sudden loud noise. Any teacher can demonstrate how this innate response remains operational in adulthood; in the midst of a droning lecture, she might suddenly and very loudly scream, "Hey!" (unconditioned stimulus). Students will jump and exhibit other signs of sympathetic nervous system arousal such as increased heart rate, respiration, and perspiration (unconditioned responses).

The remaining two components of classical conditioning are the *conditioned stimulus* and *conditioned response*. A conditioned stimulus does not innately elicit a particular conditioned response; it must be conditioned (learned) by being paired with an unconditioned stimulus. For example, the sound of an airplane overhead does not innately elicit fear. But if one hears an airplane overhead (conditioned stimulus) and very soon after hears a loud explosion nearby (unconditioned stimulus), then the next time one hears an airplane, even though no loud explosion follows, one will very likely involuntarily respond with some degree of sympathetic nervous system arousal—fear (conditioned response). The fear in the latter case is considered "conditioned" because the person acquired the response through experience. To review, in response to a loud noise (unconditioned stimulus), fear is an unconditioned response; in response to the sound of an airplane (conditioned stimulus), fear is a conditioned response. The reader may recognize a possible etiology of an aspect of posttraumatic stress disorder following combat.

The relevance of classical conditioning to the theory and practice of counseling lies in its application to client problems of not only fear and anxiety but also depression and anger. The autonomic (involuntary) branch of the peripheral nervous system consists of two branches that generally operate inversely to each other. The *sympathetic* branch is activated when one is under stress, and the *parasympathetic* branch is activated when one is at peace. From a behavioral perspective, problematic anxiety and anger involve an inappropriate overactivation of the sympathetic branch, and depression involves an inappropriate overactivation of the parasympathetic branch, of the autonomic nervous system.

Operant Conditioning

Operant conditioning is the process whereby one learns voluntary behavior. The main principle of operant conditioning is that voluntary behavior that is followed by reinforcement is likely to be repeated, whereas that which is not followed by reinforcement or is followed by punishment is not likely to be repeated. This basic principle can be summarized in the following table:

	To increase *the frequency/strength of a voluntary response*	To decrease *the frequency/strength of a voluntary response*
Using a *pleasant* consequence	Positive reinforcement	Extinction
Using an *unpleasant* consequence	Negative reinforcement	Punishment

The principle of *positive reinforcement* is that people will tend to repeat voluntary behaviors that have been followed by something pleasurable. For example, even people who are not hungry have been known to eat chocolate because it tastes good and perhaps has chemicals, or provokes the release of endogenous chemicals, that feel good. Humans also repeat voluntary behaviors that previously terminated or helped to avoid unpleasant consequences; this is the principle of *negative reinforcement.* For example, most people pay their taxes, not because anything pleasant happens when they do, but rather because paying taxes keeps aversive consequences from happening (e.g., audit, fine, jail sentence). *Prompts,* or cues from the environment, indicate the conditions whereby an operant response is likely to be reinforced such as the driver who sees a red traffic light (prompt) and then steps on the brake (voluntary response), thus avoiding a collision (negative reinforcement).

According to the principle of *extinction,* humans tend to decrease or stop voluntary behaviors that no longer are followed by something pleasurable. An example would be someone who stops attending counseling sessions after achieving the counseling goal; attendance no longer is reinforced with progress toward the goal. People also stop some voluntary behaviors because those behaviors have been followed by something aversive, that is, have been *punished.* An example would be someone who stops attending counseling because he or she has felt repeatedly judged, criticized, and blamed by the counselor.

In classical conditioning, the initial response is innate, whereas in operant conditioning, it is not. How, then, does someone come to make an operant response for the *very first time,* before the response has even had a chance to be reinforced? Imagine that someone has a newfangled camera and does not know how to open it to load the film. The person might accidentally bump the opening mechanism (*random/accidental response*), might try one thing or another until it opens (*trial and error*), or might follow directions or use the strategy that he or she observed someone else using (*imitation of a model*). All voluntary behaviors can be understood as occurring for the very first time through one of these three processes. In addition, many behaviors performed for the first time in novel situations are the product of transfer of learning from previous situations, a phenomenon that behaviorists term *generalization.* And a new complex behavior can be learned through breaking it down into component parts and reinforcing each part in succession, a process that behaviorists call *shaping.*

Principles of Conditioning

A few principles complete the broad picture of the behavioral view of how humans acquire their response repertoires. These principles apply to both classical and operant conditioning.

In *generalization,* someone will respond similarly to the classically conditioned stimulus or the operantly conditioned prompt similar to the one in the original conditioning. For example, the person classically conditioned to feel fear at the sound of an airplane probably will feel fear at the sound of a helicopter. Similarly, in operant conditioning, the child who has been reinforced by parents for behaving politely probably will behave politely in the presence of other adults.

For the remaining two principles, it is necessary to understand that in classical conditioning, the repeated pairing of a conditioned stimulus with an unconditioned stimulus also is called reinforcement. In *extinction,* in the absence of reinforcement, the person will stop emitting the conditioned response when presented repeatedly with the conditioned stimulus. Theoretically, a person will stop feeling fear at the sound of an airplane if exposed repeatedly to the sound of airplanes without that sound ever again being followed by a loud explosion. Extinction in operant conditioning was addressed earlier.

In *discrimination,* someone can learn to respond differently to two similar stimuli if the response to one stimulus is consistently reinforced and the response to the other is not. According to this principle, the person who feels fear at the sound of both an airplane and a helicopter will discontinue the latter if loud explosions continue to accompany the sound of the airplane but not the sound of the helicopter. And if politeness is reinforced at the child's own home but not at friends' homes, then the child is likely to discriminate between his or her own home and friends' homes, showing more politeness at the former and less at the latter.

Other principles related specifically to operant conditioning are too numerous to address in this brief chapter. These include *schedules of reinforcement; delay of reinforcement; spontaneous recovery;* and the concepts of *primary, secondary,* and *vicarious reinforcement.* One important principle is that in both classical and operant conditioning, a response is best learned initially through continuous reinforcement and, once learned, is best maintained through intermittent reinforcement that occurs at random intervals. These and other principles are important to the practice of behavior therapy.

Beyond the Basics of Classical and Operant Conditioning

Although classical and operant conditioning have been presented as distinct processes related to involuntary and voluntary behavior, respectively, in real life their relationship is more complex. First, *biofeedback* has bridged the two processes. In biofeedback, one can learn to voluntarily influence seemingly involuntary phenomena such as one's blood pressure, skin temperature, and heart rate. The biofeedback client is monitored for the phenomenon (e.g., with a thermometer that measures skin temperature), receives feedback for even subtle changes (e.g., a high-pitched tone when the temperature goes down and a low-pitched tone when it goes up), and uses the feedback to learn how to increasingly produce the low tone, that is, to warm one's skin. Through voluntary efforts, one can come quite reliably to produce changes in seemingly involuntary processes. Nevertheless, the term for the process involved in biofeedback, *passive volition,* implies that it is different from the "active volition" that characterizes straightforward voluntary behavior such as raising one's hand.

A second point about the real-life relationship between classical and operant conditioning is that the two processes are inextricably related. For example, phobias include aspects of both processes: classically conditioned fear about a particular environmental situation and voluntary (operant) avoidance of the situation that is negatively reinforced by escape from the fear. Because both processes are involved in day-to-day behavior, both typically are addressed in the counseling process.

Early behavioral theory included the contention that all behavior could be understood, predicted, and controlled by exclusive attention to observable overt phenomena—the environmental conditions and the person's behavior—as they related to classical and operant conditioning. Certain anomalies challenged this contention, as in the case of phobias. Behaviorists originally hypothesized that a phobia was the result of a direct experience of the traumatic pairing of an aversive unconditioned stimulus (e.g., a sudden, extremely loud noise of exploding bombs) with a previously neutral conditioned stimulus (e.g., the sound of an airplane). However, some phobias appear to have been acquired vicariously through awareness of another's traumatic experience rather than through one's own direct experience. How could one be conditioned by what one has not directly experienced? In addition, the principle of extinction would predict that most phobias eventually would extinguish; after the first traumatic experience, with repeated exposure to the conditioned stimulus (airplane noise) without the unconditioned stimulus (sudden loud noise of exploding bombs), the fear response would die out. However, clinical evidence is replete with examples of people whose phobias seem undiminished over several decades in which the original traumas never were repeated. Why did these people's fears not extinguish?

Later research affirmed the crucial role of unobservable covert phenomena—cognitions—in the conditioning process. Behaviorists have referred to this addendum to traditional behavioral learning theory as *social-cognitive theory* (Bandura, 1986). As behaviorist G. T. Wilson summarized it,

> Social-cognitive theory recognizes both the importance of awareness in learning and the person's active cognitive appraisal of environmental events. Learning is facilitated when people are aware of the rules and contingencies governing the consequences of their actions. Reinforcement does not involve an automatic strengthening of behavior. Learning is a consequence of the informative and incentive functions of rewards. . . . By symbolic representation of anticipated future outcomes of behavior, one generates the motivation to initiate and sustain current actions (Bandura, 1977). Often, people's expectations and hypotheses about what is happening to them may affect their behavior more than [does the] objective reality. (Wilson, 1995, pp. 206-207)

Regarding the preceding sentence, the originators of the various cognitive therapies could not have said it better themselves. Before addressing behavioral counseling interventions, the principles of cognitive therapy are discussed next.

Cognitive Therapy

Generic cognitive therapies share two fundamental assumptions. First, how we think about events largely determines how we feel and act in response to those events. Second, distressing feelings and actions often are the result of thinking that contains errors in logic.

The ancient Western roots of the generic cognitive therapies date back at least to the Stoic philosophers of the 1st century A.D. During the early 20th century, Alfred Adler, in his *individual psychology,* identified mistaken beliefs, or conclusions erroneously drawn in childhood and carried unchanged into later life, as the basic source of life problems (Mosak, 1995). During the middle of the century, George Kelly (1955) elaborated on the concept of *personal constructs* or cognitive formulations idiosyncratic to each person whereby the person interprets experience (Kelly, 1955). During the early 1960s, Albert Ellis developed rational emotive therapy—now called *rational emotive behavior therapy* (REBT)—in which he attributed life problems to irrational beliefs (Ellis, 1995). At about the same time, Aaron Beck developed *cognitive therapy,* in which the source of psychopathology was considered largely to be distorted cognitions (Beck & Weishaar, 1995). Beginning during the 1970s, Donald Meichenbaum developed *self-instruction* and *stress inoculation* strategies to help people overcome deficits of adaptive cognitions (Meichenbaum, 1974, 1985).

Whereas the forgoing approaches together constitute the generic cognitive therapies, Beck's (1976, 1996) specific approach, termed *cognitive therapy,* is the focus of the next section of this chapter. One reason is its collaborative approach, rather than REBT's confrontational approach, to clients; a collaborative approach is likely to be more effective for all clients in general and for clients with certain concerns in particular such as those with addictions, panic disorder, and obsessive-compulsive disorder (Spiegler & Guevremont, 1998, p. 320). Furthermore, cognitive therapy is more in line with behavior therapy than is REBT (Wilson, 1995). In addition, although among the generic cognitive therapies both Beck's cognitive therapy and Meichenbaum's stress inoculation training have had the strongest empirical research support (Spiegler & Guevremont, 1998), Beck's cognitive therapy has a wider application than does stress inoculation training, and it is founded in a more elaborated theory of personality.

In Beck's original theoretical formulation (Beck & Weishaar, 1995), he asserted that the basic human motive is to survive. To that end, each person continually scans one's external and internal environment and processes the acquired information in an attempt to minimize the threat to, and maximize the likelihood of, one's survival.

Within a few years of life, each person develops *schemata* or cognitive structures consisting of the individual's most fundamental convictions about self, others, the world, and the future (Beck & Weishaar, 1995). Any cognitive schema can be characterized as falling somewhere on a continuum; at one end are schemata characterized by an absence of bias in information processing, and at the other end are schemata characterized by severe bias in information processing. The degree of bias in a given schema is largely the result of several factors impinging on the person—innate, developmental learning history, current biological, and current environmental factors. The more biased a person's schemata, the more likely the person will feel and act in distressed or distressing ways.

Beck identified six primary forms of information processing bias (Beck & Weishaar, 1995). Each is described here in alphabetical order with an example. In *arbitrary inference,* one draws a firm conclusion in the face of insufficient or even contradictory evidence such as the worker who receives consistently good pay raises but who, after one particularly difficult day, concludes, "I'm going to be fired." In *dichotomous thinking,* one thinks in absolute black-or-white categories with no shades of gray such as the student who believes, "If I don't get an A, I've failed." In *magnification* and *minimization,* one interprets that something is far more or less important, respectively, than the evidence indicates such as the person with a clean bill of health who feels a brief slight pain in the chest and concludes, "I'm having a heart attack," or the person with a history of heart problems who feels prolonged severe pain in the chest accompanied by other symptoms of a heart attack who concludes, "I'm just having indigestion." In *overgeneralization,* one draws a broad general conclusion on the basis of one or a few isolated experiences such as the divorcee who concludes, "I'll never have a happy stable relationship." In *personalization,* one attributes causality for an event exclusively to oneself without evidence for such a conclusion such as the child who believes, "My parents are divorcing because of me." In *selective abstraction,* one focuses on a detail to the exclusion of the "whole picture" such as the employer who, when one of her best employees arrives 10 minutes late one day due to a major unanticipated traffic jam, concludes, "He's beginning to take advantage of me."

Other cognitive theorists (e.g., Burns, 1980; Freeman, Pretzer, Fleming, & Simon, 1990) have elaborated additional types of bias. In *disqualifying the positive,* positive experiences are discounted as somehow less valid than negative experiences. In *mind reading,* one applies arbitrary inference specifically to other people's perceptions of oneself. In *emotional reasoning,* one concludes that feeling a certain way means that the situation actually is that way. In *should statements,* one assumes that events, both inside and outside oneself, are supposed to conform to certain preconceived notions.

Beck further elaborated that specific types of psychological distress are characterized by specific patterns of bias in information processing (Beck & Weishaar, 1995). People who suffer from depression exemplify the cognitive triad, believing that they are inadequate, abandoned, and worthless; that the world is overwhelming and provides no satisfaction; and that the future will not be any better than the present. Suicidality is best predicted in most cases by hopelessness about the future (Weishaar, 1996). Anorexia nervosa, anxiety, mania, obsessive-compulsive disorder, panic disorder, paranoia, and phobias each involves patterns of information processing bias unique to the specific disorder. Beck and colleagues (Beck, Freeman, & Associates, 1990) and others (J. Beck, 1996; McGinn & Young, 1996; Young, 1999) have expanded on Beck's original theory to include personality disorders in which extremely rigid, polarized, pervasive schemata account for the diffused chronic nature of these disorders and call for special therapeutic interventions.

Cognitions exist at three levels, from the most general and inaccessible to awareness to the most situation specific and accessible to awareness. Schemata, one's most basic convictions, spawn *underlying assumptions,* or if-then propositions, that under certain environmental conditions yield *automatic thoughts.* Automatic thoughts are so named because, as clients soon discover in cognitive therapy, such thoughts occur almost instantaneously and, under typical circumstances, without one's awareness (or intention). An example is the cli-

ent who, when his last parent dies, becomes highly anxious. His automatic thoughts include, "I can't make it in the world without my parents; I'll die without their support." His underlying assumption is, "If I don't have support, then I'll die." His schema is, "I cannot manage on my own."

Recently, A. Beck (1996) modified and elaborated on some of his original cognitive therapy concepts. According to his current formulation, each person is born with *protoschemata* or a collection of deep structures with which one interacts with the environment to produce one's idiosyncratic schemata. One protoschema is the *orienting schema,* with which one continuously scans the internal and external environment for threats to one's ongoing achievement of the goals of bonding and survival. Emotions serve as prompts and consequences of one's actions. Pleasurable or painful emotions inform one that current conditions are supportive of or threatening to one's goals, respectively. A person develops a variety of suborganizations of personality, or *modes,* which are goal-directed complexes consisting of cognitive, affective, motivational, behavioral, and physiological schemata.

When no threat to goal achievement is perceived through the orienting schema, *minor modes* dominate, for example, one's television-watching mode or socializing-with-friends mode. When environmental conditions approach a "match" to one's cognitive construct of a threat, a *major* or *"primal"* mode is activated, beginning with cognitive schemata that appraise the threat and followed by the simultaneous activation of affective, motivational, behavioral, and physiological schemata. Beck hypothesized four basic primal modes characterized by specific phobia, general fear, hostility, and depression.

In addition to the modes, the personality contains a *conscious control system* that is capable of thinking about and acting on the modes. Normal and excessive major modes differ not in quality but rather in quantity. Compared to the less intense major mode, the more intense major mode is more easily activated, involves cognitive schemata with more biased information processing, and interferes more extensively with access to the conscious control system.

Once a mode is activated, it can set in motion a self-perpetuating cycle by increasing the likelihood of events that eventually confirm it. Consider, for example, John, for whom one schema is, "People find me boring and avoid me." The situation of conversing with someone at a party activates John's orienting schema to a threat of rejection. When John sees the other person look away momentarily, he has the automatic thought, "She's bored. She's about to leave." John's anxious (or depressed) mode is activated. In either case, he finds it increasingly difficult to concentrate on the conversation. Eventually, the other person does become bored and leaves, reinforcing John's schema. The important point is that John, by interpreting a common behavior in conversation—looking away momentarily—as a case in point of his schematic belief, inadvertently contributes to the very outcome that affirms his schema. In the alternative, he might avoid personalization and mind reading by attributing the other person's momentary lapse in attention to her seeing something temporarily distracting. Or, he might avoid arbitrary inference by concluding that even if she is bored momentarily, this is a common experience in conversation, and by predicting that despite her possible momentary boredom, she might have found most of the conversation interesting and probably would stay in the expectation that the conversation again would become interesting to her. The self-perpetuating nature of one's cognitive constructs goes a long way toward explaining how modes, once developed, are maintained.

A mode may be deactivated by targeting noncognitive schemata, as in the case of pharmacotherapy that targets the physiological schema. However, Beck and Weishaar (1995) asserted, and research tends to support, that lasting change occurs specifically as a result of targeting the cognitive schema involved in a particular mode.

A. Beck's (1996) recent theoretical modifications do not include substantial changes to the psychotherapeutic techniques he has described, although he alluded to a somewhat modified conceptualization of the mechanisms of change. However, his reference to the mode as a "suborganization of personality" and as a "complex," along with his differentiation between the modes and the conscious control system, seems to bring cognitive therapy more into alignment with theories that formerly seemed entirely unrelated. These include Assagioli's (1965) psychosynthesis, in which "subpersonalities" are a major construct, and Jung's (Douglas, 1995) and Grof's (1985) conceptualizations of the "complex" and "COEX: system of condensed experience," respectively. Assagioli's and Jung's theories, Freud's psychoanalysis (Arlow, 1995), and Berne's transactional analysis (Dusay & Dusay, 1989) include the hypothesized structure of the self, ego, and adult, respectively, that are similar to Beck's conscious control system. These developments in Beck's theory suggest interesting possibilities for the convergence of psychotherapeutic theories into one integrated theory.

Relationship Between Behavioral and Cognitive Theory and Therapy

According to Wilson (1995), contemporary behavior therapists can be understood to comprise three main camps: those who eschew the consideration of cognitive mediating processes, those who consider them, and those who rely heavily on them. Several other indications suggest that the behavioral and cognitive approaches not only are compatible but are merging. One indication is that three respected recent sources on behavior therapy (Kanfer & Goldstein, 1991; Spiegler & Guevremont, 1998; Wilson, 1995) included substantial sections on cognitive interventions. A second indication is that cognitive explanations for the effectiveness of many behavioral interventions have received empirical support, in some cases more support than behavioral explanations (Spiegler & Guevremont, 1998; Wilson, 1995).

A third indication is the similarity between a common core of seven basic concepts that all behavior therapists share (Wilson, 1995) and the basic concepts of cognitive therapists. First, therapists from both camps believe that both normal and abnormal functioning are developed and maintained by the same fundamental processes; dysfunctionality is not qualitatively but rather quantitatively different from functionality. On a related point, although both types of therapists accept the necessity of diagnosis, neither conceptualizes abnormality as illness; rather, both conceptualize abnormality as "problems in living." Third, both types of therapists address the present conditions that maintain dysfunctionality rather than historical antecedents. Even as memories are addressed in psychotherapy, they are understood as current cognitions that contribute to the maintenance of current behavior. On a related point, therapists from both camps believe that understanding the origin of dysfunction is not necessary for changing the dysfunction. Fifth, both types of therapists make extensive use of assessment to identify specific components to target in therapy. Sixth, both types of therapists tailor their interventions to the idiosyncratic needs of each individual client. Seventh, both types of therapists are committed to the scientific approach including empirical evidence for the efficacy of the approach.

In addition to Wilson's (1995) points, a few other points of similarity between behavior therapists and cognitive therapists deserve mention. Both believe the research results indicating heredity and biology as predisposing factors in personality; at the same time, both believe that within the broad limits set by heredity and biology, experience plays a profound role in personality development (A. Beck, 1996; Spiegler & Guevremont, 1998). Therapists from both theoretical camps acknowledge that therapeutic effectiveness is enhanced by seeing people not as the passive products of hereditary and environmental influences but rather as active agents who "attend to environmental stimuli, interpret them, encode them, and selectively remember them" (Wilson, 1995, p. 207). Seeing clients as active agents, both types of therapists rely on clients to be active in the therapeutic process. Based on research indicating the necessity of warmth, sincerity, and empathy in the therapeutic relationship, both types of therapists make explicit efforts to establish and maintain these qualities in their relationships with clients (Burns & Auerbach, 1996; Wilson, 1995, pp. 208-209). Both emphasize what Wilson (1995) called "corrective learning experiences" (p. 208) both in and out of the counseling session, both seek to balance directiveness with collaboration to facilitate such experiences for clients, and both encourage clients to practice new learning in their real lives between counseling sessions.

Cognitive-Behavioral Interventions

As stated previously, prior to implementing change interventions, the cognitive-behavioral counselor pursues the establishment of a facilitative relationship with the client and seeks to maintain it throughout counseling. Also during the first few sessions, the counselor conducts an assessment typically involving both an interview and the administration of assessment instruments. The counselor less frequently uses standardized instruments and more frequently uses paper-and-pencil questionnaires such as those that assess levels of depression, anxiety, or marital satisfaction. Out of the assessment, the counselor collaborates with the client in specifying the goals of counseling as well as the methods used to achieve, and the measurement of progress toward, those goals.

All cognitive-behavioral change strategies can be understood to involve aspects of classical conditioning, operant conditioning, and cognitive processes. However, most strategies emphasize one of these three aspects. The strategies described next are arbitrarily divided into categories based on the aspect emphasized in each strategy.

Change Strategies Based Primarily on Classical Conditioning

Exposure and response prevention comprise a category of interventions used for client problems involving anxiety. Prior to counseling, the client has experienced strong anxiety, presumably a classically conditioned response. To reduce the anxiety, the client has employed some operant strategy, such as avoidance in the case of phobia or repetitious behavior in the case of obsessive-compulsive disorder, and the strategy itself has become a problem. To stop the problematic strategy, the anxiety to which it is a response must be reduced. That reduction is accomplished by the client repeatedly or prolongedly exposing himself or herself to the anxiety-producing situation while preventing himself or herself from making the anxiety-reducing response.

One procedure of this type is *systematic desensitization*. The counselor and client first collaborate to develop a stimulus hierarchy or a list of anxiety-eliciting stimuli from least to most frightening. The list then is temporarily put aside while the client learns relaxation, most typically progressive relaxation, in which muscle groups of the body are progressively tensed and relaxed, starting at the head and ending at the toes. When the client can quickly achieve a state of relaxation, the least frightening stimulus from the list is encountered, either in imagery or in vivo, that is, in real life. The client reports his or her level of anxiety using a SUDs (subjective units of distress) scale from 1 (low) to 10 (high). If the client reports a SUDs of more than 1 or 2, then the client temporarily focuses on relaxation; when a SUDs of 1 or 2 is reached, the client refocuses on the anxiety-producing stimulus. After repeating this process, usually several times, the client can remain relaxed while focusing on the stimulus. Then, the next most frightening item from the list is encountered. This process is repeated until the client can focus on the previously most frightening stimulus and remain relaxed, reporting a SUDs of 1 or 2. In terms of classical conditioning, the conditioned stimulus now elicits the conditioned response of relaxation rather than anxiety.

Another procedure involving exposure and response prevention is *flooding*. Rather than gradually encountering increasingly frightening stimuli, the client agrees to attend a long counseling session in which the most frightening stimulus will be encountered continuously in imagery until anxiety dissipates. Of the two exposure and response prevention procedures, systematic desensitization tends to be favored (Spiegler & Guevremont, 1998).

Another intervention involving classical conditioning principles is for the *treatment of enuresis*. It appears that bedwetters would avoid wetting the bed if they woke up when they needed to urinate, but most fail to awaken to the rather subtle stimulus of a full bladder. To remedy this, the client sleeps on a special mattress pad that, when contacted with moisture, sets off an alarm. When the client's bladder is full and bed-wetting begins, the alarm sounds (unconditioned stimulus) and the client awakens (unconditioned response). After a few repetitions, at the sensation of a full bladder (conditioned stimulus), the client awakens (conditioned response). On awakening, the client is able to enact the operant response of going to the bathroom that already had been learned prior to the intervention.

Aversion therapy is used to help people develop negative associations to stimuli for which they have had positive associations but that have led to negative consequences. Examples include various addictions (e.g., alcohol, cigarettes, food, illicit substances) and sexual attraction to illegal or inappropriate things or people. Aversion therapy involves the use of an aversive response such as discomfort from a painful but not harmful electric shock or nausea induced by graphic description of something disgusting or by injection of the drug apomorphine. The client experiences the aversive response (unconditioned response) while attending to the conditioned stimulus, for example, seeing, smelling, and smoking a cigarette or imagining the sexual object. After repeated trials, the conditioned stimulus elicits a conditioned response of discomfort, and the client then operantly avoids the stimulus so as to avoid the discomfort. For a number of reasons, aversion therapy typically is used only as a last resort when potential negative consequences of the original condition are catastrophic and when other less distressing change interventions are not viable or have failed. A great deal of controversy surrounds the use of aversion therapy in certain cases such as persons seeking to change their homosexual orientation (Donaldson, 1998).

Change Strategies Based Primarily on Operant Conditioning

Behavioral interventions are too numerous to treat thoroughly in a brief chapter. The following strategies are among the best known. Strategies to help a client increase desirable, adaptive voluntary behavior are described first, followed by those designed to decrease unwanted behavior.

Modeling involves one person demonstrating some voluntary behavior and another person imitating the model. In counseling, clients seeking to develop certain operant responses imitate models who demonstrate the response. Models can include other people from the client's life, the counselor, or even a videotape of the client rehearsing the behavior himself or herself. Among the uses of modeling is to help people develop social skills and assertiveness (Jakubowski & Lange, 1978; Lange & Jakubowski, 1976). A related use is when a client avoids an adaptive behavior in anticipation that it will be followed by a negative consequence. The likelihood of performing a behavior can increase by observing a model who performs the behavior without negative consequences.

In *behavioral rehearsal/role-play,* a client practices a new voluntary behavior in the counseling setting before enacting it outside of counseling. The counselor often provides prompting—suggestions and directions—and positive reinforcement. If the behavior is complex or is too difficult for the client to perform all at once, then the counselor and client can use shaping to help the client develop the behavior.

A category of interventions in cognitive therapy termed *guided discovery* is based on behavioral principles. The principle of shaping is applied in *graded task assignment,* in which tasks are graded not in the sense of being evaluated but rather in the sense of progressing sequentially, from simpler to more complex or from easier to more difficult to enact. Two additional strategies can be helpful when a client feels low motivation to engage in adaptive behavior, as can be the case in clients with depression or anxiety. In *activity scheduling,* the counselor and client chart the client's daily activities for the near future. This structure helps a depressed client to counteract a tendency toward underengagement in activity or helps an anxious client to counteract a tendency toward avoidance of activity. If only the client will engage in the activities, the client likely will experience reinforcement. *Mastery and pleasure rating* are used

prior to and after the client engages in adaptive behavior. A pattern of consistently underrating how competently one performs or how much pleasure one derives from the activity helps clients to learn not to allow negative anticipation to dissuade them from engaging in adaptive behavior.

To decrease or eliminate unwanted voluntary behavior, some strategies are considered better than others. One strategy is *reinforcement of a competing response.* For example, a student is likely to stop wandering around the classroom during a lesson if the student is somehow positively reinforced for staying in his or her seat. Cognitive counselors use a form of competing response reinforcement with the strategy of *diversion.* The counselor prescribes physical activity, social contact, work, play, and/or visual imagery on the assumption that the client cannot engage in inactivity and rumination while occupied in enjoyable activity.

In some cases, reinforcement of a competing response is not a viable option for reducing an unwanted behavior. In such cases, extinction is considered a better alternative than punishment because punishment can carry adverse reactions such as distressed emotions and avoidance of the punisher. For example, according to behavioral principles, a child who interrupts while others are talking and who is criticized or slapped after he or she interrupts is more likely to exhibit negative feelings, withdrawal, and failure to learn the appropriate skill of waiting one's turn in conversation. The child probably also is more likely to imitate the aggressive behavior of the punisher when the child interacts with other people. The child is more likely to learn the skill of waiting for a pause in conversation if others prompt him or her with an "I-message" ("I would rather that you wait until the other speaker is finished talking before you begin talking"), use extinction by ignoring further interruptions, and then reinforce appropriate behavior by expressing appreciation when the child waits to talk until other speakers have finished.

The process just described is not applicable to every situation in which decrease of a voluntary response is the goal. Sometimes, the only effective strategy—and therefore the most humane one—is *punishment.* For the client capable of self-administering punishment, one of the more frequently used strategies is snapping a rubber band on one's wrist. For example, a client with trichotillomania who wants to stop pulling out her hair wears a rubber band on the wrist. When the client catches herself reaching for her hair, she snaps the rubber band.

Another application of therapeutic punishment is in cases of children with developmental disabilities whose health or actual lives are threatened by self-injurious behaviors (Spiegler & Guevremont, 1998). The counselor uses a mild electric shock comparable in discomfort to having a rubber band snapped on one's wrist. Whenever the child engages in the self-injurious behavior, he or she receives the brief shock and very quickly stops the dangerous behavior.

In most cases, less aversive strategies are viable options for decreasing unwanted behavior. In *time out,* after engaging in an unwanted behavior, the client separates from any possible source of positive reinforcement for a previously specified brief period of time. In *response cost,* the client gives up something valuable each time an undesired behavior is enacted. An example of response cost is the client with anorexia who gives the counselor a set of $25 checks made out to a political cause that the client strongly opposes. Each week in which the client succeeds in maintaining or exceeding a mutually agreed-on healthy target weight, the counselor returns one check to the client; each week in which the client fails, the counselor mails one of the checks to the political organization.

No review of behavioral strategies would be complete without mention of *token economies* used in structured settings such as schools and hospitals. The staff reinforce adaptive behavior with tokens that the clients then can use to acquire goods or privileges, and they make predominant use of less aversive strategies such as time out to decrease unwanted behaviors.

Change Strategies Based Primarily on Cognitive Principles

In cognitive therapy, change interventions are aimed at helping the client to reformulate biased information processing into more adaptive information processing that results in less distressing affect and greater potential to enact more adaptive behavior. The cognitive counselor employs two broad categories of cognitive strategies. In *Socratic dialogue,* the counselor asks a series of questions to help the client objectively assess the accuracy or adaptiveness of certain cognitions. In *collaborative empiricism,* the counselor and client together reconsider the client's cognitions as testable hypotheses and then go about testing them. Even during the first session, the counselor attempts to guide the client through a process of reformulating a distorted cognition to give the client the direct experience of reduced emotional distress and, therefore, a taste of what the client can expect. During subsequent sessions, the counselor walks the client through several strategies to examine and reformulate distorted thoughts and then reap the emotional and behavioral rewards.

The process of cognitive examination and reformulation typically involves asking the client to recall a recent situation in which he or she experienced the distressing emotion or behavior that the client would like to modify. At the moment the client was first aware of the emotion or urge to act, the counselor asks the client to "freeze the frame" and then asks the client what Beck has called the "fundamental cognitive probe for identifying automatic thoughts": "What is going through your mind right now?" (Dattilio & Padesky, 1990, p. 29). The present author has modified this question as follows: "What is going through your mind right now in the way of thoughts or images?" Once the "hot" thoughts or images (i.e., those that produce the most emotional or behavioral distress) are identified, any number of strategies may be used to reformulate the hot cognitions. Burns (1989) summarized many of these in his list of "Ten Ways to Untwist Your Thinking." For example, the client can identify the distortion(s) exemplified in the cognition. If the cognition involves all-or-nothing thinking, then the client can practice thinking in shades of gray. Or, as the result of a cost-benefit analysis, the client may discover that the disadvantages of maintaining a particular distorted cognition outweigh the advantages and then may go about modifying the cognition.

One of the most commonly used strategies to help clients identify cognitions is the *thought record*. Whenever the client feels very emotionally distressed or has behaved in a self-defeating way, the client writes down the actual event to which he or she was reacting; his or her emotions, such as fear and sadness, along with a rating of the strength of the feelings; automatic thoughts; classification of the cognitive distortion evident in the thoughts; reformulation of the thoughts into a more adaptive form along with a rating of how much the client believes the reformulated thoughts; and a re-rating of the emotions that he or she originally reported. Typically, the client experiences a reduction in intensity of the distressing emotion.

To be considered adaptive, however, a cognition must meet two criteria: It must help one to feel better, and one must consider it to fit the observable evidence more accurately. A cognition that meets the first criterion but not the second is a rationalization rather than an adaptive cognition. For example, if the client did not get a job that she had wanted and for which she had interviewed, then she would be rationalizing to think, "I didn't want that stupid job anyway," a thought that might help her to feel better but does not reflect her actual and adaptive inner experience of wanting a promising job. An adaptive cognition would be, "I have a decent chance of finding a different job that I'll like as much as the job I didn't get." This thought helps her to feel better *and* accurately reflects an actual possibility as well as increasing her motivation to behave in a way that holds the potential of actualizing that possibility.

The previous example illustrates *decatastrophizing* the belief that "I'll never find a job as satisfying as that one would have been." Through this strategy, the client discovers either that a worst-case scenario is unlikely or that it can be met with a coping strategy. Other strategies include *reattribution,* in which the client discovers that he or she is not solely responsible for some occurrence; *decentering,* a form of reattribution in which the client discovers that he or she is not the center of attention; and *redefining* a problem in a way that makes it more specific and makes the solution more achievable.

The ultimate goal of cognitive counseling is for the client to be able to initiate and successfully use cognitive strategies independently. This goal typically is met in 12 to 16 weeks of counseling (Beck & Weishaar, 1995).

The Constructivist Movement in Cognitive Therapy

A funny thing happened in the course of research on what constitutes adaptive cognition. Several studies indicated that "when they are not depressed, people are highly vulnerable to illusions including unrealistic optimism, overestimation of themselves, and an exaggerated sense of their capacity to control events. The same research indicates that depressed people's perceptions and judgments are often less biased" (Alloy, 1995, p. 4). These findings are consistent across situations involving achievement and social interaction. They suggest that validity (i.e., the extent to which one's cognitions fit the evidence) is not as adaptive as viability (i.e., the extent to which one's cognitions help to achieve desirable outcomes). Apparently, an unrealistically positive cognitive bias enhances at least two desirable outcomes: nondistressed affect and levels of motivation and activity resulting in at least occasional rewards that then sustain (reinforce) motivation and activity.

The concept of viability rather than validity of cognitions is one aspect of constructivism, an emerging paradigm in counseling in general and in the theory and practice of cognitive therapy in particular (Anderson, 1990; Hayes & Oppenheim, 1997; Lyddon, 1990). The constructivist perspective stands in contrast to the positivist perspective on which cognitive therapy originally was developed. According to positivist cognitive therapy, objective reality exists and can be known; cognitions range in their validity, that is, the accuracy with which they correspond to reality; people develop their cognitions as a result of innate and/or experiential factors; distressing affect is the result of relatively erroneous and biased cognitions; and the role of counseling is to help clients reduce emotional distress by modifying erroneous cognitions in the direction of more valid and realistic cognitions.

By contrast, according to constructivist cognitive therapy, objective reality either does not exist or cannot directly be known. Rather, reality is inherently subjective and unique to each person; it is, in fact, created by each person. Cognitions, therefore, cannot be analyzed as to their validity but can be assessed as to their viability, that is, the extent to which they enable someone to adapt or to organize experience in a way that helps to achieve desired outcomes. Distressing affect occurs when one encounters an experience in which one's cognitions are not adaptive. The role of counseling, therefore, is to explore and even amplify distressing affect and the accompanying cognitions to facilitate a transformation, an accommodation in which the client creates a cognitive reorganization that is more viable and more adaptive.

As Lyddon (1990) specified, differences between positivist and constructivist perspectives suggest at least three ways in which the counseling process is differentially conceived and undertaken. First, the positivist views client problems as dysfunctions to be eliminated, whereas the constructivist views client problems as opportunities for development. Consequently, the positivist attends exclusively to the problem and how to resolve it most efficiently, whereas the constructivist facilitates a process of exploring and transforming personal meanings "in the direction of more viable representations of experience" (p. 124). Third, positivists view painful emotion as the result of cognition, whereas constructivists view it as an accompaniment to "the emergence of higher order 'knowing structures' capable of accommodating the challenges and complexities associated with the current developmental crisis" (p. 125).

Lyddon (1990) argued that positivist cognitive therapy facilitates first-order change, or the modification of the existing cognitive system, whereas constructivist cognitive therapy facilitates second-order change, or the transformation to a new cognitive system. He urged counselors not to see each perspective as exclusive of the other but rather to see each as an alternative framework to choose depending on the type of change that counselors and their clients seek. He also emphasized that the positivist-constructivist framework "raises several questions for which no clear answers are available" (p. 126). The informed cognitive counselor is aware of the constructivist perspective as well as the fact that many as yet unanswered questions are associated with it. The present author has found substantial reconciliation of the positivist and constructivist views of emotion in psychotherapy in Greenberg and Safran (1987).

Conclusion

Since its inception, cognitive-behavioral counseling has expanded to assist a wide variety of clients with a wide variety of counseling goals. Several myths about this counseling approach have been dispelled such as the myth that emo-

tions are neither addressed nor aroused during the counseling process, the myth that the client's past is ignored, and the myth that the change strategies typically are "done to" a passive client or can be applied in a nonindividualized "cookbook" fashion. Cognitive-behavioral counselors pay as much attention to ethical considerations (Spiegler & Guevremont, 1998) and multicultural considerations (Padesky & Greenberger, 1995) as do mental health professionals aligned with other theoretical orientations.

For counselors interested in learning more about the theory and techniques of this counseling approach, numerous excellent resources now are available. In the print domain, a plethora of books exist for the practitioner. Among those not previously cited in this chapter are Freeman and Dattilio (1992); Freeman, Simon, and Beutler (1989); and Salkovskis (1996). Sources written for the general public and for clients in particular include Burns (1980, 1989) and Greenberger and Padesky (1995), respectively. Several mental health professionals have demonstrated the cognitive-behavioral process on videotape; these include Beck (Shostrom, Shostrom, & Ratner, 1986), Freeman (1995), Holden (Association for Counselor Education and Supervision, Chi Sigma Iota, Gladding, & Holden, 1993), and Padesky (Center for Cognitive Therapy, 1996). Many cognitive-behavioral practitioners, such as Burns and Padesky, are masters at presenting training workshops for counselors seeking to hone their cognitive-behavioral conceptualization and intervention skills.

The future of cognitive-behavioral counseling appears bright. The more established theory and practice are spawning new perspectives, most notably the constructivist perspective.

Many features of the more established approach, particularly its empirical validity, ensure that it will continue to be a major force in mental health for years to come.

References

Alloy, L. B. (1995, April). Depressive realism: Sadder but wiser? *The Harvard Mental Health Letter,* pp. 4-5. (74 Fenwood Road, Boston, MA 02115)

Anderson, W. T. (1990). *Reality isn't what it used to be: Theatrical politics, ready-to-wear religion, global myths, primitive chic, and other wonders of the postmodern world.* New York: Harper & Row.

Arlow, J. A. (1995). Psychoanalysis. In R. J. Corsini & D. Wedding (Eds.), *Current psychotherapies* (5th ed., pp. 15-50). Itasca, IL: F. E. Peacock.

Assagioli, R. (1965). *Psychosynthesis: A manual of principles and techniques.* New York: Viking Penguin.

Association for Counselor Education and Supervision (Co-Producer), Chi Sigma Iota (Co-Producer), Gladding, S. (Director), & Holden, J. M. (Featured Counselor and Editor). (1993). *Cognitive counseling: An instructional video* [Video]. Alexandria, VA: American Counseling Association. (5999 Stevenson Ave., Alexandria, VA 22304)

Bandura, A. (1977). *Social learning theory.* Englewood Cliffs, NJ: Prentice Hall.

Bandura, A. (1986). *Social foundations of thought and action: A social cognitive theory.* Englewood Cliffs, NJ: Prentice Hall.

Beck, A. T. (1976). *Cognitive therapy and the emotional disorders.* New York: International Universities Press.

Beck, A. T. (1996). Beyond belief: A theory of modes, personality, and psychopathology. In P. Salkovskis (Ed.), *Frontiers of cognitive therapy* (pp. 1-25). New York: Guilford.

Beck, A. T., Freeman, A. M., & Associates. (1990). *Cognitive therapy of personality disorders.* New York: Guilford.

Beck, A. T., & Weishaar, M. (1995). Cognitive therapy. In R. J. Corsini & D. Wedding (Eds.), *Current psychotherapies* (5th ed., pp. 229-261). Itasca, IL: F. E. Peacock.

Beck, J. (1996). Cognitive therapy of personality disorders. In P. Salkovskis (Ed.), *Frontiers of cognitive therapy* (pp. 165-181). New York: Guilford.

Burns, D. (1980). *Feeling good: The new mood therapy.* New York: William Morrow.

Burns, D. (1989). *The feeling good handbook: Using the new mood therapy in everyday life.* New York: William Morrow.

Burns, D. D., & Auerbach, A. (1996). Therapeutic empathy in cognitive-behavioral therapy: Does it really make a difference? In P. Salkovskis (Ed.), *Frontiers of cognitive therapy* (pp. 135-164). New York: Guilford.

Byrom, T. (1976). *Dhammapada: The sayings of the Buddha.* Boston: Shambhala.

Center for Cognitive Therapy. (1996). *Cognitive therapy training tapes* [videos]. Newport Beach, CA: Author. (1101 Dove Street, Suite 240, Newport Beach, CA 92660)

Corey, G. (1996). *Theory and practice of counseling and psychotherapy.* Pacific Grove, CA: Brooks/Cole.

Crits-Christoph, P. (1998). Training in empirically validated treatments: The Division 12 APA Task Force recommendations. In K. S. Dobson & K. D. Craig (Eds.), *Empirically supported therapies: Best practice in professional psychology* (pp. 3-25). Thousand Oaks, CA: Sage.

Dattilio, F. M., & Padesky, C. A. (1990). *Cognitive therapy with couples.* Sarasota, FL: Professional Resource Exchange.

Donaldson, S. M. (1998). Counselor bias in working with gay men and lesbians: A commentary on Barret and Barzan (1996). *Counseling and Values, 42*(2), 88-91.

Douglas, C. (1995). Analytical psychotherapy. In R. J. Corsini & D. Wedding (Eds.), *Current psychotherapies* (5th ed., pp. 95-127). Itasca, IL: F. E. Peacock.

Dusay, J. M., & Dusay, K. M. (1989). Transactional analysis. In R. J. Corsini & D. Wedding (Eds.), *Current psychotherapies* (4th ed., pp. 405-454). Itasca, IL: F. E. Peacock.

Ellis, A. (1995). Rational emotive behavior therapy. In R. J. Corsini & D. Wedding (Eds.), *Current psychotherapies* (5th ed., pp. 162-196). Itasca, IL: F. E. Peacock.

Freeman, A. M. (1995). *Depression: A cognitive therapy approach* [video]. New York: Newbridge Communications. (333 East 38th Street, New York, NY 10016)

Freeman, A. M., & Dattilio, F. M. (Ed.). (1992). *Comprehensive casebook of cognitive therapy.* New York: Plenum.

Freeman, A. M., Pretzer, J., Fleming, B., & Simon, K. M. (1990). *Clinical applications of cognitive therapy.* New York: Plenum.

Freeman, A. M., Simon, K. M., & Beutler, L. E. (Eds.). (1989). *Comprehensive handbook of cognitive therapy.* New York: Plenum.

Greenberg, L. S., & Safran, J. D. (1987). *Emotion in psychotherapy.* New York: Guilford.

Greenberger, D., & Padesky, C. A. (1995). *Mind over mood: A cognitive therapy treatment manual for clients.* New York: Guilford.

Grof, S. (1985). *Beyond the brain: Birth, death, and transcendence in psychotherapy.* Albany: State University of New York Press.

Hayes, R. L., & Oppenheim, R. (1997). Constructivism: Reality is what you make it. In T. L. Sexton & B. L. Griffin (Eds.), *Constructivist thinking in counseling practice, research, and training* (pp. 19-40). New York: Teachers College Press.

Holden, J. M. (1993). Transpersonal counseling. *Texas Counseling Association Journal, 21*(1), 7-23.

Holden, J. M., Watts, R., & Brookshire, W. (1991). Beliefs of professional counselors and clergy about depressive religious ideation. *Counseling and Values, 35*(2), 93-103.

Jakubowski, P., & Lange, A. J. (1978). *The assertive option: Your rights and responsibilities.* Champaign, IL: Research Press.

Jensen, J. P., Bergin, A. E., & Greaves, D. W. (1990). The meaning of eclecticism: New survey and analysis of components. *Professional Psychology: Research and Practice, 119,* 124-130.

Kanfer, F. H., & Goldstein, A. P. (Eds.). (1991). *Helping people change* (4th ed.). New York: Pergamon.

Kelly, G. A. (1955). *The psychology of personal constructs.* New York: Norton.

Lambert, M. J., & Cattani-Thompson, K. (1996). Current findings regarding the effectiveness of counseling: Implications for practice. *Journal of Counseling and Development, 74,* 601-608.

Lange, A. J., & Jakubowski, P. (1976). *Responsible assertive behavior: Cognitive/behavioral procedures for trainers.* Champaign, IL: Research Press.

Lyddon, W. J. (1990). First- and second-order change: Implications for rationalist and constructivist cognitive therapies. *Journal of Counseling and Development, 69,* 122-127.

McGinn, L. K., & Young, J. E. (1996). Schema-focused therapy. In P. Salkovskis (Ed.), *Frontiers of cognitive therapy* (pp. 182-207). New York: Guilford.

Meichenbaum, D. (1974). Self-instructional training: A cognitive prosthesis for the aged. *Human Development, 17,* 273-280.

Meichenbaum, D. (1985). *Stress inoculation training.* New York: Pergamon.

Mills, J. A. (1998). *Control: A history of behavioral psychology.* New York: New York University Press.

Mosak, H. H. (1995). Adlerian psychotherapy. In R. J. Corsini & D. Wedding (Eds.), *Current psychotherapies* (5th ed., pp. 51-94). Itasca, IL: F. E. Peacock.

Padesky, C. A., & Greenberger, D. (1995). *Clinician's guide to "Mind Over Mood."* New York: Guilford.

Propst, L. R. (1980). The comparative efficacy of religious and nonreligious imagery for the treatment of mild depression in religious individuals. *Cognitive Therapy and Research, 4,* 167-178.

Propst, L. R. (1988). *Psychotherapy in a religious framework: Spirituality in the emotional healing process.* New York: Human Sciences Press.

Propst, L. R. (1996). Cognitive-behavioral therapy and the religious person. In E. P. Shafranske (Ed.), *Religion and the clinical practice of psychology* (pp. 391-407). Washington, DC: American Psychological Association.

Propst, L. R., Ostrom, R., Watkins, P., Dean, T., & Mashburn, D. (1992). Comparative efficacy of religious and nonreligious cognitive-behavioral therapy for the treatment of clinical depression in religious individuals. *Journal of Consulting and Clinical Psychology, 60,* 94-103.

Richards, P. S., & Bergin, A. E. (1997). *A spiritual strategy for counseling and psychotherapy.* Washington, DC: American Psychological Association.

Salkovskis, P. M. (1996). *Frontiers in cognitive therapy.* New York: Guilford.

Sharf, R. S. (2000). *Theories of psychotherapy and counseling: Concepts and cases* (2nd ed.). Belmont, CA: Wadsworth.

Shostrom, E. T. (Executive Producer), Shostrom, S. K. (Producer), & Ratner, H. (Director). (1986). *Three approaches to psychotherapy,* Part 3: *Aaron Beck—Cognitive therapy* [Video]. Corona Del Mar, CA: Psychological and Educational Films. (PMB #252, 3334 East Coast Highway, Corona Del Mar, CA 92625)

Spiegler, M. D., & Guevremont, D. C. (1998). *Contemporary behavior therapy* (3rd ed.). Pacific Grove, CA: Brooks/Cole.

Weishaar, M. E. (1996). Cognitive risk factors in suicide. In P. Salkovskis (Ed.), *Frontiers of cognitive therapy* (pp. 226-249). New York: Guilford.

Wilson, G. T. (1995). Behavior therapy. In R. J. Corsini & D. Wedding (Eds.), *Current psychotherapies* (5th ed., pp. 197-228). Itasca, IL: F. E. Peacock.

Young, J. E. (1999). *Cognitive therapy for personality disorders: A schema-focused approach* (3rd ed.). Sarasota, FL: Professional Resource Exchange.

CHAPTER NINE

Humanistic Theories
of Counseling

RICHARD J. HAZLER

Kendra was an active 40-year-old Ph.D.-trained counselor with a successful private practice, an excellent professional reputation, a husband, and two teenage children. She seemed to have everything a person would want, so why would someone with so many positives in her life attempt suicide as she recently had done? She had professional, financial, and family success in greater measure than the vast majority of people in the world. Viewing Kendra's case from the outside as an objective observer just does not make the clean and logical sense that we might expect. What would we see differently if we were looking instead from Kendra's unique personal perspective? Would she have been understood, evaluated, and treated differently at the turn of the 20th century as opposed to the turn of the 21st century? How would she be treated if she wound up in the office of a competent humanistic counselor?

This chapter provides the reader with a case presentation of Kendra from a humanistic perspective. Key concepts in the theory are presented to help the reader understand the approach, and some attention is given to discriminating humanistic counseling from existential methods.

People Are More Than
the Sum of Their Parts

The turn of the 20th century viewed behavior, psychosexual pressures, class-consciousness boundaries, and rigid scientific thinking as the means to understanding and helping people. Scientific thinking with its origins from Aristotle, Galileo, and Isaac Newton would look for information in the one and only "real world"—the world they would physically observe surrounding Kendra. Only during the late 19th century would a new philosophical coalition begin forming that would question this "observable real world" concept and begin replacing it with a more holistic picture of humans that would take into account the world as envisioned by Kendra.

Existential philosophers in Europe during the late 19th century began successfully questioning the absolutism of concepts such as truth and fact with the idea that the whole (Gestalt) could be more than the sum of its parts (Smith, 1988). This European excitement about existentialism tended to focus on theory and philosophy, but that emphasis changed significantly as the concepts began to emerge in the United States. Leaders such as Bugental (1965), Gendlin (1962), Maslow (1954), and Rogers (1942) were among those who expanded existential philosophical ideas into more humanistic models. Their approaches put a greater emphasis on confidence in the strength, immediate potential, and positive qualities of individuals that resulted in more action-oriented techniques whereby greater responsibility was invested in individuals. These concepts challenged the behavioral view maintained by the 19th- and early 20th-century medical and scientific professions by refusing to see humans as simple objects to be understood, analyzed, and manipulated into changing (Bugental & Sterling, 1995).

This humanistic movement brought perspectives that went well beyond what the world at that time saw as scientific understanding of thinking, acting, and motivation. Humanistic concepts now are ingrained throughout a number of theories, thereby defying efforts to describe a single clear model. Instead, there exists a mixture of humanistic processes, techniques, and styles that have common themes for understanding and working with people within their personalized frames of reference. Connecting these common themes are a recognition of the subjective nature of human reality, a sense that the whole of a person is more than the sum of observable parts, and the realization that these factors cannot be as directly and objectively tested as laboratory scientists would request. The development of these philosophical concepts into a continually evolving theory of counseling has had a wide impact not only on humanistic counseling models but also on all helping professions with the integration of many concepts into modern-day general practice (Hazler & Barwick, 2001).

How would Kendra be treated in the office of a competent humanistic counselor at the beginning of the 21st century? The answer is that there could be many potential techniques used depending on the specific personality, beliefs, and abilities of her therapist but that there also would be things in common for all humanistic counselors. She would be treated as a well-meaning and resourceful person with recognized abilities. Continually emerging resources in Kendra also would be recognized as ones that will allow her to improve her effectiveness in dealing with the world around her. Her counselor would demonstrate faith in her ability to use these new self-insights to evolve productively for herself and the world around her. The counselor would provide an environment in which caring, compassion, authenticity, unconditional regard, respect, and honesty, rather than the implementation of selected techniques, were maintained as the focus of efforts (Kottler & Hazler, 2001).

Recognizing Human Potential

The outsider's view of Kendra is one of a successful counselor, businesswoman, mother, and wife. One adds up these observable facts, and her suicide attempt makes no sense at all. But inside Kendra exists a person who is afraid of not being helpful enough to her clients, who does not know all that she should know to maximize the help she wants to give, and who is fearful of the potential harm that she might do. Her efforts to spend more time improving in these areas consequently shrinks the time, thought, and caring that she can give to her husband and children, with the result that her sense of failure in those roles is increased as well. The person getting the least attention by Kendra in this situation is Kendra herself. Inadequacy, loss, and a lack of hope can easily evolve from this complex combination of observable reality mixed together with Kendra's perceived reality and inadequate attention to herself.

Understanding Kendra or any other person from a humanistic viewpoint first involves observing from a *holistic view* rather than analyzing any single aspect. Humanistic counselors see people as more than their behaviors, more than their thoughts, and more than their feelings. At a minimum, people are a combination of all these parts plus genetics, chemical makeup, spirituality, the impact of their environment, and other pieces as yet undiscovered or not clearly understood. Computers now can add faster than can humans, but no computers can yet come close to duplicating humans

in all their complexity. The result is that understanding a person in a holistic view requires attempting to view all parts of the person at once, even while recognizing that they are not all known by the counselor or even by the client. What is clear is that the more holistic the view of a person, the greater the likelihood that the combination of factors influencing who the person is, how the person acts, and how the person sees the world will become visible and, therefore, create more potential for change.

The world that is visible to the client is much more than the one that enters the body through sight, smell, sound, and touch. These senses all are filtered through people's subjective or *phenomenological* view of the world. A single mother who is without education, financially poor, and living from hand to mouth, and who has been raised in a family under similar conditions, would see Kendra's situation as a heavenly one filled with hope, love, excitement, luxury, and minimal problems. A Native American choosing to live a simple spiritual life on tribal lands might wonder why Kendra works so hard to accumulate things for herself and her family rather than living with nature and appreciating the natural order and simple gifts. Some combination of cultural worldview, developmental life stages, and individual means of perceiving serves to translate this initial information through the unique perceptions of individuals. The information may enter by the same channels and with the same initial look, but the phenomenological screening turns it into something very different for each individual. Understanding oneself or others in a humanistic way requires delving into this phenomenological world rather than presuming it from what some would call "facts."

Immediacy of awareness is needed before one can effectively understand and then purposefully act on the phenomenological perspective of oneself or others. It is no simple task because the information is internalized and ingrained for each individual to the point where people do not necessarily recognize it as unique to themselves. Awareness levels also change with time, pressures, and outside influences so that what might be current awareness for Kendra during a good day might not be available to her at another time. Increasing current awareness to outside influences, choices, strengths, weaknesses, and how one's perspective compares to others' perspectives helps to create freedom of choice along with increased personal responsibility for thoughts, feelings, and actions. Humanistic approaches seek to increase levels of current awareness so that choices can be made that reflect a person's phenomenological view as it relates to other factors.

Autonomy, genuineness, and self-trust are three closely related themes in humanistic models. *Autonomy* relates to people being able to make decisions about thoughts and actions on their own. As Frankl (1963) noted in the classic retelling of his life in a Nazi death camp, those prisoners who survived the longest and maintained their mental health were those who continued to make personal choices in an environment that sought to eliminate individual choice and one's humanity. Physical freedoms could be threatened and taken away, but the ability to make choices about how to respond—including the choice of life versus death—remained with individuals if they chose to keep it.

The acceptance that people can continually choose their thoughts and actions supports the *genuineness* theme, which encourages open and honest sharing and exploration of oneself. Gen-

uineness reaffirms the autonomous nature of people by communicating *self-trust*. The connection between these themes can be seen in Kendra's movement toward suicide where she shows an increasing personal mistrust of her own ability to choose and act. She becomes unwilling to share these troubling aspects of her perceived world even with those she loves and trusts most. Her loss of self-trust and her inability to be genuine degrade her sense of autonomy and hope for the future even further.

Hope and positive expectations for individuals are key parts of humanistic theories. They are tied to an *actualizing* theme that views people as continuously involved in self-growth by seeking to "maximize and enhance the organism" (Rogers, 1959, p. 196). This theme emphasizes the concept that motivation originates within the individual rather than from outside forces. The direction of this motivation is believed to be inherently positive, although it might not look that way to outsiders who see behaviors that often are harmful to oneself or others. These apparently negative behaviors do not appear so negative to individuals when observed through their unique phenomenological views of the people and world around them. This is why Kendra might see suicide as a positive choice at one moment and, shortly thereafter, might recognize that it does not lead in the positive direction she actually wants to pursue. It also is why the young, poor male living in a drug-infested neighborhood might view selling drugs to acquire food for his family as a positive and actualizing choice. The outsider recognizes that suicide and selling drugs are not going to move people ahead in the long run, but so long as the phenomenological view of these people supports the choices as positive, they will be making those choices with a degree of faith that they are, in fact, positive.

Human encounter is the theme that brings together the other humanistic themes in productive ways. This theme emphasizes the need for people to holistically relate with others in genuine and personalized ways. It is the vehicle for sharing information about the thoughts, perceptions, emotions, and events that make up each individual's phenomenological world. It is this information that creates a more holistic view that could not be obtained in isolation no matter how hard we tried. This personalized and, therefore, powerful new information helps to revise one's phenomenological view of the world in ways that allow for the actualizing tendency to proceed in progressively positive directions. Human encounters as the vehicle for exploring and promoting the other themes are vital in all relationships, but they also provide the purposeful foundation for the work of humanistic counselors.

Toward Growth and Adaptation

The primary emphasis of humanistic counseling is placed on the interaction between counselor and client. It is a focus on the process of connection between two humans that is central rather than any specific techniques or content. The actualizing principle provides the basis for believing that people will progress when they are involved in situations where a genuine, trusting, immediate, and empathic human relationship provides the necessary growth-producing environment.

A counseling environment that encourages *actualizing* might be viewed as analogous to a gardener who encourages seeds to grow. Given the right amounts of water, air, and nutrient-rich soil, the seeds will germinate, struggle out from the ground, and grow due to their natural actualizing tendency. The best gardeners simply do what they can to enrich that environment. They learn quickly that digging down to see whether they can help the seeds or trying to straighten the emerging seeds will only delay or kill the young plants. Provided with the right conditions, the plants will choose their own time and process for growth. A similar scenario is true in the humanistic view of counseling. People seek growth, and the first task of a counselor is to provide people with the appropriate environment for them to obtain the naturally productive development they instinctively pursue. The specifics of the situation, client strengths, and client problems might change, but providing the appropriate human relationship that can recognize and facilitate development rather than trying to create it for clients remains at the core of the process.

Recognition of people's development and, therefore, the phenomenological world in which they exist begins in part by learning who they are. A humanistic view of Kendra would extend far beyond the limited events and feelings surrounding her suicide attempt because such events do not happen in isolation. There are people, experiences, thoughts, and feelings that occur in her life that lead her to deal with the world in personalized ways. These are the origins of the *emerging personal stories* that can serve as the vehicles for conceptualizing what factors interconnect to create a holistic view of a person. So, counselors watch, listen, reflect, summarize, and share of themselves so as to better understand as much as possible of clients' phenomenological views.

The humanistic movement rejected using these stories as simple information to be registered, organized, and presented in a simplistically scientific manner. Instead, the focus was on acquiring and using the information within an integrated "I-thou" relationship with clients, making such relationships a core condition for modern practice (Buber, 1958/1970). Only this situation provides the opportunity for the full phenomenological worlds of client and counselor to intermingle, thereby influencing each other. Perls, Hefferline, and Goodman (1951/1965) stated it even more forcefully: "All contact is creative adjustment" (p. 230). All varieties of humanistic counseling, therefore, are set on the foundation of two real people sharing a wide range of thoughts, experiences, and inner feelings.

A major force in maintaining this active and personalized relationship is *immediacy* or how directly the client and therapist deal with each other in the here and now (Prouty, 1994). It is the timeliness of this factor that allows the client and therapist to know what currently is happening so that a full awareness of new information, changing perceptions, and evolving process can be maintained. A client such as Kendra, for example, might express her sense of inadequate knowledge about her clients' problems to her counselor, who might respond with personalized immediacy:

> You seem to know as much as I do about the things we are discussing, but that sense of not knowing enough is certainly one I can relate to. In fact, right now I can find myself worrying about whether I will be good enough for you or say the right things in order to help as much as I'd like.

The work of an intense I-thou relationship in which immediacy is common promotes an in-depth understanding of the other person. It is this *empathic exploration* that is critical, not the simplistic collecting of information to place people into categories or to quantify their problems. Empathic exploration focuses on learning about another person from the person's phenomenological world rather than from one's own perspective. It is a listening, feeling, and sensing of how the other person perceives the complexities of the world in general and the person's personal situation in particular. Continual reassessment of the understanding that is developing between the therapist and client and the active communication of their emerging perspectives is at the heart of this process (Prouty, 1994).

It is during the process of empathic exploration where a counselor could see that Kendra's temporary decision to commit suicide was not so irrational after all from Kendra's perspective. It was during a time when the world she could see was filled with personal inadequacy, emptiness, impossibility, and hopelessness so that leaving that world actually appeared logical for a period of time. Becoming more in touch with Kendra's full experience is what allows the counselor to understand at deeper levels what few others will. A counselor who can effectively express the depth of that empathic understanding will give Kendra a sense of being less alone in her internally experienced world, provide Kendra with new information that she is more likely to accept, help Kendra to establish greater trust in herself, and create confidence in the counselor.

The *trustworthiness* that humanistic counselors attempt to strengthen through relationships conceptually emerges from the actualizing belief that people will move toward positive forms of growth that would be supportive of themselves and others. Relationships that emphasize genuineness, empathy, and caring are among the concepts that maximize trust and, in turn, are advanced by its growth. Increasing levels of trust become connected to a greater willingness to take appropriate risks, an openness to new information, encouraging thoughts and actions toward oneself and others, and a greater general willingness to move forward in an uncertain world rather than remaining stagnant while waiting for someone else to provide answers.

Moving forward in an uncertain world involves testing new assumptions, feelings, and actions with other people. Kendra will test initial perceptions of herself and her world with the counselor. As she develops new ideas about herself, others, and life, she will be encouraged to test them again in various circumstances where she feels prepared for those risks. Some tests will work well, whereas most will need readjustments. As her phenomenological world changes, however, there will continue to be new conceptualizations to test, results to examine, and readjustments to be made. Trusting in oneself and others does not come in the nice neat package we would like. Testing perceptions in session with a counselor and also doing so in the outside world are the only ways in which to maintain appropriate trust in how well one's perceptions of the world actually facilitate life. It is the only way in which to judge who we are and how we are in our ever-changing lives as part of a continually more complex world.

Humanistic Theory During the Age of Complexity

Far more information is at our fingertips than ever before, and it is increasing at rates we cannot comprehend. Connect to the Internet, and two realities become immediately clear: There are virtually unlimited amounts of information available, and we never will be able to know it all or even be able to find it all. How will people deal with an information age that, from minute to minute, widens the gap between the knowledge available and what we as individuals can comprehend?

It is not just information alone that continues to expand the demands on people. Technological and cultural factors combine to complicate life for us as well. Global communication makes everyone neighbors, demands common languages for the necessity of interacting, and requires that we all give more attention to cultural diversity. We live less and less in the safe isolation of being with "only those people like us." Now, we have the continual press to understand the multitude of others who increasingly affect our lives on a daily basis.

Philosophy and theory began to react to these increasing complexities of the human condition as the 20th century started to wind down. Attentiveness to issues of gender, sexual orientation, and multiculturalism, among others, promoted interest in theories that emphasized multiple views of the world instead of a singular one. Chaos theory moved from science and math into the realm of human understanding as a way in which to consider the complexity and confusion of multiple realities. Postmodern philosophy and constructivism gained followers by emphasizing the central nature of differences in people's views of the world and how those views evolved. Even the highly structured field of research has given qualitative methodology increasing acceptance as the means to consider areas in which quantitative research has had less success—the uniqueness and depth of individuals, groups, and concepts.

Core themes arising from these factors affecting the future of humanity are the giving of greater attention to the unique perceptions of individuals and groups and the need to understand them in more depth. They emphasize the process of learning over ultimate final answers.

These always have been core themes of humanistic theory, and they reflect the continuing importance of the theory in a future that can only become more complex and potentially overwhelming for people.

Humanistic theory is a model that continues to give people a way of accepting these inherent and increasing pressures and a means of dealing with them in a humanistic manner through relationships with other humans. The movements toward constructivism, qualitative research, equal rights for all, and multiculturalism are basic examples of how humanistic principles have spread their influence beyond the confines of the theory alone and into societal movements that reflect conditions in a rapidly changing world.

The humanistic counselor and client bring their separate lives, bodies, minds, and experiences together in ways that allow them to share their uniquely perceived worlds and learn from the communion between them. No attempts are made to combine their worlds or to change one into the other. Instead, they meet to compare perspectives and to create better understandings of themselves as well as themselves in relation to others. Respect for differences, belief in commonalities, faith in the process, and a commitment to growth are the common categories for both the starting place and the projected outcomes of humanistic counseling. It is theory based on the assumption that we do not know all there is to know and that we need intimate and honest relationships with each other to learn more about ourselves.

The humanistic counselor is the person with more training in how to advance the struggle in positive ways, whereas the client is seeking help to implement the process. The client and counselor both will struggle to understand the other and themselves, and it is within this struggle

that growth emerges. There is no achievable end to this growth. Instead, it is a movement toward continually understanding more, an acceptance that we never will get it all, and a belief that quality life is achieved in the growth process rather than in the outcome.

References

Buber, M. (1970). *I and thou*. New York: Scribner. (Original work published 1958)

Bugental, J. F. T. (1965). *The search for authenticity*. New York: Holt, Rinehart & Winston.

Bugental, J. F. T., & Sterling, M. M. (1995). Existential-humanistic psychotherapy: New perspectives. In A. S. Gurman & S. B. Messer (Eds.), *Essential psychotherapies* (pp. 226-260). New York: Guilford.

Frankl, V. E. (1963). *Man's search for meaning: An introduction to logotherapy*. Boston: Beacon.

Gendlin, E. T. (1962). *Experiencing and the creation of meaning*. New York: Free Press.

Hazler, R. J., & Barwick, N. (2001). *The therapeutic environment: Core conditions for facilitating therapy*. London: Open University Press.

Kottler, J. A., & Hazler, R. J. (2001). Therapist as a model of humane values and humanistic behavior. In K. J. Schneider, J. F. Bugental, & J. F. Pierson (Eds.), *The handbook of humanistic psychology*. Thousand Oaks, CA: Sage.

Maslow, A. H. (1954). *Motivation and personality*. New York: Harper & Row.

Perls, F., Hefferline, R., & Goodman, P. (1965). *Gestalt therapy: Excitement and growth in the human personality*. New York: Dell (Delta Books). (Original work published 1951)

Prouty, G. (1994). *Theoretical evolutions in person-centered/experiential therapy: Applications to schizophrenic and retarded psychoses*. Westport, CT: Praeger.

Rogers, C. R. (1942). *Counseling and psychotherapy*. Boston: Houghton Mifflin.

Rogers, C. R. (1959). A theory of therapy, personality, and interpersonal relationships, as developed in the client-centered framework. In S. Koch (Ed.), *Psychology: A study of science: Vol. 3. Formulations of the person and the social context* (pp. 184-256). New York: McGraw-Hill.

Smith, B. (Ed.). (1988). *Foundations of Gestalt therapy: Hemsbach*. Munich, Germany: Philosophia Verlag Munchen Wien.

CHAPTER TEN

Existential Counseling

E. H. "MIKE" ROBINSON, III

KARYN DAYLE JONES

Existential counseling is best described as a philosophical approach to counseling. The existential approach helps people who are isolated, alienated, and not finding meaning in life to deal with their anxiety by enabling them to find meaning and purpose in life and to maintain their identity. Existential counseling does not provide a specific model of counseling; rather, it focuses on understanding a variety of humans' experiences and asks deep questions about the nature of existence. Existential counseling focuses on the importance of anxiety, freedom, meaning, death, isolation, and responsibility.

Existential counseling is considered a phenomenological approach to counseling and was developed as a reaction to the two other major models, psychoanalysis and behaviorism (Corey, 1996); thus, it is considered a third force in psychology. Psychoanalytic theory focuses on forces, drives, and past events affecting individuals' freedom, whereas behavior theory assumes that freedom is restricted by external conditioning. Existential counseling rejects the notion that our behaviors are determined or conditioned by outside sources. Clients are not viewed as sick; rather, they are seen as being sick of life and needing to recognize their ability to shape their own lives (Deurzen-Smith, 1988).

This chapter elaborates on the history of existential counseling by discussing some of the individuals who have influenced the theory and practice of the system along with key concepts associated with the approach. The chapter also describes the process of existential counseling.

History

Existential counseling draws from a major orientation in philosophy and was influenced by a number of philosophers including Kierkegaard (1813-1855), Dostoyevsky (1821-1881), Heidegger (1889-1976), Nietzsche (1844-1900), Buber (1878-1965), and Sartre (1905-1980). Existential philosophies grew out of a desire to address people who were experiencing difficulty in finding meaning and purpose in life and in maintaining their identity (Holt, 1986). May (1950, 1953, 1961, 1969, 1975, 1983) and Frankl (1963, 1965, 1969, 1978) probably are the best-known existential theorists. Moreover, existential counseling was introduced to the United States in 1958 by May. Another important figure in existential counseling is Yalom (1980), who wrote the first comprehensive textbook in existential counseling, titled *Existential Psychotherapy*.

Victor Frankl

Frankl was born in 1905 in Vienna, Austria. After receiving a medical degree in 1930 and a Ph.D. in 1949 from the University of Vienna, Frankl established and supervised youth counseling centers in Vienna. Frankl became interested in existentialism during the 1930s and began working on the manuscript for a book on a new form of counseling called *logotherapy*. Logotherapy comes from the Greek word *logos,* which can mean study, word, spirit, God, or meaning. According to logotherapy, the striving to find meaning in one's life is the primary motivational force in humans (Frankl, 1969). But Frankl's efforts were cut short by the $2\frac{1}{2}$ years he spent as a prisoner in the German concentration camps at Auschwitz and Dachau during World War II (1942-1945). The time he spent in the concentration camps crystallized his thoughts about the meaning of life and suffering, and it was partly his determination to share his beliefs that kept him alive. He believed that the will to meaning is the central drive of human existence. After the war, Frankl published many books and gave many lectures about existential counseling. His best-known books are *Man's Search for Meaning* (Frankl, 1963, 1984) and *The Will to Meaning* (Frankl, 1969). He died on September 2, 1997, at 92 years of age.

Rollo May

May is perhaps the most important figure in American existential psychology. He was born in 1909 in Ada, Ohio. After earning his bachelor's degree from Oberlin College in Ohio in 1930, May taught English at an American college in Greece. He felt a calling to study theology, returned to the United States, and in 1938 received a bachelor of divinity degree, after which he worked as a Congregationalist minister for 2 years. May then began his studies in psychology at Columbia University. While working on his doctorate and what would become his first book, *The Meaning of Anxiety* (May, 1950), he spent $1\frac{1}{2}$ years struggling with tuberculosis. In a later book, *The Discovery of Being* (May, 1983), he described how this experience moved him toward the existential viewpoint and toward his most noted work on the meaning of anxiety. May continued to lecture and write books on the subject until his death on October 22, 1994, at 85 years of age.

Key Concepts

Human Nature

Existential counseling is a dynamic approach that focuses on concerns rooted in human experience. What differentiates existential counseling from other theoretical models is its lack of emphasis on techniques and frameworks of therapy; rather, existential counseling emphasizes the need to understand the humanity of the client. Existential counselors view the client as an existing immediate person, not as a composite of drives, archetypes, and conditioning (May & Yalom, 1989). Humans in this world are in a constant state of transition, evolving, and becoming and have a capacity for awareness, freedom and responsibility, and meaning in life. Existential counselors believe that humans are capable of self-awareness. With self-awareness comes the ability for freedom in making decisions and making change.

Existential thinkers are concerned with one's "being" in this world. Heidegger (1962) best described being as follows: "Everything we talk about, everything we have in view, everything toward which we comport ourselves in any way, is Being; what we are is Being, and so is how we are. Being lies in the fact that something is, as it is, in reality" (p. 26). To be means to be present, here and now, but it also means to project oneself into the future. What is said in this moment has significance for the next moment and beyond (Moustakas, 1994, p. 19). Humans are aware of being and are able to reflect on it.

Personality theory in existentialism is based on the belief in "ultimate concerns" of existence and the anxiety resulting from awareness of these concerns. In contrast to behavior theory, existentialism does not concentrate on the outside world's influence on the personality. Unlike psychoanalytic theory, existential counseling believes that a human's basic conflict is not due to suppressed instinctual drives or to significant adults in his or her early life; rather, conflicts are caused by the individual and the "givens" or ultimate concerns of existence.

Ultimate Concerns of Existence

Yalom (1980) identified four ultimate concerns of existence as death, freedom, isolation, and meaninglessness:

> Each of us craves perdur[ability], groundedness, community, and pattern; and yet, we must all face inevitable death, groundlessness, isolation, and meaninglessness. Existential counseling is based on a model of psychopathology which posits that anxiety and its maladaptive consequences are responses to these four ultimate concerns. (p. 485)

It is the awareness of these ultimate concerns that leads to anxiety and defense mechanisms.

Death

According to existential counseling, death plays a major role in our internal experience and is a source of anxiety (May, 1961). The fear of death haunts us; it rumbles continuously under the surface just beneath the rim of consciousness (Yalom, 1980). The terror of death is of such magnitude that a considerable portion of one's life energy is consumed in the denial of death. Death is a primary source of anxiety and can result in psychopathology.

The recognition of death can play a major role in counseling. An awareness of death shifts one away from trivial preoccupations and provides life with depth and poignancy and an entirely different perspective. It can be the factor that helps individuals to transcend a stale mode of living into a more authentic one (Corey, 1996). Awareness of death can help individuals to embrace life more fully and creatively (May, 1981). In addition to fully embracing life, an awareness of death can help individuals to appreciate the countless benefits of existence, that is, the things for which they can be grateful. Ordinarily, the things that individuals do have and what they can do are forgotten, and individuals focus on what they do not have and what they cannot do. Awareness of death helps individuals to be grateful for the many things they have and experience in life.

Freedom

The concept of freedom in existential counseling is linked with the concept of responsibility (Frankl, 1978). To be aware of responsibility is to be aware of creating one's own self, destiny, life predicament, feelings, and suffering. "Freedom is man's capacity to take a hand in his own development. It is our capacity to mold ourselves" (May, 1953, p. 138). For a client who will not accept such responsibility and persists in blaming others, no real therapy is possible (Yalom, 1980). True responsibility is quite overwhelming. Existential theory assumes that nothing in the world has significance except by virtue of one's own creation. There are no rules, no ethical systems, no values, and so on. There is no grand design in the universe; it is the individual alone who is the creator or his or her

existence. People are free to choose alternatives and, therefore, have a large role in shaping their destinies (Corey, 1996).

Another aspect of freedom is "willing" or the awareness of responsibility for one's actions and the efforts to change. People often might become aware of their responsibility or aware of the freedom they have to choose their actions in a specific situation or problem. Yet, they still might not change. Willing consists of wishing and then deciding (May, 1969). Once a person fully experiences a desire or wish, he or she is faced with a decision. Thus, freedom consists of both responsibility and will.

The emphasis in existential counseling on clients' freedom and responsibility for creating their situations or problems has been criticized from a multicultural viewpoint. Some believe that the realities of racism, discrimination, oppression, and other forms of environmental circumstances that may create clients' problems are not addressed in existential theory (Corey, 1996). Existential counselors need to be aware of these factors and validate their clients' experiences while challenging clients to find areas they can change to improve their situations or problems.

Isolation

A third concern in existential theory is isolation (Yalom, 1980). *Existential isolation* is a term meaning that no matter how closely we feel to another person, each of us enters existence alone and must leave it alone. It refers to the unbridgeable gulf between oneself and any other person as well as a separation between the individual and the world. An individual never can fully share his or her consciousness with another person. It is the knowledge of death that makes one fully realize that, at the most fundamental level, dying is the loneliest human experience.

The conflict with isolation occurs between our awareness of isolation and the wish to be protected and to be part of a larger whole. Individuals who are terrified by isolation need the presence of others to affirm their existence. Individuals reach out to relationships not because they want to do so but rather because they believe that they have to do so. The relationship is based on survival and the avoidance of the anxiety caused by fear of isolation; it is not based on growth.

Meaninglessness

The fourth ultimate concern is meaninglessness (Yalom, 1980). If each person must die, if each person creates his or her own world, and if each person is alone, then what meaning is there to life? The human appears to require meaning. Thus, the questions of "What is the meaning of life?" "What is the meaning of my life?" "Why do we live?" and "What do we live for?" become instrumental in creating anxiety. Jung believed that meaninglessness inhibited fullness of life and, therefore, was "equivalent to illness" (Yalom, 1980, p. 421). He stated that one third of his cases were suffering not from any clinically definable neuroses but rather from the senselessness and aimlessness of their lives. Finding a meaning or a reason to live relieves the anxiety that comes with facing a life and world without comforting structure. However, it is up to the individual to find meaning in life (Frankl, 1978).

Anxiety

An existential counselor sees anxiety as an inevitable aspect of existence (Cohn, 1997). Anxiety arises from our personal need to survive, to preserve our being, and to assert our being (May & Yalom, 1989). Existential theory distinguishes between normal anxiety and neurotic anxiety. Normal anxiety is an appropriate response to an event being faced (Corey, 1996). This type of anxiety does not need to be repressed and can be used as motivation for change. By contrast, neurotic anxiety is out of proportion to the situation. Persons usually are unaware of this anxiety, and it can be paralyzing and can inhibit creativity. The function of therapy is not to do away with all anxiety but rather to help clients confront anxiety so as to deal with specific fears objectively.

Existential theory believes that anxiety is derived from one's confrontation with "ultimate concerns" of existence including search for meaning, awareness of death, freedom and responsibility, and awareness of isolation (Yalom, 1980). The confrontation with any one of these ultimate concerns leads to anxiety; however, the fear of death is the primary reservoir of anxiety. According to existential theory, it is anxiety that leads a person to use defense mechanisms. The existential approach retains Freud's basic structure but has a different content. The old Freudian formula of

Drive → Anxiety → Defense Mechanism

is replaced by

Awareness of Ultimate Concerns → Anxiety → Defense Mechanism.

Thus, instead of the psychoanalytic deterministic view in which drives create conflicts that lead to experiencing anxiety, existential thought proposes that it is the internal conflict brought on by the awareness of ultimate concerns that leads to anxiety. Both theories see responses to anxiety as defense mechanisms.

Defense Mechanisms

Regarding the awareness of ultimate concerns that confront individuals, Yalom (1980) described two basic forms of defense mechanisms that people use to cope with their anxiety: "specialness" and belief in an "ultimate rescuer." These beliefs can be highly adaptive, particularly when dealing with death denial. Each, however, may be overloaded and stretched thin to the point where adaptation breaks down, anxiety leaks through, the individual resorts to extreme measures to protect himself or herself, and psychopathology develops.

Specialness

Individuals have deep, powerful beliefs in invulnerability or immortality (May & Yalom, 1989). Although most people understand rationally that these beliefs are not true, many hold to the beliefs at an unconscious level that somehow we are unique and special. The belief in specialness typically wards off anxiety resulting from the reality of our vulnerability to our harsh world. It enhances our courage to encounter danger without being overwhelmed by the threat of personal extinction. For example, the sense of specialness is beneficial for those in the armed forces required to face an enemy in combat. It makes it possible for a soldier to march into danger when believing, "I won't be hurt. The other guy may get it, but I'll make it."

The belief in specialness typically is challenged when an individual learns that he or she has a serious illness such as cancer. The first reaction generally is some form of denial, usually in an effort to cope with anxiety associated with the threat to life (Yalom, 1980). When the individual really grasps that death is imminent, he or she is confronted with the reality

> that one is finite; that one's life really comes to an end; that the world will persist nonetheless; that one is one of many, no more [and] no less; that the universe does not acknowledge one's specialness; that all our lives we have carried counterfeit vouchers; and, finally, [that] certain stark immutable dimensions of existence are beyond one's influence. (p. 120)

When an individual realizes the myth of personal specialness, he or she may feel angry or betrayed. Some people believe that if they had only realized this earlier, they would have lived their lives differently. Awareness of our lack of specialness in our world helps us to realize the unimportance of trivial issues and helps us to determine what is really important in life.

The Ultimate Rescuer

The other major mechanism of defense is our belief in a personal, omnipotent servant who eternally guards and protects our welfare—who might let us get to the edge of the abyss but who always will bring us back (May & Yalom, 1989, p. 381). No early culture ever believed that humans were alone in this world. Through much of life, the belief in the ultimate rescuer provides considerable solace for a number of human difficulties including fear of death.

Most individuals remain unaware of this defense mechanism until it fails to serve its purpose. For example, when a person is confronted with a fatal illness, he or she may expend a great deal of energy believing in the ultimate rescuer, whether it is a supernatural being, medical doctor, or some other protector. Individuals may differ in the extent to which they cling to denial about the seriousness of their illness, but eventually all denial falls apart in the face of overwhelming reality.

A patient's reaction to learning that no medical or surgical cure exists is catastrophic. He or she feels angry, deceived, and betrayed. At whom can one be angry? At the cosmos? At fate? Many patients are angry at the doctor for failing them, not for failing them medically but for failing to incarnate the patient's personal myth of an ultimate deliverer. (Yalom, 1980, p. 133)

The Process of Existential Counseling

Existential counseling does not seek to cure or explain; it merely seeks to explore, describe, and clarify so as to try to understand the human predicament (Deurzen-Smith, 1997). May (1969) believed that therapists should let go of following strict methodology in favor of focusing on the richness and breadth of individuals' experiences. Existential counselors assist clients in seeing ways in which they are not fully present in counseling and in the rest of their lives. Counselors help clients to redefine themselves and develop greater genuine contact with life. Clients are encouraged to confront their anxieties and to develop more effective means of coping.

Common existential "problems" presented by clients include personal growth, facing important decisions, facing death, stage of life crises, loneliness, meaninglessness, bereavement/loss, and identity problems (Corey, 1996; May & Yalom, 1989). Other conditions associated with defenses to confrontations with existential concerns include depression, addictions, obsession, and workaholism.

Goals of Counseling

A basic goal of existential therapy is to help individuals accept their freedom to act and responsibility for their actions (Corey, 1996). Understanding the meaning of freedom means understanding our responsibility in who we are and what we do in life (Frankl, 1978). Accepting that responsibility sometimes is an awesome task. Although many believe that accepting our freedom to choose is in many ways empowering, the new freedom does bring about anxiety. It is easier to stay in the same pattern of feeling helpless while clinging to the known and familiar than to risk oneself in a less certain and more challenging life. The lack of guarantees in life is precisely what generates anxiety (Corey, 1996). Thus, existential therapy helps clients to face the anxiety of choosing for themselves and to accept the reality that they are more than mere victims of deterministic forces outside themselves.

May (1981) posited that people come to counseling believing that they are victims of their circumstances and that others can free them. Thus, the purpose of counseling is to help them become aware of what they are doing and get them out of the victim role. Existential counselors, therefore, will encourage clients to accept personal responsibility (Corey, 1996; May & Yalom, 1989). If clients say, "I can't," for example, they will be asked to substitute, "I won't" (Corey, 1996, p. 186). Counselors will challenge clients to focus on how they created their own circumstances or situations rather than placing blame on others.

Another goal of existential counseling is to help clients increase their awareness of their finiteness stemming from personal confrontations with death (May & Yalom, 1989). Individuals who are unaware of the reality of death typically postpone living until sometime in the future. These individuals rarely live in the present and may be obsessed by past events or fearful of anticipated future events. By confronting their personal deaths, individuals may "count their blessings and become aware of their natural surroundings, e.g., changing seasons, seeing, listening, touching, and loving. Petty concerns are diminished" (p. 386).

Existential counseling also may examine the issue of isolation. Clients may discover in counseling that relationships with others may reduce their feelings of isolation but not eliminate them completely. Some individuals have great difficulty in being alone and may resort to a variety of behaviors to reduce time spent alone. These behaviors may include workaholism, substance abuse, and compulsive behaviors suited to avoiding the pain of loneliness. These individuals might have difficulty in expressing love or relating to other people, but they may use others to avoid confrontation with the pain of isolation. In counseling, clients may confront isolation, learn to be alone, and learn the means to gaining appropriate support and coping skills.

For some individuals, the issue of meaninglessness is profound and pervasive (May & Yalom, 1989) and is important to address in existential counseling (Frankl, 1969). They may experience existence as a circle of daily routines needed to sustain life. May (1953) believed that the chief problem during the middle decade of the 20th century was meaninglessness or "emptiness" (p. 13). The major solution to the problem of meaninglessness is engagement (e.g., helping and caring about others; interest in ideas or projects; searching, creating, and building). To help achieve this solution, counselors might need to explore the blocks of engagement with clients and determine what prevents clients from engaging in life.

After gaining insight into the issues of isolation, meaninglessness, fear of death, and responsibility, clients clearly are encouraged to take charge of how they now choose to be in their world. Effective counseling does not stop with awareness itself; counselors encourage clients to take action based on the insights that they have learned in counseling. Clients are expected to go out into the world and decide how they will live differently.

The Counseling Relationship

Existentially oriented counselors strive toward honest, mutually open, and authentic relationships with their clients. The central task and responsibility of the counselor is to seek to understand the client as a being and as a being in his or her world. No desks are placed between the client and counselor. No "authority-aspiring" diplomas are on the walls. The counselor and client are on a first-name basis. The counselor tries to make the client as comfortable as possible with the counseling process, answering questions openly and fully. There is no attempt to bring on transference.

The counselor strives to achieve moments of authenticity by relating to the client in a genuine caring fashion. Authenticity is a behavior pattern whereby decisions stem from being true to oneself and are made through conscious awareness (Strasser & Strasser, 1997). Conversely, inauthentic behavior stems from a compulsive, out-of-awareness type of action. The counselor invites the client to grow by modeling authentic behavior. The counselor is able to be transparent when it is appropriate to the relationship, and the counselor's own humanity is the stimulus for the client to tap potentials for realness.

Existential counselors typically focus on clients' current life situations, not on helping clients to recover personal pasts. This does not mean that counselors discount clients' pasts; rather, counselors reject the notion that the past "causes" the present given that such a deterministic approach denies the ability of humans to make choices about their lives (du Plock, 1997).

Existential counselors use a variety of counseling methods and techniques, varying not only from client to client but also with the same client at different phases of the therapeutic process (Corey, 1996). In fact, no set of techniques is specified or essential in existential counseling. More important, existential counselors give central prominence to their relationships with clients. The relationships are important in themselves because they are the stimulus for positive change in clients. The counseling process is a journey undertaken by both clients and counselors. In these relationships, counselors share their reactions to clients with genuine concern and empathy as a means of deepening the therapeutic relationships.

The Counseling Process

Ultimately, the process of counseling leads clients to make changes in their behavior and to live more meaningful lives. There are three phases of the process of existential counseling (Corey, 1996). During the initial stage, counselors assist clients in becoming aware of and exploring how the clients perceive and make sense of their existence. Clients examine their values and beliefs and become aware of the ultimate concerns of their existence. Counselors teach clients how to reflect on their own existence and focus on freedom (e.g., the clients' role in creating their problems of living). During the middle stage of existential counseling, clients are encouraged to more fully examine where their value systems come from (e.g., their sources and authority). This process of self-exploration leads to clients gaining new awareness and making decisions to change or restructure their values and attitudes. The final phase of existential counseling focuses on helping clients to put what they are learning about themselves into action. Clients take responsibility for change and learn to live a more purposeful existence.

Conclusion

Existential counseling is a philosophical approach to counseling. It helps clients by focusing on the true essence of human life. Existential counseling does not rely on a strict treatment model or techniques; rather, the focus of counseling is on understanding one's being in the world and the essence of existence.

Existential thinkers view confrontation with the ultimate concerns of existence as the cause of anxiety and pathology. The ultimate concerns of death, freedom, isolation, and meaninglessness play major roles in many persons' problems of living. Individuals who are unaware of the reality of death typically do not live life to the fullest, live obsessed with past events, and may be fearful of the future. Freedom refers to the responsibility of creating one's existence and the will to change. The ultimate concern of isolation refers to the reality that no matter how much we do to avoid being alone, we ultimately enter and leave existence in isolation. In regard to meaninglessness, humans require meaning to their lives and are responsible for creating meaning.

Existential counselors do not use a specific set of techniques with clients; rather, importance is placed on the therapeutic relationship. The counselor strives toward an honest, open, and authentic relationship with the client. The counselor's primary task is to understand the client as a being and as a being in his or her own world. Finally, through self-exploration and insight, the client becomes aware of the ultimate concerns of existence and his or her freedom in choosing to make changes and live a more purposeful life.

Future of Existential Counseling

During the 21st century, the struggle for meaning in an increasingly information-rich but personally isolating society will only increase the need for individuals to find meaning in the world and in their personal existence. Approaches to counseling such as cognitive/behavioral principles will be needed in reducing symptoms and developing coping skills, but existential counseling will be essential in helping individuals to wrestle with the questions of existence and meaning. As managed care has influenced the practice of counseling in mental health settings, the future of existential counseling might come into question. Clearly, it is

not a method that lends itself to an intervention process that includes only brief therapy and few sessions. If present and future counselors wish to provide this type of counseling, then research evidence supporting the effectiveness of existential counseling outcomes will be needed, and considerations of cost-effectiveness will need to be addressed.

References

Cohn, H. W. (1997). *Existential thought and therapeutic practice: An introduction to existential psychotherapy*. London: Sage.

Corey, G. (1996). *Theory and practice of counseling and psychotherapy* (5th ed.). Pacific Grove, CA: Brooks/Cole.

du Plock, S. (Ed.). (1997). *Case examples in existential psychotherapy and counselling*. Chichester, UK: Wiley.

Deurzen-Smith, E. (1988). *Existential counselling in practice*. Newbury Park, CA: Sage.

Deurzen-Smith, E. (1997). *Everyday mysteries: Existential dimensions of psychotherapy*. London: Routledge.

Frankl, V. E. (1963). *Man's search for meaning*. Boston: Beacon.

Frankl, V. E. (1965). *The doctor and the soul*. New York: Bantam Books.

Frankl, V. E. (1969). *The will to meaning: Foundations and applications of logotherapy*. New York: New American Library.

Frankl, V. E. (1978). *The unheard cry for meaning*. New York: Simon & Schuster.

Frankl, V. E. (1984). *Man's search for meaning* (3rd ed.). New York: Washington Square Press.

Heidegger, M. (1962). *Being and time*. New York: Harper & Row.

Holt, H. (1986). Existential analysis. In I. L. Kutash & A. Wolf (Eds.), *Psychotherapist's casebook* (pp. 177-194). San Francisco: Jossey-Bass.

May, R. (1950). *The meaning of anxiety*. New York: Ronald Press.

May, R. (1953). *Man's search for himself*. New York: Norton.

May, R. (Ed.). (1961). *Existential psychology*. New York: Random House.

May, R. (1969). *Love and will*. New York: Norton.

May, R. (1975). *The courage to create*. New York: Norton.

May, R. (1981). *Freedom and destiny.* New York: Norton.

May, R. (1983). *The discovery of being: Writings in existential psychology.* New York: Norton.

May, R., & Yalom, I. (1989). Existential psychotherapy. In R. J. Corsini & D. Wedding, *Current psychotherapies* (4th ed., pp. 363-402). Itasca, IL: F. E. Peacock.

Moustakas, C. (1994). *Existential psychotherapy and the interpretation of dreams.* Northvale, NJ: Jason Aronson.

Strasser, F., & Strasser, A. (1997). *Existential time-limited therapy: The wheel of existence.* Chichester, UK: Wiley.

Yalom, I. D. (1980). *Existential psychotherapy.* New York: Basic Books.

CHAPTER ELEVEN

Adlerian Counseling Theory and Practice

JON CARLSON

LEN SPERRY

The psychological theory of Alfred Adler (Ansbacher & Ansbacher, 1956; Dinkmeyer & Sperry, 2000) is especially well suited to professional counselors. This chapter provides an overview and a description of the theoretical premises, the steps/stages, the techniques and strategies, and a case example of Adlerian counseling.

Overview of Adlerian Theory

Adler's theory applied to counseling stresses the unity of the personality and understands people as complete beings. Behavior is viewed as purposeful and goal directed. The purposeful nature of human behavior is stressed, and counselors are trained to look for where their clients' behavior is headed as opposed to where it has been in the past. Adler believed that all people have feelings of inferiority. Sometimes, these feelings can overwhelm a person, and he or she will develop an inferiority complex. More often, these feelings serve as a catalyst and motivate the individual to compensate and strive for superiority. Each individual strives to be superior. This does not mean being superior to others; rather, it means obtaining a position in life that the individual perceives as important.

Adlerians believe that people are not determined by only heredity and environment; individuals also can interpret, influence, and create events. Adlerians are more interested in what an individual does as opposed to what he or she can potentially do.

Individuals are seen as social and decision-making beings who have a unified purpose and cannot be fully known without considering the contexts that give meaning to their lives (Sherman & Dinkmeyer, 1987). Persons have their own imagined unique goals, for example, "Only when people notice me will I be important" and "It doesn't make any difference whether you are right or wrong so long as you get your way"). These goals show each person's creative power to choose what to accept as truth, how to behave, and how to interpret events.

Adlerians refer to the personality as a lifestyle. A lifestyle is the road map that a person follows to reach his or her life's goals. By striving toward goals that have meaning, each person creates a unique style of living or lifestyle (Ansbacher, 1972). It is this concept that accounts for why all behaviors fit together to provide consistency to an individual's actions. No two people develop exactly the same lifestyle. A lifestyle consists of an individual's views about self and the world as well as the distinctive habits and behaviors that the individual uses to pursue his or her goals. The following are examples:

I am . . . weak and powerless.
The world is . . . demanding.
Therefore, . . . I need others to take care of me.

I am . . . brilliant and very intelligent.
The world is . . . primitive and ignorant.
Therefore, . . . why talk to others and be bored?

I am . . . not as able as others.
The world is . . . very competitive and ruthless.
Therefore, . . . I must overachieve so that no one will know.

Adler also stressed the importance of being a part of the human community and the individual's responsibility to create a healthy social world for all those involved. Each individual attempts to find a place or niche in the social world. Everyone belongs in different ways. Someone with a high degree of social interest belongs in a way that shows empathy for others and their life conditions. The degree to which an individual shares with others and is concerned with the welfare of others is how social interest is measured. Adler believed that the more social interest an individual possesses, the more mental health he or she possesses. Problems are viewed as stemming from individuals' not belonging to their social communities or belonging in unhealthy ways. Therapy helps to connect individuals to their social world in a meaningful and socially responsible fashion. Mosak (1979) expanded the number of Adler's life tasks from three to five:

1. Relating to others (friendship)
2. Making a contribution (worth)
3. Achieving intimacy (love and family relationships)
4. Getting along with ourselves (self-acceptance)
5. Developing our spiritual dimension (including values, meaning, life goals, and our relationship with the world)

When individuals master these five life tasks, they become healthy and fully functioning. However, when they have problems in any one of these tasks, they have a functional neurosis.

Another key concept that Adler identified is that of birth order. Adler observed that people often developed their basic lifestyle beliefs as a function of the psychological situations that they experienced in their families of origin. This psychological situation is influenced by one's birth order. Adler described very clearly the differences among the oldest child, the second child, the middle child, the youngest child, and the only child. These descriptions have become part of our everyday language, and descriptions are readily available (Dinkmeyer, McKay, & Dinkmeyer, 1998; Lemen, 1995; Sulloway, 1996).

Goals of Counseling

The main goal of counseling is to develop clients' social interest. This is accomplished by increasing their self-awareness and by challenging and modifying their fundamental premises, life goals, and basic concepts (Dreikurs, 1967). This generally involves helping clients to identify mistaken goals and assumptions. The process involves reeducating clients so that they can learn to live their lives in a more functional manner. Adlerian counselors provide information, teaching, guidance, and lots of encouragement. Encouragement is the most powerful method available for changing people's beliefs (Dinkmeyer & Losoncy, 1980). Encouragement focuses on clients' strengths and raises self-esteem. According to Mosak (1995), the goals of counseling can be summarized as follows:

- Fostering social interest
- Helping clients to overcome feelings of discouragement and inferiority
- Modifying clients' views and goals, that is, changing their lifestyles
- Changing faulty motivation
- Assisting clients in feeling a sense of equality with others
- Helping clients to become contributing members of society

Steps/Stages of Counseling

Adlerian counselors focus on the cognitive aspects of the counseling process. They realize that clients are discouraged and behave ineffectively because of their faulty cognitions, that is, their beliefs and goals. Adlerian counselors believe that once clients are aware of and correct their basic mistakes, they will feel and behave better. Therefore, counselors tend to look for major mistakes in thinking involving issues such as mistrust, selfishness, underconfidence, and unrealistic expectations. Adlerian counseling is structured around four central objectives that correspond to the four phases of the therapeutic process (Dreikurs, 1967):

1. *Relationship:* Establishing an empathic relationship between counselors and clients in which clients feel understood and accepted by counselors
2. *Assessment:* Helping clients to understand their beliefs and feelings as well as the motives and goals that determine their lifestyles
3. *Insight:* Helping clients to develop insight into mistaken goals and self-defeating behaviors
4. *Reorientation:* Helping clients to consider alternatives to the problems, behaviors, or situations and to make a commitment to change

Relationship

Adlerians believe that the counseling relationship is optimal when equality and mutuality are achieved between counselors and clients. Encouragement and empowerment are both the values and strategies for bringing about change. Establishing a mutual and collaborative relationship is the first important task in counseling. Achieving such a relationship means that counselors and clients have aligned their goals for the outcome of the counseling process. Counselors are responsible for creating the necessary conditions for an effective helping relationship. Clients are not passive recipients but rather active participants in the process. Clients recognize that they are responsible for their own behavior.

Throughout this process, counselors help clients to become aware of, accept, and use their assets. Counseling does not focus on an analysis of deficits and liabilities. The most powerful tool that counselors have is that of encouragement. Encouraged clients are aware of their strengths and have the personal power to change beliefs, feelings, goals, and (ultimately) behavior. This is a positive approach that stresses assets and solutions rather than liabilities.

Assessment

To Adlerian counselors, assessment is viewed as dynamic rather than as a static event. Adlerians perform lifestyle analyses, exploring family-of-origin issues, early recollections, and the influences of birth orders. Counselors listen closely, identifying individuals' beliefs, perceptions, and feelings. This is a unique form of reflective listening. Actually, it is an active attempt to understand all of the verbal and nonverbal components of communication. Counselors also observe movement to identify beliefs and goals. All material is understood in terms of how it fits into clients' lifestyles and how it can be used to increase understanding so as to become more effective in life (Dreikurs, 1967). Once counselors are able to understand clients and their lifestyles, they are in a better position to help clients reach the same understanding by seeing how basic beliefs and perceptions influence lifestyle. True understanding of one's lifestyle is the highest form of empathy. When clients feel understood and accepted, they can confront their problematic behaviors and faulty premises and can begin to change them.

Insight

Perception is primary in organizing motives and the ensuing movement. We act on the basis of how we see things, not on the bases of others' perceptions (Dinkmeyer & Sperry, 2000).

> Individual psychology holds that behavior is always a movement toward a goal. The goals are motivated; they act as a final cause for behavior; they are the end point of intentions. Goals themselves are often unconscious or at best dimly understood. Counseling helps clients understand and change their goals. (Shulman, 1985, p. 47)

Most people go into counseling believing that they are doing something wrong. Counseling helps individuals to recognize their mistakes and ideas about tasks and to understand why they act the way they do. In other words, the goal is to have clients understand the purpose of their behavior and how that behavior helps them to achieve their goals, which often are unconscious. Counselors are empathic and accepting but also are confronting. Insight about hidden goals and purposes occurs through confrontation and encouragement as well as through interpretation and other techniques designed to facilitate self-awareness and awareness of how people interact with others. The insight into what keeps people from functioning more effectively helps clients to resolve apparent contradictions. Clients begin to give up their mistaken goals to achieve functional behavior.

Reorientation

Reorientation is the action-oriented phase of counseling that is putting insight into action. There are a variety of active techniques that are used to promote this movement. The beliefs are understood; the goals and purposes are perceived; and the feelings are accepted, clarified, and explained in light of the accompanying beliefs and goals. Attention is directed toward seeing alternatives and toward making new choices. Carlson and Slavik (1998) and Mosak and Maniacci (1998) described and illustrated the Adlerian reorientation strategies, a few of which are highlighted in what follows.

Encouragement. Encouragement is a technique that focuses on helping clients to become aware of their worth. Through encouragement, clients recognize and own their strengths and assets so that they become aware of the power they have to make decisions and choices. Encouragement focuses on beliefs and self-perceptions. It searches intensely for assets and processes feedback so that clients will become aware of their strengths. Counselors are concerned with changing clients' negative self-concepts and anticipations.

Encouragement can take many forms depending on the phase of the counseling process. For example, at the beginning, counselors let clients know that they are valued by really listening to their feelings and intentions, and counselors stimulate clients' confidence by accepting them as full and equal participants in the process. While in the assessment phase of counseling, which is designed to illuminate strengths, counselors recognize and encourage clients' growing awareness of their power to choose and their attempts to change. In the re-orientation phase, counselors promote change by stimulating clients' courage (Dinkmeyer & Sperry, 2000).

Paradoxical intention. Adler called the paradoxical intention prescribing the symptom, whereas Dreikurs called it anti-suggestion, which is a technique in which clients are encouraged to emphasize or develop their symptoms even more. For example, when a husband does not keep an agreement with his wife, the counselor might suggest that this is a good way in which to resist her authority and encourage him not to do any work that she requests. It is best to make a paradoxical recommendation for a specific period of time and to treat it as an experiment. This process of experimenting encourages the client to see what can be learned from this experience. It makes the client dramatically aware of the reality of the situation and how the client must accept the consequences of his or her behavior. Adler and Dreikurs posited that to maintain a symptom, one must fight against it. The paradox often is effective because when the client comes for help, the counselor tells the client to go back and do what he or she was doing by no longer fighting it. The client then might be free to choose giving up the undesirable behavior.

Spitting in the client's soup. This was Adler's technique and comes from the boarding school practice of getting someone's food by spitting on it. This is an application of the Adlerian strategy of changing behavior by modifying its meaning to the person who produces it. The counselor must determine the purpose and payoff for the behavior and then spoil the gain by reducing the pleasure or usefulness of the behavior in the client's eyes. For example, when the counselor learns that an alcoholic husband's father also is an alcoholic and that the husband and his father did not get along, the counselor might make the statement, "I like the way you stay loyal to your father through your drinking. It is one way that you and he can stay connected." The husband has the right to continue to drink; however, the choice is a little less palatable than it was originally once he believes that he is actually being close to someone that he does not like. This is a strategy used with clients who are reluctant to complete an activity until they are perfectly sure that it is what they want to do. It consists of suggesting that, for a specified period of time, clients can act "as if" and behave how they say they want to behave. Clients usually protest that this will only be acting and not the real people. It is helpful, however, to suggest to clients that acting might not be phony and that they might be behaving how they really would like to behave if things were going the way that they would like them to go. It is helpful to suggest a very limited task with the expectation that the plan will work.

Push-button technique. This is a strategy that was developed by Harold Mosak. This method teaches that clients are responsible for their good feelings as well as their bad feelings. This strategy emphasizes that clients really do create their own moods. In the push-button technique, clients are asked to close their eyes and visualize events in their lives that made them feel very happy such as graduations and weddings. They are asked to reexperience the good feelings they had on those occasions. Next, clients are asked to visualize unpleasant events, such as when they felt humiliated and like failures, and to experience those feelings. They again are asked to reexperience and visualize the happy incidents and to associate their posi-

tive feelings. What Adlerian counselors want their clients to learn is that they can create their feelings by the thoughts they choose to have (Mosak, 1979, 1995).

Case Study

Jeremy is a 45-year-old White male who has been married to his wife, 45-year-old Sandra, for 25 years. They have three daughters who are 20, 15, and 12 years of age. He currently works as a private practice attorney while his wife works as a family physician in a large group practice. Jeremy referred himself to treatment due to unhappiness, boredom, being out of touch with his feelings, lacking friends, and claiming, "I am a lot like my father, who wasn't very happy and then he got worse."

Jeremy and his wife both are high academic achievers who met at a prestigious college and then went on to graduate school together, he in law and she in medicine. He indicated that she was his first and only love, although he had a lot of experience socially and sexually. He reported being a "recluse" until discovering drugs and alcohol, which helped him to change his social behavior. His reliance on drugs and alcohol grew until he admitted himself to an inpatient alcohol and drug treatment program 15 years ago. He had been sober and drug free until the past 2 years, during which he has begun to have wine with meals. His oldest daughter was very rebellious and currently is away at college, whereas the two younger daughters appear to be cooperative and are attempting to please their parents.

During the initial meeting, Jeremy indicated that he has had problems for a long period of time and indicated that he now wanted to solve them for good. It was determined that treatment should begin with a comprehensive life-style assessment and that the treatment should be based on the results of his assessment. Also, he was given the Millon Clinical Multi-axial Inventory (MCMI), which provides an assessment of personality and psychopathology.

The MCMI showed no serious Axis I psychopathology. Jeremy's scores, however, indicated both avoidant and dependent personality disorders.

Lifestyle Assessment Family Constellation

The lifestyle assessment indicated that Jeremy was the youngest of two children and the only male. He found his place through the following characteristics:

Hard work
Good grades
High achievement
Persistent
Patient
Obedient
Self-reliant
Critical of self
Worried
Withdrawn
Demanding and getting his way
Chip on his shoulder
Daring
Mischievous
Covertly rebellious
Sensitive
Easily hurt
Excitement seeker
Stubborn
Shy

Jeremy indicated that his parents were not able to take care of their children, so the chil-dren spent summers with their grandparents in Maine. He enjoyed getting away to rural Maine, where he could be alone. Both he and his sister were strong students; however, his sister was more socially active. She had friends and participated in many social activities. He described his father as intelligent, neurotic, and overly sensitive, whereas he described his mother as puritanical. Both parents valued having their children do well in school. Jeremy believed that he was growing up in a "dead family." It was "good, warm, and quiet but very dull." Jeremy reported having a very ambivalent (at best) relationship with his father.

Early Recollections

Jeremy completed the following early recollections:

1. *Age 3 years:* "I was on the toilet. I was yelling for Mom to come and wipe me. She didn't come; she was next door. I got really angry." *Most vivid*—sitting there scared; I didn't know where she was.

2. *Ages 3 and 4 years:* "I was in the backyard pool. I got out and peed in the bushes. My mother yelled at me, 'Don't do that'." *Most vivid*—bushes and how green they were and feeling very ashamed.

3. *Age 5 years:* "Dad had a train set. He and my sister were playing with it. It was really Dad's. I was too young and small and couldn't touch it. I was angry as I looked up and couldn't see over the side and the train." *Most vivid*—being under the table looking up at the bottom of the table.

4. *Age 6 years:* "I was in first grade, and I had to go to the toilet and ask the teacher for a pass, and she said no. It was painful. She thought I wanted out of the room." *Most vivid*—I thought it was unfair.

These recollections seem to show someone who believed that he needed help and could not do things alone. Jeremy did not really trust other people to be there for him, and he seemed to be worried about doing something wrong and being embarrassed in front of others. There appears to be a sense of "fear" in all of his recollections. He seems to have a belief that others can enjoy life while he only can watch (at best). He appears to be very powerless in each of these memories.

Intervention

Treatment involved helping Jeremy to understand how he was finding his place in life and in his marriage. He was surprised at how similar he and his father were, and although he verbalized this as the stated problem, he did not fully understand the degree or depth of the similarity. Both were loners, worked too hard, did not know how to please, and had distant relationships with family. This insight bothered him greatly. Therefore, he wanted his treatment to achieve the following goals:

- Have friends
- Be closer to his daughters
- Develop an equal relationship with his wife

Treatment involved challenging Jeremy's belief about himself and his relationship with others. He talked to his father about their distant relationship and became more aware of his jealousy and intimidation at his mother and sister's close verbal relationship. He began to call his father on a weekly basis and usually asked for advice. He also initiated contact with his sister and mother. He changed his role from that of a respondent to their questions to one of a more equal dialogue.

Jeremy began to call his oldest daughter at college each week. He also began regular walks with his middle daughter and the family dog, and he and his youngest daughter played video games at least two times each week. This is in sharp contrast to his pre-treatment behavior of hibernating in his home office and emerging only for meals.

Six weeks into treatment, it was learned that Jeremy's wife had been having an affair with a work colleague. Initially, he expressed great anger at her; however, he eventually realized how he "drove her away through his lack of involvement with her." He and his wife entered couples therapy and have begun to explore how they have handled difference through avoidance.

Jeremy decided to join the local tennis club, although he did not much care for sports. He knew that he would have regular contacts with other people who potentially could become friends. He also joined a local social action group and offered free legal counsel one afternoon each week.

At last contact, Jeremy reported being much more optimistic and alive. He was more involved with others, and although it was not easy or comfortable for him yet, he reported some satisfaction from the contacts. Jeremy decided to stop individual treatment, and he and his wife were working with a couples therapist to help them resolve the issues in their marital relationship.

The theoretical structure allows for the treatment of a wide variety of problems in a short period of time (Carlson & Sperry, 2000; Sperry & Carlson, 1996). The approach is well suited for work with individuals, couples, or families in school, clinic, or agency settings. Counselors, as well as managed care companies, find the practical focus of this approach appealing. It is likely that Adlerian ideas will receive increased support during the new century.

Case Summary

Through an accurate assessment, it was possible for both the therapist and the client to clearly see the important clinical issues. Treatment was tailored specific to the assessment, and Jeremy was able to work toward his stated goals. The Adlerian assessment—family constellation, early recollections, and so on—was very helpful to Jeremy. He clearly was able to understand his role in his problems. Uncovering his lifestyle allowed him to challenge his distancing behaviors and learn how to become more socially connected. It is very likely that he will need further follow-up treatment, but at this point in time he is choosing to work only on couples issues.

Conclusion

The ideas of Adler seem to be most appropriate as a theoretical basis for the counseling profession. Counselors can learn this deceptively simple, socially oriented way of understanding behavior and develop some clear, effective treatment strategies that produce results in a brief period of time.

References

Ansbacher, H. L. (1972). Adlerian psychotherapy: The tradition of brief psychotherapy. *Journal of Individual Psychology, 28,* 137-151.

Ansbacher, H. L., & Ansbacher, R. R. (Eds.). (1956). *The individual psychology of Alfred Adler.* New York: Harper & Row.

Carlson, J., & Slavik, S. (Eds.). (1998). *Techniques of Adlerian psychotherapy.* Philadelphia: Taylor & Francis.

Carlson, J., & Sperry, L. (2000). *Brief therapy strategies.* Phoenix, AZ: Zeig/Tucker & Theisen.

Dinkmeyer, D., & Losoncy, L. (1980). *The encouragement book: Becoming a positive person.* Englewood Cliffs, NJ: Prentice Hall.

Dinkmeyer, D., McKay, G. D., & Dinkmeyer, D., Jr. (1998). *STEP: Parent's handbook.* Circle Pines, MN: American Guidance Service.

Dinkmeyer, D., Jr., & Sperry, L. (2000). *Counseling and psychotherapy: An integrated, individual psychology approach.* Upper Saddle River, NJ: Merrill/Prentice Hall.

Dreikurs, R. (1967). *Psychodynamics, psychotherapy, and counseling.* Chicago: Alfred Adler Institute.

Lemen, K. (1995). *The new birth order book.* Grand Rapids, MI: Feming Revell.

Mosak, H. (1979). *On purpose.* Chicago: Alfred Adler Institute.

Mosak, H. (1995). Adlerian psychotherapy. In R. J. Corsini & D. Wedding (Eds.), *Current psychotherapies* (pp. 51-94). Itasca, IL: F. E. Peacock.

Mosak, H., & Maniacci, M. (1998). *Tactics in counseling and psychotherapy.* Itasca, IL: F. E. Peacock.

Sherman, R., & Dinkmeyer, D. (1987). *Systems of family therapy.* New York: Brunner/Mazel.

Shulman, B. (1985). Cognitive therapy and the individual psychology of Alfred Adler. In M. Mahoney & A. Freeman (Eds.), *Cognition in psychotherapy* (pp. 46-62). New York: Plenum.

Sperry, L., & Carlson, J. (1996). *Psychopathology and psychotherapy: From DSM-IV diagnosis to treatment* (2nd ed.). Philadelphia: Accelerated Development/Taylor & Francis.

Sulloway, F. (1996). *Born to rebel: Birth order, family dynamics, and creative lives.* New York: Random House.

CHAPTER TWELVE

Systems Theories

PATRICIA W. STEVENS

As we enter the 21st century, there is little doubt that the world that we live in is a dramatically changed one. The world that we lived in 10 years ago—even 5 years ago—has been altered by the rapid development of technology metamorphosing the systems in which we exist. The neighborhood of our lives today is the global neighborhood. The system that we live in today is a global one.

Systems theories were developed during the early 1940s and 1950s, but the underlying foundation of these theories is as relevant for the 21st century as it was 50 years ago. Although the original systemic theories were developed as family systems theories, the constructs of family systems can be used today in working with families and the larger systems in which families exist.

This chapter provides a brief historical overview of the development of family systems theory, a discussion of general systems theory and its present application, a survey of traditional family systems theories in use today, a discussion of techniques used in systems work, and a presentation of the future of systems theories in the counseling field.

The Development of Family Systems Theories

According to Jacobson and Gurman (1986), the "history of marital therapy is defined by the historian, so there is no single tale to be told" (p. 2). Marital and family therapy developed from a variety of sources. A comprehensive review of every source and person involved in the creation of family therapy is beyond the scope of this chapter. Therefore, an overview of systems theory is presented, and by virtue of this fact alone, some of the multitude of contributors to the field might be omitted. This should be seen not as a reflection of the importance of their contributions but rather as one of space limitations. Before 1960, there were very few books or articles in the field; by the 1960s, there were about three dozen; by the 1980s, there were more than 300; and currently, the sourcebooks, manuals, books, casebooks, articles, and texts are too numerous to count.

The underpinnings of family systems theory are based on the work of biologist Ludwig von Bertalanffy and his work with general systems theory (von Bertalanffy, 1934). General systems theory describes the way in which all living systems are structured and operate. Von Bertalanffy (1968) defined a system or an organism as "composed of mutually dependent parts and processes standing in mutual interaction" (p. 33). From this work, social scientists began to develop theories of family interaction and interdependence. Family systems theories extrapolated their theories to say that families are self-regulating and self-maintaining. Furthermore, as von Bertalanffy said about living systems, family systems theorists said that change in any part of the system changes all parts of the system.

A second source of the development of family systems theory began after World War II. Researchers began to examine the role that the family played in the development and maintenance of pathology or dysfunction. As veterans returned from the war, government funding was made available to address many of the issues that these men were bringing home from the war (e.g., psychological and physical impairment) as well as issues that they were facing when they returned home (e.g., reentry into the family, women staying in the workforce, consequences of hasty or delayed marriages, changes in sexual mores). Mental health workers who in the past had dealt with individual problems or with severe psychopathology now were expected to work effectively with a variety of family-related issues. This significant increase in psychological problems created a need for briefer, more effective, and less expensive therapy. One such method originated by the National Training Laboratory was human relations training groups (T-groups) or "therapy for normals" (Goldenberg & Goldenberg, 1996). Other group therapy theories also emerged during this time period. These group theories have as their basis many of the same concepts of human interaction as does systems theory.

Another foundational concept that was beginning during this time was the study and research of cybernetic theory. Cybernetics is the study of feedback loops in communication. The Macy Foundation Conferences began this work, and it continued after World War II. Gregory Bateson, an anthropologist who studied communication theory and worked with communication patterns in schizophrenic families during the 1950s, worked extensively to apply cybernetic theory to family communication patterns (Ruesch & Bateson, 1951; Watzlawick, Beavin, & Jackson, 1967).

A fourth area that contributed to the progress of family therapy was the study of families and schizophrenia. Theodore Lidz was the primary early researcher in this area (Lidz & Lidz, 1949). Bateson, at the Mental Research Institute, applied his concepts of cybernetics to this research, enlisting the collaboration of John Weakland, Jay Haley, and William Fry. From this research came the seminal article on the double-bind theory of communication as the cause of the development of schizophrenia in these families (Bateson, Jackson, Haley, & Weakland, 1956). Murray Bowen, another early researcher of systems, worked at the Menninger Foundation in Kansas during the 1950s and later at the National Institute of Mental Health (NIMH). He studied the families of schizophrenics by having the families move into the hospital with the patients and then observing the interactions of family members, particularly the mother-child relationship (Bowen, 1960). Later, Lyman Wynne continued this research at NIMH and examined the social organization of these families (Wynne, Ryckoff, Day, & Hirsch, 1958).

A predecessor to family counseling itself was marriage counseling and the child guidance movement. Abraham and Hannah Stone, as well as Emily Mudd and Paul Popenoe, were the earliest practitioners of marriage counseling in New York during the late 1920s and 1930s. The child guidance movement began in Vienna, Austria, during the 1900s with the work of Alfred Adler (Lowe, 1982). Adler believed that treating the growing child might be the most effective way in which to avoid adult neuroses and that personal and social goals could be understood only in the environmental and social context in which they exist.

Rudolf Dreikurs expanded Adler's work and the child guidance movement to the United States, establishing clinics in Boston, Philadelphia, and New York during the 1910s and 1920s. As these clinicians worked with children, they began to see that the problems were not the obvious ones brought to the clinics but rather stresses in the families. By the 1940s, child guidance clinics had begun to bring different specialties together to work on children's problems. These teams saw other family members but saw them separately from the children.

These separate and powerful influences intertwined to form the foundation of what today is family systems theory. It is impossible (as systems theory truly reflects) to separate these factors. Furthermore, it is the integration of all these changing dynamics that creates the "emergent property" known as family systems theory.

During the 1960s and 1970s, the field was seen as emerging from research-based work to clinical work. The field expanded, with more professionals beginning to use systems work in their practice. The list of these early therapists is impressive—Jay Haley, Salvador Minuchen, Virginia Satir, Carl Whitaker, Murray Bowen, Nathan Ackerman, Ivan Boszormenyi-Nagy, and James Framo, among others.

During this time, training institutes and academic programs began to form. Professional organizations and journals were launched. The American Association of Marriage Counselors (AAMC) changed its name to the American Association of Marriage and Family Counselors (AAMFC) in 1970 and then to the American Association of Marriage and Family Therapists (AAMFT) in 1978 as an acknowledgment of the combination of marriage counseling and family therapy. AAMFC published its first journal in 1975 (Goldenberg & Goldenberg, 1996). In 1967, Virginia Satir published her nationally recognized book, *Conjoint Family Therapy* (Satir, 1967). In 1961, Don Jackson and Nathan Ackerman cofounded the journal *Family Process*. Several prominent training institutes were thriving during this period—the Mental Research Institute in Palo Alto, California; the Family Institute of New York, the Philadelphia Child Guidance Clinic, the Family Institute of Philadelphia, the Boston Family Institute, and the Institute for Family Studies in Milan, Italy (Gladding, 1998).

The 1980s continued to produce changes in the field. As clinicians were trained in the programs and universities, a growing number of "second-generation" therapists began to emerge. The early researchers and pioneers of the field were aging, and these younger therapists had "new ideas and abundant energy" (Kaslow, cited in Gladding, 1998, p. 78). During the mid- to late 1970s, many women began to emerge as leaders in the field—Monica McGoldrick, Rachel Hare-Mustin, Peggy Papp, Cloe Madanes, Fromma Walsh, and Betty Carter, among others (Gladding, 1998).

During the 1980s, the American Psychological Association (APA) formed a Family Psychology division, and the International Association of Marriage and Family Counselors (IAMFC) was formed as an interest group within the American Counseling Association (ACA). In 1990, IAMFC became a division of ACA, with a membership of more than 7,000. During the 1990s, the AAMFT membership reached more than 20,000. Outcome research also became a priority during this time. As the field has grown and with the advent of managed care, family therapists need to corroborate with families the outcome or the effectiveness of systems work (Nichols & Schwartz, 1995).

General Concepts in Systems Theories

All of the systems theories discussed in this chapter, as well as those discussed in other chapters of this volume, have as their basic foundation the concepts that are presented in what follows. These concepts provide the framework for systems in general, whether describing a family, a school, a workplace, a classroom, or a country. Understanding these concepts gives practitioners a deeper awareness of individual functioning in the family system.

To adequately understand family functioning, the individual's behavior must be examined within the context of family interactions. Satir (1967) first described this interaction using the example of a mobile. All pieces are connected yet independent to the extent that the mobile hangs in balance with pieces not touching. However, if the parts are moved—say, by a breeze—then they are shown to be interdependent because when one piece moves, it causes the other pieces to move as well. As the breeze diminishes and finally ceases, the pieces also cease movement and return to balance.

General systemic concepts of functioning form the foundation of the idea of interdependence that is systems or, for purposes of this chapter, is families. The underlying framework of family therapy/systems theory includes the following concepts:

1. All systems seek *homeostasis.*
2. All systems incorporate *feedback loops* so as to function.
3. *Hierarchy* is an integral part of systemic functioning including all the *roles, rules,* and *subsystems* necessary. *Boundaries* are necessary to facilitate the existence of roles, rules, and subsystems.
4. The system cannot be understood by reductionism (analyzing the individual parts of the system); rather, it must be examined as an entity, synthesizing the component parts into a *whole.*
5. *Change* in one part of the system creates change in all parts of the system.

Homeostasis

Jackson (1957) used the term *family homeostasis* to define the natural tendency of families to behave in such a manner as to maintain a sense of balance, structure, and stability in the face of change. Inherent in this definition is the assumption that change in one family member will create change in all other family members. Buelow and Buelow (1998) argued that the family, unlike a human body, does not have a set temperature or balance point at which it operates optimally. They indicated that homeostasis always is changing in response to the family endeavoring to meet the needs of its members. They also stated that each person in the system may be affected at "greater or lesser degrees and with vastly different consequences" (p. 183).

There will be times when change requires families to adjust. Families (systems) have a natural resistance to change, which serves as a mechanism to avoid complete chaos during the change process. During these times, families will need to renegotiate their roles, rules, and boundaries to fashion a new, more functionally balanced structure to manage these changes. If families are too resistant to change, then they become rigid and tend to entropy. Conversely, too much flexibility produces chaos.

Feedback Loops

The early interaction between researchers in cybernetics and those in social science resulted in the concept of feedback loops being applied to family therapy. The essence of systems are these feedback loops. Feedback loops are essential to the functioning of systems, providing the communication that enables the system to continue functioning and maintain homeostasis. Feedback loops provide self-regulation and self-maintenance for the system. In simple terms, *feedback loops* are the communication between parts of the system or members of the family. Feedback serves two purposes: to move the system toward change and to bring the system back to balance. *Reinforcing feedback* moves the system toward change. Sometimes called *positive feedback,* this interaction can be thought of as "heating up" the system. As feedback continues, it increases (sometimes exponentially) the system's move from the original balance. Just as a snowball gains size as it rolls down a hill, so too does reinforcing feedback move the system rapidly away from its first point of balance.

Balancing feedback (sometimes called *negative feedback*), on the other hand, brings the system back to balance. This represents the "cooling down" of the system. Balancing feedback brings the system back to its goal. The amount of dissonance between the system and its goal determines how much feedback is necessary to regain homeostasis. A good example of balancing feedback is thirst. When the body's fluids are in balance, a person has no sensation of thirst. As the person exercises or sits in the hot sun, the body's fluids become unbalanced (the experience of the sensation of thirst). The person then drinks water, and his or her body regains fluid balance. How thirsty (or out of balance) the person is determines the amount of water that he or she drink, which in turn determines the person's return to fluid balance (O'Connor & McDermott, 1997).

Hierarchy, Roles, Rules, Subsystems, and Boundaries

These systemic concepts are so interrelated that it is impossible to discuss one without discussing all of them. *Hierarchy* refers to the structure of the family—how family members are classified according to ability or by rules and role definitions within their cultural perspectives. *Roles* may be determined by individuals' behaviors in performing rights (privileges) and obligations associated with certain positions within families and usually are related to complementary expected roles of others with whom individuals are involved (Gladding, 1998). It is through these roles and their interaction that families act out the covert and overt family rules.

Although roles vary across cultures, there appear to be some generic rules that define the roles of being male, female, mother, father, husband, wife, and child within a familial structure. As children grow, they will experience childhood, adolescence, and young adulthood. In addition, throughout an individual's life cycle, the person takes on a variety of roles—child, student, worker, spouse, partner, parent, retiree, and grandparent, among others (Super, 1990). Marital and parental roles, in particular, often are derived from the family of origin. These old roles may or may not be suitable for the present family. This may create unbalance and conflict as the new family endeavors to shift and change roles. Therefore, as family members move in and out of these roles and as rules change, the family becomes unbalanced and attempts to reestablish homeostasis through the creation of a new structure.

Rules are the mutual assumptions of the family as to how members should behave toward each other and the outside world. Rules within a family may govern (a) what, when, and how family members can communicate their experiences about what they see, hear, feel, and think as well as who has permission to speak to whom about what; (b) the extent and manner in which a family member can be different; (c) what it means to be a male or a female in this family as well as how sexuality is expressed; and (d) how family members acquire self-worth and how

much self-worth a family member can experience (Fisher & Harrison, 1997; Goldenberg & Goldenberg, 1996).

Culture might not change how the family is governed but might well change the consequences of breaking the family rules. For example, a European American family might punish a child who "talks back," whereas an Asian family might use shame to correct the child who breaks the family rule.

Subsystems are the smaller systems within each system—systems within systems. A family is composed of multiple subsystems. Subsystems exist to assist the family in carrying out its day-to-day functions. Each subsystem contributes to the entire system's maintenance. Subsystems may be established by a variety of means. They may be established along generational lines (e.g., grandparents, parents, siblings) or by mutual interest (e.g., who likes to read, play ball, or shop), by sex (e.g., female-female, male-male), or by task (e.g., who cleans the house or washes the car). Within each subsystem, a family member plays a particular role that has rules and expectations that accompany it. Family members, of course, can be in more than one subsystem, requiring the person to use the appropriate role and rules for that subsystem. The clarity of the subsystem boundaries is more important than the constitution of the subsystem. For example, the partner (or marital) dyad is a primary subsystem. It is a closed system in the sense that there are certain duties and primary functions that are performed only by this partner subsystem (e.g., earning money, managing the home). With the birth of a child, this partnership changes and expands to become a parental subsystem with added duties and functions. In effect, we now have two subsystems:

the partner subsystem (with responsibilities toward the relationship itself) and the parental subsystem (with parenting duties of caretaking, discipline, scheduling of activities, and so on).

Boundaries define the subsystems. Boundaries are like fences; they keep things out, and they keep things in. Boundaries exist between family members, between subsystems, and between the family and society. The best boundary can be compared to a picket fence. It is strong enough to keep the dogs out of the garden but open enough to see the flowers across the street and to visit with friends who walk by the yard. In family systems theories, boundaries exist on a continuum from clear to unclear and from rigid to flexible. In families with overly rigid boundaries, communication is constricted and family members are disengaged or isolated. There is a lack of expressed love, a low sense of belonging, and a lack of family loyalty. Again, the clinician must be aware of cultural norms when evaluating families. In many Asian families, for example, the cultural expectation would be that the father is more disengaged. The opposite of disengagement, enmeshment, occurs when the boundaries are unclear and diffuse. Enmeshed families leave little room for difference; unity is stressed, and emotions are shared (e.g., mother cries and so does child). Again, culture colors the perspective of this term. In the Latino/Hispanic culture, an "enmeshed" mother is not only expected but also highly valued (Minuchen, 1992). However, from a Western cultural perspective, well-defined boundaries are the most functional. They allow separateness but closeness as well as freedom and flexibility, and they are based on mutual respect.

Wholeness

Another systems concept is that of *wholeness*. Systems theorists believe that one cannot understand the system by dissecting it into its individual parts. In fact, the only way in which one can understand the family is by observing the whole system. This concept of wholeness also carries with it the idea of "emergent properties" (O'Connor & McDermott, 1997). Emergent properties are the properties of the system that exist only when the system is whole and functioning; conversely, if one takes the system apart, then the emergent properties no longer exist. For example, H_2O is the chemical equation for water. When one dissects water into its component parts, the result is hydrogen and oxygen, but when one combines these elements, the result is water. Nothing in the individual elements or even in the idea of combining the elements prepares one for the wetness of water (the emergent property). The picture on a television is another example of an emergent property of a system. Take a television apart, and one will not find the picture anywhere in the parts.

In a family operating as a system, these emergent properties are the behaviors that the family exhibits. When the system is separated into individuals, these emergent properties do not exist. All of us have had the experience of talking with a friend about someone with whom the friend is involved. The dynamics of the relationship are explained through the eyes of the individual (or the part of the system). Then, when we see these two people together, the experience is very different from what has been explained. This different experience of the functioning couples system is the emergent property of the system.

Change in the System

As discussed previously, the concept of change in one part of the system (or individual) changes the other parts of the system. An important aside to this concept, especially for counseling, is to always expect side effects. With a family system, this means that change is never only one interaction or behavior; rather, it is the systemic response to one behavior change. The interconnectedness of the system requires that all parts (individuals) shift in response to any change of movement by any other part (individual). And because people are not predictable, the counselor is never sure where this change will appear.

One final concept that is important in working with family systems is that of *family values.* Family values are the composite of the rules, roles, boundaries, and subsystems in the nuclear family as well as those same concepts passed down from the family of origin. Values may be shared or valued more strongly by one partner than another. Examples of values are education, athletics, musical ability, becoming wealthy, being a good wife and mother, and being a good male provider. Conflict occurs in families when mutually exclusive values are embraced or when gender-related values cannot be fulfilled (e.g., a family that values boys has only girls). Cultural values also are superimposed on family values and affect how the family values individual members and their accomplishments and behaviors.

An important note about values is necessary here. Not only is it important for the therapist to understand the family value system, it is imperative for therapists to be aware of their own values, beliefs, and prejudices. A therapist does not leave his or her family values at the door of the therapy room. These values are apparent in each intervention, question, or comment in

therapy. The therapist's values can affect the client family system in both positive and negative ways. Therefore, it is necessary for the ethical therapist to recognize that there is no value-free therapy.

Major Traditional Theoretical Orientations in Family Therapy

During the 1950s and 1960s, four major theoretical orientations were developed in the family systems field. These theories still provide the framework for training in marriage and family work today. They are structural family therapy, strategic family therapy, experiential family therapy, and transgenerational family therapy. Each of these theories is primarily associated with a particular individual who was instrumental in the conception of the theory and is known for demonstration of the individual's work with this theory. These theories, although inspirational in their time, now are viewed as a framework for clinical work at best or as simply unsubstantiated hypotheses providing information about family functioning at worst. These theories all focus on the family system and are differentiated by what the therapist "punctuates when working with the family" (Smith, 1991, p. 3).

Structural Family Therapy

Family structure is defined as the invisible set of functional demands that organizes how family members relate to one another. Structure represents the sum of the family rules. It arranges and organizes the family's component subunits or subsystems, thereby regulating the family's day-to-day functioning.

Subsystems are an important component of family structure. The partner dyad provides the basis of the family functioning. Complementarity is emphasized, and accommodation (i.e., allowing partners to reach their potential) is considered important (Smith, 1991). The parental subsystem is another important subsystem in the family, providing the "executive" or managerial functions. This subsystem focuses on parenting the children and may or may not be the same as the marital subsystem. The third significant subsystem is the sibling subsystem. The interaction between and among siblings gives children their first interaction with peers. The relationship between these and other family subsystems forms the family structure.

Salvador Minuchen, trained as a psychoanalytic therapist, formulated structural family therapy in response to working with inner-city children at the Wiltwyck School. He found that psychoanalytic techniques were not effective with this population. Given the stressful home environment of these children and the brief period of time he was given to work with them, he believed that therapy needed to be more directive, focused on present time, shorter in length, and action oriented. Given the issues that Minuchen observed in these families, constructing a functional family structure became an important aspect of therapy (Minuchen, Montalvo, Guerney, Rosman, & Schumer, 1967).

Structural family therapy focuses on learning clear boundaries—having overt role expectations and family rules as well as the family hierarchical system and the interdependent functioning of its subsystems. Individual symptoms are best understood in the context of family transaction patterns. Minuchen believed that change in family organization or structure must take place before the symptoms are relieved. The assumption of this theory is that changes and symptom reduction will follow change in the structure; that is, as the structure is transformed, positions of individual members are altered and personal experience changes, thereby creating symptom relief.

The structural family therapist strives to change dysfunctional family transaction patterns and to realign the family structure. The goal of therapy, in addition to symptom reduction, is to assist family members in learning alternate and more satisfying ways of dealing with one another, to have appropriate boundaries, and to replace outgrown rules.

Strategic Family Therapy

Strategic family therapy is present oriented, brief, creative, directive, and positive. Jay Haley said that strategic therapists design therapy according to the presenting problem (Haley, 1973). Based on communication theory (Bateson et al., 1956; Watzlawick et al., 1967) and on Milton's metaphoric style of giving indirect suggestions or directives and his ability to create a strategy for every problem (Haley, 1973, 1976; Madanes, 1991), strategic therapy concerns itself with family communication patterns and the sequential ordering of interactions involved in the presenting problem (Goldenberg & Goldenberg, 1996). The goal of therapy is to replace these maladaptive sequences of behavior with more satisfying sequences.

There are two varieties of strategic therapy: *problem focused* and *solution focused*. In problem-focused strategic therapy, the goal is to solve the presenting problem on which the family has agreed to work (Snider, 1992), not to provide insight or understanding. To achieve this goal, strategic therapists create unique interventions that fit the presenting client problems. Directives, or assignments to be completed outside of therapy sessions, often are given to clients. The purpose of a directive is threefold: (a) to get the client to behave differently, (b) to involve the therapist in the family life outside of therapy, and (c) to gather information (Goldenberg & Goldenberg, 1996). According to Madanes (1991), directives are the "basic tool of the approach" (p. 397). Solution-focused strategic therapy looks for the exception to the problem—the times when the problem does not exist.

Strategic therapy concentrates on how the family maintains homeostasis, on how family rules are maintained, on symmetrical and complementary relationships within the family, and on the quid pro quo of family member interactions (Gladding, 1998). Strategic therapy focuses on the importance of power in relationships within the family (Haley, 1976).

Other techniques used in this modality include *reframing, pretending, positioning,* and *paradoxical intervention.* Reframing is the art of attributing different meaning to behavior, allowing the client to see the behavior in a way that is more positive. Pretending, positioning, and paradoxical intervention are methods of defining the problem creatively for the client. (See Gladding, 1998, for detailed information on these techniques.) A major strength of strategic therapy is its ability to be used with a variety of families.

Experiential Family Therapy

The most atheoretical of the theories, *experiential family therapy,* does not rely on therapy; rather, it relies on the relationship or involvement of the therapist with the family (Smith, 1991; Whitaker, 1976). As an outgrowth of phenomenology, experiential therapists believe that understanding another person requires an understanding of the individual's perception of a situation, not simply the physical reality of the situation; in other words, the perception is the reality. Behavior is determined by personal ex-

perience and individual perception rather than by external reality.

Most closely associated with Carl Whitaker's work, this therapy emphasizes free will, choice, and the human capacity for self-determination and self-fulfillment. Experience is valued over rational thought or intellectualizing. Whitaker stated that there are as many ways to provide experience for change as there are dysfunctions. Therapists are active, are self-disclosing, use a variety of evocative directive techniques, and focus on the here-and-now ongoing life experiences of families. Therapists are real, authentic people who are spontaneous, challenging, and idiosyncratic (Goldenberg & Goldenberg, 1996).

The goal of experiential therapy is growth and assisting the family in learning creative ways of coping. This goal does not necessarily imply reduction of symptomatology (Whitaker & Keith, 1981). Whitaker (1975) used what he described as the "psychotherapy of the absurd"—taking the situation to its most ludicrous outcome—to accelerate change in the family system. This change then produces growth in the system and in the individuals within the system.

Transgenerational Family Therapy

Conceived by Murray Bowen and rooted in psychodynamic and general systems theory, *transgenerational family therapy* concludes that the past is active in the present. Understanding the past, therefore, is the key to understanding the present (Smith, 1991). This multigenerational transmission process conceptualizes the family dysfunction as the "result of the family's emotional system over several generations" (Goldenberg & Goldenberg, 1996, p. 178). The major tool for discerning this pattern is the genogram. A genogram provides a visual representation of three to four generations of the family complete with relational patterns.

Another important construct in transgenerational therapy is differentiation of self. Differentiation implies that an individual distinguishes between the feeling process and the intellectual process, allowing the individual to detach from the family's emotional entanglement (Friedman, 1991).

Chronic anxiety, which comes from the "territory of living" (Friedman, 1991, p. 139), is a key component in this theory. Bowen (1978) believed that triangulation occurs when anxiety is increased, creating the smallest stable relationship system—a triangle. This triangulation is the foundation for what Bowen called the family projection process. In this process, the child's level of differentiation approximates that of the parents. Emotional cutoff, or the individual's effort to detach from unresolved family emotional ties, also occurs when anxiety is high.

The goal of therapy is for the individual and family to understand the multigenerational patterns of behavior and to gain insight into the patterns that have affected the manner in which they function in the present. In this theory, therapy is with the most differentiated of the family members or with the couple. Rarely is the whole family seen in therapy. In contrast to experiential therapy, the therapist in transgenerational theory is calm and differentiated from the family system. Objectivity and neutrality are of utmost importance (Gladding, 1998).

Common Techniques in Systems Theories

Many of the techniques used in systemic family therapy span the theories. Structural, strategic, transgenerational, or experiential therapists may use the same techniques in clinical practice. It is important to realize, however, that the reason or theoretical explanation for the use of the techniques will vary from theory to theory and that it is this focus that separates the theoretical orientations.

Reframing

Reframing is the art of attributing different meaning to behavior so that the behavior will be seen differently by the family. This changes the original perception of an event or a situation and creates a new context that has an equally plausible explanation and places the event or situation in a more positive or constructive position. Reframing allows the family to see behavior that previously has been thought of as unchangeable as voluntary and open to change. It also may allow the family to shift its perception of behavior from negative to positive. In Minuchen's work with anorectics, he frequently reframed the behavior from "sick" to "stubborn." Also, reframing a mother's questioning of a daughter's behavior as "loving" rather than "intrusive" might reduce the tension in the relationship (Smith, 1991).

The Genogram

A genogram provides a visual representation of a three-generational family or the family's emotional field. Through the use of symbols, a genogram tells the family story. Names, dates, marriages, divorces, mental illness, substance abuse, and other relevant facts are included. In addition, symbols that represent the relationship among and between family members are presented. The genogram is an informational and diagnostic tool for the therapist and is a powerful intervention for the client.

The Empty Chair

The empty chair technique has been associated with Gestalt therapy but frequently is used in family therapy. It is of particular use in expressing thoughts and feelings to absent family members. It can be used to allow a family member to express thoughts or feelings to another family member (represented by the empty chair) that they are unable to express directly to that person. In family therapy, this intervention would be used with both members present in the session whenever possible.

Family Rituals

Rituals often are "prescribed" by the therapist to improve the structure of the family. Examples might include having the family eat dinner together, having a set homework time for children, and having partners spend time alone together (or apart). Allowing the family to explore and develop their own rituals also may prove to be highly therapeutic. Specific rules and roles would be defined for these rituals. These rules might include only positive talk and no problem solving at dinnertime or during the partner time together. Other rules might dictate that there be no television or radio during homework time and that parents are available for assistance during homework time.

Couples and families frequently exhibit predictable patterns of behavior that are unproductive. Rituals that create change in these patterns are effective. For couples, caring days can be established when each of the partners is asked to act in a caring manner toward the other. In therapy, the family that is fighting and distant might be asked to plan a mini-vacation or special event. This "planning" provides information and insight for the therapist and shifts the family view of its situation from unproductive to productive (a combination of reframing a situation and prescribing a ritual).

Tracking

Tracking adopts family symbols—life themes, values, significant family events—gathered from communication and deliberately uses them in conversation. Tracking provides several advantages. It allows the therapist to enter the family and provides information about the family structure and the sequence of events that are keeping the family in a predictable behavior pattern (Smith, 1991). Furthermore, it confirms that the therapist values what the family is saying and, without soliciting information, provides a view of family dynamics through its themes, values, and events (Goldenberg & Goldenberg, 1996).

Enactment and Reenactment

It is common to ask the family to bring an outside problematic interaction into the session and to reenact the situation. The therapist then will ask the family to employ a new set of interactions with this problem. This two-part technique empowers the clients to use their knowledge of how to change the problem and strengthens their ability through action. Family members experience awareness of their own transactions and often discover more functional ways of interacting (Minuchen, 1974).

Behavioral Analysis
or Assessment

Most family therapists do engage in ongoing observation of discrete acts exchanged by family members as well as antecedent stimuli and interactional consequences of problematic behavior. Family therapists focus on the function that the behavior patterns serve in the family. It is through the understanding of the function of the behavior that the therapist and family may begin to understand what is necessary and appropriate for change to happen.

It is through assessment, or the evaluation of family behaviors, that we determine treatment plans and objectives. Assessment can be informal (using observation) or formal (using one of the more than 1,000 family assessment instruments now available) (Touliatos, Perlmutter, & Strauss, 1990). Today, assessment is a vital part of accountability for third-party reimbursement as well as for ethical and legal concerns.

Strengths and Weaknesses

Systemically oriented therapy provides the clinician with a view of family problems that is not available through any other means. Systems (families) can behave in ways that are not apparent by looking at the individual parts (people) within the systems. To fully understand the issues, it becomes necessary to apply a systemic perspective to therapy.

As stated at the beginning of this chapter, our world is becoming increasingly interconnected. Distant problems affect our lives. Not only family problems but also environmental and political problems affect how we behave. "We live in a system in a world of systems" (O'Connor & McDermott, 1997, p. xiv). The strength of systemic thinking is that it allows us to discern a sense of pattern in events and to prepare for and have influence over the future using this understanding.

This shrinking global view presents one of the main criticisms of family systems theories. The early traditional theories focused only on the family system and its interactions without accounting for the larger systems in which these families existed. So, in the early theoretical work, there was little regard for culture and gender issues. Early family therapy also focused on working with White middle-class families. Since the late 1980s, however, family therapists have become active in integrating many different family forms into their therapeutic orientations.

Another criticism of family therapy is the concept of circular causality stating that each part of the system affects the other parts of the system in the same way. This concept implies an equality of power in family systems that does not exist in reality.

A third criticism of systemic family therapy is the pathologizing of the woman/wife/mother. Many of the early theories blamed the mother/wife for the dysfunction in the family and used techniques that devalued and demeaned the role of the woman in the family.

It is appropriate to say, however, that many of the family therapy approaches have begun to recognize these weaknesses. Many therapists today use a gender and culturally sensitive perspective with their therapy, and integrative therapy addresses the impact of systems outside of the family on the family system itself. "The future of the profession depends on the ability and flexibility of professionals to work with a wide variety of families" (Gladding, 1998, p. 432). So, as in all professions, family therapy continues to develop new methods and techniques that fit contemporary families.

Perspectives on the Future

Predictions about the future of family therapy are varied. Gladding (1998) and Gurman and Kniskern (1992), experienced and knowledgeable family therapists and prolific writers in the field, provided the following picture of the future:

1. Family therapy, like all therapeutic modalities, will be more insurance driven than in the past. This will create the need for more accountability through objective goals and treatment plans and briefer therapy.

2. Family therapy theories will become more integrated. Integrated procedures and techniques will take the place of specialized theory.

3. Family therapists will focus more on specific individual psychiatric disorders.

4. Family therapy will be more influenced by research findings. Treatment will be offered based on empirical evidence rather than on intuition. There will be an integration of biological and psychological factors based on the ever-increasing technological advances in research.

In summary, it is an exciting time to be in the family therapy field. Family therapy is both a traditional field and a changing field. Family therapists need to be knowledgeable about the history, theory, practice, and process of the profession (Gladding, 1998). They must be knowledgeable about societal changes and must be aware of the variety of family arrangements that they will encounter. Family therapists need to be open to the new methods and techniques available today. In other words, they must be

systemic in their professional lives as they strive to synthesize the past and present in family systems and the larger systems in which families exist.

References

Bateson, G., Jackson, D. D., Haley, J., & Weakland, J. (1956). Toward a theory of schizophrenia. *Behavioral Science, 1,* 251-264.

Bowen, M. (1960). A family concept of schizophrenia. In D. D. Jackson (Ed.), *The etiology of schizophrenia.* New York: Basic Books.

Bowen, M. (1978). Family therapy after twenty years. In S. Arieti, D. X. Friedman, & J. E. Dyrud (Eds.), *American handbook of psychiatry: Vol. 5. Treatment* (2nd ed.). New York: Basic Books.

Buelow, G. D., & Buelow, S. A. (1998). *Psychotherapy in chemical dependence treatment.* Pacific Grove, CA: Brooks/Cole.

Fisher, G. L., & Harrison, T. C. (1997). *Substance abuse: Information for school counselors, social workers, therapists, and counselors.* Boston: Allyn & Bacon.

Friedman, E. (1991). Bowen theory and therapy. In A. S. Gurman & D. P. Kniskern (Eds.), *Handbook of family therapy* (Vol. 3). New York: Brunner/Mazel.

Gladding, S. T. (1998). *Family therapy: History, theory, and practice.* Upper Saddle River, NJ: Merrill/Prentice Hall.

Goldenberg, I., & Goldenberg, H. (1996). *Family therapy: An overview.* Pacific Grove, CA: Brooks/Cole.

Gurman, A. S., & Kniskern, D. P. (1992). The future of marital and family therapy. *Psychotherapy, 29,* 65-71.

Haley, J. (1973). *Uncommon therapy: The psychiatric techniques of Milton H. Erickson, M. D.* New York: Norton.

Haley, J. (Ed.). (1976). *Problem-solving therapy.* San Francisco: Jossey-Bass.

Jackson, D. D. (1957). The question of family homeostasis. *Psychiatric Quarterly Supplement, 31,* 79-90.

Jacobson, N. S., & Gurman, A. S. (Eds.). (1986). *Clinical handbook of marital therapy.* New York: Guilford.

Lidz, R. W., & Lidz, T. (1949). The family environment of schizophrenic patients. *American Journal of Psychiatry, 106,* 332-345.

Lowe, R. N. (1982). Adlerian/Dreikursian family counseling. In A. M. Horne & M. M. Ohlsen (Eds.), *Family counseling and therapy.* Itasca, IL: F. E. Peacock.

Madanes, C. (1991). Strategic family therapy. In A. S. Gurman & D. P. Kniskern (Eds.), *Handbook of family therapy* (Vol. 3). New York: Brunner/Mazel.

Minuchen, S. (1974). *Families and family therapy.* Cambridge, MA: Harvard University Press.

Minuchen, S. (1992). Constructing a therapeutic reality. In E. Kaufman & P. Kaufman (Eds.), *Family therapy of drug and alcohol abuse* (pp. 1-14). Boston: Allyn & Bacon.

Minuchen, S., Montalvo, B., Guerney, B. G., Rosman, B. L., & Schumer, F. (1967). *Families of the slums.* New York: Basic Books.

Nichols, M., & Schwartz, R. C. (1995). *Family therapy: Concepts and methods* (3rd ed.). Boston: Allyn & Bacon.

O'Connor, J., & McDermott, I. (1997). *The art of systems thinking.* London: Thorsons.

Ruesch, J., & Bateson, G. (1951). *Communication: The social matrix of psychiatry.* New York: Norton.

Satir, V. (1967). *Conjoint family therapy.* Palo Alto, CA: Science and Behavior Books.

Smith, R. L. (1991). Marital and family therapy: Direction, theory, and practice. *Counseling and Human Development, 23*(7), 1-12.

Snider, M. (1992). *Process family therapy.* Boston: Allyn & Bacon.

Super, D. E. (1990). A life span, life-space approach to career development. In D. Brown, L. Brooks, & Associates (Eds.), *Career choice ad development: Applying contemporary theories to practice* (2nd ed., pp. 197-261). San Francisco: Jossey-Bass.

Touliatos, J., Perlmutter, B. F., & Strauss, M. A. (Eds.). (1990). *Handbook of family measurement techniques.* Newbury Park, CA: Sage.

von Bertalanffy, L. (1934). *Modern theories of development: An introduction to theoretical biology.* London: Oxford University Press.

von Bertalanffy, L. (1968). *General systems theory.* New York: George Braziller.

Watzlawick, P., Beavin, J. H., & Jackson, D. (1967). *Pragmatics of human communication.* New York: Norton.

Whitaker, C. A. (1975). Psychotherapy of the absurd: With special emphasis on the psychotherapy of aggression. *Family Process, 14,* 1-16.

Whitaker, C. A. (1976). The hindrance of theory in clinical work. In J. Guerin (Ed.), *Family therapy: Theory and practice* (pp. 154-164). New York: Gardner.

Whitaker, C. A., & Keith, D. V. (1981). Systemic-experiential therapy. In A. S. Gurman & D. P. Kniskern (Eds.), *Handbook of family therapy* (pp. 187-225). New York: Brunner/Mazel.

Wynne, L. C., Ryckoff, I. M., Day, J., & Hirsch, S. I. (1958). Pseudomutuality in the family relationships of schizophrenics. *Psychiatry, 21,* 205-220.

Postmodern Theories
of Counseling

SANDRA A. RIGAZIO-DiGILIO

How is meaning constructed? How do our constructions influence the ways in which we experience, understand, and participate in our world? Can we use these conceptualizations to inform counseling? These are fundamental questions postmodern theorists, practitioners, and researchers are attempting to answer. Approaches emerging from their work represent an important alternative to modern counseling practice. That is, whereas modernistic assumptions purport a single, consistent, and recognizable reality that exists independent of the knower, postmodern perspectives suggest the existence of multiple realities derived from interactions between the knower and the environment that are mediated by individual, social, cultural, and temporal factors. Accord-

ingly, whereas traditional approaches view clients and client systems as nonadaptive reactors to a known environment and aim to improve their synchrony with the environment, postmodern approaches view them as active agents within the environment and seek to extend their capabilities beyond intrapersonal, interactional, and sociocultural constraints.

This chapter describes the core theoretical and applied characteristics identified by the postmodern branch of counseling. An accounting of the historical, epistemological, and philosophical trends that contributed to the emergence of postmodern perspectives provides a contextual backdrop. Foundational assumptions that inform the infrastructure for this branch and differentiate it from the traditional modernistic branch are described. Moving toward greater specificity, the distinguishing features used to classify three domains of postmodern thought are elucidated. A description of personal construct theory illustrates the principles, constructs, and practices linking these domains. Representative approaches for each domain are briefly defined to highlight the various frames of reference on which clinicians can draw to construct or extend their counseling models. Counseling methods that are common across domains are defined. A case example illustrates how postmodern theory translates to practice. Finally, the potentials and constraints of this branch are described, and future implications for expansion are discussed.

The Postmodern Transformation

The postmodern branch of counseling draws from the epistemological foundation of the same name (Botella, 1995). Originating in the works of Vico (1725/1948), Kant (1791/1969), and Hegel (1830/1975), the postmodern perspective began to gain influence as an alternative philosophical voice during the 20th century. Vailhinger (1911/1924) reinforced the idea that individuals can design creative "as if" constructions of self and environment to construct a multiplicity of interpretations and possibilities beyond those of the dominant discourse. He and others who speculated about constructed notions of reality (see Heidegger, 1927/1962; Wittgenstein, 1969) challenged the modernistic belief in a credible reality that defined a common point of reference for all. Postmodern philosophers (see Derrida, 1978; Foucault, 1980; Lyotard, 1983) convincingly deconstructed modernistic assumptions inex-

tricably intertwined in the infrastructures of various disciplines. They revealed the encapsulated nature of our knowledge structures and methods of knowledge advancement and the consequent ramification that theories and ideas, by design, emerge and gain prominence through dominant, elitist, and discriminatory practices that perpetuate traditional, unidimensional, and noninclusive power structures.

Theoretical breakthroughs in science, mathematics, aesthetics, sociology, linguistics, and psychology added credibility to the alternative voice. Kuhn's (1974) examination of the history of science provided a well-reasoned position regarding our reliance on subjective and objective images of reality to construct scientific paradigms. Einstein's deconstruction of Newtonian physics (Einstein, Lorentz, Weyl, & Minko, 1924), Hawkings's (1988) introjection of a self-regulating universe, Gleick's (1987) advancement of chaos theory, and Heisenberg's (1958) introduction of the uncertainty principle further helped to redefine the role of subjectivity in knowledge construction.

The methods of scientific discovery presumed credible also shifted from quantifiable processes aimed at reductionism, causal explanation, and prediction to qualitative methods that actively positioned the knower as a participant in the construction of personal and social realities (e.g., ethnographic analysis, hermeneutic processes, critical incident analysis). This shift represented a fundamental transformation in our ideas about the role of learning and the learner (Mahoney, 1991). "The perspective of the observer and the object of observation are inseparable; the nature of meaning is relative; phenomena are context-based; and the process of knowledge and understanding is social, inductive, hermeneutic, and qualitative" (Gergen,

1985, p. 268). The source of knowledge is based within our own thought process and is affected by the symbolic means that we use to give meaning to our reality.

Postmodern counseling also represents a rejection of modernistic practices that perpetuate positivist modes of inquiry and intervention by advancing assessment procedures that pathologize difference and treatment plans intended to ameliorate dysfunction assumed to reside within clients. Postmodern approaches instead advance multidimensional, nonpathological, and contextually contingent practices that provide ways in which to conceptualize and influence individual, relational, social, and cultural contributions to and constructions of disorder (Rigazio-DiGilio, Ivey, & Locke, 1997). Assessment practices operationalize notions of multiple perspectives, socially negotiated knowledge, and broader terrains of inquiry, and treatment plans guide clinicians to intervene within many levels of human, systemic, and cultural existence. The aim is to partner with clients to create viable personal and social constructions rather than to eliminate or revise cognitive distortions or corrective emotional experiences (Neimeyer & Harter, 1988).

Foundational Postmodern Assumptions

The postmodern branch of counseling builds on three core assumptions that extend beyond the hegemonic influences of a positivist ontology to reveal dialectic, reciprocal, and heterarchical aspects of human and systemic organization and development. First, individuals and families are self-organizing systems that are self-renewing and self-referential (Caple,

1985). Our sense of self and self-in-relation emerges within an open system of circular feedback with the environment (Steenbarger, 1991). We construct individual worldviews by participating in various contexts over time (Ivey, 2000) and construct collective worldviews by participating in resonating experiences with enduring relationships within these contexts (Rigazio-DiGilio, 1997). Second, knowledge of one's individual and collective selves and of the world is rooted within individually and socially constructed symbolic processes. Language is situated and contingent, and it actively creates and constrains new experiences, influencing what is perceived as reality (Mahoney & Lyddon, 1988). Thus, reality is relative and changeable, a function of both personal and social constructions (Lyddon, 1989). Third, morphogenic structures undergo holistic and heterarchical transformations toward broader arrangements, representing organizations of diversity that emphasize collaborative structures, distributed authority, and asset multiplicity and ambiguity. These organizational forms stand in direct contrast to the modernistic hierarchical/unidimensional structures espoused by the still dominant positivist paradigm and yet appear to be more in synchrony with our postmodern, multicultural world. In this regard, development moves toward increasing interdependence, minimal hierarchy, and organizational heterogeneity.

Differentiating Postmodern Counseling Theories

Three domains have emerged within postmodern counseling: constructivism, social constructionism, and co-constructivism. Whereas these domains draw from one another, each can be distinguished by the unique points of reference deemed primary. One distinction is the levels of reality (e.g., intrapsychic, interactional, contextual) identified as a source of resource or constraint, an origin of health or pathology, or a target of assessment and intervention (Rigazio-DiGilio et al., 1997). This distinction helps to identify models that address the terrain of investigation and methods of inquiry best suited to a client, and it cautions us against rigidly adhering to any one perspective.

Constructivist Perspectives

Constructivist theories emphasize an endogenous perspective on the nature of self and focus on internal processes of self-construction, giving less attention to the social contexts influencing individual physiology, cognitive functioning, and systemic meaning making. Radical formulations based on *ontological realism* define reality as a subjective phenomenon that exists as an extension of the knower (Maturana & Varela, 1987; von Foerster, 1984; von Glaserfeld, 1991; Watzlawick, 1984). Less radical formulations based on *hypothetical realism* posit that we live in an unknowable but nonetheless inescapable world that can enhance or constrain our ability to be self-sufficient creators of our experience (see Guidano, 1987; Howard, 1991; Kelly, 1955; Mahoney, 1991; Polkinghorne, 1994). Constructivism focuses on the process of self-construction used to define a sense of self, self-in-relation, and environment. Constructivism also asserts, with varying conditions of exception, the capacity of individuals to extend beyond constraining and oppressive con-

structions toward multiple perspectives and possibilities.

Social Constructionist Perspectives

Social constructionist theories represent variations within an exogenous perspective that emphasize social meaning-making processes (Berger & Luckmann, 1966; Burr, 1995; Hayes, 1994). How we come to understand ourselves, our relationships, and our world is assumed to emerge from linguistic constructions maintained and perpetuated in the domain of intersubjective conversation (Guterman, 1994). Therefore, our meanings reflect socially constructed concepts that are subject to change depending on the social-cultural-historical context in which we live (D'Andrea, 2000). Attention is given to identifying the cultural and contextual factors influencing discursive transactions and to assisting clients in extending beyond dominant discourses that constrain individual, interrelational, and cultural possibilities (see Anderson & Goolishian, 1988; Brown, 2000; Daniels & White, 1994; Dell, 1982; Gergen, 1991; Hoffman, 1990; Keeney, 1983; White, 1989). Whereas the focus of assessment is the wider context, less attention is given to intervening within this wider environment to loosen rigid or dominant constructions that can constrain, govern, and oppress the interactive discourse that determines reality.

Co-Constructivist Perspectives

Co-constructive theories (see Becvar & Becvar, 1994; Ivey, 2000; Neimeyer & Neimeyer, 1994) draw from endogenous and exogenous perspectives, asserting "a need to shift back and forth between environmental and organismic reference points, assigning top priority to neither" (Prawat & Floden, 1994, p. 45). How we define self, self-in-relation, and context is co-constructed in constant person-environment transactions (Ivey, Gonçalves, & Ivey, 1989) involving individuals, relationships, and the social realities that emerge from these transactions.

The person-environment dialectic is a cultural exchange process that includes issues such as gender, race, community background, physical variations, and educational levels (Ivey, 2000).

> When power differentials exist, the nature of the interaction is altered. Issues of social and economic oppression negatively influence the development of personal and collective competencies. So can any dissonance that is created when environmental demands are outside the individual's or family's physical, psychological, cultural, moral, or spiritual sense of self or self-in-relationships. (Rigazio-DiGilio, 2000b, p. 1024)

Constraining dissonance also may emerge when the environment labels a familiar way of perceiving and acting as substandard or deviant. Thus, representative models recognize a need to balance attention to internalized cognition and emotion with equal attention to the wider contexts (Rigazio-DiGilio et al., 1997). Clinicians form partnerships with clients designed to promote change in inner thoughts and feelings and in how they participate in their wider contexts. Such changes are intended to have an ameliorating effect within clients' own personal spheres and a concomitant effect on the constraining interactions that may exist in the wider sociocultural/sociopolitical context

(Ivey, 1991; Ivey, Ivey, & Simek-Morgan, 1997; Locke, 1992; Rigazio-DiGilio, 1994; Rigazio-DiGilio et al., 1997).

Representative Counseling Approaches

Although postmodern approaches are holistic and integrative, there are some distinctive features each advances within the broader postmodern frame. In this section, one model is reviewed that links constructivist, social constructionist, and co-constructivist approaches. Then, approaches representative of each perspective are highlighted.

Personal Construct Psychology: A Foundational Postmodern Approach

George Kelly built on *constructive alternativism philosophy* to explain how individuals use personal constructs to create meaning. As individuals interact with their world, they develop constructs to organize events, people, and context in ways that allow them to extract meaning. Thus, they come to know and experience reality through their active construction of it.

Personal constructs are hypotheses about events yet to be considered. Constructs suggest a wide range of opportunities and give meaning to our past and direction to our future. Although constructs are not weighted similarly, we tend to organize these hierarchically, with *superordinate constructs* being more abstract, permanent, and central to self-identity. These core constructs are the most difficult to alter. A subset of core constructs, termed *core role constructs,* is concerned with roles assumed in social interactions. Kelly elaborated his *fixed role therapy model* to help examine the opportunities and constraints associated with our familiar social roles.

Three of Kelly's core ideas, embedded in contemporary constructivists models, suggest that (a) clients construct meanings from their interactions with the world, (b) clients and practitioners co-construct counseling encounters, and (c) counselors should assume a credulous approach to client interpretations. This does not mean accepting client accountings; rather, it means knowing that what is said reveals clients' psychological realities (Fransella, 1995).

Nonrationalistic, Process-Oriented Cognitive Therapy: A Constructivist Approach

Many counseling models draw from constructivism, including solution-focused therapy (de Shazer, 1992), rational-emotive behavior therapy (REBT) (Ellis, 1979), and Adlerian counseling (Adler, 1926). A representational approach based on attachment theory is Guidano's (1991) nonrationalistic, process-oriented cognitive therapy.

Counselors working from this theory help clients to regain a self-synthesizing ability that encourages them to reconstruct their understandings of themselves and permits them to better assimilate the dialectic forces operating in their lives. The goal is to enhance client self-identity and options for dealing with life incongruities. Relying on the strength of the therapeutic alliance, counselors use techniques that help clients to examine their subjective and objective perspectives about immediate experiences and affective relationships. Self-observational techniques and orthogonal feedback from counselors encourage clients to decenter from immediate experience and to recenter on the self. This model places individual meaning-making processes at the center of treatment. The model is consistent with Martin's (1988) call for researchers to pay more attention to the relationships between counselors' and clients' theories of self, with the recognition that clinical practice can benefit from detailed accountings of what transpires in the heads of both clients and counselors.

Orthogonal Interactive Therapy: A Social Constructionist Approach

Social constructionists address how language is used to define and influence the ubiquitous power differentials that are a part of interactions between individuals and their environments. "Such a view of language-in-use leads inevitably to an analysis of power relations, whether at the level of individuals (e.g., within a marriage), groups (e.g., professional societies), or cultures (e.g., competing nations)" (Neimeyer, 1998, p. 137). The focus of social constructionist models is to surface client worldviews shared with significant others and to examine the power arrangements embedded in their languaging systems that govern their roles and identities. Helping clients to alter and modify the linguistic, power, and social contextual variables contributing to their meaning-making processes is a primary aim of this domain.

The orthogonal interactive approach (Efran, Lukens, & Lukens, 1990; Gordon & Efran, 1997) attends to ongoing diagnosis as the primary ingredient of counseling. This model is based on the assumptions that language is a form of social action and that social and linguistic processes combine to generate and/or ameliorate interpersonal and psychological problems.

> Language is what allows humans to formulate purposes, distinguish and label objects, and carve identifiable "events" out of the continuous flux of the universe. . . . Contrary to what everyone learns in school, the so-called higher cortical functions do not take place inside one's head; they take place in the community. (Efran & Cook, 2000, p. 125)

Language, therefore, is communal action taking place in a social context rather than a representation of purely internal behavior. As people use language to tell their stories, they are developing their senses of selves.

Using language in the counseling session, a clinician can create a miniculture with its own rules that can help to trigger therapeutic change. Counseling sessions take on conversational qualities to create a new social context. Central to the definition of this new context is the introduction of orthogonal interactions between the client and counselor. An orthogonal interaction is conceived as the trigger that enables a system to adapt to changing circumstances. These interactions change the relations and, therefore, generate novel adaptations and accommodations in the larger social systems to which the client belongs. Orthogonal interactions are out of the ordinary and raise questions about the inherent contradictions of client stories, illuminate reifications and paradoxes embedded in these stories, and provide opportunities for developing larger frameworks that can open up possibilities for how life might be lived.

Developmental Counseling and Therapy/Systemic Cognitive-Developmental Therapy: A Co-Constructivist Approach

Co-constructivists view individuals, families, and environments as both unique structures and interrelated systems, and they attend to both the heterarchical development and functioning of each structure and the dialectic exchanges that occur among structures. Counseling protocols offer guidelines for weighing the relevance of each structure and for facilitating change within and across structures (Rigazio-DiGilio, 2000b).

Developmental counseling and therapy (DCT) (Ivey, 2000) and systemic cognitive-developmental therapy (SCDT) (Rigazio-DiGilio, 2000a) form an integrative and transformative approach that incorporates multi-level interpretations of disorder ranging from intrapsychic phenomena to wider system narratives. Individual and collective worldviews are co-constructed in dialogic exchanges that occur within the parameters inherent in individual genetic endowment and worldview, system organization and worldview, and contextual realities and constructions. How we individually and collectively experience, understand, and participate in the world depends on these parameters, our life tasks, and our positions in wider contexts.

How individuals, families, and wider contexts contribute to and construe disorder is seen as a natural and logical consequence of developmental and contextual history (Ivey, 1991) and of the real or imagined positions of relatedness and power held by participants in the stressor experience (Rigazio-DiGilio, 1997). Distress is framed as a nonpathological response to developmental and contextual stressors that result when discrepancies or oppressive forces emerge between clients and wider contexts. Given this frame, presumed "pathological" reactions are seen as rational responses to irrational or discriminatory situations (Ivey & Ivey, 1998).

DCT/SCDT considers the territory of examination to include the disorder as it is embedded within a co-constructive dialogic process encompassing relevant biological, social, and contextual histories; the culturally defined illness ontology, the worldviews brought to bear by all participants, and the interactive discourse that emerges. DCT/SCDT suggests that the recursive and interdependent factors influencing how individuals, relationships, and wider collectives construe pathogenic experiences need to be determined, as do the factors that affect which domains have power and influence, at any given time, during interactive discourse.

By directly linking co-constructive and developmental principles to the counseling process, DCT/SCDT offers assessment and treatment strategies that can be applied during the immediacy of the counseling encounter. Assessment is linguistically based and generates discourse among individuals, systems, and institutions contributing to and construing the issues promoting treatment. This discourse uncovers identifiable language patterns in client and participant narratives that reflect particular schemata governing the expression and self-interpretation of symptomatic ideas, emotions, and actions that are used to determine where counselors can most flexibly intervene to relieve unproductive stress. Counseling focuses on co-constructing therapeutic and consultative environments within which broader narratives

emerge and become points of departure to advance multiple perspectives regarding treatment issues and to open up alternative ways for participants to understand one another and work together toward the management or dissolution of these issues. The intent is to involve relevant participants in co-constructing a broader narrative and operating within this extension.

Common Postmodern Counseling Practices

In this section, counseling practices common across most postmodern perspectives are described to demonstrate the connection between theory and practice and to distinguish postmodern methods from their modernistic counterparts. A case example is provided.

Conceptualizing Treatment Issues Defined by the Problem Narrative

Michelle (age 32 years) entered counseling when psychopharmacological intervention did not successfully reduce her depressive symptoms. Her only other depressive episode had been successfully treated in this manner. It occurred during her transition home from an extended period of inpatient rehabilitation for a cervical spinal cord injury that left her paralyzed below the neck. Due to the location of the program, she was geographically separated from her husband Robert (age 32 years) while learning to maintain her physical and emotional health using extensive technical and human assistance including a ventilator, power-chair, and health attendant. Robert's participation was significantly hampered due to the already unmanageable medical bills (considered non-reimbursable) and travel costs and responsibilities to continue the small business that represented their only source of insurance and income. Michelle's transition home required her to transfer her skills, train an attendant, and navigate her life space and functions. She experienced her first symptoms of depression during the initial months. Her physician defined this as inevitable and treated her with medication. Over the next year, her attention was devoted to mastering her environment and adjusting to a sequence of three attendants. She had just begun participating in at-home activities and a few community functions when her depressive symptoms resurfaced. She was angry that she was not responding to medications and feared that she would regress without counseling.

Counselors engage in a collaborative process with clients to co-construct viable interpretations that may account for individual, interpersonal, and wider contextual contributions to and constructions of the issues promoting treatment. Client issues do not exist independently; rather, they emanate from social narratives and self-definitions that do not yield an agency that can effectively manage tasks implicit in client narratives (Anderson & Goolishian, 1992).

Diagnostic conversations with significant participants in the illness experience revealed points of consensus. Michelle saw her symptoms as a warning to more critically examine her perhaps naive sense of confidence. She feared that she was disappointing her family and friends and was thankful that they remained patient and supportive. Robert expressed unconditional love and provided daily opportunities for her to participate with family and friends. He saw her symptoms as revealing the depression she had been stoically and unnecessarily protecting him from by remaining isolated and self-involved. This was a sign to redouble his encouragement and direction. Family and friends echoed his sentiment in words and actions. A ritualized conversation be-

tween Michelle and her brother was her timid laughter in response to his enthusiastic push to spend a week with her when she felt ready "to show him the town and eat until burstin' time," followed by talk about the van he had fixed for her to help them have fun. Conversations with family and friends were repetitions of this same theme. A ramp was built to allow Michelle access to the community center. A raffle was held to cover costs for van alterations. Invitations followed by descriptions of modifications for access were consistent and included Michelle's timid laugh and promise to accept soon. Visits to the couple's home were infrequent due to awkward modifications, an uncomfortable temperature, and a sense of intrusion on intimate routines. The reason most often expressed was the assuredness that such visits would hamper Michelle's reentry into the world. In combination, these voices revealed a narrative that defined Michelle as recognizably frail and unnecessarily self-involved, saw the counter of consistent encouragement and opportunity as essential, and focused on Michelle's return to her prior roles and relationships as the measure of success.

Opening Possibilities to Co-Construct Therapeutic Themes

The aim of the assessment phase is to move toward holistic and viable perceptions of self, self-in-relationship, experiences, and contexts so that broader perspectives and options become available. Assessment stresses identifying alternative stories and interpretations rather than narrowly locating underlying sources of psychopathology. Thus, therapeutic conversation is intended to promote perspectives that are not constrained by the treatment issues (Lyddon, 1995), instead offering multiple perspectives and options for change (Ivey, 2000).

Often, counselors introduce dialogue to unveil the constraints and potentials reflected in the narrative. This helps to construct goals that attend to these types of revelations and that fit with clients' idiosyncratic frames of reference (Guterman, 1994).

Dialogue within the frame of the dominant narrative unveiled omissions and incongruities, challenged its credibility, and opened possibilities to consider alternatives. Challenges included (a) an unacknowledged tone of sadness during encouraging conversations; (b) the deflection of dialogue testing the viability of motivational but misinformed advice; (c) the reliance on deficit-based labels of depression and isolation to explain or disregard Michelle's silence, reluctance to accept advice, or quiet expressions of discordant views; and (d) the tendency to disregard or misconstrue conversation that challenged or strayed too far from the dominant story.

Initiating Collaborative Therapeutic Dialogues and Themes

The counseling environment is a conversational context (Goolishian & Anderson, 1987) in which counselors and clients collaborate as equal members of the therapeutic alliance and as partners in a wider consultative alliance. To initiate therapeutic discourse, counselors refrain from expressing preconceived opinions and expectations and instead remain in a continued state of "being informed" by clients, helping them to broaden their journeys toward new constructions.

Themes identified as precursors for constructing therapeutic narratives included (a) an extended interpretation of *adaptation* as developmental and transactional, (b) an appreciation for the diversity and subjectivity of experiences, and (c) the need for broader definitions of success, more in synchrony with life trajectories. These themes ex-

tended the territory of investigation to include all participants contributing to and construing the problem and its management, and they changed the nature of inquiry to move beyond pathogenic dialogue and reinforce multiple interpretations and constructive solutions.

Using Interactive Language to Operationalize Co-Constructed Themes

Language is viewed as a medium in which self and social realities are constructed in ways that reveal how clients participate in their world and in relation to their life tasks. Counselors work to elicit alternative efficacious narratives by posing the traces, complements, metaphors, and contrasts revealed in dominant themes presented by clients or imposed by the environment. The client storytelling that surfaces is not just the telling of stories but also a situated action in itself (Gergen & Kaye, 1992) that generates new understandings. Language links context to relationship and elicits interaction that facilitates new interpretations. "Understanding arises not through an examination of deep structure, latent, or unconscious material, but through interaction between individuals" (Lax, 1992, p. 72).

Counseling and consultative conversation elicited ways in which to consider the implications of emerging options by drawing on the recursive nature of language and operation, as each equally informs the process of change. For example, considering the concept of *adjustment as developmental* opened possibilities to reframe Michelle's reticence to accept advice and the collective's resistance to admit uncertainty as logical consequences of the illness history and as indicators of the need for information exchange to regain reconnectedness and support that is more in synchrony with current experiences. Michelle's self-involvement now could be interpreted as where she is situated on a trajectory unfamiliar to participants. Silenced voices of sadness and uncertainty could be seen as natural responses to a tragedy and a desire to help in unfamiliar territory. These interpretations elicited discussions about isolated experiences and idiosyncratic ways of understanding, thus eliciting an emerging sense of connection and direction. It became apparent that individual experiences had promoted different life trajectories, so that rather than a sole focus on Michelle's reentry, it was clear that others would need to participate in new ways of defining themselves in relation to her including working to understand and accommodate her current condition and to respect her knowledge and expertise versus imagining that they had a superior handle on the methods and measures of success. This evolving dialogue was integrated with the component of *adjustment as transactional,* extending who was involved, and the lenses used to evaluate their involvement. This helped to expand unidimensional perceptions by welcoming less acknowledged aspects of individuals and relationships. For example, Robert's identity as an unfaltering supporter could be extended to include his own sense of isolation and uncertainty. Finally, synthesizing both components of adjustment reinforced the equal responsibilities of all participants to share information, to adapt to their own sense of self-in-relation, and to adapt to environments more welcoming for Michelle.

Addressing Contextual and Developmental Variables

The narratives that clients bring to counseling have been developing over their life spans within various contexts. These contexts have influenced their narratives, as have the particular communities, social groups, and familial contexts in which they have participated. Thus, the nature of the relationship between development and context is recursive and inextricably intertwined, making the idiosyncratic nature of development inevitable. Postmodern approaches empower clients to create viable new identities that account for contextual and cultural variables. The aim is to realign power differentials that in the past served to marginalize clients. When contextual and cultural factors are directly addressed in the therapeutic or consultative dialogue, the potential to enhance clients' sociopolitical awareness as well as to serve as a precursor to client social involvement and action is enhanced (Ellis, 1999a; Lyddon, 1995; Rigazio-DiGilio et al., 1997).

Postmodern approaches hold varying perspectives regarding which participants contributing to the meaning-making process should be included in the assessment and treatment process, but all work toward the reconstruction of personal and social narratives that are liberating (Ivey, 1995) and empowering (Lyddon, 1995).

Michelle and Robert also attended couples sessions, where they shared their disconnected experiences. This rekindled their keen sense of the consequences of this history, further consolidating the goal for collective adjustment and the use of information and participation as part of this process. These needs initiated a boundarying process that protected the integrity of their system. They began an historical recounting of the circumstances that deflected from their collective reconstruction of worldviews and minimized the personal and collective agency usually housed in such structures. Therapeutic discussions that recycled through the expanded definition of adjustment used in other consultations allowed them to access an already familiar process to deal with a less familiar territory. This work began the development of reconstructed identities. By reconstructing a story with a more comprehensive understanding of previously isolated experiences, incongruencies could be revealed. They could see that, in response to stressor events, Michelle's tendency was to increase her centripetal focus to obtain a sense of capability. Simultaneously, Robert would increase his centrifugal focus to obtain a sense of relational competence. There was no collective holding environment to interrupt this process. Their newly emerging story was the first intrusion and allowed for redirection. Michelle and Robert believed that their relationship was only beginning to move developmentally; as was the case for Robert, Michelle's competence in the management of her disability was the point of assistance. This shifted attention to centripetal activities, with Michelle welcoming Robert to learn his role in her life space, redirecting Robert's need to provide assistance and encouragement to tasks more in synchrony with the couple's development, and Michelle's redeveloping sense of personal agency. This process brought in the attendant as a player in the narrative, and the threesome dealt with issues of interference, competition, sharing, teaching, competency, coalitions, and the like, allowing the couple to experience a mini-context that was isomorphic to the history and Michelle and Robert's anticipated notions of issues they would deal with as they present to the world as a couple.

Constructing Culturally Responsive Treatment Plans

Postmodern counselors do not have an agenda that involves "curing" or "fixing" clients (McLeod, 1997). They do not attempt to help clients fit into or adapt to their environment. Rather, clinicians aim to empower clients to effect change in themselves and their world. Postmodern approaches assume the existence of a mutual and reciprocal link that ties the social realm to the interior workings of individuals, families, and wider social networks (Wentworth & Wentworth, 1997), and they view narratives as embedded stories within a community and cultural context. Treatment plans account for the idiosyncratic ways in which cli-

ents make meanings of their experiences and attend to the influences of ethnic heritage, gender, class, age, and power. Inasmuch as these factors color and direct the personal narratives of clients, they must be accounted for in new narratives that emerge from the counseling process.

Postmodern counselors help clients to examine the ways in which individual and wider systems influence the construction of their narratives. Cultural, local, familial, and personal ways of meaning making are communicated through client narratives, and counselors explicitly account for these factors throughout treatment. In this fashion, and to varying degrees, postmodern approaches design treatment plans meant, first, to address and, over time, to redress cultural forces that oppress and then to identify new cultural and community resources that can empower new self and collective identities (Sue, Ivey, & Pedersen, 1996).

Facilitating the Co-Constructive/ Restorying Process

Personal narratives or stories represent internal and social meaning-making processes. Ricoeur (1984) defined narratives as extended metaphors replete with images and events. These stories represent our view of the world and can be understood through personal schemata or scripts (McLeod, 1997). In this fashion, stories access underlying schemata and provide a therapeutic editing process whereby clients can rewrite these scripts and representations. "Narrative approaches to counseling invite clients to begin a journey of co-exploration in the search of talents and abilities that are hidden or veiled by a life problem" (Monk, 1997, p. 3).

Change or transformation in narrative schemata occurs through restorying processes based on differentiation and integration (McLeod, 1997). Through the process of differentiation, clients are assisted in generating rival narratives that are equally plausible stories about the same event. Here, multiple representations are elicited that provide new explanations and possibilities. During the integration process, clients construct new and even more compelling narratives that can help them to break free from the abstractions that have come to dominate the ways in which they experience, understand, and operate in the world (Efran, 1994; Ivey, 2000). These narrative methods introduce incongruity and conflict within client representations and use restorying methods to enable them to construct healing and normalizing theories of what happened, why it happened, and what can be done about it (Gonçalves, 1995; Martin, 1988; Meichenbaum, 1994).

By developing a more informed understanding of their history and actively working on their own treatment design, Michelle and Robert were able to implement new solutions. Conversation and participation rekindled the emotional ties and sense of competence. The emerging story was, "We are beginning to feel capable again, and part of this is due to our turn inward to remind ourselves of our own world and the intricacies of this situation. We see a different pace and a different way to decide how to manage the task of adjustment." For Robert and Michelle, this included directing the well-meaning intentions of others. They more assertively invited family and friends to engage with them in their home and be reintroduced to the couple. They made a video to say hello to the community on local television, offering their beginning presentation on their terms. When it was suggested that a community chain be coordinated to assist them in their efforts to help Michelle return to her community, it was negoti-

ated that this instead be a chain to bring in such efforts to their space. This began to occur with assistance in food preparation, home modifications, help with the business, and repairs.

Drawing From Constructivist Intervention Strategies

Regarding therapeutic interventions, most postmodern models of counseling explicate a general approach to therapy that suggests a range of techniques and a therapeutic framework that can incorporate intervention strategies from other models. For example, Kelly introduced many of the seminal strategies such as the repertory grid, loose and tight construing, the experience cycle, and the creativity cycle. Such methods were used by Kelly to help clients explore the meanings that they attach to their behaviors, feelings, and cognitions. Kelly also demonstrated how more traditional interventions—role-play, journaling, dream analysis, free association, enactment, and the like—could be used to help clients construe multiple levels of awareness.

Similarly, Ivey and Rigazio-DiGilio provided individual and collective linguistic assessment and treatment strategies that clinicians can use to structure culturally and developmentally sensitive counseling. In addition, they provided a metatheoretical classification schema that complements rather than disregards traditional theories and approaches. Counselors can use this matrix to organize traditional approaches and strategies while keeping developmental, co-constructivist, multicultural, and systemic-contextual variables at the forefront of treatment planning.

Other methods have been introduced to help clients examine the discrepancies that arise between their tightly held constructs and alternative ways of construing the same experiences. Guidano (1995) used a "moviola" technique to have clients look at the same experiences from several different points of view. "For example, he may move a client step by step through a slow-motion 'replay' of a marital quarrel, 'panning' across a series of scenes, before 'zooming in' on one that has special emotional significance" (Neimeyer, 1998, p. 144). Similarly, Atwood (1996) demonstrated how pictorial renderings can be used to analyze the personal narratives and shadow scripts that are just outside clients' awareness. Gordon and Efran (1997) used their position as "outsiders" to structure interactive discourse with clients and to provoke new perspectives and expanded views of their situations. The community genogram (Ivey et al., 1997) is another visualization tool that can be used to explore client narratives.

There also is a variety of dialectic and dialogic questioning strategies that help counselors and clients to explore issues such as meaning (Freedman & Combs, 1996), self-description (Durrant & Kowalski, 1993), exceptions (de Shazer, 1991), subjugated knowledge (White & Epston, 1990), reflections (Adams-Westcott, Dafforn, & Sterne, 1993), dominating stories (Drewery, Winslade, & Monk, 2000), and positive assets (Ivey, 1971). These can be used to help clients enhance, revise, and reconstruct new individual and collective identities.

Monitoring Client Progress

Consistent with the goals of constructivism, client progress is measured in terms of the stability of new and more viable constructions. "The goal of counseling is not the enforcement

of a particular meaning, grand narrative, or way of viewing the world, but rather the continuation of the therapeutic conversation until the co-created narrative that emerges no longer contains that which was experienced as a problem" (Lyddon, 1995, p. 582). The movement of client narratives from problem-saturated and deficit-based themes to empowered, contextually situated, and viable ones can be tracked over the course of treatment. In the beginning of treatment, the quality of the joining process will determine the level and depth of client sharing. Both counselor and client have responsibility for monitoring the complexity and rigidity of the predominant narrative. During the middle part of the treatment, the quality of the alternative perspectives that the client and counselor have co-constructed can be monitored in terms of both quantity and viability. It also is at this time that the client's sense of empowerment should be monitored at the personal, family, peer, and community levels as well. The ability of the client to maintain and hold two or more conflicting narratives is another indicator of progress. Termination is indicated not just when one narrative has replaced another but also when the client is able to participate in a continuous process of creating and transforming meaning (Gergen, 1996).

The criteria for monitoring were developed by the couple as the decision came to stop medication, diminishing contact over time. Michelle and Robert negotiated a new role with the center. The couple would be designated as the peer advocacy resource to assist injured or ill people in navigating the systems of support and intervention. They coordinated an online resource library that Michelle developed and updated through an assisted computer bought for her by the program. For themselves, Michelle and Robert hoped to gain more effectiveness in understanding financial services available to them. Legal services at the center were provided at no cost, and action was taken to challenge insurance decisions. The center also initiated a legislative action to redefine the necessity for family participation in rehabilitation services.

Concluding Treatment

The intention of postmodern approaches is to conclude counseling when clients have the sense of optimism necessary to continue as their own counselors (Viney, 1993). "During the termination phase, clients can build on their new, broader, more viable narratives and are freed (and challenged) to negotiate with others more fluid identities, striving to use the narrative resources of their communities and cultures to script more satisfying lives" (Neimeyer, 1998, p. 147). As final sessions approach, counselors co-construct scaffolds for clients to maintain and expand the more powerful and productive narratives that they have developed. The abilities to entertain multiple perspectives, isolate and maximize assets and strengths, negotiate and secure resources, and modify narratives in response to changing circumstances are typical attributes that clients will need to continue their life journeys.

Two years after the completion of counseling, Michelle and Robert were active in their advocacy role and had developed a partnership with a couple who had assisted them in maintaining their business. They had a new attendant who brought her young child into the house as well. Robert and Michelle were considering their ability to take on the task of child rearing. Although it was an interesting thought, they mentioned that being the peripheral parents to live-in children might be enough for them.

Perspectives on the Future of Postmodern Counseling Approaches

The field of counseling is at a crossroads in terms of its future impact on society. The inevitable movement toward globalization requires that theorists, researchers, and practitioners accept more open and inclusive practices to accommodate increasingly diverse clientele. If we are to navigate the transition successfully, then the field will have to reevaluate the fundamental assumptions undergirding our counseling practices. In response to this increased need to provide culturally sensitive counseling, many researchers, authors, and clinicians now acknowledge that the majority of our traditional theories emerged within the parameters of a Western, European American, individualistic framework (D'Andrea, 2000; Sue et al., 1996). Historically, the cultural influences of family, society, community, generation, politics, and institutions were relegated to noncritical background data. In addition, the focus of treatment was on assisting individuals, partners, and families to *adapt to* rather than *understand and influence* these wider contextual variables (Rigazio-DiGilio & Ivey, 1995). Postmodern concepts provide an alternative perspective of how we might want to proceed in the future.

Postmodernism confronts the intellectual hegemony of Western thought by challenging the underlying assumptions and beliefs associated with modern psychological theories, religious doctrines, and political policies (D'Andrea, 2000; Gergen, 1994a, 1994b; Sexton & Griffin, 1997). By confronting such beliefs and practices, postmodernism throws into question many pillars of the existing status quo that typically are used to repress psychological liberation and to pathologize and decontextualize persons from diverse groups and backgrounds.

Although the postmodern world of complexity and multiple voices presents us with perplexing questions, it also represents increased opportunities to build on our past with both integrative and alternative models for the future that offer more pluralist and inclusive possibilities. Such models could offer guidelines for *weighing the importance of individual, family, and wider contextual variables* when assessing and treating each client or client system who seeks our services (Rigazio-DiGilio et al., 1997). To participate in this process, the postmodern branch of counseling has much to address.

First, emerging theories need to move from reflection-on-action within an individualistic perspective to reflection-in-action within an ecosystemic perspective. Although it is generally accepted that a comprehensive postmodern theory of counseling needs to attend to the multiple realities that clients experience, we have yet to reach consensus regarding just what levels of reality warrant our primary focus. The postmodern branch still seems to represent theories that address the thought and action processes of clients but that omit action with and reflection on the wider social systems that might have contributed to or labeled the distress.

Traditional intrapsychic conceptions of disorder are being challenged by influences brought about by the postmodern world (Neimeyer & Raskin, 2000) and by changes in the predominant figures permitted to be at the mental health decision-making table (e.g., Ginter et al., 1996). However, we are far from an accepted practice that integrates the relational environments (e.g., the Global Assessment of Relational Functioning [GARF] Scale in the *DSM-IV* [*Diagnostic and Statistical Man-*

ual of Mental Disorders; American Psychiatric Association, 1994]; Kaslow, 1997) and cultural phenomena (e.g., Wentworth & Wentworth, 1997; Wynne, Shields, & Sirkin, 1992) that influence the emergence of symptomatology. It will be a very long time before we see shifts in our focus to adequately address issues such as racism, oppression, and poverty (Rigazio-DiGilio et al., 1997).

If we are committed to having a greater impact on promoting the development and well-being of larger numbers of persons in a postmodern era, then we must continue to develop and implement new intervention strategies that can be used to promote this country's mental health and spiritual well-being more effectively. We must not be limited by the traditional or even current postmodern thinking about counseling that emphasizes the importance of promoting intrapsychic changes among a relatively small number of clients. Such views continue to be commonly espoused by counselor educators who overuse individual counseling theories, including postmodernism, in their training programs (Lovell & McAuliffe, 1997). Individualistic and ethnocentric counseling frameworks also continue to be overused by many counseling theorists who promote theoretical models that inadequately address the complex ways in which clients' cultural backgrounds affect the helping process. In short, counselor educators, theorists, and practitioners all must learn to think in "bigger terms" when conceptualizing our role and purpose as human development specialists in a multicultural postmodern era (Neufeldt, 1997).

Rigazio-DiGilio and colleagues (1997) noted,

Theories of counseling and practice that perpetuate the notion of individual and family dysfunction without giving equal attention to societal dysfunction and to the dysfunctional interactions that can occur between individuals, families, and societies (e.g., intentional and unintentional power differentials) may unwittingly reinforce the oppressive paradigm. (p. 241)

Ellis (1999a) echoed this notion in an American Counseling Association (ACA) symposium when he asserted that "all systems of counseling had better give serious thought to this hypothesis and attend to both internal/individualistic and external/societal dimensions of change—as, in fact, few of them have done to date" (p. 5; see also Ellis, 1999b).

Second, the process of theory advancement must be more distributed across all levels of the profession. In the past, the gaps between theory, research, and practice influenced the development of sterile theories that were difficult to connect to the diverse realities occurring within the counseling room (Nelson & Poulin, 1997; Polkinghorne, 1992). New methods of knowledge advancement must be applied to directly link the three domains of theory, research, and practice so that credible, broad-based models can be developed. If postmodern counseling models are to emerge beyond the boundaries of our existing knowledge base, then advocates need to employ methods of inquiry that improve linkages among these three domains so that each can equally influence one another (Hoshmand & Martin, 1995; Lanning, 1994; Rigazio-DiGilio, Gonçalves, & Ivey, 1996).

Through this extended dialogue, postmodernists can begin examining the inconsistencies and limitations of our own models. For example, our appreciation of multiple perspectives may obscure our ability to recognize our own developmentally and contextually bound perspectives, thereby making it hard to identify what our approaches can and cannot do. An-

other assumption that needs to be explored more fully is how our efforts to minimize the presumed or real power differentials inherent in counseling cloud our awareness of the ways in which our voices can influence, empower, and oppress in the varied contexts within which they might be used. These types of questions cannot be investigated in a fragmented fashion with little exchange flowing across clinicians, researchers, and theorists. The advancement of the postmodern branch of counseling needs to proceed in ways that are built on its primary foundations, considering the importance of multiple perspectives across a broader territory of discourse. Rigazio-DiGilio and colleagues (1997) ask—as a primary ethical imperative—theorists, researchers, and practitioners espousing a particular counseling perspective "to clearly specify the parameters of their [approach] and to be clear about its limitations" (p. 246). Only through this expanded discussion can the tacit biases inherent in postmodern models be surfaced and addressed.

Third, the content of theory advancement will need a stronger empirical and pragmatic base that directly links constructs, practices, and methodologies. Efforts to supply empirical evidence that supports a postmodern perspective are only now beginning to emerge (see Angus, Hardtke, & Levitt, 1996; Cummings, Hallberg, & Slemon, 1994; Etringler, Hillerbrand, & Claiborn, 1995; Friedlander, Heatherington, Johnson, & Skowron, 1994; Gottman, 1994; Janko, 1994; Neimeyer, Prichard, Lyddon, & Sherrard, 1994; Rigazio-DiGilio & Ivey, 1990; Sexton & Whiston, 1994; Tamase & Rigazio-DiGilio, 1997). Developing clinical and empirical methods that are standardized yet allow room to identify and evaluate the co-constructive process that unfolds in actual sessions will be a difficult phase to navigate. This is particularly true given the skepticism that continues to plague the postmodern paradigm, specifically its emphasis on antirationalism, subjectivity, and unpredictability of environmental effects (Duncan, 1994).

"Despite the extent to which the narrative model is imbued with postmodern concepts of self-as-story and therapy as narrative revision, still greater integration with discursive principles might enhance its utility in the counseling context" (Neimeyer, 1998, p. 146). Research methods based on strategies from conversation analysis and ethnomethodology (Edwards & Potter, 1992; Freedman & Combs, 1996) and from phenomenological psychology and grounded theory (Nelson & Poulin, 1997) can be used to describe and illustrate processes of constructivist treatment. Because conversation analysis can study any social activity in a naturalistic, unobtrusive manner, it can be incorporated as an empirical tool to investigate therapeutic outcomes generated within the constructivist approach (see Gale, 1991; Kogan, 1998; Neimeyer, 1998). In addition, grounded theory and phenomenological psychology allow us to compare experience to subjective meaning by offering methods of data analysis that investigate specific situations, such as therapy, and the patterns of meaning that might emerge from these situations (Charon, 1992; Glaser & Strauss, 1967).

In summary, unless the postmodern branch of counseling attends to the current unequal development on theory and testimony and the paucity of empirical evidence, the models that are derived from this branch might lose their vitality as they continue to move toward the center of our field. If this occurs, then postmodern models no longer will be seen as an alternative to mainstream counseling practice; rather, they

may come to dominate mainstream thinking (Gergen, 1998) without simultaneously offering coherent theories and empirical bases that propel the field to apply more inclusive and multidimensional models of counseling. To counter the diminution of this approach, a concentrated effort needs to produce operationalized theoretical constructs and corresponding empirical methods to validate, modify, and teach these constructs within a multicultural and nonimperialistic fashion. The next decade will determine whether innovative methodologies will be developed for clinicians, investigators, and theoreticians to undergird their enthusiasm with sound assessments of postmodern approaches. The degree to which postmodern models will have a lasting impact depends on the systematic evaluation of the assumptions and principles of the approach (Sexton & Whiston, 1994). The question is, do we as a field have the cognitive and volitional resources to write this narrative or not?

References

Adams-Westcott, J., Dafforn, T. A., & Sterne, P. (1993). Escaping victim life stories and co-constructing personal agency. In S. Gilligan & R. Price (Eds.), *Therapeutic conversations* (pp. 258-276). New York: Norton.

Adler, A. (1926). *The neurotic constitution*. New York: Books for Libraries Press.

American Psychiatric Association. (1994). *Diagnostic and Statistical Manual of Mental Disorders* (4th ed.). Washington, DC: Author.

Anderson, H., & Goolishian, H. A. (1988). Human systems as linguistic systems: Preliminary and evolving ideas about the implications for clinical theory. *Family Process, 27*, 371-393.

Anderson, H., & Goolishian, H. A. (1992). The client is the expert. In S. McNamee & K. Gergen (Eds.), *Therapy as social construction* (pp. 25-39). Newbury Park, CA: Sage.

Angus, L., Hardtke, K., & Levitt, H. (1996). *The narrative processes coding system manual* (rev. ed.). Unpublished manuscript, York University, North York, Ontario, Canada.

Atwood, J. (1996). Social construction theory and therapy assumptions. In J. Atwood (Ed.), *Family scripts* (pp. 1-33). Philadelphia: Accelerated Development/Taylor & Francis.

Becvar, R. J., & Becvar, D. S. (1994). The ecosystemic story: A story about stories. *Journal of Mental Health Counseling, 16,* 22-32.

Berger, P., & Luckmann, T. (1966). *The social construction of reality.* Garden City, NY: Doubleday.

Botella, L. (1995). Personal construct theory, constructivism, and postmodern thought. In R. A. Neimeyer & G. J. Neimeyer (Eds.), *Advances in personal construct psychology* (Vol. 3, pp. 3-35). Greenwich, CT: JAI.

Brown, L. S. (2000). Discomforts of the powerless: Feminist constructions of distress. In R. Neimeyer & J. Raskin (Eds.), *Constructions of disorder* (pp. 287-308). Washington, DC: American Psychological Association.

Burr, V. (1995). *An introduction to social constructionism.* London: Routledge.

Caple, R. B. (1985). Counseling and the self-organization paradigm. *Journal of Counseling and Development, 64,* 173-178.

Charon, J. M. (1992). *Symbolic interactionism: An introduction, an interpretation, an integration.* Englewood Cliffs, NJ: Prentice Hall.

Cummings, A. L., Hallberg, E. T., & Slemon, A. G. (1994). Templates of client change in short-term counseling. *Journal of Counseling Psychology, 41,* 464-472.

D'Andrea, M. (2000). Postmodernism, constructivism, and multiculturalism: Three forces reshaping and expanding our thoughts about counseling. *Journal of Mental Health Counseling, 22,* 1-16.

Daniels, M. H., & White, L. J. (1994). Human systems as problem-determined linguistic systems: Relevance for training. *Journal of Mental Health Counseling, 16,* 105-119.

Dell, P. (1982). Beyond homeostasis: Toward a concept of coherence. *Family Process, 21,* 21-24.

Derrida, J. (1978). *Writing and difference.* Chicago: University of Chicago Press.

de Shazer, S. (1991). *Putting difference to work.* New York: Norton.

de Shazer, S. (1992). Doing therapy: A post-structural revision. *Journal of Marital and Family Therapy, 18,* 71-82.

Drewery, W., Winslade, J., & Monk, G. (2000). Resisting the dominating story: Toward a deeper understanding of narrative therapy. In R. Neimeyer & J. Raskin (Eds.), *Constructions of disorder* (pp. 243-263). Washington, DC: American Psychological Association.

Duncan, S. (1994). The trouble with the new contextualisms. *Collected Original Resources in Education, 18*(1). (Fiche No. 2 E01)

Durrant, M., & Kowalski, K. (1993). Enhancing views of competence. In S. Friedman (Ed.), *The new language of change: Constructive collaboration in psychotherapy* (pp. 107-137). New York: Guilford.

Edwards, D., & Potter, J. (1992). *Discursive psychology.* London: Sage.

Efran, J. S. (1994). Mystery, abstraction, and narrative psychotherapy. *Journal of Constructivist Psychology, 7,* 219-227.

Efran, J. S., & Cook, P. E. (2000). Linguistic ambiguity as a diagnostic tool. In R. Neimeyer & J. Raskin (Eds.), *Constructions of disorder* (pp. 121-144). Washington, DC: American Psychological Association.

Efran, J. S., Lukens, M. D., & Lukens, R. J. (1990). *Language, structure, and change: Frameworks of meaning in psychotherapy.* New York: Norton.

Einstein, A., Lorentz, H., Weyl, H., & Minko, H. (1924). *The principle of relativity.* New York: Dover.

Ellis, A. (1979). The theory of rational-emotive therapy. In A. Ellis & J. Whitely (Eds.), *Theoretical and empirical foundations of rational-emotive therapy* (pp. 33-60). Pacific Grove, CA: Brooks/Cole.

Ellis, A. (1999a, April). *A continuation of the dialogue on ethical issues on counseling in the postmodern era.* Paper presented at the American Counseling Association World Conference, San Diego, CA.

Ellis, A. (1999b). Rational emotive behavioral therapy as an internal control psychology. *International Journal of Reality Therapy, 19,* 4-11.

Etringler, B. D., Hillerbrand, E., & Claiborn, C. D. (1995). The transition from novice to expert counselor. *Counselor Education and Supervision, 35,* 4-17.

Foucault, M. (1980). *Power and knowledge: Selected interviews and other writings.* New York: Pantheon.

Fransella, F. (1995). *George Kelly.* London: Sage.

Freedman, J., & Combs, G. (1996). *Narrative therapy.* New York: Norton.

Friedlander, M. I., Heatherington, L., Johnson, B., & Skowron, E. A. (1994). Sustaining engagement: A change event in family therapy. *Journal of Counseling Psychology, 41,* 438-448.

Gale, J. E. (1991). *Conversation analysis of therapeutic discourse: The pursuit of a therapeutic agenda* (Advances in Discourse Processes, Vol. 41). Norwood, NJ: Ablex.

Gergen, K. J. (1985). The social constructionist movement in modern psychology. *American Psychologist, 40,* 266-275.

Gergen, K. J. (1991). *The saturated self.* New York: Basic Books.

Gergen, K. J. (1994a). Exploring the postmodern: Perils or potentials. *American Psychologist, 49,* 412-416.

Gergen, K. J. (1994b). *Toward transformation in social knowledge* (3rd ed.). Thousand Oaks, CA: Sage.

Gergen, K. J. (1996). Beyond life narratives in the therapeutic encounter. In J. Birren & G. Kenyon (Eds.), *Aging and biography: Explorations in adult development* (pp. 205-223). New York: Springer.

Gergen, K. J. (1998). Constructionist dialogues and the vicissitudes of the political. In I. Velody & R. Williams (Eds.), *The politics of constructionism* (pp. 33-48). London: Routledge.

Gergen, K. J., & Kaye, J. (1992). Beyond narrative in the negotiation of therapeutic meaning. In S. McNamee & K. J. Gergen (Eds.), *Therapy as social construction* (pp. 166-185). Newbury Park, CA: Sage.

Ginter, E. (Moderator), Ellis, A., Guterman, J., Rigazio-DiGilio, S., Ivey, A., & Locke, D. (1996, April). *Ethical issues in the postmodern era.* Paper presented at the American Counseling Association World Conference, Pittsburgh, PA.

Glaser, B., & Strauss, A. (1967). *The discovery of grounded theory: Strategies for qualitative research.* Chicago: Aldine.

Gleick, J. (1987). *Chaos: Making a new science.* New York: Penguin.

Gonçalves, O. (1995). Hermeneutics, constructivism, and cognitive-behavioral therapies: From the object to the project. In R. A. Neimeyer & M. J. Mahoney (Eds.), *Constructivism in psychotherapy* (pp. 195-230). Washington, DC: American Psychological Association.

Goolishian, H., & Anderson, A. (1987). Language systems and therapy: An evolving idea. *Psychotherapy, 24,* 529-545.

Gordon, D. E., & Efran, J. S. (1997). Therapy and the dance of language. In T. Sexton & B. Griffin (Eds.), *Constructivist thinking in counseling practice, research, and training* (pp. 101-110). New York: Teachers College Press.

Gottman, J. M. (1994). *What predicts divorce? The relationship between marital processes and marital outcomes.* Hillsdale, NJ: Lawrence Erlbaum.

Guidano, V. F. (1987). *Complexity of the self: A developmental approach to psychopathology and therapy.* New York: Guilford.

Guidano, V. F. (1991). *The self in process.* New York: Guilford.

Guidano, V. F. (1995). Self-observation in constructivist psychotherapy. In R. A. Neimeyer & M. J. Mahoney (Eds.), *Constructivism in psychotherapy* (pp. 93-108). Washington, DC: American Psychological Association.

Guterman, J. T. (1994). A social constructionist position for mental health counseling. *Journal of Mental Health Counseling, 16,* 226-244.

Hawkings, S. W. (1988). *A brief history of time: From the big bang to black holes.* New York: Bantam.

Hayes, R. L. (1994). Counseling in the postmodern world: Origins and implications of a constructivist developmental approach. *Counseling and Human Development, 26,* 1-12.

Hegel, G. W. (1975). *Logic* (W. Wallace, Trans.). Oxford, UK: Clarendon. (Original work published 1830)

Heidegger, M. (1962). *Being and time* (J. Macquarrie & E. Robinson, Eds. and Trans.). New York: Harper & Row. (Original work published 1927)

Heisenberg, W. (1958). *Physics and philosophy.* New York: Harper & Row.

Hoffman, L. (1990). Constructing realities: An art of lenses. *Family Process, 29,* 1-12.

Hoshmand, L. T., & Martin, J. (1995). Concluding comments on therapeutic psychology and the science of practice. In L. T. Hoshmand & J. Martin (Eds.), *Research as praxis* (pp. 235-241). New York: Teachers College Press.

Howard, G. S. (1991). Cultural tales: A narrative approach to thinking, cross-cultural psychology, and psychotherapy. *American Psychologist, 46,* 187-197.

Ivey, A. E. (1971). *Microcounseling: Innovations in interviewing training.* Springfield, IL: Charles C Thomas.

Ivey, A. E. (1991). *Developmental strategies for helpers: Individual, family, and network interventions.* Pacific Grove, CA: Brooks/Cole.

Ivey, A. E. (1995). Psychotherapy as liberation. In J. Ponterotto, J. Casas, L. Suzuki, & C. Alexander (Eds.), *Handbook of multicultural counseling.* Thousand Oaks, CA: Sage.

Ivey, A. E. (2000). *Developmental therapy: Theory into practice.* North Amherst, MA: Microtraining Associates.

Ivey, A. E., Gonçalves, O., & Ivey, M. (1989). Developmental therapy: Theory and practice. In O. Gonçalves (Ed.), *Advances in the cognitive therapies: The constructive-developmental approach* (pp. 91-110). Porto, Portugal: APPORT.

Ivey, A. E., & Ivey, M. B. (1998). Toward a developmental diagnostic and statistical manual: The vitality of a contextual framework. *Journal of Counseling and Development, 77,* 484-490.

Ivey, A. E., Ivey, M. B., & Simek-Morgan, L. (1997). *Counseling and psychotherapy.* Boston: Allyn & Bacon.

Ivey, A. E., & Rigazio-DiGilio, S. A. (1994). Developmental counseling and therapy: Can still another theory be useful to you? *Journal for the Professional Counselor, 9,* 23-48.

Janko, S. (1994). *Vulnerable children, vulnerable families: The social construction of child abuse.* New York: Teachers College Press.

Jankowski, P. J. (1998). A developmental constructivist framework for narrative therapy. *Family Therapy, 25,* 111-120.

Kant, I. (1969). *Critique of pure reason.* New York: St. Martin's. (Original work published 1791)

Kaslow, F. (Ed.). (1997). *Handbook of relational diagnosis and dysfunctional family patterns.* New York: John Wiley.

Keeney, B. P. (1983). *Aesthetics of change.* New York: Guilford.

Kelly, G. A. (1955). *The psychology of personal constructs.* New York: Norton.

Kogan, S. M. (1998). The politics of making meaning: Discourse analysis of a "postmodern" interview. *Journal of Marriage and Family Therapy, 20,* 229-251.

Kuhn, T. (1974). *The structure of scientific revolutions.* Chicago: University of Chicago Press.

Lanning, W. (1994). Can human systems as linguistic systems become a model for mental health counseling? *Journal of Mental Health Counseling, 16,* 125-128.

Lax, W. D. (1992). Postmodern thinking in a clinical practice. In S. McNamee & K. J. Gergen (Eds.), *Therapy as social construction* (pp. 69-85). Newbury Park, CA: Sage.

Locke, D. (1992). *Increasing multicultural understanding.* Newbury Park, CA: Sage.

Lovell, C., & McAuliffe, G. (1997). Principles of constructivist training and education. In T. Sexton & B. Griffin (Eds.), *Constructivist thinking in counseling practice, research, and training* (pp. 211-227). New York: Teachers College Press.

Lyddon, W. J. (1989). Personal epistemology and preference for counseling. *Journal of Counseling Psychology, 36,* 423-429.

Lyddon, W. J. (1995). Cognitive therapy and theories of knowing: A social constructionist view. *Journal of Counseling and Development, 73,* 579-585.

Lyotard, J. (1983). *The postmodern condition: A report on knowledge.* New York: Basic Books.

Mahoney, M. (1991). *Human change processes: Notes on the facilitation of personal development.* New York: Basic Books.

Mahoney, M. J., & Lyddon, W. J. (1988). Recent developments in cognitive approaches to counseling and psychotherapy. *Counseling Psychologist, 16,* 190-234.

Martin, J. (1988). A proposal for researching possible relationships between scientific theories and personal theo-ries and personal theories of counselors and clients. *Journal of Counseling and Development, 66,* 261-265.

Maturana, H., & Varela, F. (1987). *The tree of knowledge.* Boston: New Science Library.

McLeod, J. (1997). *Narrative and psychotherapy.* London: Sage.

Meichenbaum, D. (1994). *A clinical handbook/practical therapist manual for assessing and treating adults with post-traumatic stress disorder (PTSD).* Waterloo, Ontario, Canada: Institute Press.

Monk, G. (1997). How narrative therapy works. In G. Monk, J. Winslade, K. Crocket, & D. Epston (Eds.), *Narrative therapy in practice.* San Francisco: Jossey-Bass.

Neimeyer, G. J., & Neimeyer, R. A. (1994). Constructivist methods of marital and family therapy: A practical precis. *Journal of Mental Health Counseling, 16*(1), 85-104.

Neimeyer, G. J., Prichard, S., Lyddon, W. J., & Sherrard, P. A. (1993). The role of epistemologic style in counseling preference and orientation. *Journal of Counseling and Development, 71,* 515-523.

Neimeyer, R. A. (1998). Social constructionism in the counseling context. *Counseling Psychology Quarterly, 11,* 135-149.

Neimeyer, R. A., & Harter, S. (1988). Facilitating individual change in personal construct therapy. In G. Dunnett (Ed.), *Working with people: Clinical use of personal construct psychology* (pp. 229-269). London: Routledge.

Neimeyer, R. A., & Raskin, J. D. (Eds.). (2000). *Constructions of disorder.* Washington, DC: American Psychological Association.

Nelson, M. L., & Poulin, K. (1997). Methods of constructivist inquiry. In T. Sexton & B. Griffin (Eds.), *Constructivist thinking in counseling practice, research, and training* (pp. 157-173). New York: Teachers College Press.

Neufeldt, S. A. (1997). A social constructivist approach to counseling supervision. In T. Sexton & B. Griffin (Eds.), Constructivist thinking in counseling practice, research, and training (pp. 191-210). New York: Teachers College Press.

Polkinghorne, D. E. (1992). Postmodern epistemology of practice. In S. Kvale (Ed.), *Psychology and postmodernism* (pp. 146-165). London: Sage.

Polkinghorne, D. E. (1994). Reaction to special section on qualitative research in counseling process and outcome. *Journal of Counseling Psychology, 41,* 510-512.

Prawat, R., & Floden, R. (1994). Philosophical perspectives on constructivist views of learning. *Educational Psychology, 29,* 37-48.

Ricoeur, P. (1984). *Time and narrative* (Vol. 1). Chicago: University of Chicago Press.

Rigazio-DiGilio, S. A. (1994). A co-constructive-developmental approach to ecosystemic treatment. *Journal of Mental Health Counseling, 16*, 43-74.

Rigazio-DiGilio, S. A. (1997). From microscopes to holographs: Client development within a constructivist paradigm. In T. Sexton & B. Griffin (Eds.), *Constructivist thinking in counseling practice, research, and training* (pp. 74-100). New York: Teachers College Press.

Rigazio-DiGilio, S. A. (2000a). Reconstructing psychological distress and disorder from a relational perspective: A systemic coconstructive-developmental framework. In R. Neimeyer & J. Raskin (Eds.), *Constructions of disorder* (pp. 309-332). Washington, DC: American Psychological Association.

Rigazio-DiGilio, S. A. (2000b). Relational diagnosis: A coconstructive-developmental perspective for assessment and treatment. [Special edition: New developments in relational therapy (M. Goldfried, Ed.; J. Magnavita, Guest Ed.)]. *Journal of Clinical Psychology/In Session: Psychotherapy in Practice, 56*, 1017-1036.

Rigazio-DiGilio, S. A., Gonçalves, O. F., & Ivey, A. E. (1996). From cultural to existential diversity: The impossibility of an integrative psychotherapy within a traditional framework. *Applied and Preventative Psychology: Current Scientific Perspectives, 5*, 235-248.

Rigazio-DiGilio, S. A., & Ivey, A. E. (1990). Developmental therapy and depressive disorders: Measuring cognitive levels through patient natural language. *Professional Psychology: Research and Practice, 21*, 470-475.

Rigazio-DiGilio, S. A., & Ivey, A. E. (1995). Individual and family issues in intercultural counselling and therapy: A culturally-centered perspective. *Canadian Journal of Counselling, 29*, 244-261.

Rigazio-DiGilio, S. A., Ivey, A. E., & Locke, D. (1997). Continuing the postmodern dialogue: Enhancing and contextualizing multiple voices. *Journal of Mental Health Counseling, 19*, 233-255.

Sexton, T. L., & Griffin, B. (1997). The social and political nature of psychological science: The challenges, potentials, and future of constructivist thinking. In T. L. Sexton & B. Griffin (Eds.), *Constructivist thinking in counseling practice, research, and training* (pp. 249-262). New York: Teachers College Press.

Sexton, T. L., & Whiston, S. C. (1994). The status of the counseling relationship: An empirical review, theoretical implications, and research directions. *Counseling Psychologist, 22*, 6-78.

Steenbarger, B. N. (1991). All the world is not a stage: Emerging contextualist themes in counseling and development. *Journal of Counseling and Development, 70*, 288-296.

Sue, D. W., Ivey, A. E., & Pedersen, P. B. (1996). *A theory of multicultural counseling and therapy*. Pacific Grove, CA: Brooks/Cole.

Tamase, K., & Rigazio-DiGilio, S. A. (1997). Expanding client worldviews: Investigating developmental counseling and therapy assumptions. *International Journal for the Advancement of Counselling, 19*, 229-247.

Vailhinger, H. (1924). *The philosophy of "as if."* London: Routledge & Kegan Paul. (Original work published 1911)

Vico, G. (1948). *The new science* (T. G. Bergin & M. H. Fisch, Trans.). Ithaca, NY: Cornell University Press. (Original work published 1725)

Viney, L. L. (1993). *Life stories: Personal construct therapy with the elderly*. Chichester, UK: Wiley.

von Foerster, H. (1984). On constructing a reality. In P. Watzlawick (Ed.), *The invented reality* (pp. 40-71). New York: Norton.

von Glaserfeld, E. (1991). Knowing without metaphysics: Aspects of the radical constructivist position. In F. Steier (Ed.), *Research and reflexivity* (pp. 12-29). Newbury Park, CA: Sage.

Watzlawick, P. (Ed.). (1984). *The invented reality*. New York: Norton.

Wentworth, W., & Wentworth, C. (1997). The social construction of culture and its implications for the therapeutic mind-self. In T. L. Sexton & B. Griffin (Eds.), *Constructivist thinking in counseling practice, research, and training* (pp. 41-57). New York: Teachers College Press.

White, M. (1989). The externalizing of the problem. *Dulwich Centre Newsletter*, pp. 3-21. (Dulwich Centre Publications, Adelaide, Australia)

White, M., & Epston, D. (1990). *Narrative means to therapeutic ends*. New York: Norton.

Wittgenstein, L. (1969). *Philosophical investigations* (3rd ed.; G. Anscombe, Trans.). New York: Macmillan.

Wynne, L., Shields, C., & Sirkin, M. (1992). Illness, family theory, and family therapy: I. Conceptual issues. *Family Process, 31*, 3-18.

CHAPTER FOURTEEN

Developmental Counseling and Therapy and Multicultural Counseling and Therapy

Metatheory, Contextual Consciousness, and Action

ALLEN E. IVEY

MARY BRADFORD IVEY

This chapter describes two complementary theories developed out of the counseling orientation: developmental counseling and therapy (DCT) (Ivey, 1986/2000, 1991/1993) and multicultural counseling and therapy (MCT) (Sue, Ivey, & Pedersen, 1996). Both of these models are culture centered, have strong roots in counseling, and were developed by counselor educators.

Both DCT and MCT argue strongly that all counseling is multicultural counseling. As integrative metatheories, they point out that all clients are people-in-social-context and that contextual variables deeply affect what occurs in individuals—language, race/ethnicity, gender, sexual orientation, disability/ability, spiritual/religious orientation, and experience with trauma. In addition, life experience and multiple demographic and social constructs affect clients; again, *all counseling and therapy is multicultural*. Failing to recognize the multicultural base of the helping professions limits our effectiveness. Worse, this lack of effectiveness can and does harm clients. Our first ethical imperative is not to do harm to those whom we would serve.

MCT is organized around six major propositions, the first of which is as follows:

> MCT theory is a metatheory of counseling and psychotherapy. A theory about theories, it offers an organizational framework for understanding the numerous helping approaches that humankind has developed. It recognizes that theories of counseling and psychotherapy developed in the Western world and those helping models indigenous to non-Western cultures are neither inherently right [nor] wrong. Each theory represents a different worldview. (Sue et al., 1996, p. 13)

DCT also is an integrative metatheory and, like MCT, has many implications for both conceptualizing and facilitating the direct practice of counseling. DCT seeks to provide a working framework and rationale for integrating multiple points of view. DCT, however, rests on a neo-Piagetian developmental base with an emphasis on life-span cognitive/emotional development. The two frameworks are discussed together in this chapter, but because of space limitations, the primary emphasis is on MCT and its major propositions. DCT provides a complementary and very practical approach

that is useful in implementing many aspects of MCT.

The aim of this chapter is to provide some conceptual and practical applications for the reader (for a comprehensive view of the two approaches, see Ivey, 1986/2000, and Sue et al., 1996). MCT propositions are presented at the beginnings of key chapter segments.

The chapter discussion first focuses on the centrality of context in counseling. Second, it examines oppression as a central issue in the counseling and therapy process. Third, it presents the evolution of consciousness as a metagoal of counseling and therapy. Fourth, it explores the premises and potentials of DCT and MCT. Fifth, it presents specifics of a "liberation counseling" in which clients are encouraged to see themselves in social context. Sixth, it briefly describes the importance of adapting traditional theory so that it is more multiculturally aware and encourages the use of multiple approaches to intervention. Finally, it provides perspectives on the future of DCT and MCT.

Contextual Awareness as a Central Construct

Consciousness of self-in-social-context is central and essential to human growth and development. In DCT and MCT, the individualistic word *self* is replaced by *self-in-context, self-in-relation, person-in-community* (Ogbonnaya, 1994), and *being-in-relation* (Jordan, Kaplan, Baker Miller, Stiver, & Surrey, 1991). Both MCT and DCT point out that internal emotional distress often is related to external stressors. So-called disorder often is a reaction to disordered social conditions such as racism and oppression (Ivey & Ivey, 1998).

DCT extends the contextual framework and views various types of trauma experienced by clients as cultures deeply influenced by external conditions. For example, children of alcoholics, cancer survivors, rape survivors, and veterans of Vietnam and Gulf Wars often have experienced major trauma. Their depression, anxiety, and/or acting-out issues often are a logical result of the insane conditions through which they have lived. DCT argues that trauma survivors join particular cultures with specific norms of assimilation, rules, hierarchies, and experience. Failing to recognize the unique aspects of these cultural issues, where external (not internal) conditions are the problem, too often is a major failing of the counseling and psychotherapy field. So-called disorder is a logical response to one's developmental history (see, e.g., Ivey & Ivey, 1998).

Until counseling and therapy recognize the centrality of contextual issues and reconstruct the idea of the self, it will be difficult to work with the underlying oppression faced by many clients. MCT's proposition in this area states,

> Both counselor and client identities are formed and embedded in multiple levels of experience (individual, group, and universal) and contexts (individual, family, and cultural milieu). The totality of interrelationship of experiences and contexts must be the focus of treatment. (Sue et al., 1996, p. 15)

This important proposition of MCT reminds us that we need to see the individual in social context. Another way in which to think about this issue is whether or not the problem is *in the person* or *in the social context*. MCT and DCT argue that we cannot understand the person without an appropriate balance of person and environmental issues.

Before moving further, however, DCT and MCT are not opposed to beliefs in self-actualization and the need to recognize individual uniqueness in each client. Rather, these two models consider traditional theory to be extremely important and helpful in the change process. But traditional models of human change are incomplete and fail to consider the full complexity of the human condition. *The failure to see cultural and contextual issues actually denies and oppresses those whom we seek to help.* DCT and MCT argue that counseling without contextual awareness is more of a problem than a solution.

Both traditional individualistic thought and awareness of the fact that we are born into and live our lives in relation to others and to social context are essential. To counsel or treat any individual without awareness of unique developmental history, family background, and cultural factors—in truth—is to lessen the particularity and dignity of the person. Contextual awareness ultimately enhances individual personhood while it simultaneously facilitates relationships with others. A self-oriented counseling can end up being "self-ish." The "I" focus of most counseling theories and practices today fails to see the true complexity of men and women and their social context. Thus, both DCT and MTC endorse traditional concepts such as self-actualization and autonomy but supplement them with contextual awareness.

Oppression

One of the most important contextual issues is oppression. Locke (1998) pointed out the centrality of racism and prejudice in counseling in his book, *Increasing Multicultural Understanding*. He commented,

> *Prejudice* is defined as judging before fully examining the object of evaluation. *Racial prejudice* refers to judgement based on racial/ethnic/cultural group membership before getting to know the person. *Racism* combines prejudice with power—power to do something based on prejudiced beliefs. (p. 9, italics in original)

Oppression, particularly in the form of single or repeating instances of trauma, was described by Ivey and Ivey (1998) as perhaps the central issue in the counseling and therapy process. They commented,

> Trauma is endemic to society, and the majority of us will experience trauma in various forms as a normal part of life experience. Elliott (1997) completed a survey across the United States and found that 72% of respondents reported memory of traumatic events and 32% of these reported delayed recall. DCT argues that developmental trauma is basic and inherent to most *DSM-IV* [*Diagnostic and Statistical Manual of Mental Disorders* (American Psychiatric Association, 1994)] categories and that an understanding of incidence and implications of post-traumatic stress is basic for any meaningful work with severely distressed clients. (p. 342)

To experience trauma is to go through an oppressive event. Racism and prejudice are oppressive in a particularly traumatic way. First, there is the trauma of an instance of racism. Second, there is the continuing trauma of living in a racist and oppressive society. Duran and Duran (1995) talked of the "soul wound," a particularly pervasive type of trauma experienced over the years and in daily life by Native Americans

(and, by extension, people of color and other oppressed groups).

DCT proposes that the majority of clients experience trauma in some fashion or another. Although this may range from rape and incest to automobile accidents and war, the continuing traumas resulting from prejudice and racism as outlined by Locke (1998) are a central concern for which much more attention is required.

Ivey (1973, 1991) worked with inpatients at a veterans hospital during the final stages of the Vietnam War. Concrete skills training and reflective cognitive-behavioral techniques were important, but reconsidering the trauma and the oppressive systems related to that war was an important part of treatment. The gathering together of veterans to discuss their mutual issues and stories was vital to consciousness raising. We must recall that, eventually, it was the veterans who taught us about posttraumatic stress. Isn't it sad (and perhaps typical) that professionals and the *DSM-IV* now call their logical response to war stressors *posttraumatic stress disorder*? This is characteristic of an individualistic, noncontextual approach in which stress-related disorders are attributed to the failure of the individual. The word *disorder* might need to be stricken from the counselor and therapist vocabulary. Posttraumatic stress is nothing but a logical response to insane external conditions.

Native American theorist Carolyn Attneave provided many suggestions for action for a more inclusive counseling future (Attneave, 1969, 1982; see also Heckman-Stone, 2000). Attneave's network therapy speaks to the importance of working not only with individuals and families but also with entire communities. Duran and Duran's (1996) *Native American Postcolonial Psychology* provides a comprehensive view of culturally and contextually aware counseling and therapy.

Evolution of Consciousness: A Metagoal of Counseling

A major question remains: How do we help clients to gain consciousness of how their personal issues relate to social context? How can we help them find new ways of attributing their distress in a more balanced fashion? Some clients need to learn external attribution, others need to learn internal attribution, but most require a reasonable balance of the two. Cultural identity theory, we believe, supplies a vital connection between individualistic and contextual counseling.

Another important proposition of MCT is the following:

> Cultural identity development is a major determinant of counselor and client attitudes toward the self, others of the same group, and the dominant group. These attitudes, which may be manifested in affective and behavioral dimensions, are strongly influenced not only by cultural variables but also by the dynamics of dominant-subordinate relationships among culturally different groups. The level or stage of racial/cultural identity development will both influence how clients and counselors define the problem and dictate what they believe to be appropriate counseling/therapy goals and processes. (Sue et al., 1996, p. 17)

Cognitive/emotional development is a major goal of much of counseling, and it is perhaps even more central to DCT and MCT. Both theories recognize that, over time, people develop increased awareness of self and others, of self and context, and of the role of cultural factors in their lives. Because DCT and MCT are integrative theories, each includes other theories within its framework, and there are many shared interrelated constructs.

Let us now consider how DCT and MCT work with cultural identity theory.

The MCT Paradigm and the Evolution of Consciousness

The MCT developmental framework rests in cultural identity theory (Cross, 1971, 1991, 1995; Thomas, 1971). Cross and Thomas independently generated cultural identity theory as they observed cognitive/emotional development among African Americans who experienced the Black identity movement of the 1960s. They both recognized a Black consciousness or racial identity starting in a naive embedded awareness that then was shaken by the incongruities and discrepancies encountered in a racist society.

The most influential model has been that developed by Cross. The states or stages of the Cross model are summarized as follows:

- *Preencounter.* The individual (or group) may be locked into a White perspective and devalues or denies the vitality and importance of an African American worldview. The goal of some African Americans who take this perspective might be to be as "White" as possible.
- *Encounter.* The African American meets the realities of racism in an often emotionally jarring experience. This perturbs one's former consciousness and often leads to significant change.
- *Immersion-Emersion.* The discovery of what it means to be African American and valuing Blackness become important while often simultaneously denigrating Whites. Emotions can run strong with pride in one's culture and

anger at others. This often is a stage of action for African American rights.

- *Internalization.* A more internalized reflective sense of self-confidence develops, and emotional experience is more calm and secure. This often is featured by "psychological openness, ideological flexibility, and a general decline in strong anti-White feelings" (Parham, White, & Ajamu, 1999, p. 49). However, the strength of commitment to the African American world may be even stronger. In addition, Cross (1995) suggested a fifth stage, very similar to internalization but with the addition of a commitment to action and social change.

Cultural identity often is described sequentially, but Parham also saw cultural identity holistically and spoke of recycling (Parham et al., 1999). For example, one may achieve internalization on certain concepts but then might encounter a new form of racism. The individual then finds that although he or she might be thinking primarily from an internalization frame of reference, the new experience helps the individual to realize that parts of him or her still are at the encounter or other state of consciousness. Life is a constant state of development and change. There is no one "right" or final stage. Cross (1995) made the same point when he commented that each state or stage has value in certain situations. There is danger in thinking of one way of being as "best" at all times.

Parham made two additional important contributions to cultural identity theory. He pointed out that if children and adolescents "are exposed to and indoctrinated with parental and societal messages that are very pro-Black in orientation, then the personal identity and reference group orientation initially developed by [those] youngster[s] might be pro-Black as well" (Parham et al., 1999, p. 50). In short, from Parham's frame of reference, a circle

rather than a linear chart might be a more useful way in which to present identity development. Parham's third point was that

> identity resolution can occur in at least three ways: stagnation (failure to move beyond one's initial identity state), stagewise linear progression (movement from one identity state to another in a sequential linear fashion), and recycling (movement back through the stages once a cycle has been completed). (Parham et al., 1999, p. 53)

Cultural identity theory, then, is moving toward a broad developmental framework, and it is becoming possible to relate it to traditional life-span ego development theory (e.g., Erikson, 1950/1963). However, self-in-context, person-in-community, and being-in-relation will result in a far more culturally centered view of development than presently exists.

A large number of theorists and researchers have validated the sequential stages of cultural identity development in many cultural settings and extended it to other groups. Important among these have been Atkinson, Morten, and Sue (1993; general theory of cultural identity development), Hardiman (1982; White identity development), and Helms (1990; African American and White identity development). Although the language varies, the general sequence identified by Cross remains constant.

Both DCT and MCT seek to enhance the development of awareness of self as a cultural being. Both suggest the need for action to change that social context. Cultural identity theory, however, has focused its central effort on expanding awareness of one's racial/ethnic identity. Increasingly, we are finding identity theories focused on other multicultural issues. Cass (1979, 1984, 1990), Marszalek (1998), and Marszalek and Cashwell (1998) developed theories of gay and lesbian identity development. Ivey, Ivey, and Simek-Morgan (1997) suggested that many groups (e.g., women, cancer survivors, people with disabilities, Vietnam War veterans) go through parallel issues of identity as they discover the power of context in their individual lives.

Developmental Counseling and Therapy: The Evolution of Consciousness Through Narratives

DCT was developed from a different reference point from MCT's cultural identity theory, but there is considerable congruence around the concept of consciousness development. DCT offers a different but complementary theoretical base plus narrative specifics leading toward action to enhance identity development.

DCT's cognitive/emotional development rests in a postmodern interpretation of the Swiss developmental epistemologist, Jeanne Piaget (see especially Piaget, 1926/1963). This was partially the result of an examination of the major cognitive-developmental theories that revealed their theoretical foundations as resting on Piaget—Gilligan (1982), Kegan (1982), Kohlberg (1981), and Selman (1976). Logically, then, A. Ivey concluded that it might be wise to focus most on Piaget's development framework and move from there to find specifics for counseling and therapy.

If Piagetian thought has formed the base of so many recognized theorists, then it might be more useful to return to the originator, rather than his followers, as the foundation for integrating cognitive-developmental thought into practice. DCT points out that by joining Piagetian thinking and extensive research with a modern developmental point of view, we can move forward in a more holistic fashion. How-

ever, Piaget and most of his followers have tended to focus on the traditional individualistic self, failing to consider the person-in-context and the being-in-relation. DCT seeks to redress this error by emphasizing that development occurs over the life span—that Piagetian constructs reappear in adolescent and adult learning—but always in social context.

Whereas cultural identity theories tend to focus on specific groups, DCT takes a narrative approach to the evolution of consciousness. Individuals (and families and groups) have life stories that they tell about themselves, guiding the ways in which they think and behave.

Specifically, DCT theory asserts that clients come to counseling with varying levels of consciousness or meaning-making systems used to understand their world.[1] These consciousness orientations lead to different styles of thinking and behaving. The task of counselors is to assess and understand the cognitive/emotional ways in which clients make sense of what is happening. Then, counselors join clients where they "are" in their cognitive/emotional understandings and assist in the expansion of development both vertically and horizontally or within and across the meaning-making systems. No one type of consciousness is best, although more states and stages permit more possibilities for thought and action.

Meaning making can be equated with the development of consciousness. DCT suggests that Piagetian stages recycle again and again throughout life in a fashion similar to that suggested by Parham. DCT talks of four epistemological styles, stages, or levels of consciousness that have interesting parallels to cultural identity theory.

- *Sensorimotor consciousness.* The client or group often is embedded in direct experience.

What is seen, heard, and felt is central. External reality can direct inner experience with little or no reflective consciousness. Cognition and emotion often are not separated. The person might not be fully able to separate self from situation.

- *Concrete/situational consciousness.* The client again is focused on external reality but can talk about his or her issues with a "subject-object" orientation. Expect concrete detailed stories of issues. Emotions now are separated from cognition, but reflection is not prominent.

- *Formal/reflective consciousness.* The client or group is able to reflect on experience, cognitions, and emotions. Much traditional counseling theory rests here (e.g., "reflection of feelings"). The client is able to note and think about patterns. Action on the world, often associated with the concrete and dialectic styles, tends to be overlooked. A reflective person often is as sure of what he or she thinks and feels as is a person who is concrete, although both may fail to think about the assumptions on which their thoughts and actions are based.

- *Dialectic/systemic.* Two major concepts illustrate this style of meaning making: multiperspective thought and awareness of self-in-context. A person who thinks from this perspective is able to view information and emotions from several points of view and is able to examine and challenge his or her own assumptions. Although it is possible to become enmeshed in complex thought, action on oneself and systems often is important.

The therapeutic value of the multiple consciousness orientations of DCT is exemplified by a study of hospital inpatient clients diagnosed with depression (Rigazio-DiGilio & Ivey, 1990). All four levels of consciousness were found, and each was associated with a different narrative. Depressed clients with primary sensorimotor orientation narratives tended to present chaotic, body-oriented ways of think-

ing about their depression. Those with concrete narratives tended to describe concrete symptoms and talked in a linear fashion with sequential stories. Reflective patients tended to think about their depression abstractly. Dialectic patients saw their depression in a social context, often from multiple perspectives. Interestingly, as patients moved through a sequential discussion of their issues, they tended to move toward more systemic thinking and to attribute less responsibility to internal self-oriented conditions. In the process of examining consciousness, patients' consciousness would change.

DCT and MCT Parallels: Evolution of Consciousness

The parallels between Piagetian stages, cultural identity development, and DCT meaning-making orientations may be seen in Box 14.1. The holistic model notes that development can occur within multiple states/stages or levels/orientations/styles simultaneously. We should recall that individuals or groups can be expected to move at any time from one consciousness model to another. Types of thought, feeling, and actions vary within each consciousness model.

Openness to here-and-now experience also can represent a change in growth if, as Parham suggested, an individual is not caught in denial and stagnation. For example, concrete and specific encounter with a racist incident can perturb the individual and help him or her to move out of sensorimotor magic thinking patterns.

Encounter is so important to the change process that Cross and others usually have presented it as a separate stage. DCT traditionally has viewed this type of consciousness as late

BOX 14.1
Two Models of Holistic Consciousness Compared

Cultural Identity Theory	*Developmental Counseling and Therapy*
Preencounter	Sensorimotor
Encounter	Late sensorimotor
Immersion/emersion	Concrete
Immersion/emersion	Formal
Internalization	Dialectic/systemic

NOTE: The holistic model notes that development can occur within multiple states/stages or levels/orientations/styles simultaneously. The four types of consciousness can be thought of as a circle, rather than a linear model, indicating that individuals or groups can be expected to move at any time from one consciousness model to another. Types of thought, feeling, and action vary within each consciousness model.

sensorimotor because it opens the way to a concrete consciousness.

Immersion/emersion concepts relate to concrete and formal consciousness. The most likely result of consciousness during the encounter stage is concrete and specific awareness of racism and prejudice accompanied by anger—and, often, concrete and specific action to fight the situation. At a later time during this stage, the reflective consciousness becomes prominent, and the ability to reflect is essential if one is to operate at the internalization or dialectic/systemic level.

The reflective consciousness—thinking about thinking—is characteristic of DCT clients who think about self and of reflective individuals in cultural identity theory who reflect on cultural identity. A requirement of internalization is systemic thinking and the ability to take multiple perspectives. The self-in-relation or person-as-community requires dialectical/systemic thought. Again, Parham's model is useful here. Develop-

mentally, some African American or other minority youths might actually operate at this seemingly more sophisticated level because they may be fully aware of how oppression operates at a systemic level, yet they are able to see the perspectives of many Whites.

Thus, linear models of consciousness development do not really describe the complexity; a holistic model might be more realistic than linear stage frameworks. Young people who generally might not be reflective in cognitive/emotional development often can be found demonstrating awareness of the effect of systems.

Both the DCT model and Parham's addition to cultural identity theory suggest that higher is not necessarily better. There is value in the embeddedness of preencounter and sensorimotor approaches to reality. The ability of an individual at the encounter or concrete orientation to act on the world and tell clear stories is important. No one can deny that the formal reflective consciousness of immersion/emersion is important. And, from both the counseling/therapeutic model of DCT and the multicultural framework, it is patently clear that the ability to take multiple perspectives on reality is important. Consciousness sometimes may work in a linear fashion, but ultimately it is holistic and moving, perhaps ultimately existential and spiritual in nature. Is not our consciousness our spirit?

Moving Consciousness to New Narratives: DCT and MCT

Let us now turn to using the parallels between DCT and MCT and how they might work for the effective counselor. Another major proposition of MCT is the following:

> The effectiveness of MCT is most likely enhanced when the counselor uses modalities and defines goals consistent with the life experience and cultural values of the client. No single approach is equally effective across all populations and life situations. The ultimate goal of multicultural counselor training is to expand the repertoire of helping responses available to the professional regardless of theoretical orientation. (Sue et al., 1996, p. 19)

This assumption of MCT is a culturally appropriate restatement of traditional counseling theory and practice: *Join the client where he or she is.* Counselors and therapists are, for the most part, deeply committed to empathy and understanding clients' frames of reference. What has been missing in traditional empathic relationships and therapeutic alliance writing is cultural context and awareness of the self-in-relation.

DCT is committed to a co-constructed counseling and therapy with an emphasis on equality between counselor and client or between therapist and patient. This commitment includes awareness of the social context of both the counselor/therapist and the client consultant. The term *client consultant* emphasizes that the client can and often does have a significant impact on the helper.

Joining a client where he or she is involves diagnosing styles and levels of consciousness development, respecting that person where he or she *is,* and facilitating expansion of consciousness in consultation with the client.

The first task for a therapist focused on consciousness is to assess the client's style of meaning making. This will show most clearly in the client's verbal behavior in the interview, but it also might be manifest in behavior in the client's daily life. Both cultural identity theory and DCT suggest ways in which to assess client consciousness development.

Client narratives are particularly useful for assessment. Questions such as the following typically stimulate sufficient information:

> Could you tell me a story that occurs to you when you think about yourself as [an African American, a Korean American, a Mexican American, a Jewish American, a Polish American, a woman, a gay male, a person with AIDS, etc.]?
>
> Could you tell me about a situation in which you might have experienced or seen [prejudice, racism, sexism, heterosexism, ableism, etc.]?
>
> What does it mean to you to be [insert term here]?

DCT has generated a set of questions designed to extend narratives at each state of consciousness. Specific applications of these questions for each level of *cultural* identity theory might be as follows:

Expansion of Preencounter or Sensorimotor Consciousness

These questions are designed to encourage experiencing of what it is like to be at a specific consciousness level or orientation. They can help those at the preencounter level to expand their awareness of where they are (and perhaps prepare them to move on to other stages/states of consciousness). They also are useful for people at the immersion/emersion states who might not be fully in touch with their emotions and here-and-now experience.

The focus in the following questions is on here-and-now sensory experience related to the story. The client might be asked to generate an image of the general situation just described.

Could you think of one visual image [or auditory, kinesthetic, or other image depending on preferred sense modality of the client or group] that occurs to you that somehow strikes you as most important in that story?

Visual Perceptions
What are you seeing?
Describe in detail the scene where it happened.

Auditory perceptions:
What are you hearing?
How are people sounding?
Describe the sound in detail.

Kinesthetic perceptions:
What are you feeling in your body at this moment?
How are you feeling?
What are you feeling as this is going on?

Encouraging Movement to Another Consciousness Level

In-depth experiencing of sensorimotor experience may in itself bring about encounter and the spontaneous emergence of a new way of thinking about old ways of being. Oppression in all its forms affects the body and ultimately is a sensorimotor experience. Often, just getting fully in touch with that experience is enough to jar consciousness.

Helping the client move to a new state of consciousness often is facilitated by supportive but challenging confrontation. Pointing out discrepancies and incongruities in the client's story or situation, particularly when the story is supported by emotionally based here-and-now experience, often is helpful in moving consciousness.

Essential to the following types of supportive confrontations is, first, hearing the client carefully and listening to his or her situation

and unique perceptions and feelings. In the process of presenting what the counselor has heard, seen, or felt himself or herself, the counselor should use the client's key words so that it is the client—not the counselor—who develops the resolution (Ivey & Ivey, 1999; Ivey, Pedersen, & Ivey, 2001).

> The story is summarized with accurate paraphrasing and reflection of feeling.
>
> Important key words of the client or group are used.
>
> On the one hand, I hear you said . . ., but on the other, you said . . . .
>
> I hear you saying that you felt . . ., but then . . . .
>
> Could you point out to me the contradictions in the story and how you felt about the story now. [This type of lead may encourage more self-discovery.]

Similar questions also can be used to help people at other levels of consciousness to consider alternative perspectives. For example, a person at the immersion/emersion stage of consciousness might benefit by returning to the emotional dimensions of preencounter or by a challenge to move toward more reflective consciousness at the later stages of immersion. The person whose consciousness is at the internalization level can profit by experiencing other ways of being (e.g., the internalization stage can result in an emphasis on thinking). The internalization client may profit from the concreteness and action of the earlier stages of consciousness.

Expanding Immersion/Emersion and Concrete and Formal Consciousness

The goals at the early stage of immersion relate most closely to DCT's concrete orientation to consciousness. Formal/reflection questions are related to later stages of immersion. It also is important to note that these questions are useful in consciousness-raising groups and may help individuals to relate their experience to others in the group.

Concrete Examples Useful for the Earlier Stages of Immersion/Emersion

Could you share a story of what happened? I'd like to hear it from beginning to end.

What happened first, then what happened, and what was the consequence?

What did he or she say? What did you say? Then what was said?

What did you feel?

What do you think the other[s] felt?

Reflect feelings: "You felt . . . because . . . ."

Particularly helpful in moving to reflective thought is the summarization of two or more individual or group stories (which often will contain similar key words) and asking the individual or group how the stories are similar.

Formal Reflective Examples to Facilitate Later Stages of the Immersion/Emersion Stage

How is your story similar to stories you have told me in the past?

How is your story similar to [and different from] stories of other members of the group?

How are your feelings similar?

Is that a pattern [in the individual or group]?

What does this story say about you as a person?

What do these stories say about us all? [Identify group, e.g., a women's or gay liberation session.]

Useful in moving to internalization and dialectic/systemic thought are questions that focus on the relationship of the individual to the social context.

Expanding Internalization and Dialectic/Systemic Consciousness

Critical here is encouraging people to see themselves and their groups in systemic relation, often through multiperspectival thought. This style of consciousness can become heavily embedded in intellectual thought and abstraction. Thus, attention to action and generalizing learning to the real world through concrete action might be essential.

It often is useful to summarize major portions of an individual or group conversation. This is followed by asking people to reflect on the conversation and asking them questions such as the following:

How do you put together [or organize] all that you have told me [or the group]? What one thing stands out for you?

Often, this question or a variation will result in a broadened point of view toward the issue discussed. Other questions include the following:

How many different ways could you describe the situation? How would it look from another perspective different from your own [different ethnic group, sexual orientation, etc.]?

How would external conditions [e.g., trauma, racism, sexism, heterosexism] affect what is occurring with you [or the group]?

What rule[s] were you operating under in this situation? What rule[s] is [are] in the other person's mind?

Where did those rules come from [family, culture, etc.]?

Can you see some flaws in your own reasoning that the other person might think of? What do you see as flaws in the other person's reasoning?

Do your feelings and emotions change as you look at the situation from a new perspective?

Internalization and dialectic/systemic consciousness may become enmeshed in thought and fail to act. "Some Blacks fail to sustain a long-term interest in Black affairs. Others devote an extended period of time, if not a lifetime, to finding ways to translate their personal sense of Blackness in a plan of action or general sense of commitment" (Cross, 1995, p. 121). Both MCT and DCT would agree that thought without action is empty. Some potentially useful questions to encourage following up on these issues include the following:

What one thing might you want to do next tomorrow [or the following week] to act on what you have learned and said?

How can you put these thoughts into action?

How might you behave differently?

Let us develop an individual [or group] action plan.

It is important for the counselor or group leader to note that these all are concrete action plans and typical of what we might expect to find in the often highly motivated early stages of the concrete immersion/emersion consciousness.

And, it is important to extend this idea beyond racism to other areas of oppression. The Mothers Against Drunk Driving (MADD) organization is a personal and group statement about the effect of systemic drinking on our society. Women who march for their rights are directly attacking what many describe as an oppressive rape culture. Cancer survivors often meet in groups and take action to work with insensitive physicians or to support others in the struggle. The search for gay rights is a clear indication of taking internalization consciousness into action against heterosexism and oppression.

Action against the oppressive conditions of life can lead to better mental health. Passively sitting and discussing oppression is not enough. Action seeking to address oppressive external conditions is essential.

Each style, stage, level, or orientation to consciousness has its value. The ability to experience life directly associated with the sensorimotor and preencounter style can be useful in both survival and heightened awareness of what is happening. We need concrete narratives to describe our experience, and we need to reflect on the meaning of the narratives. Finally, dialectic/systemic internalization thought tends to help us see problems and issues in social context and, if balanced with action, can lead to significant change. So-called higher stages are not necessarily better. More useful is the ability to work with multiple levels of consciousness. Both Parham and Cross endorsed the wisdom of all states of being, but they also seemed to imply that more is better. The ability to take multiple positions seems to offer the most intentionality and perhaps the most flexibility to deal with the ultimate complexity and pervasiveness of oppressive experience.

The Liberation of Consciousness

Another major proposition of MCT theory speaks to the issues of helping clients to understand how oppression operates in their lives.

The liberation of consciousness is a basic goal of MCT theory. Whereas self-actualization, discovery of the role of the past in the present, [and] behavior change have been traditional goals of Western psychotherapy and counseling, MCT emphasizes the importance of expanding personal, family, group, and organizational consciousness of the place of self-in-relation, family-in-relation, and organization-in-relation. This results in therapy that is not only ultimately contextual in orientation, but that also draws on traditional methods of healing from many cultures. (Sue et al., 1996, p. 22)

Freire's (1972) liberation psychology has been particularly influential here. The Brazilian educator commented as follows:

True generosity consists precisely in fighting to destroy the causes which nourish false charity. False charity constrains the fearful and subdued, the "rejects of life," to extend their trembling hands. True generosity lies in striving so that these hands—whether of individuals or entire peoples—need to be extended less and less in supplication, so that more and more they become human hands which work and, [when] working, transform the world. (p. 29)

A counseling focused on liberation may use the methods of MCT and DCT to help bring individuals and groups to awareness of themselves in social context. Freire is particularly inspirational with his focus on situational and concrete change. Awareness and consciousness, as described earlier, require action leading to change.

The counseling field, individualistic in tradition, faces a major challenge in terms of social action. Is counseling interested in becoming one of those "human hands which work and, [when] working, transform the world"?

The Need for Multiple Interventions: Adapting Present Theory for Multicultural Awareness

Obviously, space does not permit full discussion of the relationships between MCT and DCT and their implications for theory and practice.

Let us summarize briefly one additional proposition of MCT as we conclude our observations:

MCT theory stresses the importance of multiple helping roles developed by many culturally different groups and societies. Besides the basic one-on-one encounter aimed at remediation in the individual, these roles often involve larger social units, systems intervention, and prevention. That is, the conventional roles of counseling and psychotherapy are only one of many others available to the helping professional. (Sue et al., 1996, p. 21)

MCT and DCT begin and end with a worldview that is contextual, one that demands more than individual, family, or group counseling alone. The counselor needs to work with all three dimensions, developing a network of change agents that together reverberate throughout the total system (Attneave, 1969, 1982).

Both MCT and DCT endorse the three early forces of counseling and therapy—psychodynamic, cognitive-behavioral, and existential-humanistic—but only if these orientations are placed in social context and broadened in their definitions and practice. Paniagua (1998) is an important example of how to use these concepts in assessment and treatment. Another attempt in this direction may be found in Ivey and colleagues (1997). These authors sought to address the "how to" of integrating multicultural issues into traditional practice with many specific exercises, particularly drawn from the internalization and dialectic/systemic orientations of DCT. MCT itself is, of course, a dialectic/systemic theory from an internalization consciousness. We would suggest that traditional theory and practice remain enmeshed in less reflective and active modes of counseling and therapy.

MCT and DCT stress the vitality of alternative approaches to therapy, particularly those drawn from other cultural frameworks (Nwachuku & Ivey, 1991). The women's movement, the gay/lesbian/bisexual/transgendered movement, and the ethnic/racial identity movement all have brought us to awareness of the importance of social context in practice. However, traditional theory and practice still have a considerable distance to go to provide culturally sensitive and aware helping.

Community counseling, intervention in systems, and encouraging changes in the workplace all are examples of an effective contextual therapy and counseling. Consultation, prevention, and training others become central roles of the competent, multiculturally aware professional.

Perspectives on the Future: DCT and MCT

We face a time of major change. MCT is leading us in a new direction. It is our hope that DCT can be part of the process supporting this change toward a new future rather than still another problem to be solved.

To put all these ideas into place, the multicultural competencies are central (Arredondo et al., 1995). Let us recall that these competencies were developed by the Association for Multicultural Counseling and Development (AMCD), a major association within the American Counseling Association (ACA). Subsequently, these competencies have been endorsed by multiple ACA divisions. The concept of specifying what it takes to be multiculturally competent is heavily reliant on the efforts of the counseling profession. Moreover, ACA members have been influential as other associations and groups within the United States and Canada, as well as other international groups, now are considering or have adopted the competencies.

Some thoughts for the future of DCT, MCT, and multicultural competence are presented for your consideration. Let us put these implications in the context of the next 50 years. The year 2050 will see our present world vastly changed. People of color are predicted to be as numerous as Whites. White privilege will perhaps be a relic of the past (McIntosh, 1989). The challenge for Whites and our present "minorities" will be to live together effectively and productively and with some sense of mutual respect and enjoyment. It might be time that we start speaking of the joys and opportunities of multiculturalism rather than considering it a problem to be solved.

Not only does White privilege need to be rolled back and ethnic/racial understanding increased, there are other matters to consider in our new, more multicultural future. All of the following (and more) can lead to a more understanding and cooperative world in 2050: We need a positive approach to language understanding, gender differences, sexual orientation and spiritual/religious differences as well as a respect for ability/disability issues.

An optimistic view of our tasks during the next decade and ensuing years with specific reference to DCT and MCT include the following:

1. Our profession will move to a contextual awareness. No longer will we think within the present individualistic frame of traditional psychodynamic, cognitive-behavioral, and existential-humanistic thought. Each of these traditional theories will remain important but will be enriched by MCT and other culturally focused frameworks such as DCT.

2. Oppression will be recognized as a central counseling construct. Counselors will include in their assessment and treatment a balance of internal and external attribution. The problem no longer will be seen as "in the individual." This will be replaced by a more sophisticated counseling in which individual, family, group,

and multiple cultural factors will be considered.

3. Facilitating the development of consciousness will become an important part of each counseling treatment plan. Counselors will be able to facilitate movement to new levels of understanding in a cooperative, co-constructive fashion with their clients. As part of this, the liberation of consciousness will become a regular part of many counseling sessions.

4. Multiple interventions co-constructed with clients will be seen as basic to any effective treatment plan. The idea of one "right" or "best" theory finally will disappear as new ways of integrating theory and practice evolve.

5. "Disorder" will cease to frame our consciousness about the deeply troubled. Rather, counseling will engage serious client "dis-stress" and not define it as "dis-ease." This means that the *DSM-IV*, if still in use, will define clients' issues and challenges as logical responses to developmental history and external social conditions. Rather than putting the difficulty in clients, counselors will enable them to balance personal and external attribution and then facilitate client internal and external *action* to produce change.

5. Counselors and the counseling profession will recognize the importance of directly attacking systemic issues that affect client development. Counseling will move toward a proactive stance rather than its present reactive position. We need not expect our clients to work alone. Counseling and counselors have an ethical imperative to work toward positive societal change.

The following is quoted and paraphrased from the final page of Ivey and colleagues' (2001) culture-centered book on group counseling:

Multicultural issues and cultural empathy underlie all forms of individual, group, and community counseling. We might coin a new term for your consideration—*multicultural intentionality*. Multi-cultural intentionality emphasizes competencies as defined by Arredondo and her colleagues (1995). Multicultural intentionality may be defined as:

1. *Awareness*—Becoming aware of your own multicultural heritage, recognizing your own biases, and [recognizing] the limits of what you can do.

2. *Knowledge*—Possessing and gaining knowledge of multicultural groups, [of] the workings of oppression, and that some traditional approaches to group work may be inappropriate or need adaptations for varying multicultural groups. This is a continuing lifelong issue and opportunity for the competent counselor and group leader, [who is] is always learning and becoming more proficient.

3. *Skills*—Possessing and constantly gaining expertise in individual and group work and their multiple orientations; developing appropriate skills to work with differing cultures; and actively seeking to prevent and eliminate prejudices, biases, and discrimination.

4. *Humility, confidence, and recovery skills*—Being aware that one does not always have the answer; that one can correct mistakes; and that one is confident in her or his ability to adapt, change, and learn. It is not your errors but [rather] your ability to recovery from them gracefully that is most important.

Let us move forward together toward a more culturally centered future for counseling.

Note

1. DCT uses multiple-language frames to discuss types of consciousness. The original term was *level*. However, consciousness ultimately is viewed as holistic. Although the term *level* remains, the complexity of human consciousness at times is better described with terms such as *stage, state, orientation, style, mode,* and *way of being. Level* and *stage* still are used but can imply that one state of being is higher than another. *State, orientation, mode, stage,* and *style* can imply nonmovement. *Way of being,* which is more holistic, is a bit vague but does suggest

movement and relationship between and among the dimensions. DCT is a holistic framework, and each language system offers a unique way in which to think about the connections and distinctions of consciousness.

References

American Psychiatric Association. (1994). *Diagnostic and statistical manual of mental disorders* (4th ed.). Washington, DC: Author.

Arredondo, P., Toporek, R., Brown, S., Jones, J., Locke, D., Sanchez, J., & Stadler, H. (1995). *Operationalization of multicultural competencies*. Washington, DC: American Counseling Association.

Atkinson, D., Morten, G., & Sue, D. W. (1993). *Counseling American minorities* (3rd ed.). Dubuque, IA: William C. Brown.

Attneave, C. (1969). Therapy in tribal settings and urban network interventions. *Family Process, 8,* 192-210.

Attneave, C. (1982). American Indian and Alaska native families: Emigrants in their own homeland. In M. McGoldrick, J. Pearce, & J. Giordano (Eds.), *Ethnicity and family therapy*. New York: Guilford.

Cass, V. C. (1979). Homosexual identity formation: A theoretical model. *Journal of Homosexuality, 4,* 219-235.

Cass, V. C. (1984). Homosexual identity formation: Testing a theoretical model. *Journal of Sex Research, 20,* 143-167.

Cass, V. C. (1990). The implications of homosexual identity formation for the Kinsey model and scale of sexual preference. In D. P. McWhirter, S. A. Sanders, & J. M. Reinisch (Eds.), *Homosexuality/heterosexuality: Concepts of sexual orientation* (pp. 239-266). New York: Oxford University Press.

Cross, W. (1971). The Negro to Black conversion experience. *Black World, 20,* 13-25.

Cross, W. (1991). *Shades of Black*. Philadelphia: Temple University Press.

Cross, W. (1995). The psychology of Nigrescence: Revising the Cross model. In J. Ponterotto, J. Casas, L. Suzuki, & C. Alexander (Eds.), *Handbook of multicultural counseling*. Thousand Oaks, CA: Sage.

Duran, E., & Duran, B. (1995). *Native American postcolonial psychology*. Albany: State University of New York Press.

Elliott, D. (1997). Traumatic events: Prevalence and delayed recall in the general population. *Journal of Consulting and Clinical Psychology, 65,* 811-820.

Erikson, E. (1963). *Childhood and society* (2nd ed.). New York: Norton. (Original work published 1950)

Freire, P. (1972). *Pedagogy of the oppressed*. New York: Herder & Herder.

Gilligan, C. (1982). *In a different voice*. Cambridge, MA: Harvard University Press.

Hardiman, R. (1982). White identity development. *Dissertation Abstracts International, 43,* 104A.

Heckman-Stone, C. (2000). A legacy of dandelions: Carolyn Lewis Attneave (1920-1992). *Journal of Multicultural Counseling and Development, 28,* 113-118.

Helms, J. (1990). *Black and White racial identity: Theory, research, and practice*. Westport, CT: Greenwood.

Ivey, A. (1973). Media therapy: Educational change planning for psychiatric patients. *Journal of Counseling Psychology, 20,* 338-343.

Ivey, A. (1991, October). *Media therapy reconsidered: Developmental counseling and therapy as a comprehensive model for treating severely distressed clients*. Paper presented at the Veterans Administration Conference, Orlando, FL.

Ivey, A. (1993). *Developmental strategies for helpers: Individual, family, and network interventions*. North Amherst, MA: Microtraining Associates. (Original work published 1991)

Ivey, A. (2000). *Developmental therapy: Theory into practice*. North Amherst, MA: Microtraining Associates. (Original work published 1986)

Ivey, A., & Ivey, M. (1998). Reframing DSM-IV: Positive strategies from developmental counseling and therapy. *Journal of Counseling and Development, 76,* 334-350.

Ivey, A., & Ivey, M. (1999). *Intentional interviewing and counseling* (4th ed.). Pacific Grove, CA: Brooks/Cole.

Ivey, A., Ivey, M., & Simek-Morgan, L. (1997). *Counseling and psychotherapy: A multicultural perspective*. Boston: Allyn & Bacon.

Ivey, A., Pedersen, P., & Ivey, M. (2001). *Intentional group counseling: A microskills approach*. Pacific Grove, CA: Brooks/Cole.

Jordan, J., Kaplan, A., Baker Miller, J., Stiver, I., & Surrey, J. (Eds.). (1991). *Women's growth in connection*. New York: Guilford.

Kegan, R. (1982). *The evolving self*. Cambridge, MA: Harvard University Press.

Kohlberg, L. (1981). *The philosophy of moral development*. San Francisco: Harper & Row.

Locke, D. C. (1998). *Increasing multicultural understanding: A comprehensive model*. Thousand Oaks, CA: Sage.

Marszalek, J. F., III. (1998). *The gay and lesbian affirmative development (GLAD) model: Testing the validity of an integrative model of gay identity development theory and Ivey's developmental counseling therapy model*. Unpublished doctoral dissertation, Mississippi State University.

Marszalek, J. F., III, & Cashwell, C. S. (1998). The gay and lesbian affirmative development (GLAD) model: Applying Ivey's developmental counseling therapy model to Cass' gay and lesbian identity development model. *Journal of Adult Development and Aging, 1* [Online]. Available: www.uncg.edu/ced/jada

McIntosh. P. (1989, July-August). White privilege: Unpacking the invisible knapsack. *Peace and Freedom,* pp. 8-10.

Nwachuku, U., & Ivey, A. (1991). Culture-specific counseling: An alternative training model. *Journal of Counseling and Development, 70,* 106-111.

Ogbonnaya, O. (1994). Person as community: An African understanding of the person as an intrapsychic community. *Journal of Black Psychology, 20,* 75-87.

Paniagua, F. (1998). *Assessing and treating culturally diverse clients: A practical guide* (2nd ed.). Thousand Oaks, CA: Sage.

Parham, T., White, J., & Ajamu, A. (1999). *The psychology of Blacks: An African centered perspective.* Upper Saddle River, NJ: Prentice Hall.

Piaget, J. (1963). *The origins of intelligence in children.* New York: Norton. (Original work published 1926)

Rigazio-DiGilio, S., & Ivey, A. (1990). Developmental therapy and depressive disorders. *Professional Psychology, 6,* 470-475.

Selman, R. (1976). A developmental approach to interpersonal and moral awareness in young children. In T. Hennessy (Ed.), *Values and human development.* New York: Paulist Press.

Sue, D. W., Ivey, A., & Pedersen, P. (1996). *A theory of multicultural counseling and therapy.* Pacific Grove, CA: Brooks/Cole.

Thomas, C. (1971). *Boys no more.* Beverly Hills, CA: Glencoe.

CHAPTER FIFTEEN

Basic Counseling Skills

JANE GOODMAN

Although most writers date the focus on using basic skills in helping to the mid-20th century, we can see precursors to this idea in the writings of early philosophers and religious leaders. (For a comprehensive look at history of counseling, see Kottler & Brown, 1996.) The Greek philosopher Socrates, in particular, was described by Plato in the dialogues as using questioning and reflection in his interactions with his students (see, e.g., Edman, 1956). Socrates taught by elucidating (literally *drawing out*) answers from his pupils rather than by didactically lecturing, as then was the custom (as it often is now). This process, today referred to as the Socratic method, implied that he believed that the pupils *already knew* the answers and that his job was to help them to become aware of that knowledge.

Counselors today who use basic helping skills usually are acting from the same prem-

ise—that their clients have the internal knowledge of how to solve their problems, make their decisions, and change their behavior and just need help in recognizing that knowledge.

Freud and other early psychoanalysts did not focus on basic skills at all. At the risk of oversimplifying, their approach can be described as one of trying to understand the internal workings—or unconscious—of their clients by encouraging them to free associate, describe dreams, and the like. The analyst's role varied, depending on the practitioner, but it basically was a "talking cure." Hackney and Cormier (1996), in discussing affective interventions in general, stated that "discussing techniques" was a contradiction in terms because affective therapists focus on the relationship between client and counselor rather than on techniques.

Rogers (1958) expanded the idea of *relationship* espoused by the psychoanalytically oriented practitioners by stipulating three core conditions for effective counseling: empathy, genuineness, and unconditional positive regard. In an earlier statement on the same topic, Rogers (1942) described the basic aspects of a counseling relationship as including (a) warmth and responsiveness, (b) permissiveness in regard to expression of feeling, (c) therapeutic limits, and (d) freedom from pressure or coercion (pp. 87-90).

Carkhuff (1969, 1972, 1987) developed a set of training methods and materials that codified basic skills and provided helpers with a set of specific instructions on how to demonstrate empathy by attending; responding to content, feelings, and meaning; facilitating understanding; and facilitating acting.

Ivey (1971) expanded these concepts into what he called *microcounseling/microskills training*. He added confrontation, focusing, and influencing to the skills described by Carkhuff (1987), as well as developing very specific strategies for learning and integrating these skills. More recently, Ivey and Ivey (1999) added multicultural skills to this list.

A beginning counselor often will seek the advice of his or her supervisor with some variation of the following: "I have learned a lot about how to conceptualize client issues. I know how to listen when clients come in and present their issues to me. But what do I say when it's my turn to speak?" It is the response to this question that we address when we teach basic skills.

The subsections that follow describe the basic skills of attending, responding, and questioning. Then, the more advanced skills of personalizing, focusing, and influencing are discussed. Next, methods for training helpers to use these basic skills and differences in using basic skills are described, including cultural differences and differences based on the experience of the therapist and the age, developmental level, and mental health of the client. Finally, the chapter closes with a few comments regarding the future of basic skills.

The Basic Skills Themselves

What are the building blocks of counselor responses? Experienced therapists usually are not aware of the individual skills that they use anymore than experienced pianists stop to consider each note that they play. They read the scores and translate the notes on the pages to their fingers on the keyboards. Perhaps an even more familiar analogy is that of learning to read. New readers see each letter and then each word as they carefully sound out sentences. Most mature readers see sentences or even paragraphs in chunks, pausing only perhaps at unfamiliar words.

Basic skills in counseling are much the same. With experience, counselors integrate the components so that they become "natural," and counselors think about them only when confronted with clients who present difficulties to them.

In the following subsections, each of the basic skills identified by one or more of the authors cited in the previous section is described. These include attending and observation, responding by reflecting thoughts and feelings, and questioning. Examples of brief dialogues illustrating reflecting and questioning are then presented. The dialogues are considered as excerpts from the middle of a counseling session; that is, there are no opening or closing sections.

Nonverbal Attending and Observation

Much of what we communicate is nonverbal. In fact, it often is suggested that the majority of our communications are nonverbal. This probably is true of many animals, not just humans. Indeed, when we are advised before hiking in the woods or walking in the city not to make eye contact with a bear or a dog, as the case may be, it is a recognition that eye contact communicates something.

Nonverbal behavior usually is described as including eye contact, head nods, facial animation, body posture, and physical distance between counselor and client (Hackney & Cormier, 1996). In addition, Carkhuff (1987) and Ivey and Ivey (1999) noted the importance of leaning, squaring, having an expressive face, and using encouraging gestures as part of nonverbal counseling behavior. Facing clients squarely often is described as having both feet on the floor, although some might describe that type of square sitting as more typical of male posture than of female posture. Inattentiveness may be demonstrated by turning away from the client, yawning, gazing around or in other directions, frowning, handling objects, or looking at one's watch frequently. It has been said that crossing one's legs or arms also may indicate being closed to communication. It often is easier to describe inattentive communication behaviors than to describe attentive ones.

We communicate attentiveness by our body posture, our head positions, and our nodding as well as by eye contact. In the case of the bear or dog mentioned earlier, eye contact is supposed to communicate aggressiveness or a desire for domination. With people, eye contact is supposed to communicate attentiveness. As is discussed later, this may differ among various cultures, but it is the standard in Western society. Nonverbal attending, however, is a delicate balance between attention and invasion. If you ever have had the experience of having someone "in your face," then you know how eye contact can be invasive. If you picture a drill sergeant, then you again will be able to imagine inappropriate eye contact. A steady but occasionally varying gaze usually is recommended. But with this, as with all of the skills to be discussed in this chapter, responsiveness to client feedback is critical. And with nonverbal attending, client feedback also may be nonverbal.

Another basic skill, therefore, may be termed *observation*. Much information may be gleaned by paying close attention to clients' behavior. In interpreting nonverbal behavior, however, it is important to see observations as hunches to be checked out, not as conclusions. Clients who lean back when counselors lean in might be telling the counselors that they are too close for the clients' comfort zones. Or, it always is possible that they might be in uncomfortable chairs or have bad backs.

If we look at the basic skills as a hierarchy, then we could say that the next step is listening. Again, this is not visible except as revealed by the attending behavior just described, but it requires considerable effort, especially for beginning helpers. It is a common experience for neophyte or even experienced therapists to be surprised, or to have family members surprised, by their fatigue at the end of their days where they "only" sat and listened. For this reason, many writers have called it "active listening" (e.g., Hackney & Cormier, 1996).

In addition to the energy required, there are other barriers to active listening. One may think to a time when he or she wanted to listen to the weather on the car radio. One turns to the correct station at a time when the weather report always is given. The next thing one knows, a voice on the radio is saying thank you to the weather person, and the person in the car has not heard a word. This person knows that he or she has not left the car. Where was this person? On a mental errand, perhaps. Thinking about whether he or she remembered to put away the milk from breakfast, thinking that he or she must remember an appointment for a haircut the next day, and thinking about a discussion with a friend all are examples of mental errands.

Another barrier to listening arises when counselors begin thinking about themselves or their own situations in response to clients' statements. For example, if a client is discussing an issue with her teenage son, then the counselor might begin to think about his or her own teenage son or about his or her own years as a teenager. If the counselor does this, then he or she probably has stopped listening at least temporarily. Or, the counselor might be thinking about himself or herself in another way, wondering how he or she is going to respond to this specific issue. This can be particularly an issue for neophyte helpers who might be less confident about their ability to handle a variety of client concerns. Even more experienced counselors might find themselves having an internal debate, for example, over whether this is a good time to confront a pattern they are seeing.

Another potential barrier to effective listening is one that is experienced by all helpers—making assumptions about what clients are going to say next. The more experience counselors have, and the better they know particular clients, the greater this danger. Counselors' assumptions often are rewarded by being right, so

counselors continue to make them, but they can get in the way of truly hearing what is being said.

Another set of listening barriers to overcome are those of not understanding what clients are saying. This might be because the messages are confusing, because counselors are not knowledgeable about the subjects they are discussing, or because counselors have been momentarily inattentive. For whatever reason, if counselors fail to ask for clarifications, then they will not adequately understand the rest of the messages. Although counselors might hesitate to interrupt clients, continuing to listen when they do not follow what is being said interrupts their ability to respond. Sometimes, in addition, sending confusing messages is central to clients' problems, and working on this issue may become part of the *content,* and not just the *process,* of counseling.

A colleague (E. Waters, personal communication, 1978) used the analogy of an umbrella stand to explain how she handled one type of distraction. She said that she imagines an umbrella stand outside of her office door into which she places all of the things on her mind as she gets ready to spend time with a client. These might be personal problems (e.g., a breakfast fight with a loved one, deadlines, paperwork to fill out before a certain date) or irritations with colleagues at work. Every issue that might be distracting goes into the umbrella stand. This is more effective than simply telling oneself not to think about whatever is on one's mind.

Try, for a moment, not thinking about *pink bunny rabbits.* I would guess that your mind now is full of the little creatures. Just as it does not work very well to push feelings down, so too does it not tend to work well to speak sternly to oneself not to think about something.

Leaving it outside—in the umbrella stand—works for my colleague because she promises herself that she can come back and get it later, at the end of the day or after this client session.

Responding

Clients, however, know only about active listening by the ways in which counselors respond. Most people categorize these responses into three main areas: minimal encouragers, reflection of thoughts and feelings, and asking questions. All of these skills lead to facilitating both understanding and action.

Minimal Encouragers

There is a category of responses that fall between nonverbal attending and actual responses, termed by Ivey and Ivey (1999) as "minimal encouragers." They are comprised of utterances such as "uh-huh," "hmn hmn," "and . . .?" and "then . . .?" Clients are encouraged to continue speaking, but without any specific directions or assurances that counselors understand. Minimal encouragers perform an important and necessary function in maintaining clients' flows of thoughts and feelings without influence from the counselors. They are not sufficient, however, for adding to clients' understanding.

Reflection of Thoughts and Feelings

For Rogers (1942, 1958), reflecting was the primary counselor response. Reflecting thoughts means responding by paraphrasing a client's statements. This often is preceded by a phrase such as "What you are saying is . . ." or "I hear you saying . . .." This verbal mirroring provides

a way for the client to know that the counselor was indeed listening and for the counselor to know that he or she heard the client correctly. It is a frequent experience at this point for the client to say, "No, what I meant was . . . ." This might be because the counselor heard the client incorrectly or because hearing the client's ideas repeated causes the client to rethink what he or she intended to communicate. Indeed, this often is a value in using this type of restatement. It provides an opportunity for clients to hear themselves as others hear them and perhaps to learn more effective ways of expressing themselves. This technique is used by many in parenting training and in couple and family counseling precisely for this reason—so that the individuals involved can hear themselves. The following vignette illustrates this point using the basic counseling skill of paraphrasing:

Client: I've had it with the situation at work. My boss hovers over me so much all day long to see what I am doing that I can't do anything. Then she criticizes me for all my mistakes and for the fact that I don't get enough done. How can I get anything done while she's watching me?

Counselor: You find that you are unproductive while she supervises you so closely.

Client: It doesn't feel like supervision; it feels like she doesn't trust me. How can I earn her trust when I don't have a chance to do my work myself?

Counselor: You don't believe that you can prove yourself unless you can work independently.

The process of simple paraphrasing in this example has helped the client to identify a core issue of her problem—that she believes herself not to have been given an appropriate opportunity to demonstrate her abilities. This has been a partial reframing from her initial complaint of her boss's scrutiny.

The next step in the process is, for many, the most critical—reflecting feelings. Here it is that a counselor most often adds to a client's self-understanding. Carkhuff (1969) introduced a useful concept in discussing reflection of feelings that described a range of responses, from those that were inaccurate, to those that exactly mirrored the client's expression in type and intensity, to those that added to the client's understanding and depth of meaning.

Feelings are reflected simply or with a re-statement of the content of a client's statements. For example, a counselor might state, "That really made you angry." Or, the counselor might say, "You were really angry when you read that letter implying that you had not been honest." Many trainers have categorized feeling words to help counselors expand their vocabularies and approach accurate reflections. Most consider there to be four categories of feelings: mad or angry, sad, glad, and scared. Others add a fifth category—confused—although some consider this to be a thought rather than a feeling or to be comprised of at least two of the other feelings. For example, a client might say that he or she is confused when feeling both angry and scared.

A helper's first job when listening to a client is to identify into which broad area the expression falls and then to identify the intensity of the feeling. There is a great difference, obviously, between furious and annoyed or between overjoyed and pleased. Having at one's command a full range of responses increases the probability of accuracy. Clients sometimes pro-

vide clues to their feelings directly by using feeling words, but often counselors have to interpret more content-focused responses. If we use Carkhuff's (1972) discrimination, then a response that is in the wrong category or at a different level of feeling intensity from that of the client will take away from both the client's perceptions of the counselor's empathy and his or her ability to grow in understanding from the interchange. According to Carkhuff (1972), particularly during the early stages of the relationship, one would attempt to match the client's expression at an *interchangeable* level. As the counseling progresses, one occasionally could intersperse a response that deepens the client's understanding, that is, through an *additive* response that *adds to* the client's understanding; however, because this often is a confronting action, one would need to rebuild trust with another series of interchangeable responses. The following is an example:

Client: The situation with my sister that I talked about last week is still going on. She calls me every morning and keeps me on the phone for 45 minutes or more telling me about all her complaints about her husband, her children, our parents, even the weather. It certainly gets my day off to a bad start.

Counselor: You are really annoyed at your sister. (*Interchangeable response*)

Client: Actually, I'm more than annoyed. My heart sinks when the phone rings around 9:00 a.m. I know it's probably her and I am in for an hour of listening to her whine.

Counselor: You feel irritated with her because she whines and angry that you have to begin your day listening to her. (*Interchangeable*)

Client: That's exactly it. If she wants to be miserable about everything, why can't she keep it to herself—or find someone else to complain to?

Counselor: It sounds like you feel trapped by these calls—that you don't see any option but to listen to her. (*Additive*)

Client: Well, I'm not really trapped, am I? I could let the phone ring or go out for my morning walk earlier.

Counselor: You feel hopeful that you could find a way to avoid these calls. (*Interchangeable*)

Client: But why should I have to leave my own house when she's the one who is bothering me?

Counselor: You feel resentful that she can control *your* schedule. (*Interchangeable*)

Client: That's exactly right. Why do I let her do this to me?

Counselor: You've told me before that your parents expected you to look out for your sister, and you still feel stuck in those old patterns. (*Additive*)

Additive responses begin the process of reflecting meaning. The counselor might help the client to understand not only how she continues to fall back on old patterns with her sister but also how she allows herself to be taken advantage of by many others in her life. This might continue to an understanding of her dependence on others' approval and lead to exploring some basic questions of self-esteem and self-worth.

This set of basic skills, therefore, can lead to facilitating understanding. Facilitating action may then be the next stage in the skills hierarchy. Questioning is the basic skill often used to help clients to not only further understanding but also change behavior, that is, act differently.

Asking Questions

Thus far, we have done without the use of questions. Carkhuff's (1969) original formulation did not consider using questions. Indeed, early training in his methods considered them to be a "no-no." Goodman (1978) evaluated the skills of paraprofessionals trained in a strict Carkhuff (1972) style and found that although they indeed had stopped using closed questions, they had not replaced them with open-ended questions. They simply did not ask questions at all. There is a difference of opinion regarding the value of questions, particularly "why" questions. But if we listen to typical counseling sessions as well as ordinary conversations, then we find that questions are a frequent part of human dialogue.

Questions usually are divided into two categories: closed and open. Closed questions are those that can be answered with a yes or a no, for example, "Did you have a good time last night?" and "Are you upset about that?" This category also may include "either/or" questions, for example, "Were you relieved or disappointed that the family reunion was canceled?" Open questions require a lengthier answer on the behalf of the responder. The most frequently used begin with an interrogative pronoun—what, how, or why. In the preceding examples, open questions might be "How was the party last night?" and "What were your thoughts and feelings when you heard that the reunion had been canceled?"

Another category of statements that usually is discussed under the rubric of questions is that of requests or gentle commands. Although grammatically these are imperative statements, they have the force of questions. For example, in the preceding situations, the counselor might say, "Tell me about the party last night" or "Give me some examples of what goes on at a typical family reunion."

This is not meant to imply that closed questions never are useful. Sometimes, it is important to clarify information, to gather demographic data, or to get a simple answer. Sometimes, it is important to help a client focus more narrowly rather than explore broadly. In situations such as these, closed questions are desirable. For example, if a client tells a counselor about an argument with his wife in which he felt criticized, which is like many other arguments the client has described in previous sessions, then the counselor might ask, "Did you tell her how you felt? Did she hear your statement without feeling blamed back? Were you able to resolve the argument?" The point is to use either closed or open questions for a purpose rather than without intent.

Bandler and Grinder (1975) used concepts from linguistics as they analyzed the work of people they identified as "gifted" therapists to examine, among other things, the role of questioning in their work. In *The Structure of Magic*, the authors discussed how these therapists, who had been seen as magical because it appeared that they could read minds, used questioning to uncover what they termed "deep structure." The idea behind this concept is that a statement such as "My father was angry" may be grammatically complete but is emotionally incom-

plete. The therapist then would ask questions such as "When was your father angry? What made him angry? What did you do when he got angry? What did you feel when he got angry? What happened to others in your family when he was angry? How do you feel today when you think about your father's anger?" These types of questions serve the function of completing the emotional content of the statement and clearly lead to a great deal more information than would be found by a simple reflection.

Although commonly used by many helpers as a part of the "when where, what, who, and why" interrogative group, "why" questions are addressed here separately. Although the use of a why question is understandable in that it helps both client and counselor to understand motivation, it also often leads to defensiveness. It is as if we catapult back to our early childhoods when "Why?" usually meant "You shouldn't have." Our parents usually were not looking for reasonable answers when they asked us why we could not sit still or why we hit younger siblings. So, for many adults, why questions are not productive. For this reason, it often is more productive to rephrase the question. For example, one might say "Tell me what was going through your mind when you agreed to go to the bar with your buddies" rather than asking "Why did you go . . .?" The former helps clients to explore their motivation without feeling a need to defend their actions.

The responding skills just described are central to all counseling interactions and should not be abandoned as helpers gains more experience. However, there are additional skills that we still might describe under the rubric of basic skills, techniques that help to move clients into greater depths of understanding and can be more effective in promoting behavioral change.

More Advanced Skills

In the following subsections, I discuss when to use these more advanced skills and then provide descriptions of each of the skills themselves—personalizing, confrontation, focusing, and influencing.

When to Use Higher-Level Skills

Higher-level skills are those that move beyond helping clients to understand their thoughts and feelings and begin the process of changing those thoughts and feelings as well as changing behavior. The first thing to remember when using higher-level skills is that it is important to maintain a basic level of trust with clients by periodically simply reflecting thoughts and feelings. This assures clients that counselors still are "with them" and that, although counselors might be pushing them to more difficult awareness and action, counselors understand clients' feelings. Carkhuff (1972) described this as returning to interchangeable responses periodically before again moving to additive responses. Others have described the process as needing to earn a certain amount of trust or "brownie points" before spending them on more advanced responses.

It also is important to assess the developmental level of clients as counselors move to more challenging interactions. In this context, the concept of developmental levels is used to look at emotional and intellectual development. Later, the relationship of age and maturity to counseling interventions is discussed. Ivey and Ivey (1999) presented one schema for looking at development. They outlined four types of client emotional experience. They stated that all four types are useful and presented suggestions for counselor interactions for each type. The four types are as follows:

1. *Sensorimotor emotional orientation.* Clients with a sensorimotor orientation "*are* their feelings. They *experience* emotions rather than naming or reflecting on them" (Ivey & Ivey, 1999, p. 138, italics in original). These clients are so connected to their emotions that they sometimes cannot distinguish thoughts from feelings. It is helpful for them to be so connected to their inner world, but they might become overwhelmed by their emotions. Focusing on their "here-and-now" feelings may help these clients to use this strength to understand themselves and their issues more clearly.

2. *Concrete emotional orientation.* Clients with a concrete emotional orientation need help in naming and clarifying feelings. They also are assisted by understanding the genesis of the feelings, for example, "You feel angry when you are left out of the decision-making loop at work." Basic reflections are the most important skill in working with concrete emotional clients.

3. *Abstract formal-operational emotional orientation.* Clients with an abstract formal-operational emotional orientation reflect about emotions but might not experience them as deeply, sometimes using an intellectualizing approach to avoid feeling. This reflection is useful in recognizing patterns of feelings and behavior, but it might be important to encourage such clients to experience their feelings more directly through strategies such as imagery and Gestalt techniques.

4. *Abstract dialectic/systemic emotional orientation.* Clients with an abstract dialectic/systemic emotional orientation analyze their feelings at a systemic level and can include several perspectives in this analysis. This level is even further from direct experiencing of emotion. It may be useful in problem solving but also may mean that clients need help in getting in touch with feelings.

Blanchard (1981) provided another paradigm for assessing the developmental level of clients. Although planned as a part of supervisor training, it has been found useful as one way of conceptualizing client readiness for more advanced work. In Blanchard's schema, there are four levels. The first represents a client probably new to counseling, perhaps new to the whole idea of personal exploration or even expressing feelings. This client often is characterized by initial excitement about the process and is labeled by Blanchard as an *enthusiastic beginner.* The counselor needs to give this client clear directions and support as the client continues in the process. The client needs to be told how to participate in counseling and perhaps shown by modeling or through use of moderate self-disclosure.

The next developmental level is one that is called the *disillusioned learner.* This person has progressed far enough to know how difficult the road is but does not yet clearly see the path to a successful outcome. At this time, the counselor needs to increase support and perhaps even decrease some of the more challenging reflections. This client needs reassurance.

The third level is that of the *reluctant contributor.* At this stage, the client is ready for more difficult work, is more autonomous, and is beginning to take responsibility for his or her own growth. The client also may exhibit resistance and regression and need to be treated accordingly, retreating to an earlier developmental level as necessary. The client at this stage, however, often is ready for more advanced interactions and might even initiate them himself or herself.

The fourth level in Blanchard's (1981) schema, the *peak performer,* is one of independence. This client may be near the end of his or her counseling experience or may actually have already terminated. The client is prepared to be self-directed in taking charge of his or her own growth and might need only periodic assistance or none at all. Goodman (1992, 1994) proposed the analogy of the "dental model" to describe the idea of the periodic checkup that often is appropriate for such an independent client. The checkup allows the client to check his or her progress and perhaps make some midcourse variations. It can encourage exploration of some new arenas or assist in managing a transition. It implies brief contact, designed to move the client quickly back into independence.

As counselors work with clients at higher levels of development, they can take advantage of clients' ability to handle more sophisticated and often more challenging interventions. The following subsections describe the skills that counselors can use to help clients progress to deeper understanding and appropriate behavior change.

The Skills Themselves

Although the basic skills described previously sometimes are sufficient to engender growth and change, it often is useful for counselors to have other skills in their repertoires that facilitate such growth and change. The following subsections describe the skills of personalizing, confrontation, focusing, and influencing.

Personalizing

Continuing with the hierarchy developed by Carkhuff (1987), we next look at skills basic to facilitating understanding using the basic skill of personalizing. According to Carkhuff, *personalizing* can be seen as a series of steps. These steps take us from the interchangeable base described earlier to personalizing meaning, personalizing problems, personalizing goals, and personalizing feelings and then to the goal of helpee understanding. Others might see all of these as components in the personalization process rather than steps to be followed in a particular order. Following these steps or using these components results in taking helpers' basic demonstration of empathy beyond reflecting thoughts and feelings to helping clients see their roles in whatever situations they are describing. Rather than saying, "You feel excited because you are going on a long dreamed of trip next week," counselors might say, "You feel excited because *you* took the initiative and planned a trip you have dreamed of for many years." Adding the "you" moves the reflection toward helping clients accept responsibility for their actions—positive or negative—and thereby increases their self-understanding. Being able to use this technique effectively requires tracking, that is, keeping track of themes or recurring patterns in clients' behavior or feelings. Another example of a personalizing statement using themes might be the following: "Whenever you tell me about your conversations with your boss, you describe yourself as feeling angry yet smiling and keeping all your discomfort

to yourself. You have said that you feel helpless to express any negative thoughts and that your conversation with your boss reminds you of how you felt when being yelled at by your father."

Confrontation

In describing personalizing in this context, it seems to move toward what many would term *confrontation*. Ivey (1994) defined confrontation as the "ability to identify incongruity, discrepancies, or mixed messages in behavior, thought, feelings, or meanings" (p. 189). Others have described confrontation as the holding of a mirror before the client to highlight behavior or thought and feeling patterns that might not be readily seen without assistance. Hackney and Cormier (1996) defined it as "a response that enables the client to face that which is being avoided" (p. 110). The avoidance might be a resistance to the client's own feelings or to another person including the counselor (and the counseling relationship). *Confrontation* is not used here in its commonsense meaning of "dukes up" or "the shoot-out at the OK Corral." It also is important to recognize that confrontation with a strength may be equally confrontive. For example, one might say to a client complaining about being unable to make friends, "You told me earlier today that you had spent an hour last night talking to the person sitting next to you at your company dinner. Does that sound to you like someone who can't make friends?" Or, one might say, "I've heard you talk about feeling isolated at work—that no one likes you. How do you explain the invitations to lunch each day by your coworkers?"

The incongruities addressed by confrontation may include discrepancies between two nonverbal behaviors, between two verbal statements, between what one says and what one does, between verbal and nonverbal behavior, or between statements and the context (Ivey, 1994; Ivey & Ivey, 1999). Some sample client statements or actions to illustrate each of these incongruities follow:

> After a welcoming statement from the counselor, the client leans forward attentively but makes no eye contact. (between two nonverbal behaviors)
>
> "I really like to spend time with my friends, but there just isn't time." (between two verbal statements)
>
> "I keep telling her I am listening, and I am. I can watch TV and still listen unless something exciting is happening on the screen. Then, I sometimes miss a bit." (between what one says and what one does)
>
> "I am *not* angry," said with clenched teeth, neck strings standing out, and jaw forward. (between verbal and nonverbal behavior)
>
> "I feel so ashamed. Being a provider has been one of my chief sources of pride, and now my wife is the one paying the bills. Why did the plant have to close?" (between statement and the context [client clearly had no control over the economic conditions that forced the plant closing, so shame is an incongruous, although real, emotion])

Confrontation often can lead the client not only to self-understanding but also to taking action. This does not always happen automatically. It often requires specific action during counseling sessions. Another way of putting it is that *insight is not enough*. Some behavioral theorists (e.g., Skinner, 1953) even believed that insight was irrelevant. Regardless of their theoretical orientations, most counselors believe that clients usually need to put their understanding into action, that is, change their behavior as they gain in understanding. Certainly, few

would dispute that helping to facilitate action is an important basic skill. We may debate whether acting leads to understanding or vice versa, but most agree that it is best when both understanding and action take place.

Carkhuff (1987) identified a series of very specific steps for facilitating action that he called *initiating:* "defin[e] goals, [develop] programs, design schedule and reinforcements, individualize steps, prepare to implement steps, initiate check steps, initiate" (p. 158). This type of very specific action planning is useful for many clients, particularly those unfamiliar with action planning or those tackling difficult issues.

Focusing

Focusing is a concept that is explained very differently by various authors. For example, Ivey and Ivey (1999) present focusing as a way of directing client attention, that is, encouraging the client to address certain areas rather than others. The idea of focusing is that the counselor chooses the arena to pursue rather than letting the client continue in a particular direction. This can have the effect of expanding the client's views of a situation as the client examines it from a variety of perspectives. Ivey and Ivey listed possible areas of focus—on the client, on the theme, on others including family or other reference group, on the counselor, and on cultural/environmental/contextual issues (pp. 226-227). The skills involved in focusing are much like those discussed earlier regarding confrontation. Focusing on a variety of perspectives serves to increase clients' understanding of the complexity of their issues and perhaps of their world in general.

For Gendlin (1981), focusing is a technique to foster attention and concentration. It is much like progressive relaxation in its instructions; however, rather paradoxically, it allows clients to intensify their feelings, and so they often experience new insights. "It is a process in which you make contact with a kind of internal bodily awareness. I call this awareness a *felt sense*" (p. 10, italics in original). Gendlin identified six steps of focusing:

1. *Clearing a space:* Relax, set aside concerns, and focus on awareness of feelings.
2. *Sensing:* Select a problem, stand back from it, and feel.
3. *Handling:* Let a word or an image describe the feeling. Stick with it until the word or image fits just right.
4. *Resonating:* Go back and forth between the felt sense and the word or image. Check for accuracy and allow either to change until it again feels just right.
5. *Asking:* Ask what it is about this problem that leads to this feeling or image. Stick with the question until there is a sense of body shift or release.
6. *Receiving:* Stay with it and experience the release.

The skill of focusing then leads "back" to other skills—reflecting the feelings expressed, asking questions about them, and so forth.

Influencing

All counselor-client interactions have the potential of influencing clients. When counselors respond to feelings, they influence clients to focus on feelings; when counselors ask questions, they determine the direction of subsequent conversations. By choosing areas to include during the summaries of sessions, counselors express their opinions about what is important. The purpose of discussing influencing as a basic skill is to make this process as conscious as possible so that counselors are not influencing out of their own unconscious needs and so that counselors can be very careful not to be manipulative in their influence.

Ivey and Ivey (1999) placed influencing at the highest point in their hierarchy of specific skills. The only skills above influencing are skill integration and determining one's own orientation and style. The authors described six influencing skills:

1. *Interpretation/reframing.* Helpers can assist clients in seeing their concerns or issues in a new way by using reframing. It is important to avoid overly optimistic or false reassurances of the order of clichés (e.g., "When you are given lemons, make lemonade"), but counselors often can see other perspectives that may be useful to clients. A client who loses her job with good severance may be helped to see it as an opportunity to retrain for a job she always has wanted. A teenager with a mean teacher can use the opportunity to prepare for working with a difficult boss.

2. *Logical consequences.* Counselors here are helping clients to understand the probabilities of certain outcomes of behavior. For example, one might say to an angry child, "If you smack your younger sister when she touches your toys, you will probably get in trouble. Is it worth it?"

3. *Self-disclosure.* This is an influencing strategy that must be used with great caution. The standard rule of thumb here is to be sure that the motivation for the disclosure is to help the client rather than to meet the counselor's needs. The purpose of self-disclosure might be

to facilitate more client self-disclosure, for example, "When that happened to me, I felt overwhelmed." Or, it might be to suggest a course of action, for example, "That happened to me when I was a new student. I made an appointment with an academic adviser and found it really helpful to have assistance in rethinking my major and my academic goals."

4. *Feedback.* This entails giving clients information on what counselors see and hear. This may be sharing the observations that counselors have made or providing information on how client statements might be received by others; it is similar to self-disclosure in this respect. Using role-playing or other rehearsal strategies may facilitate feedback, but feedback may be given at any time when counselors believe that there is enough trust developed with clients to be able to use the information. One of the advantages of group counseling is the provision of opportunities for feedback from more persons than just counselors.

5. *Information or suggestions.* There are times when counselors have information that would be useful to clients. At times such as these, it is appropriate for counselors to tell clients what they know rather than withhold the information. This information could be specific facts, for example, the phone number of an elder care referral service or a book on how to write electronic resumés. Or, it might be an idea about how to approach a situation, for example, "Why don't you try offering to work late one night a week if you can leave early on another evening to attend your daughter's baseball game?" These types of interventions move the process away from self-discovery, so they must be used with caution. But at carefully selected times, they are a critical addition to the array of helping skills. It is important, however, for helpers to remember that advice is useful only when it is sought. Even when clients say that they want ideas, they might respond with "Yes, but . . ." types of statements that are clues to counselors that the timing probably is not right. Counselors then should back off and return to reflecting and other more basic skills.

6. *Directives.* These are requests to clients to perform some actions. Counselors might give "homework" assignments to keep track of times when clients felt on the verge of losing control or to note what conditions seemed to lead to a greater sense of productivity at work. A homework assignment might be to check the want ads or to read a particular self-help book. Or, it might be an instruction to call a doctor for a checkup or to contact the financial aid office for a clarification of why a loan was refused.

Does all of this come naturally to student counselors after studying theory? Probably not. Techniques of counseling is probably as universal a course as there is in counseling programs. How it is conducted, however, has a lot of individual variation. In the following section, several methods for teaching counseling skills are described.

How to Teach the Basic and Advanced Skills

Microskills Training

As stated earlier, Carkhuff (1969) was an early advocate of skill-based training for professional and paraprofessional counselors. Ivey (1971) and Egan (1975) were other early proponents of very specific skill-building activities. Each of these systems presents skills much as one might teach a new athletic skill—artificially breaking down the components, encouraging repeated practice, and finally integrating the skills. Ivey and Ivey (1999), in addition, encouraged helpers to concentrate first on mastering the skills as presented. They suggested that helpers discover their own natural styles and then adapt the skills to those styles.

Just as skilled tennis players do not think about each movement as they play, neither do experienced counselors think about the techniques of each of their responses. But to learn tennis, one first must learn a series of independent skills including how to hold the racquet correctly, turn sideways to the ball, pull one's racquet back, swing the racquet from back to front, swing low to high, and keep one's eye on the ball. Similarly, according to the microskills training philosophy, to learn counseling, one must practice an array of artificially discrete elements.

Teaching Nonverbal Attending and Observation, Reflecting, and Questioning

In the following paragraphs, methods for teaching the basic skills are outlined. Strategies for teaching attending and observation are illustrated in detail. Similar methods can be applied to teaching reflecting and questioning, so they are described more briefly. It is important to emphasize the need for "clients" to use real issues as practices proceed. Only then will "counselors" be able to respond authentically. It is helpful to conduct a discussion with students about how to choose issues with which to practice. They probably will want to consider ahead of time issues that are real and meaningful but that do not touch on their deepest issues, that do not lead into areas they would find hard to leave as they focus on giving feedback to their helpers, and that do not disclose areas they wish to keep private. This is particularly important if the learning is taking place in classroom situations where students are graded. Even with such warnings, it is critical to emphasize confidentiality and a professional approach.

Egan (1994, pp. 16-17) provided the acronym SOLER to remember and practice the components of attending behavior. It includes instructions for counselors to face their clients *Squarely,* adopt an *Open* posture, *Lean* toward clients, maintain good *Eye* contact, and remain *Relaxed* while doing all this. In teaching SOLER attending behavior, it is helpful to have students exaggerate each of these behaviors, although that might make the relaxed part less likely. It is best to have students practice these behaviors across from others who are role-playing clients. It is difficult to face an empty chair with enthusiasm, and it certainly is not possible to make eye contact without another person's eyes. Using videotape as a feedback device is most effective at this point because students can see themselves as well as receive others' reactions.

It also is helpful to have the people role-playing clients mirror the behaviors of their counselors. That provides immediate feedback, allowing students to modify behaviors during the sessions rather than waiting for playback of the tapes and other sessions to try again. (It also is important to remember multicultural and gender differences in perceptions of attending behaviors given that the SOLER components may be most true for male North American culture. Multicultural issues are discussed more fully later in the chapter.)

One activity that has been found helpful in teaching nonverbal attending was described by Waters and Goodman (1997). Having the student (B) and the role-playing client (A) sit opposite each other,

1. "A" thinks of a problem or concern.
2. "B" nonverbally attends and observes.
3. Trainer calls time after about 30 seconds.
4. "B" describes to "A" what he or she saw during the observation.

Trainees should change roles and repeat the process. This activity helps to highlight how much of our communication is nonverbal. (pp. 1-9)

Another activity to teach observation skills also begins the process of teaching reflecting, and that is the verbatim repeat. In this scenario, A and B are seated as before, but A makes a brief statement describing some experience, and B repeats it verbatim. A gives feedback on the accuracy of the response, adding or subtracting as necessary, and then they reverse roles. Although one would not repeat verbatim in a "real" counseling situation, it is important to hear every word. As experienced counselors know, clients often imbed important comments in other statements or give them less emphasis, almost as if hoping that counselors will not notice. This artificial practice often highlights how selective hearing can interfere with true listening. Trainees often add content based on their own assumptions. Similarly, emotionally charged words frequently are left out. This can provide valuable information to trainees about their own areas of sensitivity and help them to improve the accuracy of their listening. It is common, for example, for words such as *death* and *cancer* to be transmuted into *passed on* and *ill,* respectively. Students are encouraged to practice verbatim

repeats as they listen to the radio or watch television.

In teaching reflecting, paired practice as just described is again useful. Continuing the process of breaking the response down into artificially discrete elements, it is helpful to have students first practice simply identifying the feeling expressed by the person role playing the client. Next, students tie the feeling to paraphrased or summarized content. Carkhuff (1987), Egan (1994), and Ivey and Ivey (1999) all described learning methods for developing expertise in reflecting feelings and content.

In teaching questioning, it can be helpful to have students first practice conducting interviews solely with closed questions. Role-playing clients are instructed to answer only what they are asked, not to help, for example, by expanding on a yes or no response. A few minutes usually is a long enough time to convince them that this is not effective. They then are asked to conduct second interviews on the same topic using open questions, particularly "what" and "how" questions. The result in client output is dramatic. This also helps students to see that when they ask a series of closed questions, the direction of the interviews is being determined by *them,* not the clients.

Other Teaching Methods

Although microskills teaching has become very popular, many people who train counselors take a more holistic approach. They prefer to have their students conduct longer interviews—15 to 20 minutes is typical—and then critique the entire interviews. This teaching methodology rarely looks at specific responses; rather, it focuses on conceptualizing client issues and considering the direction of the interactions as a whole. It is characteristic of this teaching strategy to look at the stages of a counseling relationship, commonly including relationship building, diagnosis or assessment, goal setting, action, and termination.

Differences in Utility of Basic Skills

Cultural Differences

The term *cultural diversity* is used in many ways. Some use more universal definitions, whereas others use narrow definitions. For the purposes of this chapter, the definition includes "a system of shared beliefs, values, symbols, artifacts, and performance styles that characterizes a group, community, or society" (Jones & Gerard, 1967, p. 710). In other words, if it feels like a culture, then it is one. Thus, most people will identify with several cultures at the same time. For example, a client may identify as young, male, Italian American, urban, Middle Western, middle class, religious Catholic, and a member of a fraternity; another client may identify as poor, female, lesbian, Chicana, rural, and of limited English proficiency.

It may be said that each individual is unique, inhabiting a unique cultural niche, defined by all of his or her individual characteristics, life experiences, life roles, life space, and so forth. The first necessity, therefore, is to pay attention to clients' phenomenological worlds, responding to both verbal and nonverbal cues as to the appropriateness or effectiveness of counselor strategies. The second requirement is to be careful not to stereotype any individual client based on expectations from the group that this client represents. Third, it is important to remember that clients are the best source of information about themselves and that counselors

can ask clients to enlighten them about cultural differences and how they translate into their own individual and unique needs.

This uniqueness notwithstanding, there are certain group differences that are worth investigating and attending to when using counseling skills. Ivey and Ivey (1999) asked Weijun Zhang, a colleague from China, to provide a series of case studies with commentaries illustrating multicultural differences in the application of counseling skills. These commentaries are integrated throughout their text. Their rationale for this approach was as follows: "After the origination of this [microskills] approach, we found that its Eurocentric ideas had to be markedly changed for use with peoples of varying cultural backgrounds" (p. 5). Examples of this include the fact that many Asian cultural groups see direct eye contact as a sign of disrespect rather than attentiveness, that African Americans often prefer more direct approaches over reflection, and that men may be more comfortable with reflection of thoughts than with reflection of feelings.

Bernard and Goodyear (1992, pp. 202-203) provided a list of areas to pursue in acquiring information about a client's singular culture. This list is not meant to be a complete one of all possible areas to pursue. Specific questions and some illustrative examples for each area are provided in what follows:

> *Historical information:* What is the history of the client's group in the country and with people of the group? For example, most African Americans' first experience in what now is the United States was as slaves to European Americans, people with disabilities often have been treated condescendingly by able-bodied people, and deaf people often have been treated as though they are mentally deficient by the hearing community.

Language: What is the client's primary language? What is the language in which the client's childhood was experienced? How do clients with limited English proficiency experience the counselor's reflections?

Social structure: What are the nature and salience of the client's nuclear and extended families? What importance does the client place on community and/or individual responsibility?

Social identity: What is the primary group identification of the client? Does the client feel part of the mainstream of society or have a distinct cultural attachment?

Religious identity: How important is religion or spirituality in the client's life? What are the client's specific beliefs about areas such as fate, God's will, sin, and responsibility?

Socioeconomic identity: What is the client's socioeconomic status, and how is it perceived? Is it markedly different from the counselor's? Is the status itself a major or minor cause of the client's problems?

Gender roles: Where is the client in terms of gender identity formation? How salient are gender issues? Is the counselor's gender a factor for the client?

Therapeutic readiness: Is the idea of therapy accepted in the client's culture? Is telling another about one's problems considered taboo?

Success orientation: How does the client define success. Is it similar to the mainstream American definition? How does your client believe success is achieved, for example, by luck or hard work?

Time orientation: Is the client's time orientation similar to the counselor's? Is promptness important? Does the client focus on the present, the past, or the future?

Differences Based on Age and Developmental Levels

Developmental levels in terms of abstraction of thinking and of experience in being a client were discussed in an earlier section. Here, we look at how differences in maturity might affect the use of basic skills. It has been said (Waters & Goodman, 1990) that older adults often prefer more consultative modes. For many of today's older adults, counseling and therapy imply serious mental illness. When their problems are more related to transitions or adjustment to life events, they often do not seek out professional help. Calling the assistance *consultation* and using a more direct and conversational approach often enables this population to take advantage of mental health services. In using basic skills, then, one would focus more on reflecting content rather than feelings, asking questions, and perhaps moving more quickly to influencing than one might with younger clients. It might well be, however, that these are age cohort issues rather than age issues and that this will change as today's young and middle-aged adults age.

Many people who work with young children find it useful to use more projective approaches. Play, art, and music therapies may be more commonly used with young children than with more mature adolescents and adults. (For a comprehensive look at the history and techniques of play therapy with children, see Muro & Kottman, 1995.) Young children, in particular, might not have vocabularies sophisticated enough to describe their feelings. Play and art often allow them to express themselves with more depth.

Differences Based on Emotional Stability

The use of basic skills in counseling is most appropriate with reasonably intact clients, those in touch with reality and not in extremely heightened emotional states. Therapists must make judgments as to whether seriously disoriented clients can benefit from this type of counseling. It might depend on clients' states at particular moments. Whether heightened emotional states are temporary or more pervasive, therapists must carefully consider their responses. It often is not prudent, for example, to reflect angry feelings to people in emotional upheavals or crises; these people might be better served by more cognitive approaches.

Differences Based on the Skill and Experience Level of the Practitioner

Students often are more dependent on "same-level" reflective responses than are experienced practitioners, who might be able to more quickly assess clients' readiness for deeper reflection. The mantra, "When in doubt, reflect," provides a comfort level for students and does not impede counseling progress.

The Future of Basic Skills

Can Basic Skills Survive During an Era of Managed Care?

The effect of managed care has been both wide and deep. Most agencies and private practice settings are dependent on insurance reimbursements for much of their incomes. And insurance is increasingly regulated as to diagnoses and lengths of approved treatments. Limits such as these often lead to more solution-focused than problem-focused treatment modalities. The personal exploration fostered by the skills described in this chapter often is seen as a luxury rather than as a necessary precursor to self-understanding.

Will Basic Skills Thrive in School and Career Counseling?

School counselors often find themselves in the same position as those responsive to managed care companies. With a typical caseload of 300 to 400 students, therapeutic help usually is limited to crisis intervention and problem- or situation-focused small groups such as groups for children of divorced parents, groups for children of alcoholics, and newcomers groups. Counselors must spend the balance of their time providing classroom guidance and consultation to parents, teachers, and administrators. The basic skills certainly are useful in problem identification, but the whole hierarchy as described earlier often cannot be followed.

Similarly, career counselors frequently are faced with clients who are not anticipating any extended contact with counselors. They usually expect a brief course of testing followed by information and perhaps advice. Although counselors might believe that more in-depth explorations of issues would be useful, these are not always feasible. Again here, the basic skills probably will be used to develop working alliances with clients, understand clients' issues, and develop plans of action. They might not be used as often to assist clients in self-understanding.

To conclude, it seems clear from the forgoing chapter that the term *basic skills* might be somewhat of a misnomer. The skills are basic in that they provide the building blocks of most interactions between client and counselor. Yet, they provide the substance of the most advanced work as well. The ability to use these skills effectively is essential for all counselors. A high level of mastery is a goal to be aimed at throughout their professional lives.

References

Bandler, R., & Grinder, J. (1975). *The structure of magic* (Vol. 1). Palo Alto, CA: Science and Behavior Books.

Bernard, J. M., & Goodyear, R. K. (1992). *Fundamentals of clinical supervision.* Boston: Allyn & Bacon.

Blanchard, K. (1981). *A situational approach to managing people.* Escondido, CA: Blanchard Training and Development.

Carkhuff, R. R. (1969). *Helping and human relations: Vol. 1. Selection and training.* New York: Holt, Rinehart & Winston.

Carkhuff, R. R. (1972). *The art of helping.* Amherst, MA: Human Resources Development Press.

Carkhuff, R. R. (1987). *The art of helping* (Vol. 6). Amherst, MA: Human Resources Development Press.

Edman, I. (Ed.). (1956). *The works of Plato.* New York: Random House.

Egan, G. (1975). *The skilled helper.* Pacific Grove, CA: Brooks/Cole.

Egan, G. (1994). *Exercises in helping skills: A manual to accompany the skilled helper.* Pacific Grove, CA: Brooks/Cole.

Gendlin, E. T. (1981). *Focusing.* New York: Bantam.

Goodman, J. (1978). *Videotape evaluation of a paraprofessional peer counselor training program.* Unpublished doctoral dissertation, Wayne State University.

Goodman, J. (1992). The key to pain prevention: The dental model for counseling. *American Counselor, 1*(2), 27-29.

Goodman, J. (1994). Career adaptability in adults: A concept whose time has come. *Career Development Quarterly, 43,* 74-84.

Hackney, H. L., & Cormier, L. S. (1996). *The professional counselor* (3rd ed.). Boston: Allyn & Bacon.

Ivey, A. E. (1971). *Microcounseling: Innovations in interviewing training.* Springfield, IL: Charles C Thomas.

Ivey, A. E. (1994). *Intentional interviewing and counseling* (3rd ed.). Pacific Grove, CA: Brooks/Cole.

Ivey, A. E., & Ivey, M. B. (1999). *Intentional interviewing and counseling* (4th ed.). Pacific Grove, CA: Brooks/Cole.

Jones, E. E., & Gerard, H. B. (1967). *Foundations of social psychology.* New York: John Wiley.

Kottler, J. A., & Brown, R. W. (1996). *Introduction to therapeutic counseling.* Pacific Grove, CA: Brooks/Cole.

Muro, J. J., & Kottman, T. (1995). *Guidance and counseling in the elementary and middle schools.* Madison, WI: Brown & Benchmark.

Rogers, C. R. (1942). *Counseling and psychotherapy.* Boston: Houghton Mifflin.

Rogers, C. R. (1958). Characteristics of a helping relationship. *Personnel and Guidance Journal, 37,* 6-16.

Skinner, B. F. (1953). *Science and human behavior.* New York: Macmillan.

Waters, E. B., & Goodman, J. (1990). *Empowering older adults: Practical strategies for counselors.* San Francisco: Jossey-Bass.

Waters, E. B., & Goodman, J. (1997). Enhancing the functioning of paraprofessionals: A key role for gerontological counselors. In J. E. Myers (Ed.), *Therapeutic strategies with the older adult.* New York: Hatherleigh.

CHAPTER SIXTEEN

Counselor Roles for the 21st Century

PATRICIA ARREDONDO

JUDY LEWIS

As citizens of the universe, Possible Persons on the threshold of a rapidly evolving global network, our vision of the Possible Profession is to: promote the wholistic development of all persons for living productively and harmoniously in the technologically complex, culturally diverse, and increasingly interdependent world of tomorrow.

—*Nejedlo, Arredondo, and Benjamin (1985, p. 1)*

Counselors are resilient professionals. The members of our profession have continuously demonstrated their capacity to broaden their perspectives, expand their repertoires of intervention techniques, and transform their roles in response to the changing needs of their clients and communities. One important factor in this creative resiliency has been, and continues to be, an abiding interest in preparing for the future, for factored into the development of counseling professionals is a worldview that embodies past, present, and future thinking.

Back to the Future

The future of the counseling profession has been an ongoing topic for decades. In 1985, for example, the Counselors of Tomorrow Interest Network, a special task force of the Association of Counselor Education and Supervision (ACES), produced a handbook outlining domestic and planetary trends, harbingers of future work environments, and specialty roles for counselors (Nejedlo et al., 1985). The interest network members considered the attitudes and values,

257

knowledge bases, and core skills that would be most important for the future. They realized that tomorrow's most successful counselors would have multicultural competency, group process skills, planning skills, and the ability to adapt their work to varying settings and to the needs of people at all stages of the life span.

The necessity of adapting counseling roles to the priorities of various settings also was emphasized by Lewis (1988) in an examination of employment trends that had brought many counselors away from the familiar territory of schools and into the new arena of community agencies:

> What do these employment changes mean for practicing counselors? It is true that a change in focus is needed. But that change should not involve turning our backs on our educational roots and creating a new profession out of whole cloth. Instead, our change of focus should allow us to use this fortuitous opportunity to build a counseling identity that can span a number of settings. (p. 223)

Lewis suggested that all counselors, regardless of settings, should consider themselves mental health professionals; that all counselors, regardless of settings, should consider themselves educators; and that all counselors, regardless of settings, should be community workers, influencing their clients' social environments as well as their personal functioning.

The idea that social issues should be a focal point for counselors also was addressed during the 1980s by Aubrey and Lewis (1983). They identified a number of emerging social issues, suggesting that the act of predicting conditions that might be problematic in the future would allow counselors to be better prepared and, therefore, more effective. Among the social issues identified were several that are

pressing concerns today including chemical dependency; crime and violence; health care practices; racism, sexism, and other forms of discrimination; pressures to respond to technological advances; and unequal distribution of resources. Aubrey and Lewis suggested that counselors could meet the heavy demands of the future by taking the following steps:

- Learning to recognize and deal with high-risk situations
- Developing models that can be applied to individuals, groups, or total populations
- Using educational approaches to build life competencies
- Becoming adept at influencing the political, social, and economic environments that affect clients
- Becoming expert in strategic planning

Herr's (1989) work during the 1980s also combined attention to the context of counseling with an emphasis on multidimensional practice:

> It is within their physical, social, and cultural environments that people negotiate their personal identity, belief systems, and life course. Such political, social, and economic contexts in which individuality is framed and is lived out change across nations, communities, and families; across racial or socioeconomic groups; and, certainly, across time. (p. 2)

In response to this recognition of context, Herr was prescient in his expectation that the counseling programs and the delivery of services of the future would need to be comprehensive in terms of settings and populations served and that counseling practices would be "described by such traits as cognitive, brief, planned, interdisciplinary, eclectic, educative, preventive, and technological" (p. 259).

Aubrey and D'Andrea (1988) were similarly prescient in their prediction of the challenges we are facing today in the realm of technology:

> Like a sudden hurricane, high technology emerged as a rampant force destined to dominate all of our lives well into the 21st century. High technology possesses not only the power and intensity of a giant hurricane, but it also contains some of its blindness and unpredictability. The "eye" of high technology may therefore appear calm and placid, but the uncontrolled forces surrounding it belie this benevolence. (p. 261)

Addressing both the "promise and plight" of technology, Aubrey and D'Andrea suggested that counselors must be knowledgeable about technology because it would have major effects on their clients and themselves. "Failure to adapt to the changes wrought by high technology could therefore have grave consequences for counselors, both personally and professionally" (p. 261).

The ideas we were considering during the 1980s are, if anything, even more relevant today than they were at that time. Recently, in fact, Herr (1999) built on his work of the 1980s, focusing on the social, political, and economic systems that affect individual behavior and the work of the counselor. If the counseling profession is to retain its tradition of resiliency, then its members will need to build on these ideas, continuing to reinvent their roles and broadening their base of competency.

Themes for the Future

Commenting about counselor roles during the 21st century is more than an abstract exercise;

in fact, it is data driven. Some might say that writing about the future is just speculation and theorizing because counselors are not fortune-tellers. However, planning and anticipating fall into our repertoire of skills, and with the available data about the past, present, and future, we *are* in a position to speak about the future for ourselves and on behalf of our profession. In fact, counselors *can* use the same skills in planning for a professional future as they use in helping clients plan for their personal futures. Consider this brief retrospective and some of the current realities.

Most would agree with Peter Drucker, a well-known management guru, who proclaimed in 1992 that we had changed profoundly in comparison to what we would have predicted during the early 1900s (Wall, Solum, & Sobol, 1992). This change certainly is apparent in our own profession. At the dawn of the 20th century, the counseling profession and counselor roles as we know them today did not even exist. Yes, there were schools in which classroom teachers assumed more than teaching roles for the thousands of newcomers at the turn of the century. There also were settlement houses staffed by social workers who primarily serviced immigrants and families. In 1909, Frank Parsons, considered the father of modern counseling, began to provide vocational assistance to men seeking work opportunities in the greater Boston area. It was not until the 1940s and 1950s, however, that the counseling profession took its place in schools of education across the United States. Not surprisingly, vocational and school counselor roles dominated through the mid-1970s. The profession's focus, based on funding through the National Defense Education Act, was to prepare school counselors and counselor educators. Since then, however, other specialty roles (family, group, and mental health counseling) and thematic perspectives (multicultural/multiracial, spiritual, and adult development/aging) have become evolving areas within counselor training programs and employment settings. We find ourselves on multiple and continuous learning curves, some more to our liking than others but all nevertheless opening new vistas and possibilities for our vocation as counselors.

With this kaleidoscope of roles, settings, and perspectives in the context of rapidly changing and challenging times, now it is more important than ever to frame new thinking about counselor competencies, both personal and professional, for the future. This discussion goes beyond just speculating about counselor roles; it is about visioning, thoughtful planning, and moving forward in uncharted territory. To remain essential as counselors, we cannot simply do what we like best or what suits our preferences about where to apply our professional skills. Rather, we must use existing data about demographic, social, economic, political, and technological issues that affect people's lives and determine the meaning and influence of these data on themes, contexts, methodology, and approaches to helping.

Consider the different phenomena that visit the lives of individuals, families, and organizations on a daily basis. During the past 3 to 5 years, we have witnessed increased school and workplace violence, natural disasters across the globe, the second biggest wave of immigrants and refugees to enter the United States, and more displaced families due to civil wars in other parts of the world. Sadly, these events have become very commonplace in the daily media. All cry out for professional helping interventions. Whether it be conflict resolution, crisis counseling, or other urgent care practices,

a counselor's helping skills are ones that can quickly be employed.

Another phenomenon with implications for the future relates to the theme of life-span development. The baby boomers are contributing to the increase in the population over 55 years of age. As life spans for women and men increase, people choose to retire later and find new ways in which to sustain their health care needs, nurture intergenerational relations, and remain potent in a society that values youth. A counselor's knowledge about health care options, medication, rehabilitation resources, and alternative non-Western ways of spirituality and healing will enable us to do gerontological counseling and more.

A third theme that hardly requires mention is the force of global technology. Technological literacy has become a requirement for counseling professionals not only for our own benefit but also as a means of communicating with others. Distance learning, particularly for adult learners, is causing many counselor educators to reevaluate tried and "proven" approaches to teaching. With our technology-centered existence, counselors have new means of access to provide career, educational, spiritual, and other forms of counseling.

Finally, the themes of multiculturalism and diversity are evident everywhere—in our classrooms, in front-page headlines, at think tanks, on government funding requests, and at international events. Cultural competency will continue to be an asset and a proficiency for all counselor roles in the new century. Witness everyday situations about human lives; the topics of diversity and multiculturalism always are embedded within them, and an important role for counselors always is there, across multiple settings and for varying issues.

Members of the counseling profession continually get involved in movements, social action and educational in nature, to respond to the needs of our diverse communities. For example, in response to the increasing population of multicultural and multiracial families (Wehrly, 1996), a group of counseling professionals has come together to examine the implications of multiracial counseling models for counselor education and practice. Gay, lesbian, bisexual, and transgendered persons continue to be visited by physical and emotional harm in an atmosphere of hate. The counseling profession is beginning to make progress in addressing this issue as well, as evidenced by the fact that the American Counseling Association (ACA) and a number of other helping organizations have joined forces to disseminate to schools throughout the nation information about sexual orientation and youth. We finally have learned that counselors cannot be true helpers without proficiency in practices relevant to multiculturalism and diversity. *We cannot be effective or ethical without multicultural competence.*

Although life forces might seem overwhelming or cause some counselors to wonder whether they ever can do good work, the upside of this thematic and contextual presentation is to emphasize that many new opportunities are there for counselors. Competencies and continuous learning and improvement will be bywords in the profession. At the same time, counselors will need to evaluate what we are doing for ourselves and will need to be congruent with the forces of change that surround our professional practice. Our heads and hearts have to be aligned, and in the words of Tao, we will require *zanshin* or the ability to flow with change (Dreher, 1995).

The 21st-Century Counselor as a Person

In counselor training, we speak of the attributes of authenticity, congruence, competency, and ethical practice as fundamental to helping the client. Engaging in textbook learning about how to counsel leaves very little room for counselors to explore their motivation and vision—what they bring to counseling. The multicultural counseling competencies literature asserts that the individual's self-awareness, self-knowledge, and personal wellness are cornerstones to assuming the role of a high-functioning and ethical counselor. Counselors often speak of high-functioning clients but rarely apply this expectation to themselves.

Being a counselor means knowing oneself, one's motivations, one's hidden agendas, and one's Achilles' heel. It is not sufficient to be a counselor so as to save the world or to help others less fortunate than oneself. According to the multicultural counseling competencies (Arredondo et al., 1996; Sue, Arredondo, & McDavis, 1992), counselors' awareness of their own attitudes and biases, knowledge, and skills with regard to their respective cultural backgrounds is fundamental. We can apply this thinking to one's initiation or continuation in the counseling profession. For what reasons? To what end? Why this profession and not something else? Consider these counselor competency statements of awareness, knowledge, and skills as they apply to self and then in relation to others:

The Self: Awareness and Knowledge

I understand my motivation for being a counselor.

I have a clear vision about my expectations for being in a counselor role.

I understand my personal biases about working in particular counselor specialty roles and not others.

I understand how I may socially influence others because of who I am (e.g., age, gender, ethnicity, race, sexual orientation, appearance).

Others: Awareness and Knowledge

I recognize that there are clients with particular sets of issues (e.g., incest victims, gamblers) with whom I would prefer not to work, but ethically, I will assist them in finding appropriate helpers and resources.

I recognize that there are culture-specific worldviews unfamiliar to me that might require additional study.

I am knowledgeable about issues of poverty and their effects on the helplessness of many clients I might serve.

Skills

I am skilled in different technological programs, enabling me to access current research on different client groups, outcome-based treatment data, the role of alternative interventions, and other resources not readily available in my work environment.

I am skilled in the use of a variety of social action interventions. For example, I know how to organize petitions and other grassroots-like actions that will benefit a particular constituency.

I am skilled in accessing various institutions that provide auxiliary services and resources to speakers of English as a second language, the physically disabled, senior citizens, the unemployed, and others seeking help from a counselor.

As we project these competencies into the 21st century, we must expect that counselors of the future will be people who are aware of their personal motivations; who know that their personal and professional experiences influence their ongoing work as counselors; who can recount the critical incidents that have changed their personal and professional worldviews; who are willing to face and overcome the fears that act as barriers to their competence; who discern that they are cultural beings with multiple cultural identities; who are knowledgeable about the effects of racism, sexism, heterosexism, and other forms of oppression on their clients and themselves; and who desire to be ethical and multiculturally proficient counselors. The counselors of the future also will be aware that they can be most helpful to their clients if they play two equally important roles: direct service provider and active advocate.

21st-Century Counseling: Direct Services

Providing direct counseling services to individuals, families, and groups always has been, and will continue to be, a part of the counselor's role. Historically, counselors have provided these services with an emphasis on the strengths and resources that each client brings to the counseling process. At times during recent years, counselors have seemed to lose sight of this positive developmental focus, forgetting the uniqueness of the counseling viewpoint in the rush to hone their skills in diagnosing and addressing pathology. We believe, however, that as the 21st century progresses, counselors will return to a professional self-concept that recognizes the uniqueness of counseling among all of the helping professions. Counselors will renew their commitment to an approach that builds on their clients' resources and that recognizes the cultural, economic, political, and spiritual contexts that shape their clients' lives.

Moreover, counselors will accomplish these tasks in the context of a highly accessible, multiresourced, multilingual service delivery system.

Strength-Based Counseling

As the 20th century edged toward its end, one of the most obvious trends affecting counselors' work involved the disparate nature of the problems and issues brought by clients. Counselors whose training took place before the last quarter of the century sometimes were taught that counselors, unlike other helping professionals, dealt with "normal" people who simply needed assistance in decision making and life planning or who were grappling with concerns of everyday living. Now, whether they work in educational institutions, community agencies, or private practice, counselors routinely see people with serious or even life-threatening problems; see people with serious mental or physical disabilities; and address issues including child abuse, domestic violence, addiction, homicide, suicide, poverty, and homelessness. The lives of the clients being served also may be characterized by oppression and poverty as the economic gap widens in U.S. society. There is every reason to believe that these trends and issues will continue and that counselors' repertoire of responsiveness will be increasingly difficult and complex. In fact, many problems may be exacerbated by the expansive feelings of uncertainty that seem to be a byproduct of the turn of the century for many individuals.

Some people might assume that predicting the presence of clients with serious problems points the way toward an emphasis on pathology. In fact, however, the more problematic a client's life appears to be, the more important it becomes for helpers to focus on the search for the client's competencies and resources. Positive approaches are most helpful for working with highly stressed individuals, families, and communities—exactly the ones whose behavior often is pathologized.

Consider, for example, the "healing attitude" that Madsen (1996) uses with families that are dealing with oppressive circumstances and multiple stressors. Realizing that these clients might feel vulnerable, disempowered, trapped, and subject to judgment by others, Madsen suggested that the helper's job is to support family functioning, not to fix dysfunction. He believes that this can happen best when the counselor is able to establish a respectful collaborative partnership with his or her clients. Rojano (1997), whose urban clients face challenges of poverty and hopelessness, also recommended a positive encouraging approach. The "diagnostic instrument" he uses focuses on issues of empowerment rather than pathology. Among the variables he tries to measure are the client's (a) knowledge of life history, (b) self-esteem level, (c) awareness of strengths and resources, (d) awareness of role in the family, (e) quality and quantity of received affection and intimacy, (f) density and use of network, (g) degree of cultural identity, (h) degree of awareness of social environment and social role, (i) knowledge and use of social support system, (j) clarity of goals and dreams, (k) ability to generate initiative, and (l) motivation for empowerment. Waters and Lawrence (1993) similarly focus on client competence, reflecting their belief "in people's need to make their world work, to grow and change and to strive for mastery both in the external world and in their internal development" (p. 7). Although a worldview of self-determination still operates strongly in counseling models, our discussion indicates that there are many individuals who might not be able to manage the gap between external forces of oppression and personal empowerment.

Accessible Services

The 21st century brings both the need for increased accessibility to services and the means for attaining them. Counselors will make it easier for people to access the help they need both by participating in improved human service systems and by using technology.

Integrated Helping Systems

The recently published surgeon general's report on mental health (U.S. Department of Health and Human Services, 1999) concluded with a "vision for the future" that emphasized the issue of access to services. Pointing out that the majority of those who need help with mental health issues do not actually seek assistance because so many barriers stand in the way, the report called for an action plan that would focus on improving public awareness of treatment; eliminating stigma; providing comprehensive integrated services; and tailoring treatment to differences based on age, gender, race, and cultural heritage. The report suggested, "The fundamental components of effective service delivery include integrated community-based services, continuity of providers and treatments, family support services (including psychoeducation), and culturally sensitive services" (p. 455). The surgeon general also stated,

All services for those with a mental disorder should be consumer oriented and focused on pro-

moting recovery. That is, the goal of services must not be limited to symptom reduction but should strive for restoration of a meaningful and productive life. (p. 455)

Just a very quick glance at the surgeon general's recommendations makes it apparent that there will be an important role for professional counselors to play in the type of integrated, consumer-oriented service system that is envisioned. Even today, counselors tend to be on the scene quickly when natural disasters or unexpected violence episodes occur. In the future, they will be even more likely to be the point of first contact, responding with finely honed skills in crisis counseling and grief counseling. What may be even more important is that counselors will be able to prevent crises of human origin by making it more routine for people to seek help at earlier points in the development of problems. The surgeon general's report stated that certain mental health services are in short supply and will be needed in the future. One of the needs identified is for multisystemic approaches that "involve the participation of the multiple health, social service, educational, and other community resources that play a role in ensuring the health and well-being of children and their families" (p. 455). A second identified need is for programs that focus on prevention and early identification of problems. Counselors, both in schools and in community agencies, will be able to fill these needs.

What will it take to reach the goal of integrated services? At local and regional levels, it will take community-based planning (Lewis, Lewis, Daniels, & D'Andrea, 1998), which involves building coalitions among policy makers, agencies, institutions, and advocacy groups for the purpose of identifying and meeting community needs. At the national and international levels, it also will take collaborations among the organizations and associations that represent the helping professions. During the 21st century, there is no room for turf wars.

Technology

The challenge faced by counselors of the 21st century is to ensure that help and services are readily available to anyone who can benefit from them. The solution will lie, at least in part, on technology-based services. There will be a time, later in this century, when cell phones, video, computers, and the Internet as we know them today will be laughably old-fashioned. Communications will take place in ways that we cannot yet imagine. In the immediate future, however, distance learning and the Internet will be important methods for providing help across time and space. Professional counselors *will* provide online counseling services, and they *will* use technological means for providing information and skills training for the purpose of prevention.

Technology will address one problem—access. At the same time, it will bring a new set of problems that we are just beginning to perceive. ACA (1999) has adopted a set of ethical standards for Internet online counseling. These standards address a number of immediate issues including the following:

Confidentiality
Protecting private communications by using secured sites and appropriate encryption technology

Informing potential clients of the limits of confidentiality

Providing informational notices about data security, software needs, and the identities of counselors who will have access to information

Executing appropriate waiver agreements

Establishment of Online Counseling Relationships
Using appropriate intake procedures for determining whether online counseling is appropriate for clients

Informing clients of the limitations, risks, and benefits of the service

Providing clients with information concerning usual response times and alternate means for emergency use

Taking licensure laws and practice expertise into account

Verifying that clients are competent to enter into counseling relationships and able to give informed consent

Legal Issues
Confirming liability insurance coverage

Checking applicable governmental, professional, certification, and licensing regulations

These guidelines offer an excellent beginning as we try to predict the future needs of online counselors and their clients. Still, these issues will have to be monitored on an ongoing basis as norms and expectations change and as technology advances. We also will have to be vigilant about balancing technology and humanity, "embracing technology that preserves our humanness and rejecting technology that intrudes upon it" (Naisbitt, Naisbitt, & Philips, 1999, p. 26). We are, after all, counselors.

21st-Century Counseling: Advocacy and Social Action

Even when direct counseling services are humane, supportive, and accessible, they never can be the whole answer for clients. Because human behavior takes place in an environmental context, positive change often requires a two-pronged effort: (a) helping clients change their own behaviors and (b) embarking on social change processes. As Lee (1998) pointed out, "Social action encompasses the professional and moral responsibility that counselors have to address the significant social, cultural, and economic challenges that have the potential to impact negatively upon psychosocial development" (p. 5).

Why do counselors, more than other citizens, bear this special responsibility to engage in social change efforts? The answer to this question lies in the nature of their daily work.

> Their work brings . . . counselors face to face with the victims of poverty, racism, sexism, and stigmatization; of political, economic, and social systems that leave individuals feeling powerless; of governing bodies that deny their responsibility to respond; [and] of social norms that encourage isolation. In the face of these realities, counselors have no choice but to promote positive changes in those systems that directly impact the psychological well-being of their clients—or to blame the victims. (Lewis et al., 1998, pp. 23-24)

Perhaps the quality of life will improve on time for the 22nd century. In the immediate future, however, counselors can expect that their clients still will be victimized by oppression. The beginning of the 21st century has seen us drifting in some troubling directions. We are told that the economy is thriving, but the gap between rich and poor continues to increase. Violence, including acts perpetrated by hate groups, perseveres. A backlash against equality shows itself in English-only movements, discrimination against immigrants, and attacks on affirmative action. The goal of universal coverage for health care seems to become more distant each year. Punitiveness toward the poor is disguised as welfare reform. Treatment for addiction is more likely to occur in prisons than in the health care system. Schools are failing to meet the needs of the children that need them most. For now, our clients and communities need to be able to count on counselors' courage and activism.

In their role as *client advocates,* 21st-century counselors will speak up on behalf of their clients and help to break down barriers to individual development. Counselors also will engage in *social/political advocacy,* addressing larger systems and policies so that the needs of whole communities or populations can be met. Among the activities that will be part of their "business as usual" will be the following:

- Making schools and communities aware of problems affecting students and community members
- Participating in alliances to work on community issues
- Acting as allies to people involved in self-help advocacy
- Lobbying for legislation that protects human rights

Counselors will not have to choose between their role as direct service providers and their role as advocates. As Cebuhar (2000) pointed out, "advocacy serves as an effective manner in which to clear the board of solvable external problems so that effective counseling can begin" (p. 138).

References

American Counseling Association. (1999). *Ethical standards for Internet on-line counseling.* Alexandria, VA: Author.

Arredondo, P., Toporek, R., Brown, S. P., Jones, J., Locke, D. C., Sanchez, J., & Stadler, H. (1996). Operationalization of the multicultural counseling competencies.

Journal of Multicultural Counseling and Development, 24, 42-78.

Aubrey, R. F., & D'Andrea, M. (1988). What counselors should know about high technology. In R. Hayes & R. Aubrey (Eds.), *New directions for counseling and human development* (pp. 261-274). Denver, CO: Love.

Aubrey, R. F., & Lewis, J. A. (1983). Social issues and the counseling profession in the 1980s and 1990s. *Counseling and Human Development, 15*(10), 1-15.

Cebuhar, J. (2000). Advocacy for people with HIV/AIDS. In J. Lewis & L. Bradley (Eds.), *Advocacy in counseling: Counselors, clients, and community* (pp. 133-138). Greensboro, NC: ERIC/CASS.

Dreher, D. (1995). *The Tao of personal leadership.* New York: HarperCollins.

Herr, E. L. (1989). *Counseling in a dynamic society: Opportunities and challenges.* Alexandria, VA: American Association for Counseling and Development.

Herr, E. L. (1999). *Counseling in a dynamic society: Contexts and practices for the 21st century.* Alexandria, VA: American Counseling Association.

Lee, C. C. (1998). Counselors as agents of social change. In C. C. Lee & G. R. Walz (Eds.), *Social action: A mandate for counselors* (pp. 3-14). Alexandria, VA: American Counseling Association and ERIC/CASS.

Lewis, J. A. (1988). From school to community mental health counseling. In R. Hayes & R. Aubrey (Eds.), *New directions for counseling and human development* (pp. 223-233). Denver, CO: Love.

Lewis, J. A., Lewis, M. D., Daniels, J. A., & D'Andrea, M. J. (1998). *Community counseling: Empowerment strategies for a diverse society.* Pacific Grove, CA: Brooks/Cole.

Madsen, W. C. (1996, October). *Brief treatment of multistressed families.* Paper presented at the annual meeting of the American Association of Marriage and Family Therapy, Toronto.

Naisbitt, J., Naisbitt, N., & Philips, D. (1999). *High tech high touch: Technology and our search for meaning.* New York: Broadway.

Nejedlo, R. J., Arredondo, P., & Benjamin, L. (1985). *Imagine: A visionary model for the counselors of tomorrow.* DeKalb, IL: George's Printing.

Rojano, R. (1997, March). *The politics of change.* Paper presented at the Family Therapy Network Symposium, Washington, DC.

Sue, D. W., Arredondo, P., & McDavis, R. J. (1992). Multicultural counseling competencies and standards: A call to the profession. *Journal of Counseling and Development, 70,* 477-483.

U.S. Department of Health and Human Services. (1999). *Mental health: A report of the surgeon general.* Rockville, MD: Author.

Wall, B., Solum, R. S., & Sobol, R. M. (1992). *The visionary leader.* Rocklin, CA: Prima.

Waters, C. B., & Lawrence, E. C. (1993). *Competence, courage, and change: An approach to family therapy.* New York: Norton.

Wehrly, B. (1996). *Counseling interracial individuals and families.* Alexandria, VA: American Counseling Association.

CHAPTER SEVENTEEN

Assessment, Diagnosis, and Treatment Planning in Counseling

THOMAS H. HOHENSHIL
HILDY GETZ

Assessment, diagnosis, and treatment planning are essential elements of the counseling process, regardless of one's theoretical orientation. *Assessment* is the process of obtaining information for use in the diagnostic process. Assessment data are collected through several formal and informal techniques including standardized tests, questionnaires, diagnostic interviews, personality measures, mental status examinations, behavioral observation, and reports by others (e.g., parents, friends, spouses, medical, educational, legal, social). As noted in this definition, standardized testing is only one of several ways in which to collect assessment information. *Diagnosis* is the meaning that is derived from assessment data when it is interpreted through the use of a diagnostic classification system. Diagnosis is a matching of the client's symptoms with the categories in a classification system to determine which category or categories best account for the presenting symptoms. Diagnosis is not a process that occurs at a fixed point in time during the counseling process, nor is it a static concept. *Treatment planning* is in large measure determined by the diagnosis and outlines the counseling goals, time lines, and techniques that will be used to assist the client. Assessment, diagnosis, and treatment planning are intertwined throughout the six stages of the counseling process as described in the following section (Hohenshil, 1996).

Integrating Assessment Throughout the Counseling Process

Stage 1: Referral

Regardless of the counseling setting, clients either self-refer or are referred by others. How a client arrives at counseling is important because it has implications for the person's motivation to change and the type of assessment information that is available to the counselor during this first stage of the counseling process. Important assessment information begins at this stage, and skilled counselors begin to formulate "diagnostic hypotheses." Referral information normally is available through self-reports by the client, information from significant others (e.g., teachers, parents, friends, spouse), and behavioral observation. Assessment and diagnostic information also might be available from various types of medical, social, educational, and legal records that are forwarded to the counselor.

Stage 2: Symptom Identification

Because most diagnostic systems are highly dependent on categorizing client symptoms, identifying these symptoms accurately is a critical part of the counseling process. As noted for Stage 1, some information about the type, duration, and severity of symptoms often is available through the referral process. Additional symptom information can be obtained through diagnostic interviews, problem checklists, mental status examinations, medical evaluation, behavioral observation, and psychological testing. Special attention needs to be given to multicultural aspects of symptom identification to ensure that the client is not inappropriately diagnosed with a mental disorder for behaviors

and attitudes that are characteristic of his or her particular subculture (Smart & Smart, 1997).

Stage 3: Diagnosis

Diagnosis generally is considered to be the process of comparing the symptoms exhibited by a client with the diagnostic criteria or categories of some type of classification system. Counselors in schools might be involved with several classification systems, the most common being that for special education services, whereas counselors in agencies and private practice would use the *DSM-IV* (*Diagnostic and Statistical Manual of Mental Disorders* [American Psychiatric Association, 1994]) classification system. Family counselors might use another type of classification system that emphasizes family dysfunction (Sporakowski, 1995).

Stage 4: Treatment Planning

The treatment plan normally includes a description of the problem, both short- and long-term treatment objectives, interventions to be used, and the prognosis for the client. Normally, counselors in private practice and agencies are required to develop comprehensive treatment plans if they are to receive third-party payments from insurance providers. School counselors also are required by special education legislation to develop well-formulated counseling treatment plans to be included as part of individual education plans. Treatment planning requires accurate diagnoses given that the intervention techniques selected should correspond to the particular developmental problem or mental disorder.

Stage 5: Treatment

The type, course, frequency, and specific counseling techniques are determined by the treatment plan developed during Stage 4. As successful treatment progresses, the diagnosis may be changed because the symptoms might be in remission, or other disorders may become evident and additional diagnoses might be necessary. There is a fluid nature to the assessment, diagnostic, and treatment process. Assessment information is especially important at this stage to determine when termination is in order or when a change in the treatment plan is necessary.

Stage 6: Follow-Up

Follow-up with the client is important to determine whether the symptoms remain in remission and whether additional counseling is required. During this stage, important assessment information might be generated through client self-reports and reports by others who know the client well through regular contact on a day-to-day basis. These reports may be provided by friends, teachers, parents, or spouse (Hohenshil, 1999).

Assessment Tools Frequently Used by Counselors

Counselors in schools, private practice, and agency settings use a variety of formal and informal assessment tools while gathering data to help clients. These include assessment in the areas of interests, aptitudes, general ability, achievement, social skills, personality, values, learning skills, and special abilities. How frequently a counselor provides assessment services in each of these areas depends on the employment setting and the needs of the client. In schools, the most frequently assessed areas are achievement, academic and career aptitudes, career interests, learning skills, and social skills. In agency and private practice settings, the most frequently assessed areas are personality, social skills, values, and general ability.

Non-Test Methods of Assessment

The manner in which non-test methods of assessment are carried out varies considerably depending on the employment setting, the client's presenting problem, and the skills of the counselor (Hood & Johnson, 1997). During intake interviews, counselors use non-test methods of assessment such as diagnostic interviewing and behavioral observation. Mental status examinations (MSEs) rely heavily on interview procedures and behavioral observation. Each of the assessment areas mentioned in the previous paragraph can be informally assessed through interview and observation procedures. For example, in the area of achievement, does the person seem to have a fund of information that is characteristic of his or her cultural background and age? How well does (or did) the client achieve in school? Career and academic expressed interests can be assessed through the interview. In other words, the client can be asked what career and academic areas he or she seems to like and dislike. Social skills represents another area that frequently is assessed with non-test methods of interviewing and observation. Does the client seem to enjoy interacting with others and to interact easily with the counselor during the interview? When observed in both natural and formal settings, does the client seem to enjoy interacting with colleagues and peers and have the necessary skills to get along socially?

The Mental Status Examination

The MSE is a special type of structured interview and behavioral observation system that is primarily used by counselors, psychologists, and psychiatrists who work in agency and private practice settings. The general purpose of the MSE is to provide a descriptive inventory of a person's behavior—a snapshot of the client at the time being seen. It normally includes the following types of observations.

General appearance, behavior, and attitude. Primary consideration with this category of the MSE is whether the client's appearance and dress are appropriate to the situation. Is the person clean and wearing clothes that are appropriate for the interview? Other characteristics considered are posture, gait, odd mannerisms, tics, activity level, and facial expression. Attitude is observed as to whether the client is cooperative, sullen, assertive, impulsive, dependent, evasive, and/or friendly.

Speech characteristics and thought processes. Speech is thought to be the best indication of the client's thought processes. Is there a sudden speech stoppage for no apparent reason and the client cannot account for the stoppage (blocking)? Is there too much unnecessary detail in the client's verbalizations, but the goal of speech is eventually reached (circumstantially)? Is there overproductivity of talk that is continuous, but ideas are fragmentary and loosely connected (flight of ideas)? Is there no verbal response, even though the client has demonstrated usable

speech in other situations (mutism)? These all are important speech characteristics to review while completing the MSE.

Emotional status and reactions. Emotional status and reactions are judged by what the client says and how he or she behaves and reacts. Key elements of this part of the MSE are observations of the client's facial expressions, whether the client is sweating or flushed, and whether the client seems to have affect that is appropriate to the situation. An example of inappropriate affect would be a client who is smiling and laughing while talking about a close friend who is gravely ill.

Content of thought. Content of thought includes an assessment of the client's thought patterns and a determination of whether they are within normal limits. A couple of examples would include delusional thinking that is defined as fixed and false beliefs that are rigidly held in spite of contradictory evidence. Delusional thinking is characteristic of several of the psychotic disorders. Obsessions are intrusive, unwanted, recurring thought patterns that may be regarded by the client as absurd, yet they persist despite efforts to get rid of them. Obsessions usually are part of the pattern of those who experience obsessive-compulsive disorder, which is one of the anxiety disorders.

Orientation and awareness. A determination of orientation and awareness is an essential component of MSEs. Here, it is important to determine whether the client is oriented to time, place, and person. This can be ascertained by asking the client his or her name (orientation to person); where the client is at the present time (orientation to place); and what day, month, and year this is (orientation to time).

Memory. Deficits to memory may be related to a lack of attention, difficulty in retention, difficulty in recalling information, or any combination of these factors. Memory is assessed using a variety of procedures. The person may be asked to describe some past and recent life experiences, for example, what elementary school experiences were like and what happened during the client's last birthday. Immediate recall can be determined by asking the person to repeat digits after the counselor and to repeat three words about 5 minutes after the counselor states them. General grasp and recall of information can be assessed by having the examiner read a short story and asking the client to immediately repeat the gist of the story with as many details as possible.

General intellectual functioning. Assessment of general intellectual functioning during the MSE usually includes four major areas. The client's fund of general information is determined by asking about information that one would expect most people living in this culture to know. For example, the client could be asked to name four presidents, the governor of the state, and/or three of the largest cities in the United States, and he or she could be asked to define some common words. Abstract thinking usually is assessed by asking the client to interpret various proverbs, for example, "What does this mean? A bird in the hand is worth two in the bush." Questions about the client's reasoning and judgment might include, for example, "What is the thing to do if you find an envelope in the street

that is sealed, addressed, and has a stamp on it?" and "In what way are a dog and horse alike?"

Insight. It is important to determine how much insight the client has about his or her current situation. For example, the counselor might ask the client to try to explain his or her own symptoms or to make suggestions for his or her own treatment.

MSE summary. In the summary section of the MSE, the counselor summarizes the important findings of the examination. This also may be followed by recommendations for further assessment procedures (e.g., psychological testing, neurological evaluation) and a "tentative" or "provisional" *DSM-IV* diagnosis. Because the MSE is influenced by cultural differences, it is important to take these into consideration when interpreting the results.

Formal Tests Used by Counselors

In many states, counselors may use any formal tests for which they are trained and have experience. In other states, there are arbitrary restrictions on certain types of testing by counselors such as projective personality testing and individual intellectual assessment. In this section, the types of tests frequently used by counselors are discussed, recognizing that not all counselors will be able to actually use all of these tests due to licensing restrictions (Clawson, 1997).

Achievement testing. Achievement testing, which deals with assessment of the level of knowledge, skill, or accomplishment in an area of endeavor, is the most popular type of testing in the world. Achievement testing focuses on the present, that is, what the client knows or can do right now. It exceeds all other types of psychological and educational measures in terms of number administered each year. School counselors are especially involved in the administration and interpretation of group achievement tests at all grade levels, whereas agency counselors and those in private practice may have access to school records that contain achievement data or may individually administer brief achievement measures. Some of the more popular achievement batteries are the California Achievement Test, Comprehensive Test of Basic Skills, Iowa Tests of Basic Skills, Metropolitan Achievement Tests, and Stanford Achievement Test Series (Aiken, 1997).

General mental ability. Tests of general mental ability (or intelligence) are available in both group and individual formats. Most counselors are not trained to administer and interpret individual intelligence tests such as the Wechsler Adult Intelligence Scale–Revised, Wechsler Intelligence Scale for Children–Third Edition, and Stanford-Binet Intelligence Scale. Normally, these are administered and interpreted by clinical and/or school psychologists and are used when very important decisions are to be made about the client's future schooling (e.g., special education placement) or work capabilities (e.g., Social Security Disability consideration). Counselors are more likely to be involved with group intelligence testing such as the Otis-Lennon School Ability Test, Cognitive Abilities Test, and Wonderlic Personnel Test. These normally are used for screening purposes to determine whether more extensive intellectual assessment might be advisable (Wodrich, 1997). Assessment of general mental ability (intelligence) is

one of the most controversial areas of testing, and care must be taken when interpreting the results of these evaluations to make sure that the results are not used in a discriminatory manner with various ethnic and cultural groups (Samuda, 1998).

Vocational aptitudes. Aptitude generally has been defined as the ability to profit from training or education in a specific field such as accounting, engineering, or auto mechanics. A variety of aptitude tests are used in schools to help students make educational and career decisions. These tests attempt to predict the area or curriculum in which a person will be successful given additional training or education. Normally, these tests are given during middle school or early high school to assist students in making decisions about their high school curriculum areas. Aptitude tests also are used with college students wishing to enter graduate schools in certain areas (e.g., medicine, dentistry, law, education) and by employment services to help businesses and clients make career decisions. Some of the more popular aptitude tests are the Differential Aptitude Tests, General Aptitude Test Battery, Armed Services Vocational Aptitude Battery, Meier Art Tests, Music Aptitude Profile, Bennett Mechanical Comprehension Test, and Computer Operator Aptitude Battery. Counselors employed in K-12 schools, community colleges, universities, employment agencies, and training centers are most involved with aptitude testing (Cohen & Swerdlik, 1999).

Interest assessment. Interest assessment refers to a client's preferences (likes and dislikes) for certain types of activities. Interest inventories most frequently are used in career counseling and are among the most frequently used assessment instruments by counselors and other mental health professionals. Interest assessment is used in middle and high schools, community colleges, universities, career training centers, the military, and public and private employment agencies as well as in private practice. Most of the inventories consist of categories of activities to which clients are asked to indicate their likes and dislikes. Then, the results are compared to the interests of persons in a wide variety of occupational areas. Some of the most frequently used interest inventories include the Strong Interest Inventory, Kuder Occupational Interest Survey, Jackson Vocational Interest Survey, Ohio Vocational Interest Survey, and Self-Directed Search (Cohen & Swerdlik, 1999).

Personality assessment. Various rating scales, checklists, interviewing procedures, and inventories, as well as behavioral observation, have contributed to the assessment and understanding of personality dynamics (Aiken, 1997). In most states, counselors can administer and interpret personality measures, with the possible exceptions of projective personality techniques (e.g., Rorschach Psychodiagnostic Technique, Holtzman Inkblot Technique, Thematic Apperception Test) and some of the more complex personality inventories (e.g., Minnesota Multiphasic Personality Inventory-2, Millon Clinical Multiaxial Inventory), which are designed to assess personality disorders and clinical syndromes. Counselors are more likely to use procedures that attempt to access more normal personality characteristics such as the California Personality Inventory and Myers-Briggs Type Indicator (Hood & Johnson, 1997).

The *DSM-IV* Diagnostic System

The *DSM-IV* (American Psychiatric Association, 1994) is among the most important diagnostic documents in the history of counseling, psychology, psychiatry, and social work. The original *DSM*, the *DSM-I* (American Psychiatric Association, 1952) and its four revisions are best viewed as evolutionary systems that have been revised periodically to reflect new research in mental health (Hohenshil, 1993). The *DSM-IV* is an important counseling tool for several reasons:

1. It provides a common language that facilitates communication among mental health personnel for purposes of diagnosis, treatment planning, treatment, and research.
2. As the most widely used system for diagnosis of mental disorders in the United States, it provides a system for diagnosing that is used by insurance companies for third-party payments; by governmental agencies for accounting purposes; and by mental health professionals practicing in agencies, private practice, schools, and hospitals.
3. The *DSM-IV* enhances the selection of treatment procedures most likely to be effective in treating specific problems or mental disorders.
4. *DSM-IV* diagnoses provide a foundation for the evaluation of counseling effectiveness when the counselor considers whether the symptoms that led to the diagnosis have been reduced and whether the client's functioning has improved.

The counseling profession clearly has recognized the importance of the *DSM-IV* by including teaching the use of the diagnostic system in counselor education programs and requiring demonstration of *DSM-IV* competencies in licensure examinations (Mead, Hohenshil, & Singh, 1997).

DSM-IV Axis System

The fundamental basis or model for the *DSM-IV* is the multiaxial evaluation system of diagnosis. All clients are evaluated on each of the five axes of the system so that no important aspects of the client's functioning are overlooked by the counselor doing the evaluation. The five axes are briefly described as follows (American Psychiatric Association, 1994):

Axis I: Includes the clinical syndromes (e.g., mood disorder, anxiety disorders) and other conditions that may be the focus of clinical attention

Axis II: Includes mental retardation and the personality disorders

Axis III: Contains a listing of general medical conditions that are relevant to the diagnosis, understanding, or management of the case (e.g., diabetes, high blood pressure, results of drug screening tests)

Axis IV: Notes psychosocial and environmental problems that may affect the diagnosis, treatment, and/or prognosis (e.g., divorce, living in poverty, loss of employment, psychological abuse by parent)

Axis V: Used to provide a global assessment of functioning (GAF) scale, which is a rating of the client's overall level of functioning, usually at the time of the evaluation

Are Counselors Diagnosticians?

There are some in the counseling profession who believe that counselors should only follow the developmental model and, therefore, not diagnose and treat pathology. They contend that the primary factor that separates counseling from psychology and psychiatry is that counselors traditionally have provided services for clients with normal developmental problems, whereas other mental health disciplines have served clients with more severe mental disorders. Furthermore, they believe that diagnosis contradicts some of the other accepted counseling models, especially the client-centered, humanistic, and family systems approaches. However, the fact of the matter is that thousands of counselors currently are employed in the private sector or by public mental health agencies, and they routinely diagnose and treat clients with both developmental problems and more serious mental disorders. One could make the case that all counselors diagnose, either formally or informally. When developmentally oriented or client-centered counselors determine that clients' behavior is not pathological and, therefore, is appropriate for their brand of counseling, this is a form of diagnosis where the only two diagnostic categories are "normal developmental problem that we can help with" and "more serious problem that we should refer to a psychologist or psychiatrist" (Hohenshil, 1996).

As noted previously, counselors are extensively involved in assessment and diagnosis as part of the overall counseling process, regardless of their employment settings. Whether counselors use a highly formalized diagnostic system (e.g., the *DSM-IV*) or a more informal system, all counselors make decisions about clients that help to guide the selection of counseling interventions. The following section deals with the development of effective treatment plans.

Treatment Planning

A treatment plan is an organized approach and intervention that can assist both the counselor and the client. Dating from the early 1960s, formalized treatment planning was important for the entire health care delivery system (Jongsma & Peterson, 1995). During the 1970s, it became especially significant in the mental health sector when clinics, psychiatric hospitals, and agencies sought accreditation from the Joint Commission on Accreditation of Healthcare Organizations (JCAHO) to qualify for third-party reimbursements. Before then, treatment providers had used minimal written plans that often were unclear or unspecific about goals, objectives, interventions, and desired outcomes for completion of therapy. During the 1980s and 1990s came the tremendous expansion of managed care systems that influenced mental health providers to move swiftly from assessment and diagnosis of problems to formulation and implementation of treatment plans.

Benefits of a Treatment Plan

Good treatment plans can benefit the client, the counselor, the treatment team, the treatment setting, and the counseling profession in general. A need for accountability and effectiveness mandates systematic treatment planning (Seligman, 1998). The client benefits when a written plan identifies the issues that are the focus of the counseling work. Treatment planning provides a structure or a road map for specific objectives that can channel work toward changes to achieve the overall goal of problem amelioration or resolution. Clients can be informed about the therapeutic direction so that therapy no longer is a vague, even mysterious process as it too often has been viewed in the past.

Counselors benefit from treatment planning because they must give considerable attention to determining what interventions will best help their clients. Third-party payers increas-ingly require clinicians to justify and clearly describe their treatment plans if payments are to be made. Therefore, the affordability for clients to receive treatment and the income for counselors to make a living is affected. Counselors also benefit from the clear documentation in treatment plans because it can provide a means of protection in case of litigation. A good clinical record with assessment and diagnosis, a treatment plan, and progress notes comprise the documentation that is an important defense against malpractice suits.

A well-developed treatment plan facilitates communication within a treatment team when the client is in a setting where there are various mental health clinicians. Pharmacological, individual, and group counseling, as well as psycho-educational group interventions, can be coordinated and enhanced when treatment planning makes clear the objectives of all interventions and who will implement them. A treatment plan also can be helpful for sharing information among professionals in different settings (e.g., school, hospital, agency). In addition to accountability, the public and the mental health profession expect results that validate the success of mental health treatment.

Components of a Treatment Plan

There are various descriptions of components of a treatment plan. Seligman (1998) organized the major elements of the treatment plan into a structured and systematic model that she termed the "client map." The acronym, DO A CLIENT MAP, is used to represent the 12 steps of the plan:

Diagnosis
Objectives of treatment

Assessments

Clinical characteristics

Location of treatment

Interventions to be used

Emphasis of treatment (e.g., level of directiveness; level of supportiveness; cognitive, behavioral, or affective emphasis)

Numbers (the number of people in treatment, whether individual, family, or group)

Timing (frequency, pacing, and duration)

Medications needed

Adjunct services

Prognosis

Makeover (1996) described assessment and formulation leading to the treatment plan that has four basic elements: aim, goals, strategies, and tactics. He viewed the *aim* as the simple most important result and the overall desired outcome. The achievement of the aim will resolve the distress that brought the client to counseling; restore the client to at least his or her previous level of functioning; and allow the client to make further progress, growth, and development. The aim is inclusive, bringing together all of the identified complaints under one encompassing idea. A *goal,* then, is a component of the aim, operationalizing it. It should be specific (concrete and relevant), realistic (achievable), and parsimonious (economy of effort). According to Makeover, the aim usually has two to four goals that represent the end points of therapeutic work. *Strategies* are therapeutic processes that can help the client to move toward a goal. Each strategy reflects a treatment orientation such as a cognitive-behavioral or insight-oriented therapy. A strategy may facilitate the accomplishment of one or more goals. *Tactics* are the specific therapeutic skills, techniques, and interventions.

According to Berman (1997), the key features in developing a treatment plan are, first, to develop long-term (major, comprehensive, and broad) goals that follow from the concepts described in the case conceptualization and, second, to develop short-term (specific, small, and measurable) goals that can be accomplished soon. Berman described five types of treatment plans. An *assumption-based plan* organizes information about the client in terms of the major assumptions of a psychological/counseling theory. An example might be that a client who comes to counseling after divorce can be viewed from assumptions of rational emotive therapy. Challenges would be made when the client predicts a self-defeating theme. The *symptom-based approach* organizes information about a client's symptoms that are presented at the beginning of therapy. An example might be that a client who presents with symptoms such as withdrawal, sleep disturbance, difficulty in concentrating, and lack of motivation would be treated as if he or she were depressed. Symptom reduction would be a focus. The *interpersonally based approach* looks at information regarding the client's relationships with others. An example might be that a client who is an acting-out teenager would be viewed from a family systems perspective. Developing a strong parental team would be a focus when it is clear that the teenager has been able to split parental authority. A *developmentally based approach* organizes information about the client's history. An example might be that a client who comes for help for her angry episodes with her child would be viewed in the context of her alcoholic family of origin. Acknowledging the anger and pain of her past would be a focus to reduce reactive anger toward her child. The *thematic or metaphorically based approach* organizes information around an important theme or metaphor characterizing the client's behavior or worldview. An example might be a client who describes "never getting anywhere" in his attempts to change his relationship with his boss. Developing a metaphor of the client as "treading water" when he might try "going with the flow" would be a path taken in treatment.

Selecting Treatments

One way of categorizing treatment selection is to differentiate whether it is therapist-based, diagnosis-based, or outcome-based treatment planning (Makeover, 1996).

Therapist-based treatment planning. Historically, therapist-based treatment has been practiced whereby the therapist has had his or her particular preferred treatment modality and theoretical perspective and has used it with most clients. Over time, different therapeutic approaches have emerged and become prominent, from a nondirective approach (Rogers, 1951) to a solution-focused approach (de Shazer, 1988). Recently, there has been less exclusive commitment to one psychotherapeutic approach, and therapists have developed eclectic or integrated approaches. Treatment planning is modeled from different theoretical viewpoints by Berman (1997). She organized these into behavioral theory, cognitive theory, process-experiential theory, family systems theory, dynamic theory, and atranstheoretical theory.

Diagnosis-based treatment planning. This approach is compatible with the *DSM-IV* (American Psychiatric Association, 1994) and was represented well by Seligman (1998) when she presented an overview of the major types of mental disorders accompanied by effective, research-based treatment models. Jongsma and Peterson (1995) wrote *The Complete Psychotherapy Treatment Planner,* which contains treatment plans for adults. This was followed by *The Child and Adolescent Psychotherapy Treatment Planner* (Jongsma, Peterson, & McInnis, 1999). Both books are devoted to specific counseling problems accompanied by behavioral definitions and possible *DSM-IV* diagnoses usually associated with clients who have those problems. A single long-term goal is stated. Objectives and relevant interventions then are indicated so that the therapist can select those that best fit the client. The American Psychiatric Association (1995) published a two-volume summary of possible treatments for most of its official diagnostic categories.

Best Practices for Therapy (Bourne, 1999) includes empirically based treatment protocols for different diagnoses. These are plans for delivering treatment that has been proven to be effective by carefully designed and replicated scientific research. The protocols usually combine several interventions in a recommended sequence, and steps actually are organized into 50-minute session outlines. Each includes a sample treatment plan that can be used by the clinician and is appropriate for external documentation.

One problem frequently noted with these types of treatment planners is that treatments are not specific to one diagnosis; rather, they often are listed repeatedly. Another issue is that diagnostically based treatment selections are labels that do not explain causative factors.

Outcome-based treatment planning. Outcome-based treatment selection involves methodology that measures continuous and usable feedback to positively influence the course of treatment. Makeover (1996) referred to this as a "top-down" approach because the therapist, in collaboration with the client, decides first what should be the final outcome. *Treatment Outcomes in Psychotherapy and Psychiatric Interventions* (Sperry, Brill, Howard, & Grissom, 1996) is a practical book written to assist mental health providers respond to the demand for cost-effective, efficient, and efficacious treatment outcomes. The authors acknowledged that determining outcomes can be difficult, but they offered several types of outcome measures, outcome monitoring systems, and outcome management systems. They promoted a paradigm shift away from treatments that are provider centered. Instead, they described prescriptive treatments that are tailored to client variables such as symptom severity, level of functioning, and readiness for change while integrating techniques from different psychotherapy systems and modalities. Maxmen and Ward (1995) also made a case that treatment selection should be based primarily on pragmatic outcome rather than on etiologic consideration. They argued that any single etiologic theory and its accompanying treatments can limit the therapist's selection of interventions.

Consideration of Human Complexity in Treatment Planning

There is some criticism that treatment plans are mass produced and used with all clients with similar problems. In response to this, Jongsma and Peterson (1995), as authors of treatment planning guides, emphasized that a client's strengths and weaknesses, unique stressors, social network, family circumstances, and symptom patterns must be considered in developing a treatment plan. Sue and Sue (1998) advocated that different cultural and subcultural groups might require different counseling processes and goals. Berman (1997) introduced and described the following "critical domains" of human complexity that she said must be considered in treatment planning: development, sexual orientation, gender, culture, and violence. She had "red flag" messages for the clinician to consider regarding each of these domains. For example, she noted that men and women have different levels of power and resources and have different realities at home and at work, factors that must be integrated into treatment planning. There are other domains of complexity—socioeconomic status, physical status, religion, and so forth—that are important to consider in treatment planning as well. Seligman (1998) addressed human complexity issues in treatment planning when she discussed four clusters of variables that seem to determine psychotherapy outcomes. She described therapist-related variables, client-related variables, and treatment variables, all of which were referred to earlier in this chapter. In addition, she emphasized the therapeutic alliance, a complex and vital aspect of therapeutic work.

Treatment Plan Example

The following is an example of a treatment plan that includes the basic information typically required. Treatment plans vary in length, and the information is provided in open-ended responses or checklists. The client information in the following treatment plan has been simulated. Therefore, any similarities between the simulated client and a real individual is coincidental.

Client Name: Sharon Jones   **Date of Birth:** 10/15/60

Social Security Number: **Insurance Policy Number:**

Presenting Problem:

Distress due to marital problems and a recent marital separation

Symptoms:

Weight loss, decreased energy, excessive anxiety and worry, loss of interest in usual activities, tense muscles, depressed mood, anger, sleep changes

Functional Impairment:

Difficulty in concentrating at work

Withdrawal from social situations

Verbally abusive conflict with estranged spouse about child visitation

Risk to Self or Others:

None

Diagnosis:

Axis I: Adjustment disorder with mixed emotional features (309.28)

Axis II: Diagnosis deferred

Axis III: Allergies, thyroid deficiency

Axis IV: Marital separation, economic problems

Axis V: GAF—55

Medications:

Xanax .5 mg as needed; Synthroid; Benadryl as needed

Alcohol and Drug Use:

Wine daily—1 glass

Proposed Treatment Modalities:

Individual therapy weekly

Figure 17.1 A Sample Treatment Plan   (continued)

Figure 17.1 Continued

<u>**Treatment Goals:**</u>

Significant reduction in anxiety and depressive reactions of the client to marital separation so that her functioning is not impaired

<u>**Treatment Objectives and Interventions:**</u>

1. To develop coping strategies to increase concentration:
   — Client will learn and use progressive muscle relaxation
   — Client will use a "worry journal" at home in which to record and leave anxieties
2. To increase social support:
   — Client will initiate contact with friends
   — Client will be referred to a divorce support group
3. To alleviate depressed mood:
   — Client will identify and challenge negative thinking and shame regarding divorce
   — Client will be referred to a physician for a medical exam and assessment of need for medication
4. To increase cooperative arrangements with husband:
   — Client will develop assertive, instead of aggressive, means to communicate with her husband
   — Client will list and process her angry feelings during individual sessions

Target date for problem reduction: 2 months and then reevaluate

Clinician's Signature: **Date:**

This initial plan would be followed with treatment updates at whatever timing is required by a third-party payer. The update likely would include the following: treatment accomplished (treatment strategies and interventions, treatment modalities), client progress (goals accomplished, symptoms, level of functioning), rationale for additional sessions (changes in condition or situation, continuation or change in treatment), and future goals (methods and target dates for achieving goals). A closing summary report likely would include the following: progress on treatment goals, remaining symptoms and problems, diagnosis at exit, referrals, and recommendations.

The Future

The use of computer technology and the Internet is having a profound influence on the way in which appraisal, diagnosis, and treatment planning are occurring. Since the first computer-based test interpretation programs were developed during the early 1960s, the use of computers to prepare clients for testing, administer the tests, and interpret test results has grown at an extraordinary pace. Today, many of the personal problem checklists, intake interviewing schedules, interest inventories, personality inventories, achievement tests, and other measures have been adapted to computers (Cohen & Swerdlik, 1999).

The World Wide Web also is having a profound effect on how counselors and clients engage in the business of assessment, diagnosis, and treatment planning. There now are Web sites in which clients can take tests and receive interpretation through the Internet, and there are literally hundreds of Web sites that deal with the topics of assessment, diagnosis, and treatment planning. There also is an online ERIC Clearinghouse on Assessment and Evaluation (www.ericae.net) that is devoted to issues of testing and assessment. The clearinghouse contains a wealth of Internet resources including an online full-text library (www.ericae.net/ftlib.htm), a test locator (www.ericae.net/testcol.htm), search capabilities (www.ericae.net/search.htm), and an online bookstore of testing materials (www.ericae.net/bstore/home2.htm).

Computerized programs also are available for psychotherapy treatment planning, as illustrated by *TheraScribe 3.5* (Jongsma, Peterson, & McInnis, 1997). This is an electronic companion to *The Complete Psychotherapy Treatment Planner* (Jongsma & Peterson, 1995), created to help clinicians to handle more quickly and efficiently the tremendous increase in paperwork involved in the treatment planning process. This software offers adult and child/adolescent libraries with a choice among thousands of prewritten treatment goals, objectives, behavior definitions, and suggested interventions. It tracks client demographic data, mental status and prognosis, treatment modality and approaches, progress, discharge criteria, and provider credentials. The treatment outcome tracking offers three-dimensional graphing, and the software is password protected to guarantee client confidentiality. It is described as more than a report generator and is considered to be a consultant in the treatment planning process. In the future, electronic data submission is likely to emerge as a requirement for clinical treatment forms. More ethical and legal issues might arise regarding the electronic storage and transfer of such extensive information on so many clients.

In addition to computer technology and the Internet, there are other influences on the future of appraisal, diagnosis, and treatment planning. Seligman (1998) described these as clinical, biological, social, historical, political, legislative, and economic influences. The next edition of the *DSM* is under way and might contain different diagnoses. Clinical experience and clinical research can lead to new diagnoses and treatment approaches. For example, as clinicians have worked with clients described as adult children of alcoholics, it has been difficult to find an accurate description of them in the *DSM-IV*, and there is interest in a new diagnosis to deal with this important area. The family systems perspective has influenced, and likely will continue to influence, clinicians in the way that they conceptualize problems and develop treatment plans. Neurological studies are linking more emotional and personality problems to biological and genetic causes. As a result, many clinicians are recognizing the need for psychopharmacological interventions.

Increasing social awareness and understanding of sexual orientation, gender, and cultural background will influence what behavior is to be diagnosed and treated. History shows that there has been great change in the interest and development of different treatment modalities and interventions. New therapeutic approaches will continue to unfold and affect treatment planning. Economic considerations have driven the managed care groups and other third-party payers toward brief counseling. In reaction, some legislatures are being pressed politically by the public to hold managed care groups more accountable when more extensive counseling treatment is needed. Legislative action in some states is creating more equity in third-party reimbursement for both mental and physical disorders, and there likely will be more clients seeking mental health treatment. More states will have "freedom of choice" legislation that requires third-party payment to any credentialed mental health provider. While the number of psychologists, clinical social workers, and licensed professional counselors is growing, the number of psychiatrists is declining. The medical model might predominate less, and a more holistic approach to mental health might continue to evolve.

References

Aiken, L. R. (1997). *Psychological testing and assessment*. Boston: Allyn & Bacon.

American Psychiatric Association. (1952). *Diagnostic and statistical manual of mental disorders*. Washington, DC: Author.

American Psychiatric Association. (1994). *Diagnostic and statistical manual of mental disorders* (4th ed.). Washington, DC: Author.

American Psychiatric Association. (1995). *Treatments of psychiatric disorders* (2nd ed.). Washington, DC: Author.

Berman, P. S. (1997). *Case conceptualization and treatment planning*. Thousand Oaks, CA: Sage.

Bourne, E. J. (1999). *Best practices for therapy*. Oakland, CA: Harbinger.

Clawson, T. W. (1997). Control of psychological testing: The threat and a response. *Journal of Counseling and Development, 76,* 90-93.

Cohen, R. J., & Swerdlik, M. E. (1999). *Psychological testing and assessment*. Mountain View, CA: Mayfield.

de Shazer, S. (1988). *Clues: Investigating solutions in brief therapy*. New York: Norton.

Hohenshil, T. H. (1993). Teaching the *DSM-III-R* in counselor education. *Counselor Education and Supervision, 32,* 267-275.

Hohenshil, T. H. (1996). Role of assessment and diagnosis in counseling. *Journal of Counseling and Development, 75,* 64-67.

Hohenshil, T. H. (1999). Diagnosing children's mental disorders using the DSM-IV. In J. S. Hinkle (Ed.), *Promoting optimum mental health through counseling* (pp. 207-211). Greensboro, NC: ERIC/CASS.

Hood, A. B., & Johnson, R. W. (1997). *Assessment in counseling: A guide to the use of psychological assessment procedures*. Alexandria, VA: American Counseling Association.

Jongsma, A. E., & Peterson, L. M. (1995). *The complete psychotherapy treatment planner*. New York: John Wiley.

Jongsma, A. E., Peterson, L. M., & McInnis, W. P. (1997). *TheraScribe 3.5*. New York: John Wiley.

Jongsma, A. E., Peterson, L. M., & McInnis, W. P. (1999). *The child and adolescent psychotherapy treatment planner*. New York: John Wiley.

Makeover, R. B. (1996). *Treatment planning for psychotherapists*. Washington, DC: American Psychiatric Association.

Maxmen, J. S., & Ward, N. G. (1995). *Essential psychopathology and its treatment* (2nd ed.). New York: Norton.

Mead, M. A., Hohenshil, T. H., & Singh, K. (1997). How the DSM system is used by clinical counselors: A national study. *Journal of Mental Health Counseling, 19,* 383-401.

Rogers, C. R. (1951). *Client-centered therapy: Its current practice, implications, and theory*. Boston: Houghton Mifflin.

Samuda, R. J. (1998). *Psychological testing of American minorities.* Thousand Oaks, CA: Sage.

Seligman, L. (1998). *Selecting effective treatments* (rev. ed.). San Francisco: Jossey-Bass.

Smart, D. W., & Smart, J. F. (1997). DSM-IV and culturally sensitive diagnosis: Some observations for counselors. *Journal of Counseling and Development, 75,* 392-399.

Sperry, L., Brill, P. L., Howard, K. I., & Grissom, G. R. (1996). *Treatment outcomes in psychotherapy and psychiatric interventions.* New York: Brunner/Mazel.

Sporakowski, M. J. (1995). Assessment and diagnosis in marriage and family counseling. *Journal of Counseling and Development, 74,* 60-64.

Sue, D. W., & Sue, D. (1998). *Counseling the culturally different: Theory and practice* (3rd ed.). New York: John Wiley.

Wodrich, D. L. (1997). *Children's psychological testing.* Baltimore, MD: Paul H. Brookes.

PART III

Settings and Interventions

CHAPTER EIGHTEEN

Counseling in Schools

STANLEY B. BAKER

EDWIN R. GERLER, JR.

This chapter examines school counseling from various perspectives. Included are discussions of the evolution of school counseling; various individual and group approaches to school counseling; consultation with teachers, parents, and others; assessment and accountability; and important issues facing school counselors during the 21st century.

Historical Perspective

School counseling appears to be a 20th-century phenomenon. Its beginnings were in the social reform movement of the late 19th and early 20th centuries. There was no master plan. School counseling evolved and seems to be continuing to evolve during the early 21st century.

As we begin the new century, school counseling appears to be in a developmental period analogous to Erikson's (1963) fifth developmental stage—identity versus role confusion. Collectively, the profession seems to be seeking to achieve a separate identity. Erikson stated, "The danger of this stage is role confusion" (p. 262). Failure to achieve an identity might prevent the profession from achieving professional maturity. What has been accomplished thus far?

The Beginnings

During the first decade of the 20th century, individuals such as Jesse B. Davis, David S. Hill, Anna Y. Reed, and Eli W. Weaver were viewed as school counseling pioneers. Independently, they introduced guidance curricula to their schools in response to local needs. These guidance classes became part of the schools' curricula and focused on vocational and moral guidance.

In the meantime, concurrent developments were generating activities that eventually would combine with and influence guidance programming in schools. For example, the work of Frank Parsons in the Boston Vocation Bureau (Parsons, 1909) spawned what has been referred to as the vocational guidance movement. His belief that providing dependable information about individuals and occupations through gathering useful information influenced the introduction of vocational guidance in some public school systems and the offering of courses in vocations in some universities.

Also, a series of events focused on assessing individuals for educational instruction (i.e., Binet's mental ability scale) and eligibility for military service during World War I (i.e., Army Alpha and Beta) led to the development of standardized psychometric instruments that also could be used in vocational and school guidance. In addition, several events occurred that created a new interest in mental health, personality, and human development (e.g., Freud's psychoanalytic ideas).

During the second and third decades of the 20th century, the number of guidance specialists in schools increased, yet there were no operational or training models. Several factors influenced what may have evolved in individual schools. First, school administrators, in many instances, defined the roles of their guidance specialists (Shaw, 1973). Second, college student personnel programs emphasizing discipline and attendance were imitated (Gibson & Mitchell, 1981). Third, attention to helping students adjust to school and plan for the future was promoted (Proctor, 1925). Fourth, a directive (i.e., trait and factor) guidance paradigm emerged as the dominant model (Aubrey, 1977). Most guidance programs were found in secondary schools. When guidance was offered at the elementary school level, it most often was a version of the secondary school model (Zaccaria, 1969).

Winds of Change

In the changing world after the World War II, the model that had emerged earlier was proving to be too restricting. Aubrey (1977) believed that a desire for more personal freedom and autonomy was occurring. The time was ripe for the writings of Carl Rogers to have a significant influence (Rogers, 1942, 1951, 1961). Viewed as a distinctively different viewpoint from the directive model that had dominated school guidance, Rogers promoted transferring the focus of counseling away from problems to individuals. He emphasized the counseling relationship and climate as well as helping individuals to resolve their own problems. Ten years after World War II ended, Smith (1955) stated that counseling had become the primary function in secondary school guidance and that Rogers's influence had moved school counselors from a directive mode to an eclectic mode. School counselors formed a national professional group known as the American School Counselor Association (ASCA). In 1953, ASCA joined with five other like-minded professional associations that had formed the American Personnel and Guidance Association (APGA) a year earlier. ASCA and another division of APGA, the Association for Counselor Education and Supervision (ACES), joined in an effort to develop and promote standards for training school counselors, thereby introducing the concept of uniformity in training and certification standards. Gradually, all states adopted certification standards by the early 1960s.

The National Defense Education Act of 1958 (NDEA) was passed in response to the threat of perceived Soviet superiority in the cold war climate after World War II. Massive levels of federal funds were provided to public schools and to institutions of higher education so that they could develop strategies to identify children in math and science careers in an effort to become superior to the Soviets educationally. Concurrently, the booming birth rate following World War II was engulfing the public schools and creating a demand for more schools, teachers, administrators, and counselors. Consequently, the number of training programs and school counseling positions proliferated, and there was more than ample federal funding to support these developments. Among the effects of this state of affairs was an increasing interest in elementary school counseling.

The decade of the 1960s is viewed as the boom era in school counseling and counselor education. Evidence of the interest at that time is found in the popularity of Wrenn's (1962) *The Counselor in a Changing World,* which sold some 60,000 copies in 4 years. Among Wrenn's ideas was a recommendation that school counselors focus more on developmental goals than on remedial goals, a theme that had other advocates as well (see Dinkmeyer, 1967; Zaccaria, 1969). Unfortunately, while the field of school counseling grew in size and stature, many identity issues remained unresolved.

Reductions in Force

The 1970s and early 1980s ushered in conditions that were troublesome for the school counseling profession. National economic problems and declining school enrollments led to re-

ductions in school staffs and a dramatic decline in openings for graduates trained to be school counselors. Counseling positions were easier to eliminate and apparently less essential than teachers and administrators. The profession became mired in defending its existence, advocating its merits, and defining its roles and functions. The boom had ended.

During this era of accountability, Arbuckle (1970) mused over whether or not schools really needed counselors. He pointed out that a gap existed between preparation and practice, that counselors did not provide unique services, and that many counselors lacked professional identities or loyalties. Many voices suggested what the role, or at least part of it, should be. For example, Menacker (1974, 1976) recommended becoming active in the schools and communities and drawing more from sociology, political science, and economics for ideas. In this model, the concept of change agent or client advocate was popularized. Others focused on the importance of preparing students for work and careers (Herr, 1969; Hoyt, Evans, Macklin, & Mangum, 1974). From this arena came the concept of career education, that is, integrating everything around a career development theme from kindergarten through 12th grade.

In addition, there were those who pointed out the importance of focusing on the personal development of students through primary prevention programming (Mosher & Sprinthall, 1970). This theme was referred to as *psychological education.* Shaw (1973) advocated a services approach in which specific functions—counseling, consultation, testing, curriculum development, provision of information, inservice training, use of records, articulation, referral, evaluation, and so forth—would define the role of school guidance personnel and would be founded on specific program goals and objectives. Finally, some recommended an eclectic paradigm, that is, blending more specific ideas into hybrids that are clearly delineated and based on accepted theory and research findings (Keat, 1974).

Changes and Challenges

APGA changed its name to the American Association for Counseling and Development (AACD) during the mid-1980s and then to the American Counseling Association (ACA) during the 1990s. These name changes reflected a continuing search for an identity. Words such as *guidance* and *development* were dropped, added, and then dropped again from the title in response to changing opinions about what the roles and functions of counselors were, opinions about which there was—and continues to be—intraprofessional disagreement.

The 1980s witnessed criticisms of the schools that indicated concern over whether or not students were being trained to be able to help the nation compete with international economic competitors. Challenges included calls for more rigorous curricula, substance abuse prevention, integration of exceptional and culturally diverse populations, reduced dropout rates, preparation for work in an increasingly complex economy and society, gender equity, and reduced or unchanged property taxes. School counseling seldom was mentioned or was not mentioned at all in these reports, leaving the profession with the challenge to recommend how it would be a player at a time when there was uncertainty about who the spokespersons were.

Challenges were coming from within the profession as well. In 1987, an AACD task force

depicted school counseling as a profession whose future was at risk, pointing out that standards varied widely across more than 300 training programs, of which only 70 were accredited by the Council for Accreditation of Counseling and Related Educational Programs (CACREP). Soon thereafter, an interdivisional task force (ACA, ASCA, and ACES) began an effort to bring about national unity in training standards and state certification/licensure requirements using the CACREP standards as a foundation (Cecil, 1990). Nearly a decade has passed without the goal being achieved.

Beliefs in what the primary focus of school counseling programs should be also varied. Because the ratios of counselors to students in most schools often are quite large, school counselors often found themselves engulfed in administrative tasks and meeting the needs of students who required help with a variety of immediate problems ranging from academic difficulties to mental health issues. Under these circumstances, counselors may be viewed by their publics as administrative associates who react to a small number of students whose needs are the greatest.

Another camp believed that school counselors should have their own curricula, devoting most of their time and energy to developmental guidance or primary prevention programming (see Gysbers & Henderson, 1994). Their primary goal would be to reach out proactively through classroom and small group activities focusing on a range of development-enhancing topics such as preparation for the transition from school to work, getting along with others, violence prevention, multicultural understanding, and coping skills training. In turn, Baker (2000) promoted a balanced approach. This approach is founded on a realization that demands for responsive services will continue to exist, whereas the focus on development and prevention is equally important.

There is insufficient space here to elaborate on all of the challenges facing school counseling in the new millennium. Suffice it to say that the challenges come from without and within the profession and that continuous efforts to respond are under way. The closing section of this chapter is devoted to those responses. In the interim, we attempt to highlight important features of the school counseling profession so as to provide an image of what the parameters of the profession are.

Childhood and Early and Middle Adolescence

Broad Spectrum View of Development During Childhood and Early Adolescence

Elementary and middle school counselors are at the core of helping young people to meet the challenges of learning in school climates that are shaped by ever-changing demands of society. Counselors' challenge is to help young people understand and manage their own complex needs within the equally complex learning environment of schools. The developmental needs of young people span a variety of areas conveniently termed the "BASIC ID" by psychologist Arnold Lazarus. Lazarus (1985) observed that cognition and learning are parts of a psychological whole in human functioning. He outlined the domains of psychological functioning with the convenient acronym, BASIC ID, which stands for the following:

Behavior
Affect
Sensation
Imagery
Cognition
Interpersonal relations
Diet/physiology

Middle Adolescence

Most secondary school students are between 14 and 18 years of age. This is a period of rapid body growth and a time when scenarios of life that have previously been relied on are questioned (Erikson, 1963). Erikson (1963) described the adolescent mind as being in a "moratorium," that is, "a psychosocial stage between childhood and adulthood and between the morality learned by the child and the ethics to be developed by the adult" (p. 262). According to Erikson, role confusion can lead to arrested development. It should be noted that writers such as Gilligan (1982) and Josselson (1987) believed that Erikson's model might be less valid for describing the development of women and people of color. Therefore, for some adolescents, arrested development may lead to both role confusion and isolation from close relationships. Prevention of arrested development or enhancement of identity and intimacy development, then, seem to be primary goals for school counseling to achieve with adolescents.

Individual Counseling

The demand for responsive services places school counselors in a position where they often find themselves engaged in one-to-one counseling relationships with student clients. Shaw (1973) suggested two types of individual counseling that may take place in schools. Early identification and treatment, or secondary pre-vention, consists of identifying problems during an early stage of development, through self-referrals and referrals from others, and trying to prevent them from becoming more serious. Remedial counseling, or tertiary prevention, involves counselors in working with student clients with serious, and perhaps chronic, problems. School counselors are challenged to be prepared to respond to student clients along a continuum of problems ranging from relatively minor to serious. Depending on the circumstances, they might be able to refer clients for more intensive help or might have to try to be of as much help as their expertise and availability allow.

School counseling did not develop its own individual counseling models. University training programs adapted models taken from other fields and disciplines to school counseling. School counselors are challenged to adapt the models they have studied to the clientele and the environment found in schools. When the clients are in elementary schools, the environment usually consists of classrooms in which the children spend most of their time. Counselors have some flexibility in scheduling individual interviews because elementary school teachers may have more flexibility in releasing their students to see counselors. When the clientele are adolescents, the environment usually consists of a school setting in which class periods last for approximately 40 to 50 minutes with bells or some other system announcing dismissal and signaling the need for students to move to the next classes on their schedules. Secondary school counselors must fit most of their individual counseling sessions into, at most, a 40- to 50-minute time frame while finding time in students' schedules to meet without intruding on their classroom time.

Counseling Children

Keat (1990) adapted the multimodal model for work with children and young adolescents. Proponents of this model believe that cognition and learning are affected by what happens in the other domains so that students who have behavior problems, emotional disturbances, interpersonal difficulties, or any number of other psychological difficulties are likely to experience learning problems.

Elementary and middle school counselors work with students who present various concerns that often are the product of dysfunction in several domains. For example, treating a school phobia might involve the counselor and student in a wide-ranging exploration of causes and solutions.

Behavioral Counseling

Whereas the multimodal approach to counseling with children and young adolescents recognizes the interaction of various aspects of human functioning, school counselors often need to focus their work on particular aspects of students' lives as starting points in dealing with presenting problems. Counselors, for example, often are called on to address behavior difficulties among students and typically employ focused behavioral strategies to alleviate behavior problems.

Counselors use behavioral counseling to help students learn or relearn behaviors that are important for success in the school environment. Counselors reinforce appropriate student behaviors and eliminate maladaptive or inappropriate behaviors by employing strategies based on certain well-established principles. If a student has a propensity for talking impulsively without permission in the classroom, for example, then a counselor might work with a classroom teacher to present positive stimuli to reinforce times when the child asks permission to talk in class. This procedure, known as *positive reinforcement,* is commonly practiced in school counseling and often is accompanied by a procedure known as *extinction,* whereby an inappropriate behavior, such as talking out of turn, is purposely ignored and not reinforced through adult attention.

Positive reinforcement and extinction are by no means the only behavior change strategies counselors employ in elementary and middle schools. Other strategies include (a) *shaping,* which induces new behaviors by reinforcing behaviors that approximate the target behavior; (b) *modeling,* which exposes students to respected individuals, either in real life or on tape, who demonstrate behaviors that the students are expected to learn; (c) *role-playing,* which engages students in simulations to practice appropriate behaviors; (d) *desensitization,* which helps to eliminate anxiety and fear, such as children's fear about attending school or about speaking in front of the class, by progressively involving the pairing of relaxing responses with incompatible, anxiety-producing stimuli to gradually eliminate the anxiety that inhibits a desirable behavior; and (e) *flooding* (the opposite of desensitization), which exposes a student repeatedly to a feared situation, such as public speaking, with the effect of wearing out the stimulus.

Both multimodal and behavioral approaches to individual counseling, although different in scope and focus, have their roots in behaviorism. Many elementary and middle school counselors, of course, base their work on other theoretical perspectives. Among the most common perspectives used at the elementary and middle school levels is Adlerian counseling.

Adlerian Counseling

This approach to counseling acknowledges that all behavior and accompanying emotions are goal directed. School counselors' approach to individual counseling, therefore, is to determine what each student wants to accomplish. Using this approach, counselors mainly look at the immediate behavior goals of students rather than at long-range goals. Adlerian counselors also attend closely to the social and family constellation of children, with an important goal of counseling being to understand the social and family dynamics that influence children's functioning.

Because school counselors often are called on to help children change inappropriate behavior, many in the profession find the Adlerian approach useful. Sweeney (1998), in particular, focused on the need to help teachers and parents understand the four goals of children's misbehavior: attention, power, revenge, and inadequacy. He recommended that adults use encouragement, natural and logical consequences to change inappropriate behavior. If a child disrupts others in the classroom, for example, then the teacher might move the child to an isolated location, preventing further disruption—a logical consequence for the misbehavior.

Adlerian approaches have been very popular among school counselors, particularly at the elementary school level. Dinkmeyer's (1973) well-known classroom program, "Developing Understanding of Self and Others" (DUSO), is Adlerian based and has been widely used by elementary school counselors. Similarly, Dinkmeyer and McKay's (1976) "Systematic Training for Effective Parenting" (STEP) for years has been among the most popular parent education programs used in school counseling. In summary, many elementary and middle school counselors find Adlerian approaches to be effective in resolving problematic behaviors in young people.

Counseling Adolescents

Adolescent clients may be difficult to motivate. Therefore, they may fail to arrive for appointments or may fail to do the things between counseling sessions that they agreed to do. Adolescent clients are more likely to be immature than are adult clients, and they may desire quick solutions. They also may have a low tolerance for lengthy sessions, continuous sessions, and self-management/self-monitoring. So, what approaches might work? Several approaches seem to have promise and can be adapted to individual counseling with secondary school adolescents. A brief overview is presented here (for more detail, see Baker, 2000).

Secondary school counselors are encouraged to view individual counseling as a developmental process that is enhanced by counselors who are empathic, genuine, respectful, and concrete in their interviews. Adolescent clients generally respond well to counselors who attend to them physically and psychologically and who can provide verbal responses that are empathic (e.g., inviting clients to talk, paraphrasing information, reflecting feelings, clarifying unclear material, summarizing information and feelings, asking appropriate questions). Adolescent clients also generally react well to intentional challenging responses that help them to move toward achieving counseling goals (e.g., mild interpretations, self-sharing, confrontation, immediacy, information, goal setting).

Many of the issues facing adolescent clients can be addressed by school counselors, who can provide assistance in the following ways: (a) providing empathic support when clients need others to listen and letting them process what they are feeling and thinking; (b) helping clients identify and evaluate their alternatives when trying to make decisions; (c) helping, or sometimes teaching, clients to think rationally about matters that are being approached irrationally; (d) helping clients to acquire skills that will enhance their development while also resolving current difficulties (e.g., learning to be appropriately assertive, to relax when under duress, and to monitor behaviors and thoughts that might need to be modified); and (e) being able to respond to crises appropriately.

Several writers have suggested a brief counseling model for school counselors (see Bruce, 1995; Littrell, 1998; Murphy, 1997). The brief model is purposely time limited so as to be efficient yet effective. In the model, counselors rely on a strong working alliance with clients and are very active (as are clients). Counselors quickly affirm clients' strengths and resources and attempt to help clients establish clear and concrete goals that are measurable and achievable. It might be the most significant new model for secondary school counselors to consider as we enter the 21st century. It appears to be very appealing on paper, and there is some empirical evidence of its merits (Bruce & Hopper, 1997; LaFountain, Garner, & Eliason, 1996; Murphy, 1997). It remains to be seen whether or not it receives widespread use and, if so, whether users find it to be a successful approach.

Group Work in Schools

Burks and Pate (1970) provided terminology to differentiate between the two arenas in which group work might occur in school counseling.

Group work designed to respond to immediate problems and to prevent arrested development is classified as *group counseling*. Groups developed for proactive curriculum programming purposes and designed to achieve primary prevention goals and enhance individual development are classified as *group guidance* (or developmental guidance). The role of the leader is to provide instruction in a manner similar to that of a classroom teacher. Goals usually are determined by leaders or curriculum planners and are based on enhancing the development of participants and preventing problems before they occur (i.e., primary prevention) or preventing at-risk individuals from suffering arrested development (i.e., secondary prevention).

Group Counseling

Many of the same skills that are required for successful individual counseling also are required in group counseling. Krieg (1988) believed that members of counseling groups are less likely to be manipulative and more likely to be honest, and Dinkmeyer (1969) asserted that these peer relationships are more realistic than individual counseling relationships with adults.

Many counselors find the leadership role in groups to be difficult to achieve and maintain, and this is not an issue in individual counseling relationships. Confidentiality also is more difficult to maintain when working with groups. Scheduling group counseling sessions is quite challenging in schools because of the demands of the academic curricula.

In his book *The Twilight of Common Dreams,* Gitlin (1995) noted, "The cultivation of difference is nothing new, but the sheer profusion of identities that claim separate political standing today is unprecedented" (p. 3). As Gitlin rightly claimed, many of us need and want to celebrate our diversity, but we also want and need to find, to accept, and to affirm what we share—in the classic words of Harry Stack Sullivan, that "we are all more simply human than otherwise" (Sullivan, 1947, p. 47). We need, in other words, to overcome our "delusions of uniqueness" (Sullivan, 1947) and to discover our common core or our shared being. The chief purpose of group counseling is to aid children and adolescents in this discovery.

The purpose here is to examine the many reasons why school counselors lead counseling groups, but always in the context of group counseling's chief purpose, that is, the search for common ground. The following are among the most common reasons for conducting counseling groups:

- Students learn about themselves and others in groups through self-disclosure.
- Students can try out new ideas and behaviors—and receive responses to them—in the relatively safe environment of a counseling group.
- Because participants outnumber counselors, groups provide security; students can be unnoticed when they need to be.
- Group counseling is an economic use of school counselors' time.
- Fellow group members can help students to make positive changes in their lives.
- Groups help students to identify concerns that might need special attention beyond group counseling.
- Groups provide "spectator therapy," that is, the opportunity for students to watch others change for the better.
- Groups give students practice in give-and-take; some students have learned how to give help but not how to receive it.
- Groups often meet students' needs for belonging, affection, and acceptance.

What follows is an elaboration of certain factors that make group counseling important for young people.

Self-Disclosure

Counseling groups that create a climate of acceptance, understanding, care, and love provide a favorable setting for encouraging students to self-disclose (Corey, 1995; Gazda, 1989). This climate provides participants with a strong sense of belonging, trust, and self-confidence, thereby diminishing defensiveness and encouraging group members to express their private thoughts and feelings (Yalom, 1985). Early in the group process, the openness exhibited by the most disclosing members, and sometimes modeled by the group leader, creates a need in members to participate actively, either by sharing personal matters or by responding with supportive and helpful comments. This process of open sharing encourages young people to trust themselves and others in the group.

Safe Environment for Reality Testing

The paths we walk in life often are uncharted. Some of us enjoy looking at unfamiliar roads and highways on maps; they always seem to hold such promise for adventure and excitement. There are some recently constructed college campuses that laid out no paths or established walkways for students until the grass became worn in specific places. Only then were the paths set in concrete.

In the adult world, it has become popular these days for many to explore uncharted pathways with relationships and human roles of various types. It is as though life has become dull, and adults need to fulfill themselves by trying

out new roads. Lacking contentment, many adults go exploring, abandoning old maps, charts, and other long-standing guides for living. Groups give children and adolescents who are being raised in this type of climate the opportunity—and the security—to explore new directions in a type of laboratory setting before they actually establish their own paths. Through group work, young people can learn how to feel some sense of security in a context of ambiguity.

As some writers have noted (Corey, 1995; Gladding, 1995; Trotzer, 1989), groups provide an arena for safe practice. Students can practice new skills and behaviors in a supportive environment before trying them in real-world contexts. Group counseling usually comes closer to replicating real life than does individual counseling. This is so because we live in a social environment that features constant interaction with people from various cultures and walks of life. Many authorities on group counseling have discussed groups as a microcosm or reflection of society (Dinkmeyer & Muro, 1971; Gazda, 1989; Yalom, 1985). Trotzer (1989) termed groups "mini-societies." While interacting with others, people experience fear, anger, doubt, worry, and jealousy. In the comparatively safe atmosphere of the group, for example, young people can experience these same emotions and can identify problems that need resolutions.

Belonging and Acceptance

Group counseling gives participants the security of being with people whose lives, like their own, have unclear destinations. The feeling of commonality that emanates from the group experience is helpful and therapeutic for most individuals and is virtually unattainable through individual counseling. Many children and adolescents, for example, carry around fears that they believe to be unique to themselves. As group members, these youngsters grow comfortable with one another and begin to take risks in sharing personal fears and other emotions.

In short, groups give us the security of knowing that we are not alone—that other people have thoughts and feeling like our own. Yalom (1985) used the term *universality* instead of *commonality* when he discussed the value of bringing people together in counseling groups, but whatever the terminology, there is nearly total agreement among group counseling experts about the benefits that accrue from sharing common experiences. These same benefits, of course, are available to adults who participate in groups led by elementary and middle school counselors. Some examples of adult groups in which shared common experiences can be helpful include parents whose children have died, victims of life-threatening illnesses, parents and teachers who recently have experienced natural disasters, parents who are having difficulty with child raising, beginning teachers who are experiencing various challenges in the classroom, and recently divorced people.

One recently divorced parent wrote in an early group session,

> I am at the point in my life where I believe I can hardly be hurt any more than I have been. When my spouse went away, I probably hurt as much as anyone can hurt. I will probably never in this life fully recover from that hurt. I think it is rather remarkable how we can delude ourselves into thinking that other humans will treat us faithfully. When I recall all the times I have treated people without caring, carelessly, without trying to under-

stand them—too tired or too lazy to do so—I surprise myself continually by dreaming about, [or] hoping for, another human being to care about me. I started to say care for me as much as I care for them. In fact, it should not surprise me at all that I have been treated the way I have considering the way I've treated so many others previously. It's hard to admit that. I absolutely feel forsaken so many times in my life. I feel that way today—absolutely alone, forsaken.

This individual obviously needed help from a group to regain her sense of belonging and acceptance. Many writers in the fields of counseling and psychology have commented on the powerful human need to belong (Adler, 1964; Berne, 1964; Maslow, 1970). This need can be satisfied, in part, by being in a group (Trotzer, 1989; Yalom, 1985). Group members often will identify with each other and, therefore, will feel part of a whole. Although intimacy and closeness are characteristics of individual counseling, only group counseling can provide social support in the form of group identity. When members experience acceptance, understanding, and cohesiveness in a group, they begin to realize their value. They believe that they need the group and are significant to the group, which characterizes the spirit of belonging. When group members—whether children, adolescents, or adults—achieve a sense of "belonging" in a group, they are free to work on improving themselves.

Here-and-Now Focus

Groups also provide security for us, in part, because they teach us how to live in the moment, that is, in the "here and now." A teacher disclosed the following about himself during a group session:

I waste a lot of my time in so-called "in-between" or interim activities, namely, activities that are getting me from here to there. For example, in my current job, it takes me about half an hour to drive to work in the morning and then back home again at night. One of the things I've learned from participating in this group is that these in-between activities consume a lot of our lives and much precious time; therefore, we need to use the time wisely, to regard these experiences as real life events and not merely transitional events getting us to what is real life.

Sometimes, in fact, parents and teachers who participate in counseling groups spend their time in sessions thinking about what they are going to be doing after the group session is over. One teacher participating in a group from 4 to 6 p.m., for example, confessed to spending at least part of the group wishing he were home eating or thinking about what he was going to eat for supper rather than concentrating on the moment in the group. "What next?" thinking takes away from the moment and robs groups of their potential for bringing joy, hope, and healing to group members.

Spectator Therapy

In many types of groups, clients frequently discuss issues that are very meaningful to other members. That is, they have the opportunity to hear others present concerns similar to their own. The positive value of vicarious learning has been discussed by a number of authors (Bandura, 1977; Corey, 1995; Yalom, 1985). Often, a group member will sit in silence yet learn a great deal by watching how fellow members resolve their personal concerns. On countless occasions, members make comments such as the following: "That problem is like mine. It helped me to watch you handle your difficulty."

Other members have said, "Hearing you has really made me aware of my own fears and concerns."

Leaders always should be aware of the vicarious learning aspects of groups. Members who are silent still can be learning important things about themselves. For example, in a group consisting of six teenagers struggling with the same math class, one member said very little throughout the eight sessions. The leader believed that he had not reached this member at all. About 6 months later, he got a short note from her saying that she had changed a number of her study habits because of watching others in the group change. She thanked the leader for allowing her to be in the group, even though she did not contribute much. This example shows that it is not always necessary to push for active participation.

In summary, spectator therapy (Dinkmeyer & Muro, 1971) affords each group member the opportunity to observe other group members work through concerns and difficulties. Thus, group members can experience the benefits of the group without revealing their own problems.

Developmental Guidance

Developmental guidance aims to promote emotional, social, and cognitive growth while preventing problems in the lives of young people. A balanced guidance program includes both primary and secondary prevention strategies. School counselors may deliver group guidance programs indirectly by helping teachers to deliver units in their classes or may do so directly by delivering units in teachers' classes or arranging to deliver their own programs. Examples of the range of programs that might be delivered in this manner include structured programs focused on teaching social problem-solving skills, helping participants to learn to cope with anxiety-provoking cognitions, providing information that will help students to succeed in the higher education admissions process, providing assistance with learning how to resist peer pressure to participate in at-risk behaviors such as substance abuse, providing training for cross-age tutors and peer counselors/helpers, and teaching conflict resolution skills.

Group guidance offers an opportunity to reach large groups of students proactively so as to try to enhance their development (i.e., developmental guidance) and prevent problems from occurring (i.e., primary prevention). On a more limited dimension, counselors can target their activities to groups of individuals who seem to be more at risk and in need of interventions so as to prevent conditions from worsening or to prevent the need for treatment services (i.e., secondary prevention).

School counselors are challenged to be adept at setting goals and objectives, researching information for their programs, recruiting and selecting participants, planning lessons, instructing groups of participants, demonstrating to groups of participants, directing participants when engaged in educational activities, helping participants to transfer training to the real world, and evaluating their programs. Indeed, group guidance is pedagogical; that is, it is a teaching endeavor.

Primary Prevention

Primary prevention strives to meet developmental needs before they occur. Advocates of a broad spectrum or multimodal approach to primary prevention, for example, have suggested that to promote cognitive development and academic success, teachers and counselors should employ innovative approaches to reach students including creative physical fitness programs (Carlson, 1990), social skills programs (Stickel, 1990), and computer interventions (Crosbie-Burnett & Pulvino, 1990).

Case studies and numerous research projects have shown the multimodal approach to influence variables important to students' learning. Case studies, for example, have demonstrated the positive effects of multimodal interventions on social and emotional development (Keat, 1985), on self-concept (Durbin, 1982), and on performance of various school-related tasks (Starr & Raykovitz, 1982). Another case study (Keat, Metzgar, Raykovitz, & McDonald, 1985) showed that a multimodal intervention improved the school attendance of boys in Grade 3. Controlled studies involving multimodal approaches in elementary schools have yielded positive results in areas such as school attendance (Gerler, 1980), classroom behavior (Anderson, Kinney, & Gerler, 1984), achievement in mathematics and language arts (Gerler, Kinney, & Anderson, 1985), and promoting on-task behavior (Morse, 1987).

The multimodal framework is a particularly useful model by which to discuss counselors' work in helping students to function effectively in the academic environment. The following are some aspects of human functioning that influence students' performance at school and that necessarily require the attention of school counselors.

Behavior. Students need to listen carefully in class to material presented by their teachers. Students also need to behave with respect toward teachers and be willing to ask for help with difficult subject matter. Counselors and teachers can make use of role models to promote appropriate learning behaviors.

Affect. Students should have positive feelings about school and about themselves as individuals. Students also should feel comfortable in school but should understand that learning sometimes might create some necessary tension and anxiety. Teachers and counselors should encourage students to express feelings openly.

Sensation. The classroom environment should be a stimulating place in which to learn. The sensory experiences provided to students, however, should be in accord with their individual needs for learning. Students need to become aware of how to use their senses in the learning process. Counselors and teachers may help relieve some of the tension involved in learning through relaxation activities involving various senses.

Imagery. Students need to be aware of the creative aspects of education. Counselors and teachers can make good use of students' mental imagery to stimulate learning and creativity. Counselors also may use students' imagery to relieve undue anxiety that sometimes occurs in the learning process.

Cognition. Students need to think positively about what they are learning and about their learning abilities. They also need to rid themselves of irrational beliefs about failure. Counselors and teachers can promote school success by helping students to learn from mistakes and to build on achievements.

Interpersonal relations. Learning involves working with others. Students need to experi-

ence cooperative educational activities with one another. Students also should work freely with teachers in the learning process without fear of unnecessary reprisals. Counselors and teachers can serve as models for cooperation in various classroom activities.

Diet/physiology. Students need to eat nutritious foods, get sufficient sleep, and exercise regularly. Students who feel well physically and who have energy for learning are likely to experience educational success. Counselors and teachers should monitor students' physical well-being and recommend changes when necessary.

Secondary Prevention

Secondary prevention works to promote growth and to prevent developmental difficulties by focusing on a selected segment of a school population. If a counselor decides to begin a dropout prevention program for middle school students, for example, then the counselor would likely involve students who are at risk, that is, students who have exhibited important indicators of leaving school early. From a broad-spectrum perspective, such indicators might include low attendance, feelings of low self-esteem, poor attitude toward school, sense of alienation, inadequate social skills, and drug abuse. School counselors often develop secondary prevention programs that target such matters.

Group Work in 21st-Century Schools

Circumstances might not change much immediately until the challenges cited heretofore are met. Technology advancements may improve the delivery of these programs if counselors have access to the needed technology and learn how to use it. On the other hand, finding opportunities to work with students in groups and wanting to do so are human factors partially controlled by school counselors and also influenced by teachers and administrators.

School Counseling Consultation

An important school counseling function is to provide assistance to individuals—teachers, administrators, students, and parents—that will benefit third parties. In these relationships, counselors serve as consultants, the individuals with whom they have direct contact are consultees, and the recipients of their indirect assistance are clients. This triangular arrangement probably has been a part of school counseling since its beginnings because school counselors are natural recipients of requests for this type of assistance. Whereas reports in the professional literature indicate that teachers are most often assisted in this manner, administrators, students, and parents may be served as well (Baker, 2000). School counselors, as consultants, generally share their expertise and use their skills in a manner that is helpful to both their consultees and the consultees' clients. Examples of these consultation relationships with a variety of consultees are provided in what follows.

Teachers as Consultees

Working with challenging students. At times, teachers are assisted by counselors when trying to determine how to work with specific students or groups of students in their classes. Examples include motivating students to perform better academically, determining the best way in which to deal with unruly or distracting class-room behavior, and seeking suggestions about how to respond to students who appear to need help yet are not seeking it.

Responding to challenging parents/guardians. Teachers might feel a need for assistance in their responses to parents who share difficult demands, questions, and personal problems. An example might be a parent who requests advice on how to motivate a student who is having difficulty in the teacher's class while also asking questions that challenge the teacher's expertise and sharing personal information indicating that the student might be living in a dysfunctional environment.

Acquiring curriculum programming assistance. Counselors may serve as consultants to teachers who are seeking assistance with units within their own curricula. For example, a health teacher might need information about adolescent development or teaching basic communication skills, social studies and business education teachers may benefit from information about career development and school-to-work transitions, and any teacher may appreciate help with ideas for enhancing their classroom presence.

Administrators as Consultees

Administrators may consult with counselors about students who present discipline or attendance challenges. Other possible consulting interactions may involve concerns about responding to parents, seeking feedback about how administrative services are working or can be enhanced, and asking for thoughts about an upcoming administrative decision. For example, an elementary school principal might consult with the counselor about the merits of a plan to change the scheduling of classes and activities so as to find out the counselor's perspective about the potential impact on students.

Parents/Guardians as Consultees

Parents may seek assistance from counselors when concerned about developmental and academic issues involving their children. They also may seek help concerning their dealings with teachers and administrators. For example, the mother of a middle school student might contact the counselor because her child is having difficulty in a class and she blames the teacher for the problem. The parent is having difficulty in determining how to approach the teacher about the situation. When engaged in consulting about the presenting problem, the parent also seeks ideas that could help her to deal with challenges that she is experiencing with the student at home (e.g., apathy toward schoolwork, rude and unruly behavior, expressing immature cognitions).

Students as Consultees

Students may seek out counselors as consultants for issues involving fellow students, parents/guardians, and teachers. An example might be three elementary school students engaged in a dispute over friendships. They are engaging in arguments, name calling, and some fighting over issues that cannot be addressed rationally among them because of their tendency to respond emotionally. With the counselor's help as a mediator, the students are better able to discuss the issues rationally.

Consulting Modes

School counseling consultation can be approached from different perspectives. Kurpius

(1978) identified four modes (prescription, provision, initiation, and collaboration), and Baker (2000) suggested that mediation is a fifth mode. *Prescription* occurs when consultants serve, more or less, as experts who analyze situations and prescribe or suggest intervention plans. For example, in the case of the teacher seeking assistance with a communications skills component in the health class cited earlier, the counselor might suggest or prescribe information and activities deemed appropriate for the situation. *Provision* takes place when consultants engage in direct services to consultees. For example, in the case of the counselor who prescribed a communication skills program for the health class, the teacher might lack the time, interest, and/or competence to use the information and activities adequately, and the counselor/consultant might then provide assistance by presenting the material, collaborating with the teacher in presenting the material, or demonstrating enough to provide a model that the teacher is able to follow.

There are times when individuals might not realize that consultation assistance is available or are unwilling to seek such assistance. Under the circumstances, counselors who recognize the need may *initiate* a consulting relationship. For example the teacher described previously who was experiencing unruly behavior in the classroom might have been overwhelmed to the point of complaining about it without seeking help. Such situations offer counselors opportunities to initiate consulting relationships by informing individuals who seem to need assistance that they are aware of the problems and available to try to help if the individuals in need are willing to give it a try. Successful initiation may then lead to employing the prescription, provision, or collaboration mode or a combination thereof.

Collaboration implies a relationship in which consultants and consultees work together to try to figure out plans of action that will serve consultees' clients. Usually, counselors/consultants provide the structure for the collaborations. For example, a teacher might approach a counselor for suggestions about making the teacher's classroom presentations more interesting to the students, a number of whom have complained about the class being boring. In turn, the counselor may consider the teacher an equal regarding teaching methods and suggest that they try to list all of the possible alternatives that they can come up with for meeting this challenge (i.e., brainstorming). The combined efforts of the two collaborators may be enhanced by seeking additional helpful information about instructional techniques. Next, the counselor/consultant recommends that the teacher consider the merits of the alternatives and use that information to make tentative implementation decisions. They can follow up by periodically discussing the effects of implementing selected ideas.

When two or more individual or groups are locked in a disagreement, counselors might be able to serve as *mediators*. As such, the individuals or groups experiencing the disagreement are at once both consultees and clients, whereas the counselor is a consultant to both parties. An example might be the three elementary school students described earlier who were fighting over friendship issues. If they agree to mediation, then the counselor/consultant probably will meet with all three students collectively and invite them to share their points of view while listening to each other, with hopes of helping them to come to a peaceful and mutually agreeable resolution. The consultant neither takes sides nor prescribes a solution.

Most of the interpersonal skills used in counseling also are appropriate when engaged in consultation. The secondary school environment provides a natural situation for school counseling consultation, causing individual teachers, administrators, students, parents, and other members of the community to seek consultation at times. The manner in which schools are structured seems to create a natural school counseling consultation model. School counselors are natural recipients of requests or opportunities for consulting relationships with students, teachers, administrators, and parents (Baker, 2000). Consequently, consultation now is an important function for school counselors and will remain so during the 21st century.

Assessment in School Counseling

The Beginnings: Trait and Factor Influence

Schools became interested in standardized testing soon after World War I, primarily as a means of classifying individuals for alternative instructional modes (e.g., special education) and evaluating the effects of instruction (i.e., achievement testing). Early efforts in vocational counseling, influenced by the trait and factor model, employed tests as sources of predictive information that could be used to inform clients about the likelihood of their being successful in educational and work endeavors. Most counselor education programs include tests and measurement among the course requirements in the preparation of school counselors.

The trait and factor approach, in which tests tend to be viewed as predictive instruments, remained in vogue into the last quarter of the 20th century, even though there were periods of changing attitudes toward testing from time to time. That is, there were times when tests generally were viewed as nearly infallible sources of information as well as times when there was considerable questioning of their value. Goldman (1972) highlighted one concern by pointing out that most tests were weak predictors for groups of people; that they were even weaker predictors for individual clients and for people outside of the mainstream population; and that, in his opinion, most counselors did not possess the knowledge and skills necessary to help clients make use of what little information was available from standardized tests. He viewed the situation as analogous to a marriage that had failed.

Others criticized testing as being biased and leading to invasions of privacy. Those who believed that tests were biased pointed out that norming groups for those tests used for making admissions decisions to colleges and universities, for awarding scholarships and other awards, and for making employment decisions had content that favored White males. This bias caused other groups, such as women and people of color, to be disadvantaged when competing for limited opportunities and, as a result, prevented them from receiving their share of the "good life."

Those concerned about invasion of privacy criticized the content of some tests as being invasive, presenting young people with questions that caused them to consider choices that their parents might not even want them to be introduced to (e.g., asking whether or not the youths had used illegal drugs) without asking parents or their children whether or not they wanted to take the tests. Other invasion of privacy concerns had to do with requiring all students to take certain tests and keeping their data in files to which persons unknown to them or their parents had access.

Broadening the Focus

Those who responded to Goldman's (1972) criticisms at the time and a decade later (see Zytowski, 1982) pointed out that changes were occurring that broadened the opportunities for counselors to move and opened the way to moving beyond the trait and factor approach and to using tests in counseling. During the last quarter of the 20th century, there was a greater likelihood of school counselors being engaged in assessment activities than of focusing more narrowly on testing. In the remainder of this section, the focus is on what assessment has to offer school counseling without claiming that what might be in effect actually *is* in effect in all schools.

The word *assessment* implies a broader, more comprehensive range of activities than does *testing*, which implies the use of standardized tests by school counselors. Examples of the use of standardized tests and test data in school counseling include (a) helping students engaged in the career decision-making process by providing information about their interests, attitudes, and academic potential from standardized tests (e.g., interest inventories, personality inventories, aptitude tests); (b) diagnosing students' status (e.g., using intelligence and achievement test data when consulting with parents or teachers about academically at-risk students); (c) helping students to gain access to information about college entrance and scholarship qualifying tests, helping them to understand the results, and helping them to decide what to do next; (d) using test data to make classification and placement decisions (e.g., placements in learning groups); (e) administering tests to groups of students in schools (e.g., achievement testing across grade levels in support of curriculum and instruction); and (f) promoting responsible use of tests as a consultant to others.

Assessment implies a broader approach to appraising students. Nonstandardized approaches are used separately or in conjunction with standardized data to achieve appraisal goals. Examples of nonstandardized assessment approaches include taking case histories, systematically observing student clients, using vocational card sorts in the career decision-making process, and collecting data about students in a classroom so as to develop a sociogram.

School counselors are encouraged to engage in assessment rather than merely engaging in testing. Engaging in assessment requires accumulating knowledge about a broader range of approaches and techniques and acquiring the requisite skills. According to data gathered by Giordano, Schwiebert, and Brotherton (1997), school counselors may believe in the broader scope of assessment but, in reality, practice within a more narrow scope.

Making a decision to engage in assessment is enhanced by several developments that have occurred recently of which school counselors can take advantage. Publishers of many standardized tests offer computer-generated data that provide counseling information suggesting what the data mean and how to use and process the information in a manner that encourages process over outcome, that is, using the information in a self-discovery process rather than predictively. Interactive computerized guidance systems such as DISCOVER are available in many schools. In addition to providing occupational information, searches for jobs and educational opportunities, and strategies for identifying occupations, these programs allow users to enter interest, aptitude, and values data in response to computer program-generated questions that, in turn, influence what is generated

by the computer program (e.g., lists of occupations to explore, interpretations, summaries). The World Wide Web now offers an assessment vehicle for school counselors. For example, the Career Key (www.ncsu.edu/careerkey) is available free to anyone who has access to the Internet. Users can take an interest inventory, receive interpretive information, and gain access to the *Occupational Outlook Handbook*. School counselors can recommend that their clients take the Career Key or make copies of the instrument and, in either case, meet with the clients after they go through the program, or while they are going through it, and help them to process what is transpiring.

The state of assessment in school counseling is not completely removed from the picture that Goldman (1972) painted in his failed marriage analogy. Many counselors still do not have the knowledge, interest, and skills that are necessary, and many schools have their counselors engaging in testing functions that are unrelated to school counseling. We have a ways to go to make efficient use of the assessment tools that are available. Fortunately, there are those who continue to push forward the frontiers in the assessment domain and whose work can be of benefit to both school counselors and their clients, so we enter the 21st century with promising opportunities in this area.

Evaluation, Accountability, and Public Relations

Evaluation and Accountability

An Important Yet Onerous Function

Evaluation and accountability are neither interchangeable nor synonymous. Each represents an important ingredient of the accountability domain, and both functions are important. Each complements the other. "Collecting information about the effectiveness of services rendered represents evaluation. Using that information to demonstrate competence is accountability" (Baker, 1983, p. 52). *Evaluation* is the act of gathering information about one's services; *accountability* is the act of reporting the results of the evaluation. Evaluation precedes accountability. Translating evaluative data into accountability information completes the process and leads to accomplishing the goals of the accountability function. (Baker, 2000, p. 300, italics in original)

Evaluation has been included as a function of school counseling in textbooks for years, whereas the inclusion of accountability as an important complement to evaluation is more recent. Accountability first received attention during the 1970s, when national economic difficulties coupled with declining school enrollments placed the profession at risk for reductions in existing school counseling positions and drastically reduced the demand for new counselors. A number of writers have attempted to provide ideas for school counselors to adapt to their work settings so as to be effective evaluators and provide accountability data for their programs (see Baker, 2000; Fairchild & Seeley, 1995; Helliwell & Jones, 1975; Krumboltz, 1974; Miller & Grisdale, 1975). Yet, Myrick (1984) spoke for many others who have experienced disappointment in evaluation/accountability efforts, or lack of effort by many school counselors, when he contended that most school counselors will agree that these are important concepts yet will detest the tasks involved and resent being held accountable.

Findings from several surveys shed some light on the matter. Fairchild and Zins (1986) found that only 55% of their respondents collected some sort of evaluation data. Although part of the problem may rightly be attributed to

school counselor attitudes and apathy, counselor educators might share in the blame. Shaffer and Atkinson (1983) found that counselor educators devoted twice as much time to instruction in scientific research competencies than was devoted to evaluation competence. Support for contending that counselor educators share the blame comes from Fairchild and Zins (1986), who found that only 41% of their respondents believed that they had learned accountability skills during their training programs.

Although school counselor attitudes and lack of sufficient training are legitimate culprits, the difficulty of the task itself also is part of the problem. Simplifying the process of evaluation and accountability is equally as important as modifying negative attitudes toward the process and improving training efforts in counselor education programs.

Simplifying the Process: A Challenge for the 21st Century

What are the challenges? Several challenges face school counselors when trying to evaluate their efforts. They usually are assigned to schools and, in many instances, are the only counselors in their schools. Their roles and functions may be loosely or vaguely defined as well as heavily influenced by the principals' and teachers' goals. Therefore, school counselors often are hard-pressed for time to engage in evaluation and accountability activities and often are confused about what to evaluate, wondering just who it is that defines what is to be evaluated.

School counselors often lack sufficient resources (e.g., secretarial and clerical assistance, reasonable caseloads, access to computers, supplies) to carry out their basic functions (e.g., counseling/advising, consulting, developmental guidance programming, referral and coordination, assessment, administrative support). Evaluation and accountability tasks usually are added to those functions already mentioned and rarely are accompanied by administrator recognition that released time and additional resources are needed or forthcoming.

Perhaps the first step in simplifying the process is for school systems to achieve clarity in defining their counselors' roles and functions and to provide sufficient support for engaging in the evaluation/accountability process. This requires support from professionals outside of the profession—particularly school principals—who seem to be key players in whether or not the evaluation/accountability process for school counselors can be simplified during the 21st century. At the present time, we do not have a solution in mind for this problem, but we are quite certain that it is a problem that needs to be resolved.

Another challenge for school counselors is to determine what data to collect, how to analyze them, and how to present them. Several recommendations have been made, although none has led to making the system so simple that a large number of school counselors have adopted it.

What data should be collected? Unfortunately, school counselors engage in a variety of functions and tasks, making the process of determining what data to collect very difficult. In addition, many of the functions and tasks are not associated with clearly stated goals and objectives, as might be the case in teachers' lesson plans. Therefore, without clearly stated goals and objectives, it is difficult to determine what outcomes to measure. For example, what do school counselors do about numerous students who refer themselves for counseling services? Are there general goals for these cases, or does each case present its own goals?

Is outcome or summative data the only type of data to collect? Probably not. Accountability theory seems to recommend consumer satisfaction and cost-effectiveness as domains of interest as well. Therefore, it appears as if school counselors also are challenged to find out what their consumers think of their services and how efficiently they are using their time.

Who are the consumers? Students, teachers, administrators, former students, parents, and the general public all have been suggested as legitimate consumers.

Keeping track of how one's time is used requires some sort of system of recording how much time is devoted to specific tasks for functions that, in turn, requires an inventory of specific legitimate functions and tasks, all of which leads to the next issue—how to analyze the data.

An alternative proposed by Schmidt (1995) is to conduct external reviews. Typically, external reviewers collect data through on-site visits, analyze the data, and make their presentations to school system representatives. This approach is time-saving for counselors and less demanding of them to have expertise in evaluation and accountability activities. On the other hand, freeing counselors from involvement may increase the likelihood that the data and process are less meaningful to them and that the reports are less accurate. Perhaps external reviewers could work with school counselors in meaningful partnerships.

How should the data be analyzed? A comprehensive plan to collect and analyze all possible outcome, consumer, and cost-effectiveness data for each school counselor is a monumental task that probably would take too much time and re-sources and would place unrealistic compe-tency expectations on counselors. Counselors and their administrators are challenged to con-sider ways in which to acquire adequate sam-ples of data and analyze those data efficiently and effectively. Possible resources are consul-tants who can set up a data collecting and analy-sis system that is manageable and programs that may be used on personal computers that are af-fordable and user-friendly.

How should the data be presented? "Although reporting systems differ, they share some basic principles that make them understandable and informative: the information is summarized and organized systematically, the presentation is clear, concise, and understandable to laypeople, and reports are as brief as possible without omitting valuable information" (Baker, 2000, p. 319). Successful presentations seem to be systematic, clearly understandable, and con-cise. Krumboltz (1974) stressed the importance of recognizing that evaluation efforts may un-cover failures and point the way to improving one's efforts. In so stating, he advocated a focus on highlighting self-improvement as well as ef-fectiveness.

Rhyne-Winkler and Wooten (1996) recom-mended displaying accountability information in a portfolio. This approach allows for com-bining traditional reporting techniques such as printed documents with samples of supporting materials.

Public Relations

Accountability information derived from evaluation activities provides opportunities to enhance public relations. A common challenge across the school counseling profession has been public perceptions or misperceptions about school counselors. Many community members, parents, guardians, colleagues, and students have vague or inaccurate perceptions about the roles and functions of school counselors. Some have had no contact with school counselors, and others have had only limited contact. Al-though they might have a pretty clear idea of what teachers and principals do, they might possess little or no accurate information about the work of school counselors.

Evaluation data may be used to provide ac-curate accountability information about school counseling, information that may enhance school counselors' reputations and provide their publics with accurate perceptions of their roles and functions. Fairchild and Seeley (1995) suggested accountability committees, confer-ences with administrators, and written reports. Committees representing cross sections of the publics being served can become informed ac-curately and, in turn, can inform others as well. Accountability conferences with administrators encourage them to become allies and enlist their support. Written reports can be dissemi-nated and will be available as references for some time thereafter. These are but a few exam-ples of ways in which school counselors might be able to enhance public relations by sharing accountability information planfully. A key point is that the information has potential that school counselors may employ to inform their publics in ways that clearly can enhance public relations for school counselors and for schools.

The Future of School Counseling: Challenges and Opportunities

School counselors have faced, and will continue to face, numerous challenges. In this closing section, we present several concerns that seem to be among the more important challenges facing school counselors during the 21st century. We also view them as opportunities for school counselors to achieve competence and enhance services to their student clients. These challenges and opportunities are achieving multicultural competence as school populations become increasingly diverse, becoming successful social activists for students, meeting the challenge of changing computer and networking technology, coping with the "echo" baby boom (discussed later) and with increasing demand for traditional and new services, providing effective counseling services when workloads are relatively high, enhancing school counseling with support personnel, helping students to make the transition from school to work in an increasingly complex world, striving for uniformity in training and licensure/certification standards so as to achieve recognition as professional counselors, and staying motivated professionally.

Achieving Multicultural Competence as School Populations Become Increasingly Diverse

During the 21st century, school counselors will be challenged to be competent in their delivery of services to a broad range of diverse students. The "multicultural competencies/standards" (Sue, Arredondo, & McDavis, 1992) provide competence criteria that hold promise for helping counselors to meet the challenges associated with delivering useful services to diverse clients. The standards encourage school counselors to be aware of their own cultural values and biases, aware of the worldviews of their clients, and able to provide culturally appropriate intervention strategies. In this vein, Herring (1997) stated that counselors are best able to serve culturally different students by employing strategies that are responsive to their goals, cultures, and environments. Therefore, school counselors are challenged to consider cultural and environmental factors in addition to being skillful counselors.

Becoming Successful Social Activists for Students

Attention to cultural and environmental factors opens the way to becoming social activists as well as skillful counselors. Lee and Sirch (1994) envisioned that the 21st century will present "a more global view of human need and potential" (p. 91). Lee and Sirch promoted adopting a sense of social responsibility and a willingness to become change agents. Therefore, school counselors will be challenged to consider a model that requires activism outside the counseling suite (e.g., striving for equal opportunity, combating racism, providing diversity-sensitive counseling for sexual-minority youths, becoming social activists). Menacker (1976) offered concrete suggestions for becoming competent social activists including (a) focusing on concrete action that objectively helps students (this is an alternative pathway to achieving empathy); (b) attempting to eliminate environmental conditions that retard student clients' goals and development; (c) attempting to capitalize on environmental conditions that enhance client development and lead to goal achievement; and (d) recognizing that systems and institutions, rather than clients, sometimes are pathological and may have goals and values that are antithetical to those of the student clients.

Meeting the Challenge of Changing Computer and Networking Technology

Multimedia is the direction of the future for preparing school counselors and for delivering many types of school counseling services. Computing systems are becoming increasingly sophisticated and now provide software tools for working with various media. Image processing, digital video capturing, graphics production, sound editing, three-dimensional modeling, and animation exist for all computer platforms. Multimedia technology offers school counselors creative possibilities for computer-assisted delivery of preventive/developmental programs to students.

The 21st century surely will mean that a school counselor with a monitor, a keyboard, and a mouse or voice command will regularly be able to observe counseling activities and programs throughout the world. The very best teaching and counseling will be available for observation. Moreover, counseling and teaching methods and products developed by professional school counselors will increasingly be shared across the world (Rust, 1995).

The problem of applying new computer technology, especially in human service areas such as counseling in schools, actually is greater than the technical problems involved in designing and creating the technology. The possibility exists that some in the profession might become so enamored with the marvels of computers that they will lose sight of how technology can be realistically applied to meeting human needs (Gerler, 1995). To those in counseling who are excited by the potential of computer technology, it is stimulating to imagine and create applications to serve clients. The challenge for leaders in technology is to make possibilities seem reasonable and workable to colleagues who are less inclined toward technology and to professionals who have had little opportunity to explore the available technology.

Coping With the Echo Baby Boom and With Increasing Demand for Traditional and New Services

The U.S. Department of Education predicts significant enrollment increases through the first 7 years of the 21st century. This phenomenon is being referred to as the baby boom echo generation. In addition to increasing diversity, school counselors will be challenged to serve larger caseloads. Successful social activists and multicultural counselors will be competent to deliver services beyond the traditional counseling functions, perhaps to larger numbers of students. Increasing enrollments seem to dictate larger counseling staffs. Unfortunately, this might not occur, especially in environments where funds are limited or school systems are devoting resources toward achieving other goals (e.g., enhancing reading skills). This appears to be an "all things to all people" challenge. Although difficult to achieve, these conditions offer school counselors opportunities to demonstrate their competence beyond the traditional, and sometimes less visible, models and to perhaps achieve support from decision makers who will increase funding for counseling positions.

Concurrent with the increasing number of students in the nation's schools, many school systems are experiencing shortages of teachers, administrators, and counselors. Insufficient numbers of students are enrolling in educational training programs, and relatively large numbers of professional educators are retiring or leaving the profession early. Among the factors causing this shortage are that (a) those counselors trained during the NDEA and baby-boomer years are reaching retirement age; (b) many schools cut back on staffs during the 1970s and 1980s, and fewer school counselors were trained; (c) some states still require school counselors to have teaching experience and, therefore, reduce their pool of prospective students significantly; (d) salaries in basic education are relatively low; (e) a booming economy attracts many people to careers in other areas; and (f) conditions such as school violence, low pay, long hours, large student-to-teacher/counselor ratios, unreasonable demands by some parents and special interest groups, increasing numbers of students who come to school from dysfunctional homes, and voters who oppose tax increases for school enhancements during times of general prosperity discourage many from pursuing careers in basic education.

The problems associated with a rising number of students enrolling in schools and a concurrent shortage of teachers, administrators, and counselors will not be resolved soon. The reasons for the shortages are numerous and very difficult to resolve. Therefore, these conditions probably will continue to challenge basic education and school counseling well into the new century.

Providing Effective Counseling Services When the Workloads Are Relatively High

Student-to-counselor ratios have been discussed for some time. Conant (1959) recommended a ratio of 250 to 300 students per counselor. Peters (1978) recommended a ratio of 200 students per counselor. Others have made their recommendations over the years as

well. Shaw's (1973) conclusion (posed more than a quarter century ago) that these ratios are determined primarily by financial conditions in school districts and the perceived values of the school counseling programs rings true today and will remain the same well into the new century. The first author of the present chapter began his school counseling career as a half-time teacher-counselor with more than 700 students to serve. This was during the baby-boomer years in an affluent community that wanted to keep property taxes as low as possible. Within 3 years, the first author was a full-time counselor, and the community had built a second high school. The number of high school counselors doubled, and the ratio became about 300 to 1, which seemed much more reasonable and made one's efforts more effective. The overcrowded circumstances that initiated the change were not related to valuing the counseling program. Yet, the fact that administrators in each of the schools requested and received the same number of counselors as were employed when there was only one high school appears to indicate that the counseling services were valued. Therefore, circumstances can lead to improvements but might be unpredictable.

Enhancing School Counseling With Support Personnel

One way in which school counselors' large workloads may be alleviated is to provide support personnel who can assume responsibility for the time-consuming nonprofessional assignments that many school counselors are given such as keeping student records up-to-date, determining whether students are meeting their graduation requirements, making corrections in student class schedules, typing letters of recommendation and other correspondence, and performing a variety of other administrative and clerical tasks. Hiring trained paraprofessionals to be responsible for these tasks has been advocated for more than 30 years, and in some instances school districts have helped their counselors in this way. Unfortunately, far too many schools still have counselors engaged in administrative and custodial tasks that keep them from adequately concentrating on their professional counselor functions. These circumstances do not appear to be on the verge of changing dramatically during the early part of the new century unless school administrators and school boards place higher value on the special competencies that school counselors possess and school counselors themselves, after having demonstrated their competence, make intelligent and convincing cases for support personnel.

Helping Students to Make the Transition From School to Work in an Increasingly Complex World

As the world and the American society become more complex, young people face increasing choices and opportunities in the world of work. Helping them to prepare for the transition has been a traditional school counseling function. School counselors are challenged to be able to help students understand the contingencies of the school-to-work process, that is, having access to useful information and help with processing it intellectually and emotionally. Students also will benefit from help in acquiring school-to-work transition skills such as evaluating recruitment materials, completing applications, taking selection tests, engaging in selection interviews, and producing resumés. In

addition, they will benefit from understanding the difference between getting selected or accepted and achieving success, developing appropriate attitudes, and expanding their horizons. To be effective in helping student clients manage the school-to-work process during the 21st century, school counselors probably will have to provide more comprehensive programs for achieving these goals than currently are in place in many schools. In these more comprehensive programs, counselors likely will be proactive planners and active participants in the process.

Striving for Uniformity in Training and Licensure/Certification Standards: Achieving Recognition as Professional Counselors

Each state has its own standards for determining whether or not to award a school counseling license or certificate. To our knowledge, none offers reciprocity to individuals holding licenses in other states. There is considerable variety in the standards as well. Some states require teaching experience, whereas others do not. The number of college course credits needed to be eligible varies as well. Some states recognize the CACREP standards, whereas others do not. Generally speaking, there is little uniformity across states or across training programs.

Many people are unfamiliar with the roles and functions of school counselors yet are quite aware of the roles and functions of school teachers and administrators. If those who train counselors and those who determine the standards for licensure/certification cannot agree on the minimum training standards, then is it any wonder that the public is uncertain about who school counselors are and what they do? CACREP clearly defines standards for professional school counselors, and three professional organizations (ACA, ACES, and ASCA) have proposed that those standards be held as the minimum for licensure/certification in all states (Cecil, 1990). Unfortunately, many training institutions are unable or unwilling to make the changes that will allow them to meet the standards, and a number of states find the standards too high for their liking. The profession has an opportunity to upgrade training and to enhance its national/local reputation by accepting and promoting the CACREP standards. This challenge, if met, may offer an opportunity for enhanced status and general clarity about who school counselors are and what they do.

Keeping Motivated to Grow Professionally

One would like to think that school counseling will be a new and shinier model during the 21st century, appearing out of the mist like Brigadoon and drastically altered. It is tempting to write about a new, almost utopian model for school counseling in the new millennium. In truth, when the calendar changed from 2000 to 2001, many school counseling positions looked similar to those during the latter part of the 20th century. That is, school counselors still are engaged in a number of non-counseling functions such as scheduling, discipline, secretarial and clerical tasks, paraprofessional tasks, and substitute teaching. They still have relatively large caseloads and find too little time to do some of the things they were trained to do. The litany of challenges is long, and most still are in place. Therefore, school counselors are chal-

lenged to keep motivated to grow professionally—for themselves and for those they serve.

Avoiding burnout will remain a challenge in the 21st century. Suggestions offered to 20th-century counselors still have merit in the new century. These include suggestions that counselors (a) accept themselves, act in good faith, and recognize their own irrational thoughts; (b) take care of their physical health; (c) be appropriately assertive; (d) try to be efficient; and (e) keep current professionally. School counselors seem to depend on significant others to help resolve a number of challenges facing them. On the other hand, the suggestions for avoiding burnout, keeping motivated, and growing professionally are within the grasp of individual school counselors.

In the opening of this chapter, school counseling was depicted as a 20th-century phenomenon. As the profession enters the 21st century, much remains unchanged. There still is no master plan, and school counseling still seems analogous to Erikson's (1963) fifth developmental stage—identity versus role confusion. The profession remains in its adolescence, seeking to achieve professional maturity. Will someone writing a similar chapter at the start of the 22nd century take a similar position? Will the profession have achieved maturity in the new century?

References

Adler, A. (1964). *Social interest: A challenge to mankind.* New York: Capricorn.

Anderson, R. F., Kinney, J., & Gerler, E. R. (1984). The effects of divorce groups on children's classroom behavior and attitude toward divorce. *Elementary School Guidance and Counseling, 19,* 70-76.

Arbuckle, D. (1970). Does the school really need counselors? *School Counselor, 17,* 325-330.

Aubrey, R. F. (1977). Historical development of guidance and counseling and implications for the future. *Personnel and Guidance Journal, 55,* 288-295.

Baker, S. B. (1983). Suggestions for guidance accountability. *Pennsylvania Journal of Counseling, 2,* 52-69.

Baker, S. B. (2000). *School counseling for the twenty-first century* (3rd ed.). Upper Saddle River, NJ: Merrill/Prentice Hall.

Bandura, A. (1977). *Social learning theory.* Englewood Cliffs, NJ: Prentice Hall.

Berne, E. (1964). *Games people play.* New York: Grove Press.

Bruce, M. A. (1995). Brief counseling: An effective model for change. *School Counselor, 42,* 353-363.

Bruce, M. A., & Hopper, G. C. (1997). Brief counseling versus traditional counseling: A comparison of effectiveness. *School Counselor, 44,* 171-184.

Burks, H., & Pate, R. H. (1970). Group procedures terminology: Babel revisited. *School Counselor, 18,* 53-60.

Carlson, J. (1990). Counseling through physical fitness and exercise. *Elementary School Guidance and Counseling, 24,* 298-302.

Cecil, J. H. (1990, Summer). Interdivisional task force on school counseling. *ACES Spectrum,* pp. 3-4. (Association for Counselor Education and Supervision)

Conant, J. B. (1959). *The American high school today.* New York: McGraw-Hill.

Corey, G. (1995). *Group counseling* (4th ed.). Pacific Grove, CA: Brooks/Cole.

Crosbie-Burnett, M., & Pulvino, C. J. (1990). Pro-tech: A multimodal group intervention for children with reluctance to use computers. *Elementary School Guidance and Counseling, 24,* 272-280.

Dinkmeyer, D. (1967). Elementary school guidance and the classroom teacher. *Elementary School Guidance and Counseling, 1,* 15-26.

Dinkmeyer, D. (1969). Group counseling theory and technique. *School Counselor, 17,* 148-152.

Dinkmeyer, D. (1973). *Developing understanding of self and others (D-2).* Circle Pines, MN: American Guidance Service.

Dinkmeyer, D., & McKay, G. (1976). *Systematic training for effective parenting.* Circle Pines, MN: American Guidance Service.

Dinkmeyer, D., & Muro, J. (1971). *Group counseling: Theory and practice.* Itasca, IL: F. E. Peacock.

Durbin, D. M. (1982). Multimodal group sessions to enhance self-concept. *Elementary School Guidance and Counseling, 16,* 288-295.

Erikson, E. H. (1963). *Childhood and society* (2nd ed.). New York: Norton.

Fairchild, T. N., & Seeley, T. J. (1995). Accountability strategies for school counselors: A baker's dozen. *School Counselor, 42,* 377-392.

Fairchild, T. N., & Zins, J. E. (1986). Accountability practices of school counselors: A national survey. *Journal of Counseling and Development, 65,* 196-199.

Gazda, G. M. (1989). *Group counseling: A developmental approach* (4th ed.). Boston: Allyn & Bacon.

Gerler, E. R. (1980). A longitudinal study of multimodal approaches to small group psychological education. *School Counselor, 27,* 184-190.

Gerler, E. R. (1995). Advancing elementary and middle school counseling through computer technology. *Elementary School Guidance and Counseling, 30,* 8-15.

Gerler, E. R., Kinney, J., & Anderson, R. F. (1985). The effects of counseling on classroom performance. *Journal of Humanistic Education and Development, 23,* 155-165.

Gibson, R. L., & Mitchell, M. H. (1981). *Introduction to guidance.* New York: Macmillan.

Gilligan, C. (1982). *In a different voice.* Cambridge, MA: Harvard University Press.

Giordano, F. G., Schwiebert, V. L., & Brotherton, D. L. (1997). School counselors' perceptions of the usefulness of standardized tests, frequency of their use, and assessment training needs. *School Counselor, 44,* 198-205.

Gitlin, T. (1995). *The twilight of common dreams.* New York: Metropolitan Books.

Gladding, S. (1995). *Group work: A counseling specialty* (2nd ed.). Englewood Cliffs, NJ: Prentice Hall.

Goldman, L. (1972). Tests and counseling: The marriage that failed. *Measurement and Evaluation in Guidance, 4,* 213-220.

Gysbers, N. C., & Henderson, P. (1994). *Developing and managing your school guidance program* (2nd ed.). Alexandria, VA: American Association for Counseling and Development.

Helliwell, C. B., & Jones, G. J. (1975). Reality considerations in guidance program evaluation. *Measurement and Evaluation in Guidance, 8,* 155-162.

Herr, E. L. (1969, March). *Unifying an entire system of education around a career development theme.* Paper presented at the National Conference on Exemplary Projects and Programs of the 1968 Vocational Education Amendments, Atlanta, GA.

Herring, R. D. (1997). *Counseling diverse and ethnic youth: Synergistic strategies and interventions for school* counselors. Fort Worth, TX: Harcourt Brace College Publishers.

Hoyt, K. B., Evans, R. N., Macklin, E. F., & Mangum, G. L. (1974). *Career education: What it is and how to do it* (2nd ed.). Salt Lake City, UT: Olympus.

Josselson, R. (1987). *Finding herself: Pathways to identity development in women.* San Francisco: Jossey-Bass.

Keat, D. B. (1974). *Fundamentals of child counseling.* Boston: Houghton Mifflin.

Keat, D. B. (1985). Child-adolescent multimodal therapy: Bud the boss. *Journal of Humanistic Education and Development, 23,* 183-192.

Keat, D. B. (1990). *Child multimodal therapy.* Norwood, NJ: Ablex.

Keat, D. B., Metzgar, K. L., Raykovitz, D., & McDonald, J. (1985). Multimodal counseling: Motivating children to attend school through friendship groups. *Journal of Humanistic Education and Development, 23,* 166-175.

Krieg, E. J. (1988). *Group leadership training and supervision manual for adolescent group counseling in schools* (3rd ed.). Muncie, IN: Accelerated Development.

Krumboltz, J. D. (1974). An accountability model for counselors. *Personnel and Guidance Journal, 52,* 639-646.

Kurpius, D. J. (1978). Consultation theory and process: An integrated model. *Personnel and Guidance Journal, 56,* 335-338.

LaFountain, R. M., Garner, N. E., & Eliason, G. T. (1996). Solution-focused counseling groups: A key for school counselors. *School Counselor, 43,* 256-266.

Lazarus, A. A. (1985). *Casebook of multimodal therapy.* New York: Guilford.

Lee, C. C., & Sirch, M. L. (1994). Counseling in an enlightened society: Values for a new millennium. *Counseling and Values, 38,* 90-97.

Littrell, J. M. (1998). *Brief counseling in action.* New York: Norton.

Maslow, A. (1970). *Motivation and personality* (2nd ed.). New York: Harper & Row.

Menacker, J. (1974). *Vitalizing guidance in urban schools.* New York: Dodd, Mead.

Menacker, J. (1976). Toward a theory of activist guidance. *Personnel and Guidance Journal, 54,* 318-321.

Miller, J. V., & Grisdale, G. A. (1975). Guidance program evaluations: What's out there? *Measurement and Evaluation in Guidance, 8,* 145-154.

Morse, L. A. (1987). Working with young procrastinators: Elementary school students who do not complete school assignments. *Elementary School Guidance and Counseling, 21,* 221-228.

Mosher, R. L., & Sprinthall, N. A. (1970). Deliberate psychological education. *Counseling Psychologist, 2*(4), 3-82.

Murphy, J. J. (1997). *Solution focused counseling in middle and high schools.* Alexandria, VA: American Counseling Association.

Myrick, R. (1984). Measurement forum: Beyond the issues of school counselor accountability. *Measurement and Evaluation in Guidance, 16,* 218-222.

Parsons, F. (1909). *Choosing a vocation.* Boston: Houghton Mifflin.

Peters, D. (1978). The practice of counseling in the secondary school. In *The status of guidance and counseling in the nation's schools* (pp. 81-100). Washington, DC: Personnel and Guidance Association.

Proctor, W. (1925). *Educational and vocational guidance: A consideration of guidance as it relates to all of the essential activities of life.* Boston: Houghton Mifflin.

Rogers, C. R. (1942). *Counseling and psychotherapy.* Boston: Houghton Mifflin.

Rogers, C. R. (1951). *Client-centered therapy.* Boston: Houghton Mifflin.

Rogers, C. R. (1961). *On becoming a person.* Boston: Houghton Mifflin.

Rhyne-Winkler, M. C., & Wooten, H. R. (1996). The school counselor portfolio: Professional development and accountability. *School Counselor, 44,* 146-150.

Rust, E. (1995). Applications of the international counselor network for elementary and middle school counseling. *Elementary School Guidance and Counseling, 30,* 16-25.

Schmidt, J. J. (1995). Assessing school counseling programs through external reviews. *School Counselor, 43,* 114-122.

Shaffer, J. L., & Atkinson, D. R. (1983). Counselor education courses in program evaluation and scientific research: Are counselors prepared for the accountability press? *Counselor Education and Supervision, 23,* 29-34.

Shaw, M. C. (1973). *School guidance systems: Objectives, functions, evaluation, and change.* Boston: Houghton Mifflin.

Smith, G. E. (1955). *Counseling in the secondary school.* New York: Macmillan.

Starr, J., & Raykovitz, J. (1982). A multimodal approach to interviewing children. *Elementary School Guidance and Counseling, 16,* 267-277.

Stickel, S. A. (1990). Using multimodal social-skills groups with kindergarten children. *Elementary School Guidance and Counseling, 24,* 281-288.

Sue, D. W., Arredondo, P., & McDavis, R. J. (1992). Multi-cultural competencies/standards: A pressing need. *Journal of Counseling and Development, 70,* 477-486.

Sullivan, H. S. (1947). *Conceptions of modern psychiatry.* Washington, DC: William Alanson White Psychiatric Foundation.

Sweeney, T. J. (1998). *Adlerian counseling.* Muncie, IN: Accelerated Development/Taylor & Francis.

Trotzer, J. (1989). *The counselor and the group* (2nd ed.). Muncie, IN: Accelerated Development.

Wrenn, C. G. (1962). *The counselor in a changing world.* Washington, DC: American Personnel and Guidance Association.

Yalom, I. D. (1985). *The theory and practice of group psychotherapy* (3rd ed.). New York: Basic Books.

Zaccaria, J. (1969). *Approaches to guidance in contemporary education.* Scranton, PA: International Textbooks.

Zytowski, D. G. (1982). Assessment in the counseling process for the 1980s. *Measurement and Evaluation in Guidance, 15,* 15-21.

CHAPTER NINETEEN

Counseling in Colleges
and Universities

MARY A. FUKUYAMA

This chapter provides an overview of mental health counseling in college and university settings. It is intended to review traditional counseling roles on campuses and to touch on current innovations and cutting-edge issues. It is important both to understand the "ground" on which counseling has been built and to be aware of the "shifting" that is significantly affecting the nature of mental health work in higher education. For some professionals, recent changes have felt like an earthquake, while others experience the tremors of change during this postmodern era. However dramatic, the fact remains that social movements and shifts in "consciousness" have influenced counseling since its inception. The following topics are discussed in five sections of this chapter: historical perspectives, contemporary counseling roles and functions, impact of rapid social change, cutting-edge issues, and perspectives for the future.

Historical Perspectives

Postsecondary education is composed of diverse settings that include 2- and 4-year colleges, technical schools, and universities. These educational institutions represent diverse demographics that may include urban commuter schools, rural private colleges, public-supported state universities, and specialized training institutes (e.g., art institutes, business schools). In this section, the historical origins of counseling in higher education are summarized, three models of counseling are identified, and current trends are discussed.

Origins of Counseling on Campuses

Counseling and student personnel roles in higher education have evolved over the past century. Historically, three distinct forces contributed to the earliest establishment of counseling services on campus:

> (1) the emergence of student personnel services as separate and specialized functions; (2) the assumption of responsibility for the health of students and the eventual provision of health services; and (3) the advent of psychiatry as a full-fledged medical specialty, the emergence of the mental hygiene movement as a social force, and the growth of psychology as a profession. (Reinhold, 1991, p. 4)

Within this latter category, the development of vocational guidance and career development as a specialty is particularly relevant to student development.

Faculty and deans originally acted in loco parentis for students and fulfilled the earliest student personnel roles. They were concerned about students' lives holistically including everything from room and board to moral development. As higher education changed from being the exclusive domain of church-supported schools to publicly supported secular education, the expectations associated with in loco parentis shifted. Student personnel roles originated during the early 20th century and became more specialized and professionalized over the subsequent 50 years.

The first health professionals (physicians) on campus can be traced to the mid-19th century.

Mental health services were introduced through physical health services, initially through psychiatry. Psychiatrists became interested in the mental health of university students during the early 1900s and are documented at Ivy League schools, such as Princeton University and Yale University, and at the University of Michigan (Archer & Cooper, 1998; Reinhold, 1991). The American Student Health Association (later renamed the American College Health Association) was established somewhat later, in 1920.

Concurrently, academic and vocational guidance developed into a specialty, with early contributors including E. G. Williamson and faculty at the University of Minnesota. Emphases on individual differences and on psychometric measurement in psychology were precursors to the career and vocational counseling movement. All of these areas expanded during the post-World War II years, when veterans entered higher education in large numbers. The counseling field became more specialized, and various professional associations were founded. The following professional organizations were established during the 1950s: Division 17 (Counseling Psychology) of the American Psychological Association (APA); the Annual Counseling Center Directors' Conference; and the merger of the National Vocational Guidance Association (NVGA), American School Counselor Association (ASCA), and National Association of Guidance Supervisors (NAGS) with the American College Personnel Association (ACPA) to form the American Personnel and Guidance Association (APGA) (Dean & Meadows, 1995). During this time of expansion, counseling centers also grew and broadened their services.

The history of *counseling centers* parallels the trends already mentioned (Archer & Cooper,

1998). During the time period before 1945, roles were less differentiated, with faculty, deans, and college physicians providing counseling and guidance. The decade between 1945 and 1955 saw the establishment of counseling centers to meet the needs of postwar veterans, and counseling for personal problems evolved further as a specialty. During the time period between 1955 and 1970, counseling centers expanded and personal counseling became as important as vocational guidance. Consultation and outreach were added as counseling center functions. From 1970 to 1982, counseling services broadened their scope to include systemic consultation and outreach functions. Since the early 1980s, counseling centers have undergone budget constrictions; at the same time, students have tended to present with more serious psychological problems. In addition, rapid social changes have affected campus environments with social problems such as violence, rape trauma, alcohol and drug abuse, racism, suicide, and the AIDS epidemic. The 1990s saw increased cultural diversity on campuses, reduced resources, and increased demands for consultation and education to deal with the fallout of these serious social ills (Stone & Archer, 1990). Next, the status quo of counseling on campuses is described, and student personnel roles are highlighted.

Three Models of Counseling

Currently, there are three models for counseling in higher education: vocational and career counseling, mental health counseling, and student personnel counseling (Dean & Meadows, 1995). On large university campuses, these functions may be designated to specific units such as a Career Counseling and Placement Center, Student Mental Health Center, Counseling and Consultation Services, and Office of Student Services. On small campuses, a few counselors may fulfill several of these functions simultaneously. On some large campuses, mental health units, which had their origin in student health services, have merged with counseling centers that had their origin in academic and career counseling. These trends parallel the growth, expansion, and contraction of the profession.

Discussion of career counseling and mental health counseling is elaborated in the next section. Student personnel work (also known as student affairs or student development) offers diverse career opportunities for counselors in higher education (Komives & Gast, 1996). The Council for Accreditation of Counseling and Related Educational Programs (CACREP) has approved a student affairs practice specialization within Counselor Education programs. Student personnel professionals are qualified to fulfill roles in admissions, recruitment and retention, orientation of new students, support services for specific populations (e.g., reentry students, persons with disabilities, veterans), study skills enhancement, judicial affairs and student conduct, student activities and programming, financial aid, residence life programs, health care, health education, multicultural programming, minority student services, and administration (deans of students). In some instances, counselors who traditionally have been trained in mental health counseling may decide to seek employment in these related student development positions. Although there are three distinct models of counseling on college and university campuses, there may be overlap in roles and functions depending on the size and resources of the institution.

Examples of professional associations that are relevant to counselors and student personnel professionals in higher education include the following (Komives & Gast, 1996):

American College Personnel Association (ACPA)
    Commission VI (Career Development)
    Commission VII (Counseling and Psychological Services)
    Commission XI (Student Development in Two-Year Colleges)
American Counseling Association (ACA)
National Career Development Association (NCDA)
American College Counseling Association (ACCA)
American Mental Health Counselors Association (AMHCA)
American College Health Association (ACHA)
American College Unions–International (ACU-I)
American Psychological Association (APA)
    Division 17 (Counseling Psychology)
Association of College and University Housing Officers–International (ACUHO-I)
National Association for Student Personnel Administrators (NASPA)
National Association for Women in Education (NAWE)
National Association of Campus Activities (NACA)
National Orientation Directors Association (NODA)

Current trends that affect student life on campuses are discussed next.

Current Trends

Bishop (1992) reviewed research articles on college campus life and summarized social changes in the college student population over the decades. In general, during the 1950s, students were traditional and conforming. During the late 1960s and early 1970s, the baby-boom generation was antiestablishment and rebellious. During the later 1970s, there was a swing back toward conservatism. The 1980s became known as the "Me Generation," and students appeared to be self-absorbed. The 1990s generation, called "Generation X," presented a mixture of despair, angst, and creative hope for preservation of the planet. The trends, according to Bishop's (1992) article, depicted students as more conservative politically, less committed to social change, and more impulsive.

Bishop (1992) summarized some shifts in values in terms of career expectations. Students were more competitive, materialistic, and financially insecure, and they expected college degrees to help them get good-paying jobs. They showed less interest in social and political issues but embraced the ideals of self-realization and freedom to achieve or to make choices (e.g., the influence of women's liberation). Inflation and the rising costs of higher education also may have affected these shifts in values.

In terms of personal behaviors, students were reported to have more problem behaviors such as cheating. Bishop (1992) cited a 1989 study reporting that between 40% and 90% of college students cheat. Other problem areas included heavy alcohol use with concomitant physical and emotional fallout, a high suicide rate among youths in general between 15 and 24 years of age, and increases in reported eating disorders. Young college women were considered vulnerable to the fad of bulimia in the college environment. In terms of interpersonal behaviors, students were more open about sexuality, more aware of AIDS, and more likely to cohabit before marriage. In addition, there were more incidents of domestic violence, courtship violence, acquaintance rape, harassment, and stalking.

Counselors need to be aware of and adapt to social change such as the increase in cultural diversity, the impact of international economy and competition, and contemporary issues (e.g., single-parent homes). Students arrive on campus with much more distressed backgrounds, which mirror the stresses of society at large. Staff have ongoing needs for professional development to improve competencies to handle these issues. Counselors also can interpret "student culture," and administrators and programmers can maintain databases of issues such as career concerns, behavioral problems, reasons for withdrawing from school, and physical health concerns. Counselors need not limit themselves to one model of student development; rather, they can take the initiative to offer programs, consultation, and leadership on campus in these areas of social change. Various counselor roles and functions are discussed in more detail in the next section.

Contemporary Counseling Roles and Functions

The primary focus of this section is on the variety of mental health counseling roles and functions on college and university campuses. Following a discussion of clinical assessment, five types of specialized services are described: career, individual, group, outreach, and peer counseling. A case study is presented to illustrate the importance of examining various demographic and cultural variables in counseling. Systemic interventions such as prevention, wellness programming, and consultation roles are highlighted. Finally, a discussion of ethical decision making regarding multiple roles is presented.

Specialized Services

Clinical Assessment

Various types of clinical assessments have been constructed and used depending on the mission of the counseling or student affairs units. Problem checklists typically are used in medium to large institution counseling centers, according to a survey conducted in a southwestern state (Zalaquett, 1996). However, the survey indicated that less than one half of the counseling centers at smaller institutions (fewer than 10,000 students) used checklists. These problem checklists were developed by counseling center staff, administered as part of the intake process, and rated as important for gathering clinical information (although not as likely to be used for research or for creating databases). The results of this survey indicated that problem checklists were completed by self-report of clients, averaged 41 items, typically took about 5 or 6 minutes to complete, were answered with Likert-type scales or check marks, and had face validity. A sample checklist is presented in Table 19.1 and is excerpted from an intake form used at the University of Florida Counseling Center.

The *cube model* of assessment was introduced in counseling centers during the 1970s (Morrill, Oetting, & Hurst, 1974) and included multilevel decision making about counseling interventions. In this model, the target of intervention is first identified (individual, primary group, associational group, institution, or community), the purpose of intervention is established (remediation, prevention, or development), and the methods are delineated (direct service, consultation and training, or media). It is not unusual for counselors to provide a multilevel approach to campus problems that include some or all of these.

TABLE 19.1   Sample Problem Checklist

Please rank order the top three (1= *most important*) concerns you would like to discuss today and check any others that apply:

___   1.   Career/major choice/future goals
___   2.   Academic progress (e.g., problems with study habits, tests, motivation)
___   3.   Math anxiety
___   4.   Stress/anxiety
___   5.   Relationship with roommate, friend, and/or partner
___   6.   Relationship with family
___   7.   Relationship issues (general)
___   8.   Loss/death of significant person
___   9.   Depression
___   10.   Personal development/identity
___   11.   Self-esteem/self-confidence
___   12.   Adult Children of Alcoholics (ACOA)
___   13.   Childhood abuse (emotional, physical, or sexual)
___   14.   Sexual assault/rape
___   15.   Physical assault/relationship violence/stalking
___   16.   Sexual identity issues
___   17.   Eating problems/body image
___   18.   Physical/health problems
___   19.   Pregnancy/abortion issues
___   20.   Religious/spiritual matters
___   21.   Oppression/discrimination
___   22.   Adjustment to the university
___   23.   Finance/money matters
___   24.   Legal/judicial problems
___   25.   Letter for petition, withdrawal, and so forth
___   26.   Other _____

Briefly state your problem/issue:

_____
_____
_____
_____

How disruptive is this problem/issue?   ___ Very disruptive   ___ Somewhat disruptive   ___ A little disruptive

SOURCE: Adapted from intake form, University of Florida Counseling Center.

Formal diagnosis and testing procedures vary from campus to campus. The use of the *DSM-IV* (*Diagnostic and Statistical Manual of Mental Disorders* [American Psychiatric Association, 1994]) depends on agency philosophy and professional expectations. For example, a *DSM-IV* diagnosis may be used routinely in a student health care center but not in a student development center. Similarly, formal testing varies by agency. Some may routinely administer the Minnesota Multiphasic Personality Inventory or Millon Clinical Multiaxial Inventory as part of an assessment battery, whereas others may rely on intake interviews. Career testing may include instruments such as the Strong Interest Inventory, the Campbell Interests and Skills Inventory, and the Myers-Briggs Type Inventory.

Career Counseling

Career counseling may be housed in a specialty unit such as career counseling and placement services, or career counseling may be an integral part of a centralized counseling service. Career assessments frequently are conducted through the use of computerized guidance programs such as SIGI-Plus and DISCOVER. Assessments of interests, values, skills, and lifestyle considerations are the cornerstones for these personal assessments. Comprehensive career counseling and placement services usually include activities such as cooperative education and internships (to gain practical experience), career "expos" whereby corporate representatives come to campus to interview prospective employees, resumé and interview preparation workshops, contact with alumni for career connections, and career resource libraries with career information (e.g., books, pamphlets, audiovisuals). Career services are increasingly relying on technology to help connect students to the corporate world through devices such as televideo interviews, online resumés, and job searches through use of the Internet.

Individual Counseling

Individual counseling or therapy typically focuses on personal issues including presenting concerns about relationships, self-esteem and identity, loss, and recovery issues. However, it is an arbitrary distinction to separate personal counseling from career counseling, as most counselors would agree that one's career choices are personal. These distinctions frequently reflect agency priorities and specialization of services. Counselors sometimes are asked to see court or judicial board referrals as part of disciplinary actions.

Stone and Lucas (1994) conducted a national survey of counseling center directors and queried them about attitudes toward providing disciplinary or mandatory counseling. Generally, the directors were ambivalent about such counseling because the therapeutic relationship is predicated on free choice. Counselors need to ask, "What is the perception of the mandatory referral?" Is it "as a cry for help . . . or as a punishment, magical problem resolution, gatekeeping function, or a last resort for 'dumping' difficulties?" (p. 238). To be therapeutic and to benefit the individual client, counseling needs to be neutral and requires free collaboration of client and counselor; that is, it is contradictory to combine counseling with coercion. Therefore, it is helpful to distinguish between disciplinary *counseling* and disciplinary *education,* where the goal is to benefit the community or public at large (vs. the individual client). Examples of such interventions might be requiring students who are under disciplinary action to attend educational workshops on topics such as anger management and peer pressure.

A recent trend in individual counseling and psychotherapy has emphasized "time-limited therapy" or "brief therapy." At one extreme, some counseling centers offer only one to three sessions and referral; at the other extreme, other centers offer time-limited therapy ranging from 6 to 20 sessions during an academic year. An extensive literature base on brief therapy includes various theoretical orientations such as psychoanalytic, cognitive-behavioral, rational emotive, and solution-focused therapy (Archer & Cooper, 1998). Counseling time limits fit naturally with the academic quarter or semester system. However, each client needs to be assessed for appropriateness of brief therapy or for referral for longer term counseling.

Group Counseling

Groups may range from general therapy groups to structured thematic groups (Metcalf, 1998). Examples of theme groups include math confidence, relationships, grief, and support groups for specific populations such as South Asian women; African American women; gay, lesbian, and bisexual students; and students older than traditional age. Group themes frequently depend on available staff to lead and interests from the student population at large.

Outreach Programming

Outreach programs usually are time limited to specific interventions such as training programs, workshops, media effort, and class presentations. Outreach typically takes the form of workshops or training sessions offered to campus groups such as residence halls, Greek system, student leadership forums, and special events (e.g., during Black Heritage Month, Cultural Diversity Week, and health fairs). Outreach usually entails a psychoeducational program organized around specific learning objectives and developed in collaboration with the requesting person or organization. Workshops may be directed at increasing personal awareness, imparting knowledge, developing skills, solving problems, or seeking systemic change (Brooks-Harris & Stock-Ward, 1999).

An example of an innovative community outreach endeavor was a "survivor art show" in which women and men who self-identified as abuse survivors contributed art pieces (e.g., sculptures, paintings, collage, poetry) to a gallery show. This project was held in conjunction with a local conference on the theme of "Women Against Violence," and the show was an important public venue to aid survivors in their recovery process (Funderburk, 1998).

Peer Counseling

Peer counseling involves training and supervising undergraduate students to provide specific services to meet developmental and educational needs of students (Cox, 1999). Examples of various peer counseling programs include counseling for deciding on academic majors, providing workshops on study skills (e.g., time management), and health-related interventions (e.g., rape prevention, AIDS education). Peer counseling is an excellent opportunity for undergraduate students to gain people-helping skills and is considered by administrators to be a cost-effective source of service delivery for specific areas of need.

Supervision of Counseling

Supervision is an essential component of providing services, and professionals might need to seek out peer supervision after they become licensed. In some settings, counselors may supervise practicum students and interns as they prepare to become professional counselors, and counselors will want to seek out peer supervision in this process as well (Holloway & Carroll, 1999). Counseling centers offer excellent training opportunities for graduate trainees to obtain a broad exposure to various counseling roles and diverse clientele.

Case Study

In this case study, various demographic and cultural variables are italicized to call the reader's attention to factors that affect assessment and choices of clinical treatment. In the discussion questions that follow, variations are suggested that may affect counselor perceptions and case decision making.

Cal is a *28-year-old White male transfer student* who is beginning his second semester at a *large state university*. His first-semester grades were a full grade point below his community college average, and he is beginning to have doubts about his *choice of major (electrical engineering)*. He always has wanted to have a "good-paying career" and thought engineering would "fit the bill." However, now he is having difficulty in getting motivated to study and tends to distract himself by watching TV or falling asleep. His *live-in girlfriend* is annoyed with him for not applying himself. She is ready to start a family and resents working to support his schooling, especially when he is not working hard enough. Cal's faculty adviser notices that he looks *depressed* and takes Cal aside to talk about his adjustment to the university. Cal admits that he does not know how

to make himself study harder. The faculty member suspects that something else is bothering him and refers him to the counseling center. Cal's *presenting problem* to his intake counselor is that he wants to know how to keep motivated so that he can raise his grade point average.

Discussion Questions

1. *Age:* Is it traditional (18 to 22 years) or nontraditional (older than average)? How does life experience affect one's experience in higher education?

2. *Ethnicity/race:* How do racial/ethnic differences affect the adjustment process to a new environment? Substitute African American, Asian American, Latino American, or another ethnicity and notice possible differences in perception.

3. *Gender:* How does gender affect expectations for counseling and interact with social norms for seeking help? Are there different pressures for traditional versus nontraditional gender-role careers? For example, substitute female. What about the case where men enter traditionally female careers such as nursing and fine arts?

4. *Class status:* What are some of the challenges for transfer students, and how do economics affect student experiences?

5. *Institutional size and resources:* What are some differences between large and small institutions? On large campuses it frequently is difficult to negotiate the bureaucracy and to locate appropriate services; counselors might need to refer and act as advocates on behalf of students. In smaller institutions, multiple professional roles might be energy draining for the helpers.

6. *Type of major:* What are counselors' biases or stereotypes about specific majors such as engineering, fine arts, psychology, business, leisure, premed, and ROTC?

7. *Sexual orientation and relationship status:* How do familial and affectionate relations affect support systems and role expecta-

tions? When would one want to recommend couples counseling?

8. *Health status:* How does one distinguish between an adjustment disorder and a more complex issue? For example, substitute an issue such as substance abuse, Adult Children of Alcoholics (ACOA), HIV status, sexual or emotional abuse survivor, recent family loss, eating disorder, or some form of physical or learning disability.

9. *Assessment:* To what extent are there previous psychological problems? What are existing support systems? How severe are the presenting symptoms?

10. *Treatment planning:* What form of interventions are appropriate and available (e.g., support group, individual counseling, referral, medication, psychiatric consultation). How do these variations affect recommendations for treatment?

Systemic Interventions

Systemic interventions focus on organizations and social institutions. Interventions discussed in this section are prevention, wellness, and consultation.

Prevention

Conyne (1997) defined preventive counseling as "programmatic, before-the-fact application of comprehensive counseling methods with healthy or at-risk groups to enhance competencies and avert dysfunction" (p. 260). Conyne summarized 10 skills clusters that are seen as important for providing preventive counseling services. Expanding an original 3 clusters (educational skills, program development skills, and change agent skills), Conyne outlined the following 10 areas:

1. The counselor adapts a "primary prevention perspective" or lens through which problems and solutions are conceptualized. From this perspective, the goal of reducing the incidence of problems is framed in a systemic ecological context. The targets of the interventions are groups—not individuals—and the techniques may be direct or indirect (e.g., using the media). The intervention is constructed through team efforts using multidisciplinary resources, and it frequently has an empowerment focus.

2. The counselor needs personal characteristics such as patience, persistence, flexibility, creativity, and organizational skills in addition to core counseling competencies. These personality characteristics are necessary because prevention often involves a longer term intervention.

3. The ethics of prevention requires the voluntary participation of the recipients of the intervention; that is, a mandatory prevention activity would be self-defeating. The counselor needs to respect the privacy of "clients," and programs should not be forced on them.

4. The counselor needs to understand how to use social marketing strategies such as "persuasion, motivation, sales, public relations, advertising, and communications." For example, an AIDS prevention campaign used TV public service spots of a popular basketball coach encouraging students to be tested for the HIV virus.

5. The counselor needs to understand cultural diversity and the relevance and appropriateness of interventions for different cultural groups. For example, some materials might need to be written for a bilingual audience.

6. The counselor needs to have good group facilitation skills and group presentation skills in order to lead psychoeducational workshops.

7. The counselor needs to be able to work collaboratively and as a team player.

8. The counselor needs to understand organization and setting dynamics such as working

in the community, neighborhoods, and other natural settings (e.g., schools, churches).

9. The counselor needs to understand cultural trends, public policy, and political dynamics of organizations and communities and be able to maneuver in the system.

10. The counselor needs to understand complex research and evaluation procedures. Prevention research is difficult because it involves demonstrating that "something bad did not happen" (p. 266). Research designs often necessitate longitudinal study and involve the community in a collaborative way. The counselor also needs to have grant-writing skills, for example, to fund programs for substance abuse prevention, high school retention, and decreasing family violence. Examples of prevention programs on campus might include AIDS awareness media spots, early-detection "free HIV testing" programs, responsible drinking programs, eating disorders peer educators, rape prevention programs, roommate conflict resolution workshops, wellness center health programs (e.g., diet, exercise), and health fairs.

Wellness

Closely linked to prevention is the concept of wellness programming and holistic counseling. Wellness, prevention, and student development are processes endorsed by ACA and embedded in many counseling centers' mission statements (Myers, Emmerling, & Leafgren, 1992). Wellness commonly involves a multidimensional schema that values balancing the various tasks of life such as vocation; family; recreation; spirituality; and physical, emotional, social, and intellectual health. Recent trends indicate that spirituality is beginning to receive more attention in the profession and is included in discussions of holistic health and multiculturalism (Fukuyama & Sevig, 1999;

Kelly, 1995). Wellness counseling may be another way of saying "whole person" counseling, which incorporates integration of mind, body, and spirit. Wellness programming may take various forms such as stress management groups and workshops, interdisciplinary forums, diversity "brown bag" lunch discussions, and spirituality and health programs.

Consultation

The history of consultation has been credited to two major sources: the organizational development literature (Gallessich, 1982) and the practice of mental health (Caplan, 1970). The role of the consultant may be defined in several ways depending on the expectations of the consultation relationship. Typically, the consultant offers expertise to the consultee for the purposes of improving services or products for a third party (e.g., client, customer). Although the consultant offers expertise, he or she establishes an equitable relationship with the consultee, and they engage as two professionals focusing on work-related issues (Brown, Kurpius, & Morris, 1988). Consultants may work with individuals, small groups, organizations, or advocates in systems (Kurpius & Brown, 1988). Consultation is a problem-solving process that includes the following components: a professional relationship, assessment, goals and strategies, interventions, and evaluation. A sample consultation project on a large university campus involved conducting a needs assessment of international student families who lived in campus housing and designing a series of programs for international wives to help them deal with cultural adjustment and isolation.

In sum, there are many variations in counseling roles and functions in mental health service delivery on campuses. Counselors typically need to negotiate their job priorities depending on multiple demands in the system. Agencies also vary in their emphases on ways in which services are delivered. For example, some counseling centers emphasize group work over individual work or specialize in consultation services on campus. Multiple role demands frequently raise the issue of "dual-role conflict," which is discussed next.

Ethical Decision Making Regarding Multiple Roles

Role boundaries are discussed at length in ethical guidelines and are clearer for counselors who have private offices than for student services professionals, who might live in residence halls and be on 24-hour call. Role boundaries become blurred when counselors wear several "hats" such as those of faculty adviser, mental health counselor, and member of a minority community. Clarification of roles and limits is necessary to protect the interests of students and clients and to prevent counselor burnout. Counselors on smaller campuses also might feel role conflicts in being mentors, friends, advisers, and administrators.

Although ethical guidelines suggest that it is prudent to refrain from dual roles, in small communities (e.g., small campuses, rural communities, minority communities), overlapping roles are common in social life through churches and community activities. Rather than prohibit or overly restrict oneself, it is helpful for each counselor to think through and discuss with colleagues how to manage dual roles. For example, how does a counselor protect confidentiality of clients when he or she runs into them at a basketball game? A counselor might need to explain in advance that in order to protect confidentiality, he or she will not initiate social conversation on campus with a client. The counselor may elect to respond to greetings but also may explain that it is better not to engage in conversation outside of counseling, thereby ensuring client privacy. Minority counselors sometimes are expected to, or want to, participate in their respective communities (e.g., gay/lesbian/bisexual, African American). They might belong to the same churches and social clubs or live in the same neighborhoods as do clients. In some cultural groups, the distinctions of professional roles may seem arbitrary and might not be understood.

Kaplan and Rothrock (1991) provided commentary on ethical guidelines that are appropriate for psychologists, counselors, mental health counselors, student affairs specialists, and university health services personnel from five sources: APA, ACA, AMHCA, ACPA, and ACHA. Kaplan and Rothrock suggested that counselors discuss potential scenarios in advance with their clients. Explaining the reasons for "boundaries" often helps to reduce client confusion or anger about such arbitrary limits. For example, one of the reasons why counseling is effective is because it is with people who are objective and not as personally involved in clients' daily lives. As such, the counseling session is a protected time and space to process intense issues.

There are frequent opportunities for overlapping professional roles in higher education settings. Counselors may be course instructors, supervisors, administrators, and employers of students. Some situations clearly might be conflicts of interest, but frequently they are ambiguous and require reflection and consultation with colleagues. Some dual-role situations, which obviously are problematic, include when the counselor-client relationship conflicts with the following:

Being a teacher-student

Being professional colleagues

Having a close social or romantic relationship

Being a supervisor-supervisee

Entering a business relationship

These are some of the more obvious cases of dual-role conflicts. Most ethical guidelines suggest that dual roles are to be avoided whenever possible. For example, it is a conflict of interest to refer students eligible for university counseling services to oneself in private practice.

Sometimes, institutions put pressure on counselors to violate confidentiality. For example, when is it appropriate to let an administrator or a faculty member know when a student who was referred has come in for counseling? APA and ACA ethical guidelines would say that this is confidential information (Kaplan & Rothrock, 1991). A signed informed consent might need to be obtained prior to revealing such information.

Dual-role situations merit an analysis that takes into account the costs (risks) and benefits of entering into dual roles. In some situations, they are unavoidable but need to be thought through and observed throughout. Counselors generally are cautioned against entering into close personal relationships or business relationships with clients or supervisees.

Herlihy and Corey (1997) provided a decision-making tree that presents a process by which to analyze a potential dual-role situation. The counselor is asked to follow a series of steps beginning with considering the question, "Is the situaion avoidable or not?" (p. 164). If the situation is avoidable, then the counselor first would need to assess the potential risks and benefits. If possible, the counselor should discuss potential problems and benefits with the client and concurrently consult with a colleague about the situation. If the risks outweigh the benefits, then it is better for the counselor to decline to enter into the relationship, to explain the reasons to the client, and to refer the client (if necessary).

However, if the situation is unavoidable, or if the benefits outweigh the risks in the preceding analysis, then the counselor should document consultation with a colleague and obtain an informed consent from the client. It is important that the counselor continues ongoing discussion with the client and self-monitors and documents the relationship. Finally, it is desirable for the counselor to obtain ongoing supervision in such situations. There are some situations in which dual roles are not necessarily wrong or harmful. For example, counselor educators may serve as mentors for students, counselors working with AIDS patients may have more community-based interactions with family members and out-of-office meetings, and counselor educators may blend didactic and experiential exercises in a group counseling class.

Herlihy and Corey (1997) summarized several key themes that occur in the realm of multiple roles. First, they suggested that multiple relationship issues affect every mental health professional, so much so that it is prudent for counselor educators to develop their own guidelines within their educational and training programs and to guide students through ethical decision making about them (following the adage of "practice what you preach"). Although ethical guidelines caution about dual-role relationships, most situations are ambiguous and are more complex than a simple "right or wrong" or "do or don't" scenario. There are few absolute answers.

The primary guiding ethic is *to do no harm* with clients, requiring counselors to enter into discussions to understand risks and benefits of dual roles. Multiple roles require counselors to examine personal motives, to know themselves, and to be self-monitoring. The question to ask is, "Whose needs are being met?" The primary objective is to seek the welfare of clients or supervisees, not just to protect themselves from censure.

In sum, counselors are advised to seek consultation prior to entering into dual-role relationships, to get help with objectivity, and to be sure that the benefits outweigh the potential risks or harm. This discussion concludes with the following case examples:

> Charles, a counselor education graduate student, comes to the (only) university counseling center for personal counseling. He thinks that he will apply to the center's practicum training program during the following year. What are the issues to explore with the client and with potential counselors or supervisors?

> Elena is the Latino student adviser and administrator for the Latino student center. Because of Latin family norms, she is perceived as a "mother figure" by many of the undergraduate students, and she develops warm relationships with many of them. However, she begins to feel responsible for them as if they were her own children, and she takes their problems home with her. Her part-time position becomes a 24-hours-a-day job, and she is expected to be available evenings and weekends to monitor and participate in the activities at the center. Some possible outcomes of this scenario include professional burnout, early termi-

nation of her position, and feelings of resentment. Question: how can Elena set boundaries in a way that respects her cultural upbringing, protects her, and is in the best interests of the students?

> Dorit, an international student from the Middle East, does not understand why she cannot enjoy a cup of coffee with her counselor in a more informal setting. She believes that a more intimate setting would be beneficial to getting to know her counselor better. How does the counselor explain differences in cultural expectations for this type of intimate relationship?

Impact of Rapid Social Change

In this section, the impact of social change on counseling is discussed. The speed of technological innovations, the increased interdependence of the global economy, and the arrival of the information age have made a significant impact on the social institutions in the United States. Shifts in demographics in the population at large and in the workplace also affect trends in student populations. Thus, the "face" of higher education is changing. In this section, multiculturalism and the effects of increased stress are discussed.

Multiculturalism

Changing demographics on campuses show increased numbers of women; visible ethnic-minority persons; adult learners; persons with disabilities; and gay, lesbian, and bisexual persons, all of whom need culturally sensitive counseling services. Much has been written in the literature about the importance of training counselors to become multiculturally competent (Sue & Sue, 1998). Predictions are that within a few years into the new millennium, one third of the U.S. population will be people of color. Multiculturalism has become a significant social force in higher education, affecting staff and students alike.

However, majority students' attitudes about "cultural differences" still reflect societal prejudice or indifference. On some campuses, racial/ethnic backlash has targeted minority groups. Kent (1996) suggested that, because of larger global economic pressures, students face increased financial worries and fewer job opportunities. Inflation and diminishing resources in general have contributed toward White people scapegoating people of color, and university campuses are no exception. Kent suggested that the United States is in a moral crisis and that "at the heart of this contemporary crisis is the collision between the American Dream's myth of individual upward mobility and the reality of the radical restructuring of the U.S. political economy" (p. 50).

Multiculturalism refers to "an individual's or an organization's commitment to increase awareness and knowledge about human diversity in ways that are translated into more respectful human interactions and effective interconnection" (D'Andrea & Daniels, 1995, p. 18). Multiculturalism is being infused into institutional life and organizations, and individual counselors are being asked to be aware of the impact of culture and oppression in their work. Counselors and student personnel professionals need to assess themselves personally and examine their work environments. Multiculturalism includes a range of attitudes, behaviors, activities, and institutional policies and procedures, from hiring practices to interior decorating.

Grieger (1996) examined the student affairs literature and identified key themes or defining principles behind multiculturalism on campuses.

She described a multicultural organization as one that

(a) is inclusive in composition of staff and constituencies served; (b) is diversity-positive in its commitment, vision, mission, values, processes, structure, policies, service delivery, and allocation of resources; (c) is permeated by a philosophy of social justice with decisions informed by consideration of ensuring fairness, ending oppression, and guaranteeing equal access to resources and opportunities for all groups; (d) regards diversity as an asset and values the contributions of all members; (e) values and rewards multicultural competencies, including diversity-positive attitudes, knowledge about salient aspects of diverse groups, and skills in interacting with and serving diverse groups effectively, sensitively, and respectfully; and (f) is fluid and responsive in adapting to ongoing diversity-related change. (pp. 563-564)

Out of Grieger's (1996) work, a comprehensive organizational checklist was developed to help professionals conduct organizational self-studies in this area. The 11 key themes are as follows: mission, leadership and advocacy, policies, recruitment and retention, expectations for multicultural competency, multicultural competency training, scholarly activities, student activities and services, internship and field placement, physical environment, and assessment/evaluation. The checklist consists of 58 items that may be used for diagnostic and goal-setting purposes. An example is Item 34: "Psychoeducational workshops, lectures, and presentations offered on campus by student affairs professionals regularly address issues of diversity and multiculturalism." (The item is answered from the following choices: *item met, item unmet, item in progress,* or *what is the timetable for completion?*) Another example is

Item 53: "Student attitudes about campus climate with regard to diversity are assessed regularly (e.g., focus groups, surveys).

Increased Stress

The shifts in global economics have increased stress in the general population of the United States through employee layoffs and corporate restructuring. Financial worries and rising costs of education increase pressures on students not only to do well but also to do well quickly. It is difficult to ignore these larger social issues when providing counseling services. Campuses have seen increases in violence, behavior problems, eating disorders, and other symptoms of stress. Students and faculty are caught in the current mood of "do more with less." Besides seeing clients who are experiencing increased stress, the counseling services themselves are being affected by time pressures. Expediency and efficiency are key words in today's managed health care marketplace. Counseling services are affected by these trends either directly or indirectly. Brief therapy has become more the standard than the exception.

Cutting-Edge Issues

Cutting-edge issues refer to new developments that are critically affecting the field. In this section, three major cutting-edge issues in higher education are discussed: the effect of the Americans with Disabilities Act, the influence of managed care, and the question of outsourcing.

Americans with Disabilities Act

Federal legislation, which serves to protect Americans with disabilities from discrimination in work and education, has made an impact in higher education. Most institutions are in the process of making "reasonable accommodations" for students who have any sorts of physical or psychological disabilities. Dean of students offices recognize that students with disabilities have specific needs and have assigned personnel to be responsible for being advocates and arranging services. Learning disabilities and attention deficit disorder (ADD) are beginning to receive attention in the counseling literature (Jackson, 1999). ADD or attention deficit hyperactivity disorder (ADHD) is a neurological disability that affects one's ability to process information and interact with others. Classroom behaviors that may indicate a problem in this area include restlessness, difficulty reading or writing, forgetfulness, mood swings, interrupting others, and excessive reactions to normal stress.

Counselors may offer individual or group counseling to students who have ADD or may intervene with teaching faculty on their behalf. Individual differences on levels of self-acceptance of ADD will influence the extent to which counselors and teachers can develop a collaborative strategy to assist students in being effective in their studies. When students have integrated an understanding of ADD, they are able to live with these limitations and use techniques to be productive. Examples of accommodations may include things such as increased test time, taking exams in separate rooms, and obtaining tutors or note takers. Counselors need to be updated on ADD and be trained to intervene with students and faculty alike (Quinn, 1994).

Influence of Managed Care

Whitaker (1997) discussed the influence of managed care on counseling services on campus. Originally, managed care was conceived as a cost-effective way in which to provide group health care and initially emphasized prevention. Health maintenance organizations (HMOs) were similar in concept to campus health care services. Although they were conceived as a way in which to control rising medical costs, profit-motivated insurance companies have severely restricted reimbursable mental health services. Some of the negative effects on mental health services include less counselor power to determine treatment plans and number of sessions, less client power (e.g., choice of counselor), less confidentiality, more paperwork, and longer waiting periods for payment. The medical model of symptom treatment has led to increased use of psychotropic drugs as a treatment of choice and a trend toward brief therapy for symptom reduction. The study of experimentally or empirically supported treatments and practice guidelines also has favored some behavioral therapies over other types of therapeutic care. How is this phenomenon affecting counseling in higher education? There is increased emphasis on short-term therapy and an increase in drug treatment. "In the old days of our college work, we would hear about parents sending their daughters off to college with birth control pills; now, they send their children off to college with Prozac and Zoloft" (Widseth, Webb, & John, 1997, p. 9). More counseling centers are referring clients into the community for care, and in some cases, counseling is being outsourced or privatized. However, this is not a one-way street. Managed care may be courting universities to provide mental health services in the name of efficiency just as administrators may be looking for privatization as a means for downsizing their bureaucracies. The issue of outsourcing is discussed next.

The Question of Outsourcing

Counseling services are not the only university services that are under scrutiny for privatization. Others include food services, health clinics, bookstores, printing, and maintenance (Eddy, Spaulding, & Murphy, 1996). It is suggested that administrators analyze the pros and cons when considering privatization of counseling. There needs to be clear and long-term cost savings while maintaining quality of care. There are other questions to consider. What happens if and when the contractor raises its fees? Is the institutional bureaucracy amenable to outside contracts? Would contracts lack flexibility to be modified if needed? Are costs and convenience to students improved? Is the mission of the institution and of student services being compromised? What are the pros and cons of an on-campus versus off-campus location? Would ethical standards be upheld, and how would student personnel professionals interact with contracted providers? What is the "bottom line" for the institution?

This concern of outsourcing or privatizing mental health counseling services is a concern nationally (Widseth et al., 1997). Phillips, Halstead, and Carpenter (1996) reported on a survey of campuses that were considering privatization of counseling services. Factors going into this decision included things such as cost comparisons, types of services being provided, missions and cultures of institutions, human resources, satisfaction with services, legal and ethical considerations, and quality and effectiveness. A small number of campuses (primarily smaller size institutions of fewer than 3,000 students) had contracted services outside of the institutions. These typically were aimed at personal/mental health counseling and often involved some fee-for-service or insurance third-party payments. Centers whose primary function was clinical counseling were more likely to be compared with outside providers, in contrast to centers that provided a breadth of functions integral to their campus communities. In some cases, outside groups provided staffing for on-campus counseling centers and provided traditional counseling functions. Positive results included factors such as access, relationship between contracted sources and college, greater quality and depth, and diversity of personnel. Reasons for dissatisfaction included discontent with service, transportation issues, and feeling that staff were not attuned to student needs.

Outsourcing raises the following question: What is the role of counseling on the college and university campus, and how does counseling fit into the missions of the institution? If mental health services are restricted to providing therapy services for diagnosable mental illness (medical model), then it is easier to envision such treatments being handled in the community. However, counselors typically have a broad and consultative role on campus, and counseling center missions take into account the full adjustment and development spectrum for students. It is important for administrators to understand these multiple roles and to value the input of student services professionals in the campus community and with individual students.

In summary, the following is a list of positive points that promote the role of counseling on campus (Widseth et al., 1997):

1. Promote strengths and professionalism of counselors, educational degrees, regional and national level of activities, national reputation, and cultural diversity. Emphasize that counselors are both generalists and specialists in working with college populations. In the private sector, what are the qualifications of a cheaper labor pool?

2. Promote the fact that counselors are experts on the social milieu of the institutional community (faculty, norms, and academic pressures).

3. Recognize broad educational and consultative roles of counselors on campus such as counselors being a part of an administrative team that addresses programs, policies, and procedures for students.

4. Note that students often like to be able to access services on campus; they prefer privacy and confidentiality of campus services. There are advantages of one-session consultations, which address more immediate needs and situational issues related to campus life.

5. Offer benefits of emergency response on campus such as with suicidal students and with those needing hospitalization.

6. Develop trauma response teams for dealing with on-campus violence and student deaths.

7. Provide consultation with administrators or faculty about problem situations and make referrals.

8. Provide leadership in developing educational programming and outreach workshops, life-skills classes, leadership skills, and peer counselor training.

9. Provide a consultative role related to the Americans with Disabilities Act, especially with regard to learning disorders and psychological disabilities that might need evaluation.

10. Recognize how counseling and student services fit into the mission statements of institutions and how they relate to holistic growth and development of students.

Perspectives on the Future

In this final section, some of the implications of technological change for counseling are considered. In contemplating perspectives on the future, the topics of the virtual university, distance learning, Webcounseling ethics, and shifting career patterns are discussed.

The Virtual University

Wulf (1995) suggested that rapidly changing information technology has the potential for radically altering institutions of higher education. Currently, some institutions are requiring computer literacy as a graduation requirement or are requiring entering freshmen to purchase personal computers. In addition, some courses now are marketed on CD-ROMs, and expanded online services offer degrees through the Internet. However, these types of technological changes go far beyond increasing speed and efficiency of information exchange. Wulf suggested the following possibilities:

1. The development of "electronic hypertext" books with animation, sound, and interactive capabilities
2. Broadening of boundaries of scholarly activities (beyond the geographic place of the university), which could lead to the concept of "cyberspace colleges"
3. Expanded databases that can include access to original works
4. Increased options for distance learning

In addition, there are many changes that have not yet been invented. This leads to a pressing question: What will be the impact of these technologies on the counseling profession? Although there is strong resistance on the part of some counselors to counseling on the Internet, this is an area that needs ongoing investigation and clarification by professional organizations (Bloom, 1999).

Sampson, Kolodinsky, and Greeno (1997) described the potential problems of the use of the Internet by counselors. Some areas of difficulty included relationship development issues and ethical concerns (e.g., confidentiality), privacy concerns, credentialing, inadequate counselor interventions, misuse of computer applications by counselors, and equality of access to Internet resources.

There are both positive and negative effects from the use of computers. On the positive side, people are connecting with people around the world. Computer users report increased feelings of intimacy because they reveal themselves in the safety of their own homes through computers more easily than in person. Online communities are being developed through shared interests. Virtual reality is a tool that may be useful to learn new behaviors or learn about new cultures. Finally, there is a feeling of equality; people can participate in online communications without formal degrees or credentialing (e.g., write an online book, establish a Web page). On the negative side, when taken to an extreme, computer users may become more socially isolated if they rely solely on the Internet for social contact, and various behavioral problems (e.g., stalking, sex addiction) have been played out on the Internet as well.

Distance Learning

Distance learning is increasingly popular, and many institutions are developing programs to reach audiences who reside at some distance from their central campuses such as through rural or statewide educational efforts. Typically, distance learning involves the use of video cameras and communication between teachers and other students through electronic communications (e.g., television, Internet, tapes). Students and instructors often feel anxious in response to the medium, and technical limitations or difficulties might be frequently encountered. Ancis (1998) explored the challenges of teaching multicultural counseling through distance education technology (interactive televised video instruction). Teaching multicultural counseling awareness and skills tends to raise students' anxiety regardless of the medium. In distance learning settings, the instructor can make use of the parallel process of learning something new through technology and learning new things about self and others through multicultural perspectives.

Teaching methodologies have to accommodate the medium and take into account the limitations of technology. For example, it is not possible to observe role-plays firsthand or to sense what is happening in the classroom related to affect. One way in which to access this information is to have students write journal entries or do "affect checks," whereby students write out lists of feelings of the moment. Ancis (1998) recommended that teachers engage students in cooperative learning exercises and activities to reduce site-specific alienation, to clarify confidentiality and include technicians and other observers in this discussion, to have backup plans when technology breaks down, and to "humanize" the experience as much as possible. It is important for the instructor to "create a climate conducive to experimentation, camaraderie, and active participation" (p. 138).

The use of computer technology in the counseling field still is in the infancy stages of development. More structured counseling-related interventions, such as computerized career guidance programs, have been in use longer, and their efficacy has been studied (Fukuyama,

Probert, Neimeyer, Nevill, & Metzler, 1988). Currently, ethical guidelines for counseling on the Web are being developed and are discussed next.

Webcounseling Ethical Guidelines

A task force under the auspices of the National Board for Certified Counselors (NBCC) is working on developing ethical guidelines exclusively for counseling on the Web. Because this is a rapidly changing area of technology, the guidelines are subject to revision, and the board is open to input and discussion (Bloom, 1999). Webcounseling is defined as "the practice of professional counseling and information delivery that occurs when client(s) and counselor are in separate or remote locations and utilize electronic means to communicate over the Internet" (Bloom, 1999). The use of counseling on the Internet more frequently has been suggested for serving rural areas. The guidelines include specific recommendations, and the following list is a sampling (Bloom, 1999):

- Ensure client confidentiality through encryption methods.
- Check on liability issues (e.g., insurance coverage).
- Inform the client how long session data will be saved.
- Check on client and counselor identities through codes.
- Verify identities of adults when consent is needed for minors.
- Establish a local on-call counselor or crisis resources.
- Screen out problems not appropriate for Webcounseling (e.g., eating disorders).
- Explain and have contingency plans if technical problems occur.

- Explain how to cope with potential misunderstandings that arise due to lack of visual clues.
- Discuss with client what to do if counselor is off-line or when there are delays in sending and receiving messages.

Because peer supervision is so important to the ethical practice of counseling, it is suggested that counselors be connected to other Web-counselors so that they can consult on issues as they arise.

Shifting Career Patterns

One of the impacts of shifts in the global economy is changing career patterns. Hansen (1997) suggested that there is a paradigm shift in career development for many people, from one of "trait and factor" job matching to consideration of a complex matrix of factors including family, gender roles, cultural diversity, global needs, spirituality, managing organizational change, and approaching career development holistically. In addition to dealing with greater cultural complexity, corporate downsizing has caused many people to reconsider their definitions of *career*. A new career pattern is emerging in which the employee is independent and directed by the needs and values of the individual more so than loyalty to one company. Named after a Greek mythological god, Proteus (who could change shape at will), the "protean career contract" is with the self rather than with an organization (Hall & Moss, 1998). This career paradigm requires individuals to be adaptable, self-directed, entrepreneurial, and willing to engage in lifelong learning. Fewer and fewer jobs exist over long periods of time due to change. There is both good news and bad news in this current trend for counselors. The good news is that many people return to college for retooling and need assistance in making career and life transitions. The bad news is that there are fewer full-time opportunities for counselors, and counselors will need to be adaptable as well. More and more graduates are putting together career packages that may draw from several sources such as part-time teaching, private practice, and organizational consulting.

Summary

This chapter has provided an overview of the diverse roles for mental health professionals in higher education. Mental health professionals have had a presence on campuses for the past 100 years. Although counselors are found in diverse units on campus, three models for counseling were presented: mental health counseling, career development counseling, and student personnel work. Counselors contribute toward the growth and development of college and university students in many different ways—individual and group counseling, psychoeducational workshops, consultation with faculty and staff, training of peer counselors, and career and life planning interventions. A discussion on ethical decision making around dual roles was included because counselors frequently engage in multiple roles with students (e.g., administrator, teacher, counselor, supervisor). As a social institution, universities and colleges have been subject to the winds of change from society at large and, as such, have been affected by increased social stress and changing demographics. Several cutting-edge issues were discussed such as the impact of the Americans with Disabilities Act, the effect of managed care, and the question of outsourcing counseling services. Perspectives on the future included exploration of the impact of computer technology on the university and on the profession of counseling, for example, the introduction of distance learning and use of the Internet. To keep up with the times, counselors who work with students to meet the challenges of the 21st century also will need to adapt to change in institutions of higher education.

References

American Psychiatric Association. (1994). *Diagnostic and statistical manual of mental disorders* (4th ed.). Washington, DC: Author.

Ancis, J. R. (1998). Cultural competency training at a distance: Challenges and strategies. *Journal of Counseling and Development, 76,* 134-143.

Archer, J., Jr., & Cooper, S. (1998). *Counseling and mental health services on campus: A handbook of contemporary practices and challenges.* San Francisco: Jossey-Bass.

Bishop, J. B. (1992). The changing student culture: Implications for counselors and administrators. *Journal of College Student Psychotherapy, 6*(3/4), 37-57.

Bloom, J. W. (1999). *Standards for the ethical practice of Webcounseling* [Online]. Available: www.nbcc.org/ethics/wcstandards.htm

Brooks-Harris, J. E., & Stock-Ward, S. R. (1999). *Workshops: Designing and facilitating experiential learning.* Thousand Oaks, CA: Sage.

Brown, D., Kurpius, D. J., & Morris, J. R. (1988). *Handbook of consultation with individuals and small groups.* Alexandria, VA: American Counseling Association.

Caplan, G. (1970). *The theory and practice of mental health consultation.* New York: Basic Books.

Conyne, R. K. (1997). Educating students in preventive counseling. *Counselor Education and Supervision, 36,* 259-269.

Cox, J. L. (1999). *A guide to peer counseling.* Northvale, NJ: Jason Aronson.

Dean, L. A., & Meadows, M. E. (1995). College counseling: Union and intersection. *Journal of Counseling and Development, 74,* 130-142.

D'Andrea, M., & Daniels, J. (1995). Promoting multiculturalism and organizational change in the counseling profession. In J. G. Ponterotto, J. M. Casas, C. A. Suzuki, & C. M. Alexander (Eds.), *Handbook of multicultural counseling* (pp. 17-33). Thousand Oaks, CA: Sage.

Eddy, J. P., Spaulding, D. J., & Murphy, S. (1996). Privatization of higher education services: Propositional pros and cons. *Education, 116,* 542, 578-579.

Fukuyama, M., Probert, B., Neimeyer, G., Nevill, D., & Metzler, A. (1988). Effects of DISCOVER on career self-efficacy and decision-making of undergraduates. *Career Development Quarterly, 37,* 56-62.

Fukuyama, M. A., & Sevig, T. D. (1999). *Integrating spirituality into multicultural counseling.* Thousand Oaks, CA: Sage.

Funderburk, J. R. (1998, March). *The survivor's art exhibit: A feminist approach to healing and recovery.* Paper presented at the Association of Women in Psychology National Conference, Baltimore, MD.

Gallessich, J. (1982). *The profession and practice of consultation.* San Francisco: Jossey-Bass.

Grieger, I. (1996). A multicultural organizational development checklist for student affairs. *Journal of College Student Development, 37,* 561-573.

Hall, D. T., & Moss, J. E. (1998). The new protean career contract: Helping organizations and employees adapt. *Organizational Dynamics, 26*(3), 23-37.

Hansen, L. S. (1997). *Integrative life planning: Critical tasks for career development and changing life patterns.* San Francisco: Jossey-Bass.

Herlihy, B., & Corey, G. (1997). *Boundary issues in counseling: Multiple roles and responsibilities.* Alexandria, VA: American Counseling Association.

Holloway, E., & Carroll, M. (1999). *Training counselling supervisors.* Thousand Oaks, CA: Sage.

Jackson, L. (1999, August). Educating in the midst of attention deficit disorder: Strategies for improved classroom management. *Innovator,* pp. 2-3. (Center for Excellence in Teaching, University of Florida)

Kaplan, D. M., & Rothrock, D. R. (1991). Ethical dilemmas in college counseling: The doctor is in! *Journal of College Student Psychotherapy, 6*(1), 15-36.

Kelly, E. W. (1995). *Spirituality and religion in counseling and psychotherapy: Diversity in theory and practice.* Alexandria, VA: American Counseling Association.

Kent, N. J. (1996). The new campus racism: What's going on? *NEA Higher Education Journal, 12,* 45-57.

Komives, S. R., & Gast, L. K. (1996). Student affairs and related careers in higher education. In B. B. Collison & N. J. Garfield (Eds.), *Careers in counseling and human services* (2nd ed., pp. 31-51). Washington, DC: Taylor & Francis.

Kurpius, D. J., & Brown, D. (Eds.). (1988). *Handbook of consultation: An intervention for advocacy and outreach.* Alexandria, VA: American Counseling Association.

Metcalf, L. (1998). *Solution focused group therapy: Ideas for groups in private practice, schools, agencies, and treatment programs.* New York: Free Press.

Morrill, W. H., Oetting, E. R., & Hurst, J. C. (1974). Dimensions of counselor functioning. *Personnel and Guidance Journal, 52,* 354-359.

Myers, J. E., Emmerling, D., & Leafgren, F. (1992). [Special issue]. Wellness throughout the life span. *Journal of Counseling and Development, 71,* 136-230.

Phillips, L., Halstead, R., & Carpenter, W. (1996). The privatization of college counseling services: A preliminary investigation. *Journal of College Student Development, 37,* 52-59.

Quinn, P. O. (1994). *ADD and the college student.* New York: Brunner/Mazel.

Reinhold, J. E. (1991). The origins and early development of mental health services in American colleges and universities. *Journal of College Student Psychotherapy, 6*(1), 3-13.

Sampson, J. P., Kolodinsky, R. W., & Greeno, B. P. (1997). Counseling on the information highway: Future possibilities and potential problems. *Journal of Counseling and Development, 75,* 203-212.

Stone, G. L., & Archer, J., Jr. (1990). College and university counseling centers in the 1990's: Challenges and limits. *Counseling Psychologist, 18,* 539-607.

Stone, G. L., & Lucas, J. (1994). Disciplinary counseling in higher education: A neglected challenge. *Journal of Counseling and Development, 72,* 234-238.

Sue, D. W., & Sue, D. (1998). *Counseling the culturally different: Theory and practice* (3rd ed.). New York: John Wiley.

Whitaker, L. C. (1997). The influence of managed care. *Journal of College Student Psychotherapy, 12*(2), 23-40.

Widseth, J. C., Webb, R. E., & John, K. B. (1997). The question of outsourcing: The roles and functions of college counseling services. *Journal of College Student Psychotherapy, 11*(4), 3-22.

Wulf, W. (1995). Warning: Information technology will transform the university. *Issues in Science and Technology, 11*(4), 46-52. (CD-ROM: Current Issues SourceFile, Record U022-1)

Zalaquett, C. P. (1996). A descriptive analysis of problem checklist utilization among college and university counseling centers in a southwestern state. *Journal of College Student Psychotherapy, 11*(2), 27-32.

CHAPTER TWENTY

Community Counseling Settings

SAMUEL T. GLADDING
MICHAEL RYAN

Counseling in community settings is both an old and a relatively new phenomenon. The practice can be traced back to one of the founders of counseling, Frank Parsons, who devised the first systematic career counseling method in the United States at the Vocational Bureau in Boston (Parsons, 1909). Other pioneers who promoted counseling in a community setting were Abraham and Hannah Stone, who began marriage counseling in New York City during the late 1920s, and clinicians who worked for the Veterans Administration both before and after World War II (Gladding, 2000).

Yet, as a common practice, counseling in community settings really did not begin until the 1960s when Congress passed the Community Mental Health Centers Act of 1963 and opened the door for large numbers of counsel-

ors to work in agency settings. This act proposed that a mental health facility be established to serve every community with a population of 100,000 or more. Along with the building of centers came the hiring of staff, many of whom were counselors.

Before the 1960s, counseling was primarily an occupation housed in educational institutions. Colleges and universities, as well as K-12 schools, employed the vast majority of counselors. Although some counselors worked in settings outside of educational institutions such as retirement communities, hospitals, and private practices, they were not numerous and often were isolated.

In this chapter, common settings in which counseling is conducted in communities are described. The skills and abilities of counselors who work in agencies also are examined. This discussion is followed by an exploration of special and unique challenges of prevalent community agencies in which counselors are employed. It is in realizing the "what" of a setting that counselors become more knowledgeable about how to work best in such environments.

Settings

Counseling is conducted in a wide variety of community settings. The physical premises range from group homes to telephone hotlines (Herr, 1998). These environments are distinguished by their diversity rather than their similarities. Individuals from all cultures are a part of the caseloads in nearly all such facilities, and counselors who work in such settings must be multicultural and developmentally astute (Locke, 1998). Problems and concerns vary from mild adjustment disorders to severe mental disturbances. The theoretical backgrounds of practitioners who conduct counseling in these environments vary as well. Thus, counselors who wish to work in community settings need to be aware that there are multiple models for operating such settings.

Unlike counseling in most educational facilities, where there is some overlap regarding problems or types of clients treated (Thompson & Rudolph, 2000), community counseling settings are noted more for their differences in missions, problems, and populations addressed. Therefore, although coursework for counselors preparing for these careers may have a number of subject areas in common, each community-based counselor faces the challenge of learning how best to operate in his or her particular agency. Such insight often comes from learning

on the job as well as learning in one's graduate counseling program. Some of the most prominent settings of community counselors are described in what follows.

Family Counseling

Counselors who work in family counseling are employed by a number of agencies. For example, counselors who work with families might actually be employees of Big Brother/Big Sister, a homeless shelter, or a center for abused women as well as practitioners in private practice or family services. The setting for such counselors is not as crucial as the way in which they deliver their services.

In most cases, family counseling is systems based (Horne, 2000). It embraces a circular causality approach and assumes that interactions within families are dynamic rather than linear, that is, rather than simply cause and effect. Therefore, community counselors who work with families see the family as a system that is imbedded within another system (i.e., the local community), which in turn is a part of even larger systems (e.g., the state, the nation, the world).

Although a systems approach might seem overwhelming at first, it actually can be quite therapeutic in letting the counselor and the family gain a larger perspective of problematic issues (e.g., rebellion of a child, abuse of a parent). This perspective tends to eliminate blame due to a single cause, thereby helping family members to explore interactions more thoroughly and to examine themselves and the systems in which they live in a more critical and constructive manner. Thus, the rebellious child might be reenacting issues that once were a part of a parent family-of-origin setting that, having never been resolved, has resurfaced in a struggle between a parent and the child. Likewise, when families understand that most abusers tend to have been victims of abuse themselves, they are freer to examine underlying factors and possible solutions from a wider and usually more creative perspective.

Popular family counseling approaches include Bowen, experiential, behavioral, structural, strategic, solution focused, and narrative. In addition, a number of community counselors work to promote marriage enrichment and help couples and families to prevent major divisive issues from arising in their households.

Outpatient and Day Care Programs

Counselors who work in community outpatient and day care programs spend the majority of their days with individuals who have severe mental, physical, or emotional problems. These people cannot function adequately in society at large without considerable support. They include among their numbers returnees from mental hospitals and rehabilitation centers or those who have disabilities. Clients who have become impaired because of developmental or traumatic situations (e.g., aging, accidents) are a part of this group as well (Herr, 1998).

Regardless of the reason for their being referred for help, community counselors face considerable challenges in helping these clients to help themselves. Some methods of treatment, however, seem to work better than others. For example, in outpatient programs, group counseling or group guidance activities seem to be one of the best therapeutic approaches. Clients who have returned from mental health facilities benefit greatly from hearing about how others are coping on their reentry to society-at-large. They also gain by working within a group to work out resolutions for problems that triggered their mental distress in the first place. In a group setting, members can bring insight into a particular situation that goes beyond what a single counselor can provide. On an individual level, on the other hand, clients may find some needed strategies or ways of adjusting to difficulties through life-skills training sessions that the counselor offers.

In day care facilities, the foci of counselors may vary more. Individuals who are in day care usually are unable to take care of themselves and need physical, mental, or even emotional support that their caregivers might have neither the time nor the skill to provide. In such settings, counselors might need to offer creative and stimulating experiences for the special needs of each client so as to help make the client's life richer and more enjoyable.

Thus, instead of operating from a traditional therapeutic perspective, the counselor in a community day care facility may offer creative arts experiences such as those involving drawing, movement, drama, writing, or music (Gladding, 1998). For example, music may be used to bring back memories and help the impaired client work through situations that otherwise have laid dormant or unresolved. Likewise, the counselor in such a situation may spend considerable time in individual counseling to help the client work through specific issues when no one else in the client's immediate environment has the time or talent to help.

Retirement Communities

There are a number of counselors who, for either personal or professional reasons, avoid working with those who are elderly and/or retired. However, the number of individuals who are retired or who will be retiring in the foreseeable future is quite large and underserved (Butler, Lewis, & Sunderland, 1991). Therefore, counselors who have chosen such communities in which to work almost always have heavy caseloads and might work long hours as well. However, there are a number of intangible benefits that come with these conditions. For example, with age often comes wisdom, kindness, and a refreshing directness that can be enlightening, inviting, and therapeutic in and of itself. Counselors are direct beneficiaries of these qualities when they work with older populations.

However, counselors who choose to work with retirees must realize that there are special concerns within this population. Retirees come with both unique and universal concerns and needs. Universal challenges include dealing with bodies that are aging and with minds that are not as sharp as they once were. Also, there may be memories or even current situations that are perplexing and unsettling for retirees such as moving to new places and having to deal with different people in a way unlike those they have previously known.

Retirees might not have had an opportunity to bring closure to turbulent situations with friends and family members including those who have died. These unresolved situations, in turn, may trigger emotional responses such as depression, guilt, and anger. In these cases, negative emotions tend to disrupt the clients' lives in a multitude of ways until they can be laid to rest. Therefore, counselors who work with retirees in day care are called on to possess multiple abilities and flexibilities. They also are required to be experts on dealing with grief and

loss. The death of a member of a client's family or of a client's friend is a frequent occurrence. Also, the death of a client is likely in some cases, and the counselor must know where to get relief and help so as to function adequately and prevent doing harm to others. Fortunately, there are opportunities for advanced training and standards for gerontological counseling that counselors in such settings can obtain (Myers, 1995).

Government and Military Posts

The word *postal* has a new meaning—it has been used during recent years to describe irrational and violent acts by disgruntled employees toward coworkers (Jaramillo, 1997). The word originated from incidents of this type in post offices. The expression "going postal" is negative and generally is used in connection with people unable to properly handle disputes or conflicts in the workplace.

Most government employees do not have incidents of inappropriate displays of anger. It is true, however, that government employees usually work in bureaucratic and hierarchical settings where they might not be well known or where their requests might be ignored. Such environments leave little room for dialogue addressing work conditions or for handling matters that could improve their personal or professional lives (getting time off or a mismatch occurring between technology and human factors).

Therefore, counselors who work in government agencies have to make sure that they know the environments of their clients. They also need to know about specific manuals and policies that dictate the jobs and responsibilities of the agencies and government employees. It is only through having such particular knowledge that counselors in these settings can truly understand the issues that clients bring them. In addition, counselors in government service must develop networks for working with clients given that government employees who engage counselors often need sources other than counseling by which to address their concerns.

Likewise, military personnel bring with them a uniqueness that counselors must understand on multiple levels (Rotter & Boveja, 1999). There are a number of issues that are special in regard to members of the armed services (e.g., frequent moves, isolation, loneliness). There also are emotions, such as fear and stress, inherent in a combat operation. Although counselors might have cognitive knowledge of these conditions, those who work best with military populations have some firsthand experience as well or become more knowledgeable by "shadowing" members of the armed forces with whom they most likely will come into contact.

Addiction Centers

Drug and substance experimentation continues to be epidemic in American society. In addition, outside of drugs, there are other addictive behaviors—even socially acceptable ones such as workaholism and gambling—that continue to be major problems in the United States (L'Abate, Farrar, & Serritella, 1992). Addictive behavior is defined as "a persistent and intense involvement with and stress upon a single behavior pattern, with a minimization or even [an] exclusion of other behaviors, both personal and interpersonal" (L'Abate, 1992a, p. 2). A primary characteristic of addicts is that they become preoccupied with one object (the addiction) that controls their behaviors. Thus, individuals who are addicted are "hooked" into limited and limiting behaviors that usually prove to be less and less satisfying over time.

Addiction and substance abuse usually are tied to the health of a community, and programs that seek to prevent them must be community-wide. Because of such an emphasis, counselors can play a leading role in both prevention and treatment of addictive behaviors. One preventive measure is the "Just Say No" campaign found in schools and public agencies sponsored by local governments. Through such programs, children learn how to be assertive and refuse offers of harmful drugs. Another form of an effective educational program involves cocaine addicts or potential cocaine addicts (Sunich & Doster, 1995). The emphasis in this program is focused on lifestyle choices, time management, nutrition, and money management. A common element in these two approaches to substance abuse and addiction prevention involves group pressure and dynamics. In setting up preventive programs, prudent counselors use their knowledge of groups.

Among the most prevalent factors affecting treatment are "motivation, denial, dual diagnosis, matching, control, and relapse" (L'Abate, 1992b, p. 11). Motivation has to do with a desire to change, which most addicts do not wish to do because of their self-centeredness and comfort. Denial is basically minimizing the effects of addiction on either oneself or others. It minimizes the harm that is being done. A dual diagnosis is one in which an addict has more than one aspect of personality that is open to labeling. For example, an addict might be impulsive or depressed in addition to being addicted. Matching concerns the right treatment for a disorder. Some addictions, such as cocaine, require specialized treatment (Washton, 1989).

Control has to do with the regulation of behavior that addicts tend to disregard. Finally, relapse is the recurrence of dysfunctional behaviors once they have been treated. It is discouraging to have addicts go through structured programs and then end up acting the ways in which they did before.

One program for treating drug addicts in jail is "Stay'n Out" in Staten Island, New York. The program is mandatory for participants who are required to attend therapy. "It's be there—or you're off to a meaner cellblock" (Alter, 1995, pp. 20-21). Although the ethical dimensions of this program are debatable, the results are a recidivism rate of only 25%, much lower than average. Treatment services also can take the form of counselors providing information. For example, a counselor might inform family members that if they are going to help the addicted individual, then they as a whole must confront the addict over the effects of his or her addiction on the family as a unit as well as on its individual members. An intervention of this type cannot be made without an intensive systems approach that involves a number of people and agencies, and that is where a counselor in a community setting can be invaluable.

Rehabilitation Agencies

Rehabilitation focuses on serving individuals with disabilities, that is, conditions that limit individuals' activities or functioning (U.S. Department of Health, Education, and Welfare, 1974). The Americans with Disabilities Act of 1990 projects that there are more than 40 million people with disabilities in the United States. Thus, there is a great need for rehabilitation services, and rehabilitation centers are eager employers of counselors.

Clients of rehabilitation counselors include people with physical, emotional, mental, and/or behavioral disabilities. They include individuals of all ages from both minority and majority cultures. Therefore, counselors who work with persons with disabilities must be versatile. They must be practical but work with a clear sense of purpose, often coordinating their activities with other professionals while simultaneously monitoring their clients' progress in gaining independence and self-control. In short, a counselor who works in a community setting doing rehabilitation "is expected to be a competent case manager as well as a skilled therapeutic counselor" (Cook, Bolton, Bellini, & Neath, 1997, p. 193).

Overall, counselors in rehabilitation settings are like counselors in a variety of other settings in that they stress the development of the whole person and focus on providing both preventive and treatment services. Yet, they are distinct in working with clients who need help in overcoming their disabilities and in coordinating their services with other professionals, especially those in the medical community.

Employee Assistance Programs

Employee assistance programs (EAPs) are found in many U.S. businesses on either an in-house or a referral basis. They are dedicated to increasing the overall functioning of individuals within companies's employment. Counselors who work in such settings provide services that are both informative and therapeutic in nature. Specific ways in which clients are served are dependent on the skills of the counselors and the needs of the populations involved.

An example of how a referral EAP program works can be found in the experience of the

Kerr-McGee Corporation, an energy company located only two blocks from the Alfred P. Murrah Federal Building in Oklahoma City, Oklahoma, that was bombed on April 19, 1995. After the bombing, the company spent a great many hours as well as tens of thousands of dollars in offering counseling and other services to employees to help them cope (Hightower, 1995). Kerr-McGee contracted with an external company, Crisis Management International (based in Atlanta, Georgia), to bring 18 counselors on-site to work with its employees. In addition, it set up a command center, held group and individual counseling sessions, and established a phone tree to update information to its workers. Problems employees had in the wake of the bombing included grief, anger, depression, fatigue, nightmares, survivor guilt, and difficulty in eating and concentrating.

Although the actions of Kerr-McGee might seem unusual or dramatic, they are not. Since the late 1970s, business, industry, government, and private/public institutions in the United States have exhibited renewed interest in the overall health of employees (Lewis & Lewis, 1986). The reasons for this interest are both humanistic and financially motivated. Through documented studies, employers have found that workers who are healthier and less stressed are better performers and subject to less absenteeism and accidents. They have further discovered that between 10% and 18% of workers normally experience some mental or emotional problems that detrimentally influence their on-the-job behavior (Masi, 1984). Thus, internal and external counseling programs have been set up by a variety of companies to help employees adversely affected by personal problems (e.g., alcoholism, drug abuse, divorce, financial pressures). In 2000, there were esti-

mated to be more than 14,000 EAPs in the United States.

"Clearly, counselors have the potential to play an important role in the EAP arena" and are doing so already (Gerstein & Bayer, 1988, p. 296). In a recent national survey of EAP programs, more than 60% of the externally administered programs reported hiring counseling graduates with master's and doctoral degrees (Hosie & Spruill, 1990). This percentage was topped only slightly by EAP programs hiring master's-level social workers. From these statistics, it is evident that the need exists for counselors to provide preventive and remedial services to employees and to train supervisors to recognize troubled workers and refer them for help. Research and conceptual development of EAP programs are other areas in which counselors can be involved in these secondary prevention operations.

Wellness Centers

During recent years, there has been an increased emphasis among counselors on positive wellness, that is, health-related activities that are both preventive and remedial and have a therapeutic value for those individuals who practice them consistently (Witmer & Sweeney, 1999). Such activities include eating natural foods, taking vitamins, going to health spas, meditating, and participating in regular exercise (O'Donnell, 1988). "For the person to be a whole, healthy, functioning organism, one must evaluate the physical, psychological, intellectual, social, emotional, and environmental processes" (Carlson & Ardell, 1988, p. 383). Signs of the holistic movement toward health and well-being are apparent everywhere and are spilling over in their impact on Americans of all ages.

Research backs up the basis for the wellness movement and in some ways continues to lead it. In an extensive review of the literature on the effectiveness of physical fitness on measures of personality, Doan and Scherman (1987) found strong support for the idea that regular exercise can have a beneficial effect on people's physical and psychological health. Their review supports counselors who prescribe health habits to accompany regular counseling practices. Other strategies for working from a wellness perspective include having counselors dwell more on positive, life-enhancing things that individuals can do and altering traditional screening to include more emphasis on overall health.

An example of a counseling approach based on the wellness model is stress inoculation training (SIT), a proactive, psychoeducational intervention that can be used with clients of all ages (Meichenbaum, 1993). In this model, individuals are helped to understand their potential problematic situations and acquire skills, through imagery or role-play, for coping with them in a positive manner. Thus, counselors who work in community settings that emphasize a wellness approach focus on prevention and education (Kleist & White, 1997). They take into account the mental, physical, and social spheres of life and in the process recognize how they can focus on avoiding or minimizing external or internal disruptive forces.

Common Skills Needed for Counselors in Community Settings

All counselors, regardless of setting, need to be able to display what Carkhuff (1969) described as "microskills." These skills include the ability to display behaviors such as empathy, joining, and closure. They are easier to discuss than to display. Yet, the majority of counselors in community settings have mastered these essential elements of the therapeutic process.

In addition to core skills, however, community-based counselors must learn to do the following.

Be flexible. A counselor in a community agency often may be asked to see a variety of clients instead of one or two special types of clients. Counselors who are open to such possibilities and are fluid in regard to learning new skills are likely to be the most successful in adjusting to the demands placed on them. For example, a counselor in a mental health facility may be asked to see individuals, groups, and families at various times and with different presenting problems. By possessing the skills and abilities to do so, the counselor is best able to serve both clients in need and the agency that makes such services possible.

Be knowledgeable. Part of counseling in a community environment is knowing what other resources are available. For example, a community counselor should be aware of what medical and emergency facilities are available in his or her environment for clients who are at risk for suicide or major depressive episodes. Likewise, the counselor needs to be aware of specialists who can respond to situations that a counselor might not be equipped to handle in depth such as the treatment of anorexia nervosa. Therefore, to be knowledgeable and ultimately effective, a counselor must learn about the community in which he or she lives, especially from clients' need perspectives.

Be connected. It is not enough, however, just to know of resources within a community. A counselor must know people in his or her environment who can be helpful at different times and in different ways. This type of knowing means having contact with such professionals on a regular basis. Opportunities for this type of contact may come through professional meetings or continuing education opportunities in which the counselor can informally converse with other specialists.

Counselors also can be proactive in inviting professionals who they know are vital to their practices to have lunch with them or to come with them to meetings of mutual interest. For example, when the first author worked in a community mental health agency, he would invite school counselors from the four different systems in his county to meet once a month with him and the agency's psychiatrist to discuss ways in which they could promote positive mental health within their environments. The meetings produced a lot of new ideas and exchanging of ideas that worked. It also made referrals and requests from the schools to the mental health center, and vice versa, much easier.

Be ready. Despite developing the best prevention and proactive programs possible, counselors in community settings inevitably must deal with crises. These events, and the chaos that often accompanies them, can be handled best if counselors have devised plans to deal with possible scenarios such as the emotional upheaval following traumatic injuries involving a violent act of nature or people. Although it is unlikely that plans of this type will be needed in the majority of the work that counselors do, such plans lessen the pain and confusion when a crisis does arise. At such a time, the counselor needs to be a member of a team within a community and not just an individual acting alone. For example, the Red Cross sends in teams of counselors who have had special training whenever a major disaster strikes. The agency realizes that there is strength in numbers and that counselors sometimes need counseling or consultation that can be generated only by having more than one counselor work in a community where a crisis has arisen.

The Future of Counseling in Community Settings

Despite some challenges, the future of counseling in community settings appears to be strong. There are multiple reasons for this.

One reason is need. Communities in the United States are changing rapidly. The diversity of people and problems that communities face is increasing. Thus, professional counselors are needed to deal with the change and chaos that might occur. Just as family medicine practitioners are the gatekeepers in managed help care and have a broad knowledge of many areas, counselors who work on a nonspecialized level in a community can be conceptualized as the generalists of the counseling profession with a breadth, if not a depth, of knowledge. As a group, these counselors are able to refer clients to specialists when appropriate. They also are able to treat clients who have less severe needs and, in so doing, prevent minor adjustment reactions from growing into severe disorders.

A second reason why counseling in community settings most likely will continue to grow is the attractiveness of these positions. Counseling in communities is both challenging and stimulating, as has been shown in this chapter. Counselors who wish to both do good and be active can choose from a wide variety of possible placements that afford them an opportunity to apply their skills in a caring, compassionate, and nonroutine manner. For example, a counselor who works in rehabilitation may see a wide variety of people and needs. Likewise, a counselor who works in an addiction center or a military post is unlikely to encounter similar situations each day. Therefore, the counselor who works in a community setting is more likely than not to be pushed to expand his or her abilities and, in the process, to grow.

Another reason why counseling in community settings is likely to expand involves funding issues. Both state and federal governments in the United States have realized during recent years that there is a need to be prepared for and prevent disasters. For example, the Department of Justice now is working on a prevention program that targets at-risk adolescents and helps to pair them up with members of their communities who not only monitor their behaviors but also serve as role models. In all probability, government on all levels will continue to expand funding such preventive efforts in an attempt to both promote health and decrease violence.

Forces that have the potential to decrease the attractiveness of counseling in community settings are not numerous but must be considered as well.

A major possible deterrent to counselors working in community settings might be the use of paraprofessionals or other professionals in these environments. Whereas counselors have much to offer communities regarding their skills and backgrounds, counseling and those who work as counselors must constantly stay alert to advocating for the profession on multi-

ple levels. In so doing, political and community leaders who ultimately make decisions will keep counselors in mind when hiring helping professionals.

Another potential detractor for counselors not working in communities might be paperwork and red tape. Like other professionals, counselors wish to be accountable but do not relish filling out complicated and/or lengthy forms. If community standards or government regulations become such that counselors must do so, then counselors are less likely to enter community work.

A final detractor for counselors working in communities is demographics. Entering professionals often want to be employed in large metropolitan areas that are saturated with professionals. The real need for counselors in community settings, however, is in underserved areas such as rural and inner-city environments. The appeal of these underserved areas is not as great as in metropolitan settings; therefore, counselors might eschew such opportunities.

Conclusion

As has been pointed out in this chapter, counseling in a community setting is full of variety in terms of who is served and how they are served. Counselors who choose the option to work in this way have a chance to serve the disabled, the addicted, the aged, the mentally disturbed, government and military personnel, employees in large companies, and people seeking positive wellness. The tasks and challenges for such professionals are numerous. Therefore, counselors in community settings must be flexible, knowledgeable, connected, and ready to respond to a number of requests.

Although the work involved in counseling in community agencies is demanding, counselors most likely will continue to be attracted to such settings because of the growing need, the challenge of these positions, and increased funding. Deterrents to the future of counseling in community settings include the increased use of paraprofessionals, red tape, and paperwork and the fact that many opportunities for employment might lie in less attractive and exciting areas of the country.

Nevertheless, counselors who wish to serve varied populations, seek to avoid routine and sameness, and strongly desire to fill a need for services will continue to be attracted to community counseling settings. It is in such environments that counseling at its best is practiced and that practitioners can truly make a difference.

References

Alter, J. (1995, May 29). What works. *Newsweek*, pp. 18-24.

Butler, R. N., Lewis, M., & Sunderland, Y. (1991). *Aging and mental health* (4th ed.). New York: Macmillan.

Carkhuff, R. R. (1969). *Helping and human relations* (Vols. 1 & 2). New York: Holt, Rinehart & Winston.

Carlson, J., & Ardell, D. B. (1988). Physical fitness as a pathway to wellness and effective counseling. In R. Hayes & R. Aubrey (Eds.), *New directions for counseling and human development* (pp. 383-396). Denver, CO: Love.

Cook, D., Bolton, B., Bellini, J., & Neath, J. (1997). A statewide investigation of the rehabilitation counselor generalist hypothesis. *Rehabilitation Counseling Bulletin, 40*, 192-201.

Doan, R. E., & Scherman, A. (1987). The therapeutic effect of physical fitness on measures of personality: A literature review. *Journal of Counseling and Development, 66*, 28-36.

Gerstein, L. H., & Bayer, G. A. (1988). Employee assistance programs: A systematic investigation of their use. *Journal of Counseling and Development, 66*, 294-297.

Gladding, S. T. (1998). *Counseling as an art: The creative arts in counseling*. Alexandria, VA: American Counseling Association.

Gladding, S. T. (2000). *Counseling: A comprehensive profession* (4th ed.). Upper Saddle River, NJ: Merrill/Prentice Hall.

Herr, E. (1998). *Counseling in a dynamic society* (2nd ed.). Alexandria, VA: American Counseling Association.

Hightower, S. (1995, May 7). Helping cope: Counselors brought to Oklahoma City company. *Winston-Salem Journal*, pp. A22, A24.

Horne, A. M. (2000). *Family counseling and therapy* (3rd ed.). Itasca, IL: F. E. Peacock.

Hosie, T., & Spruill, D. (1990, November). *Counselor employment and roles in three types of EAP organizations*. Paper presented at the Southern Association for Counselor Education and Supervision Conference, Norfolk, VA.

Jaramillo, S. (1997). *Going postal*. New York: Berkley.

Kleist, D. M., & White, L. J. (1997). The values of counseling: A disparity between a philosophy of prevention in counseling and counselor practice and training. *Counseling and Values, 41*, 128-140.

L'Abate, L. (1992a). Introduction. In L. L'Abate, J. E. Farrar, & D. A. Serritella (Eds.), *Handbook of differential treatments for addiction* (pp. 1-4). Boston: Allyn & Bacon.

L'Abate, L. (1992b). Major theoretical issues. In L. L'Abate, J. E. Farrar, & D. A. Serritella (Eds.), *Handbook of differential treatments for addiction* (pp. 5-22). Boston: Allyn & Bacon.

L'Abate, L., Farrar, J. E., & Serritella, D. A. (Eds.). (1992). *Handbook of differential treatments for addiction*. Boston: Allyn & Bacon.

Lewis, J. A., & Lewis, M. D. (1986). *Counseling programs for employees in the workplace*. Pacific Grove, CA: Brooks/Cole.

Locke, D. C. (1998). *Increasing multicultural understanding: A comprehensive model*. Thousand Oaks, CA: Sage.

Masi, D. (1984). *Developing employee assistance programs*. New York: American Management Association.

Meichenbaum, D. (1993). Changing conceptions of cognitive behavior modification: Retrospect and prospect. *Journal of Consulting and Clinical Psychology, 61*, 202-204.

Myers, J. E. (1995). From "forgotten and ignored" to standards and certification: Gerontological counseling comes of age. *Journal of Counseling and Development, 74*, 143-149.

O'Donnell, J. M. (1988). The holistic health movement: Implications for counseling theory and practice. In R. Hayes & R. Aubrey (Eds.), *New directions for counseling and human development* (pp. 365-382). Denver, CO: Love.

Parsons, F. (1909). *Choosing a vocation*. Boston: Houghton Mifflin.

Rotter, J. C., & Boveja, M. E. (1999). Counseling military families. *The Family Journal, 7,* 379-383.

Sunich, M. F., & Doster, J. (1995, June). Cocaine—Part II. *The Amethyst Journal,* pp. 1-2.

Thompson, C. L., & Rudolph, L. B. (2000). *Counseling children* (5th ed.). Pacific Grove, CA: Brooks/Cole.

U.S. Department of Health, Education, and Welfare. (1974).

Vocational rehabilitation program: Implementation provisions, rules, and regulations. *Federal Register, 39,* 42470-42507.

Washton, A. (1989). *Cocaine addiction.* New York: Norton.

Witmer, J. M., & Sweeney, T. J. (1999). Toward wellness: The goal of helping. In T. J. Sweeney (Ed.), *Adlerian counseling: A practitioner's approach* (4th ed.). Philadelphia: Accelerated Development/Taylor & Francis.

CHAPTER TWENTY-ONE

Private Practice

The Professional Counselor

EARL J. GINTER

Whereas many professional counselors work in non-private practice settings (e.g., elementary/high schools, mental health centers, hospitals, universities, rehabilitation centers, correction facilities), other professional counselors maintain either part-time or full-time private practices. With changes occurring over the past two decades in the private practice arena (e.g., insurance eligibility, number of states with licensure laws, capitation payments, case rate payments, utilization reviews), this is both an exciting and a challenging period for professional counselors who are competing with the available pool of mental health practitioners for clients.

Since 1976, when Virginia passed the first law to license counselors, professional counsel-

ors electing to practice as private practitioners have enjoyed a widening circle of recognition. Today, professional counselors are recognized through certification or licensure in nearly all jurisdictions of the United States. As private practitioners, they are working with an array of clients from whom they collect client information through interviews, assessments, and client records using the information to diagnose and establish treatment plans to assist clients in making decisions about their personal lives (e.g., personality issues, relationship issues, career decisions). While many counselors in private practice have elected to specialize (e.g., alcohol/drug abuse, pastoral, rehabilitation, community mental health), others have adopted a generalist type of approach that may involve seeing children, adolescents, or adults and working with these clients in the context of individual, couple, family, or group counseling.

To obtain a more complete understanding of who the professional counselor is, especially in terms of private practice, a number of factors must be considered—available demographics, professional organizations' views concerning professional counselors, licensure laws affecting professional counselors, diagnosis and assessment approaches used by professional counselors as well as the ways in which they approach treatment planning, the role of developmental theory in professional counseling, the effect of managed care on private practice, and special topics related to private practice counseling.

Factors Related to Private Practice

This chapter reviews the practitioner qualifications of professional counselors who work as private practitioners. It should be noted that the term *professional counselor* is used in a generic manner to refer to a certain type of mental health professional and is used in conjunction with licensure laws across the United States; as a result, it has a specific meaning depending on the jurisdiction. Also, assessment and treatment planning are discussed in relation to the *DSM-IV* (*Diagnostic and Statistical Manual of Mental Disorders* [American Psychiatric Association, 1994]) as well as alternative approaches that are based on developmental (wellness) models, and a case example is provided to highlight unique aspects of private practice counseling. Finally, the current practice environment is discussed in light of current trends related to managed care, and predictions are made concerning the future of professional counselors.

Professional Counselors and Private Practice

Demographics

The largest professional association directly affiliated with and representing the professional counselor is the American Counseling Association (ACA). Data collected by ACA on its members can be used to provide a "picture" of the professional counselor. Of course, not all professional counselors are members of this organization (it is estimated that there are 60,000 to 75,000 licensed professional counselors in the United States [Smith, 1999]), nor would all ACA members primarily identify with the label *professional counselor*. In spite of these qualifiers, one still may glean a better image of who the professional counselor is by studying ACA membership information (S. Nisenoff, personal communication, August 31, 1999).

Concerning "titles" held by ACA's members, one finds that two of the largest categories, categories frequently associated with private practice, are those of licensed professional counselor (LPC) and certified clinical mental health counselor (CCMHC). The ratio of LPCs to CCMHCs is about 14 to 1. (It should be noted that more members report national certified counselor [NCC] credentialing than LPC credentialing and that, although NCC requires 2 years of post-master's experience with 3,000 client contact hours, the certification itself is not tied solely to private practice. In many cases, the NCC designation is obtained by counselors who may or may not be seeking licensure but who still plan to work in non-private practice settings such as high schools.) Most professional counselors in private practice are master's-level practitioners, and this also is reflected in what one finds with ACA membership, where 77% of those reporting degrees report the master's as their terminal degrees. This percentage essentially matches Smith's (1999) percentage of 76% when he surveyed professional counselors maintaining private practices. Also, these master's-level professional counselors dominate two of the larger divisional organizations affiliated with ACA, the Association for Specialists in Group Work (ASGW) and the International Association of Marriage and Family Counselors (IAMFC), professional organizations that frequently are associated with private practitioners. Finally, based on ACA demographics, one may surmise that professional counseling is a field dominated by women, given that approximately 72% of the organization's membership is female.

However, simply reviewing the demographic data collected by ACA provides an incomplete picture of just who is the professional counselor. To further understand today's private practitioner, one must consider other factors such as how the term *professional counselor* has been defined by professional organizations representing such counselors and the legal restrictions (scope of practice) established by various governmental jurisdictions for the practice of counseling. Exploring each of these areas allows for drawing conclusions about the training and qualifications of the typical counselor practitioner in private practice.

Definitions

The term *professional counseling* has a specific meaning. According to ACA, the *practice of professional counseling* means "the application of mental health, psychological, or human development principles through cognitive, affective, behavioral, or systemic intervention strategies that address *wellness, personal growth,*

or *career development* as well as *pathology*" (ACA, 1997, italics added). ACA also has clarified the parameters of a professional *counseling specialty,* stating that it "is narrowly focused, requiring advanced knowledge in the field founded on the premise that all professional counselors must first meet the requirements for the general practice of professional counseling." It appears that the term *professional counselor* serves as an overarching designation that ACA views as encompassing a wide range of specialty areas.

Similar to ACA, the American Mental Health Counselors Association (AMHCA), a professional organization frequently associated with one specialty area in the field of counseling, offers a definition for its own area of practice. AMHCA (1998) adopted the following position:

> Mental health counseling is the provision of *professional counseling services* involving the application of principles of psychotherapy, human development, learning theory, group dynamics, and the etiology of mental illness and dysfunctional behavior to individuals, couples, families, and groups for the purpose of promoting optimum mental health, dealing with normal problems of living, and treating psychopathology. (p. 2, italics added)

AMHCA further stated,

> The practice of mental health counseling includes, but is not limited to, diagnosis and treatment of mental and emotional disorders; psychoeducational techniques aimed at the prevention of mental and emotional disorders; consultation to individuals, couples, families, groups, organizations, and communities; and clinical research into more effective psychotherapy techniques. (p. 2)

ACA's definition for the professional counselor "umbrellas" AMHCA's view of its own practice scope. AMHCA's definition denotes a *narrower focus* (i.e., specialty area) and suggests that professionals associated with AMHCA are primarily private practitioners who have elected to focus greater attention on the treatment of psychopathology. (It is important to keep in mind that even this specialty's focus on psychopathology is mitigated by other elements of counseling mentioned by both AMHCA and ACA, elements that are tied to wellness and developmental issues.) Whether it is mental health counseling or some other specialty, the specialty always is tied to specific training and experience that, in turn, affects the private practitioner's counseling approach. For example, a private practitioner trained as a school counselor might work with children in his or her private practice in a manner that emphasizes a psychoeducational approach to counseling, and as a result, he or she might rely much more heavily on skill-building techniques than does a private practitioner graduating from a community counseling program who might take a more traditional clinical approach to working with the same population. It is clear that the specialty training pursued by a particular professional counselor accounts for many of the perceived and actual differences encountered by a client in that counselor's private practice. In fact, the training received sometimes is the single most important factor for initially distinguishing two professional counselors starting out in private practice.

In spite of the differences that surface (e.g., definitions, specialties) within professional counseling, it is essential to realize that all of the various specialties can be traced back to the same historical roots and that common threads continue to bind all of these specialties together. One prevalent thread is that each specialty is grounded in an appreciation and understanding of how human development plays an essential role in conceptualizing clients' issues, and this appreciation and understanding play an essential role in matching appropriate interventions with those issues (Ginter, 1996).

Licensure

To fully understand the scope of private practice associated with professional counseling, one must consider the boundaries of practice that have been established by various states and the District of Columbia, all of which govern the practice of professional counselors in nearly all jurisdictions in the United States (Espina, 1998). Simply stated, even though ACA (1997) specified the scope of practice for professional counselors in terms of both general practice and specialties, a complete picture can be obtained only by reviewing and summarizing what has taken place in all those jurisdictions that recognize and control the "actual practice" of professional counseling in private practice settings. At this point in the history of professional counseling, enough states have enacted legislature to permit analysis and inferences pertaining to private practice.

As of June 4, 1999, 46 jurisdictions had issued a "general practice credential" (ACA, 1999). In most cases, the LPC designation is associated with these credentials, even when data indicate that other labels are used. ACA (1999) reported that 18 states regulate the practice of "mental health counseling," which is denoted by practice labels such as licensed mental health counselor (LMHC) and licensed clinical professional counselor (LCPC; Espina, 1998). In addition, 16 states regulate rehabilitation counseling as part of the LPC designation; others regulate rehabilitation counseling separate from the LPC designation (e.g., Louisiana, Massachusetts, New Jersey). A total of 30 jurisdictions regulate career counseling in conjunction with the LPC designation. In a few jurisdictions, the specialty areas of geriatric counseling and marriage and family counseling are regulated under the LPC title, even though in these cases the specialties might not be referred to explicitly in the specific licensure law. Many states now regulate substance abuse counseling. Finally, although some school counselors qualify for LPC designation and pursue this license, it is of no surprise that school counselors (with or without the LPC license) are overseen in all 50 states and the District of Columbia through governmental departments of education while they practice in the school settings.

The importance that licensure has played in defining and protecting the practice of professional counseling in private practice settings cannot be overstated. In terms of licensure, regardless of the specific professional counseling title (e.g., LPC, LMHC, LCPC), credential requirements frequently are part of what is called a "practice act." That is, the professional counselor must have the specified credential to practice counseling; otherwise, he or she is prohibited from practicing counseling (Espina, 1998). (It should be noted that restrictions vary. For example, the state of Colorado "registers" unlicensed therapists who are permitted to practice [J. Scalise, personal communication, January 12, 2000].) A practice act differs from a "title protection act" in that a title act prohibits only the use of that credential (e.g., LPC) as part of what one claims to be his or her job title. For example, a person who lacks the licensure/certification to be a professional counselor cannot identify himself or herself as a professional counselor. Furthermore, practice acts have an important implication for qualifying for third-party payments because they serve to "legitimize" the practice of professional counseling in the eyes of the payer. Finally, it is important to note that a number of states grant "associate" licenses/certificates to persons who are working toward meeting certain designed requirements. The professional only partially meets the requirements for licensure/certification; for example, the professional might have met the educational requirement but might not have satisfied the supervision requirements.

After careful consideration of available demographics, definitions offered by professional organizations, and the defining nature of existing licensure laws, it is reasonable to conclude the following about professional counselors in private practice:

- It is not unusual for private practitioners to align themselves with one or more specialty areas.
- Even though specialty areas differ enough in terms of general aim (e.g., prevention, enhancement, remediation) and in terms of length and content of training to warrant recognition, professional counselors as a group share a common heritage and theoretical foundation that overshadow these differences.
- Although various labels are used by this group of professionals (e.g., mental health counselor), the single most widely used label is *professional counselor*. (Although it is beyond the scope of this chapter, it is the author's opinion that a multiplicity of labels hinders wider recognition of counselors because different labels create a false impression that greater differences exist than actually do exist. Clients and other mental health professionals are confused by the multitude of labels, which obstruct an

understanding and appreciation of LPCs' competencies. Finally, although professional organizations certainly can affect the way in which the LPC designation is perceived by clients and other professionals, licensure laws using the LPC title ultimately define what the title means in a particular jurisdiction.)

- The degree of practice for the private practitioner is the master's degree (i.e., minimum entrance degree). This is reflected in all current licensure requirements and in the membership of professional organizations representing this group of practitioners.

- The most common credential self-reported by counselors that is directly related to private practice, as well as the label most frequently used in jurisdictions to legally regulate private practice, is the LPC. For the remainder of this chapter, the LPC designation is used to refer to professional counselors working in private practice settings.

LPCs' Unique Contribution to Private Practice Work

Even though the involvement of various mental health professions (e.g., clinical psychology, clinical social work) in private practice predates the existence of LPCs, it is important to note that LPCs do not represent simply another "clinical" approach that differs little from earlier established mental health professions. LPCs represent a group of uniquely trained professionals that bring a special combination of qualifications into the private practice arena. Ginter (1996) suggested that LPCs are unique because of three aspects of counseling that come together to define and provide a practice framework for these private practitioners. These three aspects are that "(a) counseling, contextually, represents an *interpersonal medium;* (b) counseling recognizes the importance of both *prevention* and *remediation;* and (c) counseling

relies on a *developmental perspective*" (p. 100, italics in original). Furthermore, the results of a qualitative study conducted by Ginter (1991) support the recognition of these aspects as distinguishing features of LPCs. According to Ginter, of primary importance is that LPCs, as compared to other mental health practitioners, focus "more on developmental issues, normality, wellness, and prevention" (p. 194). It is not surprising to discover that in Ginter's 1991 study it was found that the differences among various mental health professions are perceived to be the cause of training differences. Such differences were alluded to by David K. Brooks, one of the study's participants, who stated,

If you look at the eight areas of CACREP [Council for Accreditation of Counseling and Related Educational Programs], we share a developmental perspective to some extent with . . . psychologists of certain stripes, with social workers of certain persuasions, [and] to some extent with marriage and family therapists. We tend to be fairly well trained in group work . . ., psychologists less univerally so, and marriage and family therapists, I think almost not at all. . . . I think we know more about research than social workers do, and marriage and family therapists, and probably not as much about it as psychologists. . . . I think one thing that makes us unique is the *package of training experience* and the kinds of emphases people find in their training programs that tend to be true to some extent, [and] not true to some extent, of some other disciplines. (p. 194, italics added)

Assessment and Treatment Planning in Private Practice

LPCs are knowledgeable about the *DSM-IV* (American Psychiatric Association, 1994) diagnostic categories and developmentally based approaches to diagnosis and treatment. For example, approaches delineated by Darden, Gazda, and Ginter (1996); Ivey and Ivey (1998); McAuliffe and Eriksen (1999); Myers, Sweeney, and Witmer (2000); and Witmer, Sweeney, and Myers (1998) all have a strong developmental component. Although all of these models are different from one another, there is significant overlap and each model contains elements of what appears in ACA's definition of professional counseling, that is, working with clients by means of "cognitive, affective, behavioral, or systemic intervention strategies that address wellness, personal growth, or career development as well as pathology" (ACA, 1997). The most important feature of these models is that all of them allow LPCs to "meet" clients (during the course of counseling) anywhere the clients may "fall" along a counseling dimension that ranges from "wellness" at one end to "psychopathology" at the other.

Concerning the *DSM-IV,* it is evident that various trends can be isolated by studying the changes that have occurred in the *DSM* from revision to revision (Erk, 1995). For example, when the *DSM-III* was issued, many professionals perceived its content to reflect a postmodern move away from the dominant role still played by psychoanalytic theory in conceptualizing clients' problems. Possibly what was more important, as pointed out by Seligman (1999), was the approach taken by the American Psychiatric Association in forming committees to determine the contents of the new *DSM-III.* According to Seligman, "nonmedical mental professionals" were involved in the development of the *DSM-III*'s contents; this type of professional inclusion continued with the *DSM-IV.* Even though controversy (Ginter, 1989; Hershenson, Power, & Seligman, 1989) always has surrounded the *DSM* in terms of both its content and its use in

professional counseling, as suggested by Seligman (1999), the move to have nonmedical professionals involved in its conception marks a significant change in that the American Psychiatric Association recognizes not only that others (e.g., counselors) are relying on the *DSM* system but also that such professionals have an expertise that can contribute to the *DSM*'s validity and usability.

Seligman (1999) traced changes that have occurred in training programs over time and noted that a growing number of training programs have incorporated the topic of diagnosis to prepare counselors in private practice. According to Seligman, around the early 1990s, 79% of the 146 counselor education programs surveyed reported that instruction in use of the *DSM* was taught. Seligman maintained that it is reasonable to assume that approximately 90% of such programs are teaching the DSM today. Seligman stated, "I am confident that the importance of training in and understanding of diagnosis using the *DSM* will continue to grow and will be viewed as a necessity for all clinicians" (p. 238).

Finally, Seligman (1999) predicted that future changes in the *DSM* probably will

> include a continuing attention to the *impact of physical and medical conditions on emotional functioning,* clarification of the links among those disorders that are triggered by a history of abuse . . ., the addition of new diagnoses that describe depressive symptoms . . ., and a consideration of spectrum diagnoses, encompassing related or overlapping diagnoses. (p. 238, italics added)

Building on Seligman's (1999) predictions, it would be reasonable to assume that LPCs will need to be able to understand the "impact of physical and medical conditions on emotional functioning." Because LPCs sometimes are the "front line" of treatment for many clients (a role that can be predicted to grow), it is necessary for counselors to differentiate a "true" *DSM* disorder from conditions that "mimic" a *DSM* disorder.

Screening for Medical and Neurodevelopmental Disorders

The current state of diagnosis requires the LPC to be alert for patterns of behavior that resemble a psychological disorder but are in fact something else. According to Pollak, Levy, and Breitholtz (1999), several medical disorders are associated with symptoms that can be confused with mental disorders, and in some cases the medical conditions can even coexist with existing mental disorders but in a way that "aggravates" the existing mental disorders. Pollak and colleagues placed this particular diagnostic competency for LPC in perspective when they wrote,

> Changes in behavioral health care delivery have increased the participation and visibility of professional counselors in the intake and treatment planning process. . . . Misdiagnosis of a medical illness as a primary disorder can result in inappropriate expenditure of behavioral health care and result in potentially lethal medical complications (e.g., client with an undetected tumor). Such a diagnostic error may also dramatically increase the risk of ethics complaints and malpractice suits against counselors. . . . Greater appreciation, on the part of the professional counselor, [for] the role of medical and neurodevelopmental influences can significantly enhance an emphatic connection to the client and help to set realistic expectations and goals for intervention. (p. 351)

Pollak and colleagues maintained that LPCs should be able to recognize the presence of the following conditions that can be misidentified as other disorders (the most likely misdiagnoses appear in parentheses): hyperthyroidism (generalized anxiety disorder), hypothyroidism (depressive disorder), temporal lobe epilepsy (schizophrenic or bipolar spectrum illness, dramatic cluster personality disorder), head injury syndrome/post-concussive syndrome (anxiety disorder, mood disorder, dramatic cluster personality disorder), HIV/AIDS dementia (depressive disorder), amphetamine- or cocaine-induced disorder (schizophrenic spectrum illness, delusional disorder), frontal lobe dementia/degeneration (depressive disorder, impulse control disorder), multiple sclerosis (somatoform disorder), sleep apnea (depressive disorder), Asperger's disorder (odd/eccentric cluster personality disorder, schizophrenic disorder), nonverbal learning disability syndrome (anxious-fearful cluster personality disorder, dysthymic disorder, schizophrenic disorder), and attention deficit disorder (bipolar spectrum disorder or passive aggressive personality disorder depending on whether it is predominantly hyperactive-impulsive type or predominantly inattentive type).

Finally, LPCs should be aware of the effects of typical pharmacological treatments. It is not unusual for an LPC to discover that a client seeking counseling has had some type of medication prescribed for the condition or that the LPC's diagnosis warrants consultation and referral for such treatment. For example, an LPC arriving at a diagnosis of attention deficit disorder should inform the client that medications (e.g., Adderall, Ritalin) are available that can mitigate symptoms and should make a referral for medication if the case so warrants. Not only should the LPC refer the client when appropriate, but the LPC also should be able to explain to the client in general terms how medication can serve as an adjunct to counseling. (Of course, a specific detailed description of any prescribed medication resides with the physician who has assessed the medication needs of the client.) Simply stated, the LPC's diagnostic and treatment approach is based on recognizing the whole person. Although not always fully understood by counselors, such an approach has a long tradition in professional counseling since counselors have advocated for working with clients in terms of "mind, body, and spirit" (Burke et al., 1999). Simply stated, pharmacological treatments and psychotherapeutic treatments do not necessarily represent antithetical approaches; rather, they can represent complementary approaches that produce the best results for some clients. The role that pharmacological treatments play in private practice for LPCs was stated poignantly by Nystul (1999): "The mind and body are not separate entities but [rather] an interrelated whole. To understand one, it is essential to have knowledge of the other" (p. 130).

Infusion of a Developmental (Wellness) Perspective Into Diagnosis and Treatment Planning

Over time, the *DSM* used by LPCs has, as indicated by Seligman (1999), moved toward a broader perspective that reflects a trend toward a greater understanding that "illness" is not simply a matter confined to the person. A clear example of this is found in the *DSM*'s Global Assessment of Relational Functioning (GARF) Scale, which provides "an overall judgment of the functioning of a family or other ongoing relationship" (American Psychiatric Association, 1994, p. 758). The GARF Scale reflects a systemic approach to conceptualizing mental dis-

orders. In spite of this *DSM* trend, one should note that, for the most part, the content of the *DSM* pages prior to discussion of the GARF (i.e., 757 pages) does not represent a radical departure from the American Psychiatric Association's prior diagnostic approach to categorizing mental disorders. It is the present author's contention that professional counseling theory can make a unique contribution to diagnosis and treatment planning by complementing what is available through the *DSM*. Two models are briefly discussed to show how LPCs differ from other mental health professionals in the ways in which they can conceptualize client problems.

Ivey and Ivey (1998) developed a system based on reframing *DSM* nomenclature that provides LPCs with the means to use traditional diagnostic language (*DSM*) while simultaneously reconceptualizing that language (reframe) to work with clients from a developmentally based treatment approach. Whereas Ivey and Ivey maintained that there is a basic and inherent discrepancy between the traditional diagnostic and treatment model based on the *DSM* (which fails to move beyond a "medical model") and the position taken by ACA that endorses "a framework based on positive human development" (p. 334), those authors also concluded that "there is no necessary conflict between a developmental and pathological view" (p. 334). By reframing the *DSM* terminology, a developmental assessment and treatment plan can be achieved that pays close attention to environmental and contextual issues.

Reframing the *DSM* in terms of a developmental perspective to understand a client's depression, for example, provides the LPC with a unique means to understand the client; instead of seeing depression as something that resides within the person, depression is seen as "existing in the interaction among the individual's biological and social history, the family, and the cultural context. . . . [The depression is viewed as representing] a logical response to developmental concerns, blocks, or difficulties in one or more of these dimensions" (p. 336). Although a cursory review of Ivey and Ivey's model might lead one to believe that their position is nothing more than an issue of semantics, this is not the case. Ivey and Ivey provided a very detailed means by which the LPC can work with a client developmentally after a *DSM* diagnosis has been made.

Another developmental approach that is used by LPCs to bridge the diagnostic world of the *DSM* and the world of actual treatment is based on the work of George Gazda and colleagues. Darden, Gazda, and Ginter (1996); Ginter (1999); Ginter and Glauser (1999); and others have proposed another system of diagnosis and assessment that is not specifically tied to *DSM* nomenclature but can be used in conjunction with the *DSM*. The model rests on a foundation of developmental theory that recognizes the importance of prevention, remediation, and enhancement of clients' strengths. According to Darden, Gazda, and Ginter (1996), LPCs relying on this approach are using a comprehensive model that is founded on several assumptions about human development:

- There are several well-defined areas of human development: psychosocial, physical-sexual, vocational, cognitive, ego, moral, and affective.
- Coping behaviors that are appropriate to age and stage can be determined from these areas.
- Each area comprises identifiable stages requiring mastery in order to progress from lower to advanced stages.
- Accomplishment of developmental tasks is dependent on mastery of life-skills.

- Generally, certain life-skills are optimally learned within given age ranges.
- Individuals achieve optimal functioning when they attain operational mastery of fundamental life-skills.
- Neurosis and functional psychoses frequently result from failure to develop certain life-skills.
- Instruction and training in life-skills serve a role of preventive mental health when introduced at an appropriate developmental time.
- Counseling, therapy, or life-skills training serves the role of remediation when introduced during a time of emotional or mental disturbance of a functional nature.
- The greater the degree of functional disturbance, the greater is the likelihood that an individual will be suffering from multiple life-skills deficits. (p. 136)

The term *life-skills* should not be associated with a narrow theoretical approach, nor should it be associated with a narrow treatment approach. The term refers to "behaviors that are necessary for effective living" (Brooks, 1984, p. 6). According to Ginter (1999), a life-skills approach

can take the form of short-term intensive skill-building sessions aimed at training specific skills (e.g., assertiveness skills), and [it] can take the form of relatively long-term insight-based types of counseling that are partially aimed at revealing early developmental mishaps/disruptions and dislodging the "developmental logjam" to reinstate developmental growth and, thus, significant personality change. (p. 194)

Based on more than 30 years of work, primarily through the efforts of Gazda, four life-skills areas have been identified. These four areas are briefly defined as follows (Darden, Gazda, & Ginter, 1996):

- *Interpersonal communication/human relations skills (IC/HRS Dimension):* "This dimension includes skills necessary for effective communication (e.g., emotional perspective taking) leading to ease in establishing relationships, small and large group and community membership and participation, and management of interpersonal intimacy." (pp. 136-137)

- *Problem-solving/decision-making skills (PS/DMS Dimension):* "This dimension includes information seeking, assessment and analysis, problem identification, solution implementation and evaluation, goal setting, time management, critical thinking, and conflict resolution" (p. 137). "The term *problem solving* [is used] to denote any task with a definite right solution, whereas . . . the term *decision making* [is] appropriately applied to situations that involve issues with no definite solution." (p. 138)

- *Physical fitness/health maintenance skills (PF/HMS Dimension):* "This dimension includes skills necessary for motor development and coordination, nutritional maintenance, weight control, physical fitness, athletic participation, physiological aspects of sexuality, stress management, and leisure activity selection" (p. 138). This life-skills area is directly tied to the ability to manage stress and anxiety effectively.

- *Identity development/purpose in life skills (ID/PILS Dimension):* "This dimension incorporates the interaction of genetic endowment and feedback from the environment and contains the necessary skills for ongoing development of personal identity and emotional awareness. This includes self-monitoring, maintaining positive self-view, interpersonal intimacy, career direction, manipulation and accommodating to one's environment, clarifying values, making moral choices, sex-role development, making meaning, and certain aspects of sexuality" (p. 138). "Although identity is a continuous theme throughout the life span, with interactions with significant individuals, ethnicity, geographic origins, and vocational development influencing identity, it is essential to realize that developing a sense of identity and purpose in life is idiosyncratic." (p. 139)

A number of assessment tools have been developed to measure these four developmental dimensions for different age groups such as children (Bickham, 1993), adolescents (Darden, Ginter, & Gazda, 1996), and adults (Picklesimer & Miller, 1998; Taylor, 1991). Following a *DSM* diagnosis, the appropriate life-skills measures could be used to isolate specific developmentally related concerns (obtained by identifying "items" on the life-skills measure that were rated low). Finally, it should be emphasized that any LPC working with a client is not himself or herself "free" of the four life-skills dimensions defined here; in fact, the LPC must be aware of his or her own "place" along each of these dimensions. For example, in working with a client diagnosed with an eating disorder, it is essential for the LPC to assess his or her own functioning in terms of physical fitness/health maintenance (e.g., "Do I have unrealistic views concerning my own body image that may adversely affect the way in which I work with certain clients seeking counseling?"). Another example that would pertain to the ID/PILS Dimension is racism. Specifically, much has been written about White racial identity that White LPCs should be aware of to prevent "unconscious" racist views from negatively affecting the counseling process (Robinson & Ginter, 1999; Sue & Sue, 1999).

Case Study: An Illustration

The following case is not intended to provide a verbatim exchange; rather, its intent is to provide a general overview of the most salient factors considered in working with a client in the context of the life-skills model presented heretofore.

Joe W. was a 38-year-old male referred by his pastor for counseling. Joe had married only once and had stayed married to the same person, Ann, for 20 years until Ann informed Joe of her intention to seek a divorce. Recently, the client had taken a complete physical, and based on the doctor's summary, Joe was in "good" physical health but was told he needed to "lose about 20 pounds." Three children were born during the marriage (one female [18 years of age] and two males [13 and 10 years of age]). Joe reported that his wife became depressed after enrolling in a university to "finish her degree" but that, over time, as graduation approached, she "was less depressed and much more angry—angry all the time." A week after graduation, she asked for a divorce. After the divorce, the client discovered that his wife had been seeing another male, whom she later married. During the clinical interview, Joe reported, "I still love Ann, and my religious beliefs mean I am still married to Ann in God's eyes." Almost immediately after Ann requested a divorce, the client found himself "shattered." After the divorce itself, the client reported experiencing "a big drop in energy" and an apparent reduction in his ability to maintain an interest in what was taking place around him. Finally, the client self-reported that even though he always had been dissatisfied with his job as a computer data entry operator (receiving relatively low yearly evaluations and seeing others promoted while he remained at the same level), his performance had worsened to the point where his boss suggested that he "may be fired." When asked to summarize what he had been experiencing, the client said, "It's like the floor beneath me fell away and I just kept falling."

The clinical interview provided a constellation of depressive symptoms. Some of the most prevalent symptoms were the following:

- Joe reported diminished interest and pleasure in most activities comprising the typical day. (The client self-reported this but also stated that coworkers and family members have made the same observation about his behavior.)

- Joe indicated a gain of 20 pounds since the divorce.

- Joe reported that during some nights he could not sleep, whereas during other nights he found it very difficult to wake up in the morning; on a few occasions, he had "called in sick."

- Joe reported a loss of energy to the point where he would sit long periods at home "without moving."

- Joe indicated that he procrastinated about making decisions and found it very difficult to concentrate ("Bills are piling up; I keep getting calls about past dues").

After all relevant information was considered, the diagnosis of depression (major depressive disorder, single episode) was made and the LPC established a treatment plan with the client. Part of the treatment plan involved client education—diagnosis, prognosis, options, duration, and potential side effects of treatments (Depression Guideline Panel, 1993a, 1993b). During this phase, specific information was presented (e.g., "For depression, recovery is the rule," "There are several options for treatment that are effective, which are . . .," "The goal of counseling is symptom remission") (Depressive Guideline Panel, 1993c, pp. 9-10). In this particular case, because of the severity of the depression, a combined treatment was recommended to the client, that is, individual counseling coupled with medication. After the client agreed, the LPC consulted with a psychiatrist and then referred the client for medication and monitoring of the medication.

Based on the life-skills model, the following treatment plan/approach was developed/used by the LPC. (The treatment plan was kept flexible and was modified as needed; e.g., relationship issues became a topic of concern for the client toward the end of counseling when the client stated an interest in dating a coworker.) The four life-skills dimensions are listed next in conjunction with some of the most important points of focus during the course of counseling.

ID/PILS Dimension. During the initial stages, the LPC focused on identifying self-defeating statements (e.g., "I am worthless—just a piece of shit!") that contributed to the depression. Once identified, the LPC instructed the client in ways to self-monitor and maintain a more positive and accurate self-view. In the area of environmental changes (personal and work identity), the LPC explored with the client ways in which he might manipulate his personal and work environments to reduce feelings of depression and stress. (For example, the client reported that Ann "calls me at odd hours at home and at the office; I jump when I hear the phone ring." Following each call, the client reported a "bout of depression." These occurrences were reframed as an opportunity to establish "control" in Joe's life ["to stop the free-fall that pretty much defines who you are now"]. The decision was reached to purchase an answering machine for home and to have the secretary at work screen his calls. These solutions created a sense of control that prevented the bouts of depression from occurring.) Following the focus on negative self-talk and after assessing the client's effectiveness at using skills to significantly reduce such negative self-talk, the LPC returned to the topic of job dissatisfaction to determine its role in the client's current concerns. This led to identifying work values that did not match with the client's current job.

PF/HMS Dimension. Medication prescribed and monitored by the psychiatrist contributed to changes related to this dimension. To augment changes due to medication, the LPC taught relaxation and imagery skills to confront negative affects. Finally, basic nutritional maintenance was discussed, as were weight control and exercise. The client decided that he would consult with his family physician for recommendations about diet and exercise. A plan was developed with the physician, shared with the LPC, and followed by the client, who later claimed both "better health and better coping with stress" as a result.

PS/DMS Dimension. In this case, the client was given the Self-Directed Search (Holland, Powell, & Fritzsche, 1994) to complete. The decision was made because the "work values" identified by the client in earlier sessions did not match the characteristics of his current job and because the client decided that "it was time to move on and find a better job; there's got to be one for me." A series of career-related tasks were established tied to the results of the Self-Directed Search; for example, for the purpose of information gathering, the client contacted a friend employed in a career similar to the one he was interested in pursuing. During the course of counseling, it was discovered that the client had difficulties in completing these tasks due to poor time management skills, so the LPC initiated time management training. Throughout this stage of counseling, emphasis was placed on enhancing problem-solving and decision-making skills because the life-skills assessment completed by the client earlier had indicated that the client had a low skill level in problem solving and decision making. During the course of counseling, these particular skills were developed and reported by the client to have generalized in other areas of his life ("Before I started counseling, I couldn't decide anything; it's funny that it's so easy now").

IC/HRS Dimension. During the latter stages of counseling, as a result of "meeting someone," the client's attention turned toward dating, and the LPC followed this lead. During earlier sessions, the client had achieved insights concerning several "oppressive" beliefs held about women that the client concluded contributed to the divorce ("I always tried to fix everything before I really knew what needed fixing"). These beliefs were "revisited" during this stage in counseling (identity issues also resurfaced at this time, i.e., ID/PILS), and the focus became skill building in terms of how to communicate and interact with others, especially in situations involving intimacy and a high level of self-disclosure.

In summary, the client was "approached" as many private practitioners would approach him during the intake and diagnosis phase, but the LPC departed from these other practitioners in how a tentative treatment plan was formulated and modified over time. Simply stated, the treatment plan was based on a developmental approach to case conceptualization. The advantage of developmentally based counseling is that it rests on a solid foundation of theory, and because it relies on a "developmen-tal perspective," the LPC is able to "speak" to the client using a *normalizing* language rather than a *pathologizing* language.

Special Topics Related to Private Practice

There are many special topics of interest to LPCs including standards of care for various disorders, assessment of treatment outcome and effectiveness data, application of business skills to a private practice setting, necessary elements of record keeping, networking and consultation, and knowledge of Internet use and Web sites to gain access to useful practice information. Examples of the latter include the Web sites of ACA (www.counseling.org) and Humanistic Psychology (www.ahpweb.org). A survey found that 78.2% of professional counselors have computers for their practices and that 59.4% of those professional counselors report having established Internet connections ("Practice Trends," 1999). These topics and others have been significantly affected by the emergence of managed care organizations, which for many clients represent a key component of service delivery. The remainder of this chapter focuses on managed care and the effect that it is having on LPCs.

Over a number of years, the proliferation of managed care has created a number of variations and terms exemplifying the growth that has occurred in this area. Professional counselors are confronted with employee assistance programs (EAPs), health maintenance organizations (HMOs), independent provider organizations (IPOs), and managed mental health care organizations (MMHCOs) (Ginter, 1999). "Managed care provides many challenges for practitioners—declining incomes . . ., limits as to choice of providers, and, of course, the low number of visits being covered" (Ginter, 1999, pp. 197-198). In part because of managed care, but also because of the natural progression of any profession, greater accountability is a key issue in the practice of professional counseling. This issue of accountability can be tied to many of the special topics already mentioned.

Lawless, Ginter, and Kelly (1999) reported the findings of a qualitative study based on in-depth interviews. Participants represented a wide cross section of professionals who were involved with managed care. The professional roles represented were managed care employee, managed care publication publisher, private practitioner (member of a group practice), professional counseling association leader, counselor educator, and managed care consultant. Based on these interviews, Lawless and colleagues concluded that LPCs should possess requisite knowledge of the following: diagnostic categories of the *DSM*, existing standards of practice for different clinical problems (e.g., "Emerging Standards of Care for the Diagnosis and Treatment of Panic Disorder" [Beamish, Granello, Granello, McSteen, & Stone, 1997]), managed care terms and language, variables related to client satisfaction with services, appropriate means to receive reimbursement for services, means to ensure that services are available for the LPC's clients during one's absence (e.g., vacation), and balancing release of information to managed care organizations against confidentiality of information. Lawless and colleagues (1999) also identified requisite skills that included writing treatment plans, record keeping that met professional standards and the expectations of managed care organizations, brief-focused and solution-focused treatment

skills, collection of treatment data to provide evidence of effectiveness, basic accounting procedures, ability to explain one's treatment philosophy to clients and managed care organizations, ability to work with other service providers, and ability to interact with managed care personnel in an efficient and cooperative manner (p. 64).

Of all the areas listed by Lawless and colleagues (1999), the skill that shows the greatest variability and that potentially places an LPC in a vulnerable position is record keeping. LPCs simply do not receive enough training in this practice area. According to Scalise (2000), perhaps the most neglected area of ethical practice is record keeping. Furthermore, Scalise indicated that the significance of maintaining good client records often is appreciated and fully understood only when some sort of "crisis" situation occurs. Scalise cited examples of frequent problems related to LPCs' record keeping:

- A client emergency situation occurs when the LPC is unavailable and a colleague is unable to "find" or, if found, "decipher" the record's contents.
- A malpractice lawsuit is lodged against the LPC that requires the LPC to rely on his or her records. Difficulties arise when the client record provides little to counter the client's claim, even though the LPC provided "good" care.
- A managed care organization wants reimbursement for services that it claims were not provided and the records are incomplete, even though the LPC recalls rendering the treatment.

Records should be considered a top priority. In addition to protecting the LPC in cases such as those cited, the client record provides support for treatments rendered (i.e., that treatments provided were both necessary and tied to standards of care). Scalise (2000) maintained that, at a minimum, records should indicate that pertinent client information was obtained during intake (e.g., education level; family, employment, medical, and inpatient/outpatient treatment histories); also, a copy of the client's insurance identification card should be made. In addition to this client information, the record should note any client concerns about treatment and that necessary information was provided concerning what happens if appointments are missed (whether charged or not), emergency number to contact the LPC, collection policies used by the LPC, and whether the client is charged for phone calls to the LPC between scheduled sessions.

Also, according to Scalise (2000), the record should contain evidence that other issues were discussed such as limits of confidentiality as well as the reasons why the client is seeking treatment and the expressed goals that the client wants to achieve. Relevant client quotes should be incorporated, as should details about any homework assignments given as well as follow-up notes concerning such assignments. Scalise also believes that the initial treatment plan should be outlined and that actual interventions used during the course of treatment should be recorded. Finally, pages should be dated and numbered. Clearly, it has become necessary for LPCs to keep as detailed notes as possible.

The Future of Private Practice: A Prediction

The future of professional counseling looks bright. To a large extent because of managed care, the entire structure of private practice has been reconsidered. Master's-level LPCs have been able to secure a prominent position in the new practice environment because of their competency. Simply stated, the degree of practice is the master's for LPCs, and although an argument has revolved around the claim that a doctorate (e.g., a Ph.D. in clinical psychology) better equips a professional to deliver effective treatment, available evidence does not support this claim. Preparation and training are the deciding factors for competency, and properly trained master's-level LPCs are equal providers of services. Interestingly, some professional groups are at a disadvantage because of the fee differential that makes master's-level professional counselors more attractive to third-party payers (e.g., managed care organizations). Above all else, today's LPC has the distinct advantage of being able to provide a wider range of services because the focus of training is not restricted to remediation but rather also involves prevention and even enhancement.

Finally, although LPCs have achieved many professional gains over the past two decades, it would be foolish to believe that all "professional battles" have been fought and won. The field of counseling is dynamic and fluid in nature, and so are the needs of clients and various systems (e.g., families, schools, government agencies, courts, managed care organizations) that affect clients' welfare. Advocating for clients and advocating for the profession itself must continue to play a central role in professional counseling if LPCs are to remain in the private practice arena.

References

American Counseling Association. (1997, October). *Definition of professional counseling*. Alexandria, VA: ACA

Governing Council. (Definition adopted during Governing Council meeting)

American Counseling Association. (1999, September). *State licensure chart* [Online]. Available: www.counseling. org/resources/licensure_summary.htm

American Mental Health Counselors Association. (1998, January-February). AMHCA definition of mental health counseling. *The Advocate*, p. 2. (American Mental Health Counselors Association)

American Psychiatric Association. (1994). *Diagnostic and statistical manual of mental disorders* (4th ed.). Washington, DC: Author.

Beamish, P. M., Granello, D. H., Granello, P. F., McSteen, P. B., & Stone, D. A. (1997). Emerging standards of care for the diagnosis and treatment of panic disorder. *Journal of Mental Health Counseling, 19,* 99-113.

Bickham, P. J. (1993). *An examination of the psychometric properties of the Life-Skills Inventory–Children's Form.* Unpublished doctoral dissertation, University of Georgia.

Brooks, D. K., Jr. (1984). *A life-skills taxonomy: Defining elements of effective functioning through the use of the Delphi technique.* Unpublished doctoral dissertation, University of Georgia.

Burke, M. T., Hackney, H., Hudson, P., Miranti, J., Watts, G. A., & Epp, L. (1999). Spirituality, religion, and CACREP curriculum standards. *Journal of Counseling and Development, 77,* 251-258.

Darden, C. A., Gazda, G. M., & Ginter, E. J. (1996). Life-skills and mental health counseling. *Journal of Mental Health Counseling, 18,* 134-141.

Darden, C. A., Ginter, E. J., & Gazda, G. M. (1996). Life-Skills Development Scale—Adolescent Form: The theoretical and therapeutic relevance of life-skills. *Journal of Mental Health Counseling, 18,* 142-163.

Depression Guideline Panel. (1993a). *Depression in primary care: Vol. 1. Detection and diagnosis.* Rockville, MD: U.S. Department of Health and Human Services.

Depression Guideline Panel. (1993b). *Depression in primary care: Vol. 2. Treatment of major depression.* Rockville, MD: U.S. Department of Health and Human Services.

Depression Guideline Panel. (1993c). *Depression in primary care: Detection, diagnosis, and treatment* (reference guide for clinicians, No. 5). Rockville, MD: U.S. Department of Health and Human Services.

Erk, R. R. (1995). The conundrum of attention deficit disorder. *Journal of Mental Health Counseling, 17,* 131-145.

Espina, M. R. (1998). *Licensure chart.* Alexandria, VA: American Counseling Association.

Ginter, E. J. (1989). If you meet Moses/Jesus/Mohammed/ Buddha (or associate editors of theory) on the road, kill them! *Journal of Mental Health Counseling, 11,* 335-344.

Ginter, E. J. (1991). Mental health counselor preparation: Experts' opinions. *Journal of Mental Health Counseling, 13,* 187-203.

Ginter, E. J. (1996). Three pillars of mental health counseling: Watch in what you step. *Journal of Mental Health Counseling, 18,* 99-107.

Ginter, E. J. (1999). David K. Brooks' contribution to the developmentally based life-skills approach. *Journal of Mental Health Counseling, 21,* 191-202.

Ginter, E. J., & Glauser, A. S. (1999). *Life-skills for the university and beyond.* Dubuque, IA: Kendall/Hunt.

Hershenson, D. B., Power, P. W., & Seligman, L. (1989). Counseling theory as a projective test. *Journal of Mental Health Counseling, 11,* 273-279.

Holland, J. L., Powell, A. B., & Fritzsche, B. A. (1994). *Self-Directed Search: Professional user's guide.* Odessa, FL: Psychological Assessment Resources.

Ivey, A. E., & Ivey, M. B. (1998). Reframing DSM-IV: Positive strategies from developmental counseling and therapy. *Journal of Counseling and Development, 76,* 334-350.

Lawless, L. L., Ginter, E. J., & Kelly, K. R. (1999). Managed care: What mental health counselors need to know. *Journal of Mental Health Counseling, 21,* 50-65.

McAuliffe, G. J., & Eriksen, K. P. (1999). Toward a constructivist and developmental identity for the counseling profession: The context-phase-stage-style model. *Journal of Counseling and Development, 77,* 267-280.

Myers, J. E., Sweeney, T. J., & Witmer, J. M. (2000). Counseling for wellness: A holistic model for treatment planning. *Journal of Counseling and Development, 78,* 251-266.

Nystul, M. S. (1999). *Introduction to counseling: An art and science perspective.* Boston: Allyn & Bacon.

Picklesimer, B. K., & Miller, T. K. (1998). Life-Skills Development Inventory—College Form: An assessment measure. *Journal of College Student Development, 39,* 100-110.

Pollak, J., Levy, S., & Breitholtz, T. (1999). Screening for medical and neurodevelopmental disorders for the professional counselor. *Journal of Counseling and Development, 77,* 350-358.

Practice trends. (1999, September). *Practice Strategies: A Business Guide for Behavioral Care Providers,* pp. 1, 8. (American Association for Marriage and Family Therapy)

Robinson, T. L., & Ginter, E. J. (Eds.). (1999). [Special issue]. Racism healing its effects. *Journal of Counseling and Development, 77*(1).

Scalise, J. J. (2000). The ethical practice of marriage and family therapy. In A. M. Horne (Ed.), *Family counseling and therapy* (3rd ed., pp. 565-596). Itasca, IL: F. E. Peacock.

Seligman, L. (1999). Twenty years of diagnosis and the DSM. *Journal of Mental Health Counseling, 21,* 229-239.

Smith, H. B. (1999). Managed care: A survey of counselor educators and counselor practitioners. *Journal of Mental Health Counseling, 21,* 270-284.

Sue, D. W., & Sue, D. (1999). *Counseling the culturally different: Theory and practice.* New York: John Wiley.

Taylor, P. A. (1991). *Evidence of the validity of the Life-Skills Inventory—Adult Form.* Unpublished doctoral dissertation, University of Georgia.

Witmer, J. M., Sweeney, T. J., & Myers, J. E. (1998). *The wheel of wellness.* Model developed by the authors, Greensboro, NC.

CHAPTER TWENTY-TWO

Counseling in Medical Settings

SANDRA B. BARKER

Medical settings present a broad array of facilities, programs, and opportunities for counselors. Hospitals provide inpatient services that serve specialized populations (e.g., children, older adults) or treat specific illnesses (e.g., cancer, mental illness, brain injuries). Typically, general hospitals provide inpatient services for patients with a wide range of medical needs. They may provide behavioral health/psychiatric services. Teaching hospitals, associated with some colleges and universities, include not only direct patient care but also research and the teaching of medical students and residents specializing in a variety of medical fields. Most teaching hospitals also have affiliated specialty centers, where research and clinical care are emphasized.

With the entry of managed care into the medical arena, most hospitals have had to adjust by decreasing lengths of stay and serving only those who are acutely ill. To provide the continuity of care needed to treat many illnesses and disorders, hospitals and community agencies offer partial hospitalization programs (PHPs), intensive outpatient programs, residential programs, and outpatient clinics to which patients are referred based on their level of need when they either no longer meet, or do not meet, the acute criteria for hospital admission. PHPs provide intensive treatment to patients who do not need 24-hour nursing care but who have significant impairment due to psychiatric, emotional, behavioral, and/or addictive disorders requiring structured treatment for stabilization (Block & Lefkovitz, 1994). Such programs serve as alternatives to and prevention of hospitalization, and they may provide short-term crisis stabilization or more long-term treatment for individuals at high risk for hospitalization because of serious and chronic mental disorders. For example, a person may be discharged from an inpatient behavioral health service and admitted to a PHP because he or she no longer is suicidal but is continuing to experience auditory or visual hallucinations while medication is being adjusted and closely monitored.

Intensive outpatient programs serve more stable individuals who still need structured treatment programs. The person with alcohol dependence who has been detoxified in a more structured setting for 2 or 3 days may be referred to intensive outpatient treatment to begin work on recovery issues 3 or 4 days a week. Residential treatment programs offer supervised housing in addition to treatment programs for specific problems (e.g., substance abuse) and often have no medical staff on the premises. Outpatient clinics provide the least restrictive environment of care, with appointments made on a frequency based on individuals' needs.

In addition to these medical settings are more long-term facilities focusing on specialized treatment such as rehabilitation following spinal cord injuries or care of those with terminal or progressive illnesses (e.g., Alzheimer's disease, cancer). For terminally ill patients, hospice programs often are available to provide a team approach for providing comfort for dying patients and their families. The hospice philosophy includes not only keeping patients as free from pain as possible but also providing emotional support and creating an environment in which dying can take place in a person's familiar environment such as home (DeSpelder & Strickland, 1996).

Assessment and Treatment Planning

Working in Multidisciplinary Teams

In most inpatient medical settings, assessment and treatment planning are conducted by multidisciplinary teams, each of which is composed of a physician, nurses, and other health professionals relevant to the type of care being provided. For example, in psychiatric or behavior health services, the team might be composed of a psychiatrist, a psychiatric nurse, a social worker, a counselor, an occupational therapist, and a recreational therapist. Each team member participates in patient assessment and brings specialized information to contribute to the planning of a patient's treatment. A physician will conduct a medical assessment, a nurse will conduct a nursing assessment, and a social worker and/or counselor will conduct a psychosocial assessment. The psychosocial assessment usually includes the patient's family history, educational and occupational history, social history, and prior mental health history. These assessments usually are completed within 24 hours of the patient's admission to the hospital. The patient's diagnosis typically is determined by the physician, often with input from the other team members.

The treatment plan usually is developed, and is reviewed periodically, by the multidisciplinary team in inpatient and PHP settings. Each member of the team provides recommendations based on his or her assessment and expertise. The patient and family are included in this process whenever possible. The treatment plan includes a list of patient problems, goals with target dates, behavioral objectives, interventions and outcomes, and discharge plans. Treatment interventions on psychiatric or behavioral health services may include medication management, individual counseling, family counseling, psychoeducational groups, group therapy, occupational therapy, recreational therapy, and specialized groups (e.g., substance abuse). Depending on the hospital service, the counselor may be responsible for individual counseling, family counseling, psychoeducational groups, group therapy, or specialized groups. Although case management often is performed by social workers, the counselor also may be responsible for this aspect including discharge planning and working with community agencies to ensure continuity of patient care.

Assessment and treatment planning in PHPs is similarly performed by multidisciplinary teams. Programs designed to treat a lower level of illness severity, such as intensive outpatient programs, may offer little or no physician and nursing services. Assessment and treatment planning may be conducted by the counselor in these and other outpatient medical settings. A comprehensive assessment or initial clinical evaluation should include the presenting problem, history of the present problem (including evidence of personal distress and impaired functioning), current medications and allergies, medical history, past history of mental health problems (including treatment and outcomes), family history, social history, history of alcohol and drug use (including any treatment and outcomes), a mental status examination, and diagnosis.

Diagnosis and the DSM-IV

Counselors working in medical settings must be familiar with the *DSM-IV* (*Diagnostic and Statistical Manual of Mental Disorders* [Ameri-

can Psychiatric Association, 1994]). The *DSM-IV* is the standard manual used for diagnosing, communicating about, and studying mental disorders. Based on a multitude of research and input from experts around the world, the *DSM-IV* is used across settings (e.g., inpatient, outpatient, residential) and disciplines (e.g., psychiatrists, other physicians, nurses, social workers, occupational and recreational therapists, social workers, counselors). The disorders in the *DSM-IV* are classified into 16 major diagnostic groups such as anxiety disorders, mood disorders, and substance-related disorders. The criteria for diagnosis and a unique five-digit diagnostic code are provided for each disorder within each of the 16 major groups. Counselors working in medical settings should be trained in using the *DSM-IV* and formulating diagnoses.

Familiarity With Medical Terminology and Pharmacotherapies

In referring to the consumers of counseling, most counseling programs and texts use the term *clients* rather than *patients* in a move away from the medical model. However, in most medical settings, particularly inpatient and PHP settings, counselors will find consumers referred to as patients. Counselors might find this medical terminology uncomfortable initially and might find themselves referring to *outpatient clients* and *hospitalized patients*. Perhaps the important thought to keep in mind is to use the least confusing term for the counseling consumer and for effectively communicating with other professionals involved in the person's care.

It also is important for counselors working in medical settings to be familiar with standard medical terminology and pharmacotherapies related to the client groups with whom they are working. For example, counselors working with hospitalized psychiatric patients should be familiar with common medications used to treat depression, bipolar disorders, anxiety disorders, and psychotic disorders. Likewise, those working with patients hospitalized for substance abuse should be familiar with medications commonly used for detoxification and maintenance. Knowing the expected action of medications and the side effects can help counselors to distinguish between medication-induced symptoms and other patient problems. Knowing standard medical terminology and abbreviations (e.g., bid, tid, IV, STD) increases the effectiveness of communication between counselors and other health professionals and increases the understanding of patient medical records.

Health Care Accreditation Issues Affecting Counselors

Programs in medical settings are accredited by the Joint Commission on the Accreditation of Healthcare Organizations (www.jcaho.org), the leading evaluator of health care quality in the United States. JCAHO accredits nearly 18,000 health care organizations and programs including the following:

- General acute care hospitals and behavioral health, children's, rehabilitation, and other specialty hospitals
- Home care agencies and organizations
- Nursing homes, subacute care and dementia facilities, and other long-term care facilities
- Behavioral, chemical dependency, and mental retardation/developmental disabilities services

- Ambulatory health care providers including rehabilitation centers, group practices, and student health care centers
- Laboratories
- Health care networks, including managed care providers

Just as the Council for Accreditation of Counseling and Related Educational Programs (CACREP) develops standards that counseling programs must meet so as to be accredited, JCAHO develops standards that health care organizations must meet. Once accredited, organizations are reviewed periodically to maintain their accreditation. Standards also are reviewed and updated periodically by JCAHO.

In addition to accreditation by JCAHO, health care programs are licensed by state agencies. Behavioral health programs are licensed by the state department that oversees health, mental health, and substance abuse services. These state departments also have standards that health care organizations must meet so as to be licensed.

Different standards are established for different types of facilities and programs; standards for inpatient services differ from those for residential programs, which differ from those for outpatient programs, and so forth. Regardless of program type, there usually are standards for documentation, treatment planning, and safety. For example, most standards require that patient records include documentation of patient/family participation in the treatment planning process and patient response to participation in treatment groups. It is essential for counselors and all professional staff to be aware of the JCAHO and state licensing standards that govern their work settings.

Individual Counseling

With shorter lengths of hospital stays, individual counseling in most inpatient settings must be focused and brief if it occurs at all. The pace on most inpatient services is very quick, with patients admitted and discharged or transferred in a matter of days on many services. Depending on the reason for hospitalization, the focus in individual counseling may be on assisting spinal cord injury patients in the initial adjustment to their injuries, helping suspected victims of domestic violence identify ways in which to increase their safety, or helping those with substance abuse problems to recognize the consequences of their use. Therefore, brief counseling and crisis management strategies are important skills for counselors to acquire. Because of time constraints, in most inpatient settings it is not feasible to focus on long-term issues such as resolving child abuse issues, relationship issues, or psychological trauma. Counselors working in inpatient settings often initiate therapeutic work that will be continued in less acute settings, but rarely do they see the long-term outcomes of treatments.

More in-depth work can be accomplished in individual counseling when the length of stay in treatment programs is longer, for example, intensive outpatient programs in which clients may attend three to five times a week (4 to 6 hours a day), residential programs in which individuals live in supervised settings for months at a time, and more traditional outpatient programs. Whereas some of these less acute programs target specific clinical populations such as persons with spinal cord injuries, burns, anxiety disorders, or substance abuse disorders, others treat a broader population of persons with a variety of behavioral and physical health problems. The focus of individual counseling obviously will reflect the needs of the population being served.

Group Counseling

There are at least three basic types of groups that counselors may conduct in the medical setting: psychoeducational groups, support groups, and therapy groups. Psychoeducational groups are structured groups that focus on increasing patient knowledge and/or skills in a particular area. Such groups may address establishing a basic understanding of posttraumatic stress disorder (PTSD), understanding the risks of substance abuse during pregnancy, increasing assertiveness skills, accessing community resources (e.g., wheelchair transportation), and the like. These groups often incorporate activities and videos followed by discussions.

Counselors also may lead support groups relevant to the treatment program populations. The purpose of these types of groups is to provide emotional and social support as opposed to therapy. These groups may be for the patients and/or the patients' families/significant others. Examples of patient support groups include nicotine cessation support groups, breast cancer survivors support groups, and child abuse survivors support groups. Family support groups may be provided for parents with terminally ill children, family members/significant others of those with spinal cord injuries, or family members/significant others of those with AIDS. Counselors typically encourage the sharing of experiences, information, and support among the group members.

Like support groups, therapy groups are offered for appropriate treatment program populations. Counselors may have therapy groups composed of individuals with similar diagnoses (e.g., depression, PTSD) or individuals sharing common concerns (e.g., men's group). Therapy groups aim to help individuals function at a higher level and are either open-ended (groups that allow people to join and leave at different times) or closed (groups of individuals who begin and end the group together over a specified period of time). A substance abuse group in an inpatient setting may be open-ended to accommodate any patient admitted with substance abuse issues. An intensive outpatient program may have a closed group of female victims of domestic violence who meet for 8 consecutive weeks.

Specialized Interventions

Because of the conditions of individuals treated in medical settings, there are some specialized interventions that can help the counselor to meet patients' needs. Two of the more recognized interventions, addictions and substance abuse counseling and grief counseling, are presented in this section, followed by a more recently developed approach, eye movement desensitization and reprocessing (EMDR) for PTSD.

Addictions and Substance Abuse Counseling

It is beneficial for counselors working in medical settings to have some training in addictions and substance abuse. The Center on Addiction and Substance Abuse (1993) at Columbia University reported that 25% to 40% of general hospital beds are occupied by patients being treated for alcohol-related complications. They also estimated that $1 in every $5 spent by Medicaid on hospital care and 1 in every 5 Medicaid hospital days are for treatment related to consequences of substance abuse. Substance abuse is associated with more than 60 medical problems including pancreatic diseases, red blood cell diseases, and significant trauma (Barker, Knisely, & Dawson, 1999; Fox, Merrill, Chang, & Califano, 1995). So, it is highly likely that counselors working in medical settings will be dealing with individuals with substance abuse issues. Whereas counselors working in substance abuse treatment settings will require more extensive training and, quite likely, certification or licensing as substance abuse or addictions counselors, all counselors should have at least (a) a basic knowledge of addiction (e.g., theories of addiction, physical and psychosocial effects of substance abuse, coexistence of substance abuse with medical and psychological disorders, diagnostic criteria), (b) knowledge and skills to screen clients for addiction, and (c) knowledge of community treatment programs and support groups for referral purposes.

According to the Substance Abuse and Mental Health Services Administration (1998) publication, *Addiction Counseling Competencies*, the following competencies are deemed necessary for screening individuals for substance abuse:

1. Establish rapport including management of crisis situation and determination of need for additional professional assistance.

2. Gather data systematically from the client and other available collateral sources using screening instruments and other methods that are sensitive to age, developmental level, culture, and gender. At a minimum, data should include current and historic substance use, health, mental health, and substance-related treatment history; mental status; and current, social, environmental, and economic constraints.

3. Screen for psychoactive substance toxicity, intoxication, and withdrawal symptoms; aggression or danger to others; potential for self-inflicted harm or suicide; and coexisting mental health problems.

4. Assist the client in identifying the impact of substance use on his or her current life problems and the effects of continued harmful use or abuse.

5. Determine the client's readiness for treatment and change as well as the needs of others involved in the current situation.

6. Review the treatment options that are appropriate for the client's needs, characteristics, goals, and financial resources.

7. Apply accepted criteria for diagnosis of substance use disorders in making treatment recommendations.

8. Construct with client and appropriate others an initial action plan based on client needs, preferences, and resources available.

9. Based on initial action plan, take specific steps to initiate an admission or [a] referral and ensure follow-through. (pp. 120-121)

Counselors can acquire these competencies through university training programs and/or professional development programs.

Grief Counseling

With approximately 80% of terminal care in the United States provided by nursing homes and hospitals, grief counseling is another specialized intervention appropriate for counselors working in medical settings (DeSpelder & Strickland, 1996). Whether working in specialty settings that treat individuals with life-threatening or terminal illnesses (e.g., emergency rooms, trauma centers, cancer centers, AIDS clinics, hospice programs) or in more general medical settings, counselors are very likely to encounter patients and families dealing with issues related to death and dying. Although death is a natural process, how one deals with it is very individualized and influenced by one's culture and beliefs. Counselors must determine the most appropriate approach for their particular clients at particular times.

The medical setting has its *own culture* that affects how dying patients are treated and may complicate issues related to death. Whereas some institutions place as much importance on meeting the emotional needs of patients as on taking care of their physical needs, others avoid acknowledging and discussing death altogether, and this can result in patients and families feeling isolated (DeSpelder & Strickland, 1996).

In her popular book, *On Death and Dying,* Elisabeth Kübler-Ross outlined five stages that she observed in dying patients: denial and isolation, anger, bargaining, depression, and acceptance (Kübler-Ross, 1969). In later investigating why some people with terminal illnesses denied less and were able to move through all five stages prior to death, whereas others became stuck in the process, she found that those able to move through the stages were willing to (a) talk about their memories, thoughts, and experiences in-depth with significant others; (b) communicate with others on an equal level while sharing at a "real" level; and (c) accept the bad with the good (Kübler-Ross, 1975). Although the five stages of grief now are considered phases that individuals may experience in any order, Kübler-Ross's contributions continue to provide a useful framework for counselors working with dying individuals. Most universities offer courses on death and dying and grief counseling.

Eye Movement Desensitization and Reprocessing

Because many medical settings are specialized (i.e., serving persons with specific types of illnesses or disorders), it is important for counselors in those settings to be familiar with interventions developed and found effective with given populations. A recent example is the use of EMDR for the treatment of trauma symptoms. Developed by Francine Shapiro, EMDR is a complex eight-stage approach designed to be incorporated into an individual's treatment plan (Shapiro, 1995). EMDR is capable of rapid desensitization of traumatic events and cognitive restructuring leading to a reduction in traumatic symptoms (e.g., flashbacks, nightmares, intrusive thoughts) in a brief period of time. It has been used in both inpatient and outpatient settings and includes components of cognitive, behavioral, psychodynamic, and client-centered therapies. EMDR has been incorporated into these and other theoretical orientations such as Adlerian counseling (Barker & Hawes, 1999; Manfield, 1998).

As in deciding to implement any counseling approach, counselors need to assess clients for appropriateness. In the case of EMDR, counselors are cautioned to use this method only with client problems for which they already have been trained (e.g., depression, PTSD) and only with clients who have the internal resources

necessary to cope with intense emotions that may arise during EMDR. Clients who are psychotic, have active substance abuse problems, or have dissociative disorders are not considered appropriate for the standard application of EMDR.

A comprehensive clinical evaluation of the client is a critical first step, and this evaluation should include assessment of client appropriateness for EMDR. If EMDR is deemed appropriate, then the counselor prepares the client by educating the client about trauma reactions and EMDR, addressing client safety issues, building a therapeutic relationship, and discussing client goals and expectations of treatment. For clients lacking coping strategies to deal with intense affect, focus is placed on enhancing inner resources and further addressing other safety issues.

If the client is appropriate for EMDR, then the counselor assesses the trauma, eliciting from the client a representative image and associated negative self-belief, emotions, and physical sensations, along with a distress level assessed using Wolpe's (1991) Subjective Units of Disturbance Scale (SUDS), an 11-point visual analog scale ranging from 0 (*no disturbance or neutral*) to 10 (*the highest disturbance one can possibly imagine*). A positive belief the client would like to associate with the traumatic image then is identified along with a rating of how true the belief currently feels on the Validity of Cognitions (VOC) scale, a 7-point visual analog scale ranging from 1 (*totally false*) to 7 (*totally true*) (Shapiro, 1995). Desensitization then is undertaken by having the individual hold in mind the image of a traumatic event along with the related negative self-beliefs, emotions, and physical sensations while attending to an external left-right stimulus that may be eye movements, audio tones, or hand taps. Once the SUDS level for the traumatic memory drops to 0 to 1, the positive belief is paired with the traumatic image and the eye movements are used to strengthen the positive belief until a VOC of 6 to 7 is achieved. The client then is debriefed and subsequently reevaluated on the next visit.

Based on independent reviews of empirical research, EMDR is one of only three approaches, along with flooding and stress inoculation therapy, recognized as likely to be efficacious in treating PTSD (Chambless et al., 1998). Currently, there is more research supporting the effectiveness of EMDR than for any other treatment for PTSD (Shapiro, 1998). Such findings are important for counselors working with trauma survivors. EMDR training is provided by the EMDR Institute in Pacific Grove, California. Some universities also offer EMDR Institute-approved training.

Counseling Related to Multicultural Issues in Medical Settings

As in all settings in which counseling takes place, multicultural issues are important considerations in medical settings. Even in medical settings that specialize in treating a particular problem, the client population often is quite heterogeneous in terms of gender, cultural background, religious beliefs, and other cultural variables. It is important for counselors to be aware of multicultural issues related to their settings. For example, counselors should be aware that spiritual or religious beliefs may affect the treatment that one is willing to undergo (e.g., the Jehovah's Witness patient who refuses blood transfusions, the patient who signs a document not to be resuscitated if he or she experiences cardiac arrest). Abortion and ending life

support systems are examples of other decisions strongly influenced by religious or spiritual beliefs.

One's culture affects not only treatment-related decisions but also the patient's view of medical care, caregivers, and death. Whereas some patients may place total trust in physicians, others may view them with suspicion and fear. Such views likely will influence how compliant a patient is with medications and other treatment plans. Depending on how one's culture views death, a person may accept death as an expected and natural continuation of the life cycle or fear death as a judgment time to atone for one's sins. Thus, the Hindu patient who believes in the transmigration of the soul to another body at death may react very differently to the news of terminal illness from how an Islamic patient who has grave concerns about facing his or her final judgment may react (DeSpelder & Strickland, 1996).

Some specialty services offered in medical settings are gender specific by nature of the types of services provided. Obstetrics and gynecological services obviously are provided for females, whereas prostate cancer screening and treatment are provided for males. Counselors working in these settings will find it helpful to be knowledgeable about gender-specific issues as they relate to conditions treated by these services (e.g., unwanted pregnancies, fertility, sterility, sexual dysfunction, impotence).

Cultural issues also influence how persons view diseases and accidents. Some may believe that illness or injuries are the result of their bad deeds (i.e., punishments for past transgressions), others may believe that they are a result of weakness (i.e., if they had been smarter or stronger, then they would not be afflicted), and still others may believe that accidents can happen to good people and that it is more important to focus on recovery (DeSpelder & Strickland, 1996).

Network Interventions

Program Planning and Evaluation

Counselors responsible for program planning will find it helpful to use a model to serve as a framework and provide direction for program development. The action research model is one such model that has been found effective in mental health settings (Barker & Barker, 1994). This model represents a collaborative approach between those planning a program and those involved in or affected by the program. The model also incorporates evaluation into the program planning and development process, providing feedback from program staff and participants on which to base program revisions as well as outcome data to determine program effectiveness. The six stages of the action research model are as follows: diagnosis, data gathering, providing assessment feedback, data discussion and planning for action, action, and evaluation.

The diagnosis phase involves the initial assessment of issues to be addressed by the program. This assessment may involve observing, interviewing, or surveying key people to determine preliminary objectives for the program. An agency counselor interested in starting an intensive outpatient program for individuals with chemical dependency issues might initially talk with other counselors in the agency and colleagues in the community to get a general sense of the need for such a program.

The data gathering (or needs assessment) phase involves a more comprehensive assess-ment to determine what currently exists in terms of programs and services and to compare the current state to what programs and services are perceived to be needed. This assessment may involve current agency staff and clients or outside agencies and groups. Continuing with our agency counselor example, the counselor might develop a survey to be sent to administrators of other mental health facilities to determine the availability and client use of existing intensive outpatient programs for chemical dependency. A survey or telephone interview also may be conducted with a sample of area addictions counselors to determine their perceptions of need for such a program and the likelihood of referrals if such a program existed.

The third phase consists of providing feedback of the assessment results to appropriate groups, which may include those assessed as well as the administrators responsible for approving and funding the program. Our counselor likely would provide a summary of results to other agency staff who participated in the assessment, to those who would be affected by the new program, and to the decision makers who approve new programs.

The data discussion and planning for action phase involves all interested parties in a discussion of results and needs identified in the assessment. The group then prioritizes needs and develops an action plan to address targeted needs. In our example, the counselor and agency group might discuss the assessment results and determine that there is a need for an intensive outpatient chemical dependency group, but at a satellite location in a suburban setting. They might further agree to develop this program and to pilot test it over a 3-month period.

The action phase involves the implementation of the plans developed in the previous phase. Our counselor and agency staff would implement the intensive outpatient chemical dependency group.

The final phase is evaluation, which then becomes the initial phase as the process of planning and evaluation continues. Once the implementation has been completed, data again are gathered to determine whether the program was accepted, if it achieved its intended objectives, and what refinements are needed to improve the program. The information then provides for additional diagnosis, and the action research model continues. In our example, the counselor again would assess those affected by the program, including clients, to determine the strengths and weaknesses of the program. This information would be provided as feedback to the same group of interested agency staff and administrators so that decisions regarding program continuation and revision could be discussed. The process of program planning and evaluation using the action research model, therefore, is a continuous cycle of assessment, feedback, planning, and action.

Referring for Continuity of Care

Continuity of care refers to individuals receiving the appropriate level of treatment throughout the course of their illnesses. It is important that individuals are treated in the least restrictive environments appropriate for their conditions. Depending on their conditions, patients discharged from inpatient settings might need intensive follow-up treatment (e.g., a PHP) or less intensive treatment (e.g., weekly outpatient therapy). Similarly, there are times when outpatient treatment is not adequate and individuals need more intensive and structured treatment settings. Therefore, it is important

for counselors to be aware of resources that are more or less intense than those offered in their settings and when it is appropriate to refer to other resources. When counselors are working with uninsured client populations, they need to be aware of community resources that are available on a sliding scale or that charge no fees.

For continuity of care to be achieved effectively, treatment information must be shared among all agencies providing care. Treatment facilities have written policies governing the release of client information to comply with federal and state laws and to protect the confidentiality of clients. All health care providers must follow these policies. To release treatment information to other agencies or providers, counselor musts obtain signed release of information forms from clients. Client confidentiality may be broken in certain cases, for example, the mandatory requirement to report suspected cases of child abuse. This further emphasizes the need for counselors to be aware of their settings' policies for releasing client information as well as relevant federal and state statutes.

Outreach/Marketing

Most medical settings have personnel specifically responsible for outreach and marketing. The counselors' role might simply be to provide descriptions of services offered and numbers of clients served for the marketing staff. However, counselors often speak to public and professional audiences on counseling topics in which they have expertise. They also may write newsletter articles for civic, religious, or professional groups, and they may publish studies or concept articles in professional journals. All of these activities can serve a marketing function in letting others know of counselors' interests and expertise and of the programs available in their work settings.

Counselors may work in medical settings that have outreach teams whose primary focus is to go out into the community and serve clients not able to be adequately treated in their facilities. These teams may target the chronically mentally ill and make home visits, or they may target the homeless with substance abuse or mental health problems and search for clients on urban streets. Other programs may involve telephone outreach, that is, contacting clients to determine whether follow-up appointments are being kept, medication is being taken appropriately, and so forth.

Teaching and Research in Academic Medical Settings

Counselors working in academic medical settings likely will be involved in research and teaching as well as in direct care. Students pursuing their doctor of medicine degrees and then completing residency requirements in their chosen specializations rotate throughout academic medical settings. Whereas faculty physicians are responsible for the supervision of medical students and residents, all professional staff usually are expected to be involved in teaching activities. Teaching may be formal (e.g., lectures, seminars) or informal (e.g., one-to-one discussions between the counselor and student). Most academic medical centers accept international student populations, making awareness of multicultural issues extremely important.

Many academic medical centers are extensively involved in research funded by national, regional, or local funding sources. Counselors

may be hired with grant funds to assist in research or demonstration projects that may involve them in the grant-writing process, delivering interventions, collecting and analyzing data, and/or report writing. Depending on their interest and levels of expertise, counselors also may initiate grant proposals to secure funding for projects of interest to them.

Prevention and Wellness

Most medical settings have prevention and wellness programs. These may range from free or low-cost screenings in the community to prevention programs aimed at specific populations. Counselors may be involved in mental health screenings for depression, substance abuse, or other disorders. These screenings may be held at public schools, libraries, grocery stores, or hospitals in hopes of increasing community awareness of mental health disorders and the availability of treatment. These activities also serve as important marketing strategies.

Counselors also may be involved with developing prevention materials for specific populations such as school-age children. In addition, they may serve as expert resources for other disciplines to refer clients at risk for developing mental health problems. One example is the counselor who receives referrals from primary care physicians of patients perceived to be drinking heavily. The counselor would conduct clinical evaluations to determine whether the referred individuals have alcohol abuse or alcohol dependency problems and recommend appropriate treatment.

Case Study

J is a 27-year-old, single Caucasian male who was referred by emergency room staff to a hospital-based counselor for outpatient treatment of post-trauma symptoms. He was seen in individual counseling once a week for 12 sessions and then every 3 weeks for 3 sessions with a final session after 4 weeks. A cognitive-behavioral approach, including the use of EMDR, was used in counseling.

J was shot at work in a convenience store by two men attempting to rob the store late at night. He was admitted to the hospital with gunshot wounds to his right leg and thigh. Following surgery to remove the bullets and install a steel rod in his fractured femur, he was discharged to his home. For several weeks, J stayed at his parents' home, too fearful to return to the house he shared with a girlfriend. When he finally returned home, he barricaded himself in the house, rearranged furniture so that he never would have his back to a window, stacked his bicycle and other objects against the doors, and refused to venture outside. He was too fearful to sleep in his bedroom in the back of the house, so he slept in the living room where he could see the front and back doors and could hear if anyone was trying to break in. He also grew a beard to try to disguise his identity in case the person who shot him would try to find him.

When seen initially, J complained of frequent intrusive thoughts, flashbacks, and nightmares related to the robbery. He could not sleep at night, was easily startled, and experienced panic when he thought he heard noises outside. He tried to avoid thinking about the robbery but was triggered frequently by his surroundings, particularly loud noises and television

shows. When J appeared at the arraignment of the individual accused of shooting him, he was so afraid and anxious that he pointed to the wrong person. Therefore, the accused was set free, and as a result, J experienced increased fear.

J was raised in an intact family with two older sisters. He always was very close to his mother, who remains a strong and emotional support for him. His father was a strict disciplinarian who did not readily display affection. J lives in the same city as do his parents, and prior to his accident, he visited them frequently. He has a 12th-grade education and a consistent work history, working primarily as an auto mechanic. He wanted to try a change in occupations and began working as a convenience store night clerk 3 months prior to the shooting. He has no history of mental health treatment and no history of alcohol or drug abuse. He has no significant medical history with the exception of visible tremors in his hands that he indicates have been a problem for years. He has never been married and has no children. He and his current girlfriend have had a 9-year relationship.

Although denying suicidal ideation, J did admit to homicidal thoughts toward the man who shot him. He had no immediate plan or intent to act on those ideas.

A comprehensive clinical evaluation was completed during the first counseling session, leading to a diagnosis of PTSD. J agreed to weekly individual counseling sessions with the treatment goal of resolving his symptoms of traumatic stress. He was educated about PTSD and EMDR and agreed to participate in this treatment approach. Because of the intensity of his symptoms and severe impairment in his daily functioning, he also was referred to a psychiatrist for consideration of appropriate medications while he participates in counseling. He initially was prescribed the benzodiazepine Klonopin (1 milligram twice a day) and the antidepressant Paxil (20 milligrams once a day). The Klonopin dosage was adjusted to 0.5 milligram twice a day when J experienced negative side effects of drowsiness, excessive sleeping, and grogginess.

Early sessions with J focused on helping him to develop ways of coping with stress and intense emotions. EMDR was used to facilitate this process, and J responded well. Because J had been blind in one eye since childhood, he preferred to listen to alternating left-right audiotones delivered through stereo headphones during EMDR instead of using eye movements. Once J had the necessary coping strategies established, EMDR was used to focus on the traumatic memory of the shooting. In processing the shooting incident, J brought up the image of lying on the floor after being shot, the associated negative belief ("I am vulnerable"), and the associated feelings of fear and body disturbance in his head and heart while he listened to the audiotones. Using the SUDS (Wolpe, 1991), a visual analog scale ranging from 0 (*no disturbance or neutral*) to 10 (*highest disturbance one can imagine*), J initially rated his disturbance level for the incident at an 8.0. Following processing over three sessions, his SUDS level fell to a 1.5. Accompanying this lower level of disturbance, J reported being able to move back into his bedroom and sleeping well. He no longer was experiencing flashbacks, and he reported feeling more safe at home and able to go outside of his house. He no longer felt the need to disguise his identity, and he shaved his beard.

In spite of J's improvements, he still was afraid to go anywhere except to his appointments at the hospital, driven there by his father. He had made an attempt to go out with a friend shortly after the shooting, but he experienced a panic attack and had to be driven back home. EMDR was used to process the memory of J's panic attack, which he rated as an 8.0 on the SUDS. The image he held in mind during processing was of his body shaking and feeling panic, the associated negative belief was "I'm going to die," and the related emotion was fear accompanied by overall body tension. J again responded well to EMDR, and his SUDS level dropped to a 1.0 over the next two sessions. Although he continued to report the absence of flashbacks and nightmares as well as increased feelings of safety at home, he was not able to get out of the house, except for medical appointments and counseling, for several weeks.

During this time, J had to undergo a second surgery on his leg. Waiting at the hospital to be prepared for surgery, J became increasingly anxious and left prior to the surgery. His surgery was rescheduled, and two counseling sessions focused on helping him to prepare cognitively and emotionally for surgery. Cognitive-behavioral strategies and EMDR were used, and the client underwent successful surgery, with his leg pain greatly improved.

The client was continuing to do well, with termination of counseling planned, when J experienced an upsetting event involving a strange car pulling into his driveway several times one night. Although the event did not trigger intrusive symptoms related to the shooting, J became fearful and unable to sleep. EMDR was used to process this event, and J reported a reduction in his disturbance level from a SUDS of 5.0 to one of 1.0. The client experienced no further symptoms of PTSD, and counseling was terminated. A follow-up telephone call 6 weeks later revealed that the client's improvements were maintained, he no longer was taking any psychiatric medication, he was driving himself places without problems, and he was preparing to return to work.

In counseling this client with PTSD, EMDR was incorporated into a treatment plan to enhance the client's ability to tolerate intense emotion, desensitize him to traumatic memories of the shooting, and prepare him for further surgery. This approach was effective in resolving his symptoms of PTSD and in enhancing his positive beliefs about himself and his future.

Perspectives on the Future

Probably the single most pervasive influence on health care treatment today is the emergence of managed care. Managed health care is a growing insurance industry that dictates what treatment, how much treatment, and at what level treatment will be reimbursed by an individual's insurance company. Managed care companies rose in response to the escalating cost of health care in the United States. These companies claim to manage costs for employers while providing for quality health care. The impact on health care providers and facilities has been dramatic. As insurance companies mandate the level of acuity (severity of illness) required for inpatient reimbursement, hospital lengths of stay have been cut drastically. Requirements by insurers for preauthorization for treatment and reauthorizations for continued treatment have created a large increase in paperwork for health

care providers and a need for utilization reviewers whose primary task is to keep up with the requirements of insurers and provide the necessary information to obtain authorizations for care. Adding to the difficulty of meeting the differing requirements of various insurance companies are the numerous "carve-outs" for mental health treatment. Many insurers subcontract the management of their mental health benefits to separate companies. So, although one insurer might manage a person's health benefits, a different company might be responsible for managing the person's mental health benefits. To add to the confusion, there is little uniformity in paperwork required, information requested for authorizations, and reimbursement between companies.

We now are seeing case and capitated rates for mental health treatment, and this trend is likely to continue. Under a case rate, a facility, clinic, or health care provider is paid a prearranged sum for providing a specified service for a single episode of care for each person referred under a given policy. Thus, the provider is paid the same amount to treat a person with dissociative identity disorder (a very complex problem) as to treat a person with a simple phobia (a far less complex problem). Providers are paid retroactively based on the number of people served. Capitated rates are lump sums paid prospectively to cover a defined population, with a specified amount for each person in that population, regardless of how many persons are actually treated. Certainly, this system benefits the insurer, which can budget costs much more easily.

The impact on professional counselors is similar to that on other health care professionals—lower reimbursement rates, increased information demands, limitations on the number of providers accepted onto managed care panels, and increased time spent communicating with insurance companies. These realities are important for counselors to consider as they make career choices. Some medical settings hire counselors on a traditional salary basis, others expect counselors to see the volume of patients necessary to essentially pay their own salaries, and still others use some combination of the two. Thus, a counselor's salary may be based on the amount of reimbursement received for counseling services provided.

As the managed care environment forces competition among hospitals and clinics, the same forces trickle down to individual providers. Successful counselors in the future will be those who can carve out specialty practices that are needed and show the effectiveness of their work. Professional counselors must be able to document the effectiveness of the counseling they provide. Some counselors, or their clinics or hospitals, send outcome surveys to clients on termination. Other counselors administer standardized instruments at the initiation and termination of counseling to show improvement in their clients' functioning.

Medical settings will be exciting and challenging places for professional counselors to work in the future. Medical settings, particularly academic medical centers and specialty hospitals and clinics, often are on the cutting edge of technological advancements and preventive medical treatments leading to longer life spans as well as biomedical research into the causes and cures of many serious diseases.

The growing geriatric population resulting from Americans living longer poses challenges for behavioral and physical health providers. Professional counselors with knowledge and expertise in issues affecting aging adults likely will be in demand. Issues such as workplace adjustments for adults working longer, career opportunities for aging adults, retirement adjustments, and adult children taking care of aging parents are just a few of the issues that counselors will increasingly face.

A need for increased numbers of counselors in nursing home settings is another likely result of the growing geriatric population. Counselors will need to be skilled in working with older adults with varying degrees of dementia, depression, and other mental disorders along with declining physical health. They will need to be proficient in providing education and support to family members of nursing home residents. Grief counseling will be important to assist patients, families, other nursing home residents, and staff in coping with the loss of patients. Counselors also will need to continuously monitor their own emotional health and plan for ways in which to obtain professional support for themselves such as participating in peer consultation groups. Those counselors demonstrating experience and skills in counseling interventions that are effective with the elderly might find increasing opportunities to train other mental health providers, educate caretakers, and provide direct counseling services.

As medical treatments continue to advance, professional counselors in medical settings will have more opportunity to assist clients and their families in adjusting to life with transplanted organs or biomedically engineered body parts and to screen clients for their appropriateness for organ transplants and other advanced surgeries. Genetics research continues to uncover evidence of genetic contributions to personality, addictions, and major physical and mental illnesses. Such research will lead to new understandings, emerging medications, and new therapeutic strategies to treat a variety of problems. Clients will be increasingly more informed and misinformed about their problems and treatments as more and more individuals use Internet resources to seek information. It will be very important for professional counselors to be well informed regarding the client problems and disorders they treat as well as the effective medications and therapeutic treatments available. Innovative treatments, such as animal-assisted therapy and alternative medicine, also are important for counselors to understand. For example, a research base is growing that documents the mental and physical health benefits of interacting with companion animals (Barker, 1999; Barker & Dawson, 1998), and alternative medicine is growing in popularity as people turn to herbal remedies, traditional Native American and Chinese healing methods, acupuncture, meditation, and other alternatives to traditional medicine (Gordon, 1996).

Because the Internet provides immediate access to the latest medical and health information from around the world, counselors must become proficient in Internet use. Using the Internet, counselors can immediately access the latest information from the National Institute of Health and all of its agencies, the World Health Organization, and major medical libraries around the world and also can learn about the latest treatment developments and much, much more. The Internet also enables counselors to receive consultation from experts around the world through e-mail and professional discussion list services.

In summary, medical settings provide counselors with the opportunity to work in exciting and ever-changing environments. Counselors can choose to work in intense, fast-paced inpatient units or in longer term outpatient programs. They can specialize with particular client groups or work with more heterogeneous populations. Medical settings also provide counselors with the chance to work closely with health care professionals representing other disciplines, enabling them to learn from others while sharing their counseling perspectives.

References

American Psychiatric Association. (1994). *Diagnostic and statistical manual of mental disorders* (4th ed.). Washington, DC: Author.

Barker, S. B. (1999, February). Therapeutic aspects of the human-companion animal interaction. *Psychiatric Times*, pp. 43-45.

Barker, S. B., & Barker, R. T. (1994). Managing change in an interdisciplinary inpatient unit: An action research approach. *Journal of Mental Health Administration, 21*, 80-91.

Barker, S. B., & Dawson, K. S. (1998). The effect of animal-assisted therapy on anxiety levels of hospitalized psychiatry patients. *Psychiatric Services, 49*, 797-801.

Barker, S. B., & Hawes, E. C. (1999). Eye movement desensitization and reprocessing in Adlerian therapy. *Individual Psychology, 55*, 146-161.

Barker, S. B., Knisely, J. S., & Dawson, K. S. (1999). The evaluation of a consultation service for delivery of substance abuse services in a hospital setting. *Journal of Addictive Diseases, 18*, 73-82.

Block, B. M., & Lefkovitz, P. M. (1994). *Standards and guidelines for partial hospitalization adult programs* (2nd ed.). Alexandria, VA: American Association for Partial Hospitalization.

Center on Addiction and Substance Abuse. (1993). *The cost of substance abuse to America's health care system: Report 1. Medicaid hospital costs.* New York: Columbia University.

Chambless, D. L., Baker, M. J., Baucom, D. H., Beutler, L. E., Calhoun, K. S., Crits-Christoph, P., Daiuto, A., DeRubeis, R., Detweiler, J., Haaga, D. A. F., Bennett-Johnson, S., McCurry, S., Mueser, K. T., Pope, K. S., Sanderson, W. C., Shoham, V., Strickle, T., Williams,

D. A., & Woody, S. R. (1998). Update on empirically validated therapies (Part 2). *The Clinical Psychologist, 51*, 3-16.

DeSpelder, L. A., & Strickland, A. L. (1996). *The last dance: Encountering death and dying* (4th ed.). Mountain View, CA: Mayfield.

Fox, K., Merrill, J. C., Chang, H. H., & Califano, J. A. (1995). Estimating the costs of substance abuse to the Medicaid hospital care program. *American Journal of Public Health, 85*, 48-54.

Gordon, J. S. (1996). *Manifesto for a new medicine.* Reading, MA: Addison-Wesley.

Kübler-Ross, E. (1969). *On death and dying.* New York: Macmillan.

Kübler-Ross, E. (1975). *Death: The final stage of growth.* Englewood Cliffs, NJ: Prentice Hall.

Manfield, P. (1998). *Extending EMDR: A casebook of innovative applications.* New York: Norton.

Shapiro, F. (1995). *Eye movement desensitization and reprocessing: Basic principles, protocols, and procedures.* New York: Guilford.

Shapiro, F. (1998). Eye movement desensitization and reprocessing (EMDR): Historical context, recent research, and future directions. In L. Vandecreek, S. Knapp, & T. L. Jackson (Eds.), *Innovations in clinical practice: Vol. 16. A source book* (pp. 143-162). Sarasota, FL: Professional Resource Press.

Substance Abuse and Mental Health Services Administration. (1998). *Addiction counseling competencies: The knowledge, skills, and attitudes of professional practice* (Technical Assistance Publication Series, No. 21). Rockville, MD: Author.

Wolpe, J. (1991). *The practice of behavior therapy* (4th ed.). New York: Pergamon.

PART IV

Counselor Education
and Supervision

CHAPTER TWENTY-THREE

Counselor Education

THOMAS W. HOSIE

HARRIET L. GLOSOFF

The counseling profession has its roots deeply embedded in disciplines and movements such as those of vocational guidance, psychology, psychological testing, the early mental hygiene movement, and other social reform movements. These roots have come together in a variety of ways over the past century in response to the demands made by the industrialization and urbanization of the United States to create the counseling profession of today (Glosoff & Rockwell, 1997). Counseling, as a profession, looks quite different now from how it did nearly 50 years ago when the American Personnel and Guidance Association (APGA), now called the American Counseling Association (ACA), was formed. "Like a kaleidoscope, the form, emphasis, and brightness of various aspects of counseling have changed as society changes" (p. 4). The counseling profession has grown in size, in the types of services provided under its auspices, and in the types of clientele served by its professional members (Hollis, 1997). These changes have influenced the way in which counselors are educated. A review of these changes is beyond the scope of this chapter. The reader is referred to Sweeney's chapter in this volume (Chapter 1) and to Glosoff and Rockwell (1997) for a more detailed history of the counseling profession.

This chapter examines the credentialing of counselor education programs. The following areas are addressed:

- Terms associated with the training of professional counselors
- Selected federal legislation most directly related to the development of training standards

- A brief historical overview of the development of these standards
- A review of current accreditation standards for master's- and doctoral-level counselor education programs
- Mentoring in counselor education programs
- Counselor employment roles and functions
- Continuing education of professional counselors
- Emphases and trends in counselor education
- Perspectives on the future of counselor education

Credentialing of Counselors and Counselor Education Programs

The term *credentialing* is a coined word representing a variety of activities related to the establishment of professional training standards and regulations for practice (Bradley, 1991). It is important to distinguish between the credentialing of training programs and that of individuals. In brief, the credentials most typically associated with the practice of professional counselors include *licensure* and *certification*. Licensure is the process authorized by state legislation that regulates professions. Typically, when people refer to professional counselor licensure laws, they mean the regulation of both the practice of counseling and the use of related titles such as *professional counselor* and *professional mental health counselor*. States with such laws set forth a specific scope of practice for professional counselors and require counselors to be licensed or to meet criteria for exemption of licensing noted in those laws so as to engage in specified counseling activities. There are, however, licensing laws that only dictate who may identify themselves as *licensed counselors* or use other counseling-related titles but do not regulate the activities of people who are not licensed. These laws typi-

cally are referred to as *title acts*. Sweeney (1991) pointed out that it is essential to examine specific state laws and their accompanying regulations to determine the implications for practice.

Certification is one of the more confusing credentialing terms. It refers to the process of recognizing the competence of practitioners of a profession by officially authorizing them to use the title adopted by the profession. Certification can be awarded by federal or state agencies or state legislatures (e.g., title acts) or their designees (e.g., state departments of education, state departments of mental health). Also, professional associations (e.g., the National Board for Certified Counselors [NBCC]) can award nonstatutory certification. In most instances, noncertified individuals are not restricted in providing the services of certified individuals. In the case of state certification requirements for employment in public schools, however, individuals must be certified to hold school counseling positions. By comparison, certification by a professional organization is awarded to inform the public of those who meet the qualifications to attain the certification. Many state departments of education recently have changed from using the term *certified* to using the term *licensed* for public school teachers, counselors, and administrators. Such licensure requirements apply only to those seeking public school positions, and except for that restriction, this type of licensure is the same as certification, which involves meeting the qualifications to hold a particular title. The reader may refer to Collison's chapter in this volume (Chapter 3) for more specific information about individual credentialing.

The credentialing term most closely associated with graduate-level counselor education programs is *accreditation*. Simply defined, accreditation is the recognition and acceptance of a formal academic or training program through the approval of a professional organization on a national, regional, or state level. Accreditation now is discussed in further detail.

Promoting academic quality and informing the public of quality education programs typically is achieved through the development of training standards and the oversight of these standards by accrediting agencies. Hoyt (1962, cited in Hoyt, 1991), speaking in support of accreditation, stated,

> Accreditation as a concept in American education has consisted of decisions and judgments institutions and institutional members make regarding one another. Properly conducted, it is a valuable means of institutional self-improvement, of protecting the public from unsound, unfair, and dangerous practices, and of assuring the potential student of quality education. It allows those possessing the highest technical skills in particular educational areas to judge the degree to which quality educational opportunities in those areas are present in institutions applying for accreditation status. It is an indispensable part of American education. (p. 73)

Accreditation agencies establish specific standards or criteria that programs and institutions must meet to become accredited. Accreditation by professional groups is a voluntary process that usually involves self- and peer assessment or review. There are two types of accreditation. One is awarded by regional and national councils to entire entities such as state and private universities. The second type, specialized accreditation, is granted to specific programs within institutions such as graduate programs in counselor education (Hollis, 1997). Specialized accreditation is granted more often

through professional association credentialing groups than through governmental agencies. However, the departments of education in some states (e.g., Illinois, Iowa, Michigan, Minnesota, New York, Pennsylvania) accredit school counseling education programs. Programs seeking specialized accreditation must meet criteria established by accreditation bodies. As already noted, specialized accrediting bodies do not provide accreditation to entire academic departments. If an academic department has more than one counseling-related program, then each must be evaluated separately (Hollis, 2000).

Federal Legislation

During the past 50 years, there have been many pieces of federal legislation enacted that directly or indirectly influenced how counselors in the United States are educated. Following is a brief discussion of three of these that we believe have had the most direct impact on the *development* of training standards for professional counselors.

The Vocational Rehabilitation Act of 1954 (VRA) was a revision of earlier laws and mandated the need for counselors who specialized in assisting people with disabilities. The VRA specifically allocated funds for the training of such counselors at the master's-degree level and did *not* require that these professionals have doctoral degrees in psychology. This was a critical turn in the preparation of counselors and the later creation of the Council on Rehabilitation Education (CORE).

The National Defense Education Act of 1958 (NDEA) was passed in response to the Soviet Union's successful space program (e.g., the launching of *Sputnik* in 1957). The primary goal of the NDEA was to identify young people with scientific and mathematical talent and to encourage them to prepare themselves to go on to college and subsequently enter scientific professions. Title V of the NDEA provided grants to schools to hire counselors, whereas Title V-D authorized contracts with institutions of higher education to establish and improve training programs to produce qualified counselors to work in school settings. Approximately $20 million initially was allocated for the training of school counselors. Although the initial emphasis was on secondary schools, the NDEA was extended to include elementary school counseling in 1964 and, for a brief time later, community college counseling. By 1967, more than 24,000 counselors were trained through NDEA funding in excess of $58 million (Glosoff & Rockwell, 1997). Although the NDEA established master's-level Guidance and Counseling Institutes to train professionals to help guide bright children into fields such as math, science, and engineering, these NDEA-funded counselor education programs focused on training counselors in other domains of counseling as well (e.g., pre-college guidance and counseling). Some counselors believe that the NDEA has had a greater impact on counselor education than has any other single catalyst.

Finally, the third law that greatly changed the face of the counseling profession was the Community Mental Health Centers Act of 1963. This act mandated the creation of more than 2,000 mental health centers to provide direct counseling services to people in specified catchment areas across the country. In addition, the act directed that staff at these mental health centers provide outreach to people living in their catchment areas. The act also opened the employment arenas for counselors outside

of educational settings (Glosoff & Rockwell, 1997).

As noted previously, there have been *many* other federal laws that influenced both the provision of counseling services and the training of counselors. However, it is beyond the scope of this chapter to review all of these. The reader interested in the effects of legislation on counseling may consult Glosoff (2001).

Historical Overview

In addition to federal legislation, there have been several organizations that have influenced the credentialing of training programs for individuals who plan to provide counseling or psychotherapy. Some organizations—the American Psychological Association (APA), the National Association of Social Workers (NASW), the American Association of Pastoral Counselors, and the American Association for Marriage and Family Therapy (AAMFT), among others—have standards related to the training of professionals who may provide counseling services. However, there are only two organizations that accredit graduate education programs specifically designed for professional counselors. Following is an historical overview of these two: the Council for Accreditation of Counseling and Related Educational Programs (CACREP) and CORE.

In 1960, two divisions of the ACA—the Association for Counselor Education and Supervision (ACES) and the American School Counselors Association (ASCA)—began a joint undertaking to develop standards for the preparation of master's-level counselors. Altekruse and Wittmer (1991) noted that more than 2,500 practicing counselors and 700 counselor educators and supervisors participated in studies conducted by ACES and ASCA over a 5-year period (1958 to 1963). The results of these studies led to the creation of the following sets of guidelines for training between 1964 and 1972: "Standards for Counselor Education in the Preparation of Secondary School Counselors," "Standards for Preparation of Elementary School Counselors," "Guidelines for Graduate Programs in Student Personnel Work in Higher Education," and "Entry Preparation of Counselors and Other Personnel-Service Specialists" (Glosoff & Rockwell, 1997). By 1979, these guidelines were merged into one document: "Standards for Entry Preparation of Counselors and Other Personnel-Service Specialists."

Accreditation of graduate programs training master's-level counselors to work in environments other than school settings began during the early 1970s. CORE was established as a not-for-profit specialized accrediting body in 1972. It is comprised of representatives from the following professional organizations: the American Rehabilitation Counseling Association (a division of ACA), the National Council on Rehabilitation Education, the National Rehabilitation Counseling Association, the Council of State Administrators of Vocational Rehabilitation, and the National Council of State Agencies for the Blind. By 1981, CORE had granted full accreditation to 65 training programs and preliminary accreditation to 10 master's-level rehabilitation counselor preparation programs (Sweeney, 1995).

In 1981, ACA passed a resolution to formally oversee the work of the ACES committee on accreditation. This led to the creation of CACREP as an accrediting body sponsored by, but separate from, ACA. CACREP now accredits doctoral degree programs in counselor education and supervision as well as master's de-

gree counseling programs. The reader is referred to Sweeney's and Myers and Sweeney's chapters in this volume (Chapters 1 and 3, respectively) for further information on the history of counseling accreditation.

CACREP and CORE Accreditation Standards

CACREP and CORE provide specific criteria related to both formal coursework and supervised practice that have strongly influenced, and continue to shape, the experiences of master's and doctoral students in counselor education departments. Presented are the general requirements for CACREP and CORE accreditation. In addition to these general requirements, CACREP has specific program standards for program areas such as community counseling and school counseling. Both CACREP and CORE regularly review their standards (every 7 years and every 7 to 10 years, respectively) and make revisions based on extensive feedback from educators, supervisors, administrators, students, and practitioners. The following accreditation information is based on the 1994 CACREP standards (CACREP, 1994) and the 1997 CORE standards (CORE, 1997) that were in place at the time of this writing. As of June 2000, CACREP had approved but not published its new 2001 standards. We cautiously believe that the general requirements presented in this chapter will be representative of the 2001 standards. The reader, however, might find some differences between this presentation and the published 2001 standards and is encouraged to contact CACREP for the most current standards. The standards are on the CACREP Web page (www.counseling.org/cacrep/main.htm).

As noted previously, CACREP and CORE are two organizations that offer specialized accreditation for programs in counselor education departments or units within higher education institutions. This type of accreditation provides a means to ensure accountability and quality control for training programs. Both CACREP and CORE have obtained national recognition and acceptance as specialized accrediting agencies from the Council for Higher Education Accreditation (CHEA). CHEA, comprised of colleges and universities as well as national, regional, and specialized accreditation groups, is a national policy center and clearinghouse for the entire education community. CHEA recognition provides notification to the public that CACREP and CORE standards and procedures have been assessed by a larger outside body that recognizes their commitment to education quality. This commitment is further demonstrated by CACREP and CORE reliance on extensive input from educators, practitioners in the field, and the public at large when determining criteria for evaluation on accreditation standards. Both groups require that the institutions in which programs are located have institutional accreditation before applying for specialized accreditation.

CACREP Standards

CACREP accredits specific master's-level program areas in the counseling profession. The program areas included in the 1994 CACREP standards were community counseling, community counseling with a specialization in career counseling, community counseling with a specialization in gerontological counseling, marriage and family counseling/therapy, mental health counseling, school coun-

seling, and student affairs practice in higher education programs that contain both professional practice and college counseling emphases. All CACREP-accredited programs, regardless of program areas, share a common core of knowledge. The common core curriculum provides a foundation for students to develop more specialized knowledge. According to the 1994 CACREP standards, this core curriculum must include coursework in eight areas: *human growth and development* (theories of individual and family development, theories of learning and personality development, normal and abnormal human behavior); *social and cultural foundations* (multicultural and pluralist trends; attitudes and behavior based on factors such as age, race, religious preference, physical disability, sexual orientation, ethnicity and culture, family patterns, gender, socioeconomic status, and intellectual ability; counseling strategies with diverse populations); *helping relationships* (counseling and consultation theories including individual and systems perspectives, basic interviewing, assessment, and counseling skills; counselor or consultant and client or consultee characteristics and behaviors that influence helping processes); *group work* (principles of group dynamics; group leadership styles and approaches; theories of group counseling; group counseling methods; approaches used in other types of group work, including task groups, prevention groups, supports groups, and therapy groups); *career and lifestyle development* (career development theories and decision-making models; career, educational, and labor market information resources; career development program planning, organization, implementation, administration, and evaluation; career and educational placement, follow-up, and evaluation; assessment instruments and techniques; computer-based career development applications and strategies; career counseling processes, techniques, and resources including those applicable to specific populations); *appraisal* (theoretical and historical bases for assessment techniques; appraisal methods including environmental assessment and performance assessment; individual and group test and inventory methods; behavioral observations; psychometric statistics; cultural factors related to assessment and evaluation of individuals and groups); *research and program evaluation* (basic types of research methods to include qualitative and quantitative research designs; basic parametric and nonparametric statistics; principles, practices, and applications of needs assessment and program evaluation; uses of computers for data management and analysis); and *professional orientation* (history of helping professions, professional roles and functions, professional organizations, ethical standards, professional preparation standards, professional credentialing, public policy processes). In addition, programs are required to provide specific practica and internships within approved work settings that include both individual and group supervision. The common core of experiences and knowledge provides the foundation for each of the entry-level or master's degree programs accredited by CACREP.

Programs in all master's-level areas, except for marriage and family counseling/therapy and mental health counseling, require a minimum of 48 semester hours or 72 quarter hours for graduation. Marriage and family counseling/therapy and mental health counseling programs require 60 semester hours or 90 quarter hours. In addition to the specific coursework areas noted previously, graduates from CACREP-accredited programs are required to have a minimum of 100 clock hours of supervised practicum and 600 hours of internship. Graduates from mental health counseling programs must complete an additional 300 hours of internship (for a total of 900 hours). CACREP sets forth specific parameters for both practicum and internship experiences. For example, students must document that a minimum of 40% of their time is involved in direct client contact.

CACREP also accredits doctoral programs in counselor education and supervision to prepare students to work as counselor educators, supervisors, and advanced practitioners in academic and clinical settings. To be accredited, the doctoral program must have an entry-level program (e.g., a master's program) and show that the doctoral program is an extension of the objectives of the entry-level program and meets all of the entry-level standards. The doctoral program, including the entry-level program credit hours, must consist of a minimum of 4 academic years of graduate-level preparation. The CACREP standards stipulate a minimum credit hour requirement of 96 semester hours or 144 quarter hours for doctoral study. The doctoral program also must have specific emphasis areas (e.g., a cognate in multicultural counseling, family counseling, and organizational development) to enable students to develop areas of professional expertise and competence as advanced counseling practitioners, supervisors, and researchers. Doctoral students are required to complete a doctoral practicum and 600 hours of internship and also must complete an appropriate dissertation culminating in advancing knowledge for the counseling profession. Of note, an academic department with CACREP-accredited programs and a CORE-accredited master's program could extend that area into advanced study and include rehabilitation counseling as an emphasis area of doctoral study.

CORE Standards

CORE accredits master's programs in rehabilitation counseling. Accredited programs must consist of a minimum of 48 semester hours or 72 quarter hours of graduate-level coursework. According to CORE (1997), the required curriculum of accredited programs must include coursework in seven areas. These areas are similar to those required by CACREP and consist of the following: *foundations of rehabilitation counseling* (history of rehabilitation counseling, legal and ethical standards, trends that affect rehabilitation counseling practice); *counseling services* (individual, group, and family counseling theories and practices; diversity issues; human growth and development; environmental and attitudinal barriers to individuals with disabilities); *case management* (case management process, identification and use of community resources, computer applications and technology for caseload management); *vocational and career development* (vocational aspects of disabilities including theories and approaches to career development, occupational information, labor market trends); *assessment* (medical aspects of disabilities; psychosocial aspects of disabilities; evaluation approaches, techniques, interpretation, and vocational assessment); *job development and placement* (job analysis, work-site modification and restructuring, job development, job placement, employer contacts, disability-related legislation, supported employment); and *research* (analysis of research articles, application of research literature to guide practice, application of statistical and research methods

to guide and evaluate practice). In addition to the aforementioned curricular experiences, all students who graduate from a CORE-accredited program are expected to have a minimum of 100 clock hours of supervised practicum and 600 clock hours of supervised internship in rehabilitation settings.

Overview of Counselor Preparation Programs

More than 500 colleges and universities offer approximately 1,000 counselor education degree programs that include master's through doctorate training. In his 10th study containing detailed information about counselor education programs, Hollis (2000) cited U.S. Department of Health, Education, and Welfare data from 1964 listing 327 colleges and universities with counselor education degree programs. As of 1999, Hollis identified 542 academic departments offering one or more counseling programs. Of the 542 departments, 428 (79%) responded to his 1998 data survey designed to provide data for the 2000 publication.

Master's-Level Programs

The most frequently offered master's program in counselor education is school counseling (Hollis, 2000). A total of 314 (73%) of the departments offer school counseling graduate programs. Of the 314 programs, 120 are accredited by CACREP (2000). The vast majority (72%) of the programs require an average of approximately 47 credit hours, whereas 28% of the programs average approximately 53 credit hours for graduation. The majority of students receive master of arts (M.A.), master of science

(M.S.), or master of education (M.Ed.) degrees. According to Hollis (2000), most graduates from these programs enter elementary (30%), middle (22%), and secondary (38%) school positions, whereas 4% enter advanced graduate programs.

Hollis (2000) identified 204 master's programs in community counseling. CACREP (2000) accredits 111 of these programs. For community counseling programs, 89% averaged approximately 49 credit hours and 11% averaged approximately 56 credit hours for graduation. The majority of students receive M.S. or M.A. degrees. More than half (58%) of the graduates find employment in public agencies, whereas 13% enter individual or group private practice and 10% enter advanced graduate programs.

For marriage and family counselor/therapist preparation, there are 110 master's-level programs. CACREP (2000) has accredited 21 of these programs, and the Commission on Accreditation of Marriage and Family Therapy Education (COAMFTE) has accredited 45 programs (Hollis, 2000). Both CACREP and COAMFTE require a minimum of 60 graduate credit hours for graduation. Fully 82% of the programs average approximately 56 credit hours and 18% average approximately 68 credit hours for graduation. The majority of students receive M.A. or M.S. degrees. More than half of the graduates enter employment in public agencies, whereas 19% enter individual or group private practice during their first years after graduation.

CACREP identifies mental health counseling as a specific preparation area, distinguishing it from the community counseling area and standards. A minimum of 60 graduate credit hours are required for graduation from CACREP-accredited mental health programs, compared to the 48 graduate credits required for community counseling programs. Hollis (2000) identified 100 programs providing mental health counselor preparation. Of these programs, 20 are accredited by CACREP (2000). The majority (72%) of students receive M.A. or M.S. degrees. The programs average approximately 54 hours for completion of a degree. The majority of graduates enter public agencies after graduation, with 21% entering individual or group private practice and 12% entering managed care programs, and 9% of these graduates enter advanced graduate programs (Hollis, 2000).

As mentioned previously, CORE accredits master's-level rehabilitation counseling programs. As of August 1999, there were 82 programs accredited by CORE (CORE staff, personal communication, August 18, 1999). Of these programs, 79 responded to Hollis's 1998 survey and provided relevant data. Most (66%) of the programs award an M.S. degree, with the second most frequent degree (26%) being the M.A. On average, programs require 52 credit hours for graduation. The majority (60%) of graduates take positions in public agencies, whereas 20% find first-year employment in individual or group private practice and 5% enter advanced graduate programs.

There are two emphases in the student affairs practice in higher education area: student affairs–college counseling and student affairs–professional practice/administration. These emphases are new titles under the 1994 CACREP standards and reflect the variance in titles used across the country by college counseling and student affairs programs. Hollis (2000) identified 95 programs offering student affairs emphases. No specifics were given on types of emphases. There were 29 programs in student affairs practice in higher education accredited under the 1994 CACREP standards and 13 accredited professional practice programs (CACREP, 2000). The most often awarded degree in these areas is the M.S. (40%), followed by the M.Ed. (26%) and the M.A. (24%). Of the 95 programs identified, 80 average 46 credit hours and 15 programs average 55 credit hours for graduation. As would be expected, the vast majority (89%) of graduates take positions in student affairs areas.

Additional counselor education preparation program areas reviewed by Hollis (2000) include the following: addiction counseling (20), career counselor preparation (10), gerontological counseling (6), pastoral counseling (8), and "other areas" (28). The numbers of these programs is small compared to the primary CACREP program areas reviewed earlier. The average number of graduate credit hours for these special programs included the following: 49 for addiction counseling, 50 for career counselor preparation, 47 for gerontological counseling, 56 for pastoral counseling, and 52 for other areas. Of these programs, CACREP accredits career counseling and gerontological counseling. Both areas have few accredited programs, with 2 accredited gerontological programs and 5 accredited career counseling programs (CACREP, 2000).

In reviewing program data, Hollis (2000) noted similarities among the various types of counselor education programs including that (a) the semester hours required for a particular degree are very similar among colleges and universities; (b) admission requirements generally are similar from program to program and usually include submission of Graduate Record Examination (GRE) scores or the Miller Analogy Test (MAT) scores, undergraduate grade point average, and letters of recommendation; and (c) providing courses to meet and maintain

licensure is a common thread. To ensure high quality and employability of graduates, programs provide courses that graduates need to obtain their state licenses and to meet licensure board continuing education requirements.

Doctoral Programs

A total of 54 departments in higher education institutions with doctoral programs in counselor education and supervision responded to Hollis's 1998 request for program data. Not all responded to each question about doctoral programs. Of the 54 programs, 42 are accredited by CACREP (2000). Also of the 54 programs, 59% offer only the Ph.D., 17% offer the Ed.D., 15% offer both the Ed.D. and Ph.D., and 9% did not respond with degree information. On average, programs admit seven students a year and graduate six students a year (four females and two males). Standardized tests are used by some departments for admission. More than half (61%) of the programs require the GRE and 7% require the MAT. More than three quarters (78%) of the programs require master's degrees and 61% require relevant work experience in the field for admittance. The vast majority (91%) of the programs require letters of recommendation and 81% require personal interviews. CACREP standards require 96 credit hours or 144 quarter hours of study for graduation from doctoral programs. On average, 86% of the programs require 95 credit hours and 14% require 121 quarter hours for graduation.

Counselor education doctoral programs prepare students to work as counselor educators in higher education and as supervisors and advanced practitioners in clinical settings. CACREP doctoral program objectives are based on, and represent an extension of, the objectives of the master's-level program, including the stated common core curricular areas. As noted earlier, these areas are professional orientation, social and cultural foundations, human growth and development, career development, helping relationships, group work, appraisal, and research and program evaluation. Doctoral programs seeking accreditation must meet all of the entry-level standards, and doctoral students must complete all academic and clinical requirements of the entry-level curriculum. Many programs provide a doctorate in those same areas in which a master's degree is offered. These areas usually include emphases in both clinical practice and faculty teaching and research positions. In addition to the advanced knowledge, specialty emphasis, and research course sequences, doctoral students from CACREP-accredited programs are required to complete doctoral-level counseling internships totaling a minimum of 600 hours. These hours may include supervised experiences in clinical work, teaching, and supervision. The setting for an internship should be congruent with the student's career objectives and intended to advance the student's knowledge and practical application. A primary program obligation of doctoral programs is to prepare doctoral students to generate and advance knowledge of the counseling profession. To meet this objective, students complete advanced studies courses in theory and applications and also complete a comprehensive curriculum in research and statistics. This course and experience sequence culminates in each student completing a dissertation extending knowledge in the field of counselor education.

To become successful and assume professional leadership roles, doctoral students are expected to participate in the professional counseling organizations (e.g., ACES, ACA)

and develop collaborative relationships with program faculty in teaching, research, and service to the profession and public. Doctoral students spend much of their time in the teaching and learning environment within collaborative and mentoring relationships with faculty.

Hollis (2000) asked respondents to provide information regarding the placement of graduates from doctoral programs. Within the categories listed, the largest category of first-year placement positions was 30% for the "other" category. However, from a review of responses, Hollis found that many placements were in university faculty positions and in university counseling centers. In addition, 24% of first-year placements were in public agencies and 20% were in individual or group private practice. These percentages show a large proportion of graduates entering practitioner positions.

Mentoring in Counselor Education Programs

The 1994 CACREP standards (CACREP, 1994) and the 1997 CORE standards (CORE, 1997) have many requirements that enhance and facilitate mentoring of students. Mentoring is viewed as a common and accepted practice by major business corporations; colleges, universities, and schools; and various agencies as a formal component of career and human resource development (Gerstein, 1985). There is a variety of diverse definitions of mentoring. One often cited definition that is applicable for mentoring in higher education is from Schmidt and Wolf (1980): "Mentors are colleagues and supervisors who actively provide guidance, support, and opportunities for the protégé. The functions of a mentor consist as a role model, a consultant/adviser, and a sponsor" (p. 45). One of the most important of all the aspects of mentoring is modeling behavior for the mentee (Kottler, 1992). The purpose of a mentor is to enable a successful transition and integrate a new person into a professional role held by the mentor (Anderson & Shannon, 1988).

Counselor education accreditation standards encourage mentoring relationships through activities such as advising and collaborative research, teaching, and service (Bruce, 1995). In particular, the profession has been sensitive to mentoring women and minorities. Because there are insufficient minority faculty, Brinson and Kottler (1993) called for cross-cultural mentoring of students. Cross-cultural relationships are mutually beneficial and can provide a powerful model for cooperation of students within their learning programs and within their eventual work sites.

CACREP requires that graduate assistantships be provided to assist program faculty and to provide additional professional experiences for students. Programs also are expected to recruit students representing a multicultural and diverse society. This enables a diverse student group that provides opportunities for interaction among different types of students, thereby simulating future work environments.

The CACREP and CORE clinical instruction standards also include opportunities for mentoring and interaction with faculty in the supervision process. Both master's and doctoral students must complete practica and internship experiences with a specified amount of weekly supervision. Students work in close learning and mentoring relationships with faculty and/or field supervisors during these experiences. Tentoni (1995) specifically called for supervisors to work jointly with students in intake and therapy sessions by sponsoring, encouraging, and supporting their activities.

According to the 1994 CACREP standards, students (typically those at the doctoral level) serving as practicum supervisors are required to have training and experience in supervision and be supervised by program faculty. In addition, internship or field supervisors must hold appropriate graduate degrees, hold relevant certifications or licenses, have relevant clinical experience, and hold memberships in professional organizations. During internship experiences, students are given the opportunity to become familiar with a variety of professional experiences other than their counseling duties. Students formally evaluate faculty and site supervisors, providing feedback to program administrators and the supervisors. This procedure provides supervisors with the information required to meet supervisee needs.

Ideally, program faculty serve as models for students. Faculty in CACREP- and CORE-accredited programs must have appropriate doctoral degrees and relevant experience. In addition, they are expected to be members of appropriate professional organizations; to engage in professional development and renewal of skills; to conduct research and engage in scholarly activities; and to provide service to the profession through program presentations, workshops, consultations, and direct service. Furthermore, throughout their training, students in accredited programs must be given the opportunity and encouragement to participate in workshops, seminars, and other activities that contribute to their personal and professional development.

The CACREP standards require that doctoral students collaborate with faculty in teaching, supervision, counseling practice, research, professional writing, and service to the profession and public. Valdez (1982) emphasized the need for first-year doctoral students to decrease stress during the first years of their programs by having experienced doctoral student mentors. Also, doctoral students in CACREP-accredited programs must participate in professional organizations (e.g., ACA). Thus, students and faculty are expected to work together and collaborate to enable doctoral students to emulate the practices necessary for success in the profession.

Doctoral students also are required to complete advanced practica and internships with weekly supervision. Each student must complete one internship on a full-time basis or two internships on a half-time basis. Practica and internships enable close working relationships with supervisors and faculty. The culmination of doctoral study includes the successful completion of the doctoral dissertation. Dissertations are major works including studies that advance knowledge in the field of counselor education. Extensive collaboration of faculty and students usually is required to assist students in completing their dissertations. Writing the dissertation becomes one of the most important times for faculty to serve as mentors for students.

Counselor Employment Roles and Functions

Once counselor education students graduate, they work in a variety of different settings such as public and private schools; colleges, universities, and community colleges; federal and state agencies; business and industry; hospitals and health care facilities; residential and community support programs; and individual and group private practices (Collison & Garfield, 1996). Counselors work in elementary, middle, junior high, and high schools and in vocational technical schools serving a vast variety of student developmental needs. In some states and districts, counselors with degrees in school or community counseling work for local community counseling or mental health centers and reside in schools to serve students with special needs or disorders. Counselors also work in community college, college, and university counseling centers and in positions in student affairs in higher education. In addition to college counseling centers, counselors in higher education settings work in student services divisions such as housing, financial aid, learning assistance centers, international student centers, and dean of students offices. Counselors also may work in athletic advising programs and academic advising centers in university college divisions.

In business and industry, counselors often are employed in employee assistance programs (EAPs). The counselor can be an EAP administrator or counselor housed within the business to counsel workers or refer workers for services to outside agencies. These counselors often work for outside contract EAP agencies that serve the needs of workers in particular businesses. Most EAPs focus on employee substance abuse problems. In addition, EAP services often address family and child concerns, financial concerns, and the full range of mental disorders that may affect employees. Furthermore, many EAP counselors are hired solely to provide career counseling with an emphasis on training and retraining and outplacement counseling to enable terminated employees to find other employment.

Federal and state governments offer an array of positions for professional counselors. The more traditional positions include vocational rehabilitation and employment agency counseling. Also, many counselors are employed by the military to serve in base schools, family support service centers, and substance abuse programs and centers. Other military counselor specialties include those of transition assistance specialist (to assist in transitions to civilian life) and military education counselor (to assist in career advancement or for a post-military career) (Helwig, 1996).

Counselors also provide services in private and public hospitals and outpatient clinics. They work in hospital evaluation and short-term hospital psychiatric centers and outpatient centers as well as in hospital-attached or outpatient substance abuse centers. Counselors often work in these settings to assist in the transition of patients to independent living and work. Counselors also work in residential and community living programs to provide transition services to support and maintain client self-sufficiency.

Whereas the number of counseling licensure laws enacted across the country has increased dramatically over the past 10 to 15 years, more counselors are involved in individual and group private practices. These counselors often specialize in services for a particular developmental level (e.g., children, adolescents, adults, older adults) and client type (e.g., families, men, women, people who are gay/lesbian/bisexual, individuals from specific religious groups) with particular disorders or problems in daily living. These problems include, but are not limited to, areas such as substance abuse, eating disorders, childhood abuse, panic disorders, bereavement, retirement, parenting, adjustment to major moves, job relocations, and divorce. Many private practitioners, like other similar professionals, form group practices for cost sharing, consultation, and cross-referral. Also, counselors often enter into group practices with other mental health professionals such as psychologists, psychiatrists, or social

workers to provide comprehensive services within these practices.

A series of studies (Hosie & Mackey 1995; Hosie, Mackey, & Griffin, 1996 ; Hosie, West, & Mackey, 1988, 1990, 1993; West, Hosie, & Mackey, 1987, 1988) of master's-level counselors in college counseling centers, mental health centers, substance abuse centers and programs, and EAPs showed that counselors worked in all facets of those agencies and provided all the different types of services offered by agencies. These facets included program development and administration, peer staff supervision, and agency administration. Counselors provided intake and assessment services as well as individual, group, and marriage and family therapy in inpatient, partial hospitalization, and outpatient settings. In addition, counselors worked with all types of clients seen within the agencies including clients with *DSM-IV* (*Diagnostic and Statistical Manual of Mental Disorders*) Axis I and Axis II disorders (American Psychiatric Association, 1994).

Results of one mental health center (West et al., 1988) and one substance abuse center (Hosie et al., 1990) study showed that agency directors and supervisors viewed counselors as knowledgeable and well educated in nearly all service delivery aspects and areas. According to the respondents, the one area in which counselors could be more knowledgeable involved client medications. Substance abuse agencies were the only center type that requested that counselors have more experience with clients served by the centers. However, only 33% of the agencies made that request. Thus, counselors adequately performed serving a diverse clientele experiencing a variety of problems and disorders. The full set of studies did not specifically track the differences between doctoral- and master's-level employment and duties. An overall interpretation of the results indicates that, except for university counseling centers in large universities, most agencies employed more master's-level counselors than doctoral-level counselors. In most agencies, doctoral-level counselors served as supervisors and as program and agency directors.

Continuing Education of Professional Counselors

The education of professional counselors does not end with the completion of their academic degrees. To obtain and maintain state licensure, counselors are required to continue receiving post-master's supervised experience for 1 to 4 years. According to ACA (1999), the majority (81.6%) of jurisdictions require a minimum of 2 years of post-master's supervised experience. Depending on the jurisdiction, counselors are required to document 1,000 to 4,000 hours of post-master's supervised experience. The mean number of required hours is 2,746, and the modal number of required post-master's supervised hours is 3,000.

Most professions require or strongly encourage members to stay abreast of current information in their fields after graduation from professional training programs. In the counseling profession, for example, practitioners certified by national credentialing boards, such as NBCC and the Commission on Rehabilitation Counseling Certification (CRCC), must accrue specified numbers of approved continuing education hours every 5 years to renew their certification. NBCC and CRCC both require 100 clock hours of approved continuing education during each 5-year period.

There appears to be greater variance in the continuing education requirements associated with counselors renewing their state-regulated credentials. Many, but not all, jurisdictions require continuing education for professional counselors to maintain their licensure. Sattem (1997) conducted a study of the continuing education requirements set forth by the 43 jurisdictions that were credentialing counselors in 1997. At that time, 29 (67.4%) of the jurisdictions mandated continuing education, and two (4.6%) of the states were in the process of establishing requirements. Of the states that required counselors to obtain continuing education units to maintain their state credentials, the range was 10 to 25 hours of continuing education annually, with 45% requiring 20 hours annually. In addition, 13 states did not allow self-directed activities, supervision, and publishing as forms of continuing professional education.

Apart from mandates put forth by national certifying organizations and state regulatory boards, counselor ethical codes require counselors to maintain currency in their knowledge bases and skill levels so as to best serve their clients, students, and supervisees. The ACA (1995) code of ethics specifically directs counselors to maintain their levels of competence in the skills they use, to keep reasonable levels of awareness of scientific and professional information, and to keep current with the issues related to populations with whom they work.

In addition to staying current in their knowledge bases and skill levels, counselors are ethically obligated to recognize the boundaries of competence. To professionally serve clients from diverse cultural backgrounds who seek services for a variety of issues, counselors are well advised to stay open to new approaches and to stay current with diverse or special populations with whom they work (ACA, 1995). When expanding their services to include subject areas or skills that are new to them, professional counselors are expected to obtain appropriate education through continuing education courses and workshops. Similar to when counselors are first in training, post-academic continuing education for counselors developing new skills should include appropriate supervision to protect their clients from harm and to ensure the competency of the services provided during the learning stage (ACA, 1995).

Counselor Education: Emphases and Trends

Just as socioeconomic factors have influenced the development of the counseling profession, counselors continue to respond to societal factors. Issues such as managed care and other systems of reimbursement, technological advances, and living in an increasingly pluralist society all influence the delivery of counseling services and, therefore, counselor education.

General Trends in Graduate Preparation Programs

Hollis (2000), in comparing current data to his 1996 study data, pointed out that there appears to be some common emphasis areas and trends across the various counselor education programs. Following is an overview of those that we believe are particularly relevant as we enter the 21st century.

Hollis (2000) noted that counselor education programs appear to be establishing new and more demanding admission requirements. Not all respondents, however, clearly identified which criteria will be strengthened. Several noted grade point average requirements, the number of years of work experience preferred, and results of personal interviews. It seems that once students are admitted, they will be faced with more demanding graduation requirements. Counselor education programs have made revisions or plan on revising program requirements to ensure that graduates meet state licensure requirements, including an increase in the required credit hours for graduation to 60 semester hours (current program semester hours range from an average of 46 for student affairs counselors to 56 for marriage counselor/therapists). According to ACA (1999), 54.5% of the jurisdictions with licensure mandate that applicants have 60 graduate semester hours in counseling or a closely related field. As programs move to the requirement of 60 credit hours for graduation, they are providing additional elective specialty areas. Hollis (2000) projected that the number of doctoral programs will increase. He maintained that more specialized expertise is required to meet the demands of professional counseling positions. Requiring enhanced expertise will cause an increase in graduation requirements, and this will prompt the profession—and perhaps accreditation agencies—to increase the number of doctoral programs.

In addition to changes in the specific types of coursework required, Hollis (2000) presented trends in regard to the clinical components of training including that (a) programs are involving students with clients throughout the program rather than only in specialty or finishing courses; (b) the number of required clock hours of clinical experience appears to be increasing; (c) some programs are shifting to encouraging or requiring rotation through different types of work settings so as to provide students with exposure to diverse clientele and different clinical supervisors, whereas others are emphasizing placement in clinical settings similar to students' anticipated post-academic work settings;

(d) programs appear to be establishing closer working arrangements with clinics in which students gain experiential components; (e) more departments are creating clinics to enhance supervised student experiences; and (f) programs are entering into agreements with additional on- and off-campus clinics to enable students to have rotations among clinics. Hollis (2000) contended that licensure has influenced, and will continue to influence, such trends. He noted that licensure dictates the need for substantive clinical experiences. This, in turn, creates a need for professionally competent supervisors. Training of clinical supervisors traditionally has taken place at the doctoral level. Counselor education programs are likely to respond to an increased demand for competent supervisors, and the credentialing of supervisors by NBCC, by exploring who they will allow to take graduate courses in supervision (e.g., training advanced master's students in clinical supervision).

Hollis (2000) also noted two trends regarding students and faculty in counselor education programs. According to his data, the average age of enrolling students is increasing. In addition, more emphasis is placed on hiring faculty with different cultural and theoretical-philosophical orientations to give students a wider and more diverse set of experiences. He further noted that respondents' comments in his latest study indicate a more pronounced intent to train students to work effectively with clients from diverse cultures as compared to comments in any of his previous nine studies.

Diversity

It is almost a certainty that counselors-in-training will encounter clients who have cultural backgrounds different from their own. In fact, many leaders in counseling consider multiculturalism to be the "fourth force" in the profession (Pedersen, 1991). This force warrants a reexamination not only of assumptions underlying the delivery of traditional mental health services but also of the pedagogical foundations of counselor education. To this end, counselor educators first need to examine the efficacy of traditionally taught theories with diverse clientele and the possible constraints of how services typically are rendered (e.g., 50-minute sessions in a clinician's office; Glosoff & Rockwell, 1997). Next, counselor educators are faced with the challenge of determining how best to prepare counselors who are competent to work with clients from diverse populations. Both CACREP and CORE mandate that accredited programs include coursework in social and cultural foundations of counseling. Furthermore, specific competencies associated with counseling clients from diverse populations have been identified (Ponterotto, 1998). To date, however, these competencies have not been empirically validated (Fong, 1998). Finally, we agree with Fong (1998), who pointed out the importance of identifying "models that promote learning from a perspective that addresses diversity and culture" (p. 110). This calls for counselor educators to examine the applicability of the approaches used to teach a diverse student population, that is, to focus not only on the cultural foundations of *what* is taught but also on *how* it is taught.

Managed Care and Other Reimbursement Systems

In addition to providing services in an increasingly diverse country, the advent of managed mental health care and other systems of reimbursement has significant implications for counselor education and supervision. It will be important for educators to keep current with how managed care systems directly and indirectly influence the delivery of counseling services in the settings where their students may seek employment (e.g., community agencies, private practices, hospitals, rehabilitation facilities, nursing homes). Counselor educators will need to help students learn about how various forms of reimbursement may influence the clinical and ethical realities of working with clients (Glosoff, 1998). On the one hand, some counselors believe that working with managed care companies provides for a source of referrals and reliable reimbursement (Smith, 1999). Also, providing services in managed care organizations may help counselors to develop more time- and cost-effective practices (Smith, 1999). Furthermore, some counselors believe that their training has helped them to develop competencies (e.g., the ability to work from preventive and developmental foci, strengths in group work, mediation, crisis counseling, an emphasis on collaborative work) that can be particularly useful in managed care organizations (Smith, 1999). On the other hand, many master's-level counselors, especially those in states without licensure, find it difficult to become accepted as recognized managed care providers (Glosoff, 1998; Smith, 1999).

Regardless of whether managed care is viewed as a benefit or a drawback, it is likely that systems of managed care will continue to be an influence in the delivery of mental health services. According to the ACA (1995) code of ethics, counselor educators must prepare students to meet the clinical and ethical challenges raised by managed mental health care. Training should include focused discussion regarding the realities of how managed care systems may in-fluence students' work with clients (Glosoff, 1998). For example, because brief therapy modalities most often are identified as the treatment of choice by third-party payers, adequate training in these modalities seems to be essential for future clinicians. Therefore, counselors-in-training need to learn how to assess which clients will and will not be served effectively using a brief therapy approach as well as which individuals might be worse off with no treatment if brief therapy is the only option available (Haas & Cummings, 1991). Counselors working with managed mental health care organizations also need to be adept at writing treatment plans that are consistent with the assessments and diagnoses provided to the insurers and must include clearly stated goals that are measurable and emphasize helping clients to minimize barriers to their effective functioning in daily living (Glosoff, 1998). To do this, counselors-in-training need to become skilled at diagnosing clients' disorders. This might create difficulty for many counselors who operate from orientations that emphasize resources and strengths rather than pathology (Glosoff, 1998). It is important for counselor education programs to help their students to deal with the ethical complexities of how diagnoses influence payment for treatment. Finally, counselor educators have a responsibility to prepare students to advocate for their clients when they are denied access to appropriate treatment by managed care providers. To do this, counselors-in-training need to learn to present arguments for appropriate treatment in a language that is understood by staff in decision-making positions in managed care organizations (Glosoff, 1998).

In a survey conducted by Smith (1999), 101 counselor educators and 264 counseling practitioners were asked for specific suggestions they had for curriculum changes in counselor education programs that might improve counselors' position in managed care organizations. Their responses were categorized into the following eight suggested curriculum changes (presented in rank order): (a) increased emphasis on training in brief therapy modalities, (b) increased training related to administrative and management skills, (c) inclusion of clinical experiences in multidisciplinary managed care settings, (d) expanded coursework on the *DSM-IV,* (e) expanded coursework on current psychopharmacology, (f) inclusion of coursework on treatment planning, (g) coursework addressing organization and financing of health care delivery systems, and (h) emphasis on group therapy.

Accountability

The development of managed mental health care organizations has forced counselors to become more accountable for their services. According to a study conducted by the Ridgeland Financial Institute (1995), however, only about 20% of practitioners collect data on the effectiveness of their treatments or can speak to outcomes of their work with clients. We believe that it is important for counselor education programs to teach students how to effectively collect and present data that can demonstrate their efficacy (Glosoff, 1998).

On a different front, accredited counselor education programs must be prepared to be accountable for their training programs. CACREP and CORE mandate that accredited programs collect data on their graduates. Information gathered includes not only the types of positions in which graduates are employed but also how effective the graduates believe their training was in preparing them for such posi-

tions. Furthermore, both CACREP and CORE are members of CHEA. Providing validation of accreditation standards is a requirement for maintaining CHEA recognition as an accreditation group. Both CACREP and CORE will be active during future years in validating their counselor education standards. To meet this requirement, CACREP has established policies for board-supported and -funded grants. In addition, CACREP has formed an alliance with NBCC to conduct studies to validate accreditation standards.

Technology

We anticipate that there will be many more counselor education programs involved in distance learning media in the future. Although counselor education programs have been involved in distance learning or extension campus programs for a long time, recent technical innovations have enabled many programs to teach courses from their main campuses—through two-way interactive audio and video—to distance sites. Programs also are using two-way online (computer-based) interactions during instruction and other assisted technology such as Internet use. Courses are being offered in "real time" and supplemented in "virtual time," thereby enabling students to access course materials at their convenience. Rehabilitation programs have been at the forefront in this area. Federal and state grant support to increase the capability of state vocational rehabilitation personnel has provided the impetus for creating and teaching distance courses. The reader is referred to Eldredge and colleagues (1999) for an interesting description of five rehabilitation counseling distance learning programs. The quality of distance courses in comparison to main campus courses always is a consideration in evaluating distance courses. CACREP has acknowledged the growth and importance of distance education in counselor education and maintains the position that distance classes and programs must meet the same standards as do main campus programs. The ACES executive council, in sharing this viewpoint, endorsed its guidelines for online instruction in May 1999 (ACES, Technology Interest Network, 1999a). In addition, ACES endorsed recommended guidelines related to technical competencies that counselor education students should demonstrate before the completion of their graduate programs (ACES, Technology Interest Network, 1999b). Furthermore, ACES has created a Technology Interest Network to help examine the ramifications of technology such as e-mail, two-way video computer-based interactions, and satellite or distance learning on clinical supervision. This impetus is relatively new, and to date there appear to be few empirical studies addressing the effectiveness and difficulties of clinical training and supervision using means other than face-to-face in-person meetings.

Perspectives on the Future

The curricula of counselor education programs consistently have been shaped by societal needs and changes. Programs have been driven by the need to produce graduates who can provide high-quality services to an ever more diverse clientele. Early in the history of the counseling profession, counselors worked primarily in school and career counseling settings. Now, counselors can be found in a multitude of settings that offer a variety of services to a contin-

uum of people, from those who are functionally well to those who have severe and chronic mental illness. As the scope of counseling has expanded, educational programs have responded by developing additional curricula and coursework to adequately train counselors to meet the needs of specific types of clientele. During recent years, for example, many counselor education programs have begun to offer courses in counseling people with substance, gambling, and sexual addictions. Correspondingly, there has been a steady increase of marriage and family courses to provide additional means and methods of services to children and adults.

The advent of professional licensure and certification, and the public's acknowledgment of the quality of counseling services, has contributed to counselors entering private practices, hospitals, and inpatient and outpatient treatment programs. People in such settings work with children, adolescents, and adults from a variety of cultural backgrounds who have a variety of problems and disorders. This has influenced counselor education programs to provide extensive and in-depth coursework to adequately prepare these practitioners. Furthermore, counselors working in traditional settings such as kindergarten through postsecondary schools now are serving clients with more severe problems and crises than in the past. Counselor education programs are faced with the challenge of changing curricula to meet these ever-changing needs. We fully expect counselor education programs to provide relevant curricula and training to keep pace with societal and public demands for services.

We anticipate that other societal influences will continue to affect the academic training and continuing education of counselors. Distance learning and advanced technologies will play an increasing role in both the academic preparation of counselors and the ways in which counselors receive continuing education credits. Use of distance learning and accompanying technology to serve rural areas and specific agency needs for basic and advanced training likely will increase program enrollment. A significant amount of faculty time and energy is needed to create and maintain distance learning programs. Counselor education departments entering that arena will need to make prudent decisions related to the quality of instruction, financial costs, and faculty time and dedication to this and other areas. Regardless of whether training is provided in traditional or more technologically advanced methods, counselor educators might find themselves responding to increased pressure to be accountable for how students are prepared and, ultimately, how counseling services are provided. At present, many insurance companies require counselors to provide outcome data regarding their efficacy with clients. In the near future, accreditation agencies might require similar data to support counselor training and counselor effectiveness. Therefore, counselor education programs are advised to validate their training and educational practices and to teach students how to conduct efficacy studies to measure the effects of their work with clients.

Because managed care appears to influence nearly all venues of mental health services (e.g., private practices, federally and state-funded mental health programs), counselor education programs need to teach students about the clinical and ethical complexities involved in such systems. Furthermore, counselor education programs have a responsibility to ensure that counselors are competent in providing services to people from diverse cultural backgrounds and settings. We fully expect counselor education programs to provide relevant curricula and training to keep pace with issues related to managed care, effectively serving more diverse clients within ever-widening settings and responding to a variety of societal problems such as increased violence in schools. We anticipate that, to do this, increasing numbers of programs will lengthen master's degree requirements beyond the minimum of 48 credit hours.

Finally, considering the finite pool of resources available in colleges and universities coupled with the pressure to increase course requirements, counselor education departments likely will consolidate programs providing more in-depth instruction and experiences rather than create additional program areas. For example, there may be much similarity in client types and problem areas presented among community, clinical mental health, and college counseling areas. We anticipate that, in the future, there will be a merger of these programs with differences only in elective courses. To keep pace with the demand and finite resources, counselor education departments and programs might be forced to consolidate resources and use them in cost- and time-effective ways.

References

Altekruse, M., & Wittmer, J. (1991). Accreditation in counselor education. In F. Bradley (Ed.), *Credentialing in counseling* (pp. 53-62). Alexandria, VA: American Association for Counseling and Development.

American Counseling Association. (1995). *Code of ethics and standards of practice*. Alexandria, VA: Author.

American Counseling Association. (1999). *Counselor licensure/certification requirements* [Online]. Available: www.counseling.org/members/licensureintro.cfm

American Psychiatric Association. (1994). *Diagnostic and statistical manual of mental disorders* (4th ed.). Washington, DC: Author.

Anderson, E. M., & Shannon, A. L. (1988). Toward a conceptualization of mentoring. *Journal of Teacher Education, 39,* 38-42.

Association for Counselor Education and Supervision, Technology Interest Network. (1999a). *ACES guidelines for online instruction in counselor education.* Alexandria, VA: Association for Counselor Education and Supervision.

Association for Counselor Education and Supervision, Technology Interest Network. (1999b). *Technical competencies for counselor education students: Recommended guidelines for program development.* Alexandria, VA: Association for Counselor Education and Supervision.

Bradley, F. (1991). *Credentialing in counseling.* Alexandria, VA: American Association for Counseling and Development.

Brinson, J., & Kottler, J. (1993). Cross-cultural mentoring in counselor education. *Journal of Counselor Education and Supervision, 32,* 241-254.

Bruce, M. A. (1995). Mentoring women doctoral students: What counselor educators and supervisors can do. *Counselor Education and Supervision, 35,* 139-150.

Collison, B. B., & Garfield, N. J. (Eds.). (1996). *Careers in counseling and human services* (2nd ed.). Washington, DC: Taylor & Francis.

Council for Accreditation of Counseling and Related Educational Programs. (1994). *CACREP accreditation standards and procedures manual.* Alexandria, VA: Author.

Council for Accreditation of Counseling and Related Educational Programs. (2000). *Directory of accredited programs.* Alexandria, VA: Author. Available: www.counseling.org/cacrep/directory.html

Council on Rehabilitation Education. (1997). *Accreditation manual for rehabilitation counselor education programs.* Rolling Meadows, IL: Author.

Eldredge, G., McNamara, S., Stensrud, R., Gilbride, D., Hendren, G., Siegfried, T., & McFarlane, F. (1999). Distance education: A look at five programs. *Rehabilitation Education, 13,* 231-248.

Fong, M. (1998). Considerations of a counseling pedagogy. *Counselor Education and Supervision, 38,* 106-112.

Gerstein, M. (1985). Mentoring: An age-old practice in a knowledge-based society. *Journal of Counseling and Development, 64,* 156-157.

Glosoff, H. (1998). Managed care: A critical ethical issue for counselors. *Counseling and Human Development, 31*(3), 1-16.

Glosoff, H. L. (2001). The counseling profession: A historical perspective. In D. Capuzzi and D. Gross (Eds.), *Introduction to the counseling profession* (3rd ed.). (pp. 3-49). Boston: Allyn & Bacon.

Glosoff, H. L., & Rockwell, P. (1997). The counseling profession: A historical perspective. In D. Capuzzi & D. Gross (Eds.), *Introduction to the counseling profession* (pp. 3-44). Boston: Allyn & Bacon.

Haas, L. J., & Cummings, N. A. (1991). Managed outpatient mental health plans: Clinical, ethical, and practical guidelines for participation. *Professional Psychology: Research and Practice, 22*(1), 45-51.

Helwig, A. A. (1996). Careers in federal and state agencies. In B. B. Collison & N. J. Garfield (Eds.), *Careers in counseling and human services* (pp. 73-93). Washington, DC: Taylor & Francis.

Hollis, J. W. (1997). *Counselor preparation: Programs, faculty, trends* (9th ed.). Washington, DC: Taylor & Francis.

Hollis, J. W. (2000). *Counselor preparation: Programs, faculty, trends* (10th ed.). Philadelphia: Accelerated Development/Taylor & Francis.

Hosie, T. W., & Mackey, J. A. (1995). Employment and roles of counselors in Louisiana college counseling centers. *Louisiana Journal of Counseling, 6,* 10-17.

Hosie, T. W., Mackey, J. A., & Griffin, B. L. (1996, April). *Employment and roles of counselors in college counseling centers.* Paper presented at the American Counseling Association International Convention, Pittsburgh, PA.

Hosie, T. W., West, J. D., & Mackey, J. A. (1988). Employment and roles of mental health counselors in substance-abuse centers. *Journal of Mental Health Counseling, 10,* 188- 198.

Hosie, T. W., West, J. D., & Mackey, J. A. (1990). Perceptions of counselor performance in substance-abuse centers. *Journal of Mental Health Counseling, 12,* 199-207.

Hosie, T. W., West, J. D., & Mackey, J. A. (1993). Employment and roles of mental health counselors in employee assistance programs. *Journal of Counseling and Development, 71,* 355-359.

Hoyt, K. (1962). *An introduction to the Specialty Oriented Student Research Program.* Iowa City: University of Iowa Press.

Hoyt, K. (1991). Concerns about accreditation and credentialing: A personal view. In F. O. Bradley (Ed.), *Credentialing in counseling* (pp. 69-80). Alexandria, VA: American Counseling Association.

Kottler, J. A. (1992). Confronting our own hypocrisy: Being a model for our students and clients. *Journal of Counseling and Development, 70,* 475-476.

Pedersen, P. B. (1991). Multiculturalism as a generic approach to counseling. *Journal of Counseling and Development, 70,* 6-12.

Ponterotto, J. G. (1998). Charting a course for research in multicultural counseling training. *The Counseling Psychologist, 26,* 43-68.

Ridgeland Financial Institute. (1995, January). Fee, practice, and managed care survey. *Psychotherapy Finances,* pp. 1-8.

Sattem, L. (1997). *Mandatory continuing professional education in an emerging field: A prospectus on the counseling profession.* Doctoral dissertation, Ohio State University.

Schmidt, J. A., & Wolf, J. S. (1980). The mentor partnership: Discovery of professionalism. *NASPA Journal, 17,* 45-51. (National Association of Student Personnel Administrators)

Smith, H. B. (1999). Managed care: A survey of counselor educators and counselor practitioners. *Journal of Mental Health Counseling, 21,* 270-284.

Sweeney, T. J. (1991). Counselor credentialing: Purpose and origin. In F. Bradley (Ed.), *Credentialing in counseling* (pp. 23-52). Alexandria, VA: American Association for Counseling and Development.

Sweeney, T. J. (1995). Accreditation, credentialing, professionalization: The role of specialities. *Journal of Counseling and Development, 74,* 117-125.

Tentoni, S. C. (1995). Mentoring of counseling students: A concept in search of a paradigm. *Counselor Education and Supervision, 35,* 32-43.

Valdez, R. (1982). First year doctoral students and stress. *College Student Journal, 16,* 30-37.

West, J. D., Hosie, T. W., & Mackey, J. A. (1987). Employment and roles of counselors in mental health agencies. *Journal of Counseling and Development, 66,* 135-138.

West, J. D., Hosie, T. W., & Mackey, J. A. (1988). The counselor's role in mental health: An evaluation. *Counselor Education and Supervision, 27,* 233-239.

CHAPTER TWENTY-FOUR

Counseling Supervision

A Deliberate Educational Process

L. DIANNE BORDERS

The counseling profession has long recognized the pivotal role of counseling supervision, in terms of both counselor training and client welfare, and has been a leading force in the professionalization of the practice of counseling supervision. Accreditation standards (Council for Accreditation of Counseling and Related Educational Programs [CACREP], 1994) and licensure regulations (Sutton, Nielsen, & Essex, 1998) include requirements for substantial amounts of supervised counseling experience. Increasingly, these requirements also are addressing the conduct of supervision and the qualifications of the supervisor. During the past 20 years or so, a substantial body of literature, both conceptual and empirical, has been published. This chapter summarizes this literature in the form of principles that underlie current beliefs about what counseling supervision is and how it should be conducted. The chapter primarily focuses on the conclusions and implications of current literature for practice as opposed to providing a methodological critique of it (for thorough critiques, see Ellis & Ladany, 1997; Ellis, Ladany, Krengel, & Scholt, 1996). Even so, no handbook chapter can give adequate attention to all aspects of a topic that could, and perhaps should, be included. That limitation certainly applies here in a summary that also necessarily reflects the author's own biases and experiences as a supervisee, supervisor, supervisor trainer, supervision researcher, and participant in the profession's efforts to recognize the power and potential of the supervision enterprise.

Principles Concerning the Nature of Counseling Supervision

Counseling Supervision Is, at Its Core, an Educational Process

Although this statement might seem simplistic and obvious, the teaching-learning nature of supervision has been debated and contradicted, sometimes directly but most often indirectly. Historically, for example, supervision sometimes took on more of a clinical flavor, focused on developing the person of the counselor rather than developing the counselor's skills. Although today supervision clearly is more skill focused, it still sometimes falls short in terms of its potential as an educational process.

To be a true educational enterprise, supervision must be proactive, deliberate, intentional, and goal directed, involving active learning strategies designed to engage a particular supervisee (or group of supervisees). By most anecdotal and documented accounts (e.g., Borders & Usher, 1992), however, this crafting of the supervision session is not commonplace. Rather, it seems that some supervisors often devote little time to active preparation (e.g., reviewing tapes and designing interventions related to specified goals) for sessions. They might even spend much of the sessions detailing what to do with clients (or what *they* would do), with little attention given to helping supervisees understand the clinical interventions or making sure that supervisees know how to deliver the interventions (Borders, 1992).

As an educational process, supervision also is necessarily evaluative, a function that has been discounted or avoided as well (Bernard & Goodyear, 1998). As evaluators, supervisors are more than just responsible for assigning course grades or determining whether supervisees qualify for licenses. Evaluation itself is a key part of the educational process. Supervisors provide ongoing feedback, again crafted for particular supervisees, balancing challenge and support that invite counselor growth and development. To be effective evaluators, supervisors also must have criteria and specified goals, both of which are communicated to (or constructed with) supervisees. Too often, however, learning outcomes are vague or never actually are addressed.

Supervisors who seek to engage supervisees in an educational process use *counseling skills* not only to establish rapport but also to assess supervisees' motivations and beliefs, fears about learning and concerns about being counselors, and potential avenues for creating change. Supervisors use *teaching skills* to assess supervisees' learning needs and learning styles, as well as learning contexts (e.g., counselor education program, internship site), to design "best fit" learning strategies, that is, to determine prioritized learning outcomes and ways in which to evaluate progress toward them. Skilled supervisors integrate all of these components into a seemingly seamless educational mosaic that guides not only long-term planning but also moment-to-moment framing of responses and interventions. When all of these components come together, supervisors experience the joy of watching others unfold, awaken, and grow.

Models of Supervision Provide Highly Useful, if Somewhat Simplified, Heuristics for Understanding and Guiding the Supervision Process

Discrimination Model

Bernard's (1979, 1997) discrimination model is a particularly useful tool for helping supervisors understand that they have choices in terms of their planning and behaviors in supervision sessions. The supervisor roles of teacher, counselor, and consultant now are classic, although supervisors should be clear that they are employing skills based in these roles rather than moving into the pure role (i.e., the supervisor-as-counselor does not provide counseling for the supervisee). Supervisors also should avoid thinking in stereotypical terms about the roles, especially the teacher role. Lecturing and telling certainly are not the only methods used by teachers. In fact, these methods are the least creative and often the least effective means of teachers. The three focus areas in the discrimination model clearly illustrate the variety and breadth of supervision content necessary for full development of the counselor. Two of the focus areas emphasize skills: intervention or performance skills (i.e., what the counselor *does* in a session) and conceptual or cognitive skills (i.e., how the counselor *thinks* about the client and the counseling process). The third, personalization, emphasizes the counselor's more emotional reactions to the client and self-awareness.

Supervisors can use the model as a self-assessment tool (Am I relying on only one role or overemphasizing one focus area? If so, is this a deliberate and appropriate choice?) as well as a planning framework (What are my options in terms of role for addressing this issue? Can I really effectively address three different focus areas today? Which one needs to take priority?). Like others (Bernard, 1997), the present author also has found the model instructional for supervisees in clarifying the purposes and functions of supervision and even for writing their supervision goals (e.g., asking supervisees to write at least one goal within each focus area). The model's usefulness is reflected by several variations in which roles and/or focus areas have been further differentiated (Neufeldt, Iversen, & Juntunen, 1995). In addition, there is empirical support for the model both as a valid framework (Ellis & Dell, 1986) and as a useful teaching tool (Stenack & Dye, 1982).

Developmental Models

The various developmental models of supervision (Loganbill, Hardy, & Delworth, 1982; Stoltenberg, 1981) provide a complementary perspective to the discrimination model, giving primary emphasis to the supervisee rather than the supervisor. In fact, when the two are juxtaposed, the developmental models provide a needed rationale for determining which role(s) and focus area(s) to use with a particular supervisee.

The influence of the developmental models has been pervasive. Their publication during the early 1980s brought back to life interest in the field and spurred the development of training programs as well as academic debate (Holloway, 1987) and a relatively large body of research. In fact, for 10 years, nearly all of the supervision research was based in developmental models. Despite a number of methodological shortcomings that qualify the results, studies fairly consistently have supported the general tenets of the models (e.g., Worthington, 1987), and practitioners consistently have spoken to their commonsense value. The developmental models themselves offer key principles about the nature of supervision including the following basic ones:

- Counselors move through a progressive sequence of stages or levels as they learn the theory and skills of counseling and apply their knowledge with clients. The stages are marked by developmental changes such as a move from black-or-white thinking to more differentiated and integrated conceptualizations about clients and counseling; greater empathy and greater respect for clients' perspectives, styles, and paces of change; and increased awareness of counselors' own personal reactions to clients and the value of these reactions to the counseling process.

- Theoretically, counselors continue to develop across their professional life spans, assuming that they remain open to and seek out learning experiences, particularly supervision. This is an important point given that most master's-level counselors likely are at the middle stages of development when they graduate from their master's programs and obtain their first professional positions. This also means that counselors never "outgrow" their need for supervision.

- Counselors' rates of development through the stages, as well as the ceilings or maximum stages that can be achieved, are governed by counselors' personal attributes, particularly their general levels of development (e.g., conceptual [Harvey, Hunt, & Schroder, 1961], ego [Loevinger & Wessler, 1970]).

- Counselors' developmental levels or stages are *not* equivalent to their experience levels. The use of experience level as a proxy for developmental level has been a consistent error in supervision practice and research, despite extensive discussions of general developmental theories in presentations of the models and empirical evidence that the two are not equivalent (e.g., Borders, 1989).

- Different supervisory interventions are the most appropriate match for the various developmental levels, with a general move from more directive, instructive, and highly supportive interventions to more confrontive and consultative approaches (for more detailed descriptions of supervisory interventions by level, see Stoltenberg, 1981; Wiley & Ray, 1986).

- The task of supervisors is to provide supervision that will encourage the growth and development of supervisees. This sometimes is described as a one-half step match that challenges but does not overwhelm supervisees. Necessarily, then, supervisors must assess not only the skill levels of counselors but also counselors' general developmental capabilities and then apply that information in their supervisory approaches with supervisees.

Counseling Theory-Based Models

A third group of supervision models is counseling theory based. Historically, these were not actually models of supervision but rather descriptions of the theoretical principles and skills to be taught in supervision, often through application of the counseling theory to supervisees (e.g., attack the supervisee's irrational thoughts about the role of the counselor in rational emotive therapy supervision). More recently, authors of theory-based writings have spoken more distinctly to the supervision process per se rather than treating supervision as primarily an adjunct to counseling (Watkins, 1997). Even when supervisors do not inappropriately equate their counseling theories with their supervision approaches, the counseling theories clearly influence supervisors' beliefs about what should be addressed during supervision and, often, how this is done.

The Supervisory Relationship Is Pivotal to the Educational Process of Supervision

As in other helping and educational processes, the supervisor-supervisee relationship strongly influences how much learning and change can occur. Building rapport is the necessary but insufficient elementary building block for a productive relationship. Supervisors must carefully manage the balance of challenge and support they provide (Blocher, 1983) so that supervisees not only feel safe in being open and vulnerable about their work but also gain confidence in their ability to learn, develop, and perform. This balance differs by supervisee, client issue, supervision session, and stage of the supervisory relationship. The general underlying dynamics of the supervisory relationship have been studied most thoroughly by Holloway (1995), who identified "power" and "involvement" as core underlying constructs.

Several unique dynamics in the supervisory relationship also must be considered by supervisors. Beyond counseling interventions and case conceptualization strategies, supervisees are asked to explore their own beliefs, motivations, emotions, and experiences as these relate to their interactions with clients as well as their interactions with supervisors. In this way, the supervisory relationship itself becomes a critical vehicle for learning. In using this vehicle, supervisors must walk a narrow and often vague line between counseling supervisees and encouraging self-exploration as it directly relates

to supervisees' counseling work, being careful not to overemphasize self-awareness or to assume that counseling behaviors necessarily have personal (vs. skill-based) sources.

Supervisors' balancing act is further complicated by the evaluative nature of supervision. How do they successfully invite supervisees to be vulnerable with the individuals who will evaluate their adequacies as counselors and govern their entry into the field?

Using the supervisory relationship as a vehicle for learning is most clear in working through parallel processes, perhaps the most unique dynamic of supervision. Parallel process originally was conceived in psychodynamic terms and viewed as a reflective process in which the supervisee unknowingly portrays in supervision the client's anxiety during counseling, thereby seeking help for the supervisee's own anxiety about working with the client as well as ways in which to intervene with the client (Searles, 1955). From this perspective, the origin of the parallel process dynamic is the client. More recently, parallel process has been used to describe a counselor's manifestation of similar patterns or themes (e.g., reluctance to confront) in both counseling and supervision sessions (McNeill & Worthen, 1989). There also are indications that parallel process may emanate from the supervisor (Doehrman, 1976; Martin, Goodyear, & Newton, 1987), with the supervisee portraying during counseling the supervisor's attitudes or behaviors observed in supervision or the supervisor's in-session behavior with one supervisee reflecting issues or dynamics with another supervisee. Clearly one of the most fascinating and potentially powerful and unique interpersonal and intrapersonal dynamics of supervision, parallel process seldom has been studied by researchers. Given its highly situational nature, parallel process requires complex qualitative designs, with no guarantee that it will occur (or be detected) in a specific session. And, even when parallel process is present, an objective observer might not have the necessary background knowledge about the participants (intrapersonal aspects) or know enough about the context to be able to identify what is unique behavior and what is part of a pattern or theme in a session.

In Line With Our General Social Culture, the Supervisory Relationship Is Influenced by Gender, Race, Ethnicity, and Sexual Orientation

In addition, and also similar to our general culture, the influences of these issues might not be consciously recognized or addressed in supervision despite their pervasive and predictable effects.

In terms of gender, for example, there is consistent evidence that supervisors, whether male or female, grant more power to their male supervisees in several ways (e.g., reinforcing statements that express power, asking their opinions) (Nelson & Holloway, in press). As a result, supervisors need to learn—and consciously use—supervisory techniques that empower women (Nelson, 1997) to be confrontive and acknowledge their expertise. Similarly, male supervisees need help in being comfortable with intimacy and addressing affect (Nelson, 1997).

During the past few years, there has been a surge of literature focused on cross-cultural and multicultural supervision. Although empirical works still are quite limited, conceptual models and explorations have greatly expanded our understanding of the implications of the multicultural movement for supervision. Several conceptual models are based in developmental processes and describe progressive increases in multicultural knowledge, skills, and awareness along with guidelines for developmentally appropriate supervisory interventions such as from more to less structure (Leong & Wagner, 1994). Other writers (Cook, 1994; Fong & Lease, 1997; Leong & Wagner, 1994) have focused on racial identity models (Helms, 1995) and implications for supervision. These writers have suggested that supervisors' and supervisees' racial identity ego statuses may be more relevant to supervision dynamics than is race or ethnicity alone. In particular, the interactions of the dyad's ego statuses (whether both are parallel or one is higher than the other) could predict supervision outcomes (Cook, 1994).

Early investigations of race as a main effect in supervision were mixed (Leong & Wagner, 1994). In a more recent study (Ladany, Brittan-Powell, & Pannu, 1997), racial identity interaction (supervisees' self-reports of their own and their supervisors' racial identity) was related to supervisees' ratings of the supervisory alliance as well as their perceptions of supervisors' influence on their multicultural competence; when supervisors' racial identity was high, these outcomes were significantly greater. Even so, supervisors's race also was related to multicultural competence; supervisors of color were more influential, regardless of supervisees' race.

The Ladany and colleagues (1997) study, despite some methodological shortcomings, supported the proposed importance of racial identity in counseling supervision. The results also provided some empirical validity for the belief that supervisors should be high in racial identity and supported the need for more supervisors of color, who may encourage multicultural competence through their modeling or greater willingness to address multicultural issues. Similar conclusions seem plausible in terms of gender (Nelson & Holloway, in press) and sexual orientation, although these lack empirical support. Recently, for example, a gay male doctoral student in the author's supervision practicum helped his supervisees and his peer supervisors to become more comfortable in discussing sexual issues with gay clients. His own integrated level of identity as a gay man enabled him to do this in an informative and challenging way that was easily heard.

The Practice of Counseling Supervision

Relatively little research has been devoted to the practice of counseling supervision, so that we have few empirically based guidelines for conducting supervision. Too often, it seems, supervisors either use interventions they learned from their own experiences as supervisees or work hard to avoid those interventions because of their own negative supervision experiences. Others have relied primarily on their counseling theories for methods to teach theory-based principles and techniques. Indeed, until recently, few supervisors have had opportunities to consider and practice the wide range of supervisory interventions available to them. It should come as no surprise, then, that researchers have found few differences between experienced and novice supervisors (Worthington,

1987) and have found that supervisors overwhelmingly rely on one supervisory method—self-report (Borders & Usher, 1992). Self-report relies on supervisees' recall of what happened in counseling sessions as well as their perceptions of what issues need to be addressed during supervision. This approach may be time-efficient, but it also provides very limited—if not biased—information.

The existing literature does provide guidelines for supervision practice, although some are more implied than stated directly and all need further empirical study.

A Wide Range of Teaching, Counseling, and Consulting Methods Are Available to Counseling Supervisors

Supervisors may draw on their skills from these other roles in designing supervisory interventions (Borders & Leddick, 1987). Role-based interventions have been specified by Stenack and Dye (1982) and been expanded and illustrated by Neufeldt and colleagues (1995). In practice, role-based methods seldom are as clearly delineated as they might appear; they often have overlapping or multiple goals or are combined. Depending on the implementation, the same method can be used for more than one goal. A role-play, for example, may involve the supervisor modeling a skill and the supervisee experiencing the client's emotional frame of reference. Reversed, the supervisee role-playing the counselor may be practicing a new skill (and getting immediate feedback) or replaying a session as a first step at understanding an emotional reaction to the client. A key implication, then, is that the supervisor must be clear about the intention or goal in choosing a particular intervention and must be deliberate in its implementation (Borders & Leddick, 1987).

As suggested by role-based interventions, few supervisory methods per se are unique to supervision; it is their adaptation and application to supervision that differentiates them from other contexts. Each method has its advantages and limitations, and each is better suited for some learning goals than for others. The craft or art of supervision is in the process of choosing the appropriate method; shaping it to a particular supervisee's needs, personality, learning style, and goals; and implementing it in a well-timed intervention. Thus, supervisors need to have a repertoire of varied skills and methods from which they can choose rather than relying exclusively on their preferred approaches.

It Is Imperative That Supervisors Regularly and Consistently Employ Supervisory Interventions That Give Them Direct Knowledge of Counselors' Work

Self-reports, by definition, are limited in objectivity; regardless of supervisees' willingness or intent to provide complete and unbiased reports, they necessarily can share only what they observed or concluded from their own frames of reference about clients, themselves, and the counseling process. As a result, self-reports can be highly informative of supervisees' processing but must be supplemented by direct knowledge of clinical work. A variety of direct interventions are available including review of audiotapes and videotapes of counseling sessions, variations of live observation and live supervision methods (e.g., bug-in-the-ear, phone consultations, team supervision), and co-counseling (Bernard & Goodyear, 1992, 1998; Bor-

ders & Leddick, 1987). By combining self-reports and direct interventions, supervisors can gain valuable insights into supervisees' observation skills and/or willingness to disclose. In addition, direct methods allow supervisors to work on goals such as observing client nonverbals or reactions to counselors' interventions, timing and pacing, and rhythms of sessions. Some methods (e.g., bug-in-the-ear, consultations) also allow for immediate feedback and in-session guidance, so that supervisees are able to work with more challenging clients sooner.

One direct intervention, interpersonal process recall (IPR; Kagan, 1980; Kagan & Kagan, 1997), is perhaps the most unique supervisory method. The goal of IPR, a phenomenological and humanistic approach, is to increase supervisees' awareness of thoughts and feelings as well as clients' experiences during sessions. Supervisors take on a nonjudgmental and nonevaluative role as "inquirers" who guide supervisees' reexperiencing of sessions. The task of supervisors is to expand supervisees' awareness and to avoid providing feedback, focusing on skills, or asking leading questions (e.g., "Did you think about . . .?" "What else could you have tried?"). Staying in the inquirer role often is difficult for supervisors. IPR may be used to review a whole session or a session segment, preselected by either the supervisee or the supervisor, depending on the supervision goal. The method can be quite instructive regarding supervisees' internal experiencing and in-session thought processes (e.g., the supervisee recognized the need to confront but feared the client's response, the supervisee recognized the theme in the client's report but did not know how to use this information, the supervisee heard a husband's lack of commitment to the marriage but downplayed it in hopes that the marriage could be saved). In fact, supervisees' recall can challenge supervisors' assumptions about supervisees' insights and skills.

Direct interventions also are useful in group supervision, profiting not only supervisees and supervisors but also other group members. Supervisees often can "see" behaviors and themes in peers' work much more easily than they can in their own work, but this experience provides good practice for transferring these skills to self-observation. Review of audiotaped or videotaped segments in group can be the basis for a number of experiential teaching methods (Borders, 1991).

Much of the Work in Supervision Is Cognitive Based

To date, a comprehensive and systematic discussion of the cognitive skills and processes that need to be addressed, as well as the ways in which to address them, is lacking. In contrast to observable skills and techniques, cognitions are difficult to specify and teach, although there have been some promising efforts (e.g., Morran, Kurpius, Brack, & Brack, 1995).

Indeed, it is striking how much of the supervision literature points to supervisees' cognitions as the underlying, if not primary, focus of supervisory work. The ultimate goal of developmental models of supervision, for example, is to encourage movement toward thinking at higher conceptual levels. Blocher (1983) spoke to this goal—"a very high level of cognitive functioning"—quite cogently:

[It includes] the ability to take multiple perspectives in order to achieve empathic understanding with people who hold a variety of worldviews, value systems, and personal constructs. It includes the ability to differentiate among and manipulate a wide range and large number of relevant facts and causal factors. Finally, it involves the ability to integrate and synthesize in creative or unusual ways large amounts of such information to arrive at an understanding of the psychological identity and life situation of a wide range of other human beings. Still further, the counselor engages in this quest in active collaboration with the client and in the hope of imparting some skill and understanding of the process to the client. (p. 28)

Supervisors, then, are to be concerned with the actual thought *content* of supervisees, the ways in which supervisees *process* information, and the cognitive *schemata* underlying all cognitive activity.

Cognitive-oriented supervision strategies are scarce. Most existing cognitive-based methods are focused on clinical hypothesis formation and case conceptualization skills. Clearly, these skills are critical to counselors' ability to understand clients or families and to create appropriate treatment plans. This broad thinking, however, must be translated into moment-by-moment, deliberate, in-session thinking including what is observed, how these observations are understood, how these observations compare/contrast with observations made in previous sessions or with information from other sources (e.g., parent, spouse, teacher), and how the client's frame of reference may be influencing (e.g., limiting, coloring) his or her self-reports before moving to identifying one's options for responding and evaluating them in terms of counseling goals, level of client functioning, stage of counseling relationship and counseling process, client's pace and motivation (in this session as well as overall), client's usual reactions to various types of responses and interventions, time left in session, *and* counselor's ability to provide a particular response or intervention and other factors relevant to that particular moment. This moment-by-moment processing is, of course, ongoing throughout a session, requiring much focus and energy as it guides critical decision making for working with the client. This moment-by-moment thinking also needs to be agile and almost instantaneous, so that the counselor's in-session cognitive skills need much practice, study, and evaluation. Few have offered insights into the in-session thinking process or have suggested methods for assessing, teaching, and evaluating them in supervision. To date, the best (if not the only) intervention proposed is the "thinking aloud" approach (Borders & Leddick, 1987; Kurpius, Benjamin, & Morran, 1985) in which either the supervisee reports in-session thoughts (for assessment, intervention, and/or evaluation purposes) or the supervisor reports his or her own cognitive processing about the client or the counseling (for modeling or teaching purposes). The thinking aloud approach has some similarities to IPR, although the two interventions have very different goals.

Counselors' in-session cognitions really are the sculpting force for making counseling an art. As such, they demand much more attention from supervisors and researchers.

Never Underestimate the Power of a Carefully Worded, Well-Timed Question

The right question at the right time often is the catalyst for change. It may create cognitive dissonance that requires the supervisee to reconsider assumptions and struggle with finding ways in which to make sense of the contradic-

tions, or it may invite the supervisee to walk through a cognitive process slowly so that it may be examined. The question may spur the supervisee to take a new perspective on a client's behavior, shift the focus from the client's behavior to the supervisee's behavior, suggest another possible explanation for an event, highlight an overlooked fact or behavior, or introduce the supervisee's reactions to the client as an important consideration.

Based on experience as well as review of published transcripts (Bernard & Goodyear, 1992, Appendix D; Holloway, 1995; Neufeldt et al., 1995), it seems that a supervisor's key skill is the well-crafted question. Questions, sometimes paired with interpretations, seem to provide the critical challenges in supervision, especially when balanced by supportive reflective statements.

Supervisors Always Are Modeling, Whether Intentionally or Not

Although supervisors often deliberately model skills or techniques, or perhaps think aloud their processing about clients or issues, it should be noted that *all* of their supervisory actions become professional examples to supervisees. This modeling includes larger actions (e.g., supervisors' attitudes [whether expressed verbally or not] about clients and clients' situations) as well as "smaller" demonstrations of respect for supervisees (e.g., being on time and prepared for sessions). It is not necessary for supervisees to observe the modeling consciously for learning to take place. Supervisees learn a language and a perspective on clients and counseling from their supervisors. Supervisees may carry these forward and act them out in counseling sessions.

Group Supervision Is an Important Adjunct to Individual Supervision, Providing Complementary But Different Learning Opportunities

The advantages and unique learning opportunities of group supervision have been well described (Bernard & Goodyear, 1998; Hillerbrand, 1989; Holloway & Johnston, 1985), and a complete discussion of them is beyond the scope of this chapter.

Perhaps a key point to be made here is that, for group supervision to be complementary, supervisors need to be deliberate about their goals for their supervision groups. What can happen in group that cannot happen in individual supervision? Given the particular group (e.g., practicum vs. internship vs. post-degree practitioners, interns in a school vs. interns in a community setting), what are the appropriate goals for this supervision group? What interventions will help the group members to achieve these goals? Too often, supervisors fall into a case presentation approach, with little deliberate thought as to structure and goals beyond the outlines for the case presentations themselves. Of course, it is the responses to and processing of case presentations that is critical to learning for all of the group members, not just the supervisees who presented the cases. The selected structures also determine whether supervisees will work together as a group (assuming that this is a goal) rather than as individuals providing advice to the presenters. Clearly, supervisors' skills in leading and facilitating groups are prerequisites for structuring group supervision experiences.

It seems that group supervision also is heavily influenced by setting and context. Suggested models and interventions, for example, often grow out of supervisors' assignments within training programs and reflect the needs and parameters of those programs and their students (Borders, 1991; Neufeldt et al., 1995). This does not mean that models are not useful beyond the original groups. However, supervisors do have to give deliberate thought as to how models need to be adapted to their own groups and settings.

Although the literature on supervision groups is small, there is consistent evidence that these are more task-oriented groups than process- or counseling-oriented groups (Kruger, Cherniss, Maher, & Leichtman, 1988; Werstlein & Borders, 1997). Given the learning focus of supervision groups, this characterization seems quite appropriate. It also reinforces the demands of supervisors to be deliberate, focused, and educational in planning as well as strong group leaders.

Professional Issues: Credentialing, Ethics, and Standards

Ethical Issues

Similar to other areas in supervision, multilayered thinking is required in addressing ethical questions in counseling supervision. Supervisors have ethical obligations both to clients and to supervisees.

Supervisors, first and foremost, must consider the welfare of clients and take whatever actions are necessary (e.g., dealing directly with clients, increasing supervision regarding clients) to protect them. Clearly, supervisors also must be cognizant of all ethical issues related to the counseling process and make sure that counselors adhere to ethical standards. In addition, clients must agree to terms regarding supervision (e.g., supervisors, taping, how client confidentiality will be maintained) prior to beginning counseling as part of the informed consent procedure.

There are clear legal implications for supervisors' responsibilities to clients here. Most frequently, the principle of vicarious liability is discussed in the literature (e.g., Harrar, Vande-Creek, & Knapp, 1990). Simply stated, this principle means that supervisors are responsible for the actions of supervisees and, therefore, can be held legally liable for those actions. It is incumbent on supervisors, then, to be sure that they are informed about supervisees' clients (e.g., take steps to get the information they need) and to be sure that supervisees are informed of ethical guidelines in general and those pertinent to particular clients. There also is possible cause for direct liability (Guest & Dooley, 1999; Harrar et al., 1990). If supervisors give inappropriate or inaccurate advice about client treatment, for example, then any resulting harm to clients may be viewed as the direct result of that advice.

Supervisors have parallel obligations to supervisees. Perhaps first and foremost, supervisors should be qualified as counselors *and* as supervisors in terms of their training, supervised experience, and continuing professional development as well as the counseling areas they supervise (e.g., substance abuse, career counseling). Informed consent includes information such as the criteria for successful completion of the supervision experience, mechanics of the supervision process (e.g., supervision approaches and expectations), and professional disclosure (e.g., supervisors' qualifications as counselors *and* as supervisors) (McCarthy et al., 1995). Limits of confidentiality also need to be addressed, particularly given the evaluative nature of supervision (e.g., internship grades, recommendations for licensure or employment) and supervisors' responsibilities to the field and to supervisees' future clients. Relatedly, supervisees must be afforded due process, from timely feedback, to opportunities for remediation, to avenues to report dissatisfaction with supervision. Dual relationships may be a particularly challenging area because there is a high probability that many supervisors and supervisees will have dual relationships (e.g., also teacher-student, dissertation chair-doctoral student, or even administrator/employer-employee). Such relationships should be anticipated and, when they occur, be handled with care (Herlihy & Corey, 1997). Two dual relationships that must be avoided are that (a) supervisors do not counsel their supervisees and (b) supervisors do not have romantic or sexual relationships with their supervisees. Although the latter is fairly straightforward, there is a considerable gray area surrounding what constitutes counseling supervisees. Detailed guidelines regarding these issues are presented in ethical guidelines from the Association for Counselor Education and Supervision (ACES; Hart, Borders, Nance, & Paradise, 1995).

Professional Standards

The counseling profession has played a pivotal role in establishing counseling supervision as a professional specialty. Not only do accreditation standards for practica and internships attend to the number of hours that interns spend on-site, there also are clear expectations for face-to-face supervision of interns' counseling work (CACREP, 1994). Historically, model legislation for counselor licensure bills have included similar requirements for post-degree supervision as well as suggested qualifications for the "approved supervisor" (Glosoff, Benshoff, Hosie, & Maki, 1995). Clearly, the profession has highly valued the counseling supervision process for some time.

In an attempt to operationalize the profession's valuing of counseling supervision, the Supervision Interest Network of the ACES planned and completed a sequential set of projects designed to define the specialty and create standards for it. These projects included standards for the practice of supervision (Dye & Borders, 1990), guidelines for training supervisors (Borders et al., 1991), and the ethical practice of supervision (Hart et al., 1995). These documents encouraged state counseling licensure boards to write regulations governing supervision *and supervisors* of counselor-licensure applicants (Sutton et al., 1998) and provided the basis for a national credential for counseling supervisors awarded through the National Board of Certified Counselors (NBCC; Bernard, 1998). Perhaps the most important effect of these standards and other developments has been the elevation of counseling supervision as a professional specialty in its own right, with the accompanying emphasis on the need for thoughtful, structured, and extended training for supervisors of counselors. The counseling profession has provided a basis for enhancing our own work as well as a useful guide for other professions ready to consider supervision within their respective areas (Watkins, 1997).

Perspectives on the Future

Where do we go from here? Despite the major advancements in the field of counseling supervision over the past 20 years or so, there is, of course, still much to be done.

One increasingly important area concerns supervisor training. The advent of state regulations and a national counseling supervisor credential requiring training highlights the need for supervisor training in a pragmatic way. Therefore, we should not be surprised at the appearance of training programs designed to help practitioners fulfill these requirements including university courses and continuing education venues. Indeed, this variety of training offerings is needed and welcomed; although most training to date has been offered through doctoral-level courses, most supervisors in the field are master's-level practitioners. Although neither type of training experience is necessarily better than the other, notices of training programs indicate that they clearly vary in scope and type of experience provided. Counselors, then, are left to scrutinize the content and qualifications of trainers, perhaps using the ACES documents as their guidelines. A critical training component should be supervised experience of supervision over some time.

The field still is a fruitful area for researchers, whether experienced or new to the field. In fact, the field is in need of fresh perspectives to generate research questions that probe old and new areas of supervision practice. Developmental models provided the impetus for an incredibly productive period of supervision research that lasted 12 to 15 years. Nevertheless, we have made little progress in developing supervision-specific instruments. Instead, we often have relied on adaptations of counseling-based measures. One precursor to the development of supervision measures might be identifying what the key constructs of supervision are, particularly as they are differentiated from counseling. Current researchers are exploring more relationship and process issues in supervision as opposed to more outcome-based questions. Clearly, both types of questions are important. It is hoped that research from both perspectives—and new ones yet to be determined—will inform each other in ways that enhance not only empirical work but also the training and practice aspects of counseling supervision.

How do supervisors reflect on their work and continue their development? Similar to counselors, supervisor development is ongoing across the professional life span. Much more attention to supervisor development is needed from researchers and trainers, so that we can apply the same deliberate educational energy to supervisors' needs as we now apply to counselors. It is hoped that the counseling profession will continue to be a leading force in furthering our understanding of this and other aspects of the supervision enterprise.

References

Bernard, J. M. (1979). Supervisory training: A discrimination model. *Counselor Education and Supervision, 19,* 60-68.

Bernard, J. M. (1997). The discrimination model. In C. E. Watkins, Jr. (Ed.), *Handbook of psychotherapy supervision* (pp. 310-327). New York: John Wiley.

Bernard, J. M. (1998, Spring). Approved clinical supervisor credential. *NBCC NewsNotes,* pp. 1-2. (National Board of Certified Counselors)

Bernard, J. M., & Goodyear, R. K. (1992). *Fundamentals of clinical supervision.* Boston: Allyn & Bacon.

Bernard, J. M., & Goodyear, R. K. (1998). *Fundamentals of clinical supervision* (2nd ed.). Needham Heights, MA: Allyn & Bacon.

Blocher, D. H. (1983). Toward a cognitive developmental approach to counseling supervision. *The Counseling Psychologist, 11,* 27-34.

Borders, L. D. (1989). Developmental cognitions of first practicum supervisees. *Journal of Counseling Psychology, 36,* 163-169.

Borders, L. D. (1991). A systematic approach to peer group supervision. *Journal of Counseling and Development, 69,* 248-252.

Borders, L. D. (1992). Learning to think like a supervisor. *The Clinical Supervisor, 10,* 135-148.

Borders, L. D., Bernard, J. M., Dye, H. A., Fong, M. L., Henderson, P., & Nance, D. W. (1991). Curriculum guide for training counseling supervisors: Rationale, development, and implementation. *Counselor Education and Supervision, 31,* 58-80.

Borders, L. D., & Leddick, G. R. (1987). *Handbook of counseling supervision.* Alexandria, VA: Association for Counselor Education and Supervision.

Borders, L. D., & Usher, C. H. (1992). Post-degree supervision: Existing and preferred practices. *Journal of Counseling and Development, 70,* 594-599.

Cook, D. A. (1994). Racial identity in supervision. *Counselor Education and Supervision, 34,* 132-139.

Council for Accreditation of Counseling and Related Educational Programs. (1994). *CACREP accreditation and standards manual* (2nd ed.). Alexandria, VA: Author.

Doehrman, M. J. (1976). Parallel processes in supervision and psychotherapy. *Bulletin of the Menninger Clinic, 40,* 1-104.

Dye, H. A., & Borders, L. D. (1990). Counseling supervisors: Standards for preparation and practice. *Journal of Counseling and Development, 69,* 27-32.

Ellis, M. V., & Dell, D. M. (1986). Dimensionality of supervisor roles: Supervisors' perceptions of supervision. *Journal of Counseling Psychology, 33,* 282-291.

Ellis, M. V., & Ladany, N. (1997). Inferences concerning supervisees and clients in clinical supervision: An integrative review. In C. E. Watkins, Jr. (Ed.), *Handbook of psychotherapy supervision* (pp. 447-507). New York: John Wiley.

Ellis, M. V., Ladany, N., Krengel, M., & Scholt, D. (1996). Clinical supervision research from 1981 to 1993: A methodological critique. *Journal of Counseling Psychology, 43,* 35-50.

Fong, M. L., & Lease, S. H. (1997). Cross-cultural supervision: Issues for the White supervisor. In D. B. Pope-Davis & H. L. K. Coleman (Eds.), *Multicultural counseling competencies: Assessment, education and training, and supervision* (pp. 387-405). Thousand Oaks, CA: Sage.

Glosoff, H. L., Benshoff, J. M., Hosie, T. W., & Maki, D. R. (1995). The 1994 ACA model legislation for licensed professional counselors. *Journal of Counseling and Development, 74,* 209-220.

Guest, C. L., Jr., & Dooley, K. (1999). Supervisor malpractice: Liability to the supervisee in clinical supervision. *Counselor Education and Supervision, 38,* 269-279.

Harrar, W. R., VandeCreek, L., & Knapp, S. (1990). Ethical and legal aspects of clinical supervision. *Professional Psychology, 21,* 37-41.

Hart, G., Borders, L. D., Nance, D., & Paradise, L. (1995). Ethical guidelines for counseling supervisors. *Counselor Education and Supervision, 34,* 270-276.

Harvey, O. J., Hunt, D. E., & Schroder, H. M. (1961). *Conceptual systems and personality organization.* New York: John Wiley.

Helms, J. E. (1995). An update of Helms's White and people of color racial identity models. In J. G. Ponterotto, J. M. Casas, L. A. Suzuki, & C. M. Alexander (Eds.), *Handbook of multicultural counseling* (pp. 181-198). Thousand Oaks, CA: Sage.

Herlihy, B., & Corey, G. (1997). *Boundary issues in counseling: Multiple roles and responsibilities.* Alexandria, VA: American Counseling Association.

Hillerbrand, D. (1989). Cognitive differences between experts and novices: Implications for group supervision. *Journal of Counseling and Development, 67,* 293-296.

Holloway, E. L. (1987). Developmental models of supervision: Is it development? *Professional Psychology, 18,* 209-216.

Holloway, E. L. (1995). *Clinical supervision: A systems approach.* Thousand Oaks, CA: Sage.

Holloway, E. L., & Johnston, R. (1985). Group supervision: Widely practiced but poorly understood. *Counselor Education and Supervision, 24,* 332-340.

Kagan, H., & Kagan, N. I. (1997). Interpersonal process recall: Influencing human interaction. In C. E. Watkins, Jr. (Ed.), *Handbook of psychotherapy supervision* (pp. 296-309). New York: John Wiley.

Kagan, N. (1980). Influencing human interaction: Eighteen years with IPR. In A. K. Hess (Ed.), *Psychotherapy supervision: Theory, research, and practice* (pp. 262-283). New York: John Wiley.

Kruger, L. J., Cherniss, C., Maher, C., & Leichtman, H. (1988). Group supervision of paraprofessional counselors. *Professional Psychology, 19,* 609-616.

Kurpius, D. J., Benjamin, D., & Morran, D. K. (1985). Effects of teaching a cognitive strategy on counselor trainee internal dialogue and clinical hypothesis formulation. *Journal of Counseling Psychology, 32,* 263-271.

Ladany, N., Brittan-Powell, C. S., & Pannu, R. K. (1997). The influence of supervisory racial identity interaction and racial matching on the supervisory working alliance and supervisee multicultural competence. *Counselor Education and Supervision, 36,* 284-304.

Leong, F. T. L., & Wagner, N. S. (1994). Cross-cultural counseling supervision: What do we know? What do we need to know? *Counselor Education and Supervision, 34,* 117-131.

Loevinger, J., & Wessler, R. (1970). *Measuring ego development: Construction and use of a sentence completion test* (Vol. 1). San Francisco: Jossey-Bass.

Loganbill, C., Hardy, E., & Delworth, U. (1982). Supervision: A conceptual model. *The Counseling Psychologist, 10,* 3-42.

Martin, J. S., Goodyear, R. K., & Newton, F. B. (1987). Clinical supervision: An intensive case study. *Professional Psychology, 18,* 225-235.

McCarthy, P., Sugden, S., Koker, M., Lamendola, F., Maurer, S., & Renninger, S. (1995). A practical guide to informed consent in clinical supervision. *Counselor Education and Supervision, 35,* 130-138.

McNeill, B. W., & Worthen, V. (1989). The parallel process in psychotherapy supervision. *Professional Psychology, 20,* 329-333.

Morran, D. K., Kurpius, D. J., Brack, C. J., & Brack, G. (1995). A cognitive-skills model for counselor training and supervision. *Journal of Counseling and Development, 73,* 384-389.

Nelson, M. L. (1997). An interactional model for the empowerment of women in supervision. *Counselor Education and Supervision, 37,* 125-139.

Nelson, M. L., & Holloway E. (in press). Supervision and gender issues. In M. Carroll & E. L. Holloway (Eds.), *The practice of clinical supervision.* London: Sage.

Neufeldt, S. A., Iversen, J. N., & Juntunen, C. L. (1995). *Supervision strategies for the first practicum.* Alexandria, VA: American Counseling Association.

Searles, H. F. (1955). The informational value of the supervisor's emotional experience. *Psychiatry, 18,* 135-146.

Stenack, R. J., & Dye, H. A. (1982). Behavioral descriptions of counseling supervisor roles. *Counselor Education and Supervision, 21,* 295-304.

Stoltenberg, C. (1981). Approaching supervision from a developmental perspective: The counselor complexity model. *Journal of Counseling Psychology, 28,* 59-65.

Sutton, J. M., Nielsen, R., & Essex, M. (1998, January). *A descriptive study of the ethical standards related to supervisory behavior employed by counseling licensing boards.* Paper presented at the annual conference of the American Association of State Counseling Boards, Tucson, AZ.

Watkins, D. E., Jr. (Ed.). (1997). *Handbook of psychotherapy supervision.* New York: John Wiley.

Werstlein, P. O., & Borders, L. D. (1997). Group process variables in group supervision. *Journal of Specialists in Group Work, 22,* 120-136.

Wiley, M. O., & Ray, P. B. (1986). Counseling supervision by developmental level. *Journal of Counseling Psychology, 33,* 439-445.

Worthington, E. L., Jr. (1987). Changes in supervision as counselors and supervisors gain experience: A review. *Professional Psychology, 18,* 189-208.

CHAPTER TWENTY-FIVE

Multicultural Counselor Education

Historical Perspectives and Future Directions

MARK S. KISELICA

MARY LOU RAMSEY

Over the past 30 years, the education of counselors has been greatly influenced by the widespread belief that counselor trainees must examine their cultural heritage, values, and biases and learn about culturally diverse peoples to become competent at counseling clients who are culturally different. As evidence of this influence, the number of courses on multicultural counseling and diversity appreciation offered in graduate programs in counseling increased significantly during the 1980s (Ponterotto & Casas, 1991) and continued to grow during the 1990s (Ponterotto, 1997).

The growing emphasis on multicultural counseling training (MCT) represents a radical transformation of attitudes about the role of culture and diversity in understanding and helping clients in counseling. Prior to the 1960s, culture and diversity were largely ignored as important counseling process variables by the counseling profession. According to Sue, Ivey, and Pedersen (1996), this neglect fostered the failure of most counselors to recognize the harmful effects of their culturally biased assumptions on the well-being of culturally different clients. Since the 1960s, however, the counseling profession has gradually recognized the influence of culture and diversity on the entire counseling process, especially the impact of counselor bias on clients (Kiselica, Maben, & Locke, 1999). As we enter the 21st century, consideration of culture and diversity in counseling now is so widespread that multiculturalism is considered by many counseling authorities to be one of the major forces in the counseling profession (Herring, 1997; Lee, 1989; Locke, 1998; Pedersen, 1991; Sue et at., 1996).

The purpose of this chapter is to describe this transformation of counselor education by examining the past, present, and future of MCT. First, we provide an historical overview of MCT, explaining the neglect, emergence, and proliferation of MCT over three distinct historical periods. Next, we describe the current status of the practice of MCT and discuss the dominant principles of MCT. We conclude with an assessment of the future of MCT.

History of MCT

According to Wehrly (1995), the evolution of MCT has occurred over three successive and discernible eras: the Monoculturalism Era, the Cross-Culturalism Era, and the Multiculturalism Era. Employing Wehrly's historical framework, this section discusses the sociopolitical issues and themes, professional association and organizational developments, dominant cultural themes in the counseling literature, and major training issues and foci for each era. Considering each of these topics for the three eras of MCT provides a contextual understanding of the forces that shaped the development of MCT and the changes in the content of MCT that have occurred over time.

The Monoculturalism Era (pre-1960s)

Sociopolitical issues and themes. Prior to the 1950s, a prevailing societal view was that the United States was a melting pot of cultures. A basic assumption associated with the melting pot perspective was that cultural homogeneity (assimilation) was a success and that cultural heterogeneity was a failure. Mainstream society expected culturally different people to forsake their unique cultural identities and "melt in" with the dominant culture (Vacc, Wittmer, & DeVaney, 1988). People who appeared or acted different from prevailing Anglo-Saxon norms (e.g., African Americans, Asian Americans, Hispanics) were looked down on and often were the targets of discrimination. Outright expression of racism was common, and most of the laws and institutions of the United States supported the oppression of people of color (Pettigrew, Fredrickson, Knobel, Glazer, & Ueda, 1982).

Professional association and organizational developments. Prior to the 1950s, there was no effective organization representing the interests of counselors in the United States (Gladding, 1992). In 1952, the American Personnel and Guidance Association (APGA, later renamed the American Counseling Association [ACA]) was formed "with the purpose of more formally organizing groups interested in guidance, counseling, and personnel matters" (p. 14). Originally consisting of a few thousand members, APGA expanded its membership and underwent several name changes over the subsequent few decades as it became recognized as the official organization for professional counselors. As was the case with most other institutions in the country during the 1950s, APGA was primarily a White organization with few members who were people of color. Most ethnic-minority people who were members of APGA neither held key positions in the association nor had any substantive input into the construction and establishment of APGA bylaws or professional standards. Also, issues pertaining to culture and diversity were not a priority of the organization (Ponterotto & Casas, 1991).

Dominant cultural themes in the counseling literature. Although a few early pioneers (Du Bois, 1903; Frazier, 1939/1966; Horney, 1937; Sanchez, 1932; Stonequist, 1937) recognized the importance of cultural factors in understanding human behavior, until the 1960s most psychological theorists, researchers, and practitioners rarely acknowledged culture as playing a major role in personality dynamics or as influencing the psychotherapeutic process. Instead, counseling and psychology were used as a tool for maintaining the power dominance of White, European American men in the United States during the 1800s and the first half of this century. For example, according to Sue (1981), much of the early literature in psychology stereotyped ethnic minorities in this country as being deficient in certain desirable attributes (e.g., intelligence) or as being culturally deprived. In addition, White psychologists and counselors tended to try to persuade their culturally different clients to assimilate into White culture, a practice that was an expression of "the 'melting pot' notion of creating one idealized national culture" (Wehrly, 1995, p. 24). Overall, the dis-

paraging treatment of people of color by the mental health professions was a manifestation of the racism and discrimination of White society, supported structural inequality and racial segregation, and alienated ethnic minorities from mental health professionals (Sue, 1981).

Major training issues and foci. Prior to the 1960s, counseling students were almost exclusively taught models of counseling that were developed by White, European, and European American males. These models were assumed by most counselor educators to have universal application, and the relevance of culture to the counseling process rarely was discussed in counselor training programs (Sue, 1981).

The Cross-Culturalism Era (1960s-1970s)

Sociopolitical Issues and Themes

The 1960s and 1970s were a period of great social unrest in the United States. The Vietnam War and the civil rights, women's rights, and disabled awareness movements were leading factors in sparking widespread interest in social problems and a questioning of long-standing societal values and conventions (Baker, 2000). The passage of landmark legislation (e.g., the Civil Rights Act of 1964, Title IX of the Education Amendments of 1972, the Education of All Handicapped Children Act of 1975) designed to support the ideals of equality, equity, and equal opportunity indicated that large numbers of White Americans had become sensitive to issues of race, prejudice, discrimination, and privilege (Baker, 2000). Cultural pluralism, or the belief that people of diverse ethnic and racial identities should retain their separate identities within the framework of the larger society and that society benefited from the coexistence and interaction of different cultural groups, was embraced by many who opposed the melting pot/cultural assimilation perspective (Axelson, 1999).

During this same period, similar developments occurred in the counseling profession. "This sensitization took the form of concern over the profession's failure to provide 'guidance for all'—that is, counseling that addresses the diverse needs of all the people who seek it" (Jackson, 1995, p. 9). In addition, there was a growing respect among counseling professionals for the uniqueness of culturally different clients. This change in attitude was reflected in several developments in professional counseling associations, the counseling literature, and counseling training.

Professional Association and Organizational Developments

Cultural awareness began to take shape in the form of several initiatives within formal counseling organizations during this era. In 1965, APGA formed the Human Rights Commission, whose mission was to assess and be an advocate for the needs of culturally unique groups and individuals (Ponterotto & Casas, 1991). At the 1966 APGA convention, special policies calling for the counseling of "culturally disadvantaged" persons were enacted. In 1969, the National Office of Non-White Concerns was created to coordinate APGA policies and positions regarding non-White groups and interests (Ponterotto & Casas, 1991). In 1972, the Association for Non-White Concerns in Personnel and Guidance (later renamed the Association for Multicultural Counseling and Development [AMCD]), was established as a division

of APGA (Gladding, 1992). In its 1977 position paper on non-White concerns, the Association for Counselor Education and Supervision (ACES) called for the development of training programs that would encompass the unique needs and aspirations of non-Whites (Ponterotto & Casas, 1991).

Increased organizational sensitivity also was demonstrated by the election of people of color to executive positions in APGA. For example, Thelma Daly was the first African American elected as the president of APGA and served during 1975-1976 (Jackson, 1995).

Although some of these developments continued to reflect cultural insensitivity (e.g., the use of the term *culturally disadvantaged* implies that minorities are culturally impoverished [Sue, 1981]), APGA and its divisions had taken major steps forward in recognizing the importance of culture and diversity in its policies, organizational structure, and leadership.

Dominant Cultural Themes in the Counseling Literature

Although the well-intended but offensive reference to people of color as culturally disadvantaged continued to be printed in the counseling literature, new terminology such as *cross-cultural counseling* and *multicultural counseling* began to appear (Jackson, 1995). Influential writers, such as Clement Vontress and Gilbert Wrenn, addressed factors that influence the counseling relationship when the cultures of counselors and clients differ (Wehrly, 1995). In many of the primary scholarly counseling journals, increased attention was devoted to topics such as the cultural barriers to effective counseling (e.g., language differences, culture-bound attitudes) and the relationship between these barriers and the underuse and early termination of counseling by ethnic-minority clients (Ponterotto & Casas, 1991). New scholarly journals (e.g., the *Journal of Non-White Concerns* [later renamed the *Journal of Multicultural Counseling and Development*]), dedicated to the study of ethnic-minority concerns and the counseling of the culturally different, were launched.

Major Training Issues and Foci

Although counselor educators continued to emphasize White, European American concepts about counseling, interest in preparing counselors for the challenges involved in crossing cultural boundaries during counseling with the culturally different emerged. Hence, the terms *cross-cultural counseling* and *cross-cultural training* began to filter down through counselor education programs during the 1970s (Jackson, 1995). New courses on cross-cultural counseling were introduced in counselor education programs across the country, although multicultural training still was not required in most programs (Ponterotto & Casas, 1991). New models of counselor training designed to prepare counselors for working with culturally different clients were developed. For example, the triad training model, which is one of the earliest and most frequently cited models of multicultural training, was introduced by Pedersen (1977) during the late 1970s. This model consists of simulated cross-cultural counseling sessions that require counselor trainees to work in teams of three. One trainee acts as the counselor, another as the "anti-counselor" or "procounselor," and a third as the client. The anti-counselor closely matches the client culturally and is deliberately subversive in attempting to exaggerate culturally related mistakes by the counselor during the interview. The pro-counselor is similarly culturally matched with the client but emphasizes the positive messages between the client and the counselor. "As the counselor becomes more familiar with the positive and negative messages that a culturally different client might be thinking but not saying, the counselor will be able to incorporate those messages into the counseling interview itself" (Pedersen, 1999, p. 118) and, consequently, develop competence as a cross-cultural counselor (Pedersen, 1977). The incorporation of the triad model and notions of cross-cultural counseling into counselor education programs represented the springboard for an explosion of multicultural counseling, training, and research over the last two decades of the 20th century.

The Multiculturalism Era (1980s-1990s)

Sociopolitical Issues and Themes

As questioning of the melting pot perspective and an appreciation for cultural pluralism continued into the 1980s and 1990s (Wehrly, 1995), many proponents of cultural pluralism adopted a broadened definition of culture that included considerations of ethnicity, race, and religion as well as other variables such as gender, sexual orientation, and socioeconomic status (Pedersen, 1991). Support for cultural and diversity appreciation education grew and multicultural and diversity training spread widely throughout industry and every level of our nation's educational system (Stimpson, 1997).

According to Ridley and Thompson (1999), the heightened American consciousness and broadened view about issues of diversity has had many positive and visible consequences:

Books about issues of gender, race and ethnicity, the aged, and sexual orientation . . . can now be found in sections of mainstream bookstores and libraries. Within business and organizational settings, the number of people from diverse backgrounds has increased at all levels of hierarchy, men and women are more diversified into occupations that were formerly primarily divided by gender, and the number of physically challenged persons in work settings has risen. . . . Media images are more representative of the nation's diversity, and the perspectives of those who were once considered outside of society's "moral community" (Opotow, 1990) are included in news, film, and journal productions. To continue the work of promoting fairness and equality among Americans from various walks of life, efforts are being made in all aspects of public life to remedy the problems of America's troubled past. As recently as 1997, the president of the United States, William Clinton, issued an initiative on race and reconciliation to examine continued problems of racism in American society. (pp. 9-10)

In contrast to these pro-diversity developments, there were indicators that legions of people in the United States opposed multiculturalism. A neoconservative movement emerged during the 1980s and maintained a powerful presence during the 1990s. Led by political leaders (e.g., Ronald Reagan, Pat Buchanan) and media celebrities (e.g., Rush Limbaugh), the neoconservatives charged that cultural pluralism, affirmative action policies, and recent immigration trends threatened the national identity and well-being of the nation. According to Ridley and Thompson (1999), covert and codified forms of sexism, racism, homophobia, and other forms of prejudice continued to manifest themselves during the 1980s and 1990s at all levels of our society and to create divisions among culturally different people.

Professional Association and Organizational Developments

During the late 1980s and throughout the 1990s, the counseling profession gradually replaced terms such as *minority counseling* and *cross-cultural counseling* with the term *multicultural counseling* to describe topics and activities pertaining to culture and counseling. This change in terminology represented new perspectives about the relationships between culture and the counseling process. First, *multicultural counseling*

> could describe interactions not only between majority group counselors and minority group clients but also between minority group counselors and majority group clients or between counselors and clients who belonged to different minorities. By shifting the focus away from minority groups exclusively, these terms challenged majority group counselors to become aware of the role that their own cultural assumptions played in their interactions with clients. (Jackson, 1995, p. 11)

Second, *multicultural* replaced *cross-cultural* as an expression of the emerging belief that people had multiple, rather than single, cultural identities that are defined by demographic variables (e.g., age, gender), status variables (e.g., educational, economic), and affiliations (formal and informal) as well as by ethnographic variables (e.g., nationality, ethnicity, language, religion) (Pedersen, 1991).

Several notable changes in the names of professional organizations also occurred during the 1980s and 1990s. APGA became the American Association for Counseling and Development (AACD) in 1983, and AACD became the American Counseling Association in 1992.

These changes were prompted by the belief that the name of the umbrella organization for professional counselors should better reflect what counselors do (i.e., counsel people and help them with their developmental concerns, hence AACD) and better represent the diverse array of professionals whose work involves counseling (hence ACA). In 1985, the Association for Non-White Concerns in Personnel and Guidance also changed its name. Its new name, the Association for Multicultural Counseling and Development, reflected both the work that counselors do and the new preference for the term *multicultural* described previously.

In addition to terminology and name changes, the profession intensified its commitment to issues of culture and diversity during the 1980s and 1990s. For example, in 1987, AACD approved and published a position paper on human rights that reaffirmed the ideals of the APGA Human Rights Commission of 1965. Many women and several people of color were elected president of AACD/ACA, and celebrations of diversity were held at most AACD/ACA conventions during this era. And revisions of the ethical standards of AACD/ACA and several of its divisions included standards mandating counselors to respect the human rights and cultural uniqueness of clients and to develop multicultural competence.

Dominant Themes in the Counseling Literature

The year 1981 marked the publication of Derald Wing Sue's provocative and classic text, *Counseling the Culturally Different* (Sue, 1981), in which he challenged the counseling profession to examine its contribution to the oppression of people of color, to understand the effects of cultural variables on the counseling process, and to develop culturally sensitive skills in working with the culturally different. Since the publication of Sue's landmark book, there was a growing presence of articles and books on multiculturalism during the 1980s and an explosion of them during the 1990s.

Across these many publications, several themes emerged. First, there has been an ongoing debate about what constitutes the domains of multiculturalism (Herring, 1997). As mentioned earlier, the definition of culture was broadened by many writers to include a host of variables such as gender, sexual orientation, and life span (Baruth & Manning, 1999), although some authorities, such as Lee and Richardson (1991), argued that the ever-expanding view of culture adopted by the profession was so inclusive that the profession was in danger of rendering *multicultural counseling* to be a meaningless term. Jackson (1995) added that the important and sensitive subject of racism will be ignored if variables such as gender, age, and disability are included in the definition of multiculturalism. In an effort to mediate these differences of opinion and clarify the language used in counseling, Arredondo and colleagues (1996) made a distinction between *multiculturalism* (which refers to ethnicity, race, and culture) and *diversity* (which refers to other characteristics by which individuals may prefer to self-define such as age, gender, sexual identity, religious/ spiritual identification, social/economic class, and residential location [i.e., urban/rural]).

While this debate over terminology continued, the growing interest in cultural issues and an expanded view of culture contributed to the development of numerous models of cultural identity development. Some of the models, such as the Black identity models proposed by Cross (1991) and Helms (1990), accounted for one form of cultural identity development such as race. Other models, such as those designed by Arredondo and Glauner (1992), Ibrahim and Kahn (1987) and Ramsey (1994), attempted to explain multiple identifications as a function of several cultural and diversity variables. Research examining cultural identity assessment devices and the relationship between cultural identity and other variables was conducted regularly and appeared frequently in the literature, thereby making cultural identity development a dominant theme of the Multiculturalism Era.

A third theme, which can be considered an offshoot of the first two themes, was the growing awareness that all counseling is, to some extent, multicultural. If one considers age, lifestyle, socioeconomic status, and gender differences in addition to ethnic and national differences, then it quickly becomes apparent that there is a multicultural dimension in every counseling relationship (Pedersen, 1991).

A fourth and final theme pertains to the burgeoning influence of multicultural counseling and the breadth of topics that are of interest to multicultural scholars. In the September-October 1991 special issue of the *Journal of Counseling and Development,* Paul Pedersen, the issue editor, proclaimed multiculturalism to be a "fourth force" position in counseling, "complementary to the other three forces of psychodynamic, behavioral, and humanistic explanations of human behavior" (Pedersen, 1991, p. 6). The special issue featured 10 articles pertaining to conceptual frameworks for multicultural counseling, 11 articles on multicultural education and training, 9 articles on

multicultural research, and 7 articles on multicultural service delivery. This issue was one of many works published during the 1990s that featured contributions by numerous scholars on a variety of topics pertaining to multiculturalism. Perhaps the most famous of these works was the massive volume, *Handbook of Multicultural Counseling* (Ponterotto, Casas, Suzuki, & Alexander, 1995), which was so comprehensive in its scope and so popular in its appeal that it signified that multiculturalism is indeed a force in counseling that is here to stay. As significant was the publication of another special issue of the *Journal of Counseling and Development* in 1999 that featured 17 personal narratives on racism, followed by 3 qualitative analyses of the narratives and 5 other articles addressing theoretical, research, and training issues pertaining to the reduction of racism (Robinson & Ginter, 1999). This special issue communicated that the profession had moved from ignoring racism to making the topic the complete focus of an issue of the flagship journal of ACA.

Major Training Issues and Foci

The multicultural movement also became a major force in counselor education during this era. Numerous models of multicultural training were proposed (Bowman, 1996; Pedersen, 1988; Sue, Akutsu, & Higashi, 1985; Sue & Sue, 1990). Collectively, these models were designed to promote the following: (a) self-knowledge, especially an awareness of one's own cultural biases; (b) knowledge about the statuses and cultures of different cultural groups; (c) skills to make culturally appropriate interventions including a readiness to use alternative counseling strategies that better match the cultures of clients; and (d) actual experiences in counseling culturally different clients.

Gradually, counselor educators added to their curricula courses on multicultural counseling that were designed to increase multicultural awareness. Survey data collected by Hills and Strozier (1992) indicated that only 59% of counselor education programs responding to their survey conducted in 1989 required all students to take a multicultural course. By 1995, however, 89% of the programs responding to a survey by Ponterotto (1997) had this requirement. Other survey data reported by Hollis and Wantz (1994) indicated that new multicultural counseling courses were being added to existing counseling curricula at a rapid pace. This growth was prompted in part by (a) a revision of the accreditation standards established by the Council for Accreditation of Counseling and Related Educational Programs (CACREP, 1994), which required accredited graduate programs in counseling to include the study of the social and cultural foundations of counseling as a core component of the curriculum; (b) new ethical standards of ACA (1995), which stated that it now is an ethical responsibility of counselors to learn "how the counselor's own cultural/ethnic/racial identity impacts her/his values and beliefs about the counseling process" (p. 2); and (c) similar accreditation and ethical standards of the American Psychological Association (APA) pertaining to multicultural considerations (Ponterotto & Casas, 1991).

As more and more counselors sought training in multicultural counseling, a variety of texts on the subject emerged. Some of these texts, such as *Increasing Multicultural Under-standing* (Locke, 1998), provided culture-specific information for counseling a variety of ethnic populations including African Americans, Hispanics, and the Amish. Other texts, such as *Pathways to Multicultural Counseling Competence* (Wehrly, 1995), were designed to take students through a variety of cognitive and affective experiences believed to be important for the development of multicultural counseling competence. Still other books, such as *Consciousness-Raising* (Parker, 1988) and *Improving Intercultural Interactions* (Brislin & Yoshida, 1994), are manuals filled with experiential exercises whose purpose is to foster affective learning and cultural empathy.

The proliferation of MCT texts was accompanied by an emerging literature pertaining to the pedagogy of MCT. For example, Vasquez (1997) argued that syllabi covering a wide range of diversity topics and readings should be a foundation for MCT courses. Ridley, Esperlage, and Rubinstein (1997) discussed the process of developing an effective course on multicultural counseling. A variety of innovative methods that multicultural educators can employ to help trainees achieve higher levels of consciousness about oppression and cultural identity also were developed during the Multiculturalism Era and are described in Kiselica (1999b). This pedagogical literature has helped counselor educators to better define both the content and the process of MCT.

In summary, by the end of the 1990s, frameworks for teaching MCT had been developed, MCT had become widespread, and a wide variety of texts on MCT had been published in the counselor education literature. The burgeoning literature on MCT helped counselor educators to refine the pedagogy of MCT.

The Current Status of the Practice of MCT

In his recent analysis of the MCT literature, Kiselica (1999c) identified several converging themes regarding the current status of the practice of MCT. They are, in paraphrased form, as follows.

MCT requires organizational support. Multicultural educators continue to experience organizational opposition to MCT that can undermine the efforts of those educators. Institutions of higher education must support multicultural educators by mandating that MCT is a priority, making an honest effort to recruit, employ, and retain a culturally diverse faculty who value MCT and by developing and enforcing antiracist policies.

MCT focused on providing knowledge about the culturally different, examining cultural biases, and developing culturally appropriate skills appears to reduce ethnocentrism and prejudice. Although most of the research studies investigating the effectiveness of MCT have been hampered by methodological problems, the findings of these studies have yielded the consistent impression that multicultural education and diversity appreciation training help counselor trainees to reduce their prejudices.

A climate of trust must be established before emotionally charged subjects, such as racism and sexism, are confronted during MCT. Examining prejudice is difficult—or, for many students, impossible—in an atmosphere void of trust. Therefore, multicultural educators must take measures to help students feel safe about exploring their own imperfections.

Discomfort is a necessary but manageable aspect of MCT. Although efforts should be made to minimize the level of discomfort felt in the classroom, some degree of uneasiness is required for students to confront their biases and move toward more tolerant thinking and behavior.

MCT educational strategies and processes must be adjusted according to the differing developmental levels of students. Students enrolled in multicultural education courses differ in terms of their psychological and multicultural development. Some students are racist and naive, whereas others are tolerant and sophisticated. Counselor educators must give students individualized assignments that are tailored to each student's developmental level. Furthermore, multicultural educators must be able to negotiate different opinions about sensitive topics (e.g., racism) among students throughout the training process.

The cultural and racial identity of the instructor will influence the dynamics and outcomes of MCT. Instructors also vary in terms of their racial backgrounds and racial identity development, and these variations will influence the dynamics and outcomes of multicultural training. MCT instructors should be individuals who have achieved high levels of racial identity consciousness, are able to recognize and empathize with the fears and struggles of students, and yet are capable of confronting ethnocentrism and prejudice in a caring but effective manner.

Experiential and clinical learning activities are central to comprehensive multicultural education. Didactic instruction alone cannot prepare students for the highly human experiences of crossing cultural boundaries and learning about culturally different people. Experiential training exercises can prepare students for multicultural encounters by sensitizing students to the affective reactions evoked by such encounters. Didactic and experiential learning must be followed by actual supervised work in counseling the culturally different so as to ensure that students have opportunities to transfer their multicultural counseling knowledge and skills from the classroom to clinical settings.

The Future of MCT

We predict that several trends pertaining to the practice of MCT and research on MCT will occur during the first few decades of the new millennium, as follows.

Continuing education, with a focus on MCT, will target counselor educators and practicing professionals. As this historical analysis has shown, MCT did not become widespread until the 1990s. Therefore, a significant number of current counselor educators who were trained prior to the 1980s did not graduate from programs requiring MCT. The profession will have to provide extensive continuing education opportunities for counselor educators who wish to learn multicultural counseling skills for the first time and, as Lee (1991) noted, for practicing counselors who wish to upgrade and refine their skills.

MCT will be infused throughout counselor education curricula. Many scholars of multiculturalism (Grottkau & Nicholai-Mays, 1989; Lee, 1991; Locke & Faubert, 1999; Ponterotto, 1997; Ridley, Mendoza, & Kanitz, 1994;

Tomlinson-Clarke & Ota Wang, 1999) have suggested that exposure to multicultural training across the curriculum over time, rather than in one course, might be necessary so as to significantly increase the multicultural counseling competencies of students. Heppner and O'Brien (1994) added that additional training beyond one course probably is necessary to help students integrate changes in thinking with actual counseling skills. These considerations suggest that MCT is likely to be infused throughout counseling curricula in the future. That is, many counselor educators are likely to address cultural issues in all counseling courses, not just in multicultural counseling classes. As this occurs, counselor educators will have to investigate whether or not MCT infusion curricula are more effective than single courses on MCT in promoting multicultural counseling competencies.

Multicultural immersion experiences will become more common. A handful of counselor education programs now require their students to engage in semester- or year-long "multicultural immersion experiences." According to Pope-Davis, Breaux, and Liu (1997), students participating in these experiences become involved or immersed in a culturally different group for a defined period of time, attending group or individual meetings and social gatherings in which the group is involved. In theory, as a result of completing an immersion experience, students gain a deep appreciation for—and an understanding of—the norms, values, and perspectives of that cultural group. We predict that multicultural immersion experiences will grow in popularity during the next decade. Although preliminary case study data (Kiselica, 1991) and program evaluation data (Pope-

Davis et al., 1997) indicate that multicultural immersion experiences increase multicultural counseling competencies, additional research evaluating the efficacy of this approach to MCT is needed.

Programs will be expected to demonstrate that their students are competent multicultural counselors. Several recent publications have been devoted to defining the variables constituting multicultural counseling competence and developing measures to assess those variables (Arredondo et al., 1996; DeLucia-Waack, 1996; Pope-Davis & Coleman, 1997; Sue, Arredondo, & McDavis, 1992). Once the profession reaches a consensus about the dimensions of multicultural counseling competence and which instruments best measure those dimensions, there will be pressure on counselor educators to demonstrate that their students have achieved some minimal standards of multicultural counseling competence. Research on the assessment of multicultural counseling competence and evaluations of these competencies in counselor education programs will continue into the future.

Faculty and students in counseling will become more culturally diverse. Although the majority of faculty and students in counseling are primarily non-Hispanic Whites, the profession will continue to encourage departments of counselor education to recruit more culturally diverse faculty and students. Such diversity is viewed as necessary so as to train counselors who are representative of our culturally diverse nation and to expose counselors-in-training to a variety of cultural perspectives in the classroom. Atkinson, Brown, Casas, and Zane (1996) argued that continued diversification

should increase until ethnic parity is achieved in counselor education programs, and Ponterotto (1997) recommended that counselor education programs strive to achieve a critical mass of at least 30% ethnic/racial-minority faculty and students. The impact of such diversification on the dynamics within, and on the outcomes of, MCT must be explored in future research (Ponterotto, 1998).

Effective and constructive means for confronting biases will be identified and refined. Helping students to identify, confront, and eradicate their cultural biases is one of the most important, and yet delicate, challenges of MCT (Kiselica, 1999d). Because this process requires trainees to discover and confront imperfections about themselves, many react to the training with fear, ambivalence, and varying degrees of resistance (Reynolds, 1995). Drawing from the writings of Sanford (1963), Reynolds (1995) argued that MCT should be designed and conducted with a balance of challenge and support so as to facilitate learning. "Too much challenge causes trainees to withdraw because they feel overwhelmed. Too much support leads to complacency and detachment because there is nothing testing or challenging the trainees" (p. 318). But how do counselor educators and supervisors achieve this balance? What specific conditions facilitate the examination of ethnocentrism and racism? Although recent work has attempted to address these questions (Kiselica, 1999b), counselor educators must continue to refine the process of confronting the prejudices of both White, European American students and students of color in a constructive and effective manner (Kiselica, 1999e; Locke & Kiselica, 1999; Rooney, Flores, & Mercier, 1998). According to Ponterotto (1998), through empirical research, counselor educators should tackle the following questions. What forms of confrontation facilitate the racial identity development of the trainee? What forms or level of confrontation are counterproductive to the training process?

More emphasis will be placed on the joyful aspects of multiculturalism. Although confronting ethnocentrism and racism is a critical component to multicultural training, an overemphasis on these tasks can obscure what might be the most enriching aspect of cross-cultural counseling—experiencing the beauty of different cultures and sensing one's personal development toward a multicultural identity. The multicultural training literature has done little to adequately emphasize the potential for mental health professionals to discover these joys that are inherent in multicultural counseling (Kiselica, 1998). Yet, anecdotal data indicate that several MCT authorities do incorporate joyful exercises and experiences into their multicultural courses as a means of promoting appreciation of different cultures and MCT (Kiselica, 1999c). These latter findings suggest that, while counselor educators will continue the important work of helping students to confront their own prejudices, more attention will be devoted to the joys of multiculturalism in the multicultural literature and throughout the multicultural training process.

Procedures for dealing with students whose extreme prejudices are harmful to clients will be developed. Historically, self-examination of prejudice was not a common activity in counseling programs. As a result, students harboring rigid biases against the culturally different were unlikely to be identified. However, the recent proliferation of MCT has required more and more students to address their prejudices in class. This process has resulted in the exposing of some students whose prejudices are so strong that they might be harmful to their clients if the students are allowed to enter clinical practice. The profession will have to develop guidelines and criteria for evaluating whether or not particular student biases warrant an evaluation of a student's appropriateness for continued study in the field. This will be no easy task. The profession must sponsor a careful and thoughtful discussion of this issue. Any guidelines that are developed as a result of this dialogue should be guided by fairness and the sincere belief that extremely prejudicial students need help rather than punishment (Kiselica, 1999e).

The efficacy of MCT will be evaluated through experimental empirical research. Although research findings suggest that students participating in MCT perceive themselves to experience increased multicultural knowledge and awareness, cause-and-effect inferences regarding the relationship between MCT and multicultural counseling competence are somewhat limited because of the absence of experimental studies evaluating this relationship (Kiselica et al., 1999). Future experimental research will be conducted to assess the efficacy of MCT. The results of this research either will provide counselor educators with increased confidence that their training methods are having a positive effect on their students or will indicate that changes in training procedures are required to enhance MCT efforts.

Future research will include component analyses of MCT. Future research will include investigations that are designed to evaluate the relative contributions of different components of MCT to multicultural counseling competence. Most prior studies have examined MCT that has included didactic instruction, experiential exercises, and skills training. Although practitioners have argued in favor of the efficacy of all three components, in light of the extant research literature, we do not know which component or combination of components is the critical mechanism for effecting multicultural counseling competence (Kiselica et al., 1999). Future research will gradually shed light on this issue (Kiselica et al., 1999) and will identify the key training factors involved in the stimulation of the racial identity development of students (Ponterotto, 1998).

The characteristics of an effective multicultural mentor will be identified. In several personal narratives about multicultural identity development, Kiselica (1991, 1998, 1999a), Rooney and colleagues (1998), and Lark and Paul (1998) acknowledged that mentors played an important role in the respective authors' choices to pursue multicultural specializations. Collectively, the mentors described in these publications were caring role models who were willing to share stories about their own multicultural journeys and who challenged and supported their students to examine their cultural biases and develop multicultural sensitivity. Locke and Kiselica (1999) added that counselor educators can be effective multicultural mentors by being available to students after class for informal conversations about issues that are raised during class and by inviting students to complete additional readings, conduct conference presentations, and investigate research on multicultural topics. Future research should evaluate the validity of these propositions. On a re-

lated note, Ponterotto (1998) recommended that future research address the following questions:

> What are the characteristics of effective multicultural mentors?
>
> Do most training programs have multicultural mentors?
>
> Should all faculty and supervisors be multicultural mentors? Is that possible?
>
> What role does race or minority status have in mentoring?
>
> What is the relationship between mentor/trainee self-disclosure of racial identity struggles/issues and the racial identity development of the trainee?
>
> How do effective mentors incorporate the joyful aspects of multiculturalism into their courses? (p. 59)

Tensions pertaining to the boundaries of MCT will continue and then abate. For the past 40 years, there has been considerable strife among counselors about MCT. Because cultural issues were ignored by most White, European American counselors for so long, several pioneering ethnic-minority scholars—Derald Wing Sue, Don C. Locke, John McFadden, and Courtland Lee, among others—challenged the profession to recognize the harmful effects of cultural encapsulation on the counseling process. Although many White counselors initially reacted to these confrontations defensively, they gradually recognized the perspectives of ethnic-minority scholars and began to support the multicultural movement in counseling. Over time, a spirit of collaboration and mutual appreciation developed between many White and non-White leaders in the field, fostering an embracing of multiculturalism by the profession.

But has the profession really embraced multiculturalism in spite of the clear presence of MCT in counselor education programs to-day? As is illustrated by recent commentaries by Sue (1996) and Ivey, Ivey, D'Andrea, and Daniels (1997), ethnic-minority veterans of multicultural battles and several of their White supporters continue to be leery about what lies ahead, fearful that hard-fought gains in MCT will be lost unless continued pressure to address issues of culture and diversity is applied to the power structure of ACA. Applying the heat on the profession is necessary to make White counselors more aware of racial matters (Sue, 1996) and to offset the potential influence of a strong neoconservative movement in the United States on counselors (Ridley & Thompson, 1999).

The role of White multicultural educators and researchers in MCT is another fear and source of resentment for ethnic/racial-minority scholars. As Whites become more involved in the research and teaching of multiculturalism, where will that leave ethnic/racial-minority scholars and educators who fought White opposition to MCT for years and were largely responsible for the birth and adoption of MCT by the profession (Parham, 1993)? Lee (1989) suggested that the struggle for leadership of MCT is entangled in the larger power struggle between people of color and the dominant White majority in the United States. Sue (1993) urged both minority and majority researchers to make a genuine and concerted effort to reach out to one another and understand the historical perspectives underlying this debate. Only then will we begin to transcend the mistrust that permeates tensions between White and non-White counselor educators.

Other controversies pertain to the limitations and trade-offs associated with the growth of MCT. Have the fears of the proponents of multiculturalism and their efforts to thrust multiculturalism into the mainstream of counselor education overextended the promise and boundaries of MCT? In an attempt to redress the cultural insensitivity of White counselors to ethnic/racial-minority perspectives (Sue et al., 1996) and the absence of cultural emphasis in prevalent theories (Nuttall, Webber, & Sanchez, 1996), multicultural scholars might have overplayed the role of cultural influences on human behavior (Nuttall et al., 1996). As Nuttall and colleagues (1996) observed,

> Not all psychological problems stem from cultural issues; personality and individual differences also play an important part in social development. For instance, an extroverted Asian child may have an easier time adjusting to an American classroom than an introverted one with the same cultural background. (p. 127)

In this example, a student who ignores this issue of a child's temperament while searching only for cultural explanations for classroom adjustment may proceed to implement an inappropriate intervention. In light of such a possibility, we must entertain the question: Will an overemphasis on MCT by some counselor educators result in the neglect of other training topics and contribute to new skills deficits among trainees? Or, as asked by Weinrach and Thomas (1996): Does MCT overemphasize between-group differences to the point of fostering overgeneralizations about specific cultural groups and missing important differences within those groups?

Another issue that the profession must address in the future has to do with where the boundaries of MCT will end. When will counselor educators be able to say that we have devoted sufficient attention to MCT in our training programs? When all programs teach a course on the subject? When all programs infuse multiculturalism throughout the entire curriculum? When all programs require every student to participate in a cultural immersion program? When a critical mass of graduating students demonstrate multicultural competence?

These questions and the issues discussed in this section illustrate the lingering tensions and growing pains that are part of the evolution of MCT. Lee (1995) commented that, because there still is no real consensus among counselor educators about what the content or process of multicultural counseling pedagogy should be, further discussion and inquiry into the nature of MCT should continue. We predict that the profession will continue to struggle with these issues pertaining to the boundaries and legitimacy of multiculturalism for some time to come. However, we are convinced that enough Whites, people of color, and people from other diverse groups (e.g., gay/lesbian/bisexual individuals, disabled people) will continue to engage in productive negotiations about multiculturalism and that, over time, these negotiations will result in ever more diverse faculty and student bodies, greater harmony between culturally diverse faculty and students, and genuine acceptance of MCT in counselor education programs by the majority of its faculty and students. Once these achievements are realized, there will be fewer disagreements and a clearer consensus about the boundaries and domains of MCT.

Conclusion

As we reflect on the information that we reviewed for this chapter, we are encouraged by the changing attitudes toward multiculturalism within counselor education. MCT, once a neglected topic, now is a major component of counselor education in the United States. All indicators suggest that MCT is here to stay, and we predict that the counseling profession's knowledge and valuing of MCT will continue to grow into the next millennium. We applaud and celebrate this trend, for it is a sign that counselors will play an important role in promoting an appreciation for the many beautiful people who comprise our multicultural nation.

References

American Counseling Association. (1995). *Code of ethics and standards of practice*. Alexandria, VA: Author.

Arredondo, P., & Glauner, T. (1992). *Personal dimensions of identity development model*. Boston: Empowerment Workshops.

Arredondo, P., Toporek, R., Brown, S. P., Jones, J., Locke, D. C., Sanchez, J., & Stadler, H. (1996). Operationalization of the multicultural counseling competencies. *Journal of Multicultural Counseling and Development, 24*, 42-78.

Atkinson, D. R., Brown, M. T., Casas, J. M., & Zane, N. W. S. (1996). Achieving ethnic parity in counseling psychology. *The Counseling Psychologist, 24*, 230-258.

Axelson, J. A. (1999). *Counseling and development in a multicultural society* (3rd ed.). Pacific Grove, CA: Brooks/Cole.

Baker, S. B. (2000). *School counseling for the twenty-first century* (3rd ed.). Upper Saddle River, NJ: Merrill/Prentice Hall.

Baruth, L. G., & Manning, M. L. (1999). *Multicultural counseling and psychotherapy: A lifespan perspective*. Upper Saddle River, NJ: Merrill/Prentice Hall.

Bowman, V. E. (1996). Counselor self-awareness and ethnic self-knowledge as a critical component of MCT. In J. L. DeLucia-Waack (Ed.), *Multicultural counseling competencies: Implications for training and practice* (pp. 7-30). Alexandria, VA: Association for Counselor Education and Supervision.

Brislin, R. W., & Yoshida, T. (1994). *Improving intercultural interactions: Modules for cross-cultural training programs*. Thousand Oaks, CA: Sage.

Council for Accreditation of Counseling and Related Educational Programs. (1994). *Accreditation standards and procedures manual*. Alexandria, VA: Author.

Cross, W. E. (1991). *Shades of Black: Diversity in African-American identity*. Philadelphia: Temple University Press.

DeLucia-Waack, J. L. (Ed.). (1996). *Multicultural counseling competencies: Implications for training and practice*. Alexandria, VA: Association for Counselor Education and Supervision.

Du Bois, W. E. B. (1903). *The souls of Black folk*. Chicago: McClurg.

Frazier, E. F. (1966). *The Negro family in the United States* (rev. ed.). Chicago: University of Chicago Press. (Original work published 1939)

Gladding, S. T. (1992). *Counseling: A comprehensive profession* (2nd ed.). Columbus, OH: Merrill.

Grottkau, B. J., & Nicholai-Mays, S. (1989). An empirical analysis of a multicultural education paradigm for preservice teachers. *Educational Research Quarterly, 13*, 27-33.

Helms, J. E. (1990). Toward a model of White racial identity development. In J. E. Helms (Ed.), *Black and White racial identity: Theory, research, and practice* (pp. 49-66). Westport, CT: Greenwood.

Heppner, M. J., & O'Brien, K. M. (1994). Multicultural counselor training: Students' perceptions of helpful and hindering events. *Counselor Education and Supervision, 34*, 4-18.

Herring, R. D. (1997). *Multicultural counseling in schools: A synergetic approach*. Alexandria, VA: American Counseling Association.

Hills, H. I., & Strozier, A. L. (1992). Multicultural training in APA-approved counseling psychology programs: A survey. *Professional Psychology, 23*, 43-51.

Hollis, J. W., & Wantz, R. A. (1994). *Counselor preparation 1990-1992: Programs, personnel, trends* (8th ed.). Washington, DC: Taylor & Francis.

Horney, K. (1937). *The neurotic personality of our time*. New York: Norton.

Ibrahim, F. A., & Kahn, H. (1987). Assessment of worldviews. *Psychological Reports, 60*, 163-176.

Ivey, M. B., Ivey, A. E., D'Andrea, M., & Daniels, J. (1997, Summer). White privilege: Implications of counselor education multicultural identity. *ACES Spectrum*, pp. 3-6. (Association for Counselor Education and Supervision)

Jackson, M. L. (1995). Multicultural counseling: Historical perspectives. In J. G. Ponterotto, J. M. Casas, L. A. Suzuki, & C. M. Alexander (Eds.), *Handbook of multicultural counseling* (pp. 3-16). Thousand Oaks, CA: Sage.

Kiselica, M. S. (1991). Reflections on a multicultural internship experience. *Journal of Counseling and Development, 70*, 126-130.

Kiselica, M. S. (1998). Preparing Anglos for the challenges and joys of multiculturalism. *The Counseling Psychologist, 26*, 5-21.

Kiselica, M. S. (1999a). Confronting my own ethnocentrism and racism: A process of pain and growth. *Journal of Counseling and Development, 77*, 14-17.

Kiselica, M. S. (1999b). (Ed.). *Confronting prejudice and racism during multicultural training*. Alexandria, VA: American Counseling Association.

Kiselica, M. S. (1999c). Confronting prejudice: Converging themes and future directions. In M. S. Kiselica (Ed.), *Confronting prejudice and racism during multicultural training* (pp. 187-198). Alexandria, VA: American Counseling Association.

Kiselica, M. S. (1999d). Preface: How can we help students confront and reduce their own prejudices? In M. S. Kiselica (Ed.), *Confronting prejudice and racism during multicultural training* (pp. ix-xii). Alexandria, VA: American Counseling Association.

Kiselica, M. S. (1999e). Reducing prejudice: The role of the empathic-confrontive instructor. In M. S. Kiselica (Ed.), *Confronting prejudice and racism during multicultural training* (pp. 137-154). Alexandria, VA: American Counseling Association.

Kiselica, M. S., Maben, P., & Locke, D. C. (1999). Do multicultural education and diversity appreciation training reduce prejudice among counselor trainees? *Journal of Mental Health Counseling, 21*, 240-254.

Lark, J. S., & Paul, B. D. (1998). Beyond multicultural training: Mentoring stories from two White American doctoral students. *The Counseling Psychologist, 26*, 33-42.

Lee, C. C. (1989). AMCD: The next generation. *Journal of Multicultural Counseling and Development, 17*, 165-170.

Lee, C. C. (1991). New approaches to diversity: Implications for multicultural counselor training and research. In C. C. Lee & B. L. Richardson (Eds.), *Multicultural issues in counseling: New approaches to diversity* (pp. 209-214). Alexandria, VA: American Association for Counseling and Development.

Lee, C. C. (1995). Reflections of a multicultural road warrior: A response to Smart and Smart; Chambers, Lewis, and Kerezsi; and Ho. *The Counseling Psychologist, 23*, 79-81.

Lee, C. C., & Richardson, B. L. (1991). Promise and pitfalls of multicultural counseling. In C. C. Lee & B. L. Richardson (Eds.), *Multicultural issues in counseling: New approaches to diversity* (pp. 3-9). Alexandria, VA: American Counseling Association.

Locke, D. C. (1998). *Increasing multicultural understanding: A comprehensive model* (2nd ed.). Thousand Oaks, CA: Sage.

Locke, D. C., & Faubert, M. (1999). Innovative pedagogy for critical consciousness in counselor education. In M. S. Kiselica (Ed.), *Confronting prejudice and racism during multicultural training* (pp. 43-58). Alexandria, VA: American Counseling Association.

Locke, D. C., & Kiselica, M. S. (1999). Pedagogy of possibilities: Teaching about racism in multicultural counseling courses. *Journal of Counseling and Development, 77,* 80-86.

Nuttall, E. V., Webber, J. J., & Sanchez, W. (1996). MCT theory and implications for training. In D. W. Sue, A. E. Ivey, & P. B. Pedersen (Eds.), *A theory of multicultural counseling and therapy.* Pacific Grove, CA: Brooks/Cole.

Opotow, S. (1990). Moral exclusion and injustice: An introduction. *Journal of Social Issues, 46,* 1-20.

Parham, T. A. (1993). White researchers conducting multicultural counseling research: Can their effort be "mo betta"? *The Counseling Psychologist, 21,* 250-256.

Parker, W. M. (1988). *Counsciousness-raising: A primer for multicultural counseling.* Springfield, IL: Charles C Thomas.

Pedersen, P. B. (1977). The triad model of cross-cultural counseling training. *Personnel and Guidance Journal, 56,* 480-484.

Pedersen, P. (1988). *A handbook for developing multicultural awareness.* Alexandria, VA: American Association for Counseling and Development.

Pedersen, P. B. (1991). Multiculturalism as a generic approach to counseling. *Journal of Counseling and Development, 70,* 6-12.

Pedersen, P. B. (1999). Confronting racism through increased awareness, knowledge, and skill as a culture-centered primary prevention strategy. In M. S. Kiselica (Ed.), *Confronting prejudice and racism during multicultural training* (pp. 107-122). Alexandria, VA: American Counseling Association.

Pettigrew, T., Fredrickson, G., Knobel, D., Glazer, N., & Ueda, R. (1982). *Prejudice.* Cambridge, MA: Harvard University Press.

Ponterotto, J. G. (1997). Multicultural counseling training: A competency model and national survey. In D. B. Pope-Davis & H. L. K. Coleman (Eds.), *Multicultural counseling competencies: Assessment, education, training, and supervision* (pp. 111-130). Thousand Oaks, CA: Sage.

Ponterotto, J. G. (1998). Charting a course for research on multicultural counseling training. *The Counseling Psychologist, 26,* 43-68.

Ponterotto, J. G., & Casas, J. M. (1991). *Handbook of racial/ethnic minority counseling research.* Springfield, IL: Charles C Thomas.

Ponterotto, J. G., Casas, J. M., Suzuki, L. A., & Alexander, C. M. (Eds.). (1995). *Handbook of multicultural counseling.* Thousand Oaks, CA: Sage.

Pope-Davis, D. B., Breaux, C., & Liu, W. M. (1997). A multicultural immersion experience: Filling the void in multicultural training. In D. B. Pope-Davis & H. L. K. Coleman (Eds.), *Multicultural counseling competencies: Assessment, education, training, and supervision* (pp. 227-241). Thousand Oaks, CA: Sage.

Pope-Davis, D. B., & Coleman, H. L. K. (Eds.). (1997). *Multicultural counseling competencies: Assessment, education and training, and supervision.* Thousand Oaks, CA: Sage.

Ramsey, M. L. (1994). Use of a personal cultural perspective profile (PCPP) in developing multicultural competence. *International Journal for the Advancement of Counseling, 17,* 1-8.

Reynolds, A. L. (1995). Challenges and strategies for teaching multicultural counseling courses. In J. G. Ponterotto, J. M. Casas, L. A. Suzuki, & C. M. Alexander (Eds.), *Handbook of multicultural counseling* (pp. 312-330). Thousand Oaks, CA: Sage.

Ridley, C. R., Esperlage, D. L., & Rubinstein, K. J. (1997). Course development in multicultural counseling. In D. B. Pope-Davis & H. L. K. Coleman (Eds.), *Multicultural counseling competencies: Assessment, education, training, and supervision* (pp. 131-158). Thousand Oaks, CA: Sage.

Ridley, C. R., Mendoza, D. W., & Kanitz, B. E. (1994). Multicultural training: Reexamination, operationalism, and integration. *The Counseling Psychologist, 22,* 227-289.

Ridley, C. R., & Thompson, C. E. (1999). Managing resistance to diversity training: A social systems perspective. In M. S. Kiselica (Ed.), *Confronting prejudice and racism during multicultural training* (pp. 3-24). Alexandria, VA: American Counseling Association.

Robinson, T. L., & Ginter, E. J. (1999). Introduction to special issue on racism. *Journal of Counseling and Development, 77,* 3.

Rooney, S. C., Flores, L. Y., & Mercier, C. A. (1998). Making multicultural education effective for everyone. *The Counseling Psychologist, 26,* 22-32.

Sanchez, G. I. (1932). Group differences and Spanish-speaking children: A critical review. *Journal of Applied Psychology, 16,* 549-558.

Sanford, N. (1963). Factors related to the effectiveness of student interaction with the college social system. In B. Barger & E. E. Hall (Eds.), *Higher education and mental health* (pp. 8-26). Gainesville: University of Florida Press.

Stimpson, C. R. (1997). Introduction. In J. Kramer, *Whose art is it?* (pp. 1-35). Durham, NC: Duke University Press.

Stonequist, E. V. (1937). *The marginal man.* New York: Scribner.

Sue, D. W. (1981). *Counseling the culturally different: Theory and practice.* New York: John Wiley.

Sue, D. W. (1993). Confronting ourselves: The White and racial/ethnic-minority researcher. *The Counseling Psychologist, 21,* 244-249.

Sue, D. W. (1996, Fall). ACES endorsement of the multicultural counseling competencies: Do we have the courage? *ACES Spectrum,* pp. 9-10. (Association for Counselor Education and Supervision)

Sue, D. W., Arredondo, P., & McDavis, R. J. (1992). Multicultural competencies/standards: A pressing need. *Journal of Counseling and Development, 70,* 477-486.

Sue, D. W., Ivey, A. E., & Pedersen, P. B. (1996). Preface. In D. W. Sue, A. E. Ivey, & P. B. Pedersen (Eds.), *A theory of multicultural counseling and therapy* (pp. xvii-xx). Pacific Grove, CA: Brooks/Cole.

Sue, D. W., & Sue, D. (1990). *Counseling the culturally different: Theory and practice* (2nd ed.). New York: John Wiley.

Sue, S., Akutsu, P. D., & Higashi, C. (1985). Training issues in conducting therapy with ethnic-minority group clients. In P. Pedersen (Ed.), *Handbook of cross-cultural counseling and therapy* (pp. 275-280). Westport, CT: Greenwood.

Tomlinson-Clarke, S., & Ota Wang, V. O. (1999). A paradigm for racial-cultural training in the development of counselor cultural competencies. In M. S. Kiselica (Ed.), *Confronting prejudice and racism during multicultural training* (pp. 155-168). Alexandria, VA: American Counseling Association.

Vacc, N., Wittmer, J., & DeVaney, S. B. (1988). *Experiencing and counseling multicultural and diverse populations.* Muncie, IN: Accelerated Development.

Vasquez, L. A. (1997). A systemic multicultural curriculum model: The pedagogical process. In D. B. Pope-Davis & H. L. K. Coleman (Eds.), *Multicultural counseling competencies: Assessment, education, training, and supervision* (pp. 159-179). Thousand Oaks, CA: Sage.

Wehrly, B. (1995). *Pathways to multicultural counseling competence: A developmental journey.* Pacific Grove, CA: Brooks/Cole.

Weinrach, S. G., & Thomas, K. R. (1996). The counseling profession's commitment to diversity-sensitive counseling: A critical reassessment. *Journal of Counseling and Development, 74,* 472-477.

PART V

Research in Counseling

CHAPTER TWENTY-SIX

Epistemological and Methodological Issues in Counseling

EDNA MORA SZYMANSKI

RANDALL M. PARKER

Epistemology is a branch of philosophy that addresses the question, "What is true?" In other words, it is the study of the nature and origin of knowledge. The epistemological question just stated and two others form the foundational foci of philosophy. The two other questions "What is real?" and "What is good?" are the philosophical domains of ontology and axiology, respectively (Morris, 1961; *New College Dictionary,* 1999). This chapter speaks specifically to epistemology and its ramifications for counseling research methodology.

How professional counselors view the source and character of knowledge shapes their worldview. Moreover, knowledge institutionalized in individuals is a key element of professions (Abbott, 1988). In addition, access to and control of knowledge are key elements of social power (Friere, 1973). Because the counseling profession applies knowledge to social issues, the profession must examine, rather than take for granted, its knowledge foundation. Consequently, the chapter explores (a) key questions of counseling, (b) paradigms of knowing, (c) methodologies of knowing, (d) connections between research and practice, and (e) perspectives on the future of counseling research.

Key Questions of Counseling Research

Key research questions regarding counseling, because of the immediate focus and ultimate goals of the counseling process, must first emphasize clients and clients' welfare. The paramount goal of counseling research must be to identify interventions, broadly speaking, that facilitate positive changes in clients. In many respects, this goal could be likened to the search for the Holy Grail, a quest for an ultimately unattainable treasure. Researchers have been frustrated in securing their prize because of the complexity of variables obscuring and distorting their vision of "reality."

The research process must, implicitly or explicitly, take a stance on the nature of reality. Scarr (1985) presented an intriguing perspective, suggesting that reality is "constrained only by imagination and a few precious rules of the scientific game" (p. 512). Furthermore, Scarr stated,

> The psychological world in which we conduct research is, in my view, a cloud of correlated events to which we as human observers give meaning. In the swirling cloud of interacting organisms and environments, most events nearly co-occur. As investigators, we construct a story (often called a theory) about relations among events. We select a few elements and put them into a study. By doing so, we necessarily eliminate other variables a priori from possible analysis, and we preconstrue causal relations among the events. One cannot avoid either the theoretical preconceptions or the selection of variables to study, but one can avoid exaggerated claims for the causal status of one's favorite model. (p. 502)

The cloud of correlated events in counseling is daunting. Among the manifold variables are clients' characteristics (e.g., age, gender, marital status, culture, socioeconomic status, personal history, attitudes) as well as presenting problems, all of which are examples of contextual variables in counseling research. In addition, counselor variables must be measured and incorporated into research data. Counselor variables include not only age, gender, and professional training and experience but also things such as theoretical stance, communication style, and physical appearance. Similarly, intervention or treatment protocols must be identified, standardized, and carefully applied to the research sample. The helping process, including interactional and reciprocal aspects of counseling, also must be assessed. Finally, relevant outcome variables must be measured and input as data. Clearly, the researcher must account for the variance of an incredible number of relevant variables, indeed a formidable task.

The multiplicity of variables in counseling, the multivariate nature of the counseling encounter, leads to *the* central issue of counseling research. In fact, the critical methodological issue of all social, psychological, and educational research is the issue of control. Control refers to managing the tangled web of variables that invariably exists in social, psychological, and educational research. Consequently, managing all relevant variables, whether they are of primary interest or not, is the major methodological issue in identifying valid causes of gain or positive outcomes in counseling. Particularly vexing is the control of extraneous or nuisance variables, the ones that are not of primary interest. The purpose of research design is to identify strategies for limiting or eliminating extraneous variance, which in turn limits rival hypotheses or explanations concerning the results of addressing research questions (Cook & Campbell, 1979; Cook, Campbell, & Peracchio, 1990; Parker, 1993).

The multidimensional nature of counseling research is conveyed by the familiar question (modified from Paul, 1967), "What counseling interventions are effective with what kinds of clients treated in which settings by what counselors using what approaches?" Despite the confusing tangle of myriad variables, research addressing this question fills volumes.

Three landmark counseling outcome studies, selected from among thousands because of their discordant methodologies and concordant findings, are presented to illustrate this genre of research: Smith, Glass, and Miller (1980); Luborsky, Crits-Christoph, Mintz, and Auerbach (1988); and Seligman (1995). Using meta-analysis, Smith and colleagues (1980) aggregated the effects reported in 475 controlled psychotherapy outcome studies. Statistically, the average effect of psychotherapy, based on the 475 controlled studies containing 1,766 measured effects on tens of thousands of persons, is 0.85 standard deviation unit. This translates to the treated individual being better off at the end of therapy than 80% of those who are untreated but who need therapy. More recent publications on meta-analysis research of counseling outcomes include Crits-Christoph (1997); Sexton, Whiston, Bleuer, and Walz (1997); and Wampold and colleagues (1997).

The 20-year Penn Psychotherapy Project conducted by Luborsky and colleagues (1988) found that psychotherapy had even larger effects. Luborsky and colleagues reported an average effect size of 1.05 standard deviation unit. Translated into ratings of clients' benefits by therapists, 22% of clients attained large improvement, 43% attained moderate improvement, 27% attained some improvement, 7% showed no change, and 1% were worse off.

In 1995, Seligman reported the results of a survey of *Consumer Reports* readers regarding the effects of therapy from mental health service providers. Of the estimated 180,000 readers who were mailed the 1994 annual questionnaire, nearly 22,000 of the total sample responded (12% response rate). The sample of interest was the approximately 4,100 individuals (19% of respondents) who had consulted mental health professionals, support groups, or family physicians for stress or emotional problems within the previous 3 years (Seligman, 1995). The results revealed that 87% of those who said that they felt *very poor* at the beginning of therapy were feeling *very good, good,* or *so-so* at the time of the survey. Of those feeling *fairly poor* at the beginning of therapy, 92% reported feeling *very good, good,* or *so-so* at the time of the survey.

In summary, Smith and colleagues (1980), Luborsky and colleagues (1988), and Seligman (1995) presented evidence for the positive effects of counseling and psychotherapy. Despite these positive results, critics of counseling and psychotherapy outcome research abound because of the difficulties in controlling the multitude of extraneous variables noted earlier (Dawes, 1994; Lambert & Bergin, 1994; Lambert & Hill, 1994; VandenBos, 1996).

Paradigms of Knowing

A paradigm is a basic set of beliefs or worldview that guides the researcher's inquiries in ontologically and epistemologically fundamental ways (Creswell, 1998; Guba & Lincoln, 1994). It is the lens through which the world is both viewed and interpreted. Paradigms have evolved over time, and many currently coexist. Four major paradigms affecting counseling research are positivism, postpositivism, constructivism, and critical theory.

Positivism

Positivism is the paradigm that assumes a reality that can be understood. Findings from research studies can be considered definitive, and hypotheses can be verified (Guba & Lincoln, 1994; Hammersley, 1989; Lincoln & Guba, 1985). In positivism, reality is objective and not influenced by the beliefs of individuals (Firestone, 1987). Consider the parable of the "blind men" attempting to describe an elephant. A positivist studying elephants, for example, would choose a suitable theory to test, hypothesize about the nature of the elephant, gather data, and if the data supported the hypothesis, draw firm conclusions about the nature of the elephant.

Postpositivism

In postpositivism, "reality is assumed to exist but to be only imperfectly apprehensible because of basically flawed human intellectual mechanisms and the fundamentally intractable nature of the phenomena" (Guba & Lincoln, 1994, p. 110). Cook and Campbell (1979) referred to this approach as *critical realism*. Rather than verifying hypotheses, significance tests are used to falsify or "render implausible only *one* of the many plausible threats to validity that are continually arising" (p. 93, italics in original). To deal with the relatively fuzzy nature of reality, postpositivists gather a variety of data from different angles to bolster their conclusions (Cook & Campbell, 1979), which are only probably true (Guba & Lincoln, 1994;

Lincoln & Guba, 1985). Like positivists, they still test theories through hypotheses. A postpositivist studying elephants would consider theory, hypothesize or speculate, plan data collection accordingly, collect data from multiple sources and angles, and advance tentative conclusions about the nature of elephants.

Constructivism

To the constructivist, reality is truly in the mind of the beholder.

> Realities are apprehensible in the form of multiple, intangible mental constructions, socially and experientially based, local and specific in nature (although elements are often shared among many individuals and even across cultures), and dependent for their form and content on individual persons or groups holding the constructions. (Guba & Lincoln, 1994, pp. 110-111)

There is a connection between the researcher and the research subjects, and both are involved in constructing the findings (Mertens, 1998). "The final aim is to distill a consensus construction that is more informed and sophisticated than any of the predecessor constructions (including, of course, the etic construction of the investigator)" (p. 111). A constructivist studying elephants might live among the herd, conduct multiple interviews with herd members, and engage members of the herd in constructing the findings.

Critical Theory

The critical theorist holds that reality, over time, has been "shaped by a congeries of social, political, cultural, economic, ethnic, and gender factors and then crystallized (reified) into a series of structures that are now (inappropriately) taken as 'real' " (Guba & Lincoln, 1994, p. 110). The researcher and subjects are connected, and

> what can be known is inextricably intertwined with the interaction between a *particular* investigator and a *particular* object group. . . . [It] requires a dialogue between the investigator and the subjects of the inquiry; that dialogue must be dialectical in nature to transform ignorance and misapprehensions (accepting historically mediated structures as immutable) into more informed consciousness. (p. 110)

Like the constructivist, the critical theorist would live with the herd. However, rather than simply transmitting findings relating to poor living conditions resulting from human encroachment, the critical theorist might teach the elephants how to negotiate for better game preserves.

Paradigms of knowledge actually are at the heart of the counseling profession. For example, are the counselor's diagnostic impressions, guided by the *DSM-IV* (*Diagnostic and Statistical Manual of Mental Disorders*), reality (American Psychiatric Association, 1994)? To what extent is normalcy a political and social construction (Stubbins, 1988)? And, to what extent do professional interventions, based on one perception of reality, become disabling (Illich, Zola, McKnight, Caplan, & Shaiken, 1977). Clearly, beliefs about reality guide both research and professional practice. In the next section, we present the link between paradigms and methodologies for approaching problems.

Methodologies of Knowing

According to Skrtic (1991), professionalism is inherently positivist. Professional autonomy "implies that professionals know best what is good for their clients because they have access to the profession's specialized knowledge and skills" (p. 90). In fact, professions are based on the assumption that there is a distinct apprehensible knowledge or reality that can be institutionalized in individuals (Abbott, 1988; Rothman, 1987). Although this positivist assumption is, or should be, open to critical inquiry, it has nonetheless formed the backdrop of current counseling research. Thus, it is not surprising that much of counseling research has tended toward positivist and postpositivist paradigms.

Positivism is associated with quantitative methods, and postpositivism is associated with both quantitative and qualitative methods (Guba & Lincoln, 1994; Lincoln & Guba, 1985). Constructivism and critical theory are associated primarily with qualitative methods.

Quantitative and qualitative methods depend not only on different types of data but also on different types of reasoning. A full discussion of qualitative and quantitative methods is beyond the scope of this chapter. The reader is referred to chapters by Elmore and Bradley (Chapter 27 on quantitative methods) and Paisley and Reeves (Chapter 28 on qualitative methods) in this volume. Rather, we provide a brief overview and contrast through discussion of (a) definitions of quantitative and qualitative methods, (b) data collection and analysis, (c) the role of the researcher, and (d) differential utility.

Definitions of Quantitative and Qualitative Methods

Quantitative research examines natural phenomena or behaviors through "objective measurement and quantitative analysis" (Firestone, 1987, p. 16). Much of quantitative research is devoted to testing theories and currently uses a postpositivist paradigm. "Experimental results never 'confirm' or 'prove' a theory—rather, the successful theory is tested and escapes being disconfirmed" (Campbell & Stanley, 1963, p. 35). And, "qualitative, contextual information (as well as quantitative information on tangential variables)" (Cook & Campbell, 1979, p. 93) is important to interpreting hypothesis testing. Quantitative researchers who collect and examine such additional data conform to postpositivist tenets, whereas those who do not tend more toward positivism and naive realism.

Qualitative research, on the other hand, is "multimethod in focus, involving an interpretive, naturalistic approach to its subject matter. In other words, qualitative researchers study things in their natural settings, attempting to make sense of, or interpret, phenomena in terms of meanings people bring to them" (Denzin & Lincoln, 1994, p. 2). Although qualitative research tends toward constructivism or critical theory, it also can be regarded as postpositivist if its intent is to illuminate a supposed reality from multiple perspectives.

Data Collection and Analysis

Quantitative and qualitative methods differ both on types of data and analytic reasoning. Specifically, quantitative data are measurable and usually can be reduced to numbers for statistical description or manipulation (Creswell, 1994). Qualitative data, on the other hand, often involve multiple forms of soft data such as participant observation, in-depth interviewing, and document review. Field notes and researcher memos (Bogdan & Biklen, 1992; Creswell, 1994) usually supplement these forms.

Quantitative studies involve deductive reasoning, that is, hypothesizing and gathering data to test the hypotheses. Hypotheses, which are conjectures about the relationships among variables (Kerlinger, 1986), are derived from theory. Variables are operationalized through instruments, which are used to gather data. Significance tests then are applied to test the hypotheses (Creswell, 1994; Kerlinger, 1986). The quantitative researcher studying elephants would (a) use theory to hypothesize about elephant behavior; (b) devise an instrument to collect data on the variables of interest in the hypothesis (e.g., an elephant behavior checklist); (c) use statistical procedures to analyze the data and apply significance tests; and (d) make conclusions in relation to support, modify, or not support the original theory.

By contrast, qualitative data analysis is inductive. Researchers "do not search out data of evidence to prove or disprove hypotheses they hold before entering the study; rather, the abstractions are built as the particulars that have been gathered are grouped together" (Bogdan & Biklen, 1992, p. 31). Data collection and data analysis are interwoven. Although the researcher may start with questions to guide data collection, he or she is open to surprises and patterns that emerge from the data. From these patterns, theories or pictures of the phenomena emerge (Strauss & Corbin, 1990). The qualitative researcher studying elephants might (a) set out with some vague guiding questions about elephant behavior, (b) collect a great deal of different data about elephant behavior, (c) do some initial analysis of the data and refine the initial guiding questions, (d) set out to collect yet more data to further refine the emerging patterns, and (e) present a theory grounded in the data collected on elephant behavior.

The Role of the Researcher

The role of the researcher clearly is different in qualitative and quantitative methods, although there might be some blurring in the postpositivist genre. Quantitative researchers remain detached and avoid introducing their own biases, whereas qualitative researchers often are very involved with their participants (Firestone, 1987). They are, in essence, an instrument of data collection (Creswell, 1994) bringing their inherent biases, which must be identified (Hammersley, 1989). Whereas the quantitative researcher would observe elephants from a concealed blind, the qualitative researcher would be likely to live among them.

Differential Utility

Quantitative and qualitative methods differ in the types of knowledge they bring to counseling. For example, quantitative methods have been used to examine (a) the effects of counseling interventions (Lambert & Cattani-Thompson, 1996; Luborsky et al., 1988; Merz & Szymanski, 1997; Seligman, 1995; Sexton et al., 1997; Smith et al., 1980; Wampold et al., 1997); (b) the relationship of client characteristics to outcome (Garfield, 1994; Garfield & Bergin, 1986); (c) the importance of counselor characteristics such as professional qualifications and personal attributes (Barrett & Wright, 1984; Beutler, Machado, & Neufeldt, 1994); and (d) what occurs within the counseling process (Hill, 1982; Orlinsky, Grawe, & Parks, 1994).

Similarly, qualitative methods historically have been used to better understand and treat client problems ranging from severe psychological difficulties (e.g., clinical case studies by Breuer & Freud, 1936) to the everyday problems faced by individuals with developmental disabilities (Edgerton, 1967).

Both types of methods clearly are important in informing counseling practice. Quantitative methods tend to provide information about intervention effectiveness and description and comparison of measurable aspects of the population (e.g., student academic achievement). Qualitative methods, on the other hand, help counselors to better understand the specific nature or context of behaviors and to glimpse situations from the perspectives of those most involved. We view the two approaches as two sides of a coin or, perhaps, as ends of a methodological continuum; both are essential to move knowledge in the field forward.

Connections Between Research and Practice

A considerable body of literature exists on the relatively weak connections between research and practice (Tracey, 1991). For example, there is a disconnect between career theory, which is tied to research, and the practice of career counseling (Savickas & Walsh, 1996). And, according to Tracey (1991), the "typical practitioner does not engage in research . . . or read research . . . and generally holds negative attitudes about research" (p. 5). In this section, we explore the connections between research and practice through discussion of the following topics: (a) limited methodological diversity, (b) the importance of research to practice, (c) the scientist-practitioner model, (d) the reflective practice model, and (e) research instruction.

Limited Methodological Diversity

Although other fields, such as education, have embraced qualitative research more readily (Conrad, Neumann, Haworth, & Scott, 1993), change has been slow to come in counseling (Polkinghorne, 1991). Polkinghorne (1991) suggested that this reluctance might relate to ties with academic psychology, which espouses closer ties to the natural sciences. Heppner, Kivlighan, and Wampold (1999) attributed this situation to a hierarchy in which experimental studies were perceived as most valuable. In opposing the hierarchy, they proposed that "the selection of the research method must fit the phenomenon under investigation and the type of information being sought" (p. 10). Consequently, descriptive studies, including clinical case studies, often are more instructive than research based on null hypothesis significance testing.

Increasing methodological diversity in counselor training may decrease the rift between research and practice. "One of the advantages of including instruction in qualitative procedures as part of scientific training is that the conceptual skills required to carry out these procedures are closely related to those required to work successfully with clients" (Polkinghorne, 1991, p. 169).

The Importance of Research to Practice

Research is necessary to both guide and evaluate practice. In guiding practice, research not only can influence the choice of a particular technique but also can influence the way in which the clinician thinks about and approaches practice (Polkinghorne, 1991). This influence can be provided by all four of the knowledge paradigms discussed earlier.

Although some have questioned the importance of the link between research and practice, clinical judgment, uninformed by research, has proved to be fallible (Tracey, 1991). Furthermore, the trust placed in professionals by society (Rothman, 1987) and the power differential in the counseling process (Bersoff, 1995) demand the systematic application of some type of scrutiny. Such scrutiny can and should come in many forms including the positivist and postpositivist hypothetical and deductive approach, the constructivist qualitative and inductive approach, and the value explicit critical theory approach.

The Scientist-Practitioner Model

Counseling has long wrestled with the connections of research and practice. The scientist-practitioner model was advanced in 1950 to address the relationships of research and practice in the training of clinical and counseling psychologists (Hayes, Barlow, & Nelson-Gray, 1999; Heppner et al., 1999). The positivist roots of the model still are apparent.

> The skilled practitioner engages in the exact same processes as the researcher: problem definition, using appropriate theory in hypothesis generation, operationalization of constructs, application of intervention, and assessment of effects. The main difference between the researcher and practitioner is the generalization sought. (Tracey, 1991, p. 21)

Despite its positivist beginnings, the scientist-practitioner model is amenable to various epistemologies. However, although this pedagogical model consists of training students broadly in both scientific and practitioner domains, the emphasis tends to be on traditional quantitative approaches (Hayes et al., 1999; Heppner et al., 1999). As counselor education programs begin to include more studies in qualitative methodologies, the utility of the model will expand. Until then, the reader is recommended to consider alternative models such as the reflective practitioner model espoused by Schön (1983).

The Reflective Practice Model

The reflective practice model appears to have evolved in reaction to the positivist traditions of the relation of knowledge to professional practice (Schön, 1983). This model leans more toward the constructive and critical theory epistemologies and away from the positivist conceptualization of professional-as-expert.

In the reflective practice model, the counselor and client engage together in discovery of solutions in the context of the client's real-life problems. "Research is an activity of practitioners. It is triggered by features of the practice situation, undertaken on the spot, and immediately linked to action" (Schön, 1983, p. 308). Reflection enables the practitioner to "surface and criticize the tacit understandings that have grown up around the repetitive experiences of a specialized practice and can make new sense of the situations of uncertainty or uniqueness" (p. 61).

The reflective practice model should not substitute for or compete with the scientist-practitioner model. Rather, as the counseling profession moves more toward necessary methodological diversity, it provides an alternative method of linking research and practice.

Research Instruction

Now that we have discussed the need for and problems of the linkage of research to practice, we turn our attention to research instruction, which is a relatively recent area of inquiry (Gelso & Lent, 2000). Although increasing epistemological and methodological diversity has been recommended to bridge the rift between research and practice (Heppner et al., 1999), it has been slow to take hold. Heppner and colleagues (1999) noted the pervasive belief among academic departments today in the superiority of quantitative approaches. In addition, as noted by Polkinghorne (1991), many professors who conduct and teach research today were educated solely in the positivist (or, at best, postpositivist) traditions and often exclusively teach in those modes.

Problems in research instruction are not due solely to epistemology and methodology. Instruction also plays a role (Heppner et al., 1999). Nonetheless, research in rehabilitation counseling has shown that methodologically diverse, contextualized instruction can decrease anxiety about research and increase confidence in research ability in master's students (Szymanski, Swett, Watson, Lin, & Chan, 1998). Similarly, Gelso and Lent (2000) reported on a variety of recent studies in research instruction and presented recommendations, including methodological diversity, in the context of the research training environment theory.

Perspectives for the Future of Counseling Research

Epistemological and methodological diversity is necessary for responsible growth of the counseling profession. In fact, Schön (1983) and

Lincoln and Guba (1993) questioned positivist approaches on ethical grounds. In addition, increasing understanding of diversity has called into question the classic models of theoretical application (Szymanski & Hershenson, 1998). Thus, positivism, alternatively termed *naive realism* (Guba & Lincoln, 1994), no longer can be the major lens guiding counseling practice. Epistemological and methodological diversity must be approached on two fronts: research and scholarly publication and academic preparation.

Research and Scholarly Publication

High-quality methodologically diverse research must reach the field and inform practice. To achieve this goal, the scholarly community must (a) conduct practically relevant, high-quality research and (b) ensure that editorial processes do not privilege or marginalize specific epistemologies and methodologies.

If practitioners are to read research, then they must find it practically relevant as well as understandable. The quest for practically relevant research is not new. Techniques, such as participatory action research (Whyte, 1991), have been advanced to better link the activities of researchers and practitioners. In addition, qualitative methods, by their very nature, are likely to be more accessible and relevant to professional practice (Polkinghorne, 1991).

Furthermore, high-quality, methodologically diverse research must reach practitioners. This can be a problem due to the fact that many members of editorial boards were educated solely in quantitative methods (Polkinghorne, 1991) and might privilege those methods. Alternatively, in an effort to promote diversity, naive reviewers might support poor-quality qualitative research. It is important for editors to make concerted efforts to seek out expertise in various qualitative methodologies.

Academic Preparation

Counseling students still are receiving research instruction that either omits or marginalizes qualitative methods. This situation must change to further advance the profession and to improve the link between research and practice. To this end, professional associations should recommend inclusion of epistemological and methodological diversity in research instruction in their accreditation standards. In accordance with this belief, we applaud the proposed Council for Accreditation of Counseling and Related Educational Programs (CACREP) year 2001 standards for recognizing both quantitative and qualitative methodologies as essential in counselor preparation (CACREP, 1999).

In summary, increasing epistemological and methodological diversity is absolutely critical to the future of the counseling profession. Returning to our elephant analogies, epistemological and methodological diversity is necessary to gain a better understanding of elephants. It enables consideration of multiple facets of elephant behavior from multiple perspectives and with critical examination of inherent values. The current situation, which privileges one approach, limits inquiry in a way similar to just studying fossils of extinct members of the elephant family so as to understand elephant behavior.

References

Abbott, A. (1988). *The system of professions: An essay on the division of expert labor.* Chicago: University of Chicago Press.

American Psychiatric Association. (1994). *Diagnostic and statistical manual of mental disorders* (4th ed.). Washington, DC: Author.

Barrett, C., & Wright, J. (1984). Therapist variables. In M. Hersen, L. Michelson, & A. Bellack (Eds.), *Issues in psychotherapy research* (pp. 361-392). New York: Plenum.

Bersoff, D. N. (1995). Multiple relationships. In D. N. Bersoff (Ed.), *Ethical conflicts in psychology* (pp. 207-208). Washington, DC: American Psychological Association.

Beutler, L. E., Machado, P., & Neufeldt, S. (1994). Therapist variables. In A. E. Bergin & S. L. Garfield (Eds.), *Handbook of psychotherapy and behavior change* (4th ed., pp. 229-269). New York: John Wiley.

Bogdan, R. C., & Biklen, S. K. (1992). *Qualitative research for education: An introduction to theory and methods* (2nd ed.). Boston: Allyn & Bacon.

Breuer, J., & Freud, S. (1936). *Studies in hysteria.* New York: Nervous and Mental Disease Publishing.

Campbell, D. T., & Stanley, J. C. (1963). *Experimental and quasi-experimental designs for research.* Chicago: Rand McNally.

Conrad, C., Neumann, A., Haworth, J. G., & Scott, P. (Eds.). (1993). *Qualitative research in higher education: Experiencing alternative perspectives and approaches* (ASHE Reader Series). Needham Heights, MA: Ginn.

Cook, T. D., & Campbell, D. T. (1979). *Quasi-experimentation: Design and analysis issues for field settings.* Boston: Houghton Mifflin.

Cook, T. D., Campbell, D., & Peracchio, L. (1990). Quasi-experimentation. In M. Dunnette & L. Hough (Eds.), *Handbook of industrial and organizational psychology* (2nd ed., Vol. 1, pp. 491-576). Palo Alto, CA: Consulting Psychologists Press.

Council for Accreditation of Counseling and Related Educational Programs. (1999). *2001 CACREP accreditation standards and procedures manual* (Draft 3). Alexandria, VA: Author.

Creswell, J. W. (1994). *Research design: qualitative and quantitative approaches.* Thousand Oaks, CA: Sage.

Creswell, J. W. (1998). *Qualitative inquiry and research design: Choosing among five traditions.* Thousand Oaks, CA: Sage.

Crits-Christoph, P. (1997). Limitations of the dodo bird verdict and the role of clinical trials in psychotherapy research: Comment on Wampold et al. *Psychological Bulletin, 122,* 216-220.

Dawes, R. M. (1994). *House of cards: Psychology and psychotherapy built on myth.* New York: Free Press.

Denzin, N. K., & Lincoln, Y. S. (1994). Introduction: Entering the field of qualitative research. In N. K. Denzin & Y. S. Lincoln (Eds.), *Handbook of qualitative research* (pp. 1-17). Thousand Oaks, CA: Sage.

Edgerton, R. B. (1967). *The cloak of competence: Stigma in the lives of the mentally retarded.* Berkeley: University of California Press.

Firestone, W. A. (1987). Meaning in method: The rhetoric of quantitative and qualitative research. *Educational Researcher, 16*(7), 16-21.

Friere, P. (1973). *Pedagogy of the oppressed.* New York: Seabury.

Garfield, S. L. (1994). Research on client variables in psychotherapy. In A. E. Bergin & S. L. Garfield (Eds.), *Handbook of psychotherapy and behavior change* (4th ed., pp. 190-228). New York: John Wiley.

Garfield, S. L., & Bergin, A. E. (Eds.). (1986). *Handbook of psychotherapy and behavior change* (3rd ed.). New York: John Wiley.

Gelso, C., & Lent, R. (2000). Scientific training and scholarly productivity: The person, the training environment, and their interaction. In S. D. Brown & R. W. Lent (Eds.), *Handbook of counseling psychology* (3rd ed., pp. 109-139). New York: John Wiley.

Guba, E. G., & Lincoln, Y. S. (1994). Competing paradigms in qualitative research. In N. K. Denzin & Y. S. Lincoln (Eds.), *Handbook of qualitative research* (pp. 105-117). Thousand Oaks, CA: Sage.

Hammersley, M. (1989). *The dilemma of qualitative method: Herbert Blumer and the Chicago tradition.* New York: Routledge.

Hayes, S. C., Barlow, D. H., & Nelson-Gray, R. O. (1999). *The scientist practitioner: Research and accountability in the age of managed care.* Boston: Allyn & Bacon.

Heppner, P. P., Kivlighan, D. M., & Wampold, B. E. (1999). *Research design in counseling* (2nd ed.). Pacific Grove, CA: Brooks/Cole.

Hill, C. (1982). Counseling process research: Philosophical and methodological dilemmas. *The Counseling Psychologist, 10,* 7-20.

Illich, I., Zola, I. K., McKnight, J., Caplan, J., & Shaiken, H. (1977). *Disabling professions.* London: Marion Boyars.

Kerlinger, F. N. (1986). *Foundations of behavioral research* (3rd ed.). New York: Holt, Rinehart & Winston.

Lambert, M. J., & Bergin, A. E. (1994). The effectiveness of psychotherapy. In A. E Bergin & S. L. Garfield (Eds.), *Handbook of psychotherapy and behavior change* (4th ed., pp. 143-189). New York: John Wiley.

Lambert, M. J., & Cattani-Thompson, K. (1996). Current findings regarding the effectiveness of counseling: Implications for practice. *Journal of Counseling and Development, 74,* 601-608.

Lambert, M. J., & Hill, C. E. (1994). Assessing psychotherapy outcomes and process. In A. E. Bergin & S. L.

Garfield (Eds.), *Handbook of psychotherapy and behavior change* (4th ed., pp. 72-113). New York: John Wiley.

Lincoln, Y. S., & Guba, E. G. (1985). *Naturalistic inquiry.* Beverly Hills, CA: Sage.

Lincoln, Y. S., & Guba, E. G. (1993). Ethics: The failure of positivist science. In C. Conrad, A. Neumann, J. G. Haworth, & P. Scott (Eds.), *Qualitative research in higher education: Experiencing alternative perspectives and approaches* (ASHE Reader Series, pp. 417-428). Needham Heights, MA: Ginn.

Luborsky, L., Crits-Christoph, P., Mintz, J., & Auerbach, A. (1988). *Who will benefit from psychotherapy? Predicting psychotherapeutic outcomes.* New York: Basic Books.

Mertens, D. (1998). *Research methods in education and psychology.* Thousand Oaks, CA: Sage.

Merz, M. A., & Szymanski, E. M. (1997). The effects of a vocational rehabilitation based career workshop on commitment to career choice. *Rehabilitation Counseling Bulletin, 41,* 88-104.

Morris, V. C. (1961). *Philosophy and the American school: An introduction to the philosophy of education.* Boston: Houghton Mifflin.

New college dictionary. (1999). Boston: Houghton Mifflin. Author.

Orlinsky, D., Grawe, K., & Parks, B. (1994). Process and outcome in psychotherapy—Noch einmal. In A. E. Bergin & S. L. Garfield (Eds.), *Handbook of psychotherapy and behavior change* (4th ed., pp. 270-376). New York: John Wiley.

Parker, R. (1993). Editorial: Threats to the validity of research. *Rehabilitation Counseling Bulletin, 36,* 130-138.

Paul, G. (1967). Strategy of outcome research in psychotherapy. *Journal of Consulting Psychology, 31,* 109-118.

Polkinghorne, D. E. (1991). Qualitative procedures for counseling research. In C. E. Watkins, Jr., & L. J. Schneider (Eds.), *Research in counseling* (pp. 163-204). Hillsdale, NJ: Lawrence Erlbaum.

Rothman, R. A. (1987). *Working: Sociological perspectives.* Englewood Cliffs, NJ: Prentice Hall.

Savickas, M. L., & Walsh, W. B. (1996). Toward convergence between career theory and practice. In M. L. Savickas & W. B. Walsh (Eds.), *Handbook of career counseling theory and practice* (pp. xi-xvi). Palo Alto, CA: Davies-Black.

Scarr, S. (1985). Constructing psychology: Making facts and fables for our times. *American Psychologist, 40,* 499-512.

Schön, D. A. (1983). *The reflective practitioner: How professionals think in action.* New York: Basic Books.

Seligman, M. E. P. (1995). The effectiveness of psychotherapy: The *Consumer Reports* study. *American Psychologist, 50,* 965-974.

Sexton, T. L., Whiston, S. C., Bleuer, J. C., & Walz, G. R. (1997). *Integrating outcome research in counseling practice.* Alexandria, VA: American Counseling Association.

Skrtic, T. M. (1991). *Behind special education: A critical analysis of professional culture and school organization.* Denver, CO: Love.

Smith, M. L., Glass, G., & Miller, T. (1980). *The benefits of psychotherapy.* Baltimore, MD: Johns Hopkins University Press.

Strauss, A., & Corbin, J. (1990). *Basics of qualitative research: Grounded theory procedures and techniques.* Newbury Park, CA: Sage.

Stubbins, J. (1988). The politics of disability. In H. E. Yuker (Ed.), *Attitudes toward persons with disabilities* (pp. 22-32). New York: Springer.

Szymanski, E. M., & Hershenson, D. B. (1998). Career development of people with disabilities: An ecological model. In R. M. Parker & E. M. Szymanski (Eds.), *Rehabilitation counseling: Basics and beyond* (3rd ed., 327-378). Austin, TX: Pro-Ed.

Szymanski, E. M., Swett, E. A., Watson, E. A., Lin, S. L., & Chan, S. Y. (1998). The effects of contextualized research instruction on research anxiety, perceived utility of research, and confidence in research ability. *Rehabilitation Education, 12,* 347-360.

Tracey, T. J. (1991). Counseling research as an applied science. In C. E. Watkins, Jr., & L. J. Schneider (Eds.), *Research in counseling* (pp. 3-31). Hillsdale, NJ: Lawrence Erlbaum.

VandenBos, G. R. (Ed.). (1996). Outcome assessment of psychotherapy [Special issue]. *American Psychologist, 51*(10).

Wampold, B. E., Mondin, G. W., Moody, M., Stich, F., Benson, K., & Ahn, H. (1997). A meta-analysis of outcome studies comparing bona fide psychotherapies: Empirically, "all must have prizes." *Psychological Bulletin, 122,* 203-215.

Whyte, W. F. (Ed.). (1991). *Participatory action research.* Newbury Park, CA: Sage.

CHAPTER TWENTY-SEVEN

Quantitative Research Methods

PATRICIA B. ELMORE

RICHARD W. BRADLEY

Counselors who question are researchers. They ponder problems and set out to resolve them. They solve puzzles, and the puzzles on which they concentrate are those they believe can be both stated and solved within an existing tradition. One such tradition in the history of science is labeled *quantitative*. Quantitative methods were derived from the word *quantity,* which means that something is measurable and that a number representing the quantity can be determined. This approach to research provides counselors with tools to organize and communicate information effectively.

To understand quantitative research methods, one needs to consider philosophical assumptions underlying the approaches. This methodology, as taught in most graduate counselor training programs, has been based on the positivism tradition of reductionism (Hoshmand, 1989). Key to this approach are the principles that "truth" exists, it can be observed and measured, and the experimenter is an objective observer of phenomena who does not affect the search for truth. The positivism paradigm was replaced with postpositivism, which also believes in a "real" world and that the goal of research is to discover the truth. However, there is recognition that the truth probably never can be fully known. So, "at best, we make probabilistic statements rather than absolute statements about truth" (Heppner, Kivlighan, & Wampold, 1999, p. 237). Postpositivism, with its quantitative approach, is the dominant research orientation in universities.

Quantitative research methods provide the processes that enable researchers to communicate information simply and effectively. Researchers are particularly interested in variables. Variables are characteristics of individuals or objects that change from person to person or over time. Variables are classified as continuous if they are real numbers that can be measured to a finer degree of precision (e.g., chronological age, weight, height, annual income). Variables are classified as discrete if they are integers and can only take separated values (e.g., number of children, gender, religious affiliation, *DSM-IV* [*Diagnostic and Statistical Manual of Mental Disorders*] diagnosis [American Psychiatric Association, 1994]).

Scales of Measurement

The first step in any research project is the determination of the constructs or variables to be studied and measured. The scale of measurement chosen for the variables will affect the statistics or quantitative methods available to researchers. The lowest level or scale of measurement is the nominal scale that involves naming or distinctness. Most counselors work with clients and identify them by number for confidentiality. Michael Jordan wore a Chicago Bulls jersey with the number 23. Certainly, the number 23 identified him, but it did not have meaning in terms of his skill or level of performance. Other examples of variables measured using a nominal scale include gender, treatment group membership, and religious affiliation.

The ordinal scale includes distinctness like the nominal scale but also involves order and allows researchers to specify more or less of some trait or characteristic but not how much more or less. Examples of variables measured using an ordinal scale include *DSM-IV* diagnoses ordered by severity, number of children, rank in high school or college graduating class, class year (freshman, sophomore, junior, or senior), and military rank. During the summer of 1998, two baseball players broke Roger Maris's record of 61 home runs in one season. Mark McGwire (who wears St. Louis Cardinals jersey number 25) hit the highest number of home runs, and Sammy Sosa (who wears Chicago Cubs jersey number 21) hit the second highest number of home runs that year. Their jersey numbers are nominal, and their ranks in terms of home runs hit—1 and 2—are ordinal.

In counseling research, most of our data are at best ordinal. However, some variables are measured on an interval or ratio scale. The interval scale of measurement includes the characteristics of the nominal and ordinal scales plus equal units of measure along the scale but an arbitrary zero. Similarly, the ratio scale of measurement includes the characteristics of the nominal, ordinal, and interval scales plus an absolute zero. Examples of variables measured on an interval scale include calendar time, chronological age, and degrees Celsius or Fahrenheit. Examples of variables measured on a ratio scale include height in inches, feet, or centimeters; weight in pounds or grams; dosage of a drug in milligrams; time in minutes or hours; and annual income in dollars or other currency.

Continuous variables tend to be measured using the interval and ratio scales of measurement, and discrete or categorical variables tend to be measured using the nominal and ordinal scales of measurement. In counseling, we construct instruments and obtain scores. Some examples include attitude instruments using Likert scales from *strongly agree* to *strongly disagree,* intelligence tests with scores ranging from 55 to 145 and with an average of 100, and college admission tests such as the ACT (American College Test, with scores ranging from 1 to 36) and the SAT (Scholastic Assessment Test) and GRE (Graduate Record Examination), with scores ranging from 200 to 800. These test scores certainly have properties above an ordinal scale but are not interval or ratio. Researchers in the social sciences tend to use statistical analyses such as *t* tests, multiple regression, and analysis of variance that require sums, differences, multiplication, or division of score values to analyze test scores, assuming that the test scores are measured on a continuous scale with interval or ratio properties.

Reliability and Validity

Measurement concepts of reliability and validity of test scores from instruments developed by counseling researchers are discussed prior to the five-step scientific method and statistical analyses used by counseling researchers.

Reliability

Possible synonyms for reliability in this context are consistency and stability. The three types of reliability used in counseling research are test-retest (stability), parallel forms (equivalence), and internal consistency. Test-retest reliability is assessed when the same instrument is administered at two different times. It should be used in a study when the instrument measures a stable trait that is not affected by carry-over effects such as memory and practice. Paral-

lel forms reliability is assessed when two different test forms are administered at the same time. For ACT, GRE, SAT, and TOEFL (Test of English as a Foreign Language) test administrations, different test forms measuring the same content are essential. Actually stability and equivalence can be assessed at the same time when two different forms of an instrument are administered at two different times.

Internal consistency reliability coefficients (e.g., split half, Cronbach's alpha, Kuder-Richardson 20 and 21) provide evidence of the unidimensionality of the trait or construct measured by the instrument. Because Cronbach's alpha is the average of all split halves, the split-half coefficient seldom is reported. Cronbach's alpha is used with rating scales that have more than two categories or instruments that do not have a correct answer. Examples include Likert scales with responses ranging between *strongly agree* and *strongly disagree* frequently used to measure self-concept or self-efficacy. The Kuder-Richardson 20 is used when the instrument is scored correct/incorrect or has dichotomous rating categories. Examples include a test with questions that have correct answers and a rating scale indicating the presence or absence of some characteristic for diagnosis. The Kuder-Richardson 20 is preferred over the Kuder-Richardson 21, which assumes that all the items are equally difficult and does not require item responses for calculation.

Validity

Evidence of validity should provide information about *what* characteristic or construct an instrument measures and *how accurate* the measurement is. Traditionally, validity has been grouped into three categories: content, criterion related, and construct.

Content validity usually refers to the degree to which items on the instrument are representative of the domain to be measured and is determined by experts in the field.

Criterion-related validity often is classified into two types: concurrent and predictive. When criterion-related evidence is obtained, it is required that the criterion be reliable, appropriate for the setting, and free of contamination. For concurrent validity, the instrument being studied and the criterion are obtained simultaneously; for predictive validity, the criterion is obtained some time after the instrument being studied. Predictive validity could be assessed when predicting performance in a position following college graduation from cumulative college grade point average (GPA). Concurrent validity could be assessed by determining the relationship between two different measures of mathematics attitudes when the two instruments were administered during orientation week prior to the freshman year in college.

Construct validity is concerned with obtaining evidence that some theoretical construction about human behavior exists. Methods of obtaining such evidence include group differences, change after some intervention, and the dimensionality of the construct. Types of construct validity include convergent and discriminant validity obtained using the multitrait-multimethod technique and factorial validity from factor analysis. Convergent validity is demonstrated by high correlations between scores on tests measuring the same trait by different methods. Discriminant validity is demonstrated by low correlations between scores on tests measuring different traits, especially when using the same methods. Examples of constructs include cognitive abilities (e.g., verbal, quantitative, spatial), attitudes (e.g., liberal vs. conservative), and personality characteristics (e.g., state and trait anxiety).

Measurement researchers (Cronbach, 1991; Ellis & Blustein, 1991a, 1991b; Messick, 1995; Moss, 1995; Schafer, 1991) have questioned whether all validity is construct validity. Messick (1995) offered a unified concept of validity by providing a comprehensive theory of construct validity that addresses score meaning and the social consequences of score use. Messick concluded, "Thus, validity and values are one imperative, not two, and test validation implicates both the science and the ethics of assessment, which is why validity has force as a social value" (p. 749).

Researchers need to keep in mind that validation is a continuing, never-ending process. The use of a test or scale may be validated for a specific sample of participants in a particular setting using a particular research design and statistical analysis. Researchers should obtain reliability and validity evidence for each use of a test, scale, or instrument.

The Scientific Method: Using Descriptive and Inferential Statistics

Counselors doing research in the behavioral sciences need to be familiar with quantitative methods used to describe data and with inferential techniques used to generalize from a sample to a population. Some definitions may be helpful. A population is the universe or totality of individuals to whom researchers want to generalize. A sample is a subset of the population. Seldom can counselors observe or test all individuals in the population about whom they wish to generalize; therefore, most quantitative research in counseling requires sampling. The most common sampling procedure is simple random sampling, where each individual in the population has the same chance of being chosen. For survey research, proportional stratified random sampling usually is used to allow individuals to be selected from the strata (e.g., gender, ethnicity) in the same proportions as in the population.

If the population is accessible and available for study, then researchers need only to calculate descriptive statistics. If a sampling study is conducted, then inferential techniques are required. Even if inferential statistical techniques are used, researchers have an obligation to provide the readers of their findings with information that describes the participants in their studies. Thus, descriptive statistical techniques are used in both studies of populations and studies of samples.

An Historical Outcome Study

The overriding question most often asked in counseling research is, "Does it work?" This question has been asked in a variety of ways over the history of our profession. Rothney's (1958) classic book, *Guidance Practices and Results,* opened with the following paragraph:

> This is a report of an attempt to counsel students and to determine its effectiveness. Eight hundred and seventy students in all the sophomore classes in four representative high schools were distributed randomly into control and experimental groups. No counseling was provided for the members of the control group, but the experimental subjects were counseled throughout their remaining years in high school. In order to determine the effectiveness of the counseling and to

learn about the problems that youth and young adults meet in the process of coming of age, all of the 690 students who remained to graduate were followed up six months, two and one-half years, and five years after they completed their high school careers. (p. 1)

Conducting such an ambitious study over 8 years (3 in high school through 5 years after high school graduation) required careful enunciation of the logic employed and attention to detail. Rothney (1958) specified the decision rules, which touch on a recurrent dilemma when conducting counseling research from a quantitative orientation. That is, we never want to lose sight of individuals, but we generally analyze on the basis of group data. Therefore, he listed the following criteria:

1. Any datum about an individual that assists in the understanding of his [or her] behavior must be given due consideration. (p. 67)
2. Conceptualization must be continuous as each separately evaluated datum is added to the study of the individual. (p. 68)
3. Any datum about an individual that is to be used in his [or her] counseling must be appraised in terms of its accuracy and economy. (p. 69)

This means that all variables or scores from instruments must be subjected to considerations of reliability and validity.

After presentation of one's logic, the next step is to outline methods and procedures followed and to define the independent (treatment) and dependent (outcome) variables. The investigator has control over the treatments (in this case, defining the counseling process) and must explain the effect on the outcome measures. So far, what has been described about the

Rothney (1958) study can be summarized as the first three steps of a five-step scientific method.

Step 1 is a statement of the problem, which in this case might be reframed as follows: Does counseling bring about measurable differences in individuals later in life?

Step 2 takes aspects of the problem and breaks them down into component parts. Just what is counseling? What do previous researchers/theorists say? What do we need to check on to confirm that counseling is being conducted in the specified manner? Step 2 defines the independent variable(s).

Step 3 defines how information will be collected in trying to address the problem. This step begins with defining the constructs or criteria to be used and how they will be measured. What differences will be examined later in life, and how are these measured?

In terms of quantitative research methods, Steps 2 and 3 are loaded with measurement issues. Probably most important are issues associated with reliability, validity, and scales of measurement. Researchers need to provide evidence of reliability and validity for their variables for the participants in their studies before moving to the next step in the scientific method.

Step 4 is the way in which one analyzes the data obtained in Steps 2 and 3. With a study done more than 40 years ago (Rothney, 1958), before the use of computers for statistical analysis, most of the follow-up results were presented by percentages of the number of participants who responded to questionnaires or from data collected about the participants. From inspection of the percentages reported by Rothney (p. 323), one can observe the trend toward superiority by those counseled. More than twice as many won honors, more graduated from college in 4 years, and fewer were dropped for low grades. Yet, when analyzed by the chi-square test, the obtained differences did not reach statistical significance at the .05 level.

When considering Step 5 of the scientific method, to draw conclusions, Rothney (1958) found that the counseled students generally achieved slightly higher academic records in high school and college, were more likely to go on for higher education, were more consistent with their career aspirations, made more progress in employment, participated in more self-improvement activities, and were more satisfied with postsecondary education and their status 5 years after high school graduation. These conclusions reflect the three general criteria used for years to measure outcomes: changes in academic performance, career development, and self-reported personal reactions. Let us fast forward 40 years to the 1990s and look at some more outcome studies.

Present-Day Outcome Studies

Whiston and Sexton (1998) located and summarized 50 school counseling outcome studies published between 1988 and 1995. Interestingly, 43 (86%) of these were classified as quantitative, and the majority used statistical tests to analyze data. The other categories of studies were evaluations (which we would categorize as quantitative and statistical) and qualitative (which included descriptive statistics). Among these 50 studies, the most ambitious, classified as an evaluation, was conducted by Lapan, Gysbers, and Sun (1997).

The Lapan and colleagues (1997) study looked at the relationship between guidance program concepts and selected outcomes for students attending 236 Missouri high schools. Gysbers and Henderson's (1994) model of school guidance included the following counseling program concepts or treatments, the independent variables: a classroom or group counseling curriculum; activities designed to assist students in developing and implementing personal, educational, and career plans; services designed to provide special assistance to students facing personal, social, or educational problems; and management activities that maintain and enhance the program. This list illustrates, as did the analogous list in Rothney's (1958) study, that any quantitative research study must fully explain what constitutes the counseling provided. Consumers of the research must know what was being done to influence outcomes.

Even though nearly 40 years lapsed between the studies conducted by Rothney (1958) and Lapan and colleagues (1997), there was little change in sophistication of outcome variables during that time. All student outcome and attitude variables were measured on a self-report questionnaire. Items included self-reported grades on an 8-point scale (1 = *below D* to 8 = *mostly A*). In addition, 5-point Likert scales were employed for students to rate quality of their educations, liking for schools, perceptions about being safe, and feelings of belonging in their schools. The similarity in outcome variables and how they were measured points out an old problem. Rothney and Farwell (1960) wrote about what they labeled the *criterion problem.*

> Researchers were plagued with the problem of securing adequate terminal measures of attempts to provide guidance services. . . . It is evident that the problem of selecting and securing adequate measures of criteria against which guidance services are to be assessed has not been solved. (pp. 168-169)

Lapan and colleagues (1997) did better than many researchers in defining variables. Yet, we must recognize that measurement of treatment and outcome variables is a critical component of a research study and affects the results obtained.

Where the Lapan and colleagues (1997) and Rothney (1958) studies really differ is in the sophistication of data analysis. In Lapan and colleagues (1997), there were approximately 100 randomly selected students from the 236 high schools for a total of 22,964 students. In addition, 434 counselors answered questions regarding implementation of the counseling programs, and data were obtained about each school's size, socioeconomic level, and percentage of minority students. Multiple linear regression analysis is an inferential statistical analysis technique that allows researchers to analyze one continuous or dichotomous dependent variable and a number of continuous or categorical independent variables simultaneously. It was used to predict outcome measures (e.g., grades) as a function of particular student characteristics (e.g., school size, student perceptions of the school climate). We refer the reader to that article for elaboration of the statistical techniques and findings.

So far, the examples of outcome studies have used high school participants. Similar studies can be located in most American Counseling Association (ACA) division journals. Counseling researchers employed with all types of agencies and serving all types of clientele want to check whether their services are working. When reading the Spring 1999 issue of the *Journal of College Counseling,* we noted that the first research article, titled "Evaluating Therapy Outcome at a University Counseling Center With the College Adjustment Scales" (Nafziger,

Couillard, & Smith, 1999), was another big question outcome study.

With the initiation of a time-limited brief therapy policy (up to 10 sessions), this counseling center found that the average number of counseling sessions for clients during the 1990s was between six and seven. Nafziger and colleagues (1999) refined the big question, "Does counseling work?" to "Does brief therapy reduce clients' self-reported symptomatology after six individual sessions?" To answer this question, they administered a pretest before the intake interview and a posttest after the sixth session to determine whether brief therapy delivered over 30 months by the 5 professional staff members and a yearly cadre of 7 graduate assistants and 15 practicum students had an effect on symptomatology. All we know for sure about this brief therapy was the number of sessions; nothing was reported about what went on during these sessions. More than 1,000 potential clients completed the pretest. There were 423 participants in six or more sessions, yet only 333 completed the posttest. We must conclude that Step 2 of the scientific method, the specification of the independent variable, was not adequately described in this study.

By contrast, the dependent variables that were scores on the nine College Adjustment Scales were well described. Nafziger and colleagues (1999) built a case for why these scales are appropriate for college students and reported evidence of reliability and validity for scores from the College Adjustment Scales for participants in their study. All three—the supporting logic, consistency data, and construct support—are necessary when explaining dependent variable selection. Step 3 of the scientific method was accomplished.

The analysis phase of this study, Step 4 of the scientific method, used a repeated measures multivariate analysis of variance (MANOVA) and found statistically significant decreases from pretest to posttest on all nine College Adjustment Scales. Many times with relatively large samples (and 333 is a large sample size for a counseling study, even though it is dwarfed by the 22,964 in the Lapan et al. [1997] study), slight mean differences can result in statistically significant findings. So, researchers have devised a way to check for how important the differences are, called *effect size*. An effect size was calculated "by subtracting the mean score at intake from the mean score after the sixth session of counseling and then dividing by the standard deviation (at intake)" (Nafziger et al., 1999, p. 7) for all nine College Adjustment Scales. Basically, this procedure can be thought of as telling about how many standard deviation units were changed across sample participants. A 50% standard deviation drop was considered moderate, an 80% drop was considered large, and a 20% drop was considered small. Nafziger and colleagues (1999) provided an interesting discussion of the differences, leading to Step 5 in the scientific method, that is, drawing conclusions.

What, then, may be concluded from the Nafziger and colleagues (1999) study? From a postpositivism perspective, we probably never will know "the truth" relative to the big question, "Does counseling work?" Scholarship and research are processes adding to our body of knowledge. Nafziger and colleagues (1999) convinced us that there was a statistically significant decrease in self-reported symptomatology among the 333 college counseling center clients who completed the pretest and posttest. Was this the result of the brief therapy they received? We still are searching for this answer.

Researchers continue to be interested in outcomes of counseling, but counseling seldom was looked at as such an ubiquitous entity. Instead, the individual differences movement began to exert influence on counseling research. The question was modified from the general "Does counseling work?" to "Under what conditions or with what populations does counseling work?"

Counseling Individuals With Special Needs

The overriding question, "Does counseling work?" often is refined to "Does counseling work with these people with these problems or under these conditions?" Instead of investigating a generalized brief therapy approach in a college counseling center as was done by Nafziger and colleagues (1999), Wlazelek and Coulter (1999), in the same issue of the *Journal of College Counseling,* investigated "The Role of Counseling Services for Students in Academic Jeopardy."

Target participants were 414 rural northeastern university students who did not earn a cumulative 2.0 GPA at the end of an academic year and returned the following semester. They were sent letters by the provost's office about being in academic jeopardy and were directed to "schedule academic counseling through the counseling center" (p. 36).

The number of contacts that these students had with the counseling center the following summer and fall semesters was the independent variable for this study. Contacts were divided into three categories: no involvement, one session, and more than one academic counseling session. Academic counseling provided was described clearly by Wlazelek and Coulter (1999), but there were no reported checks to verify that counseling was conducted in the specified manner. Thus, simply stated, this study asked, "Does a type of treatment (academic counseling) work for a particular group (college students) with an identified problem (being in academic jeopardy) as measured by a yet to be defined criterion?"

The criterion or dependent variable examined in this study was the score obtained by subtracting the cumulative GPA at the end of one academic year from the cumulative GPA obtained the subsequent fall semester. It is interesting to note that nearly 40 years after Rothney and Farwell (1960) discussed problems of securing adequate terminal measures of counseling services, Wlazelek and Coulter (1999) used changes in GPA even though we know that difference scores tend to be more unreliable than the scores entering into the difference (Allen & Yen, 1979). It is important for researchers to determine whether groups differ on pretest scores before selecting a statistical technique to use to compare change for the groups. There have been numerous articles written concerning the problems encountered when dealing with difference or change scores and how to analyze them appropriately. We recommend that the reader consult Cronbach and Furby (1970) and Linn and Slinde (1977).

It is important for researchers to recognize that the questions asked and definitions used for variables almost always dictate the type of analysis. Beginning students of research often operate the other way around. They learn a statistic and search for a question or define variables so as to use the acquired method of analysis. As an example, Wlazelek and Coulter (1999) defined the independent variable as three categories of contact with the counseling center: none, one, and more than one academic counseling session. When researchers are comparing mean scores on a continuous dependent variable (e.g., GPA), for three or more groups, an analysis of variance (ANOVA) is appropriate. If the ANOVA is significant, then it also is useful to conduct an after-the-fact or post hoc analysis, such as the Tukey or Scheffé multiple comparison procedure, to determine which groups differ. Results indicated a statistically significant difference among groups on the measure of academic performance. Students in academic jeopardy who attended one or more academic counseling sessions showed significantly greater improvements in GPA than did students not involved in academic counseling.

Remember that the truth about anything never can be fully known from a postpositivism perspective. Consequently, researchers make additional efforts to rule out alternative explanations. This generally involves addressing possible threats to validity using a framework such as the one formulated by Cook and Campbell (1979). They created a taxonomy that classifies validity into four types: statistical conclusion, internal, construct, and external. Discussion of these leads researchers from Step 4 of the scientific method to Step 5, that is, drawing conclusions.

Research adds to our scientific understanding. When studying issues as complex as how counseling can bring about change in human behavior, often all researchers can say is that these findings are promising. Researchers-in-training should not become discouraged by the realization that we seldom have definitive re-

sults. Promising results often are very exciting such as in the study conducted by Fall, Balvanz, Johnson, and Nelson (1999):

> This research study suggests that children's self-efficacy may be increased with a half-hour play therapy intervention once a week for 6 weeks. This is an important finding. If we can intervene with young children before they lose the natural love of learning that they come to school with, we will be making a difference that could have potential effects throughout school careers. (p. 203)

In addition to a promising outcome, Fall and colleagues (1999) seem to represent a collaborative team approach to research that we encourage. From the biographical lines listed in *Professional School Counseling,* we surmise that the first author of the article (Fall), a counselor educator, may have contributed research expertise. The next three authors, listed in alphabetical order, all are school counselors who probably provided the play therapy treatment and were identified as Counselors 1, 2, and 3 in the article. The big question was, "Do children who are exposed to a brief play therapy intervention exhibit improved classroom learning behaviors and beliefs of self-efficacy?" (p. 194).

Step 1 of the scientific method involves not only the question asked but also the theoretical and empirical rationale for the variables to be studied. But it involves even more. Fall and colleagues (1999) began their article by discussing students who are disruptive to learning and are referred by classroom teachers to school counselors. Because of language deficiencies, many of these children are unable to participate in talk therapy. This leads to a discussion of conceptions about play therapy and prior research on client change as a function of counseling. Fall and colleagues set the stage for Step 2 and eventual description of play therapy as the independent variable. But their introduction also set the stage for Step 3 by discussing the outcome variables noted in their research question, that is, "improved classroom behaviors and beliefs of self efficacy." They concluded their theoretical framework with the following reframe:

> Accordingly, this study asks, "Does a 6 week, once a week, half-hour play therapy intervention with K-3 grade level students in the schools make a difference in children's learning (as measured by teacher report), self-efficacy (as measured by the Self-Efficacy Scale for Children Grades K-3 . . . and audiotapes), and classroom learning behaviors (as measured by the Conners Teacher Rating Scale . . . and classroom observations)?" (p. 196)

Step 4 of the scientific method is the way one analyzes the data. Fall and colleagues (1999) used a randomized experimental-control groups pretest-posttest design. Although this is quite a long title, it explains clearly what was done. First, to select participants, counselors in several elementary schools asked teachers to identify children "whose coping mechanisms did not facilitate learning" (e.g., acting out or being shy, withdrawn, easily frustrated, or unwilling to take risks). From a list of such children, participants were randomly assigned to the experimental group (whose members received the play therapy treatment) or the control group (whose members did not receive this treatment but were evaluated in the same manner as the experimental group). Both groups were evaluated using the three dependent measure observational techniques before (pretest) and again after (posttest) the experimental group members' six play therapy sessions. Thus, all aspects of the design title were covered. This mixed design is powerful because it can control both be-

tween- and within-subject effects (Heppner et al., 1999).

Perspectives on the Future

The measurement issues and topics discussed in this chapter will continue to be a concern. An excellent reference for counseling researchers is the 1999 *Standards for Educational and Psychological Testing* (American Educational Research Association, American Psychological Association, & National Council on Measurement in Education, 1999). This edition contains a revised conceptualization of validity, an expanded discussion on fairness in testing and test use, a separate chapter on testing individuals with disabilities, and numerous chapters of interest and importance to counseling researchers. The introduction to the standards states,

> Educational and psychological testing and assessment are among the most important contributions of behavioral science to our society, providing fundamental and significant improvements over previous practices. Although not all tests are well developed nor are all testing practices wise and beneficial, there is extensive evidence documenting the effectiveness of well-constructed tests for uses supported by validity evidence. The proper use of tests can result in wiser decisions about individuals and programs than would be the case without their use and also can provide a route to broader and more equitable access to education and employment. (p. 1)

The quantitative research methods used in the future by counseling researchers will include techniques with which we are familiar and new techniques not yet developed. How, then, can researchers keep up with current developments? The Association for Assessment in

Counseling, a division of ACA, sponsors the journal *Measurement and Evaluation in Counseling and Development* (*MECD*). A special section of that journal titled "Methods Plainly Speaking" publishes articles that present state-of-the-art statistical and measurement procedures with heuristic examples for use by counselors and counselor educators in teaching and for their professional development.

Counseling researchers often use structural equation modeling, including confirmatory factor analysis, to study latent constructs such as family socioeconomic status given that observable variables such as mother's or father's education are imperfect indicators of the latent construct. These techniques require researchers to theorize an underlying structure prior to using a computer program such as LISREL (Jöreskog & Sörbom, 1993) or EQS (Bentler, 1993) to determine how well the observed data fit the proposed model. The Methods Plainly Speaking section of *MECD* has included a primer describing the use and interpretation of structural equation models by Baldwin (1989) and an article on hierarchical modeling and measures of fit by Buczynski (1994). Similarly, item response theory is a measurement model used by counseling researchers to describe the relationship between a latent trait (mathematics ability) and an observed measure of mathematics ability (ACT mathematics score). The Methods Plainly Speaking section also has included an introduction by McKinley (1989) to item response theory models appropriate for dichotomous items and an introduction by DeAyala (1993) to polytomous item response theory models appropriate for Likert scales. Recent topics in the Methods Plainly Speaking section have included standard-setting techniques (Stephenson, Elmore, & Evens, 2000), a review

of procedural and statistical methods for handling attrition and missing data in clinical research (Mason, 1999), an overview of meta-analysis (Schafer, 1999), an introduction to logistic regression (Cizek & Fitzgerald, 1999), and an article on misinterpreting interaction effects in analysis of variance (Harwell, 1998).

As researchers, we conduct studies and report our findings to the profession through papers presented at conferences and articles published in professional journals. Current editorial policies of many journals, including *MECD*, require that effect sizes and statistical test results be included when reporting results of empirical research studies. A special Methods Plainly Speaking section of the April 1998 issue of *MECD* contained three articles on this topic (Biskin, 1998; Vacha-Haase & Nilsson, 1998; Vacha-Haase & Thompson, 1998).

Counseling researchers certainly will continue to conduct studies using quantitative research methods. How to report their findings ethically and responsibly has become an important area of concern for all researchers in the behavioral sciences.

References

Allen, M. J., & Yen, W. M. (1979). *Introduction to measurement theory*. Pacific Grove, CA: Brooks/Cole.

American Educational Research Association, American Psychological Association, & National Council on Measurement in Education. (1999). *Standards for educational and psychological testing*. Washington, DC: AERA.

American Psychiatric Association. (1994). *Diagnostic and statistical manual of mental disorders* (4th ed.). Washington, DC: Author.

Baldwin, B. (1989). A primer in the use and interpretation of structural equation models. *Measurement and Evaluation in Counseling and Development, 22*(2), 100-112.

Bentler, P. M. (1993). *EQS: Structural equations program manual*. Los Angeles: BMDP Statistical Software.

Biskin, B. H. (1998). Comment on significance testing. *Measurement and Evaluation in Counseling and Development, 31*(1), 58-62.

Buczynski, P. L. (1994). Using hierarchical modeling and practical measures of fit to evaluate structural equation models. *Measurement and Evaluation in Counseling and Development, 27*(1), 328-339.

Cizek, G. J., & Fitzgerald, S. M. (1999). An introduction to logistic regression. *Measurement and Evaluation in Counseling and Development, 31*(1), 223-245.

Cook, T. D., & Campbell, D. T. (1979). *Quasi-experimentation: Design and analysis issues for field settings.* Boston: Houghton Mifflin.

Cronbach, L. J. (1991). A moderate view: Response to Ellis and Blustein. *Journal of Counseling and Development, 69,* 556-557.

Cronbach, L. J., & Furby, L. (1970). How we should measure "change"—Or should we? *Psychological Bulletin, 74,* 68-80. (Errata, Vol. 74, p. 218)

DeAyala, R. J. (1993). An introduction to polytomous item response theory models. *Measurement and Evaluation in Counseling and Development, 25*(4), 172-189.

Ellis, M. V., & Blustein, D. L. (1991a). Developing and using educational and psychological tests and measures: The unificationist perspective. *Journal of Counseling and Development, 69,* 550-555.

Ellis, M. V., & Blustein, D. L. (1991b). The unificationist view: A context for validity. *Journal of Counseling and Development, 69,* 561-563.

Fall, M., Balvanz, J., Johnson, L., & Nelson, L. (1999). A play therapy intervention and its relationship to self-efficacy and learning behaviors. *Professional School Counseling, 2,* 194-204.

Gysbers, N. C., & Henderson, P. (1994). *Developing and managing your school guidance program* (2nd ed.). Alexandria, VA: American Counseling Association.

Harwell, M. (1998). Misinterpreting interaction effects in analysis of variance. *Measurement and Evaluation in Counseling and Development, 31*(2), 125-136.

Heppner, P. P., Kivlighan, D. M., Jr., & Wampold, B. E. (1999). *Research design in counseling* (2nd ed.). Belmont, CA: Wadsworth.

Hoshmand, L. L. S. T. (1989). Alternate research paradigms: A review and teaching proposal. *The Counseling Psychologist, 17,* 3-79.

Jöreskog, K. G., & Sörbom, D. (1993). *LISREL 8 user's reference guide.* Chicago: Scientific Software International.

Lapan, R. T., Gysbers, N. C., & Sun, Y. (1997). The impact of more fully implemented guidance programs on the school experiences of high school students: A statewide evaluation study. *Journal of Counseling and Development, 75,* 292-302.

Linn, R. L., & Slinde, J. A. (1977). The determination of the significance of change between pre- and posttesting periods. *Review of Educational Research, 47,* 121-150.

Mason, M. J. (1999). A review of procedural and statistical methods for handling attrition and missing data in clinical research. *Measurement and Evaluation in Counseling and Development, 32*(2), 111-118.

McKinley, R. L. (1989). An introduction to item response theory. *Measurement and Evaluation in Counseling and Development, 22*(1), 37-57.

Messick, S. (1995). Validity of psychological assessment: Validity of inferences from a person's responses and performances as scientific inquiry into score meaning. *American Psychologist, 50,* 741-749.

Moss, P. A. (1995). Themes and variations in validity theory. *Educational Measurement: Issues and Practice, 14*(2), 5-13.

Nafziger, M. A., Couillard, G. C., & Smith, T. B. (1999). Evaluating therapy outcomes at a university counseling center with the College Adjustment Scales. *Journal of College Counseling, 2,* 3-13.

Rothney, J. W. M. (1958). *Guidance practices and results.* New York: Harper & Row.

Rothney, J. W. M., & Farwell, G. F. (1960). The evaluation of guidance and personnel services. *Review of Educational Services, 30,* 168-175.

Schafer, W. D. (1991). Validity and inference: A reaction to the unificationist perspective. *Journal of Counseling and Development, 69,* 558-560.

Schafer, W. D. (1999). An overview of meta-analysis. *Measurement and Evaluation in Counseling and Development, 32*(1), 43-61.

Stephenson, A. S., Elmore, P. B., & Evens, J. A. (2000). Standard-setting techniques: An application for counseling programs. *Measurement and Evaluation in Counseling and Development, 32*(4), 229-244.

Vacha-Haase, T., & Nilsson, J. (1998). Statistical significance reporting: Current trends and uses in *MECD. Measurement and Evaluation in Counseling and Development, 31*(1), 46-57.

Vacha-Haase, T., & Thompson, B. (1998). Further comments on statistical significance tests. *Measurement and Evaluation in Counseling and Development, 31*(1), 63-67.

Whiston, S. C., & Sexton, T. L. (1998). A review of school counseling outcomes research: Implications for practice. *Journal of Counseling and Development, 76,* 412-426.

Wlazelek, B. G., & Coulter, L. P. (1999). The role of counseling services for students in academic jeopardy: A preliminary study. *Journal of College Counseling, 2,* 33-41.

CHAPTER TWENTY-EIGHT

Qualitative Research
in Counseling

PAMELA O. PAISLEY

PATRICIA M. REEVES

As counseling comes of age as a discipline and as we as counselors acknowledge the diversity of our experience and our different ways of knowing, we must also come to a place where we can honor both empirical data and the power of personal narrative. To limit ourselves professionally to one approach limits our definition of who we are and who we can become . . ., [for] our profession will be known not only by theory and research but also by the practice of individual counselors, supervisors, and counselor educators. More importantly, perhaps, we will be defined by the stories we tell— by how, when, and why we tell them and by what we give significance to.

—Paisley (1997, pp. 4-5)

One of the shifts in scholarly inquiry that has occurred within the past 20 years begins to acknowledge this different way of knowing and defining our profession. In *Research in Counseling and Therapy,* Loesch and Vacc (1997) suggested that research "must evolve from reliance on traditional, primarily quantitative perspectives to encompass greater recognition and acceptance of newer, primarily qualitative perspectives . . . [as] a means of aligning research methodology with the philosophical underpinnings of the helping professions" (p. vi). Today, this paradigm shift from positivist quantitative methodologies to more interpretive qualitative designs is under way not only in counseling and other helping professions such as social work but also in disciplines traditionally rooted in a strict positivist tradition (e.g., business, marketing). It is important to remember, however, that movement toward a more inclusive view of acceptable research procedures should not be interpreted as an attempt to diminish the significance of quantification. Instead, this movement illuminates the social construction of meaning from the perspectives of those who have "lived" a particular phenomenon. The emphasis, consequently, is on understanding rather than on explanation (McLeod, 1996). Perhaps Patton (1987) said it best in noting that, in qualitative research, the intent is not necessarily to be "anti-numbers" but rather to be "pro-meaning."

The purpose of this chapter is twofold. First, we introduce the reader to the basic tenets, assumptions, and methods associated with qualitative research. Second, we consider how they can be applied in counseling research and practice.

Defining Qualitative Research

Although numerous definitions of qualitative research can be found in the literature, we believe that Patton's (1985) explication of this research methodology best captures its essential characteristics. According to Patton, qualitative research is an

> effort to understand situations in their uniqueness as part of a particular context and the interactions there. This understanding is an end in itself, so that it is not attempting to predict what may happen in the future necessarily, but to understand the nature of that setting—what it means for participants to be in that setting, what their lives are like, what's going on for them, what their meanings are, what the world looks like in that particular setting—and in the analysis to be able to communicate that faithfully to others who are interested in that setting.... The analysis strives for depth of understanding. (p. 1)

Other terms used interchangeably with *qualitative research* include *naturalistic inquiry, interpretive research, field study, participant observation, inductive research, case study,* and *ethnography* (Merriam, 1998).

Unlike quantitative approaches that seek to control and predict, qualitative research focuses on description, analysis, and understanding. The qualitative researcher

> assumes that understanding (analyzing and interpreting) and representing (interpreting and writing about) are filtered through [his or] her own personal biography that is situated in a specific sociopolitical, historical moment. Through this lens, the researcher tries to make sense of what [he or] she has learned; the researcher interprets the world [he or] she has entered. (Rossman & Rallis, 1998, p. 10)

In short, the qualitative researcher *is* the instrument for both data collection and analysis. The mediation of data by a person, rather than through an inanimate instrument such as a survey, allows the researcher to be responsive to contextual considerations and to immediately seek clarification or follow other avenues of inquiry. The collection of qualitative data commonly involves extensive fieldwork—"going to the people" for interviews, observations, and documents. Because qualitative research developed, in part, as a critique of the artificial setting of a laboratory, "doing research in the field—rather than in the laboratory or through a mailed questionnaire—became an important, complementary, and legitimate approach to social science" (p. 8).

Another distinguishing feature of qualitative research concerns the role of subjectivity in the research process. Although "detachment" is considered the ideal state for a researcher according to the positivist quantitative tradition, a qualitative approach to inquiry values "immersion." Peshkin (1988) asserted, "One's subjectivity is like a garment that cannot be removed. It is insistently present in both the research and non-research aspects of our life" (p. 17). Moreover, he concluded,

> The subjectivity that originally I had taken as an affliction, something to bear because it could not be foregone, could, to the contrary, be taken as "virtuous." My subjectivity is the basis for the story that I am able to tell. It is a strength on which I build. It makes me who I am as a person *and* as a researcher, equipped me with the perspectives and insights that shape all that I do as a researcher, from the selection of topics clear through to the emphases I make in my writing. Seen as virtuous, subjectivity is something to capitalize on rather than to exorcise. (Glesne & Peshkin, 1992, p. 104, italics in original)

By acknowledging the existence of subjectivity in their work and being mindful of it—"monitoring and managing it"—qualitative researchers can "escape the thwarting biases that subjectivity engenders" (Peshkin, 1988, p. 21) while "making a distinctive contribution, one that results from the unique configuration of their personal qualities joined to the data they have collected" (p. 18).

In applying this recent interpretivist approach to inquiry in counseling, certain underlying assumptions and tenets are worth noting. From this perspective, counseling is viewed as both a process and a lived experience. It is interactive, influencing both client and counselor and both individuals and systems. Gaining knowledge about this process requires understanding the meaning of the experience for the individuals involved. In addition, because meaning is

seen as socially constructed, multiple realities are possible. For the interpretivist, there is not a fixed, easily quantifiable external reality "out there" waiting to discovered; instead, there exists a fluid, co-constructed social reality (McLeod, 1996). According to Merriam (1998), the belief that "reality is constructed by individuals interacting with their social worlds" (p. 6) is the key philosophical assumption of all types of qualitative research. Because of this belief, qualitative researchers do not impose a rigid a priori framework on the social world; they do not generate formal hypotheses that are to be tested. Instead, they "want to learn what constitute important questions about the participants' lives from them" (Rossman & Rallis, 1998, p. 9).

Types of Qualitative Research

Although there are many types of qualitative studies, Merriam (1998) identifies five as most likely to be used within education. These same approaches have the most potential for use in counseling as well. These five types are the basic or generic qualitative study, ethnography, phenomenology, grounded theory, and case study. It should be noted that Creswell (1998) offered a similar typology in which he replaced the basic or generic qualitative study with biography.

Basic or Generic Qualitative Study

The basic or generic study is the most common form of qualitative research in counseling and education, and it exemplifies the characteristics of qualitative research in general. The basic or generic study seeks to discover and understand a phenomenon, a process, or the perspectives and worldviews of the people involved. Data most often are collected through interviews, observations, and document analysis (any one means or a mixture of the three), and the results (or findings) usually are presented as a combination of description and analysis. Data analysis focuses on the identification of patterns or themes that cut across the data or that in some way delineate a process.

Ethnography

This methodology, most often used in anthropology, involves the study of human society and culture and refers to both a set of methods used to collect data *and* the written report as the product of using these methods (Merriam, 1998). Although observations provide the cornerstone for the data collection process, other techniques used include interviewing, examining life histories, creating investigator diaries, and conducting documentary analysis. The distinguishing characteristic of ethnography is the focus on cultural context and, subsequently, sociocultural interpretation. It also should be noted that ethnographic research requires sustained time in the field and that, because of this requirement, it is not seen as frequently in the education and counseling literature as are other approaches to qualitative inquiry. Most ethnographers would agree that a minimum of 6 months of fieldwork is needed to acquire an understanding of the roles, attitudes, values, and behaviors that govern a particular culture.

Phenomenology

Phenomenology, a school of philosophical thought that underpins all qualitative research, focuses on the essence of experience—the essential invariant structure or central underlying meaning of experience. It highlights the lived experience of specific individuals rather than the individuals themselves, and it acknowledges the intentionality of our interaction within the world in which we live (Leitner, 1999). Intentionality refers to the idea that "consciousness always is directed toward an object. Reality of an object, then, is inextricably related to one's consciousness of it. . . . It is only perceived within the meaning of the experience of an individual" (Creswell, 1998, p. 53).

Data collection in a phenomenological inquiry involves in-depth interviews with 5 to 25 individuals (Polkinghorne, 1989) and commonly involves a series of three interviews with each individual. A phenomenological study adheres to a strict procedural process in which the concept of *epoche* is key. Epoche involves bracketing one's preconceived ideas about the phenomenon being studied to understand it from the perspectives (and through the voices) of those who have lived the experience (Field & Morse, 1985). Bracketing can be achieved in one of three ways. In one, the interviewer can describe specifically why he or she is interested in the study. In a second way, the researcher can complete a personal statement related to the topic. In a third way, the interviewer can be interviewed. Bracketing is not used to ensure objectivity or remove bias but rather is used to raise researcher consciousness (Leitner, 1999).

The findings from a phenomenological study consist of rich descriptions of particular phenomena that provide plausible pictures of experience. A reader of a phenomenological study understands the essence of the experience and recognizes that there is a single unifying meaning for the experience. This means that "all experiences have an underlying 'structure' ([e.g.,] grief is the same whether the loved one is a puppy, a parakeet, or a child)" (Creswell, 1998, p. 55). After reading a phenomenology, a person should be left with the feeling that "I understand better what it is like to experience that" (Polkinghorne, 1989, p. 46).

Grounded Theory

Unlike a phenomenological study, which emphasizes the meaning of an experience for individuals, grounded theory targets theory development. Glaser and Strauss (1967), who first conceptualized this approach to inquiry, maintained that theories should be "grounded" in data from the field, particularly in the actions, interactions, and social process of individuals. The theory that is developed, substantive theory (rather than formal or "grand" theory), is related to the context of the phenomenon being studied. That is, it "has as its referent specific, everyday-world situations. . . . [It] has a specificity and hence usefulness to practice often lacking in theories that cover more global concerns" (Merriam, 1998, p. 17).

In a grounded theory study, it is customary for the researcher to conduct 20 to 30 interviews, and the "participants interviewed are theoretically chosen—in theoretical sampling—to help the researcher best form the theory" (Creswell, 1998, p. 57). Data are analyzed according to the constant comparative method (Glaser & Strauss, 1967) using a systematic and highly structured coding process that involves three levels of coding: open, axial, and selective. The substantive theory that emerges from the analytic process consists of categories, properties, and hypotheses. According to Merriam (1998),

> Categories, and the properties that define or illuminate the categories, are conceptual elements of the theory. Hypotheses are the relationships drawn among categories and properties. These

hypotheses are tentative and are derived from the study. They are not set out at the beginning of the study to be tested, as is true in quantitative research. (p. 18)

Grounded theory studies do more than identify common themes and patterns that cut through a preponderance of the data; they also provide the "conceptual links" between these themes and patterns and, in so doing, generate theories with explanatory power.

Case Study

A case study is an intensive description and analysis of a single, clearly defined ("bounded") unit. It is used to gain an in-depth understanding of a particular situation or context as well as the meaning that it has for those who are a part of it. In case study research, the "interest is in process rather than outcomes, in context rather than a specific variable, in discovery rather than confirmation" (Merriam, 1998, p. 19). Case study research necessitates an extensive, detailed data collection process that involves multiple sources of data including observations, interviews, documents, archival records, and physical artifacts (Creswell, 1998). Examples of case studies can be seen in research focused on an individual, a program, an event, a group, an intervention, or a community (Merriam, 1998).

As with ethnography, the term *case study* can refer to both the process for conducting the study and the end product. Merriam (1998) used the term *case study* to refer to a methodology, whereas Stake (1995) considered the *case* as the object of study. Merriam (1998) characterized the case study as particularistic, descriptive, and heuristic. *Particularistic* refers to the specificity of focus on practical problems, whereas *descriptive* depicts the full rich description of the experience studied. Case studies "use prose and literary techniques to describe, elicit images, and analyze situations" (Wilson, 1979, p. 448). The *heuristic* component of the case study refers to the new or confirmed knowledge that is generated by the inquiry.

Developing a Qualitative Research Design

A research design is simply a plan or a purposefully constructed means to accomplish the goal of one's research. Initial considerations in developing a research plan include (a) determining a question or focus to guide the researcher's inquiry; (b) assessing the researcher's emotional attachment to the topic that he or she has selected; and (c) considering practical issues such as time, place, and money. Rossman and Rallis (1998) offered three somewhat similar considerations to guide the complex research design process: *do-ability* (the feasibility of the project), *want-to-do-ability* (a reflection of one's personal interests), and *should-do-ability* (the significance and ethics of the study). What is absolutely essential is for the topic or problem to be something that intrigues the researcher, that is, something that the researcher wants to learn more about. It must be a problem capable of sustaining the researcher's interest when obstacles arise, as they inevitably will. Ideas for a research problem can come from many different places including personal experience, theoretical gaps, reviewed literature, and current social and political issues.

Theoretical Framework

The theoretical framework for one's study provides the structure for how the researcher will proceed, and it is based on the orientation or philosophical stance that the researcher brings to the study. It also is known as the conceptual context of the study—"the system of concepts, assumptions, expectations, beliefs, and theories that supports and informs your research" (Maxwell, 1996, p. 25). Furthermore, Maxwell (1996) noted,

> The most important thing to understand about your conceptual context is that it is a formulation of what you think is *going on* with the phenomena you are studying—a tentative *theory* of what is happening and why. The function of this theory is to inform the rest of your design—to help you to assess your purposes, develop and select realistic and relevant research questions and methods, and identify potential validity threats to your conclusions. (p. 25, italics in original)

Although a review of existing literature informs the construction of a study's theoretical (or conceptual) framework, reviewed literature is not synonymous with the theoretical framework of a study. A theoretical framework must be constructed, not discovered. "While it is important for you to pay attention to existing theories and research that are relevant to what you plan to study," one also must remember that these "theories and results are sometimes misleading or flawed, and you will need to critically examine each piece of existing material to see if it is a valid and useful module for constructing the theory that will best inform your study" (Maxwell, 1996, p. 27). Maxwell (1996) offered four sources that aid in the construction on a conceptual context or theoretical framework: one's own experiential knowledge, existing theory and research, pilot and exploratory research, and thought experiments.

It is interesting to note that any given topic can be approached from different theoretical perspectives. The problem will be "shaped to reflect a particular perspective," and this in turn "determines what the purpose of the study will be; what questions . . . will be fashioned; and how data will be collected, analyzed, and interpreted" (Merriam & Simpson, 1995, p. 24). A recent publication on adult development theory (Clark & Caffarella, 1999) illustrated how the same topic can be approached from different perspectives. Reeves's (1999) article, for example, presented a psychological perspective of adult development, illustrating how classical theories of psychological development—stage, phase, life events, and transitions—are being challenged and how more context-sensitive theories are being proposed. In another article on the biological development of adults, Mott (1999) highlighted the multiple factors that shape the aging process, noting that recent interest in mind-body interaction is especially intriguing and promising. A research study from either of these perspectives would be

> drawing from a different literature base, would be using concepts and terms unique to that orientation, and would shape the problem and study purpose to reflect the particular assumptions and concerns of the theoretical base. This is what is meant by a theoretical or conceptual framework of a study. (Merriam & Simpson, 1995, pp. 24-25)

The Problem Statement

A problem statement is simply a carefully crafted essay, usually no more than one and a half pages in length, that lays out the logic of the research study. Although one will not see a section titled "Problem Statement" in a qualitative journal article (even though the inclusion of this section is a common practice in qualitative dissertations), writing a problem statement at the

outset of a study is an extremely useful practice. It forces the researcher to progressively (and logically) narrow the scope of the research to a clear, one-sentence statement of the purpose of the study. Merriam and Simpson (1995) suggested "funnel thinking" as a guide in constructing a problem statement:

> Consider the funnel shape. It is wide at the top and gets progressively narrower as you move to the bottom. Similarly, in setting up the research problem, the essay begins broadly, identifying for the reader the general area of interest. . . . The next step in the narrowing process is to identify specifically what *aspect* of the topic you are particularly concerned with. This is where you might point out the lack of information on this particular aspect of the topic. . . . You have essentially led the reader to the point where it is obvious what needs to be done. What needs to be done is the *purpose* of your study. A purpose statement is a direct response to the problem that you have carefully identified. (pp. 18-19, italics in original)

It also should be noted that the problem statement establishes the significance of one's research, clearly communicating why knowledge is needed in a particular area. Furthermore, it includes the definitions of key concepts and terms used in shaping the study.

The purpose statement, or the one-sentence culmination of the problem statement, often is followed by research questions. The research questions are "derived from the problem statement and reflect the researcher's judgment of the most significant factors to study" (Merriam & Simpson, 1995, p. 21). They specifically explain what one's study will attempt to learn or understand, help the researcher to focus the study, and provide guidance on how to conduct it (Maxwell, 1996). In qualitative research, questions generally are focused on process and understanding (Merriam, 1998). *How* and *what* questions are far more likely to be asked than are *why* questions. *How* did something happen? *What* happened? *What* does it mean?

Evaluating the Research Design

Good qualitative studies have a number of characteristics in common (Merriam, 1998). The studies are framed within the assumptions and identifying characteristics of qualitative research, and they begin with a single focus. They also employ rigorous data collection procedures including detailed methods related to analysis and writing. A detailed explication of methods is absolutely essential in qualitative studies because, unlike in quantitative studies, there is no prescribed way of conducting the research. Data analyses are conducted using multiple levels of abstraction, and the subsequent writing of results is thorough and persuasive, so that the reader has a sense of "being there"—what Richardson (1994) referred to as "verisimilitude" (p. 521). The reader must be engaged in the presentation of the study and also convinced that what the researcher is reporting "rings true." To engage the reader, the researcher's work must be "exploring, playful, metaphorical, insightful, and creative" (Patton, 1990, p. 433); to be convincing, the researcher must demonstrate that his or her approach to the research has been "systematic, analytical, rigorous, disciplined, and critical in perspective" (p. 433).

Cobb and Hagemaster (1987) suggested nine criteria for developing and evaluating a research plan:

1. One's expertise in doing what is proposed
2. The research problem and research questions
3. The purpose and significance of the research
4. A review of the literature
5. The context
6. The sampling design
7. The data collection methods
8. The data processing and analysis methods
9. The provision for the use of human subjects

Sample Selection

One of the first steps in research after the problem has been identified is to determine the sample. This involves the selection of a research site, time, people, and events. Unlike quantitative researchers, who rely on probability and random sampling, qualitative researchers are more interested in purposeful sampling, that is, selecting individuals who can provide the richest information in regard to the purpose of the study. This method of sample selection is consistent with the goal of qualitative research—to gain an in-depth understanding of a few individuals rather than a "surface" understanding of many. "The phrase that quantitative research is 'a mile wide and an inch deep' and [that] qualitative research is 'an inch wide and a mile deep' holds a grain of truth when it comes to sampling" (Padgett, 1998, p. 50).

Given that it is not possible to study everything and everyone, the qualitative researcher must consider carefully the research questions guiding the study and then develop criteria to select participants who can provide the most information-rich data. If the logic that underpins the criteria for inclusion in the sample is not evident, then the researcher must share this with the reader. There are many different purposeful sampling strategies including typical, unique, maximum variation, convenience, snowball, chain, and network sampling (Merriam, 1998).

An additional form of sampling used less commonly in qualitative research is theoretical sampling. Mentioned earlier in this chapter and used in conjunction with grounded theory studies, theoretical sampling involves an ongoing, evolving sample selection process that occurs simultaneously with data collection (Merriam, 1998). The process begins like purposeful sampling, but unlike in purposeful sampling, the entire sample is not selected at the beginning of the study. Instead, each set of data that is collected leads the researcher to the next source of data, with an individual's ability to contribute to the development of the theory as the basis for inclusion in the sample.

Data Collection

A widespread misconception regarding data is that they are endowed with magical properties "out there" waiting to be collected. Merriam (1998) maintained that data are "nothing more than ordinary bits and pieces of information found in the environment" (p. 69). Unless data first are noticed by the researcher and treated as such "for purposes of his or her research" (Dey, 1993, p. 15), they never transcend their commonplace characteristics. "The data collection techniques used, as well as the specific information considered to be 'data' in a study, are determined by the researcher's theoretical orientation, by the problem and purpose of the study, and by the sample selected" (Merriam, 1998, p. 70).

Bogdan and Biklen (1998) used the term *data* to refer to the "rough materials researchers collect from the world they are studying; they are the particulars that form the basis of analysis" (p. 106). They went on to say that

data are both the evidence and the clues. Gathered carefully, they serve as the stubborn facts that save the writing that you will do from unfounded speculation. Data ground you to the empirical world and, when systematically and rigorously collected, link qualitative research to other forms of science. (p. 106)

In quantitative research, data usually are reported numerically. In qualitative research, however, words comprise the data for a study. Qualitative data consist of "direct quotations from people about their experiences, opinions, feelings, and knowledge" obtained through *interviews;* "detailed descriptions of people's activities, behaviors, and actions" recorded in *observations;* and "excerpts, quotations, or entire passages" extracted from various types of *documents* (Patton, cited in Merriam, 1998, p. 69).

As a cautionary note, Glesne and Peshkin (1992) informed the researcher what to anticipate during the process of data collection:

Expect to feel—all at the same time or in close sequence—that you are not learning enough, that you are learning more than you can ever deal with, that you are not learning the right stuff, and that you are learning great stuff but do now know where it will lead or how it will all fit together. (p. 36)

Interviews

Interviews are the most common form of data collection in qualitative studies in education and counseling. As conversations "with a purpose" (Dexter, 1970, p. 136), interviews allow the researcher to gather descriptive data in the words of study participants so that insights can be developed as to how they interpret "some piece of the world" (Bogdan & Biklen, 1998, p. 94). According to Patton (1990),

We interview people to find out from them those things we cannot directly observe. . . . We cannot observe feelings, thoughts, and intentions. We cannot observe behaviors that took place at some previous point in time. We cannot observe situations that preclude the presence of an observer. We cannot observe how people organized the world and the meaning they attach to what goes on in the world. We have to ask people questions about those things. The purpose of interviewing, then, is to allow us to enter into the other person's perspective. (p. 196).

Interviews range in structure from highly structured to unstructured, based on the purpose of the study, the information to be collected, and the nature of the researcher's knowledge about the phenomenon.

Structure

Highly structured interviews consist of predetermined questions asked in a fixed sequence and closely resemble an oral version of a written survey. It is rare to see an entire interview conducted according to a highly structured protocol because it does not permit a participant to tell a story in his or her own words. Some even would argue that an interview protocol that is rigidly structured "falls outside of the qualitative range" (Bogdan & Biklen, 1998, p. 94) because it is not consistent with the goal of qualitative research, that is, to gain an understanding of a phenomenon or situation from the perspectives (and using the words) of those who have experienced it.

In a highly structured interview, the researcher rigidly controls the content and flow and operates under the assumption that the words that he or she uses have the same meaning for the participant as they do for the researcher. More commonly seen in qualitative

research is the use of a highly structured protocol in a *portion* of an interview, for example, when the researcher wants to collect specific information from the participant such as sociodemographic data.

Semistructured interviews, the type most commonly employed in qualitative research, allow some flexibility in the wording of the questions, and the sequence in which the questions are asked is not predetermined. Consequently, these interviews are less rigid, often consist of a mix of both more and less open-ended questions, and are not based on the assumption that the researcher and participant share a common vocabulary. In addition, they "offer the interviewer considerable latitude to pursue a range of topics" and also provide the participant with a "chance to shape the content of the interview" (Bogdan & Biklen, 1998, p. 94).

At the opposite end of the structured-unstructured continuum is the very open-ended interview. In this type of interview, the participant plays a much more prominent role in defining the content of the interview and the direction of the study (Mischler, 1991). This type of interview is particularly appropriate when a study still is in the exploratory stages, that is, when the researcher is trying to learn more about a particular topic including areas to investigate and pertinent questions to ask in subsequent interviews (Merriam, 1998). The very nature of this type of interview requires a skilled researcher who is comfortable with a high degree of ambiguity.

Although the type of interview that the researcher uses should reflect the goal of his or her research, it certainly is appropriate to use different types of interviews at different stages in the same study (Bogdan & Biklen, 1998). For example, at the beginning of the study, it might be important to use the more free-flowing, exploratory interview because your purpose at that point is to get a general understanding of a range of perspectives on a topic. After the investigatory work has been done, you might want to structure interviews more in order to get comparable data across a larger sample or to focus on particular topics that emerged during the preliminary interviews. (p. 95)

Questions

The key to obtaining good data resides in the construction of good questions, and different types of questions yield different types of information. "People being interviewed have a tendency to offer a quick run-through of events. [They] can be taught to respond to meet the interviewer's interest in the particulars, the details. They need encouragement to elaborate" (Bogdan & Biklen, 1998, p. 95). Carefully constructed questions provide this encouragement. For example, the researcher should avoid asking several questions at the same time, asking questions that "lead" the participant to a particular answer, and asking questions that can be answered with a yes/no response. Also, the researcher is more likely to elicit a rich response from the participant if the questions are phrased in language that is familiar to the participant. Skilled researchers regularly use pilot interviews to check for clarity and depth in their interview questions.

Good interview questions tend to fall into four major categories: (a) hypothetical, (b) devil's advocate, (c) ideal position, and (d) interpretive (Merriam, 1998). Hypothetical questions ask what the participant might do or what it might be like in a particular situation and usually begin with "What if" or "Suppose" (e.g., "Suppose that you were to find yourself faced with unemployment. What would you do in this situation?"). Devil's advocate questions are particularly useful in addressing controversial topics and ask interviewees to consider an opposing view (e.g., "Some people might say that the recreational use of drugs during adolescence leads to addiction in adulthood. How would you respond to that statement?"). Ideal position questions, on the other hand, elicit both information and opinion and ask participants to describe an ideal situation (e.g., "Assuming that time and money were no object, what would the 'perfect weekend' look like for you?"). Finally, interpretive questions "provide a check on what you think you are understanding as well as provide an opportunity for yet more information, opinions, and feelings to be revealed" (Merriam, 1998, p. 78) (e.g., "Would you say that leaving the agency where you worked and going into private practice has proved to be different from what you expected?").

Other Issues

The researcher's ability to collect good data also is dependent on the rapport that he or she establishes with the participants, and this is facilitated by the researcher communicating, from the very start, respect for those individuals who have agreed to let the researcher "enter their lives." At the beginning of an interview, it is important to deal with the logistics of the study and to make sure that the researcher and the participant are in agreement as to what participation in the study entails. Issues to be discussed might include things such as the number and length of interviews to be conducted, the use of electronic recording devices, and any incentives offered for participation in the study. The purpose of the study, as well as the researcher's intentions (e.g., to publish the findings), should be discussed as well. Other topics to be addressed include the use of a pseudonym to protect the identity of the participant and the determination of who (researcher or participant) will have the final say over the contents of the study.

Observations

Although interviews comprise the primary source of data for most qualitative studies, observations are commonly used as well. In some types of qualitative studies (e.g., ethnography), observations serve as the main source of data. Observations allow the interviewer to be a part of the social setting.

> You will learn firsthand how the actions of your others correspond to their words, see patterns of behavior, experience the unexpected as well as the expected, and develop a quality of trust with your others that motivates them to tell you what they might not. Interview questions that develop through participant observation are connected to known behavior, and their answers can therefore be better interpreted. (Glesne & Peshkin, 1992, p. 39)

Merriam (1998) discussed several reasons why a researcher might want to gather data through observations. For one, as an outsider, an observer will notice things that have become commonplace for the participants themselves—things that might lead to a better understanding of the context of the research as well as things that they might never think to discuss in interviews. "Observations are also conducted to triangulate findings; that is, they are used in conjunction with interviewing and document analysis to substantiate the findings" (p. 96). In

addition, observations permit the researcher to record behavior as it is taking place, "to see things firsthand," and to use one's "own knowledge and experience in interpreting what is observed rather than relying upon once-removed accounts from interviews" (p. 96). Finally, observations serve as a source of data in some situations when people are unable or unwilling to talk about particular topics.

Throughout the observation process, the goal is to make the strange familiar and to make the familiar strange (Erickson, 1973). By understanding a situation, the strange becomes familiar. However, making the familiar strange is harder to accomplish because

> you must continually question your own assumptions and perceptions: Why is it this way and not different? Overcome your disposition to settle into a way of seeing and understanding that gives you the comfort of closure at the price of shutting down thought. (Glesne & Peshkin, 1992, p. 42)

In making the strange familiar and in making the familiar strange, the researcher can adopt a range of positions, from mostly observation to mostly participation. It is common for the researcher to occupy different points at different places in the data collection process, and it should be noted that ethical considerations often influence one's stance as well. Merriam (1998, pp. 100-101) delineated several positions that are possible for the researcher-as-observer including the following:

- *Complete participant:* The researcher is a member of the group and conceals the observer role.
- *Participant-as-observer:* The researcher's observer role is known to the group but is subordinate to the role as participant.

- *Observer-as-participant:* The researcher's observer role is known to the group and is primary to the role as a participant.
- *Complete observer:* The researcher is either hidden from the group or in a completely public setting.
- *Collaborative partner:* The researcher is closest to being a complete participant, but his or her identity is clearly known to everyone involved.

Whatever the position adopted by the researcher-as-observer, the goal of collecting data through observations is the same—to understand the research setting, its participants, and the participants' behavior. The process of understanding is facilitated through field notes or "the written account of what the researcher hears, sees, experiences, and thinks in the course of collecting and reflecting on the data in a qualitative study" (Bogdan & Biklen, 1998, pp. 107-108). Field notes are the record of an observation, just as a transcript is the record of an interview.

Documents

Documents provide data that fulfill both an "historical and [a] contextual dimension" (Glesne & Peshkin, 1992, p. 54) and have been an underused source of information in qualitative studies in counseling and education. Merriam (1998) used the word *documents* as "an umbrella term to refer to a wide range of written, visual, and physical material relevant to the study at hand" (p. 112). According to Merriam, there are three types of documents available to the researcher: public records, personal documents, and physical materials. Public records refer to the ongoing records of a society. Personal documents include any first-person

accounts that describe an individual's actions, experiences, and beliefs. Physical materials, often referred to as artifacts, consist of physical objects found within the study setting. Although documents usually are produced for reasons other than to inform the research at hand, it is not uncommon for researchers to generate documents (e.g., asking participants to keep journals that they would be willing to share).

Documents have both strengths and limitations. On the plus side, many are easily accessible, are free, and contain information that otherwise would take an inordinate amount of time and energy to gather. In addition, they are both stable and grounded in the real-world context in which they were produced (and are not affected by the researcher's presence, as is the case with interviews and observations). On the minus side, documents may be incomplete or inaccurate. Even when their comprehensiveness or authenticity is not contested, it might be that the information provided through documents is not in a form that is useful to the researcher (Merriam, 1998).

Data Analysis

Data analysis, simply put, is "what researchers do to answer their particular research question[s]" (Langenbach, Vaughn, & Aagaard, 1994, p. 237). Bogdan and Biklen (1998) described the process of data analysis as

> systematically searching and arranging the interview transcripts, fieldnotes, and other materials that you accumulate to increase your own understanding of them and to enable you to present what you have discovered to others. Analysis involves working with data, organizing them, breaking them into manageable units, synthesiz-

ing them, searching for patterns, discovering what is important and what is to be learned, and deciding what you will tell others. (p. 157)

Data analysis involves meticulous attention to detail. However, "the point of data analysis is not simply to find a concept or label to neatly tie together the data. What is important is understanding the people studied" (Patton, 1990, p. 392).

In qualitative research, the process of data collection and analysis is dynamic and recursive. "Data analysis is one of the few facets, perhaps the only facet, of doing qualitative research in which there is a right way and a wrong way. . . . The right way . . . is to do it *simultaneously* with data collection" (Merriam, 1998, p. 162, italics in original). Simultaneous collection and analysis yields data that are "parsimonious and illuminating" (p. 162).

Although a variety of data analysis strategies can be used in qualitative research including ethnographic, narrative, and phenomenological techniques as well as content analysis and analytic induction (Merriam, 1998), by far the most commonly employed strategy is the constant comparative method (Glaser & Strauss, 1967). "The basic strategy of the method is to do just what its name implies—constantly compare" (Merriam, 1998, p. 159). This involves comparing a particular incident from a data set to another incident in the same set of data or in another set. A rough classification scheme emerges from this comparison. Further analysis of the data transforms the classification scheme into categories and properties that reflect the purpose of the study.

Qualitative inquiry "gives credence to the contextual nature of social phenomena, that is, to the fact that they are protean, shaped by and embodying passions and values that are expressed variably in time and place" (Langenbach et al., 1994, p. 274). These reasons account for the ability of a qualitative design to capture the "surprise, disorder, and contradictions of a phenomenon" (p. 274). These reasons also account for why data analysis, or "making sense out of data" (Merriam, 1998, p. 178), can be particularly challenging.

Writing Qualitative Research Reports

In qualitative research, a major challenge arises at "the point where rich data, careful analysis, and lofty ideas meet the iron discipline of writing" (Woods, 1985, p. 104). We can promise the reader one thing at this point in the research process: Every pencil on the researcher's desk will be sharpened, and every desk accessory will be neatly aligned—all done in service to avoid the actual process of writing. This is because most researchers never are "ready" to write. They must make the conscious decision to quit sharpening those pencils and aligning those accessories and, instead, commit this energy to putting words on paper. Then, they must have the discipline to follow through. Bogdan and Biklen (1998), in relaying one person's comments about writing, noted, "Writing is easy; all you do is sit staring at the blank sheet of paper until drops of blood form on your forehead" (p. 208).

Part of the challenge in writing up a qualitative study stems from the fact that there is not a specific time when everything else stops and writing begins (Merriam, 1998). Compounding this situation is the fact that there often is a "great amount of qualitative data [that] needs to be sorted through, selected, and woven into a coherent narrative" (p. 230). Finally, there is no standard or preferred way in which to report the data. "Qualitative field research seems distinct in the degree to which its practitioners lack a public, shared, and codified conception of how what they do is done and how what they report should be formulated" (Lofland, 1974, p. 101).

These challenges notwithstanding, there are ways in which to facilitate the writing process. Merriam (1998) suggested three ways: determining the audience, selecting a focus, and outlining the report. As in quantitative studies, the writing must address specific components—a discussion of the nature of the problem, an explanation of the way in which the study was conducted, and a thorough examination of the findings. Although it still is considered technically optional, a description of the researcher is becoming increasingly common in the write-ups of qualitative reports. Next, one simply has to sit down and begin.

Although writing up qualitative research is a challenging part of the research process, the researcher should not lose sight of the fact that "writing is a political act" (Glesne & Peshkin, 1992, p. 171) as well. It is important to "carefully think through both the intended and the unintended consequences of your words. Your first responsibility is to your research respondents, those persons whose cooperation is the basis of your research" (p. 171).

Implications for Counseling

What does this methodology mean for counseling? We believe that it means a great deal. Counseling and psychology have tended to rely on quantitative research studies to align themselves with the hard sciences and to justify our professional existence. We, in no way, intend to dismiss the need for outcome studies that contribute to our knowledge of efficacy and comparison of treatments. There certainly are important research questions to be asked that are most appropriately answered by quantitative methodologies—methodologies that lend themselves to generalizability. Unfortunately, if we remain wedded to only one way of seeing and understanding our world and the lived experience of those who travel in it, we will miss many important questions and the corresponding directions we might discover.

Research methods should be driven by research questions. Within the counseling process, some questions can be answered by surveys, experimental designs, and carefully constructed statistical analyses. In other cases, the questions do not lend themselves to these avenues of discovery. Instead, the research questions themselves require us to look for answers in different ways. In some cases, even when a quantitative design has provided initial information regarding change, we have a need to look inside a complex, interpersonal, interactive process such as counseling to understand what contributed to the difference. Quantitative methods may allow us to generalize in the statistical sense, but qualitative approaches allow us to explore the richness of the personal experience of our profession for both counselors and those individuals who reach out to us for help. These strategies allow us to examine the impact of our profession on individuals, families, and systems through interviews, observations, examination of our artifacts, and focused group discussions.

Qualitative approaches to inquiry already are emerging in our field. Applications of qualitative methods are available in counseling and psychology in response to a variety of research questions:

1. What is the client experience of the therapy hour? (Rennie, 1992)

2. How do family members evaluate family therapy? (Howe, 1989)

3. What are the patterns of client change in short-term counseling? (Cummings, Hallberg, & Sleman, 1994)

4. What is the process of problem formulation in therapy? (Davis, 1986)

5. What are the processes and issues surrounding lesbian disclosure of sexual orientation to health care professionals? (Hitchcock & Wilson, 1992)

6. What is the experience of being schizophrenic? (Laing, 1960, 1961)

7. What are the barriers and challenges in cross-cultural supervision in counseling? (Daniels, D'Andrea, & Kim, 1999)

8. What are roles for school counselors as multicultural advocates and community-family liaisons for Chicano/Latino students to prevent dropping out of school? (Aviles, Guerrero, Howarth, & Thomas, 1999)

These are important questions that can be thoroughly answered only through qualitative designs. Such approaches to these questions require a commitment on the part of the researcher to personal self-reflection and involvement. Qualitative studies are time-intensive and always must acknowledge the perspectives and participation of the persons conducting the studies. As we look inside the process of counseling to understand with whom, how, and under what circumstances it "works," we must understand the experiences and perspectives of the participants involved. Answers to these issues address not only whether behaviors were

modified or pain was alleviated but also what those processes or experiences were like for the persons involved as well as what the critical incidences were that informed change.

Qualitative approaches in counseling and psychology are relatively new. We can learn lessons from our colleagues in anthropology and education who have pointed to a direction for counseling research. Although few qualitative studies have been published in our journals, there is increased interest in posing and answering questions from this perspective. The qualitative method "respects the complexity of the phenomenon being studied, invites the active participation of informants, and takes as its goal the enhancement of understanding" (McLeod, 1996, p. 82). This respect, invitational stance, and search for understanding are very much in keeping with the values and principles of counseling.

Acknowledging this correspondence of values and principles, we can end as we began. If counseling, as a discipline, is to come of age, and if we, as counselors, are to acknowledge the diversity of our experiences and our different ways of knowing, then we must come to a place where we can honor both quantitative *and* qualitative studies. If we fail to do so, then we will unintentionally limit our professional potential—the research questions we could ask, the answers and themes that might emerge, and the meanings we might co-construct.

References

Aviles, R. M., Guerrero, M. P., Howarth, H. B., & Thomas, G. (1999). Perceptions of Chicano/Latino students who have dropped out of school. *Journal of Counseling and Development, 77*, 465-473.

Bogdan, R. C., & Biklen, S. K. (1998). *Qualitative research for education: An introduction to theory and methods* (3rd ed.). Boston: Allyn & Bacon.

Clark, M. C., & Caffarella, R. S. (Eds.). (1999). *An update on adult development theory: New ways of thinking about the life course.* San Francisco: Jossey-Bass.

Cobb, A., & Hagemaster, J. (1987). Ten criteria for evaluating qualitative research proposals. *Journal of Nursing Education, 26*(4), 138-143.

Creswell, J. W. (1998). *Qualitative inquiry and research design: Choosing among five traditions.* Thousand Oaks, CA: Sage.

Cummings, A. L., Hallberg, E. T., & Slemon, A. G. (1994). Templates of client change in short-term counseling. *Journal of Counseling Psychology, 41,* 464-472.

Daniels, J., D'Andrea, M., & Kim, B. S. K. (1999). Assessing the barriers and changes of cross-cultural supervision: A case study. *Counselor Education and Supervision, 38,* 191-204.

Davis, K. (1986). The process of problem (re)formulation in psychotherapy. *Sociology of Health and Illness, 8,* 44-74.

Dexter, L. A. (1970). *Elite and specialized interviewing.* Evanston, IL: Northwestern University Press.

Dey, I. (1993). *Qualitative data analysis.* London: Routledge.

Erickson, F. (1973). What makes school ethnography "ethnographic"? *Council on Anthropology and Education Newsletter, 4*(2), 10-19.

Field, P. A., & Morse, J. M. (1985). *Nursing research: The application of qualitative approaches.* Rockville, MD: Aspen Systems.

Glaser, B. G., & Strauss, A. L. (1967). *Discovery of grounded theory: Strategies for qualitative research.* Chicago: Aldine.

Glesne, C., & Peshkin, A. (1992). *Becoming qualitative researchers: An introduction.* New York: Longman.

Hitchcock, J. M., & Wilson, H. S. (1992). Personal risking: Lesbian self-disclosure of sexual orientation to professional health care providers. *Nursing Research, 41,* 178-183.

Howe, D. (1989). *The consumer's view of family therapy.* Aldershot, UK: Gower.

Laing, R. D. (1960). *The divided self: An existential study in sanity and madness.* London: Tavistock.

Laing, R. D. (1961). *Self and others.* London: Tavistock.

Langenbach, M., Vaughn, C., & Aagaard, L. (1994). *An introduction to educational research.* Boston: Allyn & Bacon.

Leitner, D. (1999). *It is OK to be this way: A phenomenological study of the experience of being a lesbian adolescent.* Unpublished doctoral dissertation, University of Georgia.

Loesch, L. C., & Vacc, N. A. (1997). *Research in counseling and therapy.* Greensboro, NC: ERIC/CASS.

Lofland, J. (1974). Styles of reporting qualitative field research. *American Sociologist, 9,* 101-111.

Maxwell, J. A. (1996). *Qualitative research design: An interactive approach.* Thousand Oaks, CA: Sage.

McLeod, J. (1996). Qualitative research methods in counselling psychology. In R. Woolfe & W. Dryden (Eds.), *Handbook of counselling psychology* (pp. 64-86). London: Sage.

Merriam, S. B. (1998). *Qualitative research and case study applications in education.* San Francisco: Jossey-Bass.

Merriam, S. B., & Simpson, E. L. (1995). *A guide to research for educators and trainers of adults* (2nd ed.). Malabar, FL: Krieger.

Mischler, E. G. (1991). *Research interviewing: Context and narrative.* Cambridge, MA: Harvard University Press.

Mott, V. W. (1999). Our complex human body: Biological development explored. In M. C. Clark & R. S. Caffarella (Eds.), *Adult development: Capturing new ways of thinking about the life course* (pp. 9-17). San Francisco: Jossey-Bass.

Padgett, D. K. (1998). *Qualitative methods in social work research: Challenges and rewards.* Thousand Oaks, CA: Sage.

Paisley, P. O. (1997). Personalizing our history: Profiles of theorists, researchers, practitioners, and issues. *Journal of Counseling and Development, 76,* 4-5.

Patton, M. Q. (1985, April). *Quality in qualitative research: Methodological principles and recent developments.* Invited address delivered at the annual meeting of the American Educational Research Association, Chicago.

Patton, M. Q. (1987). *How to use qualitative methods in evaluation.* Newbury Park, CA: Sage.

Patton, M. Q. (1990). *Qualitative evaluation and research methods* (2nd ed.). Newbury Park, CA: Sage.

Peshkin, A. (1988). In search of subjectivity—One's own. *Educational Researcher, 17*(7), 17-22.

Polkinghorne, D. E. (1989). Phenomenological research methods. In R. S. Valle & S. Halling (Eds.), *Existential-phenomenological perspectives in psychology* (pp. 41-60). New York: Plenum.

Reeves, P. M. (1999). Psychological development: Becoming a person. In M. C. Clark & R. S. Caffarella (Eds.), *Adult development: Capturing new ways of thinking about the life course* (pp. 19-28). San Francisco: Jossey-Bass.

Rennie, D. L. (1992). Qualitative analysis of the client's experience of psychotherapy: The unfolding of reflexivity. In S. G. Toukmanian & D. L. Rennie (Eds.), *Psychotherapy process research: Paradigmatic and narrative approaches.* London: Sage.

Richardson, L. (1994). Writing: A method of inquiry. In N. K. Denzin & Y. S. Lincoln (Eds.), *Handbook of qualitative research* (pp. 516-529). Thousand Oaks, CA: Sage.

Rossman, G. B., & Rallis, S. F. (1998). *Learning in the field: An introduction to qualitative research.* Thousand Oaks, CA: Sage.

Stake, R. (1995). *The art of case study research.* Thousand Oaks, CA: Sage.

Wilson, S. (1979). Explorations of the usefulness of case study evaluations. *Evaluation Quarterly, 3,* 446-459.

Woods, P. (1985). New songs played skillfully: Creativity and technique in writing up qualitative research. In R. G. Burgess (Ed.), *Issues in educational research: Qualitative methods* (pp. 86-106). London: Falmer.

CHAPTER TWENTY-NINE

Evidence-Based Counseling Intervention Programs

Practicing "Best Practices"

THOMAS L. SEXTON

Professional counselors, the counseling profession, and the client population that we serve always have had, in their own ways, an interest in what "works." Early on, our efforts at identifying the most effective practices, or "best practices," focused on the development of theoretical models. Over the past decade, there has been an emerging definition of best practices that is quite different. It is a definition influenced by the growth in available research evidence, the realization that there are common factors at work in successful counseling regardless of theory, and increasing calls for accountable counseling. This new definition of best practices is one based on the existence of *research evidence* to support the effectiveness of a systematic intervention program.

As best practices in counseling increasingly become defined as research based, the field is quickly moving toward evidence-based counseling practice. Unfortunately, this move has been, and continues to be, a struggle within counseling. Despite improvements in research relevance and increased calls for integration, the well-documented research-practice gap remains. As a result, the many valuable and informative results of research efforts rarely have an impact on mainstream counseling practice.

Regardless of the struggles, tensions, and debates (e.g., art vs. science, experience vs. evidence), research now is a major factor in the real-world "practice" of counseling. Therefore, counselors, counselor educators, policy makers, and theory developers will increasingly need to focus on research as a primary source of clinical decision making.

The goals of this chapter are to consider the ways in which evidence-based practice actually may serve as an important and valuable new direction in professional counseling that can both improve practice and enhance the direction of the profession. On a practical level, the chapter identifies ways in which research can become an integral part of practitioners' clinical decision making. To this end, I first consider the role that process and outcome research may play in evidence-based counseling. Second, I look at some of the lessons learned from the literature as examples of ways in which research can affect counseling. Third, I review some of the current evidence-based counseling protocols. Finally, I discuss ways in which evidence-based counseling may change the future of professional counseling through the emerging definitions of best practices. It is important to note that this chapter is intended not as a review of the outcome and process literature but rather as an example of the ways in which evidence is becoming the foundation for professional counseling.

The Role of Process and Outcome Research in Evidence-Based Counseling

One of the reasons for the gap between research and practice is that there is a common misunderstanding of the *role* that research can and should play and what to *expect* from the research results (Sexton & Whiston, 1996). To understand the issues of role and expectation, it first is important to understand the basic assumption of evidence-based counseling practice: Clinical decision making requires multiple data sources, from multiple perspectives, to bring the best knowledge to bear on helping clients to change (Sexton, Whiston, Bleuer, & Walz, 1997). Whereas each of these data sources (e.g., clinical experience, theoretical orientation) has its advantages, research knowledge, above all others, offers a reliable source of guidance from a broad sample of evidence (Sexton et al., 1997).

There are two types of research that inform counseling practice. *Outcome* research focuses on the final result of counseling efforts and has the ability to inform what interventions and approaches may work best for which desired outcomes. Thus, outcome research tells the clinician what type of approach to choose for a particular client problem. *Process* research has a focus on the mechanisms of change and informs the clinician regarding the most probable routes to achieve the desired outcomes.

The current knowledge base of process and outcome research is such that general trends can be identified regarding the common factors that contribute to successful counseling. These trends are sufficient enough to *inform* clinical decisions in practice, curricular decisions in training, and relevant future research. The outcome research is not complete enough, however, for all clinical decisions to be made solely on these findings. What research knowledge can do is serve as the basis for informing practice by identifying trends and similarities in counselor characteristics, client characteristics, and treatment interventions. These process elements contribute to successful counseling through the matching of protocols to client issues and problems. The central features of research (explicit procedures, reliability, and validity) are the ideal complement to clinical decisions in that they help to overcome the well-documented biases in human decision making (Dawes, 1994). Thus, research knowledge, combined with experienced clinical judgment, can serve as the basis for treatment plans with the highest probability of success.

The emergence of systematic research-based intervention models (protocols) is likely to even further strengthen evidence-based practices. These protocols are organized approaches to a specialized form of clinical intervention. More than a set of techniques, intervention protocols are "maps" of clinical practice based on a comprehensive conceptual framework that allows successful matching of clients to interventions. A systematic protocol includes a set of core clinical principles based on clearly articulated change mechanisms identifying interventions that address those change goals in a stage-based, systematic manner (Alexander, Sexton, & Robbins, in press). To be research based, a protocol not only would need to be a comprehensive change model but also would need to include outcome studies that confirm the success of the protocol with a particular client problem area while including general research themes. It is these programs that are most likely to meet the criteria for best practices noted subsequently.

Thus, during the new era of evidence-based practice, counseling research has a critical role in every part of the counseling domain (clinical decision-making process, program development, theory/model development, and training). The development of conceptual models draws on trends from the research knowledge base. Clinical practice draws on existing evidence-based clinical protocols and knowledge to determine appropriate interventions and to match protocols with client needs. Counselor training is based on practice techniques and knowledge supported by the literature. Each of these domains, in turn, uses the research methods to conduct ongoing evaluation. The role of process and outcome research is a primary but not exclusive one in the clinical and policy decision-making processes. As a result, research consumers can expect guidance but not definitive answers in regard to these same decisions.

Lessons From the Literature

Over the past 100 years, the research knowledge base for counseling practice has continually grown, evolved, and improved (Sexton, 1996). Within the outcome research, there are findings that have been so consistently supported over time and across various clinical situations that they now have taken the form of general principles (Sexton et al., 1997). There are other areas in which the knowledge is more limited and findings are inconsistent. Some of these limitations are due to inadequacies of methodology inherent in the applied nature of counseling outcome research. These areas also are "holes" in our understandings that are important because they generate new questions and future research efforts.

Until recently, most of the available research findings focused on isolated common factors (e.g., client/counselor factors, techniques) rather than on systematic intervention programs. For example, we know a great deal about the counseling relationship, but as of yet we do not know its importance within some specific intervention program that targets a specific client problem. It is important to note that general research trends, isolated from a program of intervention, do not constitute best practices. As discussed subsequently, the current definitions of best practices require systematic intervention programs with significant outcome research that demonstrate positive outcomes and process research that delineates the active change mechanisms that account for those successful changes. The good news is that the field is accumulating a significant body of process and outcome research-focused systematic intervention programs.

There are numerous reviews of the outcome literature currently available for use in guiding practice. Important contributions include Bergin and Garfield's (1994) *Handbook of Psychotherapy and Behavior Change;* Sexton and colleagues' (1997) process model review; and Roth, Fonagy, Parry, and Target's (1996) review of the most effective treatments for various common psychological disorders. In addition, various sources publish lists of best practices (Chambless et al., 1996; Elliott, 1998). The intent here is not to repeat the content of those primary sources but rather to illustrate the ways in which the well-established common trends in the outcome literature and the focused research on systematic intervention can contribute to evidence-based clinical decision making.

Common Factors Across Counseling Approaches

Throughout its history, one of the major thrusts of counseling outcome research has been the quest to identify the "best theory." To that end, numerous studies have examined whether one theoretical approach is superior to others. Surprisingly, with the exception of a small advantage found for some approaches in specific circumstances (e.g., cognitive, cognitive-behavioral), the major theoretical approaches are relatively equal in their effectiveness. Initially, it was assumed that the lack of differential effectiveness was due to the "dodo bird" phenomenon ("Everyone has won and all must have prizes" [Luborsky, Singer, & Luborsky, 1975]), in which it was the common factors shared by these theoretical approaches that accounted for change. Common factors are those elements that are part of all effective counseling regardless of the counselor, theory, or technique. It probably is the case that there are great differences among various approaches to counseling but that theoretical models are not specific enough to account for those differences. In the future, the systematic intervention programs that are emerging finally might help us to find the differences among approaches.

We now can safely conclude that there are common factors among counseling approaches that account for a substantial amount of client improvement. If one were to *broadly* determine the percentage of improvement in clients as a function of different factors, 40% would be due to change factors outside of counseling, 15% would be due to expectancy or placebo effects, 15% would be due to specific psychological techniques, and 30% would be due to common factors evident in all therapies regardless of the counselor's theoretical orientation (Lambert, 1991). If this analysis is correct, then the impact of these common factors is twice that of specific psychological techniques.

Our best current understanding of common factors is that they likely are organized around three categories. The first category, *support fac-*

tors, includes catharsis, positive relationship with the counselor, a therapeutic alliance, counselor warmth, respect, empathy, and trust. The second category, *learning factors,* includes advice, affective experiencing, corrective emotional experiencing, feedback, and assimilation of problematic experience. The third category, *action factors,* includes behavioral regulation, cognitive mastery, facing fears, and successful experiences. These common factors provide for a cooperative working alliance that leads to successful change (Lambert & Cattani-Thompson, 1996). The most useful clinical guidance would be to identify clinical protocols that include these common factors.

Although informative, such broad and general findings do not help practitioners to know exactly which intervention programs to apply to which clients. A successful counseling outcome is at least somewhat dependent on matching the client's interpersonal style and presenting problems (Beutler & Clarkin, 1990). It probably is the case that successful intervention programs contain, in some fashion, the critical common factors while adding the unique intervention methods to further enhance successful intervention with specific client problems. These common factors are likely to be made up of research regarding the counseling relationship, client and counselor factors, and common techniques and interventions.

With the evolution of systematic intervention programs, however, our thinking about common factors is beginning to change. We now know that certain systematic intervention programs are more successful in certain client areas (Alexander et al., in press; Roth et al., 1996). For example, the systematic research reviews by Gurman, Kniskern, and Pinsof (1986) concluded that family-based interventions were successful across a variety of client problems including adolescent behavior problems, antisocial children, and schizophrenic behaviors. Furthermore, we now know that career counseling is effective for a variety of concerns including indecision and facilitating career maturity (Whiston, Sexton, & Lasoff, 1998). We know that individual counseling is helpful for problems ranging from depression to anxiety, depending on the specific approach.

Counseling Relationship

Of all the techniques, client-counselor characteristics, and procedures studied, the counseling relationship remains unequivocally the most significant factor in successful counseling (Sexton & Whiston, 1994). The research has overwhelmingly confirmed that any successful therapeutic endeavor has at its very core the participants establishing an open, mutual, trusting, collaborative relationship. Two major reviews, spanning four decades of research, found that 80% of the studies indicated that a positive therapeutic relationship was significantly related to successful therapeutic outcomes (Orlinsky, Grawe, & Parks, 1994). The failure to form a quality relationship in therapy is associated with client noncompliance (Eisenthal, Emery, Lazare, & Udin, 1979), premature termination (Tracey, 1977), and poor outcomes (Alexander & Luborsky, 1986).

Although it seems an intuitively simple question to ask, it has been more difficult than one might imagine answering the question, "What is therapeutic about the relationship between the client and the counselor?" Early in the history of our profession, the counseling relationship became synonymous with the necessary and sufficient counselor-offered conditions proposed by the person-centered perspective. These conditions became collectively referred to as the "core conditions" of counseling and grew to be the very embodiment of what was most therapeutic about a counseling relationship. Although a number of early reviews found support for the therapeutic effectiveness of some of these conditions (Gurman, 1977), recent comprehensive reviews have not found these commonly accepted conditions to be particularly important when compared to other aspects of the relationship (Beutler, Crago, & Ariznendi, 1986; Sexton & Whiston, 1994). Sexton and Whiston (1994) suggested that the nature of the relationship could be explained only when a multidimensional perspective is adopted. In this regard, it probably is more promising to look at specific elements that comprise a therapeutic alliance regardless of its theoretical label. Thus, any systematic protocol would need to consider a broad multidimensional view of the therapeutic relationship both theoretically and practically.

The Counselor Contribution

It is interesting that within the entire body of counseling outcome research, there probably is no other aspect of counseling more actively studied than the counselor factors that contribute to successful outcomes. We know from the major studies of counseling outcomes that some counselors produce positive results more consistently than do others (Lafferty, Beutler, & Crago, 1989). As research has progressed, it has become increasingly apparent that there is no single profile of an effective counselor (Sexton et al., 1997). This does not mean, however, that we have not gained some interesting insight into important demographic (e.g., age, sex, ethnicity), professional (e.g., experience, training,

discipline), therapeutic skill (e.g., therapeutic orientation, skillfulness), and personal (e.g., relational style, personality type, emotional well-being) characteristics of counselors that are important ingredients in successful counseling.

A number of these findings are particularly interesting for this discussion. In general, there seems to be little difference in outcomes based on professional discipline. For example, the results from meta-analyses range from moderate support for the differential efficacy of psychologists (Smith, Glass, & Miller, 1980) to negligible effects across disciplines (Prioleau, Murdock, & Brody, 1983). The findings associated with those from meta-analytic reviews generally agree that professionally trained counselors have no systematic advantage over nonprofessional therapists. In a meta-analysis of dynamic-oriented therapists, Svartberg and Stiles (1991) found that therapeutic efficacy decreased with experience. There are two notable exceptions to this trend, Crits-Christoph and Mintz (1991) found experience level of the therapist to be significantly (and positively) related to counseling outcomes when studies specifically accounted for therapist experience. Similarly, Lyons and Woods (1991) countered earlier findings with results showing that as the experience of the counselor increased, so did the effect size.

We currently know little about the relationship between therapist skill and counseling outcomes. This dearth of studies is perplexing given that one of the major approaches to counselor education is skill acquisition. Mocher and Prinz (1991) concluded from their review of more than 350 outcome studies that most had either ignored or failed to adequately control for therapist competence and skill. When skill has been considered, it seems to have been an extremely important contributor to successful outcomes. In their extensive qualitative review of the outcome literature, Orlinsky and colleagues (1994) found therapist skillfulness to be among the most salient variables that contribute to successful therapeutic outcomes. Furthermore, high levels of therapist skill were found to promote successful counseling interventions and positive outcomes (Crits-Christoph, Cooper, & Luborsky, 1988).

Although seemingly confusing, the findings regarding experience, skillfulness, and outcomes do make sense. Experience does not necessarily imply skillfulness. In turn, skillfulness does not mean that what is being offered to a client is what would be most helpful. Evidence-based protocols include specific methods to guide counselors to be conceptually complex, relationally responsive, and skillful within the goals of the specific protocol. As a result, the protocol is necessary to determine the operational definition of skillful and to understand the ways in which experience may positively contribute to resolving the client's concerns. Thus, it probably is the case that experience is helpful only when applied within a successful intervention program. Future research that looks at the skillful application of established intervention programs probably will give us a better read on the value of clinical experience, training, and skill.

The Client Contribution

The efforts to identify client contributions to successful counseling have resulted in inconsistent findings. For example, whereas specific domains (e.g., educational level, intelligence) are positively associated with outcomes, others (e.g., social class, age) are not (Luborsky, Crits-Christoph, Mintz, & Auerbach, 1988). Other demographic areas are more complex. For example, whereas females are more likely than males to enter a counseling relationship, males most often will remain in counseling longer after entering the relationship (Carpenter & Range, 1983).

Although the empirical data are inconclusive, the client's level of disturbance or initial level of anxiety does seem to be significantly related to counseling outcomes. In fact, it seems as if there is an inverse relationship between severity of disturbance and outcome (i.e., high level of disturbance and low level of positive outcome). In some cases, disturbance level has been defined as suitability for treatment. Orlinsky and colleagues (1994) suggested that when it was defined as the degree to which a client could benefit from counseling, client suitability was a significant variable in more than 68% of studies completed over the past 40 years.

Although the findings regarding client diagnoses and outcomes appear empirically and intuitively appealing, they are compromised by the imprecision in our current methods of diagnostic classification. In some well-defined diagnostic areas (e.g., depression), we can confidently say that clients most depressed prior to treatment remain most depressed even after psychotherapy. Although the findings related to depression have demonstrated its stability relative to the initial symptoms, this consistent trend is lacking with other clinical populations where the symptom profiles are less than stable. Unfortunate as the case may be, few diagnostic categories, outside of depression and some forms of anxiety disorders, seem to be robust and reliable enough to aid us in these efforts (Garfield & Bergin, 1994).

A recent trend in this area has focused on matching characteristics of the client with either characteristics of the counselor, the counseling process, or both. Early work in this area focused on simple client-therapist matching in regard to characteristics such as attitudes, beliefs, and personal characteristics. Although initially seen as promising, the study of these relationships did not turn out to be an avenue that was helpful in identifying successful counseling. In an early example of matching protocol to client, Beutler and Bergin (1991) investigated the interaction among three different types of therapy (cognitive, experiential, and supportive self-directed) and either the coping style (externalization) or the resistance potential of the client. Those clients applying an externalizing coping style improved more with cognitive therapy, whereas a supportive self-directed therapy benefited the nonexternalizing and resistant clients. Low-resistant clients, on the other hand, benefited more from cognitive therapy than from a self-directed modality. These findings also lend support to the work of Tracey (1987), in which the counseling outcome was seen as more or less dependent on the development of a complementary relationship pattern between client and counselor. Client involvement remains one of the most important in-session variables related to future research in the area of relational interaction.

It seems that any evidence-based protocol would need to consider matching the protocols with a systematic approach toward the presenting problems of the client. This approach would need to be presented in ways that match the client's relational and interpersonal style such that a positive expectation for success is developed.

Common Techniques and Interventions

It has not been uncommon for the research literature to focus on common techniques in an attempt to determine the best technique. The assumption behind this research is that technique exists separate from the common factors (e.g., relationship) and the intervention program. Numerous therapeutic interventions have been investigated, but few garner the empirical support necessary to have great confidence in their efficacy. Moreover, when these interventions are linked to outcomes, their success often appears dependent on some mediating variable such as client distress level, therapist skillfulness, the counseling relationship, or the cumulative effect of an intervention program. The available evidence suggests that the study of isolated techniques might not yield an informed perspective on the best practices in counseling. Thus, theory development and future research should take a more complete view, examining intervention programs within comprehensive conceptual models rather than isolated techniques and eclectic approaches.

Evidence-Based Protocols

During the current era of evidence-based practices, it is not enough to make clinical decisions based on general research trends such as those presented previously. In addition to knowing about research trends, it is important that clinical decisions be cohesively linked and justified by an overarching conceptual model (Roth et al., 1996). Without an organizing model, it would be difficult to understand the change mechanisms of effective counseling and to use those mechanisms effectively. By definition, evidence-based intervention programs should incorporate the broad trends regarding the counselor, the client, and common factors related to successful counseling. In addition, comprehensive intervention programs should address the specific techniques that apply to the client population for which they were developed, a systematic procedure for implementing these techniques, and a method for comprehensive treatment planning. Thus, systematic intervention programs help to bring us closer to having programs that we can apply to specific clients in specific situations with specific problems.

To be evidence based (or best practices), an intervention program must have "enough" research to make the counselor feel confident that the intervention, if delivered correctly, will replicate the positive results demonstrated in highly controlled laboratory conditions. The obvious question is, "What is enough?" Until recently, we have been restricted to talking about very broad areas of counseling practice. Unfortunately, such general outcome data cannot guide the multitude of specific clinical decisions that must be made in helping clients.

Currently, there are three different approaches to defining best practices. Within these definitions, there now is a range of specific, well-documented treatments with established efficacy that can be used with various client problems. These models fall along a continuum defined by the assumptions on which they are based. At one end of the continuum is the empirically validated treatment/empirically supported treatment (EVT/EST) model. The EVT/EST approach is based on the assumption that it is the reliability of research methodology that is most important. By definition, the most reliable research is based on the logical positivist tradition.

The EVT/EST model was developed by Division 12 (Clinical Psychology) of the American Psychological Association (APA) during the early 1990s. Designation as an EVT/EST is based on the following criteria: (a) a standardized or manualized treatment of a specific disorder that has been shown to be (b) superior to placebo or other treatments or (c) equal to a previously established treatment in at least two

studies conducted by different investigators. The first publication of the EVT/EST list included 25 treatments, the second publication increased the well-established list to 47 treatments, and the most recent publication pushed the list to 71 treatments (Chambless et al., 1996). Based on the EVT/EST criteria, we now can say that depression, anxiety, panic disorders, and obsessive compulsive disorders are better treated by some techniques than by others (for a complete analysis of which techniques are most effective with which specific client concerns, see Roth et al., 1996).

At the other end of the continuum is an approach based on assumptions of validity. The blueprint model (Elliott, 1998) requires high methodological standards but values independent replication and demonstrated ability of the program to be implemented in local communities. The primary goal is to find effective programs that can be implemented successfully in local communities, thereby guaranteeing ecological validity. The blueprint model evolved from a national initiative to identify the most effective intervention programs for violent, drug-abusing, delinquent, and other multi-problem adolescents and their families. Through the efforts of Elliott at the Center for the Study and Prevention of Violence, the Centers for Disease Control, and the National Institute of Justice, a set of criteria was developed to help communities and practitioners to determine the appropriate standard for programs that might work.

Four criteria need to be met for a program to receive blueprint status:

- A strong research record that has demonstrated the effectiveness of the program is required. The research needs to include both randomized clinical trials and community-based effectiveness studies published in the professional literature. These studies need to demonstrate that the intervention program is effective, compared to no treatment and alternative treatments.

- Independent research replications conducted by investigators other than the program originators are required. The intent is to eliminate researcher bias.

- Multisite replications need to demonstrate that the program has been effective in a variety of practice settings with varying types of clients as applied by different interventionists.

- The program has to be replicable as demonstrated by a clear articulation and description (e.g., a manual).

In the area of youth violence and related behavioral problems, 500 different programs were identified. Of these, only 10 met the blueprint criteria, and only 2 of these are counseling-type approaches. Both counseling approaches are family based (functional family therapy and multisystemic therapy).

The middle position of the best practices continuum is defined by the assumptions of reliability and validity. The Principles for Empirically Supported Intervention Programs (PESIP) (Wampold, Lictenburg, & Waehler, in press) suggest that effective programs are those that have empirical support at a variety of levels of evidence. Division 17 (Counseling Psychology) of APA developed the model based on the assumptions that (a) it would be impossible to identify all treatments for all types of persons, (b) traditional *DSM-IV* (*Diagnostic and Statistical Manual of Mental Disorders* [American Psychiatric Association, 1994]) diagnosis does not reflect the orientation of counseling because clients often do not present with unitary and well-defined problems, (c) outcome measures should recognize the various perspectives of the

therapist and client, (d) meta-analytic review of outcome studies is a more rigorous test than are other measures to review the literature, and (e) effectiveness and safety (no negative effect) are the most important criteria.

The resulting criteria are a set of seven principles that provide a decision-making scheme rather than a dichotomous decision. Thus, the counseling practitioner is left to determine whether an intervention program might be useful by surveying various levels of increasing specific evidence. The final decision is left to the practitioner (Wampold et al., in press).

These criteria share at least one common factor that will affect counseling practitioners— the use of treatment manuals as a common feature in the world of counseling. Treatment manuals specifically outline the details of particular types of intervention, thereby standardizing delivery of the psychotherapeutic approaches. As such, they serve as a mechanism to transfer the technology of effective programs into practice. Treatment manuals have been found to increase the intervention delivery consistency among counselors (Crits-Christoph & Mintz, 1991), resulting in a significant positive relationship between therapist compliance with the manuals and positive outcomes (Luborsky et al., 1975). Treatment manuals vary in their makeup. Some read like cookbooks, with specific step-by-step instructions. According to Henry (1998), manuals of this type are not applicable to "real" clinical practice. Alexander and colleagues (in press) described a contingently directed type of treatment manual that overcomes many of the problems of clinical relevance. This type of manual allows for specific process goals, providing guiding therapeutic principles and requiring the counselor to respond contingently to the interpersonal events in a given counseling session to reach the manual's prescribed goals.

A study by Henggeler and colleagues (1997) linked treatment adherence (via manuals) and clinical outcomes. In this study, the level of therapist adherence was significantly related to absolute outcomes such as rearrest and incarceration rates. High adherence predicted favorable outcomes, whereas low adherence predicted poor outcomes. Although technical proficiency was increased with manualized treatment, relationship skill and supportiveness tended to decline (Henry, 1998). This decline might, however, be evident only immediately following counseling. For example, Robinson, Berman, and Neimeyer (1990) found negligible differences in effect sizes for those studies with and without manual-based treatments. Following a 1-year follow-up, however, clients treated by counselors trained with treatment manuals experienced fewer symptoms and problems than did those treated by therapists without manualized training.

Perspectives on the Future of Evidence-Based Counseling

In a climate of evidence-based practice, findings such as those presented in this chapter can serve as the foundation for clinical decision making, counselor training, and future research agendas. These findings are, however, only a beginning. It is unfortunate that we have been unable to determine the most effective treatments for a wider array of client problems. As the sophistication of outcome research grows, however, we will become better at identifying the most effec-

tive treatments for a broad spectrum of client concerns. Based on the findings of outcome research, an effective model of counseling would need to incorporate the research-supported treatment protocols matched to the appropriate client problem. Over time, research will identify an increasing number of successful intervention programs with clearly articulated change mechanisms that are relevant for the day-to-day clinical decision making of the counseling practitioner.

On a broader level, it is likely that the future of professional counseling will be forever altered by the emergence, during the current era, of best practices defined by evidence-based intervention programs. On the one hand, such a movement will make even further inroads into eliminating the research-practice gap in counseling and will help us to develop an even stronger evidence base for our practices. On the other hand, the criteria will dramatically alter the ways in which counselors practice, what counselor educators teach, and the research agendas of clinical investigators. Thus, as a profession, we need to support a definition of best practices that fits with the roles, traditions, and practices of counseling professionals. Some have suggested that the medical model approach of the EVT/EST movement (Henry, 1998) supports the more medical model-oriented professions. The PESIP model seems to be broader and more inclusive of both methodological and philosophical plurality. The blueprint model, probably more than any other model, conveys a concern for implementation and dissemination of research programs to local communities.

As we move in the direction of evidence-based practice, it also is important to remember that the research process is an inclusive one that involves practitioners, researchers, and educators. The future of evidence-based counseling will require an integration of these roles around the development, use, and dissemination of knowledge. We no longer can view practitioners as just users of the knowledge base; instead, we must view them as professionals who play a crucial and unique role in the development of the knowledge base. Because practitioners are the ones in the "trenches," they are best suited to identify pertinent and relevant clinical questions. Furthermore, counselors can become "local scientists" (Stricker & Trierweiler, 1995) who evaluate the effectiveness of clinical protocols. As a pragmatic activity, practice also is the breeding ground for the implementation of innovative practice that would spawn new research questions. Furthermore, practice is the arena in which research findings are tested and new questions about the clinical application of research themes are generated. Along the way, counseling practitioners develop local databases that might be used to promote and guide their individual practices. Thus, counseling practitioners would not just be consumers of research; they also would be researchers who gather information about their own practices. In this way, the gap between research consumers and research producers will fall away.

Educators play a role in translating research findings into curricula that prepare counselors for practice. Perhaps more important, educators can help most by creating a new identity for professional counselors. This identity would be one that embraces the knowledge base of research through an attitude of inclusion rather than rejection of research findings.

Finally, these standards will create a tension that will spark an important professional debate regarding the appropriate model for integrating research into professional practice. Regardless of the outcome, the debate will benefit the profession in that it will force a further articulation of the philosophical principles that will guide future efforts toward research and practice integration. Thus, as a relevant guide to evaluate clinical research, a way in which to stimulate intervention program development, and a stimulus for professional debate, the development and discussion of these models is an important stage in the development of our profession. The future will require counselors to understand the issues surrounding these models in such a way that the models might be advocated and implemented in an informed manner.

References

Alexander, J. F., Sexton, T. L., & Robbins, M. A. (in press). The developmental status of family therapy in family psychology intervention science. In H. A. Liddle (Ed.), *Family psychology intervention science.* Washington, DC: American Psychological Association.

Alexander, L. B., & Luborsky, L. (1986). The Penn Helping Alliance Scales. In L. S. Greenberg & W. M. Pinsof (Eds.), *The psychotherapeutic process* (pp. 325-366). New York: Guilford.

American Psychiatric Association. (1994). *Diagnostic and statistical manual of mental disorders* (4th ed.). Washington, DC: Author.

Bergin, A. E., & Garfield, S. L. (Eds.). (1994). *Handbook of psychotherapy and behavior change* (4th ed.). New York: John Wiley.

Beutler, L. E., & Bergin, J. (1991). Value change in counseling and psychotherapy: A search for scientific credibility. *Journal of Counseling Psychology, 38,* 16-24.

Beutler, L. E., & Clarkin, J. (1990). *Systematic treatment selection: Toward targeted therapeutic interventions.* New York: Brunner/Mazel.

Beutler, L. E., Crago, M., & Ariznendi, T. G. (1986). Research on therapist variables in psychotherapy. In S. L. Garfield & A. E. Bergin (Eds.), *Handbook of psychotherapy and behavior change* (pp. 257-310). New York: John Wiley.

Carpenter, P. J., & Range, L. M. (1983). The effects of patients' fee payment source on the duration of outpatient psychotherapy. *Journal of Clinical Psychology, 39,* 304-306.

Chambless, L. D., Sanderson, W. C., Shoham, B., Bennett-Johnson, S., Pope, K. S., Crits-Christoph, P., Baker, M., Johnson, B., Woody, S. R., Sue, S., Beutler, L., Williams, D. A., & McCurry, S. (1996). An update on empirically validated therapies. *The Clinical Psychologist, 49*(2), 5-18.

Crits-Christoph, P., Cooper, A., & Luborsky, L. (1988). The accuracy of therapists' interpretations and the outcome of dynamic psychotherapy. *Journal of Consulting and Clinical Psychology, 56,* 490-495.

Crits-Christoph, P., & Mintz, J. (1991). Implications of therapist effects for the design and analysis of comparative studies of psychotherapies. *Journal of Consulting and Clinical Psychology, 59,* 20-26.

Dawes, R. M. (1994). *House of cards: Psychology and psychotherapy built on myth.* New York: Free Press.

Eisenthal, S., Emery, R., Lazare, A., & Udin, H. (1979). "Adherence" and the negotiated approach to patienthood. *Archives of General Psychiatry, 36,* 393-398.

Elliott, D. S. (1998). Editor's introduction. In D. Elliott (Series Ed.), *Book Three: Blueprints for violence prevention* (pp. xi-xxi). Golden, CO: Venture.

Garfield, S. L., & Bergin, A. E. (1994). Introduction and historical overview. In A. E. Bergin & S. L. Garfield (Eds.), *Handbook of psychotherapy and behavior change* (pp. 3-18). New York: John Wiley.

Gurman, A. S. (1977). The patient's perceptions of the therapeutic relationship. In A. S. Gurman & A. M. Razin (Eds.), *Effective psychotherapy* (pp. 503-545). New York: Pergamon.

Gurman, A. S., Kniskern, D. P., & Pinsof, W. M. (1986). Research on marital and family therapies. In S. L. Garfield & A. E. Bergin (Eds.), *Handbook of psychotherapy and behavior change* (3rd ed., pp. 565-624). New York: John Wiley.

Henggeler, S. W., Rowland, M. D., Pickrel, S. G., Miller, S. L., Cunningham, P. B., Santos, A. B., Schoenwald, S. K., Randall, J., & Edwards, J. E. (1997). Investigating family-based alternatives to institution-based mental health services for youth: Lessons learned from the pilot study of a randomized field trial. *Journal of Clinical Child Psychology, 26,* 226-233.

Henry, W. (1998). Science, politics, and the politics of science: The use and misuse of empirically validated treatment research. *Psychotherapy Research, 8,* 126-140.

Lafferty, P., Beutler, L. E., & Crago, M. (1989). Differences between more or less effective psycho-therapists: A study of select therapist variables. *Journal of Consulting and Clinical Psychology, 57,* 76-80.

Lambert, M. J. (1991). Introduction to psychotherapy research. In L. E. Beutler & M. Crago (Eds.), *Psychotherapy research: An international review of programmatic studies* (pp. 1-23). Washington, DC: American Psychological Association.

Lambert, M. J., & Cattani-Thompson, K. (1996). Current findings regarding the effectiveness of counseling: Implications for practice. *Journal of Counseling and Development, 74,* 601-608.

Luborsky, L., Crits-Christoph, P., Mintz, J., & Auerbach, A. (1988). *Who will benefit from psychotherapy? Predicting therapeutic outcomes.* New York: Basic Books.

Luborsky, L., Singer, B., & Luborsky, L. (1975). Comparative studies of psychotherapies: Is it true that "everyone has won and all must have prizes"? *Archives of General Psychiatry, 32,* 995-1008.

Lyons, L. C., & Woods, P. J. (1991). The efficacy of rational-emotive therapy: A quantitative review of the outcome research. *Clinical Psychology Review, 11,* 357-369.

Mocher, F. J., & Prinz, R. J. (1991). Treatment fidelity in outcome studies. *Clinical Psychology Review, 11,* 247-266.

Orlinsky, D. E., Grawe, K., & Parks, B. K. (1994). Process and outcome in psychotherapy—Noch einmal. In A. E. Bergin & S. L. Garfield (Eds.), *Handbook of psychotherapy and behavior change* (pp. 270-378). New York: John Wiley.

Prioleau, L., Murdock, M., & Brody, N. (1983). An analysis of psychotherapy versus placebo studies. *Behavioral and Brain Sciences, 6,* 275-310.

Robinson, L. A., Berman, J. S., & Neimeyer, R. A. (1990). Psychotherapy for the treatment of depression: A comprehensive review of controlled outcome research. *Psychological Bulletin, 108,* 30-49.

Roth, A., Fonagy, P., Parry, G. P., & Target, M. (1996). *What works for whom? A critical review of psychotherapy research.* New York: Guilford.

Sexton, T. L. (1996). The relevance of counseling outcome research: Current trends and practical implications. *Journal of Counseling and Development, 74,* 590-600.

Sexton, T. L., & Whiston, S. C. (1994). The status of the counseling relationship: An empirical review, theoretical implications, and research directions. *The Counseling Psychologist, 22,* 6-78.

Sexton, T. L., & Whiston, S. C. (1996). Integrating counseling research and practice. *Journal of Counseling and Development, 74,* 588-589.

Sexton, T. L., Whiston, J. C., Bleuer, J. C., & Walz, G. R. (1997). *Integrating outcome research into counseling practice and training.* Alexandria, VA: American Counseling Association.

Smith, M. L., Glass, G. V., & Miller, T. I. (1980). *The bene-fits of psychotherapy*. Baltimore, MD: Johns Hopkins University Press.

Stricker, G., & Trierweiler, S. J. (1995). The local scientist: A bridge between science and practice. *American Psychologist, 50,* 995-1002.

Svartberg, M., & Stiles, T. C. (1991). Comparative effects of short-term psychodynamic psychotherapy: A meta-analysis. *Journal of Consulting and Clinical Psychology, 59,* 704-714.

Tracey, T. J. (1977). Impact of intake procedures upon client attrition in a community mental health center. *Journal of Consulting and Clinical Psychology, 45,* 192-195.

Tracey, T. J. (1987). Stage differences in the dependencies of topic initiation and topic following behavior. *Journal of Counseling Psychology, 34,* 123-131.

Wampold, B. E., Lictenburg J. W., & Waehler, C. A. (in press). Principles of empirically supported intervention programs in counseling psychology. *The Counseling Psychologist.*

Whiston, S. C., Sexton, T. L., & Lasoff, D. (1998). Career-intervention outcome: A replication and extension of Oliver and Spokane. *Journal of Counseling Psychology, 45,* 150-165.

CHAPTER THIRTY

Counseling Program Evaluation

Inside and Outside the Box

LARRY C. LOESCH

Counseling program evaluation (CPE) may be broadly defined as the collection of information to allow appraisal of the quality of and assist decision making about counseling program service delivery (Gredler, 1996; Hadley & Mitchell, 1995; Houser, 1998). The purpose of CPE is to maximize the efficiency and effectiveness of service delivery through careful and systematic examination of program components, methodologies, and outcomes. It is *not* the purpose of CPE simply to provide a rationale for what currently exists or is being done. Rather, CPE is used primarily to *change* counseling service delivery for the better.

A catchphrase of the 1990s was "thinking outside the box," which meant thinking creatively to accomplish goals and objectives. Unfortunately, it appears that this catchphrase has not found a niche in the realm of CPE. Indeed, examples of the creative practice of CPE are relatively rare. Perhaps CPE is not highly valued in the counseling profession. If it is not valued, then there is little likelihood that its processes and outcomes have been closely scrutinized. Stevens and Dial (1994) wrote, "The misuse of evaluation means that an evaluation has been used for the wrong purpose or that the results of an evaluation have been misapplied or used improperly" (p. 3). To the extent that CPE is not valued sufficiently in the counseling profession, the potential for misuse is great. Although the counseling profession has not yet enjoyed the benefits of good CPE (i.e., it has not been thinking about CPE outside the box), there remains strong potential for using CPE creatively to build more effective counseling programs. Achievement of this potential, however, will require careful attention to CPE as an integral component of counseling service delivery programs.

The Box: Program Evaluation Stakeholders

As a "major player" in the helping professions, counseling service delivery programs obviously are *intended* to do good for the people they serve. Unfortunately, even though the need for CPE has been recognized (Hadley & Mitchell, 1995; Hosie, 1994; Houser, 1998), too many counseling service providers have interpreted that perspective to mean that there is no substantive reason to *demonstrate* that counseling programs do good. Thus, many counseling service programs seem to operate on the assumption that the inherent worth of counseling services provided is self-evident. However, this assumption does great injustice to the programs, the counseling profession, and (most important) the stakeholders for counseling services.

It is difficult to argue against the proposition that the primary stakeholders in counseling programs are the people to whom the services are delivered. After all, counseling programs exist simply to provide counseling services to clients, so clients certainly have a right to the best possible services. Thus, clients obviously have a large stake in wanting counseling services to be both efficient and effective, which are the likely results of good CPE. However, it would be a mistake to assume that all clients

have the same interests in and needs for CPE. For example, Stockdill, Duhon-Sells, Olson, and Patton (1992) wrote,

> An important new direction for program evaluation is to seek ways of actively involving people of color in evaluation processes. This means adding a multicultural perspective to stakeholder involvement processes. Stakeholders do not just represent power positions, program constituencies, and key influences. Different stakeholders also bring varied cultural perspectives to evaluation. (p. 17)

Similarly, other stakeholders varying on other characteristics have different vested interests in and contributions to good CPE.

Although not thought of as readily, there also are other important counseling program stakeholders. For example, there are many *economic* stakeholders. Counseling services are *not free*, even though they might appear to be. Various government entities, private businesses, educational systems, charitable organizations, and other agencies are likely to pay in some way for the provision of counseling services, even if clients are not charged directly. Thus, these funding entities have an important stake in good CPE.

The general public also is a counseling stakeholder. Society at large does not function as well as it might if the people of the society do not function well. Counseling is intended to help people to function well, and if it is effective, society is better for it. Therefore, society in general benefits from good CPE.

Finally, professional counselors themselves also are major stakeholders in counseling service delivery. Burnout among counselors is common, and not without ready explanation. Counseling is a challenging job, one possibly fraught with difficulties, frustrations, and unfulfilled expectations. However, counseling can be a highly rewarding and satisfying job *if* the counseling services provided are effective. One of the ways in which counselors can help to ensure that counseling is a good and enjoyable job is to engage in sound, credible, and appropriate CPE.

Each of these stakeholders has a part in the determination of how CPE is conducted. Sometimes their respective CPE needs are in concert, and sometimes they are not. Some may be most interested in formative (process) evaluation, others in summative (outcome) evaluation, and still others in cost-benefit evaluation. However, they all are relevant stakeholders because they all help to determine the nature of effective CPE practices.

Inside the Box: Common Approaches to Program Evaluation

Although many different program evaluation approaches have been presented, 10 appear to be the most credible based on the frequency with which they are referenced in the professional literature. These 10 may be aligned within three broad perspectives for discussion clarity: product function, utilitarian, and intuitionist/pluralist.

The Product Function Perspective

The oldest approach applied to evaluation of human service programs is the input/output model, sometimes known as the *production factor concept*. Application of this model assumes a parallel between production in manufacturing and the delivery of human services. Key assumptions in this model are that (a) individuals

and organizations act to maximize identifiable outcomes, (b) consensus exists about desired outcomes, (c) human service programs can be defined fully in terms of funding and other resources, and (d) the "production function" between inputs and outputs can be quantified (Gredler, 1996).

Because of the assumed production function relationship between resources expended and products delivered, CPE based on this model would be conceived of as the attempt to answer two questions: "What did the program have to work with?" (e.g., monetary, personnel, physical, and other resources or inputs) and "What were the program's products?" (e.g., number of clients served, types of client problems solved, or other outputs).

Although widely used, there are substantive problems in applying this model to evaluation of human service programs. In general, the production factor concept is a poor fit with the social and other "realities" of human service programs (Gredler, 1996). For example, the assumption of a direct link between inputs and outputs is tenuous at best. In addition, the model does not allow for different conceptual foundations, nor does it allow for differential purposes and goals across programs. Furthermore, the model allows only for evaluation of readily quantified outputs and does not give consideration to more abstract but also desirable outcomes. Finally, the model assumes that outputs will be evaluated from only one perspective (e.g., that of program administrators or managers), and again this is most commonly an untenable assumption.

Problems inherent in the production factor concept spawned new program evaluation models, many of which originated during the 1970s. These newer approaches generally can be divided into the utilitarian and intuitionist/ pluralist perspectives.

The Utilitarian Perspectives

The utilitarian perspectives sometimes are referred to as *preordinate* because they rely on specific designs, identifiable objectives, operational definitions of variables, and numeric data (Gredler, 1996). These approaches share with the production factor concept the assumptions that the users of the evaluation results are the (only) decision makers, there exist predetermined standards for program utility, and the results apply to the program as opposed to persons in or components of it.

The Provus discrepancy model was among the first developed within the utilitarian perspective. Its purpose is to yield a singular decision—maintain, improve, or terminate a program (Gredler, 1996). Emphasized in this model are program definition and installation as important parts of the overall evaluation. The four major components of the model are (a) establishment and evaluation of program definition, (b) evaluation of program installation, (c) evaluation of relationships between programmatic processes and outcomes, and (d) evaluation of program outcomes. Gredler (1996) wrote, "The program is often referred to as a discrepancy model because, at each of the four stages, program performance is compared with selected standards to determine the discrepancy" (p. 43).

Major strengths of the Provus model include that it emphasizes program definition, careful analysis of program definitions, and use of databases to link service recipient characteristics and program processes and outcomes. Limitations of the model include the extensive time

needed to implement it and the need to specify carefully both intermediate and terminal objectives. The Provus model is particularly well suited to evaluation of innovative programs because of its emphasis on evaluation of initial program components. However, it requires that substantial personnel resources be assigned to the evaluation process, so it typically can be used only in programs that have such resources available.

The CIPP model, generally attributed to Stufflebeam, was developed during the early 1970s and has enjoyed a degree of popularity for CPE (Hadley & Mitchell, 1995). CIPP is an acronym for *c*ontext, *i*nput, *p*rocess, and *p*roduct evaluations. The CIPP model's purpose is to provide information for decision making.

The original focus of context evaluation was to provide a rationale for setting objectives. Thus, in CPE, context evaluation was roughly synonymous with needs assessment. More recently, context evaluation also includes careful consideration of the program's environment, personnel and other resources, and target population.

Input evaluation is used to examine potential approaches to goal achievement as well as barriers or constraints to effective implementation of the program. It also allows evaluation of current and needed resources and of what procedural plans are best suited to the program.

The focus of process evaluation is determination of whether changes are needed in the program activities currently being implemented. Process evaluation information also can be used effectively to provide information about the program to external audiences and to facilitate interpretation of program outcomes.

Product evaluation is intended to identify the extent to which programmatic needs have been met and which program goals have been achieved. Product evaluation usually is considered as synonymous with outcomes evaluation.

Although the CIPP model is helpful in that it identifies four primary aspects of effective CPE, it does not delineate specific activities needed or to be implemented. Thus, it is a very general model, one that is implemented in widely varying ways.

Stake's (1981) *countenance* approach is not so much an evaluation model as a method of systematic consideration of the three different types of data that exist in any program. *Antecedents* are data that reflect the conditions existing prior to program implementation and that may be related to program outcomes. *Transactions* are data that reflect the dynamic interactions and encounters among the various persons associated with the program. *Outcomes* are data that reflect the effects of the program on the various persons associated with it including both program service providers and recipients.

Stake's (1981) countenance approach includes consideration of both descriptive and judgmental information. Relationships among the data are examined for logical (i.e., theoretically sound) consistencies and congruence among elements. The descriptive information examined often is numeric and voluminous (e.g., information from clients' records, required funding and/or service provider documentation, regulatory agency databases). The judgmental information often is anecdotal (e.g., information from counselors' case notes or client feedback solicitations). Therefore, the major limitation of this approach is that the large complex data sets to be considered and evaluated are difficult to interpret.

The primary purpose of Scriven's (1973) *goal-free* perspective is to reduce bias in inquiry,

not to delineate a particular set of evaluation procedures. Scriven considered the consumer to be the primary recipient of evaluation results, so his perspective sometimes is known as *consumer-based evaluation*. In Scriven's approach, evaluations of a variety of criteria ultimately are summarized in an overall judgment of program worth.

A major focus of Scriven's (1973) approach is to identify *all* the effects of a program, whether they be positive or negative. Thus, this model addresses more than just "what worked." This model also encourages use of a wide variety of methods—especially methods other than experimental design—to determine causal relationships between all of the various elements of the program and the program's outcomes.

A primary benefit of using Scriven's (1973) approach is heightened sensitivity to the wide variety of possible program effects and, in particular, to unanticipated effects. Another benefit is the freedom to use diverse methods to explain causal relationships among program elements. Unfortunately, however, the approach is not prescriptive as to the types of methods that should be used. Therefore, there is substantial potential for misinterpretation of global programmatic results if the methods used to derive conclusions are not examined critically. In addition, it is debatable whether consumers (as opposed to, say, program managers or funding administrators) *always* should be the primary audience for program evaluation results.

The Intuitionist/Pluralist Perspectives

The intuitionist/pluralist perspectives differ from the previous perspectives in their assumptions concerning to whom the evaluation results are most valuable. The intuitionist/pluralist approaches view evaluation results as most useful to persons associated with implementation of the program and with much less emphasis on use of results for (management and/or external) decision making. These approaches also assume that a program may be valued differently by different groups and that differential characteristics of persons associated with the program are important factors in its evaluation.

Both the *judicial* and *adversary* models are based on the assumption that human judgment and testimony are important sources of information given that they are obtained systematically and understood in an appropriate context (Gredler, 1996).

The judicial model consists of four stages: (a) issue generation, (b) issue selection, (c) preparation of arguments, and (d) the clarification forum. After a pertinent set of issues has been selected, the pros and cons of an issue are presented to a panel of policy makers (e.g., representatives of a funding agency or another decision-making body, such as school board members). This model has appeal for CPE because it relies heavily on interpersonal interactions for decision making and typically yields recommendations for improvements. However, it is not well suited for situations in which there are distinct ideological differences about program purposes.

The adversary model is similar but addresses a finite question, "Should the program be continued?" This *high-stakes* approach usually involves stringent "cross-examination" of position and/or information presenters. Unfortunately, because it is not a legal process, there are no stipulated rules for how the process proceeds.

The judicial and adversary models have the advantage of allowing for inputs from a wide variety of persons. Unfortunately, however, the results often are determined more by the oratorical skills of the presenters than by the evidence.

Eisner's (1977) *connoisseurship and criticism* model is distinctive in its emphasis on analytic study of interactions among program participants. Eisner viewed his approach as a supplement, not an alternative, to other, more scientific approaches to program evaluation. His advocacy for the approach was based on his belief that the complexity of program events is greater than can be measured effectively by traditional measurement tools.

In Eisner's (1977) approach, connoisseurship is judgment based on experience and knowledge to understand the different qualities of the program. Criticism, in Eisner's model, is vivid description, interpretation, and evaluation of programmatic events. Criticism in this context is not meant to have a negative connotation; rather, it is meant to imply rich description of evaluative judgments. Criticisms often are presented as narratives that attempt to explain phenomena observed and evaluations made about them.

An advantage of this model is that it includes a description of aspects of programs by actual participants, and generally in relatively easily understood language. However, it is limited in that the exact criteria on which judgments are made are delineated only infrequently.

Identified limitations of Stake's (1981) countenance approach described earlier included that it did not address the various roles of persons associated with the program being evaluated or the types of information that should be reported. Stake developed his *responsive evaluation* approach to address these limitations. A key concept in this approach is *social plurality,* which means that there is no single true value for a program but rather different values for different people for different purposes (Stake, 1990). In responsive evaluation, therefore, a primary purpose is to make the evaluation useful to any and all program stakeholders.

The three primary activities in responsive evaluation are (a) initial planning and focusing, (b) conducting observations, and (c) organizing and reporting results. In this approach, it is important for the evaluator(s) to become completely familiar with the program, primarily by interacting with the various persons associated with the program. However, the approach should not be construed to be only qualitative inquiry because both qualitative and quantitative data may be considered in the evaluation process (Gredler, 1996).

An advantage of the responsive evaluation approach is that it facilitates understanding of the complexities of programs and is responsive to all stakeholders. A disadvantage, however, is that stakeholder involvement that is too extensive may result in overlooked information or decreased evaluation quality.

Parlett's (1990) *illuminative evaluation* approach shares with the responsive evaluation approach an emphasis on sensitivity to the needs and concerns of various stakeholders. However, it differs in that it is a *holistic* approach intended to describe (or illuminate) the entire network of interrelationships among elements of a program. This approach involves application of anthropological methods to evaluation, in particular, that the nature of the problem defines the methods to be used. However, it is a broader, more integrated approach than typical qualitative inquiry and includes consideration of both qualitative and quantitative data.

The first stage is the immersion period, during which the evaluator becomes thoroughly familiar with the program. The next stage allows determination of themes to guide the direction, and perhaps methods, for the program evaluation process. The third stage is directed toward identifying patterns of cause and effect and toward placing specific findings in a broad explanatory context. The primary techniques used for data collection include observation, document analyses, and unstructured interviews.

The primary advantage of this approach is the progressive focusing on themes to be explored and, in the process, the development of plans for subsequent inquiries. Unfortunately, this approach requires that the evaluator have especially good anthropological investigation skills including good qualitative investigation and interpersonal skills. In addition, this approach is subject to criticism for being overly subjective in both the gathering of data and the interpretation of findings.

Evaluation Tools

Just as there are a variety of perspectives in which CPE can be couched, so too are there a variety of tools (or techniques) that can be used in CPE processes to obtain information and data. For discussion, these may be divided into four commonly used group and two commonly used individual approaches.

Group Approaches for Data Gathering

A *focus group interview* (FGI) is an information-gathering technique intended to discover participants' perceptions and feelings about a particular topic (e.g., counseling program). It is not a brainstorming session, intended to achieve consensus, or designed to facilitate decision making. The FGI usually is used to develop ideas for further, more structured data collection; to identify potential problems in a program; or to provide insights into program functioning.

A good FGI includes 7 to 10 participants, fewer than 10 specific questions, a discussion moderator, an appropriate environment, and an organized method of data analysis (e.g., content analysis). Participants are instructed to provide emotional reactions (i.e., feelings) to topics as opposed to "rationales" for opinions held or positions taken.

FGIs have the advantage of providing relatively specific feedback and reactions quickly and at relatively little cost. They also allow participants to generate additional ideas based on the comments of others and thereby provide more complete responses. The difficulty in using FGIs is that the data derived are complex, owing to the open-ended questions asked.

In contrast to the FGI, the *nominal group technique* (NGT) is intended to facilitate decision making, using procedures in which the group actually makes the decisions. The word *nominal* in the term refers to the fact that the participants are a group in name only. That is, the participants usually are diverse in regard to their personal characteristics and situations, the nature of their association with the program being evaluated, and their vested interest in the results. A key characteristic of the technique is that each participant's input is viewed as being as valuable as that of any other participant; evaluations of participants' responses are not permitted. The NGT usually is used to address a single question, although the question is broad enough to allow for multiple perspectives to be expressed. It also often is used early in the pro-

gram evaluation process to help develop focal points for subsequent activities.

The actual NGT group usually consists of 7 to 10 participants. The question to be addressed is created by the evaluator. Initially, each participant (silently) creates a personal response to the question, and then the various responses are listed for all to view. Responses are explained but not debated. Then, each participant is instructed to select three to five "top" items from the list and to prioritize his or her list. Then, the "votes" are tallied across items, and the results are shared with the group. Finally, each participant rates the three to five items receiving the most votes, the ratings are tallied, and a final rank order is determined.

The primary advantage of the NGT is that the result is a prioritized list generated from a disparate group of individual perspectives. In addition, the technique allows for identification of problems that might be difficult to document in other ways. The primary disadvantage of the NGT is that many responses might lack quality or relevance but still have to be considered.

The *Delphi* technique is another method developed to facilitate decision making based on group consensus. The procedure usually is implemented by policy decision makers as opposed to others who might wish to influence decisions but who do not actually have the authority to do so. It can be used to identify program problem areas or to set goals and objectives. The Delphi technique is most appropriate when respondents otherwise would be unlikely to have the opportunity to provide input.

In a typical Delphi procedure, the policy makers first develop a set of open-ended questions for consideration. Next, participants' responses are presented as items that can be evaluated (i.e., rated), usually through the use of a

Likert-type response scale. After the items are rated in the first round, the results are summarized and provided as feedback to respondents, and then the respondents rate the items again. This procedure is repeated for a third and final round. Then, the items are prioritized by average item ranking.

Historically, the time and costs necessary for a three-round Delphi technique often were substantial. However, the increasing use of thermofax and electronic mail systems and the Internet (e.g., posting the items and related information on a Web site) has greatly reduced both the time and the costs needed for the procedures.

A significant advantage of the Delphi technique is that it allows participants to respond at times when they can focus their attention fully on the task. Another is that it avoids undue social pressure or persuasion to respond in particular ways. It also avoids problems associated with "one-shot" evaluations. However, the second- and/or third-round tasks may be discomforting to respondents who hold opinions strongly at odds with the feedback data provided from previous rounds. Also, the implementation time period may be long if traditional mailing methods are used.

The *opinion survey* is perhaps the most commonly used data-gathering technique in CPE, primarily because it generally is viewed as the easiest way to get information as well as the easiest way to get information from relatively large groups of people. Opinion surveys are similar to, but not exactly the same as, attitude measures. Opinion surveys are used to obtain group data (i.e., average opinions) related to relatively specific topics such as issues; policies; program characteristics; and institutional needs, goals, or priorities. They also often are used to obtain opinion data about program effectiveness.

Effective opinion surveying typically includes six stages: (a) generation of issues or topics, (b) item construction and pilot testing, (c) selection of sample(s), (d) administration, (e) data analyses, and (e) dissemination of results. A variety of response formats may be used, but Likert-type response scales are used most often. Appropriate data analyses range from relatively simple descriptive statistics to factor analyses.

The major advantage of using an opinion survey is that information can be obtained efficiently from a large respondent group. A major disadvantage of opinion surveys is that the items must be constructed with great care so that all respondents interpret them as equally and uniformly as possible. In addition, it is not always easy to establish response priorities, especially when multiple items apply to the same issue or topic.

Individual Approaches to Data Gathering

Applications of *alternative assessments,* sometimes called *authentic assessments,* in educational contexts have gained widespread popularity during recent years. In general, the term *alternative* refers to any of a variety of assessment procedures other than the use of so-called traditional (e.g., paper-and-pencil) tests. In educational contexts, alternative assessment usually implies evaluation of actual applications of learning such as giving a speech after having been instructed in principles of public speaking. The popularity of alternative assessment lies in the perception that it focuses on the "end result" of instruction as opposed to the methods or components of instruction. Although alternative assessments still are used primarily in educational contexts, more recently they have been used in other contexts including program evaluation (Gredler, 1996).

Performance assessment and *portfolio assessment* are two types of alternative assessments that have at least limited potential for use within the context of CPE. Performance assessment is literally what the term implies, that is, assessment (and evaluation) of how a person actually performs, acts, or behaves. For example, suppose that a goal of a counseling process is to enable the client to be more assertive. A performance assessment of the effectiveness of the counseling might involve the client being observed (i.e., assessed for assertiveness) in a situation where the client has the opportunity to be assertive. Data might be obtained from any persons who have the skills and opportunity to assess the client's performance in the situation.

In educational contexts, portfolio assessment starts with a student quite literally creating a portfolio that contains any of a variety of types of "evidence" that the student considers to be indicative of learning in various areas of instruction. In counseling, a client might be asked to create a portfolio of materials to indicate the effects of counseling. In response, the client might include materials such as a personal diary showing changes in mood or affect over time, testimonial statements about client change from friends or relatives, and a calendar showing changes in specific behaviors over time.

Both the performance assessment and portfolio assessment techniques are potentially innovative ways in which to obtain data in the context of CPE. They have a degree of appeal because they yield data from actual recipients of program services (as opposed to program administrators or counselors as service providers). They also have the advantage of permitting evaluation of observable phenomena as op-posed to judgmental interpretations of rather abstract constructs. In addition, they allow clients to play an important role in determining what is examined and when. Unfortunately, however, each of these techniques still is in the early stages of refinement as useful approaches to measurement. As is true for students in educational contexts, there is great variation in clients' abilities to create substantive portfolios. In regard to psychometric properties, both techniques are notoriously unreliable, and this in turn raises significant issues about their validity. They both also require substantial investments of human time and effort, and they often are impractical to implement.

Outside the Box: The Future of Counseling Program Evaluation

As society in general and various components of it change, current realities rapidly become old realties. For example, advances in psychopharmacology and/or other medical technology have impacts on how certain psychological conditions are treated, who provides the treatment and at what cost, and what constitutes effective treatment. Thus, the boundaries of what is considered appropriate CPE practice must be flexible and adaptive, as must the counselors who conduct it.

No constellation of changes has greater potential for profound impact on counseling service delivery than do those in the realm of computer-related technologies. Changes in this realm affect current counseling service delivery modalities and also open broad vistas for new modalities. Consider, for example, counselors' record-keeping functions. Sophisticated computers now both greatly enhance what can be placed into records *and* decrease (but do not eliminate) the time involved in record keeping. Similarly, advances in technologies such as telecommunications and the Internet have greatly broadened counselors' potential service delivery modalities, resources, clientele, and spheres of influence in general. These changes are happening now. Ignoring their impact or using old approaches to evaluate their impact will not serve the counseling profession well. Consideration of these changes must be incorporated into CPE practices.

Does managed care and its influences on the counseling profession even need to be mentioned here? Managed care is the manifestation of what happens when CPE practices are imposed externally.

The general result of coupling the interests of multiple stakeholders with rapidly changing ways of life is increased pressure on counselors both to engage in more CPE and to develop more—and more effective—CPE practices. In so doing, all stakeholders will benefit and the profession will be enhanced.

Is there a need for new CPE paradigms? The answer is a definite yes and no. The answer certainly is yes *if* new paradigms will increase the amount of CPE actually being conducted by professionals associated with counseling program service delivery. The foremost problem with CPE practice today is that not much of it is being done. The lack of CPE *may* be a function of confusion about program evaluation and accountability, which are related but not synonymous concepts. Gredler (1996) wrote,

> The major difference between evaluation and accountability is that the purpose of accountability systems typically is to assign responsibility for outcomes among a program's operators. Ac-

countability is thus a measure of control. This perspective is a restricted view of the reasons for program success or failure. (p. 15)

Accountability is a *really scary idea* if there is an attempt to assign unilateral links between specific program outcomes and particular persons. No wonder counselors (and many other professionals) avoid it. However, good CPE practice does not use such simplistic interpretations of person-outcome linkages; instead, it seeks to explain how the complexities of the program yield various outcomes. If new CPE models will foster greater clarification of what good CPE is and how it should be implemented, then new models should be developed—and quickly.

From a practical perspective, new CPE paradigms are not needed. What is needed is greater creativity and innovation in the application of existing program evaluation approaches. Most program evaluation approaches initially were developed to be applied to educational programs (Popham, 1993). Although there are similarities between educational and counseling programs, they clearly are not exactly the same. Therefore, available models should (and can) be *adapted* so as to be effective for CPE.

There are many different evaluation approaches and data-gathering techniques potentially suitable for use in CPE. The selection and adaptation process should begin with careful consideration of the stakeholders for whom the CPE is to be conducted. This crucial initial decision should be followed by equally careful consideration of which of the existing evaluation approaches is most likely to yield good information *for a particular purpose for a particular stakeholder group in regard to a particular program.* The next focal point should be the identification of appropriate data-gathering methodologies. Finally, minimal modifications should be made to an existing evaluation paradigm so as to maintain the integrity of the CPE process to the greatest extent possible.

This call for more frequent, and better, CPE will go unheeded if there is not first a more fundamental change in the counseling profession. Specifically, CPE must become an expected and accepted part of the professional counselor's functioning. Unfortunately, CPE is consistently given minimal attention, and indeed often appears to be an afterthought, in the counseling literature. Typically, CPE is obfuscated under the general rubric of research (Hadley & Mitchell, 1995; Houser, 1998), a tactic that gives the erroneous impression that research and CPE are synonymous. For example, although the Council for Accreditation of Counseling and Related Educational Program's (CACREP) professional preparation standards for counselors appear to call for training and skill development in program evaluation by virtue of its inclusion as part of a "core curriculum" area title (i.e., II-J-7: Research and Program Evaluation), CPE is not referred to at all in the general description of that curriculum area, and the only standard in which it is referred to (II-J-7-c) is so vague as to be relatively meaningless (CACREP, 1994). A similar situation exists for data-gathering techniques. Here, too, the data-gathering techniques best suited for effective CPE are conspicuous by their lack of attention in the professional literature (Drummond, 1996; Hood & Johnson, 1997).

Diminished recognition of CPE pervades other aspects of the counseling profession as well. For example, although ethical practice is heavily emphasized in the counseling profession, how many counselors are even aware that there is substantive literature on the ethical conduct of program evaluation (Newman & Brown, 1996)? Finally, how many counselors are even aware of the various professional standards for program evaluation implementation (American Evaluation Association, Task Force on Guiding Principles for Evaluators, 1995; Joint Committee on Standards, 1994)? Ignorance of good CPE practices does great injustice to both counselors and the counseling profession, and it certainly limits our ability to reap the potential benefits of CPE.

Conclusion

Evaluation is not a popular topic in the counseling profession, most likely because evaluation necessarily involves application of judgments, and most counselors strive to be nonjudgmental in their counseling and other professional activities. Unfortunately, however, ignoring *good* evaluation does not serve the profession well. Most, if not all, of the various stakeholders in counseling service delivery programs want, and often demand, evaluative information. They have every right to make such demands because, by definition, they are affected by, and have vested interests in, those programs. If the counseling profession ignores the wants and demands of its stakeholders, then its perceived value among its stakeholders, as well as among others in society, never can be as high as it should be.

Fortunately, there are a variety of perspectives and methods that have strong potential to yield effective and useful CPE results. Each approach and data-gathering method has its strong points; therefore, each merits consideration as a way in which to help any counseling program demonstrate that, indeed, good things result from conduct of the program. However, the best and most favorably received results most likely will be achieved through application of unique combinations of approaches and techniques. That is, if each counseling program is evaluated in multiple ways, and in ways that are not threatening to the individual professionals associated with the program, then the collective information derived will benefit everyone associated with the program. It follows that if good CPE becomes relatively standard practice, then all stakeholders in counseling service delivery programs, the counseling profession, and society will benefit greatly.

References

American Evaluation Association, Task Force on Guiding Principles for Evaluators. (1995). Guiding principles for evaluators. In D. L. Shadish Newman, M. A. Scheirer, & C. Wye (Eds.), *Guiding principles for evaluators* (New Directions in Program Evaluation, Vol. 66, pp. 91-126). San Francisco: Jossey-Bass.

Council for Accreditation of Counseling and Related Educational Programs. (1994). *Accreditation standards and procedures manual.* Alexandria, VA: Author.

Drummond, R. J. (1996). *Appraisal procedures for counselors and helping professionals* (3rd ed.). Columbus, OH: Merrill.

Eisner, E. (1977). On the uses of educational connoisseurship and criticism for evaluating classroom life. *Teachers College Record, 78,* 345-358.

Gredler, M. E. (1996). *Program evaluation.* Englewood Cliffs, NJ: Prentice Hall.

Hadley, R. G., & Mitchell, L. K. (1995). *Counseling research and program evaluation.* Pacific Grove, CA: Brooks/Cole.

Hood, A. B., & Johnson, R. W. (1997). *Assessment in counseling: A guide to the use of psychological assessment procedures* (2nd ed.). Alexandria, VA: American Counseling Association.

Hosie, T. (1994). Program evaluation: A potential area of expertise for counselors. *Counselor Education and Supervision, 33,* 349-355.

Houser, R. (1998). *Counseling and educational research.* Thousand Oaks, CA: Sage.

Joint Committee on Standards. (1994). *Program evaluation standards* (2nd ed.). Thousand Oaks, CA: Sage.

Newman, D. L., & Brown, R. D. (1996). *Applied ethics for program evaluation.* Thousand Oaks, CA: Sage.

Parlett, M. E. (1990). Illuminative evaluation. In H. J. Walberg & G. D. Haertel (Eds.), *The international encyclopedia of educational evaluation* (pp. 68-73). Columbus, OH: Merrill.

Popham, W. J. (1993). *Educational evaluation* (3rd ed.). Boston: Allyn & Bacon.

Scriven, M. (1973). Goal-free evaluation. *Evaluation Comment, 3*(4), 1-4.

Stake, R. (1981). Persuasions, not models. *Educational Evaluation and Policy Analysis, 3*(1), 83-84.

Stake, R. (1990). Responsive evaluation. In H. J. Walberg & G. D. Haertel (Eds.), *The international encyclopedia of educational evaluation* (pp. 75-77). Columbus, OH: Merrill.

Stevens, C. J., & Dial, M. (1994). What constitutes misuse? In C. J. Stevens & M. Dial (Eds.), *Preventing the misuse of evaluation* (New Directions in Program Evaluation, Vol. 64, pp. 3-14). San Francisco: Jossey-Bass.

Stockdill, S. H., Duhon-Sells, R. M., Olson, R. A., & Patton, M. Q. (1992). Voices in design and evaluation of a multicultural education program: A developmental approach. In A. M. Madison (Ed.), *Minority issues in program evaluation* (New Directions in Program Evaluation, Vol. 53, pp. 17-34). San Francisco: Jossey-Bass.

PART VI

Critical Issues and Emerging Topics

CHAPTER THIRTY-ONE

Facing the Changing Demographic Structure of Our Society

MICHAEL D'ANDREA
JUDY DANIELS

Despite the far-reaching impact that the multicultural movement is having on the field, it is important to note that most of the criticisms and suggestions that multicultural advocates have made regarding the importance of promoting cultural sensitivity and competence in the profession are based on data that were generated from population studies conducted during the 1980s and early 1990s (Atkinson, Morten, & Sue, 1993; Locke, 1992; Sue & Sue, 1990). Because these data are a decade old, it could reasonably be argued that the demographic changes that were predicted to occur in

the United States might not match the actual modifications that have taken place in the makeup of this nation's citizenry over the past 10 years. In extending this argument further, one could hypothesize that earlier population studies might have either overestimated or underestimated the demographic changes that were expected to occur in this country over the past decade.

To accurately understand the changing structure of our society, it is important that professional counselors periodically update their knowledge of the current demographic makeup of our nation's citizenry. Besides checking the accuracy of the predictions that were made several years ago, updating our understanding of the demographic changes that recently have taken place in our society can lead counselors to reflect on the types of challenges that the profession faces if it is to effectively and ethically promote the development of persons from a broad range of cultural, ethnic, and racial groups.

With this backdrop in mind, this chapter is designed to serve a twofold purpose. First, to help counselors gain an accurate and updated understanding of the changes that are occurring in our society, we present information generated from recent population studies in the United States (Russell, 1998; U.S. Bureau of the Census, 1998). In so doing, we have specifically chosen to focus on recent research on the five major cultural/racial groups in the United States. This includes providing brief updated reports on persons from (a) non-Hispanic, White European backgrounds; (b) African Americans; (c) Asian Americans; (d) Hispanics/Latinos/Latinas; and (e) Native persons including Native Americans, Alaska Natives, and Native Hawaiians. Second, using the recent demographic research findings as a guide, we outline several major challenges that counselors must face if they are to remain a relevant and viable part of a mental health care system that is designed to meet the needs of a culturally and racially diverse populace during the 21st century.

Persons From Non-Hispanic, White European Backgrounds

Overall Population

The dominant cultural/racial group in the United States historically has been comprised of non-Hispanic White persons who come from a variety of Western European backgrounds. Of the approximately 270 million persons who currently live in the United States, it is reported that 192 million individuals come from non-Hispanic, White European backgrounds. This represents 71% of the country's total population (U.S. Bureau of the Census, 1998). As was predicted from earlier population studies (U.S. Bureau of the Census, 1989), the growth rate for persons in this cultural/racial group slowed considerably during the past decade. More specifically, it has been noted that the total number of non-Hispanic White persons from European backgrounds living in the United States grew by only 2% from 1990 to 1997 (Russell, 1998). This continued slow growth trend within the dominant cultural/racial group in the United States has led researchers to predict that the total percentage of persons who come from non-Hispanic, White European backgrounds will be reduced from 71% of the U.S. population in 1998 to 64% by 2020 (Russell, 1998).

Population Changes

A closer analysis of the demographic changes that are taking place among non-Hispanic White persons in the United States indicates that this group accounts for a smaller share of persons in younger age groups but is increasingly represented among the expanding number of older persons who live in this country (Myers, 1995). Based on recent population projections provided by the U.S. Bureau of the Census (1998), it is expected that the number of children from non-Hispanic, White European backgrounds who are under 5 years of age is expected to grow by only 4.6% while the numbers of children between 5 and 9 years of age and between 10 and 14 years of age will increase by

5.2% and 2.0%, respectively, between 2000 and 2010.

Similar slow growth rates have been calculated for young and middle-aged adults from White European backgrounds. In this regard, it has been reported that the number of persons in the dominant cultural/racial group in the United States between 30 and 34 years of age decreased by 12.5% between 1993 and 1997. It also is projected that the total numbers of persons in the dominant cultural/racial group between 35 and 39 years of age and between 40 and 44 years of age will decrease by 19% and 13%, respectively, between 2000 and 2010 (U.S. Bureau of the Census, 1998).

Risk Factors and Counseling Challenges

The projected decreases in the numbers of children and young and middle-aged adults who come from non-Hispanic, White European backgrounds in the United States are in sharp contrast to the rapid increases in the numbers of older persons who live in this country. This increase is reflected in the 25.1% and 20.0% growth rates that were reported among White persons from non-Hispanic European backgrounds between 50 and 54 years of age and between 55 and 59 years of age, respectively, between 1990 and 1997 (U.S. Bureau of the Census, 1998). Given the broad range of risk factors that older persons commonly experience in their lives (Myers, 1995), counselors will be increasingly pressed to acquire a host of gerontological competencies that will enable them to work effectively and ethically with the disproportionate number of persons from non-Hispanic, White European backgrounds who will constitute a sizable percentage of the total population of the United States during the 21st century.

Asian Americans

Overall Population

Approximately 10.5 million Asian Americans lived in the United States in 1998. This represents approximately 4% of the total U.S. population. This figure also reflects a 10% increase in the total number of persons from Asian decent living in the United States since 1995, when 9.3 million Asian Americans resided in this country (Russell, 1998). The rapid increase in the Asian American population in the United States has led demographers to project that the number of persons in this country who come from different Asian backgrounds will increase by 20.2% between 1995 and 2000 (from approximately 9.3 million to 11.2 million). It is further predicted that the Asian American population will increase by 35.7% between 2000 and 2010 (from 11.2 million to 15.2 million) (U.S. Bureau of the Census, 1998).

Population Changes

The single most important factor contributing to the significant growth rates of persons of Asian descent in the United States is immigration. In terms of recent immigration trends, it has been reported that 34% of all persons who immigrated to the United States in 1996 came from Asian countries (U.S. Bureau of the Census, 1997). Of all the Asian American persons currently living in this country, 63% are foreign born. A closer look at this figure indicates that most foreign-born Asian American persons came from Vietnam, India, Korea, China (including Hong Kong), and the Philippines (Russell, 1998), whereas Japanese Americans are the least likely to be foreign born at the present time (U.S. Bureau of the Census, 1997). Although there continues to be substantial growth in the number of Asian Americans in the United States, Russell (1998) noted, "Asians will account for just 6 percent of the U.S. population in 2020, as Blacks and Hispanics will continue to greatly outnumber Asians for decades to come" (p. 54).

Risk Factors and Counseling Challenges

Counselors need to avoid falling prey to the "model minority" stereotype (Baruth & Manning, 1999, p. 177) that many people have adopted about Asian Americans. Although many Asian Americans have achieved considerable academic and financial success that should not be understated, many persons from different Asian backgrounds experience heightened levels of stress and failure in various areas of their lives. As Baruth and Manning (1999) noted, language problems, dismal employment opportunities for unskilled Asian workers, and conflicting familial roles and expectations represent serious risk factors that compromise the mental health and sense of well-being of many persons from Asian descent who live in the United States.

It also is important that counselors gain knowledge of the rich cultural diversity that characterizes persons from different Asian backgrounds. It is particularly important to realize, for example, that being knowledgeable of the values, language, traditions, and worldviews that characterize many Japanese persons will not be very useful when working with Filipino clients whose lives are strongly influenced by traditional Filipino values and traditions.

African Americans

Overall Population

Recent demographic reports indicate that there are approximately 35.4 million African Americans living in the United States. This figure represents approximately 13% of the total U.S. population (Russell, 1998). Unlike Asian Americans, Hispanics/Latinos/Latinas, and Native Americans, all of whom tend to be concentrated in certain geographical parts of this country, African Americans represent a sizable segment of the population across much of the United States. Despite their geographical dispersion, a substantial number of persons of African descent continue to reside in the southeastern part of the country, where they account for 19% of the total number of individuals living in that region (Russell, 1998). Although an increasing number of African Americans have immigrated to the United States from various Caribbean countries over the past three decades, all Black persons in the Western Hemisphere have their roots in Africa.

Population Changes

The 35.4 million African persons who currently reside in the United States represent an 11% increase over the 30.8 million African persons who lived in this country in 1991 (Locke, 1992) and a 33% increase over the 26.4 million African persons who resided in this country in 1980 (U.S. Bureau of the Census, 1986). Projected population studies suggest that the number of African Americans will increase to 37.8 million by 2005. Census reports also indicate that a sizable percentage of the expanding number of African Americans will be teenagers. More specifically, it is expected that the

2,285,000 African American persons between 14 and 17 years of age who presently live in the United States will increase to 2,431,000 by 2005 (U.S. Bureau of the Census, 1995). It should be particularly alarming to counselors that a disproportionate number of these youths will grow up in severely poor economic conditions characterized by a host of problems (including being routinely subjected to various forms of racism in their daily lives) that commonly compromise their mental health and sense of well-being.

Risk Factors and Counseling Challenges

Although significant numbers of persons in this cultural/racial group have moved into the middle class during the past 30 years (Cose, 1993), African Americans continue to be disproportionately represented among the total number of poor persons in the United States (U.S. Bureau of the Census, 1998). Given the clearly established link that exists between individuals' socioeconomic status and other health-related problems, researchers have noted that millions of poor African Americans continue to be at risk for a host of psychosocial and physical health difficulties that are directly tied to their economic disenfranchisement in our society. In commenting on the risk factors that African Americans commonly experience in their lives, Sue and Sue (1999) pointed out,

> The poverty rate for African Americans remains nearly three times higher than that of White Americans (33.1% versus 12.2%) and the unemployment rate twice as high (11% versus 5%) (U.S. Bureau of the Census, 1995). Their disadvantaged status, as well as racism and poverty,

contribute to the following statistics. About [one third] of African American men in their 20s are in jail, on probation, or on parole. This rate has increased by over [one third] during the past five years. The life span of African Americans is five to seven years shorter than that of White Americans. (pp. 235-236)

Given the multifaceted problems that many African Americans encounter as a result of being subjected to racism, poverty, and other forms of social and political disadvantage, multiculturalists have urged counselors to reassess the ways in which they can most effectively help foster the psychological health and personal well-being of persons in this cultural/racial group (Parham, White, & Ajamu, 1999). Besides calling on counselors to develop new individual counseling competencies that reflect greater sensitivity and respect for the African experience in the United States, these advocates have urged mental health professionals to take a more proactive stance by working to eradicate those toxic environmental conditions that undermine Black clients' sense of mental health and personal well-being.

The Hispanic/Latino/Latina Population

Total Population

The term *Hispanic/Latino/Latina* population denotes the rich cultural/ethnic diversity that characterizes persons from Mexican, Puerto Rican, Cuban, Spanish, and Central and South American descent who live in the United States. Recent findings indicate that a little more than 30 million individuals in this diverse cultural/racial group currently live in this country, making them the second largest non-White group in this nation (African American persons presently outnumber Hispanic/Latino/Latina persons) (Sue & Sue, 1999).

Population Changes

The recently calculated number of Hispanic/Latino/Latina persons currently living in the United States (30.2 million) represents a 77% increase in the total population of this group since 1985, when 16.9 million individuals of Hispanic descent resided in this country (U.S. Bureau of the Census, 1986). Based on the relatively high birthrate among Hispanic/Latino/Latina persons and the increasing number of persons immigrating to the United States from Mexico and other Latin countries, this cultural/racial group is projected to expand from 30 million persons in 1998 to more than 52 million by 2020. It also is worth noting that by 2009, persons of Hispanic descent are predicted to outnumber Black Americans and become the largest non-White group in this country (Russell, 1998).

Risk Factors and Counseling Challenges

Like many African Americans, Hispanic/Latino/Latina persons are considered largely to be a disadvantaged group in terms of their educational, health, and socioeconomic status in the United States. In listing some of the disadvantages that characterize the lives of many persons in this group, Russell (1998) pointed out the following:

- Many Hispanic/Latino/Latina persons lag far behind the total population in educational attainment because they are recent immigrants who came to the United States as adults with little schooling.

- Hispanics are more likely to be without health insurance than is any other racial/ethnic group in the United States. In 1996, 34% of all Hispanic/Latino/Latina persons did not have health insurance.

- Hispanic women are less likely to be in the labor force than are Black, White, or Asian women. Consequently, only 48% of Hispanic couples are dual earners.

- The median net worth of Hispanic households in 1997 was $16,500, well below the $56,400 median for all households in the United States.

Native People: Native American Indians/Alaskan Natives/ Native Hawaiians

The terms *Native American Indians, Alaskan Natives,* and *Native Hawaiians* are used in this chapter to describe the Native people of the United States. Numbering 2.3 million persons in 1998, these Native persons represent the smallest non-White, non-European group in this country (Russell, 1998). Although relatively small in number compared to persons from other cultural/racial groups in the United States, Native people have greatly increased their numbers since 1980, when approximately 1.5 million Native persons resided in this country (U.S. Bureau of the Census, 1986). By 2020, the total number of Native people is expected to increase to 3.1 million, which will represent about 1% of the total U.S. population.

Native American Indians, Alaskan Natives, and Native Hawaiians are culturally heterogeneous, geographically dispersed, and remarkably young (LaFromboise, 1993). A closer look at the demographic profile of these people indicates that 39% are under 29 years of age, compared to 29% of the total U.S. population in this age group. Fewer Native people are high school graduates relative to the general population

(66% vs. 75%). The annual income level of Native people as a group is only 62% of the U.S. average, and the poverty rate is nearly three times higher than that of persons with non-Hispanic, White European backgrounds (Sue & Sue, 1999; U.S. Bureau of the Census, 1995).

Although Native people suffer many of the same problems and issues that lead others to seek counseling, traditional counseling interventions have largely been ineffective in terms of promoting positive psychological outcomes among Native people. Duran and Duran (1995) suggested that some of the reasons why traditional counseling services fail to result in more positive outcomes with larger numbers of Native people include the following:

- Counselors' lack of understanding of Native people's traditions, values, and worldviews
- The failure of mental health professionals to include spiritual beliefs in the therapeutic process
- The lack of outreach to Native people who are at high risk for psychological problems but lack the resources (e.g., money, transportation) to access the mental health care system
- The unwillingness of counselors to address contextual factors (e.g., cultural oppression, racism) that compromise the mental health of many Native people

Do Early Predictions Match Current Demographic Realities?

The multicultural counseling movement has largely been fueled by the belief that the United States is undergoing a radical cultural/racial transformation in the makeup of this country's citizenry. However, because multicultural advocates have relied on data generated by population studies conducted more than a decade ago, it is reasonable to question whether the pre-dictions regarding the changing demographics of the United States have been manifested as expected.

In short, researchers predicted that there would be a decrease in the overall percentage of persons who traditionally have constituted the dominant cultural/racial group in the United States (i.e., non-Hispanic White persons from European backgrounds) and an increase in the percentage of persons from non-White, non-European groups. An updated review of the changes that have occurred in the cultural/racial makeup of this country's citizenry indicates that predictions based on population studies conducted during the 1980s and early 1990s are consistent with the actual alterations that have taken place in the current demographic structure of our society. While the growth rate of persons in the dominant cultural/racial group slowed significantly during the 1990s, substantial increases occurred in the actual numbers and percentages of African Americans, Asian Americans, Hispanic/Latino/Latina persons, and Native people residing in the United States. Furthermore, whereas persons in the dominant cultural/racial group comprise a disproportionate number of middle- and upper-class older adults who currently reside in the United States, individuals from non-White, non-European backgrounds generally are found to be younger and poorer.

Charting Future Challenges for the Counseling Profession

A review of the updated information regarding the continuing cultural/racial transformation of the United States underscores the need for professional counselors to reflect on the specific changes that they will need to make if the counseling profession is to remain a relevant and viable part of this country's mental health care system. This section briefly describes some of the challenges that professional counselors face as they strive to (a) work effectively and ethically with clients from diverse cultural/racial populations and (b) foster the continuing viability and relevance of the counseling profession within the context of a culturally and racially diverse 21st-century society.

Developing New Counseling Competencies

To work effectively and ethically with persons from diverse cultural/racial/ethnic populations, counselors will need to acquire a host of new multicultural counseling competencies. The Association for Multicultural Counseling and Development (AMCD) (see Appendix A, this volume) has endorsed a set of 31 counseling competencies that every counselor is urged to acquire before working with culturally and racially different clients. These competencies are divided into three major headings describing the types of multicultural awareness, knowledge, and skills that practitioners need to possess so as to provide services to culturally different clients in an effective and respectful manner. Counselors have been encouraged to (a) use the AMCD competencies to assess their own levels of cultural competence and (b) plan ways in which to enhance their own levels of multicultural competence by intentionally working to improve their areas of greatest weakness (Arredondo & D'Andrea, 2000).

Organizational Support for Multicultural Competence

Besides having individual counselors make the commitment to develop new counseling competencies that will enhance their effectiveness when working with persons from diverse client populations, professional organizations such as the American Counseling Association (ACA) must demonstrate their commitment to respond to the changing demographic structure of society. It is important to have professional organizations demonstrate a commitment to values that support diversity and multiculturalism. This support may be demonstrated in a variety of ways such as endorsement of the multicultural competencies (see Appendix A, this volume).

Striving to Gain a More Comprehensive and Accurate Understanding of Human Development

It is increasingly being recognized that the counseling theories that have been commonly used by counselor educators and practitioners during the 20th century are embedded in Eurocentric beliefs about mental health and human development (D'Andrea, 2000; Sue & Sue, 1999). Although such theories are useful when implemented among persons from non-Hispanic, White European backgrounds, they often are less effective and can even be harmful when used among persons from non-White, non-European groups (Sue & Sue, 1999).

Thus, by failing to incorporate cultural considerations into the epistemological frameworks that counselor educators and practitioners use in their work, these professionals operate from an incomplete and inaccurate understanding of human development (Pedersen, Draguns, Lonner, & Trimble, 1996). For this reason, it is imperative that (a) counseling researchers make the commitment to incorporate cultural factors as central considerations in future research endeavors and (b) counseling theorists work to promote a more accurate understanding of human development and mental health from a cultural perspective. In terms of this latter challenge, D'Andrea, Daniels, and Parham (2000) urged counselors to do the following:

1. Revise existing theoretical models that have failed to include cultural diversity as an important consideration in the past.

2. Develop new conceptual frameworks that incorporate different ways in which persons from cultural and racially different groups construct meaning of foundational constructs such as "mental health," "psychological maturity," "personal well-being," "human development," and "helping strategies."

By making these changes in the profession, counselors will be better able to move beyond the ethnocentric biases that currently characterize the existing knowledge base in the field and gain a more complete, accurate, and culturally respectful understanding of human development.

Acknowledging the Convergence of Multiple Personal Identities in Counseling

The multicultural counseling movement not only has helped counselors to become more aware of the ways in which clients' cultural, racial, and ethnic backgrounds affect their sense of psychological well-being, but also has sensitized mental health professionals to the different ways in which other types of group-referenced identities (e.g., a person's religious/spiritual group identity, sexual identity, or socioeconomic class identity) influence human development. When discussing these group-referenced considerations, it is important to note that much controversy has existed among many persons in the profession regarding the definition of multicultural counseling. Whereas some counselors have advocated for a narrow definition of the term *multicultural,* others have called for a broad definition that includes women, gays/lesbians/bisexual/transgendered persons, physically challenged individuals, poor persons, and older adults, to name a few groups (Fukuyama, 1990; Pedersen, 1991). Although this controversy has been instrumental in shaping the evolution of the multicultural counseling movement in the past, Arredondo and D'Andrea (2000) suggested that the time has come for counselors to move beyond focusing on single group-referenced factors as they strive to grapple with the more complex issue of how the convergence of multiple group-referenced identities affect human development in general and their clients' psychological health in particular. In discussing the need to focus on the convergence of multiple identities in counseling, Arredondo and D'Andrea suggested that counselors rarely work with African American, Asian American, gay, or poor clients per se. Counselors more typically interact with clients whose constructions of themselves and the world are substantially influenced by the interface of multiple group-referenced identities (e.g., being a gay African American male who is poor and physically challenged).

The challenge of dealing with the convergence of multiple group-referenced identities has numerous implications for the counseling profession. This includes the need for the following:

1. Researchers to develop more complex investigative approaches that will enhance their ability to study the convergence of multiple group-referenced identities and their influence in the developmental process

2. Counselor educators to implement new training models that direct attention to the ways in which multiple group-referenced identities affect clients' development and sense of well-being

3. Counseling practitioners to accept new roles and responsibilities reflecting a greater commitment to foster positive environmental changes that result in a greater level of acceptance, respect, and affirmation of the various group-referenced identities that clients acquire during their lives

Embracing New Professional Roles and Responsibilities

Besides helping counselors to gain a more complete and accurate understanding of how the convergence of multiple personal identities affects human development, multiculturalism emphasizes the need for mental health professionals to move beyond the overuse of the individual, intrapsychic counseling approaches that dominated the profession during the past century (Lewis, Lewis, Daniels, & D'Andrea, 1998). More specifically, multicultural advocates have pointed out repeatedly that although toxic environmental conditions that are associated with the perpetuation of racism, sexism, classism, and poverty continue to compromise the psychological well-being of large numbers of persons from diverse groups in our society, professional counselors generally have failed to effectively address these broader social issues in their work.

It has been further noted that if the counseling profession is to remain a relevant and viable part of the U.S. health care system during the coming decades, counselor educators and practitioners will need to direct more time and energy toward addressing the negative contextual factors that undermine the mental health of many persons from non-White, non-European backgrounds in professional training programs and clinical settings (Pedersen et al., 1996; Sue, Ivey, & Pedersen, 1996). This will require an expansion of the traditional way in which counselors have thought about their role as mental health professionals to include accepting the responsibility to implement client advocacy services, organizational development initiatives, and social change strategies in their daily work (Lewis et al., 1998).

It should be noted that expanding professional counselors' role to include these types of activities continues to be a source of controversy for some persons in the profession. However, unless counselors expand the way in which they traditionally have conceptualized their responsibilities as mental health professionals, and unless they work toward addressing the toxic contextual and environmental conditions that adversely affect the lives of millions of persons from diverse groups in this country, counselors will run the risk of undermining their own relevance and respectability in the minds of many persons who continue to be victimized by such external conditions.

In conclusion, it is clear that the counseling profession will need to continue to evolve to meet the challenges associated with the changing demographic structure of society. Counselors will increasingly be pressed to move beyond the monocultural ethnocentric values and biases that characterize traditional counseling theories and intervention strategies during the 21st century. The challenges outlined in this chapter represent some of the important considerations that counselors need to keep in mind if they are to help the profession become more responsive to the changing demographic structure of our society. By successfully responding to these challenges, counselors will be able to implement more effective and ethical counseling and development services among culturally and racially different clients as well as contribute to the evolution of a more just, democratic, accepting, and respectful society.

References

Arredondo, P., & D'Andrea, M. (2000, January). Resolutions for the new millennium: Meeting the challenge of multiculturalism. *Counseling Today,* pp. 31-32.

Atkinson, D. R., Morten, G., & Sue, D. W. (Eds.). (1993). *Counseling American minorities: A cross-cultural perspective* (4th ed.). Madison, WI: Brown & Benchmark.

Baruth, L. G., & Manning, M. L. (1999). *Multicultural counseling and psychotherapy: A lifespan perspective* (2nd ed.). Englewood Cliffs, NJ: Merrill/Prentice Hall.

Cose, E. (1993). *The rage of a privileged class: Why are middle-class Blacks angry? Why should America care?* New York: HarperCollins.

D'Andrea, M. (2000). Postmodernism, constructivism, and multiculturalism: Three forces that are reshaping and expanding our thoughts about counseling. *Journal of Mental Health Counseling, 22,* 1-16.

D'Andrea, M., Daniels, J., & Parham, T. (2000). *Challenges counselor educators, practitioners, and researchers face in a postmodern, multicultural, 21st century society.* Unpublished manuscript, University of Hawaii.

Duran, E., & Duran, B. (1995). *Native American postcolonial psychology.* Albany: State University of New York Press.

Fukuyama, M. (1990). Taking a universal approach to multicultural counseling. *Counselor Education and Supervision, 30,* 6-17.

LaFromboise, T. D. (1993). American Indian mental health policy. In D. R. Atkinson, G. Morten, & D. W. Sue (Eds.), *Counseling American minorities: A cross-cultural perspective* (4th ed., pp. 123-144). Madison, WI: Brown & Benchmark.

Lewis, J. A., Lewis, M. D., Daniels, J. A., & D'Andrea, M. J. (1998). *Community counseling: Empowerment strategies for a diverse society* (2nd ed.). Pacific Grove, CA: Brooks/Cole.

Locke, D. C. (1992). *Increasing multicultural understanding: A comprehensive model.* Newbury Park, CA: Sage.

Myers, J. E. (1995). From "forgotten and ignored" to standards and certification: Gerontological counseling comes of age. *Journal of Counseling and Development, 74,* 143-149.

Parham, T. A., White, J. L., & Ajamu, A. (1999). *The psychology of Blacks: An African centered perspective* (3rd ed.). Upper Saddle River, NJ: Merrill/Prentice Hall.

Pedersen, P. (1991). Multiculturalism as a fourth force in counseling [special issue]. *Journal of Counseling and Development, 70.*

Pedersen, P. B., Draguns, J. G., Lonner, W. J., & Trimble, J. E. (Eds.). (1996). *Counseling across cultures* (4th ed.). Thousand Oaks, CA: Sage.

Russell, C. (1998). *Racial and ethnic diversity* (2nd ed.). Ithaca, NY: New Strategist Publications.

Sue, D. W., Ivey, A. E., & Pedersen, P. B. (Eds.). (1996). *A theory of multicultural counseling and therapy.* Pacific Grove, CA: Brooks/Cole.

Sue, D. W., & Sue, D. (1990). *Counseling the culturally different: Theory and practice* (2nd ed.). New York: John Wiley.

Sue, D. W., & Sue, D. (1999). *Counseling the culturally different: Theory and practice* (3rd ed.). New York: John Wiley.

U.S. Bureau of the Census. (1986, 1989, 1995, 1998). *Population profile of the United States.* Washington, DC: Government Printing Office.

U.S. Bureau of the Census. (1997). *Source and accuracy statement for the foreign born population: 1997.* Washington, DC: Government Printing Office.

CHAPTER THIRTY-TWO

Working With Survivors of Trauma and People at Risk

MICHAEL TLANUSTA GARRETT

In the midst of sorrow, sickness, death, or misfortune of any kind, silence was the mark
of respect. More powerful than words was silence.

—*Luther Standing Bear (Lakota) (quoted in Padilla, 1994, p. 43)*

It probably is both a blessing and a curse that we cannot look directly into the hearts of others. We are limited to the use of words that create images of themes and patterns, details of experiences and interpretations, subjective perceptions, cognitive processes, and sequential events being played out in our minds for us by the people with whom we talk. Oh, we have "hunches" alright. We often are "hunched" over someone with the vague, sometimes nagging feeling of familiarity, like somehow we understand or are beginning to understand some truth that lies before us in all its glory and power. What would it be like if we could look right into the hearts of others in that silence re-

quiring no words? What would we understand then? What would it be like to look into the eyes of other persons and know their stories immediately? What types of tales would that silence tell us? Where would those stories take us? What is it like to feel with other persons' skins or to breathe with their breaths? Would that silence take us to the darkest, most endless night? Or, would it take us to the very edge of the brilliance of some emerging newborn dawn?

We are counselors, and we are healers. We listen, we receive, we create or recreate, we intervene, we support, we invite, we challenge, and we try to help others find "home." Some of us never will truly know the pain of living that others have gone through. Some of us know all too well the pain of living that others go through. Either way, we constantly are faced with a reality of the world in which we live where people suffer, and we are challenged to help them find their way back "home" again.

The purpose of this chapter is to explore the experiences and needs of survivors of trauma and people at risk as well as implications for counseling. First, the reality of violence and victimization in our society is illustrated through statistics. Second, the journey of those who suffer is explored. Third, an assessment tool useful for working with survivors of trauma is offered. Fourth, effective interventions for creating the healing process are discussed. Finally, perspectives on the future are explored as a way of helping us to get a sense of where we are heading as a counseling profession with regard to these populations and issues.

The Reality

Power is used and abused. People get hurt. It is not always that simple, especially for those who have experienced some sort of trauma. However, these are a reality of human interaction. Although it always is important to look not only at the bad side of things, could it be that a reality of violence and conflict exists in our nation today? The following is a fairly comprehensive list of statistics presented by categories to illustrate the present state of affairs regarding trauma and violence in our society. The reader should sit with this list of quantified information and allow it to tell its story. Then, the reader should consider this story of the big picture as well as the impact on the lives of our individual clients or potential clients.

General

1. There was one violent crime every 19 seconds in 1997 (Federal Bureau of Investigation [FBI], 1998).

2. In the United States, there are more than 3,400 animal protection shelters and only about 1,200 shelters for battered women (Buel, 1994).

3. It has been estimated that domestic violence kills approximately 58,000 people every 5 years, the same number of Americans lost in the Vietnam War (Gardner, 1992).

4. An estimated five out of six people will be victims of either completed or attempted violent crimes at least once in their lives (Koppel, 1987).

Child Abuse

1. Approximately 1 million children were identified as victims of substantiated or indicated abuse or neglect in 1996 (U.S. Department of Health and Human Services, Children's Bureau, 1998).

2. A survey of adolescent boys' health revealed that one in eight high school boys (13%) had been physically or sexually abused or both. Two thirds (66%) of boys who reported physical abuse said that it had occurred at home, and 68% reported that the abuser was a family member. Nearly half (48%) of physically or sexually abused boys said that they had not talked to anyone about their abuse (Schoen & Davis, 1998).

3. One in five high school girls (21%) surveyed reported that she had been physically or sexually abused. The majority of the abuse occurred at home (53%) and more than once (65%). Nearly one third (29%) of girls who had been physically or sexually abused had not told

anyone about the abuse. Abused girls also are at double the risk for signs of eating disorders (Commonwealth Fund, 1997).

Elder Abuse

1. Experts estimate that only 1 in 14 domestic elder abuse incidents come to the attention of authorities (National Center on Elder Abuse, 1998).

2. Neglect is the most common form of elder maltreatment in domestic settings. Of the non-self-neglect reports substantiated in 1996, 55.0% involved neglect. That same year, physical abuse accounted for 14.6%, and financial/material exploitation represented 12.3% of the substantiated reports (National Center on Elder Abuse, 1998).

Hate Crimes

1. The most common bias motivation behind hate crimes in 1996 was race (63%), followed by religion (14%), sexual orientation (12%), and ethnicity (11%; FBI, 1997).

2. There were 474 hate groups documented in 1997. Of these, 127 were Ku Klux Klan organizations and their chapters, 100 were neo-Nazi groups, 42 were Skinhead groups, 81 were Christian Identity (a racist religion) groups, 12 were Black separatist groups, and 112 followed hate-based doctrines and ideologies (Southern Poverty Law Center, 1998).

3. There were 268 documented incidents motivated in whole or in part by hatred, fear, and ignorance about HIV/AIDS in 1997 (National Coalition of Anti-Violence Programs [NCAVP], 1997).

4. A study that surveyed a small sample of lesbian, gay, and bisexual adults found that 41% reported being victims of hate crimes since 16

years of age. These hate crime victims also reported experiencing higher levels of depression, anxiety, anger, and posttraumatic stress symptoms (Herek, Gillis, Cogan, & Glunt, 1997).

Relationship Violence

1. Nearly one in four American women between 18 and 65 years of age has experienced domestic violence (Body Shop, 1998).

2. In 1996, there were nearly 1 million female victims and about 150,000 male victims of intimate violence (Greenfield & Rand, 1998).

3. Only about 1 in 10 women victimized by a violent intimate sought professional medical treatment in 1996 (Greenfield & Rand, 1998).

4. There were 2,352 documented cases of lesbian, gay, bisexual, and transgender domestic violence victimization in 1996 (NCAVP, 1997).

5. In 1996, 30% of female murder victims were killed by their husbands or boyfriends, and 3% of male murder victims were killed by their wives or girlfriends (FBI, 1997).

Sexual Assault

1. In 1996, the rape/sexual assault rate for females was 2.3 per 1,000 persons age 12 years or over. The rape/sexual assault rate for males was 0.4 per 1,000 persons age 12 years or over (Ringel, 1997).

2. Results from the National Women's Study showed that 26.6% of women suffering from bulimia nervosa were raped at some point in their lives, whereas only 13.3% of women who do not have binge eating disorders or bulimia nervosa have been raped (Dansky, Brewerton, Kilpatrick, & O'Neil, 1997).

Stalking

1. Approximately 1 in 12 women and 1 in 45 men have been stalked at some times in their lives, according to a 1998 study (Tjaden & Thoennes, 1998).

School Violence

1. More than half (57%) of U.S. public schools reportedly experienced at least one crime (violent or nonviolent) during the 1996-1997 school year (Heaviside, 1998).

- During the 1996-1997 school year, schools reported experiencing approximately 4,000 rapes or other types of sexual battery, approximately 11,000 physical attacks or fights in which weapons were used, and approximately 7,000 robberies (Heaviside, 1998).

Youth Violence

1. Each day in the United States, 14 children die as a result of guns (Children's Defense Fund, 1997).

2. Juveniles between 12 and 17 years of age commit about one quarter of serious violent crimes, a category that covers rape, robbery, aggravated assault, and homicide (Bureau of Justice Statistics, 1997).

3. More than 23,388 youth gangs were reported as active in 1995. California had the most (4,927), followed by Texas (3,276), Illinois (1,363), and Colorado (1,304) (Office of Juvenile Justice and Delinquency Prevention, 1997).

Mental Health Consequences

1. Crime victims are estimated to represent 20% to 25% of the total client population of mental health care professionals (Cohen & Miller, 1998).

2. More than half of the victims seeking mental health care are adult survivors of child sexual or physical abuse (Cohen & Miller, 1998).

3. In 1991, an estimated 3,100,000 to 4,700,000 people received mental health counseling primarily as a result of criminal victimization (Cohen & Miller, 1998).

A Survivor's Story

Angelique sought counseling in a nonprofit community agency to deal with the effects of incest from childhood. Angelique was a 20-year-old, married, biracial (African American and European American) female whose motivation for coming to counseling was "recurrent nightmares and difficulty dealing with the rage I feel inside." The nightmares and series of flashbacks had been occurring recently and seemed to be intensifying. Angelique had not been to counseling previously. However, a family doctor had prescribed medication for depression, which Angelique described as "not working worth shit." Angelique and her husband of 2 years still lived in the household with her parents. Their combined annual income totaled approximately $14,600, thereby limiting their options.

Angelique's perception of the problem was that the anger she felt about her gradually emerging knowledge of childhood sexual victimization by her father scared and confused her, and it was affecting the quality of her life as well as her interactions with others. Angelique reported that she frequently was "blowing up" at her husband and friends, spending time alone crying uncontrollably, having difficulty in keeping a steady job due to flashbacks and recurrent dreams that made it difficult to sleep, and having a hard time being sexually or emotionally intimate with her husband. Her main goal was "to not be afraid of what I don't know happened to me as a child" and to deal with the current effects of that experience. Coping strategies that Angelique described as working well for her so far in her daily life were creative writing and reading; strategies that she described as not working well so far were leaving home and communicating her feelings of anger and mistrust to her father and mother. Among the things Angelique wanted to do were the following:

- "Feel that people support me"
- "Not be afraid"
- "Feel safe"
- "Feel safe around other people"
- "Be understood"
- "Remember what happened"
- "Understand why he did this to me"
- "Understand why I eat when I'm not hungry"
- "Have a better sexual relationship with my husband"
- "Be able to keep a steady job"
- "Be able to move out of their [her parents'] house"
- "Feel again"

The Journey of Those Who Suffer

Who Are Survivors of Trauma and People at Risk?

So, who are survivors of trauma and people at risk? That is a good question. Survivors of trauma and/or people at risk could include the following: people of color; people who are gay, lesbian, or bisexual; people with HIV/AIDS; people with disabilities; survivors of violence; survivors of rape and sexual assault; refugees; survivors of catastrophic events; war veterans; homeless persons; older adults; children and adolescents; and the non-beautiful (McWhirter, 1994). These groups represent people who historically have been marginalized by society through systematic oppression and victimization or who have endured intense, stressful, or life-threatening circumstances.

Time to Intervene or Time to Prevent?

When we talk about people who are "at risk," those two words can imply so many different forms and origins of suffering. It also implies a time factor that certain people may be more likely to experience certain forms of suffering than are others but that it might not occur or might not have occurred yet. If trauma already has occurred, then intervention is appropriate and usually takes the form of either crisis counseling or long-term remediation. If trauma has not yet occurred, then we as counselors have to be aware that members of certain populations (e.g., elders, children, adolescents) could experience trauma in the future, and we have an opportunity to facilitate prevention through psychoeducation and/or social advocacy work.

Victims Versus Survivors

Usually, the people who are most likely to be at risk are those who, due to certain characteristics or experiences, possess less power in society, whether it be social, economic, political, or psychological. If we are working with people in counseling who possess less power (for whatever reason), then it is our responsibility to be mindful of the fact that when we refer to those clients as "victims," we are reinforcing and becoming part of the victimization process.

Therefore, it becomes important and extremely therapeutic to remind people who have experienced trauma that they are in fact survivors, so that they never forget the inner power that they possess no matter the circumstances. Likewise, people who are at risk also should be reminded that they are survivors of the difficult circumstances in which they exist, so that they are less likely to become disheartened by the idea that they have little power.

Understanding the Drama of Trauma

When we hear clients describe shocking, overwhelming, painful experiences or sets of experiences, it is as if we are watching movies in our minds that we create to help us have some sense of what those persons have been through. As we watch the movies that we create in our minds, it is important to remember that we are watching movies that we directed but that those movies are based on the screenplays that the clients have given to us. Our interpretations may or may not accurately portray through images what was given to us in words and suggested movements. It is difficult to know what it is like to experience trauma until we directly experience it ourselves. Yet, what makes it even more complicated is the fact that different people perceive and respond differently to different traumatic experiences. In a strange paradox, one person's limitation is another person's opportunity.

There are many sources of trauma including, but not limited to, violence, abuse, neglect, assault, loss, rejection, and oppression, all of which could be specifically defined here but probably are best defined by the client himself or herself. In the extreme, the phenomenon known as posttraumatic stress disorder (American Psychiatric Association, 1994) can be expe-rienced by survivors of trauma demonstrated by a combination of the following reactions: recurrent distressing memories of the event; recurrent dreams of the event; flashback episodes; inability to recall important aspects of the trauma; lack of interest in activities; feelings of detachment; sense of foreshortened future; difficulty in sleeping; irritability or outbursts of anger; difficulty in concentrating; exaggerated startled response; sense of guilt about the event; excessive sweating; paleness; rapid or irregular heartbeat sensations; headache; fever; fainting; dizziness; anxiety, stress, and tension; and agitation. All of these "symptoms" represent descent of the survivor into a world of darkness, confusion, desperation, and turbulent silence. How may we as professional counselors enter this world to help our clients emerge from their long painful silences and give voice to the experiences of their lives?

Respecting Silence, Giving Voice to Silence

It is difficult to sit with someone who is in pain. If the reader ever has just sat with someone while the person cried, then the reader will know how difficult it is to see someone hurt. The reader will know how difficult it is to not want to just take away the person's suffering and make everything okay. In counseling, the client's pain can hang like a cloud of tension in the room, and it takes a patient, wise, and compassionate person to know how to honor that pain and the person who is experiencing it. So often in day-to-day life, people avoid pain, talk around pain, or avoid other people experiencing pain. Because it is uncomfortable, we do not always know what to do with pain, and it reminds us of our own vulnerability. So often, fear or shame prevents those who are living in pain from giving voice to their experiences. Silently, these people go on suffering day after day. Some make it, and some do not.

In a society that does not always deal effectively with pain or teach people how to deal well with their suffering, how can we as counselors respect the silence of survivors of traumatic experiences while also encouraging them to give voice to their experiences? It is a difficult balance at best. As members of this society, we are taught "not to pry," and as counselors, we are taught to "delve into issues" so as to help people express and deal with the things in life that create obstacles or difficulties. Sometimes, one of the most powerful things we ever can do with clients who feel powerless or with survivors of trauma is to help them find the courage to speak their truths while maintaining respect for where they may be in their understandings of themselves, their traumatic experiences, and their journeys. Sometimes, wisdom in counselors involves finding the courage to be still and to sit with clients when they need us the most.

Turning Powerlessness to Empowerment

Empowerment was referred to by McWhirter (1994) as the

> process by which people, organizations, or groups who are powerless or marginalized (a) become aware of the power dynamics at work in their life context, (b) develop the skills and capacity for gaining some reasonable control over their lives, (c) which they exercise, (d) without infringing on the rights of others, and (e) which coincides with actively supporting the empowerment of others in the community. (p. 12)

McWhirter went on to say that people who are powerless are those who experience difficulty in directing their lives "due to societal conditions, power dynamics, lack of skills, and/or lack of belief" (p. 12) that they have the ability to change their lives and make choices for themselves. In addition, the fact that these people often also are marginalized means that they have been excluded socially, politically, and/or economically from positions of power. Thus, our job as counselors becomes that of working to help our clients regain some sense of direction and control over themselves, their relationships with others, and their own lives. In a sense, we seek to help them become the authors of their own stories with the story lines and outcomes they prefer.

Shedding Light in Darkness: TRIADS

In dealing with any survivor of trauma, it is important to do an assessment that will help direct us as counselors in implementing interventions and therapeutic treatment planning. A helpful assessment technique in understanding the intensity of trauma suffered by a survivor is known as the TRIADS model (Brown, 1991). TRIADS assesses the following areas in helping counselors to gain a better understanding of the nature and extent of trauma experienced by survivors:

Type of abuse: Physical, sexual, psychological

Role relationship of survivor to offender: Intrafamilial, extrafamilial

Intensity of abuse: Number of acts, number of abuses

Affective state: Expressed style (e.g., anxious, angry, sad), controlled style (e.g., blank, calm, denial)

Duration: Length of time

Style of abuse: Blitz, repetitive patterned, ritualistic/ceremonial

Emerging From Silence

All too often, we as counselors look to talk therapy as a cure-all for the mental, emotional, and spiritual needs of our clients. When it comes to working with survivors of trauma or people at risk, we must remind ourselves to make sure that the basic needs (e.g., food, shelter, clothing, safety) of our clients are met first. Then, we can move into other modalities of intervention.

In helping clients to emerge from the uncomfortable silence of their suffering, a number of therapies have proven effective. Among those helpful in promoting the healing process are interventions that allow clients to give voice to their experiences through creative expression. Examples of these approaches include art therapy, clay modeling, sand tray work, masking, music, dance and movement, journaling, and play therapy (Brown, 1991). Of course, there always are the traditional modes of therapeutic process such as individual and group counseling and support groups. During recent times, however, other forms of therapeutic process also have gained much popularity including wilderness retreats (e.g., ropes courses), recreational therapy, and inner healing represented through alternative approaches to healing that focus on connecting with one's sense of spirituality and personal peace.

Perspectives on the Future

When we look back at what has gone before us, we see a past of human history in which, at no known time, have we as humans ever existed during a time that was without wars or conflict of some kind. When we look at the present, we see an existence in a society that is replete with, and even glorifies, resolution of conflict through violence and aggression. When we look to the future, what might we see? In the midst of all the rapid social, political, and economic changes, as well as the climatic and environmental changes, it is difficult to say. However, according to Brown (1991), there are certain social trends that remain:

- One out of four girls has been or will be sexually molested by 18 years of age.
- One out of seven boys has been or will be sexually molested by 18 years of age.
- Violence will occur at least once in two thirds of all marriages.
- A murder will occur about every 25 minutes.

What does this tell us? There always have been survivors of trauma and groups of people who are at risk for experiencing trauma. Our work, as counselors working with these groups of people, may or may not ever be finished. As we offer our therapeutic skills in helping people to deal with the suffering inherent in life, we also must ask ourselves not only what our responsibility is for responding to the ailments of members of our society but also what our role might need to be in changing that society so as to prevent people at risk from being at risk (Lee & Walz, 1998). Do we as counselors not have a responsibility to challenge and change systems that allow, ignore, encourage, or promote injustices that demean the human spirit and body through oppression, abuse of privilege, and outright harm?

We as counselors are taught to have compassion for all of our clients, but we also must have a passion for ensuring that our clients and potential clients do not suffer needlessly. Organizations such as Counselors for Social Justice, the newest division of the American Counseling

Association (ACA), give voice to the responsibility we have to advocate for social change. We must make it a point to be actively involved in a variety of organizations that advocate for the rights of disadvantaged persons and/or survivors of traumatic experiences, and we must encourage others to do the same.

There are many people who suffer in silence. We must ask ourselves how we as a profession can balance our role in giving voice to the silence of those who suffer while using whatever power we possess to educate, influence, and influence the very foundations of American society. We are reminded to observe and learn from the mistakes of the past:

> Yonder sky that has wept tears of compassion upon my people for centuries untold, and that which to us appears changeless and eternal, may change.
>
> —*Seattle (Suquamish)*
> (quoted in Hilfer, 1996, p. 345)

References

American Psychiatric Association. (1994). *Diagnostic and statistical manual of mental disorders* (4th ed.). Washington, DC: Author.

Body Shop. (1998). *The many faces of domestic violence and its impact on the workplace.* New York: Savvy Management.

Brown, S. (1991). *Counseling victims of violence.* Alexandria, VA: American Counseling Association.

Buel, S. (1994). *Hearing on domestic violence, February 1, 1993.* Washington, DC: Government Printing Office.

Bureau of Justice Statistics. (1997). *Perceived age of offenders chart* [Online]. Available: www.ojp.usdoj.gov/bjs/glance/offage.htm

Children's Defense Fund. (1997). Child gun deaths drop for first time in more than a decade. *CDF Reports, 18,* 1.

Cohen, M., & Miller, T. (1998). The cost of mental health care for victims of crime. *Journal of Interpersonal Violence, 13,* 93-110.

Commonwealth Fund. (1997). *The Commonwealth Fund survey of the health of adolescent girls: Highlights and methodology.* New York: Author.

Dansky, B., Brewerton, T., Kilpatrick, D., & O'Neil, P. (1997). The national women's study: Relationship of victimization and posttraumatic stress disorder to bulimia nervosa. *International Journal of Eating Disorders, 21,* 213-228.

Federal Bureau of Investigation. (1997). *Crime in the United States 1996.* Washington, DC: U.S. Department of Justice.

Federal Bureau of Investigation. (1998). *Crime in the United States 1997.* Washington, DC: U.S. Department of Justice.

Gardner, M. (1992). Restraining hearts too full of violence. *Christian Science Monitor, 84,* 13.

Greenfield, L. A., & Rand, M. R. (1998). *Violence by intimates: Analysis of data on crimes by current or former spouses, boyfriends, and girlfriends.* Washington, DC: U.S. Department of Justice.

Heaviside, S. (1998). *Violence and discipline problems in U.S. public schools: 1996-97.* Washington, DC: U.S. Department of Education.

Herek, G., Gillis, R., Cogan, J., & Glunt, E. (1997). Hate crime victimization among lesbian, gay, and bisexual adults. *Journal of Interpersonal Violence, 12,* 195-215.

Hilfer, J. S. (1996). *A Cherokee feast of days* (Vol. 2). Tulsa, OK: Council Oak Books.

Koppel, H. (1987). *Lifetime likelihood of victimization.* Washington, DC: U.S. Department of Justice.

Lee, C. C., & Walz, G. R. (1998). *Social action: A mandate for counselors.* Alexandria, VA: American Counseling Association.

McWhirter, E. H. (1994). *Counseling for empowerment.* Alexandria, VA: American Counseling Association.

National Center on Elder Abuse. (1998). *Elder abuse in domestic settings* [Online]. Available: www.gwjapan.com/ncea/statistics/index.html

National Coalition of Anti-Violence Programs. (1997). *1997 report on lesbian, gay, bisexual, and transgender domestic violence.* New York: Author.

Office of Juvenile Justice and Delinquency Prevention. (1997). *1995 National Youth Gang Survey: Program summary.* Washington, DC: U.S. Department of Justice.

Padilla, S. (1994). *A natural education: Native American ideas and thoughts.* Summertown, TN: Book Publishing.

Ringel, C. (1997). *Criminal victimization 1996: Changes 1995-96 with trends 1993-96.* Washington, DC: U.S. Department of Justice.

Schoen, C., & Davis, K. (1998). *The health of adolescent boys: Commonwealth Fund survey findings.* New York: Commonwealth Fund.

Southern Poverty Law Center. (1998). *SPLC: Intelligence report, Winter 1998* [Online]. Available: www.splcenter.org/klanwatch/kw-4e.html

Tjaden, P., & Thoennes, N. (1998). *Stalking in America: Findings from the National Violence Against Women Survey*. Washington, DC: U.S. Department of Justice.

U.S. Department of Health and Human Services, Children's Bureau. (1998). *Child maltreatment 1996: Reports from the states to the National Child Abuse and Neglect Data System*. Washington DC: Author.

CHAPTER THIRTY-THREE

A Model Substance Abuse Prevention Program

JOHN D. SWISHER

LORI BECHTEL

KIMBERLEY L. HENRY

JUDITH R. VICARY

ED SMITH

This chapter presents an overview of a strategy for implementing an effective substance abuse prevention program in a school under the leadership of school counselors. In the substance abuse literature, this strategy has been labeled *infusion,* whereas in education, it is known as *curricular integration.* The essence of this substance abuse prevention approach is that the content and skills to be learned are spread across several different subject areas, thereby reducing the burden on any one teacher

for implementing a program. In addition, if the integration is done in the context of the subject being taught, then it is possible to teach two learning objectives simultaneously. For example, an English teacher might teach spelling and integrate knowledge of the risk of chewing tobacco using a spelling list of words such as *carcinogen.* Similarly, a social studies teacher might teach personal decision-making steps in relationship to critical decisions made at some point in history. This type of integration does not require additional time to achieve the counseling objective of substance abuse prevention and allows the teacher time to accomplish his or her current academic subject matter objective simultaneously. Furthermore, many of the effective substance abuse prevention program components—decision making, social skills, coping skills, assertive skills, and the like—overlap substantially with the skills development that is part of a comprehensive developmental guidance program. Consequently, the school counselor has an opportunity to provide leadership in accomplishing multiple tasks and goals for the guidance program.

This model is similar to the infusion of career development content and skills into the curriculum (Herr & Cramer, 1996). The material for this chapter is based on a current 5-year research project, Adoption of Drug Abuse Training (Project ADAPT), to assess the effectiveness of integrating prevention into academic subjects. The problems and pitfalls of an infusion approach are discussed along with strategies to offset these problems.

Effective Substance Abuse Prevention

Several prevention programs have been evaluated over time and shown to be effective. Some of the most notable include Project ALERT (Ellickson & Bell, 1990), Project STAR (Pentz et al., 1989), All Stars (Hansen, 2000), SMART Leaders (St. Pierre, Marks, Kaltrider, & Aikin, 1997), and Life-Skills Training (LST; Botvin, Baker, Dusenbury, Botvin, & Diaz, 1995). However, other prevention programs have been found to be ineffective or have minimal support. For example, the status of prevention programs in schools indicates that Drug Abuse

Resistance Education (DARE) is in approximately 75% of schools and has been shown to be ineffective (Ennett, Tobler, Ringwalt, & Flewelling, 1994). Furthermore, Here's Looking at You 2000 claims to be in approximately 25% of schools and has only small-scale, short-term evaluations for its support (Swisher, Doebler, Babbitt, & Walton, 1991).

One major component of Project ADAPT is to study how schools adopt such an innovation. In this instance, LST (Botvin et al., 1995) was selected as the program to be diffused as an innovation, and the integration approach is the major experimental variable in this 5-year study. The hypothesis is that schools will adopt and maintain an effective substance abuse program if it can be implemented in an integrative or infused mode.

Rationale for Integration

The major strategy for facilitating the adoption of LST by Project ADAPT has been to assist teachers with the integration of LST into their normal teaching. Such an approach has been labeled constructivist (Gatewood, 1998), which also is seen as a multidisciplinary or interdisciplinary approach. The assumption made is that optimal learning occurs when information is embedded in meaningful contexts, applications and multiple representations are provided, metaphors and analogies are created, and opportunities for learners to generate personally relevant questions are given. Similarly, Jacobs (1989) described integration as an approach that consciously applies content from more than one discipline to examine a central theme or issue, which in this case was substance abuse prevention.

The ideal form of integration centers the curriculum on life itself rather than on the mastery of fragmented information within the boundaries of academic subject areas (Beane, 1995). In the field of substance abuse prevention, the term *infusion* often is used to describe the integration of prevention content and processes into the standard academic subjects of a school curriculum. This requires the active involvement of teachers in the design and delivery of the prevention content and its implementation in their regular subjects and classes. Infusion becomes more than using guest speakers or fragmenting a prevention program into blocks spread among several teachers. Rather, infusion requires teachers to work with others to creatively weave prevention content and process into a unit that fits well within the total curriculum of the school.

The skills being integrated into the regular classes are best presented in an interactive mode (Tobler, 2000), and many teachers need assistance with this approach to teaching. An interactive approach actively engages students in the learning process by including them in hands-on, student-centered learning activities. Students may participate in group discussions and role-play activities that allow them to practice life-skills. Students who participate in these types of learning activities need to receive coaching and direction from teachers. It is important that teachers carefully plan all activities and facilitate their implementation to ensure that the activities are effective in helping students to achieve the goals of the lessons. To address this potential problem, Project ADAPT staff employed a step-by-step approach to curriculum integration (Cinelli, Rose-Colley, & Bechtel, 1995) that identified and linked key objectives in middle school academic subjects

and key objectives from LST. This model provided a structure for teachers to create integrated lesson plans and also assisted teachers with identifying the best interactive teaching approaches (e.g., role-playing simulations, decision-making scenarios, student-centered discussions) for accomplishing these dual objectives.

Diffusion Theory as a Guide to Adoption and Integration

Project ADAPT, a National Institute for Drug Abuse-funded initiative being implemented in 10 rural Pennsylvania schools, used Rogers's (1983) theory of diffusion and adoption of innovations to enhance the use and acceptance of the ADAPT model. Diffusion and adoption theory is composed of five stages: innovation development, dissemination, adoption, implementation, and maintenance.

Rogers (1983) described *innovation development* as the planning stage that occurs early in the development of an innovation. Project ADAPT was developed from a model suggesting that an infused or integrated method of drug abuse prevention programming could be as effective as, or more effective than, traditional separate prevention curricula (e.g., LST) and could provide schools with a more flexible and integrated approach. The project aim is to infuse or integrate into academic courses LST including resistance skills, decision making, coping behaviors, drug knowledge, self-improvement, advertising myths, normative education, communication skills, social skills, and assertiveness training. This method has several hypothesized benefits. First, it avoids engaging in a "time out for drug abuse prevention," allowing the message to become an infused and integral part of the regular curriculum and learning process. Second, it allows for a higher "dosage" or experience of the program as the students learn the skills in multiple subjects and under various situations. Project ADAPT also includes a parent homework component. This randomized study compares the effectiveness of (a) the standard implementation of LST in three schools (LST schools), (b) the integrated implementation of LST in three schools (I-LST schools), and (c) no implementation of new programs in three schools (control schools).

In the second stage (i.e., *dissemination*), Rogers (1983) recommended a direct approach involving the researchers with the professionals who will be responsible for delivering the innovation. ADAPT staff began by introducing the program to school administrators and teachers in each school district through meetings and presentations so as to elicit their understanding, participation, and support. Once acceptance was achieved, the LST teachers participated in structured prevention training, follow-up workshops, and individual meetings to maximize their use of the LST curriculum in an infused setting. I-LST teachers also received two 4-hour initial training sessions led by project staff demonstrating effective teaching methods including facilitation, coaching, and role-playing. The curriculum was described in depth in a step-by-step manual given to each teacher, and a resource library also was created for each school.

During the *adoption* stage, which involves the level of acceptance of the program by the school administration and teachers, careful consideration was given to Rogers' (1983) five adopter categories that describe the conditions and extent to which people accept innovation: innovators, early adopters, early majority adopters, late majority adopters, and laggards. The

project maximizes adoption categorization through individually tailored attention at both the school and teacher levels. Process evaluation reveals varying levels of program acceptance; therefore, project staff then initiate different tactics with each level in working toward optimal program adoption. For example, in this study, several teachers indicated that their interest in participating in the LST program stemmed from personal concerns about substance abuse and the consequences that their students had experienced. In identifying early adopters, it is useful to ascertain which teachers have a deeper concern than other teachers about alcohol, tobacco, and other drugs.

Rogers's (1983) stage of adoption categorization at the school level was attended to by allowing the recruitment of teachers to vary at each school, thereby allowing the dynamics of the school culture to dictate the optimal strategy in teacher selection. The adoption categorization of the individual teachers also was carefully considered. Teacher training took place at each individual school, encouraging a self-driven and facilitative environment. Teachers were encouraged to choose their own topics within their subjects and to integrate the material into the courses that they considered most appropriate. Ongoing support from the project staff also has had a personalized nature, using teachers' attitudes, strengths, and needs to guide interactions.

The *implementation* stage focuses on the actual use of the new program and lessons by the teachers. Orlandi, Landers, Weston, and Haley (1990) noted the importance of a linkage agent who assists with the process of training and problem solving. The school counselor in a given school can greatly assist with this stage of the total process. The school counselor will know the local issues and personalities and will greatly facilitate a successful implementation. ADAPT has a staff member serving as school coordinator who fills this role, acting as a single point of contact for all participating schools. In addition, each school selected a participating teacher or counselor to serve as the school team coordinator, thereby providing another point of contact for teachers.

The *maintenance* stage of adoption also is of prime importance, and ADAPT has taken every opportunity to ensure that the program is maintained after the initial implementation. Strategies for enhancing maintenance include continued administrative support as well as update and replacement training. The nature of integration allows this process to be more cost- and time-effective than other packaged prevention programs given that expensive materials and books are not required. The lessons and activities are infused into what already is taking place in the classroom; therefore, special workbooks and time set aside from the standard curriculum are not needed. Process evaluation and year-end focus groups have provided project staff with information useful in improving the training and overall delivery of the program. The intent is that each school will have a comprehensive institutionalized program by the end of the funding period that will be easily continued without direct support from an external source.

Overview of LST

LST was developed by Botvin (1998), a leading expert on drug abuse prevention among adolescents. LST is a substance abuse prevention and competency enhancement program designed to focus on the major social and psychological factors that offset substance use and abuse. LST provides students with skills to achieve the following outcomes (Botvin et al., 1995):

1. Resist social pressures to use alcohol, tobacco, and other drugs
2. Develop greater self-direction
3. Cope with anxiety
4. Improve decision-making skills
5. Improve basic communication and social skills
6. Increase knowledge of the risks associated with the use of alcohol, tobacco, and other drugs
7. Promote the development of healthy normative beliefs and attitudes consistent with non-substance use

Rigorous empirical testing has found the LST program to be effective in preventing or delaying onset of tobacco, alcohol, and marijuana use (Botvin et al., 1995). The program consists of a 3-year prevention curriculum initiated in Grade 6 or 7 and typically includes one or two teachers who implement the LST curriculum, consisting of 15 lessons during the first year, 10 lessons during the second year, and 5 lessons during the third year. A variety of subject matter teachers have been involved including teachers of science, English, social studies, geography, math, and reading. Health teachers often participate, and they have been helpful in covering in their courses critical components that the other teachers are unable to integrate.

Evaluation

Formative evaluation is used extensively in Project ADAPT to ensure optimal program fidelity. Several evaluation checkpoints are employed including lesson plan assessment, teacher self-survey of lesson plan implementation, on-site teacher observations, and a year-end focus group.

All teachers submit copies of their lesson plans to project staff for review, and suggestions for improving the lessons are made before implementation. Based on the suggestions, teachers make any necessary changes to their lessons before using them in their classrooms. The majority of the suggestions made by ADAPT staff have reflected a need for emphasizing more interactive activities (e.g., student-centered discussions, role-playing) to demonstrate competency in using various skills (e.g., assertiveness, decision making).

One of the five lessons led by each teacher is observed by a staff member of Project ADAPT. In observing the lesson, the project staff member assesses the teacher's attitudes and enthusiasm toward the program, use of effective teaching strategies (role-playing, coaching, and facilitating), and ability to stimulate discussion. Likewise, the staff member observes student responses to the lesson including participation, understanding, questioning, and interest. Based on the observations, it appears that the teachers have adopted the program and methods very well. They lead excellent lessons that are both thought provoking and useful. As a result, the students have responded with interest and enthusiasm.

During the initial training, teachers develop a matrix of LST components matched with their subjects. Table 33.1 is an actual matrix for one of the Project ADAPT I-LST schools, and as can be seen, a complete program of LST components was offered through the different subjects. One advantage to the project in this school was the inclusion of a course in personal development, and this teacher was very willing to use the components of LST that paralleled the course. The health teacher also helped to complete the matrix in areas where the other teachers had difficulty with integration of a particular component. Several major conclusions were drawn from this matrix including the following:

1. A complete LST program was infused for all students at the targeted grade level in this school.
2. Approximately 30 lessons were implemented, as compared to the standard 15 LST lessons, without additional time taken from the school day.
3. Teachers were creative in the design of their lesson plans that integrated the program (I-LST).

At the end of the school year, all teachers completed a survey and participated in focus groups so that Project ADAPT staff could better understand the adoption process of the integrated LST program, uncover any problems the teachers might be experiencing, and gain valuable suggestions for subsequent years. Based on the survey and focus groups, it was concluded that teachers easily and enthusiastically grasped the integration approach and generally implemented the program in a desired manner. A great deal of creativity and initiative has been observed in most of the project teachers. In addition, they reported that, as a result of integrating the LST program, their students were more engaged in the lessons and eager to participate. They did express some concerns about the amount of work that was required to develop their lessons and about the work involved in the research. Project ADAPT staff will modify the workshops to give the teachers more lesson plan development time and attempt to clarify the expectations at the outset.

TABLE 33.1   Lesson Matrix Based on Submitted Lesson Plans for One School With an Integrated Model Program

Life Skills Training Component	School Subject				
	English	Geography	Earth Science	Personal Development	Health
Self-image and self-improvement	Essay: Goal setting and strategies for achieving a goal	Family cultures and their role in shaping self-identity		Self-confidence for success	Development of a positive self-image
Decision making		Map travel: Choosing routes	Space travel: Weighing pros and cons	Steps in personal decision making	
Knowledge of risk	Vocabulary and use in a sentence			Knowledge of risk	Knowledge of risk
Normative education				Clarifying misperceptions of peer relationships	
Analyzing advertisements	Student creation of television ads to attract customers	Newspapers during Education Week			Alcohol, tobacco, and other drug advertisements
Coping with anxiety	Impromptu speech: Gaining skills to cope and perform		Coping with test-taking anxiety	Managing emotions	
Communication skills		Presentation of travel brochure	Mineral identification and presentation in small groups		Communication skills: Conflict resolution
Social skills	Telling a joke: Developing public speaking and listening skills		Working effectively in project groups		Asking for a date and communicating with the opposite sex
Assertiveness				Improving peer relationships: Learning to express feelings	Refusing alcohol and tobacco, and other drug role-plays

Key Roles for School Counselors

Implementing a program of this nature draws on the strengths that school counselors bring to the integrative context in several ways. Counselors are aware of developmental guidance objectives and can help to select effective substance abuse prevention programs that are consistent with such goals. The LST program outlined here clearly is consistent with developmental guidance objectives. Counselors also can assist with judging the ease with which these programs can be integrated into the existing curriculum of a particular school. A counselor's knowledge of strong teachers who have good interpersonal skills and positive relationships with students can help to guide the recruitment of teachers for the integration team. Furthermore, effective delivery of prevention programs through any means requires that the students be engaged in an interactive participatory and problem-solving process (Tobler, 2000). The facilitation skills essential to this type of delivery are similar to the group process and counseling skills that counselors have in their repertoires.

Summary and Conclusions

Facilitating the integration of substance abuse prevention programs into academic courses is a strategy that school counselors can employ to further guidance aims and involve greater numbers of teachers in the total process. A decentralized strategy requires delegation of responsibility and monitoring of adequacy of delivery, and this takes time from counselors' schedules. Conversely, if the implementation of the integrated program is well managed, then counselors will be indirectly providing far more services to students than they ever could in their offices.

In the future, as pressures increase for school reform and for academic standards enforced by state or federal standardized achievement tests, school counselors will need to find effective and complementary means for providing comprehensive guidance services. If selected guidance objectives can be effectively woven into the academic fabric of the schools without "extra time" from academic subjects, such a process would allow counselors to plan more complete and effective mechanisms for providing their services. Prevention is an arena in which interactive learning can be enhanced through the individual and group communication skills of school counselors. The future of prevention programming also would be well served by the integration of life-skills into the mainstream curriculum.

References

Beane, J. A. (1995). Curriculum integration and the disciplines of knowledge. *Phi Delta Kappan, 76,* 616-662.

Botvin, G. J. (1998). *Life Skills Training: Promoting health and personal development.* Princeton, NJ: Princeton Health Press.

Botvin, G. J., Baker, E., Dusenbury, L., Botvin, E. M., & Diaz, T. (1995). Long-term follow-up results of a randomized drug abuse prevention trial in a White middle-class population. *Journal of the American Medical Association, 273,* 1106-1112.

Cinelli, B., Rose-Colley, M., & Bechtel, L. J. (1995). A strategy for the facilitation of curriculum integration. *The Health Educator, 26*(2), 27-31.

Ellickson, P. L., & Bell, R. M. (1990). Drug prevention in junior high: A multi-site longitudinal test. *Science, 247,* 1299-1305.

Ennett, S. T., Tobler, N. S., Ringwalt, C. L., & Flewelling, R. L. (1994). How effective is drug abuse resistance education? A meta-analysis of Project D.A.R.E. outcome evaluations. *American Journal of Public Health, 84,* 1394-1401.

Gatewood, T. (1998). Integrated curriculum in today's middle schools? *Education Digest, 63,* 24-28.

Hansen, W. B. (2000). *Evaluation of all stars* [Online]. Available: www.tanglewood.org

Herr, E. L., & Cramer, J. H. (1996). *Career guidance and counseling through the lifespan: Systematic approaches* (5th ed.). New York: HarperCollins.

Jacobs, H. H. (1989). *Interdisciplinary curriculum: Design and implementation.* Alexandria, VA: Association for Supervision and Curriculum Development.

Orlandi, M. A., Landers, C., Weston, R., & Haley, N. (1990). Diffusion of health promotion innovations. In K. Glanz, F. M. Lewis, & B. K. Rimer (Eds.), *Health behavior and health education: Theory, research, and practice.* San Francisco: Jossey-Bass.

Pentz, M. A., Dwyer, H. H., MacKinnon, D. P., Flay, B. R., Hansen, W. B., Wang E. Y. I., & Johnson, C. A. (1989). A multicommunity trial for primary prevention of adolescent drug abuse: Effects on drug use prevalence. *Journal of the American Medical Association, 261,* 3259-3266.

Rogers, E. M. (1983). *Diffusion of innovations* (3rd ed.). New York: Free Press.

St. Pierre, T. L., Marks, M. M., Kaltrider, D. L., & Aikin, K. J. (1997). Involving parents of high-risk youth in drug prevention: A three-year longitudinal study in Boys and Girls Clubs. *Journal of Early Adolescence, 17,* 21-50.

Swisher, J. D., Doebler, M. K., Babbitt, M. E., & Walton, H. (1991). *Here's looking at you, 2000: A review of evaluations and a conceptual critique.* Unpublished research report, Pennsylvania State University.

Tobler, N. (2000). Lessons learned. *Journal of Primary Prevention, 16,* 261-274.

CHAPTER THIRTY-FOUR

Changing Demographics
of the Profession

RICHARD YEP
DON C. LOCKE

As society has evolved over the past century, the profession of counseling has seen significant changes so as to meet the needs of individuals, couples, and families. Professional counselors have moved from being primarily employed in educational and employment service settings to being employed in community agencies, corporate organizations, and private practice (Herr, 1999). Expansion into private practice and community agencies also has been stimulated by various societal factors that encompass the longer life spans of individuals, evolving nontraditional family structures, violence, changing racial/ethnic demographics, and the movement toward deinstitutionalization of individuals. By working in these areas,

the counseling profession internally has increased its knowledge base, raised the standards of practice, developed stronger ethical standards, and pursued the benefits of continuing professional development.

Changes in society, relative to a greater understanding and acceptance of mental health services, and the role of the government in mandating services or standards are some of the most significant external forces in expanding the role and work of professional counselors. For example, with the support of former First Ladies Betty Ford and Roslyn Carter, substance abuse and mental health issues during the late 1970s and early 1980s were given more prominence, thereby serving to reduce the stigma associated with these concerns. Also during this time, both the federal government and state governments made several policy-making decisions that broadened the work conducted by professional counselors. These factors drove fundamental changes in the demographics of those who provide counseling services.

This chapter presents an historical perspective on the counseling profession, information on the growth of school counseling during the last half of the 20th century, an overview of federal legislation affecting counselors, data on clinically trained counselors, and a profile of members of the American Counseling Association (ACA). The chapter concludes with a section on how counselor demographics may affect the future of the counseling profession.

Historical Perspective: 1900 to 1950

In exploring the changing demographics of the profession, it is helpful to have an historical perspective on those internal and external actions that influenced counseling during the 20th century. It first must be understood that the main body of formal research, study, evaluation, and practice of counseling began during the early 1900s. When Frank Parsons and his colleagues began using guidance-focused activities in 1908 to help immigrants and young men in Boston find gainful employment, the belief was that providing such direction was consistent with helping individuals to realize their full potentials, an underlying principle that has remained constant through the years. Counselors were responsible for working with clients to help them define what type of work was "best suited" to their interests and skills. With the success of Parsons' methods, the Boston public schools adopted his model by identifying teach-

ers to serve as vocational counselors. Many who provided counseling and guidance services during the early 1900s focused on employment-related guidance with either youths or adults.

With the outbreak of World War I, the U.S. military needed a way in which to predict how individuals might perform in battle. The development of these tests led to the development of other aptitude and interest instruments (Aubrey, 1982). The end of World War I led to the military's use of vocational rehabilitation and counseling for veterans. So, in addition to working with youths and new immigrants who were looking for employment, counselors now took on counseling and guidance activities that focused on career guidance services for veterans.

As the United States headed into the Great Depression during the early 1930s, an even greater emphasis on career counseling with adults took place when thousands of Americans sought some type of work and needed to learn new skills. Professional counselors of this era likely had studied the vocational counseling work of Parsons and E. G. Williamson (who modified Parsons' work so that it could be applied to high school and college students). Williamson also described a theory he called *clinical counseling,* something he applied at the nation's first student counseling center at the University of Minnesota.

Counselors who practiced during the first 30 years of the 20th century most likely used a counselor-centered approach to working with students and adults, and most counseling continued to be practiced within educational and employment settings. Although "child guidance clinics" were organized as early as 1921 (Goldenberg & Goldenberg, 1991), there were no professional counselors who practiced within this environment per se given their traditional calling to serve within education and employment settings. However, the publication of Carl Rogers's *Counseling and Psychotherapy* during the early 1940s, which featured his theories of a nondirective client-centered approach, provided one of the profession's major shifts (Rogers, 1942). Rather than use a prescriptive approach to working with individuals, Rogers suggested an approach that focused on the individual rather than on the problem. His theory was based on the counselor developing a trusting relationship with the client so that the individual is able to better explore his or her feelings and insights. Rogers believed that his client-centered theory could be applied to areas of guidance such as education and employment. Counselors who studied and embraced Rogers's theories were the first to meld education and psychology into the practice of counseling. With the advent and evolution of Rogers's theories, professional counselors made another major shift in how they traditionally had provided services during the first three decades of the 20th century.

World War II created a need for the development of instruments that would assist mental health professionals with the problems faced by returning veterans. Educational benefits, readjustment, and career guidance were provided through the Veterans Administration (VA). Funding from the VA also resulted in the establishment of counseling centers at many institutions of higher education. This effort by the VA led to the need for more counselors who could staff these counseling centers (Nugent, 2000). So, in addition to working in vocational and secondary school settings, professional counselors of this era began working on college campuses.

Clearly, the need for counselors to service veterans, and the emergence of Rogers's theories on client-centered counseling, led to the growth of professional counselors practicing outside the traditional areas of education and career guidance. Again, the role of the federal government cannot be understated in looking at the changing demographics of the professional counselor. For example, without the government's focus on assisting World War II veterans using readjustment services and placement on college campuses of counseling offices, it might have taken many more years before professional counselors moved out of their traditional place within high schools and employment agencies.

Growth in School Counseling

During the last half of the 20th century, the first major growth of professional counselors occurred in conjunction with the enactment of yet another government-led initiative, the National Defense Education Act of 1958 (NDEA). When the Soviet Union launched the space satellite known as *Sputnik,* the U.S. Congress responded with legislation that would encourage talented individuals to pursue careers in math and science. To attract, transition, and retain these students, the NDEA called for career guidance and counseling at the high school and college levels as a step toward competing with the Soviet Union in the space race. Included in the new law was the appropriation of $20 million to hire guidance counselors in the nation's public schools as well as funds to establish training programs for school counselors (Lanning, Forrest, & Carey, 1984).

NDEA funds were used to train more than 25,000 counselors during the first 8 years of the program. Eventually, nearly $59 million was spent during those first 8 years in support of counseling personnel for schools. By 1965, it was estimated that there were at least 30,000 counselors in high schools alone (Aubrey, 1982), with another 24,000 at other education levels. Again, the federal government's decision to compete with the Soviet Union in the space race was what triggered this drive to recruit and train school counselors.

The features that remained constant within school counseling from the 1950s through the 1990s were that an overwhelming majority of school counselors hold master's degrees and that more than 50% of professional school counselors are female. There are various reasons for the dominance of women in the field of professional school counseling, one of which is the fact that many school counselors who were trained had come from classroom teaching (also primarily female over the past 50 years).

Impact of Legislation

The development of the counseling profession is tied to national legislation. Among the federal legislation during the first 60 years of the 20th century having major impacts on counseling were the following:

- The Federal Board for Vocational Education was formed in 1917 to administer federal grants under the Smith-Hughes Act.
- The Civilian Rehabilitation (Smith-Fess) Act of 1920 provided vocational rehabilitation services for civilians through federal grants to states.
- The Vocational Rehabilitation Act Amendments of 1943 (Barden-LaFollette Act) extended eligibility for vocational rehabilitation to include "emotionally disturbed and mentally retarded persons" (Wright, 1980, p. 139).

Administrative expenditures included costs for counseling and placement.

- The National Mental Health Act of 1946 established the National Institute of Mental Health, which marked the beginning of publicly funded mental health services.
- The Vocational Rehabilitation Act Amendments of 1954 (Hill-Burton Act) included among its provisions (a) extension and improvement of state programs, (b) authorization of federal support of research for new knowledge and demonstration projects to spread better methods of treatment, and (c) authorization of training grants for the preparation of rehabilitation professional personnel.

The government's role in helping to develop and expand the scope of the counseling profession is represented with four other major pieces of legislation passed by Congress during the first 4 years of the 1960s: the Manpower Development and Training Act of 1962, the Vocational Education Act of 1963, the Community Mental Health Centers Act of 1963, and the Economic Opportunity Act of 1964. Each of these acts had the effect of establishing additional places in which professional counselors could be trained and/or could work.

By the end of the 1960s, most counselors were working in one of three general areas: education, employment services, or rehabilitation. According to the U.S. Department of Labor (1970), of the approximately 71,000 counselors working in the United States in 1968, the overwhelming majority (75%) were school based, followed by 16% in rehabilitation and another 7% in employment-related areas. In 1972, or 4 years later, the government reported that the number of professional counselors in these areas was approaching 78,000, with the relative percentages remaining about the same.

Private Practice and Community-Based Service

Whereas a profound shift began to occur in the demographics of professional counselors during the early 1970s, a precursor to this shift was the passage of the Community Mental Health Centers Act. Whereas three of the acts (Manpower Development and Training Act, Vocational Education Act, and Economic Opportunity Act) had a strong focus on education or employment issues, the Community Mental Health Centers Act helped to move professional counselors into community-based settings. This act is cited as one of the key elements in the ability of the U.S. government to confront and address the mental health needs of its citizens (Ohlsen, 1983). The act provided for the establishment of mental health centers in areas that encompassed between 75,000 and 200,000 individuals.

By the early 1970s, a growing number of professional counselors were choosing to pursue private practice and community-based service. During this period, government action at the state level also was significant as registry, certification, and licensure laws initially were enacted. Government action at the federal level helped to create more jobs for counselors as the Vietnam War ended and returning veterans were in need of many types of services that could be provided by professional counselors who focused on mental health issues.

During the final 20 years of the 20th century, the counseling profession continued to change as the number of counselors grew larger among those who entered private practice and other noneducational settings. With the increase of private practice and community-based services came an increase in the number of professional counselors who entered the profession without teaching experience. Some states even relaxed the requirement of teaching experience as a prerequisite for school counselor certification.

The Substance Abuse and Mental Health Services Administration (SAMHSA) published data on mental health professions in *Mental Health, United States, 1998* (Manderscheid & Henderson, 1998). SAMHSA updates the data every 2 years. Although the data are hard to compare in some instances because they come from different sources and sometimes from different years, they offer what might be the best picture available of who is providing mental health services in the United States.

SAMHSA found 29,906 counselor trainees during the 1994-1995 academic year. There were 28,270 master's degree students and 1,636 doctoral students.

SAMHSA reported that 96,263 clinically trained counselors were employed full-time and part-time in the United States in 1996. Counselors providing direct services to clients represented 73% of the total and were distributed by primary employment setting percentages as follows: 30% clinics, 28% individual practice, 9% academic settings (colleges, universities, elementary schools, and secondary schools), and 6% hospitals. Those not providing direct services to clients were engaged in teaching (9%), administration (7%), research (0.1%), and other activities (e.g., consultation) (11%).

The total number of clinically trained counselors included 28,137 males and 68,126 females. These counselors were distributed ethnically as follows: 91.8% White (not Hispanic), 3.7% Black (not Hispanic), 1.8% Hispanic, 0.7% Asian/Pacific Islander, 0.6% American Indian/Alaska Native, and 1.4% not specified.

Working Within Managed Care

Those counselors who work in private practice or community mental health centers also have had to significantly increase their knowledge of managed care issues. During the early 1980s, there were few managed health care organizations. Although the number of different managed care organizations grew significantly during that decade, there were changes in the health care delivery system during the mid-1990s that required professional counselors in private or group practice to become more knowledgeable of the managed care arena. Currently, the push by managed care organizations to reduce costs has, in some cases, helped mental health counselors because they traditionally have charged less than psychiatrists and psychologists. The main competition for mental health counselors within the managed care arena are social workers. It has been reported that social workers provide 50% of mental health services in the United States (Clay, 1998). Another changing demographic is that professional counselors need to know how best to work within a team of mental health professionals so as to provide cost-efficient services that will be covered under managed care.

The fact that approximately six companies cover 140 million Americans for behavioral health issues means that mental health counselors need to understand how case management works within these companies. The case manager who works for a managed care organization has the ability to determine the course of treatment or therapy that clients will receive. It is imperative, then, that today's professional counselors understand how managed care works, how best to negotiate the intricacies of the system, and how to educate the case manager as to what is being suggested.

Professional counselors who work in private practice or community mental health centers are faced with having to engage in much more brief therapy. Some counselors have had to reduce the length of sessions, whereas others are choosing to leave this type of counseling in favor of working within education or other careers altogether.

Profile of ACA Members

Although ACA does not represent all professional counselors in the United States, it is the largest organization of its type in the world. As of May 2000, ACA had 51,637 members. By looking at historical and current membership data, the opportunity exists to see trends in the demographics of professional counselors over a given period of time.

For many years, ACA has collected data on its membership. Those who identify themselves as school-based counselors (i.e., elementary, middle, secondary, parochial, or vocational school; community college) comprise the largest percentage of overall ACA membership. However, certain shifts have been occurring gradually. In 1990, 30% of all members who reported occupational categories identified themselves as school-based counselors, a figure that remained constant through 1995 but that dropped to 23% in 2000. Those who identified themselves as working in private practice settings in 1990 comprised 25% of all who reported occupational categories. The private practice group grew to 31% of all who reported in 1995, a figure that stayed constant through 2000. In the most recent data collection of 30,143 ACA members (from a total of just over 51,000), nearly 67% of those who responded indicated that their highest academic degree was a master's degree. This fact seems to be consistent with the counseling population-at-large in the United States.

As of 2000, 38% of ACA members were between 50 and 59 years of age. This fact is especially illuminating for a number of reasons. First, this group of counselors would have "come of age" professionally during the time when the federal government was enacting the NDEA and the Community Mental Health Centers Act, thereby showing the impact of the role of government on the counseling profession. Also, because the 50- to 59-year age group comprises the largest proportion of members in ACA, this points to a "graying" of the profession. As retirement approaches, there is likely to be a number of counseling positions opening for younger professionals.

Just over one third (34%) of those who responded reported making $40,000 or more per year. Of those who answered the question on gender, 72% were female and 28% were male. The gender breakdown appears to be higher than the overall population of professional counselors (ACA and non-ACA combined), although the profession is predominantly comprised of females, as noted earlier.

Perspectives on the Future

According to the *Occupational Outlook Handbook* (U.S. Department of Labor, 2000), professional counseling positions will continue to increase beyond the average rate of other occupations through 2008. The 182,000 counselors employed in 1998 is projected to increase by 25% (46,000) by 2008. The reasons for the increase include larger school enrollment, a move for more elementary school counselors, the increased role that counselors play in crisis situa-

tions (school and community), reimbursement for counselors in private practice, and the realization that people with physical and emotional disabilities are in need of assistance (which may or may not be funded through government programs).

Manderscheid and Henderson (1998) pointed out that their data on clinical mental health counselors were based on conservative estimates extrapolated from a variety of sources. The collection of these data has "pointed out the immediate need for the counseling profession to collect systematic and equivalent data with other mental health professionals" (p. 287). Additional information is needed on characteristics of the providers, clientele served, actual services delivered, sources of referrals, and relationships with other health and social service professionals.

A number of population demographics also will affect the role of professional counselors during the first 10 years of the 21st century. Four examples of what counselors might expect in the future are as follows:

1. Because the United States is becoming increasingly diverse from a racial/ethnic perspective, counselors will have to be well grounded in multiculturalism. It is projected that Hispanics will outnumber African Americans in the United States by the year 2010. The need to understand languages other than English will be important for those counselors who work in ethnically diverse areas.

2. As many professional counselors are nearing retirement age, a number of position vacancies will mean that those who completed their academic studies during the 1990s will be hired to fill senior positions within academia-, education-, and community-based organizations.

3. With advances in medicine, people are living longer. This parallels many issues that professional counselors may be called on to address

with clients, such as the needs of the elderly and those of their children who take care of them.

4. As elementary, middle, and secondary schools increasingly become "one-stop shops" in which educational and emotional needs are addressed, the school counselor of the 21st century will have a distinctively different role from that of his or her colleagues who were trained under the NDEA during the late 1950s and early 1960s.

The demographics of the counseling profession of the future will include a much more even distribution of males to females. There will be more counselors involved in private practice or community mental health centers providing counseling services as psychiatrists and psychologists look to other venues and types of services (e.g., psychopharmacology). In fact, it appears that psychiatry already has begun a move away from psychotherapy.

The counselor of the future will work collaboratively with many different professionals to enhance the services that are provided to children and adults. In fact, in keeping with the traditional "gatekeeper" role to other helping professions, the counselor of the future may be called on to replace the caseworker found in many of today's managed care organizations who have little or no background in mental health issues.

Clearly, the counselor of tomorrow will need to be Internet savvy. Regardless of those who insist that counseling cannot take place unless it is face-to-face, technology is evolving so quickly that counseling over the Internet will be a common practice and will include the ability to communicate verbally and nonverbally (via streaming video). ACA adopted Internet guidelines for counseling in 1999 to address this growing area of communication.

Another demographic change in the future of counseling will be the increasingly important role of the paraprofessional. Whereas academic, accreditation, and licensing standards were developed during the latter half of the 20th century, the profession will need to address the role for paraprofessionals who work closely with counseling professionals. Standards and codes of ethics will need to be developed for those who will serve in this area.

References

Aubrey, R. F. (1982). A house divided: Guidance and counseling in 20th-century America. *Personnel and Guidance Journal, 61,* 1-8.

Clay, R. A. (1998, September). Mental health professions vie for position in the next decade. *APA Monitor,* p. 21.

Goldenberg, I., & Goldenberg, H. (1991). *Family therapy: An overview* (3rd ed.). Pacific Grove, CA: Brooks/Cole.

Herr, E. L. (1999). *Counseling in a dynamic society: Contexts and practices for the 21st century.* Alexandria, VA: American Counseling Association.

Lanning, W., Forrest, D., & Carey, J. (1984). Counselor educators: Comparing NDEA and non-NDEA participants. *Counselor Education and Supervision, 24,* 107-113.

Manderscheid, R. W., & Henderson, M. J. (1998). *Mental health, United States, 1998.* Rockville, MD: U.S. Department of Health and Human Services, Substance Abuse and Mental Health Services Administration.

Nugent, F. A. (2000). *Introduction to the profession of counseling* (3rd ed.). Upper Saddle River, NJ: Merrill/ Prentice Hall.

Ohlsen, M. M. (1983). *Introduction to counseling.* Itasca, IL: F. E. Peacock.

Rogers, C. R. (1942). *Counseling and psychotherapy.* Boston: Houghton Mifflin.

U.S. Department of Labor. (1970). *College educated workers, 1968-80.* Washington, DC: Government Printing Office.

U.S. Department of Labor. (2000). *Occupational outlook handbook, 2000-01.* Washington, DC: Government Printing Office.

Wright, G. N. (1980). *Total rehabilitation.* Boston: Little, Brown.

Professional Identity
for Counselors

HOWARD B. SMITH

Defining a profession is of extreme importance for a number of reasons. First, it sets the parameters on what laypersons expect from that profession. Second, without clearly identified parameters, practitioners themselves suffer from a lack of professional identity and direction, standards of practice, and a clear and precise sense of mission or calling. Without definitive parameters, a specific profession is set adrift in a world full of professions—one in a field of many. When there are a number of closely related professions, as is the case with the mental health care provider arena, it is even more critical for the lines of distinction to be clearly drawn around each of the related professions. Failure to do so results in unnecessary confusion on the part of consumers and in professional turf battles that almost always are counterproductive for all parties.

The counseling profession is but one of many professions that provide mental health care. At nearly 50 years of age and still being one of the youngest of those professions, we have an identity crisis. Some authors have written accounts of the roots extending back as far as Pillippe Pinel and his bringing "liberty, equality, and fraternity" to his job as director of the Bicetre, a mental institution in Paris, in 1793 (Brooks & Weikel, 1996). Or, another account points to the 1952 merging of four professional counseling and guidance organizations into a single association structured to permit them to retain their separate identities as the real beginning of the profession of counseling (Brooks, 1996).

Or, perhaps the reader might prefer the opinion, as Aubrey (1986) pointed out, that the successful launching of the *Sputnik* satellite by the Soviet Union and the subsequent National Defense Education Act of 1958 was a major event signifying the beginning of the profession. It was that piece of legislation that provided the funding and focus for the birth of many of today's counselor education programs.

There also have been several shifts in the mission and focus of the counseling profession over the years. Lopez Levers (1999) wrote that during the "early years" of the profession, counselors focused on guidance and vocational issues in schools and on the rehabilitation arena. She mentioned several other shifts in the profession. For example, counselors soon began to (a) move from institutional settings into community settings, (b) work with psychosocial and clinical issues, and (c) move from a client-centered therapy and other individual therapies to more systemic and ecological views of the individual.

Aubrey and Lewis (1983) stated that many of these shifts were made in an attempt to remain responsive to an ever-changing society. They noted that the issues characterizing the social and political upheavals of the 1960s rendered counselors' methods and approaches ineffective and inappropriate responses. The impact of the Vietnam War, the women's liberation movement, the presence of many counter-culture groups, and other societal factors forced the counseling profession to make shifts in its focus.

Suffice it to say, the lack of a single, linear developmental history of the profession has contributed to the difficulty in identifying who counselors are, where they practice the profession, what they do, and how they do it. In this

chapter, some of the difficult issues that affect the identity of professional counselors from both the internal and external domains are identified. Some perspectives on the future and suggestions for what we might do to overcome these problematic issues are discussed.

Issues From the Internal Domain

As Lopez Levers (1999) pointed out, the profession of counseling evolved from a very diverse root system. This system is the result of much more than tracing our roots back to the field of psychology. Lopez Levers posited that our evolution has been affected by many disciplines including but not limited to anthropology, education, ethics, history, law, medical sciences, philosophy, psychology, and sociology. One could argue the various magnitudes of the effects from each of these disciplines. The point here is that counseling, as a profession, has evolved from a highly interdisciplinary framework.

It could be argued further that we maintain an interdisciplinary quality in that our graduate counseling programs welcome students from a variety of undergraduate disciplines. These individuals come to the graduate counseling programs bringing educational backgrounds from a variety of academic disciplines with them. Some would argue that a student entering a master's degree program in counseling whose undergraduate degree is in literature is perhaps better prepared to comprehend human nature and to deal with the vast panorama of human behavior, having studied literature throughout history, than is a graduate from one of the behavioral sciences such as psychology or sociology. In light of this, it seems that one of the qualities the profession has, but fails to appreciate, is the history of and unintentional continuation of its interdisciplinary nature.

Another dimension that has posed problems in defining the identity of professional counselors from the beginning of the profession is the confusion over whether counseling is a profession by and of itself or whether it is a group of professions. Given the historical accounts listed previously, it is little wonder not only that the identification of counselors has been difficult but also that the definition of professional counseling itself, in clear and concise terms, has been elusive.

In support of the opinion that the counseling profession is a group of professions, we have only to look at history. Three of the four professional associations that came together in 1952 to form the American Personnel and Guidance Association (APGA)—the National Vocational Guidance Association (NVGA), the Association of Counselor Education and Supervision (ACES), and the Association for Humanistic Education And Development (AHEAD)—have maintained their identity as separate associations as well as divisions of the American Counseling Association (ACA). The fourth Division, the American College Personnel Association (ACPA), disaffiliated in 1992 and currently is separate from ACA.

To further complicate the matter, over the years, the number of divisions in ACA has risen to the current 17, all of which have their own separate identities. So, a strong argument can be launched that what we call the counseling profession today actually is a group of several separate professions, each of which has carved out its own unique corner of the larger whole, that is, its specialization. How does one identify such a complex profession?

Others would say, however, that if one takes a critical look at these areas of specialization, then it soon would become obvious that many, if not most, of the ACA divisions do much of the same thing as did the original four, and it is more a matter of emphasis, rather than uniqueness, that sets one division or specialty apart from the others. They would argue that what we have is one, admittedly somewhat complex, profession. Furthermore, they would argue that the profession would be better served by adopting a pluralist and inclusive identity that would embrace the things held in common by the various divisions.

This struggle—stressing the similarities versus the differences within the profession—has led us to abort organized, strategic, and serious attempts at advocacy for the counseling profession as a whole through benign neglect (Smith, 2000, p. 154). These efforts at advocacy for the respective specialty areas or divisions of ACA abound (Covin, 1994; Glauser, 1996; Griffin, 1993; Henderson & Gysbers, 1998).

The danger in this approach has been, and remains, that of primary loyalty versus secondary loyalty. As Liteman and Liteman (1998) pointed out, when one's primary loyalty is given to a subgroup, much needed energy for the larger group is dissipated, the priorities of the whole are distorted (depending, e.g., on which of the subgroups is doing more advocating), and progress toward any overarching goal is weakened or disrupted. Unfortunately, the counseling profession currently finds itself in just such a situation.

As a point in fact, the largest, single professional organization for counselors, ACA, did not take formal action on a definition that attempted to embrace all facets of the profession until 1997. Rather, what has happened for the most part is that the various specialty areas have engaged in advocacy efforts for their respective specialties and developed clear and concise definitions for the practice of those specialties while avoiding addressing the counseling profession as a whole.

The final issue from the internal domain to be discussed in this chapter has to do with the way in which we prepare new professionals for entrance into the field. The curriculum in counselor education programs has tried not only to educate and train graduates to be competent for entering the profession but also to offer specialized training at a master's degree level within the confines of a program requiring 48 semester hours. Remember, the incoming students have degrees in a variety of disciplines, so we can make few, if any, assumptions about background preparation.

This points to a related area of concern—the degree of variability in curricula in counselor education programs across the country. There will need to be difficult decisions made regarding the continued existence of programs that are not professionally accredited and are unable to become accredited. Allowing this difficult issue to go unresolved only exacerbates the problem. Master's-level counselor education simply cannot continue to operate in the current fashion if the profession is to survive, much less thrive, in the competitive marketplace of today.

Most other professions require students entering graduate education to possess undergraduate degrees in those specific disciplines (e.g., psychology, engineering, biology). This allows the master's-level curricula to build on those degrees with the firm knowledge that all enrollees have substantial and significant background knowledge of the disciplines to which the graduate-level educations add depth and

breadth. Many other disciplines require that discipline-specific standardized examinations be passed before entering graduate-level programs.

Still others do not allow specialization until doctoral-level educations are taken and often require breaks between master's-level and doctoral-level educations to enable individuals to gain some experience prior to completing their terminal degrees. There are examples of doctoral-level counseling students who never have had full-time "profession-related" jobs (or any full-time employment, for that matter). To be sure, they have completed the requisite supervised clinical components of their degree programs. The point here, however, is that they have known nothing of the profession other than what they learned from their role as students.

These statements might sound harsh. However, until the counseling profession adequately addresses some of these issues, it will continue to struggle with obtaining a clear and concise definition around which there are several areas of specialization and an equally clear identity for its members.

In summary, the issues affecting the identity of professional counselors from the internal domain are long-standing, significant, and extremely complex. Some would say that they defy resolution.

Issues From the External Domain

The external domain holds many challenges for the identity of professional counselors as well. The first of these issues has to do with the other mental health care providers in the marketplace. Because they preceded us into the mental health care arena, we are faced with several problems. First, we must decide whether we want our identity to be similar to any or all of those older professions (e.g., psychology, social work) or whether we want to set our identity to be different from them.

If we were to adopt the first alternative, then we would want to select the strongest qualities of these other professions and try to emulate as many of them as we can without looking like a cheap reproduction. The public, public policy makers, and third-party payers are, by definition, players in the marketplace and already know these other professions. If counselors can convince this marketplace audience that we are very much like these other mental health care providers, then we should be recognized and afforded all of the rights and privileges that accompany that recognition.

There obviously are some problems with this course of action. Professional counselors are not psychologists or social workers. We have our own unique history as a profession. Whereas our profession's history is complex and does not necessarily lend itself well to a single interpretation, it differs from the other professions' histories in many ways, not the least of which is its interdisciplinary and diverse nature. There are other, perhaps more significant differences as well.

Figure 35.1 represents a mental health continuum that has high-level wellness at one end and severe and persistent mental illness at the other. Somewhere along that continuum, there is a point that divides the population into the more mentally healthy people and the more mentally ill people. Obviously, on the side toward the high-level wellness end is a mentally healthy description, and on the other side—the one closer to the severe and persistently ill end—is the less than mentally healthy description.

It is important to understand the nature and significance of that dividing point and the role it plays in the identity of professional counselors. It was placed there as a vitally important part of the traditional medical model, a model designed by the medical profession to treat and effect cures on the individuals who fall to the left of that point. There is precious little of medical interest to the right of that point in the minds of traditional medicine. Stated slightly differently, that tradition treats pathology and has little, if any, interest in wellness.

The health insurance industry is based on that same concept. If a person is well, then he or she cannot file a claim, even for preventive or self-improvement efforts. If a person meets certain diagnostic criteria that place him or her to the left of that point, then the person's claims against the insurance company will be received and paid.

By way of further clarification, all individuals exist at some point on this continuum at any given moment. In addition, all individuals have a range on this continuum that would be descriptive of their composite beings—their range of "normal" behavior, affect, and cognition. These ranges are unique to those particular individuals and can be broadened either toward

| Severe and Persistently Mentally Ill | ———————— • ———————— | High-Level Wellness |

Figure 35.1. Mental Health Continuum

the health or illness end of the continuum by life circumstances including biochemical shifts and, in some instances, by individuals deciding to commit, and subsequently committing, to such changes. Admittedly, individuals often need assistance in making these commitments.

The medical profession traditionally has focused on applying its medical knowledge and the products of medical science to those individuals who are ill, with the clear intent of making them healthy. Several of the professions that provide mental health care choose to align themselves with this model. In so doing, they are saying, in essence, that this is one way in which they are like the medical profession; they work with sick people to make them well, and therefore, they should be recognized as health care professionals and be reimbursed through the same third-party payer system.

The counseling profession, however, has a great deal of interest on both sides of that point on the continuum. Much of the counseling profession is, in fact, focused to the right of that point. Stated differently, the counseling profession believes that one does not have to be ill to get better. For example, a professional counselor who works in a school setting and is engaged in classroom guidance activities in which he or she is attempting to enhance the self-esteem of the elementary students is engaged in a preventive counseling activity. The school counselor is using much the same training and education as is a professional counselor who practices in an inpatient facility working with a group of depressed clients attempting to enhance self-esteem and who is engaged in a remedial counseling activity. In one setting, the profession is being applied to wellness, and in the other, it is being applied to illness; it is, nonetheless, the same profession.

While acknowledging that there are certain predispositions to mental illness (e.g., biochemical imbalances, long-standing and persistent environmental influences) that can contribute in a negative way developmentally, professional counselors also want to identify the strengths within their clients and assist the clients with transferring those strengths to address their levels of discomfort and, yes, even their pathology. Again, the broad parameters of the profession make identity a problem.

A second issue in the external domain is that counselors are not consistently recognized in state and federal legislation. Public policy makers, for the large part, remain innocently ignorant, if not confused, about our identity. A majority of the responsibility for their ignorance or confusion lies with the counseling profession itself. We have been less than clear about our identity and have not spoken with one clear voice about who we are and what we do.

We need the recognition and support of these public policy makers at the federal level as they write the legislation that names the various professions who will be recognized as providers of mental health care programs receiving federal funding (e.g., Medicare, Medicaid, long-term care). Beyond that, the federal government provides insurance coverage for federal employees covering a significant portion of the population (e.g., CHAMPUS, federal employee health benefit package). In addition, it is from the federal legislation that many insurance companies and managed care organizations take their cue as to who is eligible for reimbursement. This issue is addressed in greater detail later.

We need recognition by state legislatures as they make decisions regarding the practice of many professions, including mental health professions, within their state boundaries. They do their best to ensure that citizens of their states have a certain quality of life. Regulating physical and mental health care is one way in which they do that. Even with the 46 entities (45 states and the District of Columbia) that currently have counselor licensure laws on the books, there is a great deal of variability in what professional counselors are allowed to do across the country.

When the policy makers at these levels receive mixed messages about the identity of professional counselors, we cannot expect them to comprehend, much less appreciate, who we are and what we do—our interdisciplinary nature. Stated slightly differently, the counseling profession undoubtedly would make better progress toward recognition as a serious contender in the mental health care provider arena if we were able to have one clearly articulated statement about who we are and what we do.

Third-party payers, major players in the marketplace of the mental health care services delivery systems, pose a special problem for professionals whose identity is unclear and for a profession as loosely defined as the counseling profession. Not to be disrespectful, but third-party payers are in the business world. That being the case, they make decisions based on the principles of business rather than on any altruistic motivation. Being part of that business environment, they expect professions to have crisp, clear, and concise definitions of who they are and what they are trained to do.

Any profession being proffered without that definition and identity will not be given favorable consideration for reimbursement by these groups. What the counseling profession must keep in mind is that other mental health care provider professions have offered such crisp, clear, and concise definitions. If we want to be on a level playing field, we must do our part to present ourselves in such a way that the chances for our success are as great as we can make them.

The issue is further clouded by the fact that the professions providing mental health care that have preceded us into the marketplace are known and trusted by these groups, whereas we are not. We have to live down the less than favorable comparisons that other professions have made between professional counselors and themselves in addition to being clear about who we are. In other words, we must sell third-party payers not only on who we are but also on who we are not.

We must be very clear that we as a profession are driven by a code of ethics that prohibits us from practicing beyond the scope of our education and training, have a significant and substantial knowledge base to support our identity, and possess the competency to practice effectively. We must be very careful not to make claims that we cannot support (e.g., claiming a certain level of education or training for all counselors that, in fact, is true for only those counselors trained in certain specialty areas).

The final major issue facing the counseling profession from the external domain to be covered here is the increased consumer knowledge relative to health care. Consumers in this country expect quality health care. Whereas they are capable of and willing to tolerate, if not embrace, homeopathic approaches, they expect health care to be delivered by professionals who are educated and trained in the healing arts or sciences and who practice the same in an ethical manner. If consumers are not satisfied with their care, then they do not hesitate to pursue satisfaction, including monetary restitution.

Evidence of this exists in the increase in litigation against health care providers who fail to effect cures for whatever might be bothering clients. The message here for the counseling profession is that we must be clear about what people can rightfully expect to receive when they come to see us. It is more than just practicing ethically. The quality of care that we deliver is measured client by client. The incompetence or poor judgment of one professional counselor with any one client can call into question the progress that the profession has made toward attaining and maintaining a reputation as a major mental health care provider. This is equally true whether that counselor practices in a K-12 school setting, an institution or agency funded by private or public funds, or a private practice setting.

Looking to the Future

In view of the issues stated heretofore and the awareness that there are many additional issues not addressed in this chapter, one might conclude that all is lost and that it is foolish to attempt to continue as one more in a parade of many mental health care professions. That would be extremely shortsighted. Many of these issues are being addressed in an aggressive and ongoing manner. For example, in 1997, the ACA Governing Council did make a valiant attempt at defining this interdisciplinary and diverse profession. Although the definition of *professional counseling* that eventually was adopted should not be seen as the final word, it should be seen as a very important step in the developmental journey of an evolving profession. A second example is that the Council for Accreditation of Counseling and Related Educational

Programs (CACREP), as our professional accreditation body, is studying different delivery models in its current efforts to revise the curriculum and standards of preparation for the field.

We also must understand that, because of the nature and magnitude of the challenge, solutions will not come by any single act. Rather, solutions will come as the result of continuous efforts of a dedicated community of professional counselors who take themselves and their profession seriously and maintain integrity, dedication, and dignity in the face of adversity. The success that they attain will be meted out in developmental increments. The evolution of a profession is a slow process if it is to be inclusive of the efforts of its members.

The largest difficulty that the profession has is in coming to an agreement on how to best address our identity crisis. Obviously, although we all might have solutions in mind, if we attempt to implement all of them independently, then we will have chaos and will worsen our condition. Even if we develop subgroups around specific aspects of the profession (which we already have in the form of the 17 ACA divisions mentioned earlier), there are inherent dangers. As Liteman and Liteman (1998) pointed out, it is very difficult to avoid the tar pit of focusing so narrowly and surgically precisely on the efforts of the subgroup that the overarching goals of the whole either are left unattended or go down to defeat due to dissipated energies.

The point is that solutions will come to the major issues articulated here only through the organized, collaborative, and cooperative efforts of the profession as a whole. The operative phrase here is *as a whole.* ACA provides the best single vehicle today through which these combined efforts can be channeled. An important step was taken by the ACA Governing Council in 1997 when it adopted a definition of professional counseling. That definition, which in and of itself is not a panacea, attempts to establish an identity for professional counselors and to embrace the diversity and multidisciplinary issues mentioned previously. It did not come easily, and it was adopted only because of the sustained efforts of leaders in the profession over time. That definition of the practice of professional counseling reads "the application of mental health, psychological, or human development principles, through cognitive, affective, behavioral, or systemic intervention strategies, that address wellness, personal growth, or career development as well as pathology" (ACA Governing Council minutes, October 17-19, 1997, p. 8). At that same meeting, the Governing Council adopted the definition of a *professional counseling specialty* as "narrowly focused, requiring advanced knowledge in the field founded on the premise that all professional counselors must first meet the requirements for the general practice of professional counseling" (p. 8).

It also should be pointed out that any profession's identity or definition needs to be seen as a snapshot of the profession at a specific point in time. There always needs to be an ongoing and continuous reaffirmation/revision process in place that keeps the definition and identity a dynamic and accurate reflection of the constant struggle of staying current without being subject to the influence of momentary whims or issues that come along. Metaphorically, the definition, or identity statement, should serve as the rudder that determines the course of the profession.

To address the issues raised in the earlier discussion of the internal domain, the counseling profession somehow must learn to accommodate its own interdisciplinary nature. We have struggled with trying to simplify something that defies simplification. We need to find ways in which to accept our complexity in such a manner that a single identity can be embraced by all of the divisions and specialties within the profession.

We need to be clear about the nature of specialties. As individual members of the profession, we must be absolutely clear that our primary loyalty lies with the profession and that our secondary loyalty, no matter how strong, lies with the area within that profession in which we have chosen to specialize. This certainly is implied in the definitions adopted by the ACA Governing Council.

Also, from the internal domain—from an individual counselor's perspective as opposed to our composite identity—we must understand the seriousness of our individual professional identity. Collison (2000) pointed out that each member of the profession must examine issues of his or her own identity from the views of clients, the general public, colleagues, and the profession as a whole. Without each individual professional counselor holding himself or herself to the highest standards of both pre-degree education and post-degree continuing education, the entire profession suffers.

To summarize what is necessary in the future to address the issues in the internal domain, professional identity is a function of professionalism. The point here is that all individual counselors must make certain that they are engaged in ongoing preparation for the profession by continuing their educations as new research brings new evidence forward. As individual practitioners, they must hold themselves to the highest standards of credentialing and must understand that their involvement in their own growth and professional development is an on-going process. As we hold ourselves to that higher standard, there also must be a prevailing attitude of cooperation and collaboration with colleagues regardless of one's area of specialization.

Regarding the future of issues from the external domain, it would seem prudent to offer a more united picture of the profession relative to our multidisciplinary nature. We own our pluralist nature and incorporate it as a strength as opposed to a weakness. It requires a higher level of intellectual skill to comprehend and accommodate a complex concept such as this, but we have no choice. It is who we are, and it is how and where we practice our profession.

It is essential that we not only tolerate but also actively promote a united front to the external domain as individual professionals and as a profession. We must be able to speak with one voice to public policy makers, third-party payers, the general public, and our respective client populations. Without this form of advocacy, we will not succeed.

These issues from the external domain are arguably as important to the professional identity of counselors as those from the internal domain. Whereas the internal domain issues must be dealt with first, those from the external domain will continue to plague our identity until we as a profession move decisively to address them. They require that counselors move forward with a united front.

Assuming a united front that recognizes our pluralism and interdisciplinary nature, the issue then becomes one of what we must do and how we must do it. At the very least, the counseling profession must address any misinformation that exists about us in the marketplace and must promote accurate information about who we are and what we do. We must advocate for the wellness philosophy that is part of our unique niche among the mental health professions. Consumers may actively seek our services to prevent dysfunction as well as to treat it if we as a profession become our own strong and effective advocates.

There is cause for optimism regarding the identity of professional counselors. To be sure, the profession and those of us in it are going through some growing pains. On the other hand, these growing pains also make it possible for us as individual professional counselors to influence and shape the profession and, thereby, position the profession to be not only a major player but also the player of choice in the mental health care arena.

How successful we are in doing this will depend on each individual counselor advocating for the highest possible standards for himself or herself as well as for the profession. One cannot do this by being a member who merely "pays the dues and reads the news." The identity of professional counselors must be built on professionalism. It requires active participation in the ongoing life of the profession.

References

Aubrey, R. F. (1986). The professionalization of counseling. In M. D. Lewis, R. L. Hayes, & J. A. Lewis (Eds.), *An introduction to the counseling profession* (pp. 1-35). Itasca, IL: F. E. Peacock.

Aubrey, R. F., & Lewis, J. (1983). Social issues and the counseling profession in the 1980s and 1990s. *Counseling and Human Development, 15*(10), 1-15.

Brooks, D. K., Jr. (1996). Credentialing of mental health counselors. In W. J. Weikel & A. J. Palmo (Eds.), *Foundations of mental health counseling* (2nd ed., pp. 259-275). Springfield, IL: Charles C Thomas.

Brooks, D. K., Jr., & Weikel, W. J. (1996). Mental health counseling: The first twenty years. In W. J. Weikel & A. J. Palmo (Eds.), *Foundations of mental health coun-*

seling (2nd ed., pp. 5-29). Springfield, IL: Charles C Thomas.

Collison, B. B. (2000). The counselor's professional identity. In H. Hackney (Ed.), *Practice issues for the beginning counselor* (pp. 9-22). Boston: Allyn & Bacon.

Covin, T. M. (1994, February). Freedom of choice and advocacy. *AMHCA Advocate,* p. 5. (American Mental Health Counselors Association)

Glauser, A. (1996). A hub for mental health counselor practitioners: The untapped potential. *Journal of Mental Health Counseling, 18,* 312-315.

Griffin, B. (1993). ACES: Promoting professionalism, collaboration, and advocacy. *Counselor Education and Supervision, 33,* 2-9.

Henderson, P., & Gysbers, N. C. (1998). *Leading and managing your school guidance program staff: A manual for school administrators and directors of guidance.* Alexandria, VA: American Counseling Association.

Liteman, M., & Liteman, J. (1998, December). Turf battles. *Executive Update,* pp. 26-29. (Greater Washington Society of Association Executives)

Lopez Levers, L. (1999). *Coming to terms with identity politics: Counselor identity, professionalization, and the rhizome.* Unpublished manuscript, University of Rochester.

Smith, H. B. (2000). Counselor advocacy: Promoting the profession. In H. Hackney (Ed.), *Practice issues for the beginning counselor* (pp. 153-169). Boston: Allyn & Bacon.

CHAPTER THIRTY-SIX

Defining and Responding to Racial and Ethnic Diversity

COURTLAND C. LEE

The constructs of race and ethnicity have been mainstays in the counseling literature for the past 30 years. Ever since Clemmont Vontress's landmark article, "Counseling Blacks," in the *Personnel and Guidance Journal* in 1970, where he contended that Blacks have developed unique environmental perceptions, values, and attitudes, making it difficult for counselors to establish and maintain rapport, the counseling profession has been on notice that sensitivity to issues of racial and ethnic diversity must be factored in as an important variable in counseling theory, practice, and research (Vontress, 1970). Significantly, the discipline of multicultural counseling that has emerged over the past two decades rests on a foundation of

ideas and principles about race and ethnic group membership.

At the beginning of the 21st century, demographic realities make it imperative that the profession of counseling reconsider its traditional definition of and responses to racial and ethnic diversity. Population projections for the new century suggest that those U.S. citizens from historically minority racial/ethnic groups will supplant those citizens of European origin, traditionally identified racially as "White," as the majority of the country's population (Spencer, 1989). This chapter offers a 21st-century analysis of the constructs of race and ethnicity and presents a counseling paradigm for responding to the challenges of, and maximizing the opportunities inherent in, ethnic diversity among client populations.

Race Versus Ethnicity: A Contemporary View

The terms *race* and *ethnicity* (ethnic group) generally are used interchangeably. Often, they both are used to refer to groups of people who share similar physiological traits and/or personality characteristics. These traits and characteristics either are genetically transferred or have become reinforced through group association over long periods of time. However, these terms are not synonymous. Mio, Trimble, Arredondo, Cheatham, and Sue (1999) defined *race* as a system based on "hair texture, skin color, eye color, and facial features" to

> categorize people into one of four groups: Asian, Black, White, or American Indian. Although many educational, governmental, and military institutions still use racial classifications and identities, new data on genetics make such classifications scientifically meaningless. (p. 218)

Mio and colleagues defined *ethnic* as "derived from the ancient Greek word *ethnos,* which referred to a range of situations in which a group of people lived and acted together. It refers to one's values and general lifestyle that is shared" (p. 110).

In reviewing these two definitions, it can be argued that race has become an archaic anthropological/biological classification of human differences that historically has been used as part of political, social, cultural, and economic brutality and exploitation in many parts of the world. Such a definition of race historically has formed the core of the heinous phenomenon

known as *racism.* A classic example of this is Adolf Hitler's labeling of Judaism, which is a religion and ethnic/cultural tradition, as a race, thereby perpetrating the Holocaust of the last century.

What is most important from a mental health perspective, however, are not genetically transferred physiological/biological traits but rather personality characteristics among people that become reinforced through association over time. It is these long-standing dynamics of thinking, feeling, and behaving that form the cultural basis of *ethnicity* or an *ethnic group.* This makes implicit the significance of the concept of ethnicity as an important counseling construct (Lee, 1997). In considering a new counseling paradigm for changing population dynamics, therefore, it is important that the focus is on the importance of ethnicity and ethnic diversity in the relationship between counselor and client. In other words, rather than using the U.S. Bureau of the Census's (1990) racial terminology of Black, White, Asian, American Indian, or Hispanic as a frame of reference for a diverse American society, it makes more sense and provides more meaning to people's lives to consider their realities in terms of ethnic group membership (e.g., African American, Jamaican American, Irish American, Italian American, Korean American, Chinese American, Navajo, Lakota).

The two definitions and the reconceptualization of race as ethnicity underscore an important question facing the counseling profession: How do we get beyond classical racism to a model of counseling that incorporates and validates this ethnic diversity? As Robinson and Ginter (1999) made excruciatingly explicit in the Winter 1999 issue of the *Journal of Counseling and Development,* race and ethnic diversity were powerful and problematic constructs during the 20th century. They negatively affected the psychosocial development of scores of people. For this reason, counselors must address issues of ethnic diversity in a responsive manner.

Ethnic Identity Development: A Crucial Factor in Responding to Diversity

Certainly, an answer to the preceding question and the accompanying challenges of racism lies in an understanding of ethnic identity development. The basis of any counseling paradigm that responds to ethnic diversity must be predicated on an appreciation of ethnic identity development. Ethnic identity has been referred to as an individual's sense of belonging to an ethnic group and that part of an individual's personality that is attributable to ethnic group membership (Rotheram & Phinney, 1987). Ethnic identity may be considered as the interior vision that a person possesses of himself or herself as a member of an ethnic group. It forms the core of the beliefs, social forms, and personality dimensions that characterize distinct cultural realities for an individual (Lee, 1997).

The development of ethnic identity traditionally has been conceptualized as an evolutionary linear stage process (Atkinson, Morten, & Sue, 1993; Cross, 1995) or, more recently, as a dynamic personality status process in which racial/ethnic information is simultaneously interpreted and internalized at a variety of levels (Helms, 1995). During the 20th century, ethnic identity development occurred in a milieu characterized by complex social interaction among individuals from ethnic-minority groups and the ethnic groups comprising the European American cultural majority in the United States. It is important to point out, therefore, that most models of ethnic identity development in the United States have been developed in a context where people of European ethnic origins have been in a position of social and cultural dominance with respect to other ethnic groups. In this country, European Americans generally have enjoyed cultural privilege in their relationship with members of other ethnic groups (McIntosh, 1989). This cultural privilege has profoundly influenced the attitudes of European Americans toward members of ethnic-minority groups (Helms, 1990, 1995). Likewise, the perceptions of this cultural privilege held by people from ethnic-minority groups has profoundly influenced attitudes that they hold of themselves and European Americans as racial/ethnic beings (Atkinson et al., 1993; Helms, 1990, 1995).

Ethnically Responsive Counseling: A 21st-Century Counseling Paradigm

If counselors are to be effective with clients from a variety of ethnic backgrounds, then they must approach the helping process from a perspective that simultaneously acknowledges human difference and celebrates human similarity. They must adopt a philosophy that promotes the ability to view each client as a unique individual while, at the same time, taking into consideration the client's common experiences as a human (i.e., the universal developmental challenges that face all people regardless of ethnic background) and the specific experiences that come from his or her ethnic background. It is important, therefore, that counselors consider each client as a unique individual within an ethnic group context and a broader global human perspective.

This perspective, to a certain extent, underlies the work of Sue, Arredondo, and McDavis (1992), who provided a set of competencies for counseling practice in a multicultural society. These competencies are based on the premise that counselors who are responsive to clients from diverse cultural backgrounds have heightened self-awareness, have an expanded knowledge base, and use helping skills in a culturally responsive manner. This premise provides a framework for a 21st-century paradigm for ethnically responsive counseling.

It is imperative that ethnically responsive counselors build a repertoire of relevant skills. They should be able to use counseling strategies and techniques that are consistent with the life experiences and cultural values of clients from diverse ethnic backgrounds. To develop and implement such skills, however, counselors first must have awareness and knowledge related to issues of ethnic diversity.

Self-Awareness

The prerequisite for ethnically responsive counseling is self-awareness. It is crucial that counselors fully experience themselves as racial/ethnic beings. Individuals who expect to work with clients from ethnically diverse backgrounds first must be anchored in perceptions of their own ethnic realities. This process should start with explorations of how their own ethnic backgrounds have influenced their psychosocial development. It is of the utmost importance that individuals consider the role that ethnic heritage and customs play in shaping their personality characteristics.

It also is crucial that individuals assess their levels or stages of ethnic identity development. The crucial questions that one must ask in this regard are "How do I see myself as a member of Ethnic Group X?" "How do I see other members of Ethnic Group X?" and "How do I perceive people of other ethnic backgrounds?"

As part of this self-exploration process, it also is important that counselors evaluate the influences that have shaped the development of their attitudes and beliefs about people from different ethnic backgrounds. It is important to evaluate the explicit, as well as the often subtle, messages that they have received throughout their lives about people who are ethnically "different." Counselors must evaluate how their personal attitudes and beliefs about people from different ethnic groups may facilitate or hamper counseling effectiveness.

Although much of this has been previously advocated in the counseling literature, little direction has been provided about how to actually operationalize such a self-awareness process among counselors. As we proceed into the 21st century, it is important that opportunities be provided at both the pre- and in-service levels for individuals to self-segregate for self-exploration. Forums must be established for counselors and counselors-in-training to be in safe, supportive, and validating experiences with peers from their respective ethnic groups to explore the challenging issues and questions discussed here.

An important follow-up to such experiences should be integrated forums in which counselors and those in counselor training programs have the opportunity to dialogue with peers across ethnic lines. Again, in a safe and supportive environment, individuals should be provided opportunities to discuss aspects of their new levels of consciousness with ethnically diverse groups of peers.

Ethnically responsive counselors explore personal issues and questions, no matter how uncomfortable or distasteful, in an attempt to discern how their own ethnic heritages, values, and biases might affect the counseling process. Self-exploration leads to self-awareness, which is crucial in developing a set of personal attitudes and beliefs to guide ethnically responsive counseling practice. Ethnically responsive counselors are sensitive to ethnic group differences because they are aware of their own identity as ethnic beings.

Acquiring Knowledge

It is imperative that ethnically responsive counselors have knowledge bases from which to plan, implement, and evaluate their services. First, they must have an understanding of how economic, social, and political systems operate with respect to their treatment of ethnically diverse groups. For example, counselors should have an understanding of the historical impact of social forces (e.g., poverty, discrimination) on the psychosocial development of many ethnic-minority groups.

Second, counselors who are responsive to diverse ethnic realities acquire working knowledge and information about specific groups of people. This should include general knowledge about the histories, experiences, customs, and values of ethnically diverse groups. From such knowledge should come an understanding of specific ethnic contexts and how they may influence personal and social development.

Again, the literature often has been vague about how this knowledge acquisition process should be operationalized. The obvious answer is to upgrade graduate-level coursework and in-service professional development experiences on multicultural issues in counseling. However, a 21st-century paradigm for ethnically responsive counseling calls for new and creative ways in which to help professionals and emerging professionals acquire knowledge about ethnic diversity. This certainly would entail increased use of media. Counselors should enhance their personal growth and professional development by reading the literature and exposing themselves to other forms of artistic expression (e.g., television programs and documentaries, films, artwork) of ethnically diverse groups. A great deal of information about lifestyles, customs, traditions, language patterns, values, and histories, as well as their impact on human development and personality, can be gained from such forms of artistic expression. The Internet can be an important aid in exposing counselors to important information about ethnically diverse groups of people.

Counselors also should go out and experience ethnic diversity firsthand. There is a limit to how much can be learned about different ethnic groups from classes, workshops, books, and films. Much more can be learned by actually being among people from diverse ethnic groups and interacting with them in their cultural environments. Professional development initiatives should be planned and implemented to visit with people at family gatherings, religious services/ceremonies, ethnic festivals, and the like. Such in vivo experiences can raise levels of awareness, increase knowledge, and provide important dimensions to empathic style in counseling interventions.

Building Skills

The essence of counseling is the ability to help people with problem resolution or decision making. Ethnically responsive counselors should have skills repertoires that will allow them to help people solve problems or make decisions in a manner that is consistent with and affirms the integrity of clients' ethnic realities.

Ethnically responsive counseling skills should be based on the following premises. First, ethnic group diversity is real and should not be ignored. Second, ethnic group differences are just that—differences. They are not necessarily deficiencies or pathological deviations. This means having the ability to meet clients where they are, despite any obvious cultural gaps spawned by ethnic differences between helpers and helpees. Third, when working with clients from diverse ethnic groups, it is important to avoid stereotypes and a monolithic perspective. It is crucial that counselors consider clients as individuals within an ethnic group context.

In this ethnically responsive paradigm, a number of skills should be included in counselors' repertoires. It is important that counselors' styles be eclectic enough that they can use a variety of helping approaches. These approaches should incorporate diverse ethnic group views and practices with respect to a number of important concepts including the following.

Kinship influences. The influence of kinship may include immediate and extended family, friends, or community resources. Kinship support can be crucial in providing help with problem resolution or decision making. Ethnically responsive counseling should be based on an understanding of and appreciation for the role of kinship dynamics in human development. As appropriate, counselors should find ways in which to make use of the kinship system in the counseling process.

Language preference. Ethnically responsive counseling should be based on an appreciation of and sensitivity to client language preference. This might encompass ethnic group differences in language fluency, accent, dialect, and nonverbal communication. Counselors must be skilled in allowing clients to "tell their stories" in languages and communication styles that are most appropriate and comfortable for them.

Sex-role socialization. Counselors should be aware of how gender-based differences in academic, career, and personal-social expectations are manifested in problem resolution and decision making among the males and females of diverse ethnic groups. Counseling interventions might need to be conducted with sensitivity to sex-role socialization practices.

Religious/spiritual influences. For many ethnic groups, there is little distinction between religious/spiritual and secular lives. Counseling may be enhanced, therefore, if the influences of religion and/or spirituality are considered a crucial dynamic in the helping process. As appropriate, it might be necessary to form consultative relationships with religious/spiritual leaders or other indigenous helpers/healers for the benefit of clients.

Help-seeking attitudes and behavior. Counselors must be cognizant of the fact that there is great ethnic group variability with respect to help-seeking attitudes and behaviors. Not all ethnic groups traditionally value or understand the nature of formal counseling as a source of help with problem resolution and decision making. It might be necessary, therefore, to step outside the confines of the traditional counseling setting to offer services. Counselors might need to think creatively in terms of how they provide services to clients for whom the counseling process might be a totally alien experience.

In addition to a sensitivity to such dynamics in their skill repertoires, it also is important for ethnically responsive counselors to understand and be willing to assume the role of systemic change agents or advocates for many clients. When working with many clients from ethnically diverse groups, counselors might need to consider the negative effects of phenomena such as racism and other forms of cultural, economic, or social oppression on growth and development. The etiology of problems often is not in clients but rather in intolerant or restrictive environments. The only way in which clients will be able to solve problems or make decisions is to eradicate these systemic impediments. Ethnically responsive counselors often must assume the role of systemic change agents and help clients to challenge such impediments.

The components of this paradigm not only are the basis of ethnically responsive counseling but also can be considered as the foundation of quality counseling in general. As counselors strive to be aware of and responsive to the needs of ethnically diverse client groups, they raise the standard of the profession for all.

Looking to the Future

As the paradigm for ethnically responsive counseling becomes the standard for quality counseling, two intriguing issues present themselves to the profession. These issues underscore the ongoing challenges associated with the concepts of race and ethnic diversity as the profession of counseling and the nation enter the 21st century.

The first issue is addressing the complex notion of "White" as a racial/ethnic identity and what it means to be a member of a White ethnic group in the United States. As mentioned previously, the ethnic groups of European origin in this country that comprise the cultural group collectively known as Whites historically have enjoyed privilege based largely on skin color in their relationships with members of other ethnic groups. Because of this, it often has been easy for White Americans not to have to deal with racial/ethnic issues in other than a minimal fashion. Quite often, they have not had to experience themselves as racial/ethnic beings (Kiselica, 1999).

The future of ethnically responsive counseling will need to include forums and processes that allow members of these ethnic groups to experience themselves as ethnic beings and explore the nature of their cultural privilege. This will be particularly important as demographic shifts place members of these groups into the numerical minority. It also will be important if constructive dialogues are to take place across ethnic group lines as has been called for by the country's leadership.

The second important issue is fully addressing the challenges associated with interracial or bicultural identity development. In spite of dramatic increases in the number of people from mixed racial/ethnic backgrounds in the United States over the past two decades, the counseling profession has given minimal attention to this population (Wehrly, 1996). It is important that the profession understand the challenges that this growing group of individuals face in dealing with the "other" racial/ethnic identification status so often seen as a racial/ethnic demographic designation (Fukuyama, 1999; Williams, 1999). Counselors need to develop self-awareness about their personal attitudes and behaviors toward this growing population. In addition, they need information to understand the challenges that children, adolescents, and adults from biracial/bicultural backgrounds face in developing ethnic identities (Kerwin & Ponterotto, 1995; Poston, 1990). Finally, the counseling profession needs to continue developing guidelines for responsive counseling with interracial individuals and their families.

Conclusion

As a new century dawns and population demographics continue to shift, there appears to be a window of opportunity for the country to conquer one of its worst historical enemies—racism. The profession of counseling can help in the battle against this foe by ensuring that counseling theory, research, and especially practice are responsive to diverse ethnic realities. Counselors must, therefore, develop skills that will allow them to communicate responsively and effectively with clients from diverse ethnic backgrounds.

References

Atkinson, D. R., Morten, G., & Sue, D. W. (1993). *Counseling American minorities: A cross-cultural perspective* (4th ed.). Madison, WI: Brown & Benchmark.

Cross, W. E. (1995). The psychology of Nigrescence: Revisiting the Cross model. In J. G. Ponterotto, J. M. Casas, L. A. Suzuki, & C. M. Alexander (Eds.), *Handbook of multicultural counseling* (pp. 93-122). Thousand Oaks, CA: Sage.

Fukuyama, M. A. (1999). Personal narrative: Growing up biracial. *Journal of Counseling and Development, 77,* 12-14.

Helms, J. E. (1990). *Black and White racial identity: Theory, research, and practice.* Westport, CT: Greenwood.

Helms, J. E. (1995). An update of Helms's White and People of Color racial identity models. In J. G. Ponterotto, J. M. Casas, L. A. Suzuki, & C. M. Alexander (Eds.),

Handbook of multicultural counseling (pp. 181-198). Thousand Oaks, CA: Sage.

Kerwin, C., & Ponterotto, J. G. (1995). Biracial identity development: Theory and research. In J. G. Ponterotto, J. M. Casas, L. A. Suzuki, & C. M. Alexander (Eds.), *Handbook of multicultural counseling* (pp. 199-217). Thousand Oaks, CA: Sage.

Kiselica, M. S. (1999). Confronting my own ethnocentrism and racism: A process of pain and growth. *Journal of Counseling and Development, 77,* 14-17.

Lee, C. C. (1997). Cultural dynamics: Their importance in culturally responsive counseling. In C. C. Lee (Ed.), *Multicultural issues in counseling: New approaches to diversity* (pp. 15-30). Alexandria, VA: American Counseling Association.

McIntosh, P. (1989, July). White privilege: Unpacking the invisible knapsack. *Peace and Freedom, 2,* 10-12.

Mio, J. S., Trimble, J. E., Arredondo, P., Cheatham, H. E., & Sue, D. (1999). *Key words in multicultural interventions: A dictionary.* Westport, CT: Greenwood.

Poston, W. S. C. (1990). The biracial identity development model: A needed addition. *Journal of Counseling and Development, 69,* 152-155.

Robinson, T. L., & Ginter, E. J. (Eds.). (1999). [Special issue]. Racism—healing its effects. *Journal of Counseling and Development, 77.*

Rotheram, M. J., & Phinney, J. S. (1987). Introduction: Definitions and perspectives in the study of children's ethnic socialization. In J. S. Phinney & M. J. Rotheram (Eds.), *Children's ethnic socialization* (pp. 10-31). Newbury Park, CA: Sage.

Spencer, G. (1989). *Projections of the population of the United States by age, sex, and race: 1988-2080* (U.S. Bureau of the Census, Current Population Reports, Series P-25, No. 1018). Washington, DC: Government Printing Office.

Sue, D. W., Arredondo, P., & McDavis, R. J. (1992). Multicultural counseling competencies and standards: A call to the profession. *Journal of Counseling and Development, 70,* 477- 486.

U.S. Bureau of the Census. (1990). *Race and Hispanic origin population density of the United States: 1990* (GE-90, No. 6). Washington, DC: Government Printing Office.

Vontress, C. E. (1970). Counseling Blacks. *Personnel and Guidance Journal, 48,* 713-719.

Wehrly, B. (1996). *Counseling interracial individuals and families.* Alexandria, VA: American Counseling Association.

Williams, C. B. (1999). Claiming a biracial identity: Resisting social constructions of race and culture. *Journal of Counseling and Development, 77,* 32-35.

CHAPTER THIRTY-SEVEN

"Where No One Goes Begging"

Converging Gender, Sexuality, and Religious Diversity in Counseling

TRACY L. ROBINSON

SHERRY K. WATT

In each person's life, both visible and invisible identities exist. These identities are multiple and simultaneous, and they work in conjunction. Traditionally, the multicultural counseling literature has focused on three identity constructs—race, ethnicity, and culture—with the goal of enhancing the counseling process, particularly when the client and counselor are of different racial/cultural backgrounds. Although differences in and of themselves are not problematic, they can create conflict within racially dissimilar client-counselor dyads, leading to ineffective service delivery and undesirable counseling outcomes (Locke, 1998). This focus often was warranted given cross-racial differences in values, communication styles, sociopolitical histories in America, and experiences with racism.

Robinson and Howard-Hamilton (2000) presented the first comprehensive effort in the counselor education literature to attend to mul-

AUTHORS' NOTE: The title of this chapter is adapted from T. L. Jewell (Ed.), *The Black Woman's Gumbo Ya-Ya: Quotations by Black Women* (Freedom, CA: Crossing Press, 1993). The quotation is that of L. Reese, "i be/long where no woman goes begging," from "Introduction."

tiple identities and their collective simultaneous roles in psychosocial identity development. Identity constructs such as religion, sexuality, and gender are prominent in a client's psychosocial development, problem presentation, and its subsequent resolve. Thus, an exclusive focus on a specific identity construct to the exclusion of others does not allow the counselor to relate to the client as a whole person and communicates to the client that particular identities and realities are outside the domain of counseling.

In the course of normal adult development, gender, sexuality, and religion occupy space in everyone's life; are basic to personhood; and can be the source of crises. These include, but are not limited to, infertility; sexual attraction to same-sex or different-sex persons within marriage; keeping faith amid life's seeming injustice (e.g., the death of a child); choosing to neither marry nor have children; sexual problems in relationships due to childhood incest; changes in one's physical appearance due to prostate, breast, or other forms of cancer; the impact of normal aging and illness on sexual functioning or body image; and one's role as a financial provider after being downsized. How do counselors successfully integrate gender, sexuality, and religion into their work toward seeing clients as whole persons? The goal of this chapter is to leave "no one begging" by unpacking gender, sexuality, and religious diversity. These core identities and the way in which they converge in psychosocial identity development often are ignored within the counseling literature. Another aim of this work is to enhance counselors' effectiveness when addressing these intersecting constructs. First, definitions are provided.

Phenomenological Definitions

Gender and Sex

Gender and sex are different. A "uniformity myth," or the assumption that biological sex is the same as gender roles, has existed in counseling literature (Mintz & O'Neil, 1990). *Biological sex* refers to the possession of an XY chromosome for a genetically healthy male and an XX chromosome for a genetically healthy female, along with the corresponding anatomical, hormonal, and physiological parts (Renzetti & Curran, 1992). Cook (1987) referred to gender as a multidimensional construct that encompasses more than just biological sex. It is a social construction that describes interactions, relationships, and behaviors associated with being male and female in a society. *Gender* describes the socially constructed masculine and feminine roles that women and men play based on biological sex. It is an all-encompassing term that speaks to the cultural phenomenon of male and female behavior. *Gender roles* for women and men are heavily prescribed and include expectations, behaviors, and attitudes created by society (Mintz & O'Neil, 1990) such as provider, homemaker, caretaker, and war hero. *Sex roles* include functions associated with one's biological sex such as menstruation, pregnancy, erection, ovulation, ejaculation, and lactation (Robinson & Howard-Hamilton, 2000). A distinction is also made among gender, masculinity, femininity, and androgyny. *Masculinity* is associated with characteristics traditionally viewed as performed by men (e.g., fierce independence, strong-willed, and emotional restraint). *Femininity* is associated with behaviors and traits traditionally expected to be performed by women (e.g., nurturance, caretaking, not using harsh language). Although none of these characteristics is exclusively performed by men or women, society historically has associated these behaviors with biological sex.

Heterosexuality, Bisexuality, and Homosexuality

Arredondo (1994) conceptualized sexual orientation as an "A" dimension or the ones into which people are born. This point is controversial, particularly in many traditional religious contexts where homosexuality is regarded as an immoral and sinful choice. Homosexuality is a religious and ethical dilemma for some, but it is a natural and necessary experience for others. *Sexuality* refers to how humans relate to self and others as sexual beings. Defined on a continuum, sexuality includes the socially constructed meanings of being heterosexual, bisexual, and homosexual. A person who is heterosexual is an individual whose sexual and affective orientation is toward the different biological sex. However, a heterosexual closer to bisexuality on the sexuality continuum may be a man who has sex only with his wife but who fantasizes about and desires to be sexual with another man. A gay person, traditionally referred to as homosexual, is attracted sexually and affectionally to someone of the same biological sex. A person who is bisexual is attracted to both women and men.

Instead of multiple points on the line as a continuum suggests, heterosexuality and homosexuality are socially constructed as two bipolar dimensions. There are a few exceptions to the conceptualization of sexuality as dichotomous and mutually exclusive categories. Kinsey's work, which is inclusive of the experiences of homosexuals, bisexuals, and heterosexuals, has six stages that describe the physical/sexual and affectional attraction at each level (Kinsey, Pomeroy, & Martin, 1948; Kinsey, Pomeroy, Martin, & Gebhard, 1953). There are six points on the continuum from heterosexual to homosexual. An individual who is a 0 (zero) has no physical contact that results in erotic arousal with members of the same sex. There also is no psychic response to individuals of one's own sex. Sociosexual contact and responses are exclusively with members of the opposite sex. A person who is a 1 on the continuum has only incidental homosexual contact, which involves physical or psychic response or incidental psychic response. There also is a greater preponderance of sociosexual experience and reaction with the opposite sex. Having a 2 on the continuum means that the person has more than incidental same-sex experience and/or responds to homosexual stimuli. Heterosexual experience still surpasses homosexual experience, although both types of contact might be frequent. Specific arousal from homosexual stimuli occurs, but heterosexual responses are stronger. A 3 on the continuum has equally overt heterosexual and homosexual experiences and psychic reactions. This person accepts and enjoys both types of contacts and has no strong preference for one or the other. An individual who is a 4 on the continuum engages in more overt activity and psychic reactions to same-sex stimuli but also experiences a fair amount of heterosexual activity and/or psychic response. This position is the reverse of the 2 position. A 5 on the continuum suggests that a person engages in almost all homosexual activity and psychic reactions. However, there may be incidental psychic experiences with the opposite sex as well as psychic reactions to the opposite sex. This position is the reverse of the 1 position. A person who is a 6 on the continuum is considered to be exclusively homosexual in regard to both overt experience and psychic reactions. This position is the reverse of the 0 position.

Whereas a person's sexual orientation can fall anywhere on the continuum, the gender to which one identifies could differ from biological sex. Thus, a distinction is made between sexual orientation and gender identity. Known as transgender, a person may be biologically female yet identify within the body and psyche as a male who is attracted to women.

Religion and Spirituality

Although related, religion, faith, and spirituality are operationalized differently. Spirit comes from the Latin word *spiritus,* meaning "breath of life" (Kelly, 1995). *Spirituality* is internally and experientially defined, transcends the tangible, and connects one to the whole, which includes the universe and all organisms. It offers life direction and meaning, and it represents the core of people's lives (McDonald, 1990). *Religion* is the practice of one's beliefs regarding a higher being. It involves behaviors, rituals, and routines related to the experience of worship. One of the purposes of religion is to be in the company of believers. Religion tends to be associated with a particular denomination, and it "has come to represent an institutionalized set of beliefs and practices by which groups and individuals relate to the ultimate" (Burke et al., 1999, p. 252). These institutionalized practices include chanting, confessing, baptizing, praying at particular times during the day and night, meditating, fasting, building an altar, wearing particular clothing, liturgical

reading, lighting candles, and burning incense. World religions include Buddhism, Christianity, Confucianism, Islam, Judaism, Hinduism, Shintoism, Taoism, and Tribal beliefs (Wehrly, 1995).

The Socially Constructed Cultural Context of Gender, Sexuality, and Religion

Discourses

Social constructionism represents a way of viewing the world by exploring assumptions about knowledge and attending to subtle and blatant uses of language. The way in which society in general and counselors in particular learn to talk or not talk about gender, sexuality, and religion is linked to socially constructed dominant discourses or uses of language and verbal exchanges of ideas that operate as forms of social practice to communicate and perpetuate particular meanings (Monk, Winslade, Crocket, & Epston, 1997).

Through a child's fairy tale, the dominant discourses of androcentrism and heterosexism are revealed. Cinderella, a beautiful young girl with a wicked stepmother and two unattractive stepsisters with large feet, is required to work all day long. A grand social affair, the ball, is announced by the prince's family members, who presume that it is time for this young single man to be married. In a scurry of excitement, Cinderella's sisters prepare for the ball. Cinderella's attendance at this festive and elitist event is not considered. However, the miraculous arrival of a fairy godmother changes everything. With the aid of a pumpkin and a mouse (or not, depending on which version), Cinderella is transformed into a beautiful belle, prepared for the ball with a gorgeous gown for her petite and delicate frame, complete with glass slippers for her small feet. She and the prince dance for hours as he is stricken by this nameless beauty. At midnight, the transformation hour, Cinderella flees the ballroom and, in so doing, leaves behind her glass slipper, the only object with which the prince has to find his lovely lady. He diligently searches throughout the town, subjecting the single women who went to the ball to the test—trying on the tiny and dainty glass slipper to see whether it fits. Again, by some miracle, Cinderella is allowed to try the slipper on, and it fits perfectly. She and the prince marry, and they live happily ever after.

There are many dominant discourses in this seemingly innocuous child's story: Blended families are dysfunctional; single women want to get married, and single men should get married; women need miracles outside of themselves to flee difficult situations; handsome princes are rich, able-bodied, and heterosexual, and they can choose any women they want; unattractive women are mean and fat; women compete with each other for men; marriage is an escape route out of a bad situation, and it solves everything.

Androcentrism and Heterosexism

Androcentrism refers to the centrality of the male experience for all humans, independent of sexual and gender diversity (Bem, 1993). Men—and this term applies primarily to heterosexual men given that true manhood is predicated on either being heterosexual or not acting gay—have unearned yet normative advantage accorded to them by societal institutions such as religious, educational, corporate, and family institutions. Males come into the world as the

preferred sex; they earn more money than do women for comparable work; they are not expected to change their names when they marry, and it is assumed that their offspring will automatically take their names; nearly all human development models have been created by males and have been patterned primarily on their experience; and men own the majority of the world's capital despite the volume of nonremunerated women's work around the world.

Dominant discourses teach men to scrutinize their lives and other men's lives to ensure rigid adherence to an austere masculine and homophobic-driven code that

> demands more than they can deliver; that is, to be regarded as adequately masculine, men must be powerful and competitive; not show vulnerability, emotions, or weakness; control themselves, others, and their environments; be consistently rational; be sexually skilled; and be successful in their work. (Good, Robertson, Fitzgerald, Stevens, & Bartels, 1996, p. 45)

Despite these discourses, men often feel like workhorses, and many are ill equipped to comfortably experience and express a full range of emotions such as fear, dependence, sadness, and uncertainty.

Western culture is masculine and associated with an instrumental orientation or a cognitive focus on completing tasks. Competition, materialism, independence, and assertiveness are held in high esteem and are synonymous with being a rugged, middle-class American. Admittedly, women benefit from androcentrism, particularly when in masculine contexts they adapt allowable expressions of masculinity, which has social utility for them as well as for men (Burnett, Anderson, & Heppner, 1996). Nonetheless, women recognize that excessive masculinity (e.g., self-reliance, assertiveness) is inconsistent with femininity and may be evidence of homosexuality or bitchiness. Women often are socialized that being a woman means catering to other people's needs first, particularly men's needs, and that physical beauty is their greatest source of power. With it, marriage and eventually motherhood, quintessential markers of womanhood, can be achieved.

Heterosexism has been defined as a worldview, a value system that prizes heterosexuality, assumes that it is the only appropriate manifestation of love and sexuality, devalues all that is not completely heterosexual, and supports the belief that heterosexual relationships are necessary for the preservation of the nuclear family. It refers to the belief that everyone is or should be heterosexual because such relationships are morally superior and are sanctioned by many major religions (Robinson & Howard-Hamilton, 2000).

Critical Themes and Essential Dialogue

Sexuality, religion, and gender are status variables because "they possess rank, have value, and are constructed hierarchically" (Robinson, 1999, p. 73). Because of the androcentric and heterosexist context in which gender, sexuality, and religion are located, critical dialogue about these constructs in counseling can be eclipsed. For example, many religious institutions do not discuss single adults' sexuality other than to communicate that it is wrong and inadmissible and that it should be avoided. This has particular relevance for women who should safeguard their sexual reputations. A dominant religious discourse that intersects with gender and sexuality is that men, by virtue of their centrality in

the human experience and their socially assigned status as providers and leaders, choose virtuous women to marry. Women wait for men to propose marriage, lest they be labeled aggressive and/or desperate. Upon marriage, they are among those who have permissible and acceptable sexual relations. Despite the fact that sexual desire is an experience that people enjoy independent of sexual orientation, religion, gender, and marital status, heterosexism stipulates that sex is reserved exclusively for married and heterosexual persons. There are persons who are sexually active, consider themselves religious, and are single and/or gay. The silence among many traditional religious institutions about this sizable number of people throughout the developmental pipeline denies them opportunities for established, albeit meaningful, dialogue and insight about their multiple identities as sexual, religious, and gendered beings.

The socially endorsed experience of heterosexuality and the unconscious and unearned privilege afforded heterosexuals often deems them unaware of the importance to transition through sexual identity formation. It is presumed that sexual identity formation pertains to gay people only. Normal human development includes crises and dissonance and presupposes that heterosexuals examine their sexual identities, lest their assertions of heterosexuality reflect foreclosure (Marcia, 1981) or the making of commitments without experiencing and successfully resolving crises. Heterosexist and androcentric structures suppress the reality that some heterosexuals explore and clarify their sexual identities in adulthood through contemplation, therapy, prayer, group work, periods of voluntary celibacy, sexual experimentation, or other means of gaining insight.

Integrating Gender, Sexuality, and Religious Diversity Into Therapeutic Spaces

Case Study

The following case study presents multiple identities within a client:

Mecca is a 32-year-old, physically healthy Lebanese woman living in California with her 34-year-old husband, Saim. He also is Lebanese. Mecca works part-time in her uncle's restaurant during the day and also is working on her bachelor's degree in journalism. Saim is a manager in the family restaurant, earns a good salary, and is the primary breadwinner in the family. They have two school-age children and a close extended family nearby. They both are Muslims and are involved in their mosque. Saim has noticed that Mecca has been spending several evenings a week away from the home with a woman friend from college. When he confronted Mecca, she told him that they were studying. The couple's lovemaking has become infrequent, and Saim believes that the relationship is strained. He suggested that they speak to their minister, and Mecca told him that she could not talk to him. When asked why she could not talk to their minister of 8 years, Mecca told Saim that she was having a sexual relationship with her female friend from college and had been having these feelings before they married but knew that they were wrong. She figured that marriage would "take care of those abnormal and confusing thoughts." She prays for the feelings to go away, but they have not. Although he kept it a secret until Mecca's confession, Saim had an extramarital affair with a woman he met at the gym during the first years of their marriage.

Converging identities in counseling means that the counselor considers the constellation of a client's identities. In so doing, an exclusive focus on one identity is not maintained, but the simultaneous identities occurring in a client's life are embraced. The counselor activated by a social constructionist perspective realizes that Mecca is wrestling with sexual identity issues but also realizes that one's sexual identity is not determined by sexual behavior and that sexual orientation may be an evolving component of identity for some people (Haldeman, 1994). In addition, the counselor does not allow this one identity to eclipse other identities in Mecca's life as an able-bodied, Lebanese Muslim woman who also is a mother, a wife, a daughter, a sister, a niece, a friend, an employee, and a student.

Mecca's presenting issues and the counselor's approach to them are influenced, be it consciously or unconsciously, by dominant cultural discourses regarding the exalted statuses of maleness and heterosexuality. In light of this, is Saim's heterosexual infidelity more easy to forgive than Mecca's homosexual infidelity? The rewards and consequences for complying with or straying outside of appropriate sexual and gender boundaries are influenced by religion and differ for men and women.

Independent of its religious diversity, much of the values and structures of American society evolved from an androcentric Judeo-Christian heritage. And although the majority of religious Americans profess a Christian faith, not all Americans are Christians. Within any given faith, there is tremendous variety. As religious and spiritual beings, counselors may face times when they are unable to explore certain themes or help clients with particular issues because of their own strong beliefs, which may be dissimilar to their clients' beliefs, or because of unresolved spiritual issues in their personal lives (Miranti & Burke, 1995). If Mecca's counselor is unable to offer effective services due to differences in religious beliefs or judgments about Mecca's life, then the counselor needs to refer

Mecca to a helping professional who can offer the empathic services to which she is entitled. Furthermore, the counselor's strong religious convictions about the immorality of Mecca's same-sex sexual behavior could result in greater comfort with Mecca's remorse than with her resolve about being in a lesbian relationship. Although it is important for counselors to be aware of their religious belief systems and their own sexual identities, some heterosexual counselors, particularly those in lower stages of sexual identity development (Chojnacki & Gelberg, 1995), are limited in their ability to counsel gay, lesbian, or bisexual clients. The reasons may include being threatened by differences between themselves and their clients, disdain for homosexuality, anxieties about their own sexuality, and fears related to the intimations of their association.

Mecca's sexuality may encourage exploration of spiritual or religious beliefs that differ from the mainstream or institutionalized practices to which she is accustomed. Although she is Muslim, "the three moral choices gay men and lesbians perceive as offered to them by traditional Judeo-Christian religions (i.e., conversion/repentance, celibacy, or an often spurious heterosexual marriage) are frequently perceived as deeply offensive and contrary to their desire for wholeness" (Ritter & O'Neill, 1995, p. 129). Because they do not find safety or feel acceptance in traditional religions, some gay men and lesbians, as well as some heterosexuals, cultivate spiritual beliefs that provide their lives with meaning and purpose.

Whereas religion is a source of empowerment for some clients, it represents oppression and bondage for others. The effective counselor considers the power of faith in both enhancing and restricting clients' lives. Bishop (1992) stated, "Counselors who fail to directly assess the client's religious values run the risk of overlooking potentially important aspects of the client's cultural background and current cultural experience" (p. 181). If Mecca's counselor is not knowledgeable about the basic tenets of Islam, then conducting some research, talking with Muslims, and/or visiting a mosque would be helpful.

Mecca's answer to the basic question of "Who am I?" has its genesis in multiple identities and could affect her marriage, mosque, and community participation. Toward helping Mecca to clarify gender, sexual, and religious identities, dichotomized dominant discourses need to be examined. For example, good mothers are heterosexuals. Muslim women are not lesbians. Muslim daughters do not bring shame and dishonor to the family by divorcing their husbands. A confusing array of emotions such as guilt, relief, shame, and fulfillment require acknowledgment and release. The counselor can help Mecca to unravel the guilt and shame associated with disrupting her children's stable lives, her infidelity, and/or violating familial and cultural expectations of a Lebanese daughter from, perhaps, her feelings of contentment experienced in her relationship with a woman. In addition to talk therapy, bibliotherapy (i.e., reading the stories of other women who have discovered their sexuality as lesbians while being married) could reduce Mecca's feelings of alienation and isolation. Group work, marriage counseling, prayer, and counseling with a minister or an understanding elder in the community may prove to be beneficial.

Narrative therapists operate within a social constructionist paradigm, and many use externalizing conversations in working with clients. In so doing, perceived problems are externalized and not seen as inherent in the client. A narrative therapist might ask Mecca, "What effect has Islam had on you as a woman and the acknowledgment and expression of your sexuality?" This question is different from "How long has the conflict between your sexuality and religion been a problem for you?" In the former, the problem is externalized. In the latter, the problem is seen as internal to Mecca, and this may encourage self-blame and recrimination (Monk et al., 1997).

Converging Multiple Identities

Multiple identity development is an emerging theme in the literature. It has become more apparent to practitioners and counselor educators that therapeutic interventions need to consider the multiple aspects of personal identity such as religion, gender, and sexuality. The existing psychosocial literature on identity (Erikson, 1968; Marcia, 1981) does not address how one aspect of identity (e.g., occupational identity) could be achieved, whereas another area (e.g., interpersonal relationships) could be in a state of moratorium.

Scholarly research in counseling that examines the convergence of gender, sexuality, and religion is limited (Robinson, 1999; Robinson & Howard-Hamilton, 2000). The empirical investigations have depended on qualitative research designs in three primary categories: (a) sexual abuse survivors, (b) 12-step programs, and (c) sexual minorities. Abstract constructions are difficult to define as independent concepts, and it is even a greater challenge to explore them as converging ideas. Thus, a review of the research literature reveals emerging theoretical frameworks and implications for practice.

In addition to race and culture and the oppressive practices related to these identities, the multicultural competencies (Arredondo, 1999) include a statement to counselors regarding various dimensions of identity. It states, "Culturally skilled counselors should attend to, as well as work to eliminate, biases, prejudices, and discriminatory contexts in conducting evaluations and providing interventions and should develop sensitivity to issues of oppression, sexism, heterosexism, elitism, and racism" (p. 108). Given how culture influences dominant values such as religion, this competency seems to apply to gender, sexual, and religious oppression.

Convergence of Gender, Sexuality, and Religious Diversity: Future Issues

This chapter has explored the social and political implications of the intersections among gender, sexuality, and religion within counseling. With respect to future issues, two overarching factors as they relate to these constructs were articulated. First, this chapter covered new territory. Although these constructs have been examined independently numerous times in the literature, this chapter is one of only a few to look closely at the convergence of these identities. Second, this chapter gave voice to the idea that there are multiple identities within an individual and considered, albeit indirectly, the impact that other identity constructs (e.g., race, culture, ethnicity) have on the convergence of gender, sexuality, and religion, both individually and interpersonally. Future practice, education, and research must consider these overarching issues.

Future Directions
For Practitioners

Practitioners who provide service to a diverse American population must understand that clients are on a lifelong search for identity. A human constantly is asking the question, "Who am I?" and consistently changing his or her responses to this question over time. Practitioners must be current on the emerging literature regarding multiple identity development in clients. This includes not only reading the literature but also engaging in dialogue with colleagues. Workshops need to be conducted that allow space for multiple aspects of clients' identities to be discussed. Similarly, this space needs to be honored when in session with clients.

The interpretation of assessment measures traditionally used in counseling is affected by gender, religious, and sexuality discourses. Because clients come to counseling with presenting problems, the profession needs to view the complexity of clients' issues rather than focusing on a single domain. This paradigm shift is critical for practitioners who wish to honor multiple aspects of identity.

Future Directions for
Counselor Educators

On a national level, counselor education programs typically engage in a peripheral discussion of gender, sexuality, and religion in multicultural counseling courses. In addition to competence in race and culture, counselors need to develop competence when dealing with gender, sexuality, and religion as well. Multicultural counseling courses must go beyond helping future counselors to understand specific populations (e.g., European, African,

American, Asian, Latino, Native American Indian) and help them to examine the sociopolitical context in which assumptions about gender, sexuality, and religion are located. Doing so will better ensure that when counselor trainees are released to practice, they will be educated within a framework that allows for multiple identities to be explored.

Future Directions
for Research

Gender, sexuality, and religion are difficult constructs to research because they are challenging to quantify. Although this has implications for the establishment of construct validity, these concepts are central to our day-to-day interactions and take on meaning between individuals within relationships. Given this challenge, studies that examine the convergence of gender, sexuality, and religion must depend on qualitative research designs. Although quantifying the data is important, qualitative designs that focus on how individuals make meaning of their experiences are needed to expand our understanding of these three critical aspects of human functioning.

Conclusions

This chapter has examined the convergence of gender, sexuality, and religious diversity in counseling. Each construct was explored from the perspective of its intersection with other components of identity. Given the considerable diversity that exists across gender, sexuality, and religion, it is imperative that counselors know how to approach each client with respect for his or her unique and individual story. To leave "no one begging," counselors must be able to speak about the unspeakable. The aim of this work was to prepare counselors to be more attuned to each client's view of the world and interact within it toward accurately and respectfully reflecting empathy, the essential counseling tool.

References

Arredondo, P. (1994). *Cultural considerations for working more effectively with Latin Americans* [Video]. North Amherst, MA: Microtraining Associates. (Box 9641, North Amherst, MA 01059-9641)

Arredondo, P. (1999). Multicultural counseling competencies as tools to address oppression and racism. *Journal of Counseling and Development, 77*, 102-108.

Bem, S. L. (1993). *The lenses of gender: Transforming the debate on sexuality inequality.* New Haven, CT: Yale University Press.

Bishop, D. R. (1992). Religious values as cross-cultural issues in counseling. *Counseling and Values, 36*, 179-189.

Burke, M. T., Hackney, H., Hudson, P., Miranti, J., Watts, G. A., & Epp, L. (1999). Spirituality, religion, and CACREP curriculum standards. *Journal of Counseling and Development, 77*, 251-257.

Burnett, J. W., Anderson, W. P., & Heppner, P. P. (1996). Gender roles and self-esteem: A consideration of environmental factors. *Journal of Counseling and Development, 73*, 323-326.

Chojnacki, J. T., & Gelberg, S. (1995). The facilitation of a gay/lesbian/bisexual support-therapy group by heterosexual counselors. *Journal of Counseling and Development, 73*, 352-354.

Cook, E. P. (1987). Psychological androgyny: A review of the research. *The Counseling Psychologist, 15*, 471-513.

Erikson, E. (1968). *Identity: Youth and crisis.* New York: Norton.

Good, G. E., Robertson, J. M., Fitzgerald, L. F., Stevens, M., & Bartels, K. M. (1996). The relation between masculine role conflict and psychological distress in male university counseling center clients. *Journal of Counseling and Development, 75*, 44-49.

Haldeman, D. C. (1994). The practice and ethics of sexual orientation conversion therapy. *Journal of Consulting and Clinical Psychology, 62*, 221-227.

Kelly, E. W. (1995). *Spirituality and religion in counseling and psychotherapy.* Alexandria, VA: American Counseling Association.

Kinsey, A. C., Pomeroy, W. B., & Martin, C. E. (1948). *Sexual behavior in the human male.* Philadelphia: W. B. Saunders.

Kinsey, A. C., Pomeroy, W. B., Martin, C. E., & Gebhard, P. H. (1953). *Sexual behavior in the human female.* Philadelphia: W. B. Saunders.

Locke, D. C. (1998). *Increasing multicultural understanding: A comprehensive model.* Thousand Oaks, CA: Sage.

Marcia, J. E. (1981). Identity in adolescence. In J. Adelson (Ed.), *Handbook of adolescent psychology* (pp. 197-243). New York: John Wiley.

McDonald, A. L. (1990). Living with our deepest differences. *Journal of Law and Religion, 8*, 237-239.

Mintz, L. B., & O'Neil, J. M. (1990). Gender roles, sex, and the process of psychotherapy: Many questions and few answers. *Journal of Counseling and Development, 68*, 381-387.

Miranti, J., & Burke, M. T. (1995). Spirituality: An integral component of the counseling process. In M. T. Burke & J. G. Miranti (Eds.), *Counseling: The spiritual dimension* (pp. 1-3). Alexandria, VA: American Counseling Association.

Monk, G., Winslade, J., Crocket, K., & Epston, D. (1997). *Narrative therapy in practice: The archaeology of hope.* San Francisco: Jossey-Bass.

Renzetti, C. M., & Curran, D. J. (1992). *Women, men, and society.* Boston: Allyn & Bacon.

Ritter, K. Y., & O'Neill, C. W. (1995). Moving through loss: The spiritual journey of gay men and lesbian women. In M. T. Burke & J. G. Miranti (Eds.), *Counseling: The spiritual dimension* (pp. 127-142). Alexandria, VA: American Counseling Association.

Robinson, T. L. (1999). The intersections of dominant discourses across race, gender, and other identities. *Journal of Counseling and Development, 77*, 73-79.

Robinson, T. L., & Howard-Hamilton, M. F. (2000). *The convergence of race, ethnicity, and gender: Multiple identities in counseling.* Upper Saddle River, NJ: Merrill/Prentice Hall.

Wehrly, B. (1995). *Pathways to multicultural counseling competence: A developmental journey.* Pacific Grove, CA: Brooks/Cole.

CHAPTER THIRTY-EIGHT

The Spiritual and Religious Dimensions of Counseling

MARY THOMAS BURKE
JUDY MIRANTI

Spirituality in counseling encompasses various dimensions and approaches directed at assisting clients in exploring meaning and purpose in life. Therefore, establishing a trusting relationship is crucial whenever a client wishes to explore religious or spiritual issues, which usually are sacred to the individual. An openness and respect for this aspect of the client's life builds on the empathic understanding that counselors are expected to show for clients' diversity. As clients express their religious and spiritual needs, counselors must listen actively to themes and narratives that will become the substance of the counseling process.

Emphasis on the spiritual dimensions of counseling has achieved national recognition over the past decade, as evidenced by the numerous publications on the topic (Burke & Miranti, 1995; Kelly, 1995; Richards & Bergin, 1997). Critics have expressed concerns that counselors who incorporate the spiritual dimensions in the counseling process might be likely to violate ethical guidelines by imposing their values on clients (Richards & Potts, 1995). However, there are no professional ethical guidelines that prohibit counselors from discussing religious issues or using spiritual interventions with clients. Rather, the ethical guidelines encourage adherence to respect individual differences in values (American Counseling Association [ACA], 1995; American Association of Marriage and Family Therapy [AAMFT],

1985; American Psychological Association [APA], 1992). A counselor who incorporates the spiritual dimension is no more likely to violate a client's value autonomy than is one who does not. Clearly, sensitivity and respect for the diversity of religious and spiritual traditions as well as multicultural dimensions are ethical behaviors expected of all counselors (Lee & Sirch, 1994). To do otherwise would violate the ethical code of the counseling profession.

This chapter adds to the body of knowledge regarding spirituality in counseling by focusing on the competencies needed by counselors and the advantages of incorporating the spiritual dimension into the therapeutic process. The impact on the future preparation of counselors—including assessment, training implications, and research findings—is addressed.

The Importance of Including Spirituality in Counseling

As we approach this topic, it may be helpful to distinguish between the words *religion* and *spirituality*. The *American Heritage Dictionary of the English Language* (1992) defines *spirituality* as "of concern with or affecting the soul . . . in relation to God" (p. 1238). Spirituality refers to a way of being in the world that acknowledges the existence of, and the desire to be in relationship with, a transcendent dimension or higher power. This spiritual tendency is believed to move the individual toward knowledge, hope, love, transcendence, connectedness, and compassion. "Spirituality includes one's capacity for creativity, growth, and the development of a value system" ("Spirituality Competencies," 1995, p. 30).

The *American Heritage Dictionary of the English Language* (1992) defines *religious* as "having or showing belief in and reverence for God or a deity and of, concerned with, or teaching religion" (p. 1525). Religion refers to the social or organized means by which a person expresses his or her spirituality. In this sense, religion is expressed through Christianity, Judaism, Islam, Hinduism, Buddhism, Confucianism, and Taoism as well as the many institutionalized variations within each of these world religions (Kelly, 1995).

Thus, the terms *religious* and *spiritual* are interrelated, but they can be distinguished from each other along several dimensions. Religious expressions tend to be denominational, external, cognitive, behavioral, and public. Spiritual experiences tend to be universal, internal, spontaneous, ecumenical, and private. It is possible to be religious without being spiritual and to be spiritual without being religious (Richards & Bergin, 1997).

Spirituality is an integral part of every human, and the counselor must address the spiritual needs of the client who comes for counseling. One may argue that the spiritual dimension is omitted because one cannot adequately measure the spiritual or prove that it exists. Yet, much has been written about psychological constructs, even though these are not concrete or measurable (Bergin & Payne, 1991; Ingersoll, 1994). So, the argument that we must ignore the spiritual is a moot point. Is it not then feasible that much of the depression, anger, guilt, and/or sadness that the client brings to counseling sessions had their origins in a lack of connectedness or meaning in the client's life? This lack of connectedness or meaning creates a vacuum that can be filled by a depth dimension referred to as spirituality (Worthington, 1989).

If there is a depth dimension or a spiritual dimension in each life, then why would a counselor refuse to explore spirituality with a client?

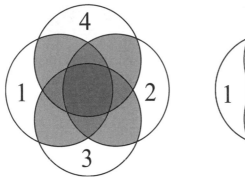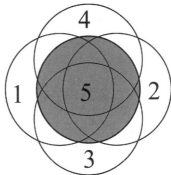

Figure 38.1. Spirituality: The Unifying Dimension of Personhood

Is there any other issue introduced by a client that a qualified professional counselor would ignore or, even worse, would refuse to address because the counselor does not know what to do or how to respond? Why the hesitancies?

Importance of Addressing All Needs in a Person's Life

Most of the counselor education programs, and all Council for Accreditation of Counseling and Related Educational Programs (CACREP)-accredited counselor education programs, require that human growth and development be included as an integral part of every student's program. Thus, the physical, emotional, intellectual, and social needs of the person are fully explored and studied. The interrelationship among these needs is illustrated in Figure 38.1 by using a Venn diagram of four circles representing the (1) physical, (2) emotional, (3) social, and (4) intellectual dimensions of every human.

Each dimension of the human person intersects with the other. If the physical needs of the person are unmet, then the whole person suffers. Likewise, if the emotional, social, or intel-

lectual needs of the person are unmet, then the impact is felt on the entire person. There are times, however, when a client presents symptoms that do not fall under any one of these four areas. A more comprehensive model of human behavior includes a fifth dimension, the spiritual, which integrates and gives meaning to the other dimensions. Physicians, psychologists, counselors, and even the business community now are acknowledging the importance of the fifth dimension in maintaining the health and wellness of the whole person.

The spiritual essence of the person is at the core, integrating and uniting all parts with equal force and bringing meaning and depth to human behavior. Emphasis on the holistic model allows counselors to acknowledge that spiritual and religious dimensions of client needs are at the core of wellness (Witmer, Sweeney, & Myers, 1994). Wellness may be defined as the level of functioning at which individuals feel comfortable and are considered healthy for themselves and for society (Theodore, 1984). To prepare counselors to address this issue in their practice, counselor education programs must train counselors in this area. In his national survey of 525 counselor education programs in which he examined the role of religion and spirituality in counselor education, Kelly (1994) reported that only a minority of programs included the religious and spiritual dimensions. Survey respondents, mostly heads of departments, considered these issues to be important. Few counselor education programs, however, address these issues. This leaves a significant gap in the education of future counselors. To meet this training component, the spiritual needs must be addressed with the same seriousness as the physical, emotional, and social, as well as the intellectual, needs of clients.

Miranti (1998, p. 118) summarized some practical reasons for incorporating the spiritual dimension of counseling:

- Incorporating the spiritual dimension provides the practitioner with a type of metaphor or road map for better understanding the worldview of the client.

- Religious identity often is as strongly influential as either racial or cultural identity (Worthington, 1989).

- The multicultural perspective includes variables such as religion, nationality, ethnicity, language, gender, age locale, social, economic, and educational factors and affiliations (Pedersen, 1990).

Sensitivity to client diversity necessitates that all aspects of a client's worldview be important in the counseling process. Counselor education programs are remiss if they fail to train counselors to effectively explore with clients the spiritual and religious issues presented either directly or indirectly in the counseling process. The counseling profession and counselor educators need to engage more deeply in professional dialogue about ways in which to incorporate the religious and spiritual dimen-sions into the counseling process so as to meet clients' needs.

Hesitancies to Address the Spiritual Dimension

There are at least four reasons why counselors hesitate to address spiritual issues in counseling:

- A fear of imposing personal values
- The counselor's attitude toward spirituality
- A lack of knowledge of spiritual concerns
- A lack of facilitative theoretical models for working with spiritual issues

Each of these issues is addressed separately in what follows.

Fear of imposing values on the client often is stated as the primary reason why counselors hesitate to respond to the spiritual issues that a client brings to the session. As the counseling profession emerged, the philosophical and theoretical biases against spiritual perspectives adopted by the early contributors became deeply imbedded in clinical practice. The continual influence of these biases is one of the main reasons why spiritual perspectives are not more fully integrated into the practice of counseling (Bergin & Garfield, 1994). A counselor who addresses spiritual concerns is not more likely to violate a client's rights than he or she would be if the client were dealing with a marriage problem or any other problem.

Another reason why counselors hesitate to address the spiritual issues of clients may be counselors' own feelings about religion and spirituality. Some counselors may have had negative experiences with their churches or synagogues during their formative years and, therefore, do not feel comfortable in discussing these issues with their clients. To address the spiritual dimension adequately in their clients' lives, counselors first must examine their own biases and prejudices. They need to be familiar and comfortable with their own spirituality so that they can encourage and support this dimension in the lives of their clients (Ingersoll, 1994). Mandatory ethics requires that counselors respect diversity. However, aspirational ethics, which calls for counselors to practice the highest standards of care, inspires counselors to look beyond the immediacy of the particular situation and to encourage client growth and development in ways that foster clients' interest and welfare (Herlihy & Corey, 1996).

For others, a lack of knowledge of spiritual issues may keep them from addressing the spiritual dimension (Lovinger, 1990). Insufficient knowledge indicates a need for education. Counselors must keep expanding their knowledge to serve their clients. Workshops on emerging issues always are available.

Perhaps the lack of facilitative models or the lack of integrating spiritual issues into their theoretical models would cause counselors to be fearful of addressing the spiritual concerns of their clients. Counselors in the past, fearing that they lacked the training or expertise, often referred their clients to ministers, priests, or rabbis to help resolve the clients' religious and spiritual issues. Today, the counseling profession is acknowledging that these issues can best be addressed by professional counselors. Several authors have documented their successes and provided examples of the incorporation of spirituality into the counseling process. Chandler, Holden, and Kolander (1992) described specific strategies (e.g., meditation, visualization, yoga) that can be used to foster spiritual devel-

opment. Smith (1993) explored the religious and spiritual needs of dying persons in the counseling process. Prest and Keller (1993) provided several clinical examples in their incorporation of spirituality into family therapy. Hinterkopf (1994) provided a way of integrating spirituality into the counseling process using Gendlin's (1981) experiential focusing method. Frame and Williams (1996) discussed different ways of integrating spirituality into counseling African American clients. Finally, Curtis and Davis (1999) discussed how spirituality can be integrated into Lazarus's multimodal therapy.

Advantages of Integrating Spirituality Into Counseling

There are many advantages to integrating spirituality into counseling. In comparing counseling with spirituality, one becomes aware that both are attempting to help the client to (a) learn to accept self; (b) forgive others and self; (c) acknowledge his or her shortcomings; (d) accept personal responsibility; (e) let go of hurts and resentments; (f) deal with guilt; and (g) modify self-destructive patterns of thinking, feeling, and acting. These are the issues that clients bring to counselors, and all have spiritual and/or religious dimensions to them (Gladding, 1995).

A majority of Americans reported in a poll that active religious beliefs and/or spiritual awareness are integral to their lives (Gallup & Begilla, 1994). The data from the poll suggest the possibility that many of these individuals will seek counseling to resolve their deep spiritual and/or religious issues. The common denominator of spirituality and counseling is human suffering. Few clients come for counseling when everything is going well, and many persons turn to their spiritual and religious beliefs when things go wrong. In dealing with these clients, counselors must recognize the importance of spiritual issues and communicate a willingness to explore them in an empathic and understanding manner. In addition, counselors must be skillful in discerning healthy practices from unhealthy practices in clients' belief systems. For example, a client's description of a personal problem might focus excessively on guilt-oriented thoughts or depression that might be directly related to his or her belief system. In cases such as this, it is imperative for the counselor to conceptualize these feelings and behaviors in an effective manner so as to select the appropriate therapeutic approach (Faiver & O'Brien, 1993).

Frequently, the issues presented initially might not be at the root of the expressed concerns. These might not surface until the third or fourth session. A clinical assessment or structured intake may facilitate the surfacing of the root problem much sooner. If the counselor is skilled in interpreting unexpressed needs, then the intervention selected may help the client to articulate the concerns that brought him or her to counseling.

Clinical Considerations for Counselors

Counselors who choose to ignore the spiritual dimension might (a) be in violation of the ACA (1995) code of ethics that regulates the profession of counseling and (b) fail to promote the growth of their clients. If a counselor does not feel qualified to address the spiritual and religious needs of a client, then the counselor would have an ethical responsibility to refer the client.

A client who brings up spiritual issues may attempt to get specific answers to spiritual and religious questions from the counselor. If this occurs, then the counselor needs to respond as he or she would to any other questions posed by the client. One caution that needs to be raised is that of a counselor displaying religious symbols that would indicate his or her own belief system. The displaying of any religious symbol needs to be avoided unless a person is practicing in a religious setting. It is inevitable that clients and counselors will become aware that they have differences with regard to certain beliefs and social values (Corey, Corey, & Callanan, 1993). Care must be exercised to make sure that a counselor, who is perceived as the individual with the power, does not in any way (verbally or nonverbally) impose his or her values on a client, thereby violating the trust, respect, and confidence that the client has placed in the counselor.

Some spiritual interventions, such as discussing religious or theological concepts, religious relaxation, or religious imagery, are inappropriate in a nonreligious setting. Such interventions may be perceived as being in violation of the separation of church and state, and they would require the informed consent of the client. In general, it is safest to be open with clients, colleagues, and supervisors about the spiritual aspect of one's work (Richards & Bergin, 1997).

Research Findings

Recent attention to diversity issues in counseling has underscored the need for training counselors to respond to the unique spiritual and religious needs of their clients. Myers and Truluck (1998) replicated a study conducted by Bergin and Jensen (1990) using a sample of professional counselors. Two primary research questions were addressed:

- Are professional counselors' perceptions of the relation of religion to mental health the same as those of other mental health professionals?
- Are professional counselors' perceptions of the role of values in counseling the same as those of other mental health professionals?

The findings from this study have important implications for counselor preparation and the delivery of counseling services to clients. Myers and Truluck (1998) reported that counselors differed from other mental health providers in every area measured. In every instance, including both the perceptions of counselors regarding the importance of religious beliefs and values in their own lives and the perceived importance of those values in guiding the process of counseling with clients, professional counselors rated the items as being more important than did the other mental health providers. The study concluded that clients with spiritual needs might have a greater chance of having those needs met if they choose professional counselors rather than other mental health professionals for their spiritual and religious concerns.

Competencies Needed

Counselor educators have begun to give serious attention to training counselors in the spiritual dimension by developing competencies and outlining the advantages of incorporating the spiritual dimension into the counseling process. The Summit on Spirituality ("Spirituality Competencies," 1995), endorsed by the Association for Ethical, Religious, and Values Issues in Counseling, was held in Charlotte, North Carolina, in October 1995. The proceedings were published in *Counseling Today,* the ACA newsletter. A list of competencies was developed by participants at the Summit on Spirituality and endorsed by the Association for Spiritual, Ethical, and Religious Values in Counseling. To address the spiritual and religious needs of clients, a professional counselor must be able to do the following:

- Explain the relationship between religion and spirituality including both similarities and differences.
- Describe religious and spiritual beliefs and practices in a cultural context.
- Engage in self-exploration of one's religious and spiritual beliefs so as to increase sensitivity, understanding, and acceptance of one's belief system.
- Demonstrate sensitivity and acceptance of a variety of religious and spiritual expressions in client communication.
- Identify limits of one's understanding of a client's religious and spiritual expression and demonstrate appropriate referral skills and possible referral sources.
- Assess the relevance of religious and spiritual themes in the counseling process as befits each client's expressed preference.
- Use a client's religious and spiritual beliefs in the pursuit of the client's therapeutic goals as befits his or her expressed preference.

To assess the relevance of religious and spiritual domains in the client's therapeutic issues, the counselor will need some assessment tools early in the counseling process.

Assessment Component in Training

Viewed comprehensively, assessment involves ways in which counselors facilitate understanding of clients' belief systems that are relevant to the resolution of issues that the clients bring to counseling. Counselors, however, are taught in the assessment course that formal or informal assessment results can be used for the purpose of assisting clients' decision making, self-exploration, understanding, and action planning (Kelly, 1995). In assisting clients with spiritual issues, counselor trainees need to be taught to select those tools that are appropriate for clients of diverse religious and spiritual beliefs and affiliations. In conducting informal assessments, counselors should collect information that could enable them to understand their clients' spiritual worldviews and also help counselors to decide whether their clients' spiritual and religious backgrounds are relevant to their expressed concerns and issues.

The following global assessment questions, formulated by Richards and Bergin (1997), are offered as suggestions that might help a counselor to understand the worldview of a client:

- What is the client's metaphysical worldview (e.g., Western, Eastern, naturalistic-atheistic, naturalistic-agnostic)?

- What were the client's childhood religious affiliation and experiences?

- What is the client's current religious affiliation?

- What is the client's level of devoutness?

- Does the client believe that his or her spiritual beliefs and lifestyle are contributing to the client's problems and concerns in any way?

- Does the client have any religious and spiritual concerns and needs?

- Is the client willing to explore his or her religious and spiritual issues?

- Does the client perceive that his or her religious and spiritual beliefs are a potential source of strength and assistance?

The following questions also may be used in the intake interview to assist the counselor in determining the client's spiritual worldview and belief system (Miranti & Burke, 1998):

- When you want to feel strength, where do you go or whom do you see?

- When you want to feel comfort, where do you go or whom do you see?

- What one goal do you have that is most important to you right now?

- In one sentence, how would you describe the purpose of your life?

- What one goal do you have that is most important to you right now?

Taking the client's spiritual inventory and assessing for spiritual strengths might require training programs to develop (a) curricula that would include models of spiritual development, (b) comparative religious studies of the major religious systems, and (c) scenarios in which trainees work with spiritual and religious issues. Because values often are influenced by spiritual and religious beliefs, training programs will need to provide opportunities for students to articulate their own values and beliefs so as to be aware of how to use them appropriately in counseling. The models of spiritual development will help counselors to understand the role that spirituality plays in normal human development. The spiritual inventory also could provide an overview of how spiritual beliefs are developed and facilitated over the life span. Comparative religious studies give counselors an overview of the major religious systems that they may encounter in the counseling process. A major focus of counselor training programs needs to be developing and upgrading skills to intervene effectively in the lives of clients from a variety of cultural backgrounds, including the religious and spiritual components, as well as incorporating into the training models holistic approaches that help clients to view their lives from a transcendent point of view (Lee & Sirch, 1994).

Shafranske and Malony (1996) recommended that graduate programs should provide direct training and supervision including assessment of spirituality and religion as variables in mental wellness and exposure to implicit and explicit models of addressing this issue in the counseling process. By being open to the role that religion and spirituality play in a client's life, the counselor can facilitate the exploration of issues presented by the client.

Training Implications

For counselors, the challenge is not whether the issue of spirituality and counseling should be addressed, but rather how it can best be addressed by well-prepared and sensitive professionals. The following are some ways in which these dimensions can be included:

- Include spiritual competencies in all counselor education programs.
- Develop resources and materials to assist counselor educators in training programs.
- Use references to different religious and spiritual traditions when using case studies in training.

- Emphasize the infusion of religious and spiritual sensitivity in all counseling sessions.
- Include religious and spiritual diversity in multicultural courses.
- Guard against the promulgation of only the Judeo-Christian perspectives in ethical concerns.
- Ensure that all religious and spiritual traditions are acknowledged in discussions.
- Be familiar with current research and scholarly works about religion and spirituality in counseling and mental health journals.
- Obtain specialized training in dealing with spiritual issues in counseling if such training was not a part of the counselor's education repertoire.
- Continue to seek supervision and/or consultation from colleagues when clients present challenging spiritual issues that the counselor has not yet encountered.

Future Directions

Empirical research on religious and spiritual issues in counseling has mushroomed during the past decade. As spiritual intervention strategies are developed and integrated into the counselor education curriculum, there will be an ongoing need for additional outcome studies solidly grounded in and supported by both quantitative and qualitative empirical research.

In the future, all counselor education programs must include adequate training on addressing clients' spirituality. A balanced and thoughtful infusion of this topic into students' curriculum is a reasonable and sound approach to preparing counselors to work ethically and effectively with these issues in secular counseling settings (Burke et al., 1999).

Although theory and research relevant to the spiritual dimension of counseling have increased during the past decade, there is still a need for the following (Richards & Bergin, 1997; Worthington, 1989):

- More outcome studies with actual clients on specific spiritual interventions
- Studies that document the effectiveness of spiritual approaches
- More theory and research on how religion and spiritual beliefs and practices influence people's personality development and functioning
- More research on religiously and culturally diverse groups
- An integrative spiritual strategy for counseling
- Religious and spiritual development across the life span
- Research methodologies, procedures, and designs that allow researchers to study spiritual phenomena validly

From Case Conceptualization to Application

As clients' present issues and begin the process of exploring solutions or alternatives, counselors conceptualize the issues and begin the process of selecting the appropriate theoretical approaches or models. The counselor educator guides students in the conceptualization of a case and then allows the trainees to discuss the case from several theoretical approaches. The following case is complex in nature and is followed by several suggestions for application.

A Case Study

Mary is a 36-year-old mother of three children. She and her husband, Bob, have been married for 16 years. Mary reports that she lacks meaning in her life and dreads getting up each day. She says that she feels guilty because she has three beautiful children and a committed husband. She admits that she has gotten overly involved in her work at the law firm and has taken on additional cases that prevent her from having quality time with her family. Her husband does not complain because he believes that, because her salary is higher than his, he would be acting unappreciatively. However, Mary and Bob have not been intimate for several months, and although Bob denies being attracted to other women, he has entertained thoughts of "going out with the boys" and having "fun." The couple's marriage is strained, and they have been discussing the possibility of a separation. Mary is opposed to the separation and thinks that her husband is putting undue pressure on her. Her church does not allow divorce, and she says that separations frequently lead to divorce.

How does the spiritual dimension apply in this case? Mary is expressing a sense of meaninglessness in her life and a feeling of disconnectedness from her husband and children. In addition to the types of theoretical approaches that may be used, the element of spirituality could be introduced by asking several questions such as the following. When you want to feel strength, where do you go or whom do you see? What goal do you have that is most important to you at this time? Mary is so caught up in "doing" that she has lost a sense of "being." It might be appropriate to ask Mary what gives her feelings of self-worth or what some of her beliefs are about God given that she has indicated a religious affiliation. Mary is at a point in her life where she is questioning her role as mother and wife. Thus, she might be seeking new meaning for her relationships. The counselor indicates that he or she is willing to journey with Mary and help her to explore and reclaim meaning and purpose in her life.

Suggestions for Application

This case is complex and can be approached from several theoretical models, taking into consideration the cultural context, family-of-origin issues, traditional family role functions, and so on. Trainees would select a theoretical approach or a combination of theories and would incorporate the spiritual dimension. For example, if they selected the Adlerian approach, then family constellation, early childhood recollections, and use of the lifestyle assessment would facilitate the deeper exploration of the issues. The counselor educator could have the trainees apply this case to each theory, infusing the spiritual dimension and emphasizing the competencies for incorporating this perspective.

Conclusion

The need for skilled counselors who can efficiently facilitate life-enhancing change is becoming increasingly apparent as we enter the new millennium. Now, more than ever, the emphases on purpose and meaning—the essence of spirituality—are within the grasp and scope of helping professionals. Counselors must constantly seek to understand their own prejudices and limitations so as not to impose their values on their clients. It is of the utmost importance that counselors equip themselves with the knowledge and skills they need to address all the dimensions of human behavior. Counselors then will become more proactive in helping to shape a new society, one in which people realize the importance of the mind, body, and spirit connection. By doing this, spirituality—the essence of meaning in our lives—will emerge from the confines of religious doctrine and become the driving force that truly binds the human family together (Lee & Sirch, 1994).

References

American Association of Marriage and Family Therapy. (1985). *Code of ethical principles for marriage and family therapists.* Washington, DC: Author.

American Counseling Association. (1995). *Code of ethics and standards of practice.* Alexandria, VA: Author.

American heritage dictionary of the English language (3rd ed.). (1992). Boston: Houghton Mifflin.

American Psychological Association. (1992). *Ethical principles of psychologists* (rev. ed.). Washington, DC: Author.

Bergin, A. E., & Garfield, S. L. (Eds.). (1994). *Handbook of psychotherapy and behavior change* (4th ed.). New York: John Wiley.

Bergin, A. E., & Jensen, J. P. (1990). Religiosity of psychotherapists: A national survey. *Psychotherapy, 27,* 3-7.

Bergin, A. E., & Payne, I. R. (1991). Proposed agenda for a spiritual strategy in personality and psychotherapy. *Journal of Psychology and Christianity, 10,* 197-210.

Burke, M. T., Hackney, H., Hudson, P., Miranti, J., Watts, G., & Epp, L. (1999). Spirituality, religion, and CACREP curriculum standards. *Journal of Counseling and Development, 77,* 251-257.

Burke, M. T., & Miranti, J. G. (1995). *Counseling: The spiritual dimension.* Alexandria, VA: American Counseling Association.

Chandler, C. K., Holden, J. M., & Kolander, C. A. (1992). Counseling and spiritual wellness. *Journal of Counseling and Development, 71,* 168-176.

Corey, G., Corey, M. S., & Callanan, P. (1993). *Issues and ethics in the helping professions* (4th ed.). Pacific Grove, CA: Brooks/Cole.

Curtis, R. C., & Davis, K. M. (1999). Spirituality and multimodal therapy: A practical approach to incorporating spirituality in counseling. *Counseling and Values, 43,* 199-210.

Faiver, C. M., & O'Brien, E. M. (1993). Assessment of religious beliefs form. *Counseling and Values, 37,* 176-178.

Frame, M. W., & Williams, C. B. (1996). Counseling African Americans: Integrating spirituality in therapy. *Counseling and Values, 41,* 16-28.

Gallup, G. H., Jr., & Begilla, R. (1994, January 20). More find religion important. *The Washington Post,* p. G10.

Gendlin, E. T. (1981). *Focusing.* New York: Bantam.

Gladding, S. (1995). Unpublished paper delivered at the North Carolina Association for Spiritual, Ethical, and

Religious Values in Counseling Conference, Greensboro, NC.

Herlihy, B., & Corey, G. (1996). *ACA ethical standards casebook*. Alexandria, VA: American Counseling Association.

Hinterkopf, E. (1994). Integrating spiritual experiences in counseling. *Counseling and Values, 38,* 165-175.

Ingersoll, R. E. (1994). Spirituality, religion, and counseling: Dimensions and relationships. *Counseling and Values, 38,* 98-112.

Kelly, E. W., Jr. (1994). Counselor preparation: The role of religion and spirituality in counselor education: A national survey. *Counselor Education and Supervision, 33,* 227-237.

Kelly, E. W. (1995). *Spirituality and religion in counseling and psychotherapy*. Alexandria, VA: American Counseling Association.

Lee, C. C., & Sirch, M. L. (1994). Counseling in an enlightened society: Values for a new millennium. *Counseling and Values, 38,* 90-97.

Lovinger, R. J. (1990). *Religion and counseling*. New York: Continuum.

Miranti, J. G. (1998). The spiritual/religious dimension of counseling: A multicultural perspective. In P. B. Pedersen & D. C. Locke (Eds.), *Cultural and diversity issues in counseling* (pp. 117-120). Alexandria, VA: American Counseling Association.

Miranti, J. G., & Burke, M. T. (1998). Spirituality: A source for social change. In C. C. Lee & G. R. Walz (Eds.), *Social action: A mandate for counselors* (pp. 161-176). Alexandria, VA: American Counseling Association.

Myers, J. E., & Truluck, M. (1998). Health beliefs, religious values, and the counseling process: A comparison of counselors and other mental health professionals. *Counseling and Values, 42,* 106-123.

Pedersen, P. (1990). Multiculturalism as a fourth force in counseling. *Journal of Mental Health Counseling, 12,* 93-95.

Prest, L. A., & Keller, J. F. (1993). Spirituality and family therapy: Spiritual beliefs, myths, and metaphors. *Journal of Marital and Family Therapy, 19,* 137-148.

Richards, P. S., & Bergin, A. E. (1997). *A spiritual strategy for counseling and psychotherapy*. Washington, DC: American Psychological Association.

Richards, P. S., & Potts, R. (1995). Using spiritual interventions in psychotherapy: Practices, successes, failures, and ethical concerns of Morman psychotherapists. *Professional Psychology, 26,* 163-170.

Shafranske, E. P., & Malony, H. N. (1996). *Religion and the clinical practice of psychology: A case for inclusion*. Washington, DC: American Psychological Association.

Smith, D. C. (1993). Exploring the religious-spiritual needs of the dying. *Counseling and Values, 41,* 16-28.

Spirituality competencies for counselors. (1995, December). *Counseling Today,* p. 30. (American Counseling Association)

Theodore, R. M. (1984). Utilization of spiritual values in counseling: An ignored dimension. *Counseling and Values, 28*(4), 162-168.

Witmer, J. M., Sweeney, T. J., & Myers, J. E. (1994). A holistic model of wellness and prevention over the life span. *Journal of Counseling and Development, 71,* 140-148.

Worthington, E. L., Jr. (1989). Religious faith across the lifespan: Implications for counseling and research. *The Counseling Psychologist, 17,* 555-612.

CHAPTER THIRTY-NINE

The Potential for Success and Failure of Computer Applications in Counseling and Guidance

JAMES P. SAMPSON, JR.
JOHN W. BLOOM

Computers have been used in counseling for more than three decades. During the 1960s, tests were scored, database searches were completed, and information was delivered through the computer technology of the day. As the cost-effectiveness of computing improved, more diverse applications were developed over time. Today, computers are an essential component of counseling and guidance practice. Applications include assessment; career guidance; maintenance of client records; preparation of case notes, reports, and correspondence; delivery of public presentations, and practice management, to name a few. Newer applications are emerging such as cyber-counseling (Bloom & Walz, 2000) and distance guidance (Sampson, 1999). In addition, the natural higher education extension of guidance into online student affairs and services—including orientation, academic advising, counseling, judicial services, and student activities—also is occurring (Ford, 2000). Instead of focusing on all current computer applications, this chapter deals with applications that are used by clients. Applications related to practice management and student services other than counseling are not covered in this chapter. The chapter begins with an exploration of how computer applications used by clients can contribute to effective counseling and guidance outcomes as well as an exploration of the role of the counselor in computer-assisted service delivery. The chapter continues with an examination of why computer applications tend to succeed or fail. It ends with a description of future actions needed to maximize success and minimize failure.

Potential Contributions of Computer Applications to Counseling and Guidance

Before exploring the potential contributions of computer applications to counseling and guidance, it is important to clarify what is meant by counseling and guidance in this chapter. *Counseling* is used here to imply that a relationship is established between a client and a counselor over time on an individual or group basis for the purpose of helping the client (or groups of clients) to solve or prevent problems. Although guidance also aims to help individuals (or groups of individuals) solve or prevent problems, guidance may or may not involve the establishment of an ongoing relationship between a counselor and a client. *Guidance* is used in this chapter to include the creation and delivery of text, graphic, audio, and video resources in a self-help mode to individuals without counselor intervention as well as the use of resources in a counselor-supported mode as part of a guidance intervention.

Consider the case of Ann, a woman who is working in a rapidly changing industry for an employer that is experiencing increasing global competition. Employee job stress in this situa-

tion generally has increased as a result of increasing work demands from company downsizing.

- Ann may seek individual counseling from a private practitioner to better cope with the stress associated with her job (counseling intervention).

- Ann may seek group counseling on stress management delivered through the employee assistance program offered by her employer (counseling intervention).

- Ann may seek self-help resources on stress management as she experiences the work environment becoming more stressful (self-help guidance intervention).

- After completing an interest and ability self-assessment at a local community college career center library to explore the possibility of a career change to reduce stress, Ann may seek assistance from a counselor to answer questions about subsequent steps in exploring her options (counselor-supported, reactive guidance intervention).

- After asking Ann whether she was finding the information she needed in the community college career center library, a counselor may intervene if and when it is apparent that she was not able to integrate her career self-assessment results into an appropriate plan of action to explore less stressful career options (counselor-supported, proactive guidance intervention).

Counseling and guidance are not mutually exclusive and may be combined in several ways. Information resources that originally were designed for use in a self-help mode also may be used as homework in counseling. After termination in counseling, the client may be encouraged to use self-help resources to continue learning how to cope successfully with complex problems. Receiving information from self-help guidance resources on the circumstances when counseling typically is needed may encourage individuals to seek counseling at appropriate times. Computer applications may become more proactive, indicating to the individual that their pattern of software use differs from typical patterns of effective use and that a brief session with a practitioner may be appropriate (Offer & Sampson, 1999). Such quick and easy access to counseling while using software—the "teachable moment"—may significantly improve the effectiveness of computer applications. Teachable moments occur *while* individuals are using assessment, information, or instructional resources, providing counselors with the opportunity to help individuals immediately process and apply what they are learning to problems they face and decisions they are making. By interacting *during* learning, as opposed to helping individuals reconstruct and clarify issues at subsequently scheduled counseling appointments, counselors participate in more immediate and robust learning experiences with individuals. This is not to suggest that reflection time between the use of resources and counseling no longer is needed; rather, it suggests that adding counselor-client interaction during the teachable moment to existing counseling strategies is a promising opportunity to be explored.

In summary, the use of information is a key element in problem solving. Whereas some individuals can use information resources to solve problems effectively on their own, other individuals need helping relationships with counselors to obtain and use information effectively in problem solving. For the individuals who need counseling, some require only very brief counseling interventions, whereas others need substantial assistance in problem solving. Computer applications can be used to deliver information in both counselor-supported and self-

help modes. The following subsections deal with the potential contribution of computer applications to counseling and guidance.

Computer Applications in Counseling

Computer applications have the potential to contribute to counseling by maximizing the human dimension in counseling and by improving access to counseling services.

Maximizing the Human Dimension in Counseling

Counselors, as humans, possess a mixture of assets and limitations. The typical personality characteristics and the emotional and intellectual capabilities of counselors allow them to develop helping relationships quickly with diverse clients, to conceptualize complex client problems from a variety of theoretical perspectives, and to develop counseling interventions that are designed to meet a variety of evolving client needs. These same counselor characteristics, however, make it difficult to complete simple repetitive tasks. Humans often have difficulty in concentrating when doing repetitive tasks, resulting in less competent performances. For example, consider the difficulty in hand scoring and profiling the hundreds of scales contained in some current interest inventories. The problem is magnified when scoring and profiling inventories for groups of clients, resulting in the need to process information from thousands of scales. In addition to being less competent, humans also get bored easily when completing repetitive tasks. Consider the examples of client orientation to counseling and the delivery of information or instruction that clients need to solve problems. Both of these tasks can involve presenting virtually the same information to many different clients. The problem is that clients might be unable to differentiate between counselors being bored with repetitive tasks and counselors being bored with them as clients, resulting in potential relationship development problems. Repetitive information processing and instructional tasks are better completed by a computer that does not make random information processing errors and does not get bored. Computers have been shown to be effective in completing repetitive tasks in assessment (Sampson, 2000a) and career guidance (Harris-Bowlsbey & Sampson, in press). Because computers also perform repetitive functions at less cost, this use of technology makes more socially responsible use of the limited funds available for counseling. By incorporating computers into the counseling process, counselors can become more fully human by spending more time performing the tasks that are uniquely suited to their characteristics and capabilities and by avoiding tasks that are better suited for computers to complete.

Considering the case of Ann discussed earlier, the counselor's effectiveness was improved by having Ann complete a computer-based orientation to counseling prior to or after their first session, as is done at the *Therapy Online* Web site (www.therapyonline.ca), which offers potential clients a description of services available and answers to questions regarding accessibility, effectiveness, anonymity, results, quality assurance, and research. Completing a computer-based orientation leaves more time with the counselor for clarifying her problem and relationship development. By using the computer to deliver instruction on theory-based principles of stress management, the counselor had more time available to help Ann explore how

family-of-origin issues make it difficult for her to apply the stress management principles she has learned (Sampson & Krumboltz, 1991). By using the computer to administer and score a stress management inventory, as well as to develop a score profile and a narrative description of the results, potential scoring and profiling errors were eliminated and the counselor had more time available to think about how the results of the instrument could be used to clarify the nature of Ann's problems and develop appropriate intervention strategies (Sampson, 2000a).

Improving Access to Counseling Services

The Internet has given people unprecedented access to diverse information and has fostered inexpensive communication worldwide. Counseling delivered through the Internet, also known interchangeably as *cybercounseling* (Bloom & Walz, 2000) or *Webcounseling* (National Board for Certified Counselors [NBCC] and Council for Credentialing and Education, 1997), has the potential to improve clients' access to counseling. Webcounseling has been defined as "the practice of professional counseling and information delivery that occurs when client(s) and counselor are in separate or remote locations and utilize electronic means to communicate over the Internet" (p. 1). Access to counseling services is potentially improved in several ways (Krumboltz & Winzelberg, 1997; Offer & Watts, 1997; Sampson, 1998a, 1999, 2000b; Sampson, Kolodinsky, & Greeno, 1997). Individuals who have difficulty in accessing counseling services because they live in geographically remote areas or have disabilities that reduce their mobility can use the Internet to interact with counselors. Counselors with specialized expertise who are not available locally can be used as therapists or co-therapists to meet unique client needs. The anonymity and convenience afforded by the Internet also may encourage some individuals, who have been reluctant to seek assistance in the past, to now seek the services they need. Once engaged in a cybercounseling process, both client and counselor can interact more frequently and more rapidly than ever was possible when face-to-face appointments had to be scheduled weeks in advance. Finally, the consultation process is facilitated by the Internet in that counselors have much more rapid access to referral sources and consultations even can include client, counselor, and consultant when a medium such as instant messaging is incorporated.

This interaction between counselor and client also can be either asynchronous (via e-mail) or synchronous (via teleconferencing or videoconferencing). Whereas e-mail interaction has the obvious disadvantage of omitting important nonverbal information, the asynchronous nature of the communication has some advantages including providing time between interactions for the client and counselor to reflect on what they read as they consider their responses, the ability to communicate at convenient times during the week as opposed to one scheduled appointment, the creation of a permanent record of the session, and a degree of anonymity that may encourage reluctant clients to seek counseling when they might not have done so if they had to present themselves at counselors' offices (Murphy & Mitchell, 1998).

Cybercounseling using videoconferencing technology more closely approximates traditional face-to-face counseling, allowing both a counselor and a client to perceive and respond to verbal and nonverbal communication. Ques-

tions have been raised about the impact of cybercounseling on the development of the counseling relationship and whether or not face-to-face counseling is equivalent to cybercounseling (Sampson et al., 1997). Determining whether remote videoconference interaction between a counselor and a client in a helping relationship is equivalent to face-to-face interaction is an interesting, but not essential, question. Given our current knowledge, the answer likely is no; face-to-face interaction and videoconferencing are distinct forms of communication. A far more important question is whether remote videoconference interaction between a counselor and a client in a helping relationship assists the client in solving his or her problems effectively (Sampson, 2000b).

The use of synchronous communication over distances to facilitate counselor-client interaction actually has been used successfully for decades in the form of telephone counseling and crisis hotlines. No one has suggested that telephone counseling should completely replace traditional face-to-face counseling, just as no one has suggested that cybercounseling should replace face-to-face counseling. Both telephone counseling and cybercounseling have an appropriate role to play in the overall delivery of counseling services. Our task as a profession is to determine how client characteristics and circumstances interact with the capabilities and limitations of various counseling delivery options (i.e., face-to-face, telephone, and Internet) and to select the delivery option that is most likely to meet client needs.

It is important to note, however, that despite the considerable attention that cybercounseling has received among counselors recently, only a small fraction of current counseling services are delivered over the Internet. An Internet search for the words *online counseling* identified only 93 sites, 46% of which had counseling content, 19% consulting content, 13% therapy content, and 22% "other" content (Welfel, Heinlen, & Rak, 2000). Three reasons likely account for the current limited use of the Internet in delivering counseling services. First, limitations in current data transmission capabilities of the Internet make videoconferencing impractical for many users. This problem likely will improve dramatically in the near future as the technical capacities of the Internet improve. Second, even with ongoing improvements in technology, individuals with limited incomes have difficulty in gaining access to the Internet. Third, potential ethical and legal problems (described later in this chapter) are likely to be at least partially responsible for keeping counselors and clients from widely using this new technology.

Again considering the case of Ann, she could receive counseling for her job stress through cybercounseling. Ann selected a credentialed counselor, specializing in occupational stress and career counseling and residing in a large city, from an Internet-based international counselor directory. Ann accessed the counselor's Web site to help her make a decision about the appropriateness of this counselor given her needs. She received information about the counselor's credentials, the type of issues that clients typically bring to counseling, and how cybercounseling functions including a short video in which the counselor described his theoretical approach to counseling. She also accessed an online verification center, such as *Credential Check* (www.mentalhelp.net/check), to confirm the credentials of the online therapist. After making a decision to proceed, she used her home computer equipped with a television camera to schedule and complete a brief session with the counselor so as to mutually determine whether cybercounseling was, in fact, appropriate in her case. After determining that cybercounseling was appropriate, Ann returned to the counselor's Web site to complete an informed consent form and to schedule her initial session. Counseling then proceeded, with the counselor receiving distance supervision (Christie, 2000; Coursol & Lewis, 2000; Schnieders, 2000) as agreed in the informed consent signed by Ann (Sampson et al., 1997).

Computer Applications in Guidance

Computer applications have the potential to contribute to guidance by maximizing opportunities for learning and by improving access to guidance resources.

Maximizing Opportunities for Learning

Computer applications contribute to individual learning as a result of the interactivity and flexibility of the medium. In comparing the outcomes of using interactive media (e.g., a computer) to those using noninteractive media (e.g., linear print materials, videos), interactive media are more motivational to use because the individual maintains at least partial control over the selection and sequencing of information (Peterson, Sampson, & Reardon, 1991). Guidance resources can be helpful only when they actually are used; therefore, maintaining user motivation is essential if these resources are to be used effectively. Computer applications also contribute to learning by the flexible options that users have for obtaining information. For example, many computer-assisted career guidance systems present information in multiple text, graphic, audio, and video formats, allowing users to select not only the information they want but also the media for receiving the information (Sampson, Reardon, et al., 1998). Fully featured, computer-based guidance resources allow individuals to select the media formats that best fit their typical learning styles, further contributing to the potential effectiveness of these resources.

At present, personal computer (PC)-based computer applications typically are more interactive and fully featured than their Internet-based computer counterparts. The more sophisticated programming and the full integration of text, graphics, audio, and video available on many PC-based guidance applications enhance the motivational features and learning flexibility of this technology relative to Internet-based applications, which currently are dominated by simple programming and the delivery of flat text and graphic files. At present, time delays often encountered in downloading files can reduce user motivation to access these resources. These differences are likely to be only temporary, however, as the technical capacity of the Internet improves, allowing the downloading of sophisticated software with flexible multimedia features.

Returning to the case of Ann, she could obtain self-help resources on the Internet using the local community college career center Web site resources on strategies for coping with job stress. She also could use the same Web site to obtain information on determining when it is appropriate to change jobs. After using this information, she decided to search for another position. The Web site also indicated circumstances when adults typically need assistance to resolve their career problems. Based on this information, Ann decided to go to the commu-

nity college career center to have her resumé critiqued prior to applying for a new position (Sampson, 1999).

Improving Access to Guidance Resources

While the use of the Internet to deliver counseling is minimal and controversial at present, the use of the Internet to deliver resources in guidance is extensive and relatively noncontroversial. Career guidance, where information historically has played a key role, has made extensive use of PC-based software (Harris-Bowlsbey & Sampson, in press). Numerous Internet Web sites exist for career guidance (Riley-Dikel, 1998; Sampson, Lumsden, Carr, & Rudd, 1999). Exploring employment and career options has become one of the most common uses of the Internet. Assessment, another typically information-intensive function, also has made considerable use of PC-based computer applications (Sampson, 2000a). Although slower to develop than career guidance, assessment resources are beginning to emerge on the Internet (Oliver & Zack, 1999). As with counseling, this improved access to guidance resources means that geographic distance, mobility limitations, and reluctance to be seen accessing resources no longer are barriers to obtaining resources. Rather than needing to travel to a career center, a public library, or a bookstore, individuals now can access assessment, information, and instructional resources through the Internet from their places of residence or work. Ethically, however, cybercounselors always must keep in mind the debilitating aspects of the "digital divide," as evidenced by U.S. Department of Commerce data indicating that households with incomes of $75,000 or higher are 20 times more likely to have access to the

Internet, and 9 times more likely to have computers at home, than are households at the lowest income levels (Lee, 2000).

Assessments, information, and instruction are delivered on the Internet through Web sites. A Web site is the total collection of Web resources, including a home page and external links, for either an organization or an individual (Sampson et al., 1997). Web sites provide access to resources and links, and they can be categorized as integrated or independent. An integrated Web site is the distance guidance component of an organization delivering guidance services in one or more actual physical locations. An integrated Web site extends the traditional resources and services available to individuals. Whereas some integrated Web sites provide only advertisements of traditional services and limited downloading of flat text files, other integrated Web sites clearly identify the intended audience, the potential needs of users, and the delivery of resources or links to independent Web sites that provide the resources needed. Independent Web sites offer virtual career resources and services that are not associated with a specific service delivery organization in one or more locations (Sampson, 1999). Examples of independent Internet Web sites may be found in Riley-Dikel (1998) and Sampson and colleagues (1999).

Well-designed Internet Web sites operate equally well in self-help and counselor-supported modes. Higher functioning individuals can use the navigation aids and descriptions of resources to locate the information they need, seeking assistance from counselors when they have difficulty in locating or using the information they need. With lower functioning individuals, counselors provide readiness assessment screening, orientation to the software applications, and follow-up to ensure appropriate use of the applications by clients.

Recalling again the case of Ann, she could have learned of the availability of the local community college career center from the human resources department of her employer. After reviewing descriptions of the services available for adults considering career changes, she completed an Internet-based career self-assessment measure. Bringing her assessment results with her to the career center, she asked a staff member for assistance in locating information to help her further explore occupational and employment options that would be satisfying yet less stressful than her current job. While subsequently using information on resumé preparation in the career center, a staff member noticed that Ann appeared confused when the staff member asked whether Ann was finding the information she needed. After reviewing her needs, Ann and the staff member collaboratively decided that counseling was needed to help Ann deal with family-of-origin and self-esteem issues associated with articulating her skills on her resumé (Sampson, Peterson, Reardon, & Lenz, in press).

The Role of the Counselor in Computer-Assisted Resource and Service Delivery

The role of the counselor in computer-assisted resource and service delivery is to ensure, to the greatest extent possible, that clients have access to quality computer applications that meet well-defined needs and are used in an effective manner. Three key counselor behaviors that contribute to the effectiveness of computer-assisted counseling are (a) screening clients to ensure that they are reasonably capable of benefiting from computer applications, (b) orienting clients who need counseling support to the features of computer applications so that they learn how systems can be best used to meet their needs, and (c) following up with clients who need support to verify that systems have been used effectively and that they have plans for applying what they have learned in problem solving and decision making (Sampson, 1997). Additional counselor roles in promoting effective computer-assisted resource and service delivery include ensuring that (a) the software is valid and reliable in terms of the assessment, information, and instruction delivered; (b) the software contains no inherent bias that would have any adverse impact on a particular group of individuals; (c) the lack of financial resources does not impose an unreasonable barrier to accessing counseling resources or services; (d) adequate precautions have been taken to maintain the confidentiality of any client data that are transmitted or stored on a computer; (e) the system is implemented within the organization responsible for delivering resources and services so that staff use the software in a cost-effective manner; and (f) the design and use of the system are evaluated regularly (Sampson, 1998a; Sampson & Pyle, 1983; Walz, 1984; Watts, 1986).

Potential Reasons Why Computer Applications Will Succeed

There are several reasons why computer applications are likely to succeed in contributing to counseling and guidance outcomes. These reasons include freedom of access by individuals, the evolution of the Internet into the "information highway," the apparent effectiveness of existing applications, and the growth of distance learning. These reasons highlight just a few key factors and are not exhaustive. Before exploring these potential reasons for success, it is important to briefly describe the computer applications that likely will be in use in the future. Current computer applications in counseling tend to be primarily PC or Internet based. This distinction between PC- and Internet-based applications likely will disappear as the Internet and PCs merge, with perishable data and software upgrades delivered over the Internet and with rapidly accessible stable data and installed software residing on PCs.

Freedom of Access by Individuals

With PC-based software, individuals had to physically go to counseling service delivery organizations to gain access to software. The Internet substantially improves access to counseling and guidance software by allowing easy access to self-help resources and counseling services from individuals' workplaces or residences. This freedom of access, coupled with the existing demand for employment and career development information on the Internet, may create an increasing demand for software. This public demand for accessing software applications on the Internet may create an increased willingness on the part of policy makers and private sector developers to invest in the development of quality resources and services to meet public needs.

The Evolution of the Internet Into the Information Highway

Individuals with PCs at their workplaces or residences tend to be affluent and well educated. Despite the enormous popularity of PCs, this technology still is not used by the general public. The PC is viewed as "something different" that requires computer skills to use. This situation is changing as the Internet evolves into the information highway. Made possible by the ongoing improvement of computing and communication capabilities, the information highway integrates the Internet with multimedia-based PCs, cable television networks, and wired and wireless telephone networks (Sampson et al., 1997). As individuals use their televisions to communicate using both audio and video and to interactively obtain information along with their favorite shows, the information highway will provide access to the Internet for the vast majority of our society. As was the case with cable television, improved technology will create demand for additional content. Again, public demand for self-help resources and counseling services may create an awareness of the need to fund the development of Internet-based resources and services.

Apparent Effectiveness of Existing Applications

Despite initial predictions by counselors that clients would not like, or benefit from, computer applications in counseling, computers have been shown to be an effective element of computer-assisted career guidance (Sampson, Rudd, & Reardon, 1998) and testing (Sampson, 2000a). The general public perception that computer applications can be a good

resource for obtaining and using information increases demand for this technology. Again, consistent public demand is a key element in obtaining the capital investment necessary to develop and deliver quality Internet-based guidance resources and counseling services.

The Growth of Distance Learning

Distance learning involves the delivery of instruction at a distance to students using multimedia technology to present course content. It also involves the use of communication technology to promote group discussions among students and an instructor as well as promote individual discussions between a student and an instructor. Students use the Internet to submit assignments, complete examinations, and engage in collaborative work on group assignments with other students. Distance learning may include student contact with a local learning mentor to provide encouragement, foster motivation, and help students explore issues and answer questions related to course content. Distance learning is being advocated for the same reasons that cybercounseling is being advocated, namely, increasing access to previously underserved populations. Distance learning is being advocated far more strongly than is cybercounseling due to economic considerations. Some educators and policy makers view distance learning as a strategy for saving money by not having to build additional facilities to serve the increasing number of students seeking higher education.

Computer applications in counseling and guidance will be increasingly in demand as a result of distance learning. Distance learning necessitates distance guidance. *Distance guidance* can be defined as "the delivery of self-assessment, information, and instruction in remote locations, with or without practitioner assistance, for the purpose of assisting individuals in making informed career, educational, training, and employment decisions" (Sampson, 1999, p. 244). Distance guidance can be used to serve both distance learning and traditional, classroom-based learning. The same guidance site that serves a student in a distant city can serve a student in his or her room in the residence hall. Whereas many distance learning systems provide academic advising and auditing programs that match courses taken with programs of study available, distance guidance software and cybercounseling are needed for helping students to relate programs of study to career options and, subsequently, to follow through with their choices by seeking employment or further education. Understanding how programs of study relate to future goals is critical to maintaining motivation for students at a distance who might be isolated from the traditional supportive environment provided on campus. Again, the demand for distance guidance may create a willingness to invest in counseling and guidance software necessary for the effectiveness of distance learning. For this to occur, however, counselors need to be proactive in helping policy makers to understand how distance guidance potentially contributes to positive outcomes in distance learning.

Potential Reasons Why Computer Applications Will Fail

Just as there are reasons why computer applications are likely to succeed, there are equally compelling reasons why this technology will fail or at least not achieve the potential that is possible. These reasons include implementation problems and various ethical concerns about the design and use of computer applications.

Implementation Problems

Irrespective of the innate quality of software, the ultimate effectiveness of computer applications in counseling and guidance is constrained by the quality of the process used by an organization to implement technology. Common implementation problems that limit effectiveness include a lack of staff participation in decision making, poor integration of new computer applications with existing resources and services, inadequate staff training, and poor evaluation (Sampson, 1996, 2000a; Sampson & Norris, 1997). Software that is poorly implemented will not meet the intended needs of users. Users typically are unable to differentiate between bad software design and bad software implementation. Users may conclude that a particular software application (or category of software application) is ineffective when in fact the application is adequate but the implementation is poor. Such negative feedback from users may cause policy makers and private sector developers to mistakenly discontinue investing financial resources in software that could be very useful with proper implementation.

Ethical Concerns

A variety of ethical concerns have been noted related to PC- and Internet-based computer applications in counseling and guidance. The confidentiality of client records and data transmission can be breached when inappropriate individuals gain access to client data. Assessments, information, and instruction may be attractively presented but inherently invalid and potentially harmful. Clients might be unable to differentiate valid and invalid software, especially given the general positive public perceptions about the accuracy of computer-based information. Whereas some individuals need no assistance in using software, other individuals might need, and might not receive, the assistance they require to make effective use of software. Counselors who are overworked or inadequately trained might misuse or become dependent on software such as computer-based test interpretation. Individuals might have difficulty in gaining access to computer applications as a result of having limited financial resources. In cybercounseling, the counselor might be unaware of important location-specific circumstances in a remote location and might misinterpret client data or fail to recognize relevant issues. Some resource and service providers on the Internet fail to indicate appropriate credentials necessary for the client to distinguish between qualified and unqualified practitioners. Most self-help resources provide no recommendations regarding the circumstances when self-help is inappropriate and counseling is needed. Individuals may use self-help resources, experience difficulty, and then inappropriately conclude that they cannot be helped when in fact counseling might have been effective. Also, accessing the Internet from a residence shared with other persons might not provide the auditory and visual privacy necessary for establishing and maintaining a counseling relationship (Bartram, 1997; Bloom, 2000; Carson & Cartwright, 1997; Krumboltz & Winzelberg, 1997; Lee, 2000; Offer & Watts, 1997; Oliver & Zack, 1999; Robson & Robson, 1998; Sampson, 1998b, 1999; Sampson et al., 1997).

Future Actions Needed to Maximize the Potential for Success

Whereas computer applications appear to have been more of a success than a failure to date, the following actions are recommended to maximize success and minimize failure. First, counselors should expend the most effort on cybercounseling activities that have the greatest potential for success. Delivering brief cybercounseling interventions in response to individual concerns that arise while using Internet-based self-help software would be less controversial and more likely to be financially supported than would cybercounseling that aims to replace traditional scheduled counseling appointments. Initial experimentation in this area could use telephone counseling with the cost borne by the users or an organization with a mission to support specific users. Fully developed cybercounseling then could begin as soon as enough videoconferencing capacity is generally available to support establishing the service. Counselors would need to be fully credentialed in traditional counseling as well as trained in the resource being used by the client and trained in the cybercounseling process. Experimentation with cybercounseling that replaces traditional scheduled appointments should be linked to distance learning to increase the chances for financial support afforded by the strong interest among policy makers in distance learning. By linking cybercounseling development and evaluation with existing resources and policy initiatives, there is a greater chance that the funding will be available to adequately explore the capacity of this technology in counseling.

Second, counselors need to take the initiative in contributing to software development in counseling and guidance. This is particularly important now in view of the rapid growth of the Internet. Counselors' first priority should be contributing to the development of integrated Web sites for the organizations and clients they serve. Counselors' second priority should be contributing to self-help information access delivered through PCs and independent Internet Web sites (Sampson, 1999). Given current public demand for resources and services, especially Internet-based resources and services, software will be created with or without counselor input. Software will be much more likely to integrate successfully with counseling if counselors are actively involved in the design.

Third, counselors need to evaluate both the design and use of computer applications. There is a need to operationally define successful and unsuccessful outcomes and then evaluate system design and use in relation to these outcomes. Good evaluation will contribute to improved software designs and enhanced strategies for integrating software into counseling and guidance. If adequate evaluation data are not available, then policy makers and private sector developers will be less likely to invest at levels necessary for the development of quality software.

Fourth, counselors need to evaluate and revise the initial standards that have been developed for the design and delivery of computer applications (Bloom, 1998; Offer & Sampson, 1999). Issues that initially were anticipated as potentially serious might not be significant problems and vice versa. Standards need to offer reasonable protection to the public while not being so restrictive as to limit innovation in the development of new resources and services.

Fifth, counselors need to acquire and refine the competencies necessary to use computer ap-

plications effectively. Counselor training needs to be established at both pre-service and in-service levels (Bloom, 2000; Sampson, 1999, 2000a, 2000b). Ongoing in-service training is particularly important given the rapid developments that are taking place with the Internet. Training content needs to include the design and content of typical computer applications, strategies for integrating software into counseling and guidance, and evolving standards for software design and use.

Sixth, counselors also need to take an active part in discussions regarding the credentialing required for cybercounseling. The information available to consumers on the credentials of practitioners delivering cybercounseling varies from comprehensive to nonexistent (Bloom, 2000; Sampson et al., 1997). Counselors need to be proactive in promoting credentialing standards that offer reasonable protection to the public from incompetent or fraudulent practitioners while not taking a protectionist stance that unnecessarily restricts client access to services.

References

Bartram, D. (1997). Distance assessment: Psychological assessment through the Internet. *Selection and Development Review, 13,* 15-19.

Bloom, J. W. (1998). The ethical practice of Webcounseling. *British Journal of Guidance and Counselling, 26,* 53-59.

Bloom, J. W. (2000). Technology and Webcounseling. In H. Hackney (Ed.), *Practice issues for the beginning counselor* (pp. 183-202). Boston: Allyn & Bacon.

Bloom, J., & Walz, G. (Eds.). (2000). *Cybercounseling and cyberlearning: Strategies and resources for the millennium.* Alexandria, VA: American Counseling Association.

Carson, A. D., & Cartwright, G. F. (1997). Fifth-generation computer-assisted career guidance systems. *Career Planning and Adult Development Journal, 13,* 19-40.

Christie, B. S. (2000). *Theoretical tenets of cybersupervision: Implications and outcomes* [Online]. Available: cybercounsel.uncg.edu

Coursol, D., & Lewis, J. (2000). *Cybersupervision: Close encounters in the new millennium* [Online]. Available: cybercounsel.uncg.edu

Ford, D. (2000, April). Providing student services online. *Counseling Today*, p. 5. (American Counseling Association)

Harris-Bowlsbey, J., & Sampson, J. P., Jr. (in press). Computer-based career planning systems: Dreams and realities. *Career Development Quarterly.*

Krumboltz, J. D., & Winzelberg, A. (1997). Technology applied to learning and group support for career-related concerns. *Career Planning and Adult Development Journal, 13,* 101-110.

Lee, C. (2000). Cybercounseling and empowerment: Bridging the digital divide. In J. Bloom & G. Walz (Eds.), *Cybercounseling and cyberlearning: Resources and strategies for the millennium* (pp. 85-93). Alexandria, VA: American Counseling Association.

Murphy, L., & Mitchell, D. (1998). When writing helps to heal: E-mail as therapy. *British Journal of Guidance and Counselling, 26,* 21-32.

National Board for Certified Counselors and Council for Credentialing and Education. (1997). *Standards for the ethical practice of Webcounseling* [Online]. Available: www.nbcc.org/ethics/wcstandards.htm

Offer, M., & Sampson, J. P., Jr. (1999). Quality in the content and use of information and communications technology in guidance. *British Journal of Guidance and Counselling, 27,* 501-516.

Offer, M., & Watts, A. G. (1997). The Internet and careers work. *NICEC Briefing.* Available: www.crac.org.uk (National Institute for Careers Education and Counselling, Cambridge, UK)

Oliver, L. W., & Zack, J. S. (1999). Career assessment on the Internet: An exploratory study. *Journal of Career Assessment, 7,* 323-356.

Peterson, G. W., Sampson, J. P., Jr., & Reardon, R. C. (1991). *Career development and services: A cognitive approach.* Pacific Grove, CA: Brooks/Cole.

Riley-Dikel, M. (1998). Exemplary Web sites. In J. Harris-Bowlsbey, M. Riley-Dikel, & J. P. Sampson, Jr. (Eds.), *The Internet: A tool for career planning* (pp. 11-28). Columbus, OH: National Career Development Association.

Robson, D., & Robson, M. (1998). Intimacy and computer communication. *British Journal of Guidance and Counselling, 26,* 33-41.

Sampson, J. P., Jr. (1996). *Effective computer-assisted career guidance* (Occasional Paper No. 2, 2nd ed.). Tallahas-

see: Florida State University, Center for the Study of Technology in Counseling and Career Development.

Sampson, J. P., Jr. (1997, April). *Helping clients get the most from computer-assisted career guidance systems.* Adapted from a paper presented at the Australian Association of Career Counselors Seventh National/International Conference, Brisbane, Australia. Available: www.career. fsu.edu/techcenter/councda1.html

Sampson, J. P., Jr. (1998a). The Internet as a potential force for social change. In C. C. Lee & G. R. Walz (Eds.), *Social action: A mandate for counselors* (pp. 213-225). Greensboro, NC: ERIC/CASS.

Sampson, J. P., Jr. (1998b). Potential problems and ethical concerns. In J. Harris-Bowlsbey, M. Riley-Dikel, & J. P. Sampson, Jr. (Eds.), *The Internet: A tool for career planning* (pp. 31-37). Columbus, OH: National Career Development Association.

Sampson, J. P., Jr. (1999). Integrating Internet-based distance guidance with services provided in career centers. *Career Development Quarterly, 47,* 243-254.

Sampson, J. P., Jr. (2000a). Computer applications. In C. E. Watkins, Jr., & V. L. Campbell (Eds.), *Testing and assessment in counseling practice* (2nd ed., pp. 517-544). Mahwah, NJ: Lawrence Erlbaum.

Sampson, J. P., Jr. (2000b). Using the Internet to enhance testing in counseling. *Journal of Counseling and Development, 78,* 348-356.

Sampson, J. P., Jr., Kolodinsky, R. W., & Greeno, B. P. (1997). Counseling on the information highway: Future possibilities and potential problems. *Journal of Counseling and Development, 75,* 203-212.

Sampson, J. P., Jr., & Krumboltz, J. D. (1991). Computer-assisted instruction: A missing link in counseling. *Journal of Counseling and Development, 69,* 395-397.

Sampson, J. P., Jr., Lumsden, J. A., Carr, D. L., & Rudd, E. A. (1999). *A differential feature-cost analysis of seven Internet-based career information delivery systems (CIDS)* (Technical Report No. 24). Tallahassee: Florida State University, Center for the Study of Technology in Counseling and Career Development. Available: www.career.fsu.edu/techcenter/computerapplications_ feature-cost.html

Sampson, J. P., Jr., & Norris, D. S. (1997). An evaluation of computer-assisted career guidance implementation effectiveness. *Career Planning and Adult Development Journal, 13,* 75-86.

Sampson, J. P., Jr., Peterson, G. W., Reardon, R. C., & Lenz, J. G. (in press). Using readiness assessment to improve career services: A cognitive information processing approach. *Career Development Quarterly.*

Sampson, J. P., Jr., & Pyle, K. R. (1983). Ethical issues involved with the use of computer-assisted counseling, testing, and guidance systems. *Personnel and Guidance Journal, 61,* 283-287.

Sampson, J. P., Jr., Reardon, R. C., Reed, C., Rudd, E., Lumsden, J., Epstein, S., Folsom, B., Herbert, S. M., Johnson, S., Simmons, A., Odell, J., Rush, D., Wright, L., Lenz, J. G., Peterson, G. W., & Greeno, B. P. (1998). *A differential feature-cost analysis of seventeen computer-assisted career guidance systems* (Technical Report No. 10, 8th ed.). Tallahassee: Florida State University, Center for the Study of Technology in Counseling and Career Development. Available: www.career.fsu.edu/techcenter/computerapplications_feature-cost.html

Sampson, J. P., Jr., Rudd, E., & Reardon, R. C. (1998). *Computer-assisted career guidance: Research and evaluation bibliography.* Tallahassee: Florida State University, Center for the Study of Technology in Counseling and Career Development. Available: www.career.fsu.edu/techcenter/resbibnew.html

Schnieders, L. (2000). *From a bug in the ear to a byte in the eye* [Online]. Available: cybercounsel.uncg.edu

Walz, G. R. (1984). Role of the counselor with computers. *Journal of Counseling and Development, 63,* 135-138.

Watts, A. G. (1986). The role of the computer in careers guidance. *International Journal for the Advancement of Counselling, 9,* 145-158.

Welfel, E., Heinlen, K., & Rak, C. (2000, March). *Buyer beware: Data on Webcounselors' (non)compliance with ethical standards.* Paper presented at the annual conference of the American Counseling Association, Washington, DC.

CHAPTER FORTY

Character, Personal Responsibility, Emotional Intelligence, and Self-Esteem

Preventive Approaches to Counseling

EDWIN L. HERR

SPENCER G. NILES

Counseling during the past century has become more comprehensive in the settings where it is provided, the problems that it addresses, and the populations that it serves. In parallel, the theories of counseling that evolved during the 20th century also have grown in complexity as they have sought to explain the formation of personality, self-classification mechanisms, motivation, anxiety and depression, and the process of decision making. Many variables have been used to explain why people do what they do and ignore other actions. Often, the influences of values, genetics, aptitudes, interests, instrumental and associative learning, environmental reinforcements, family belief systems, and/or experiences with peer groups are used as the mechanisms to explain why persons have problems in living and, therefore, their need to have access to counselors.

Within such a context, this chapter reviews some emerging explanatory systems for at-risk behavior, including a resurgence of concern about personal character and responsibility as it affects individual choice as well as new perspectives on life-role salience, personal competence, and emotional intelligence. Related to these concepts, relevant counseling roles, the use of psychoeducational models and preventive approaches, pertinent assessment devices, and related techniques are discussed in the chapter.

Personal Character and Responsibility

One of the recurring issues explicit in counseling theory has to do with the role of personal character and responsibility in the decisions people make and in the actions that result. Increasingly, this issue arises in the areas of alcohol and drug abuse, AIDS, road rage, violence, and other contemporary phenomena. Explanations for the involvement of persons in such problems of living stress that most of the problems that people bring to counselors are not pathological or organic. Rather, they are seen as matters of personal competence and the degree to which people have knowledge or skills that permit them to cope with or master the various developmental tasks, transitions, or crises they face across the life span. Relevant to such issues is that one of the rationales for mental health counseling, in particular, is that when the 10 major causes of death are considered in rank order, at least 7 of these causes are directly related to lifestyle, personal behavior, and/or personal choices. Examples of such causes of death are

motor vehicle accidents, accidents other than those involving motor vehicles, cirrhosis of the liver, suicide, AIDS, and heart disease (Herr, 1998). One also could argue that although road rage, violence and battering, teenage pregnancy, sexually transmitted disease, and alcohol and drug dependence are not necessarily leading causes of death, they are in fact major social problems in which personal behavior, personal choices, and lifestyles are implicated.

Indeed, in arguing for improved behavioral health in schools, Kolbe, Collins, and Cortese (1997) of the Centers for Disease Control and Prevention stated,

> The most serious and expensive health and social problems that afflict the United States today are caused in large part by behavioral patterns established during youth (e.g., tobacco use, high-fat diets, drug and alcohol abuse, violence, and sexual risk behaviors). Health problems spawned by these behaviors fuel unnecessary health care costs, and unattended health and social problems among America's young people seriously erode their health status, educational achievement, and quality of life. Young people who suffer from physical illness or injury, mental health problems, hunger, pregnancy, alcohol and drug use, or fear of violence are less likely to learn irrespective of efforts to improve educational methods, standards, or organizations. (p. 256)

Whether or not one wishes to consider many of the causes of death, social dysfunction, or problems of living as issues of character, they are, at some level, issues of personal responsibility for one's physical and psychological health and for that of others. In such instances, counseling intersects with concepts of behavioral health and cross-cultural perspectives that suggest that wellness and unwellness, illness and many accidents, and interpersonal conflict and violence are linked to one's feelings of self-esteem, depression, or other mind-body connections.

As attempts to understand individual problems of living shift from the external environments that people occupy to their internal environments—their attitudes, values, impulse control, worldviews, interpersonal sensitivity, and so on—there is a new and growing respect for individual responsibility, for what the individual does, for achievements, and for self-care and concern for others.

Essentially, the qualities of individual responsibility and behavior point to the importance of developing "good character." Aristotle suggested that good character involves displaying qualities such as self-control, moderation, generosity, and compassion. In referring to character education in the schools, Lickona (1991) noted,

> When we think about the kind of character we want for our children, it's clear that we want them to be able to judge what is right, care deeply about what is right, and then do what they believe to be right—even in the face of pressure from without and temptation from within. (p. 51)

The two values essential for developing good character are respect and responsibility. Lickona noted that respect primarily provides direction regarding what we *should not* do (e.g., do not hurt others), whereas responsibility provides direction concerning what we *should* do (e.g., do help others). Respect and responsibility are values that are a matter of moral obligation, rather than mere preference, around which good character is formed.

During the late 1980s and early 1990s, many school systems attempted to remain value neutral. Many educators thought that a value-neutral stance was the most appropriate response to cultural pluralism. Discussions of values education typically led to heated arguments concerning *whose values* should be taught. The escalation in problems of living experienced by youths (e.g., vandalism, stealing, bullying, bigotry) has led many to reconsider the value-neutral stance taken by many schools. Many parents and educators, whether liberals or conservatives, now realize that there is no such thing as value-free education. Each interaction and every behavior serves as a concrete manifestation of individual values and beliefs. When values associated with developing good character and personal responsibility are not espoused by counselors and teachers, the values vacuum often will be filled with conflict and confusion. Thus, many school systems now focus on which values will be taught and how well these values will be taught. In most instances, the values identified emanate from universal moral values such as treating all people with respect, respecting equality, and treating all people justly. Universal values such as these provide a moral compass that guides individual behavior and enhances respect and personal responsibility toward self and others. Moreover, these values provide fertile ground for developing positive self-esteem and emotional intelligence as well as a coherent framework for making individual choices.

Individual Choice

As totalitarian approaches to government decrease around the world, it is assumed that individual power to choose and to be responsible become more possible and more powerful. Individual quests for spirituality, for uniqueness, for creativity, and for an enhanced quality of living are seen as growing by many contemporary observers, but so is meanness to others, a lack of civility, violence, and other socially dysfunctional behaviors. Thus, an increase in personal power to choose how one will react to others, to the larger society, or to one's own well-being can be manifested in positive or negative ways.

As individual freedom to choose becomes more available across gender, racial, ethnic, and age groups in the United States, so does one's responsibility to choose prudently and to do so with respect for others. Bennett (1993) suggested that one has options from which to choose.

> To respond is to answer. . . . Correspondingly, to be "responsible" is to be "answerable," to be "accountable." . . . Taking responsibility—being responsible—is a sign of maturity. . . . In the end, we are answerable for the kinds of persons we have made of ourselves. (p. 185)

According to Bennett,

> "That's just the way I am!" is not an excuse for inconsiderate or vile behavior, nor is it even an accurate description, for we are never "just" what we are. As Aristotle was among the first to insist, we "become" what we are as persons by the decisions that we ourselves make. . . . Responsible persons are mature persons who have taken charge of themselves and their conduct, who "own" their actions and "own up" to them—who "answer" for them. (pp. 185-186)

Decisions that persons make about the daily behavioral options with which they are faced tend not to be spontaneous and unconnected but rather are linked to their philosophies of life, to their views of their own internal or external loci of control, to their sense of self-efficacy to cope with the daily onslaught of personal encounters, and to the types of options that require them to take action. At the root of such challenges are recurring allusions in the professional literature to self-esteem, personal responsibility, and control. In a major sense, these terms are interactive; when individuals feel good about themselves, they are able to accept their characteristics, to systematically attempt to understand and improve selected ones, to be optimistic and resilient in their approach to life, and to believe that they are in control. Of equal importance, people of high self-esteem are likely to exhibit personal responsibility for themselves and toward others. They are able to exert control over their lives and to accept personal responsibility for how they behave.

Self-Esteem

Self-esteem, as an important ingredient of individual responsibility and choice making, has been defined in many ways. One of the interesting perspectives available is to consider self-esteem as a major aspect of individual cognitive regulation. As Ford (1987) suggested,

> Every problem-solving activity, decision, or choice requires selection from among options representing alternative goals or means for controlling behavior. This implies that there must be criteria for making such selections. Evaluative thoughts provide such criteria. . . . Three major kinds of evaluative thoughts have been studied. One kind is self-evaluative thoughts. Every behavior episode provides people with information about themselves. From such information, people develop concepts and propositions about themselves as parts of their behavior episode schemata. These concepts and propositions are often termed the *self-concept* or *self-system* of which self-evaluations are components. Self-

evaluations of one's ability or opportunity to function as a causal agent are sometimes called *self-efficacy expectations, causal-attributions,* or *control beliefs.* Self-evaluations of one's self- or social acceptability are often termed *self-worth* or *self-esteem.* (pp. 31-32, italics in original)

Dealing with issues of self-esteem may involve the counselor with the application of cognitive behavior therapy or client-centered counseling or, indeed, a constructivist approach that allows individuals to clarify their own search for meaning and to reframe and rescript their views of personal responsibility for their actions. Because a lack of self-esteem frequently stems from an individual's negative evaluations of self-worth, such evaluations and the bases for them might need to be confronted and alternative ways of viewing himself or herself must be examined. Because self-esteem is so fundamental to an individual's way of viewing others, the world, and the utility of an individual's continuing to live and be purposeful, the counselor must create in his or her communication with the client a relationship that is characterized by caring, trust, understanding, honesty, sincerity, acceptance, liking, and interest. These relationship variables might sound so familiar that they are passed over lightly as old and dated concepts; however, the point is that these types of interpersonal elements are precisely what has been missing from the client's life and have brought him or her to a lack of self-esteem or self-worth. These types of counseling variables are the healing ingredients by which people can be helped to self-disclose, exhibit trust in others, and communicate the feelings of pain and loneliness that underlie and presage dealing with problems of self-esteem.

Johnson (1986) indicated that "the human species seems to have a *relationship imperative:* we desire and seek out relationships with oth-ers, and we have personal needs that can be satisfied only through interacting with other humans" (p. 1, italics in original). Johnson extended the point to suggest that the basis for personal well-being is effective interpersonal skills. In his view, human development follows a pattern of expansion of interdependence with others, individual identity is built out of our relationships with other people, and psychological health depends almost entirely on the quality of relationships with others. Johnson also contended that each of us needs to be confirmed as a person by other people.

Confirmation consists of responses from other people in ways that indicate that we are normal, healthy, and worthwhile. Being disconfirmed consists of responses from other people suggesting that we are ignorant, inept, unhealthy, unimportant, or of no value and, at worst, that we do not exist. (p. 3)

A basic truth associated with nearly all activities is that the degree of success associated with any activity is directly proportional to how well the people who are involved in it get along with each other. Thus, those people who lack interpersonal skills are likely to experience high rates of failure in their activities. That the leading cause of death for young men is gunshot wounds rather than disease or accidents provides clear evidence that many people have not learned how to interact constructively with others. By providing relationships characterized by caring, trust, empathic understanding, and the like, counselors model the types of behaviors their clients need to learn to interact effectively with others, enhance the probability that they will be successful in their activities, and increase their self-esteem.

In a world of loneliness, rapid change, discrimination, complex stressors, and psychological and physical abuse, many individuals never have learned or been systematically exposed to interpersonal skills that allow them to develop self-worth, identity, and effective relationships with others. Thus, their behavioral repertoires may be very limited in how to act in an interdependent world, or they may feel so limited in their internal locus of control—their ability to manage their lives—that they attribute everything that happens to them to fate or external control by other people. The sense of stress, powerlessness, frustration, and lack of personal worth that results frequently may be manifested in vandalism, aggressiveness, uncontrolled anger, violence, bullying, chemical abuse, and other self-destructive or antisocial acts.

In counseling those for whom life is a negative experience and for whom relationships with others do not lead to feelings of personal confirmation or a sense of community, a major counselor role is to help in the acquisition of the basic interpersonal skills by which to initiate, develop, and maintain caring and productive relationships.

The learning of interpersonal skills typically is accomplished by the application of a psychoeducational model. Whether implemented on an individual basis or in a group context, clients have to be helped to understand why the basic skills to be learned about interpersonal behavior are important in alleviating the problems they are experiencing, what the basic components of the skills are, the need to practice such skills and get feedback about their progress in implementing the skills, and the persistence required to make it an authentic part of their personal behavior. In implementing such a psychoeducational approach to interpersonal development, counselors likely will use modeling, reinforcement, homework, and other techniques to sustain clients' motivation to learn these skills so as to alter the feelings of poor self-esteem and unworthiness that are central motivations for whatever self-destructive or antisocial behaviors are exhibited.

The lack of self-esteem or effective interpersonal relationships, in addition to resulting in self-destructive or antisocial acts, may be reflected in emotional manifestations such as shyness, anxiety, a reluctance to take risks, and an unwillingness to be accountable for one's behavior. These and similar feelings restrict people from being who they want to be. The way to control such feelings is to take charge of behavior that will alter these feelings or stimulate action that is managed and self-directed. Every individual operates within the limits of time, resources, and other restrictions on what can be done. However, the only limits on attitudes or purposeful behavior within whatever external constraints exist are those that are self-imposed. *Doing* changes attitudes. This perspective, too, becomes a major ingredient of building self-esteem. It is the essence of what Glasser (1984) called *control theory.*

The central notion of control theory is that regardless of how people feel, they have some control over what they do. The underlying perspective is as follows: "Nothing we do is caused by what happens outside of us. If we believe that what we do is caused by forces outside of us, we are acting like dead machines, not living people" (Glasser, 1984, p. 1). Thus, people have the opportunity to choose how they will feel and how they will react or behave in response to life's unfolding events. If individuals want to change total behaviors, then they must choose what to *do* and what to *think* differently.

As individuals do so, their *feelings* about themselves, about the situation, and about others also are likely to change.

The key in such behavior change is acknowledging the freedom of choice involved in how one thinks, feels, and behaves. Once this is acknowledged, people can shift from what Glasser (1998) called an *external control psychology* (in which people blame others for their situations and try to control others, often through guilt, punishment, and shame) to *choice theory* (in which people take responsibility for their thoughts, feelings, and behaviors).

Counseling Techniques

As suggested earlier, within or as adjuncts to individual counseling of persons for individual responsibility, there are techniques that counselors can use. One of the major approaches is the use of psychoeducational models focused on remediation or prevention.

Psychoeducational models can be used for remediation of skill deficits already apparent in the dysfunctional behavior of adolescents and adults or for the prevention of behavioral disorders likely to ensue in the absence of appropriate social behavior, planning skills, or other skills. Such intervention strategies rest on conceptualizations of mental dysfunctions as other than organic, as behavioral and learned, and as either susceptible to change or preventable.

There are many approaches to the implementation of psychoeducational models. Each such approach involves the counselor's provision of structured learning including the teaching of skills; homework and practice; the use of films, videos, and other audiovisual materials; simulations and direct participation in information seeking; and role-playing. One of the classic approaches to psychoeducational models is that of Goldstein, Sprafkin, Gershaw, and Klein (1980), who proposed the following:

> Structured learning consists of (1) modeling, (2) role-playing, (3) performance feedback, and (4) transfer of training. The trainee is shown numerous specific and detailed examples (either live or on audiotape, videotape, film, or filmstrip) of a person (the model) performing the skill behaviors we wish the trainee to learn (i.e., modeling). The trainee is given considerable opportunity and encouragement to rehearse or practice the behaviors that have been modeled (i.e., role-playing) and provided with positive feedback, approval, or praise as the role-playing of the behaviors becomes more and more similar to the behavior of the model (i.e., performance feedback). Finally, the trainee is exposed to procedures which are designed to increase the likelihood that the newly learned behaviors will in fact actually be applied in an able manner in class, at home, at work, or elsewhere (i.e., transfer of training). (p. 15)

Such an approach to psychoeducational structured learning lends itself to helping persons make concrete the ingredients of character, responsibility, self-esteem, and control so that they not only can talk about such behaviors but also can practice and implement them. Psychoeducational approaches and notions of prevention as an important mental health strategy have become prominent at similar points of history and continue to be important national issues.

Albee (1982), a major spokesman for preventive rather than remedial approaches to problems in living, suggested the following nearly 20 years ago:

> If your purpose is to reduce the incidence of the different conditions or lifestyles we refer to as mental disorders . . ., there are several strategies

for accomplishing our purpose. The first of these is to prevent, to minimize, or to reduce the amounts of the organic factors that sometimes do play a role in causation (e.g., lead poisoning, brain damage from automobile accidents). . . . A second strategy . . . involves the reduction of stress. (p. 1046) . . . Another area . . . involves increasing the competence of young people to deal with life's problems, particularly with the problems of social interactions, and the development of a wide range of coping skills. . . . Increases in support systems and self-esteem have been shown to reduce psychopathology. (p. 1045) . . . Those who argue against the concept of mental illness do not deny the existence of behavior that can be called abnormal or pathological. They simply hold that abnormal behavior can be learned through perfectly normal processes—and what can be learned can be unlearned or prevented. (p. 1050)

Albee (1982) also argued that a competence model must replace the defect or illness model of mental disturbance. A competence model contends that all individuals, whether youths or adults, have adaptive potential and competencies that can be enhanced by mental health professionals by strengthening individual coping skills, self-esteem, and social support systems.

The importance of devising interventions to implement the strategies identified by Albee (1982) cannot be overstated. The issues identified earlier (e.g., substance abuse, incidents of violent behavior, teen pregnancy) make it clear that many adults and young people lack important coping skills and have not developed their adaptive potential and competencies. It can be argued that many of the inter- and intrapersonal difficulties that people experience result from attempts to participate in life roles for which they are not developmentally prepared. Thus, psychoeducational and preventive approaches can be applied to helping clients develop their readiness for effective life-role participation.

Life-role readiness can be defined as the possession of the knowledge, attitudes, and skills necessary for effective life-role participation (Niles, 1998). For example, effective parenting requires possessing basic knowledge about child development, possessing a positive attitude toward parenting as a life role, and possessing the skills necessary for providing basic child care. Likewise, life-role readiness related to the leisure role requires possessing basic knowledge about specific leisure activities, possessing a positive attitude toward leisure as a life role, and possessing the basic skills necessary for participation in specific leisure activities.

Counseling for Life-Role Readiness

The "social elements that constitute a life are arranged in a pattern of core and peripheral roles" (Super, Savickas, & Super, 1996, p. 128). The core roles played by an individual provide the primary outlets for identity development and are essential to the individual's life satisfaction. To foster the development of life-role readiness, counselors can encourage their clients to identify the life roles that are important to them (i.e., their life-role salience) and to increase their awareness concerning the contextual factors (e.g., family, culture, economics, new occupational options) influencing their life-role salience (Super, Sverko, & Super, 1995).

Life Role Salience

Encouraging clients to increase their self-awareness concerning life-role salience is useful because life-role salience provides the motivating force behind the development of life-role readiness (Super et al., 1996). That is, if a life role is important to someone, then it is likely that the individual will engage in the behaviors necessary to become prepared for taking on that life role. Likewise, when salience is low, there often is little motivation for developing the requisite behaviors for effective participation in that role. Developing life-role readiness requires clients to identify their salient life roles and to examine the relationship between their goals and their current life-role activities. When life-role readiness "gaps" exist (i.e., when individuals are playing roles for which they are not prepared), counselors can draw on the psychoeducational interventions (e.g., structured learning) to help their clients acquire the skills necessary for more effective life-role participation. For example, counselors can model effective disciplinary techniques for parents lacking skills related to disciplining their children. When there is low participation in life roles that are important to clients, counselors can explore the reasons for low participation and, when appropriate, use cognitive-behavioral techniques to encourage the clients to consider increasing participation in the salient life roles.

Counselors can begin the process of exploring life-role salience by asking clients to respond to questions such as the following. How do you spend your time during a typical week? How important are the different roles of life to you? What do you like about participating in each of the life roles? What life roles do you think will be important to you in the future? What do you hope to accomplish in each of the life roles that will be important to you in the future? What life roles do members of your family play? What do your family members expect you to accomplish in each of the life roles?

Counselors also can use the Salience Inventory (Super & Nevill, 1986) as a starting point for initiating a discussion of life-role salience. The Salience Inventory measures the relative importance of five life roles (student, worker, citizen, homemaker, and leisurite) on three dimensions (one behavioral and two affective). The behavioral component, Participation, assesses what the individual does or has done recently in each of the life roles. The first affective component, Commitment, requires the inventory taker to indicate how he or she feels about each of the five life roles. The second affective component, Values Expectations, requires the respondent to indicate the degree to which there will be opportunities, at present or in the future, to express important values in each of the life roles.

Once information about life-role salience is acquired, counselors can help clients to construct strategies for preparing for their salient life roles. For example, if the life role of a parent is expected to be salient in the future, then ways in which to plan and prepare for that role can be identified. Counselors also can encourage clients to examine areas of potential role conflict and discuss strategies for coping with excessive demands from multiple life roles.

Contextual Factors Influencing Life-Role Salience

Obviously, patterns of life-role salience are significantly influenced by immediate (e.g., family, cultural heritage, level of acculturation) and distal contextual factors (e.g., economics, environmental opportunities for life-role participation; Blustein, 1994). However, many people lack an awareness of the ways in which contextual factors (e.g., the dominant culture, the individual's culture of origin) interact with identity development to shape life-role salience (Blustein, 1994).

The Influence of the Dominant Culture

Often, people simply "inherit" patterns of life-role salience that are passed on from the dominant culture. Such inheritances can be problematic when they are embedded with beliefs based on gender and racial stereotypes. For example, researchers have consistently found gender differences that coincide with traditional sex-role expectations in life-role salience (e.g., women participating more in home and family and expecting more from this life role than do men [Niles & Goodnough, 1996]). Women who have high salience for the worker role are placed at an obvious disadvantage in the workforce by such traditional expectations. Also, men limit their opportunities for participating in the home and family when they adhere to traditional expectations for life-role salience. Raising clients' awareness of the influence of the dominant culture on life-role salience will make them less likely to allow beliefs reflecting racist and sexist attitudes to influence their beliefs about life-role salience.

The Influence of Culture of Origin

Discussions related to the influence of the dominant culture on life-role salience also can lead to discussions that focus on how clients' cultural backgrounds influence their viewpoints on life-role salience. By discussing the ways in which culture influences life-role salience, clients become aware of how their cul-

tural backgrounds influence their life-role salience and learn about differing patterns in role salience across cultures. In these discussions, clients can identify how they perceive and interpret the role expectations emanating from their cultures of origin and how these expectations influence their decisions as to whether particular life roles are important. Particular attention can be paid to exploring how these expectations influence clients' understanding of the behaviors required for effective role performance.

One specific activity that may provide opportunities for discussing these topics was suggested by Borodovsky and Ponterotto (1994). They identified the family genogram as a useful tool for exploring the interaction among family background, cultural prescriptions, and career planning. The genogram provides a tool for tracking career decisions across generations and for identifying sources of important career beliefs and life themes that students have acquired.

Personal Competence and Emotional Intelligence

From the view taken in this chapter, most of the problems that people bring to counselors are matters of personal competence and the degree to which people have knowledge or skills that permit them to cope with or master the various developmental tasks, transitions, and crises they face across the life span. Personal competence can be labeled and described in many ways. Goleman (1995) recently described *emotional intelligence* as fundamental to personal competence and responsibility to self and others. He argued that the abilities that make up emotional intelligence should be taught to children and should be the subject of prevention programs and, certainly, of counseling. In Goleman's view, an expanded model of what it means to be intelligent puts emotions at the center of aptitudes for living. They are the mediating variables that allow individuals to pursue other cognitive forms of intelligence appropriately and effectively. In essence, emotional intelligence is a different way of being smart. It includes self-awareness and impulse control, persistence, zeal and self-motivation, and empathy and social deftness. Goleman contended that these are the qualities that mark people who excel in real life, whose intimate relationships flourish, and who are stars in the workplace. These also are the hallmarks of character and self-discipline, of altruism and compassion, and of maturity and responsibility. Emotional intelligence can be taught to children, adolescents, and adults in specific courses, psychoeducational approaches, and individual counseling.

One can find parallels between concepts of emotional intelligence and terms such as *personal flexibility, life development skills, life-role readiness, deliberate psychological education,* and particularly *personal competence.*

Amundson (1989), a Canadian counseling psychologist, suggested, "Competence refers to a state of being as well as a state of doing. A competent person is one who has the capacity (or power) to adequately deal with emerging situations" (p. 1). Amundson's model of competence has eight components. Competency in almost any job demands some capability in (a) sense of purpose; (b) self-other and organizational understanding; (c) communication and problem-solving skills; (d) theoretical knowledge and understanding of facts and procedures; (e) practical experience; (f) a supportive organization context that, at a minimum, has

elements that allow people to achieve without wasting time and resources; (g) a support network that allows competent people to give and receive help as part of maintaining their competency; and (h) self-confidence including acceptance of oneself, the strength to learn from mistakes, and perseverance.

In essence, then, a preventive approach to counseling, whether group or individual, presupposes that the elements of personal competence, emotional intelligence, the skills needed to handle problems in living, and the behaviors on which relationship enhancement or positive interpersonal relationships rest can be known and understood. Such a notion implies that the knowledge, attitudes, and skills central to life coping skills or to personal responsibility can be identified; used as the content of preventive structured learning or psychoeducational approaches or as targets of other therapeutic interventions; and thereby learned, changed, or strengthened. These assumptions are implicit in models of the increasingly common counseling language of assertiveness training, anger management, stress inoculation, obesity or smoking control, decision-making training, and other forms of planned psychosocial development.

Conclusions

This chapter has examined the emerging attention to personal character and personal responsibility in individual decision making. It discussed the important implications of concepts such as emotional intelligence, self-esteem, life-role readiness, and personal competence as mediators of the choices that people consider and make. The chapter also discussed the applications of individual counseling, psychoeducational models, and preventive approaches to advancing the development of skills underlying personal character and responsibility.

References

Albee, G. W. (1982). Preventing psychopathology and promoting human potential. *American Psychologist, 37,* 1043-1050.

Amundson, N. E. (1989). *Competence: Components and development.* Unpublished manuscript, University of British Columbia.

Bennett, W. S. (Ed.). (1993). *The book of virtues: A treasury of great moral stories.* New York: Simon & Schuster.

Blustein, D. (1994). "Who am I?" The question of self and identity in career development. In M. L. Savickas & R. W. Lent (Eds.), *Convergence in career development theories* (pp. 139-154). Palo Alto, CA: Consulting Psychologists Press.

Borodovsky, L. G., & Ponterotto, J. G. (1994). A family-based approach to multicultural career development. In P. Pedersen & J. Carey (Eds.), *Multicultural counseling in schools* (pp. 195-206). Boston: Allyn & Bacon.

Ford, D. H. (1987). *Humans as self-constructing living systems: A developmental perspective on behavior and personality.* Hillsdale, NJ: Lawrence Erlbaum.

Glasser, W. (1984). *Control theory: A new explanation of how we control our lives.* New York: Harper & Row.

Glasser, W. (1998). *Choice theory: A new psychology of personal freedom.* New York: HarperCollins.

Goldstein, L. P., Sprafkin, R. P., Gershaw, N. J., & Klein, P. (1980). *Skill-streaming the adolescent: A structured learning approach to teaching prosocial skills.* Champaign, IL: Research Press.

Goleman, D. (1995). *Emotional intelligence.* New York: Bantam.

Herr, E. L. (1998). *Counseling in a dynamic society: Contexts and practices for the 21st century.* Alexandria, VA: American Counseling Association.

Johnson, D. W. (1986). *Reaching out: Interpersonal effectiveness and self actualization.* Englewood Cliffs, NJ: Prentice Hall.

Kolbe, L. J., Collins, J., & Cortese, P. (1997). Building the capacity of schools to improve the health of the nation: A call for assistance from psychologists. *American Psychologist, 52,* 256-265.

Lickona, T. (1991). *Educating for character.* New York: Bantam.

Niles, S. G. (1998). Developing life-role readiness in a multicultural society: Topics to consider. *International Journal for the Advancement of Counselling, 20,* 71-77.

Niles, S. G., & Goodnough, G. E. (1996). Life-role salience and values: A review of recent research. *Career Development Quarterly, 45,* 65-86.

Super, D. E., & Nevill, D. D. (1986). *The Salience Inventory.* Palo Alto, CA: Consulting Psychologists Press.

Super, D. E., Savickas, M. L., & Super, C. M. (1996). The life-span, life-space approach to careers. In D. Brown & L. Brooks (Eds.), *Career choice and development: Applying contemporary theories to practice* (3rd ed., pp. 121-178). San Francisco: Jossey-Bass.

Super, D. E., Sverko, B., & Super, C. M. (Eds.). (1995). *Life roles, values, and careers: International findings of the work importance study.* San Francisco: Jossey-Bass.

CHAPTER FORTY-ONE

Optimization of Behavior

Promotion of Wellness

JANE E. MYERS

THOMAS J. SWEENEY

J. MELVIN WITMER

Although counseling as an activity has been traced from antiquity, counseling as a formal profession emerged as recently as the latter part of the 20th century (for a review of the historical development of the profession, see Sweeney's chapter in this volume [Chapter 1]). Antecedents to the emergence of the profession included societal needs, reformer movements in education and mental health, federal legislation directed to serve specific populations, and the coalition of organizations concerned with the guidance movement in this country. As early as the late 19th and early 20th centuries, there were calls for addressing vocational, educational, and mental health needs in a more systematic planned way. Although there have been positive steps toward achieving a more universal acceptance of proactive developmental interventions in the lives of both young and older persons (e.g., *Healthy People 2010* [U.S. Department of Health and Human Services, 2000), it is far from common in practice.

During the last decades of the 20th century, the changing and complex nature of society, increases in violence and person abuse (see Garrett's chapter in this volume [Chapter 32]), and competition in the mental health market-place led to an increasing adoption of a medical, illness-based model among health care professionals, including counselors. Frustration with the failure of the illness-based model for both monetary and human suffering reasons, however, has called attention to a need for alternative approaches. New advocates for change are being found among business, industry, insurance, and government agency personnel who see rising costs as a compelling reason to seek relief.

Research suggesting the life span impact of negative events on human development, coupled with a myriad of empirical studies emphasizing the importance of prevention, led some leaders in the counseling profession to reclaim our developmental roots. In so doing, the philosophies of development and prevention have been combined in a new paradigm—*wellness*.

Myers (1992) defined wellness as the cornerstone of the counseling profession. Although many authors have written about this concept, it was Sweeney and Witmer (1991) and Witmer and Sweeney (1992) who integrated cross-disciplinary research with counseling paradigms to define the meaning of wellness for counselors. Through the development of a theoretical model and an assessment instrument, research, and practice, these authors defined and promoted a practical approach to helping people optimize their behavior and achieve wellness across the life span (Myers, Sweeney, & Witmer, 2000).

In this chapter, wellness is defined and the roots of wellness are explored. A model of wellness based in counseling theory is described, and the application of this model in clinical practice is discussed. Finally, the significance of wellness as an emerging paradigm for service delivery is examined, and the importance of wellness as the future paradigm for counseling is presented.

Defining Wellness

The term *wellness* has roots in ancient Greek philosophy, where the concepts of cure and hygiene were personified by Panaceia and Hygeia, each representing an approach to health. Panaceia represented treatment of illness through the use of medicine, and Hygeia represented the ways of preventing illness through healthy living (Witmer, 1996). The concept of mind and body unity has been found in both ancient Greek and Eastern philosophies. For example, the Greek word *halos* (i.e., holistic) posits the idea of wholeness and wellness and, hence, the term *holistic wellness*.

Dunn (1961), who is widely credited as being the "architect" of the modern wellness movement, defined wellness as "an integrated method of functioning which is oriented toward maximizing the potential of which the individual is capable" (p. 4). He also suggested that counselors were in a unique position to help individuals achieve high-level wellness (Dunn, 1977). However, physicians and public health educators have been perceived to be at the forefront in this arena. For example, Hettler (1984), a public health physician, is viewed by some as the father of the modern wellness movement. Hettler views wellness as a process whereby individuals make choices for a successful existence. Similarly, Ardell (1988) defined wellness as a proactive approach to life that optimizes one's potential.

Archer, Probert, and Gage (1987), writing from a psychological perspective, defined wellness as "the process and state of a quest for maximum human functioning that involves the body, mind, and spirit" (p. 311) or what Maslow (1970) would term an intrinsic motivation toward self-actualization and fulfillment. More recently, Myers and colleagues (2000) defined wellness as

> a way of life oriented toward optimal health and well-being in which body, mind, and spirit are integrated by the individual to live life more fully within the human and natural community. Ideally, it is the optimum state of health and well-being that each individual is capable of achieving. (p. 252)

Clearly, what is common across definitions of wellness is a concern for optimizing human behavior and functioning and for integrating body, mind, and spirit as part of this process. To the extent that counselors choose philosophies of wellness, they also must infuse strategies for optimizing development throughout their clinical practices.

Models of Wellness as a Foundation for Practice

A number of models have been proposed to explain the myriad of factors that combine to create healthy functioning. Most such models are based in physical health professions and place primary emphasis, although by no means sole emphasis, on physiological aspects of development. As such, they provide only minimal guidance for counselors. The Wheel of Wellness, however, is based in Adler's individual psychology and incorporates a holistic perspective that counselors may find most useful (Myers et al., 2000). The wheel is described next, followed

by a discussion of strategies for applying the model in clinical practice.

Sweeney and Witmer (1991) and Witmer and Sweeney (1992) first proposed a holistic model of wellness and prevention over the life span based on the writings of Adler (1927/ 1954), Maslow (1970), and others who studied characteristics of healthy persons. This model incorporates the results of research and theoretical perspectives from personality, social, clinical, health, and developmental psychology as well as stress management, behavioral medicine, psychoneuroimmunology, ecology, and contextualism.

The Wheel of Wellness model proposes the significance of five life tasks as central to healthy functioning. These tasks are depicted in a wheel with spokes that are interrelated and interconnected. The five tasks are (1) spirituality, (2) self-direction, (3) work and leisure, (4) friendship, and (5) love. The life task of self-direction includes 12 additional components: sense of worth, sense of control, realistic beliefs, emotional awareness and coping, problem solving and creativity, sense of humor, physical fitness, nutrition, self-care, stress management, gender identity, and cultural identity. The model is ecological in that the life tasks interact dynamically with a variety of life forces including, but not limited to, family, community, religion, education, government, media, and business/industry. Global events, whether of natural (e.g., floods, famines) or human (e.g., wars) origin, have an impact on the life forces and life tasks depicted in the model. The model is shown graphically in Figure 41.1, and the various components are described in what follows. Support for the definitions and more extensive descriptions of research studies and results are found in Myers and colleagues (2000).

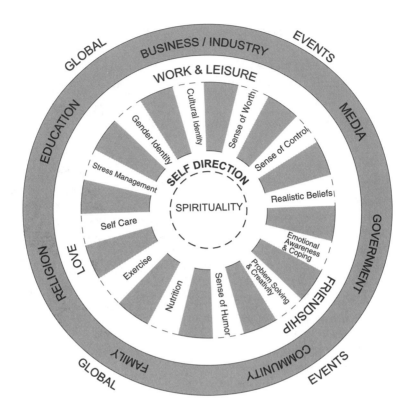

Figure 41.1. The Wheel of Wellness
SOURCE: © 1998, J. M. Witmer, T. J. Sweeney, & J. E. Myers.

Changes in one area of wellness affect other areas in both positive and negative directions. Several recent studies provide empirical support for the interaction among various components of the Wheel of Wellness (Seaward, 1995) as well as evidence that different components of wellness are more or less salient at different points in the life span (Ryff & Heidrich, 1997). Healthy functioning occurs on a developmental continuum, and healthy behaviors at any one point in life affect subsequent development and functioning as well. Gender differences in many of the components of wellness and cultural differences also have been identified. Thus, although the life tasks are presented here as discrete, a concern for holism suggests that they be considered together in understanding healthy behavior. The definitions here are necessarily brief, and the interested reader is referred to Myers and colleagues (2000) for more extended discussions of each concept.

Life Task 1: Spirituality

Spirituality is defined as an awareness of a being or force that transcends the material aspects of life and gives a deep sense of wholeness or connectedness to the universe. A distinction is made between spirituality (a broad concept representing personal beliefs and values) and religiosity (a narrower concept that refers to institutional beliefs and behaviors). Religiosity is a public matter, often expressed in group religious participation, whereas spirituality is more of a private issue that may or may not be expressed publicly. Recent studies suggest that there is a significant positive relationship among spirituality (of which religion is only one part), mental health, physical health, life satisfaction, and wellness (Lindgren & Coursey, 1995; Westgate, 1996).

Life Task 2: Self-Direction

Self-direction is the manner in which an individual regulates, disciplines, and directs the self in daily activities and in pursuit of long-range goals. It refers to a sense of mindfulness and intentionality in meeting the major tasks of life.

Sense of worth. Sense of worth is variously referred to in the literature as self-concept, self-esteem, and self-worth. High self-esteem results when "we consider aspects of our life as important and . . . we have the confidence to fulfill our expectations" (Hattie, 1992, p. 54).

Sense of control. The results of numerous studies (e.g., Beckingham & Watt, 1995; Daniels & Guppy, 1994) indicate that people experience positive outcomes when they perceive themselves as having an impact on what happens to them and experience negative outcomes (e.g., depression) when they perceive a lack of personal control. Perceived control is associated with emotional well-being, successful coping with stress, better physical health, and better mental health over the life span.

Realistic beliefs. Epictetus stated that "people are disturbed not by things but by the view which they take of them" (quoted in Ellis, 1984, p. 200). Healthy people are able to process information accurately and perceive reality as it is rather than as they wish it to be. People who have realistic beliefs are able to accept themselves as imperfect.

Emotional awareness and coping. Self-actualizing people have been described as spontaneous in their behavior and emotions and are able to experience a range of both positive and negative affect such as anger, anxiety (fear), sadness, guilt, shame, disgust, interest/excitement, love/compassion, and happiness/joy.

Problem solving and creativity. Intellectual stimulation, including problem solving and creativity, is necessary for healthy brain functioning and, hence, quality of life across the life span (i.e., "use it or lose it"). Problem-solving appraisal has been correlated with anxiety, depression, and overall psychological adjustment. Creativity has been identified as a universal characteristic of self-actualizing people, all of whom demonstrate originality, a special type of creativeness, inventiveness, and problem-solving ability (Maslow, 1970).

Sense of humor. Humor, a cognitive and emotional process, includes both recognition and appreciation of humorous stimuli and creation of humorous stimuli. Especially when accompanied by laughter, humor causes the skeletal muscles to relax, boosts the immune system, increases heart rate, stimulates circulation, oxygenates the blood, massages the vital organs, aids digestion, and releases chemicals (endorphins) into the brain that enhance a sense of well-being. Humor facilitates the enjoyment of positive life experiences and has a positive effect on physical health.

Nutrition. There is a clear relationship between what we eat and our health, moods, performance, and longevity. The eating and drinking habits of Americans have been implicated in 6 of the 10 leading causes of death including the fact that one in three Americans is considered to be overweight.

Exercise. Regular physical activity is viewed as essential in the prevention of disease and enhancement of health as well as for healthy aging. Exercise increases strength as well as self-confidence and self-esteem.

Self-care. Choosing to develop safety habits (e.g., exercising, preventive medical and dental care, wearing seat belts, avoiding harmful substances including those in the environment) improves quality of life and extends longevity, whereas failure to engage in these preventive health habits leads to declines in physical functioning and increased mortality.

Stress management. Stress affects both psychological and physiological functioning and has a specific depressant effect on immune system functioning. Persons who are stress resistant experience more positive and beneficial immune system responses, greater resistance to psychosocial stressors, a more internal locus of control, more positive mental health, and greater physical health.

Gender identity. Gender identity refers to subjective feelings of maleness or femaleness and is culturally constructed or defined. Gender-role socialization, a process that begins at birth and continues throughout the life span, results in culturally appropriate gender-role behaviors being rewarded for both males and females. Gender differences in gender-role behavior have been linked to both wellness and illness in adulthood.

Cultural identity. Culture may be broadly defined as "a multidimensional concept that encompasses the collective reality of a group of people" (Lee, 1996, p. 11). Cultural identity, a concept that incorporates racial identity, acculturation, and an appreciation for the unique aspects of one's culture, is positively related to well-being. Cultural identity affects self-perceived health and wellness given that concepts of health differ according to culture.

Life Task 3: Work and Leisure

Work serves the major functions of economic purposes, psychological purposes, and social benefits (Herr & Cramer, 1996) and was considered by Adler (1927/1954) to be the most important task for maintenance of life. Adler further defined work as any activity that is useful to the community, whether for monetary gain or otherwise. Work satisfaction—comprised of challenge, financial reward, co-worker relations, and working conditions—is one of the best predictors of longevity and perceived quality of life. Leisure activities (e.g., physical, social, intellectual, volunteer, creative) have a positive effect on self-esteem and perceived wellness. Life satisfaction also is influenced by leisure congruence, defined as the selection of leisure activities consistent with one's personality type.

Life Task 4: Friendship

Adler (1927/1954) considered social interest as innate to human nature, noting that we all are born with the capacity and need to be connected with each other. This motivation is reflected in the need for frequent positive interactions with the same persons and the search for a long-term, stable, and caring support network. There is a strong positive connection between friendship quality and sense of well-being including both physical and mental health.

Life Task 5: Love

Characteristics of healthy love relationships include the ability to be intimate, trusting, and self-disclosing with another person as well as the ability to both receive and express affection with significant others. The life task of love also necessitates having a family or family-like support system that has the following nine characteristics: shared coping and problem-solving skills; commitment to the family; good communication; encouragement of individuals; expression of appreciation; religious/spiritual orientation; social connectedness; clear roles; and shared interests, values, and time.

Applying the Wheel of Wellness in Counseling

Our suggestions for using the Wheel of Wellness in counseling arise from years of clinical experience and from use of the wheel in workshops, seminars, and classes with counselors and other professionals. We have found that four phases or steps comprise a natural process that affects self-understanding and helps to commit clients to choosing healthy behaviors: (1) introduction of the Wheel of Wellness model including a life-span focus; (2) formal and/or informal assessment based on the model; (3) intentional interventions to enhance wellness in selected areas of the wheel; and (4) evaluation, follow-up, and continuation of Phases 2 through 4.

Phase 1: Introduction of the Wheel of Wellness Model

The first step in use of the Wheel of Wellness typically is to define wellness, introduce the model, and explain how a focus on healthy living can contribute to overall well-being. The interaction of the components of the model is an important concept when presenting the wheel. Change in any one area can contribute to or create changes in other areas, and these changes can be for the better or for the worst. We emphasize the point that wellness is a choice and that each choice made toward wellness empowers the client toward even greater happiness and life satisfaction by enhancing overall well-being.

We encourage our clients to view the model as a round sphere or globe with spirituality in the center. If one's sense of spirituality is healthy, then the middle of the sphere is round and full and provides a firm foundation or core for the rest of the components of wellness. If one's sense of spirituality somehow is flat, then the rest of the sphere cannot be firm and round. Similarly, the tasks of self-direction function metaphorically like the spokes in a wheel. So long as they are strong, the wheel can roll along solidly through time and space. If one or more spokes are defective, as in the broken spokes of a bicycle, then the wheel is unable to move smoothly through time and space. It is, in effect, similar to a wheel that is out of balance as it travels roughly along the continua of time and space.

The Wheel of Wellness represents the components of wellness over the life span, and attention to each component has consequences that multiply over time. For those who make wellness choices, the cumulative effect over the life span is one of increasing wellness in all dimensions, thereby contributing to quality of life and longevity. We encourage clients to take a life-span perspective on their total wellness, reviewing the impact of prior choices in each dimension of wellness and projecting the future impact of choices made at this time.

Phase 2: Informal and Formal Assessment of the Components of the Wheel of Wellness

Assessment of the components of the Wheel of Wellness requires a procedure for systematically viewing each dimension and measuring one's wellness on a continuum from not well to high-level wellness. We consider health to be a neutral state in which disease is absent. High-level wellness, on the other hand, is a deliberate state in which the process of making choices toward greater wellness becomes self-perpetuating. The purpose of assessment is to provide a basis for developing a personal wellness plan and beginning the process of ensuring that change is for the better, with any lifestyle changes designed to contribute to greater total wellness.

A global self-report assessment of a client's functioning in each of the components of the Wheel of Wellness can be obtained by asking the client to rate his or her overall wellness in each dimension on a scale of 1 to 10, with 1 being a *very low* level of wellness and 10 being a *high* level of wellness. Once clients have completed their self-ratings, we ask them to reflect on the scores to determine themes and patterns and to confirm that these ratings are accurate in terms of how they see their wellness at this point in time.

In addition to or in place of an informal assessment, wellness in each dimension may be assessed using the Wellness Evaluation of Lifestyle (Myers, Sweeney, Witmer, & Hattie, 1998), a paper-and-pencil measure that assesses each of the dimensions of wellness and provides composite scores for the tasks of self-direction and total wellness. The Wellness Evaluation of Lifestyle has been normed on more than 6,000 persons—including adolescents, young and midlife adults, and older adults—and has good psychometric properties (Hattie, Myers, & Sweeney, 2000). Profiles may be plotted showing graphically the relationship between scores on each dimension. Clients are encouraged to reflect on their scores, determine how representative the scores are of their total wellness (i.e., how well the scores reflect their perceptions of their total wellness), and then reflect on the patterns of their high and low scores. They are encouraged to select one or more of their low scores as areas for which they would like to develop personal wellness plans. We attempt to build on assets found within the profile by emphasizing attributes that can help to strengthen those found less satisfactory by clients.

Phase 3: Intentional Interventions to Enhance Wellness—Developing a Personal Wellness Plan

Once wellness in each dimension has been assessed either informally or formally, we ask clients to choose one or more areas of wellness that they would like to change and improve. We then work to co-construct a personal wellness plan in each targeted area. The plan begins with a restatement of the definition of wellness for that particular dimension, followed by a rating scale consisting of the numbers 1 through 10. Clients are asked to circle (in writing) the number reflecting their wellness in this area. The next step is the development of a written behavioral wellness plan. Included are objectives for change, methods to be used to effect change, and resources that will be employed as the plan is implemented. If other persons are to be involved in the plan in some way, then that fact is noted. For example, if a client chooses to increase his or her level of exercise but does not enjoy exercising alone, then we would discuss ways in which to select and involve a partner in the exercise plan.

Phase 4: Evaluation and Follow-Up

Finally, a discussion of evaluation procedures and time lines is an important part of the behavioral plan. The client should be encouraged to commit to an ongoing plan for regular and systematic evaluation, with identified markers that signify progress in making change. For wellness dimensions such as exercise, nutrition, and self-care, it might be easier to list and identify markers of change (e.g., exercised three times this week for 20 minutes each time,

ate breakfast daily, lost 2 pounds per week). For other areas, it might be more difficult to identify the process and outcomes of the change process. We have found, for example, that feedback from friends and family is a good indicator that efforts to enhance one's sense of humor are having positive results, whereas feedback from clients themselves is necessary to determine when cognitive techniques (e.g., thought stopping, challenging one's irrational thoughts) are having an impact on irrational belief systems. We encourage clients to develop both short- and long-range plans to improve their wellness and to use their counselors as resources for enhancing the change process.

Wellness and Counseling in the Future: The Case for a New Paradigm

More than half, and as many as two thirds, of all premature deaths in the United States are due to lifestyle factors that can be modified (Shannon & Pyle, 1993; U.S. Department of Health and Human Services, 1990, 2000). Although more than 75% of health care dollars are spent to treat people with chronic diseases, less than 1% of federal funds and 2% of state funds are spent to prevent these diseases from occurring (National Association of Social Workers, 1995). In fact, the total costs of illness increased from 5% to 12% of the gross national product during the 30-year period from 1960 to 1990 (U.S. Department of Health and Human Services, 2000). There is increasing recognition that the high cost of illness can be largely offset through an emphasis on prevention.

The federal response to escalating health care costs was described in the reports, *Healthy*

People 2000 and *Healthy People 2010,* which set health promotion and disease prevention goals for the nation (U.S. Department of Health and Human Services, 1990, 2000). By 1996, only two thirds of the original goals had shown any improvement, and none had been totally met (Kaufmann, 1997). Clearly, there is a need for wellness-oriented paradigms to emerge as alternatives to the medical model. In fact, wellness is increasingly emphasized in business and industry as a cost-saving measure while also being a strategy to enhance human potential.

Advocacy for this paradigm, however, no longer is for professional counselors alone to claim. Nurses, psychologists, social workers, health educators, and others have their own rationales for why they are the logical practitioners to whom others should turn for expertise in the evolving political area of health care. We have witnessed presentations by all of these groups—some in hospital settings, others in educational and community meetings—advocating for their versions of what wellness represents and how they can meet the needs of others through wellness programming. The question for us is the following: Are we to work under the leadership and supervision of others in these settings, or shall we take a leadership role in educating and implementing a developmental, comprehensive model applicable to persons of all ages and in all settings?

We have at least three compelling reasons for embracing a proactive stance toward the wellness paradigm such as that described in this chapter. First, the failure of the current health care delivery system to meet the needs of Americans and the public pressure for health care reform are well documented (Zis, Jacobs, & Shapiro, 1996). Traditional delivery systems have failed both economically and in terms of

care to meet the needs of millions of individuals who are uninsured or underinsured. Congress, state legislatures, and insurers are desperate to find a way out of the current dilemma.

Second, in response to these conditions, a variety of programs have emerged that represent new directions. In medical care, for example, Dean Ornish has successfully promoted a nonsurgical, nonpharmacological approach to reversing heart disease, a program that has been so successful as to receive funding from Medicare (Sternberg, 1997). The success of this program lies in the use of nontraditional "therapies" including stress management, techniques for improving communication and interpersonal relationships, modification of lifestyle factors (e.g., exercise, diet), meditation, and communication with a personally defined higher power. Ornish's program has been credited with savings of up to $10,000 per patient in addition to saving lives. Our challenge is to promote counseling programs that can show similar effectiveness in other areas of wellness that have equally valuable results.

Third, and perhaps most important to counselors, is the fact that the emerging paradigm in health care stresses prevention, early intervention, and alternative methods of remediation, strategies that are within the purview of skills of professionals in our field. It is noteworthy that Smith (1999), in a recent national survey of counselors' participation in managed care, identified several unique competencies of professional counselors that are "particularly useful in the managed care environment" (p. 277). These include a prevention focus that incorporates a wellness, holistic, and developmental orientation as well as treatment planning that builds on the strengths and assets of our clients.

Finally, we believe that it is essential for counselors in all settings to emphasize how their training is different from that of other disciplines. In addition to the differences in philosophical and fundamental values of counselors, we must note that our national standards require preparation and at least minimal competence in positive human development in all dimensions of wellness over the life span—cultural diversity; career development; individual appraisal and assessment; and methods for working with individuals, families, couples, and groups. For example, school counselors educated to provide a comprehensive, developmental counseling program are well prepared to embrace this paradigm. As a result, we believe that the Wheel of Wellness provides a comprehensive model into which specific methods can be incorporated within counselors' existing repertoires of knowledge and skills. In so doing, they will be even more effective providers in all settings. Equally important, they will become a part of the solution to the ills of our society rather than a part of the problem. If implemented in cooperation with others in the legislative and related political arenas, this can be a future of our own creation that is derived from our heritage as a profession.

References

Adler, A. (1954). *Understanding human nature* (W. B. Wolf, Trans.). New York: Fawcett. (Original work published 1927)

Archer, J., Probert, B. S., & Gage, L. (1987). College students' attitudes toward wellness. *Journal of College Student Personnel, 28,* 311-323.

Ardell, D. B. (1988). The history and future of the wellness movement. In J. P. Opatz (Ed.), *Wellness promotion strategies: Selected proceedings of the eighth annual National Wellness Conference.* Dubuque, IA: Kendall/Hunt.

Beckingham, A. C., & Watt, S. (1995). Daring to grow old: Lessons in aging and empowerment. *Educational Gerontology, 21,* 479-495.

Daniels, K., & Guppy, A. (1994). Occupational stress, social support, job control, and psychological well-being. *Human Relations, 47,* 1523-1544.

Dunn, H. L. (1961). *High-level wellness.* Arlington, VA: R. W. Beatty.

Dunn, H. L. (1977). What high level wellness means. *Health Values: Achieving High Level Wellness, 1,* 9-16.

Ellis, A. (1984). Rational emotive therapy. In R. J. Corsini (Ed.), *Current psychotherapies* (3rd ed., pp. 196-238). Itasca, IL: F. E. Peacock.

Hattie, J. A. (1992). *Self-concept.* Hillsdale, NJ: Lawrence Erlbaum.

Hattie, J. A., Myers, J. E., & Sweeney, T. J. (2000). *A Multidisciplinary model of wellness: The development of the Wellness Evaluation of Lifestyle.* Model developed by the authors, Greensboro, NC.

Herr, E. L., & Cramer, S. H. (1996). *Career guidance and counseling through the lifespan: Systematic approaches* (5th ed.). New York: HarperCollins.

Hettler, W. (1984). Wellness: Encouraging a lifetime pursuit of excellence. *Health Values: Achieving High Level Wellness, 8,* 13-17.

Kaufmann, M. A. (1997). Wellness for people 65 years and older. *Journal of Gerontological Nursing, 23,* 7-9.

Lee, C. C. (1996). MCT theory and implications for indigenous healing. In D. W. Sue, A. E. Ivey, & P. B. Pedersen (Eds.), *A theory of multicultural counseling and therapy* (pp. 86-98). Pacific Grove, CA: Brooks/Cole.

Lindgren, K. N., & Coursey, R. D. (1995). Spirituality and serious mental illness: A two-part study. *Psychosocial Rehabilitation Journal, 18,* 93-111.

Maslow, A. (1970). *Motivation and personality* (2nd ed.). New York: Harper & Row.

Myers, J. E. (1992). Wellness, prevention, development: The cornerstone of the profession. *Journal of Counseling and Development, 71,* 136-139.

Myers, J. E., Sweeney, T. J., & Witmer, J. M. (2000). The wheel of wellness: Counseling for wellness: A holistic model for treatment planning. *Journal of Counseling and Development, 78,* 251-266.

Myers, J. E., Sweeney, T. J., Witmer, J. M., & Hattie, J. A. (1998). *The Wellness Evaluation of Lifestyle* [Model]. Greensboro, NC: Authors.

National Association of Social Workers. (1995). *Encyclopedia of social work* (19th ed.). Washington, DC: Author.

Ryff, C. D., & Heidrich, S. M. (1997). Experience and well-being: Explorations on domains of life and how they matter. *International Journal of Behavioral Development, 20,* 193-206.

Seaward, B. L. (1995). Reflections on human spirituality for the worksite. *American Journal of Health Promotion, 9,* 165-168.

Shannon, G. W., & Pyle, G. F. (1993). *Disease and medical care in the United States: A medical atlas of the twentieth century.* New York: Macmillan.

Smith, H. B. (1999). Managed care: A survey of counselor educators and counselor practitioners. *Journal of Mental Health Counseling, 21,* 270-284.

Sternberg, S. (1997, September 10). Medicare gives preventive Ornish heart program a try. *USA Today,* p. D1.

Sweeney, T. J., & Witmer, J. M. (1991). Beyond social interest: Striving toward optimal health and wellness. *Individual Psychology, 47,* 527-540.

U.S. Department of Health and Human Services. (1990). *Healthy People 2000: National health promotion and disease prevention objectives.* Washington, DC: Government Printing Office.

U.S. Department of Health and Human Services. (2000). *Healthy People 2010: Understanding and improving health.* Washington, DC: Government Printing Office.

Westgate, C. E. (1996). Spiritual wellness and depression. *Journal of Counseling and Development, 75,* 26-35.

Witmer, J. M. (1996). *Reaching Toward Wellness: A holistic model for personal growth and counseling.* Model developed by the author, Athens, OH.

Witmer, J. M., & Sweeney, T. J. (1992). A holistic model for wellness and prevention over the lifespan. *Journal of Counseling and Development, 71,* 140-148.

Zis, M., Jacobs, L. R., & Shapiro, R. Y. (1996). The elusive common ground: The politics of public opinion and healthcare reform (Where is healthcare headed?). *Generations, 20*(6), 1-5.

CHAPTER FORTY-TWO

The Independent Practice
of Mental Health Counseling

Past, Present, and Future

ARTIS J. PALMO

MICHAEL J. SHOSH

WILLIAM J. WEIKEL

Although it might seem that the independent practice of mental health counseling has been around for many decades, this is far from the truth. Counseling can be traced to the early 1900s (Gladding, 1988); however, it was not until the late 1960s and early 1970s that the independent practice of counseling and psychology truly began. At that time, several important events occurred that drastically changed the manner in which mental health services were provided to the general public.

There might seem to be a long history of mental health practice as we now know it, but this is simply not the case. The past 30 years have shown major shifts in the way in which the general public views mental health services and the manner in which these services are provided (Palmo, 1996). When attempting to forecast the future of mental health service delivery systems, it is important to have an historical perspective to more fully understand the forces directing the present systems.

Historical Perspective on Mental Health Professionals in Independent Practice

Even though the history of organized mental health services can be traced to the late 18th century (Brooks & Weikel, 1996), the major changes and advances have occurred over the past 50 years. The following discussion provides a perspective on the rapidity with which service delivery systems for mental health have changed during that period of time, especially during the past 20 years.

Growth of Independent Practitioners During the 1960s and 1970s

Beginning during the 1960s, the general public became much more accepting of the use of counseling and psychotherapy to assist individuals with personal problems affecting their mental health (Palmo, 1996). Importantly, the overwhelming impact of the works of Carl Rogers (Aubrey, 1977, 1983) drastically shifted mental health services from the medical model of psychiatry to the more humanistic aspects of counseling espoused by Rogers. By the 1960s, the stigma attached to someone seeking mental health services was significantly reduced as more and more people sought these services.

As counseling and psychotherapy began to shift to a more humanistic perspective, there were major changes in where the services were provided and by whom. Up until the late 1960s, psychiatrists controlled the direction of mental health services, using either hospital-based programs or their own private practices. The use of medication by psychiatrists was common practice, with the primary "talking" treatment being psychoanalysis (Brooks & Weikel, 1996).

There was little opportunity for the less affluent to use psychoanalysis because of cost restrictions and the need for immediate assistance with their concerns and problems. However, by the 1960s, the impact of Rogers's (1942) work on the training and development of mental health professionals took hold. Not only did Rogers effect changes in the procedures and practices of mental health professionals, his works also drastically changed the negative and sometimes suspicious views held by the general public toward counseling and psychotherapy.

Growth of Marriage and Family Counseling

The popularity of mental health programs and self-help books for treating dysfunctional couples or families can be directly related to the social unrest of the 1960s. For example, Berne's (1964) classic *Games People Play* is one of the original paperback books that popularized the use of psychological concepts and ideas for use by the general public. The popular writings created an atmosphere in which it became acceptable for members of the general public to pursue counseling for problems in their marriages or in other areas of their lives.

The social unrest and the willingness of couples and families to seek treatment for their psychological difficulties created a new marketplace for mental health professionals. Counselors and psychologists began to provide services for the general public through private independent practices. Within a four-decade period, the general public became open to psychological treatment and had a choice of professionals from whom to choose treatment for the problems they faced at home, at work, or in the community.

Employee Assistance Programs

Along with the shift by the general public toward greater acceptance of counseling assistance, employers began to develop behavioral health programs to reduce the impact of mental health problems on productivity and profit (Patricelli & Lee, 1996). Whereas the first programs focused on alcohol abuse, often using recovering employees to assist other workers, by the 1970s the employee assistance programs (EAPs) had become more diversified in their approaches. In addition to the problems of alcohol abuse, EAPs began to focus on other issues that were severely affecting employee job performance such as marital issues, home finance problems, and family issues. EAPs signified the acceptance of psychological services by business and industry.

Licensure of Mental Health Professionals

The greatest single event for mental health professionals was the initiation of licensure during the 1970s (Brooks, 1996). Licensure regulates "both the use of the professional title and the scope of practice" (p. 262), permitting the professional to practice independently, without supervision from any other person or professional group. No longer were counselors, social workers, and psychologists beholden to psychiatry. Each professional group could treat individuals, families, and groups on its own so long as its members practiced within the confines of their training.

With licensure, mental health professionals throughout the country established independent practices, attracting a broad array of clientele. No longer was psychological treatment restricted to those few individuals who could

financially afford services. By the 1970s, anyone could find affordable and readily available services for themselves or their families. Some of the stigma associated with seeking assistance from mental health professionals was reduced because clients no longer were being viewed as mentally ill; rather, they were viewed as "suffering normal developmental conflicts faced by everyone" (Palmo, 1999, p. 217).

Licensure opened the door for both clients and professionals. Clients had the opportunity to seek professional assistance from a broad array of mental health professionals in the community while being assured that these professionals had met the requirements of licensure. Professionals no longer had to be restricted in where they practiced. The avoidance of the medical model was key to the success of the early practitioners, who found their success in treating clients pragmatically and with respect (Weikel & Palmo, 1989). For mental health professionals, licensure was the single greatest factor in changing the availability of mental health services.

Expansion of Health Care Coverage for Mental Health

Following licensure, the second major event that would change the face of mental health was the initiation of health care insurance coverage for the mentally ill that would pay nonmedical professionals for treatment. Psychologists, social workers, and marriage and family therapists began treating clients and were paid either partially or fully by the clients' medical insurance companies. The insurance companies made payment either directly to the practitioners or, most frequently, to the clients, who had to submit their claims under major medical and wait for reimbursement. Payment for non-medical mental health professionals provided a major breakthrough to independent practitioners by reducing the financial burden placed on their clients and providing greater availability of services to the general public.

Major Medical

For many independently practicing professionals, the event that signified the most important change in how they operated their practice was the day they received their insurance provider numbers. For example, in Pennsylvania during the 1970s, psychologists were given Blue Shield numbers and packages of reimbursement forms, just like those provided to physicians (Palmo, 1999). This event was taking place all over the country and involved not only psychologists but other mental health professionals as well. From the 1970s through the end of the 1980s, independently practicing mental health professionals were able to benefit and profit from this association with medical insurers.

Once mental health professionals began to pursue and accept medical insurance payments, the demands on the profession changed immediately. No longer was the humanistic model the only directing force within the treatment process (Palmo, 1999); now, the medical model again had an overriding influence. Payment for services required that practitioners give medical diagnoses of clients' maladies. Nonmedical mental health professionals found themselves in a real dilemma—provide diagnoses for payment but provide treatment based on acceptance of clients having normal developmental difficulties.

Once mental health professionals began accepting medical payments, their independent style of practicing began to change because officials controlling the medical payments wanted more and more of a say in the process. Kovacs (1998) argued that many mental health professionals have "sold out" to belong to the medical establishment, creating a situation in which mental health professionals now are beholden to the insurance companies. To maintain their businesses, according to Kovacs, mental health professionals must follow the rules of the insurers and, therefore, make decisions based on the needs of the insurers and not their clients. Kovacs believes that the decline in income ("Therapists' Fees," 1997) being experienced by mental health professionals today can be traced directly to the participation of non-medical professionals (i.e., insurers) in medical health insurance plans.

According to Kovacs (1998), once mental health professionals began to accept medical payments, the general public began to expect and demand that the costs of counseling and psychotherapy be covered by insurance. Now, the members of the public rely on insurers to cover the costs of treatment, no longer expecting to pay for services on their own as they did during the early days of independent practices. Therefore, according to Kovacs, the benefit of being connected to the medical model was very short-lived given that independent practitioners now are dependent on insurers for their financial survival.

Clients as Patients

One final note related to the shift in practice from self-pay to reliance on medical payments needs to be made. There has been a not-so-subtle shift in the way that those seeking psychological services have gone from being seen as clients to being seen as patients. This shift has caused a major change in treatment to occur, where individuals with "normal developmental conflicts" (Palmo, 1999, p. 217) have been transformed into individuals with more pathological diagnoses. In many instances, mental health professionals are required to document the *medical necessity* (Lehigh Valley Hospital Center, 1999) of patients' presenting problems before insurance-covered treatments are permitted to continue. There is a greater emphasis being placed on the *pathology* of *patients* than on the developmental and prevention focus of many therapeutic approaches to counseling and psychotherapy.

Managed Care and Practitioners During the 1980s and 1990s

Toward the end of the 1980s, a major shift in the manner in which clients and practitioners were reimbursed for services began. This shift would bring a very abrupt end to the reimbursement practices of the previous 15 years, whereby independently practicing mental health professionals were paid for services with little or no involvement from the insurers. Rates for services provided were determined by the professionals, and clients had coverage through major medical or indemnity insurance policies. These policies would reimburse either the clients or the practitioners at rates equal or nearly equal to the rates being charged. It was a relatively easy system, with few questions asked by insurers. At that time, psychiatric hospitals had free rein on charges and lengths of stay for patients.

Like independently practicing professionals, hospitals had little interference from the insurers. By 1990, all of the accepted practices for reimbursement changed.

Practice Management by Insurance Carriers

As independently practicing professionals moved into the 1990s, they found an entirely new set of expectations being placed on their practices. No longer was the contract for services between the professionals and the clients. Now, the insurers became directly involved through managed care (Palmo, 1999). The various managed care organizations (MCOs) selected specific professionals who would be able to treat clients, thereby restricting where the clients could go to receive mental health services. Those mental health professionals chosen by the MCOs were on the insurers' panels, and those not selected were excluded from the panels—or, in today's terminology, were *out-of-network*.

Being selected by an MCO meant that a mental health professional was required to follow the rules and regulations established by the insurer, especially fee structures. MCOs established fees for psychotherapy services that initially were below the typical fees charged by independent practitioners. However, the MCOs soon began to significantly lower their fees to approximately half the normally accepted fees. For example, a psychologist typically might charge a client $100 per 50-minute individual psychotherapy session. With Aetna/USHealthcare (Lehigh Valley Hospital Center, 1999), the approved provider would receive only $50 for the same amount of work. Needless to say, this drastically reduced the incomes of independent practitioners.

In addition, a practitioner was faced with several other new and intrusive features introduced by MCOs. First, the number of sessions permitted by the insurer was controlled from the beginning of the process. Second, the practitioner was required to complete certain forms designating the identified problem and the treatment goal. The primary care physician was provided with a report and became the gatekeeper for the entire process. Third, if the practitioner needed more sessions to complete the treatment, then a detailed treatment plan had to be filed with the MCO. Once a case manager read the request for additional sessions, the manager would determine the *medical necessity* for more sessions.

Exclusion of Practitioners
From Certain MCOs

By the early 1990s, mental health professionals found themselves in the "greatest resocialization" (Cummings, 1995, p. 10) of mental health practices faced since the days following the tremendous growth and acceptance of counseling and psychotherapy. According to Cummings (1995), the resocialization forced mental health professionals to immediately confront changes that they were not ready to accept. Cummings reported that five major changes occurred with (a) practitioners joining together to form comprehensive groups so as to be accepted by MCOs, (b) brief psychotherapy techniques being accepted as useful and productive, (c) the role of practitioners as helpers being redefined and redirected to meet the demands of MCOs, (d) group practices being required to show that they are not only efficient

but also effective, and (e) the MCOs recognizing prime providers that can offer a broad array of treatment alternatives and diagnostics within the restricted financial criteria established.

With the initiation of MCOs came the development of provider panels or the lists of professionals accepted by the MCOs and approved to provide treatment. Those providers accepted by MCOs were referred to as *preferred providers*. Individuals seeking treatment were directed to them for services. Anyone not approved for the MCO panels was referred to as out-of-network. Being out-of-network severely restricted the ability to offer services to individuals seeking services. The MCOs did not stop their insured clients from using out-of-network providers, but there were severe financial consequences for these clients. Instead of small co-payment fees (e.g., $10), clients would have to pay double or triple the copayment fees to see out-of-network professionals. MCO-insured individuals learned very quickly to use the preferred providers because the fees were drastically reduced. Unfortunately, practitioners not acceptable to the MCOs saw their practices significantly curtailed.

Clients Given Limited
Choice of Practitioners

While practitioners were trying to adapt to the new restrictions and rejections of the MCOs, clients also were facing new challenges. Those seeking counseling services were forced to seek services from professionals identified as acceptable by the MCOs rather than being allowed to choose whomever they wanted. Similar to general medicine insurance policies, the behavioral health care regulations restricted choice by giving preferred providers the financial advantage over out-of-network providers. Although the MCOs insisted that they were not restrictive in their policies given that individuals could choose any professionals they desired, in reality they were very restrictive. Clients insured by MCOs really had no choice because choosing professionals in-network simply was much less expensive for the clients. Technically, clients were not restricted from seeking services from whomever they desired, but the financial penalties for seeking out-of-network providers meant that, pragmatically, such choices were prohibitive.

Increased Costs for Inpatient Treatment

The one major factor that created the atmosphere for change was the rapid increase in costs for inpatient psychiatric treatment and for inpatient drug and alcohol treatment (Patricelli & Lee, 1996). Through the 1980s and early 1990s, the accepted inpatient treatment time was 30 days for psychiatric admissions and 28 days for drug and alcohol treatment. The costs of such treatments were significant. For example, the first author had a client referred to him in 1993 by an inpatient treatment facility following treatment for depression and suicidal ideation. The client remained in the hospital for 30 days at a total cost of $33,000. Needless to say, the insurance industry would not continue to pay such rates without more control over the treatment process and established rates for treatment.

Inpatient facilities were the first to feel the effects of the restrictions of managed care. No longer would insurers accept 30 days as the accepted length of stay for inpatient treatment, requiring the facilities to have clear and defined criteria for admissions of patients. For many in-surers, the distinction between an individual who was admitted to an inpatient facility and one who was not was the level of lethality exhibited by the individual. If the individual was very likely to do harm to himself or herself or to someone else, then he or she would be hospitalized. However, the length of stay for the individual might be for only 2 or 3 days. Patients then were referred to various outpatient programs that were much cheaper to operate for the insurers.

The resultant effect of the financial cuts for inpatient care immediately began to change reimbursement for outpatient services and private practitioners. Even though outpatient costs and reimbursements were only a fraction of the costs being assessed against insurance companies when compared to inpatient costs, insurers became much more restrictive, once again attempting to control costs and increase their own profits (Miller, 1997).

Summary

The purpose of this section was to make several important points. First, the mental health delivery system, as we know it today, really has a very short history. With the initiation of comprehensive treatment programs during the late 1960s and early 1970s, mental health treatment has grown by enormous proportions in a very short time. Second, funding for mental health services has had a major impact on the manner in which services are provided as well as on the amount of services that individuals can have covered by insurance. Third, the financial structure used to cover mental health services has been developed only recently, and the final structure for coverage of services still is in question.

Multidisciplinary Practices

Beginning during the early 1990s, major changes occurred in the manner in which mental health practitioners operated their practices. Phelps, Eisman, and Kohout (1998) spoke for most psychologists when they maintained, "Marketplace-driven demands for integrated services, large and diversified group practices, and greater accountability have created obstacles and declining market opportunities that threaten the very existence of traditional psychological practice" (p. 35). Independent practitioners from counseling, psychology, social work, and marriage and family therapy were forced to change their office procedures, adjust their payment scales, become more flexible, and (in some instances) change their therapeutic styles (Steenbarger, 1994).

Reduced Profitability and Flexibility

The development of MCOs created many concerns for practitioners, but the two most critical problems were (a) reduced income and profitability and (b) reduced flexibility in treating clients. As noted earlier ("Therapists' Fees," 1997), from the early 1990s through the present, mental health practitioners have seen a significant drop in their incomes. The drop in incomes can be attributed to two factors: facing reduced per-session fees controlled by MCOs and being dropped from various MCO provider panels (resulting in fewer new client referrals). Over a period of just a few years, independent practitioners watched their incomes decrease in significant increments, with many practitioners choosing to change their employment.

Even though many practitioners reported increased hours spent in clinical activities and assessment (Phelps et al., 1998), the amount of income continued to decrease. Practitioners found that they had to increase their hours and reduce their session times so as to combat the loss of income.

For those practitioners not accepted by MCO panels, maintaining their practices became a challenge. Referrals were decreased, clients could find *cheaper* counseling services with other practitioners, and greater effort was being expended to achieve the financial goals of previous years. It was next to impossible to maintain a viable active practice as an independent practitioner without being connected to one or more MCOs.

Independent Contractors Versus Employees

One important set of regulations controlling the status of independent practitioners who practiced under the Internal Revenue Service (IRS) designation as an *independent contractor* (Duckworth, 1997) has had a significant effect on the way in which professionals practice. The IRS outlined 20 criteria that "are to be used to determine whether a worker is an employee or [an] independent contractor" (p. 2). Of the 20 factors, the most important criterion used to define the difference between an employee and an independent contractor was how much control existed over the professional. In many instances, independent contractors in reality were employees of organizations and, therefore, subject to different IRS regulations.

For independent contractors working alone, the IRS distinction usually was not a concern.

However, some independent contractors worked for professional groups where they relied completely on these groups for referrals and billings. In these instances, independent contractors were more closely defined as employees, a concern that the IRS began to police more closely. Many independently practicing professionals heading group practices found themselves faced with a very difficult dilemma regarding whether or not to continue to use independent contractors, better define the relationship among contractors, or simply take on employees or become employees themselves.

The shift from using independent contractors to hiring employees to provide counseling services for large mental health professional groups has drastically changed the ways in which services are provided and professionals are paid. This transition will continue to take place as we move further into the 21st century. Maintaining a solo practice or continuing to function as an independent contractor will become more and more difficult for a professional wanting to maintain a full-time counseling practice.

Effect of MCOs on Individual Practitioners

One final point about the effect of MCOs needs mentioning. As MCOs have grown in impact (Cummings, Budman, & Thomas, 1998), individual practitioners have been faced with drastic cuts in the numbers and types of referrals they are able to garner. Cummings and colleagues stated, "During the heyday of indemnity-reimbursed solo practice, 20% of the patients could absorb 70% of the expenditures. Now all of that has drastically changed"

(p. 463). The typical solo practice has been unable to continue under the previous format of the 1970s and 1980s and has been required to lower costs for treatment, join panels when permitted, and/or find a different type of work setting in which to practice.

Practitioners Organizing to Reduce Costs and Increase Services

Several major trends have occurred over the past 10 years in the way that mental health professionals operate their practices. Because of the numerous changes created by managed care, mental health professionals have begun a stampede into a broad variety of services beyond the traditional one-on-one counseling business. In addition, mental health professionals have taken steps to join forces by establishing group practices with multidisciplinary professionals. In some corners, professionals even have advocated the development of unions to stem the tide of reduced fees (Lundeen, 1999). In this section, we take a brief look at the transition to group practices to meet the demands of today's mental health marketplace.

Group Practices

The primary reason for the movement of mental health professionals from individual practices to group practices is cost containment. Managed care placed critical factors—quality of care, consumer needs, long-term benefits of therapy, and the like—in a secondary position to controlling costs (Frasure, 1996). Therefore, practitioners are faced with severe cuts in their incomes and attempt to control these losses by joining various forms of group practices. In addition, when joined as groups, these professionals can attract contracts from the MCOs that are increasingly selective in choosing groups over individual practitioners.

As MCOs began to restrict the growth of treatment at inpatient hospital programs, new growth occurred in outpatient programming (Miller, 1996; Rosenberg, 1996). Because costs are significantly decreased in outpatient programs, both hospitals and practitioners expanded services by forming groups of multidisciplinary professionals to meet the demands of MCOs. Although presented by the MCOs as a new and more effective delivery system, in reality the system of using groups is simply more cost-effective. According to Hersch (1995), managed care created a situation in which practitioners had to adapt to the changes or not survive in their practices, whether inpatient or outpatient.

Cost Factors

The primary motivation for the establishment of any type of multidisciplinary group is the cost containment benefit (Hersch, 1995) for both professionals and MCOs. Benefits derived from multidisciplinary groups include a broader client base for referrals, more effective networking, professional enrichment, and reduced costs for the services provided. Severely reduced fee structures, limited sessions for clients, and increased provider costs all have created a situation in which professionals are *expanding* services in looking for ways of saving or generating money while MCOs are *reducing* services as a way of saving money. Professionals with long-established practices are the ones most likely to survive the cost-cutting of the MCOs; therefore, the greatest concern is for

new professionals entering the field of mental health (Phelps et al., 1998). Increasingly, MCOs are using master's-level professionals to provide services while ignoring doctoral-level professionals (Cummings, 1995).

Growth of Alternative Delivery Systems in Behavioral Health

With the rapid changes in behavioral health care funding, professionals faced with the responsibility of caring for clients are confronted with the dilemma of how to meet client needs in a financially sound manner. The health maintenance organizations (HMOs) and MCOs have continued a trend of placing the financial risks on the providers or institutions (Patricelli & Lee, 1996) rather than on themselves. For example, MCOs have begun to establish fixed rates for certain diagnoses, and providers have the responsibility of assisting clients within these cost restrictions. If a provider requires more time with a client, then the financial burden rests with the provider, and not the insurer, to ensure that the client's issues are resolved. The shift of financial responsibility to providers has significantly affected the manner in which mental health services are provided.

Managed Behavioral Health Organizations

The development of various forms of managed behavioral health organizations (MBHOs) began in earnest during the late 1980s and early 1990s. According to Patricelli and Lee (1996), "Americans spent approximately $80 billion on the direct costs of treating mental illness and chemical dependence in 1994" (p. 325). The cost to insure workers was one of the primary forces causing employers to reassess how they paid for mental health care benefits. As noted earlier, the escalating costs of inpatient care during the early 1990s created a situation in which alternatives had to be found to reduce the financial burden on employers and insurers.

As a result of escalating costs, the number of people covered by MCOs has risen drastically over a 6-year period. M. E. Oss, writing in *Open Minds* (cited in Patricelli & Lee, 1996), reported that there were 78 million people covered by MCOs in 1993. In 1999, *Open Minds* reported that 176.8 million people were covered by MCOs ("Getting Bigger," 1999). This number represented 72% of insured Americans.

Provider Panels and the Lives of Practitioners

The growth of MBHOs has changed the professional lives of independent practitioners. As noted earlier, the changes facing practitioners are numerous and varied. Three of the changes appear to be the most critical. First, independent practitioners have had to come to terms with being accepted by MBHOs as preferred providers (Palmo, 1999). In light of the overabundance of mental health professionals available, MBHOs concerned about cost containment can be selective in choosing providers for their panels. Because MBHOs have the prerogative of choice, many practitioners are being forced to make difficult decisions about their careers. To date, many mental health professionals have not faced this professional predicament, believing or hoping that the mental health payment system will return to some semblance of its form during the 1980s. This seems highly unlikely.

Second, practitioners have had to face the intrusion of care managers into the treatment process with clients (Palmo, 1999). Because independent practitioners in outpatient practices and mental health professionals in inpatient facilities could not, or would not, function in a financially responsible manner, MBHOs developed and prospered.

Third, the traditional therapy conditions of congruence, unconditional positive regard, and empathy are being threatened by the new MBHO procedures (Palmo, 1999). With the MBHO emphasis being placed on problem resolution, shorter forms of treatment that do not rely on the traditional core conditions have been introduced.

Survival During the 21st Century

When examining the drastic changes that have occurred in the mental health delivery system over the past 25 years, it is difficult to imagine what will happen during the next 25 years. In this section, we take a look into the future of the mental health professions and mental health care delivery systems and try to predict some of the trends of the future. The changes are affecting not only the mental health delivery system but also training programs, accreditation, licensure, and certification. The future could be seen as frightening, but we look toward the future with excitement.

Traditional Delivery Systems Versus Future Models

Much of what professionals have known as the *traditional delivery system* will not exist under the control of MBHOs. With 72% of the country enrolled in some form of a MBHO ("Getting Bigger," 1999), there is no likelihood that clients will be able to have traditional 30-day paid stays at inpatient facilities or twice-weekly individual paid analytic psychotherapy sessions. Traditional treatment programs, whether inpatient or outpatient, will exist only for those people who have the ability to pay for their treatments on their own.

Problem Resolution Versus Personal Growth

There is no likelihood that insurers will return to the system of paying for long-term counseling for developmental purposes. Any long-term counseling will involve only those clients with the most severe diagnoses (Knapp, 1999). Anyone can seek help with developmental issues, but any long-term counseling will have to be paid by the individual, not the insurer. The emphasis for MBHOs will be on problem resolution within a brief therapeutic approach. Practitioners will be facing the issues of *medical necessity* in defining the need for therapy, with more and more restrictive definitions being used over the next decade.

Availability of Care for Consumers

The most important aspect of the changes in the mental health delivery system has been the increased availability of care to a greater number of people. Although professionals have complained about reduced earnings, more paperwork, intrusive case managers, and restrictive treatments, in reality more clients have some form of low-cost counseling services available. With significantly reduced out-of-pocket copayments for individuals wanting

mental health assistance, counseling has become affordable to more people than ever before.

The process of finding mental health services usually is quite simple. Because the out-of-pocket expenditures are so minimal, even the most financially restricted individuals usually can find help. As noted throughout this chapter, there are many unique difficulties with and concerns about the present system offered by MBHOs. However, there is much promise for a future mental health delivery system that will be available for all people and not just those who can afford the cash outlays for exclusive private practitioners.

EAPs and Employee Coordinated Health Programs

When examining the future for mental health delivery systems, one of the present programs that offers much promise is the EAP. Delivery systems will be tied more and more directly to employers over the next 5 years *because employers are paying the mental health bills.* To obtain more effective and financially prudent mental health services, employers are demanding greater control of the provider services. Professionals are realizing the need to adapt their services to meet the needs of employers (Heller, 1999), who want to increase their companies' effectiveness and be able to manage health care costs.

EAPs have offered a cost-efficient method of handling problem employees; however, greater health care program coordination seems to be necessary. We are referring to this as *employee coordinated health programs* (ECHPs). The problem with managing health care treatment and costs has been the disjointed manner in which the programs are administered. For example, an employee might be out of work and on disability for a work-related injury but never be seen by a mental health professional. In our experience, workers on disability tend to have numerous personal issues and problems besides their medical problems.

If the mental health delivery system of the future is to be effective and efficient, then it will have to be a coordinated system including every aspect of medical care. ECHPs of the future would consolidate the services to be provided to ensure that individuals are receiving the best of care while also ensuring that the most financially responsible approaches are being used. Programs will be employer based because the increasing costs of health care fall onto employers. Accountability will be based on effective services to clients and financially sound decisions about treatments.

Mental Health Training Programs

Graduate training programs in mental health have been slow to respond to the drastic changes that have taken place in the mental health delivery system (Cummings, 1995). Although coursework has been developed to handle the increased demands placed on mental health professionals, there continues to be a need for professionals who can (a) be outstanding diagnosticians, (b) understand and use brief therapeutic approaches, (c) work with a broad array of clientele, (d) offer different therapeutic modalities to match client needs, (e) be effective group therapists, and (f) be good teachers and group communicators.

According to Cummings (1995), mental health professionals of the future will have to face a new and diverse way in which to offer services. Cummings believes that 25% of the

psychotherapy of the future will be individual, 25% will be group therapy, and 50% will be "structured psychoeducational programs" (p. 14). He also believes that the impetus to reach a 25:25:50 ratio will be based on proven outcome studies showing that psychoeducational programming is effective and is not simply a cost containment method.

If Cummings (1995) and others are correct (Hersch, 1995; Phelps et al., 1998), then mental health professionals of the future will need to be good clinicians and effective educators. Mental health professionals of the future will need to be comfortable with a broad array of professional environments including health care, psychopharmacology, employer-based programming, diverse treatment models, and niche programs (e.g., weight loss, smoking cessation).

Accreditation and Graduate Program Development

At this point in time, accreditation programs for counseling, psychology, psychiatry, and social work seem to be a necessity for professional credentialing and licensure; however, programs historically have been developed to meet the needs of the old model of mental health service delivery. As noted in the previous section, training programs are going to need major overhauls to meet the needs of the present system and of future delivery systems.

Conclusions

The intent of this chapter has been to present the history of mental health delivery systems so as to understand the present system. Rapid changes over the past 10 years have created a great deal of havoc for mental health professionals because they were totally unprepared for the changes. Graduate training and supervision did not prepare new professionals for the demands of managed care, and many veteran independent practitioners would not face the obvious, opting instead to hold onto the archaic system of the past. The system needed to change and continues to need to develop if it is to provide the highest quality of service in a cost-effective and efficient manner. Typical mental health practices of the 1970s and 1980s will become a memory as new, more streamlined models are developed that can match the needs of clients receiving services and the organizational clients who pay for the services. The "upside" in this major shift is that more persons than ever before will have ready access for mental health services that are easy to access and affordable for most of the population.

References

Aubrey, R. F. (1977). Historical development of guidance and counseling and implications for the future. *Personnel and Guidance Journal, 55,* 288-295.

Aubrey, R. F. (1983). The odyssey of counseling and images of the future. *Personnel and Guidance Journal, 62,* 78-82.

Berne, E. (1964). *Games people play.* New York: Grove Press.

Brooks, D. K. (1996). The impact of credentialing on mental health counseling. In W. J. Weikel & A. J. Palmo (Eds.), *Foundations of mental health counseling* (2nd ed., pp. 259-275). Springfield, IL: Charles C Thomas.

Brooks, D. K., & Weikel, W. J. (1996). Mental health counseling: The first twenty years. In W. J. Weikel & A. J. Palmo (Eds.), *Foundations of mental health counseling* (2nd ed., pp. 5-29). Springfield, IL: Charles C Thomas.

Cummings, N. A. (1995). Impact of managed care on employment and training: A primer for survival. *Professional Psychology: Research and Practice, 26,* 10-15.

Cummings, N. A., Budman, S. H., & Thomas, J. L. (1998). Efficient psychotherapy as a viable response to scarce resources and rationing of treatment. *Professional Psychology: Research and Practice, 29,* 460-469.

Duckworth, T. J. (1997). *Classification of employee vs. independent contractor.* Report prepared by law offices of Margolis Duckworth & Funt for Bethlehem Counseling Associates, Bethlehem, PA.

Frasure, J. S. (1996). All that glitters is not always gold: Medical offset effects and managed behavioral health care. *Professional Psychology: Research and Practice, 27,* 335-344.

Getting bigger. (1999, August). *Psychotherapy Finances,* p. 8.

Gladding, S. T. (1988). *Counseling: A comprehensive profession.* Columbus, OH: Merrill.

Heller, K. M. (1999). The business of practice network (BOPN). *The Independent Practitioner, 19,* 212-213.

Hersch, L. (1995). Adapting to health care reform and managed care: Three strategies for survival and growth. *Professional Psychology: Research and Practice, 26,* 16-26.

Knapp, S. (1999). Legislative committee evaluates health care in Pennsylvania: Existing consumer protections should be strengthened. *The Pennsylvania Psychologist, 59*(7), 2-3.

Kovacs, A. (1998, March). *Surviving and thriving in a managed care era: New strategies for independent practice.* Program presented to the Lehigh Valley Psychological Association, Bethlehem, PA.

Lehigh Valley Hospital Center. (1999). *PennCARE Behavioral System manual.* Allentown, PA: Author.

Lundeen, E. J. (1999). Unions in Pennsylvania. *The Pennsylvania Psychologist, 59*(2), 10.

Miller, I. J. (1996). Managed care is harmful to outpatient mental health services: A call for accountability. *Professional Psychology: Research and Practice, 27,* 349-363.

Miller, I. J. (1997). Beware of a Trojan horse from managed care: Dangerous provisions in parity legislation. *The Independent Practitioner, 17,* 138-143.

Palmo, A. J. (1996). Professional identity of the mental health counselor. In W. J. Weikel & A. J. Palmo (Eds.), *Foundations of mental health counseling* (2nd ed., pp. 51-69). Springfield, IL: Charles C Thomas.

Palmo, A. J. (1999). The MHC reaches maturity: Does the child seem short for its age? *Journal of Mental Health Counseling, 21,* 215-228.

Patricelli, R. E., & Lee, F. C. (1996). Employer-based innovations in behavioral health benefits. *Professional Psychology: Research and Practice, 27,* 325-334.

Phelps, R., Eisman, E. J., & Kohout, J. (1998). Psychological practice and managed care: Results of the CAPP practitioner survey. *Professional Psychology: Research and Practice, 29,* 31-36.

Rogers, C. R. (1942). *Counseling and psychotherapy.* Boston: Houghton Mifflin.

Rosenberg, S. (1996). Health maintenance organization penetration and general hospital psychiatric services: Expenditure and utilization trends. *Professional Psychology: Research and Practice, 27,* 345-348.

Steenbarger, B. N. (1994). Duration and outcome in psychotherapy: An integrative review. *Professional Psychology: Research and Practice, 25,* 111-119.

Therapists' fees and incomes are under growing pressure. (1997, May). *Psychotherapy Finances,* pp. 1-12.

Weikel, W. J., & Palmo, A. J. (1989). The evolution and practice of mental health counseling. *Journal of Mental Health Counseling, 11,* 7-25.

CHAPTER FORTY-THREE

The Costs, Cost-Effectiveness, and Cost-Benefit of School and Community Counseling Services

JOHN D. SWISHER

The relative importance, effectiveness, and costs of school and community counseling services have become issues for many schools and counseling services offered in the community. For example, the state of Virginia passed legislation changing the school regulations so that school districts could choose between reading specialists and school counselors. If the schools cannot afford both types of "specialists," then how do they make their decisions? Similarly, managed care organizations have begun to set limits for counseling services through community agencies and private providers. Evidence about costs, cost-effectiveness, and cost-benefit of counseling would provide leverage in restoring, maintaining, and/or enhancing counseling services. This chapter provides counselors with some data to help them justify their positions in economic terms. An important point of the chapter is that these economic justifications are based on the effectiveness studies provided to the profession by researchers studying the impact of school guidance and other counseling services (e.g., Lambert & Cattani-Thompson, 1996; Lapan, Gysbers, & Sun, 1997; Nathan, 1998).

The four major reasons for being concerned with costs and benefits of school and community counseling services are as follows:

1. To be accountable for the use of public and private funds
2. To know what it costs to achieve an effect
3. To compare the economic advantages of alternative services
4. To understand the short- and long-term economic benefits derived from counseling services

Counselors need to maintain "audits" (Myrick, 1993) of the services they deliver because one of the assumptions of this chapter is that counselors can account for their "time on tasks." Other chapters in this volume help with comprehensive evaluation and accountability procedures that include needs assessment, services delivered, and outcomes of those services. Given the availability of such information, counselors need to be good consumers of the outcome literature and change their practices to be consistent with the evidence-based practices in the profession. One of the major sections of this chapter focuses on the outcomes of the Missouri Developmental Guidance Approach (Lapan et al., 1997), which clearly indicated how school counseling services should be arrayed to achieve maximum benefit for the students. Another section focuses on an effective approach to one area of counseling services, substance abuse prevention, and is based on a program known as Life Skills Training (LST; Botvin, Baker, Dusenbury, Botvin, & Diaz, 1995). These are used for illustrative purposes in the context of their economic implications, but they also point to the types of counseling services that should be provided as counselors strive to be maximally effective. The processes and techniques used in this chapter, although applied to the schools and to school counselors, can be used in any of the other settings in which counselors

work—colleges and universities, community agencies, private practices, and the workplace.

It is important to point out that many of the outcomes of counseling services cannot be defined in economic terms. For example, if a private practice offers a program on effective parenting and is able to demonstrate that parenting skills have improved, then how can monetary values be attached to these outcomes? These outcomes may include better communication between parents and children, use of consistent and reasonable disciplinary actions, provision of more family rituals, and increased parent-child bonding through parent participation in children's activities (Kaltrider & St. Pierre, 1995; Klein & Swisher, 1983). It might be possible to follow the children of these families for many years to determine whether there were other outcomes (e.g., increased graduation rates) to which monetary values can be attached, but this type of research is extremely rare. The important point is that not all desirable outcomes can be reduced to monetary values, and school and agency counselors would be well advised not to focus solely on economic issues but instead to continue to build part of the justification for their services around quality-of-life outcomes for students, families, and communities. Furthermore, as Plotnick (1994) pointed out, not all policy decisions can or should be based on cost issues given that political, ethical, and/or moral issues often are involved.

Definitions of Costs, Cost-Effectiveness, and Cost-Benefit

The economic literature uses a variety of definitions for these terms, but for purposes of this chapter, each of these terms is defined as follows (Hu, Swisher, & McDonnell, 1978):

- *Costs* are defined as the expenditures to deliver services and the expenditures to receive services.
- *Cost-effectiveness* is defined as the expenditures required to achieve a level effect (Hurley, 1990).
- *Cost-benefit* in social terms is defined as the ratio between the expenditures required to achieve an effect and the social costs reduced (e.g., the cost of increasing graduation rates vs. the costs of welfare).

In general, costs can be classified as public costs, private costs, and social costs. Public costs are the dollars expended by governmental bodies (federal, state, and local school districts) to provide for guidance and counseling services. Private costs are the often intangible costs incurred by students and their parents while receiving services. The latter can include, for example, transportation costs to participate in a program and potential loss of earnings while at school at night (lost opportunity costs). There often are fees charged to clients associated with special events (fees for taking tests or for materials for the program). Finally, contributions often are solicited. Taken together, public and private costs are included in the more general term of *social costs*. Social costs are the total public and private costs, and they reflect more accurately what the costs are to society for guidance services.

Cost-effectiveness is focused on the total investment required to achieve a particular effect. The ultimate purpose is to discover the most effective approach requiring the fewest expenditures. In guidance and counseling terms, we might ask how much effort is required to retain an individual in school. An example of this issue was the adoption by Pennsylvania of an approach to student assistance programs (SAPs) that used existing school personnel to implement an SAP. The objectives of this program were to identify students whose behaviors were inconsistent with school policies or detrimental to academic success and, in turn, to match these students with necessary school or community services. The assumption was made that this was the least costly approach to delivering SAP services (Swisher et al., 1993) compared to contracting for SAP services from an external provider. This example is discussed in detail in the next section. Suffice it to point out here that whereas teachers, counselors, and administrators already are salaried, their time on the SAP team takes away from other potential services that they might be providing such as teaching.

Costs of Counseling

In general, estimating the costs of services makes the assumption that other agencies attempting to replicate a service need to know the total social costs that will be required. A comment such as "This program did not cost anything because we had a grant, the school let us use its building, and we had several volunteers" is misrepresenting the actual total social costs.

Within a school or an agency, the costs of counseling can be classified as operating or capital costs (Mitchel, Hu, McDonnell, & Swisher, 1984). Operational costs include personnel, travel, communication, and maintenance. Capital costs include facilities and equipment. Any administrator with budget experience might view these costs as easy to calculate. However, there are several sets of assumptions that need to be clarified including those related to the following:

- Budgetary expenditures versus economic costs
- Allocation of shared costs
- Treatment of capital costs
- Estimating opportunity costs
- Time periods

Budgetary expenditures versus economic costs. The terms *costs* and *expenditures* are not the same from an economic perspective. Some expenditures are consumed over time, and their costs should be prorated across programs. If other agencies contribute time to a program, such as an agency mental health expert serving on a student assistance team, then that time also must be accounted for as a cost even though the school did not have an expenditure for this individual's time.

Shared costs. Shared costs occur when two or more programs use the same facility or the same staff. For example, if the group guidance class meets in the same room as do other classes, then the costs for that facility should be prorated. Similarly, if teachers provide part of the comprehensive guidance program, then their time on task should be attributed to the program.

Capital costs. Capital costs include land, facilities, improvement, and equipment. These costs need to be prorated across all activities in a school or an agency, but they need to be prorated and depreciated or appreciated using basic assumptions. Straight-line depreciation generally is an acceptable approach but might be difficult to calculate due to establishing original or replacement costs, making assumptions about rates of inflation, and having variable rates of depreciation for facilities and equipment. Another approach is to use equivalent rental rates for space used for a program. Other capital costs are depreciated faster. For example, the value of a computer is short-lived compared to the value of a building.

Opportunity costs. Opportunity costs are the losses of potential income or resources while using a facility or personnel for one program versus another. Similarly, participation in counseling services might take time away from potential earnings. The potential loss of revenue from rent while a facility is freely given to a program is a clear example of a cost that should be imputed for calculating total costs. Another example is the loss of potential income from volunteer time of parents or participants in evening or weekend programs. These individuals could work during those times and, accordingly, have lost the opportunity to earn income while participating in any particular program.

Time periods. The accounting period of a particular service or cluster of services also should be considered when assessing costs. If a special program is offered within a month of a school year (9 or 10 months), then the costs should be proportionate for that time period regardless of the annual salary of the counselor or the annual taxes on the facilities (e.g., 1:9, 1:10, 1:12).

Although many of these costs have been borne by existing agencies or schools, they are real costs and should be acknowledged in a comprehensive assessment of costs to a program that is operating in one of these settings. If these costs are not attributed to the total costs of a program, then the rationale for not estimating them should be acknowledged. Many of the types of school or agency services that counselors provide are mandated by regulatory bodies, and one could argue that the position is required by law and that any particular activity within the position is a marginal cost rather than a direct cost. Marginal costs are those that result from an activity added on to an existing role or function rather than requiring additional resources.

Cost of Services

This section details the costs for conducting an SAP, which is a typical program component found in many schools today. The question is simple: What does this service or cluster of services cost? Then, it would be possible to compare one set of costs to alternative costs, but not in terms of which service is more effective.

SAPs are designed to identify students experiencing difficulty and to help them receive specialized services (Swisher et al., 1993). Consistent with the workplace model of employee assistance programs, teachers are trained to monitor behavior (both academic and personal). When a student's behavior appears to have changed in a negative direction, the teacher refers the student in question to the SAP counselor or team. In turn, the SAP staff monitor the individual's behavior in other contexts to confirm the pattern. When clear evidence of a problem exists, the student's parents are contacted and often become involved in the plan for resolving the problem. It also is common for the SAP staff to refer the student in question to specialized services in the community (e.g.,

mental health, substance abuse). At no time are teachers expected to make a diagnosis in making their referral. The basis for the referral is a change in a student's academic or personal behavior. Training for teachers for this type of program should emphasize the point that it is inappropriate for teachers to make a diagnosis because it is not their role and is a form of malpractice. For example, it is difficult to differentiate the flu from a hangover in a student, but the fact that something is wrong and persistent or frequent may be the basis for a referral.

Several basic approaches to providing SAPs include the following:

- Hiring an external contractor who places staff in the school
- Hiring internal specialized staff to serve in this capacity
- Reassigning regular staff (teachers, counselors, and administrators) to serve in this capacity

Pennsylvania's approach was to reassign regular staff to an SAP team, referred to as the Core Team Model (Swisher et al., 1993). One of the assumptions of this approach was that, because all of these personnel were on salary, there were no additional costs for operating the SAP program. However, as discussed later in this section, the members of the SAP team were given released time from teaching and so their time devoted to the SAP was viewed as a cost.

Table 43.1 outlines the costs for the components of operating an SAP program following the Core Team Model. This illustration assumes that a senior high school has 1,000 students and that 10% of the students would be referred to the SAP team. This illustration also assumes that the school and community personnel

TABLE 43.1   Costs of a Student Assistance Program Operating for 1 School Year (in dollars)

Costs	Total Costs	Average Costs per Student
Costs incurred directly by the program		
Personnel (at 5% time)		
School counselor ($45,000)	2,225	
4 teachers (average $40,000)	8,000	
School principal ($50,000)	2,500	
2 community counselors (average $30,000)	3,000	
Travel	300	
Equipment (assumes depreciation)	300	
Telephone	250	
Supplies	100	
Facilities (meeting and work space at $10 per square foot for 200 square feet at 5% for 10 months)	1,000	
Subtotal	14,675	
Per student		146.80
Costs contributed by other sources		
Training	3,550	
Costs incurred by participants and parents		
Travel ($0.30 per mile times 2,000 miles)	600	
Parents' opportunity costs ($10 per hour for 50 parents times 2 hours)	1,000	
Community agency counseling (50 students for 5 hours times $50 per hour)	12,500	
Total social costs	31,425	
Per student		314.25

NOTE: Program size: 100 referrals.

involved spend 5% of their time on this activity. Other assumptions were made regarding average salaries, rent, parent lost opportunity costs, and so on to arrive at these costs. This example is hypothetical, but it was extrapolated from real patterns of program delivery (Swisher et al., 1993).

Table 43.1 illustrates the costs associated with operating an SAP if certain assumptions are made. The cost items would need to be de-termined for each school district as a function of the actual salaries and fees charged for services in the community. It also would be important to determine exactly how many parents were involved, how often, and so on. One could argue that the parents were not losing income by attending a meeting or that a minimum wage should be used. In fact, nearly every assumption in this illustration could be modified to fit local circumstances. However, for purposes of making planning decisions, these costs could be compared to the cost of hiring an external contractor to perform the same services. The components of each element in Table 43.1 would need to be revised according to the contractor's bid, but this type of information is crucial to decision makers. Pennsylvania's model might have been less expensive than other options, but there were both social costs and direct costs associated with this approach, as there are with any other approach.

Cost-Effectiveness

This section illustrates the costs required to produce a level of effect, for example, the cost of an increment of improved school achievement. The preceding section asked whether the costs justify the returns (costs vs. benefits). The Missouri Comprehensive Guidance Program (MCGP) and the research results obtained are the basis for this section on cost-effectiveness (Lapan et al., 1997).

Lapan and colleagues (1997) analyzed the differential effectiveness of more fully implemented guidance and counseling programs versus less fully implemented programs. Their effectiveness criteria were differences in school grades, student perceptions of how well they were prepared for the future, and student perceptions of how much they liked school. The 236 schools being compared all were implementing the MCGP, which emphasizes three program components:

1. Developmental competencies for students including career planning, knowledge of self and others, and educational and vocational development

2. Overall organizational plan including a philosophy and a budget

3. Identification of human, material, and political resources necessary to implement the program

The research design called for randomly sampling 100 students from each of the 236 schools, resulting in a total sample of 22,964 students. All students were administered the Secondary Student Questionnaire that included self-reported grades, perceptions of the adequacy of their preparation for the future, and the degree to which they liked school. School counselors from the 236 schools rated their guidance and counseling programs on a 32-item scale according to the extent to which they were implementing the MCGP elements and were receiving fiscal support for their programs. Each school was assigned a mean rating reflecting the degree of implementation of the MCGP.

The statistical analyses employed in this study controlled for school size, socioeconomic status, and minority representation. The findings indicated that schools with more fully implemented school guidance and counseling programs produced students with higher self-reported grade averages (half As and Bs vs. Bs or lower) and students who felt better prepared for the future. However, these programs did not influence how students felt about their schools.

In the MCGP study, there were approximately two counselors per school at an average salary of $34,188 per year. Teachers also are involved in the schools where the MCGP is more fully implemented, and their time devoted to the program also needs to be considered as a cost (Table 43.2). However, no data were pro-

TABLE 43.2   Costs of a Comprehensive Guidance Program Operating for 1 School Year to Achieve the Effect of Half a Letter Grade Improvement (in dollars)

Costs	Total Costs	Average Costs per Student
Costs incurred directly by the program		
Personnel		
2 school counselors ($34,188)	68,376	
20 teachers (average $30,000 at 1% time)	6,000	
School principal ($50,000 at 10% time)	5,000	
1 staff member ($15,000 at 50% time)	7,500	
Travel	2,000	
Equipment (assumes depreciation)	1,600	
Telephone	1,600	
Supplies	1,600	
Facilities (meeting and work space at $10 per square foot for 300 square feet at 100% for 10 months)	30,000	
Subtotal	123,676	
Per student		123.68
Costs contributed by other sources		
Training (in-service)	1,000	
Costs incurred by participants and parents		
Parents' opportunity costs (evenings and student assistance program at $10 per hour for 500 parents times 1 hour)	5,000	
Travel (250 cars times $0.30 per mile for 2,500 miles)	750	
Total social costs	137,426	
Per participant		130.43
Minus counselor salaries	(68,376)	
Adjusted social costs	69,050	
Adjusted per participant		69.05

NOTE: Program size: 1,000 students.

vided regarding the numbers of teachers per school, and assumptions are made regarding the numbers of teachers and the extent of their participation. Also, the higher implementing schools contributed more resources for travel and equipment, but detailed information on these items was not included and so assumptions also were made regarding these additional costs. In general, a 10% estimate was added to the basic counselor salaries for their travel, supplies, equipment, and phones ($6,800).

If a school with 1,000 students had no school counselors and wanted to achieve the effects as defined by Lapan and colleagues (1997), then it would need to spend approximately $123.68 per student per year to enhance academic performance by half a letter grade and to have students feel better prepared for their futures. If a school already has two school counselors, then these are not additional costs. Furthermore, if it is assumed that the additional costs are in the form of in-service training and staff support, then the additional costs would be $69.05 per student per year to achieve these outcomes. These same expenditures also will give students greater confidence in their preparation for the future. This type of self-efficacy also is important to future success (Herr & Cramer, 1988). These outcomes may help students obtain higher levels of postsecondary education that, in turn, lead to higher lifetime earnings (benefits). However, the illustration in this section is focused only on what it cost to achieve this level of improvement in grades and greater confidence regarding the future. These costs could be compared to those of other types of programs attempting to foster improvement in achievement and self-confidence to determine relative cost-effectiveness.

Cost-Benefit

Cost-benefit ratios are based on the knowledge of program costs, program effectiveness, and costs saved or revenues generated as a result of a program. This type of research usually requires longitudinal data through which one can observe outcomes such as lower rates of use of social services and higher levels of income.

Short-term benefits (i.e., 5 years) have been documented for a substance abuse prevention program (Pentz, 1998) known as the Midwestern Prevention Project (MPP), a comprehensive program that included five components introduced into schools and communities over a 5-year period. The components involved mass media programming of 31 programs per year for the first 3 years; a school program of 18 sessions during the first year, 13 during the second year, and 5 during the third year; a parent program operating from the third year on; a community task force operating from the third year on; and local policy changes during the fourth and fifth years (Pentz et al., 1989).

This program was implemented in a large metropolitan area and was estimated to cost $30 per family unit per year (Table 43.3). In a follow-up of a sample of the participants and controls, it was determined that in the short term (i.e., 3 years), there was an estimated reduction in health care costs. The cost-benefit ratio for this program was 1.00:8.12, indicating that for every $1.00 spent on prevention, there was a savings of $8.12 per family. Long-term benefits also were calculated for reduced daily smoking (8% less in the experimental group) and were estimated at 1.00:67.63, indicating that for every $1.00 spent, $67.63 was saved in reduced morbidity and mortality costs over a lifetime.

Another look at long-term benefits can be seen through the LST program (Botvin & Tortu, 1988) that has repeatedly been shown to be effective and to have its effectiveness endure for up to 3 years after the end of the program (Botvin et al., 1995). This program typically is delivered by counselors or teachers and requires special training as well as leader and student workbooks. The program is designed to increase an individual's abilities in several domains including goal-setting skills, decision-making skills, knowledge of risks associated with substance use, coping skills, normative awareness, communication skills, social skills, and refusal (assertiveness) skills. The program

TABLE 43.3 Costs and Cost-Benefit Ratio for Project Star: 1989-1990 (in dollars)

Prevention Component	Direct Costs	Donated Costs
Program development		90,000
Training	100,000	76,000
Implementation	715,000	150,000
Institutionalization	88,000	
Research/evaluation	846,000	79,000
Total (direct and donated)	2,144,000	
Per family unit	30	
Cost-benefit ratio for smoking reduction	1.00:8.12	

NOTE: Program size: 26,000 families.

also entails 18 sessions, usually beginning in Grade 6 or 7, and 10 sessions in each of 2 subsequent years. The costs of this type of program (Table 43.4) are fairly straightforward, and as will be seen, the long-term benefits are very positive (Table 43.4). Botvin and colleagues (1995) reported 30% fewer pack-a-day smokers for the experimental group. This would be the equivalent of 40 fewer pack-a-day smokers in the hypothetical school of 1,000 students.

Table 43.4 indicates that the cost per student for LST is $114 over a 3-year period. From a cost-effectiveness standpoint, $114 per student in additional costs would be required to reduce smoking. It should be noted that this program also reduced drunkenness, marijuana use, and polydrug use (Botvin et al., 1995).

The estimated cost-benefit ratio is based on 3-year costs divided by the number of affected individuals and would be $1:10.65. Dollars in this estimate were neither discounted nor inflated. This is based on the assumption that

$56,000 is the lifetime costs and losses per smoker. Oster, Colditz, and Kelly (1984) estimated this cost at $28,000 in 1984, and even at a low rate of inflation, this figure probably would have doubled by 2000.

It would cost approximately $1.0 billion to implement LST-type programs for all 12- to 15-year-olds through schools and community agencies across the country. The potential savings for 30% fewer smokers would reduce the social costs of smoking ($138 billion) by $41.0 billion. For alcohol benefits, the potential savings would be $47.5 billion, and the savings for drug abuse would be $46.0 billion. The cost-benefit ratio for this scenario would be 1:134, indicating that for every $1 spent on junior high school students, there would be a total social cost savings of $134 per person over their lifetimes.

Conclusions

Costs in this chapter have been defined more comprehensively than counselors in schools and communities usually consider. These include all expenditures to provide services as well as costs to participate in services (e.g., time, travel). Cost-effectiveness was described as the costs required to achieve a level of effect. At this juncture, policy makers can compare services in terms of cost-effectiveness. Cost-benefit was defined as the total social cost required to derive savings in reduced demand for services. Examples were given indicating short- and long-term cost-benefit ratios. It is clear that the costs of counseling services can be justified with reference to their ability to save society other costs, particularly in the health care domain.

TABLE 43.4   Costs of a Life-Skills Training Substance Abuse Prevention Program Operating for 1 School Year (in dollars)

Costs	Total Costs	Average Costs per Student
Costs incurred directly by the program		
Personnel (at 5% time)		
2 school counselors ($45,000)	4,500	
10 teachers (average $40,000)	20,000	
Training	3,000	
Travel	300	
Equipment (assumes depreciation)	300	
Telephone	300	
Supplies (student workbooks)	6,000	
Facilities (Classrooms—no opportunity costs imputed)		
Subtotal	34,400	
Per participant		34.40
Costs contributed by other sources		
Costs incurred by participants and parents		
Travel (at $0.30 per mile times 2,000 miles)	600	
Parents' opportunity costs ($10 per hour for 500 parents times 1 hour for homework)	5,000	
Total social costs	40,000	
Per participant		40.00
3-year costs	114,000	
3-year costs per affected participant		114.00
Cost-benefit ratio for smoking reduction: 1.00:19.65		
(40 students were prevented from pack-a-day smoking. Lifetime benefits are $56,000 ÷ $2,850)		

NOTE: Program size: 1,000 students and families.

In the future, counselors in schools and community agencies will need to be more sophisticated regarding real total costs, the cost-effectiveness of various interventions, and the ultimate cost-benefit to their clientele. The managed care movement already has begun to emphasize cost considerations in its planning, and the counseling profession would be better positioned to negotiate if data were available supporting counseling services as cost-effective and cost-beneficial. The lack of these cost data as a basis for planning has created an opportunity for decisions to be made on other bases. Schools also are becoming more cost conscious as a result of drains on their budgets from vouchers and alternative tax bases. School counselors also will be asked to justify their efforts in the context of value added.

References

Botvin, G. J., Baker, E., Dusenbury, L., Botvin, E. M., & Diaz, T. (1995). Long-term follow-up results of a randomized drug abuse prevention trial in a White middle-class population. *Journal of the American Medical Association, 273,* 1106-1112.

Botvin, G. J., & Tortu, S. (1988). Prevention of adolescent substance abuse through Life Skills Training. In R. Price, E. Cowen, R. Lorion, & J. Ramos-McKay (Eds.), *14 ounces of prevention* (pp. 98-110). Washington, DC: American Psychological Association.

Herr, E. L., & Cramer, S. H. (1988). *Career guidance and counseling through the life span: Systematic approaches* (3rd ed.). New York: HarperCollins.

Hu, T. W., Swisher, J. D., & McDonnell, N. (1978). *Cost/effectiveness study of drug prevention programs.* Research report by the Institute for Policy Research and Evaluation, Pennsylvania State University, for the National Institute on Drug Abuse.

Hurley, S. (1990). A review of cost-effectiveness analyses. *Medical Journal of Australia, 153,* S20-S23.

Kaltrider, D. L., & St. Pierre, T. L. (1995). Beyond the schools: Strategies for implementing successful drug prevention programs in community youth-serving organizations. *Journal of Drug Education, 25,* 223-237.

Klein, M., & Swisher, J. (1983). A statewide evaluation of a communication and parenting skills program. *Journal of Drug Education, 13,* 73-82.

Lambert, M. J., & Cattani-Thompson, K. (1996). Current findings regarding the effectiveness of counseling: Implications for practice. *Journal of Counseling and Development, 74,* 601-608.

Lapan, R. T., Gysbers, N. C., & Sun, Y. (1997). The impact of more fully implemented guidance programs on the school experiences of high school students: A statewide evaluation study. *Journal of Counseling and Development, 75,* 292-302.

Mitchel, M., Hu, T., McDonnell, N., & Swisher, J. (1984). Cost-effectiveness analysis of an educational drug abuse prevention program. *Journal of Drug Education, 14,* 271-292.

Myrick, R. D. (1993). *Developmental guidance and counseling: A practical approach.* Minneapolis, MN: Educational Media Corporation.

Nathan, P. E. (1998). Practice guidelines: Not yet ideal. *American Psychologist, 53,* 290-299.

Oster, G., Colditz, G. A., & Kelly, N. L. (1984). *The economic costs of smoking and benefits of quitting.* Lexington, MA: D. C. Heath.

Pentz, M. A. (1998). Costs, benefits, and cost effectiveness of comprehensive drug abuse prevention. In W. Bukoski & R. Evans (Eds.), *Cost-benefit/cost-effectiveness research of drug abuse prevention: Implications for programming and policy* (Research Monograph Series, No. 176, pp. 111-129). Rockville, MD: National Institute on Drug Abuse.

Pentz, M. A., Dwyer, H. H., MacKinnon, D. P., Flay, B. R., Hansen, W. B., Wang E. Y. I., & Johnson, C. A. (1989). A multicommunity trial for primary prevention of adolescent drug abuse: Effects on drug use prevalence. *Journal of the American Medical Association, 261,* 3259-3266.

Plotnick, R. D. (1994). Applying benefit-cost analyses to substance use prevention programs. *International Journal of the Addictions, 29,* 339-359.

Swisher, J., Baker, S., Barnes, J., Doebler, M., Haldeman, D., & Kophazi, K. (1993). An evaluation of student assistance programs in Pennsylvania. *Journal of Alcohol and Drug Education, 39,* 1-33.

PART VII

Conclusion

CHAPTER FORTY-FOUR

Counseling and the Future

DON C. LOCKE

JANE E. MYERS

EDWIN L. HERR

We had a number of goals in mind when we set out to develop this handbook. The foremost of these goals was to provide the reader with access to that unique body of knowledge that defines the profession of counseling. Our intent was to describe the state of the art in our profession as it exists at the present time including the history, conceptual models, and practices of counseling. Furthermore, we sought to project the challenges for the future that face us as a profession.

The plan for this handbook arose from a need to provide, in a single volume, a comprehensive overview of the profession of counseling. Such a treatment is needed to reflect the changing policies, demographics, and social and economic environment of the United States as well as the challenges for counselors produced by these processes. Because we wanted the content of the handbook to be of the best quality possible, we carefully selected a diverse group of professional counselors to serve as contributing authors. These practitioners, researchers, and theorists helped us to achieve our goal of developing a handbook devoted exclusively to our profession. The handbook has been designed to provide a comprehensive understanding of the profession of counseling, foundations of counseling, counseling settings and interventions, counselor education and supervision, research in counseling, and critical issues and emerging topics.

In this chapter, current trends and projections in the profession of counseling are identified and discussed. Similarly, selected social and environmental factors that influence the profession of counseling are reviewed. Examination of the future possibilities of and challenges to the profession of counseling is one of the central methods through which professional counselors bring order to their understanding of our present and give meaning to the past. Based on the contributions to this handbook, the future of the profession of counseling is bright. However, in this chapter, discussion is in order about how professional counselors might prepare for the changes that the future will bring and the anticipated value conflicts accompanying those changes for the profession and its future mission in society.

History, Conceptual Models, Practices, and Practitioners

Sweeney (Chapter 1) explained how counseling evolved from an educational guidance perspective early in the 20th century to become a distinct mental health profession by the end of that century. Bradley and Cox (Chapter 2) provided further support for the evolution of the profession through a discussion of school, community, mental health, and marriage and family counseling emphases. Our history is based, in large part, on the individual and collective energies of special interests and specialties, which comprise both a source of strength and diversity and a challenge to unity as a single profession in the marketplace and community (Myers & Sweeney, Chapter 3).

Counseling shares much in common with other mental health professions, yet the philosophy on which we base our practice differs in important ways, as discussed by numerous authors in this handbook, notably Sweeney (Chapter 1); Myers and Sweeney (Chapter 3); Engels and Bradley (Chapter 6); Smith (Chapter 35); Herr and Niles (Chapter 40); and Palmo, Shosh, and Weikel (Chapter 42). As counselors, we apply strategies of prevention and holism based on developmental principles both to normal developmental processes and to aid in the understanding of pathology. Traditional approaches to working with clients, including humanistic (Hazler, Chapter 8) and existential (Robinson & Jones, Chapter 10) as well as cognitive-behavioral (Holden, Chapter 8) and Adlerian (Carlson & Sperry, Chapter 11) counseling, are as fundamental to the preparation of professional counselors as are the basic counseling skills described by Goodman (Chapter 15). Increasingly, new metatheories are becoming essential to the repertoire of effective counseling. Such approaches include cognitive developmental stage theories (Sprinthall, Peace, & Kennington, Chapter 7), development counseling and therapy (Ivey & Ivey, Chapter 14), and other methods subsumed under the rubric of "postmodern theories" of counseling as described by Rigazio-DiGilio (Chapter 13).

The practice of counseling has been defined as "the application of mental health, psychological, or human development principles, through cognitive, affective, behavioral, or systemic intervention strategies, that address wellness, personal growth, or career development as well as pathology" (American Counseling Association [ACA] Governing Council minutes, October 17-19, 1997, p. 8).

Engels and Bradley (Chapter 6) discussed counseling as a distinguished and distinctive caring profession, promoting the worth, dignity, uniqueness, and potential of all individuals including those in underserved, vulnerable, and oppressed populations and meriting equivalent status with other caring professions. As social, economic, and political changes occur, so too do the problems that clients bring to counselors. Therefore, counseling constantly strives to serve all persons and all institutions in a rapidly changing, industrialized, technologically based society. Such an effort requires the development of new approaches to new problems and new issues. The old theories and techniques might not be adequate for the challenges presented by life during the 21st century.

Throughout the 20th century, particularly the latter 50 years, the number of professional counselors grew quite rapidly. Hosie and Glosoff (Chapter 23) reported that more than 500 colleges and universities offer approximately 1,000 counselor education degree programs in the United States including master's through doctoral training. Engels and Bradley (Chapter 6) reported some 135 schools with nationally accredited counselor education programs, 65,000 state credentialed professional counselors, more than 45,000 nationally credentialed professional counselors, and more than 110,000 members of state and national counselor associations. Myers and Sweeney (Chapter 2) and Yep and Locke (Chapter 34) noted statistics from the *Occupational Outlook Handbook* suggesting that more than 200,000 professional counselors are practicing in the United States. Clearly, there are many more counselors functioning than are officially recorded by professional organizations. Many of those professional counselors who are counted are graduates of institutions accredited by the Council for Accreditation of Counseling and Related Educational Programs (CACREP), are licensed in their home states, and are certified by the national counselor certifying organization. Many who do not meet these professional standards are seeking to meet the standards set by the profession. With so many in practice, it seems rather obvious that there is a need for the services that professional counselors provide. We would do well to ask ourselves the basis of that need.

The Need for Professional Counseling: A Parable

Janet Poppendieck used a parable in her book, *Sweet Charity? Emergency Food and the End of Entitlement,* that may be interpreted as providing a sound basis for the existence of the profession of counseling (Poppendieck, 1998). In the parable, there is a community along a river and everything is going along just fine until, one day, a baby comes floating downstream. Everyone is appalled and alarmed. They all rush out to save the baby, finding clothes to swaddle it in, food to feed it, and a warm home and family to take it in from the cold. At the end of the day, everyone celebrates and pats each other on the back for helping out. The warm glow of a good deed done settles over the entire community.

But then, the next day, another baby comes floating down the river and everyone is galvanized back into action. And again, they succeed and save the baby. But the day after that, another baby comes, and the subsequent day, two babies come down the river. Pretty soon, babies are coming down the river every day, sometimes as many as a half dozen at a time. It does not take long for the community to realize that it needs to get organized if it is going to succeed at saving all of these babies. So, dozens of baby-saving organizations are created, some targeting low-income babies, others serving babies with learning disabilities, and still others helping babies only from rural areas; bylaws and policies and procedures are written, and boards and committees are created; professional consultants are hired to give workshops on effective baby-saving techniques; baby-saving newsletters are published; the local community college develops a professional certification program for baby savers; foundations establish baby saving as a new priority funding area and conduct grant-writing sessions across the region; employee benefits programs and pension plans are developed to attract and retain high-caliber professional baby savers; a coalition of all the baby-saving organizations is created so that, what with resources being so scarce, a baby that receives help from one organization will not accidentally receive help from another; the local media run heartwarming stories about how committed the community is to saving babies; and an annual awards banquet is held to honor the best baby savers.

However, during all of this frenzied activity, no one makes the effort to venture upstream and find out what is causing all of these babies to end up in the river in the first place. There are a lot of reasons for this. First, all of this baby saving has endowed the community with an altruistic glow; everyone has put aside their old antagonisms to come together and do a good deed, and they feel good about themselves. They are saving babies. What could be better than that? Second, much of the community's economy during recent years has been built up on all of this baby saving. An awful lot of money is being spent on payroll, rent, telephone, postage, printing, and all the other expenses involved in the baby-saving effort. Third, people are afraid that if they go upstream, they will find out that the problem that is causing all these ba-

bies to come down the river is far too big and complicated to solve. They might even find out that the basic assumptions and principles by which they currently live their lives actually are the root causes of this problem. "Better we just stick with what we know," they conclude, "saving babies as they float down into our town."

This parable has meaning for professional counselors in that the policies that support counseling and the decisions of individual counselors determine where the profession of counseling places its focus—preparing and supervising counselors who possess finely tuned counseling strategies for helping clients to deal with all the challenges they face in life or preparing and supervising counselors who find out why these challenges exist in the first place.

The Distinctive Characteristics of the Counseling Profession

The profession of counseling has made a commitment to distinguish itself from other mental health professions and to create a particular field of practice that facilitates change from within the profession, as described by Palmo, Shosh, and Weikel (Chapter 42); from societal issues (e.g., spirituality), as described by Burke and Miranti (Chapter 38); or from individual needs for help with their choice options and their lack of information, negative emotions, and irrational beliefs. These authors and others in the handbook argued for system changes so that the highest quality of service can be provided in a cost-effective, efficient, and caring way. For example, Stevens (Chapter 12) predicted that family therapists will use more integrated procedures and techniques, will focus more on specific individual psychiatric disorders, will be more insurance driven, and will be influenced by research findings. Swisher (Chapter 43) called for counselors to be more sophisticated regarding real total costs of services, the cost-effectiveness of various interventions, and the ultimate cost-benefit to their clients. He argued that it is out of this commitment to prevention that counseling has established itself as unique in the mental health field.

Even so, counselors do many of the same things as do other mental health professionals. Educated with a strong background in growth and development, professional counselors distinguish themselves in the prevention and wellness arena. Myers, Sweeney, and Witmer (Chapter 41) reported that some two-thirds of all premature deaths in the United States are due to lifestyle factors that can be modified. Furthermore, whereas more than 75% of health care dollars are spent to treat people with chronic diseases, less than 1% of federal funds and 2% of state funds are spent to prevent these diseases from occurring. These authors argued that professional counselors should take a leadership role in educating and implementing a developmental, comprehensive model applicable to persons of all ages and in all settings. In public education efforts, the profession of counseling must emphasize how the training of professional counselors differs from the training of other mental health professionals.

Professional counselors must affirm that national standards in counseling require preparation in human development, cultural diversity, career development, and individual appraisal and assessment; methods for working with individuals, families, couples, and groups; and methods for working with college students (Collison, Chapter 4; Hosie & Glosoff, Chapter 23). Furthermore, supervised training in clinical practice is a foundation of counselor training and, at the same time, a growing area of

emphasis and professional concern (Borders, Chapter 24). Counselors are trained to seek guidance in decision making from our ethical standards and in the future will benefit from turning to the standards for help in increasingly complex and challenging ethical dilemmas, as discussed by Herlihy and Remley (Chapter 5).

Professional counselors can use their training in support of the emerging paradigm in health care that stresses prevention, early intervention, and alternative methods of remediation. Sprinthall, Peace, and Kennington (Chapter 7) expect the demands on and the expectations of professional counselors to grow in both complexity and degree. Factors such as continuing demographic changes, new immigrants, economic discrepancies, disenfranchised adolescents, and managed care require professional counselors to broaden their ideas about helping. Emphasis on human growth and development can be used to guide professional counselor practice that responds effectively to future client and societal needs. Lee (Chapter 36) sees ethnically responsive counseling, with special attention to bicultural identity development, as one specific response to the changing demographics from which future clients will come—growing numbers of women, persons of color, and immigrants. Robinson and Watt (Chapter 37) give voice to the idea that the multiple identities of gender, sexuality, and religion, as well as their intersection with other identity constructs, provide important insight for intra- and interpersonal issue exploration for many client populations.

Research in the Counseling Profession

Major advances in the prevention of problems in several areas of mental health have led to an increased awareness of the promise of prevention in the overall scheme of life enhancement. What is needed is a research agenda designed to expand the knowledge base for preventive interventions, more rigorous evaluation, and coordinated research efforts across disciplines. Szymanski and Parker (Chapter 26) posited that epistemological and methodological diversity is necessary for responsible growth of the counseling profession. High-quality methodologically diverse research must reach the field and inform practice. To achieve this goal, the counseling community must conduct practically relevant, high-quality research and ensure that editorial processes do not accept specific epistemologies and methodologies while they marginalize others.

Elmore and Bradley (Chapter 27) and Paisley and Reeves (Chapter 28) argued that research methods must be driven by research questions. As questions are generated from changes in the dynamics of counseling, so too will the approaches used to answer these new questions. If counseling is to come of age, then we must come to a place where we honor multiple question styles and multiple methods of answering those questions. Hohenshil and Getz (Chapter 17) suggested that clinical research could lead to new diagnoses and treatment approaches that can be reflected in publications such as the *Diagnostic and Statistical Manual of Mental Disorders* (American Psychiatric Association, 1994). A growing knowledge base asserts that increasing social awareness and understanding of sexual orientation, gender, and cultural background will have an impact on what behavior is to be diagnosed and treated. The medical model focused on pathology may decline, and more holistic approaches to using an individual's strengths may continue to evolve, providing opportunities for new research ques-

tions. Loesch (Chapter 30) suggested that evaluation is not a popular topic in the counseling profession, even when the various stakeholders for counseling service delivery demand evaluative information. He supported the application of unique combinations of approaches and techniques to achieve useful evaluative information. He also recommended that each counseling program be evaluated in multiple ways. Hohenshil and Getz (Chapter 17) identified the ERIC Clearinghouse on Assessment and Evaluation as a source for information on testing and assessment. The clearinghouse includes an online test library, search capabilities, and an online bookstore of testing materials. The use of such strategies and information will benefit both the profession and society in general. Clearly, there is a critical need for counseling practice to be based on empirically tested data—what Sexton (Chapter 29) called *evidence-based practice*—with counselors expected to demonstrate expertise about treatments likely to work with different presenting problems. The case management of each and every client will need to take the form of a mini-research design, with the resulting information being used to further improve the counseling practice with clients with similar concerns and emotional responses.

The Settings for Counseling

Currently, the principal settings for the delivery of professional counseling are schools, colleges and universities, community agencies, medical settings, and private practice. Professional counseling practices in these environments use a variety of delivery systems; operate from specific counseling theories; and serve children, adolescents, adults, and families.

Arredondo and Lewis (Chapter 16) reminded us that the future of the counseling profession has been an ongoing topic for decades. Counseling roles must be adapted to the priorities of various work settings. The idea that social issues should be included in the role of counselors emerged during the 1980s. These authors suggested that counselors can become prepared for the future by learning to recognize and deal with high-risk situations; using educational approaches to build life competencies; becoming adept at influencing the political, social, and economic environments that affect clients; lobbying for legislation that protects human rights; and becoming experts in strategic planning. These roles can be developed in any of the settings in which counselors work.

Baker and Gerler (Chapter 18) reported that school counselors will continue to face numerous challenges—achieving multicultural competence as school populations become increasingly diverse, becoming successful social activists for students, meeting the challenge of changing computer and networking technology, coping with the "echo" baby boom and with increasing demand for new services, providing effective services with relatively high workloads, and helping students to make the transition from school to work in an increasingly complex world. The substance of school counseling is expected to remain a 21st-century challenge with identity and role confusion issues.

Fukuyama (Chapter 19) identified a number of challenges that will be faced by college and university counselors—the introduction of distance learning, the use of the Internet, the effects of managed care, and the question of outsourcing counseling services. College and university counselors will continue to contribute to the growth and development of college students in many different ways—individual

and group counseling, psychoeducational workshops, consultation with faculty and staff, training of peer counselors, and career and life planning interventions.

Barker (Chapter 22) reported that professional counselors who work in medical settings experience job-related challenges similar to those experienced by other health care professionals—lower reimbursement rates, increased information demands, limitations on the number of providers accepted on managed care panels, and increased time spent communicating with insurance companies. These challenges exist alongside the need for increased numbers of counselors in nursing homes, the need for counselors to assist clients and their families in adjusting to life with transplanted organs or biomedically engineered body parts, and the need for counselors to screen clients for their appropriateness for organ transplants and other advanced surgeries.

Professional counselors in community settings, as reported by Gladding and Ryan (Chapter 20), will see an increasing need for their services. As communities change and as diversity increases, so too will the need for counselors to deal with the change and chaos that may occur. Counseling in community settings remains quite attractive, and this attraction is expected to grow as counselors find these positions to be both challenging and stimulating. These authors reported an expectation of increased funding for preventive efforts in an attempt to both promote health and decrease violence within individual communities.

Ginter (Chapter 21) predicted a bright future for professional counselors in private practice in spite of the growth of managed care. Master's-level professional counselors have been able to secure a prominent position in the new practice environment because of their competency, the fee differential between them and doctoral-level professionals, and the wide range of services they can provide (e.g., remediation, prevention, enhancement).

Emerging Issues

Based on what the contributing authors wrote in this handbook, it is clear that the profession of counseling will face several major hurdles in the near future. Politically, there is concern about national leadership and how the program emphases identified as significant by counselors will fare in budget deliberations. Socially, according to the demographic projections by D'Andrea and Daniels (Chapter 31), the rapid growth in the sheer numbers of citizens in at-risk categories will require that counselors direct more time and energy toward the negative contextual factors that undermine the mental health of persons in these categories. An increasing focus on factors and issues outside counselors' offices may be seen by some as an inappropriate role and function, but it surely is seen by many as a proper place for counselors to be devoting time and attention. Unless counselors develop and implement strategies to change the contextual and environmental conditions that adversely affect the lives of many citizens, they run the risk of undermining their relevance and respectability in the minds of many who are victimized by such external conditions.

Garrett (Chapter 32) argued that counselors have a responsibility to challenge and change systems that allow, ignore, encourage, or promote injustices that demean the human spirit and body through oppression, abuse of privilege, and/or outright harm. Among the contextual and environmental conditions of continuing concern are racism in a growing multicultural nation. Kiselica and Ramsey (Chapter 25) identified several trends pertaining to the practice of multicultural counseling theory, practice, and research. They anticipate multicultural training becoming infused throughout counselor education curricula. This infusion increasingly will occur as counselor educators who were trained prior to the emphasis on multiculturalism phase into retirement and more recently trained professional counselors assume roles as counselor educators. The new counselor educators represent a more culturally diverse group, and their students are participating in multicultural immersion experiences as part of their training. This new faculty will themselves mentor a more diverse group of students while they demonstrate the efficacy of multicultural counseling and training through experimental empirical research.

A separate chapter on substance abuse (Swisher, Bechtel, Henry, Vicary, & Smith, Chapter 33) was included in this handbook because of the dramatic statistics on addiction and substance abuse in the United States. Joseph Califano, president of the Center on Addiction and Substance Abuse at Columbia University, reported that substance abuse and addiction accounts for at least $140 billion of the $1 trillion that Americans were expected to spend on health care in 1994 (Califano, 1993). He went on to speculate that drugs and alcohol are implicated in at least three fourths of the nation's homicides, suicides, assaults, rapes, and child molestations; fully 80% of state and local prisoners are incarcerated for drug- and alcohol-related crimes. Most of the homeless are victims of alcohol and drug abuse.

Because the Internet provides immediate access to the latest information on an unending list of topics, Sampson and Bloom (Chapter 39) argued that professional counselors must become proficient in Internet use. Using the Internet, counselors can immediately access the latest information from major libraries, agencies, and organizations from around the world, and using this information, they can develop the latest treatment strategies. The Internet also enables counselors to receive consultations from experts around the world through e-mail and professional discussion list services. Hohenshil and Getz (Chapter 17) identified computerized programs available for treatment planning that track client demographic data, mental status and prognosis, treatment modality and approaches, progress, discharge criteria, and provider credentials. Professional counselors of tomorrow must be prepared to work within an information society where the amount of information is doubling every year. Professional counselors must learn how to learn and must not be intimidated by change as more emphasis is placed on learning concepts and problem solving.

Professional counselors will need a broad knowledge base to deliver comprehensive counseling services and also will need specialized knowledge to cope with changes in client conditions. Changes in client populations were predicted by a number of contributing authors in this handbook. These changes are assumed to affect all areas of the counseling profession. The announcement that scientists have unstrung the human genome, biology's basic book of life, heralds the dawn of a new mental health era ("Genetic Map," 2000). New mental illnesses will be differentiated as medical research continues. Additional research will focus on biochemical causes of mental and emotional illnesses and symptom complexes not previously labeled. Counseling research will continue to focus on mental health diagnoses and the most effective interventions for clients demonstrating specific diagnoses as well as developmental

and wellness emphases that will prevent these problems from occurring.

Counselors will be functioning on a more professional level as a result of changes in the practice environments and will expect to be treated as colleagues rather than as the subordinates of the past. An increasing need for counselors to more clearly articulate their role in the delivery of mental health care will support this new collaborative level of relationships. Commonly understood descriptions of what counselors do for clients are essential if counseling is to be recognized as a principal contributor to mental health care. Counselors need to work in collaboration, not in competition, with other mental health care providers to increase the effectiveness of mental health delivery systems.

This handbook does not offer a single vision for the future; rather, it offers several alternative visions. All are based on the optimal development of counselors as individuals, as described by Herr and Niles (Chapter 40) in their discussion of character and personal responsibility. It is the hope of the editors and the contributing authors that the counseling profession will be able to apply the insights contained here to shape a better future both for the profession and for those we serve. Such an outcome is both the legacy and the promise of counseling.

References

American Psychiatric Association. (1994). *Diagnostic and statistical manual of mental disorders* (4th ed.). Washington, DC: Author.

Califano, J. A., Jr. (1993, November 14). America in denial. *The Washington Post*, p. C7.

Genetic map is hailed as new power. (2000, June 27). *USA Today*, p. A1.

Poppendieck, J. (1998). *Sweet charity? Emergency food and the end of entitlement*. New York: Viking.

APPENDIX A

American Counseling Association Divisions

Association for Assessment in Counseling (AAC). Originally the Association for Measurement and Evaluation in Guidance, AAC was chartered in 1965. The purpose of AAC is to promote the effective use of assessment in the counseling profession. Membership: 1,077

Association for Adult Development and Aging (AADA). Chartered in 1986, AADA serves as a focal point for information sharing, professional development, and advocacy related to adult development and aging issues. AADA addresses counseling concerns across the life span. Membership: 1,156

American College Counseling Association (ACCA). ACCA is one of the newest divisions of the American Counseling Association (ACA). Chartered in 1991, the focus of ACCA is on fostering student development in colleges, universities, and community colleges. Membership: 1,874

Association for Counselors and Educators in Government (ACEG). Originally the Military Educators and Counselors Association, ACEG was chartered in 1984. ACEG is dedicated to counseling clients and their families in local, state, and federal government or in military-related agencies. Membership: 367

Association for Counselor Education and Supervision (ACES). Originally the National Association of Guidance and Counselor Trainers, ACES was a founding association of ACA in 1952. ACES emphasizes the need for quality education and supervision of counselors for all work settings. Membership: 2,456

Association for Gay, Lesbian, and Bisexual Issues in Counseling (AGLBIC). AGLBIC educates

EDITORS' NOTE: Memberships are as of December 31, 2000.

693

counselors about the unique needs of client identity development and a nonthreatening counseling environment by aiding in the reduction of stereotypical thinking and homo-prejudice. Membership: 877

Association for Multicultural Counseling and Development (AMCD). Originally the Association of Non-White Concerns in Personnel and Guidance, AMCD was chartered in 1972. AMCD strives to improve cultural, ethnic, and racial empathy and understanding by programs to advance and sustain personal growth. Membership: 2,060

American Mental Health Counselors Association (AMHCA). Chartered in 1978, AMHCA represents mental health counselors, advocating for client access to quality services within the health care industry. Membership: 6,000+

American Rehabilitation Counseling Association (ARCA). Chartered in 1958, ARCA is concerned with helping people with physical, mental, and/or emotional disabilities to improve their lives. Membership: 944

American School Counselors Association (ASCA). Chartered in 1953, ASCA promotes school counseling professionals and interest in activities that affect the personal, educational, and career development of students. ASCA members also work with parents, educators, and community members to provide a positive learning environment. Membership: 11,000+

Association for Spiritual, Ethical, and Religious Values in Counseling (ASERVIC). Originally the National Catholic Guidance Conference, ASERVIC was chartered in 1974. ASERVIC is devoted to professionals who believe that spiritual, ethical, religious, and other human values

are essential to the full development of the person and to the discipline of counseling. Membership: 2,705

Association for Specialists in Group Work (ASGW). Chartered in 1973, ASGW provides professional leadership in the field of group work, establishes standards for professional training, and supports research and the dissemination of knowledge. Membership: 2,073

Counseling Association for Humanistic Education and Development (C-AHEAD). C-AHEAD, a founding association of ACA in 1952, provides a forum for the exchange of information about humanistically oriented counseling practices, and promotes changes that reflect the growing body of knowledge about humanistic principles applied to human development and potential. Membership: 688

Counselors for Social Justice (CSJ). CSJ actively promotes individual and collective social responsibility as well as the eradication of oppressive systems of power and privilege. CSJ develops and implements social action strategies through collaborative alliances with ACA entities, community organizations, and the community-at-large. Membership: 413

International Association of Addiction and Offender Counselors (IAAOC). Originally the Public Offender Counselors Association, IAAOC was chartered in 1972. Members of IAAOC advocate the development of effective counseling and rehabilitation programs for people with substance abuse problems, other addictions, and adult and/or juvenile public offenders. Membership: 1,684

International Association of Marriage and Family Counselors (IAMFC). Chartered in 1989,

IAMFC helps to develop healthy family systems through prevention, education, and therapy. Membership: 4,002

National Career Development Association (NCDA). Originally the National Vocational Guidance Association, NCDA was one of the founding associations of ACA in 1952. The mission of NCDA is to promote career development for all people across the life span through public information, member services, conferences, and publications. Membership: 2,731

National Employment Counseling Association (NECA). NECA originally was the National Employment Counselors Association and was chartered in 1966. The commitment of NECA is to offer professional leadership to people who counsel in employment and/or career development settings. Membership: 686

List of Abbreviations

This appendix includes abbreviations/acronyms frequently used by counselors. Many of these are used in the chapters in this handbook. All acronyms of associations and divisions are spelled out on their first use in every chapter. Other abbreviations/acronyms are considered to be important enough to be included in this appendix.

AAC	Association for Assessment in Counseling
AACD	American Association for Counseling and Development
AADA	Association for Adult Development and Aging
AAMFT	American Association for Marriage and Family Therapy
AAPC	American Association of Pastoral Counselors
AASCB	American Association of State Counseling Boards
AATA	American Art Therapy Association
ACA	American Counseling Association
ACCA	American College Counseling Association
ACEG	Association for Counselors and Educators in Government
ACES	Association for Counselor Education and Supervision
ACGPA	American Council of Guidance and Personnel Association
ACPA	American College Personnel Association
ACT	American College Testing Project
ADTA	American Dance Therapy Association

AERA	American Educational Research Association	ASGW	Association for Specialists in Group Work
AFTA	American Family Therapy Association	CAAP	Comprehensive Academic Achievement Program
AGLBIC	Association for Gay, Lesbian, and Bisexual Issues in Counseling	CACD	Connecticut Association for Counseling and Development
AHEAD	Association for Humanistic Education and Development	CACREP	Council for Accreditation of Counseling and Related Educational Programs
AMCD	Association for Multicultural Counseling and Development	C-AHEAD	Counseling Association for Humanistic Education and Development
AMECD	Association for Measurement and Evaluation in Counseling and Development	CCMHC	Certified Clinical Mental Health Counselor
AMEG	Association for Measurement and Evaluation in Guidance	CGPA	Counsel of Guidance and Personnel Association
AMHCA	American Mental Health Counselors Association	COPA	Council on Postsecondary Accreditation
ANWC	Association for Non-White Concerns in Personnel and Guidance	CSI	Chi Sigma Iota Honor Society
		CSJ	Counselors for Social Justice
APA	American Psychological Association	DCT	Developmental Counseling and Therapy
APGA	American Personnel and Guidance Association	DOT	Dictionary of Occupational Titles
ARCA	American Rehabilitation Counseling Association	DSM-IV	Diagnostic and Statistical Manual of Mental Disorders (4th ed.)
ASCA	American School Counselors Association	ERIC	Educational Resource Information Center
ASERVIC	Association for Spiritual, Ethical, and Religious Values in Counseling	IAAOC	International Association of Addictions and Offender Counselors

IAIC	International Alliance for Invitational Counseling	NCACES	North Central Association for Counselor Education and Supervision
IAMFC	International Association of Marriage and Family Counselors	NCATA	National Coalition of Art Therapies Association
MCI	Multicultural Counseling Inventory	NCATE	National Council for Accreditation of Teacher Education
MECA	Military Educators and Counselors Association	NCBLPC	North Carolina Board of Licensed Professional Counselors
NACAC	National Association of College Admission Counselors	NCC	National Certified Counslor
NACBT	National Association of Cognitive Behavioral Therapists	NCCC	National Certified Career Counselor
NACCMHC	National Academy of Certified Clinical Mental Health Counselors	NCDA	National Career Development Association
NACFT	National Academy for Certified Family Therapists	NCGC	National Certified Gerontological Counselor
NAEP	National Assessment of Educational Progress	NCIS	National Career Information System
NASP	National Association of School Psychologists	NCSC	National Certified School Counselor
NASW	National Association of Social Workers	NECA	National Employment Counselors Association
NAWDAC	National Association for Women Deans, Administrators, and Counselors	NIMH	National Institute of Mental Health
		NOICC	National Occupational Information Coordinating Committee
NBCC	National Board for Certified Counselors	NVGA	National Vocational Guidance Association
NCAA	National Collegiate Athletic Association	PGA	Personnel and Guidance Association

Don C. Locke, Ed.D., is Director of the Asheville Graduate Center and Director of the North Carolina State University (NCSU) doctoral program in Adult and Community College Education at the Asheville Graduate Center. Prior to moving to the Asheville Graduate Center, he was a professor and head of the Department of Counselor Education at NCSU. He earned a B.S. in history and an M.Ed. in history education from Tennessee State University. He began his career as a high school social studies teacher in Fort Wayne, Indiana, where he also worked as a high school counselor for 2 years. He earned his doctorate at Ball State University and currently serves on the Teachers College board of visitors at Ball State. He has been active in state, regional, and national counseling organizations. Prior professional service includes stints as president of the North Carolina Counseling Association, chair of the Southern Region Branch of the American Counseling Association (ACA), president of the Southern Association of Counselor Education and Supervision, member of ACA's Governing Council, chair of the Counseling and Human Development Foundation, associate editor of the *Mental Health Counselors Journal,* president of Chi Sigma Iota, and president of the Association for Counselor Education and Supervision. He is a recipient of the Ella Stephens Barrett Leadership Award from the North Carolina Counseling Association, the Professional Development Award from ACA, and the Professional Recognition Award from the ACA Foundation. He is the author or coauthor of more than 60 publications, with a current focus on multicultural issues. His 1992 book, *Increasing Multicultural Understanding,* was a Sage Publications best-seller, and the second edition was released in 1998. The second edition of *Psychological Techniques for Teachers* was published in 1995. His coauthored book, *Culture and Diversity Issues in Counseling,* was published in 1996.

Jane E. Myers, Ph.D., is Professor of Counselor Education at the University of North Carolina at Greensboro. She received her master's in rehabilitation counseling (specialist in counseling and educational administration) and doctorate in counselor education (with certificate in gerontology) from the University of Florida. She has worked as a rehabilitation counselor and an administrator of state service programs for older persons. She also directed five national grant projects on aging for the American Counseling Association (ACA), with funding in excess of $1 million, that developed curriculum materials and competencies for training counselors to work with older persons. She is a former president of the American Association for Counseling and Development (now ACA). She is a former president of two ACA divisions, the Association for Assessment in Counseling and the Association for Adult Development and Aging, for which she served as founding president. She has been an officer, a member, and a committee chair for national and division committees of ACA; has served on the editorial boards of ACA journals; and was selected as the founding editor of the *Journal of Adult Devel-*

755

opment and Aging. She also has served as president of both Chi Sigma Iota and Rho Chi Sigma. She has been chair of the Counseling and Human Development Foundation, the ACA Executive Director Search Committee, and the Council for Accreditation of Counseling and Related Educational Programs. She has written or edited more than 180 publications and has coproduced 7 training videotapes for gerontological counseling. Her recent books include *Adult Children and Aging Parents* and *Competencies for Gerontological Counseling.* She also is a coauthor of a model of wellness and an assessment instrument designed to promote individual evaluation and enhancement of holistic wellness across the life span.

Edwin L. Herr, Ed.D., is Distinguished Professor of Education (Counselor Education and Counseling Psychology); Associate Dean for Graduate Studies, Research, and Faculty Development; and Interim Department Head for Adult Education, Instructional Systems, and Workforce Education and Development in the College of Education at Pennsylvania State University. Prior to 1992, he served as head of the Department of Counselor Education, Counseling Psychology, and Rehabilitation Services Education or earlier department iterations for 24 years. He received his B.S. in business education from Shippensburg State College and received his M.A. in psychological foundations, professional diploma in coordination of guidance services, and Ed.D. in counseling and student personnel administration from Teachers College, Columbia University, where he was an alumni fellow. A former business teacher, school counselor, and director of guidance, he previously served as assistant and associate professor of counselor education at the State University of New York at Buffalo and as the first director of the Bureau of Guidance Services and the Bureau of Pupil Personnel Services in the Pennsylvania Department of Education. He has been a visiting professor, researcher, or coordinator of international conferences at some 20 European universities as well as those in Africa, Canada, Japan, and Taiwan. He is a past president of the American Association for Counseling and Development, past president of the National Vocational Guidance Association, and past president of the Association for Counselor Education and Supervision. He also served as president of Chi Sigma Iota during 2000-2001. He is the author or coauthor of more than 275 articles and book chapters as well as 31 books and monographs. He is a past editor of the *Journal of Counseling and Development* and of *Counselor Education and Supervision.* He is a member of several other editorial boards including that of the *British Journal of Guidance and Counselling.* He is a recipient of the Eminent Career Award of the National Career Development Association, the ACA Distinguished Professional Service Award, and the ACES 50th Anniversary Leadership Award.

Patricia Arredondo, Ed.D., is Associate Professor at Arizona State University and founder and president of Empowerment Workshops in Boston. She is known for her leadership in multicultural counseling competencies, the woman factor in multicultural counseling, reshaping counselor education, and Latino perspectives in counseling. She has served as president of the Association of Multicultural Counseling and Development and of the Society for the Psychological Study of Ethnic and Racial Minority Issues.

Sandra B. Barker, Ph.D., is Associate Professor of Psychiatry, Internal Medicine, and Anesthesiology in the Medical College of Virginia at Virginia Commonwealth University, where she serves as Associate Director of Inpatient Psychiatry Programs. She is also Adjunct Professor of Small Animal Clinical Sciences at Virginia-Maryland Regional College of Veterinary Medicine. Her research and clinical interests include trauma resolution, substance abuse, and the human-companion animal interaction. She has published and presented extensively in these areas. She is president of the Research and Assessment Corporation for Counseling board of advisers and is a past president of the International Association of Addictions and Offender Counselors (IAAOC), past chair of the Addictions Academy of the National Board of Certified Counselors, and recipient of the Distinguished Service Award and President's Award from IAAOC.

Stanley B. Baker, Ph.D., is Professor of Counselor Education and Head of the Department of Educational Research and Leadership and Counselor Education at North Carolina State University. A former school counselor, he has supervised school counseling interns and published research related to school counseling for nearly 30 years. His book, *School Counseling for the Twenty-First Century,* is used as a text for training school counselors in a number of training programs. From 1993 to 1999, he was the field editor of *The School Counselor* and *Professional School Counseling.*

Lori Bechtel, Ph.D., is Professor of Biobehavioral Health and Department Head of the Division of Education, Human Development, and Social Sciences at Altoona College of Pennsylvania State University. She has published widely in health education and has conducted numerous workshops for teachers that involve the integration of health into school curricula. She is a coinvestigator on Project ADAPT (Adoption of Drug Abuse Prevention Training), a National Institute on Drug Abuse-funded research study focusing on rural adolescent drug use.

John W. Bloom, Ph.D., is Professor of Counselor Education at Butler University. Previously, he taught at Northern Arizona University for 19 years. He has edited and authored books and articles related to technology applications in counseling and teaching. He currently is a member of the editorial board of the *Journal of*

Technology in Counseling and is professional editor of a Web site (www.cybercounsel.uncg. edu). He is a former chair of the board of directors of the National Board for Certified Counselors, former member of the Governing Council of the American Counseling Association, and former member of the board of directors of the American School Counselors Association.

L. DiAnne Borders, Ph.D., is Professor and Chair of the Department of Counseling and Educational Development at the University of North Carolina at Greensboro. She is coauthor of the *Handbook of Counseling Supervision,* has published numerous conceptual and empirical works on supervision practice and supervisor training, and has received several awards for her work. She has conducted supervision workshops for counselor educators and counseling practitioners across the United States and in Australia. She also has published extensively on professional issues, school counseling, and adoptive children and their families.

Loretta J. Bradley, Ph.D., is Professor of Counselor Education and past chair of the Division of Educational Psychology and Leadership at Texas Tech University. She was president of the American Counseling Association in 1998-99 and president of the Association for Counselor Education and Supervision in 1995-96. Previously, she was Associate Professor of Human Development Counseling at Peabody College of Vanderbilt University and an assistant dean of the College of Education at Temple University. She received the ACES Publication Award for the second edition of her book, *Counselor Supervision: Principles, Process, and Practice.* She is a recipient of the ACA Research Award and of the Association for Counselor Education Research Award. She was chair of the editorial board of the American Counselor and was a member of editorial boards for several other journals. She has authored or coauthored six

books and numerous manuscripts and book chapters.

Richard W. Bradley, Ph.D., is Emeritus Professor in the Department of Educational Psychology and Special Education at Southern Illinois University, Carbondale. He has authored or coauthored more than 75 publications and recently was recognized as among the top 1% of contributors to the *Journal of Counseling and Development* and the *Career Development Quarterly.* He has served on several American Counseling Association journal editorial boards and was the editor for four volumes of *Counselor Education and Supervision.* He was awarded the first American Association for Counseling and Development Extended Research Award for "Career Patterns of School Counselors: A 15-year Follow-Up" published in *Vocational Guidance Quarterly.*

Mary Thomas Burke, Ph.D., is Professor and Coordinator of Counseling at the University of North Carolina at Charlotte. She is the author or coauthor of numerous journal articles and has coedited two books on spirituality in counseling. She has served as president of Chi Sigma Iota, as president of the Association of Spiritual Ethical and Religious Values in Counseling, and as chair of the Council for Accreditation of Counseling and Related Educational Programs. She is a recipient of the Counselor of the Year Award from the American Counseling Association.

Jon Carlson, Psy.D., Ed.D., is Professor of Psychology and Counseling at Governors State University in Illinois and Psychologist at the Lake Geneva Wellness Clinic in Wisconsin. He is a past president of the International Association of Marriage and Family Counselors, the founding editor of *The Family Journal,* and a former editor of the *Journal of Individual Psychology.* He holds a diplomate in family psychology and in marital and family therapy. He has authored 25 books and 120 articles.

Brooke B. Collison, Ph.D., is Professor Emeritus of Counselor Education at Oregon State University. He is a past president of the American Counseling Association (ACA) and has published work in the areas of counselors as social advocates, school counseling, and counseling men. He is a former editorial board member of the *Journal of Counseling and Development* and is a recipient of the David Brooks Distinguished Mentor Award from the ACA Foundation. He and his spouse, Joan, are corecipients of the Joe Norton Service Award from the Association for Gay, Lesbian, and Bisexual Issues in Counseling.

Jane A. Cox, Ph.D., is Assistant Professor in the Department of Educational Psychology and Special Education at Southern Illinois University at Carbondale. Her areas of research and scholarly interest include the use of social construction concepts in counseling practice and training (including collaborative methods for supervision of counselors-in-training) and counseling with couples and families. She is active in the Association for Counselor Education and Supervision (ACES) and currently is chair of the ACES Doctoral Program Interest Network and as secretary of North Central ACES (NCACES). She also has served as the NCACES Conference program chair and as secretary for the Illinois Counselor Educators and Supervisors.

Michael D'Andrea, Ed.D., is Professor in the Department of Counselor Education at the University of Hawaii. He has authored or coauthored more than 100 journal articles, book chapters, books, and other scholarly works on a broad range of issues related to multicultural counseling. In addition to his extensive research in the area of multicultural counseling,

he is best known for his political and social activism in the counseling profession.

Judy Daniels, Ed.D., is Professor in the Department of Counselor Education at the University of Hawaii. Her research and publications focus primarily on issues related to multicultural counseling, the needs of homeless children, and the psychology of White racism. She is well-known for her efforts to promote changes in the counseling profession that reflect an increased level of understanding, sensitivity, and respect for cultural differences.

Patricia B. Elmore, Ph.D., is Associate Dean for Administrative Services in the College of Education and Professor in the Department of Educational Psychology and Special Education at Southern Illinois University, Carbondale. She specializes in educational measurement and statistics. She is a past president of the Association for Assessment in Counseling and is a recipient (with Ruth B. Ekstrom and Esther E. Diamond) of the American Counseling Association Research Award. She is editor of *Measurement and Evaluation in Counseling and Development* and is on the editorial boards of *Applied Measurement in Education* and *Educational and Psychological Measurement*. She coauthored *Basic Statistics* with Paula L. Woehlke.

Dennis W. Engels, Ph.D., is Regents Professor of Counselor Education at the University of North Texas at Denton. He teaches or supervises courses in career counseling, counseling theory and methods, counseling pre-practicum, ethics, life career development, and school counseling internship. His research and scholarly interests center on career development, decision making, ethics, human resource development, multipotentiality, and organizational and disciplinary history. He has published extensively in books, refereed journals, and other publications. He has held numerous offices and chairs in state and national professional organizations, has served as a consulting editor on several nationally refereed journals, has consulted with public and private sector organizations and agencies throughout the United States, and serves as editor of *Counseling and Values.* He is a past president of the National Career Development Association, was chair-elect of the American Counseling Association's Council of Journal Editors in 2000, and has served as president of the Texas Counseling Association.

Mary A. Fukuyama, Ph.D., is Clinical Professor and Psychologist at the University of Florida Counseling Center, where she has devoted most of her professional career to working with college students. Her other professional interests include training and teaching in the Department of Counselor Education. She is coauthor (with Todd Sevig) of *Integrating Spirituality Into Multicultural Counseling* and teaches a newly developed course on spiritual issues in counseling.

Michael Tlanusta Garrett, Ph.D., Eastern Band of Cherokee, is Assistant Professor of counseling in the Department of Human Services at Western Carolina University. He is the author of numerous articles and chapters dealing with wellness, spirituality, and cultural issues of counseling Native Americans. He also authored the book, *Walking on the Wind: Cherokee Teachings for Harmony and Balance,* and coauthored the book, *Medicine of the Cherokee: The Way of Right Relationship.* His experience with Native people, both professionally and personally, lends a unique perspective and expertise with Native American issues and concerns. He has worked with children and adolescents in the schools, with Native American and other minority students in higher education, as an individual and group therapist in a community agency setting, and as a project director in an urban Indian center serving the local Native American community.

Edwin R. Gerler, Jr., Ed.D., is Professor of Counselor Education and recently served as Associate Dean for Research and External Affairs in the College of Education of Psychology at North Carolina State University. A former elementary school counselor, he has published extensively in the counseling literature and has been the editor of two national counseling journals. He is the founding coeditor of *Meridian,* an online journal for professionals interested in middle school computer technologies (www.ncsu.edu/meridian), and the codirector of *MEGA,* an online computer technologies network for middle school educators (www.ncsu.edu/mega).

Hildy Getz, Ed.D., is Assistant Professor of Counselor Education at Virginia Tech. She has made numerous presentations and published on the topic of clinical supervision and is developing clinical supervision distance education courses and training. A focus of the courses she teaches is treatment planning and evaluation. She is a licensed professional counselor and marriage and family therapist in Virginia with many years of experience in community and private practice settings.

Earl J. Ginter, Ph.D., is Professor at the University of Georgia. He currently is editor of the *Journal of Counseling and Development,* the official journal of the American Counseling Association. His publications focus primarily on issues that comprise the theoretical and practice base of counseling. His research and assessment interests pertain to the application of developmental-based approaches to working with individuals, couples, families, and groups. He is a licensed professional counselor and a licensed marriage and family therapist affiliated with Psych-Health Associates in Athens, Georgia.

Samuel T. Gladding, Ph.D., is Professor and Director of the Counselor Education Program at Wake Forest University. His previous academic appointments were at the University of Alabama at Birmingham and at Fairfield University in Connecticut. He also has worked in mental health counseling. He is the author of more than 100 counseling publications, including 8 books. He is a former editor of the *Journal for Specialists in Group Work* and a past president of the Association for Counselor Education and Supervision, the Association for Specialists in Group Work, and Chi Sigma Iota.

Harriet L. Glosoff, Ph.D., is Associate Professor of Counselor Education and Director of the Counseling and School Psychology Lab at Mississippi State University. In addition to being a counselor educator, she has extensive experience in clinical supervision and more than 20 years experience in the provision of counseling services in diverse settings such as community agencies, psychiatric facilities, public schools, and the private sector. Her primary research interests are in the areas of professional ethics, clinical supervision, and process variables related to treatment outcomes. She is the author of several book chapters and articles on professional ethics and on issues related to the counseling profession and credentialing.

Jane Goodman, Ph.D., is Associate Professor of Counseling and Director of the Adult Career Counseling Center at Oakland University in Rochester, Michigan. She is the 2001-2002 president of the American Counseling Association and a past president of the National Career Development Association. She has written in the area of career development, adult transitions, and basic counseling skills.

Richard J. Hazler, Ph.D., is Professor of Counselor Education at Ohio University. His professional experience has spanned more than 30 years as a faculty member; as a counselor in schools, prisons, the military, and private practice; and as a public school teacher. His current research focuses on the development, intervention, and prevention of youth violence as well as on the human factors involved in the counseling profession. He is a former editor of the *Journal of Humanistic Education and Development* and has authored or coauthored numerous humanistically oriented articles as well as current books, including *Core Conditions of the Facilitative Environment, Helping in the Hallways, What You Never Learned in Graduate School, The Emerging Professional Counselor,* and *Breaking the Cycle of Violence.*

Kimberly L. Henry, M.S., is a doctoral student of biobehavioral health at Pennsylvania State University. Her interests include program evaluation of intervention and prevention programs; adolescent health; and issues surrounding alcohol, tobacco, and other drug use. She currently works as a research assistant on Project ADAPT (Adoption of Drug Abuse Prevention Training), a National Institute on Drug Abuse-funded research study focusing on rural adolescent drug use. She also serves as a research assistant for the Penn State-Pennsylvania Liquor Control Board Partnership for Prevention, a coalition dedicated to preventing binge drinking.

Barbara Herlihy, Ph.D., is Professor in the Counseling Graduate Program at the University of New Orleans. Her scholarly work has focused on the area of counseling ethics. She is a former chair of the American Counseling Association (ACA) Ethics Committee and is a coauthor of the ethics casebook published by ACA. She conducts workshops nationally in the area of ethical issues in counseling and has written numerous journal articles, book chapters, and books on the topic. She has served on the editorial boards of the *Journal of Counseling and Development, Directions in Mental Health,* and *The School Counselor.* She also has served as editor of *The Wisconsin Counselor* and the *Texas Counseling Association Journal.* She is a licensed professional counselor and a national certified counselor.

Thomas H. Hohenshil, Ph.D., is Professor of Counselor Education and Psychology at Virginia Tech. He is experienced as a counselor and psychologist in community mental health settings and in the public schools. He is widely published and has presented numerous workshops on the diagnosis and treatment of mental disorders throughout the United States, Europe, and Canada. He is associate editor of the *Journal of Counseling and Development* and has served on the editorial boards of seven other national journals in counseling and psychology. He is a licensed professional counselor in Virginia and a licensed professional clinical counselor in Ohio.

Janice Miner Holden, Ed.D., is Associate Professor of Counseling at the University of North Texas, where she is Coordinator of the Counseling Program. She is the featured counselor in the video, *Cognitive Counseling: An Educational Video,* produced by the Association for Counselor Education and Supervision and Chi Sigma Iota. Most of her professional publications and presentations have addressed her primary area of professional interest—the role of transpersonal experiences in psychospiritual development. She also is interested in the interface between cognitive counseling and the transpersonal perspective in counseling.

Thomas W. Hosie, Ph.D., is Professor and Chair of the Department of Counselor Education and Educational Psychology at Mississippi State University. He also is a professor emeritus at Louisiana State University. He is the author or coauthor of more than 50 journal articles and book chapters. He has national research awards from the American Counseling Association (ACA), the Association of Counselor Education and Supervision (ACES), and the American Mental Health Counselors Association for his published research studies on counselor training and employment roles. He also has served as ACES president and treasurer, as editor of *Counselor Education and Supervision,* as an ACA Governing Council member, as a Council for Accreditation of Counseling and Related Educational Programs member, and as a member and chair of the Louisiana Professional Counselors board of examiners.

Allen E. Ivey, Ed.D., is Distinguished University Professor (Emeritus) at the University of Massachusetts, Amherst. He is president of Microtraining Associates, an educational publishing firm. He also serves on the board of directors of the National Institute for Multicultural Competence. He received his undergraduate degree from Stanford University, followed by a year as a Fulbright scholar at the University of Copenhagen in Denmark. He earned his doctorate at Harvard University. He is the author or coauthor of more than 25 books and 200 articles and chapters, translated into at least 16 languages. He is the originator of the influential microskills approach to counselor training. A past president of the Division of Counseling Psychology of the American Psychological Association (APA), he is a fellow of APA and a diplomate of the American Board of Professional Psychology. He also is a fellow of APA's Society for the Study of Ethnic and Minority Psychology. A lifetime member of the American Counseling Association, he is a recipient of its Professional Development Award.

Mary Bradford Ivey, Ed.D., is Vice President of Microtraining Associates, an educational publishing firm, and is a former school counselor in Amherst, Massachusetts. She has served as a visiting professor or counselor at Amherst College; the University of Massachusetts, Amherst; the University of Hawaii, Manoa; and Keene State College. She is on the board of directors of the National Institute for Multicultural Competence. She is the author or coauthor of 8 books, several articles and chapters, and more than 10 counseling videotapes translated into multiple languages. She has presented workshops and keynote lectures throughout the world. She received national recognition in 1988 when her elementary counseling program at the Fort River School was named one of the 10 best in the nation at the Christa McAullife Conference. She also is a recipient of the O'Hana Award of the American Counseling Association for her work in multicultural counseling in the schools.

Karyn Dayle Jones, Ph.D., is Assistant Professor in the Counselor Education Program at the University of Central Florida. She has published research articles and book chapters in the area of child abuse and counselor education. She has many years of counseling experience working with children, adolescents, adults, and families, particularly in the field of child abuse and sexual trauma. She is a national certified counselor and a licensed mental health counselor in the state of Florida. She also is on the board of the Counseling Association of Humanistic Education and Development.

Patricia Anne Davis Kennington, Ph.D., is Assistant Director, Success Programs, Division of Student Affairs, Georgia Institute of Technology, Atlanta. She specializes in teaching and training from a primary prevention and psychological development perspective. Her work focuses on academic support and counseling, and she is faculty advisor for One to One Tutoring, SPAARC, a peer advising student organization,

and the Team Leader Advisory Board, a student group composed of peer leaders for the first-year experience seminar. She has extensive experience in training and curriculum development for programs with adult groups representing the mentally disabled, the homeless, and agency volunteers. With a particular focus on spirituality and counseling and women's issues, she is cofounder of the Center for Spiritual Formation at St. James' Episcopal Church in Marietta, Georgia, providing spiritual direction, retreats, and classes on spirituality issues.

Mark S. Kiselica, Ph.D., is Associate Professor and Chair of the Department of Counselor Education at the College of New Jersey. He has conducted 52 convention presentations and is the author or editor of 45 refereed publications, including *Multicultural Counseling With Teenage Fathers: A Practical Guide; Confronting Prejudice and Racism During Multicultural Training;* and *Handbook of Counseling Boys and Adolescent Males: A Practitioner's Guide.* He is a former consulting scholar to the Clinton administration's federal Fatherhood Initiative and is a past president of the Society for the Psychological Study of Men and Masculinity (American Psychological Association [APA], Division 51). He has been named Counselor Educator of the Year and Researcher of the Year by the American Mental Health Counselors Association, is a recipient of the Publication in Counselor Education and Supervision Award, and has been named an APA fellow.

Courtland C. Lee, Ph.D., is Dean of the School of Education and Professor of Counselor Education at Hunter College of the City University of New York. He is the author, editor, or coeditor of four books on multicultural counseling and the author of two books on counseling African American males. He has published numerous book chapters and articles on adolescent development and counseling across cultures. He is a past president of the American Counseling Association, the Association for Multicultural Counseling and Development, and Chi Sigma Iota (CSI). He is a charter member of CSI's Academy of Leaders for Excellence. He is a former editor of the *Journal of Multicultural Counseling and Development* and the *Journal of African American Men*. He serves on the editorial boards of the *International Journal for the Advancement of Counselling* and *Career Development Quarterly*. A former teacher and school counselor, he has served as an educational consultant in both the United States and abroad.

Judy Lewis, Ph.D., is Professor in the College of Health Professions at Governors State University in Illinois. She is the 2000-2001 president of the American Counseling Association as well as a past president of the International Association of Marriage and Family Counselors. She has published books on adolescent, family, community, substance abuse, employee assistance, health, and women's counseling. Her current consultation and training efforts focus on diversity initiatives and innovative helping strategies.

Larry C. Loesch, Ph.D., is Professor in the Department of Counselor Education at the University of Florida. His research and writing interests are focused on measurement and evaluation as well as counselor preparation and credentialing. He has served as measurement and research consultant for the National Board for Certified Counselors since 1981. Among other professional recognitions, he is a co-recipient of the American Counseling Association's (ACA) Research Award and of the ACA Hitchcock Distinguished Professional Service Award. He is a past president of Chi Sigma Iota and a current member of its Academy of Leaders for Excellence.

Judy Miranti, Ed.D., is Professor of Counselor Education and an Academic Dean at Our Lady of Holy Cross College in Louisiana. She has published articles and book chapters and has coedited texts on the topic of spirituality in counseling. She is on the board of the Council for Accreditation of Counseling and Related Educational Programs and has held leadership positions at the state and national levels. She has presented nationally and internationally and is a frequent presenter of workshops on the spiritual dimensions of counseling.

Spencer G. Niles, Ed.D., is Professor-in-Charge of the Counselor Education Program at Pennsylvania State University. Previously, he served as a professor and an assistant dean at the University of Virginia. He is a licensed professional counselor and licensed psychologist. He currently serves as editor of *Career Development Quarterly* and is on the editorial boards of the *Journal of Career Development, International Journal of Educational and Vocational Guidance, International Journal of Counselling, Journal of College Student Development,* and *International Career Journal.*

Pamela O. Paisley, Ed.D., is Associate Professor and School Counseling Program Coordinator at the University of Georgia. She is a past president of the Association for Counselor Education and Supervision and currently serves as an associate editor of the *Journal of Counseling and Development*. She is the principal investigator for a national grant focused on transforming school counseling. She has written and consulted nationally and internationally on school counseling program development. Her research, using both qualitative and quantitative methodologies, focuses on restructuring school counseling preparation and practice, applications of developmental theory, and efficacy of interventions with children and adolescents.

Artis J. Palmo, Ed.D., is a full-time private practitioner and chief executive officer of Bethlehem Counseling Associates in Pennsylvania. Prior to full-time practice, he served as a professor of counseling psychology at Lehigh University. He specializes in the treatment of individuals and couples facing issues such as divorce, remarriage, parenting, stepparenting, and relationship problems. He has published extensively on a wide range of topics including important issues facing mental health professionals in the future, blended families, adolescent and children's problems, and group counseling.

Randall M. Parker, Ph.D., is Melissa Elizabeth Stuart Centennial Professor of Education, Professor of Special Education, and Director of Rehabilitation Counselor Education at the University of Texas at Austin. He is a fellow of the American Psychological Association, Division 17 (Counseling Psychology) and Division 22 (Rehabilitation Psychology). He is coeditor of the *Rehabilitation Counseling Bulletin* and is a past president of the American Rehabilitation Counseling Association and the Texas Psychological Association. He is a recipient of the University of Wisconsin–Madison School of Education Alumni Achievement Award, the University of Texas at Austin College of Education Outstanding Faculty Award, and the American Rehabilitation Counseling Association James F. Garrett Award for Career Research.

Sandra DeAngelis Peace, Ed.D., is Associate Director of the Model Clinical Teaching Program at North Carolina State University. She has held counselor education faculty appointments at North Carolina Central University (as department chair) and at North Carolina State University. She has been a school counselor in New York City and North Carolina. Her research and publications have focused on school coun-

selor developmental supervision and on promoting counselor and teacher development.

Mary Lou Ramsey, Ed.D., is Professor and Coordinator of the School Counseling Program in the Department of Counselor Education at the College of New Jersey. She is a national train-the-trainer of the Association for Multicultural Counseling and Development and is a member of the curriculum development committee of the Counselors for Social Justice. Her scholarly achievements include 15 state and federal grants, 25 refereed publications, and more than 100 professional conference and workshop presentations, many of which are devoted to issues of diversity and multiculturalism.

Patricia M. Reeves, Ph.D., is Assistant Professor of Social Work at the University of Georgia. She serves as an adviser to several local/state social service agencies. Her research interests include coping and adapting in marginalized populations, empowerment fostered by the use of information technologies, and school social work. She is investigating how access to information through the Internet challenges the traditional relationship between physicians and HIV-AIDS patients as well as the mental health needs/issues of women in a homeless shelter.

Theodore P. Remley, Jr., Ph.D., is Coordinator of the Counseling Graduate Program at the University of New Orleans. He is a member of the bar in Virginia and Florida and is a licensed professional counselor in Virginia, Mississippi, and Louisiana. He is a member of the counselor licensure board in Louisiana and also has served on the licensure boards in the District of Columbia as well as in Mississippi and Virginia. He is a former executive director of the American Counseling Association and was the founding president of the American Association of State Counseling Boards. He conducts workshops nationally in the area of legal issues in mental health and has written numerous journal articles, book chapters, and books on the topic.

Sandra Rigazio-DiGilio, Ph.D., is Associate Professor in the Commission on Accreditation of Marriage and Family Therapy Education master's and doctoral programs at the University of Connecticut, Storrs. She is a licensed psychologist, a licensed marriage and family therapist, and an American Association of Marriage and Family Therapy-approved supervisor. She is associate editor of the Teachers College Press Book Series in Counseling and Development, has served as associate editor of the Practice section of the *Journal of Mental Health Counseling,* and has served on the editorial board of the *Journal of Counseling and Development.* She has written numerous articles and chapters on a co-constructive-developmental model of therapy and supervision and has presented internationally and nationally on these topics.

E. H. "Mike" Robinson, III, Ph.D., is Professor in the Department of Human Service and Wellness at the University of Central Florida (UCF), where he also serves as Coordinator of Counselor Education Programs and as Graduate Director of the Ph.D. Program in the College of Education. He is the founder and codirector of the Consortium for Social Responsibility and has received grants for his work in the consortium with children and adults from the AT&T Foundation; The Celebration Company; and the UCF Academy for Teaching, Learning, and Leadership. His research has focused on the human relationships in counseling and teaching and on the developmental nature of fear and anxiety. He has served on the boards of a number of professional associations including the American Counseling Association. He is a recipient of the Distinguished Mentor Award

from the Association for Counselor Education and Supervision.

Tracy L. Robinson, Ed.D., is Professor of Counselor Education at North Carolina State University (NCSU). Prior experience includes stints as director of research for the Quality Education for Minorities Project at the Massachusetts Institute of Technology, research associate with the New England Research Institute, and director of the Counseling and Testing Center at Johnson C. Smith University in North Carolina. She recently participated in an invited sabbatical at the University of Waikato in New Zealand. She is a recipient of the NCSU College of Education and Psychology Board of Governors' Excellence in Teaching Award. She is a coauthor of *The Convergence of Race, Ethnicity, and Gender: Multiple Identities in Counseling* and serves as an associate editor of the *Journal of Counseling and Development.*

Michael Ryan is a graduate student at Wake Forest University specializing in school counseling. This is his first publication. He is working on a variety of projects including a team council project for middle schools using praise and encouragement with children and the use of rational emotive behavior therapy with teenagers.

James P. Sampson, Jr., Ph.D., is Professor in the Psychological Services in Education Program and coDirector of the Center for the Study of Technology in Counseling and Career Development at Florida State University. He is a national certified counselor and a national certified career counselor. He is a member of the American Counseling Association, the Association for Assessment in Counseling, the Association for Counselor Education and Supervision, the National Career Development Association, the American Psychological Association (Counseling Psychology and Psychology of Religion divisions), and the Association of Computer-Based Systems for Career Information. His areas of interest are computer applications in counseling and human services as well as career decision making and the delivery of career services.

Thomas L. Sexton, Ph.D., is Professor in the Department of Counseling and Educational Psychology at Indiana University, where he is Director of the Clinical Training Center, is Director of the Centor for Adolescent and Family Studies, and teaches in the nationally accredited Counseling Psychology Program. He has written extensively in the areas of outcome research and its implications for clinical practice and training. He is a national expert on family-based treatment interventions for at-risk adolescents. He is the author of 4 books and more than 35 professional articles and chapters in the areas of marriage and family therapy and counseling outcome research. As the clinical training and externship coordinator for the Functional Family Therapy Project, he has presented workshops on functional family therapy both nationally and internationally. He is a licensed psychologist, a member of both the American Psychological Association and the American Counseling Association, and an approved supervisor in the American Association of Marriage and Family Therapy.

Michael J. Shosh, M.S., is Director of Training and Business Development at Bethlehem Counseling Associates in Pennsylvania. He has more than 20 years experience as a human resources/organizational development consultant. His work has focused on maximizing individual and organizational performance and on managing problem employees. His expertise extends to the issues of employee drug testing and critical incident management. He has authored articles on a variety of topics and a book chapter on counseling in business and industry.

Ed Smith, D.P.H., is Director of Evaluation Research in the Prevention Research Center at Pennsylvania State University. Previously, he was a faculty member at Johns Hopkins University, the University of Waterloo in Ontario, the University of North Carolina, and the University of Georgia. He has authored more than 70 articles, book chapters, and reports centered around preventing unwanted teenage pregnancy, repeat pregnancy, substance use, and the promotion of healthy lifestyles. For the past 20 years, he has been concerned with the design, implementation, and evaluation of programs aimed at improving the lives of adolescents and young adults. As part of this area of study, he works with program providers, developers, and administrators to improve programs by incorporating pragmatic evaluation findings. The settings for these programs have included schools, health clinics, camps, and community and recreation centers.

Howard B. Smith, Ed.D., is Senior Director for Professional Affairs of the American Counseling Association (ACA). Previously, he served as head of the Educational Leadership and Counseling Department at the University of Louisiana–Monroe. Prior to that, he served as department head of Counseling and Human Resource Development at South Dakota State University. He has held national, regional, and state elected and appointed offices within ACA, its divisions, and its state branches during his career.

Len Sperry, Ph.D., is Professor and Vice Chair of the Department of Psychiatry and Behavioral Medicine at the Medical College of Wisconsin. He also holds appointments as Professor of Family and Community Medicine and as Professor of Preventive Medicine. He is board certified in clinical psychology, preventive medicine, and psychiatry and is a fellow of both the American Psychological Association and the American Psychiatric Association. He is a member of the American Family Therapy Academy, the American College of Preventive Medicine, and the American College of Psychiatry. He has published 28 professional books, including *The Disordered Couple,* and more than 200 chapters and journal articles. He is on the editorial boards of 10 professional journals including the *American Journal of Family Therapy* and *The Family Journal.*

Norman A. Sprinthall, Ed.D., is Professor Emeritus at North Carolina State University, where he served as department head. Previously, he held faculty appointments at the University of Minnesota and Harvard University. He has authored a number of textbooks as well as numerous book chapters and research articles. His main interests always have been to promote a preventive developmental model for counseling.

Patricia W. Stevens, Ph.D., is Director of the Marriage and Family Training Program at the University of Colorado at Denver. She currently is president of the International Association of Marriage and Family Counselors and is a past chair of its Ethics Committee. She is a past cochair of the Women's Mentoring and Interest Network of the Association for Counselor Education and Supervision. She is a clinical member and approved supervisor with the American Association for Marriage and Family Therapy, a certified family therapist, a licensed professional counselor, a licensed marriage and family therapist, and a licensed clinical supervisor. She has written and presented extensively at the local, regional, national, and international levels in the areas of marriage and family training, substance abuse, gender issues, and ethical and legal issues in marriage and family therapy. She

is a recent recipient of a Fulbright scholarship and traveled to Malaysia, where she assisted the National University in developing a marriage and family training program.

Thomas J. Sweeney, Ph.D., is Professor Emeritus in Counseling and Higher Education at Ohio University and is Executive Director of Chi Sigma Iota (CSI) and a member of its Academy of Leaders for Excellence. He is a past president of the American Counseling Association (ACA), the Association for Counselor Education and Supervision, and CSI, and he was the founding chair of CACREP. He is a recipient of the ACA Carl Perkins Legislative Award and the Arthur A. Hitchcock Distinguished Professional Service Award. His professional interests include the theory and practice of the individual psychology of Alfred Adler, child guidance, marriage and family counseling, career counseling, group work, and counselor education.

John D. Swisher, Ph.D., is Professor Emeritus of Education at Pennsylvania State University. His research specialty has been the evaluation of prevention programs for schools and colleges. He has been a school counselor and counselor educator, and most recently he was the department head for programs in counselor education, counseling psychology, and rehabilitation. He was co-principal investigator for a research grant from the National Institute on Drug Abuse that evaluated the cost-effectiveness of prevention programs. He has been involved in several projects focusing on the integration of prevention programs in schools. He currently is a senior research scientist on Project ADAPT (Adoption of Drug Abuse Prevention Training) through the Institute for Policy Research and Evaluation at Penn State.

Edna Mora Szymanski, Ph.D., is Dean of the College of Education at the University of Maryland, College Park. Previously, she served in a variety of capacities at the University of Wisconsin–Madison including professor in the Department of Rehabilitation Psychology and Special Education, department chair, associate dean, director of the Rehabilitation Research and Training Center on Career Development and Advancement, and chair of the campus committees on retirement and disability. Her major areas of scholarship have focused on disability and career development, rehabilitation counselor education, and research instruction. Her most influential research has demonstrated the relationship of rehabilitation counselor education to employment outcomes of people with severe disabilities. She has authored or coauthored numerous refereed articles and book chapters and has received national recognition for her research, including awards from the American Counseling Association, the American Rehabilitation Counseling Association, the American Association of Counselor Education and Supervision, and the National Council on Rehabilitation Education.

Judith R. Vicary, Ph.D., is Professor of Biobehavioral Health at Pennsylvania State University and recently served as Senior Research Fellow at the Robert Wood Johnson Foundation. She has conducted research and published in the area of substance abuse prevention in school, community, and workplace settings. She was the principal investigator for a Center for Substance Abuse Prevention community health project targeting alcohol, tobacco, and other drug use by pregnant and parenting young adult women that received the National Exemplary Prevention Program Award. She also has been the principal investigator for a longitudinal study of adolescent development and health, focusing on both teen pregnancy and substance abuse, following the participants for 14 years into young adulthood. She has been a National Institute on Drug Abuse postdoctoral fellow. She has served for 3 years as chair of the

Planning Committee for the Penn State-Pennsylvania Liquor Control Board Partnership for Prevention, developing campus-community partnerships at the 20 Penn State campuses.

Sherry K. Watt, Ph.D., is Assistant Professor at the University of Iowa. Previously, she held a faculty appointment at Radford University. She is a licensed professional counselor in the state of North Carolina. She has varied experience in the student affairs administration and community agency field. Over the past 10 years, she has held a variety of positions in student affairs administration including career counselor, resident director, and college instructor. She founded and operated a private consulting firm through which she provided individual and group counseling; conducted programmatic evaluations; and facilitated a wide range of workshops on topics such as adolescent development, diversity, time management, and community building. She is a recipient of the Annuit Coeptis Award for Emerging Professionals from the American College Personnel Association and of the Chi Sigma Iota Outstanding Teacher Award from Radford University. Her teaching and research interests include administrative operations in student affairs, identity development, student development, racial identity development, gender issues, and spirituality development.

William J. Weikel, Ph.D., is Professor in the Counseling Program at Morehead State University and has been in private practice for more than 20 years. He is a past president of the American Mental Health Counselors Association and of the Kentucky Counseling Association. He is the author of numerous journal articles and books in the field of mental health.

J. Melvin Witmer, Ph.D., is Professor Emeritus at Ohio University, where he taught in Counselor Education for 32 years. He is a professional clinical counselor, consultant, and workshop leader in counseling and human development. His 1985 book, *Pathways to Personal Growth,* and subsequent publications describe the process of developing one's potential, striving for wellness, and coping with stress. His application of a model of wellness has been presented throughout the United States and overseas to groups in education, mental health, community agencies, and business and industry. He continues to refine the wellness model in collaboration with colleagues Thomas Sweeney and Jane Myers.

Richard Yep, M.P.A., is Executive Director of the American Counseling Association (ACA). Prior to his current appointment, he served in a variety of positions with ACA including director of government relations and associate exec-

utive director for corporate planning. He has been involved in education and human services work for more than 20 years. He began his career in a human services agency by working with the Native American population as a Volunteer in Service to America (VISTA). He went on to do direct service work in the TRIO programs focusing on youths from underrepresented populations as they transitioned from high school to postsecondary education. He served as project director for an Asian American AIDS education program. He worked in the California state legislature and in the U.S. Congress as a legislative assistant, focusing on education, human services, and civil rights issues. He received his bachelor's degree from the University of California, Santa Barbara, and his master's degree from the University of Southern California.